C Unleashed

Richard Heathfield
Lawrence Kirby
et al.

SAMS

A Division of Macmillan USA
201 West 103rd Street
Indianapolis, Indiana 46290

C Unleashed

International Standard Book Number: 0-672-31896-2

Library of Congress Catalog Card Number: 99-068209

Printed in the United States of America

First Printing: July 2000

02 01 00 4 3 2 1

Trademarks

This publication was produced using the Advent 3B2 Publishing System.

Warning and Disclaimer

Executive Editor
Rosemarie Graham

Acquisitions Editor
Carol Ackerman

Development Editor
Gus A. Miklos

Managing Editor
Matt Purcell

Senior Editor
Karen A. Walsh

Copy Editor
Kim Cofer

Indexer
Diane Brenner

Proofreaders
Juli Cook
Candice Hightower
Matt Wynalda

Technical Editors
Steve Krattiger
Peter Seebach
Vinay Pai

Software Development Specialist
William C. Eland Jr.

Interior Design
Gary Adair

Cover Design
Aren Howell

Copy Writer
Eric Borgert

3B2 Design
Michelle Mitchell
Daniela Raderstorf

About the Authors

Richard Heathfield is a software developer for (and owner of) Eton Computer Systems Ltd. Having written code for several insurance companies, a health authority, a bank, and an airline, he is beginning to wonder if he'll ever find a client using C++ Builder. He currently lives near Potterspury, Northamptonshire (in the UK) with his wife, three wonderful children, network of five PCs, and more C compilers than he knows what to do with. He stopped voiding `main()` shortly before becoming a regular contributor to `comp.lang.c`, a fact for which he is eternally grateful. Richard spends far too much time in Yahoo! Chat, rejoicing in the "nick" of `C_Dreamer`, and would like to use this opportunity to say "hi" to everyone in the Programming room there. His current interests are TCP/IP programming, automated C code generation, C99, and coffee. When he's not programming, chatting about programming, or writing about programming (or drinking coffee), he plays keyboards and electric guitar far too loudly. Richard can be reached at `http://users.powernet.co.uk/eton`.

Lawrence Kirby, a graduate of Cambridge University, England, has been programming in C for more than 10 years. He is a co-founder of Netactive Systems Ltd, a company specializing in communications and financial market information. Previously he worked at British Telecom for several years on network service and information systems. He enjoys being a regular contributor to Usenet newsgroups such as `comp.lang.c` and finds both the experience of helping others with C problems and sharing experience with other C programmers (from novice to C standard committee members) extremely helpful.

Dann Corbit has a degree in Numerical Analysis from the University of Washington and has been a computer programmer since 1976. A partial listing of computer-related work can be found at `ftp://38.168.214.175/pub/C.A.P.%20Biographies/DannCorbit.htm#_Toc441048186`

Dann has been programming in C since the mid 1980s and has taught the C programming language at Olympic College in Bremerton, Washington. He has written magazine articles for *Dr. Dobb's Journal* and co-authored scientific papers on the Bowhead whale (Balaena mysticetus) for the North Slope Borough that were presented to the IWC. He is the founder and manager of the international Chess Analysis Project, which uses computer programs to analyze chess board positions and catalog the results in a database. The Chess Analysis Project FAQ can be found at `ftp://38.168.214.175/pub/Chess%20Analysis%20Project%20FAQ.htm`.

As a regular contributor to `news:comp.lang.c`, Dann can frequently be found there, posting away in his eccentric style. Long interested in mathematics and science, he won first place in the Mid Columbia Science Fair and was a finalist at the International Science Fair for his project *An Analysis of a Solid Solution*.

Chad Dixon, a network engineer for the past seven years, has dealt with many wide-ranging technologies in the computing field. Along the way, he began to implement solutions for his clients ranging from Client/Server Application development and database solutions to Network Monitoring enterprise systems. Working with companies and organizations such as NASA, Lyondell, Olin, Arco Chemical, and British Petroleum has granted him considerable experience in cross-platform network-aware application development. Chad lives in Houston, Texas with his lovely wife Veronica and Snowball, their pet rabbit. Chad can be contacted at `http://www.loopy.org`.

William Fishburne graduated from the University of Maryland in 1989 with a Bachelor of Science Degree in Computer Science. He is currently a senior consultant for Alphatech Corporation. William has also taught at Prince George's Community College in Maryland and is currently a member of the Association of C and C++ Users (ACCU).

William has been programming in C since graduating and worked in such diverse areas as satellite communications, document imaging, and financial accounting systems. He has worked on a wide variety of UNIX platforms and was an early participant in porting Microsoft Windows NT to multi-processor platforms. William has written articles for popular programming magazines such as *Dr. Dobb's Journal*. In addition, he has been involved in volunteer activities such as Project Gutenberg. (The project preserves books that are no longer copyrighted and distributes them electronically for free.)

You can reach William on the Internet at `wfishburne@atcnet.com` and visit Project Gutenberg at `http://www.gutenberg.net`.

Scott Fluhrer has been programming in C since 1979. He is currently a Development Engineer at Cisco Systems. His other interests include science fiction and cryptography.

Sam Hobbs has been involved in computing since 1966 beginning with 25-bit serial computers with drum memory and 196 words of core memory where the only programming language was machine language. Since then, he has worked in FORTRAN, Basic, FOCAL, C, C++ and various scripting languages (primarily AWK and Perl) as well as with some database languages. He began working with C in 1985. His primary experience has been in the electric utility industry (primarily in commercial nuclear power) in technical, supervisory, and management roles. He currently works as an engineering and management consultant in the nuclear power industry.

Ian Kelly is a computer systems consultant who first programmed professionally in 1963. He has progressed from giving technical programming help at the main electricity generation company in the UK, through designing and managing the writing of an operating system (ADAM), constructing numerous compilers, to writing reports for the European Commission on the portability of software. He holds a Bachelor's Special degree in mathematics, and has been looking for some excuse to do something mathematical for the past 35 years—and failing. Instead, he has picked up (by using) more than twenty computer languages in many different environments. Currently, he advises on how mixed-language systems can be improved and extended.

With the (mistaken) belief that French would be as easy as Cobol, in the late 1970s, he became interested in Machine Translation (MT), has written two books and several papers on the topic, and was (for more than 15 years) the chairman of the BCS specialist group for MT.

Ian lives in Surrey, England next door to a pub. He plays the organ in a 1,000-year-old church and arranges music for the ladies' choir he conducts. Happily married for more than 30 years with two children, a guinea-pig, and a chinchilla, Ian promises that he'll get round to mowing the lawn—next week.

Jack Klein has been involved in programming desktop computers and primarily in designing and programming embedded systems since 1980. He has been involved in products using many different 8-, 16-, and 32-bit processors, programming them in their native assembly languages and, since 1983, in the C programming language.

Specializing in process control, motion control, and communications, Jack has designed and programmed embedded systems for use in industrial, medical, consumer, and office equipment.

Jack is currently a Senior Principal Engineer for the Nuclear Medicine Group of Siemens Medical Systems, where he works on embedded processor circuit design and on motion control, patient safety, and image acquisition software for medical imaging devices.

Michael Lee has been programming since 1979 and has many years of experience with the PL/I and C programming languages. The primary focus of his career has been custom database system development. A recent effort of note was grafting an SQL interface onto a database originally implemented in FORTRAN.

Perhaps his most rewarding project was a query optimizer, a piece of code that analyzed an incoming database query and transformed it into an equivalent but more efficient query that made better use of the database's links and indexes. Side projects include a comprehensive Web page on optimization tricks and techniques and software to generate top 10 lists for Usenet newsgroups.

When not programming, Mike likes to mountain bike in the hills near his California home, definitely preferring downhill to uphill.

Ben Pfaff is a student in electrical engineering at Michigan State University, where he is on the MSU fencing team. After graduation, he hopes to find a job designing digital integrated circuits. Ben has been working with computers for 14 years, 10 in the C programming language. His interests outside computers include French, Japanese, science fiction, and world travel. On the Internet, you can often find him answering questions on Usenet's `comp.lang.c` forum. Ben is also a maintainer for Debian GNU/Linux (`www.debian.org`) and a software author with the Free Software Foundation (`www.fsf.org`). Ben can be contacted through email as `pfaffben@msu.edu`.

Peter Seebach is a C hobbyist. He learned to read C from paper printouts, and eventually learned to write it, too. He is on the ANSI/ISO C standards committee "because it sounded like fun." He moderates `comp.lang.c.moderated`. He mostly programs because it's the best way to cheat at video games.

Steve Summit is a veteran C programmer, author, and teacher. For 20 years, he has programmed almost exclusively in C. He is the maintainer of the `comp.lang.c` FAQ list. His programming interests are varied, but they all tend to revolve around the themes of cleanliness, usability, portability, and implicit correctness.

Mathew Watson wrote his first machine code (because high-level languages ran so slowly on the first 8-bit micros) program at the age of 10 and has been hooked on computers ever since. He studied computer science at the University of London and has worked for various computer firms and has seen first-hand how you need a software project to see how things can really go wrong. Mathew is currently waiting for his first child to be born so that he/she can show him how to program whatever will be the equivalent of the video recorder in the 21st century—just as he did for his dad.

Stephan Wilms is a professional software developer with experience in the fields of industrial picture processing and medical systems for cardiac research and treatment. In his career, he has worked with highly parallel Embedded Systems and developed complex end-user Windows applications.

Ian Woods has been programming professionally for six years and is currently working for a research company writing real-time embedded software. He specializes in C and various assembly languages. Many of his projects rely upon heavy knowledge of discrete mathematics and signal processing. He is currently learning a spoken language called Lojban, an engineered logical language with a formal grammar which greatly simplifies speech generation and processing. Most of his interest lies in researching his strange ideas, which encompass many areas of software development.

Mike Wright is Chief Technologist of Innovative Systems Architect, a Utah-based corporation that earned an impressive reputation supporting the technical needs of the U.S. Department of Defense's test and training range community. He has directed the design and development of advanced mission analysis and visualization tool suites for the Nevada "Black" Range. Mike thoroughly enjoys the challenges of his job, constantly pushing the envelope and investigating new advances in software engineering. He can be reached at `mike_wisdom@yahoo.com`.

Dedication

To Nicky, the most beautiful woman in the world. IDLY.

—Richard Heathfield

Acknowledgments

So many people to thank! The co-authors, naturally, come first. Without them, no book. But special mentions go to Dann Corbit and Ben Pfaff, whose skilled dissection of my source code killed a lot of nasal demons; to Chad Dixon, a very present help in time of trouble; and to Ian Kelly, surely the UK's answer to Donald Knuth.

At Sams, many thanks to Carol Ackerman, who must take much of the credit for making this thing happen; to Gus Miklos, a steady hand at the helm; and to all the other people at Sams who worked so hard to turn this book from an idea into reality.

A number of other people gave freely of their time, energy, ideas, and resources, too; thanks to Ola Angelsmark, Nick Cramer, Mark Dean, Jonathan George, Matt Gessner, Stephen Heathfield, John Hixson, Leibish Mermelstein, Edmund Stephen-Smith, and Bryan Williams.

Finally, a very quick mention for the best bunch of hackers in the world, the denizens of that deep, dark, and clueful jungle known as `comp.lang.c`, who provided expert technical help accidentally, by answering questions asked by other people, who thus saved me the trouble of asking them myself.

—Richard Heathfield

Tell Us What You Think!

As the reader of this book, *you* are our most important critic and commentator. We value your opinion and want to know what we're doing right, what we could do better, what areas you'd like to see us publish in, and any other words of wisdom you're willing to pass our way.

As Associate Publisher for Sams, I welcome your comments. You can fax, email, or write me directly to let me know what you did or didn't like about this book—as well as what we can do to make our books stronger.

Please note that I cannot help you with technical problems related to the topic of this book, and that due to the high volume of mail I receive, I might not be able to reply to every message.

When you write, please be sure to include this book's title and author as well as your name and phone or fax number. I will carefully review your comments and share them with the authors and editors who worked on the book.

Fax: 317-581-4770

Email: `opsys@mcp.com`

Mail: Michael Stephens
Sams Publishing
201 West 103rd Street
Indianapolis, IN 46290 USA

The C Language Revisited

Part I

In This Part

CHAPTER 1

C Programmer Unleashed!

by Richard Heathfield

In This Chapter

Welcome to *C Unleashed*!

Sams has run the *Unleashed* series of computing books for quite a while now, and there are *Unleashed* books for almost every language and compiler under the sun. But there was one wide, in fact yawning, gap: There was no book in the series devoted entirely to C. That gap has now been filled, and you hold the result in your hands.

There are dozens of books on C. (I should know; I think I've bought most of them.) Every facet of the language has been covered by multitudinous tomes, each scrabbling for your attention in a crowded marketplace. So what aspects of C can we possibly unleash that have not been thoroughly loosened, untied, and set free already? What parts of the language are still in thrall, and have yet to be released on an unsuspecting world?

None, obviously. C is a simple but extremely powerful language; it has been used to implement operating systems, video games, microwave ovens, word processors, and in fact pretty well any modern electronic gadget you can think of. If C had any serious limitations, not only would it not be so popular as it undoubtedly is, but also this book would probably be quite short. For tradition's sake this book is called *C Unleashed*, but I think I would almost have preferred to call it *C Programmer Unleashed*. We don't need to unleash the language, because it isn't leashed in the first place. Our aim is to unleash you, the C programmer.

Why do you need to be unleashed? Here's one reason why:

> Q: I'm trying to do some calculations where accuracy is important. I need 500 digits of accuracy, but I can only seem to get 15 or so. How do I get more accuracy?
>
> A: You can't do that in C. The number of digits of precision of a `double` is defined by `DBL_DIG` in `<float.h>`, and is typically 15 on modern systems. Are you sure you need 500 digits?

Although I just invented this question and answer, it's typical of the kind of answer you might get if you were to pose this question on Usenet. For far too long, people have been saying "You can't do that in C and you shouldn't want to anyway." In this book, we will show you how you *can* do that in C. It takes a bit of work and a bit of thought, but it can be done.

We'll show that it is possible to sort data faster than QuickSort could do it. It is possible to process human languages effectively. It is possible to automatically detect memory leaks. It is possible to multiply two arrays together. In fact, almost anything is possible in C.

Unfortunately, not everything can be done in pure, ANSI-defined C. The idea of ANSI C is that it should be portable to all platforms. As a result, desirable features, which you would think should be standard in any language, are often missing for the simple reason that there is no guarantee that all platforms support those features. For example, you can't clear the screen in C! Why not? Because not all systems have a screen. My own Linux system is, most of the time, devoid of screen and keyboard, but still manages to do useful work. As a rule of thumb, anything that relies on particular hardware (such as a laser printer, or indeed a printer of any kind at all), or the vagaries of a particular operating system paradigm (the concept of a directory structure, for example) is unlikely to be possible in ANSI C. At times like this, we must turn to the additional functions provided by our particular implementation.

Even given that restriction, however, there are many things you can do in C that most people seem to think you can't do. All it takes is a little thought (sometimes a lot of thought) and some hard work. We've tried to do the thinking and the hard work for you, as far as we can, so that you can enjoy the gain without suffering the pain.

Who Should Read This Book?

C Unleashed is intended for C programmers who have already acquired at least a year's experience in the language and are either using it daily in their job or studying it thoroughly as part of a course in higher education, and have been doing so for at least a year. Newcomers will find it heavy going, and would be well advised to first consider turning their attention to one of the many excellent introductory C language books. If you want a recommendation, I suggest *C Programming: A Modern Approach* by K.N. King, published by W.W. Norton & Company, 1996; the ISBN is 0-393-96945-2.

If you're interested in making your C programs go more quickly, read this book (don't forget to buy it first).

If you're interested in making your C programs more portable, read this book.

If you're interested in how modern, fast, efficient algorithms can be implemented in C, read this book.

If you don't care two hoots about any of the above, read this book to find out why you should care.

If you're a C++ programmer who picked this book up by mistake and you're too embarrassed to ask the shop for a refund, have no fear. All of the ideas and most of the code in this book will work just fine in C++ with only a few very minor changes.

Finally, if you're a cute little old lady who picked this book up at random as a potential birthday present for your grandson and are wondering if he'd like it, the answer is undoubtedly YES; take it to the cashier right away. If you ask nicely, I expect they'll gift-wrap it while you wait. (While you're at it, why not buy him an introductory book on C, a C compiler, and a computer?)

What Knowledge Is Assumed?

In writing this book, we've assumed that you have a working knowledge of the core C language. If you have a reasonably thorough grasp of types, operators, expressions, control flow, function syntax, pointers, arrays, structures, unions, stream input and output, string handling, scope, visibility, and basic preprocessor syntax, you're going to do just fine.

Of these areas, perhaps the one that most people find difficult to understand, including people whose knowledge of C is otherwise relatively sophisticated, is the idea of *pointers*. With this in mind, here's a whistle-stop tour of elementary pointer theory. Those who already understand pointers thoroughly can skip right ahead to the next section.

A pointer is a variable. That's the most important idea you need to grasp. Once you know this, almost everything else falls into place fairly easily.

Okay, so it's a variable. But of course it's a special type of variable, in that the values it holds are *addresses*. A pointer variable can hold the address of another variable. If we don't have a variable whose address we want it to hold right now, we can point it at the special location `NULL`.

We assign a pointer to an object's address using the `&` operator. We get at the object pointed to by using the `*` operator.

Note

In C, an *object* is simply a named region of storage, and is not to be confused with the C++ idea of an object being an instance of a class.

The most important fact to remember about pointers is that they must point to somewhere valid before being dereferenced. Thus, we can't just say:

```
char *p;
strcpy(p, "Hello world");
```

We must first allocate space. We can do this generously ("Hey, let's get more space than we'll ever need") or parsimoniously ("No, let's get exactly enough space for our purposes"). Both techniques are shown in Listing 1.1 (and yes, the purpose of the code is entirely illustrative—I don't really write `"hello world"` programs for a living):

LISTING 1.1 Providing a Place to which Pointers Can Point

```
#include <stdio.h>
#include <string.h>
#include <stdlib.h>

int main(void)
{
  char *p;
#ifdef SCROOGE
  /* Allocate exactly enough space, including
   * one for the '\0'-terminator.
   */
  p = malloc(strlen("Hello world") + 1);
#else
  /* Allocate plenty of space */
  p = malloc(1000);
#endif
  /* note: malloc returns NULL if there
   * is not enough memory available.
   */
  if(p != NULL)
  {
    strcpy(p, "Hello world");
    printf("%s\n", p);
    free(p);
    /* note: we always free memory when
     * we've finished with it.
     */
  }
  return 0;
}
```

There is a special kind of pointer, called a *void pointer* (or pointer to void), which points to some data type unknown to the compiler. Given some pointer P to type T, we can use a void pointer V to point at the same object that P points to, but we can't do any serious work with that pointer. It's just a place-marker in memory. (And this is very useful, as we will see.) To do anything useful with the memory we're pointing to, we must use a pointer of the correct type. Thus, this is legal:

```
T *p;
void *v;
T *q;

p = malloc(sizeof *p);

if(p != NULL)
{
  v = p;
  /* ... */
  q = v;
  /* ... do something to the memory using q ... */
  free(q);
}
```

Notice the complete absence of casts. Casts are nearly always a Bad Thing in C. Here, they are completely unnecessary.

If all that was terribly easy for you, good! We're going to do just fine from here on in. If it wasn't so obvious, perhaps you need to brush up on pointers first, using any good introductory C book.

How to Get the Most from This Book

To get the best out of this book, I strongly recommend that you read it. I only say this because I have at least a hundred books on computing on my bookshelves, totaling perhaps 50,000 pages. I doubt if I've actually read more than about 10,000 of those pages, at the very outside. So I haven't got the best out of my book collection by any means. Don't let that happen to you!

This book covers many techniques that you possibly haven't happened upon before, or that you thought didn't apply to your particular programming needs. Many people underestimate the power of "classical" data structures and algorithms, thinking they are somehow old-fashioned, and having some vague idea that modern computers are so powerful that it doesn't really matter what algorithm you use because even the slowest method will be quick enough. This is simply not true. Yes, computers are quick nowadays. But have you ever sat in front of a PC impatiently waiting for it to do something? I know I have. Therefore, computers are not quick enough to patch over the inadequacies of our programs. So, until they are, we should write our programs intelligently. And because the faster computers get, the more work we expect them to do, they will never be fast enough to turn a bad algorithm into a good one.

So, read the book. We've tried to pitch it at two levels: *interested* and *lazy*. We hope you are interested enough in intermediate/advanced C programming to study the text and the source code carefully, understand it, and learn how to apply what you learn in your daily programming tasks. But we fully recognize that you might not have time to be interested. (Regrettably, I myself fall into this category all too often.) Your boss wants a program from you tomorrow, and your program needs a really quick sort routine now, and you don't have time to mess around with actually understanding this stuff—you just want to plug it into your program and watch it fly! That's fine by us. We've tried to arrange the text so that you can get a reasonable idea of what's going on without having to study every single word on every single page. Naturally, we hope that you'll come back to the text later and read up on the subject more thoroughly. So, if you want to be lazy, or don't have time to be as interested as you'd like, relax—grab what you need, ignore what you don't need.

You'll be glad to hear that you don't need to read this book cover-to-cover! Each chapter stands more or less by itself, so it's ideal for "evening swim" reading. Jump into whichever pool of knowledge takes your fancy, immerse yourself thoroughly, swim a few lengths, then emerge exhilarated, breathless, and needing a stiff drink.

Why Another Book About C?

C is used by many tens of thousands of programmers on a daily basis because it is fast, solid, fairly easy to use, and portable. Although it is true that C++ has gained a solid foothold in the marketplace, C has a well-established and well-deserved place in the programming world. It has become the *lingua franca* of the development community, and has a very healthy following among modern programmers.

C is not a perfect language; its most ardent supporters are usually the first to moan about its flaws. Nevertheless, it has stood the test of time, and stood it well.

This book seeks to enable you to be a better C programmer by sharing in the tips and tricks of experts who've been around the block a few times. We will be showing you what works. We know it works because we've tried it. We'll be handing you source code that you can plug straight into your own applications.

Why ANSI C?

Many books on C make certain assumptions about the platform you are using. Some books cover specific compilers or operating systems; an obvious example would be a book covering Windows programming or Borland C++. (It gets worse—some books only cover certain versions of certain compilers!) Sometimes it's more subtle, such as the assumption that you are using the ASCII collating sequence. This is particularly frustrating for those of us who are forced, through no fault of our own, to use EBCDIC occasionally.

In this book, we discuss ANSI C almost entirely because, by adhering to standard C, we maximize the portability of our advice and our source code. This book is not intended just for Windows C programmers or just DOS C programmers or just UNIX C programmers, but for *everyone*. We'll be looking at binary trees you can use on your platform, no matter what that platform may be. We'll be looking at natural language processing that you can use in your LE/370 programs, your UNIX programs, or your Windows programs. Or all three together. Or some totally different platform. And we'll be looking at sorting techniques that work for you, no matter where you do your work. As long as you have an ANSI C compiler, we're in business.

It's not always possible, however, to write your entire program in ANSI C. There are always going to be irritating customers who insist on your program performing devious and unholy tricks such as—ahem—clearing the screen. The ANSI C standard doesn't even require that you *have* a screen, so clearing the screen in ANSI C is tricky. (In fact, there is no 100% portable solution to this problem.) Likewise, there is no completely portable way to get a keystroke from the user without echo (as when, for example, capturing a password). So there will often be times when you need to step outside the standard, and use implementation-specific extensions. C purists will balk at this, but it's inevitable for some applications. After all, although it's undoubtedly possible to write a word processing application entirely in ANSI C, I doubt whether it would sell very well. As a rule of thumb, then, be portable when you can, and be non-portable when you must. This is the approach we've adopted in this book. As much of the book as possible is written using ANSI C code. Where we've had to step outside the standard, we've drawn attention to that fact.

If you find our insistence on using the standard core of the language as much as possible rather limiting, you're right. It is. The code in this book, rather than being free to exploit all the various powerful options of one particular version of one particular compiler for one particular operating system, is restricted to only being suited to all the ANSI C compilers on all the operating systems in the world. We think we can live with that limitation.

By Murphy's Law or some corollary thereof, you will find that the very next time you write some non-portable code, not only will it be in a huge application, but also you'll have to port it to some totally alien platform the very next week. It would ease the task enormously if you could isolate non-portable code for easy replacement when it's time to move platforms. So we'll be discussing ways to do this, taking socket programming as our example.

What Platforms Does This Book Cover?

All of them!

This book, for the most part, describes programming in ANSI C. (Strictly, ANSI/ISO C.) Therefore, it covers all platforms and none. You will find very little platform-specific source code in this book. Most particularly, this book does not cover Windows or UNIX programming, although it does provide useful transferable knowledge and plug-in source code that can be used on those platforms (and many more). Also, we briefly discuss the Linux kernel, multi-threading, multi-processing, and embedded systems.

About the Source Code in This Book

Almost all the source code in this book will work on any ANSI C compiler for any platform, provided sufficient resources (such as memory) are available at runtime. There are a few exceptions, such as the portability case study previously mentioned.

I've already touched on the difference between interested and lazy reading. We've designed the source code to be useful to you in either case. If you're interested, you'll find plenty to absorb you here, and you'll win lots of kudos from us. If you lack the time or energy to be interested, simply study the driver code, see how to use the functions, rip out the driver, and you have a library you can use right away. (Actually, you shouldn't even need to rip out the driver because it will be in a separate file to the library code. But, if at all possible, you should at least study the driver to see how the library works.)

Code Quality

It's not unusual, in books of this nature, to see demonstration code such as this:

```
void cat3(char *s, char *t, char *u)
{
  strcat(s, t);
  strcat(s, u);
}
```

This is fine as far as it goes and, undoubtedly, will work much of the time. What if one or more of the pointers is NULL, though? This could easily be checked, but the author hasn't bothered, thinking perhaps that pedantic (that is, cautious) readers can insert the validation themselves.

The authors of this book believe that caution is a virtue, not a sin. Our aim has been to write solid, reliable, robust code, without compromising on performance. How far we have succeeded in this respect, only time will tell. If you have any comments about the quality of the code in this book, or if you find any bugs, please let us know.

In the case of a discrepancy between the source in the book and the source on the CD, believe the CD. We've tried very hard to make sure that the code in the book is correct, but people are people and mistakes happen. The code on the CD has, at least, been compiled and tested. Ever tried getting a C compiler to read a piece of paper? It's not easy.

How This Book Is Organized

It is our hope that this book will help you to make the leap from Intermediate C programmer to Advanced C programmer, by showing you a few things (okay, a lot of things) you didn't know before—things that distinguish the expert from the professional.

We've divided the book into three parts—"The C Language Revisited," "Data Organization," and "Advanced Topics."

In Part I, "The C Language Revisited," we examine some areas of C programming that should be obvious but, all too often, aren't. We start off by visiting some of the thorny coding style issues and technical traps that can cause many an argument in a development team, looking particularly at what's important and what's merely interesting about particular programming styles.

So let's examine this area of programming styles and standards more closely, and try to identify which aspects of programming style *are* important and which are simply irrelevant, and perhaps we can arbitrate a peaceful settlement to the Holy Wars (or at least a cease-fire). We'll start off with a topic dear to every C programmer's heart: bracing styles.

Bracing Styles

There are four widely recognized bracing styles in use in the C community today. No doubt you will have your own opinion as to which one is "right." Let's look at each in turn.

1TBS

1TBS is an abbreviation for the One True Bracing Style. It's given such a fanciful name because it is the style used by Kernighan and Ritchie in their classic text, *The C Programming Language*. Kernighan and Ritchie (K&R from now on, throughout this book) are considered "demigods" by C programmers, so the One True Bracing Style has a suitably religious tone. Some people prefer to call it K&R style, or kernel style. Proponents typically use indents of eight spaces, but this is not universal.

Here's a code snippet illustrating 1TBS:

```
for(j = 0; j < MAX_LEN; j++) {
        foo();
}
```

The most commonly suggested advantage of this style is its economy with vertical space. The downside is that it can be hard to spot the {, tucked away at the end of a line.

Allman

Eric Allman wrote BSD utilities in this style, which is therefore called "BSD style" by some aficionados. Indents for Allman style are usually, but not always, four spaces.

```
for(j = 0; j < MAX_LEN; j++)
{
    foo();
}
```

This style (and those that follow) uses more vertical space than 1TBS. Supporters of this style argue that it makes the scope of a block statement clear, and associates it visually with its control statement.

Whitesmith

Once upon a time there was a C compiler called Whitesmiths C. Its documentation supplied examples formatted like this:

```
for(j = 0; j < MAX_LEN; j++)
    {
    foo( );
    }
```

This has the advantage of associating the braces more closely with the code they enclose and delimit, at the expense of making them slightly harder to find when visually scanning the source. Four-space indents are common.

GNU

The Free Software Foundation's GNU writers (particularly in the GNU EMACS code) use a hybrid of Allman and Whitesmith. (By the way, GNU stands for "GNU's Not UNIX," and EMACS is derived from "Editing MACroS"—it's a UNIX text editor, but to call it *just* a UNIX text editor would be like calling a computer an adding machine.)

```
for(j = 0; j < MAX_LEN; j++)
    {
        foo( );
    }
```

It's hard to say whether this combines the advantages of Allman and Whitesmith, or the disadvantages.

It's tempting to ask the question, "Which is the right way?" but of course they are *all* correct. The most important thing is not to mix them all into one program. Pick a style and stick to it. It may not even be up to you. If you are working in a formal development environment, you are almost certainly working to some kind of coding standards document, usually an authoritarian treatise with little in the way of common sense to back it up. Nevertheless, it's a lot easier to read code that's all in one style than code that uses several different styles simultaneously. Consider the following ghastly code, which takes mixed styles quite close to the limit:

```
for(j = 0; j < MAX_LEN; j++) {
    for(k = 0; k < MAX_WIDTH; k++)
        {
        for(m = 0; m < MAX_HEIGHT; m++)
        {
            for(n = 0; n < MAX_TIME; n++)
                {
```

```
                foo(j, k, m, n);
                }
        }
        }
}
```

The compiler will be quite happy with that code, but you shouldn't have to put up with it, and nor should your fellow team members. So if your guidelines suggest a style, stick to them, and try to persuade your less perceptive team members to do the same (if they were perceptive, they'd be reading this book too, so you wouldn't need to tell them). If your guidelines don't mention a house style for braces, they should. It doesn't really matter *which* style they suggest. Whichever it is, use that style for that project, and your fellow programmers (and maintenance team!) will love you forever.

If you aren't working on a team project and therefore have no guidelines, that's fine. Just pick the bracing style you feel most comfortable with, and use it consistently.

While we're on the subject of braces, consider a `for`, `do`, `while`, `if`, or `else`, with a single statement following it:

```
if(condition)
    foo();
```

This is, of course, quite legal. Now consider the following modification to the code:

```
if(condition)
    foo();
    bar();
```

Note the indentation. So, did the programmer intend the new function call to be dependent on the condition, or not? It's impossible to tell. For this reason, standards documents often recommend that you *always* use block statement syntax:

```
if(condition)
{
    foo();
}
```

This technique undoubtedly helps prevent bugs. Nevertheless, many C programmers think it's too verbose. In my own code, I tend to use the full block statement syntax even for single statements because I think it's clearer; in code fragments in this book, I'll often omit optional braces in the interest of economy with vertical space.

Use of Whitespace

Bracing styles aren't the only battlefield on which Holy Wars are fought. The way in which you use whitespace greatly affects the readability of your code. If you thought there must surely be one whitespace style that everyone considers to maximize your code's readability, I'm afraid you'd be mistaken. There are almost as many whitespace styles as there are C programmers.

Indentation

What are the "right" settings for tab and indent? The most common choices are two, three, four, eight, and no columns. I hope you'll agree that we can dismiss the zero option as rendering the code completely unreadable, but all the others are perfectly readable choices. Most programmers start by using the default tab setting, which is often eight columns wide (but not necessarily; this depends on your text editor). After a time this begins to look a little stretched, especially with multiple indentation levels:

```
int foo(int arr[A][B][C])
{
        int a, b, c, total = 0;
        for(a = 0; a < A; a++)
        {
                for(b = 0; b < B; b++)
                {
                        for(c = 0; c < C; c++)
                        {
                                total += arr[a][b][c];
                        }
                }
        }

        return total;
}
```

Therefore, many people drop down to four spaces:

```
int foo(int bar[A][B][C])
{
    int a, b, c, total = 0;
    for(a = 0; a < A; a++)
    {
        for(b = 0; b < B; b++)
        {
```

```
            for(c = 0; c < C; c++)
            {
                total += bar[a][b][c];
            }
        }
    }

    return total;
}
```


This was my own preferred choice for many years. More recently, I've found that two spaces are perfectly adequate for my needs. This was a setting from which I would have recoiled not so long ago. I got the two-space habit when I started regularly posting Usenet articles. Not only was the tab setting on my newsreader far too wide for source code, but also I didn't like the idea of embedding tabs in Usenet postings, so I used the spacebar instead. Once that decision was made, I rapidly discovered that pressing the space character twelve times for a three-level indent was not a good use of my time, so I started using a two-space indent. To my surprise, I found that I liked it better than four spaces, so now I use it all the time.

A three-space indent seems a little unnatural to many C programmers. Nevertheless, it is used at some sites and doesn't look too bad.

Which is the *correct* setting for your tab and indent? You're ahead of me, I know—there is no one correct level. Unless your project coding standards stipulate the setting you should use, pick the level you think looks most readable, use it consistently throughout your program, and be prepared to review your opinion over time.

Tabs and Mainframe Compilers

Some mainframe C compilers don't respond well to embedded tab characters in source files. If you do find yourself trapped in a dinosaur pen, it may be worth your while to invest time (or money) in a software tool to replace tabs with spaces. In fact, you may already have such a tool. For example, Microsoft Visual C++'s editor has this capability.

Whitespace Around Tokens

It's a good idea to be creative in your use of whitespace to enhance the readability of your code. Again, there is no single *right* way to use whitespace, but there are plenty of wrong ways. Here's an example of poor use of whitespace:

```
#include   <stdlib.h>
#include    <stdio.h>
#define   P    printf
```

```
#define   I      atoi
int main(int a,char*v
[]){int r=5, i;if(a>1
) r=I(v[1]); if(r<=0)
r=5;if(r%2==0)++r;for
(i=0; i<r*r; P(i/r==(
3*r)/2-(i%r+1)||i/r==
r/2 - i%r||i/r==r/2+i
%r||i/r==i%r-r/2?"*":
" "),i++, i % r==0?P(
"\n") : 0);return 0;}
```

(In case you're wondering, I didn't pinch that from the International Obfuscated C Coding Competition. I wrote it myself, so that I can post it in IRC [Internet Relay Chat] whenever someone poses the rather common homework question to which it relates. Working out what it does is left as an exercise for you. Running it first is cheating.)

Probably the most effective way to increase the readability of code is to place whitespace around binary operators. Consider

```
a=b+c*d/e%f;
```

and

```
a = b + c * d / e % f;
```

Which do you find easier to read? So do I.

Some people also like to place whitespace around parentheses:

```
for ( foo = 0; foo < bar; foo++ )
```

and even brackets:

```
a [ baz ] = 0;
```

Personally, I think this is an over-zealous use of whitespace, but it is a style you will see occasionally.

Cosmetic Code Fixes

For some people it's very tempting, when maintaining code you didn't write yourself, to adjust bracing styles and whitespace to suit the project guidelines or even your own preferences. I've never done this myself, of course (at least, not when anyone's looking).

Unless you have been asked by a project manager specifically to do this, it's probably a bad idea. It's often useful to be able to compare two versions of a source file; the current version, and the previous, relatively bug-free, version, to see what's changed and therefore where the bug might be. If somebody's been playing with whitespace, you get a lot of false positives, which slows you down and is therefore counterproductive (not to mention downright annoying). If you don't keep revision histories of your code, it doesn't really matter, of course, but it does mean you should consider introducing a revision history or version control system.

It's perhaps worth mentioning at this point that there is a utility called `indent`, which can format code in a consistent manner. If the team can agree on a style, and always runs code through `indent` before checking it into version control, much whitespace pain can be avoided. The `indent` utility is included in Linux distributions. You can find the source code at `ftp://ftp.gnu.org/gnu/indent` (but check `http://www.gnu.org` first to find out whether there is a local mirror site you can use instead. It will be quicker to download that way).

Structured Programming

Ever since Djikstra published his famous paper, "Goto Statement Considered Harmful," people have been fighting over structured programming techniques. A complete description of structured programming is beyond the scope of this book, but there are certain issues that regularly crop up in coding standards documents, so let's take a look at them.

goto

It isn't just Djikstra who complains about `goto`. On page 65 of K&R2, we find Brian Kernighan's lament that "C provides the infinitely-abusable `goto` statement." (In case you're wondering how I know it was him rather than Dennis Ritchie, the general consensus is that most of the first part of the book—the tutorial section—is Kernighan's work, with Ritchie doing most or all of the reference section.)

Using `goto` can make the control flow of your code seriously difficult to follow. Source code containing many `goto` statements is often graphically described as "spaghetti code," which is why most project coding standards documents deprecate it.

It's usually fairly easy, given a few moments thought, to find an alternative to `goto`. This process will frequently involve using an extra status variable, which is why programmers of embedded systems use `goto` more than the average—memory can be extremely tight in embedded systems.

The best reason usually given for using goto is that it enables you to escape from deeply nested code quickly in the event of an error. This justification is perfectly defensible, so we're not going to be dogmatic and say never use goto. Nevertheless, it's probably wisest to look first at other solutions. If you do decide that goto is for you, bear in mind that it's generally easier to follow control flow *down* the code, so try to ensure that you jump *forward* through the code, not backward.

break

The break statement is very useful within switch statements. Some people also like to use it within loops, to provide early exit from the loop. This isn't a particularly structured use of the statement, which is why I never use break in this way. I'm not going to make the mistake of saying that early exit from loops is the Wrong Thing, though. I know of many highly skilled and thoughtful programmers who are of the opinion that your code should reflect your intention, so if your intention is to break out of the loop early, your code should show that intention clearly. It's a powerful argument, which happens not to fit into the way I like to structure my programs. If you are going to use break in loops, you might consider adding a short explanatory comment to the source, especially if the code is tight.

continue

Like break, continue can be used to modify the flow of loops in a way that would have a structured programming purist breaking out in coughing fits (although it's not as bad as the ALTER statement in COBOL, which alters the destination of a goto!). Unlike break, continue doesn't have the virtue of being associated with the switch statement. So, what good is it?

I only use continue in empty loops as an indication to the maintenance programmer that the loop is deliberately empty, like so:

```
while(*s++ = *t++)
{
  continue;
}
```

I'd like to recommend that you restrict your use of continue in the same way, but I can't. Proponents of the continue statement put forward cases like this one:

```
while(fgets(buffer, sizeof buffer, fp) != NULL)
{
  if(strchr(";#/", buffer[0]) != NULL)
  {
    /* it's a comment line - starts with a
     * semicolon, hash, or slash, so skip
```

```
    * it and go on to the next line
    */
   continue;
  }

  /* large block of code goes here */
}
```

Here, the `continue` statement simplifies the code by dismissing an unusual condition immediately and getting straight on with the next iteration of the loop, avoiding the necessity to add an `else` and an extra level of indentation to the large block of code following the `if` block. So, again, there are perfectly valid reasons both for using the `continue` statement and for not using it.

Let common sense prevail; before using `continue`, stop and think "Am I using this statement because it's quicker and easier than adopting a more structured approach, or am I genuinely contributing to the readability of the program?" If the latter case is true, by all means use `continue`.

while(1)

This is a common construct. Almost invariably, its loop body contains a break or return or even a call to `exit()`. So the loop header is saying "this loop runs forever" and the loop body contradicts it. Clearly the loop body is going to win every time, but that's not really the point. If we are in the business of making our code easy to read, we can do that by documenting the purpose of the `while` loop, in the loop header, by a suitable choice of termination condition. For example, we might write

```
int more = GetFirstItem(&foo);
while(more)
{
  Process(&foo);
  more = GetNextItem(&foo);
}
```

rather than

```
if(GetFirstItem(&foo))
  while(1)
  {
    Process(&foo);
    if(!GetNextItem(&foo))
      break;
  }
```

which, although trying to be terse, actually takes one more line of code than the long-winded example using a status variable.

Sometimes, we really and truly need an infinite loop, which is genuinely intended to run until the dusk of time (or at least until someone unplugs the microwave oven). Under these circumstances, of course, `while(1)` is perfectly reasonable. There is a case, however, for using

```
for(;;)
{
  /* ... */
}
```

because this will almost certainly not generate the diagnostic that some compilers provide for `while(1)`—something along the lines of "conditional expression is constant."

I had to say "almost certainly not" because an ANSI C compiler can generate as many diagnostics as it likes, including

```
"warning: line 37: your mandarin needs a new coat
➥of yellow paint and two coffee cups."
```

or, more worryingly:

```
"warning: line 1: you have had this compiler for WEEKS now,
➥so why not buy an upgrade? You know you want to."
```

as long as it correctly compiles correct code and correctly diagnoses syntax errors and constraint violations.

return

One of the tenets of structured programming is that routines should have one entry point and one exit point. It's easy, in C, to construct a routine with many exit points. Unfortunately, it's also quite easy to construct a routine like this (don't worry about trying to work out what it means! Its only purpose is illustrative):

```
char *foo(char *s, char *t)
{
  switch(*s)
  {
    case 0:
      return s;
    case 1:
      return t;
```

```
    case 2:
      return t - s;
    case 4:
      return s - t;
    case 8:
      return s + sizeof(long);
    case 16:
      return t + sizeof(double);
    default:
      break;
  }
}
```

It doesn't take a genius to spot that, in the default case, no value is returned. In a much larger function, however, with many more branches of control flow, maybe even a genius wouldn't see the error. Fortunately, most compilers will warn about this, but it isn't a constraint violation or a syntax error, so the Standard doesn't *require* a diagnostic message. If, however, the calling function uses the return value of the called function, where no return value was actually provided, the behavior is undefined. Furthermore, functions with multiple `return` statements are harder to read than functions that just have one `return` statement at the end.

Of course, real life is never that simple, and there are good reasons to have multiple `return` statements within some functions. For example, a routine for searching a binary tree can be written much more simply if we allow multiple return values:

```
TREE *SearchTree(TREE *node, char *s)
{
  int diff;
  if(node == NULL)
    return NULL;
  if(s == NULL)
    return NULL;

  diff = strcmp(s, node->data);

  if(diff == 0)
    return node;
  else if(diff < 0)
    return SearchTree(node->left, s);
  return SearchTree(node->right, s);
}
```

It's pretty easy to follow the flow of control here. Comments would help a little, but the code is more or less self-explanatory (at least from the point of view of control flow. If you're not happy with the concept of a function calling itself, don't panic—we will be discussing recursion later on). In fact, this code is much shorter than the equivalent code with only one `return` statement.

My own binary tree library does in fact have just one `return` statement per function, perhaps because I'm a closet purist. There are good arguments on both sides, so use common sense as your guide.

Insane Function Pointers

A few projects ago, I was working at a site where the coding standards said "don't use `goto`." The project was a quotations system for an insurance company, and consisted to some extent of rewriting old QBASIC programs in C, but the programmers didn't have access to the QBASIC programs. The actuaries did, and they translated the programs into specifications. The actuaries said they didn't want to make any assumptions about the language features available in C, so they unstitched all the QBASIC program's `for` loops. Thus, instead of saying, for example, "Loop through the clients, working out their retirement ages from their dates of birth" they would say something like

1.4.9.3	Set `ClientID` to 1
1.4.9.4	Work out retirement age of Client with index of `ClientID`, using date of birth and system date
1.4.9.5	Store retirement age in `RetAge` field of `Client` with index of `ClientID`
1.4.9.6	Add 1 to `ClientID`
1.4.9.7	If `ClientID` exceeds number of clients for this quotation, proceed from step 1.4.9.9
1.4.9.8	Proceed from step 1.4.9.4

Furthermore, since the actuaries were experts in actuarial work (and we programmers weren't) we were under strict instructions to follow the specifications exactly. Now, most of us thought the actuaries were just messing around (and indeed one of them confessed to me later that that was *exactly* what they were doing), so naturally we ignored our strict instructions and rolled code such as this into a proper loop. One rather pedantic programmer (usually the best kind, but not always!) had a different idea. He had a relatively simple spec that happened to contain a lot of this kind of actuarial playfulness, and decided to obey both tenets ("Follow the spec exactly," "don't use `goto`") to the letter. Wherever he met a `goto` statement in the spec, he wrote a function to handle the code for that loop. The function would return a pointer to the next function to be executed!

The driver for all this code looked positively fiendish. Debugging the code, and modifying it to meet changing requirements, were an educational experience. (The actual author of the code should have been debugging it, but of course he'd left the company by then.) Eventually, I resolved to map out the network of function pointers and document my findings in a diagram, which ended up being the third scariest diagram of my career.

Once I had diagrammed the code, it didn't seem quite so bad because at least we now had a clue where the code would jump next. But when an actuary showed me the original QBASIC program, I was startled to see how simple the code was, and how clearly and easily it could have been implemented using loops. Insane function pointers are tremendous fun to play with, but have no place in production code. (I have no problem with *sane* function pointers, though.)

All generalizations are false (including this one) but, even so, I'm going to make the general point that, the more structured your approach to programming, the fewer bugs you'll have. The more highly structured your code, the easier it is to read. Code that is easy to read is easier to understand than code that is difficult to read. Code that is easy to understand is more likely to be modified correctly than code that is difficult to understand, and hence will have fewer bugs.

Initialization

C has hidden depths. Even something as apparently simple as initialization can be tricky to get right. It's not just a matter of style; portable initialization is not as easy as it seems.

Multiple Definitions on One Line

As you know, C allows you to define many objects of the same type, and pointers to objects of that type, on one logical line. You've probably become used to doing this, and I'm not going to make the mistake of asking you to stop doing it. I invite you to consider, however, that there are advantages to defining one variable per line. Consider this code:

```
int foo(char *s, char *t, size_t len)
{
  float PiTo2DecimalPlaces = 3.14, q, CircleRadius = 1.0;

  /*                   input file    output file */
  FILE *               fpIn,         fpOut;

  /* ... */
}
```

First, if we want to modify q's type to (say) `double`, we end up needing to put it on a separate line anyway, so why not put it on a line of its own to start with? Second, it's hard to spot among its long-named neighbors. Third, the bug in `fpOut`'s type (it should be `FILE *` but is actually just `FILE`) happens all too often.

Initialization at Definition

C allows you to choose, when defining an object, whether to initialize it. Apart from the obvious benefit of saving you the trouble of giving the variable a start value later on, initializing the variable at definition time gives you the important subsidiary advantage of ensuring that the function begins execution in a known state. For example, setting a pointer to `NULL` at definition might not stop your functions from having pointer bugs in them, but it will certainly make those bugs easier to find and fix.

On the other hand, if you don't give a value to a variable at definition, the compiler is much better placed to detect subsequent usage of that variable before a value has been assigned to it in the code. Also, some compilers will produce a warning if you assign a value to a variable that is then subsequently overwritten by another assignment, as in:

```
int a = 0;

for(a = 0; a < 10; a++)
```

Experienced programmers like to get a clean compilation whenever possible because even trivial warnings (like the one the preceding code would generate), if allowed to proliferate, soon obscure other, more important warnings, making them harder to find and rectify.

So yet again, it's unwise to be dogmatic. A mixed strategy is probably best. Certainly it's a good idea to initialize pointers to `NULL`. Also, the convenience of initializing an array or struct using `{0}` is not to be underestimated. It's quite common for programmers to "zero out" an array or a `struct` like this:

```
struct FOO foo;

memset(&foo, 0, sizeof foo);
```

Unfortunately, this is not guaranteed to have the desired effect if the structure definition of `FOO` contains floating point numbers (`float`, `double`, `long double`) or pointers, where the representation of zero is not guaranteed to be all-bits-zero. For example, there's nothing in the C Standard to prevent an implementation using the bit pattern 0x80000000, under the hood, to represent a `NULL` pointer, provided that appropriate conversions are made for code such as


```
char *foo = 0;
```

Our oddball compiler can detect such assignments and initializations, and load the pointer with the appropriate bit pattern, 0x80000000, behind the scenes. Unfortunately, it *can't* intercept `memset` in the same way; the ANSI C standard doesn't permit this. Much the same line of reasoning applies to floating point numbers.

Most compilers don't need to indulge in this kind of trickery, but you have no guarantees that your compiler (or possibly the next compiler on which you'll build your code) is obliging enough to use all-bits-zero for 0.0 and `NULL`. Fortunately, there is a simple way to initialize all members of a `struct` to their appropriate default values.

```
struct FOO
{
  double d;
  int num;
  double e;
  float f;
  char *p;
};

struct FOO foo = {0};
```

When you initialize a `struct` in this way (and the same applies to arrays), the initialization is incomplete. Here's what the Standard has to say about partial initializations:

"The initialization shall occur in initializer list order, each initializer provided for a particular subobject overriding any previously listed initializer for the same subobject; all subobjects that are not initialized explicitly shall be initialized implicitly the same as objects that have static storage duration." (C9X Standard, section 6.7.8, Jan 1999 draft).

Translation: in the definition

```
struct FOO foo = {0};
```

`foo.d` picks up the 0 in the braces (which is converted to 0.0), `foo.num` gets initialized to 0, `foo.e` gets initialized to 0.0, `foo.f` gets initialized to 0.0F, and `foo.p` gets initialized to NULL, regardless of the internal representation of floating point numbers and pointers. Thus we have a totally portable technique for initializing structs and arrays.

Statics and Globals

There are two kinds of file scope identifiers: file scope identifiers with internal linkage (static objects and functions) and file scope identifiers with external linkage (extern objects and functions). The latter are commonly known as *globals* (although the only mention of global variables that I can find in the ANSI Standard is in connection with the floating point environment's flags and modes). Project coding standards documents frequently recommend or even insist that global variables are not used, and programmers just as frequently ignore those recommendations. Who is right?

Note

In C, an object is a named region of storage, variables being the most obvious example. They should not to be confused with C++'s class instances, which are also called objects.

On this occasion, I'm going to cheer for the standards document. Here's just one example of why. It's regrettably common for applications developers, in the teeth of a Force 9 deadline, to throw structure and modularity to the winds in an effort to get the code in on time. The result is often that very long functions are produced.

Consider the implications of a particularly long function using a fistful of global variables. The code was written just before the last deadline, and is being maintained just before the next one. A new calculation is needed. The programmer needs a new integer, so he adds one at the top of the function: `double PresentValueOfFutureProfits = 0.0`. He uses this variable in a couple of places, in accordance with the program specification's new requirements.

What he fails to notice, not having visited this code before, is that his local definition of `PresentValueOfFutureProfits` has inadvertently masked out a variable with file scope and external linkage (a global), visible in the same source file. That variable happened to be a `double` too. He didn't spot it, and the code went to unit test, which it passed with flying colors. The integration test came and went with the program's reputation intact.

Fortunately, the bug was eventually caught—in User Acceptance Testing! It took the better part of a day to track down the actual cause. Once it was found, the fix was trivial (change the name of the local variable, although even then a review of the function's version control history had to be conducted to ensure that *only* the correct references to the name were changed). I'm not making this up—I was that maintenance programmer. I won't trouble you with the details of my reaction when I discovered that I'd been bitten by a global variable (explicitly forbidden by the project's coding standards); I'll leave you to guess.

If you must use variables with file scope (whether with internal or external linkage), consider restricting access to them by writing access functions. But before you do, there's something else to consider.

Problems with Re-use

Let's take a simple stack library. Our design is very simple—we want a push, a pop, and something to push items onto and from which we can pop those items. Because we have two functions that access the stack, we need to share information between them. Enter the file scope variable. Because we don't need to share the information with other functions, however, we put `push()` and `pop()` into their own source file, which contains no other functions but these two, and make our stack `static`. This is good practice in terms of information hiding.

```
#define MAX_STACK 1024

int stack[MAX_STACK];
int stackptr;

int push(int i)
{
  int failed = 1;
  if(stackptr < MAX_STACK - 1)
  {
    stack[stackptr++] = i;
    failed = 0;
  }
  return failed;
}

int pop(int *i)
{
```

```
  int failed = 1;
  if(stackptr > 0)
  {
    *i = stack[--stackptr];
    failed = 0;
  }
  return failed;
}
```

And hey, presto! One stack library. Unfortunately, it has several problems, of which just one is of concern to us at present—programs can only use this library to create and manipulate *one* stack. There's only one stack pointer, and there's only one stack so we can only use one stack at a time. If our programs require more than one stack at once, we must find a better way. Of course, human ingenuity is unbounded, and it wouldn't be too difficult to write a stack library that had complete data hiding and yet could handle multiple stacks. But it would be *more* difficult, and there are easier methods to do this using simple structure-passing techniques.

A further problem with `static` variables is that they can bite you in multithreaded environments. C doesn't support threading, but implementations frequently provide it. In a typical threaded environment, `static` variables are at risk from being accessed and updated by more than one thread at the same time.

None of this is intended to discourage you from using static variables, but it is important to remember that there are issues with statics other than simple scoping rules.

Identifier Names

Naming conventions are frequently the source of heated debate. I don't propose to mandate any particular convention, since that would simply be another salvo in the Holy War. The following observations are based on experience, but other experienced programmers have different viewpoints.

Length

The length of an identifier name is, of course, proportional to its descriptiveness. If you plan on using a variable a lot, it's a good idea to give it a meaningful name, and that generally means a long name. If, on the other hand, you just need a simple loop counter, a long name is probably unnecessary. Many people use `i`, `j`, and `k` for loop counters. If they are simple loops, this is fine. If you are populating an array of array of array of some `struct`, however, you might well want to choose more helpful names for the loop counters, to give a reminder of what each index of the array actually means.

There are limitations on the *significant* length of identifiers. You can make identifiers as long as you like, but they are only guaranteed to be significant to 31 characters. Actually, 31 is plenty. The names of identifiers with external linkage, however, are only *guaranteed* to be unique to six characters. And it gets worse—there is no guarantee that the linker can distinguish external identifiers by case. Thus, a linker may well consider:

```
int NotableValue;
int notablevalue;
int NoTableFound;
int NotAbleToExecute;
int NotABlankSpace;
```

to all refer to the same identifier. This is a serious limitation, which has been alleviated to some extent in the latest release of the ANSI/ISO C Standard. Until such time as C99 compilers become commonplace, however, it's yet another reason to avoid external linkage wherever possible. Note that this limitation applies to external identifiers in general, not just variables. Thus, function names not qualified with the `static` keyword are only guaranteed to be significant to six characters.

Intelligibility

When choosing a name, bear three things in mind. You are going to have to type it a lot. That shadowy figure, the maintenance programmer, is going to have to read it a lot. And, of course, you and he both need to know what it means. Therefore, it makes sense to choose names that are easy to read, easy to type, and unambiguous in meaning.

C is traditionally a lowercase language, but there is nothing to stop you from using mixed case. Here are a few common styles:

```
all_lower_case_with_underscores_to_separate_words
lowerCaseFirstLetterThenMixedCase
AllMixedCase
UPPERCASENOSEPARATOR
UPPER_CASE_WITH_SEPARATOR
```

Although C does distinguish between cases, using identifier names distinguished *only* by case is problematical. Quite apart from the inability of some linkers to distinguish case, there is the problem of readability:

```
int foo(int Foo)
{
  int fOo, FoO, foO, FoO = FOO;
  /* ... */
}
```

This may have a place in the IOCCC, but not in production code!

Smtmes it's ncssry to abbrvte idntfrs, often by omitting vwls. For example, the best name for a variable may be rather long:

```
double PresentValueOfFutureProfitsCalculatedGross;
double PresentValueOfFutureProfitsCalculatedNet;
```

Quite apart from the fact that these names are so long as to be practically untypeable, they fall foul of the rule that only 31 characters are guaranteed to be significant.

The abbreviations

```
double PrsntVlfFtrPrftsClcltdGrss;
double PrsntVlfFtrPrftsClcltdNt;
```

certainly disambiguate the two identifiers from the compiler's point of view, but have we really improved matters? I don't think so. These variable names look positively ghastly.

These are better, even though slightly longer, abbreviations:

```
double PresentValFutureProfitsGross;
double PresentValFutureProfitsNet;
```

although they are still a little too long for comfort. In this case, it would be perfectly reasonable to shorten them to

```
double GrossPVFP;
double NetPVFP;
```

because PVFP is a recognized abbreviation. By all means use abbreviations recognized within your application domain when appropriate. A good general principle is that different variables in the code should be easily distinguishable to the reader.

Reserved Names

What is wrong with this header file?

```
#ifndef __RAGBAG_H__
#define __RAGBAG_H__
extern double strength;
extern char memorandum[1024];
extern int isotope;
extern float tolerance;
#endif
```

Give up?

It may come as a shock when I tell you that all the identifiers in that header file, including the symbolic constants, violate the ANSI standard!

Because C has so few keywords, and a relatively small standard library, many programmers commonly assume that they can call their identifiers almost anything they like. This is not quite true.

First, any identifier beginning with a leading underscore and then followed either by an uppercase letter or another underscore is reserved for use by the implementation. This is to provide the implementation with a way to define functions and variables without getting in your way and invading your namespace. It's a really good idea to stay out of the implementation's namespace too! The safest course is not to start any identifier with an underscore. Trailing_ underscores_ are_ okay_ though_.

Implementations typically put inclusion guards around their headers, which is a good thing. It's a good thing for user-programmers, too. Regrettably, the habit of copying the implementor's `__NAME_H__` convention has become widespread. (Implementors are allowed to use leading underscores. The whole point of the restriction is to prevent your identifiers from clashing with those of the implementation.) By all means use trailing underscores but, if you want your program to be portable, don't use a leading underscore.

This is a good way to provide inclusion guards:

```
#ifndef NAME_H__
#define NAME_H__
/* Header stuff goes here */
/* ... */
#endif
```

But what about the declarations in that header file? Why aren't they legal?

It's all to do with extensibility. The ANSI committee recognizes that languages grow or die. The recent update to the C standard, for example, introduces several powerful new techniques (which we cover later in the book). Specifically, the committee wanted to make room for new functions in the standard library, while minimizing the possibility of breaking existing code. To that end, they reserve certain letter combinations that are particularly likely to form the start of new function names. For example, anything beginning with "str" is reserved because, although there are already plenty of standard library functions beginning with "str", there is certainly much more useful functionality that could be provided for string-handling. To allow for this, the letter combination "str" is reserved. The same applies to "is" and "to" (to allow `<ctype.h>` to be extended), "mem" (for extra memory manipulation functions), "SIG" (for new signals) and a number of other prefixes.

Here is an abridged list of all the identifiers you *can't* use. In the interests of space, I've omitted most of the standard library functions and other identifiers, in the firm belief that anyone clever enough to buy this book is also clever enough not to use those symbols. But I have included some of the weirder, less commonly known ones.

Note

I've used regular expression syntax to further shorten the list. [A-Z] means any character in the uppercase alphabet; [0-9] means any digit; * means anything at all, and so on.

So, without further ado, *don't use these identifiers*:

```
E[0-9]*        E[A-Z]*        is[a-z]*
LC[A-Z]*       mem[a-z]*      NDEBUG
Offsetof       raise          SIG[A-Z]*
str[a-z]*      to[a-z]*       wcs[a-z]*
_*
```

And what if you do? What if you have a variable with external linkage, called `total`? Where's the harm in that?

Strictly speaking, the harm is that your program can no longer be guaranteed to work. It might look as if it's working, and it might even sail through its testing phase, but the C standard doesn't *guarantee* it to work at any point.

Prefixes: the "Transylvanian Heresy"

A few years ago Charles Simonyi, who later became a notable programmer for Microsoft, devised a prefix-based naming convention that came to be called "Hungarian notation" in his honor. His idea was to give each identifier a prefix according to the sort of thing it represented. Microsoft later adapted this idea, giving each identifier a prefix indicating its data type. Thus, `ints` would be prefixed with `n`, long `ints` with `nl`, arrays of `char` would start `ca`, and strings (arrays of `char` terminated by a null character) would start `sz`. These names could get quite bizarre. For example, `lpszFoo` would mean "Foo, which is a long (meaning 32-bit or 'far', under Intel/DOS segmented memory architecture) pointer to string terminated by zero (the null character)."

This convention gave you the advantage of being able to identify a variable's type simply by looking at its name, without having to look up its definition. Unfortunately, not only did it lead to completely unpronounceable names, but also it made the task of changing a variable's type considerably harder. In Windows 3.1, `int`s are 16 bits wide. If you started off with an `int` but discovered, after passing this `int` to 30 or 40 functions, that an `int` would not, after all, be big enough for your purposes, you'd have to change not only your variable's type, but also its name, in 30 or 40 functions!

Hungarian notation fell into disuse, except by some die-hard Windows programmers, because it was impractical. (That's the cue for 30 or 40 angry emails from around the world assuring me it's still used and loved.) No doubt there are a few sites where it is still extant, but most people have now abandoned it. Type prefixes are, generally speaking, a bad idea because they bind the variable too closely to its type. For a similar reason, experienced programmers use this construct for `malloc` (where `T` is some type):


```
T *p;
p = malloc(sizeof *p);
```

rather than

```
T *p;
p = malloc(sizeof(T));
```

With the second technique, changing the type of `p` introduces an inconsistency that needs to be fixed, a problem that simply does not arise with the first example.

One relic of Hungarian notation that has survived is the practice of preceding a pointer with `p`, a pointer to pointer with `pp`, and so on, so that a pointer to pointer to a variable of type `FOO` might be defined as

```
FOO **ppFoo;
```

I'll leave you to make up your own mind whether this is a good idea or a bad one.

Naming Variables

The name of a variable should reflect its purpose. By long-standing convention, most sites accept that for loop counters used in small, tight loops, it's perfectly all right to use `i`, `j`, `k`, `m`, `n`. The letter `l` is best left out of that list because it's too easy to confuse with the digit 1, and `o` is best left unused for a similar reason. Since `p` is often used for a scratch pointer, it's best not to use it for loop counters. In graphics programs, it's not uncommon to see loops controlled by `x` and `y`.

For more persistent variables, more meaningful names should be used. Well-chosen variable names are important (in fact, I actually believe that choosing good names for identifiers is one of the most important and difficult aspects of programming).

For variables representing properties (such as color, height, balance, and so on) the appropriate noun is the best choice. Sometimes you'll need a qualifier, such as BackColor and ForeColor.

Variables that represent Boolean states should take names that reflect which state is current. It's tempting to use the word "Is" for this purpose. And you can, provided you are using local variables. Thus, `IsInComment` might be a good variable name in a source parsing program, and would presumably have the value 1 if the program is currently looking at a character in a comment, and 0 otherwise.

Naming Constants

Most C programmers like to give symbolic constants uppercase names. I do too. Personally, though, I find names like, say, `DIRECTVIDEODISK` harder to read than `DIRECT_VIDEO_DISK`—when using all one case (either upper or lower), underscore separators aid clarity.

Constants, types, and macros are all traditionally named in UPPERCASE. In theory, this could mean they get confused with each other but, in practice (at least in my own experience) context always disambiguates them. Since I never use `#define` for type aliasing, I know that an uppercase token in a definition or declaration or cast, or as an operand to `sizeof`, is a type alias. Pretty well anything else in uppercase is a macro or a symbolic constant.

Naming Types

Nouns make the best type names. Try to pick a noun that correctly describes the type at the right level of generality. For example, `MAN` is a better type name than `SIMON`, and for most applications `PERSON` is better still.

Sometimes you'll want to use `typedefs` to simplify a declaration. In these cases, naming is still important but it's less important that the name be an easily readable noun. The name should at the very least reflect the purpose of the type.

For example, let's define a pointer to an array of 25 pointers to function taking `double` and pointer to function taking `char *` and returning `int`, and returning `int (!)`. The array will be used, say, for mortgage calculations.

First of all, let's define a type alias for a pointer to a function taking `char *` and returning `int`.

```
typedef int (*I_PF_STR)(char *);
```

Here, I've used `I_` to represent the return type of the function pointed to by an instance of the type, `PF` for pointer to function, and `_STR` to represent the parameter list. Shades of Hungarian notation—but then we are naming a *type*, not a variable, and a type's name should reflect its nature (which is why integers are called `int`s, not `zog`s).

Our problem has now become simplified—we want a pointer to an array of 25 pointers to functions taking `double` and `I_PF_STR`, and returning `int`. So let's define a type alias for this new kind of pointer to function:

```
typedef int (*I_PF_DBL_I_PF_STR)(double, I_PF_STR);
```

Now we want an array of 25 of those:

```
typedef I_PF_DBL_I_PF_STR MORTGAGE_ARRAY[25];
```

And now we want a pointer to that array:

```
MORTGAGE_ARRAY *p;
```

The intermediate type names are ghastly, aren't they? If we were going to use them a lot, we would spend much more time thinking about their names. Since they are only used for deriving the readable type at the end, they aren't so important.

Naming Macros

I've already covered the naming of symbolic constants; here I'm talking about function-like macros. If you must use them, please use uppercase for them. There are inherent dangers in using function-like macros; these can be mitigated to some extent by warning the programmer that he is in fact using a macro rather than a function. By the same token, don't use uppercase for function names (mixed case is fine). The case is a visual clue, and a highly effective one.

Naming Functions

Function naming is really important. Good function names can greatly enhance the readability of a program, and poor function names can greatly obscure an otherwise clear program.

A function is for doing things, so it seems natural to give it a verb in its name. Furthermore, functions rarely exist in a vacuum. Not only does a function do things, but frequently it does things *to something*. When this is the case, it is a good idea to include an appropriate noun in the function name too.

Thus, `strcpy()` is a good name for a function that copies a string.

My own preference is for the form `Verb[Noun]()`, using mixed case with the verb first, optionally followed by an appropriate noun (and maybe an adjective too). Some examples:

```
Wait();
PollTimer();
PrintReport();
CalcGrossInterest();
```

If your implementation's library uses this style, you may consider choosing a different style, or a unique prefix not present in your implementation API, to avoid the possibility of a clash.

Writing Useful Comments

Regrettably, programmers often give comments too low a priority. It is true that comments make no difference whatsoever to a compiler because the preprocessor strips them out. Nevertheless, comments can be invaluable to maintenance programmers, if written carefully.

Comments Are Useful—If You Read Them!

A year or two ago, I was doing some Year 2000 preventive maintenance work for a bank. One day, a guy from the bank's software development department asked me why I'd changed a particular function, which calculated whether a year was a leap year.

I'd changed it from

```
int IsLeapYear(int Year)
{
  return Year % 4 == 0 &&
    (Year % 100 != 0 || Year % 400 == 0);
}
```

to something along these lines:

```
int IsLeapYear(int Year)
{
  if(Year <= 100)
    return Year % 4 == 0;
```

```
    return Year % 4 == 0 &&
      (Year % 100 != 0 || Year % 400 == 0);
}
```

So, why did I change it? I couldn't remember for the life of me. I even called in a colleague who had been working on the same module; together we stared at the code for about an hour (honestly!), and we were just on the point of deciding that I appeared to have introduced a pointless change.

Then, finally, I noticed that I'd written a comment just above the code. It pointed out that `IsLeapYear()` was called, usually, with a two-digit date but was occasionally passed a `tm_year` member from a `struct tm`. As you know, `struct tm` stores the years since 1900. Thus, the full leap year test would have resulted in a failure for the year 2000 if stored in a `struct tm`'s `tm_year` member, which is why I'd changed the function. If I'd not inserted the comment when I changed the code, I would probably have believed my change had been pointless and would have backed out the change, re-introducing the bug. So the comment saved the day, and I learned something as well—comments are not just for writing, but for reading too!

In recounting this, I am reminded of two other things about the function: First, that the original function was clearly written to expect four-digit dates, although in fact it was only passed two- or three-digit dates. Second, the function's name violates the Standard because it's an external identifier beginning with the characters "is" (remember, external identifiers are not guaranteed to be case sensitive, because some linkers are not case sensitive).

Comment Layout Styles

```
/*********************************
 *                               *
 *   This is a boxed comment.    *
 *   A real pain to maintain.    *
 *                               *
 *********************************/
```

The trouble with this style is that you can't easily update it without spending (wasting) time keeping the `*` columns nicely lined up. (It is possible, however, to write code to do the formatting, and some editors already do this for you anyway.)

Sometimes the maintenance problem of boxed comments is sidestepped, like this:

```
/*********************************
 *
 * This is a boxed comment with
```

```
 * the right hand column of stars
 * removed.
 *
 *********************************/
```

This is much better because you get almost all the aesthetic and attention-grabbing benefit of the box without the maintenance headache. Some people use a thoroughly minimalist box:

```
/*
   This is a boxed comment with
   the right hand column of stars
   removed.
                                 */
```

There are almost as many styles for multi-line comments as there are programmers.

```
/*
 * This is my own preferred method for
 * multi-line comments. It keeps the easily
 * distinguishable column of asterisks, but
 * avoids the necessity to put comment syntax
 * (asterisk and hyphen) outside the first three
 * columns of the current indent; thus, in my
 * opinion, it's quick, easy, and effective.
 * Your mileage may vary.
 */
/* Winged comments look like this, and are good... */
int foo; /* ...for adding comments to the right of code. */
int bar; // here's another single-line comment
```

Please note that this latter style, beloved of BCPL and C++ programmers, was not legal in the C89 Standard—it became part of the C language in October 1999 when C9X was ratified, and became the C99 Standard. So if your compiler doesn't support C99, you shouldn't really be using // comments.

Also, beware of using // comments when your comment ends in a backslash.

```
foo(path); // works on C:\MYAPP\
bar(path);
baz(path);
```

Line splicing occurs before comment removal, so this code is preprocessed into

```
foo(path); // works on C:\MYAPPbar(path);
baz(path);
```

Next, the comments are removed, and thus `bar()` never gets called at all. This is a vicious bug and, in my opinion, enough reason not to use // comments at all. But, of course, you must make up your own mind.

When Not to Comment

Where does this comment belong?

```
i++; /* add 1 to i */
```

If you answered "the bit bucket," you get six points. If you answered "a C tutorial book" you get ten points and a free grape (while stocks last; I only have one bunch, and my children love grapes).

There's no need to add a comment to every line of code. If the intent of the code would be quite clear to a maintenance programmer, there's no point in commenting it. For example:

```
int i = 0;
while(IDNumber != client[i].IDNumber && i < MAX_CLIENTS)
{
  i++;
}
```

It's reasonably clear what this is doing, so there's no real need for a comment.

Comment What the Code Does

Good comments reflect the code's intent, not its mechanism. After all, the mechanism may change over time, as new and improved ways of doing things are discovered. If, however, the program's intent changes, it's effectively a new program needing new source code (and new comments).

```
/* save current head of the list */
temp = *list;
/* move list pointer to next item in the list */
*list = (*list)->next;
/* copy the data from the current list item */
memcpy(dataptr, temp->data, sizeof *dataptr);
```

These comments document the mechanism, not the intent. Far better to have a comment along the lines of

```
/* get this client, and make next client current */
temp = *list;
*list = (*list)->next;
memcpy(dataptr, temp->data, sizeof *dataptr);
```

This comment is much better—when we decide to rip out the list and use a simple array instead, we don't have to rewrite the comments.

Comment Complex Code

There are times, however, when we do need to document the mechanism. It's generally a good idea to write simple code whenever possible but, sometimes, it's just not possible to combine simplicity with speed. When you write complex code, do the maintenance programmer a favor and explain how it works.

"If it was hard to write, it should be hard to read." Stuff and nonsense. If it was hard to write, it's vital that it should be as easy as possible to read, because otherwise the cost of maintaining it will be much higher than necessary, and the chance of it breaking under maintenance is greatly increased.

Comment Closing Braces

When your deadline is approaching and your functions are far too large, it can be tricky to identify which `}` matches to which `{`. Some editors provide keystroke macros to help you find matching braces, which is fine if you happen to be near your editor. Unfortunately, I know of no paper supply company supplying such functionality for printouts. Therefore, in large programs it can be a good idea to comment your closing braces:

```
if(IncomingMissile == TRUE)
{
  /* ... 20 lines of code ... */
  while(PhaseOfMoon == FULL_MOON)
  {
    /* ... 40 more lines of code */
  } /* end while(PhaseOfMoon == FULL_MOON) */
} /* end if(IncomingMissile) */
```

Coding standards that insist that you do this at the end of every single block statement (as some do) are just being pointlessly authoritarian:

```
if(p == '-')
{
  sign = NEG;
  ++p;
} /* end if(p == '-') */
```

is just plain silly.

Don't "Comment Out" Code

The trouble with "commenting out" code is that it's so hard to comment it back in again! Because C doesn't allow nested comments, using comments to remove code *containing* comments can be a real trial of patience. Re-enabling the code is a pain, too, because you have to re-stitch all the comments you unstitched when you started the whole process. (If you are either cheating or using a C99 compiler, you may be using // comments, in which case this process is a lot easier.)

There's a much simpler and more convenient way, which is far superior in every respect to commenting out: the preprocessor. It was tailor-made for this task.

When you comment out code, what you are really doing is temporarily removing it from the compilation phase (either because you don't require its functionality after all but are loath to delete it in case the spec changes back again, or because you're on a bug hunt).

The preprocessor does a first class job of removing code from the compilation phase. Here's an example:

```
#include <stdio.h>

int main(void)
{
#if 0 /* having problems with this printf */
  /* fetch name from environment */
  printf("Hello %s and ", getenv("NAME"));
#endif
  printf("hello everyone else.\n");
  return 0;
}
```

This technique is superior because, first, it's really easy to re-enable the code (by changing `#if 0` to `#if 1`) and, second, it's easy to get rid of the preprocessing altogether when you're done with it, by simply deleting the `#if 0` and the `#endif` lines.

Common Errors and Misunderstandings

The next few sections cover some miscellaneous common C programming errors and misunderstandings.

The `void main` Heresy

The `main()` function returns `int`. If you already know this, by all means move on to the next section if you wish.

If you give `main()` a return type other than `int`, in pre-C99 compilers you get undefined behavior. In C99 compilers you get unspecified behavior if the implementation says so, or undefined behavior if it doesn't. Do you want to trust your program to either one?

Many people simply don't believe me when I tell them this (just as I didn't believe it when I was first told). This is partly because several widely read C tutorial books, and at least one big-league compiler's sample programs, use `void main()` with alarming regularity. Here's the wording of the C99 Standard (which is actually a bit more lenient than the C89 Standard you are probably more used to):

"5.1.2.2.1 Program startup

[#1] The function called at program startup is named main. The implementation declares no prototype for this function. It shall be defined with a return type of int and with no parameters:

```
int main(void) { /* ... */ }
```

or with two parameters (referred to here as argc and argv, though any names may be used, as they are local to the function in which they are declared):

```
int main(int argc, char *argv[]) { /* ... */ }
```

or equivalent; or in some other implementation-defined manner."

A little further on, we read about program termination.

"5.1.2.2.3 Program termination [#1] If the return type of the main function is a type compatible with int, a return from the initial call to the main function is equivalent to calling the exit function with the value returned by the main function as its argument; reaching the } that terminates the main function returns a value of 0. If the return type is not compatible with int, the termination status returned to the host environment is unspecified."

In this context, "unspecified" means that the Standard does not require any specific behavior from the compiler, which is free to return any status it likes to the host environment (typically the operating system), and this only applies if the implementation documents the fact that it supports other return types from `main()` other than `int`. If you void `main()` and you're writing code for a nuclear reactor or a military aircraft, you're probably feeling a little unsettled right now, and I don't blame you. Furthermore, defining main() to return void is not a syntax error or a constraint violation, so the compiler is under no obligation to generate a diagnostic message.

Let's look at this from a slightly different angle. Consider the fourth argument to qsort. This is specified as a pointer to function taking two const void * as arguments, and returning int. The qsort function calls the function pointed to, and uses the return value to establish the relationship between two objects in the array to be sorted. Now, what if you write a comparison function like this?

```
void CompInts(const void *p1, const void *p2)
{
  const int *n1 = p1;
  const int *n2 = p2;
  int diff;
  if(*n1 > *n2)
    diff = 1;
  else if(*n1 == *n2)
    diff = 0;
  else
    diff = -1;
}
```

That's really dumb, right? There's no way qsort can get at the information it needs. It is not up to you to specify the prototype of the comparison function—you must stick to qsort's rules if you want qsort to do what you expect it to do.

Okay, back to main(). It's exactly the same situation. You're not responsible for defining main()'s interface. The caller is. Who calls main()? It's not you (although in fact you may call main() if you want, just as you can call your qsort comparison function if you want); but the primary customer for main() is the startup code. How can the startup code determine whether the program succeeded, if you don't tell it? Somewhere deep in the bowels of the system is a call along the lines of

```
int returnstatus;
returnstatus = main(argc, argv);
```

(I'm simplifying a bit.)

If you void main(), a number of interesting possibilities arise:

- The program may work exactly as you expected.
- returnstatus may end up with a trap representation, and crash the program (or the whole machine).

- The startup code may send the spurious return code to the operating system, which then decides to roll back a database transaction because the program didn't return a success value.
- Worst of all, the startup code may reach out to your nose and start extracting demons from it.

The `main()` function returns `int`. There are exactly three portable values you can return from `main()`. They are:

```
0
EXIT_SUCCESS
EXIT_FAILURE
```

The last two are both defined in `<stdlib.h>`, and their actual values vary from system to system. (In other words, it's not a great idea to look up the value in `<stdlib.h>` and hardcode it into your program.)

If you return 0, the startup code will tell the operating system or other host environment that your program succeeded, translating the 0 into some other value if necessary.

Number of Arguments for `main( )`

Actually, `main()` can be defined in an implementation-defined way. Therefore, it's not necessarily illegal to define `main` as

```
int main(int argc)
```

or

```
int main(int argc, char **argv, char **env)
```

but you should be aware that no compiler is obliged to support either of these two definitions; they are only legal for compilers that document these alternative forms, which certainly doesn't include *all* compilers.

Here are the portable definitions of `main`:

- `int main(void)`
- `int main(int argc, char **argv)`
- `int main(int argc, char *argv[])`
- Any definition exactly equivalent to any one of the above

Thus, you can use different variable names for `argc` and `argv`, you can use `FOO` if the definition is preceded by `typedef int FOO`, and so on. But to be portable, you must return `int` from `main` and you must take either no arguments or the two specified by the standard.

If you need to access the environment in a portable way, you can of course use `getenv()`.

Integer Math Versus Floating Point Math

"Everybody knows that integer math is faster than floating point math, which is one reason why professionals do calculations in integers whenever possible." This used to be true. In the last few years, however, math co-processors have become almost obligatory in new desktop machines. As a result, it may well be the case nowadays that floating point operations are sometimes faster than their integer equivalents. The old rule of thumb no longer applies all the time.

This is just one aspect of a more general point about performance. The C standard doesn't specify how fast C functions execute, either absolutely or relative to each other. Given any two algorithms of the same time complexity (described in more detail in Chapter 3, "Optimization"), you simply can't tell whether one programming technique will outperform another. For example, there is no guarantee that

```
int ch;
ch = fgetc(fp);
if(ch != EOF)
{
  /* ... */
```

will be faster (or slower) than

```
unsigned char c;
if(fread(&c, 1, 1, fp) > 0)
{
  /* ... */
```

The only way to find out is to try it and see. Even when you've done that, your findings are not portable to another machine, operating system, or implementation (or even to a different version of the same compiler). It's worth investing in a good code profiler if performance is key to your application. (If performance isn't key to your application, why are you worrying about performance in the first place?) For most applications, performance only matters when the program is running like a dog with one leg. In these circumstances, you are much more likely to get significant performance gains by reviewing your choice of algorithm than by saving a cycle here and a cycle there.

If your coding standards document says integer math is faster than floating point math, your reply should be "prove it!"

Signal Handling

Whenever I see a supposedly portable program that uses signal handling, I get suspicious. Most programs that handle signals do so incorrectly. In your signal-handling function, you're actually not allowed (except in certain, rather limited circumstances) to refer to any static object unless it's been declared as having the type `volatile sig_atomic_t`. (An atomic variable is, loosely speaking, one that can be referenced in a single machine operation.) Most C programmers I know have never heard of the `sig_atomic_t` type, yet many of them continue to add signal handling to their programs.

Furthermore, you're not allowed to call any standard library function (or cause any such function to be called, such as calling a function that calls a standard library function) from within a signal handler (except for `abort()` and, under certain circumstances, `signal()`). That doesn't stop people from doing it, of course, but it is non-portable and should be avoided in a portable program.

In practice, many programs use signals, and not just for catching floating point exceptions. For example, signals are frequently employed in UNIX networking applications. My point is simply that such usage relies on the implementation allowing and supporting it, so you should be wary. (Strictly, you are relying on undefined behavior, but if your vendor documents the behavior and you can trust your vendor, you should be all right, at least until the next version of your compiler is released.)

Passing by Value

We all know we can't swap two `int`s like this:

```
void swap(int a, int b)
{
  int t;
  t = a, a = b, b = t;
}
```

because C is pass-by-value. Unfortunately, some C tutorial books suggest that you pass by reference instead:

```
void swap(int *a, int *b)
{
  int t;
  t = *a, *a = *b, *b = t;
}
```

Sure, this works. But it isn't pass-by-reference. There is quite literally no such thing in C. What is actually happening here is that the addresses of `a` and `b` are being passed—by value! We can see this most clearly with a simple demonstration program:

```
#include <stdio.h>
void increment(char *p)
{
  ++p;
}

int main(void)
{
  char *s = "Hello world";
  increment(s);
  printf("%s\n", s);
  return 0;
}
```

If C passed pointers by reference, this program would print

```
ello world
```

But it doesn't. It prints

```
Hello world
```

This indicates that the modification of `p` by the `increment()` function has no effect on the original pointer `s`. This is exactly the behavior we would expect of pass-by-value. For precisely the same reason, this code doesn't work (and in fact results in undefined behavior):

```
#include <stdio.h>

int openfile(char *s, FILE *fp)
{
  fp = fopen(s, "r");
  return fp ? 1 : 0;
}

int main(void)
{
  FILE *fp;
  char buffer[1024];
  if(openfile("readme", fp))
  {
    while(fgets(buffer, sizeof buffer, fp))
```

```
      printf("%s", buffer);
    fclose(fp);
    printf("\n");
  }
  return 0;
}
```

If, then, you want to change the thing a pointer points to, within a function, how do you do it?

The technique is exactly the same as for a variable: You pass a pointer to the thing you want to change. In the preceding example, we wanted to make a pointer point to `fopen`'s return value. Here is a modified program that will work correctly:

```
#include <stdio.h>

#define MAX_BUFF 1024

int openfile(char *s, FILE **fp)
{
  *fp = fopen(s, "r");
  return *fp ? 1 : 0;
}

int main(void)
{
  FILE *fp;
  char buffer[MAX_BUFF];
  if(openfile("readme", &fp))
  {
    while(fgets(buffer, sizeof buffer, fp))
      printf("%s", buffer);
    fclose(fp);
    printf("\n");
  }
  return 0;
}
```

Similarly, if you need to change a variable `ppt` of type `T**` (where `T` is some type), you need to pass `&ppt` to your function, which would be prototyped something like this:

```
int foo(T *** pppT);
```

(And yes, it can get even sillier than that. I've had to use five asterisks before, in real live code. Fortunately, that's a rare requirement.)

Problems with Unions

Some machines store numbers with the most significant byte first. These are known as *big-endian* machines. Others store the least significant byte first, because that arrangement happens to be more efficient for their particular architecture. Sometimes it's necessary to determine which "endianness" a particular machine has.

Here's a commonly used technique for determining whether a machine is big-endian or little-endian:

```
#include <stdio.h>

union U
{
  long  bignum;
  short littlenum[2];
};

int main(void)
{
  union U u = {1L};

  if(u.littlenum[0] == 1)
  {
    printf("Little-endian\n");
  }
  else
  {
    printf("Big-endian.\n");
  }
  return 0;
}
```

Unfortunately, this technique is not guaranteed to work (strictly, whether it works is implementation-defined in the old C standard, and undefined in C99). You can only take out of a union what you put into it. If you put a `long int` in, you can only take a `long int` out.

It may seem picky to say that this code's behavior is implementation-defined or undefined, but its very nature *requires* that it be portable. Why would anyone bother (other than as a one-off exercise) to write a routine to determine at runtime whether a machine has a particular representation if they are only ever going to run it on one implementation on one machine?

There's an exception to this union rule that has to do with structs with common initial sequences. It's a lot easier to show than to tell. I've laid out the following definitions horizontally not just to save space, but to highlight their common initial sequence:

```
typedef struct FOO { int i;   double j;  long k;  } FOO;
typedef struct BAR { int a;   double b;  char c;  } BAR;
typedef struct BAZ { int d;   double e;  FOO f;   } BAZ;

typedef union QUUX
{
  FOO foo;
  BAR bar;
  BAZ baz;
} QUUX;

FOO first = { 3, 3.14, 42 };
QUUX q;
q.foo = first;
printf("%d  %f\n", q.bar.a, q.baz.e);
```

Because `FOO`, `BAR`, and `BAZ` share the common initial sequence int, `double`, it is legal to examine any member of that sequence using either `q.foo`, `q.bar`, or `q.baz`. But if you store a value in a member not in that common initial sequence (for example`q.foo.first.k = 9;`) it is not portable to read that information via `q.bar.c` or `q.baz.f`.

The `sizeof` Operator

`sizeof` is an operator, not a function. This surprises some people. The `sizeof` operator yields the size of an object-typed expression (or a type) at compile time. It's a unary operator, so it takes just one object, or just one object-typed expression, or type. Thus,

```
FOO foo;
size_t size = sizeof foo;
```

is legal. If you need to give it a type instead, you do need the parentheses, but that doesn't make it a function.

```
size_t othersize = sizeof(FOO);
```

Here's a trick we really wish would work:

```
void foo(int *array)
{
```

```
    printf("array is stored in %u bytes.\n",
           (unsigned) sizeof array);
    printf("It has %u elements.\n",
           (unsigned)(sizeof array / sizeof(int)));
}
```

Unfortunately, `sizeof array` will not give us the size of the array here, only the size of a pointer to `int`. Furthermore, the preceding code fragment will always report the same number for the number of elements in the array. That value is implementation-dependent, but on many systems it would print 1 because a pointer often takes the same storage as an `int`.

The `return` Keyword

The `return` keyword is not a function, so it doesn't need parentheses. You can use them if you like, but you don't have to.

Understanding Declarations, Definitions, and Prototypes

C programmers often have trouble telling the difference between declarations, definitions, and prototypes. What exactly *are* they?

Declarations

A declaration gives the compiler information about the type of an identifier. (Strictly, "a declaration specifies the interpretation and attributes of a set of identifiers.") A definition is a declaration, but a declaration isn't necessarily a definition. For example, a file scope variable with external linkage may be defined only once in a program, but you can declare it as many times as you like. Thus, in source file A we might have

```
int GlobalX = 0;
```

defined at file scope. In source files B, C, and D we could legitimately declare

```
extern int GlobalX;
```

Furthermore, we can place this declaration into A as well, without affecting the legitimacy of the definition already there.

Definitions

Defining an object (such as a variable, for example) means allocating storage for it and (optionally) giving it a value. An object should be defined exactly once within a program.

An object may also be *tentatively* defined. A tentative definition is a definition at file scope without an initializer and without storage qualifiers (or with the `static` storage qualifier). I'd love to be able to tell you how useful this is, but I can see no point whatsoever in tentative definitions.

Defining a function means giving it a function body. So a function definition includes the function body. Thus, a C program can be thought of as a collection of definitions.

Prototypes

According to the Standard, a function prototype is "a declaration of a function that declares the types of its parameters."

A prototype is always a declaration, and can be a definition, of a function. Prototypes are used by the compiler to validate argument lists in calls to prototyped functions. I'm sure you already know about prototypes as declarations, so here's an example of how a function definition can also be a prototype:

```
#include <stdio.h>
#include <string.h>

int foo(char *s)
{
  return (int)strlen(s);
}

int main(void)
{
  char *hi = "Hello world";
  printf("The string %s is %d bytes long\n", hi, foo(hi));
  return 0;
}
```

Here, the line

```
int foo(char *s)
```

is not just the first line of a function definition; it is also a full prototype.

The Importance of Portability

One of the biggest hurdles to overcome when moving from "kindergarten" C to the real world is that of portability. There is an understandable tendency to assume that "the compiler is the language." It's quite a shock to the system when you discover that `getch()` is not part of the C language!

Ones and Twos Complement

C doesn't assume you are working on a twos complement machine. This is why the ANSI Standard requires implementors to make `INT_MIN` at least 32767 in magnitude (it must be negative, of course) rather than 32768. In ones complement, you can't store -32768 in 16 bits (although you do gain the ability to distinguish between 0 and -0). Because of the different bit patterns used by ones complement and twos complement machines to store negative numbers, the result of shifting a negative number is implementation-defined at best (as is any shift operation involving the sign bit) and undefined at worst. When shifting bits, then, it's safest to stick with unsigned types.

Defining Undefined Behavior

Here's what the C standard has to say about undefined behavior:

"3.18 [#1] undefined behavior [is] behavior, upon use of a nonportable or erroneous program construct, of erroneous data, or of indeterminately valued objects, for which this International Standard imposes no requirements."

Here is a C program that contains no syntax errors or constraint violations. (In other words, ANSI C compilers are allowed to compile this program without issuing any diagnostic messages.)

```
void main()
{
  printf("Hello world\n");
}
```

From the C Standard's point of view, this program can do anything at all. The most likely outcome is that it will print

```
Hello world
```

on the standard output, but there is absolutely no guarantee of that. There are two reasons for this. First, the function incorrectly specifies `main()` as returning `void`; in C, `main()` must return `int`. The second reason is that `printf`, a variadic function, has been called without a full prototype for it being in scope.

Now, it may well work on your machine. That does not mean it will work on the next machine you compile it on. It doesn't mean it will work on a different compiler, even if it's for the same operating system. In fact, it doesn't even mean that it will work on a previous version, or a subsequent version, of your own compiler. Denizens of `comp.lang.c` will point out that there is nothing to stop the implementation pulling demons out of your nose (and in fact, "nasal demons" is an alias for undefined behavior in that newsgroup). Of course, demonographic rhinology is not the only possible outcome. If you have the right hardware, this program could walk your computer over to the window and hurl it out, or send an email to your boss notifying him of your resignation, or format all your local disks, or even launch a thermonuclear attack against the Isle of Wight.

Flushing Input Buffers

Here's a commonly used technique for getting rid of unwanted characters in an input stream:

```
printf("Enter age:");
scanf("%d", &age);        /* get age from the user */
printf("Enter shoesize:");
fflush(stdin);            /* get rid of line feed */
scanf("%d", &shoesize); /* get shoe size from the user */
```

Here's what the standard has to say about it (from section 7.19.5.2):

```
#include <stdio.h>
int fflush(FILE *stream);
```

"[#2] If stream points to an output stream or an update stream in which the most recent operation was not input, the fflush function causes any unwritten data for that stream to be delivered to the host environment to be written to the file; otherwise, the behavior is undefined."

If you want to get rid of spurious characters between calls to `scanf`, you can do it like this instead:

```
printf("Enter age:");
fflush(stdout);
scanf("%d", &age);        /* get age from the user */
printf("Enter shoesize:");
fflush(stdout);
scanf(" %d", &shoesize); /* note the leading space */
```

(As you can see, I've taken the opportunity to demonstrate that you can portably gather input on the same line as the previous output, by judicious use of `fflush()`.)

In fact, it's best not to use `scanf()` for getting data interactively. It's intended to read formatted data from `stdin`, and human beings aren't the best source of formatted data.

Using scanf() works much better when stdin is, for example, redirected from a file with a carefully defined format.

If you're accustomed to using scanf() and would now like an alternative suggestion, take a long, hard look at fgets(), which is ideal for gathering data from the user.

is() and to()

The is*() and to*() functions in <ctype.h> (isupper, tolower, and so on) take an int as their argument, but that argument must be either EOF or a value representable as an unsigned char. Any other value invokes undefined behavior. If you want to be totally safe using these functions, cast the argument to unsigned char on the way in. (This will cause problems with EOF itself, but you can always design your algorithm so that passing EOF into the function simply doesn't happen.) Your casting to unsigned char will ensure that the operation is safe, and the compiler will take care of promoting the value back to an int for you.

This is only an issue when your string might have characters in it that might be represented by values not in the range 0 to UCHAR_MAX. For example, your program might be running on a system such as DOS, where char is typically signed by default, and the user may have used ALT in conjunction with the numeric keypad, to enter a character not in the ASCII character set. In such circumstances, you need to be careful. Here's an illustration of how you can ensure that your code is robust:

```
void MakeStringUpperCase(char *s)
{
  while(*s)
  {
    *s = toupper((unsigned char)*s);
    ++s;
  }
}
}
```

String Reversal

Here's a common trick to exchange two integers without using a temporary variable:

```
a ^= b ^= a ^= b;
```

This trick may look cute, but it's impossible to use it correctly. Here's one way it's often used:

```
void strrev(char *s)
{
  int len = strlen(s);
  int i, j;
  for(i = 0, j = len - 1; i < j; i++, j--)
    s[i] ^= s[j] ^= s[i] ^= s[j];
}
```

If you think that looks terribly scary, you're right. Not only that, but it's wrong. Because the code modifies the value of an object twice between sequence points, it results in undefined behavior. In comparison, the failure to include `<string.h>` for `strlen`, the wrong type for `len` (it should be `size_t`), and the namespace violation (`strrev`) seem relatively trivial. (By the way, if you do make `len` a `size_t` type, you should add a check for the special case when the string is zero bytes long.)

What's more, none of these errors is a syntax error or a constraint violation, so no diagnostic is required!

In case you're interested, the code could be legally written like this:

```
#include <string.h>

void revstr(char *s)
{
  size_t len = strlen(s);
  size_t i, j;
  if(len > 0)
    for(i = 0, j = len - 1; i < j; i++, j--)
      s[i] ^= s[j], s[j] ^= s[i], s[i] ^= s[j];
}
```

This is fine because the commas introduce sequence points into the code. (It's still fairly horrible, but at least it's legal C. A better, clearer solution would be to use a temporary variable.)

Nasal Demons

The two most dramatic results of undefined behavior I have personally witnessed both involved leaving insufficient room in a `char` array for the terminating null character of a string.

The first occasion was in 1989, and the victim was my brother, Steve. He (ahem) drew my attention to his screen, which was displaying a message asking him to confirm that he wanted to format his hard disk. He was lucky—he was asked.

A year or so later, a colleague of mine (hi, Kevin) wasn't quite so lucky. The first sign of his program's undefined behavior was that his machine hung. The second sign was that it wouldn't reboot! He had to spend quite some time nursing the machine back to health using the diagnostic floppies supplied by the manufacturer.

I've never had anything that bad happen to me. In a way, I've been unfortunate. I would love to bring you a really embarrassing first-hand account of how I brought down a major government by dereferencing a `NULL` pointer or flooded a city by passing `(UCHAR_MAX + 1)` to `isupper()`. My own bugs have been far less dramatic. Sorry to disappoint you.

Sizes of Integer Types

Strictly speaking, a long int is `sizeof(long int)` bytes in size. You know it's at least 32 bits because it has to be able to represent all the integers between -2147483647 and +2147483647. It may be more than 32 bits, either because `LONG_MAX` is higher on your particular implementation or because padding bits have been used (these are not required but compilers are allowed to use them if they so choose). For the purposes of determining storage requirements, work from `sizeof(long int)`. For the purpose of working out how big a number can be stored in a `long int`, use `LONG_MAX`. On current systems, long ints are typically 32 bits long.

The same reasoning can be applied to `short int`, which is `sizeof(short int)` bytes long, and at least 16 bits because it has to be able to represent all the integers between -32767 and +32767. It may be more than 16 bits, of course, again because your compiler may have higher implementation limits than strictly required (which is quite legal), or because of padding bits. On current systems, short ints are typically 16 bits long.

When we come to `int`, we can still apply the same reasoning. `INT_MAX` must be at least 32767 (and `INT_MIN` must be at most -32767), so we know an `int` is 16 bits at least. In older operating systems (and in newer operating systems when they are in emulation mode to support software from the older ones) `int` is typically, but not universally, 16 bits. In newer operating systems, `int` is typically 32 bits.

It's a bad idea, however, to take any of these values for granted. There is at least one computer in this world (a Cray) that uses 8 bits for a char and 64 bits for a short, 64 bits for an int, and 64 bits for a long.

The point I'm making is that

```
#include <stdio.h>
int main(void)
{
  printf("%d\n", (int)sizeof(int));
  return 0;
}
```

may well print 2 on your machine. Or it may print 4. Or it may print 8, if you happen to be using a Cray (as I'm sure practically all of you are). Whatever value it prints, it's asking for trouble if you assume it'll be the same on the next machine on which you compile this code.

Structure Padding

Structures are a wonderful way to store items of related data together. You may not be aware, however, that compilers are not required to store their members contiguously in memory. It's quite allowable for a compiler to insert padding bits (as many as it likes) between members of a structure, and at the end of a structure (but not at the start). Not only are compilers allowed to do this, but they *do* do this; it's a very handy way of aligning data for efficient access.

Thus, this code:

```
struct FOO
{
  char a;
  char b;
  char c;
  char d;
  char e;
  char f;
};

FOO foo = {0};

char *p;
char q[] = "hello";
int i;

p = (char *)&foo;
for(p = &foo.a, i = 0; q[i] != '\0'; i++, p++)
```

```
  *p = q[i];

printf("%s\n", &foo.a);
```

quite apart from being terrible code, is absolutely not guaranteed by the Standard to print `"hello"`.

You should be particularly wary of structure padding when communicating data between two different machines, which may well be using different alignment strategies.

Macros

You know this already, but I can't really leave it out just in case you don't. Beware of macros and their side-effects.

The simple, cute-looking

```
#define SQ(x) x * x
```

breaks with the code

```
a = SQ(b + c);
```

because this expands to

```
a = b + c * b + c;
```

which is almost certainly not what was intended.

Let's mend it:

```
#define SQ(x) ((x) * (x))
```

Now we can break it a different way:

```
a = SQ(++b);
```

Not only will this not give the intended result, but it also results in undefined behavior. The expansion:

```
a = ((++b) * (++b));
```

modifies an object's value more than once between sequence points, which is a naughty no-no.

If you must use macros, please ensure that they are, at the very least, named in uppercase, to give the user-programmer a visual reminder that "here be dragons."

C Versus C++

C and C++ are different languages, for different people. C is a procedural language, whereas C++ is an object-oriented language. The things that make you a good C programmer can be obstacles to your learning effective C++ programming. Similarly, C++ programmers sometimes find it difficult to make the transition to C. It is possible to master both languages, but it's harder than you might think.

Arguments about which language is better are, of course, futile. The languages are different, and have different strengths and weaknesses.

Those who claim "C++ is a better C" are wrong.

(I'm not anti-C++; I'm a big fan of C++ Builder, which makes the combination of rapid Windows development and high performance possible at last.)

C++ is a different C. C has moved on from the point where C++ branched off from it, especially with the recent (October 1999) ratification of the C99 Standard. C++, too, has evolved. Neither language is a subset of the other.

Nevertheless, they do have much in common—and that's a good thing because it means that much of your C knowledge is transferable to C++. Sometimes that can be a real lifesaver. For example, when I'm writing C++, I use the `FILE *` functions for file access because I find the iostream stuff too fiddly. I know I'm not the only one who does this; several C++ aficionados of my acquaintance confess privately that they do the same whenever they think they can get away with it (I won't name and shame them here—they know who they are).

Now, this book is about C, so we're not going to talk much more about C++. One important point, however: Many C compilers on sale today are also capable of compiling C++. That's a Good Thing. Unfortunately, at least in the world of Windows, it does seem that most of the combined compilers come complete with text editors that like to default their file types to `.cpp` rather than `.c`, with the result that (if you're not careful) you can end up compiling your C code as if it were C++. Since the two languages are different, that's a Bad Thing. For example, the following code:

```
#include <stdlib.h>
#include <stdio.h>
#include <string.h>

int main(void)
{
  char *p = malloc(1024);
  if(p)
```

```
  {
    strcpy(p, "Hello world.");
    printf("%s\n", p);
    free(p);
  }
  return 0;
}
```

is perfectly legal C, but under C++ you'll get a diagnostic message because of the conversion of `malloc`'s `void *` return value to char *.

So a word to the wise: When using such compilers, pay particular attention to the default file extension.

Summary

Project coding standards play an important role in the life of a software development project. They can only be truly effective, however, if you follow their recommendations. Being a good and conscientious programmer, you won't follow their recommendations if those recommendations are wrong-headed or misguided.

I hope you're now in a better position to examine such documents critically, with an eye to improving them for your own benefit and that of the other people on your project.

We've also looked at a few of the problems of writing portable code. Portability is particularly important in a book about C, because we, the authors, haven't the faintest idea what platform you're running on. So we will keep coming back to this theme of writing code that will run not just on our platform, but on yours too, whether you are running AmigaDOS, MVS, MacOS, or some lesser known operating system such as UNIX or Windows. For example, we certainly don't assume you're using EBCDIC; all the example code in this book also supports other C-compatible character sets (such as ASCII).

CHAPTER 3

Optimization

by Michael Lee

In This Chapter

Ever since there have been machines, there have been people trying to make them go faster. The information age has taken this pastime to a new level, from days and weeks down to milliseconds and microseconds. Often, functions written in a high-level language perform so quickly that the time spent is imperceptible. It is only through repetition over millions of calls that a change in speed becomes noticeable. These vast scales, beyond normal day-to-day human counting, demand a sense of proportion tuned specifically to computer program optimization. The goal of this chapter is to give you that sense.

To that end, we will look at ways to *analyze* the performance of algorithms using O-notation, ways to *measure* the performance of programs using profilers, and we will also examine some strategies for *improving* the performance of programs in light of our measurement and analysis.

The Appeal of Optimization and Some Ancient History

Optimization got off to a funny start. For the first two decades of digital computing, computer time was considered more valuable than programmer time. Institutions such as service bureaus and universities literally charged users for machine use, often dollars per minute. Programmers had a strong incentive to make each microsecond count and had to consider not only the run time of their programs but also the costs of loading, compiling, and printing results. Even the time of day the job was run had to be considered.

Those days are over for most of us, but some challenges remain. Commercial software often must meet specific benchmark requirements. Three-dimensional games compete in the marketplace on frame rates and texture mapping quality. Ambitious scientific projects analyze intricate details of nuclear collisions or radio waves from distant galaxies. While computers have gotten faster, applications for them have grown to process more data in more detail.

Time Well Spent

Optimization usually involves studying your program carefully. In my own experience, I've discovered many latent (and some not so latent) errors in my logic or implementation that came to my attention while analyzing my code and its performance. While it may seem more productive to finish what you're doing and start on another project as soon as possible, it is important to spend some time pondering what you've already written. When you're thinking about the efficiency of your code is a good time to ponder its accuracy as well.

C Is Already a Very Fast Language

C has been categorized by many as a "high-level assembly language." This reputation is supported by the ease of mapping many basic types and many basic operations directly into simple machine instructions. Ints, floats, and pointers can and should fit in single machine registers. Assignment, arithmetic, array indexing, and dereferencing map directly into simple machine instructions on those registers. Of course, as you use more complex types such as lists and multidimensional arrays or more sophisticated library functions such as `qsort`, you can no longer expect the one-to-one mapping of C constructs to machine level to be maintained. But you will find that, in C, the transition from simple types and operations to more complicated types and operations is very gradual and emphasizes performance whenever possible.

The standard C library and include files contain several features to enhance performance:

- The `stdio` functions use buffered input and output. Many of the functions that write to these buffers are allowed to be macros (such as `putc` and `getc`), which in the absence of inlining are generally faster than function calls.
- `memcpy`'s existence isn't strictly necessary, but it is often faster than its more general counterpart, `memmove`.
- The `assert` macro is designed to have zero overhead when `NDEBUG` is `#defined`.
- Both single- and double-precision versions of mathematical operators are allowed to exist. This gives the compiler the option of using a faster single-precision floating-point operation when appropriate (though it is not required).
- A select few high-level functions like `bsearch` and `qsort` are provided so that the C implementation can choose to take advantage of machine-specific hacks without rendering users' programs nonportable.
- Perhaps the most daring speed-related feature of the C library is the lack of an imposed I/O paradigm. Other languages go to some effort to isolate the programmer from the details of bits and bytes that are read and written. (C provides `printf` and `scanf` for formatted I/O but does not require their use.)

Because of C's emphasis on performance, it seems to have been chosen as a language to which to apply the most sophisticated compile-time optimizations. Only FORTRAN has received similar attention from compiler writers. Of course, because of shared backends, other languages benefit from this attention, but some constructs (such as unformatted I/O and machine-specific `qsort` or `memcpy` optimizations) simply may not be accessible from other languages.

The Importance of Measurements

In the end, speed is a strictly measurable quantity. Every lap of a racecar, every marathon, and every bobsled run is held to the impartial judging of a stopwatch. But the stopwatch has a limitation—it measures only the time as you cross the finish line. We programmers are blessed by the invention of profiling tools. Not only can we time how long it takes to finish the run, we can also examine the speed of individual modules and functions in our program to look for specific areas that can be optimized further, and our changes to those areas can be measured independently of the rest of the program to establish the exact benefits. A profiler is a powerful tool for the C programmer interested in speed.

Note

Profiling is covered in more detail in the appropriately named "Profiling" section later in this chapter.

Thinking About Performance

This section discusses the nature of time and space. Mostly time.

A Sense of Perspective

If your goal is a speedy program, you need to have an idea of how long each operator or library function takes to complete. You might suspect that a call to `qsort` could take a lot longer than adding two integers, but where in between those two extremes do all the other operators and functions fall? If an operator or function does not take a constant amount of time under all circumstances, what does it depend on?

Which is faster, `malloc` or `free`?

What takes more time, `fseek` or `rand`?

Could `exit` take longer than `system`? Vice versa?

Table 3.1 shows relative speeds of selected operations and library functions on a somewhat old (but still functioning) Sun SPARCstation 2. It was constructed by performing operations a couple of million times, calculating the time that took, and then dividing by the number of iterations.

The program that generated this table appears on the examples CD as `speed.c`.

The first column indicates the operation or function that was timed. The second column is how long the operation took in microseconds. The table is sorted in order of increasing time, with the fastest operations at the top and the slowest at the bottom.

TABLE 3.1 Sample Timings for Basic Operations in C

Sample Operation	*Time (in usec)*
`int - int`	0.013
`deref pointer`	0.025
`array index`	0.026
`int =`	0.036
`bit shift`	0.037
`(int) float`	0.038
`float * float`	0.049
`float + float`	0.049
`int ^ int`	0.050
`empty func()`	0.058
`int + int`	0.063
`if-then-else`	0.086
`float / float`	0.118
`int * int`	0.198
`rand()`	0.268
`int / int`	0.391
`sqrt()`	0.399
`strcmp()`	0.556
`strcpy()`	0.665
`malloc/free`	2.834
`fopen/fclose`	30.908
`system()`	25949.621

The basic operations take increasingly small amounts of time in absolute terms, but relative to each other you can see, for example, that integer division takes seven times as long as addition. At the extreme, `fopen` is very slow, and `system()` takes an incredible amount of time!

The Memory Hierarchy and Its Effect on Performance

The first subsystem to be concerned about is the memory hierarchy. Even a function that performs no I/O or multitasking can still be affected by this. In most computers, there is a strict hierarchy of memory access speed and, the farther down you go, the longer it will take to access your data:

- *CPU registers*—Almost instantaneous.
- *L1 cache*—Very fast, only a few clock cycles.
- *L2 cache*—Also very fast, but a few more clock cycles.
- *RAM*—Pretty fast, but it can take many clock cycles to get something from RAM.
- *ROM*—Slightly slower than RAM, not accessed much except for booting.
- *Virtual memory*—Rather slow. It can take thousands of clock cycles.

The implication is that if you want your program to run fast and your program uses a lot of memory, you should have your program access memory as high up in the memory hierarchy as possible. To do this you need to understand some of the characteristics of the different levels.

CPU registers are a precious resource. Often there are as few as three useful ones available to your program. They are often used for loop counters or to hold pointers being used to access arrays. These are actually under control of the compiler; user programs don't usually have direct control over register use.

An L1 cache and an L2 cache are similar (and yes, there is such a thing as an L3 cache, it's just not used very often). The function of the cache is to store a copy of a portion of what's in RAM. As your program accesses data, it will eventually ask for something that isn't in the cache or for more than the cache can hold. This is when your array-crunching program can get bogged down. Not all machines have cache (older CPUs were so slow that RAM was fast enough). The tricky thing about cache is that it is sensitive to the patterns in which you access memory.

If you access data in a pattern that repeats over intervals similar to the size of the cache lines, successive accesses to memory may all get mapped to the same cache line. This underutilizes the cache.

The second problem is that cache doesn't necessarily do anything to speed up long linear accessing of memory. If you're scanning through 24MB of memory, it all has to be read eventually, and it all has to fit through the same system bus limitations.

Of course, RAM is what most people mean when they talk about memory. Of interest is that lately the different types of memory are often named or defined by their speed—70ns SIMMs or PC-133 SDRAM, for example. These designations give clues to the speed and frequency of operation, respectively.

Most computers have only an inconsequential amount of ROM and so the average program doesn't waste much time on it. ROM is considered slightly slower than RAM, but this is generally ignored except during OS booting. A trick that is sometimes used on computers where ROM is frequently accessed is to copy the contents of the ROM into RAM where it can be accessed faster. As long as this copy of the ROM is protected from being destroyed by application software, most programs won't be able to tell the difference.

Virtual Memory

You can cause disk activity even if your program doesn't do any I/O! If your program needs more memory than actual RAM available and your OS supports virtual memory, some of your data is going to be placed on a swap disk. Assuming you actually need to use that data at some point, it will be extremely slow to access, compared to data stored in RAM or cache. If you use such a large amount of data (more than will fit into RAM) and access it frequently or randomly, many attempts to access RAM will instead access the swap disk. This is called *thrashing*. In this condition, almost nothing gets done and your program can slow down by a factor of a thousand or more.

O-Notation

O-notation is a widely used method for gauging the speed of an algorithm or function. The O-notation for an algorithm is a formula that gives the upper bound of a resource used by an algorithm, after factoring out constants and time spent other than in the inner loop of the algorithm. Most often it describes the time required for the algorithm to run, but it can also be used to describe the memory space needed or some other resource. O-notation can alternately be called the "complexity" or "big-O" of an algorithm.

As an exercise, here's an example program that has been exhaustively examined and found to take exactly this long to execute (in milliseconds), given `N` number of input records:

$$4N + 2.1*N^2 + 48$$

In other words, given 100 input records, the program takes 21448 milliseconds to finish. O-notation simplifies this by first removing the coefficients and constants, leaving

$$N + N^2$$

It then further simplifies by retaining only the fastest-increasing term, in this case N^2. Now we can state the algorithm's O-notation as

$$O(N^2)$$

This is useful because the other terms (`4N` and `48`) and the constant factor on the significant term (`2.1`) would become nearly irrelevant as `N` increases. For example, if `N` were 10,000,000, the N^2 term would overwhelm any other part of the formula in terms of affecting the resulting time taken by the algorithm. We can use O-notation to compare this algorithm to other algorithms and establish which is superior for large values of `N`.

Oddly, given the incredible richness of programming and mathematics, most algorithms have O-notations that fall into a few broad categories, and some of these categories have widely used names. We present this list in order of best O-notation to worst, in the sense that an O(1) algorithm is preferable to an $O(N^2)$ algorithm, given that they both perform adequately otherwise.

- *O(1)*—Often referred to as *constant time*, this algorithm takes the same amount of time to finish regardless of the size of the input set. There is no free lunch even in computer science, so this probably means the algorithm isn't processing the entire input set. For example, it might simply be averaging the first five elements and ignoring the rest.
- *O(log N)*—Often referred to as *logarithmic*, the logarithmic base is factored out (it ends up being a constant). Many searching algorithms are O(log N). For example, a binary target search on sorted input would be O(log N).
- *O(N)*—Often referred to as *linear*, this algorithm takes time in direct proportion to the size of the input set. Basically any algorithm that needs to look at each data item only once will fall into this category.
- *O(N log N)*—This one is significant because many sort algorithms fall into this category, including quick sort, heap sort, and merge sort.
- *$O(N^2)$*—This is often called *quadratic*. Some sort algorithms such as bubble sort are quadratic time. Some others, notably quick sort, are quadratic time only for certain pathological input cases, for example input that is already sorted or that contains identical records.
- *$O(N^x)$*—where *X* is an integer greater than two. This is often called *polynomial*. Of course, there is a significant difference between $O(N^5)$ and $O(N^{17})$, but any algorithm that is slower than quadratic becomes unusable even for small input sets. For example, an $O(N^5)$ algorithm would require on the order of 10 billion steps to process only 100 input items!
- *$O(X^N)$*—Often called *exponential* or *geometric*, not many widely used algorithms fall into this category. It is still possible for an exponential algorithm to be useful, such as if the base (X in the formula) is very small (for instance, 1.0001).
- *O(N!)*—Called *factorial time*, algorithms that explore permutations and combinations of data can become ungainly with large input sets. For the same set of 100 input

items, the time taken by a factorial time algorithm would be somewhere near 10^{158}, a remarkable number by most standards.

FIGURE 3.1
A chart of common O-notation categories.

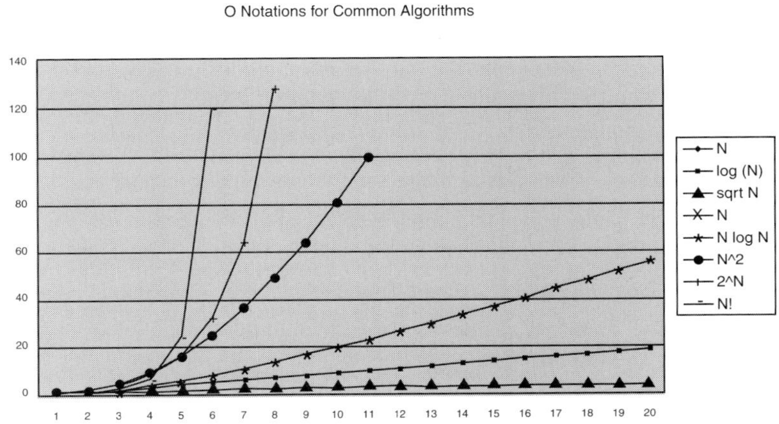

Clearly, if you have a choice of algorithms or can change your algorithm significantly, you should arrange that it have an O-notation closer to constant time than to exponential time. And of course, there are some in-between measures such as O(sqrt(N)) and O(log log N).

A note on best case/worst case behavior: Many algorithms behave differently if given some property of the set of input items. For example, if the items are in a certain order or are chosen from a certain set of values, this can make your algorithm take less or more time. One instance would be a sort function that normally takes O(N log N) time but can check to see if the input is already in the proper order in a single pass and then finish in linear time. If an algorithm is sensitive like this, its description may give as many as three different O-notations for it: best case, worst case, and average case. If only one is given, you can probably assume it's the average case.

When analyzing your own functions and algorithms, you might need to take into account hidden loops that are implicit in library calls, for example `strlen` or `memcpy`. To be completely picky about it, for extremely large input sets you'd need data of length log N simply to differentiate one item from another. For example, if you are sorting students by last name for a class assignment, perhaps only the first three or four characters are all that's need for `strcmp` to do its job. If you expand to include more students (a whole school district, for example), you'll have to also take into account first name and middle initial, and `strcmp` may have to look at several successive characters in each name before it can make a determination.

A Little Bit of Arithmetic

In the real world, your C program is likely to be a collection of several unrelated algorithms. How can you establish what the O-notation is for your whole program, or for the parts of your program that use multiple algorithms? First, establish what is represented by the N in the formula. If you are processing payroll records, perhaps N is the number of employees. If you are transmitting data across a network, perhaps N is the number of bytes being sent. Examine the basic parts of your algorithms for inner loops and establish their individual O-notations in relation to your chosen N.

Now you are in a position to combine the O-notations from different parts of your program to get an overall value. There are three meaningful ways to combine O-notations: sequential, nested, and parallel.

- *Sequential Operations*—The O-notation of two algorithms completed in sequence, one after the other, is the larger of their individual O-notations. In other words

  O(f(N)) *in sequence with* O(g(N)) = O(max(f(N), g(N))

  For example, if f(N) was larger than g(N), the combined O-notation would be f(N).
- *Nested Operations*—When an algorithm contains a call to another algorithm inside it, the resulting O-notation is found by multiplying the O-notations of the individual algorithms.

  O(f(N)) *calls* O(g(N)) = O(f(N) * g(N))

  For example, if O(f(N)) was simply N (linear), and O(g(N)) was N^2 (quadratic), the result of nesting the two algorithms would be $O(N^3)$.
- *Parallel Operations*—Of course, you're thinking that C doesn't support parallel operations, and you're right. But for the record, the combined O-notation for two algorithms that operate in parallel is the larger of the two algorithms' O-notations.

  O(f(N)) *in parallel with* O(g(N)) = O(max(f(N), g(N))

But wait, isn't that exactly the same as for sequential algorithms? Yep, it is. Ideally, the gains from parallelizing an algorithm come from spreading the task over several processors. For any given machine, the number of processors available is a constant, and since O-notation factors out constants, we get the (somewhat startling) result above.

Okay, so we're just programmers and we're not all so hot at math. What's the bottom line of all this? What it comes down to is that O-notation takes to heart the idea that it's the innermost loop of the most critical part of your algorithm that matters the most. If you are satisfied that you have the right algorithm, you know that you'll have to start fiddling with that inner loop if you want to speed things up!

This section was about how to think about performance. In order to make good decisions about how to optimize your program, you need good intuition at the detail level about how long various operations and library functions in C take to execute, a general idea of how different subsystems of your computer are being used and, at the highest level of abstraction, an idea of the O-notation for your algorithm.

Profiling

Profiling is the automated analysis of how much time is spent in different parts of your program. A good profiler will give you detailed breakdowns on the number of calls and the amount of CPU time taken by each function. This is called a *flat profiler*. A really good profiler will go the extra mile and analyze the calling sequences and tell you which functions call which other functions the most, again by time and number of calls. This is called a *graphing profiler*.

Profilers almost exclusively measure CPU time and number of calls but fail to measure I/O time, network delays, cache latency, and a large number of other possible problems. However, in many cases these delays can be inferred by what is often called a library function associated with that task. For example, a lot of calls to `fread` might indicate your program is I/O bound and CPU time isn't an issue. Pay special attention when the total CPU time indicated by the profiler is only a fraction of the observed wall-clock time spent by your program, because this indicates that the bottleneck is in some other subsystem, perhaps memory, disk, or network activity.

Profiling requires instrumentation. Tracking and counting calls and time spent takes work and isn't usually enabled by default, so you need to set the proper switches in your programming environment to enable profiling of your code, then recompile. What this does is tell the compiler to insert some extra code into each function to count calls and CPU time and, in the case of graphing profilers, the caller stack. After your program is run, the statistics are dumped to a file. If the file contains raw binary data, you'll need to run a program afterward to analyze this data and present it in a readable format.

Note

A little disclaimer: There is no ANSI/ISO standard for C profiling tools, and the current state of the art is for each programming environment to have its own tools producing profiling output in its own particular format. The discussion in this chapter will use as examples the *prof* and *gprof* facilities from the UNIX programming environment, but these are just examples. You may have to break out the documentation for your own programming environment to figure out what tools you have available. The abstract concepts presented should apply to all profiling environments, though the details will differ significantly.

Flat Profiling

This is the most common profiling format and the easiest to interpret. Each function is timed (based on CPU usage), and the most time-consuming functions are listed in order. The following profile was taken from a program that reads in a file then sorts it using bubble sort and a case-insensitive string comparison.

% Time	Cumulative Seconds	Self Seconds	Calls	Self ms/Call	Total ms/Call	Name
52.9	67.71	67.71				internal_mcount
22.1	96.03	28.32	2739025	0.01	0.02	compare
13.2	112.93	16.90	208082387	0.00	0.00	toupper
2.5	116.17	3.24	5481361	0.00	0.00	strlen
1.7	118.36	2.19				mcount (249)
1.5	120.25	1.89	4630519	0.00	0.00	realfree
1.2	121.79	1.54	5479717	0.00	0.00	malloc_unlocked
1.1	123.25	1.46	5478052	0.00	0.00	free_unlocked
0.6	123.99	0.74	3007715	0.00	0.00	cleanfree
0.6	124.72	0.73	2739025	0.00	0.00	strcmp
0.5	125.32	0.60	5479709	0.00	0.00	malloc
0.4	125.84	0.52	10957790	0.00	0.00	mutex_unlock_stub
0.4	126.35	0.51	1	510.00	58166.22	bubblesort
0.4	126.85	0.50	3842815	0.00	0.00	t_delete
0.4	127.31	0.46	10957791	0.00	0.00	mutex_lock_stub
0.3	127.73	0.42	5478052	0.00	0.00	free
0.1	127.87	0.14	661494	0.00	0.00	t_splay
0.1	127.98	0.11	786934	0.00	0.00	smalloc
0.1	128.07	0.09	466318	0.00	0.00	swap
0.0	128.08	0.01	1663	0.01	0.01	memccpy

Here's how to interpret the columns in this particular sample:

1. The first column indicates what percentage of the total time was spent in this function, and it is also the sort order of the list. The higher in the list a function appears, the more likely it is that optimizing it will pay off.
2. *Cumulative Seconds* is a running total of the seconds taken for all functions up to this point. Note that this is the total for all calls to the function, not the per-call cost.
3. *Self Seconds* is how many seconds each function took in total. Again, this is the total for all calls to the function, not the per-call cost.

4. The fourth column is simply the number of times the function was called.
5. *Self ms/Call* is how much time was spent inside each call to the function, in milliseconds. Hopefully, your profiler is a little more with the times and can measure in microseconds instead of milliseconds!
6. *Total ms/Call* is an extension of Self ms/Call that includes time spent in subroutines.
7. The last column is the name of the function.

Some things to note. The original program only had three functions defined, `compare`, `bubblesort`, and `main`. The profiling report shows many other irrelevant functions. The primary one to ignore is `internal_mcount`, which is an artifact of the measurement process.

Some of the other functions are recognizable as library functions or their derivatives. You should note calls to `fread` or `fwrite` or other standard library I/O functions as possible indications that your program's speed may be determined primarily by I/O speed and not computation and should be optimized according to that criterion instead.

What the profile is telling us is that we should spend most of our optimization efforts on the `compare` function. In particular, we should look for calls to `strlen` or `toupper` that could be reduced in number or eliminated.

What the profile *doesn't* tell us is that the real problem with this program is that it uses `bubblesort` (a poor algorithm choice), and it doesn't tell us *which* calls to `strlen` or `toupper` are significant, since they could be called from many places in the program.

Graphing Profilers

Graphing profilers are not as common as flat profilers, but they do come in handy for larger programs in which it isn't always obvious where a standard library or your own general-purpose utility function is being called from. In this context, graphing doesn't mean that the output is a graph or picture of any sort. It means that the profiler makes a mathematical graph in memory of what functions call what other functions and correlates that data to help spot optimization issues that cross functions.

Here is a snippet from the output of a graphing profiler. (Some of the irrelevant portions have been skipped in the interest of saving space. The original report was about 15 pages long.)

```
Called/Total         Parents
Index  %Time     Self Descendents  Called+Self     Name         Index
                                   Called/Total       Children


                 0.00       58.19        1/1           _start [2]
```

```
[3]      46.2    0.00        58.19        1          main [3]
                 0.51        57.66        1/1            bubblesort [4]
                 0.00         0.01     1657/1657         fgets [21]
                 0.00         0.01     1655/1655         printf [25]
                 0.00         0.00     1656/5479709      malloc [7]
                 0.00         0.00     1656/5481361      strlen [9]
                 0.00         0.00        1/1            fclose [32]
                 0.00         0.00        1/1            calloc [36]
                 0.00         0.00        1/5478052      free [12]
                 0.00         0.00     1656/1656         strcpy [40]
                 0.00         0.00        1/1            fopen [45]
                 0.00         0.00        1/1            memset [128]

----------------------------------------

                 0.51        57.66        1/1            main [3]
[4]      46.2    0.51        57.66        1          bubblesort [4]
                28.32        29.25 2739025/2739025       compare [5]
                 0.09         0.00   466318/466318       swap [20]

----------------------------------------

                28.32        29.25 2739025/2739025       bubblesort [4]
[5]      45.7   28.32        29.25 2739025           compare [5]
                16.90         0.00 208082387/208082387 toupper [6]
                 0.60         5.41 5478050/5479709       malloc [7]
                 3.24         0.00 5478050/5481361       strlen [9]
                 0.42         1.69 5478050/5478052       free [12]
                 0.73         0.00 2739025/2739025       strcmp [14]
```

The preceding profile consists of three sections that are summaries of the execution time and call counts for the `main`, `bubblesort`, and `compare` functions. Each section is identified by the indented function name in the "Name" column (column six). Within each section, subroutines called are listed below the function's line and callers are listed above the line, in order of contribution to the time spent.

The meanings of the individual columns are as follows:

1. The first column is an index number and is otherwise not very significant.
2. *%Time* is the total amount of time taken by this function and all the functions it calls (and the functions they in turn call, and so on). Since everything is originally called from `main`, it always appears at or near the top of a report like this, but that doesn't mean it should be the target of optimizations.

3. *Self* is the total number of seconds spent in this function, not including time spent in subroutines. In other words, even though `main` accounted for 46.2% of the time spent in the program, 0 seconds of it was actually in `main` alone, and the rest was in the subroutines that `main` called.
4. *Descendents* is the total number of seconds spent in functions called by this function.
5. *Called/Total* is the ratio of times this function was called from a particular parent function or performed calls to child functions.
6. *Name* with parents and children indented. These are the function names in question. Functions that appear above the function that the summary is centered on are callers, those appearing below are callees.

The graphing profiler lets you think about optimization across calls and across modules. Unlike the flat profile, it shows `bubblesort` contributing to excessive calls to the `compare` function, even though very little time is spent in `bubblesort` itself.

It's not shown in the above sample, but graphing profilers are also good at identifying time spent in recursion. It would appear as *Called+Self* in the above format.

Other Profiling Methods

Another common profile format is the *test coverage* profile. Typically this will incorporate a listing of the function with numbers next to each statement showing how many times it was executed, either per call, per the whole run of the program, or both. It is very useful if you have already narrowed your optimization efforts to one particular function.

Don't have a profiler or can't figure out how to use it? If you have a debugger handy, you can start a long run of your program and interrupt it every so often and do a stack trace. Write down the top two functions on the stack, then let the program run some more. Interrupt your program again and write down the new functions that appear or put a check mark next to those you've already seen. After five to ten stack traces, you should have a clear idea which functions your program is spending the most time in, with a cute histogram representation of check marks showing the most time-consuming functions.

Profilers provide objective evidence of the location and nature of bottlenecks in your program. You should use this information to target your optimization efforts precisely on the problem areas in your program.

Algorithmic Strategies for Optimization

When creating your program, you were probably faced with several choices about which algorithms to use. Now would be a good time to revisit your choices for their relevance to your optimization goals and consider replacing them with others.

The most straightforward decisions on algorithm choice are centered around sorting. The subject has been studied in great detail (and even occupies a whole chapter in this book). Thankfully, C provides the `qsort` library function, which is good enough for most sorting situations that no further work needs to be done beyond replacing your own sort function (`bubblesort` or whatnot) with a call to `qsort`. Keep in mind that `qsort` doesn't have to be implemented as `quicksort`, though it often is.

There are some circumstances in which a particular sort algorithm is likely to be more appropriate than just calling `qsort`. Please see Chapter 13, "Rapid Sorting Techniques," for specific information about sort algorithm choices.

There are many kinds of algorithms other than those just for sorting. Do a little Web research and visit some programmer-oriented Web sites to see if they have some bits of code that are appropriate for your task. Many areas are well represented in books and journals. For example, there are dozens of books and journals on computer graphics, and nearly every significant algorithm in the subject area has been documented. Regardless of topic, being able to start with an algorithm that someone else has tested and optimized is a great headstart; you should by all means take advantage of the contributions of others.

The next step is to examine your chosen algorithm. The following discusses ways to speed things up on an algorithmic level.

Loops within loops (within loops, and so on). Each level of a nested loop increases the exponent in the O-notation for your algorithm (a very bad thing). Unfortunately, I can't give you any hard-and-fast rules about how to reduce the nesting level of algorithms in general. Each algorithm has to be taken on its own terms and sometimes nothing can be done. But at the very least, eliminate any loops that are unrelated to the work of the algorithm itself.

Here's an example. Suppose you need to sort a list of words without regard to the case of the letters. In your initial attempt, you call `qsort` and give it a comparison function that converts the words to uppercase before returning a result. Each time `qsort` calls your comparison function, the conversion happens again. Assuming your library `qsort` is O(N log N), you will be converting words to uppercase O(N log N) times. A better alternative is to convert the words to uppercase before doing the sort. By converting beforehand, it can be done exactly once per word, making it O(N).

Here's another example. Let's say you have two lists of words to compare to see which words both lists have in common. The simplest thing is to loop over each word in the first list then compare it to each word in the second list. That algorithm contains two loops over the input, one nested inside the other, so it would be $O(N^2)$. We can make an improvement by sorting the two lists beforehand, which will allow us to do the comparison in a single pass. This new algorithm would have an O-notation of only O(N log N) accounted for in the time spent sorting.

Reality Check

Optimizing an algorithm on an abstract level is actually quite hard. Furthermore, your program may contain many algorithms interacting in complex ways that make it difficult to guess at possible improvements. But fear not.

It is still valuable to think about the real task that your program is trying to accomplish. You may be inspired to rewrite it, so as to center it around fewer, simpler, or better-known algorithms. The important thing is to avoid algorithms with disadvantageous O-notations like $O(N^3)$ and replace them with better ones that have lower O-notations like O(N), or at least O(N log N).

Implementation Strategies for Optimization, or Micro-Optimizations

This section discusses some ways to tweak your code to make it just a bit faster. The justification for this is that O-notation analysis of algorithms factors out the constants and lower-order contributions to time taken by an algorithm. By addressing optimization on this level, we can make some gains that, while less dramatic than eliminating loops, are still worthwhile.

Also, this is where the profiler comes in handy. First, you use it to find the inner loops in functions that are called most often; you do the micro-optimization there first. Then, run the profiler again to verify that the change you made actually was an improvement!

A gentle reminder: Some of these micro-optimizations are tasks that a sophisticated compiler can already do automatically when you set it to "optimize" mode. Spending a moment reading the compiler documentation could save you the effort of rewriting your code.

Inlining

Inlining is the replacement of a call to a function with the actual code of the called function. Many older compilers are capable of inlining small functions automatically, and newer compilers that support C++ or C99 are required to support the `inline` keyword in the language. Some compilers are quite enthusiastic about inlining and will even do recursive inlining.

But if necessary, very small functions can be recoded as macros to obtain similar speedups on compilers without inlining capability. This should be done after the code is completely debugged. All debuggers that I've seen are incapable of displaying or stepping through the expanded macro text, which can get quite complex.

Consider the following example code before optimization:

```
int foo(a, b)
{
    a = a - b;
    b++;
    a = a * b;
    return a;
}
```

Here is an example of equivalent code that has been inlined via macros:

```
#define foo(a, b) (((a)-(b)) * ((b)+1))
```

The extra parentheses in the macro are necessary to preserve grouping in case `foo` is used in an expression with higher precedence than `*` or in case `a` or `b` contains subexpressions with lower precedence than `+` or `-`.

Comma expressions and `do { ... } while(0)` can be used for more complicated functions, with some restrictions. The `do-while` style of macro lets you create local variables for use in the macro, but you can't return a value to the expression the macro is used in. The opposite is true for macros using comma expressions.

Caution

Making every function in sight into a macro leads to code bloat and can dramatically increase the amount of memory your program needs. The larger a program is, the less likely it is to fit entirely into cache or some other layer of physical memory, undoing the hoped-for gains.

Macros in C "evaluate" their arguments each time the argument is mentioned inside the macro. If the argument actually passed to the macro is a complicated expression or function call, the net result may very well be an increase in CPU time. Creating multiple side effects the caller did not expect will almost certainly make the program buggy.

Because these macros can contain complicated statements, optimizers have a hard time figuring them out and may give up. Also, don't forget that there's a limit on how many characters a macro can have.

Profilers don't see macros, so it's hard to optimize any further once you've done this.

Loop Unrolling

When the time spent on iteration and looping itself becomes significant compared to the time spent on the instructions within the loop, you can use *loop unrolling* to unleash economies of scale. Repeat the body of the loop a few times (5 to 10 is a good start) and insert the minimal code necessary to adjust the loop counter or other conditions of the loop.

Many compilers will do loop unrolling for you automatically but, if you know yours doesn't, you can try it yourself.

Consider this example with a single-statement `for` loop:

```
for (i = 0; i < 100; i++)
{
    code(i);
}
```

After optimization by loop unrolling by 10, it looks like this:

```
for (i = 0; i < 100; )
{
    code(i); i++;
    code(i); i++;
    code(i); i++;
    code(i); i++;
    code(i); i++;
    code(i); i++;
    code(i); i++;
    code(i); i++;
```

```
        code(i); i++;
        code(i); i++;
    }
```

In this way the test for `i < 100` and the branch back to the top of the loop are executed only 11 times rather than 101. Loop unrolling works best when the loop is executed a fixed, non-prime number of times and the iteration variable is only modified in one place (aside from its initialization).

Furthermore, if `code()` didn't make use of `i`, all the little `i++`'s could be replaced by a single `i += 10`. Rearranging the `for` loop into a `do-while` loop can make the 11 into 10. If the loop went only to 5 rather than 100, you could unroll the loop completely and eliminate the branching and testing entirely.

For computations that converge on some result, compilers will often refuse to unroll on the grounds that unrolling will change the result. If the application is not sensitive to excess precision, you can arrange to test the convergence less often by duplicating the interior of the loop. This is especially useful if the test for convergence is expensive in relation to the calculation of the result.

Caution

An unrolled loop is larger than the "rolled" version and so may no longer fit into the instruction cache (on machines that have them). This will make the unrolled version slower. Also, in this example, the call to `code` probably overshadows the cost of the loop, so any savings from loop unrolling are insignificant in comparison to what you'd achieve from inlining in this case.

If you happen to be using a vectorizing compiler on a supercomputer, loop unrolling can interfere with vector optimization. Consult the compiler manual for specific advice on how to write loops to take full advantage of your particular machine's strengths.

Loop Jamming

The idea of loop jamming is to combine adjacent loops that loop over the same range of the same variable. Assuming nothing in the second loop indexes forward (for example `array[i+3]`), you can do loop jamming optimization.

Here is an example of code with separate loops:

```
for (i = 0; i < MAX; i++)    /* initialize 2d array to 0's */
    for (j = 0; j < MAX; j++)
        a[i][j] = 0.0;
for (i = 0; i < MAX; i++)    /* put 1's along the diagonal */
    a[i][i] = 1.0;
```

The same code after loop jamming optimization:

```
for (i = 0; i < MAX; i++)
{
    for (j = 0; j < MAX; j++)
        a[i][j] = 0.0;       /* initialize 2d array to 0's */
    a[i][i] = 1.0;           /* put 1's along the diagonal */
}
```

This way, the incrementing and testing of `i` are done only half as often. Under some circumstances, locality of reference (defined later) may be better, improving cache behavior. (This example is credited to Aho and Ullman.)

Loop Inversion

Some machines have a special instruction for decrementing and comparing with zero. By rewriting your loops to count down instead of up and by stopping the loop at 0 instead of some maximum, you have given your compiler a strong hint that now would be a good time to use one of those special instructions, if applicable.

Assuming the loop is insensitive to direction, try this simple replacement.

Here is a typical `for` loop in C:

```
for (i = 1; i <= MAX; i++)
{
    ...
}
```

After optimization by loop inversion, it looks like the following:

```
i = MAX+1;
while (--i)
{
    ...
}
```

If you plan on doing this optimization in combination with pointer arithmetic, take heed that while ANSI C has a special rule that allows you to set a pointer to one element past the end of the array, there is no similar rule for one element before the *beginning* of the array.

Strength Reduction

Strength reduction is the replacement of an expression by a different expression that yields the same value but is cheaper to compute. (Many compilers will do this for you automatically.) The classic examples follow, with the rationale for each strength reduction optimization in comments.

Here is the unoptimized code:

```
x = w % 8;
y = pow(x, 2.0);
z = y * 33;
for (i = 0; i < MAX; i++)
{
    h = 14 * i;
    printf("%d", h);
}
```

After optimization by strength reduction, it could look like the following:

```
x = w & 7;              /* bit-and cheaper than remainder */
y = x * x;              /* mult is cheaper than power-of */
z = (y << 5) + y;       /* shift & add cheaper than mult */
for (i = h = 0; i < MAX; i++)
{
    printf("%d", h);
    h += 14;            /* addition cheaper than mult */
}
```

Also note that array indexing in C is basically a multiplication and an addition. The multiplication part can be subjected to strength reduction under some circumstances, notably when looping through an array.

Loop Invariant Computations

Any part of a computation that does not depend on the loop variable and is not subject to side effects can be moved out of the loop entirely. Most compilers are pretty good at doing this by themselves, but try to keep the computations within the loop simple anyway and be prepared to move invariant computations out yourself. (There may be some situations in which you know the value won't vary, but the compiler is playing it safe in case of side effects.) "Computation" here doesn't mean just arithmetic; it also applies to array indexing, pointer dereferencing, and calls to pure functions; all are possible candidates for moving out of the loop.

In a loop that calls other functions, you might be able to get some speedup by ripping the subroutines apart and figuring out which parts are loop invariant *for that particular loop in its caller* and calling those parts ahead of time. This is not very easy and seldom leads to much improvement unless you're calling subroutines that open and close files repeatedly or you `malloc` and `free` large amounts of memory on each call or do something else drastic.

Expression Grouping

Older C compilers were allowed to regroup arithmetic expressions to some extent. ANSI codified that arithmetic expressions are evaluated as they are grouped so as to avoid any unwanted surprises. What this means is that:

```
float a, b, c, d, f, g;
...
a = b / c * d;
f = b * g / c;
```

will not be seen as having the common subexpression `b / c`. If you rewrite the second expression, like so:

```
float a, b, c, d, f, g;
...
a = b / c * d;
f = b / c * g;
```

an ANSI C compiler is now free to compute `b / c` only once. Note that the new code may behave differently for overflow or provide slightly different results with floating point.

Tail Recursion Elimination

When a recursive function calls itself, an optimizer can, under some conditions, replace the call with an assembly level equivalent of a "goto" back to the top of the function. This saves the effort of growing the stack, saving and restoring registers, and any other function call overhead. For very small recursive functions that make zillions of recursive calls, tail recursion elimination (TRE for short) can result in a substantial speedup. With proper design, the TRE can take a recursive function and turn it into whatever is the fastest form of loop for the machine.

TRE has been around for a long time. It originated with functional languages such as LISP that do so much recursion that TRE is a necessity. C, C++, and the Pascal-like languages fall into the "imperative" language category; extremely efficient programs, recursive or not, can be written and compiled without the benefit of TRE and still perform on a par with (and often better than) a similar LISP program. What I'm leading up to is that TRE is not automatically present in every modern optimizer, though many certainly do have it.

Back to the conditions mentioned earlier. In order for TRE to be a safe optimization, the function must return the value of the recursive call without any further computation.

Consider this sample of code:

```
int isemptystr(char * str)
{
  if (*str == '\0') return 1;
  else if (! isspace(*str)) return 0;
  else return isemptystr(++str);
}
```

The above can have TRE applied to the final `return` statement because the returned value from this invocation of `isemptystr` will be exactly that of invocation n+1 with no further computation.

This is an example of when TRE cannot be applied:

```
int factorial(int num)
{
  if (num == 0) return 1;
  else return num * factorial(num - 1);
}
```

The above cannot have TRE applied because the returned value is not used directly. It is multiplied by `num` after the call, so the state of that invocation must be maintained until after the `return`. Even a compiler that supports TRE cannot use it here.

This is a rewrite to allow TRE optimization:

```
int factorial(int num, int factor)
{
  if (num == 0) return factor;
  else return factorial(num - 1, factor * num);
}
```

What we have done is move the multiplication by `num` down into the caller by passing `num` as the second parameter.

In my experience, the optimizers for languages like C don't bother to perform this sort of rewriting. However, even if your compiler implements TRE optimization, you should not assume that it automatically has done so for you. You may have to rewrite even the simplest recursive function before TRE can be applied. If doing so reduces the readability of the function significantly, the effort is highly questionable.

There is a large subset of recursive algorithms that have simple iterative counterparts. C compilers are very, very good at optimizing loops and can do so without the sometimes onerous conditions that TRE requires. If you must optimize at the source level, consider using plain iteration before TRE-friendly rewriting.

Finally, if the recursive function contains loops or large amounts of code, TRE will be only marginally helpful, since TRE optimizes only the recursion, nothing about the algorithm itself. Function calls are very fast, and optimizing something that is already very fast will quickly run into the law of diminishing returns.

Table Lookup

Consider using lookup tables, especially if a computation is iterative or recursive, for example, convergent series or factorials. Calculations that take constant time can often be recomputed faster than they can be retrieved from memory, and so do not always benefit from table lookup.

Here is a widely used example, a recursive function that calculates the factorial of a number:

```
long factorial(int i)
{
    if (i == 0)
        return 1;
    else
        return i * factorial(i - 1);
}
```

After optimization by table lookup, it would look like this:

```
static long factorial_table[] =
    {1, 1, 2, 6, 24, 120, 720 /* etc */};

long factorial(int i)
{
    return factorial_table[i];
}
```

If the table is too large to type, you can have some initialization code compute all the values on startup or have a second program generate the table and `printf` it out in a form suitable for including in a source file. At some point, the size of the table will have a noticeable effect on paging space. You could have the table cover the first N cases, then augment this with a function to compute the rest. As long as a significant number of the values requested are in the table, there will be a net win.

String Operations

Most of the C library character and byte string functions operate in time proportional to the length(s) of the string(s) they are given. It's quite easy to loop over calls to these and wind up with a significant bottleneck. Some things that may ease the situation are as follows:

- Avoid calling `strlen` during a loop involving the string itself. Even if you're modifying the string, it should be possible to rewrite it so that you set `x = strlen()` before the loop and then `x++` or `x--` when you add or remove a character.

- When building up a large string in memory using `strcat`, it will scan the full (current) length of the string on each call. If you've been keeping track of the length anyway (see above), you can index directly to the end of the string and `strcpy` or `memcpy` to there.

- For `strcmp`, you can save a little time by checking the first characters of the strings in question before doing the call. Obviously, if the first characters differ, there's no reason to call `strcmp` to check the rest. Because of the non-uniform distribution of letters in natural languages, the payoff is not 26:1 but more like 15:1 for typical uppercase data.

  Here is a simple replacement for `strcmp` that implements this idea:

  ```
  #define QUICKIE_STRCMP(a, b)  (*(a) != *(b) ? \
    (int) ((unsigned char) *(a)- \
           (unsigned char) *(b)) : \
    strcmp((a), (b)))
  ```

- An entirely different way to speed up `strcmp` is to place all your strings into a single array, in order. Then you only have to compare the pointers, not the strings. If the point of all the calls to `strcmp` is to search for a value from a large, known set and you expect that you'll be doing many such searches, then you'll want to invest in a hash table.

- Empty string tests are commonly implemented as `strlen(s) == 0`, and even experienced programmers may use `strlen` for this purpose. But if the strings you are working with are of substantial size, `strlen` will dutifully check each character until it finds the NULL terminator. Replacing with `*s == '\0'` saves the function call overhead, and it has to check only the first character. There can be a substantial improvement if your character strings are fairly long.

- Instead of `strcpy(s, "")`, try `*s = '\0'`. That will also save an unnecessary function call.
- Be aware that `strncpy` pads short strings with zeros. Except for the first one, which terminates the string, the extra zeros are typically never used, so some time is wasted, though typically not very much.
- Generally, `memcpy` is faster than `memmove` because it can assume that its arguments don't overlap. If you are tempted to replace these with your own versions, be sure to verify that your version works and is faster.

Variables

Avoid referring to global or static variables inside the tightest loops. Don't use the `volatile` qualifier unless you really mean it. Most compilers take it to mean roughly the opposite of `register`, and they will deliberately not optimize expressions involving `volatile` variables.

Avoid passing addresses of your variables to other functions. The optimizer has to assume that the called function is capable of stashing a pointer to this variable somewhere, and so the variable could get modified as a side effect of calling what seems like a totally unrelated function. At less intense levels of optimization, the optimizer may even assume that a signal handler could modify the variable at any time. These cases interfere with placing variables in registers, which is very important to optimization. For example

```
a = b();
c(&d);
```

Because `d` has had its address passed to another function, the compiler can no longer leave it in a register across function calls. However, it can leave the variable `a` in a register. The `register` keyword can be used to track down problems like this; if `d` had been declared `register`, the compiler would have to warn that its address had been taken.

Use of Floating Point

It wasn't that long ago that floating point operations were quite slow compared to integer operations. Within the last few years, floating point operations have have become just as fast as their integer counterparts.

By making proper use of floating point arithmetic in your program you can achieve two optimization goals:

1. Use floating point expressions and variables without mixing integer expressions or variables until the final stages of the computation. Often the cost of converting from integer to floating point or back again several times within an expression takes more CPU time than just doing the entire computation in floating point in the first place.
2. The very latest processors are quite good at keeping themselves busy with other tasks while floating point operations are proceeding. Some can even do multiple floating point operations at once. This is a form of free parallelism that you should not hesitate to take advantage of.

Locality of Reference

The foremost consideration when optimizing memory access, whether for virtual memory (VM) or cache considerations, is *locality of reference*. A program displays good locality of reference by using memory addresses that are near (in both time and location) to other recent references to memory. The main difference between optimizing for VM and optimizing for cache is scale: VM pages can be anywhere from 0.5KB to 8KB and beyond and can take tens of milliseconds to read in from disk. Cache blocks typically range from 16 bytes to 256 bytes and are read in at a rate in tens of microseconds. A program that forces many VM pages or cache lines to load in quick succession is said to be “thrashing.”

You can affect locality of reference by changing the order in which you access and allocate memory objects such as arrays or by splitting your data structures into “frequently used” and “infrequently used” segments and allocating all the “frequently used” stuff together. Don’t fool yourself into thinking that `malloc` always allocates adjacent chunks of memory on each successive call. You have to allocate one giant chunk and dole it out yourself to be certain. But this can lead to other problems.

Search and sort algorithms differ widely in their patterns of accessing memory. Merge sort is often considered to have the best locality of reference. Search algorithms may take into consideration that the last few steps of the search are likely to take place in the same page of memory and select a different algorithm at that point.

Row-Major Addressing

When stepping through multidimensional arrays, be sure to increment the rightmost index first. This is natural for C programmers but backward for FORTRAN programmers. If you find yourself writing C code like this, you can switch the array indexes to speed things up, as seen in the following:

```
float array[20][100];
int i, j;

for (j = 0; j < 100; j++)  /* note j is outer */
```

```
{
  for (i = 0; i < 20; i++)   /* note i is inner */
  {
    array[i][j] = 0.0;
  }
}
```

After row-major optimization the two `for` loops switch places, like this:

```
float array[20][100];
int i, j;

for (i = 0; i < 20; i++)   /* note i is outer now */
{
  for (j = 0; j < 100; j++)   /* note j is inner now */
  {
    array[i][j] = 0.0;
  }
}
```


Some Additional Optimization Strategies

If you are desperate for a little more speed but have exhausted the avenues of algorithm choice and implementation optimization, you might have to think about optimization outside the comfortable context of the C programming language.

One approach that some people swear by is to rewrite the most time-critical sections of code in assembly language. I will stand off from this advice a bit, because unless you are good enough as a programmer to write high-quality assembly language code that competes with the capabilities of a good compiler, you probably shouldn't be fiddling with assembly language. Mind you, it's not magic incantations only for high priests, but there are enough pitfalls that you will soon appreciate how tough a compiler's job really is.

If you feel up to trying it out, I suggest you optimize your code as far as possible in C then use your compiler to generate an assembly language listing of your function, which you can use as a starting point for experimentation. As a practical matter, keep the amount of assembly language code to a minimum to reduce the pain from porting your code to other platforms and processors in the future.

Another time-honored way of speeding up a program is simply to throw money in the general direction of hardware vendors. Depending on the source of the bottleneck, consider upgrading your CPU, adding co-processors, upgrading your Internet connection speed, or installing a high-speed RAID disk array. One drastic (and expensive) solution is to port your code to a supercomputer.

You can also throw money at software vendors. One simple approach is to install compilers from several different vendors and compile all your time-critical functions with each and profile them separately to see which compiler generates the fastest code for you. Typical variations between top-quality compilers are on the order of 2% to 5% in speed of the generated code (more as a matter of what circumstances the compiler authors have chosen to optimize for rather than any general failing). Another software-based solution is to use an appropriate commercial product such as a database package or a numerical analysis library. This lets you take advantage of heavily optimized software that wouldn't normally be at your disposal and that may contain some proprietary speedups that would never have occurred to you or me.

But we aren't all made of money and aren't all destined to become legendary assembly language hotshots. What simple and affordable strategy can we use? Patience. Thanks to Moore's law, computing power doubles approximately every 18 months. If your code is too slow by a factor of four, simply wait 36 months and your code will be up to spec without your having to lift a finger. That may seem facetious, but there are two interesting ramifications.

Given that computing power increases exponentially over time, algorithms with exponential or better O-notations are actually linear with a large constant. All that is required is that their progress can be checkpointed and transferred to an upgraded CPU every so often.

On a more mundane level, someone has to choose how often to upgrade to newer, faster hardware, which presents some conflicts. Given a limited but ongoing budget, one could purchase an expensive, top-of-the-line machine every few years. But by the time you can afford to replace it, the old machine that was fast in its day will be quite slow. Another strategy would be to buy lower end or midrange machines that are cheaper so that you can afford to replace them more often. That way you're never too far from the current state of the art.

Cooperative and Parallel Optimizations

There was a time when computers came with minimal operating systems capable of running only one program at a time. For these primitive systems, programmers could afford to make less than the best use of the resources of the machine (disk, memory, I/O controllers). Essentially, sloppy use of resources hurt only their own program, but as long as some useful work was being done by at least one subsystem, making some other subsystem do its job more efficiently didn't often pay off, since devices would just sit idle if they finished their tasks early. (Lest this seem like ancient history, I remind you that all the traits just mentioned apply to MS-DOS.)

Multitasking, multiuser, and server operating systems have changed this a bit. When your program finishes using a resource, another task that has been waiting can now proceed. That's good. But now, inefficient use of the resource no longer means merely less idle time during your program's run, it means that you might actually be preventing some other program from running. And users can exacerbate the problem by running the same program at the same time, forcing competition for the same resources.

The final twist is that under these multitasking OSs it's possible for different programs running at the same time to communicate with each other. If one program needs to receive a reply from the other program before proceeding (which they often do), the program making the request has to wait. What has happened is that not only do programs *use* resources, they in fact *are* resources.

Some New Measurements

So far, we've measured in O-notation, which implicitly measures the time taken by an algorithm, and we've measured by actual milliseconds and microseconds by using a profiler on a program. There are some other measurements useful for describing the performance of resources on a system (or network):

- *Throughput*—The amount of data that can be transmitted in an interval of time. Typically measured in bits per second (bps).
- *Latency*—The delay between issuing a request to a resource and the action starting to be performed. Typically measured in milliseconds or microseconds.
- *Burstiness*—The tendency of demands for a resource to be in quick succession with pauses of inactivity between them.
- *Duty Cycle*—The proportion of time a resource is being used. Usually measured as a percentage.

Client/Server and Parallelism

You would think that if you had two computers, one running a client program and the other running a server program, when the two programs communicated they would be running in parallel in some sense and would finish twice as fast as a single program attempting to do the work of both. The answer depends on an aspect of the protocol used to communicate between them, whether it is *blocking* or *non-blocking*.

Many Internet protocols are blocking protocols. For example, if you receive or send mail though an SMTP or POP server, the client program you use must stop and wait for a response from the server, since the protocols demand that a reply be received before the client can continue.

There are a couple of ways to allow the hoped-for parallelism to work. Unfortunately, both fall outside the strict confines of ANSI C.

The simplest is to use a non-blocking protocol in the first place. This is the approach used by the X11 Window System, for example. In this protocol, requests (usually to draw on the screen) are sent off, and the client program continues running without having to check for a reply or result in most cases. In fact, several requests can be generated in quick succession, and the X11 client-side library can package them up and send them together for maximum efficiency. In any case, the requests are processed by the server as they come in, and the client, if it is running on another processor, can still be doing other useful work, perhaps generating more requests. The X11 Window System API was also designed to have the advantage that the non-ANSI C details that support this scheme are hidden in library code—the programmer making use of it feels like he is writing normal function calls.

Another solution is to use a multithreading package to allow one part of your client program to wait for a reply from a server (using a blocking protocol) but let other threads in your client continue productively. This is a method used by many Web browsers to allow downloads of multiple pages and multiple images at the same time, even though the underlying protocol, HTTP, is a blocking protocol. This approach has the disadvantage that lots of your code may have to be rewritten to follow the model of threads controlling execution of your program, and there are several features of C that behave differently or unpredictably in a multithreaded program.

To be fair, there is no client/server overhead in C, and there is no parallelism, and there is no interprocess communication. None of these facilities are built into the language or the standard library. However, when such facilities are provided by the operating system, they are almost always available with a C header file to include and a precompiled library to link to. A well-rounded C programmer knows where the line is between ANSI C and OS-specific libraries, and he crosses it as few times as necessary.

Implicit Parallelism

There is ample opportunity for parallel processing in even the most mundane of computers. Each input/output device has a controller with a tiny little dedicated CPU inside it. It's possible to have data being sent out to a modem, records being written to disk, sections of RAM being read into cache, and pixels being written onto the screen, all on the same computer, all at the same time, with the main CPU actually being available through the whole process to do floating-point and integer computations.

Of course, this level of I/O parallelism can't be achieved at all times. But you can write your code to allow it to happen. Consider a simple program that

1. Reads a large number of records from a file.
2. Makes some changes to them while in memory.
3. Writes them to a new file.

As it is, each phase of the process makes full use of only one device at a time, and the rest are idle. No overlap of operations can take place. Now let's make two simple changes.

First, we consider the natural work sizes of the devices. For a disk, that natural size is usually a moderate number like 512 or 1024 bytes. Figure out how many records (from your file) are needed to fill a single disk block (let's say it's 8) and that gives you an idea of the smallest unit of work that will make full use of reading the disk. We will go a bit further and assume that there is a level or two of buffering going on in the OS or in the disk drive and that it can actually handle several requests being queued up. But we aren't here to saturate the drive to a 100% duty cycle. We just need to give it enough work that we can start work somewhere else while the disk is busy reading. What we're trying to avoid is giving it so much work that the entire program has to wait for it to finish.

So, we rewrite our program to

1. Read a small number of records from a file.
2. Make some changes to them while they are in memory.
3. Write them to a new file.
4. Repeat until the entire file is processed.

Even at this point we have two advantages. Many OSs will do read-ahead so that, if you're reading the file sequentially (as opposed to randomly), they can read a couple of blocks ahead so that when your program gets around to asking for the next bunch of records, they're all ready to go. Also, by having fewer records in memory at once, there is a better chance of them all fitting into the cache and less risk of having virtual memory swapping pages out, which of course adds to the load on the disk.

When we write out the records to a new file, we may be able to arrange, by careful choice of filename if nothing else, that the new file is written to a different disk than the one the original file is read from. If the second disk is on a different bus or controller, all the better. Now we have the following process:

1. Read a small number of records from a file on one disk.
2. Make some changes to them while in memory.
3. Write them to a new file on a different disk.
4. Repeat until the entire file is processed.

Such a program isn't going to run as if it were on a supercomputer, but it will make it possible for a good OS to distribute the processing load much better.

User Interface Considerations for Time-Consuming Algorithms

Okay, our 3-phase disk record copying function runs noticeably faster than it did before, but maybe it still takes up to a minute to finish. If it were being called from a program that had a graphical user interface, our program would be unresponsive to input, the user wouldn't know if or when it would become responsive again, and he would become more tempted with each passing moment to terminate the program.

The simplest thing is to change the cursor to a watch or hourglass to let the user know the program isn't freezing, that we're doing this intentionally. The next step is to estimate how much work there is to be done and how far along it is. These can be embellished with estimates of completion time and performance numbers that the user can use to evaluate hardware upgrades.

There is a complication to progress bars, and that is that not all algorithms proceed from start to finish at an even rate in a straight line. Here are some guidelines for dealing with this:

- If possible, put the slower and more random parts of the algorithm at the beginning, so that performance appears to improve or steady as time goes on. The user does not want to see things getting worse!
- Have one and only one progress bar up for the entire time the program is processing. It is quite disappointing watching a progress bar make it all the way over, only to be shown another one starting from scratch.
- The progress bar should never move backward. (Yes, I've seen it happen, but I couldn't get mad because it was my own code!)

Consider providing a Cancel (or Stop) button. This has the advantage that, should the user lose patience, your program will be the first to know, and you will have an opportunity to respond. For example, you might update any partially completed records or remove temporary files, or even indicate that the operation will be completed later, when the user isn't around and won't be bothered. Without a Cancel button, the user will have to terminate your program forcefully, and that could leave data in an inconsistent or garbage state.

If by any chance you follow all this advice about progress bars and Cancel buttons, you may happen upon an unpleasant fact. There is time and effort spent by the computer in updating the screen, checking for the user pressing the Cancel button, and having your program call upon the OS to check and process these even if nothing needs be done yet. This extra work can slow your program down significantly.

From experimentation, I've found that a good compromise between checking too often (and wasting time) and checking too seldom (and causing sluggishness) is about 200 milliseconds. But here's the final catch: Checking the system clock every time through the loop in your algorithm can also waste time. Listing 3.1 shows a pseudocode sample of how to write a loop inside your algorithm that doesn't incur too much overhead from any of the above GUI-friendly suggestions.

LISTING 3.1 Pseudocode for Cancel/Progress Algorithm

```
unsigned int count = 1;
timetype_t lastcheck = -1;
/* can't use time_t, as millisecond
resolution not guaranteed */

while (whatever)
{
  if (count % 100 == 0)
  {
     now = timecheck();
     if (now - lastcheck > 200 milliseconds)
     {
        if (cancel button pressed)
        {
           change dialog to say "cancelling...";
           clean up temp files and whatever else
             needs to be done;
           break;
        }
        update progress bar;
```

LISTING 3.1 continued

```
            lastcheck = now;
        }
    }
    /* do actual processing here
    each time through the loop */
    count++;
}
```

When Not to Optimize

As compelling as it is to try to make things go faster, remember that optimization should usually be the *last* stage of the development process, and generally should be subordinate to other software goals.

Here are some final "Words of Wisdom" that could save you a lot of time and effort during your optimization efforts.

Premature Optimization Is the Root of All Evil

The worst time to optimize is the instant you start writing code. Of course, that's the time you should be making algorithm choices that are efficient. But the code you're writing should not be tarnished by any thoughts of saving machine cycles. If it is, what you'll end up with is code that is difficult to maintain and harder to optimize later, because it won't be as easy to understand.

What you should do is write straightforward code that implements the right algorithm as clearly as possible. For a large, multiperson project, all the usual demands for documentation and comments and coding guidelines should not be given short shrift in the name of optimization. If anything, it is now more important that other programmers be able to understand your code, so that when it is finally time to optimize, everyone will have a clear idea of what the code is doing, rather than having to puzzle it out or ask you to explain some unusual line of code.

And of course, the most premature optimization is the one you do without using a profiler or other measurement tool first.

It is Easier to Make a Correct Program Fast Than a Fast Program Correct

It is far better to start with a working piece of code and try to improve it than to start with a broken piece of code and try to make it unbroken.

- Any shortcuts or quirky program statements made in the name of optimization are prime territory for bugs to hide in.
- In many (if not most) programming environments, setting the compiler to generate the fastest possible code turns off the generation of debugging information.
- By having a correct (but slow) copy of the code, you can run comprehensive regression tests on optimized versions to verify that the optimization process has not introduced any new bugs.

Don't Optimize Away Portability

Moore's law was inspired by the decrease in size (and corresponding increase in number) of transistors on silicon chips over time. But some of the gains in computer power over the years have also come from significant shifts in computer architecture. From mainframe to micro, from CISC to RISC, from batch mode to multithreading, each brought a new level of computer power and tested the portability of many applications.

By writing your programs to be portable to the latest and fastest machines, even a less than optimal program may run substantially faster than a very nicely optimized one that was designed for outdated hardware.

The Lazy Way to Optimization

Over the years I have accumulated a small library of personal utility programs that I never bothered to optimize. All of them are fairly portable ANSI C, (with a little POSIX here and there), and upgrades to newer machines usually are painless. Each time I try out my programs on new hardware, I am amazed at how snappy and quick my old unoptimized code has become over the years, with no effort on my part other than an occasional recompilation.

Let the Compiler Do It

This advice started out good and keeps getting better. Not only does hardware get faster, but the compilers that generate object code get better, too. Take a moment to look through your compiler documentation to see what optimizations it can perform all by itself, so you won't be tempted to duplicate its efforts. Find out what switches or command-line options need to be set to get maximum optimization.

Most modern compilers can be expected to perform at least these optimizations:

- Inlining
- Loop unrolling
- Loop inversion (on machines for which that would help)
- Strength reduction
- Loop invariant code removal
- Register assignment

Summary

I hope you've gotten a sense from this chapter that optimization isn't about "code tweaks" at all. Instead it's about choosing efficient algorithms based on O-notation, implementing those algorithms correctly, and then using profilers to evaluate your program for hotspots where some micro-optimizations would be appropriate, while respecting other programming goals like readability and portability throughout the process.

CHAPTER 4

Dealing with Dates

by Lawrence Kirby

In This Chapter

Date handling on computers has had a lot of press recently, notably concerning the millennium bug. The new millennium has already started as you read this so you will have some idea as to what effect it really had. However, the problems that caused the millennium bug haven't gone away. It is still important to be aware of the problems and code date handling to avoid them. But first we should look at what date and time facilities are provided by C.

Date and Time Functions

C's standard C library contains a set of date and time handling functions declared in the header `<time.h>`. These are shown in Listing 4.1. They make use of three types also defined in the header: `time_t`, `struct tm`, and `clock_t`.

LISTING 4.1 C's Time Functions Declared in `<time.h>`

```
time_t time(time_t *timer);
double difftime(time_t time1, time_t time2);
struct tm *gmtime(const time_t *timer);
struct tm *localtime(const time_t *timer);
char *asctime(const struct tm *timeptr)
char *ctime(const time_t *timer);
size_t strftime(char *s, size_t maxsize, const char *format,
                const struct tm *timeptr);
time_t mktime(struct tm *timeptr);
clock_t clock(void);
```

Basic Date and Time Functions

The `time()` function is declared as

```
time_t time(time_t *timer);
```

and gives the current date and time represented as a `time_t` value. You can either use the return value directly or pass it a pointer to a `time_t` variable where it will write the time value. If you don't pass it a pointer to a `time_t` variable, you must pass it a null pointer. `time_t` is defined as an arithmetic type capable of representing times. That means it can be an integer type such as `signed` or `unsigned`, `int` or `long`, or a floating point type such as `double`. C doesn't specify how `time_t` represents times. A portable program should not try to manipulate `time_t` values directly, but should use the standard library functions to do so.

It is common practice for compilers to define `time_t` as `int` or `long` and to store dates represented as seconds since January 1, 1970. The latter is specified in the POSIX standard but is not required by the C language, and it is best to avoid assumptions like this where possible. Even between systems that use seconds since January 1, 1970, there can be other differences such as the time zone (UTC or local time).

The `difftime()` function is declared as

```
double difftime(time_t time1, time_t time2);
```

and calculates the interval between two `time_t` values, giving an answer in seconds. If `time1` is later than `time2` the result is positive; if it is earlier the result is negative. `difftime()` allows us to measure a time interval in seconds even when `time_t` doesn't represent seconds. Listing 4.2 demonstrates this.

LISTING 4.2 Measuring Time Intervals Using `time()` and `difftime()`

```
#include <stdio.h>
#include <stdlib.h>
#include <time.h>

int main(void)
{
    time_t start, end;

    start = time(NULL);
    if (start == (time_t)-1) {
        printf("Sorry, the time is unavailable on this system\n");
        exit(EXIT_FAILURE);
    }

    printf("Please wait a few seconds and then press your ENTER/RETURN key");
    fflush(stdout);

    getchar();

    end = time(NULL);
    printf("\nThe interval was %.2f seconds\n", difftime(end, start));

    return 0;
}
```

Note that the code neither knows nor cares what type and representation `time_t` has; the details are always handled by standard library functions. The code checks whether `start` is `(time_t)-1`, which is the value `time()` returns if no time is available.

The program outputs the result to two decimal places. Typically `time_t` represents times in whole seconds, in which case there will be no fractional part. However, C allows an implementation to store partial second information in `time_t` if it wants.

Breaking Dates and Times into Useful Quantities

The type `struct tm` represents a date and time broken down into conventional components according to the Gregorian calendar. Table 4.1 shows its members.

TABLE 4.1 The Members of a `struct tm`

Member	*Description*
`int tm_sec`	Seconds after the minute (0–60)
`int tm_min`	Minutes after the hour (0–59)
`int tm_hour`	Hours since midnight (0–23)
`int tm_mday`	Day of the month (1–31)
`int tm_mon`	Month of the year (0(Jan)–11(Dec))
`int tm_year`	Years since 1900
`int tm_wday`	Day of the week (0(Sun)–6(Sat))
`int tm_yday`	Day of the year (0–365)
`int tm_isdst`	Daylight saving time indicator

The members and ranges are generally self-explanatory, but here are a few additional points:

- `tm_sec` is normally in the range 0–59 but can be 60 for a leap second, which is occasionally inserted to keep days in synchronization with the Earth's rotation.
- `tm_mon` starts at 0 rather than 1 for January. This often means it has to be adjusted by 1 in date conversions. `tm_mday` starts at 1, so it doesn't have the same problem.
- `tm_year` represents years since 1900. That means to represent the year 2000 it will contain the value 100. It does not contain just the last two digits of the year.
- `tm_yday` starts at 0 for January 1. December 31 is 364, or 365 in a leap year.
- `tm_isdst` indicates whether daylight saving time is taken into account for the specified time:

positive	Daylight saving time is in effect
zero	Daylight saving time is not in effect
negative	Information not available

C has two functions to convert a `time_t` value to a `struct tm`: `localtime()` and `gmtime()`, which are declared as

```
struct tm *gmtime(const time_t *timer);
struct tm *localtime(const time_t *timer);
```

They both take a pointer to a `time_t` variable holding the value to be converted (why they take a pointer is a historical accident, possibly because `time_t` may not always have been a type guaranteed passable as a function argument). The `time_t` variable is not modified, but both functions return a pointer to an internal static `struct tm` object containing the appropriate values. The difference between `localtime()` and `gmtime()` is that `localtime()` gives a result represented in the program's local time zone, whereas `gmtime()` gives the result represented as GMT (or more correctly these days UTC—Coordinated Universal Time).

How time zones are managed varies considerably between systems; C doesn't attempt to standardize this. A common method is to use an environment variable `TZ` to specify time zone information. Typically, setting up `TZ` is a system administration problem and the C program itself need not be concerned about it. The standard library does not provide a way to set time zone information. All you can do is get the current time zone name (see `strftime()` later on) and determine whether daylight saving time is in effect.

Simple Time String Formatting

The `asctime()` and `ctime()` functions generate a string representing the specified time in a fixed format, for example

```
Tue Feb 29 23:59:59 2000\n
```

Where `\n` is the normal newline character. Having the newline character is often a nuisance because in many cases you have to remove it afterward. The declarations of `asctime()` and `ctime()` are

```
char *asctime(const struct tm *timeptr)
char *ctime(const time_t *timer);
```

They are the same except that `asctime()` takes a pointer to a `struct tm` object, whereas `ctime()` takes a pointer to a `time_t` object. `ctime()` is defined to output a local time and `ctime(timer)` is equivalent to `asctime(localtime(timer))`. Listing 4.3 demonstrates the use of these functions to output the current time on local and UTC forms.

LISTING 4.3 Using `asctime()` and `ctime()` to Create Simple Date Strings

```
#include <stdio.h>
#include <stdlib.h>
#include <time.h>

int main(void)
```

LISTING 4.3 continued

```
{
    time_t timeval;
    struct tm *tmptr;

    timeval = time(NULL);

    printf("Time as local time is %s", ctime(&timeval));

    if ((tmptr = gmtime(&timeval)) == NULL)
        printf("UTC time not available\n");
    else
        printf("Time as UTC time is %s", asctime(tmptr));

    return 0;
}
```

`asctime()` and `ctime()` return pointers to internal static storage that holds the resulting strings. Multiple calls to these functions can overwrite the same object, so it is important to have finished with the string before calling one of the functions again. `gmtime()` can return a null pointer if no conversion to UTC is possible, so the program checks for this.

Complex Time Formatting

The `strftime()` function uses a format string in the style of `printf()` (but with different conversion specifications) to provide a flexible way of specifying formats. The declaration for `strftime()` is

```
size_t strftime(char *s, size_t maxsize,
                const char *format,
                const struct tm *timeptr);
```

`s` is a pointer to a caller-defined array of characters where the resulting string will be stored. `maxsize` is the maximum number of characters that `strftime()` can write, including the null character (typically the size of the array). `format` is the format string and `timeptr` is a pointer to a filled out `struct tm`. `strftime()` copies characters from the format string to the array pointed at by `s`, converting two character sequences starting with `%` to time fields. The function returns the number of characters written to the character array, including the null character. If the output won't fit (that is, would be longer than `maxsize`), `strftime()` returns 0 and you should not assume anything about the contents of the array; it might have been partially written. Table 4.2 summarizes the conversion specifiers.

TABLE 4.2 `strftime` **Conversion Specifiers (* indicates locale-specific)**

Specifier	*Replaced by*
`%a *`	Abbreviated weekday name
`%A *`	Full weekday name
`%b *`	Abbreviated month name
`%B *`	Full month name
`%c *`	Full date and time
`%d`	Day of the month (01–31)
`%H`	Hour (24 hour clock) (00–23)
`%I`	Hour (12 hour clock) (01–12)
`%j`	Day of the year (001–366)
`%m`	Month (01–12)
`%M`	Minute (00–59)
`%p *`	AM/PM designation for a 12 hour clock
`%S`	Second (00–60)
`%U`	Week number (Sunday-based)
`%w`	Weekday (0(Sun)–6(Sat))
`%W`	Week number (Monday-based)
`%x *`	Full date representation
`%X *`	Full time of day representation
`%y`	Year without century (00–99)
`%Y`	Full year including century
`%Z`	Time zone name or abbreviation (or empty if no time zone information available)
`%%`	A single `%` character

The starred items in the table are locale-specific (that is, their output can vary depending on what locale is in effect). This allows the same code to support the different date formats used in different regions of the world. Different locales can be set using the `setlocale()` function, which is declared in `<locale.h>`. For example the call

```
setlocale(LC_TIME, "");
```

will set time-related parts of the program's locale to whatever default environment the system specifies. The second argument can be `C`, which is the environment that C programs initially start with. The implementation can support other values for the string, but the exact forms are implementation-specific. Other points concerning Table 4.2 are

- Many of the conversion specifiers clearly relate to a particular `struct tm` member (for example, `%M` outputs the value of the `tm_min` member), but `%j` and `%m` adjust the values from `tm_yday` and `tm_mon` by 1 for more natural ranges.

- Field sizes for locale-specific conversions are not specified. This makes it tricky to know what size of character array to supply for the result. Be generous with the buffer size when using these and always check the return value to make sure the result fits.
- `%U` and `%W` give week numbers. With `%U`, the first Sunday of the year is defined as the first day of week 1; with `%W` it is the first Monday. Any day prior to this is considered to be in week 0. Unfortunately, there are various ways in use of specifying week numbers so if you have a particular application for week numbers, these may not be the ones you need. We will look at another definition of week numbers later on.

Listing 4.4 shows a sample program that lets you experiment with `strftime()` formats. The program looks for an environment variable `LOCALE` and if found, sets the time locale to that specified. How you set environment variables varies from system to system. If you have difficulty with this, the program could easily be changed to take an environment argument from the command line. Strictly using an invalid conversion specifier (that is, one not defined in the table) is an error that could even crash the program. So allowing the user to specify format strings like this is not a good idea for a real-world program. The `timestr` array is made deliberately small so you can see the effects of making the string too long.

LISTING 4.4 Experimenting with `strftime()` Format Strings

```
#include <stdio.h>
#include <stdlib.h>
#include <locale.h>
#include <time.h>

int main(void)
{
    time_t timeval;
    struct tm *tmptr;
    char *localename, *category;
    char format[100];
    char timestr[30];

    if ((localename = getenv("LOCALE")) != NULL) {
        if ((category = setlocale(LC_TIME, localename)) == NULL)
            printf("Warning - locale change failed\n");
        else
            printf("Locale changed to %s (%s)\n", localename, category);
    }
```

LISTING 4.4 continued

```
    for (;;) {
        printf("Enter a strftime() format string or q to quit\n");
        fflush(stdout);
        if (fgets(format, sizeof format, stdin) == NULL)
            break;
        if (format[0] == 'q' && format[1] == '\n')
            break;

        timeval = time(NULL);
        tmptr = localtime(&timeval);
        if (strftime(timestr, sizeof timestr, format, tmptr) == 0)
            printf("The timestr array isn't big enough\n");
        else
            printf("%s", timestr);
    }
    return 0;
}
```

Reading and Manipulating Dates and Times

`mktime()` is essentially the opposite of the `localtime()` function. It takes a filled out `struct tm` and converts it to a `time_t` value. Additionally, it modifies the `struct tm` members so that they are all in their correct ranges. The declaration for `mktime()` is

```
time_t mktime(struct tm *timeptr);
```

It takes a pointer to a `struct tm` object that it can both read and modify and returns the `time_t` value. It returns `(time_t)-1` if the time in the `struct tm` cannot be represented as a `time_t` value. All of the members listed in Table 4.1 are used as input except `tm_wday` and `tm_yday`, which are simply set based on the values in the other members. The `struct tm` is taken to represent a local time; there is no `mktime()` equivalent to `gmtime()`.

`mktime()` serves two main purposes: to help input and encode dates and to perform date arithmetic. There is no standard equivalent to `strftime()` for reading dates (some compilers support a `strptime()` function but it is not standard C); however, the `*scanf()` functions (`scanf()`, `fscanf()`, `sscanf()` plus others in C99) provide a reasonable way to read date strings, especially numerically encoded ones. Listing 4.5 gives an example of this. It reads date strings from the user and shows how they are interpreted by re-creating a date string with `asctime()`. The `tm_year` and `tm_mon` are adjusted as previously noted and `tm_isdst` is set to -1, indicating that whether daylight saving is in effect or not is unknown.

LISTING 4.5 Reading Date Strings

```
#include <stdio.h>
#include <time.h>

int main(void)
{
    time_t timeval;
    struct tm tmval;
    char inbuff[30];

    for (;;) {
        printf("\nEnter a date and time formatted as YYYY/MM/DD HH:MM:SS\n");
        printf("or q to quit\n");
        fflush(stdout);
        if (fgets(inbuff, sizeof inbuff, stdin) == NULL)
            break;
        if (inbuff[0] == 'q' && inbuff[1] == '\n')
            break;

        if (sscanf(inbuff, "%d/%d/%d %d:%d:%d",
                   &tmval.tm_year, &tmval.tm_mon, &tmval.tm_mday,
                   &tmval.tm_hour, &tmval.tm_min, &tmval.tm_sec) != 6) {
            printf("Invalid date format\n");
            continue;
        }
        tmval.tm_year -= 1900;
        tmval.tm_mon--;
        tmval.tm_isdst = -1;

        if ((timeval = mktime(&tmval)) == (time_t)-1) {
            printf("time_t cannot represent that date and time\n");
            continue;
        }

        printf("The date and time you entered is %s", asctime(&tmval));
    }

    return 0;
}
```

mktime() can also be used for date arithmetic. For example, if you run the code in Listing 4.5 with the date 2000/01/33 12:00:00, which is essentially two days after Jan 31, 2000, the program should output

```
Wed Feb 02 12:00:00 2000
```

If you give 2000/03/01 -1:00:00, the program should output

```
Tue Feb 29 23:00:00
```

That is, one hour before the start of March 2000. In general, you can adjust the members of a struct tm by specific time intervals and then call mktime() to adjust the members back to their correct ranges. Be careful with changes of daylight saving time (that is, clocks moving forward or backward an hour); some days are 23 or 25 hours long. If you are performing day calculations, set the time to midday to avoid any problem of hour changes spilling into a different day.

Measuring Execution Time

The final function in <time.h> is clock(). It is unlike the other functions in that it isn't truly date related, but I mention it here for completeness. clock() doesn't measure "wall-clock" time; rather, it measures CPU execution time. It is declared as

```
clock_t clock(void);
```

The <time.h> header in addition defines the type clock_t and a macro CLOCKS_PER_SEC. clock() returns values that measure time in units of 1/CLOCKS_PER_SEC seconds. In other words, to convert the interval between two clock() calls to seconds, you divide the difference by CLOCKS_PER_SEC. clock() is useful for measuring the CPU execution time of code. Listing 4.6 demonstrates a correct approach for using clock().

LISTING 4.6 A Wrapper to Measure Code Execution Time

```
#include <stdio.h>
#include <time.h>

int main(void)
{
    clock_t start, end;

    start = clock();

    /* The code you want timed goes here */

    end = clock();
```

LISTING 4.6 continued

```
    printf("Interval = %.2f seconds\n", (double)(end-start) /
                                        (double)CLOCKS_PER_SEC);

    return 0;
}
```

The most important thing to note is that a single `clock()` value is meaningless; only the difference between two `clock()` values is a useful quantity. This is because what point in time corresponds to a zero return value is unspecified. On some implementations that might be the start of the program, but you cannot assume this. Other points are

- Like `time_t`, `clock_t` can be any arithmetic type, integer or floating point. The code therefore casts the difference and `CLOCKS_PER_SEC` to `double` to give a known type for the division and result.
- `clock()` can typically measure to sub-second resolution, although C doesn't require any specific resolution and it can vary greatly from compiler to compiler. `CLOCKS_PER_SEC` is not an indication of the available resolution. One common implementation is to set `CLOCKS_PER_SEC` to `1000000` (one million) but the resolution is only 1/100 of a second, so the return value of `clock()` would increase in multiples of 10000.
- `clock_t` is often a 32-bit integer with a maximum value of `2147483647`. Couple that with a `CLOCKS_PER_SEC` value of `1000000` and you have only about 2147 seconds or just over 35 minutes of execution time before it overflows. So take care when trying to time programs with long execution times; it may work on some systems but not on others.

Because the resolution of `clock()` can be quite limited, often not even down to the millisecond level, it won't measure short execution times directly. One way around this is to run the code to be tested many times on a loop, measure the overall execution time, and calculate the time for a single execution.

The Millennium Bug: Date-Related Problems

There are many problems attributed to the millennium (or Y2K—Year 2000) bug, but the main one occurs with code that manipulates or stores dates using just the last two digits of the year. As the year changed from 1999 to 2000, two-digit dates appeared to change from 99 to 00 (that is, a 99 year decrease rather than a 1 year increase). This can produce the wrong results for programs that calculate time intervals or sort data by date, or programs may simply display the wrong date (for example, by prefixing 19 to give 1900 rather than 2000). Luckily, C's date-handling functions don't inherently suffer from these sorts of problems. The important things to remember are that the `tm_year` member of a `struct tm` represents years since 1900, not the last two digits of the year. Also, when using `strftime()`, use `%Y` rather than `%y` so that the full year is output.

Even though standard library functions don't suffer from Y2K problems, user code still can. Storing dates as `time_t` values where possible avoids Y2K problems, although it can create others. If you have to provide your own date format, make sure the full year is included. There are cases where you can get away with not doing this. For example, credit cards typically still show only a two-digit year for expiry dates. This works because such dates can only be valid for a limited period close to the current date. If you know the current year, you can calculate the full year such a two-digit year relates to using a limited capture range. Listing 4.7 demonstrates this.

LISTING 4.7 Determining a Full Year Using a Capture Range

```
int resolve_year(int year2dig, int yearnow)
{
    int result = yearnow - yearnow%100 + year2dig;

    if (result >= yearnow) {
    if (result > yearnow+50)
            result -= 100;
    } else {
        if (result <= yearnow-50)
            result += 100;
    }

    return result;
}
```

This will return a year whose last two digits are the same as `year2dig`, but which is within plus or minus 50 years of `yearnow`. This sort of technique can be useful when dealing with existing data that doesn't contain century information, but should be adapted to use whatever you know about the data. New code and data formats should include century information.

The biggest potential problem with C's date and time handling functions is the range of dates that `time_t` can represent. C doesn't specify any minimum ranges; however, a common representation for `time_t` is specified in the POSIX standard and is seconds since

Jan 1, 1970. If `time_t` is an unsigned integer type, this cannot represent dates before 1970 (and possibly not even if it is a signed integer type). If `time_t` is a 32-bit signed integer type it can represent up to 2147483647 seconds after 1 Jan 1970. That means it runs out on January 19, 2038. Should we worry about this? Probably not unduly, but we should be aware of it. Simply ignoring the issue is what caused the millennium bug in the first place. As far as compilers go, they will have the opportunity to change `time_t` to a wider (such as 64-bit) type long before that. Programs should be written so that they are insensitive to changes to `time_t` as well as other standard types. The biggest problem here is in stored data formats. Storing dates in files simply as `time_t` fields is dangerous because `time_t` can vary from compiler to compiler. There are various possibilities, including

- Store dates as an unsigned 32-bit value representing seconds since Jan 1, 1970. This pushes the expiration date to 2106. This doesn't quite solve the problem but remains largely compatible with existing 32-bit time formats.
- Allocate a wider field, such as 64 bits, to store a seconds since Jan 1,1970, value. This does effectively solve the problem, although it may seem wasteful of space.
- If you don't need down to the second resolution, storing the values as counts of days, hours, or even minutes can increase the date range enough to effectively eliminate the problem for most practical purposes.
- Use other formats such as text strings to represent dates. Although not space efficient, the most basic YYYYMMDD format requires eight bytes. It is simple and the obvious choice for text files.

It all ultimately depends on what you are trying to do. 2038 may already be inadequate for some financial contracts. `time_t` has always been hopelessly inadequate for cosmologists or even historians.

Useful Bits and Pieces

This section describes two functions that can be useful in date and time operations: determining whether a year is a leap year and calculating ISO 8601 week numbers.

Leap Years

One of the simplest questions about dates is whether a year is a leap year. Currently the calendar in widest use (and assumed by C's `<time.h>` functions) is the Gregorian calendar. In this a year is a leap year if it is divisible by 4 except where it is divisible by 100. Years divisible by 400 are, however, leap years. Those are the only rules (I've heard talk about 1000 or 4000 year rules but currently they don't exist). 2000 in particular is (or was) a leap year; in fact, all years between 1901 and 2099 divisible by 4 are leap years. Some code has used this simplified formula, but the full one isn't that complex and there is no good reason not to use it. The function `is_leap` demonstrates this:

```
int is_leap(int year)
{
    return year %4 == 0 && (year % 100 != 0 || year % 400 == 0);
}
```

ISO 8601: Date Formats and Week Numbers

Different parts of the world tend to use different date definitions and formats. Probably the most classic example is that in the U.S. the basic date format is MM/DD/YYYY, whereas in other parts of the world, such as the UK, it is DD/MM/YYYY. So 01/02/2000 is February 1 in the UK but January 2 in the U.S. There is, however, an international standard concerning dates called ISO 8601. It defines various things such as standard date formats and a standard week number. Although not always adopted for everyday use, it provides a basis for portable date formats. The full ISO 8601 date format is

```
CCYY-MM-DDThh:mm:ss
```

where `CC` is the century and `T` is literally the letter `T`; for example, 2000-02-29T12:00:00 is midday on Feb 29, 2000. You can express simpler variants of this, such as 2000-02-29. The obvious feature here is that the year and century are placed first, which with a four digit year makes this format unambiguous with the U.S. and UK formats. It also means, incidentally, that it will sort correctly using normal string comparison.

If you recall, `strftime()` has the `%U` and `%W` conversion specifiers for producing week numbers. However, ISO 8601 has its own definition of week numbers, which is in common use in some parts of the world. Listing 4.8 shows a function that calculates ISO 8601 and also explains the rules.

LISTING 4.8 Calculating ISO 8601 Week Numbers

```
/*****************************************************************************
 * weeknum_ISO8601.c       December 1999       L.Kirby
 *
 * Calculates the week number of a day in the year based on the ISO8601 week
 * numbering scheme. The arguments are:
 *
 * t - a pointer to a struct tm in which the following members must be set and
 *     normalised to the standard ranges specified (as standard library
 *     functions gmtime, localtime and mktime should do):
 *
 *     tm_wday - The day of the week of the day in question:
```

LISTING 4.8 continued

```
 *               0-Sunday -> 6-Saturday
 *
 *     tm_yday - The day of the year of the day in question: 0 -> 365
 *               January 1st is day 0.
 *
 *     tm_year - The year since 1900.
 *
 * firstDOW - This defines the day of the week on which a week starts:
 *            0-Sunday -> 6-Saturday. Normal ISO8601 weeks start on
 *            a Monday in which case this should be 1.
 *
 ********************************************************************************
 *
 * The week number is a value between 1 and 53 inclusive defined according to
 * the following rules:
 *
 * 1. The Gregorian calendar is assumed.
 *
 * 2. There are always 7 consecutive days with the same week number.
 *
 * 3. January 4th is defined to be in week 1. Equivalently week 1 is the
 *    first week of the year which has at least 4 days in that year.
 *
 * 4. firstDOW defines the day of the week which starts a new week i.e. has
 *    a different week number from the previous day.
 *
 * 5. Week numbers increase in sequence from week 1 until the week that is
 *    defined to be week 1 of the following year.
 *
 * It follows that:
 *
 * 6. Up to January 3rd may be in either week 1 of the current year or in
 *    weeks 52 or 53 of the previous year.
 *
 * 7. 29th December onwards may be in either weeks 52 or 53 of the current
 *    year or week 1 of the following year.
 *
 * XPG4 specifies a slight difference to the ISO rules which is implemented
 * if the XPG4_WEEKNUMS macro is defined
 *
 ********************************************************************************
 */
```

LISTING 4.8 continued

```
#include <time.h>

#define is_leap(year) (!((year) % 4) && (((year) % 100) || !((year) % 400)))

int weeknum_ISO8601(const struct tm *t, int firstDOW)
{
    const int tmp1 = firstDOW - t->tm_wday;
    const int tmp2 = t->tm_yday + ((tmp1 > 0) ? 3 : 10) + tmp1;
    const int fourthdaynum = tmp2 % 7;
    int       weeknum = tmp2 / 7;

    if (weeknum == 0) {
#ifdef XPG4_WEEKNUMS
        weeknum = 53;
#else
        const int yearnum = t->tm_year + (1900 % 400)-1;

        weeknum = (fourthdaynum + is_leap(yearnum) >= 6) ? 53 : 52;
#endif
    } else if (weeknum == 53) {
        const int yearnum = t->tm_year + (1900 % 400);

        if (fourthdaynum > is_leap(yearnum))
            weeknum = 1;
    }

    return weeknum;
}
```

Summary

In this chapter we have covered C's standard functions for dealing with dates and times, as well as the `clock()` function. We've covered how to use them for inputting, outputting, and manipulating dates and times, as well as common pitfalls (notably the millennium bug) including problems in storing dates and times. Finally, we've covered leap year calculations and looked briefly at ISO 8601, notably with regard to ISO week numbers.

There is nothing particularly complex in all this, but I hope you now have a better idea of what C's date and time handling routines are capable of and how to avoid some of the pitfalls that have trapped other programmers in the past.

CHAPTER 5

Playing with Bits and Bytes

by Lawrence Kirby

IN THIS CHAPTER

This chapter looks at how to manipulate bits and bytes using C. We will develop some useful techniques that involve bit and byte manipulation and look at particular code examples.

TABLE 5.1 C's Bitwise Operators

Operator	*Description*
&	Bitwise AND
|	Bitwise OR
^	Bitwise Exclusive-OR
~	Bitwise complement
<<	Bitwise left shift
>>	Bitwise right shift

Other than ~, these are all binary operators. That is, they take two operands and have corresponding assignment forms. For example, `a &= b` is equivalent to `a = a & b`, except that `a` is only evaluated once.

Representation of Values in C

C is a language designed to run on binary computers, and various binary characteristics show through in the language. Integer types in particular have a strong binary flavor. Perhaps most obvious is the maximum and minimum values that any integer type can hold. The actual values vary from compiler to compiler but typical maximum values for signed types are `127`, `32767`, and `2147483647` and for unsigned types typical values are `255`, `65535`, and `4294967295`. These look odd in decimal but always correspond to one less than a power of two. Writing these numbers in hexadecimal shows this more clearly: `0x7f`, `0x7fff`, and `0x7fffffff` for the signed values; `0xff`, `0xffff`, and `0xffffffff` for the unsigned values.

Integer values (and for that matter any other sort of value) are stored as a collection of bits in memory. The number of distinct values that a type can represent is limited by the number of bits it contains. For N bits the maximum is 2^N (2 to the power of N) states. So one bit can represent two states, two bits can represent four states, three bits can represent eight states, and so on. With unsigned integer types these states can all be used for positive values and zero. With signed integer types the states have to be shared between positive and negative values. Typically, the largest value of a signed type will be about half that of the corresponding unsigned type.

Bits are grouped into units called bytes. A byte is the smallest unit of memory that can be used to build objects. It is also the smallest generally addressable unit of memory, ignoring bit-fields, which we will cover later in the chapter. A byte consists of a fixed number of bits, usually eight. C guarantees that an implementation will make this at least eight (it can be more). The actual value used by an implementation is given by the macro `CHAR_BIT` in the header `<limits.h>`. In C a byte is the unit of storage occupied by a `char`.

The term *byte* is very common in computing and is used to specify system disk and memory sizes and even data transfer rates for storage and communications devices. C's definition of a byte is independent of these, although they usually do correspond. When I use the term byte, I always refer to C's definition. That is, the size of a `char`, `CHAR_BIT` bits, which is also the smallest unit of allocation and addressability defined by C.

The Representation of Integer Values

C's bit manipulation operators, `&` `|` `^` `~` `<<` and `>>`, along with their assignment counterparts, `&=` `|=` `^=` `<<=` and `>>=`, all work only on operands having an integer type to give an integer result. Because these operators manipulate the underlying bits of integer values, we should consider how these values are represented.

Unsigned integers are the simplest and are represented in a simple binary format where each bit position represents a power of two (1, 2, 4, 8...) referred to as its *weighting*. The weightings of all of the 1 bits are added together to form the overall value.

Signed integers are more complex because there are several ways to represent negative numbers. The formats that are possible in C are called twos complement, ones complement, and sign-magnitude (or signed magnitude or similar variants). These formats all use a bit to indicate the "sign" of the value, with 0 indicating a positive sign, 1 negative. For positive numbers, the format is the same as for unsigned integers. For negative numbers, the three formats take different approaches.

- Sign-magnitude corresponds most closely to the normal method of writing numbers in decimal. To get the representation of a negative number you take the representation of the corresponding positive number and simply set the sign bit.
- Ones complement represents negative numbers by inverting all of the bits of the corresponding positive number.
- Twos complement represents negative numbers by inverting all of the bits of the corresponding positive number and then adding 1.

Table 5.2 shows some examples of negative values represented in each of these three ways. The examples use an eight-bit format. The top bit always represents the sign bit, so the remaining seven bits represent size information.

TABLE 5.2 Representing Negative Values Using Signed Integer Formats

Decimal Value	*Sign-Magnitude*	*Ones Complement*	*Twos Complement*
0	00000000	00000000	00000000
-0	10000000	11111111	(00000000)
1	00000001	00000001	00000001
-1	10000001	11111110	11111111
16	00010000	00010000	00010000
-16	10010000	11101111	11110000
127	01111111	01111111	01111111
-127	11111111	10000000	10000001
128		-	-
-128		-	10000000

Some things to note from Table 5.2 are

- All formats use the same representation for positive numbers, which is also the same representation used by the corresponding unsigned format.
- Sign-magnitude and ones complement have separate representations for +0 and -0. This is generally not useful for integer operations but does have implications for bitwise operations that will be discussed later on.
- Twos complement has only one representation for zero but can represent an extra negative value (-128 in the eight-bit example even though it cannot represent 128).

Of the three signed integer formats, twos complement is by far the most commonly used. Nevertheless, you should at least be aware of the other formats. Although "invert all of the bits and then add 1" sounds odd, it turns out to have some nice properties both in terms of implementing it and using it. Other than overflow and carry conditions, the hardware operations required to implement twos complement arithmetic are the same as those required to implement unsigned arithmetic, when the result is represented in a form no wider than the input values. Table 5.3 shows some examples of adding bit patterns and the values concerned when interpreted as unsigned and twos complement values.

TABLE 5.3 Examples of 8-bit Unsigned and Twos Complement Addition

Binary Representation	*Unsigned Value*	*Twos Complement Value*
00001001	9	9
+ 00010011	19	19

TABLE 5.3 continued

Binary Representation	*Unsigned Value*	*Twos Complement Value*
= 00011100	28	28
10001001	137	-119
+ 00010011	19	19
= 10011100	156	-100
11001001	201	-55
+ 11010011	211	-45
= 10011100	156	-100

Table 5.3 also demonstrates that the same bit pattern can represent different values, even when representing integer values in the same program. In C, the type of the variable is the extra piece of information needed to determine fully what value a bit pattern represents. The last case in the table demonstrates a sum whose unsigned result cannot be represented. 201+211 should be 402 but the ninth bit is effectively lost, which reduces the result by 256 giving a result of 156.

C allows for integer representations to have "holes," which are unused bits that do not contribute to the integer value. The only exception is unsigned `char` where all bits are guaranteed to contribute to the value. This means that if, for example, an `int` is 32 bits wide, that does not guarantee that it can represent values up to `2147483647`. To find the true range that an integer type can represent, look at the `*_MIN` and `*_MAX` macros defined in the standard header `<limits.h>`. For example, `INT_MAX` defines the largest value that `int` can represent on that particular compiler.

Using Unsigned Type for Bit Manipulation

The preceding section shows that signed integers can be represented in various different formats with differing properties. To avoid many problems associated with this, it is usually best to use unsigned types to perform integer operations.

- The two representations for zero in ones complement and sign-magnitude representations can cause problems because most operations in C work in terms of values. With two representations for zero, the compiler can pretty much convert between them at will, which is very bad indeed if the state of particular bits is important.
- Because there are different ways of representing negative numbers, the same bit pattern on different systems can represent different values, and changing a bit can have a different effect on a value. For example, changing a bit other than the sign bit

in a negative number from 0 to 1 could either increase or decrease the magnitude of the number (sign-magnitude versus the others). Some bit tricks, as we will see later, simply won't work on some signed representations.

- Just changing the sign bit has very different effects on the value between the different representations—look at the bit patterns `01111111` and `11111111` in Table 5.2, for example.

In short, negative numbers are trouble when it comes to bitwise operations. It is possible to use signed integer types and restrict yourself to positive operands and results. However, it is still safer to stick to unsigned types. One word of caution: `char` and `short` values are promoted to at least `int` before any operation is performed on them. That means that even if you start off with an unsigned type, such as `unsigned char` or `unsigned short`, you can end up performing the operation on int (and therefore signed) values. With shift operations in particular this can produce unexpected results if data is moved into the sign bit.

Bit Shifting

Bit shifting is arguably one of the simplest operations that a computer can perform: moving the data in each bit in a value to another bit. For something so simple it can be used to do some surprisingly powerful operations, such as multiplication and division.

In decimal, you can multiply by 10 by adding another 0 on the right of a whole number value, or more generally by moving the decimal point one place to the right. Another way of looking at it is that you keep the decimal point fixed and move all the digits in the number one place to the left, supplying zeros at the right-hand end as necessary. So left shifting by one place multiplies the value by 10. This operation can be repeated so left shifting two places multiplies the value by 100, three places by 1000, and so on. On binary systems shifting multiplies by 2 rather than 10 at each step, giving multiplication factors of powers of 2 (2, 4, 8, 16, and so on).

When left shifting unsigned values, you will sooner or later shift 1 bits off the left-hand end. These bits are discarded so the result no longer corresponds to simply multiplication but a "truncated" version of the result.

When left shifting signed values, you have in addition the problem that either the original value, the result, or both can be negative because bits are shifted in and out of the sign bit. I've already covered the perils of interpreting bit patterns that represent negative values. Unfortunately, this means that the technique of left shifting an integer to multiply it by a power of 2 doesn't always work for negative numbers, although it does work for twos complement representations.

Since left shifting can be used to multiply by a power of 2, right shifting can be used to divide by a power of 2. Bits "shifted off" the right-hand end are lost, and this corresponds to discarding any remainder from the division. As before, this works smoothly for positive values but breaks down for negative values. In addition to all the representation problems, right shifting creates a new problem: What gets shifted in at the left-hand end? If a positive value is being shifted, the answer is simple: 0s are shifted in and this will give the expected result. For negative values it is less clear. In ones and twos complement representations, the compiler can preserve the division property by shifting 1 bits in on the left. Where the division is inexact, this causes the result to be rounded down (toward zero) for ones complement representations and up (toward negative infinity) for twos complement. C doesn't specify what the result will be when a negative value is right shifted; it is implementation-defined so the compiler gets to decide whether ones or zeros get shifted in on the left. This severely limits the usefulness of shifts on signed integers.

Note that while you can implement multiplication and division by a power of 2 using shifts, your compiler can do this too. Most compilers are quite capable of optimizing, say, a multiplication by 8 to a left shift of 3 places, where that would be more efficient. The best approach in code is to be clear and use a multiplication when you want to multiply and a shift when you want to shift bits. Nevertheless, it is useful to be aware of the correspondence, and that some multiplications and divisions by constant values can be much more efficient than others. For multiplication this doesn't necessarily have to be a power of 2. For example

```
X + (X << 3)
```

multiplies the value of `X` by 9 (because `9*X` can be broken down into `X + 8*X`). Again, most compilers can perform this sort of optimization automatically.

Other Bit Operators

If you think about it, all operations on a binary computer manipulate bits. In cases like general multiplication and division, the manipulations involved are complex. However, integer addition and subtraction are relatively simple and at the most basic level they take a collection of bits as input and produce a collection of bits as output. Certainly, they are defined in terms of values (for example, from Table 5.3, 9+19 must produce the answer 28 whatever bit pattern that happens to be). However, for unsigned integer operations in particular we can determine precisely what bit operations are required in order to produce the correct result. For our purposes here we will look at three simple cases:

- Adding 1 (incrementing)
- Subtracting 1 (decrementing)
- Negating the value

When you add 1 to a binary value you start at the lowest order bit. If it is 0 you set it to 1 and then stop. If it is 1 you set it to 0 and then move on to the next higher bit, in effect performing a "carry." You repeat this process for each bit in turn until a zero bit stops it or you run out of bits. For example:

```
 01001111
+       1
 --------
 01010000
```

The overall effect is that a sequence of ones starting at the lowest order bit is set to 0 and the first 0 bit encountered is set to 1. In the case of all ones (11111111), the result is that everything is converted to 0s: 00000000.

Subtracting 1 from a binary value works in a similar way. The difference is that the process stops when you encounter a 1 bit rather than a 0 bit. In effect, subtracting 1 from a 0 bit causes a "borrow" to occur, rather than the carry that occurs when you add 1 to a 1 bit. For example:

```
....10110000
   -       1
    --------
    10101111
```

The overall effect of decrementing is that a sequence of 0s starting at the lowest order bit is set to 1 and the first 1 bit is set to 0. In the case of all 0s (00000000), the result is that everything is converted to 1s: 11111111.

Negating an unsigned value sounds odd at first, but it does turn out to be a precisely defined operation. -X can be viewed as a shorthand for 0-X. C has the rule that if the result of an unsigned operation would be out of range for the unsigned type, the result is reduced modulo MAX+1 where MAX is the largest number the type can represent. "Reduced modulo" means the effect is the same as if MAX+1 was added or subtracted as many times as necessary to bring the value back into range. If you check back to Table 5.3 you will see this happening for 201+211. The result (412) exceeds MAX (255) so MAX+1 (256) is subtracted to give a result (156), which is then in range. Table 5.4 gives some more examples of this.

TABLE 5.4 Modulo Reduction on Unsigned Numbers

Starting Value	*Result*	
0	0	
255	255	
256	0	(256-256)
257	1	(257-256)
512	0	(512-256-256)
-1	255	(-1+256)
-255	1	(-255+256)
-256	0	(-256+256)

In the case of negation, we start with a value in range (in this case a value from 0 to 255) and negate it, giving a value from 0 to -255. -1 to -255 is out of range for an unsigned type so we reduce that by adding MAX+1 (256 in this case). We end up with -X+256 or just 256-X. In general the result of -X can be calculated by MAX+1-X, which also works for 0 since the result MAX+1 is reduced back to 0. We can rewrite MAX+1-X as (MAX-X)+1. This is significant because MAX is the maximum value representable by our unsigned variable (that is, the value represented by all 1 bits). Subtracting another unsigned value from this cannot generate any borrows. It just causes the bits in the original number to be inverted, for example:

```
....11111111
   -10010110
    --------
    01101001
```

In short, MAX-X is another way of writing ~X, and -X (that is, (MAX-X)+1) is equivalent to (~X)+1. This isn't surprising because it is how twos complement negation is defined, and we already know that the bit operations of unsigned and twos complement arithmetic correspond. The overall effect of unsigned negation at the bit level is to invert all of the bits above the lowest order 1 bit in the number. An example will demonstrate this more clearly:

```
    X          10010000
   ~X          01101111
 (~x)+1        01110000
                  ^
```

Note the position that corresponds to the lowest order 1 bit in the original X. In the result this remains as 1, all bits to the right of it remain as 0, and all bits to the left of it have been inverted.

We now have bit-level definitions for the unsigned integer operations increment, decrement, and negation. They all show behavior based on the position of the lowest order 1 bit (or 0 bit in the case of increment). With one more step we can produce results that are made use of later on in this chapter.

Consider the expression X & -X. For example:

```
  X        10010000
 -X        01110000
X & -X     00010000
```

The result is that all bits except the lowest order 1 bit have been cleared. Now consider X & (X-1):

```
  X        10010000
X-1        10001111
X & (X-1)  10000000
              ^
```

The result here is that the lowest order 1 bit has been cleared. Other combinations of arithmetic and bitwise operator are possible, and Table 5.5 shows some of these. However, these first two tend to be the most useful.

TABLE 5.5 Lowest Set/Clear Bit Manipulation Expressions

Expression	*Effect*
X & (X-1)	Clears the lowest 1 bit in X
X & -X	Clears all bits except the lowest order 1 bit of X
X | (X+1)	Sets the lowest order 0 bit in X
X | (~X-1)	Sets all bits except the lowest order 0 bit in X

Enough background; it is time to look at some applications of bit and byte manipulations. However, we will be making use of these expressions later on.

Bit Arrays (Bit Maps)

C doesn't have any built-in way to access individual bits organized into an array. However, C's bit operations allow us to simulate bit arrays using a few simple macros. The basic requirements for a bit array are

- A data structure that can hold the bit array.
- An ability to create and destroy bit array objects. This might be done by either directly declaring them or allocating them dynamically using `malloc` and related functions.

- A way to set the bit array to a known state, such as all bits clear.
- Ways to set, clear, and test a specified bit.

This section demonstrates how to meet these requirements using a set of macro definitions and a type definition. More complex bit operations could be added using functions. The definitions that follow can be found on the CD in the header file `bitarray.h`. The first thing we need is a data structure, and for that we will use an array of unsigned integers to hold the bits. We already know that unsigned integers are the best types for bit operations, but we have a choice of `unsigned char` right through to `unsigned long` (and other choices in C99). The good news is that we don't have to commit the code to one type. We can use a `typedef` to select one and if we want to use a different one later on, we can just change the `typedef`.

```
typedef unsigned char BARR_ELTYPE;
```

I have chosen `unsigned char` here because it is the simplest and is guaranteed to use all of the bits in each byte. Notice that this definition and all subsequent ones are given a name starting with `BARR_`. This makes them easily recognizable as related bit array operations.

For a general bit array we are going to need more than one integer's worth of bits, so the overall data structure for holding the bit array will be an array of `BARR_ELTYPE` elements. Next, we can define some useful quantities relating to the array, which can be used by other macros.

```
#define BARR_ELBITS (CHAR_BIT * sizeof(BARR_ELTYPE))
```

`BARR_ELBITS` specifies the number of bits in an element of the array—that is, the number of bits in a `BARR_ELTYPE` object. This is calculated by multiplying the size of the type `BARR_ELTYPE` in bytes by the number of bits in a byte (`CHAR_BIT`, which is defined in the standard header `<limits.h>`). Strictly, what we need here is the number of bits in the type that are used to hold its value. Since types other than `unsigned char` can have unused bits, this could overstate the number of value bits. However, we will simply specify that `BARR_ELTYPE` should be defined as a type that has no unused bits, and failing anything else `unsigned char` has that property.

```
#define BARR_ARRAYSIZE(N) (((N) + BARR_ELBITS-1) / BARR_ELBITS)
```

`BARR_ARRAYSIZE(N)` evaluates to the number of `BARR_ELTYPE` elements we need in the array to be able to hold `N` bits. This calculates the result of `N/BARR_ELBITS` rounded up so that any bits left over still have a place in the array. A simple way of "rounding up" any remainder in the integer expression A/B is to write (A+B-1)/B. This works when all values are non-negative and A+B doesn't overflow.

The first step to using a bit array in a program is to create one. The simplest way is to define an array as a program variable. For example, to create an array of `SIZE` bits we can now write

```
BARR_ELTYPE bitarray[BARR_ARRAYSIZE(SIZE)];
```

`BARR_ARRAY(SIZE)` is a constant expression as long as `SIZE` itself is, which means we can use it to specify the size in an array declaration. As with any other type of data structure, we might want to create a bit array dynamically. This can be done by calling `malloc`. The messy details of this can be hidden in a macro:

```
#define BARR_MALLOC(N) \
        ((BARR_ELTYPE *)malloc(BARR_ARRAYSIZE(N) * sizeof(BARR_ELTYPE)))
```

The \ at the end of the first line is a standard C way of splicing lines together, which in this case allows the macro definition to be split across multiple lines. Notice that `malloc()` allocates the specified number of *bytes*, so we need to allocate the number of `BARR_ELTYPE` elements in the array multiplied by the number of bytes in each `BARR_ELTYPE` element. You don't need to cast the return type of `malloc`, and generally it is a bad idea to do so because it can prevent the compiler diagnosing the error of calling `malloc` without having included `<stdlib.h>`. In this case, the cast is useful because it ensures that the code using the macro assigns the result to a variable of appropriate type. You can choose to omit the cast or not. To use this macro we could write, for example

```
BARR_ELTYPE *bitarray;
If ((bitarray = BARR_MALLOC(size)) == NULL) {
    /* Deal with the allocation failure */
}
```

This behaves just like any normal `malloc` call; `bitarray` is now defined as a pointer and the return value needs to be checked for allocation failure. A `malloc` operation needs a corresponding `free` operation. We could call `free` directly; however, it is better to use a corresponding `BARR_FREE` macro. This creates a consistent interface and provides the flexibility of being able to change the internal details later on without breaking code that uses the bit array macros.

```
#define BARR_FREE(barr) free(barr)
```

Any bit array created using `BARR_MALLOC` should be destroyed using `BARR_FREE`. A usable bit array needs to be in a known state, the simplest being all bits clear. For a declared array, the language provides a simple way of achieving this in the form of an initializer. For example

```
BARR_ELTYPE bitarray[BARR_ARRAYSIZE(SIZE)] = { 0 };
```

This causes the whole array to be initialized to zero. If you want to clear the array later on or clear an array created using BAR_MALLOC, you can use the standard memset function. Again, we can hide the messy details behind a macro definition:

```
#define BARR_CLEARARRAY(barr, N) \
        memset(barr, 0, BARR_ARRAYSIZE(N) * sizeof(BARR_ELTYPE))
```

This requires the caller to specify the size of the array in bits. This should only be used to clear the whole array. Specifying a smaller value for N may clear more than just the initial N bits. This could be corrected, but at the cost of complexity (it would probably need a function).

Finally, we can consider the operations that make bit arrays useful: bit setting, clearing, and testing. First, we define a couple more helper macros:

```
#define BARR_ELNUM(N) ((N) / BARR_ELBITS)
```

BARR_ELNUM specifies the index of the BARR_ELTYPE element that contains bit N.

```
#define BARR_BITNUM(N) ((N) % BARR_ELBITS)
```

BARR_BITNUM specifies which bit of the BARR_ELTYPE element holds bit N. This gives a value between 0 (indicates the least significant bit) and BARR_ELBITS-1.

```
#define BARR_SET(barr, N) \
        ((barr)[BARR_ELNUM(N)] |= (BARR_ELTYPE)1 << BARR_BITNUM(N))
```

BARR_SET sets the Nth bit in the bit array barr. A 1 is shifted left by BARR_BITNUM(N) places and this is bitwise ORed with element BARR_ELNUM(N) of the bit array, which results in the corresponding bit being set. The (BARR_ELTYPE) cast is to ensure that the shift is performed on an appropriately sized type. For example, if BARR_ELTYPE was unsigned long, an unsigned long shift is required.

```
#define BARR_CLEAR(barr, N) \
        ((barr)[BARR_ELNUM(N)] &= ~((BARR_ELTYPE)1 << BARR_BITNUM(N)))
```

BARR_CLEAR clears the Nth bit in the bit array barr. It is similar to BARR_SET except that to clear a bit it bitwise ANDs the BAR_ELTYPE element with the inverse of the shifted value. That is, one where all bits except the one we want to clear are 1.

```
#define BARR_TEST(barr, N)  \
        ((barr)[BARR_ELNUM(N)] & ((BARR_ELTYPE)1 << BARR_BITNUM(N)))
```

BARR_TEST tests whether the Nth bit in barr is set. It evaluates to a non-zero value if it is set, otherwise zero. It works in a similar way to BARR_SET except that it bitwise ANDs the shifted 1 with the array data to mask out all other bits. The bit array is not modified, but the result can be used by the program.

The result is not necessarily 1 if the bit is set; it is some non-zero value. The macro could have been written to produce a 1 result, but to specify this might impair efficiency (which is a consideration for a general bit array implementation) for no great gain.

Finally, it turns out to be easy to write a macro to invert a specified bit in the bit array. Here it is:

```
#define BARR_FLIP(barr, N) \
        ((barr)[BARR_ELNUM(N)] ^= (BARR_ELTYPE)1 << BARR_BITNUM(N))
```

This uses the bitwise exclusive-OR operator to invert the Nth bit in `barr`. Listing 5.1 contains the complete list of bit array definitions.

LISTING 5.1 The Definitions in `bitarray.h`

```
typedef unsigned char BARR_ELTYPE;
#define BARR_ELBITS (CHAR_BIT * sizeof(BARR_ELTYPE))
#define BARR_ARRAYSIZE(N) (((N) + BARR_ELBITS-1) / BARR_ELBITS)

#define BARR_MALLOC(N) \
        ((BARR_ELTYPE *)malloc(BARR_ARRAYSIZE(N) * sizeof(BARR_ELTYPE)))
#define BARR_REALLOC(barr, N) \
        ((BARR_ELTYPE *)realloc(barr, BARR_ARRAYSIZE(N) * sizeof(BARR_ELTYPE)))
#define BARR_FREE(barr) free(barr)
#define BARR_CLEARARRAY(barr, N) \
        memset(barr, 0, BARR_ARRAYSIZE(N) * sizeof(BARR_ELTYPE))

#define BARR_ELNUM(N) ((N) / BARR_ELBITS)
#define BARR_BITNUM(N) ((N) % BARR_ELBITS)
#define BARR_SET(barr, N) \
        ((barr)[BARR_ELNUM(N)] |= (BARR_ELTYPE)1 << BARR_BITNUM(N))
#define BARR_CLEAR(barr, N) \
        ((barr)[BARR_ELNUM(N)] &= ~((BARR_ELTYPE)1 << BARR_BITNUM(N)))
#define BARR_FLIP(barr, N) \
        ((barr)[BARR_ELNUM(N)] ^= (BARR_ELTYPE)1 << BARR_BITNUM(N))
#define BARR_TEST(barr, N)  \
        ((barr)[BARR_ELNUM(N)] & ((BARR_ELTYPE)1 << BARR_BITNUM(N)))
```

Bit Counting

This section looks at how to solve a simple problem: how to count the number of 1 bits in an integer value. Many of the algorithms used in this and subsequent sections need to know the overall number of bits in the integer value concerned. They will refer to a macro called

VALUE_BITS. This will often be required to be the number of bits in the integer type being used, so it could be defined, for example, as (assuming unsigned long)

```
#define VALUE_BITS (CHAR_BIT * sizeof(unsigned long))
```

Because unsigned long can have "holes" (unused bits), this may have to be adjusted for some systems. In other cases it may be preferable to specify an exact number of bits, in which case VALUE_BITS can be defined or substituted for the appropriate value. You may decide instead to supply the value as an extra argument to the function.

Probably the simplest way to count the number of 1 bits in a value is to check each bit in sequence to see if it is 1.

```
unsigned long bit_count1(unsigned long value)
{
    int count = 0;
    int bit;

    for (bit = 0; bit < VALUE_BITS; bit++) {
        if (value & 1)
            count++;
        value >>= 1;
    }

    return count;
}
```

This tests the state of bit 0 (the lowest order bit) and then shifts all bits in value one place to the right. After VALUE_BITS iterations of the loop, all of the original bits in value have been shifted through bit zero and been tested.

This approach is simple and it works. The only reason to look for alternatives is efficiency. In many cases that won't matter; it still takes a very small amount of time to execute. However, if it executed a large number of times the time can add up to something significant. So for a general solution, it is useful to look for improvements.

The problem with bit_count1 is that it will always loop VALUE_BITS times. We can do better than this on average by noting that if value is or becomes zero, there are no more 1 bits to test for and the loop can terminate immediately. bit_count2 changes the test condition accordingly:

```
unsigned long bit_count2(unsigned long value)
{
    int count = 0;
```

```
    while (value != 0) {
        if (value & 1)
            count++;
        value >>= 1;
    }

    return count;
}
```

The number of times around the loop is now only related to the position of the highest order 1 bit in the original value. This will show an improvement for small values. Another property of this approach is that it does not depend on `VALUE_BITS`; it will simply check all of the bits in the value passed.

We have already encountered methods of testing and clearing the lowest order 1 bit of an unsigned integer. In particular, X & (X-1) clears the lowest order 1 bit. We can use this so that each time around the loop the code clears one bit, and so just needs to test how many bits need to be cleared before the value becomes zero. `bit_count3` demonstrates this method:

```
unsigned long bit_count3(unsigned long value)
{
    int count = 0;

    while (value != 0) {
        count++;
        value &= value-1;   /* Clear lowest order 1 bit */
    }

    return count;
}
```

The `value &= value-1` line is something of a clever trick and is not obvious if you don't know it. Therefore, a comment is appropriate here.

`bit_count4` demonstrates another approach that doesn't use a loop at all:

```
unsigned long bit_count4(unsigned long value)
{
    value = (value & 0x55555555) + ((value >>  1) & 0x55555555);
    value = (value & 0x33333333) + ((value >>  2) & 0x33333333);
    value = (value & 0x0f0f0f0f) + ((value >>  4) & 0x0f0f0f0f);
    value = (value & 0x00ff00ff) + ((value >>  8) & 0x00ff00ff);
    value = (value & 0x0000ffff) + ((value >> 16) & 0x0000ffff);
```

```
    return (int)value;
}
```

It is based on the idea of splitting the value first into small and then increasingly larger groups of bits. The example is designed for a fixed input data size of 32 bits. The first line uses a mask value of `0x55555555`, which has the bit pattern 01010101... (that is, alternate ones and zeros). This is applied to the value itself and to the value shifted right by one position. So given an initial bit pattern of

```
ABCDEFGH...
```

we end up with two values

```
0B0D0F0H...
```

```
0A0C0E0G...
```

which are added together to form groups of two-bit values

```
¦A+B¦C+D¦E+F¦G+H¦...
```

Each group of 2 bits contains the number of 1 bits contained in those two bits originally. The next line uses a mask of `0x33333333`, which has the bit pattern 00110011.... The shifting and masking produces the two values

```
¦00¦C+D¦00¦G+H¦...
```

```
..¦00¦A+B¦00¦E+F¦...
```

which are added together to form groups of four-bit values

```
¦A+B+C+D¦E+F+G+H¦...
```

Notice that in each step there are enough zero bits to the left of each value to hold any carry in the addition. The process repeats doubling the field width at each step until just a count of the total number of 1 bits is left in `value`. This is then returned.

Finally, `bit_count5` demonstrates a simple but often very effective approach to writing efficient code, which is to use a lookup table:

```
unsigned long bit_count5(unsigned long value)
{
    static const unsigned char count_table[] = {
        0,1,1,2,1,2,2,3,1,2,2,3,2,3,3,4,1,2,2,3,2,3,3,4,2,3,3,4,3,4,4,5,
        1,2,2,3,2,3,3,4,2,3,3,4,3,4,4,5,2,3,3,4,3,4,4,5,3,4,4,5,4,5,5,6,
        1,2,2,3,2,3,3,4,2,3,3,4,3,4,4,5,2,3,3,4,3,4,4,5,3,4,4,5,4,5,5,6,
        2,3,3,4,3,4,4,5,3,4,4,5,4,5,5,6,3,4,4,5,4,5,5,6,4,5,5,6,5,6,6,7,
        1,2,2,3,2,3,3,4,2,3,3,4,3,4,4,5,2,3,3,4,3,4,4,5,3,4,4,5,4,5,5,6,
        2,3,3,4,3,4,4,5,3,4,4,5,4,5,5,6,3,4,4,5,4,5,5,6,4,5,5,6,5,6,6,7,
```

```
        2,3,3,4,3,4,4,5,3,4,4,5,4,5,5,6,3,4,4,5,4,5,5,6,4,5,5,6,5,6,6,7,
        3,4,4,5,4,5,5,6,4,5,5,6,5,6,6,7,4,5,5,6,5,6,6,7,5,6,6,7,6,7,7,8
    };

    int count = 0;

    while (value != 0) {
        count += count_table[value & 0xff];
        value >>= 8;
    }

    return count;
}
```

The table contains 256 elements and contains counts of the 1 bits in every number from 0 to 255. The code simply splits `value` into eight-bit chunks and adds up the number of bits in each chunk. It is possible to adjust the table size to taste. For example, by using seven-bit chunks the table size can be halved to 128 elements. That may result in more loop iterations, however.

There are often many ways of solving a particular problem, usually with different tradeoffs between simplicity and efficiency. Efficiency can often depend on the expected form of the input data. For example, `bit_count3` will work well for values with a small number of 1 bits but poorly when there are many, whereas `bit_count4` and `bit_count5` do the same amount of work for any input data. Whether `bit_count4` or `bit_count5` is more efficient will depend on the compiler and system the code is being run on.

The different techniques employed in the bit count functions (bit-by-bit analysis, multiple bit operations, table lookup) are applicable to many problems.

Bit Mirroring

Another simple problem is how to reverse the order of all of the bits in a value. Several of the solutions here bear a strong resemblance to solutions for the bit counting problem. `bit_rev1` demonstrates a simple approach where `value` is shifted right repeatedly, and at each step the low order bit of `value` is moved to the low order bit of `result`, which is repeatedly left shifted. The code expects `VALUE_BITS` to be defined as explained earlier in the chapter.

```
unsigned long bit_rev1(unsigned long value)
{
    unsigned long result;
    int i;
```

```
    result = 0;
    for (i = 0; i < VALUE_BITS; i++) {
        result = (result << 1) | (value & 1);
        value >>= 1;
    }

    return result;
}
```

bit_rev2 demonstrates a more curious approach where corresponding left and right bits are swapped in place.

```
unsigned long bitrev2(unsigned long value)
{
    unsigned long lbit, rbit, mask;

    for (lbit = 1UL << (VALUE_BITS-1), rbit = 1UL;
         lbit > rbit;
         lbit >>=1, rbit <<= 1) {
        mask = lbit|rbit;
        if ((value & mask) != 0 && (value & mask) != mask)
            value ^= mask;
    }

    return value;
}
```

lbit and rbit are 1-bit masks that start off at the leftmost and rightmost bits respectively. At each iteration of the loop they move in one bit until they finally meet or cross. mask is the bitwise OR of lbit and rbit; that is, the two bits that are to be tested. If these two bits are the same (both 0 or both 1), swapping them has no effect and nothing needs to be done. If they are different, swapping them will cause both to be inverted, which is performed by value ^= mask.

bit_rev3 works by swapping adjacent bits, then adjacent groups of two bits, then adjacent groups of four bits, and so on until adjacent groups of 16 bits are swapped. This is very similar to the bit_count4 algorithm and similarly assumes the data width is 32 bits. To see how this works consider an 8-bit example consisting of the bits

```
A B C D E F G H
```

First, adjacent bits are swapped to give

```
B A D C F E H G
```

Then adjacent pairs of bits are swapped to give

```
D C B A H G F E
```

Then adjacent groups of four bits are swapped to give the result, which has all of the bits in reverse order:

```
H G F E D C B A
```

```
unsigned long bit_rev3(unsigned long value)
{
    value = ((value & 0x55555555) <<  1) | ((value >>  1) & 0x55555555);
    value = ((value & 0x33333333) <<  2) | ((value >>  2) & 0x33333333);
    value = ((value & 0x0f0f0f0f) <<  4) | ((value >>  4) & 0x0f0f0f0f);
    value = ((value & 0x00ff00ff) <<  8) | ((value >>  8) & 0x00ff00ff);
    value = ((value & 0x0000ffff) << 16) | (value >> 16);

    return value;
}
```

Strictly speaking, if `unsigned long` is known to be exactly 32 bits wide, the `0x0000ffff` mask in the last step is not necessary. However, this isn't guaranteed to be true in general. The code as it stands will work for 32-bit values even if `unsigned long` is wider than 32 bits.

Finally, `bit_rev4` demonstrates a table lookup technique. The table contains 256 entries containing the result of bit reversing each 8-bit value. The program works much like `bit_rev1` except that it works eight bits at a time rather than one. In this case, the width of the value to be reversed must be a multiple of eight.

```
unsigned long bit_rev4(unsigned long value)
{
    static const reverse_table[] = {
        0x00,0x80,0x40,0xc0,0x20,0xa0,0x60,0xe0,
        0x10,0x90,0x50,0xd0,0x30,0xb0,0x70,0xf0,
        0x08,0x88,0x48,0xc8,0x28,0xa8,0x68,0xe8,
        0x18,0x98,0x58,0xd8,0x38,0xb8,0x78,0xf8,
        0x04,0x84,0x44,0xc4,0x24,0xa4,0x64,0xe4,
        0x14,0x94,0x54,0xd4,0x34,0xb4,0x74,0xf4,
        0x0c,0x8c,0x4c,0xcc,0x2c,0xac,0x6c,0xec,
        0x1c,0x9c,0x5c,0xdc,0x3c,0xbc,0x7c,0xfc,
        0x02,0x82,0x42,0xc2,0x22,0xa2,0x62,0xe2,
        0x12,0x92,0x52,0xd2,0x32,0xb2,0x72,0xf2,
        0x0a,0x8a,0x4a,0xca,0x2a,0xaa,0x6a,0xea,
        0x1a,0x9a,0x5a,0xda,0x3a,0xba,0x7a,0xfa,
        0x06,0x86,0x46,0xc6,0x26,0xa6,0x66,0xe6,
```

```
        0x16,0x96,0x56,0xd6,0x36,0xb6,0x76,0xf6,
        0x0e,0x8e,0x4e,0xce,0x2e,0xae,0x6e,0xee,
        0x1e,0x9e,0x5e,0xde,0x3e,0xbe,0x7e,0xfe,
        0x01,0x81,0x41,0xc1,0x21,0xa1,0x61,0xe1,
        0x11,0x91,0x51,0xd1,0x31,0xb1,0x71,0xf1,
        0x09,0x89,0x49,0xc9,0x29,0xa9,0x69,0xe9,
        0x19,0x99,0x59,0xd9,0x39,0xb9,0x79,0xf9,
        0x05,0x85,0x45,0xc5,0x25,0xa5,0x65,0xe5,
        0x15,0x95,0x55,0xd5,0x35,0xb5,0x75,0xf5,
        0x0d,0x8d,0x4d,0xcd,0x2d,0xad,0x6d,0xed,
        0x1d,0x9d,0x5d,0xdd,0x3d,0xbd,0x7d,0xfd,
        0x03,0x83,0x43,0xc3,0x23,0xa3,0x63,0xe3,
        0x13,0x93,0x53,0xd3,0x33,0xb3,0x73,0xf3,
        0x0b,0x8b,0x4b,0xcb,0x2b,0xab,0x6b,0xeb,
        0x1b,0x9b,0x5b,0xdb,0x3b,0xbb,0x7b,0xfb,
        0x07,0x87,0x47,0xc7,0x27,0xa7,0x67,0xe7,
        0x17,0x97,0x57,0xd7,0x37,0xb7,0x77,0xf7,
        0x0f,0x8f,0x4f,0xcf,0x2f,0xaf,0x6f,0xef,
        0x1f,0x9f,0x5f,0xdf,0x3f,0xbf,0x7f,0xff
    };
    unsigned long result;
    int i;

    result = 0;
    for (i = 0; i < VALUE_BITS; i += 8) {
        result = (result << 8) | reverse_table[value & 0xff];
        value >>= 8;
    }

    return result;
}
```

Bit-Fields

Structures and unions can have members defined as bit-fields. A bit-field is defined with one of the type `int`, `signed int`, or `unsigned int` and is given in addition a width value. For example

```
struct Bitfield {
    int field1 : 10;
    signed field2 : 8;
    unsigned field3 : 6;
};
```

defines a structure with three bit-field members. `field1` has type `int` and is 10 bits wide, `field2` has type `signed int` and is 8 bits wide, `field3` has type `unsigned int` and is 6 bits wide. Some compilers allow types other than `int`, `signed int`, and `unsigned int`, but these are not portable. The bit-field size is given by the number specified, not the type.

Bit-fields defined as `signed int` or `unsigned int` are explicitly signed (can hold negative values) or unsigned (cannot hold negative values). *Plain* `int` is strictly a signed type (in fact, it is exactly the same type as `signed int` and behaves the same in all other circumstances). However, a bit-field effectively represents a sub-range of the type and the compiler is allowed in the case of `int` to choose whether this sub-range is positive only or contains both positive and negative values. When using bit-fields, you should use `signed int` or `unsigned int` rather than plain `int` to ensure consistent behavior between compilers.

At a first glance, bit-fields look as if they might be a good way to manipulate parts of an integer value. Unfortunately, C specifies very little about how bit-fields are laid out by the compiler. There is some sort of allocation unit but the compiler can allocate bit-fields starting from the high order bits or the low order bits. If a bit-field will not fit in the space left, the compiler can either split it across two allocation units or move it completely to a new allocation unit leaving unused bits in the first. The size of the allocation unit is also up to the compiler. It must be a multiple of a byte, so you can't use bit-fields to create arrays of single bits in memory. The structure

```
struct Onebit {
    unsigned bit : 1;
};
```

will take up at least one byte in memory, and possibly more. If, for example, the allocation unit is 32 bits, this will be 32 bits wide. Some compilers allow the size of the allocation unit to be controlled (for example, by allowing other field types such as `unsigned char` to be specified), but you cannot rely on this.

The purpose of bit-fields is to allow you to efficiently store a number of small integer values in a structure. They are simply a space-saving device, which can be useful if you are creating a large data structure in memory. Bit-fields have been employed within some operating systems and embedded systems to access individual parts of hardware registers. With this sort of application, portability is less of an issue; however, using C's bit operations, possibly with some macros to hide the details, is probably a better approach. These days, even hardware can be moved between different types of systems.

Looking at Portability

Any object in C can be viewed as a sequence of bytes (except perhaps register variables, which don't have addresses). Individual bytes can be accessed by viewing the object as an array of `unsigned char`; functions such as `memcpy` depend on this property. Consider Listing 5.2, which outputs the individual bytes of a variable `value` in the order they appear in memory.

LISTING 5.2 Viewing an Object as a Byte Array

```
#include <stdio.h>

int main(void)
{
    unsigned value = 0x1234;
    unsigned char *ptr = (unsigned char *)&value;
    int i;

    for (i = 0; i < sizeof value; i++)
        printf(" %02x", ptr[i]);

    putchar('\n');

    return 0;
}
```

Different compilers can represent integers in different ways; for example, any of the byte size, byte order, and number of bytes in the object can change. There might be unused bits that suddenly become visible when viewed this way. On most compilers, bytes are eight bits wide and there are no unused bits, so I'll assume these for now. Even so, various outputs for the program are possible, as Table 5.6 shows.

TABLE 5.6 Possible Outputs from Listing 5.2 on Eight-bit/byte Systems

Program Output	*Unsigned* `int` *Format*
34 12	2 byte little endian
12 34	2 byte big endian
34 12 00 00	4 byte little endian
00 00 12 34	4 byte big endian
12 34 00 00	4 byte mixed endian
00 00 34 12	4 byte mixed endian

The term *little endian* means the bytes are arranged from lowest order at the lowest address to highest order at the highest address. *Big endian* means the bytes are arranged in the opposite order, high first to low last. *Mixed endian* just means a mixture of the two. Intel x86 processors used in PC compatibles are little endian, but others are big endian, such as Macintoshes and some workstations.

This creates an immediate problem if you want to transfer binary data between different types of system or even, in some cases, programs compiled with different compilers or compiler settings. Binary data written by one program may be interpreted differently when read by another. Probably the simplest way to solve this problem is to avoid binary data completely and read or write data as text. This has the advantage of fairly consistent interpretation between systems. Where that isn't the case, for example different line termination characters, it is usually easy enough to convert; there may even be tools available to do it.

To make binary data portable between systems, we need to define an external data format that is independent of the platform or compiler the program is being run on. This means specifying it down to the byte level. There are portable data format definitions and libraries available on many systems that implement them (for example, XDR and ASN.1). Bytes can be of different sizes, and there isn't much we can do about this. C guarantees that bytes are at least eight bits wide, which is a common minimum that happens to be used by most systems. This means we can define a byte as a data unit capable of holding at least eight bits worth of data; that is, the values 0 to 255. Consider the following structure:

```
struct Container {
    unsigned length;              /* Up to 10000 */
    unsigned long capacity;       /* Up to 10000000 */
    unsigned char colour;         /* 0 to 7 */
    int position;                 /* from -1000 to 1000 */
    double weight;
};
```

This specifies information about some sort of container. We want to write this information to a file and then read it on another system. The simplest and often best way would be to write the data out in text format, maybe on a line as a comma-separated list. We could have a simple function that takes a pointer to a container and writes it as a line to a text file:

```
int write_container(FILE *fp, const struct Container *container)
{
    return fprintf(fp, "%u,%lu,%d,%d,%.2f\n",
                   container->length, container->capacity,
                   container->colour, container->position,
```

```
                    container->weight);

}
```

Then, a corresponding function that reads a line from a text file and fills in a `Container` structure:

```
int read_containter(FILE *fp, struct Container *container)
{
    char buffer[100];
    int colour;

    if (fgets(buffer, sizeof buffer, fp) == NULL)
        return -1;

    if (sscanf(buffer, "%u,%lu,%d,%d,%lf",
                   &container->length, &container->capacity,
                   &colour, &container->position,
                   &container->weight) != 5)
        return 0;

    container->colour = colour;
    return 1;
}
```

These will write and read lines such as

```
5000,2000000,5,-300,42.53
```

To write a portable binary format, we need to specify the external representation carefully. Irrespective of how they are stored in the structure (for example, `int` is often 32 bits wide), we know the possible ranges of the values and therefore how many bytes are required to store them. The exception is weight, which needs to be treated slightly differently. Table 5.7 shows the sizes and offsets we will use in the external format.

TABLE 5.7 Field Sizes and Positions for an External Representation of `struct Container`

Structure Member	*Size (bytes)*	*Offset*
length	2	0
capacity	4	2
colour	1	6
position	2	7
weight	8	9

Finally, we need to decide on a byte order that the multi-byte values will be stored in. For this example I'll use big endian (high order byte first). Listing 5.3 shows functions to write and read this data in binary format.

LISTING 5.3 Writing and Reading `struct Container` as Binary Data

```
#include <stdio.h>
#include <stdlib.h>

int writebin_container(FILE *fp, const struct Container *container)
{
    unsigned char buffer[17];

    buffer[0] = (container->length >> 8) & 0xff;
    buffer[1] = container->length & 0xff;

    buffer[2] = (container->capacity >> 24) & 0xff;
    buffer[3] = (container->capacity >> 16) & 0xff;
    buffer[4] = (container->capacity >>  8) & 0xff;
    buffer[5] = container->capacity & 0xff;

    buffer[6] = container->colour;

    buffer[7] = (container->position >> 8) & 0xff;
    buffer[8] = container->position & 0xff;

    memcpy(&buffer[9], &container->weight, 8);

    if (fwrite(buffer, 1, sizeof buffer, fp) != sizeof buffer)
        return -1;

    return 0;
}


int readbin_container(FILE *fp, struct Container *container)
{
    unsigned char buffer[17];

    if (fread(buffer, 1, sizeof buffer, fp) != sizeof buffer)
        return -1;

    container->length = ((unsigned)buffer[0] << 8) | buffer[1];
```

LISTING 5.3 continued

```
    container->capacity = ((unsigned long)buffer[2] << 24) |
                          ((unsigned long)buffer[3] << 16) |
                          ((unsigned long)buffer[4] <<  8) |
                          buffer[5];

    container->colour = buffer[6];

    container->position = ((int)buffer[7] << 8) | buffer[8];

    memcpy(&container->weight, &buffer[9], 8);

    return 1;
}
```

The functions work by making use of bit shift and mask operations. There are a number of points to consider:

- An array of `unsigned char` is used to hold the external data.
- Values are split into eight-bit quantities, irrespective of what the byte size (`CHAR_BIT`) on that system happens to be. In `writebin_container`, byte values are masked with `0xff` to ensure that just eight bits worth of data is written.
- In `readbin_container`, a byte value is cast to the target type before being shifted. This ensures that the shifting takes place at an appropriate width.

The position member is a signed integer. Signed integers can have different representations (twos complement, ones complement, sign-magnitude), so the code only works between systems that use the same representation. This is okay most of the time because most platforms use twos complement. It is possible to write code that works across different types of systems. One way is to write all integer data as unsigned values. When the writer needs to store a signed value, it first converts it to an unsigned value and writes that. The reader reads the unsigned value and converts it back to the corresponding signed value.

```
    int signed_value;
    unsigned unsigned_value;

/* Encode a signed value between -32767 and 32767 to an
   unsigned value between 0 and 65535 */

    unsigned_value = signed_value >= 0
                         ? signed_value
```

```
                         : signed_value + 65536U;

/* Decode an unsigned value between 0 and 65535 to a
   signed value between -32767 and 32767 */

    signed_value = unsigned_value <= 32767
                        ? (int)unsigned_value
                        : (int)(unsigned_value-32768)-32767-1;
```

These expressions encode and decode any `int` value to and from an unsigned value that is consistent with whatever signed integer format the compiler uses. The unsigned value is formatted like a twos complement number. The strange combination of numbers in the last line is to ensure that no signed integer operation overflows (remember ints are only guaranteed to be able to represent numbers in the range -32767 to 32767). The compiler will probably be able to optimize this significantly.

The final problem is the weight member, which has double type. There can be a great variety in the way floating point numbers are represented. If you need ultimate portability here, a text format is very likely the best option. However, many systems these days use standard formats defined by the ANSI/IEEE-754 document. An IEEE float is 32 bits wide, and an IEEE double is 64 bits wide. The remaining portability problems are byte size (we'll assume 8 bits) and byte order. Typically, byte order will be either big endian or little endian. Code portable between these types of systems needs to be able to copy the bytes of the floating point object directly or to reverse their order. Listing 5.3 demonstrated a direct copy using `memcpy`. A byte reversal would require a loop such as

```
   For (i = 0; i < 8; i++)
         Buffer[n+i] = ((unsigned char *)container->weight)[7-i];
```

The process of converting a large structure to and from an external data format can consist of a lot of fiddly operations. We can improve matters by defining a set of helper functions, for example

```
/* Encode a signed value into a 2 byte big endian field */

void encode_s2(unsigned char *field, int value)
{
    unsigned uvalue = value >= 0
                         ? value
                         : value + 65536U;

    field[0] = (uvalue >> 8) & 0xff;
    field[1] = value & 0xff;
}
```

```
int decode_s2(unsigned char *field)
{
    unsigned uvalue = ((unsigned)field[0]) | field[1];

    return uvalue <= 32767
             ? (int)uvalue
             : (int)(uvalue-32768)-32767-1;
}
```

Summary

C supports some rather low level bit- and byte-based operations. This chapter demonstrated some useful techniques that use bit and byte manipulations, as well as some caveats as to what operations may not be portable. In particular, signed integers can have various representations and it is better to avoid them where bit operations are concerned.

The chapter also covered approaches for implementing bit arrays, bit counting, and bit reversal. These are simple operations in themselves, but demonstrate a number of significantly different techniques. Finally, this chapter covered how bit and byte manipulation can be used to create binary data formats, which can be accessed using the same code on different platforms.

CHAPTER 6

Offline Data Storage and Retrieval

by Steve Summit

In This Chapter

Generally speaking, whenever we have data to be read in from or written out to the outside world, we use some kind of data file format. This chapter covers various techniques for reading and writing data files effectively, and discusses some of the issues that guide the selection or design of the file formats used.

The chapter begins with some background covering the choice of data file formats and the general techniques for reading and writing them and moves on to some more concrete examples. If you already understand or aren't interested in all the background, you can jump to the "Basic Techniques" section for some "building blocks" for reading and writing individual data objects within data files, or to the "Generic Formats" section for some sample code for reading popular file formats such as TDF (tab-delimited fields), CSV (comma-separated values), and `.ini` (sectioned initialization) files.

Goals and Applications

Data files come in many guises. An application that lets the user create documents, whether text, graphics, or other, saves those documents in some kind of data file. Any program that needs to save its state between invocations does so in a data file and, as you'll see, a program's configuration files can also be thought of as data files. Data acquisition programs emit their acquired data in some data file format; that data may then be read in by various data manipulation programs. Most networking protocols involve the transmission of structured data which can be thought of as a data file format.

Data file format design is a topic unto itself, which we won't attempt to explore thoroughly. But the format chosen for a data file obviously has a defining relationship with the code written to maintain that format; the format and the code are often inextricably linked. So we can't talk about file-writing or file-reading code in isolation, and we'll therefore have occasion to touch on several format design issues throughout the chapter.

There are quite a few goals we might have in the selection of a data file format. We might require that data files be as compact as possible or that they can be read and written as efficiently as possible. We might prefer that the code for reading and writing the files be easy to write, or that the work can be performed entirely by prewritten libraries. We might want the files to be human-readable, or on the other hand, we might want to hide or even encrypt certain data. We might want the format to be extensible, or backward-compatible with some format that has been used in the past. We might want the data files to be portable between different machines. Overriding all these concerns, we might have a data file format forced on us by some external entity; we don't always have the luxury of defining our own. In any case, though some of these goals are contradictory, we'll see ways of satisfying most of them.

At one level, reading and writing data files is conceptually quite simple. The data file is merely one representation of some abstract data, and that data can also be represented in memory using some kind of data structure. The data file writing process is simply one of converting the in-memory representation to the external representation while writing the data out to the file. Reading a data file involves the inverse process of reading and interpreting the bytes of the external representation and reconstructing the in-memory representation. We will find that the facilities of C's `<stdio.h>` library are generally adequate for all aspects of both tasks; as is so often the case, "the devil is in the details."

It is extremely important to recognize, however, that the internal ("in-memory") and external representations of data are generally different. The writing and reading processes generally do involve some conversion, and it is virtually always appropriate to hide the details of the conversion, reading, and writing process behind an interface—that is, to define data file reading and writing as abstractions. As we'll see, it's possible to define the layout of a data file as being "just like the data is laid out in memory," but this approach ends up having some significant drawbacks.

Text and Binary Formats

There are two main classes of data file formats. *Text* formats encode data as plain text, generally human-readable. Text data file formats are designed so that, in addition to their structured and stylized use by the particular programs that are designed to read and write them, the files can also be read and written by ordinary text file utilities—text editors, file printers, and utilities such as the UNIX `grep` program. Text files generally consist of only ordinary, printable characters, plus spaces, newlines, and maybe tabs. In a text file, for example, the integer 1850 might be represented by the four characters 1, 8, 5, and 0, which placed next to each other in the file would look like the string "1850". In ASCII, these four characters would have the byte values 0x31, 0x38, 0x35, and 0x30. These points may seem too obvious to be worth belaboring, but it's very important to compare the ways data is encoded in text versus binary files.

In a *binary* data file, on the other hand, data values are encoded in more the way they are in memory. A binary data file typically contains bytes with arbitrary values such that not all of them are printable, and attempting to view or manipulate a binary data file using an ordinary text-file utility will result in meaningless gibberish. For example, the integer 1850 has the hexadecimal value 0x073a, so its representation in a binary data file would include bytes with the values 0x07 and 0x3a. Figure 6.1 shows the byte-by-byte representation of the integer 1850 in text and binary formats.

FIGURE 6.1
Representations of the integer 1850 as a string in an ASCII text data file, and as a two-byte little-endian integer in a binary data file

```
           '1'    '8'    '5'    '0'
         +------+------+------+------+
text:    | 0x31 | 0x38 | 0x35 | 0x30 |
         +------+------+------+------+

         +------+------+
binary:  | 0x3a | 0x07 |
         +------+------+
```

Structural Issues

When describing a binary data file format, we also have to consider the *size* and *byte order* of the objects encoded in it. The size of an object (for example, the number of digits in an integer) is often implicit in a text file, but it is never so in a binary file. Going back to the integer 1850, is it stored in the data file as two bytes or four bytes or some other number of bytes? If we were to inspect the file sequentially as individual bytes, would the 0x07 come first, or would 0x3a? Unless we define these details carefully, we won't generally be able to read and write binary data files reliably.

Binary data files tend to be more compact, and it tends to be faster to read and write them. It can also be very easy to write simple code that reads and writes binary files, although as you'll see, the simple code has a number of serious problems.

The big problem with binary data files is that it is hard to make them portable. Precisely because the byte layout in the data file is identical, in the simple case, to the representation of data in memory, simple binary data files end up being intimately tied to the machine architectures and perhaps even the particular compiler that was used to create them. It is possible to design portable data file formats, as youll see later in this chapter, but the code to read and write them ends up being considerably more elaborate, and not always as blazingly efficient.

Though they tend to be somewhat larger and somewhat slower to read and write, text data files have a number of significant advantages. The primary one is simply that they are human readable, and this fact ends up paying several dividends. You can look at a text data file and see what's in it; you don't need to use special binary file viewers or editors. You can manipulate text data files using generic, off-the-shelf tools. Text files are easier to debug, too: When a data file isn't working right, you can look at the file and immediately pinpoint the problem, or at least determine whether the writer or the reader is at fault. Another advantage is that the numeric representations we tend to use in text data files (that is, the representations we use for encoding integer and floating-point data) tend to be automatically insensitive to the details of size and representation of these types on different machines. Text data files therefore tend to be very portable.

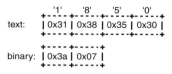

The code required to read and write text data files is not as blisteringly simple as the simpleminded code for reading and writing binary files, but in this chapter we'll see how to make it easy enough. Moreover, as mentioned, the simpleminded techniques for reading and writing binary data lead to data files that are nonportable. The code for reading and writing *portable* binary data files ends up being at least as complicated as that for text data files.

For most purposes, text data files are perfectly adequate, and recommended. Unless you have particularly high performance requirements, you won't generally need to concern yourself with the intricacies of trying to read and write binary data files.

Format Design Issues

Sometimes you have the luxury (or the burden—it isn't always a privilege) of defining your own data file formats, and if you do, you can lay them out in the way that makes the most sense to you, or that you find easiest to read and write. Other times, however, a format is imposed on you by some external entity or specification, and you have to figure out how to match that existing format exactly. If you're lucky, the format will be defined in terms of the bits and bytes in the file: "The heading is stored in a 4-byte field, in least-significant-byte-first order, starting at offset 120." If you're not so lucky, the format might be defined implicitly by the particular program, running on a particular machine, which creates it. In that case, you might have to do a certain amount of reverse engineering to determine all the details of the file format, and it may be a challenge to write some independent code that can read and write files compatible with those of the original program, especially if the new code must run on a different machine.

Besides the actual data in a data file, it's often useful for a data file format to contain some information describing the data file itself. For example, many data files begin with a *magic number*, a bit pattern that identifies the particular kind of data file and can be used by a reader to verify that the input is the right kind of file. It's extremely useful if data files contain a *format version number*, so that if the file format evolves, software can cleanly determine whether an old-format or new-format file is in use. It's often useful, especially for text data files, if a data file can contain additional human-readable comments that describe the file or its data but which are ignored by the programs that read the data.

Another defining characteristic of data file formats that's useful to consider is whether the various pieces of data in the file are laid out in what we might call a fixed or variable format. In a fixed-format file, we always write the same pieces of data in the same order; the meaning of each piece of data is essentially defined by its position in the file. In a variable-format file, on the other hand, the data might appear in different orders in different instances of the file, and some data might be optional, not necessarily appearing in every file. Generally, variable-format data files use some kind of an explicit *tag* next to each piece of data, to unambiguously specify what kind of data it is. Variable-format data files are also called *self-describing data files*.

Fixed-format files are obviously somewhat less flexible. If we ever need to add new data to the format, we can do so only at the end, unless we're willing to invalidate all existing files, or to write some conversion software that can handle multiple variants. A variable-format file, on the other hand, is much more flexible; we can add new data pretty much anywhere in it, at any time. The flexibility comes at a price, however, since the explicit tags take up extra space in the file.

Text data files often use variable formats, and binary data files usually use fixed formats, but it is also possible to have fixed-format text files and variable-format binary files.

Basic Techniques

This section looks at some basic, low-level techniques for storing individual objects in data files. We'll use these techniques as "building blocks" when writing larger pieces of code to read and write entire data files. Since the techniques for reading and writing text versus binary files are so different, they will be covered in separate sections.

Text Files

The text file is one of the few truly ubiquitous, cross-platform, universal, generic entities in computing. Virtually every computer system has the notion of a "text file," and although different systems might represent text files slightly differently, it is just about always possible to convert text file formats between machines without knowing what data they contain. Indeed, text file format conversion is usually taken care of more or less automatically by any program that claims to be able to transfer files between heterogeneous machines. Therefore, our programs rarely need to worry about any platform-specific details when reading and writing text data files; we can use the generic model of a text file presented to us by the C language and let the C runtime library and the underlying operating system worry about the platform-specific details.

Platform Specifics

The principal difference between text files on different platforms is the end-of-line representation. UNIX terminates lines in text files using a single linefeed (LF) character; MS-DOS and Microsoft Windows use a carriage-return/linefeed (CRLF) pair. Perhaps just to be different, Macintosh systems use single carriage returns. But no matter what end-of-line representation the operating system uses, within a C program the newline sequence is always represented by the single character `'\n'`. When we write a text file, we indicate end-of-line by writing a `'\n'` character, and when reading a file, we know we've reached the end of a line when we see a `'\n'`. The C runtime library translates between `'\n'` and the local operating system's end-of-line representation, and we can generally assume that a file transfer program has taken care of translating the end-of-line representation, and any other text file format details, if data files were transferred between machines. Therefore, it's usually easy to ignore these platform dependencies when working with text files.

One other platform dependency which might be an issue in otherwise generic text files is the character set used. Data files that don't contain lots of human-readable strings generally don't need to worry about the character set and can let any translation (perhaps between ASCII and EBCDIC, if that's ever necessary) be taken care of by external programs, such as the cross-system file transfer utility. However, when data files *do* contain human-readable strings, and especially if the strings could contain non-ASCII, international characters, character set issues can become very significant. However, a full treatment of international character sets is beyond the scope of this chapter.

Data Representation

The basic representation of numeric data in a text data file is a string of digits. Strings of digits representing numeric quantities are very easy to generate—this is precisely what `printf` formats such as `%d` and `%f` do. In fact, it's so easy to use `%d` in `printf` to generate the string of digits corresponding to an integer that it's easy to forget that there's a big difference between the integer 1850 and the string of digits 1 8 5 0. But that difference is crucial to understanding the difference between text and binary data file formats.

Writing to Text Data Files

Writing text data files is usually extremely easy and straightforward. We just use `printf` or `fprintf` to write the data out to the file in whatever format we've chosen. (Youll see several examples later in this chapter.) We have several choices when reading the data back in—we can attempt to use `scanf` or `fscanf` as the logical inverses of `printf` and `fprintf`, or we can read text from a file a character or a line at a time and convert selected numeric data using functions such as `atoi`, `atol`, `atof`, `strtol`, `strtod`, or perhaps `sscanf`. (The `scanf` function has a deservedly poor reputation in terms of its suitability for robust interactive user input, but `fscanf` and `sscanf` can be perfectly appropriate for use in reading data files, as long as their return values are checked.)

Numeric Data

For example, if we had a fixed-format data file consisting of an integer on the first line, a floating-point number on the second line, and an integer, a long integer, and a floating-point number on the third line, like this

```
123
456.789
1234 567890 123.456
```

we would have quite a few choices for reading the various numbers. (In the code fragments that follow, we'll assume that the stream variable `ifp` is open for reading on the data file in each case.)

To read the number on the first line, we could call

```
int i1;
fscanf(ifp, "%d", &i1);
```

Or, we could read the line using `fgets` and convert the integer using `atoi`:

```
#define MAXLINE 100
char line[MAXLINE];
fgets(line, MAXLINE, ifp);
i1 = atoi(line);
```

(Obviously the value chosen for `MAXLINE` could be significant; 100 is only an example. Instead of `atoi`, we could use `strtol` or `sscanf`, as in the following examples.)

For the second line, we could call

```
float f1;
fscanf(ifp, "%f", &f1);
```

Or, we could read the line using `fgets` and convert the number using `strtod`:

```
fgets(line, MAXLINE, ifp);
f1 = strtod(line, NULL);
```

Instead of `strtod`, we could use `atof` or `sscanf`.

For the third line, we could call

```
int i2; long int i3; double f2;
fscanf(ifp, "%d %ld %lf", &i2, &i3, &f2);
```

Or, we could read the line using `fgets` and convert the three numbers using `sscanf`:

```
fgets(line, MAXLINE, ifp);
sscanf(line, "%d %ld %lf", &i2, &i3, &f2);
```

Or, having read the line, we could convert the numbers one at a time, using `strtol` and `strtod`:

```
char *p;
i2 = strtol(line, &p, 10);
```

```
i3 = strtol(p, &p, 10);
f2 = strtod(p, NULL);
```

Since `strtol` and `strtod` can optionally return, via their second argument, a pointer to the character just past the end of the number they convert, it's straightforward to chain together a sequence of calls to convert several adjacent numbers from the same string. Yet another option (described in the section "Whitespace- or Tab-Delimited Files") is to break the line apart into whitespace-separated "words" and deal with each component individually.

There are few hard-and-fast rules governing which of these conversion alternatives to prefer. Some of the choices have to do with personal preference, some have to do with error handling (which we haven't considered yet), and some are truly arbitrary. One significant decision point is whether the input is line-based or freeform. The `scanf` functions work pretty well for freeform input, because for the most part they treat a newline as just another whitespace character. To read line-based input, it's usually most convenient to read an entire line, using `fgets` or the equivalent, and then parse the line. This two-step strategy is especially useful when the file format contains optional or alternative elements, when you want to respond definitively to failures in your attempt to parse the line, either by trying an alternative strategy, or reporting the error.

In the preceding fragments, we dealt with data of types `int`, `long int`, `float`, and `double`. (Note that `i3` was `long int` and `f2` was `double`.) Due to the various implicit conversions that C performs, we can use `%f` format when printing values of type `float` or `double`, and the `strtol` function when converting values of type `int` or `long int`, and the `strtod` function when converting values of type `float` or `double`. But in general we have to be more careful that the types match exactly: For example, we must match `%d` to type `int` and `%ld` to `long int` with both `printf` and `scanf`, and we must match `%f` to type `float` and `%lf` to `double` with `scanf`.

The following table summarizes some appropriate `printf` formats, `scanf` formats, and other conversion functions appropriate for various basic data types:

Data Type	`Printf` *Format*	`Scanf` *Format*	*Other Functions*
`char`	`%c`	`%c`	
`short int`	`%d`	`%hd`	`atoi`, `strtol`
`int`	`%d`	`%d`	`atoi`, `strtol`
`long int`	`%ld`	`%ld`	`atol`, `strtol`
`float`	`%e`,`%f`,`%g`	`%f`	`atof`, `strtod`
`double`	`%e`,`%f`,`%g`	`%lf`	`atof`, `strtod`
string	`%s`	-	

If a variable of an unsigned type must be stored in a data file, we can use %u or %lu format or the strtoul function. We could also use bases other than 10, using the %o or %x formats, or by using a value other than 10 as the third argument to strtol or strtoul.

String Data

Strings must be handled a bit more carefully. They can be printed straightforwardly using %s, but scanf's %s format is not always appropriate, because it stops scanning at the first whitespace character. In other words, strings that might contain whitespace cannot be scanned using a single %s format specifier with one of the scanf functions. When strings that might contain whitespace are to be read from a data file, you must either use some more complicated format specifier (generally %[...]), or not use the scanf family of functions at all.

Dates and Time

One more data type that's worth thinking about how to store in a data file is a date/time stamp. Because C defines the standard type time_t for representing dates and times, and because time_t is *usually* (but not always!) a long int, it's tempting to store a raw time_t value as a long int, perhaps using %ld. But this is a bad idea, because it leads to another kind of nonportability in the data file. If the data file is ever read on a machine whose operating system or C runtime library uses a different definition of time_t, the timestamps in the data file won't make sense.

A better way to store dates and times, in keeping with the theme of this chapter, is in a platform-independent format. For a text file, it's natural to use some unambiguous but human-readable format; a good choice would be one of the ISO 8601 standard representations. For example, here is a little function to write a time_t value to a file in the ISO 8601–suggested combined date/time format. The work is all done by the C library function strftime:

```
#include <stdio.h>
#include <time.h>

void
timetprint(time_t t, FILE *ofp)
{
char buf[25];
struct tm *tp = localtime(&t);
strftime(buf, sizeof(buf), "%Y-%m-%dT%H:%M:%S", tp);
fputs(buf, ofp);
}
```

This function would write the time 12:34:56 on March 10, 2000 as 2000-03-10T12:34:56.

To convert one of these strings back to a time_t when reading a data file, we can write a function based on the standard library function mktime:

```
time_t
timetparse(char *str)
{
int y, mo, d;
int h, m, s = 0;
struct tm tm = {0};

if(sscanf(str, "%d-%d-%dT%d:%d:%d", &y, &mo, &d, &h, &m, &s)
    < 5 && sscanf(str, "%4d%2d%2dT%2d%2d%2d",
            &y, &mo, &d, &h, &m, &s) < 5)
    return (time_t)(-1);

tm.tm_year = y - 1900; tm.tm_mon = mo - 1; tm.tm_mday = d;
tm.tm_hour = h; tm.tm_min = m; tm.tm_sec = s;

return mktime(&tm);
}
```

This function is slightly robust: Besides the format generated by timetprint, it also accepts a condensed representation, also sanctioned by ISO 8601, which omits the extra punctuation. Also, in either case, it allows the seconds to be omitted, and defaulted to 0.

As written, the timetprint and timetparse functions store the time using the local timezone. Often, especially in data-interchange formats, it's preferable to use a locale-independent time zone, namely GMT. Unfortunately, that's trickier, because the standard C library doesn't give us all the tools we need. (We could use gmtime instead of localtime in timetprint, but unfortunately a standard GMT-using analog to mktime is not yet widespread.)

Mixed Formats

We will close this section with a slightly more involved (though somewhat artificial) example. Suppose that we want to store a single integer, an array of up to 10 integers, and an instance of the structure

```
struct s
    {
    int i;
    float f;
    char str[20];
    };
```

to one data file, using a mix of fixed- and variable-format techniques. Generally, mixtures like this are awkward and should be avoided; we're using both techniques here only so that we can demonstrate them both at the same time.

The first line of the data file will contain the word `sampdata` to identify the data file format, followed by a version number. The second line will contain the single integer. The third line will contain the array of up to 10 integers, all on one line, separated by spaces. The remainder of the file will contain the elements of the structure, one per line, tagged at the beginning of each line with an identifier matching the structure member name. For example, a complete data file might look like this:

```
sampdata 1
42
1 2 3 10 9 8
i 100
f 3.14
str Hello, world!
```

The digit `1` at the end of the first line marks this as data file format version number 1. The array on the third line evidently contained 6 elements at the time this data file was written.

Here is a function for writing an instance of this data file. The function accepts a stream (`FILE *`) argument which is assumed to be open on the data file to be written; the caller is responsible for opening the file. The function also accepts the three pieces of data to be written. The array parameter `a` is accompanied by a parameter `na` indicating the number of elements in the array.

```
void txtwrite(FILE *ofp, int i, int a[], int na, struct s *s)
{
    int j;
    fprintf(ofp, "sampdata %d\n", 1);
    fprintf(ofp, "%d\n", i);
    for(j = 0; j < na; j++)
        fprintf(ofp, "%d ", a[j]);
    fprintf(ofp, "\n");
    fprintf(ofp, "i %d\n", s->i);
    fprintf(ofp, "f %g\n", s->f);
    fprintf(ofp, "str %s\n", s->str);
}
```

The function is perfectly straightforward; it simply uses a sequence of `fprintf` calls to build up the required data in the file. To save floating-point values to data files, `%e` or `%g` are both good choices, but if you need high accuracy, you might also want to increase the precision, perhaps by using `%.10g`. Note that the correspondence between the tag in the data file and the structure member name is explicitly embodied in the `fprintf` calls and their format strings; there's no way to ask the compiler to put a structure's member names into a data file automatically.

Reading the file back in is not much more difficult; Listing 6.1 presents a function to do it. Again, it accepts a file pointer opened on the data file to be read; this time the file pointer is for reading. The `i` and `na` parameters are passed as pointers (that is, C's form of "pass by reference") so that the function can return their new values to the caller.

(The `na` parameter is read-write: On input it is taken to be the maximum size of the destination array, and on output it is filled in with the number of array elements actually read from the file.)

LISTING 6.1 Function `txtread()` for Reading a Text Data File

```
#define MAXLINE 100
#define TRUE 1
#define FALSE 0

int txtread(FILE *ifp, int *i, int a[], int *na, struct s *s)
{
    char line[MAXLINE], tmpstr[10];
    int j;
    char *p, *p2;

    if(fgets(line, sizeof(line), ifp) == NULL)
        return FALSE;
    if(sscanf(line, "%10s %d", tmpstr, &j) != 2 ||
            strcmp(tmpstr, "sampdata") != 0)
        return FALSE;    /* data file format error */
    if(j != 1)
        return FALSE;    /* version number mismatch */
    if(fgets(line, sizeof(line), ifp) == NULL)
        return FALSE;
    *i = atoi(line);
    /* read and parse array line */
    if(fgets(line, sizeof(line), ifp) == NULL)
        return FALSE;
    for(j = 0, p = line; j < *na && *p != '\0'; j++, p=p2)
        {
        a[j] = strtol(p, &p2, 10);
        if(p2 == p)
            break;
        }
```

LISTING 6.1 continued

```
    *na = j;
    /* remainder of file is variable-format */
    while(fgets(line, sizeof(line), ifp) != NULL)
        {
        /* split tag from data */
        p = strpbrk(line, " \t");
        if(p == NULL)
            continue;
        *p++ = '\0';
        p += strspn(p, " \t");
        /* p now points to data, */
        /* tag isolated at beginning of line */
        if(strcmp(line, "i") == 0)
            s->i = atoi(p);
        else if(strcmp(line, "f") == 0)
            s->f = atof(p);
        else if(strcmp(line, "str") == 0)
            {
            if((p2 = strrchr(p, '\n')) != NULL)
                *p2 = '\0';
            strncpy(s->str, p, sizeof(s->str));
            }
        /* unrecognized fields ignored */
        }
    return TRUE;
}
```

The code in Listing 6.1, too, is mostly straightforward, but a few points deserve mentioning. The function returns `FALSE` (that is, zero) on a serious data file error, such as a version number mismatch. The line containing the array elements (the second line) is parsed using repeated calls to `strtol`. There's an extra test to remove the trailing `\n` from the input line when necessary, since `fgets` leaves it there. The function's error handling is not exhaustive; it quietly ignores a few other potential errors, such as nonnumeric data on the second or third line, or malformed data in the variable-format section. You might choose to check for errors more stringently in your own code.

The most interesting aspect of this code is its parsing of the variable-format data. For each line, it separates the tag at the beginning of the line, by looking for the first whitespace character, and treats the remainder of the line as data. If the code does not recognize a tag, it does not complain; the assumption is that an unrecognized tag represents newer data which this program does not know about and can safely ignore. Separating the tag and data "by hand" with `strpbrk` is a bit of a nuisance; we'll see a cleaner way of dealing with whitespace-delimited data in the section "Whitespace- or Tab-Delimited Files."

This code's parsing of the variable-format data is more robust than it might strictly need to be: The tag and data can be separated by arbitrarily many spaces and tabs. On the other hand, this strategy means that saved strings cannot contain leading whitespace and be read back in identically. Also, the assumption that unrecognized data can be ignored does not necessarily hold in all circumstances, so it's an issue you might want to think about for your own data files.

It's worth saying a few more words about error handling when reading data files. Because data files are a "real world" input, you should plan for the possibility of errors in them, no matter how strongly you believe that it was your own perfect code that created the file being read. It's graceless for a program to crash because of a garbled input file; data file–reading code should perform enough sanity checks that it can print a meaningful error message if it encounters an improperly formatted file. If you're using any of the `scanf` functions in your data file reading or parsing code, one basic test—which should be considered mandatory—is to check `scanf`'s return value to see whether the expected number of items were converted.

This section has demonstrated just about all the techniques you'll need to read and write text data files reasonably conveniently. It's worth noting that the handling of the variable-format, tagged data scheme used in the last example is essentially equivalent to the way command lines and scripts are parsed: The first "word" on the line tells what the line is or does, and the remainder of the line consists of "arguments" that are interpreted in the context of the first word. Stated another way, reading and interpreting this particular kind of data file requires, at one level, just about exactly the same kind of code as is typically used to interpret simple command scripts, and also the same kind of code as is used to interpret simple command/argument or tag/value configuration files.

It's fair to ask how the text data files of this section measure up against the qualities we listed at the beginning of this chapter. These data files are, of course, very portable, and the code to read and write them doesn't have to be that difficult to write, either. But we must admit that they are not usually as compact as binary data files can be, nor are they necessarily as efficient to read and write. Disk space keeps getting cheaper so file size may not be so much of a concern, but I/O speed can matter, especially for huge files. If you're worried about efficiency but committed to using text data files, it's probably worth using hexadecimal (`%x`) formats instead of decimal (`%d`), since the various conversion functions may be able to implement hexadecimal conversions more efficiently than decimal conversions, which require multiplications and divisions by 10. For floating point, C99 adds a new hexadecimal floating point format, `%a`.

Another concern when dealing with large text data files (or any large variable-format data files, for that matter) is simply locating the desired information. One way to avoid having to search through a large file sequentially is to use an index, either stored in a separate file or within the data file itself. Youll see an example of this technique in the "Indexing" section, later in the chapter.

Binary Files

Our treatment of binary files will parallel that for text files in the previous section, and we'll see a few similarities, but for the most part, binary data files are almost completely different, as is the code we write for dealing with them.

The first thing to be careful of when using binary data files is to open them correctly. Since they are, by definition, not text files, we do not want the C runtime library to do any translation of carriage return or linefeed characters. Nor do we want it to treat a control-Z character as an in-band end-of-file indication under MS-DOS or Microsoft Windows. The way to request that the `stdio` library not do any of these translations is to open the file in binary mode, by including a `b` character in the mode string that is the second argument to `fopen`. That is, to open a binary file for reading, use `rb`, and for writing, use `wb`.

As a point of departure (but *not* because they're recommended), we'll first look at the some simplistic techniques for doing binary I/O. These techniques are simple indeed, and involve the `fread` and `fwrite` functions. Both functions accept a pointer to some data, a data object size, a count of data elements, and a stream pointer. The functions are designed to copy bytes of data directly between a file and memory. They can be used with text files, but their more common use is with binary data files.

If we had an integer `i`, we could write it out to a binary data file by calling

```
fwrite(&i, sizeof(int), 1, ofp);
```

If we had an array of integers `arr`, containing `na` elements, we could write it out by calling

```
fwrite(arr, sizeof(int), na, ofp);
```

If we had a structure `s`, we could write it out by calling

```
fwrite(&s, sizeof(s), na, ofp);
```

In each case, we use `sizeof` to compute the size, in bytes, of the data object being written; this size is exactly what `fwrite`'s second argument is supposed to be. The first argument is a pointer to the data to be written, and the third argument is a count of the number of elements.

Reading data back in is equally straightforward. Three `fread` calls, corresponding to the `fwrite` calls, might look like this:

```
fread(&i, sizeof(int), 1, ifp);
na = fread(arr, sizeof(int), 10, ifp);
fread(&s, sizeof(s), na, ifp);
```

(In the second line, we assume that the destination array `arr` is declared as size 10, and we assign `na` to hold the number of elements actually read.)

The good news is that these `fwrite` and `fread` invocations are very easy to code. But the bad news is that the data files they produce are about as nonportable as they can be. Since the data file layout is a one-to-one map of the individual in-memory data structures that were written, the file layout ends up depending on all sorts of platform-specific details. The number of bytes written for objects of types such as `int` and `float` (and indeed for any type) can vary from machine to machine. For multibyte quantities, the order of the bytes varies: On "big-endian" machines, the most-significant byte of a multibyte quantity is stored "first" in memory and ends up being written first to the file, whereas on "little-endian" machines the reverse is true. Most machines today represent negative integers using twos complement, but ones complement and sign-magnitude representations are theoretically possible. Floating-point formats have more variety still: Besides size and byte order, different machines allocate different numbers of bits to the exponent and fraction parts, and some machines use 10 or 16 as the base. Many machines do use the IEEE-754 floating point formats, but not all do. Finally, when it comes to structures, different compilers allocate different amounts of *padding* between members, to keep them properly aligned for efficient access. So under different compilers, the overall size of a structure will often vary even though it contains the same members in the same order.

The differences in object size, byte order, floating-point format, and structure padding mean that binary data files written using `fwrite` on one machine using one compiler may not be readable when transported to another machine. There will obviously be problems if that other machine has a different word size or byte order or if its compiler pads structures differently, but the same problems can also arise when using different compilers on the same machine, or different versions of the same compiler, or even the same compiler when invoked with different option settings. The bottom line is that if data files must be portable, the oh-so-simple reading and writing techniques involving `fread` and `fwrite` cannot generally be used.

It is possible to write and read binary data files portably, but we must take more direct control over the writing and reading of the individual bytes of the file, rather than delegating it to the compiler. Unfortunately, when we write and read data files a byte at a time, we lose some of the code simplicity and read/write efficiency advantages that made binary data files attractive in the first place.

The basic technique is indeed to manipulate the file's data a byte at a time. For example, suppose we have an `int` value that we want to write to a portable data file. We must first know how many bytes the value should occupy in the file, and in which order the bytes should be. (We have to know this because the whole point is not to let the machine or compiler make these choices for us.) Suppose we decide that the `int` as represented in the data file will be two bytes in little-endian order, that is, with the least-significant byte first. We could write the `int` out like this:

```
putc(i & 0xff, ofp);
putc((i >> 8) & 0xff, ofp);
```

The expression `i & 0xff` selects the least-significant byte, and the expression `(i >> 8) & 0xff` selects the one above that. Key point number one here is that we're extracting these bytes explicitly, based on their arithmetic significance, *not* based on their (machine-dependent) relative positions in memory. Key point number two is that we're not concerned with how big an `int` happens to be on this machine; our hypothetical portable data file format specifies that the size of this particular integer in the file is two bytes, period.

If we choose to write the two-byte integer in big-endian order instead, the modification is obvious:

```
putc((i >> 8) & 0xff, ofp);
putc(i & 0xff, ofp);
```

Although we've been harping on the issue of portability, and although this basic method of writing integers to a binary data file looks pretty good, we must admit that it's still not perfect for negative numbers, since it essentially imposes the native machine's choice of negative number representation (ones complement, twos complement, or sign-magnitude) on the data file. It's certainly reasonable to define a data file format as using twos complement, but to read and write the files on ones complement or sign-magnitude machines would require extra code which explicitly performed those conversions.

Reading a two-byte integer back in is almost as straightforward. Again, we have to take care to read the bytes back in in the correct order while reassembling them. To read in two little-endian bytes, we could use

```
i = getc(ifp);
i |= getc(ifp) << 8;
```

Or, to read two big-endian bytes, simply

```
i = getc(ifp) << 8;
i |= getc(ifp);
```

It's worth noting, however, that we could *not* compress either of these two fragments down to a single expression. For example,

```
i = getc(ifp) | (getc(ifp) << 8);      /* WRONG */
```

Does this expression read a little-endian or big-endian integer? The answer depends on which of the two `getc` calls is made first, and it turns out that the compiler is free to arrange to call either of them first. There's no guarantee in C that expressions in general are evaluated from left to right.

Using the preceding code fragments as a model, it's easy to see how to start reading and writing other data types. Here is code to write a 4-byte integer, `i2`, in little-endian order:

```
putc(i2 & 0xff, ofp);
putc((i2 >> 8) & 0xff, ofp);
putc((i2 >> 16) & 0xff, ofp);
putc((i2 >> 24) & 0xff, ofp);
```

And here is code to read it back in:

```
i2 = getc(ifp);
i2 |= (unsigned long)getc(ifp) << 8;
i2 |= (unsigned long)getc(ifp) << 16;
i2 |= (unsigned long)getc(ifp) << 24;
```

(All three casts to `(unsigned long)` are significant, to avoid precision loss and inadvertent sign extension of intermediate results.)

So far we've discussed integers, but how can we write other types of data to binary data files? Characters can be written as themselves; strings can be written either zero-terminated as in C, or preceded by a 1- or 2-byte length, or padded to some fixed length. (As mentioned earlier, however, international character sets can pose special problems for string data.) The general technique for reading or writing a structure is to handle it one member at a time, using methods appropriate for each member's type. We don't generally worry about storing pointers in data files. It's almost never appropriate to do so, since there's very rarely any guarantee that the pointed-to data will be in memory at all, let alone at the same address, when the data file is read back in later.

The previous section mentioned the possibility of treating date/time data specially, and it's worth considering this issue in the context of binary data files as well. In a binary data file, it's perhaps even more tempting to store a `time_t` value as a raw integer. But doing so is particularly dangerous for binary files—and quite aside from the possibility that `time_t` is not an integer at all. Many of the `time_t` values in use on today's machines are 32-bit integers that count seconds since some "epoch" (January 1, 1970, for UNIX), and these values "run out" sometime near the year 2040. By then, most machines will probably be using 64-bit timestamps, but there will still be many, many legacy data file formats in use which allocated only 32 bits for a date/time stamp. There will be a "Y2.038K" problem just about as nasty as the Y2K problem we just went through, and today's programmers will be the ones getting the bad press for perpetrating the problem on the world by "only allocating 4 bytes for a date/time stamp." To spare your successors (and your own reputation) this anguish, make sure that your data file formats do not lock in a range for `time_t` values which, though barely adequate for today and the next few years, will start breaking down in only a few more.

What can we do instead, especially if the machines we're working with today are still using 32-bit timestamps? One possibility is to allocate a few more bytes in the data file than we need, and write the reading and writing code in such a way that it will automatically keep working on the day when our code is ported to an environment where `time_t` values have more than 32 bits. For example, a 6-byte field would give us 48 bits, and 2^{48} seconds is almost nine million years. We'll see some sample code for writing such an expanded format later in this section.

Perhaps the trickiest data to handle in binary data files is floating point. It's not sufficient to nail down just the size and byte order, nor is it even clear whether "byte order" means the same thing for floating-point data as it does for integers. Different machines have completely different floating-point formats that use different numbers of bits for the exponent and fraction parts, and although the IEEE-754 formats are widespread, they are not universal. One approach, analogous to the one we just used for integers, is to use a particular well-defined floating-point format in the data file, converting back and forth between that format and the machine's native format when reading and writing. We'll see how to do it, using an IEEE-754 format, in the next example.

To put all these ideas together, we'll now show how to write and read a binary version of the sample data file from the section "text data files." (To recapitulate, that file contained a magic number, a version number, an integer, an array of integers, and a structure.) Here is a function for writing the same data out to a binary data file:

```
void binwrite(FILE *ofp, int i, int a[], int na, struct s *s)
{
    int j;
    putint(12543, ofp);     /* magic number */
    putc(1, ofp);          /* version number */
    putint(i, ofp);
    putint(na, ofp);
    for(j = 0; j < na; j++)
        putint(a[j], ofp);
    putc('i', ofp); putint(s->i, ofp);
```

```
    putc('f', ofp); putfloat(s->f, ofp);
    putc('s', ofp); fwrite(s->str, 1, 20, ofp);
}
```

When we wrote a text data file, we were able to let the standard library function `fprintf` do most of the work. For portable binary data files, we're not so lucky. We've deferred much of the work to our own functions `putint` and `putfloat`, which we'll see how to write in a minute.

Reading the binary data file back in is analogous:

```
int binread(FILE *ifp, int *i, int a[], int *na, struct s *s)
{
    int x, x2, j, j2, tag;

    if(!getint(&x, ifp) || x != 12543)    /* magic # */
        return FALSE;
    if((x = getc(ifp)) == EOF || x != 1)    /* version # */
        return FALSE;
    getint(i, ifp);
    getint(&x, ifp);
    for(j = j2 = 0; j < x; j++)
        {
        getint(&x2, ifp);
        if(j2 < *na) a[j2++] = x2;
        }
    *na = j2;
    /* remainder of file is variable-format */
    while((tag = getc(ifp)) != EOF)
        {
        switch(tag)
            {
            case 'i':
                getint(&s->i, ifp);
                break;
            case 'f':
                getfloat(&s->f, ifp);
                break;
            case 's':
                fread(s->str, 1, 20, ifp);
                break;
            /* unrecognized fields ignored */
            }
        }
```

```
    return TRUE;
}
```

Again, we've deferred much of the work to functions `getint` and `getfloat`.

The `putint` and `getint` functions are simple to write; we've seen the complete details of `putint` already, and for `getint`, we merely need to add a bit of error checking.

```
void putint(int i, FILE *ofp)
{
    putc(i & 0xff, ofp);
    putc((i >> 8) & 0xff, ofp);
}

int getint(int *ip, FILE *ifp)
{
    int i;
    int c;
    if((c = getc(ifp)) == EOF)
        return FALSE;
    i = c;
    if((c = getc(ifp)) == EOF)
        return FALSE;
    i |= c << 8;
    *ip = i;
    return TRUE;
}
```

It's now time to start dealing with floating-point data. Here is a simplified implementation of a function for writing a C float to a portable binary data file. The function writes four bytes, in IEEE-754 single format, with the least-significant byte first.

```
void putfloat(float f, FILE *ofp)
{
    double mantf;
    unsigned long mantl;
    int e, s = 0;

    mantf = frexp(f, &e);
    if(mantf < 0)
        { s = 1; mantf = -mantf; }

    mantl = ldexp(mantf, 24);
    mantl &= ~(1L << 23);       /* zap implicit leading 1 */
```

```
    mantl |= ((unsigned long)s << 31) |
        ((unsigned long)(e+126 & 0xff) << 23);

    putc(mantl & 0xff, ofp);
    putc((mantl >> 8) & 0xff, ofp);
    putc((mantl >> 16) & 0xff, ofp);
    putc((mantl >> 24) & 0xff, ofp);
}
```

The heart of this implementation of `putfloat` is the C library function frexp from `<math.h>`, which splits a floating-point number into its exponent and fraction parts. The fraction is returned as a floating-point number between 0 and 1; we turn around and hand it to another `<math.h>` function, `ldexp`, to multiply it by 2^{24}, effectively shifting it to the left by 24 bits so that we can treat it as an integer. Because the high-order bit of a normalized nonzero fraction is always 1, IEEE-754 formats do not store it, so we clear that bit. We paste in the exponent and sign bits in their proper places, and finally write out the four bytes.

This version of `putfloat` is not complete, since it doesn't deal with denormalized numbers, nor does it deal with infinities or `NaN`s. The CD-ROM accompanying this book contains a fuller implementation.

Here is an implementation of the companion `getfloat` function:

```
int getfloat(float *fp, FILE *ifp)
{
    unsigned char buf[4];
    unsigned long mant;
    int e, s;

    if(fread(buf, 1, 4, ifp) != 4)
        return FALSE;

    mant = buf[0];
    mant |= (unsigned long)buf[1] << 8;
    mant |= (unsigned long)(buf[2] & 0x7f) << 16;

    e = ((buf[3] & 0x7f) << 1) | ((buf[2] >> 7) & 0x01);

    s = buf[3] & 0x80;

    mant |= (1L << 23);          /* restore leading 1 */
```

```
    *fp = ldexp(mant, e-127-23);

    if(s)    *fp = -(*fp);

    return TRUE;
}
```

The C library `frexp` function is used again, this time for its intended purpose of reassembling the exponent and fraction parts. The casts to `(unsigned long)` in the construction of the `mant` variable are needed for the same reason as they were in our earlier discussion of reading 4-byte integers, namely to avoid precision loss and inadvertent sign extension. This version of `getfloat`, like that of `putfloat`, is simplified: It does not deal with denormalized numbers, and it does not always return a correctly rounded result. Again, the CD-ROM accompanying this book contains a fuller implementation. The CD also contains code for reading and writing C `double` values in IEEE-754 `double` format.

Returning to the question of storing dates and times, here is a function that writes a `time_t` value to a binary data file as a 6-byte little-endian integer. It is the obvious analog to the `putint` function, using a loop to extend it to six bytes:

```
void puttime(time_t t, FILE *ofp)
{
    int i;
    for(i = 0; i < 6; i++)
        {
        putc(t & 0xff, ofp);
        t >>= 8;
        }
}
```

Here is the corresponding function for reading the `time_t` back in:

```
int gettime(time_t *tp, FILE *ifp)
{
    time_t t;
    char buf[6];
    int i;
    if(fread(buf, 1, 6, ifp) != 6)
        return FALSE;
    t = buf[5];     /* sign extend, probably */
    for(i = 5-1; i >= 0; i--)
        t = (t << 8) | (buf[i] & 0xff);
    *tp = t;
    return TRUE;
}
```

Both of these functions will work correctly whether `time_t` is a 32-bit type, or larger. (There is an explicit though relatively innocuous assumption that `time_t` is signed, as it tends to be on most UNIX systems.) When using these functions, you'll still have to worry about portability of your data files to operating systems that use a different epoch or `time_t` mapping, but at least you won't constrain the timestamps in your data files to 32 bits.

With the exception of the preliminary `fread` and `fwrite` examples, all the code we've presented in this section is nicely portable. It must be admitted, however, that reading and writing binary data files a byte at a time is laborious and less than maximally efficient, especially when the size and byte order of the values being read or written does happen to match the native formats of the machine in use just now. We'll close this section by mentioning two compromise approaches which might be appreciably more efficient.

If we have large numbers of adjacent, same-sized integers to read or write, and if we can somehow guarantee that one of C's integer data types has a size matching those in the file, we can read or write the integers all at once using `fread` or `fwrite`, and swap the bytes only if necessary. For example, if we have an array `arr` of two-byte integers, we might choose to write them out using code like this:

```
#ifdef BIGENDIAN
swap2bytes(arr, na);
#endif
fwrite(arr, 2, na, ofp);
```

where the `swap2bytes` function is something like

```
void swap2bytes(void *buf, size_t n)
{
    unsigned char *p = buf, tmp;
    size_t i;
    for(i = 0; i < 2 * n; i += 2)
        {
        tmp = p[i];
        p[i] = p[i+1];
        p[i+1] = tmp;
        }
}
```

For this technique to work, we have to make sure that the underlying C data type has the right size. It's tempting to assume that `short int` is a safe type to use to guarantee two bytes and that `long int` is a good choice for four bytes. However, 64-bit machines, with 8-byte `long ints`, are becoming more and more popular. (The assumption that `sizeof(short int) == 2` isn't guaranteed, either, although if you want to play the odds, it's probably a safer bet.) Therefore, the use of suitably chosen `typedefs`, with definitions that vary depending on the machine or compiler in use, is a necessity. Under the new C99 standard, the header `<inttypes.h>` defines a number of fixed-size types which would be appropriate for this purpose.

Reading the array back in is similar to writing it:

```
n = fread(arr, 2, na, ifp);
#ifdef BIGENDIAN
if(n > 0)
    swap2bytes(arr, n);
#endif
```

The disadvantage here, for both the reading and writing cases, is that the code is no longer so portable: Wherever and whenever we compile it, we have to ensure that the data type chosen matches the integer size in the file exactly, and we have to make sure that the preprocessor macro `BIGENDIAN` is set appropriately—either defined or not defined, depending on the endianness of the machine in use. Coding styles that require settings such as these (type size, byte order, and so on) to be chosen exactly are a real bane to portability, so these styles should not be adopted lightly.

Another aspect of concern when binary data files are defined portably (that is, with the byte order specified independently, as part of the data file format) is that if a file happens to be both written and read on machines with the "wrong order," the data ends up being swapped twice. We can minimize redundant swapping, at the cost of some additional complexity, by always writing data files using the native byte order of the writing machine, but tagging the data file in such a way that the reader knows what ordering a particular instance of the data file uses and hence whether the reader will have to swap or not. For example, if we were to write the constant 2-byte value 0x0102 or the 4-byte value 0x01020304 somewhere in the header, and if the program reading the file finds itself reading them back as 0x0201 or 0x04030201, it knows it will have to swap the data while reading, but otherwise, it can read the data file natively, and presumably more efficiently.

The disadvantage here is the extra complexity; in the worst case each program has to carry around two sets of file-reading routines, a fast native-order set and a slower byte-swapping set. Also, we're still faced with the problem of keeping the sizes of the integers compatible, with all the maintenance headaches which that task can imply.

Generic Formats

The previous sections looked at data file formats we designed ourselves, where all we cared about was that our special-purpose data file reader could read what the special-purpose data file writer had written. This section considers the problem of writing files in generic, industry-standard formats that other programs might be able to read, and similarly of writing code to read files in generic formats that other programs have written.

Whitespace- or Tab-Delimited Files

Perhaps the most generic and widely applicable data file format, especially in the UNIX world, is a text file with whitespace-separated columns of numbers. Writing some utility code for handling whitespace-separated fields is a great idea, because it ends up being useful in many more situations than just reading data files *per se*.

One such piece of utility code is this function for breaking a string up into a series of whitespace-separated "words." This function actually performs a task similar to that performed by the library function `strtok`, but with a different interface.

```
#include <stddef.h>
#include <ctype.h>

int getwords(char *line, char *words[], int maxwords)
{
char *p = line;
int nwords = 0;

while(1)
    {
    while(isspace(*p)) p++;
    if(*p == '\0') return nwords;
    words[nwords++] = p;
    while(!isspace(*p) && *p != '\0') p++;
    if(*p == '\0') return nwords;
    if(nwords >= maxwords) return nwords;
    *p++ = '\0';
    }
}
```

This function breaks the text line up in-place, by inserting `'\0'` characters, and places pointers to the beginning of each word into a caller-supplied array. That is, `words[0]` is left pointing at the first word, `words[1]` at the second word, and so on. If we had a data file consisting of three columns—one integer, one floating-point, and one string—we could read it into an array of structures using this code, where the structure definition is the same as in the section "Text Files"):

```
#define MAXLINE 100
#define MAXARRAY 50

struct s sarray[MAXARRAY];
char line[MAXLINE];
char *p, *words[3];
int nw, na = 0;
struct s s;

while(fgets(line, sizeof(line), ifp) != NULL)
    {
    if(*line == '#') continue;
    nw = getwords(line, words, 3);
    if(nw < 3) continue;
    if(na >= MAXARRAY) break;
    s.i = atoi(words[0]);
    s.f = atof(words[1]);
    if((p = strrchr(words[2], '\n')) != NULL)
        *p = '\0';
    strncpy(s.str, words[2], sizeof(s.str));
    sarray[na++] = s;
    }
```

This code also introduces a few other niceties: Lines beginning with a # character are taken to be comments and are skipped; blank lines are also skipped.

As mentioned earlier, when we store strings in text files we often have to be careful if the strings could contain whitespace or other text delimiters. For this example, what if one of the strings in the third column contained a space? Would that make it look like four columns? In this case, we take advantage of a (deliberate) quirk in the `getwords` implementation: If the caller's `words` array is insufficient to contain the number of words actually found on the line, the excess words are not split apart, but are all placed into the final element of the caller's `words` array, with their intervening whitespace intact. Here, by passing `getwords`'s third argument as 3, we ensure that the string from the "third" column—whether it contains whitespace or not—will end up in `words[2]`, and hence in `s.str`.

This `getwords` function ends up being useful for more than just reading columnar data files; it's an excellent addition to any programmer's toolbox. For example, here is the last loop from the `txtread` function of the "Text File" section, rewritten to use `getwords` to separate the tag from the rest of the data on each line in the variable-format portion of the file:

```
while(fgets(line, sizeof(line), ifp) != NULL)
    {
    nw = getwords(line, words, 2);
    if(nw < 1)
        continue;
    if(strcmp(words[0], "i") == 0)
        s->i = atoi(words[1]);
    else if(strcmp(words[0], "f") == 0)
        s->f = atof(words[1]);
    else if(strcmp(words[0], "str") == 0)
        {
        if((p2 = strrchr(words[1], '\n')) != NULL)
            *p2 = '\0';
        strncpy(s->str, words[1], sizeof(s->str));
        }
    /* unrecognized fields ignored */
    }
```

When we arrange that columns can be separated by arbitrary whitespace, we obviously cannot allow arbitrary whitespace within arbitrary columns. (The trick of the preceding example works only for the last column.) Another approach, of course, is to pick exactly one delimiter and use exactly one of it to separate each column. One very common choice of delimiter is the tab character; a text data file containing tab-delimited fields is often referred to as TDF. If we adopt the rigid policy that exactly one tab separates each column, we can then accommodate other whitespace within any column, and we can also handle leading and trailing spaces on columns, or even empty columns.

Here is a function for splitting a line into columns more rigidly, based on any single delimiter, which is passed as a parameter. The library function `strchr` from `<string.h>` does all the work; the rest is just bookkeeping.

```
#include <string.h>

int getcols(char *line, char *words[], int maxwords, int delim)
{
char *p = line, *p2;
int nwords = 0;

while(*p != '\0')
    {
    words[nwords++] = p;
```

```
    if(nwords >= maxwords)
        return nwords;
    p2 = strchr(p, delim);
    if(p2 == NULL)
        break;
    *p2 = '\0';
    p = p2 + 1;
    }
return nwords;
}
```

Usage of `getcols` is equivalent to `getwords`; they're nearly drop-in replacements for each other, depending on which column-splitting behavior is required.

Turning from the reading problem back to writing, here is a general-purpose function for writing a line of data to a rigidly delimited file. (Again, the particular delimiter character chosen is passed as a parameter.)

```
void writecols(char *cols[], int ncols, FILE *ofp, int delim)
{
    int i;
    char *p;
    for(i = 0; i < ncols; i++)
        {
        for(p = cols[i]; *p != '\0'; p++)
            {
            if(*p != delim && *p != '
}n')
                putc(*p, ofp);
            else    putc(' ', ofp);
            }
        putc(i < ncols-1 ? delim : '\n', ofp);
        }
}
```

This function accepts an array of strings, and prints them all on one line, separated by the specified delimiter. It double-checks to make sure none of the strings contains the delimiter, since embedded delimiters would otherwise mess up the columnar arrangement. If any string contains the delimiter, occurrences of the delimiter within the string are quietly replaced with spaces. (The code also checks for any embedded newlines in the strings, which would obviously mess up the file even more.)

Comma-Separated Values (CSV)

Another popular data file format consists of comma-separated values, and is often known as a CSV file. Simplistically, we could read and write CSV files using the `getcols` and `writecols` functions of the previous section, specifying a comma character as the delimiter. But `getcols` and `writecols` would not handle the quoting mechanism which CSV files introduce to solve the problem of fields containing delimiters—in this case, the possibility that a value field contains a comma. If one of the comma-separated fields is enclosed in double quotes, commas within that field are assumed to be field data, not separators. As soon as double quotes are introduced as a special character, however, we naturally also have to worry about the possibility that a field contains a literal double quote character. This problem is typically solved in CSV files by doubling a literal double quote; when a CSV file reader is parsing a double-quoted field, a doubled double quote is converted to a single double quote but does not terminate the quoted field.

(Note that the doubled double-quote convention is different from the one used in C's double-quoted string literals—in C, of course, the way to get a literal double quote in a double-quoted string literal is to use the escape sequence `\"` instead.)

Parsing CSV files is not quite as easy as the whitespace-separated files of the previous section; it's a bit tricky to handle the quoting right. Here's a function for breaking up a line of text into comma-separated values. Like the `getwords` and `getcols` functions of the previous chapter, it assumes that the caller has taken care of actually reading the line, which is passed in as a string. The function returns the individual values as pointers into the original string, in place. (One difference is that since doubled double quotes in double-quoted fields must be mapped to single double quotes, characters must sometimes be moved around in the line buffer; it's not sufficient to simply overwrite the trailing delimiters with `\0`, as `getwords` and `getcols` did.)

```
#include <stddef.h>

csvburst(char *line, char *arr[], int narr)
{
    char *p;
    int na = 0;
    char prevc = ',';    /* force recognizing first field */
    char *dp = NULL;
    int inquote = FALSE;

    for(p = line; *p != '\0'; prevc = *p, p++)
        {
        if(prevc == ',' && !inquote)
            {
```

```
                /* start new field */
                if(dp != NULL)
                    *dp = '\0';  /*terminate prev*/
                if(na >= narr)
                    return na;
                arr[na++] = p;
                dp = p;
                if(*p == '"')
                    {
                    inquote = TRUE;
                    continue;      /* skip quote */
                    }
                }

            if(inquote && *p == '"')
                {
                /* doubled quote goes to one quote; */
                /* otherwise quote ends quote mode */
                if(*(p+1) != '"')
                    inquote = FALSE;
                p++;        /* skip first quote */
                }

            if(*p != ',' || inquote)
                *dp++ = *p;
            }

        if(dp != NULL)
            *dp = '\0';

        if(na < narr)
            arr[na] = NULL;

        return na;
}
```

Although the code flow may look a bit tangled at first, this function basically does three things:

- It copies characters, using the assignment `*dp++ = *p`, in the value currently being scanned. (The use of two pointers ensures that characters can be shifted, if necessary, when quoted quotes are converted.)

- It looks for the commas separating values, and when it finds one, it writes a `\0` to terminate the previous value, and records the start of the new one.
- It looks for double quotes, both at the beginning of a value and within a value. At the beginning of a value, a quote enables "quote mode" for that value. Within a value, a quote is either the first of two quotes which represent one literal quote, or else it is the closing quote which ends quote mode.

Here is a companion function for writing a line of comma-separated values to a text file. Like the `writecols` function of the previous section, it takes care of checking for special characters and quoting a field, if necessary.

```
#include <stdio.h>
#include <string.h>

void csvwrite(char *arr[], int narr, FILE *ofp)
{
    int i;
    for(i = 0; i < narr; i++)
        {
        if(strpbrk(arr[i], ",\"\n") == NULL)
            fputs(arr[i], ofp);
        else    {
            char *p;
            putc('"', ofp);
            for(p = arr[i]; *p != '\0'; p++)
                {
                if(*p == '"')
                    fputs("\"\"", ofp);
                else if(*p == '\n')
                    putc(' ', ofp);
                else    putc(*p, ofp);
                }
            putc('"', ofp);
            }
        putc(i < narr-1 ? ',' : '\n', ofp);
        }
}
```

The standard library function `strpbrk` returns non-`NULL` if (in this case) the string to be printed contains a comma, double quote, or newline.

As a demonstration of the use of these two functions, here is a scrap of code that copies one CSV file to another, extracting selected columns. The `selcols` array contains the indices of the columns to be extracted; in this example it requests extraction of the columns numbered 1, 3, and 5.

```
int selcols[] = {1, 3, 5};
int nselcols = 3;
char line[MAXLINE], *p;
char *arr1[MAXCOLS], *arr2[MAXCOLS];
int na, i;
while(fgets(line, sizeof(line), ifp) != NULL)
    {
    if((p = strrchr(line, '\n')) != NULL)
        *p = '\0';
    na = csvburst(line, arr1, MAXCOLS);
    for(i = 0; i < nselcols; i++)
        {
        if(selcols[i] < na)
            arr2[i] = arr1[selcols[i]];
        else    arr2[i] = "";
        }
    csvwrite(arr2, nselcols, ofp);
    }
```

`.ini` Files

Another common data file format is the `.ini` file.

An `.ini` file is a text file containing configuration variable settings, optionally divided into sections, with each section containing configuration variables for a different subsystem within a program, or perhaps (especially on Windows systems) for a different program. For example, the file

```
[A]
b=1
c=2
[B]
b=2
d=3
```

contains configuration variables for two facilities or subsystems, A and B. Listing 6.2 shows a function for fetching a configuration variable from a `.ini` file. The function takes three parameters: the `.ini` filename, the section, and the configuration variable name, or "key." The function takes care of opening the file, finding the requested section, and finding the key within that section. If there are any problems (the file cannot be opened, or the requested section or key cannot be found) the function returns `NULL`.

LISTING 6.2 Getting a Configuration Variable from an `.ini` File

```
#include <stdio.h>
#include <string.h>

#define MAXLINE 1000

char *
inifetch(const char *file, const char *sect, const char *key)
{
FILE *fp;
static char line[MAXLINE];
char *p, *retp = NULL;
int len;

if((fp = fopen(file, "r")) == NULL)
    return NULL;

/* search for section */
len = strlen(sect);
while((p = fgets(line, MAXLINE, fp)) != NULL)
    {
    if(*line != '[')
        continue;
    if(strncmp(&line[1], sect, len) == 0 &&
                line[1+len] == ']')
        break;
    }

if(p != NULL)    /* found it */
    {
    /* search for key */
    len = strlen(key);
    while(fgets(line, MAXLINE, fp) != NULL)
        {
        if(*line == '[')
            break;
        if(strncmp(line, key, len) == 0 &&
                line[len] == '=')
            {
            retp = &line[len+1];
            if((p = strrchr(retp, '\n')) != NULL)
                *p = '\0';
            break;
```

LISTING 6.2 continued

```
            }
        }
    }

fclose(fp);

return retp;
}
```

Since C's `strncmp` function is used to match section and variable names, these names are case sensitive. Typically, however, the names in `.ini` files should not be case sensitive. You can remove `csvburst`'s case sensitivity by replacing one or both calls to `strncmp` with calls to some caseless variant, such as the `strnicmp` or `strncasecmp` functions provided as extensions on many systems.

The code in Listing 6.2 demonstrates a basic method of reading these files, although in practice, if we had several configuration variables to read, we'd prefer not to reopen the file and search for the correct section, again, once for each variable. The CD-ROM packaged with this book contains an expanded version of `inifetch`, which avoids doing so much reopening and rescanning.

Advanced Techniques

So far we've talked about writing data files and reading them back in again, but we haven't talked about updating them. In the general case, we can't usually update a data file in-place, because C's I/O model, in keeping with the basic one provided by virtually all operating systems, does not give us any way of inserting or deleting bytes in the middle of a file. Therefore, in the general case, the only way to update a data file is to rewrite it. The usual technique is to write the revised data out to a temporary file, and when the writing process has completed successfully, delete the original data file while renaming the temporary file to the original data filename.

It is possible to overwrite some number of bytes in the middle of a text file, which allows us to update a data file as long as the new information we're writing to the file is of exactly the same length (in bytes) as the old data it replaces. This section talks about overwriting data in pursuit of two different goals: updating a data record, and building an in-place index to allow records in variable-format data files to be looked up easily.

Updating Records

Sometimes it is necessary to read through a data file looking for a particular record and, when it is found, to update it with some new data. The following code fragment illustrates this technique. We suppose that the file pointer `fp` is open on a data file that contains many consecutive instances of our three-element structure (`int`, `float`, string), written one after the other using `putint`, `putfloat`, and `fwrite` for the string. In other words, we're using a fixed-format scheme, almost as if we'd used `fwrite` on whole structures or on the array of structures; we are not using the `binwrite` function shown earlier in the chapter. Because this is a binary file and we're going to be both reading and writing from it, `fp` must have been opened using the mode string `r+b` or its equivalent.

```
struct s s;
long int offset;

while(1)
    {
    offset = ftell(fp);
    if(!getint(&s.i, fp))
        break;
    getfloat(&s.f, fp);
    fread(s.str, 1, 20, fp);
    if(s.i == 3)
        {
        strcpy(s.str, "changed");
        fseek(fp, offset, SEEK_SET);
        putint(s.i, fp);
        putfloat(s.f, fp);
        fwrite(s.str, 1, 20, fp);
        break;
        }
    }
```

Since each record was written using `putint`, `putfloat`, and `fwrite`, we read records back in by calling `getint`, `getfloat`, and `fread`. Just before we read each record, we call `ftell` to record our current offset in the file. When we find the record we're looking for, we update the string value in our in-memory copy of the structure, call `fseek` to seek back to the spot where we read this record, and write the modified record out. In this example, the record to be updated is, artificially, just one with the `int` member `i` set to 3.

There are two important things to notice here. One is our use of `fseek`; in the `r+` and `w+` modes, an explicit seek is one of the ways that the `stdio` library can be informed that a switch from reading to writing may be about to take place. In our case, of course, the seek is natural anyway, to return to the spot where we read the record to be rewritten.

The second aspect of note is that we neither inserted nor deleted information, but overwrote it. As mentioned, it's generally impossible to insert or delete data without rewriting the entire file. In some cases it is possible to achieve about the same effect as deleting data by overwriting it with a modified record (again, of the same size) that contains some bit or other flag which marks it as deleted. Though the record is still there, if all code which reads the file is programmed to ignore a marked-as-deleted record, it will be effectively invisible. Another possibility, if a data file uses its own index to allow efficient random access, may be to write a new copy of an updated record elsewhere in a file while updating the index to point to it, leaving the old, superseded data unreachable. We'll look at an example of such an index (though without using it to update data in this way) next.

Indexing

Earlier we mentioned that one way to improve the efficiency of variable-format files is with an index. Our last example will be a variable-format text data file, similar to the last example in the "Binary Files" section, but this time containing multiple records. The first part of the file will be an easy-to-read index permitting the full records in the rest of the file to be located efficiently. But since we won't know the offsets of the individual records until the instant we write them, we'll have to go back and fill in the offsets in the index later.

Here is some code for writing the file. First it writes a dummy index, and then it writes the records, keeping track of the file offset of the beginning of each one, by calling `ftell`, and storing the result in a temporary index structure. Then it rewinds the file pointer and writes the index a second time, this time containing the real offsets, namely the ones recorded during the first pass. Since the dummy index contained strings of `0`s of known length, as written by the `fprintf` formats `%06d` and `%015ld`, it should be possible to overwrite them exactly.

```
struct s data[MAXARRAY];
int na;

struct index
    {
    int key;
    long int offset;
    };

struct index ix[MAXARRAY];
```

```
/* write dummy index */
for(i = 0; i < na; i++)
    fprintf(ofp, "%06d %015ld\n", 0, 0L);

fprintf(ofp, "[end of index]\n\n");

for(i = 0; i < na; i++)
    {
    ix[i].key = data[i].i;
    ix[i].offset = ftell(ofp);
    fprintf(ofp, "i %d\n", data[i].i);
    fprintf(ofp, "f %g\n", data[i].f);
    fprintf(ofp, "str %s\n\n", data[i].str);
    }

rewind(ofp);

for(i = 0; i < na; i++)
    fprintf(ofp, "%06d %015ld\n", ix[i].key, ix[i].offset);
```

Here is code for reading the index later, prior to looking up individual records. This index starts at the beginning of the file, and ends at the line containing `"[end of index]"`.

```
na = 0;
while(fgets(line, sizeof(line), ifp) != NULL)
    {
    if(strncmp(line, "[end of", 7) == 0)
        break;
    nw = getwords(line, words, 3);
    if(nw == 2)
        {
        ix[na].key = atoi(words[0]);
        ix[na].offset = atol(words[1]);
        na++;
        }
    }
```

Finally, here is a skeleton of some code for seeking to and reading a selected record. We presume that the index has been read into the `ix` array by the preceding code. The record being looked for is the one matching the integer value contained in the variable `seekval`.

```
    struct index *ixp = NULL;
    for(i = 0; i < na; i++)
        {
```

```
        if(ix[i].key == seekval)
            {
            ixp = &ix[i];
            break;
            }
        }

    if(ixp == NULL)
        return;     /* not found */

    fseek(ifp, ixp->offset, SEEK_SET);

    while(fgets(line, sizeof(line), ifp) != NULL)
        {
        nw = getwords(line, words, 2);
        if(nw == 0)
            break;
        if(strcmp(words[0], "i") == 0)
            s.i = atoi(words[1]);
        else if(strcmp(words[0], "f") == 0)
            s.f = atof(words[1]);
        else if(strcmp(words[0], "str") == 0)
            {
            char *p2 = strrchr(words[1], '\n');
            if(p2 != NULL)
                *p2 = '\0';
            strncpy(s.str, words[1], sizeof(s.str));
            }
        }
```

The offset found in the index tells us where the record begins, so we seek to that point and start reading. The record ends at the next blank line.

Related Topics

This chapter has focused mostly on designing and implementing your own data files, but to some extent, the world doesn't need any more data file formats. There are quite a few formats out there already, some special-purpose, some general-purpose, some with prewritten code libraries you can use to manipulate them. You might choose to learn about and use one of these, rather than inventing your own format. This section contains references to several of these formats, along with a few other resources relating to data file formats in general. (Unfortunately, tutorials on these formats or on the code for reading or writing them are beyond the scope of this chapter.)

The Hierarchical Data Format (HDF) has a home page at `http://hdf.ncsa.uiuc.edu/`.

The Common Data Format (CDF) has a home page at `http://nssdc.gsfc.nasa.gov/cdf/cdf_home.html`.

The netCDF project (network Common Data Form, a cousin of CDF) has a home page at `http://www.unidata.ucar.edu/packages/netcdf/index.html`.

Sun's External Data Representation (XDR) is described in RFC 1014 and RFC 1832.

The Basic Encoding Rules (BER) are described, along with the related ASN.1 (Abstract Syntax Notation) in the X.409 and ISO 8825 standards.

If you're interested in compressed data file formats, an excellent resource is Jean-loup Gailly's compression FAQ, available on the Internet in the usual FAQ list repositories.

For graphics file formats, an excellent reference is James D. Murray's Graphics File Formats FAQ list at `http://www.ora.com/centers/gff/gff-faq/index.htm`.

A huge repository of file format information (for files of all types) is at the site `http://www.wotsit.org/`.

Note

These URLs were accurate in March 2000, as this chapter was being written, but some might have changed by the time you read this. You can check this book's home page/errata list at `http://users.powernet.co.uk/eton/unleashed/errata/index.html` for updates.

Finally, if you need fast random access to large amounts of data, or if you need true insert and delete operations, or if you have truly huge amounts of data, you'll do well to look into the possibility of storing it in a true database, rather than a simple data file.

Summary

In this chapter you've seen how to design, write, and read formatted data files, using both text and binary methods. Binary data files can be smaller and faster to read and write, whereas text files are somewhat more flexible and (due to their human readability) can be quite convenient to use in practice.

Carefully designed data files are portable between machines. They contain features such as embedded version numbers so that they can be manipulated gracefully even as programs and file formats evolve. Well-designed code for reading data files checks a file's version number and other structural details as the file is being read, so that it can print useful error messages rather than crashing if a file contains unexpected data.

In general, the data in a data file is represented differently than it is in memory. Therefore, reading and writing data files generally involves certain data format conversions. Though our focus has been on reading and writing data files, many of the same techniques for writing, reading, and encoding structured data are also applicable to tasks such as reading configuration files, or implementing network protocols.

Text data files are generally written using `fprintf`, and read using combinations of file-reading functions such as `fgets` and data-converting functions such as `strtol`. The only standard functions suitable for reading and writing binary data files are `fread` and `fwrite`, but they generally result in nonportable data files, so we wrote our own utility functions (including `putint` and `getint`) to conveniently write and read various data types to and from binary data files portably, in a bytewise fashion.

Finally, you saw how to read and write some industry-standard generic file formats, namely TDF, CSV, and INI. You saw how to update records in a data file in-place, and how to build an index to streamline the lookup of records in a variable-format file.

CHAPTER 7

When Things Go Wrong: Code-Mending

by Richard Heathfield

In This Chapter

Programming is an inherently difficult activity, possibly the most difficult mental task routinely undertaken every day by large numbers of people. Because it's difficult, mistakes in programs are inevitable. It is also true that the longer a mistake goes unnoticed, the more costly it is to fix. I won't try to prove this, but I can very simply illustrate it: If a bug is discovered in User Acceptance Testing, it is necessary not only to fix the code, but also to do a whole batch of regression tests to ensure that the fix didn't break anything else. Clearly, if the bug had been spotted at development time, the regression tests would not have been necessary. As a matter of pure economics, we need to adopt development strategies that will catch mistakes as soon as possible in the development life cycle.

In this chapter, we'll be exploring some ways we can catch bugs early. We'll start by looking at compiler diagnostics. Then we'll examine some common characteristics of debugging software. We will also develop a code tracing library, and consider a few common classes of bugs. The chapter winds up with a truly dreadful program that demonstrates a number of typical programming errors.

Dealing with Diagnostics

Our first line of defense against program errors (apart from our own brains, of course) is the compiler. All ANSI C compilers are required to produce at least one diagnostic message if they encounter a constraint violation or syntax error. Here's an example of a constraint violation:

```
typedef struct FOO
{
  unsigned int i: 1;
  unsigned int j: 1;
} FOO;

FOO foo;

unsigned int *p;

p = &foo.j;
```

This violates the constraint that the operand of the `&` operator must not be a bit-field, so the compiler is required to issue a diagnostic message. I won't trouble you with an example of a syntax error; you've undoubtedly seen a few thousand of those already.

There is a plethora of other information the compiler can gather as it wends its merry way through your code, but it doesn't *have* to tell you any of this extra information. Fortunately, good compilers do provide far more diagnostic information than they have to. This is very helpful, enabling you to improve the quality of your code even as you are writing it.

Some people think you should write your program completely before compiling it for the first time. There is some justification for this attitude in time-shared systems such as mainframe environments, where compilations can take quite a while to execute. This is especially true if it is a large program comprising many modules, with compilation being controlled by a versioning system; this can have an impact on the machine power available to other users, merely by taking up processor cycles. Certainly you should design your program long before you touch your compiler, irrespective of your hardware circumstances. Once you have started the process of cutting code on a standalone machine, however, it's best to compile regularly. That way, you can fix your typographical errors as you go, which is less tiresome than doing them in one big purgatorial editing session at the end.

Furthermore, some modern integrated editors have a "code completion" feature, prompting you for each argument to a function, and presenting you with a selection of fields for the structure whose name you just typed in. This is a big time-saver, lends a certain decadent air to the task of programming, and is tremendous fun, too, especially when it goes wrong. It's not uncommon for the code completion database to be built at compilation time. So compiling frequently can save you the time and effort of looking up your own function prototypes and structure information.

There's nothing new under the sun. Undoubtedly you've often been in the situation where you've hit a problem that reminds you vaguely of a similar bug you encountered a year or so ago. This isn't much help unless you can remember how you fixed it last time! Keeping a diary of your bugs, and how you solved them, is an excellent idea and I recommend it to you. It could save you many hours of head scratching.

Use Warnings Wisely

Compiler diagnostics are there to help you. Most compilers split their diagnostics into two kinds—errors and warnings. Very few programmers would consider forcing a compiler to build a program even though it contained errors. I've met many programmers, however, who have no problem with releasing code into the production environment even though it generates many, many warnings.

It's wise to remember that every single warning is there for a very simple reason—to help you write better code. Probably the simplest way you can become an even better programmer is to start taking notice of each and every single warning. Track down the cause of each warning, and consider long and hard whether there is a simple way to write this code more robustly.

Sometimes, tolerating warnings is very tempting. When you recall that the ANSI standard allows a compiler to issue any diagnostics it likes, as long as it correctly compiles correct code, it's not surprising that some compilers issue diagnostics for code which you consider to be perfectly all right. For example, Borland's compiler will issue a diagnostic for the code in Listing 7.1.

LISTING 7.1 Generating Compiler Diagnostics

```
#include <stdio.h>
#include <string.h>

int main(void)
{
  size_t len = 0;
  char buffer[1024] = {0};
  if(fgets(buffer, sizeof buffer, stdin) != NULL)
  {
    len = strlen(buffer);
    printf("The input string is %u bytes long.\n",
           (unsigned)len);
  }

  return 0;
}
```

When I compiled this using Borland C++ 5.2, I got the following warning:

```
Warning foo.c 6: 'len' is assigned a value that is never used in function main
```

Now, I have a penchant for initializing all my variables at definition. There are arguments for and against this style, as discussed in Chapter 2, "Holy Wars: Programming Standards—Causes and Cures," and clearly one of the arguments against my preferred style is that it produces this warning!

This warning really annoys me. I know exactly what it means and why it's there, and I can see how the warning would be of benefit to someone with a style different than mine. The trouble is that, if I just ignore it, I end up with quite a few warnings in every program I write. The problem there is that these "harmless" warnings tend to accumulate, to the point where I can't easily spot the warnings I really want to know about.

I could probably use a compiler-specific pragma to turn off the warning, but pragmas tend to cause far more problems than they solve. For example, the Borland C++ pragma to turn off this warning is

```
#pragma warn -aus
```

This suppresses the warning, but there are three objections to such an approach. First, you have to either turn the warning on, and then off, for each function, or just accept that you'll never get a warning for a genuinely useless assignment. Second, pragmas are compiler-specific by definition; in theory, a compiler is supposed to ignore pragmas it doesn't recognize, but in practice some don't. And what if that pragma means something different in a different compiler? The pragma ties the code to a particular compiler, and that's bad for portability. In my line of work, portability is usually a requirement, so that's not a valid solution. Third, using pragmas to suppress warnings sets a bad precedent. Once your less punctilious teammates see an example in your code, they might just start suppressing warnings in this way themselves—and that way chaos lies.

I could use a different compiler, of course, and for many years I did exactly that. The trouble is that the Borland compiler, while not perfect by any means, is one of the better compilers for PCs, and I'm in the process of migrating *to* it, rather than *from* it.

Or perhaps I could do something like this:

```
void sink(void *p, int i)
{
  if(i > 0)
    sink(p, 0);
}
```

and call it like this:

```
  size_t len = 0;
  char buffer[1024];

  sink(&len, 0);
  if(fgets(buffer, sizeof buffer, stdin) != NULL)
  {
    len = strlen(buffer);
  /* ... */
```

But that would be going a little far, perhaps. I'd have to call the `sink()` function once for each variable I planned to use—hardly a good use of programming resource, even if I arranged matters such that `sink()` was conditionally compiled out of production code.

Another possible solution is to change my programming style—and in fact this is what's happening. It wasn't a conscious decision, but I have noticed that I've started getting less pernickety about initializing variables at definition since I started using the Borland compiler more frequently.

If you ever find a style that will, for any program, produce no warnings at all under *all* ANSI C compilers at their pickiest warning level, the world would be very glad to hear from you.

Use More than One Compiler

Implementations may produce as many or as few diagnostics as they like (subject to the requirement to diagnose syntax errors and constraint violations), provided they correctly compile correct code. Using more than one compiler can help you to identify problems with your code. Of course, this suggestion presupposes that your code is portable from one compiler to another, which is only likely to be true if you are writing pure ANSI C.

Using at least two compilers, if possible, can sometimes help you prove to whoever needs convincing (usually yourself) that a particular problem is indeed with your code, and is not a bug in the compiler; after all, it's unlikely that two competing compiler-writers made exactly the same mistake. Also, it's perfectly possible for one compiler to be more forgiving than another. For example, there's nothing in the ANSI standard to stop a compiler from initializing local variables to `NULL`, 0, or 0.0 if it likes. If your favorite compiler does this but your second compiler doesn't, the code may exhibit completely different behavior depending on which compiler you used this time around. (If this is the case, your code definitely has a bug, in which case using a second compiler just saved you from unnecessary embarrassment at the testing stage.) Furthermore, the Standard permits quite a range of more tangible difference between compilers; for example, `INT_MAX` (the highest value that an int can store) must be at least 32767, is often 2147483647, and can be any of many other values. Thus, using different compilers can help to show up portability problems with your code.

Choosing a Warning Level

If we agree that warnings are helpful, clearly it's beneficial to get as many warnings as a compiler is able to give us for any particular piece of code. Some programmers take the opposite tack. They want a clean compilation, so they turn their warning level *down*! This ostrich-like attitude is not going to help them in the long run. Burning your telephone bill doesn't mean you don't owe the phone company money; it only means you don't know how much you owe. Just turning off the warnings doesn't make the problems go away. If there's a problem with the code, the sooner we know about it, the better. Set up your compiler to be as grumpy and pernickety as it can be. If it has a "curmudgeonly" setting, use it.

Some authors recommend that you use the switch provided by many compilers, to treat all warnings as errors. I wouldn't go that far. After all, some compilers generate warnings on what many of us would consider to be style issues. Furthermore, there are times when we just want to write a quick and fairly trivial use-once-throw-away program, when speed is more important than code perfection (as long as the program actually works, of course), and when it would be annoying to have to plough through the compiler options twice, once to turn 'warnings as errors' off and once to turn it on again. But you should certainly aim for a clean compilation at the highest warning level available when writing production code.

If you do decide to tolerate warnings, you should do so from knowledge, rather than ignorance. As far as is possible, C trusts you to know what you are doing. Make sure that you do! Tolerating a warning is not something to be done lightly. Investigate each warning thoroughly. If, having done so, you are quite happy in your own mind that you understand the reason for the warning and know for a fact that in this case your code is fine and the warning is a well-meaning canard, and if you are confident of justifying this to your team members at peer review, by all means tolerate it. It would be wise to document the code that is causing the warning, though, with a clear comment explaining exactly why you have decided to put up with it. If it turns out later on that your decision was wrong, whoever is maintaining the code will at least have some clue to help him start off his debugging investigation. And that someone could be you.

Use ANSI Settings

It would be most naive of me to assume that everyone reading this book programs purely in ANSI C. If you are writing a program that must run on more than one system, however, you are in all likelihood striving for ANSI C code, in which case turning on the ANSI C option on your compiler is most important. Modern compilers can warn you about all kinds of non-portable constructs, if you instruct them to do so.

This book isn't about particular platforms or compilers. Nevertheless, here are the ANSI switches (and maximum warning levels) for a handful of the more popular current microcomputer compilers:

- Borland C++ 5.2: `bcc32 -A -w foo.c`
- Microsoft Visual C++ 5.0/6.0: `cl -Za -W4 foo.c`
- GNU C/Delorie C: `gcc -W -Wall -ansi -pedantic foo.c`

Top-down Approach

Compilers can get really confused by poor syntax, to the extent that they can generate thirty or fifty or a hundred spurious errors, simply because you forgot a closing brace on a `while` loop, or typed a colon instead of a semicolon at the end of a statement. Because of this, and because I am blessed with a relatively quick machine, I have a tendency to fix just a few errors at a time, starting each time at the top of the list. My most common error message is probably `unknown identifier`—I get a lot of those because I tend not to declare variables until after I've fully decided how (or indeed *whether*) I'm going to use them. I can fix fifty `unknown identifier` errors in one go. If, however, I see errors such as these:

```
For statement missing ; in function main
Function should return a value in function main
'i' is assigned a value that is never used in function main
```

I know that I've got one of those errors that has a knock-on effect on the compiler. The clue is that missing semicolon which, together with mismatched parentheses, braces, or brackets, is an excellent way to befuddle a compiler. At this point, it's wise to start fixing just one error at a time. If, in this case, I had ignored the first diagnostic, I would have been scratching my head in consternation for quite some time over the other two. This is not surprising because the diagnostics themselves were spurious. So in this circumstance it's best to fix the first error, and then compile the program again.

This phenomenon isn't unique to C, by the way. Many years ago, a friend of mine complained that his COBOL compiler had generated over three thousand error messages because he'd misspelled ENVIRONMENT in one single place in his program. Fixing this misspelling reduced the number of error messages to a much more manageable number (three hundred).

Lint Is Your Friend

Many years ago, someone decided to move code quality analysis techniques out of the C compiler and into a separate utility, in an effort to speed up compilation. The separate utility was called `lint`, the idea being that you could compile your program quickly until it was more or less working, then use `lint` to get the "pocket-fluff" out of the program.

This strategy was possibly a mistake. By divorcing the process of cleaning up code from the process of producing it, it may have diminished the perceived importance of robust code in the minds of some programmers. It did, however, have the desired effect of speeding up the development cycle. Modern compilers have taken advantage of the massive speed increases of recent years to re-incorporate basic `lint` functionality into the compiler. This is clearly a good move. Nevertheless, some `lint` programs are incredibly fussy and, as such, can tell you a lot about your code that you thought you already knew.

The lint I use myself is called LCLint, which is legally downloadable from the World Wide Web; it's one of the most vicious lints I've ever come across. Here's a sample of its output (I've included the input first to give you an idea of how picky this program is):

```
#include <stdio.h>

int main(void)
{
  printf("Hello world\n");
  return 0;
}
```

What could possibly be wrong with that program? Let's find out. Here's the output from LCLint, using its +strict setting:

```
hello.c: (in function main)

hello.c:5:3: Called procedure printf may access file system state, but globals
list does not include globals fileSystem

A called function uses internal state, but the globals list for the function
being checked does not include internalState (-internalglobs will suppress
message)

hello.c:5:3: Undocumented modification of file system state possible from
call to printf: printf("Hello world\n")

report undocumented file system modifications (applies to unspecified functions
if modnomods is set) (-modfilesys will suppress message)

Finished LCLint checking --- 413 code errors found
```

(I snipped out the other 411 errors it found, which were all in stdio.h! Many referred to unused constants or function prototypes.)

Reducing LCLint's severity level from +strict to +checks showed a corresponding reduction in the number of stdio.h problems to a mere 230, and no problems in hello.c.

A good lint really does improve your code quality, if you manage to find a setting that is strict enough, without being discouragingly severe. On LCLint, I use +checks, which I understand to be about halfway between a straightforward syntax check and the pedantry of +strict. (Apparently there's a little something on offer from the LCLint guys if you manage to write a real program that produces no messages at the +strict level. There's a challenge for you.)

The benefits are immediate. If you pay any attention to lint output (and if you don't, why run it at all?) you will almost certainly find a few flaws in your programming style. As you begin to correct these, your `lint` output will become correspondingly less verbose; this usually corresponds to a real increase in the quality of your code—which is the whole point, of course.

There is a particular kind of programmer who likes nit-picking other people's code (okay, okay, I confess!). `Lint` is great for nitpickers, and some people wield it almost like a weapon (for example, on Usenet). Oddly enough, it's a weapon which brings great benefits to a perceptive "victim," who is wise enough to see past the minor humiliation of having his code ripped apart in public, and realizes that here is an opportunity to become a better programmer.

I'm not advocating LCLint particularly—that just happens to be the one I use. But I do advocate `lint` programs in general; I strongly recommend that you find a good one for your particular platform and use it on all new source code (and old source code if you have the time, energy, and enthusiasm to go back and fix it).

Debugging Common Errors

Let's draw a distinction right away between testing and debugging. Both are complex arts, both are necessary, and each is very different from the other. Here are a couple of working definitions:

Testing is the art of trying to break your program when you think it works.

Debugging is the art of trying to mend your program when you know it's broken.

(I coined these definitions myself, so it was with mixed feelings that I recently noticed more or less identical definitions in *The Practice of Programming* by Kernighan and Pike. There's nothing new under the sun.)

When you complete (or think you have completed) your first cut of any non-trivial program, you can bet your shirt that it's broken. It has truly been said that all non-trivial programs contain at least one bug. So debugging comes before testing, as well as after it. It's an iterative process, of course.

This chapter is about debugging, not testing, but I think a quick word about testing is in order. You shouldn't really test your own code. If your organization is large enough, testing should be done by an independent person who had little or nothing to do with the development process. It's difficult to view your own code objectively. Naturally, you're proud of your code, you believe it to be bug-free, and you think it's ready to go into production. (If not, why is it being tested?) So you're not really in the right frame of mind to rip it apart, are you? And until it's proved that it can stand up to being ripped apart, it's not really ready for the real world. An independent tester will not share your blind spots on the code, and will subject your code to far more rigorous testing than you can possibly give it.

Of course, a program continues to be tested for as long as it is in actual use—not by the tester, but by real users. The more thorough the initial testing, the more likely it is that the program will continue to be used for a long time.

It's not very pleasant to be told by a tester that your program is broken, so it's worth spending time doing your best to make sure it isn't. Of course, when the program is only just written, it's bound to have bugs (unless it's a really trivial program, in which case it's only extremely likely to have bugs), so it's a good idea to run the program a few times to see if it does what you wanted it to do. This may sound really obvious, but it's not. Some programmers really do check their source code back in to their version control systems without even compiling it. They are asking for trouble, and trouble will undoubtedly follow. (I know this is true because, shame on me, I've done it myself.)

When you've run your program for the first time, you'll probably notice one or two things wrong. Write them down. Write down everything you noticed about your program that was either unexpected or just plain wrong. The natural reaction is to go fix the first problem. If you do this, however, you're likely to forget about the other problems you noticed, and they might not be readily apparent on subsequent runs. By writing them down, you ensure that you have a chance to examine *all* potential trouble spots.

This is an N-pass process, of course. Run program, write down anything odd you notice, go fix the code, run program...

When do you stop? When you run out of problems, of course. That doesn't mean your program is now bug-free, but it does mean it's ready for testing.

Just a moment. If you were paying attention just then, you'll have spotted that I said "go fix the code." What a handwave! *How* do you go fix the code? Specifically, how do you identify and correct a subtle flaw?

The best strategy is to divide and conquer. After all, if you know where the problem *isn't*, that's almost as good as knowing where the problem *is*, especially if you can quickly identify large areas of your code that are known not to be the cause of the problem.

Modular design helps out a lot here. If you have designed your program as a great interconnected mass of spaghetti, full of gotos and globals and `longjmp()` calls, it's going to be a lot harder to debug than a carefully designed, modular program. If your program is divided into modules, each of which bears responsibility for one particular aspect of your program, it's going to be much easier to find a problem than if responsibility for a given process is split across multiple functions or even source files.

Modular design has other important benefits too. For example, if you isolate non-portable parts of your program into their own modules, and communicate with those modules only via their well-defined interfaces, porting your program to another platform is going to be relatively simple and trouble-free.

Once you've identified which module the problem is likely to be in, the obvious first step is to look at the source code. Probably 90% of bugs are spotted in this way. But don't spend too long on it—if you haven't spotted the bug in the source code itself within a couple of minutes, you don't really know where it is. Set your watch. If you can't find the bug through trial and error within two or possibly three minutes, spending longer is a waste of time, and a more methodical approach will save you that time. By all means try the random approach, but don't rely on it.

So, if you haven't found your problem by chance, how are you going to locate the troublesome code?

First, try to reproduce the error in a controlled way. If you can, that tells you something important about the nature of the error. If you can't, that tells you something equally important.

If the error is reproducible for a known set of inputs, try a slightly different set of inputs. Does the error still occur? Again, both possible answers to that question yield useful information. If you can reproduce the error in a variety of ways, you are very close to identifying the cause of the problem. What is the minimum change you can make to the input data which results in the bug *not* manifesting itself? Once you have established this, you can probably go right to the offending code.

What if there is apparently only one input that causes your problem? Some people might be tempted to fix it like this:

```
foo = bar(baz);
if(baz == 9)
  foo = 13.4;
```

The technical term for this so-called fix is "bodge." It looks wrong, feels wrong, smells wrong. The programmer has fixed the symptom, not the cause. The real problem presumably lies in the `bar()` function, so the `bar()` function should be inspected, and the true cause of the error identified and fixed.

Once you've established a set of inputs that exercise the error, and a set of slightly different inputs that don't, you are in a position to hypothesize. Don't be tempted to make just one hypothesis. Now is the time for pencil and paper (or text editor and fingers). Without trying to evaluate them, try to think up at least half a dozen possible causes of the error.

Once you have your list of hypotheses, you can establish a set of test conditions that will uniquely test each hypothesis. This may involve simply examining your source code, or it may require designing a new test case.

You may be able to reduce your workload here, especially when testing big systems with a lot of input data, by extracting the module in question and placing it into a specially written test program, which basically consists of `main()`, the suspected routine, and as little else as possible. Then you can concentrate purely on the inputs to the troublesome routine. This is obviously much less practical if you have many global variables or other unmodular constructs, and that's a good reason for writing your code in a modular fashion.

Now is the time for single-stepping through the code or examining trace files. With good modern debuggers, you should be able to get to the right module very quickly, using step-over and trace-into functionality. If you are using trace files instead, use a code-scanning utility such as `grep` to get you to approximately the right place.

The general idea is to keep a close eye on your program's behavior, to identify the first place where it appears to be misbehaving. One way to do this is simply to place a breakpoint roughly halfway through your program, execute to that point, and check out the state of your variables. If all seems well, put another breakpoint three-quarters of the way through your code, and let the code run. Otherwise, stop debugging, put a breakpoint a quarter of the way through your code, and let the code run to there. This is a straightforward application of the binary chop principle. If you have a one million line program, careful choice of breakpoints can reduce the number of iterations of this idea to only twenty or so, before you've identified the approximate line of code that is causing the problem.

Ask Teddy

Don't feel that you have to solve the problem all in one go, or all on your own. Sometimes taking a break works wonders. If you've ever quit work for the day without having found your bug, only to work it out in the car on the way home, you'll already know the value of standing back from the problem. (This method doesn't just work for debugging. It's a well-known crossword-solving technique too.)

Consulting your colleagues is also a useful way to get a clearer perspective on your code. The very act of clearly explaining the problem to another human being, in sufficient detail to give them a chance of being able to help you, is frequently enough to kickstart your brain. If you're short of human beings to try this on, use a teddy bear. It still works! As long as you can convince yourself, however temporarily, that your audience can listen to and understand you, that's all that matters. Their role is purely maieutic; they don't need to say a word.

My teddy bear is called Clint (The Bear With No Name). A (so-called) friend of mine insists on consulting me *before* he talks to Clint, because he doesn't want to waste the bear's valuable time. Hmmmm. If you feel stupid talking to a dumb teddy bear, find a spare pair of spectacles (sunglasses will do) and put them on the bear. Now you're talking to an (apparently) *intelligent* teddy bear, and that can make all the difference. I don't know why this works, but it does. A good friend of mine to whom I suggested this laughed at the very idea, but I persuaded him to try it. He didn't have a teddy bear, but he did have a toy elephant that apparently looks really cool in Ray-Bans. Now the elephant is an intrinsic part of his debugging strategy. Why? Because it works.

It doesn't work all the time, of course. If you don't solve your problem this way, and want to consult a real human being, that's fine. We've all done it, and it's not an admission of failure, merely another tool in your toolbox.

To minimize the time your colleague has to spend helping you, it's a good idea to construct a minimal program that reproduces the problem you're having. Make a safe copy of the code, and remove all extraneous and irrelevant material from your program. Once that's done, run it to make sure it still reproduces the bug. This simplification process may in itself reveal to you the cause of the problem. If it doesn't, you will at least have eased your colleague's tasks of understanding and then (hopefully) explaining the problem.

Once you've localized the problem to a particular line, or perhaps to a particular loop or function, you will in most cases see the problem straight away, and the fix will often be obvious.

Unfortunately, there is no algorithm for finding a bug. No step-by-step guide is going to guarantee that you can find your programming error merely by following that guide. Even so, many bugs are very common. Let's have a look at a few of the most common errors; "know your enemy" is the watchword. Later on in this chapter we'll be looking at bugs from a diagnostic viewpoint. At the moment, our aim is to look at some common *causes* of errors.

Off-by-One Errors

```
char *strdup(char *s)
{
  return strcpy(malloc(strlen(s)), s);
}
```

This code exhibits a number of problems. It invades implementation namespace, for a start. Also, it uses the return value of `malloc` without first checking that the allocation request was honored, and it blithely assumes that `s` is non-`NULL`. Ninety-seven times out of 100 (yes, I made that figure up), none of these problems will cause a particular program run to fail. But there is another problem. Insufficient space has been allocated for `s`. This is because `strlen` returns the number of characters in a string, not including its null terminating character. Therefore, `strcpy` is updating memory the program doesn't own. This is a classic off-by-one error. Here's another:

```
int CalcTotal(int *arr, size_t numelems)
{
  size_t i;
  int total = 0;

  for(i = 0; i <= numelems; i++)
  {
    total += *arr++;
  }
  return total;
}
```

The bug here is in the loop control statement's relational operator. It should be <, not <=. This is, you might think, an obvious error. And so it is. So why do we make this mistake so often?

Fencepost Errors

Sometimes we are concerned not so much with data objects themselves as with the relationships between them, at which point we are particularly susceptible to a fencepost error. For example, if we want to calculate the sum of differences between adjacent items in an array, we might do it like this:

```
int CalcDiffSum(int *arr, size_t numelems)
{
  int Sum = 0;
  size_t i;
  for(i = 0; i < numelems; i++)
```

```
  {
    Sum += *arr - *(arr + 1);
  }

  return Sum;
}
```

The problem here is in the loop condition statement. It *looks* right, doesn't it? But of course, it isn't. It should be

```
  for(i = 0; i < numelems - 1; i++)
```

For maximum robustness, `numelems` should be checked before we ever go into the loop, to ensure that it is not 0 or 1.

This is a variant of the off-by-one error. All fencepost errors are off-by-one errors, although not all off-by-one errors are fencepost errors. Unfortunately, this particular error almost invariably involves accessing memory we don't own, so it is often a cause of seemingly random behavior.

Infinite Loops

When you consider that loops are a stock-in-trade of the professional (and indeed, the amateur) programmer, it's surprising how often our loops become tangles. We all know that our loops should terminate at some point. But often, they don't. Here's a fairly subtle example:

```
void WriteCharacterSet(char *filename)
{
  unsigned char ch;
  FILE *fp = fopen(filename, "wb");
  for(ch = 0; ch < 256; ch++)
  {
    fwrite(&ch, 1, 1, fp);
  }
  fclose(fp);
}
```

This is fairly typical "quick-and-dirty" code, of the kind that many programmers write in a few seconds to do one small, well-defined job. You might use this routine to get yourself a quick EBCDIC or extended ASCII table, suitable for browsing in a hex editor, so that you can find out visually the collating sequence order of a particular character. Except that the routine doesn't work. We'll skip over the complete absence of error-checking (worrying as it is) and instead focus, again, on the loop.

It looks harmless enough, but in fact this program will run (in theory) forever on implementations where CHAR_BIT is 8 (that is, most implementations). Given that CHAR_BIT is 8, the unsigned char type can hold the values 0 through 255. When ch is at 255, and ch++ is executed, ch has a notional value of 256, and this is reduced to fit within the data type's range (this is not a case of overflow causing undefined behavior; such reduction is defined by the Standard for unsigned types). So ch goes from 256 to 0 (because 256 % 256 is 0), and the loop continues. In practice, the program may shudder to a halt when the disk fills up. If you're lucky, that is.

Assignment Instead of Comparison

This is a nasty bug. In C, every non-void expression has a value, and that value can be used in other expressions. This can lead to the following problem:

```
NODE *AddNode(NODE *root, char *data)
{
  diff = strcmp(data, root->data);
  if(diff > 0)
  {
    if(root->left = NULL)
    {
      root->left = malloc(sizeof *root->left);

/* ... */
```

It's pretty clear that this particular tree is going to be little more than a blade of grass for the rest of its life. The trouble is with that equality sign, which is actually an assignment operator. The programmer meant to type ==, but he missed an = sign. It's easily done.

This bug can be prevented much of the time by a simple rearrangement of terms. In a test for equality it makes no difference which way around the arguments are, from the point of view of the compiler. If both sides are variable, you just have to be careful to get the right number of = signs. If, however, one side is a constant, there's a positive thing you can do to prevent bugs.

Why not accustom yourself to putting the constant on the *left* side of the comparison operator? That way, if you leave off one of the = signs, you are guaranteed a compilation error (can't assign to a constant, you see).

In our example, we could have typed:

```
  if(NULL = root->left)
  {
    /* ... */
```

The same typographical error is there but, this time, the code will simply not compile. It's better to catch a bug at compile time than at run-time, as I am sure you will agree.

Those with compilers who warn against assignment statements inside `if()` and `while()` expressions often say that it's better to write clear code and trust the compiler to warn you about typos, and claim that `(root->left == NULL)` is easier to read than `(NULL == root->left)`. Those who use more than one compiler regularly are less convinced about this. Some compilers simply don't perform this kind of checking.

Buffer Overflow

Beginning C programmers quickly learn that you can't do this:

```
#include <stdio.h>
#include <string.h>
int main(void)
{
  char *s;
  strcpy(s, "Hello world!");
  printf("%s\n", s);
  return 0;
}
```

because of course `s` doesn't point to a region of storage owned by the program. An appropriate fix would be to make `s` an array of 13 or more characters.

So, how about this?

```
#include <stdio.h>

int main(void)
{
  char s[13];
  printf("Please type in your name\n");
  gets(s);
  printf("Your name is %s\n", s);
  return 0;
}
```

This program contains an intermittent bug. It will work just fine, provided the user doesn't type more than 12 characters. But how do you control the user? You can't. If he types in a fifty-character name, you're in big trouble. If he types in a thirteen-character name, you're still in big trouble.

The `gets()` function cannot be used safely. The `fgets()` function is recommended instead, but even this function is not a panacea because you have to take care to match the middle argument to the buffer size carefully. Although `fgets()` is certainly more robust than `gets()`, it's not magical; you do need to get the arguments right.

Of course, sometimes buffer overflow comes in more subtle ways, as shown in Listing 7.2.

LISTING 7.2 Buffer Overflow

```
#include <stdio.h>
#include <string.h>

int main(void)
{
  char Name[12];
  char First[12];
  char Second[12];

  printf("First name?\n");
  fgets(First, sizeof First, stdin);
  printf("Last name?\n");
  fgets(Second, sizeof Second, stdin);

  strcat(Name, First);
  strcat(Name, " ");
  strcat(Name, Second);

  printf("Full name: %s\n", Name);

  return 0;
}
```

The first problem here is that `Name` has not been initialized, so the `strcat` call may well overflow its buffer. You might be lucky. The first byte of `strcat` might be 0, and all is well (for now). You might be even luckier. The first few bytes of `strcat` might be printable characters, such as "XzR3kg59ED", followed by 0. This way, your program will not only work in a reasonably well-behaved manner, but will also produce output showing clearly that you have a bug, which gives you a chance to fix it before handing it over for testing.

The second problem is that there is insufficient space in the `Name` array for some possible combinations of inputs into the `First` array and the `Second` array. For example, the name "Winston Churchill", while overflowing neither `First` nor `Second`, *will* overflow the `Name` array when copied into it.

Array Bounds Violation

Buffer overflow is a special case of array bounds violation. C arrays may be divided into two kinds. The first is the array whose bounds are decided at compile time and, of course, the second is the array whose size is determined at run-time, using a routine such as `malloc` to allocate the memory.

(The new C99 Standard introduces variable-length array syntax, but I am presuming that you are using a C89 compiler for the time being.)

Listing 7.3 is an example of a simple fixed-length array bounds violation.

LISTING 7.3 Fixed-length Array Bounds Violation

```
#include <stdio.h>

int main(void)
{
  char CharacterSet[128] = {0}; /* init array to all 0 */
  int ch;
  int i;

  while((ch = getchar()) != EOF)
  {
    ++CharacterSet[ch];
  }

  printf("Char  Frequency\n");
  printf("----  ---------\n");
  for(i = 0; i < sizeof CharacterSet; i++)
  {
    printf("%3d  %d\n", i, CharacterSet[i]);
  }
  return 0;
}
```

This program has quite an interesting history. It was first written on a system using ASCII. It was tested on that system, using files that contained only ASCII characters (in the range 0 to 127). Later, it was ported to a system using EBCDIC. Nobody noticed that the program assumed a file using the 7-bit ASCII character set. On EBCDIC systems, `char` is typically unsigned (whether "vanilla" `char` is signed or unsigned is an implementation issue), because EBCDIC is an 8-bit character set. Of course, with the very first character of input, the program broke.

The bug is an array bounds violation, but the cause was a false assumption about the execution character set.

Missing Arguments

C's prototyping, neatly purloined from C++ when nobody was looking, has gone a long way toward ensuring that our function calls have the right number of arguments. Unfortunately, prototyping does not help us when we use variadic functions. Well, it helps a bit. It means we get type checking on the return value of the function, and on those types that *are* referenced in the prototype. But as soon as the ellipsis is reached, prototype checking stops.

Here's one of my favorite bugs:

```
#include <stdio.h>

int main(void)
{
  char *s = "string";
  int d = 42;
  double f = 3.14;
  printf("String is %s, int is %d, double is %f\n");
  return 0;
}
```

Well, yes. It's a glaring error. But the compiler can't (or at least, certainly is not obliged to) catch it. Certainly there isn't enough information in the prototype. For a compiler to catch this problem, it has to rely on special knowledge of the `printf` function. Furthermore, it's not impossible for the format string to be derived (in fact, in real world programs, deriving the format string is quite common), in which case the compiler certainly would not be able to trap this error.

Why is this my favorite bug? Perhaps because I make this mistake so often. It's an easy mistake to make, especially when I'm in a hurry. Fortunately, it's usually quite easy to catch, and it invariably produces embarrassing output. I once managed to display, for an insurance premium of only £30 (that's about $50) per month, a "sum assured" which would have bankrupted every single nation in the world, had it ever been claimed.

Pointers

I firmly believe that a true C programmer can be identified easily by his attitude to pointers. Those who love C, love pointers. Those who don't love pointers are never going to love C, no matter how hard they try. C programmers love pointers because they are so simple and yet so powerful. Those who loathe pointers think they are unnecessarily complicated. One thing is certain: pointer bugs are the hardest to track down and fix.

If we understand pointers, we are most likely to encounter pointer problems when we don't think sufficiently carefully about end conditions. Those who do not understand pointers can, of course, encounter problems with them at more or less any time.

Let's look at a common rookie error in Listing 7.4, where the programmer uses memory he doesn't own:

LISTING 7.4 Memory Allocation Error

```
#include <stdio.h>
#include <stdlib.h>

int main(void)
{
  char *filename;
  FILE *fp;
  int Result = EXIT_SUCCESS;
  int i;

  printf("This program calculates perfect squares.\n");
  printf("Please enter a filename for the output:\n");

  fgets(filename, 13, stdin);
  fp = fopen(filename, "w");
  if(fp != NULL)
  {
    fprintf(fp, "Perfect squares\n");
    for(i = 0; i < 100; i++)
    {
      fprintf(fp, "%2d   %4d\n", i, i * i);
    }
    fclose(fp);
  }
  else
  {
    printf("Couldn't open file %s\n", filename);
```

LISTING 7.4 continued

```
    Result = EXIT_FAILURE;
  }
  return Result;
}
```

Quite apart from the fact that it wrongly assumes that filenames can only be up to 13 characters long and does not check the return value from `fgets()`, this program also uses space it doesn't own. The `filename` variable is a pointer. It has not been initialized, and consequently has a "garbage" value. The `fgets()` function has no way of knowing that it has been passed a meaningless address, and will write up to 13 characters of data into the 13 bytes beginning at that meaningless address. What will happen as a result? We can't tell. It's entirely possible that the program will work anyway but, of course, that's far from certain. This is an example of undefined behavior.

A related error occurs when memory is correctly allocated, then freed, and then used again. Once you have freed memory, it is immediately unavailable to you, and accessing it results in undefined behavior. This code fragment illustrates the bug:

```
while(p->Next != NULL)
{
  free(p);
  free(p->Data);
  p = p->Next;
}
```

I found that code in a monthly batch program which had been in production for over a year; the program was a constant source of trouble, and I had been asked to glance over it with a fine-toothed comb, in case there was anything obviously wrong with it. This was only one of many errors I found in that program. Fixing this one was the biggest win, though, because it meant that the operator would no longer have to start the batch run off again after running this program.

The misconception that led to this bug was simple. "I've only just freed that memory. The value of the data stored there won't have changed in the few microseconds before I refer to it, so all will be well. I can still access it for now." This is false. When you free your memory, it must be forever, starting immediately. If you want to refer to that data again, don't free the memory in the first place. If you want the memory back for some other purpose, call `malloc()` again.

Another pointer-related mistake is to free memory more than once. Two strategies for preventing this problem spring to mind. First, we can assign `NULL` to a pointer after freeing the memory to which it points. After all, the ANSI Standard guarantees to us that

```
free(NULL);
```

is harmless; therefore, setting pointers to `NULL` prevents damage from occurring if they are subsequently passed to `free()`. This is a valuable safeguard, but you may consider it to be weak as a form of protection. A more robust approach is possible, but needs to be in place at the design stage; the program should only free memory in the right place, and there should only be one right place. Ideally, a module that allocates memory should be responsible for freeing that memory.

Less harmful than any of these, but still a major problem, is the issue of the so-called memory leak. This sounds like a serious hardware problem but is, in fact, merely the failure to free memory when it's finished with. Listing 7.5 shows a good way to leak memory.

LISTING 7.5 Leaking Memory

```
#include <stdio.h>
#include <stdlib.h>
#include <time.h>

int main(void)
{
  clock_t start, end;

  unsigned long count = 0;
  start = clock();

  while(malloc(1024))
  {
    ++count;
    if(count % 16 == 0)
    {
      end = clock();

      printf("%7f CPU seconds: %d kilobytes allocated\n",
             (double)(end - start) / CLOCKS_PER_SEC,
             count);
    }
  }
  printf("Out of memory (no more kilobytes).\n");
  return 0;
}
```

It can be instructive to actually run this program, leaks and all, simply to get an idea of the performance hit that your program takes as the operating system starts to scratch around for more memory. You may need to re-start your machine afterwards, depending on your operating system. Bear in mind that memory leaks don't affect your process alone; they can reduce the time and memory available for other processes running on the same machine at the same time.

Many C programmers have been taught that pointers and arrays are the same. They certainly share many common characteristics, but they are not the same. Confusing pointers and arrays can be a cause of bugs. For example:

```
int GetLoginNameFromUser(char *buffer)
{
  int Result = 0;
  if(fgets(buffer, sizeof buffer, stdin) == NULL)
  {
    Result = -1;
  }
  return Result;
}
```

The problem with this bug is that it looks correct. The construction of the `fgets` call would work superbly if only `buffer` were an array of `char`. It isn't. The longest login name you are likely to get this way is `sizeof(char *) -1` bytes.

What if we changed the parameter like this?

```
int GetLoginNameFromUser(char buffer[100])
/* ... */
```

This doesn't help! The `buffer` variable is still a pointer to `char`, because the compiler decays it from an array to a pointer. If you doubt it, run this program:

```
#include <stdio.h>

int foo(char *p)
{
  return (int)sizeof(p);
}

int bar(char s[100])
{
  return (int)sizeof(s);
}
```

```
int main(void)
{
  char baz[100];

  printf("sizeof char[100] in main() = %d\n",
          (int)sizeof baz);
  printf("sizeof char * in foo()     = %d\n", foo(baz));
  printf("sizeof char[100] in bar()  = %d\n", bar(baz));
return 0;
}
```

The output from this program clearly demonstrates two points: arrays are not pointers, and arrays decay to pointers when passed as parameters to a function.

Keeping pointers straight can be difficult sometimes. If a pointer is pointing somewhere other than its intended target, it can land you in a lot of trouble. The most common place to find pointer misdirection is in groups of related dynamically allocated data structures (linked lists and all their kin). For the rest of this discussion, I'll refer to linked lists, but the principles apply to any similar data structures, such as queues, stacks, and trees.

Problems arise when the programmer fails to take into account all the possible permutations when adding a new item to a list (or other data structure), deleting an item, looking up an item, or moving an item. Consider exchanging two items in a double-linked list. Your strategy for exchanging them must take into account each of these possibilities: that one item is at the end of the list; that both items are at one end or other of the list; that the items are adjacent; that the items are not adjacent; that the items are separated by one other item.

These are just the cases you need to consider for a double-linked list. More complex data structures require more complex case analysis. Rotating a sub-tree when deleting a node in a binary tree, for example, needs even more careful consideration.

When this case analysis is not done correctly and completely, we are quite likely to run into problems. To discover and correct these problems requires a lot of patient detective work. Here's a method that takes a long time, but which is known to work. Using either a debugger or trace code to establish pointer values, we can build a picture of the data structure on paper. Using boxes to represent discrete blocks of data, and arrows to represent pointers, we can begin to visualize what is actually happening in our program. If we have a clear idea of what is *meant* to happen, this technique will always give us much better information about the problem and how to fix it. Unfortunately, it's a painstaking method, and very slow, not unlike solving a large simply-connected maze by keeping one hand on the left-hand wall—you go everywhere it's possible to go, but if you stick to the task diligently, you'll get there in the end. We can often minimize the pain by identifying in advance a relatively small set of test data that reliably reproduces the bug.

The biggest problem with this technique has to do with human nature. After you've tracked about a hundred different pointer assignments, you'll probably be pretty bored with the whole thing, and there's a very real temptation to rush ahead on the off-chance that you will notice something odd. Patience, I'm afraid, is a virtue.

Debugging Software

If only there were a program that could debug your code for you. Well, there isn't (at least, not yet). The best we can manage right now is a program that gathers information to help *you* debug. This is called debugging software, mainly for want of a better term. It doesn't do any debugging—you do. Even so, debugging software is certainly very valuable, in that it provides you with the right information for identifying the problem (if only you can work out which information you need to ask it for).

There are two kinds of software: programs you write and programs other people write. The same is true of debugging software. Let's take a look at both kinds.

Commercial Debuggers

Good debuggers are a godsend—they can make your life amazingly easy. If you've never used a debugger, get one, and learn how to use it. A good debugger has these facilities as a minimum:

- Set and clear breakpoints
- Execute the code up to the current cursor position
- Step through the code one line at a time
- Trace into functions
- Display the values of whichever variables you select
- Display the current call stack

There are many excellent debuggers on the market, not least those which are included with popular commercial compilers. Learn to use them effectively, and you will save yourself many thousands of hours. We'll be looking at effective debugger usage later on in this chapter.

Although the best debugger in the world is no substitute for clear thinking, intelligent use of a good debugger is probably the best debugging method there is.

Trace Macros

Before we had interactive debuggers, we used to sprinkle output statements throughout our code. If the output statements were chosen and placed carefully, they were a real boon in problem-solving. Nevertheless, we were extremely grateful for interactive debuggers when they finally arrived on the scene.

And yet, sometimes a debugger cannot, by its very nature, solve your problem. This is especially true in real-time code, responding to real-time events. For example, consider a program that sends packets asynchronously on a TCP/IP socket. What you don't know, and are trying to find out, is that the program is sending too many packets too quickly over a slow link. Single-stepping through your source code is a slow process, even if you do it as quickly as you can (that is, too quickly), when you compare it to the speed with which your program executes outside the debugger. Therefore, when you are single-stepping through this TCP/IP code, it works fine. When you execute it at normal speed, it doesn't work at all. What we need in this situation is for our program to give us internal information about its state, while it is running at full speed outside the debugger. It's at times like this that we fall back on trace code.

What do we want from trace code?

We certainly don't want the trace code to be included in our production release. We are likely to produce quite large traces (the smaller the better, but they'll certainly start off big). If our program is a command-line program, trace code would be intrusive to the end user if we placed it in the standard output or standard error stream. If our program is GUI-based, there may not even be a convenient standard output stream to which to send the output! If we place it in a file (a better option), it won't be long before our trace files fill up the user's entire storage medium. So we have to be able to remove the trace code easily. Of course, we also have to be able to put it back easily. This sounds like a job for conditional compilation. We don't want to use our usual debug macros, however—we should be able to toggle the trace code on and off independently of other debugging subsystems we might have.

We want our trace code to be separate from our standard output and error streams if at all possible. So we'll use a file.

Should we use the same file every time? No. To be able to compare trace files from different runs of the program is a clear advantage that we should allow if at all possible. Ideally, the filename should be chosen automatically, and should be different on each run. One possible technique would be to make the filename depend on the date and time.

We want our trace code to be simple to use. We'd like to have a simple way of tracing the current value of a single variable. We'd also like to be able to output the values of several variables at once, and specify our own format string. We'd even like to be able to write trace-specific code sometimes.

It would be really helpful if each trace statement's filename and line number could be included in the trace. And we'd like to know, just from looking at the trace file, from which function each trace output originates.

Finally, the trace code must be clear, comprehensible and, subject to those constraints, tight. We want its presence to affect the program as little as possible, and we don't want to pollute our namespace too much, so we should use no global variables, and as few functions as possible.

Here's a tried-and-tested set of trace macros and functions fulfilling all the above criteria; it's short enough to quote here in its entirety, and of course the source is also available on the CD-ROM. I know it's tried and tested because I've used it myself on several projects. I'm sure I've got all but one of the bugs out of it. It may even be completely free of bugs! (If there is a bug, it's likely to be in the date-handling code. To paraphrase Peter van der Linden, anyone who thinks date programming is easy has never done any.) For the purposes of this book, I've renamed it `CFollow` (after a quick search of the Web eliminated a few more obvious names as having been used already). First, the header in Listing 7.6.

LISTING 7.6 Trace Macros Header

```
#ifndef CFOLLOW_H__
#define CFOLLOW_H__

#define CFOLLOW_MAXLINE 100000L /* Max lines that will
                                 * appear in trace file
                                 */

 header file (trace macros)>
/* Tracing is turned off by default. To enable it, you
 * could change #if 0 to #if 1 (below) but a better
 * way, if available, is to use your compiler's command
 * line #define capability.
 * Typically, -DCFOLLOW_ON__ would be the Right Thing,
 * but of course it may be different for your compiler.
 */

#if 0
#define CFOLLOW_ON__
#endif
```

LISTING 7.6 continued

```
#ifdef CFOLLOW_ON__

/* S for string */
#define S_FOLLOW(svar) CFollow(__FILE__,\
                               __LINE__,\
                               0,\
                               #svar"=[%s]",\
                               svar)

/* A for array (of char, not necessarily terminated) */
#define A_FOLLOW(avar, bytes) CFollow(__FILE__,\
                                      __LINE__,\
                                      0,\
                #avar"(first %d bytes) =[%*.*s]",\
                                      (int)bytes,\
                                      (int)bytes,\
                                      (int)bytes,\
                                      avar)
/* I for Int */
#define I_FOLLOW(ivar) CFollow(__FILE__,\
                               __LINE__,\
                               0,\
                               #ivar"=[%d]",\
                               ivar)
/* U for Unsigned int */
#define U_FOLLOW(uvar) CFollow(__FILE__,\
                               __LINE__,\
                               0,\
                               #uvar"=[%u]",\
                               uvar)
/* HI for sHort Int */
#define HI_FOLLOW(sivar) CFollow(__FILE__,\
                                 __LINE__,\
                                 0,\
                                 #sivar"=[%hd]",\
                                 sivar)
/* HU sHort Unsigned int */
#define HU_FOLLOW(suvar) CFollow(__FILE__,\
                                 __LINE__,\
                                 0,\
                                 #suvar"=[%hu]",\
```

LISTING 7.6 continued

```
                                  suvar)
/* LI for Long Int */
#define LI_FOLLOW(lvar) CFollow(__FILE__,\
                                __LINE__,\
                                0,\
                                #lvar"=[%ld]",\
                                lvar)
/* LU for long unsigned int */
#define LU_FOLLOW(ulvar) CFollow(__FILE__,\
                                 __LINE__,\
                                 0,\
                                 #ulvar"=[%lu]",\
                                 ulvar)

/* D for Double */
#define D_FOLLOW(dvar) CFollow(__FILE__,\
                               __LINE__,\
                               0,\
                               #dvar"=[%f]",\
                               dvar)
/* B for Boolean condition (true/false) */
#define B_FOLLOW(cond) CFollow(__FILE__,\
                               __LINE__,\
                               0,\
                               "Condition "#cond" = %s",\
                               (cond) ? "TRUE" : "FALSE")
/* P for pointer */
#define P_FOLLOW(ptr) CFollow(__FILE__,\
                              __LINE__,\
                              0,\
                              "Pointer "#ptr" = %p",\
                              (void *)(ptr))
/* F for user-specified Format
 * integer suffix indicates
 * number of extra args
 */
#define F_FOLLOW0(s) CFollow(__FILE__,\
                             __LINE__,\
                             0,\
                             s)
#define F_FOLLOW1(format, a) \
                        CFollow(__FILE__,\
```

LISTING 7.6 continued

```
                                __LINE__,\
                                0,\
                                format,\
                                a)
#define F_FOLLOW2(format, a, b) \
                        CFollow(__FILE__,\
                                __LINE__,\
                                0,\
                                format,\
                                a, b)
#define F_FOLLOW3(format, a, b, c) \
                        CFollow(__FILE__,\
                                __LINE__,\
                                0,\
                                format,\
                                a, b, c)
#define F_FOLLOW4(format, a, b, c, d) \
                        CFollow(__FILE__,\
                                __LINE__,\
                                0,\
                                format,\
                                a, b, c, d)
#define F_FOLLOW5(format, a, b, c, d, e) \
                        CFollow(__FILE__,\
                                __LINE__,\
                                0,\
                                format,\
                                a, b, c, d, e)

#define CF_CODE(code) code
#define CF_FUNCIN(funcname) CFollow(__FILE__,\
                                    __LINE__,\
                                    1,\
         "Function %s() entry point.",\
                                    #funcname)

#define CF_FUNCOUT(funcname, typespec, rval) \
                    CFollow(__FILE__,\
                            __LINE__,\
                            -1,\
         "Function %s() returns [%"#typespec"].",\
                            #funcname,\
```

LISTING 7.6 continued

```
                            rval)
#define CFOLLOW_CLOSEDOWN CFollow(NULL, 0, 0, NULL)

void CFollow(char *FileName,
             int   LineNumber,
             int   DepthModifier,
             char *FormatString,
             ...);

#else

#define S_FOLLOW(svar)
#define A_FOLLOW(avar, bytes)
#define I_FOLLOW(ivar)
#define U_FOLLOW(uvar)
#define HI_FOLLOW(sivar)
#define HU_FOLLOW(suvar)
#define LI_FOLLOW(lvar)
#define LU_FOLLOW(ulvar)
#define D_FOLLOW(dvar)
#define B_FOLLOW(cond)
#define P_FOLLOW(ptr)
#define F_FOLLOW0(s)
#define F_FOLLOW1(format, a)
#define F_FOLLOW2(format, a, b)
#define F_FOLLOW3(format, a, b, c)
#define F_FOLLOW4(format, a, b, c, d)
#define F_FOLLOW5(format, a, b, c, d, e)

#define CF_CODE(code) /* no code! */
#define CF_FUNCIN(funcname)
#define CF_FUNCOUT(funcname, typespec, rval)

#define CFOLLOW_CLOSEDOWN

#endif /* Trace statements are on/off */

#endif /* CFOLLOW_H__ */
```

And now the source code in Listing 7.7.

LISTING 7.7 Trace Macro Code

```
#include <stdio.h>
#include <stdarg.h>
#include <time.h>
#include <string.h>

#include "cfollow.h"

/*
 * GetOutputFileName():
 * This function retrieves a filename for use by fopen.
 * It's static, so it won't pollute your namespace.
 *
 * This function, although a conforming ANSI C routine, is
 * nevertheless platform-specific, because it builds
 * a filename. The filename it builds works perfectly
 * well for:
 *
 * MS-DOS     Windows   Unix
 * Linux      AmigaDOS  TOS (Atari ST)
 *
 * systems, but you may have problems if you are running
 * it on some other system. If you are running MVS, I
 * suggest you simply use an ordinary DDNAME as a
 * filename, and control the filename itself via JCL.
 * If you are running some other system, you may want
 * to tweak the sprintf to get a format appropriate to
 * your system.
 *
 * If your implementation uses 32-bit time_t epoched
 * at 1/1/1970, this code breaks in 2038. By then,
 * hopefully, you'll be using 64-bit time_t - so just
 * recompile.
 */

static void GetOutputFileName(char *OutFileName)
{
  time_t    CurrentTime;
  struct tm Now;
  long      DaysSince1999;
  long      YearsSince1999;
  time(&CurrentTime);
```

LISTING 7.7 continued

```
  memcpy(&Now, localtime(&CurrentTime), sizeof Now);

  YearsSince1999 = (long)(Now.tm_year - 99);

  DaysSince1999 = YearsSince1999 * 365 +
               (YearsSince1999 + 3) / 4;

  /* 2100, 2200, etc are not leap years */
  if(YearsSince1999 > 100)
  {
    DaysSince1999 -= YearsSince1999 % 100;
  }
  /* 2400, 2800, etc are leap years */
  if(YearsSince1999 > 400)
  {
    DaysSince1999 += YearsSince1999 % 400;
  }

  DaysSince1999 += Now.tm_yday + 1;

  /* ensure the number fits into 4 digits */
  DaysSince1999 %= 10000;

  sprintf(OutFileName,
          "C%04ld%02d%01d.%01d%02d",
          DaysSince1999,
          Now.tm_hour,
          Now.tm_min / 10,
          Now.tm_min % 10,
          Now.tm_sec);
}


void CFollow(char * InFileName,
             int    LineNumber,
             int    DepthModifier,
             char * FormatString,
             ...)
{
  static FILE *fp = NULL;
  static long Counter = 0;
  static int Depth = 0;
```

LISTING 7.7 continued

```
const int TabWidth = 4;
static char OutFileName[FILENAME_MAX] = "";
int i;
static int CounterWidth = 0;
long cwloop;

va_list ArgList;

if(DepthModifier < 0)
{
  Depth += DepthModifier;
}

va_start(ArgList, FormatString);

if(NULL == fp)
{
  GetOutputFileName(OutFileName);
  fp = fopen(OutFileName, "w");
  if(NULL == fp)
  {
    /* We can't record in a file.
     * Bite the bullet and use stdout.
     */
    fp = stdout;
  }
  CounterWidth = 0;
  for(cwloop = 1;
      cwloop <= CFOLLOW_MAXLINE;
      cwloop *= 10L)
  {
    ++CounterWidth;
  }
}

if(NULL == FormatString)
{
  if(fp != stdout)
  {
    fclose(fp);
  }
}
```

LISTING 7.7 continued

```
  else
  {
    if(Counter < CFOLLOW_MAXLINE)
    {
      fprintf(fp,
          "%0*ld %12s (%5d) : ",
          CounterWidth,
          ++Counter,
          InFileName,
          LineNumber);

      for(i = 0; i < TabWidth * Depth; i++)
      {
        fprintf(fp, " ");
      }

      vfprintf(fp, FormatString, ArgList);
      fprintf(fp, "\n");
      fflush(fp);
    }
  }

  if(DepthModifier > 0)
  {
    Depth += DepthModifier;
  }

  va_end(ArgList);
}

/* end of cfollow.c */
```

On the CD-ROM, you'll find a simple driver program that illustrates the use of each of these macros. Perfectionists will note that it's a good idea to call the `CFOLLOW_CLOSEDOWN` macro to close the trace file at the end of `main()`.

The macros for tracing individual variables are simple enough. They use the preprocessor stringizing operator, `#`, to turn variable names into strings; this saves you a bit of typing.

It would have been pleasant to be able to include a generic `fprintf`-type macro. If we had been using `printf`, this would have been fairly easy to do, albeit at the expense of odd-looking code. I can explain this more easily by simply showing you what I mean:

```
#define PRINT(x) printf x
```

This can be used as follows:

```
  /* ... some code ... */

  PRINT(("foo = %s, bar = %d, baz = %f", foo, bar, baz));

  /* ... code continues ... */
```

The oddity here is that we need two sets of parentheses, which does look a little odd. Unfortunately, this is necessary, because C89 macros can't take a variable number of parameters. (C99 macros can, but I can't take it for granted that you have a C99 compiler yet.)

The trouble is, we're using a trace file, not `stdout`. We can only use this technique for `fprintf` if we are prepared to surface the file pointer used by the trace function, and this I was loathe to do because it would interfere with the user's namespace and thus introduce a potential bug.

So I reluctantly rejected that idea, and instead provided a set of macros taking more and more arguments. This works quite well, although of course you have to be just as careful to match the format string and argument tail as you do when using `fprintf` in the normal way. The preprocessor should save you from using the wrong number of arguments in a macro, though, which is an unexpected but welcome benefit.

Sometimes it's handy to introduce trace loops. If, for instance, we want to dump all the contents of an array, it would be nice to have a loop in order to do that. No doubt, there will be other circumstances in which we want trace-only code. Therefore, I introduced the simple `CF_CODE` macro, which allows us to enclose code as follows:

```
CF_CODE({)
CF_CODE(  int i);
CF_CODE(  for(i = 0; i < 10; i++))
CF_CODE(    F_FOLLOW2("arr[%d] = [%d]\n", i, arr[i]);)
CF_CODE(})
```

You might prefer to simply write:

```
#ifdef CFOLLOW_ON__
  {
    int i;
```

```
    for(i = 0; i < 10; i++)
      F_FOLLOW2("arr[%d] = [%d]\n", i, arr[i]);
  }
#endif
```

The choice is yours.

When writing programs that behave asynchronously (for example, Windows sockets programs) I have found the CF_FUNCIN and CF_FUNCOUT macros to be extraordinarily useful insofar as they make it clear which functions happen in which order! You'd think this would be fairly basic information, but it's alarmingly easy to get confused. These macros assist greatly in my understanding of such programs. Furthermore, they utilize the CFollow() DepthModifier variable to indent at entry into a function and then outdent on exit from that function. If you remember to "top and tail" a function with these macros, the trace output file is much easier to read.

I've set the maximum number of lines of output to 100,000. If you want more output than this, the first thing to do is consider whether you are really going to use all that information. If you actually do have a need for that many lines of trace, the second thing to do is to simply change the appropriate #define, CFOLLOW_MAXLINE, in cfollow.h.

Plan to Succeed by Expecting to Fail

The failure rate of software projects is alarmingly high. Success can be measured in terms of budget, delivery date, and quality of implementation. Most projects fail to meet at least one out of these three criteria. So we are in no position, as an industry, to say that we never make mistakes. If you assume right from the outset that you are going to make mistakes, you can plan to deal with them in advance, and thus minimize their impact. Many valuable techniques exist for catching bugs as early as possible, including proper objective-setting, prototyping, rewarding programmers who deliver robust code, sensible testing strategies, peer review, iterative design methodologies, modular design, change control procedures, and so on. All of these are important, but none of them is exclusively relevant to C programming, so I won't cover them here. If you want to read further on the topic of general code quality, I can thoroughly recommend to you Steve McConnell's excellent book, *Code Complete*. Instead, I will focus on how we can plan to succeed in C programming, by using techniques that anticipate, and help us to obviate, failure. Let's look specifically at debug-only code and assertion statements, which are the two most useful weapons in our armory.

Debug-only Code

Sometimes we want our program to give us information to assist us in debugging. Our users will never need this information, but it's rather useful for us. Our trace macros are a fairly typical example of debug-only code, but by no means the only example.

We usually control debug-only code by conditional compilation, by defining a macro when we want to turn the debugging on, and not defining it when we want to turn it off again. This works rather well, and it's a shame that we don't have a standard macro we can all use to mean the same thing. In a way, however, there is such a standard macro, although with the opposite sense: `NDEBUG`. The `assert()` macro (discussed next) is pre-processed out of existence if `NDEBUG` is defined. So we could write debug code like this:

```
#ifndef NDEBUG
  DebugDumpList(&Root);
#endif
```

I've never been on a project where this is done, though. Most people seem to prefer rolling their own macro. That's fine too, of course.

Kernighan and Pike aren't keen on the `#ifdef DEBUG` approach, pointing out that it makes testing more problematic. They recommend this instead:

```
enum { DEBUG = 0 };

if(DEBUG)
  printf(....
```

They claim that many compilers will not produce code for the debugging statements when `DEBUG` is set to 0, but will nevertheless do a syntax check for you (a benefit you lose with conditional compilation). While I can see their point of view, I can find no guarantee in the ANSI C standard that a compiler will not and must not generate code for unreachable branches of the program. Their technique may well work for your compiler (in which case, by all means use it). However, where portability is an issue (as it must be in a book that's about C, rather than UNIX C or mainframe C or DOS C), we *know* that conditional compilation will not generate code for unreached branches, so that's the method I have to recommend.

Even if you've never used debug-only code before, you've had a taste of it with the `CFollow` macros. But trace code isn't the only thing you can do to make your development task easier. Some programmers have developed entire debugging sub-systems that they plug into each new project. `CFollow` is one example of this, and we'll be seeing another in the chapter on memory management later on in this book.

The most important thing to remember about debug code is that it should be extra code, not an essential part of the program. Counter-intuitively, good debug code can often add quite a performance hit to a product (extra information cannot always be produced in zero time, no matter how much we'd like it to be). Furthermore, it often utilizes resources specific to the developer's system or network (the original version of `CFollow` was written on a Windows 95 machine, but always wrote its trace files to a UNIX box that happened to be hanging around on the LAN). We can't just leave that code in place; at shipping time it has to be removed. So we do need to ensure that we aren't removing important production code at the same time.

What debug code you write is up to you. The most generally useful is trace code, but many other possibilities spring to mind. In a highly structured environment, it may be beneficial for the program to insert a record into a database every time it's run, storing details such as program version number, date, time, machine and user IDs, command-line arguments, test data filename, performance statistics, and any of a thousand other useful bits and bobs. Of course, this could not be done in ANSI C alone, so I won't go into details here. But imagine the benefits of being able, for example, to compare the performance of different versions of your program with a simple SQL query on an automatically-generated database. The usefulness of debug code is limited only by common sense and your imagination.

Using Assertion Statements

Assertion statements validate your program's logic. The idea is to call `assert()`, giving it a condition that must be true if the program is working as designed. If the condition is false, `assert()` stops the program. The `assert()` macro is a debug-only macro—if `NDEBUG` is defined at the time `<assert.h>` is included, `assert()` is preprocessed out of existence. So it has no impact on performance in a production environment.

This is a wonderful idea! It means that you can perform all kinds of in-code tests to ascertain whether your code is written the way you think it is. Take full advantage of this feature, and you will not regret it.

`assert()` Is Not Always a Cert

On a recent project, I put quite a few assertions and other debug-specific stuff into the source code. In due course, the code went for system test, and our debugging macros were all switched off. The people setting up and executing the compilation JCL weren't C programmers, however, and they neglected to define `NDEBUG` (and this wasn't the kind of compiler to do it for you!). As a result, all the assertions were left in place! Fortunately, this didn't matter too much because my code failed to compile. Defining `NDEBUG` fixed it, of course.

Don't use `assert()` to validate your data. Its only appropriate role is to evaluate program logic. For example, consider this code:

```
  char *p;

  p = malloc(len);

  foomem(p);

  /* ... */
}

void foomem(char *p)
{
  assert(p != NULL);
  dosomethingwith(p);
}
```

This is a perfectly reasonable use of `assert`. Clearly, `foomem()` does something to the buffer passed to it, and (in production) assumes that the buffer is valid. That's okay because anyone who calls `malloc` checks their return value, to the extent where it could be considered an error not to do this. Thus, when the program is tested with `len` set to four thousand million, we can be relatively sure that the assertion will fail, aborting the program, with a brief message on `stderr` (typically with full information on the source filename and line number where the assertion occurred).

What you should most definitely *not* use `assert()` for is data validation. An assertion failure basically translates to "the programmer made a mistake in his logic, which is mitigated to some extent by the fact that he bothered to assert his logic." To do this for data is meaningless. If the program's input data causes problems for the program, that's a matter for whoever is responsible for putting data into the program. The following code misuses `assert()`:

```
#include <stdio.h>
#include <assert.h>

int main(void)
{
  char buff[32];
  printf("Type your name\n");
  assert(NULL != fgets(buff, sizeof buff, stdin));
  printf("Your name is %s\n", buff);
  return 0;
}
```

There are several problems here: First, `assert()` is a macro, and it's usually a bad idea to call functions within macro parentheses, lest the argument be evaluated twice. Second, it's a particularly bad idea to write a vital part of the program inside an assertion—if `NDEBUG` is defined, this code will be removed completely! Third, the assertion is being used to detect whether the user managed to avoid entering data by pressing some key combination signaling end-of-data to the operating system (for example, control-Z in DOS, or control-D in UNIX). This assertion has nothing to do with the program logic's correctness or otherwise, and thus is inappropriate.

Asserting That Data Validation Modules Work

Having said all that, there is one scenario where you would want to use `assert()` to validate data, and that is where the data *should already have been validated*.

Programs need data. The data has to come from somewhere, and only the most limited programs contain all the data they need. So in the majority of cases, that data must come from outside the program. If you're an exponent of modular design, your eyes probably just lit up. Wouldn't it be a great idea to have one module whose sole responsibility is to gather *correct* data from the user? That module would be responsible for validating that the input given to it was correct. (Alternatively, there could be two co-operating modules, one of which gathered data and passed it to the other for validation.)

This is good design at work. If the responsibility for ensuring that input data is valid is given entirely to one module, there is no need whatsoever for any other module to validate that data. You can imagine the data validation module to be a protective ring around the inner core of the program. In a perfect world, the data validation module can validate the data once, so the inner routines (which are possibly called many times over) can trust the data they receive; this could be a big performance win.

Unfortunately, this is not a perfect world. Nobody guaranteed that the data validation module would be bug-free, did they? Hopefully it will be, one day. In the meantime, it would be foolish to write a routine like this:

```
double CalcMetresPerSecond(double miles, double hour)
{
  return miles * 0.447 / hour;
}
```

What if our data validation routine has a bug in it, which allows `hour` to be 0.0?

If there were no data validation module, we'd need to add a test such as:

```
if(fabs(hour) > DBL_MIN)
/* ... */
```

But there *is* a data validation module; we just don't trust it yet. But we will trust it one day, and so what we really want is a way of validating the data only at the debugging stage, on the assumption that when the production code is shipped, the validation module will be fixed. In the meantime, if it's broken, we want to know about it.

By having a validating `assert()`,

```
assert(fabs(hour) > DBL_MIN);
```

we solve all these problems. We add robustness to our debug code, we provide an alarm facility in case the data validation code has a bug, and we have a simple way to compile away the validation.

There's one minor gotcha in the `assert()` macro; you must give it an integer expression as its argument. Strictly, in C89 this code:

```
int foo(char *bar)
{
  assert(bar);
  /* ... */
}
```

invokes undefined behavior! This code, however:

```
int foo(char *bar)
{
  assert(bar != NULL);
  /* ... */
}
```

is fine, because relational operators yield an integer result (in this case, 0 if the operands are equal, and 1 if they are not). In C99 this is no longer an issue because `assert()` can be passed an expression of scalar type, such as a pointer.

Compile-time Assertions

Sometimes you don't want to wait until run-time, but want (under certain conditions) to generate a compile-time error. For example, you may be including two project headers (say, `foo.h` and `bar.h`) which both contain structs, perhaps `struct FOO` and `struct BAR`. For the purposes of your code, it's important that they are both the same size—yet you know they are both subject to constant independent modification. Have they been updated correctly, in step with each other? Here's one way to find out:

```
char dummy[sizeof(FOO) == sizeof(BAR) ? 1 : -1];
```

Because you need to use `sizeof`, you can't do this at preprocessing time, but you can do it at compile time because, naturally, `sizeof` is resolved at that point. Clearly, if the structures are not equal in size, you will be declaring an array with a negative number of members, which is illegal and requires a diagnostic message. This is a rather neat trick (it's amazing what you can pick up on Usenet), although somewhat limited in scope; you'll probably never use it. Still, it's there if you need it.

The Debugging Process

To debug our program, we need to know what it's meant to do, and we need to be able to examine its actual behavior, to see how this differs from its intended behavior. If we can classify bugs according to their effect on programs, this can help us to establish the cause of this difference.

Knowing What Is Meant to Happen

To mend your program, you need to understand what your program is doing and how it is doing it. If you fully understood your program, you would have written it without bugs, it wouldn't be broken, and you wouldn't be debugging it. So debugging can be thought of as improving your knowledge about your own program. Nevertheless, unless you have an exact knowledge of what the program is *meant* to do, and how, your debugging task is very unlikely to succeed.

Watching It Happen

Simply running your program can give you some insight into problems in the code. Maybe things don't quite look right. Maybe there's a big pause between two outputs, where you weren't expecting one. Or maybe the program runs too quickly. These are all hints that something might be wrong. Watching your code can teach you a lot about the difference between what you wanted from your program and what you actually got.

If at all possible, set up your program to accept input from file. (The `stdin` stream is fine.) Then you can automate your runs. You don't need to sit there typing in data. You can redirect your input from a file. (Not all operating systems allow this, but many do.) That way, you spend your time watching and thinking about your code, rather than feeding it.

Identifying Where It Breaks

Stepping through your code (or reading through your trace files) is the simplest way to identify where the first symptom appears, but the symptom is not the cause, merely the effect. To locate the cause, you do need to find the location of the first symptom, simply because it limits your search for the cause. The trick is to look at your symptom, and scratch around for an immediate cause of that symptom. For example, let's say we have a `printf` that's writing nonsense to the output stream. Eventually, we track it down in the debugger, and find that it is printing a string. Could the character pointer be `NULL`? So we add some trace code (or ask the debugger for the pointer's value) and find that it isn't `NULL`. But the data is nonsense. Inspection of the routine shows that this pointer is passed into the current function as a parameter. So the next step is to look at the stack trace to find out where this function was called from. Working backward in this way, we should be able to identify the cause of the data corruption quite quickly. Don't let your bugs intimidate you. They are traceable, and thus vulnerable.

You don't have to step through every single line of code every time. Use your debugger's breakpoint capability to set points in the code to which you can let your program run unhindered. Then you can single-step and watch the values of variables from that point on. Some debuggers have a "run to cursor" option that runs your program at normal speed, stopping at the point where your cursor is currently located, as if a temporary breakpoint had been inserted at that point. This is a useful shortcut, especially when you're deep in a set of nested loops that you really didn't want to go into in any detail. Simply place the cursor beyond the loop and press the "run to cursor" key or keys.

Core Dumps

Some operating systems provide a core dump when a program goes sufficiently wrong to merit the intervention of the system itself. Where core dumps are available, there is usually some tool for interpreting them. For example, Linux developers have access to the GNU debugger, gdb. If you get a core dump in Linux then, provided you compiled with debugging on (`-g`) you can find out the exact line on which the program dumped core, using gdb. If your executable program filename is `crash`, and core was dumped to a file called `coredump`, you'd simply type:

```
gdb crash coredump
```

This is a very helpful shortcut if your implementation software supports it.

Once you have identified where it breaks, you ought to be able to fix the code. If you can't, you don't understand your program well enough, in which case it may be worth rewriting in a simpler (possibly more long-winded) way.

Debugging is all about understanding your code. If you understood your code perfectly, it would have no bugs. But you don't have to wait until a bug appears before you start debugging. Why not single-step through all new code, as you write it? This is a good way to verify that your program is following the same basic execution thread that you intended for it, and can highlight some problems very early, before they have a chance to cost real money.

Types of Bugs

Once your program actually compiles, there are only two real ways it can go wrong. Either your program didn't follow your specification, or your program somehow failed to run successfully to completion (through some kind of segmentation fault or access violation or general protection fault or user application error or abend—isn't it odd how many words we have for "crash"?), or your program worked as you wanted it to. For our current purposes, working code is totally uninteresting, so we will airily dismiss it and focus on application logic bugs, and crash bugs.

Application logic bugs are, fortunately, fairly easy to put right, provided of course that you understand your specification. Crash bugs can be harder, because it is rare for their cause to be immediately apparent.

The Jargon File

The Jargon File is an entertaining and valuable lexicography of hacker terminology ancient and modern. It dates back to 1975, and was begun by Raphael Finkel at Stanford University. It is to some extent based on the TMRC Dictionary compiled by Pete Samson in 1959. Within its covers are thousands of jargon terms used by the hacker community, including such gems as D.E.D. (Dark Emitting Diode) and S.E.D. (Smoke Emitting Diode), to name just two of my favorites.

If I told you where to find it, you'd waste hours of otherwise productive time browsing through it, and we can't have that, can we?

Oh, all right. Fire up your Web browser, and point it at `http://www.tuxedo.org`.

Or, if you are one of these strange people who likes spending money, order it from your local bookstore:

The New Hacker's Dictionary 3rd Edition, compiled by Eric S Raymond, published by The MIT Press, ISBN 0-262-68092-0.

The Jargon File contains four amusing terms for different kinds of bugs, all named after famous scientists (Niels Bohr, Werner Heisenberg, Benoit Mandelbrot, and Erwin Schroedinger). These are classified more according to their symptoms than their causes. When you realize you have a bug, you are far more likely to be aware of the symptom than the cause, so they are actually quite a useful set of categories. Let's have a look at each of them, and investigate some techniques for uncovering their various causes.

Bohr Bugs

A Bohr bug is a bug that has a simple (although possibly unknown) cause. If the cause is detected and removed or appropriately modified in some way, the bug will go away. Deterministic errors are the easiest bugs to find and fix. Fortunately, most bugs fall into this category. For example, an output statement with the wrong text in it is a deterministic error. If you meant to type

```
puts("This is correct.");
```

but you actually typed

```
puts("This is incorrect.");
```

then you have a deterministic error.

The Bug Bites

Perhaps the most famous Bohr bug in history was Grace Murray Hopper's moth. Just after World War II, Hopper was working on the Harvard Mark II for the U.S. Navy. On September 9, 1947, a technician traced a problem on the Mark II to a moth (sadly, deceased) positioned between the contacts on one of the machine's relays. The incident was written up in the log book as "First actual case of bug being found." (Hopper was careful to admit that she was not actually there at the time, but she used to dine out on the story, so it is traditionally associated with her.) As far as I am aware, the bug itself, and the logbook, are now in the Smithsonian's History of American Technology Museum. This story is widely known, but many people mistakenly believe that the word "bug" was coined in connection with this incident. It wasn't. The term bug was current at least 100 years previously, and was apparently widely used in the early days of telegraphy.

If you think this kind of bug could never happen to you, think again! Have you noticed that, in recent years, PC expansion slot blanking plates have been of the "snap-off" variety? If you fit a new card to your machine and then, at some later point, remove it, you have a hole in the back of your PC. I've never found a moth in any of my machines, but spiders are a regular problem (which perhaps explains the absence of moths). I live in hope that they will one day discover the World Wide Web and vanish out of my life forever.

Bohr bugs typically turn out to be simple application logic bugs, simple off-by-one errors not usually involving array bounds, typographical errors that happen to result in valid code (for example, = where == is meant), accidentally commented-out code, and other mundane issues.

Heisenbugs

This is an excellent name for a class of bug and I really wish I had invented it. The pun is most apt; I am no physicist but, if I recall correctly, Heisenberg's Uncertainty Principle (somewhat freely translated) says something like "you can't observe a phenomenon without changing it." That's annoying enough to quantum physicists, I imagine, but to programmers it's really very frustrating. Your program doesn't work. Okay, get the debugger out. You know it doesn't work, so you single-step it carefully. It works. Excellent. So you run it outside the debugger again. It doesn't work. Oh. So you run it inside the debugger again, this time cruising through without single-stepping. It works. Argh! It only works when you're trying to track down the fault! (Heisenbugs often lead to programmers using an excessive number of exclamation marks.)

No doubt you've had this experience yourself. The two questions that spring to mind are:

- Why does it happen?
- What can I do about it?

Heisenbugs usually turn out to be memory violations of one kind or another. Either some pointer is pointing somewhere it shouldn't, or some array index is wrong. If we access memory we don't own (whether for reading or writing) we are invoking undefined behavior, and the trouble with undefined behavior is that we can't define it, so we shouldn't really be surprised at *anything* our program does. Sad but true. Now, consider the case of an uninitialized pointer:

```
char *p;
```

and the effect of this statement:

```
strcpy(p, q);
```

where `q` is some valid pointer, pointing to a relatively long string. Now, the compiler allocates some memory for the pointer `p`, just as it allocates memory for any variable. Whatever the contents of that memory location happen to be will be the address to which `p` points. What are the chances that `p` points somewhere safe? Well, it's incalculable. Maybe `p` points somewhere safe and maybe it doesn't. You can't tell.

A Heisenbug happens when `p` is pointing somewhere unsafe, causing the program to fail, so you load up the debugger, thus causing the operating system to move data around in memory, the end result of which is that `p` happens to point somewhere harmless.

So what can we do about it? My first line of attack is to initialize all pointers to `NULL` at declaration, to the point where it's a habit for me now. This is one place where I won't compromise with the compiler. If I get a warning for this, so be it. Initializing ints at definition may not be too important compared to a clean compilation, but for pointers the initialization is vital, warning or no warning.

When that isn't enough, it's time to use the debugger or, if it's a program where real-time events are an issue, the trace code.

As usual, finding the symptom is the first step. In my experience, it's not uncommon for the problem to be manifested in a standard library function, often one of the `printf` family. Some implementations include the source code for their standard library, and it can be disconcerting to be dumped right in the middle of the source code to the `printf` function. But the rules are the same—work backwards. The stack trace will take you to the place where the `printf` was called from your own code, and from then on it's all down to patience and care. (The first time I was slung into `printf` source by the debugger, I got all hung up on the possibility of a bug in `printf`. This cost me several pointless hours; I'd broken the first rule of debugging—"Blame the compiler last!")

If you're debugging a complex data structure such as an object tree, you'll probably end up following each pointer assignment and comparison, as described earlier in the chapter. It's a long and thankless task, but it does get results.

Mandelbugs

Some bugs seem to be completely random. Their underlying causes appear incomprehensibly complex, just like the legendary Mandelbrot set after which they have been named. You can't seem to reproduce them consistently. The program works 70% of the time (for given inputs), or only works outside the debugger (the reverse of the Heisenbug), or produces spurious results on Wednesdays, or only works on Joe's machine, or only breaks on Kate's machine.

The most annoying Mandelbug is the one that stops your program from even executing. This can be particularly frustrating when you know that your program works perfectly, on a different platform. I recently started to port a networking library from Windows to Linux. The first module I tried to port was a module for managing binary trees. I wrote a test driver to exercise the tree library, and tested it on the Windows machine. It all worked swimmingly well. I copied it over to the Linux machine and re-compiled it. It segfaulted and dumped core. I couldn't understand this. It didn't seem to make any kind of sense. Lacking experience of gdb, I added some trace code. The program still segfaulted, without a single line of output. So I added a trace statement right at the top of `main()`, as the very first line in the program. I still got a segfault, and still no output!

Faced with this situation, two possibilities spring to mind. Some of the program is right, and some is wrong. So we could start off with an empty `main` function, and add code one section at a time, testing as we go. Eventually, we will insert the bug, at which point the program will stop working. This locates the bug. Or we could start off with the complete program, and *remove* modules, functions, lines, whatever. At some point, the program will start to work again, in the sense that it will run without segfaulting. Again, this gives us a handle on the problem. As long as we have a complete backup of our source, these are both zero-risk strategies.

Once we have identified the subset of code that seems to cause the problem, we're back to patient detective work.

Schroedinbugs

Well, this one's a bit of a stretch, but there are apparent reported cases of Schroedinbugs. In Schroedinger's famous "Cat" thought experiment, a (hypothetical) cat is placed in a closed box in circumstances that have the remarkable consequence of causing the cat to be both alive and dead at the same time. Looking in the box collapses the two probabilities into one certainty. Schroedinger devised this thought experiment in order to illustrate what he considered to be a fallacy inherent in quantum theory.

A Schroedinbug is, roughly speaking, a bug that lies dormant in a program. The program serves well for many years. Then someone notices the bug while reading through a musty, yellowing source listing. At this point, the program stops working, and will not run again until the bug has been fixed. The act of examining the source code collapses the probabilities of there being or not being a bug into the hard certainty that there is one.

It sounds impossible, doesn't it? Yet, as I have said, there are reported cases. I'm not superstitious, so I can't help looking for a rational explanation. My guess is that the bug in question is either in a little-used part of the program or affects the output of the program in a non-critical way; the bug has always been there, but nobody ever noticed it before. Once you notice the bug in the listing and start looking for the errant behavior, you find it.

Genuine Schroedinbugs are interesting but hardly challenging. By definition, you know where in the source the problem lies, so it's just a question of fixing it.

Maintaining old code can of course be a challenge all by itself. If you have the source code, that's always a bonus. I was actually asked a couple of years ago to prepare a Year 2000 compliance analysis report on a mission-critical in-house program to which the source code had been lost. It was a lot more difficult than it need have been, as a direct result of the lack of source.

There isn't a lot you can do about mending old code if you don't have the right resources available to you. Solving such problems will require ingenuity and great care. What you can do, though, is ensure that your code, currently brand new, lends itself to trouble-free maintenance when its time comes. Here's how to make your maintainer love you to bits, ten years down the line, instead of cursing your name. Make sure the following are safely locked away, ready to be made available to him when he needs them:

- A machine running the right operating system
- The compiler you used—never throw away old compiler CDs!
- A list of the compiler options and switches you used
- The source code, including header files
- As much documentation as you can
- Test scripts, conditions, data
- Expected results of the tests

Given all these, a skilled maintainer should have no real problem maintaining your code.

A Programmer's Nightmare

To wind up this chapter, I'd like to present a gem of a program developed by Edmund Stephen-Smith, a New Zealand programming consultant, and reproduced here with his permission. The program in Listing 7.8 compiles (with warnings but no errors). The game is to count the bugs. Edmund developed this program as an interview test. Most people manage to find four or even five problems with it. How many can you spot? Play fair; don't read the notes that follow the listing until you've arrived at a figure yourself.

(The numbers down the left-hand side are there purely for reference, and are not part of the code. The version on the CD-ROM doesn't have these numbers.)

LISTING 7.8 Counting the Bugs

```
#include <stdio.h>
#include <assert.h>

#define  SWAP(x, y)  x^= y^= x;

int
main()
{
    char *s="uvwxyz";
    char *t;
    unsigned long a, b, c;
    int i;

    printf("String: %s (%d entries).\n"
           "Change which character to '1'? ", s,
           strlen(s));
    scanf("%d", &a);

    assert((0 <= a) && (a < strlen(s)));
    s[a]= '1';

    printf("Original changed to %s\n", s);
    printf("Reverse which range of characters (from-to)? ",
           b, c);

    scanf("%lu%lu", &a, &b);
    assert(a<=b);

    t= malloc(strlen(s+1));
```

LISTING 7.8 continued

```
30
31     strcpy(t, s);
32     for (i=b; i<(b+c)/2; i++)
33         SWAP(t[b+i], t[c-i]);
34
35     printf("Result of reverse is %s -> %s\n", s, t);
36     return 0;
37 }
```

Before reading on, try to find as many errors as you can. How many did you find? How many did I find? I'm not sure that I caught all the problems, but this is my list:

Right at the top of the source, we're missing `<stdlib.h>` and `<string.h>` (for `malloc` and `strcpy`). That's two errors, at least one of which results in undefined behavior.

In line 4, we have a rather fudged attempt at an XOR swap. It's hard to say how many errors there are here. First, the semicolon on the end is probably a bad idea but not actually wrong. Then we have the bug that two XORs don't actually swap the two variables. Finally, if we corrected this by adding an XOR in the same style as the others, we'd have undefined behavior caused by the modification of a variable twice between two sequence points. Let's call the whole thing one ghastly error, making three so far. A better solution would be:

```
#define SWAP(x, y) do{unsigned long tmp;\
                      tmp = x;\
                      x = y;\
                      y = tmp;} while(0)
```

Splitting `int main()` over two lines looks odd but is legal.

In the `printf` beginning on line 14, the string literal is split over two lines. This is fine—they'll be concatenated. But `strlen`'s return value is matched against a `%d` in the format string, as if it were an int, whereas `strlen` actually returns `size_t`. Thus, a cast to `int` is required. Better would be to make the format string read `%u` instead. Even so, a cast to `unsigned int` would be required because there is no guarantee that `size_t` is an `unsigned int`. It might be an `unsigned long int`, for example. One more error, making four up till now.

In line 17, `scanf` takes the address of `a` as an argument, and `a` is an `unsigned long`, so the format string should be `%lu`. That's five errors.

Because the return value of `scanf` is not checked, we have no guarantee that the value of `a` is determinate. Therefore, it can't be safely used in the subsequent `assert` call (unless

`NDEBUG` is not defined). That's six errors. In line 20, the program modifies one of the elements of the string literal array pointed to by `s`. This results in undefined behavior. Seven errors.

In the `printf` call starting on line 23, the arguments `b` and `c` are superfluous. I'm not going to count that as an error, but it was a close call.

In line 26, `a` and `b` are passed to `scanf`, but inspection of later code reveals that `b` and `c` were intended. That's a logic error. Eight so far. We'll assume for the rest of this analysis that we have corrected this line. Also, the return value of `scanf` isn't checked, but I'm not going to count that error again.

The assertion in line 27 raises my hackles a little. Of course, the check should be for `b <= 0`. If we're going to validate that, we might as well validate `c < strlen(s)` too. The erroneous check makes a running total of nine errors.

In line 29, `malloc`'s argument is `strlen(s + 1)` but should in fact be `strlen(s) + 1`. Ten.

Line 30 contains a hard-to-spot bug. The line is empty! It should of course contain a check for whether the call to `malloc` did in fact yield the memory we requested. Eleven errors.

The loop in line 32, and its body in line 33, are completely wrong, in a classic case (were this to be a real program) of a programmer trying to be too clever, and failing to be clever enough. Better would be to have two loop counters, one ascending from `b` and one descending from `c`, with the test being `b < c`. Twelve errors.

Finally, the space allocated by `malloc` is not released by the program. You could argue that this isn't a bug because the memory will all be cleaned up for us at the end anyway. So it isn't, strictly speaking, an error.

So my score is twelve. You may well have scored more, by being stricter than me. Did I miss any altogether?

This program is quite beautiful in its own hideous way. You may wish to incorporate something similar into your own interview process.

Summary

In this chapter we've looked at some useful debugging strategies. We've looked at ideas like bug diaries, long-suffering debug teddy bears, and debug-only code. We've classified some common bugs according to their symptoms and their causes. And you now have a new trace code library, `CFollow`, to help you on your way.

Debugging is a difficult task; of that there is no doubt. But with patience and diligence, and a little ingenuity, any given bug can be identified and fixed. The most important lesson we can learn is, "Don't give up." There's a way to fix this bug. We just have to find out what that way is.

CHAPTER 8

Managing Memory

by Richard Heathfield

In This Chapter

This chapter is not about implementing C's memory management functions (`malloc`, `calloc`, `realloc`, and `free`), as I'm sure you'll be relieved to hear, but about using them in a robust and efficient way. Also, we'll be examining how to track memory allocation and release, with the objective of preventing memory leaks in our programs.

What Is Memory Management?

Memory is a scarce resource. No matter how much there is, we can always find use for more. In these days of multitasking operating systems and ever-larger "bloatware" applications, the demands on our computers' memory are increasing exponentially. Every now and then, someone posts a question to Usenet along these lines: "How can I allocate more than 2 gigabytes of memory?" The usual answer is another question: "Are you sure you need two gigabytes? Perhaps you should reconsider your design." It's a fair response, because most computable problems can be solved using considerably less memory than this.

Furthermore, the physical size of computers is shrinking. More and more applications are being shoehorned into miniscule boxes, many of them smaller than your hand. There is a physical limit to the number of RAM chips these computers can hold. This problem may be alleviated by advances in miniaturization technology, but we can't count on that. Therefore, we cannot assume now, any more than we ever could, that the amount of memory in a host environment will constantly grow.

It is our responsibility as programmers to use memory wisely and economically. As with any jointly managed scarce resource, we should be considerate when requesting memory from the system, because there are likely to be other processes running at the same time as our program, and we are frequently in no position to assess the importance of our program to the user in relation to those other processes. We should use what we need, of course, but we shouldn't take morethan we need without very good reason (and there may be good reasons why we might take a little more memory than we strictly need, as we will see).

Common Memory Usage Errors

Unfortunately for an author, much of the topic of memory management consists of what you shouldn't do, which sounds very negative, whereas I'd really like to sound upbeat and positive. So let's look at it this way—this section describes blunders that will positively get you beaten up by your peer reviewers. And you don't need that kind of unhappiness, so pay close attention.

Using Memory You Didn't Allocate

C Unleashed is not a book for beginners. Therefore, this little section should not really be necessary. Regrettably, there are C programmers out there in the big wide world who claim to have many years of experience using the language, are earning considerable amounts of money (often at consultancy rates) in return for offering their expertise, and yet cannot see anything wrong with this code:

```
char *p;

strcpy(p, "Hello world.");
```

I'm sad to say I know some of these people personally. I won't name and shame them here, but this section is for them and for people like them. If reading that code fragment made you spray this book with a mouthful of coffee, please clean the page carefully and skip forward a page or so.

To those of you who are still reading—please listen, because this is really important. Pointers are for storing and accessing the locations of objects. That doesn't mean, though, that they are born knowing where objects are located. They have to be pointed to the right place.

Sometimes, we use pointers to `char` as if they are arrays of `char`, and sometimes we use arrays of `char` as if they are pointers to `char`. But pointers and arrays are notequivalent. Pointers are not arrays, and arrays are not pointers. It just happens that they aresyntactically equivalentas formal parameters in a function declaration, purely because the compiler decays array notation to pointer notation, and this is what may have led to a certain amount of confusion among C programmers.

It's extremely important to pay careful attention to how your code and the standard library use memory. For example, a function such as `strcpy`, while being prototyped as taking `char*` for its first argument, in fact needs to be given the address of the first element of an array of `char` big enough to hold a copy of the source string specified in the second argument. Simply handing over an uninitialized `char *` variable (or, as I occasionally see on the Web, the address of a single character!) is just not good enough.

Here's another example of memory abuse, this time straight from the annals of Usenet (lightly edited to disguise the handiwork of the guilty), this time involving `sprintf`. The question was along these lines: "I have a `char` array and I would like to append an `int` to the `char` array, something like `int d = 42; char *s = "some text" + d;`. Obviously, this will not work... but is there a way to do it?" Here's the answer some bright spark came up with:

> Have you tried
>
> ```
> int d = 42;
> char *s;
> sprintf(s, "some text %", d);
> ```

This betrays a fundamental misunderstanding of how to use memory. The pointer `s` has not been initialized. It has no particular value (its value is *indeterminate*). It doesn't point anywhere legal and useful. No memory has been allocated in which `sprintf` may store its output legally.

Note

While we are on the subject of `sprintf`, it may be worth pointing out that this common construction

```
sprintf(mystring, "%s%d%s%f", mystring, j, otherstring, d);
```

results in undefined behavior, because the compiler is allowed to start writing into `mystring` straight away if it likes, perhaps starting off at the right side of the expression. Or it might not.

If you find yourself wanting to do this, use another string as a temporary holding area.

```
sprintf(thirdstring, "%s%d%s%f", mystring, j, otherstring, d);
strcpy(mystring, thirdstring);
```

So how should you allocate memory for a string? Here are a couple of ways:

```
char s[13];

strcpy(s, "Hello world.");
```

and

```
char *p;
p = malloc(13);
if(p != NULL)
{
  strcpy(p, "Hello world.");
```

```
    /* here, do whatever you need to do with the string */

    free(p);
  }
```

Note that, to use `strcpy`, you should `#include <string.h>`, and to use `malloc` and `free`, you should `#include <stdlib.h>`.

In the `sprintf` example, our would-be Usenet expert would have been wise to consider how much storage the resulting string would take up, including space for a null terminator, and to allocate at least that much space (the example requires 13 bytes).

`gets()` Function Considered Harmful

There is one function for which you will never be able to allocate enough memory to make it safe to use: `gets()`. This function is, quite simply, a bug waiting to happen. Worse still, on many systems it is possible to exploit a `gets()`-ridden program to gain access to a system. The infamous Internet Worm was based on just such an attack on `gets()`.

The `gets()` function takes as its sole argument a pointer to `char`. Starting at that `char`, it will probably fill memory with data from `stdin` until a newline is encountered, at which point `gets()` will probably null-terminate the string and probably return control to its caller. If, by some miracle, `stdin` contains a newline character within the first *N* characters, where *N* is the size of the supplied buffer, then you can remove all the references to *probably* from that sentence—for that one call. If there isn't a newline early enough, however, `gets()` will start to trample over memory that it shouldn't be touching, with undefined results.

On stack-based systems (in other words, most systems), it's fairly easy to give `gets()` an input string that deliberately overwrites the return address on the stack, substituting the address of a hostile, invasive routine. What can this invasive routine do? Anything a cracker wants it to do, really. That's not good for system security. Don't use `gets()`, ever. (Much the same line of argument also applies to `scanf()` when reading string data, the difference between the two functions being that it is possible, with care, to use `scanf()` correctly.) As a rule of thumb, use `fgets()` instead.

Failing to Store the Address

When you call a memory allocation function, you need to store its return value. You know this already, right? Code like this

```
strcpy(malloc(13), "Hello world.");
```

is not the kind of code you want to be seen writing at this stage in your career! (If you had a good chuckle just then, be scared. I've seen source not too dissimilar to this in production code. And if you didn't get the joke, be very scared indeed.)

That doesn't mean, however, that you necessarily have to keep the pointer pointing to that address all the time. For example:

```
char *p;
int i;

p = malloc(N);
if(p != NULL)
{
  for(i = 0; i < N; i++)
  {
    *p++ = '\0';
  }
  /* ... */
```

This looks unsafe, because we've allocated memory and then changed the pointer value that was storing the base address of that allocated memory. In fact, though, it's perfectly safe, because all we need to do is rewind the pointer: `p -= N;` to get back the value we need. (Alternatively, we could have simply assigned to some other variable the value that `p` held before the loop.) I'm not saying this is a good way to write code, but it is not actually wrong.

As another example of what I mean, consider a double-linked list like this:

```
typedef struct doublelist
{
  struct doublelist *next;
  struct doublelist *prev;
  struct FOO payload;
} doublelist;
```

To build this list, you would start with a `doublelist *`, to which you would assign the result of a call to `malloc`. The results of subsequent calls to `malloc` for further links in the list would be assigned to various instances of `next` and `prev` pointers. Since you can use these pointers to navigate to any item in the list, there is no particular need to keep the original pointer, as long as you have a pointer to somewhere in the list.

Not Checking Return Values

The most annoying aspect of memory allocation is that it doesn't always work. As a result, we have to check the return value of `malloc`, `calloc`, and `realloc` every single time we call them. If they do fail, we should take appropriate action. (More on this later.)

Bear in mind that they all return `NULL` on failure. Just about the first thing you do to memory after requesting it is to put something in it. And it's illegal to write to a `NULL` pointer. (We covered the consequences of undefined behavior earlier in the book, so I won't point out yet again all the terrible things that might happen.)

Therefore, if you fail to check a memory allocation function for the `NULL` return value, the very next thing your program does is completely undefined and unknowable, from the C abstract machine's point of view.

Some people omit the test for `malloc()` failure because they consider the performance gained by dropping the test to outweigh the corresponding loss in safety. This is like driving down a country lane and hurtling far too fast around a corner you know well, on the grounds that you've never before met anyone coming the other way. One day, you'll regret it.

Not Using a Spare Pointer for `realloc`

Listing 8.1 presents a little nightmare for you.

LISTING 8.1 A Poor Use of `realloc`

```
char *ReadTextFile(FILE *fp)
{
  size_t size = 0;
  size_t len;
  char *p = NULL;

  char buffer[128];

  while(fgets(buffer, sizeof buffer, fp))
  {
    len = strlen(buffer);
    p = realloc(p, size + len);
    strcpy(p + size, buffer);
    size += len;
  }
  return p;
}
```

This function reads a file into memory. It may be, however, that it can't allocate sufficient memory to read the whole file. In that case, it may be appropriate to allow the user to edit the portion of the file that could be read and to save it under a different filename, or some similar approach. Unfortunately, he won't ever get the chance, because the code allows the return value, `NULL` in the event of memory allocation failure, to overwrite the information stored in `p`—the address of the original buffer.

Listing 8.2 shows a much better way to do it.

LISTING 8.2 Using `realloc` Properly

```
char *ReadTextFile(FILE *fp, int *Error)
{
  size_t size = 0;
  size_t len;
  char *p = NULL;
  char *q;
  char buffer[128];

  *Error = 0;

  while(fgets(buffer, sizeof buffer, fp))
  {
    len = strlen(buffer);
    q = realloc(p, size + len);
    if(q != NULL)
    {
      p = q;
      strcpy(p + size, buffer);
      size += len;
    }
    else
    {
      *Error = 1;
    }
  }
  return p;
}
```

This function returns a pointer to an in-memory copy of as much as possible of the input file (or `NULL` if the very first allocation went awry). In the event of an incomplete read, it sets the content of an error variable to non-zero. At no time does it leak memory (although, of course, it's the calling function's responsibility to arrange for the memory to be freed at an appropriate time).

Using Memory You No Longer Own

I don't know why, but many programmers think they can do this:

```
while(p != NULL)
{
  free(p);
  p = p->next;
}
```

Their reasoning seems to be "I know what p pointed to just before I called free(), and I haven't done anything to change it, and all free() does is muck about with a list somewhere. The assignment will happen a nanosecond or so after the free() call, so there hasn't been time for the system to use that memory for anything else. I should still be able to access that memory to get to the next pointer; so I will."

It's hard to argue with this kind of attitude, especially when (in many cases) these programmers can show you that their reasoning is correct (even though it isn't). But argue we must. Those who suffer allergic reactions to analogies should now skip two paragraphs.

It's a bit like buying and then selling a house. Once you have bought it, you can do more or less what you like with it. You can put whatever you like in it, and you can live in it quite happily, for as long as you wish, right up to the moment when you sell it.

Once you have soldthe house, you no longer have the right to live there. You don't even have the right to go in. You may well have a spare key (analogous to the pointer p), but that's beside the point. It's notyour house any more. From the moment you hand over the title deed to the new owner, you are not entitled to be in that house for any reason. If you accidentally left something extremely valuable in the attic, you might be tempted to go back to get it, but you'd have no right to be there. In some countries, the owner might even be within his rights to shoot you dead if he found you (a rather extreme case of undefined behavior). It's far safer to check that you've saved everything you need *before* handing over possession.

It's only an illustration; as Bjarne Stroustrup says, "proof by analogy is fraud." If it doesn't satisfy you, then consider section 7.20.3 of the C Standard, which says that "the value of a pointer that refers to freed space is indeterminate." In other words, to refer to freed space results in undefined behavior. To put it yet another way, you can't guarantee how your program will behave and, in theory, it can make the computer do anything it is physically capable of doing, including all kinds of creative email-to-your-boss possibilities about which I really don't wish to alarm you.

Here's how you can solve the above conundrum without raising the grisly specter of undefined behavior:

```
T *q; /* same type as p */

while(p != NULL)
  {
    q = p->next;
    free(p);
    p = q;
  }
```

A similar problem arises in functions like this:

```
char *BuildPhoneNumber(int code, int num)
{
  char telno[16];
  sprintf(telno, "(%05d) %d", code, num);
  return telno;
}
```

The `telno` variable is local to the `BuildPhoneNumber()` function. Therefore, its contents cannot be relied upon, once the function has returned.

To solve this little puzzle, either turn `telno` into a `static` variable or pass in an array of sufficient `char` or dynamically allocate space and return a pointer to the allocated memory (remembering to free it when you're done with it).

Relying on the OS to Reclaim Memory

The C Standard has nothing to say on what happens to dynamically allocated memory that remains allocated at the end of the program. After all, the program may be in C, but there's no requirement that its caller is written in C, is there? What happens just after the C program ends is beyond the scope of the C Standard. It's a common belief that the operating system reclaims memory used by a program when that program terminates. For many operating systems, this is true; in fact, it's extremely likely to be true for the operating systems in most common use. But the C Standard provides no guarantee that it is true.

It is good programming practice to do your own housekeeping, to leave the computer as you found it, so to speak. Returning dynamically allocated memory is part of this process. If this (stylistic) argument convinces you, however, you are already convinced, and if it doesn't, I doubt I'll change your mind now. So allow me to turn to a more pragmatic reason for always releasing your memory—code reuse.

Good programs get reused. Sometimes, an entire program is converted into a library routine. When I was working at a life assurance company recently, a projection roll-up application (several thousand lines of code) that I had helped to develop was turned into a library routine; it changed from being the program to being just a function (or rather, a whole suite of functions having one function as its entry point), and this function was now to be called many times during one program run. It was unfortunate that the application allocated memory but did not free it up when it finished with that memory—and what had been perfectly acceptable to many people when the application was a program became a classic memory leak after conversion to a library routine. Clearly, it had to be fixed. Equally clearly, a lot of time and therefore money could have been saved if the program had been designed from the start to free its memory properly.

Plan to reuse your code. Release memory when you finish using it. Your colleagues will think you're a pedant, but the guys who have to maintain your code 10 years down the line will love you. They'll still call you names (all maintenance programmers do this), but the names won't be quite as unpleasant, and that's like money in the bank.

When a Memory Allocation Function Fails

This kind of error-handling code is very common:

```
p = malloc(bytes);
if(p == NULL)
{
  printf("Can't allocate enough memory. Aborting.\n");
  exit(EXIT_FAILURE);
}
```

For "student" code, this is fine. The check is necessary, because `malloc` might fail. In practice, correctly written student code rarely fails to allocate sufficient memory, because the amount requested tends to be a few hundred bytes at most, and no more than a handful of such blocks are requested on any given run (unless the professor is in a foul mood). Even if a conscientious student decides to "stress-test" his application by asking it to use more memory than it can possibly get, he is likely to be smugly satisfied with the resulting `printf`. His program draws to a premature close, failing by design.

Note

It isn't only students who can get away with this. It seems to have become traditional for those who teach C, either in college or on Usenet or in other instructional channels, to abort applications when memory allocation fails. Recovery from a memory allocation error seems to be left as an exercise for the graduate student, rather than explored thoroughly as a natural requirement of a real program. There is some value in this, provided that the student is given to understand that `exit(EXIT_FAILURE);` should really be read as shorthand for "Insert your recovery mechanism here."

In the real world, life isn't that simple. Imagine that you've just spent the past hour working on a document, when your favorite word processor suddenly tries to allocate 20 or 30 bytes for a new font instance, fails, writes a quick explanation to `stdout`, and terminates. No opportunity to cancel the action that caused the memory allocation request, no option to save your work, just a matter-of-fact "whoops, isn't that tragic, never mind, goodbye" message (if you're lucky!), and an hour's work down the tubes. Would it remain your favorite word processor for very much longer?

What action can we take in the event of a failure? To a large extent, of course, it depends on the application, but we can make some general observations, depending on the exact nature of our memory requirements.

Break Down the Memory Requirement

Does the memory we requested have to be in one contiguous block? If the answer is no, then perhaps we can split it into two requests. That way, `malloc` may be able to squeeze in both requests. When you call `malloc`, it attempts to find a single block of free memory big enough to satisfy your request. If it can find a big enough block, it will return a pointer to it. If it can't, it will return `NULL`. By asking for two smaller blocks, you are making `malloc`'s life easier, and it may indeed be able to cope with the two requests.

Use Less Memory

Did we ask for more memory than we really needed? This isn't necessarily a bad thing, if you consider the constant trade-off between size and speed. For example, we may have a dynamic buffer that we occasionally need to resize; it makes sense to allocate considerably more than we need when we resize. Doing so will reduce the number of times we have to call `realloc`, and thus our program's performance won't suffer quite as much as it might otherwise. Some people go so far as to say that we should double the buffer size at each request, as Listing 8.3 shows:

LISTING 8.3 Minimizing `realloc` Calls

```
static char *buffer = NULL;
static size_t bufsize = 0;
while(strlen(s) >= bufsize)
{
  p = realloc(buffer, bufsize * 2);
  if(p != NULL)
  {
    bufsize *= 2;
    buffer = p;
  }
  else
  {
    printf("er...now what?\n");
  }
}
```

There is scope here for a corrective strategy in the event of a memory allocation failure. After all, it may well be that the buffer is almost big enough already. Listing 8.4 shows how we might make an attempt to recover from such a failure.

LISTING 8.4 Recovering from `realloc` Failure

```
static char *buffer = NULL;
static size_t bufsize = 0;
size_t len = strlen(s) + 1;

while(len > bufsize)
{
  p = realloc(buffer, bufsize * 2);
  if(p != NULL)
  {
    bufsize *= 2;
    buffer = p;
  }
  else
  {
    p = realloc(buffer, len);
    if(p != NULL)
    {
      bufsize = len;
      buffer = p;
    }
```

LISTING 8.4 continued

```
      else
      {
        /* What to do next depends very heavily
         * on the nature of the application.
         */
        printf("What we need here is a design decision!\n");
      }
    }
  }
```

This code is better. It makes an attempt to recover from the allocation failure, but it still leaves unanswered the question of what to do if the second attempt fails. Probably the right thing for this function to do is to either release all the memory and tell the calling function that the whole shooting match went wrong, or take an extra parameter, a pointer to a status variable, and set it to indicate that not all the data could be stored correctly because of memory constraints, but that the part that could be stored is now available. Which is correct depends on the application. The most important point to make here is that it is not a subsidiary function's job to decide to abort the application. That decision properly belongs at an application level, not at a utility function level. This is because utility functions, if genuinely useful, will be used in many different kinds of applications, which will almost certainly have a variety of required reactions to failure.

Use a Fixed Length Buffer

Consider a simple copying program, which copies a file from one place to another. If the input file size can be determined in advance (perhaps via an implementation-defined extension such as `filelength()`, which some well-known compilers provide), the program could allocate that many bytes, read the input file into that buffer, and write it out again from that buffer. Simple and quick. If it fails, though, it's no big deal. The program need not rely on the dynamic buffer; if worst comes to worst, it can make do with a buffer of just one byte, and it could almost certainly use a small automatic buffer, an array of `unsigned char`.

I recently wrote a program that had to process a text file to do an elementary "search and replace." I wanted a large buffer but could make do with a smaller one if need be. I defined a small buffer and a `char *`. I tried allocating eight kilobytes of space dynamically. If that failed, I tried for half that much, and half again, and half again, until either the allocation was successful or the amount of memory I was requesting was no more than the size of the automatically allocated buffer, at which point I would give up and point to the automatic buffer instead. Needless to say, I haven't yet had that function fail to allocate the full eight kilobytes on the first attempt. But, when it does eventually fail, I'll be ready!

Allocate an Emergency Reserve

It may well be that the design of your program is such that you cannot failsafe your program after a memory allocation failure, because you need to allocate memory to do so(!) and the memory just isn't there to be allocated. This is a design issue. If you encounter this situation, consider redesigning your program so that it allocates the memory it needs for a graceful failure right at the start of the program when, presumably, there's plenty of memory to go around. It's true that you might not need this memory unless you need to fail gracefully, but it's also true that this is the time you are most likely to get it—waiting until it's too late is perhaps not a good plan. This is another example of allocating memory that you may not *need*, strictly speaking, but that you grab anyway in the name of robustness.

Using Disk Space

You may be able to use some other kind of storage as a supplement to main memory. Many operating systems already use such a *virtual memory* technique as standard; when short on RAM, they find some memory that doesn't seem to be needed immediately and write it to a disk, to make room for your allocation request. If your operating system does this, you are unlikely to get dynamic memory allocation failures, unless your program is extremely demanding or is bug ridden to the extent that it corrupts the implementation's memory allocation subsystem.

Winding Up Windows

When testing some memory management code a couple of years ago, I managed to get Windows NT to hand me 1.5 gigabytes of memory, using lots of comparatively small allocations in a loop. It took over 90 minutes to free it all up again!

If your operating system does not provide virtual memory, it's relatively easy to provide it yourself. All you need to do is create a large file on your main storage device, be it disk, tape, or rewritable CD-ROM. I'll assume you'll be using a disk; for the purpose of this discussion there is little or no difference in principle between disks, tapes, rewritable CD-ROMs, and yellow sticky notes.

How large the file should be depends partly on how much disk space you have and partly on how much memory you need. Fortunately, disk space is a lot cheaper than RAM, so you are likely to have access to as much disk space as you need for this purpose.

The idea is simple. First, allocate a buffer of a reasonable size early on in your program, when memory is most plentiful. Then, if an allocation fails, find some block of dynamically allocated memory that you don't need for a while, and write it to the disk file. Then you can reuse the memory for some other purpose. When you need the original contents of the buffer, they can be reread from the file. (If you still need the newer data, you can write it to a different part of the file before loading the older data.) You may want to write some management functions to handle all this for you. They are so simple to write, and there are so few mainstream operating systems nowadays that don't use virtual memory, that I won't cut the code for you here.

Using one or more of these strategies should mean that you need never again lose data because of memory constraints.

What to Do when `calloc` Succeeds

The `calloc` function, I used to think, is marvelous. It doesn't just allocate memory (I used to think) in convenient rectangular blocks suitable for arrays; I used to think that it also initializes all its array elements to zero.

Are you ahead of me? I used to think *wrong*, at least in regard to these aspects of `calloc`'s behavior. For a start, this vague idea I had about rectangular memory, which had its origins in `calloc`'s two arguments (*length* and *breadth*, so to speak), now leaves me squirming with embarrassment, and I only mention it here because I've met several other people who had the same kind of misconception. In case you're one of those people, that's not how memory works, okay? It's best just to think of it as one long line of cardboard boxes with little octal or hexadecimal numbers painted on the sides. And keep taking those little tablets the doctor gave you. Mine are green.

More important (because it's more dangerous) is the other misconception; `calloc` does *not* necessarily initialize all elements of the array to zero. Worse still, it probably will but it might not, so it's more likely than most C traps to catch you unaware.

You're okay with integers (`char` and the various flavors of `int`), be they `signed` or `unsigned`. They will be set to zero. And you might be okay with pointers and with floating-point numbers (`float`, `double`, and `long double`). But you might not. C does *not* guarantee that all-bits-zero is the zero representation for either pointers (`NULL`) or floating-point numbers (0.0). This frequently is the case, but you can never be *sure* that it's the case. This isn't something I want to cover in detail right now, especially since it's more to do with data types than with memory management, so let this warning suffice; if portability is important to you, don't rely on `calloc` to initialize your variables to zero. If pointers or floating-point numbers constitute elements of your array (or you are building an array of structures or unions containing floating-point numbers or pointers), do the initialization yourself, in a loop.

In fact, you might as well use `malloc`. If your structures are large, this might seem like a huge inconvenience. Notationally, however, it's not difficult to find a shortcut, at the expense of an extra instance of your structure:

```
FOO f = {0};
FOO *p;

p = malloc(n * sizeof *p);
if(p != NULL)
{
  for(i = 0; i < N; i++)
    p[i] = f;
}
```

This code does what we really would have preferred `calloc` to do for us. It sacrifices efficiency to gain clarity and brevity. If you are looking to squeeze the very last unnecessary byte from your code, you probably will prefer to use the longhand method instead.

Staying in Control

Control is what memory management is all about. To make memory work for you, you need to know (or be able to derive) the location of every block of memory allocated to your program, without fail, so that you can always get to the memory when you need it (and so that you can clean up properly when you're done). You also need to know how big each block is, so that you can ensure that you don't write to memory you don't own.

A few years ago, I was working on a program that allocated and reallocated a lot of memory. I was concerned about memory leaks; I wanted to minimize the chance of the program being unable to complete its task because of allocation failure. To ensure that I handled the memory correctly, I wrote a set of wrapper functions to call `malloc` and such and to track all memory allocations and releases. I tried to make these functions more useful than their C library equivalents, too; for example, they all matched my personal convention of the time by returning `int`, with `0` indicating success. The wrapper for `realloc` was a definite improvement; I would never again have to remember to use a spare pointer, as it would do that for me, returning a failure status code (and leaving the original pointer intact) if anything went wrong. To achieve this magic (as I then considered it), I had to pass a pointer to pointer into each allocation function.

Tracking consisted of loading information about the allocations into a binary tree, together with `__FILE__` and `__LINE__` information. The primary information I stored was the pointer itself. I used this as the key.

What I hadn't appreciated was that the operating system in question started to allocate memory from low addresses first, increasing the returned address by some amount with each new allocation. As a result, my binary tree began to look more like a unary telegraph pole—a most expensive simulation of a sorted list. Performance took a nosedive.

To solve the performance issue, I subjected the whole suite of functions to conditional compilation. It would only be included if I wanted. Otherwise, simpler production functions would be used. That way, I could track memory in development, fix the leaks, and then recompile for production. I'd put up with a slow application in development for the assurance it gave me of the solidity of the production code.

Amazingly, the code worked. I developed my application, it sold exactly zero copies (ah well), and the code fell into disuse.

I dug it out a few days ago, knowing full well that my code was good enough for this book and hoping that this excellent library would at last prove to be of some real benefit to the human race. Much to my astonishment, however, it wasn't anywhere near good enough; it needed a *lot* of work to bring it up to scratch. For a start, it was about as portable as a coal mine (have you ever tried to move one?). I was appalled. Since I couldn't possibly write code that badly, I could only assume that it had rotted. I'm sure you know what I mean. So the next time you take a horrified look at code you wrote several years ago, spare me a thought.

Tip

If you're concerned about code portability, it's a really good idea to use more than one compiler. If at all possible, compile and test your code on more than one operating system, too. I like to use Windows and Linux as my usual test operating systems, although it's not unknown for me to use OS/2 and OS390 (a mainframe operating system). Running your code on a mainframe really tests your notion of portability!

Anyway, I did the necessary work and came up with the revised source that I'll be showing you here. The library comprises a header (`memtrack.h`) and a source file (`memtrack.c`). The `memtrkmn.c` file is a simple driver. In addition to showing you how to track memory, I'll be pointing out my mistakes (and the solutions to those mistakes) along the way, partly for your amusement but mainly in the hope that you, gentle reader, might profit from my mistakes by not making them yourself.

Memory Tracking Header File

Listing 8.5 describes the interface.

LISTING 8.5 Memory Tracking Header

```
#ifndef MEMTRACK_H__
#define MEMTRACK_H__
```

Here was my very first mistake. Yes, already! In my original source, this inclusion guard had two leading underscores (`__MEMTRACK_H__`), which looks really cool but is in fact an invasion of the implementation's namespace.

```
#define MEMTRACK_FILENAME "MEMTRACK.TXT"
```

Mistake number two. This time, a design error. Instead of allowing the user to specify the logfile name at runtime, I used a hard-coded filename for the logfile. I haven't changed the design (because it would involve a radical change to the interface that wouldn't teach us anything about memory management), but I have at least moved the string literal into the header file, where it's easier to locate if you want to change it.

The next step is to define a number of function names, which are in fact preprocessor directives. Depending on whether or not we are tracking memory, these will be replaced by the names of either tracking functions or non-tracking functions.

Names are important. I thought long and hard about the wisdom of naming these macros `malloc`, `realloc`, and so on. To do so would make the user-programmer's code appear much more normal, which, on the face of it, would be an advantage. On the other hand, it would obscure the use of the memory tracker, and this obscurity would be a Bad Thing. Also, it would mean having a separate header for these macros, because they would otherwise clash with the standard library calls to `malloc` and so on in the memory tracking source itself. Furthermore, these macro names would clash with the prototypes given in `<stdlib.h>`, which would cause all sorts of difficulties. It simply would not be good enough. So I had to use different names. I considered naming the macros `xmalloc`, `xrealloc`, and so on. As these names are already quite popular as unofficial extensions, though, I elected to use descriptive, mixed-case names, which are unlikely to clash with popular extant functions.

```
#ifdef MEMTRACK

#define AllocMemory(size)     \
```

```
DebugAllocMemory(size, __FILE__, __LINE__)

#define AllocCopyString(s)        \
DebugAllocCopyString(s, __FILE__, __LINE__)

#define ReAllocMemory(p, newsize) \
DebugReAllocMemory(p, newsize, __FILE__, __LINE__)

#define ReleaseMemory(p)          \
DebugReleaseMemory(p, __FILE__, __LINE__)

#define MEMTRK_MEMALLOC   1
#define MEMTRK_MEMFREE    2
#define MEMTRK_REPORT     3
#define MEMTRK_DESTROY    4

#ifndef TYP_MEMTRK_MSG
#define TYP_MEMTRK_MSG
typedef int MEMTRK_MSG;
#endif
```

We have four different tasks for the memory tracking function to perform. We want to record the allocation of memory, remove outdated records (when memory is freed), provide a report on request, and destroy all the records (at the end of the program). I did have a fifth, `MEMTRK_INIT`, but it turned out to unnecessarily complicate the application code, so I threw it away. The `TrackMemory()` function uses these constants in its `switch()` statement.

The `typedef` is interesting. We still don't have a `#ifntypedef` directive in C, a lack which I find annoying. For example, it's not uncommon to `typedef int BOOL`. Precisely because it's not uncommon, the chances are high of a collision between two type definitions with the same name in the headers to two different utility libraries. (In this particular case, the new C99 Standard provides us with a `_Bool` type, but the principle remains the same for other common user-defined types, and I've experienced the same difficulty with a couple of particularly obscure user-defined types in corporate development work.) Here is one possible way to hack around the problem that `#ifntypedef` would solve properly, if only it existed: a header-style inclusion guard around every `typedef`. Unfortunately, to fix all our `typedef`s this way would be prohibitively expensive. And although I'd made a start, it's pretty obvious that I didn't keep up the habit. Nevertheless, I've left the guard code in place in case you think it's a good idea and want to take it on board. If you don't, simply forget all about it.

Now we come to a very important type, `ALIGN`. Let's take a look at it first, and then I'll explain.

```
#ifndef TYP_ALIGN
#define TYP_ALIGN

typedef union
{
  long l; /* if C99, consider using intmax_t instead */
  unsigned long lu;
  double f;
  long double lf;
  void *vp;
  void (*fp)(void);
} ALIGN;

#endif
```

The first version of this library stored copies of the pointers returned by the various dynamic allocation functions in a binary tree. To find the right place in the tree to store the pointer, it was necessary to compare pointer values relationally. Since many operating systems assign addresses in ascending order, at least for a while, this technique is quite likely to result in a tree thinner than a ballpoint pen on a diet. Of course, we could solve this problem by somehow turning the pointer into an integer and hashing that integer to give us a better tree.

But we have a more serious and fundamental problem in comparing pointers. It is perfectly permissible in a C program for two pointers with different bit patterns to point to the same object. They can have the same object representation even though they have different values. The infamous segmented memory architecture of early Intel 80x86 processors is a classic example of this oddity. On these processors, the bit patterns `0x100400A0` and `0x100000E0` refer to the same address. This is highly counterintuitive, but it's correct. We could turn a pointer into an integer (probably via an array of `unsigned char`) and store that integer as our key. But we can't guarantee that the user's program will hand us back the same bit pattern for freeing the pointer that we handed over immediately after allocation.

And we can't just shrug and say we're not going to bother supporting any platform that creative with addressing. This is *C Unleashed*, not *C for Linear Addressing Platforms Unleashed*! So we must search for a better solution.

Well, okay, if we can't compare pointers conveniently, perhaps we can compare something else instead? What if we assign a unique value to each memory allocation and use that value as the tree's key?

The trouble with this idea is that to ensure that each allocation has a moderately firm guarantee of being unique, it's probably best to assign an index that is incremented with each allocation. That's all right (up to a somewhat distant point) except that it leads to a grossly inefficient tree structure. How can we get around this problem?

One possible solution, as I hinted earlier, is hashing. If we can design a way of mangling the key in a predictable (or, at least, reproducible) way, that should give us a much flatter and fatter tree. This saves us from writing tree-balancing code, which we won't be doing for a few chapters yet. What's more, we don't even need to store the hashed value. We can simply recalculate it whenever we need it, if we can only find a way to store the key itself. This is especially useful if we end up using more than one hash value.

Tip

Remember that a hashing algorithm should be crafted for a particular set of data and for your particular requirements. You may want to have (or must not exceed) a few "buckets" or you may want many. You may have a constraint on the number of collisions you can allow for a given number of input items. In the current case, we want no collisions at all, and it's usually good to have no more than a reasonable number of collisions. What constitutes "reasonable" will vary from one application to the next.

How can you know what your collision rates are? How can you know whether all the available buckets are being used? It's worth writing a program to read sample data and print out a hash table population chart, so that you can get this information and use it to assess your hashing algorithm quantitatively.

To store the key, we need memory. As it happens, though, we only need a new key precisely at the time when we're allocating memory anyway. So all we need to do is allocate a little extra in which to jot down the key value for a given allocation.

It wouldn't be very convenient for our calling code to have to skip past the key when using dynamically allocated memory, however—especially since it would have to be dependent on whether `MEMTRACK` were defined or not. The pointer we return should be a pointer to just past the extra memory we reserved for the key. But how much memory should we reserve for the key? Does it depend on how many allocations we will be doing?

It may come as a surprise, but the key size is not the main issue here. The most important thing to ensure is that we return to the user-programmer a pointer that is suitably aligned for storing any kind of data. If we don't do this, the user-programmer's code could end up segfaulting (or GPF-ing, or crashing, or whatever your operating system calls it) without his code having anything visibly wrong with it. That would not be good. So we ensure that the pointer to memory that we return to the user-programmer is suitably aligned for whatever he wants. In order to ensure this, we store our key in a `union` comprising a hatful of big data types—the bigger the better. The likes of `char` aren't really likely to be widest type, but `long int` and `long double` and pointers to function are all potential candidates, so we simply use a `union` of all of them (and a few others). Hence the `ALIGN` type. It will easily store an `unsigned long`, which is going to be enough for a memory allocation counter.

In passing, I should perhaps mention that we don't intend to use more than one field in the `union`. We are using a `union` purely to force the compiler to align our memory in the way we want—the most flexible way.

Now we need a type for describing the details of an allocation. Specifically, we would like to store the address returned to the user, the amount of memory allocated, and—most vitally—the place in the user-programmer's source code where the allocation occurred (filename and line number). Armed with this information, the user-programmer should be able to track down most memory leaks. We won't store the key in this structure, because it really has nothing to do with the allocation—it's just a number for helping us keep track of this data. It could be any data.


```
#ifndef TYP_PAYLOAD
#define TYP_PAYLOAD

typedef struct PAYLOAD
{
  void *Ptr;
  size_t Size;
  char *FileName;
  int LineNumber;
} PAYLOAD;

#endif
```

It would have been quite convenient for us if any of this information had been suitable for using as a unique key. None of it is, though. We've already discussed why the most promising candidate, `void *Ptr`, isn't suitable. You might like to spend a moment rejecting the other possibilities, too. You might have to think more carefully about `LineNumber` than about the others.

Now let's wrap that type up in a structure type suitable for being a node in a binary tree. This is not intended to be a binary tree demonstration, I hasten to add. The tree code used here is very simple, as you will see. It doesn't support balancing, for example.

```
#define MEM_LEFTCHILD     0
#define MEM_RIGHTCHILD    1
#define MEM_MAX_CHILDREN  2

#ifndef TYP_MEMTREE
#define TYP_MEMTREE

typedef struct MEMTREE
{
  struct MEMTREE *Child[MEM_MAX_CHILDREN];
  unsigned long Key;
  PAYLOAD Payload;
} MEMTREE;

#endif
```

(To save space, I've removed the function prototypes from this listing, but of course you can find them on the CD-ROM.)

The interface definition winds up by specifying what will happen if `MEMTRACK` is not defined.

```
#else
#define AllocMemory     malloc
#define AllocCopyString CopyString
#define ReAllocMemory   realloc
#define ReleaseMemory   free
#define TrackMemory(a, b, c, d, e, f)

#endif

#endif
```

Implementing the Memory Tracking Library

So much for the interface. Now let's have a look at how the code actually works. Listing 8.6 (which, I'm afraid, is quite long) shows the implementation:

LISTING 8.6 Memory Tracking Library Source

```
#include <stdio.h>
#include <stdlib.h>
#include <string.h>
#include <time.h>

#include <assert.h>

#include "memtrack.h"
```

The `strdup()` function is not part of the ANSI C standard library. It is, however, widely used. Since `strdup()` is traditionally implemented by many compilers as a way of allocating storage for a string and then copying the string into that storage, I considered it wise to include a way of tracking `strdup()`-type allocations. I can't use the name `strdup()` for this function, unfortunately, because that would violate the Standard's "future directions" convention, which reserves all external identifiers beginning `str` followed by a lowercase letter for its own future use.

This function doesn't track the memory allocations it invokes, but it's a necessary non-tracking analogue to the tracking version.

```
char *CopyString(char *InString)
{
  char *p = NULL;

  if(InString != NULL)
  {
    p = malloc(strlen(InString) + 1);
    if(NULL != p)
    {
      strcpy(p, InString);
    }
  }

  return p;
}

#ifdef MEMTRACK

/* Tracking versions */
```

Whenever we allocate memory, we need to record the fact. By allocating a few extra bytes, we make enough space to store our key. The actual key handling is done by `TrackMemory()`.

The function `DebugAllocMemory()` is almost a drop-in `malloc()` replacement. It takes a couple of extra parameters, `FileName` and `LineNumber`. The user-programmer doesn't have to worry about these, though, because they are supplied by the macro mask for the function.

```
void *DebugAllocMemory(size_t Size,
                       char *FileName,
                       int LineNumber)
{
  void *ptr;
  char *p;

  ptr = malloc(Size + sizeof(ALIGN));
  if(ptr != NULL)
  {
    TrackMemory(MEMTRK_MEMALLOC,
                0,
                ptr,
                Size,
                FileName,
                LineNumber);
```

Our extra memory must be transparent to the calling function, so we need to report an address `sizeof(ALIGN)` bytes higher than the one returned by `malloc`. But we can't do pointer arithmetic on pointers to incomplete type (`void` pointers). To get around this, we use a temporary `char *` so that we can find the appropriate address.

```
    p = ptr;
    p += sizeof(ALIGN);
    ptr = p;
  }

  return ptr;
}

char *DebugAllocCopyString(char *String,
                           char *FileName,
                           int   LineNumber)
{
  char *p = NULL;
  int ErrorStatus = 0;
```

```
  size_t Length = strlen(String) + 1;

  p = malloc(Length + sizeof(ALIGN));
  if(0 == ErrorStatus)
  {
    strcpy(p + sizeof(ALIGN), String);
    TrackMemory(MEMTRK_MEMALLOC,
                0,
                p,
                Length,
                FileName,
                LineNumber);

    p += sizeof(ALIGN);
  }
  return p;
}
```

We can't call our `strdup()` clone directly because it won't allocate enough memory for the key stored by `TrackMemory()`. We could do something ugly with `#ifdef`, but I think it's clearer in this case simply to re-engineer a copy of the code that includes tracking. (Originally, I had done this for `malloc`, `calloc`, and `realloc`, too, but I discovered I could save quite a few lines of code by simply throwing out the non-tracking versions of the wrappers for these functions, without loss of functionality.)

Redesigning `realloc`

The next task is to take care of tracking all the calls to the `realloc` wrapper. This function, like the other wrapper functions, used to take `void **` as its first parameter. This was a really good idea. Instead of slavishly following the `realloc` interface, I could improve upon it. After all, it was very clear to me that the ANSI committee, or Dennis Ritchie, or whoever it was, had not considered the design of the `realloc` function as carefully as they should have done. So, how to improve it?

I could pass the address of the old pointer, rather than its value, and update it within the wrapper function if and onlyifthe internal `realloc` call succeeded. The function would return not a pointer but an integer representing success or failure, in accordance with my normal practice at that time. Therefore, the `ptr = realloc(ptr, newsize)` bug would be squashed forever! I was really rather pleased with this idea, and I lost little time in coding it. It worked rather well, too.

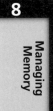

You're right. As I discovered when recompiling and retesting the code for this book, it's not a portable technique. While it is true that you can assign any object pointer to a `void *` pointer without loss of information, the same does not necessarily apply to a `void **` pointer! It worked fine in the compiler I was using at the time, but that's the best that can be said about it. In order to force it to work in ANSI C, I'd have to cast, in the call, something like this:

```
DidItWork = ReallocMemory(&(void *)p, newsize);
```

Sometimes casting is necessary (as here), but it's always ugly. If your function's design requires that the user must always or nearly always cast his arguments to that function, then you have to think seriously about whether you have the right design.

Having thought seriously about whether I had the right design, I concluded that I didn't. I had no desire to write `&(void *)` anywhere in my source code, ever. So I considered some other possibilities. One idea was to wrap the pointer in a structure. The trouble with that idea, though, was that I'd have to wrap up the pointer, pass the structure, dig out the pointer within the wrapper, do the allocation, update the pointer, and then let the calling function dig out the pointer again, so that it could actually be used. That sounded like a lot of hard work, especially for the user-programmer—something I try to avoid if I can; I like the library to do the work whenever possible. I was determined, though, to come up with the best possible design, rather than just meekly copy the ANSI method.

Finally, I established a foolproof technique. Well, almost foolproof. It would mean trusting the calling function a bit, though. If I simply took a normal `void *`, I would avoid the casting problem. Of course, the fact that C always passes parameters by value would mean that I couldn't (effectively) update the pointer, so I'd have to return a pointer from the function instead of a status code. That would be all right, though, because I could use `NULL` to indicate failure. Admittedly, that would place the onus on the user-programmer to use a spare pointer in case of failure, but that was a small price to pay for the cleaner technique.

I took a step back to admire my handiwork and discovered that I had just re-implemented ANSI C's `realloc` design! There's a time to fight and a time to accept the inevitable, so I gave in; it seems that whoever designed `realloc` did know what they were doing, after all. There's a lesson there somewhere for overzealous and arrogant wheel inventors.

Unredesigning `realloc`

Here's how the wrapper ended up, after a number of changes:

```
void *DebugReAllocMemory(void *pOldMem,
                         size_t NewSize,
                         char *FileName,
                         int LineNumber)
```

```
{
  void *NewPtr = NULL;
  int ItWasntNull = 0;
  char *p;

  ALIGN KeyStore;

  if(pOldMem != NULL)
  {
    ItWasntNull = 1;
```

If we are being passed a non-NULL pointer, we assume that the pointer points to memory previously allocated with a wrapper function from this library. After all, if the user-programmer were allocating his own memory, he wouldn't be using this library. Therefore, we can go and dig out the key from the bytes immediately preceding the address we were given.

```
    p = pOldMem;

    p -= sizeof(ALIGN);

    memcpy(&KeyStore.lu, p, sizeof(ALIGN));
  }

  NewPtr = realloc(pOldMem,
                   NewSize +
                   (NewSize > 0  ?
                   sizeof(ALIGN) :
                   0));

  if(NULL != NewPtr)
  {
    if(ItWasntNull)
    {
```

The C Standard guarantees that `realloc` will correctly copy data (if necessary) from the old block to the new block, so it's not quite the same as a call to `free` followed by `malloc`. Nevertheless, from a memory tracking point of view, it amounts to the same thing, so that's how we record it. As a result, under most circumstances this function will call `TrackMemory` twice.

```
      TrackMemory(MEMTRK_MEMFREE,
                  KeyStore.lu,
                  NULL,
```

```
                    0,
                    FileName,
                    LineNumber);
    }

    if(NewSize > 0)
    {
      TrackMemory(MEMTRK_MEMALLOC,
                  0,
                  NewPtr,
                  NewSize,
                  FileName,
                  LineNumber);

      p = NewPtr;
      p += sizeof(ALIGN);
      NewPtr = p;
    }
  }

  return NewPtr;
}
```

The object of the exercise is to discover whether we have allocated any memory that we haven't subsequently released. As well as tracking allocations, then, we need to track releases. This function is a simple wrapper for `free`, which first calls `TrackMemory` to tell it about the memory release.

```
void DebugReleaseMemory(void *pSource,
                        char *FileName,
                        int LineNumber)
{
  char *p;
  ALIGN KeyStore;

  if(pSource != NULL)
  {
    p = pSource;
    p -= sizeof(ALIGN);
    memcpy(&KeyStore.lu, p, sizeof(ALIGN));

    TrackMemory(MEMTRK_MEMFREE,
                KeyStore.lu,
                NULL,
```

```
                0,
                FileName,
                LineNumber);

    free(p);
  }
}
```

Hash Key Design

As we have already established, pointers to `void` make unsuitable tree keys, so we are going to use a hashed index instead. The index is stored with the allocated memory and passed to `MemTrkCmp`, which in turn passes it to the `hash1` and `hash2` functions.

These two functions look very similar. All that differs is the constants. The first is designed with tree balance in mind. I have deliberately refrained from giving the tree perfect balance, because that would distract us from our primary objective for this chapter, which is to discuss memory management. (If you want to learn how to balance trees, don't worry. It's covered in Chapter 12, "Binary Search Trees.") So `hash1` is intended to give us a relatively well-balanced tree, without getting overly concerned about it. Unfortunately, this means that many key values are duplicated. I spent a lot of time looking for constants that would give me lots of unique keys and good tree balance, but I didn't find any that I considered good enough, which is why I decided to use two hashes.

Our second hashing routine sorts out any collisions caused by the first algorithm and is based on the assumption that no more than 2,147,483,647 memory allocations are going to be performed within the course of any one test run. I would argue that this is a reasonable assumption. (If the program allocated an average of one thousand memory blocks per second, it would take over three weeks to exhaust all our unique hash values.) For a library intended to be used in production, we'd need to consider this more carefully. Since this is a debugging library, I feel quite safe. If your requirements are particularly demanding, however, here's a possible plan for modification: Add a third hash function and compare against that if the first two hash algorithms both fail to distinguish between two keys. Ensure that the constants you use for the third hash function are large and that they are co-prime with the existing constants.

```
unsigned long hash1(unsigned long value)
{
  return ((value * 179424601UL + 71UL) % 167UL);
}
```

```
unsigned long hash2(unsigned long value)
{
  return ((value * 179424673UL + 257UL) % 2147483647UL);
}
```

The MemTrkCmp function simply compares two keys by hashing them and comparing the hash values. It could compare the keys directly, of course, but that would give us a terribly inefficient tree.

```
int MemTrkCmp(unsigned long key1,
              unsigned long key2)
{
  int diff = 0;

  unsigned long hv1, hv2;

  hv1 = hash1(key1);
  hv2 = hash1(key2);

  if(hv1 > hv2)
  {
    diff = 1;
  }
  else if(hv1 < hv2)
  {
    diff = -1;
  }
  else
  {
    hv1 = hash2(key1);
    hv2 = hash2(key2);
    if(hv1 > hv2)
    {
      diff = 1;
    }
    else if(hv1 < hv2)
    {
      diff = -1;
    }
    else
    {
```

If the assertion ever failed, I'd be astonished. The only way I can think of for it to fail is if you have run a three-and-a-half-week test allocating a thousand blocks a second, in which case you might wish to consider a third hash function, as I suggested earlier.

```
      assert(key1 == key2);
    }
  }

  return diff;
}
```

Reporting Current Memory Allocations

At the end of the program run (or, in fact, at any time during the run), we'd like to see how much memory has been allocated and not released. This function displays the information for one allocation.

```
int MemPrintAllocs(const PAYLOAD *p1, void *p2)
{
  FILE *fp = p2;

  fprintf(fp,
          "\n%8p allocated %7u byt%s "
          "at Line %5d of File %s.",
          p1->Ptr,
          (unsigned int)p1->Size,
          p1->Size == 1 ? "e " : "es",
          p1->LineNumber,
          p1->FileName);

  return 0;
}
```

Now let's take a look at `TrackMemory`, which actually does the tracking. The first thing to note is that we are passed either a key value or a pointer. Ideally we'd like the key both times, because the key is our way to find the right place in the tree. If we are recording that memory has just been allocated, though, we don't have a key yet. In fact, it is the task of this function to decide what that key should be. So when we are recording an allocation, we make do with a pointer. If we are recording the release of memory, however, the key is known, so we use it.

This function uses quite a lot of `static` variables. I am not a fan of `statics`; I've used them here reluctantly. I would have preferred the user's code to keep a structure containing the necessary information, and to pass it into this function when necessary via the memory allocation functions. Unfortunately, the user-programmer is probably not accustomed to passing allocation information structures to memory allocation functions. Furthermore, the structure would not be needed when MEMTRACK is not defined; managing that complexity at a user-programmer level would have made use of these library functions intolerably complex. So I went with `static` variables, even though they are not thread safe. Please bear this in mind if you are a multithreading kind of person.

You'll also notice that I've initialized all the `static` variables explicitly to their appropriate zero values. Since C does this already for `static` variables, this precaution can only be either provision against a later change in storage qualifiers or incipient paranoia. I'll let you decide which.

```
int TrackMemory(MEMTRK_MSG    Msg,
                unsigned long Key,
                void *        Ptr,
                int           Size,
                char *        FileName,
                int           LineNumber)
{
  int ErrorStatus = 0;
  static FILE *fp = NULL;
  static unsigned long MemTrackIdx = 0;

  PAYLOAD EntryBuilder = {0};
  MEMTREE *NodePtr = NULL;
  unsigned long ThisKey = 0;
  PAYLOAD *EntryFinder = NULL;
  ALIGN KeyStore = {0};

  static MEMTREE *MemTree = NULL;
  static int IveBeenInitialised = 0;
  static unsigned long MaxAlloc = 0;
  static unsigned long CurrAlloc = 0;

  time_t tt = {0};
  struct tm *tmt = NULL;

  if(!IveBeenInitialised)
  {
```

The first time in, we need to open a file in which to dump the allocation reports. It's confession time again. When I first wrote this code, I opened the file in "wt" mode, meaning "create a text file." I knew that "w" would achieve the same thing, but I thought I was being thorough. In fact, I was being nonportable. Don't use "wt" when you mean "w".

Our allocation report file pointer provides a good example of how it is not always necessary to abandon a program when some resource request fails. Since we know we're in a test library, not a production system, we have a little freedom. We not only can change the destination of our output, but we can even scribble a message on stderr to let the user know we're having problems.

```
    fp = fopen(MEMTRACK_FILENAME, "w");
    if(NULL == fp)
    {
      fprintf(stderr,
              "Can't create file %s\n",
              MEMTRACK_FILENAME);
      fprintf(stderr,
              "Using stdout instead.\n");
      fp = stdout;
    }
    IveBeenInitialised = 1;
  }
```


We'd like to store the location of the line of code that was responsible for the allocation. Our wrapper macros have provided us with __FILE__ and __LINE__ information, which works well.

Storing a copy of the filename would involve us in significant overhead. We could live with that, but it's unnecessary. As long as we never try to change its contents, we can point our FileName pointer at the address represented by __FILE__ quite happily.

```
  EntryBuilder.FileName = FileName;
  EntryBuilder.LineNumber = LineNumber;

  switch(Msg)
  {
    case MEMTRK_MEMALLOC:
```

We're now recording an allocation. This involves saving the address at which the new memory block resides (from the user-programmer's point of view, not our own, so we need to correct for the extra block we use for our own purposes), the size of the block, and the key (which we allocate from an index that we increment on each allocation).

```
      EntryBuilder.Ptr = (char *)Ptr + sizeof(ALIGN);
      EntryBuilder.Size = Size;
      ThisKey = MemTrackIdx++;
```

```
        KeyStore.lu = ThisKey;
        memcpy(Ptr, &KeyStore, sizeof KeyStore);

        if(NULL == AddMemNode(&MemTree,
                              ThisKey,
                              &EntryBuilder))
        {
          fprintf(fp,
                  "ERROR in debugging code - "
                  "failed to add node to memory tree.\n");
          fflush(fp);
        }
        else
        {
```

Having successfully added a record of the allocation to the tree, we can usefully keep track of the allocations another way, too; we can count how many bytes the user thinks he has allocated and also the maximum amount of memory allocated at any one time.

```
          CurrAlloc += Size;
          if(CurrAlloc > MaxAlloc)
          {
            MaxAlloc = CurrAlloc;
          }
        }

        break;

      case MEMTRK_MEMFREE:

        NodePtr = FindMemNode(MemTree, Key);
        if(NULL != NodePtr)
        {
          EntryFinder = &NodePtr->Payload;
          CurrAlloc -= EntryFinder->Size;
          if(CurrAlloc < 0)
          {
            fprintf(fp,
                    "ERROR: More memory released "
                    "than allocated!\n");
            fflush(fp);
          }
```

```
      DeleteMemNode(&MemTree, Key);
    }
    else
    {
      /* Tried to free an entry
       * that was never allocated.
       */
      fprintf(fp,
              "Attempted to free unallocated "
              "block %p at Line %d of File %s.\n",
              EntryBuilder.Ptr,
              EntryBuilder.LineNumber,
              EntryBuilder.FileName);
      fflush(fp);
    }

    break;

  case MEMTRK_REPORT:

    fprintf(fp,
            "\nMemory Tracker Report\n");
    fprintf(fp,
            "---------------------\n\n");
```


Our report is fairly simple to write; nothing too strenuous here. It would be pleasantly convenient for the user if we were to date and time stamp the report. So we'll do that (provided `localtime` doesn't return an error, of course).

```
    tt = time(NULL);
    tmt = localtime(&tt);
    if(tmt != NULL)
    {
      char timebuffer[64] = {0};

      strftime(timebuffer,
               sizeof timebuffer,
               "%H:%M:%S %Z on %A %d %B %Y",
               tmt);
      fprintf(fp, "\n%s\n\n", timebuffer);
    }
```

```
        fprintf(fp,
                "Current Allocation: %lu byt%s.\n",
                CurrAlloc,
                CurrAlloc == 1 ? "e" : "es");

        fprintf(fp,
                "Maximum Allocation: %lu byt%s.\n",
                MaxAlloc,
                MaxAlloc == 1 ? "e" : "es");

        fprintf(fp,
                "Nodes currently allocated:\n\n");
```

To fathom out whether any memory remains allocated, we recursively walk through the tree, visiting every node. Each node represents a block of memory allocated but not yet released.

```
        WalkMemTree(MemTree, MemPrintAllocs, fp);
        if(CurrAlloc == 0)
        {
          fprintf(fp, "None! (Well done!)");
        }
        fprintf(fp, "\n");
        fflush(fp);
        break;
      case MEMTRK_DESTROY:
        DestroyMemTree(&MemTree);
```

I don't know whether you noticed, but I've been writing rather a lot of information to the log file, and I haven't checked any of the `fprintf` statements to ensure that they worked. Let's take care of that now, by calling `ferror`, so that we are informed of any problem with the output (and if you're guessing that the original code didn't bother to do this, you have far too much time on your hands):

```
        if(ferror(fp))
        {
          fprintf(stderr, "Error writing to log file.\n");
        }
        fclose(fp);
        break;
      default:
        break;
    }
```

```
  return ErrorStatus;
}

/* binary search tree functions omitted for brevity; you'll find
 * them at this point in the code, in memtrack.c on the CD-ROM
 */
```

We're done. All that remains is to discuss the tree library functions themselves.

Well, perhaps that's a little disingenuous. The tree library functions gave me the biggest trouble of all the source in this chapter. The tree functions I'd written originally were not portable and were not well suited to the sweeping changes I had to make to the code to bring it up to publishable quality. I had to rewrite them from scratch, with not a little help from Ben Pfaff and Chad Dixon (but any bugs are mine, not theirs). I'm now fairly pleased with them. I haven't published the source here because this chapter is about memory management, not trees! Of course, you can find my tree code on the CD-ROM, but please don't use it as a basis for your own tree library. Ben's implementations of red-black and AVL trees are far more suitable for that.

While you're hunting around on the CD-ROM, you'll also find a driver program that just allocates a lot of memory and then releases it. Compile with `MEMTRACK` defined if you want to track memory and without it if you don't.

Summary

Using memory correctly is a vital part of C programming. In this chapter, we have recounted many common errors in memory management, explored ways of recovering from memory allocation failures, and developed a memory leak detection program.

As applications get more complex, proper memory management becomes more and more awkward. Once we have a reasonable set of tools at our disposal for handling this, however, the task is no longer difficult. It can even be fun!

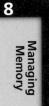

CHAPTER 9

Simulations and Controllers

by Mathew Watson

In This Chapter

Controllers are all around us. Before the existence of computers, control mechanisms were implemented in hardware. Today, with the advent of inexpensive microprocessors, software controllers are ubiquitous.

At the end of the twentieth century, people expressed surprise that elevators, cars, and heating systems would all need to be checked for Year 2000 compliance. C is often the language of choice for embedded controllers, due to its speed and compactness. Imagine a real-time system such as air-traffic control being written in COBOL in a batch environment!

The following topics are covered in this chapter:

- What a finite state machine is and how it is used.
- How to translate state diagrams into C code.
- How to simulate real-world entities. Many applications in the real-world utilize finite state machine properties.
- Why controllers are vitally important and what can happen when they go wrong.
- How more complex scenarios are simulated.

Finite State Machines Overview

A finite state machine (FSM) is, as the name suggests, a model that contains a finite number of states. At any moment in time, the machine will be in a given state. When an input is received into the machine, it can move to a different state, as shown in Figure 9.1.

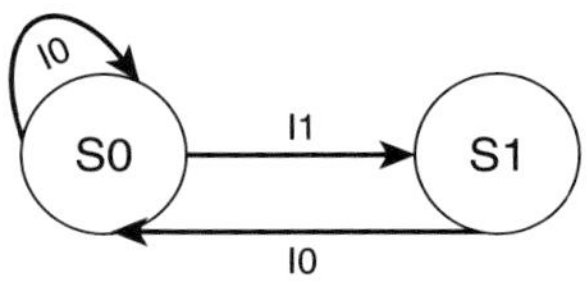

FIGURE 9.1
State transition diagram.

An input is said to cause a *transition* from one state to another. An input will not always cause this transition if, for example, the machine is already in a particular state.

Finite state machines often provide the best model for many real-world machines. Particular examples include elevators, traffic lights, and vending machines, where a discrete set of states and inputs exists.

Finite state machines are useful in the development of programs by helping to formalize the system. They also aid in maintenance and future expansion by providing an exact model of the behavior of the system. This can only be a good thing! In software development, frequently the code will reach a point where the programmer no longer understands exactly why a program works. At this stage, interactions are not fully understood and it is hard to conceptualize precisely the various states that the program moves through. Using an FSM avoids this.

Light Switch Example

Take, as an extremely simple example, the light switch. This machine has two possible states: off and on (see Figure 9.2). We will name these states S_0 and S_1. There are two possible inputs: switch-on and switch-off. These will be called I_0 and I_1.

FIGURE 9.2
A light switch has only two possible states.

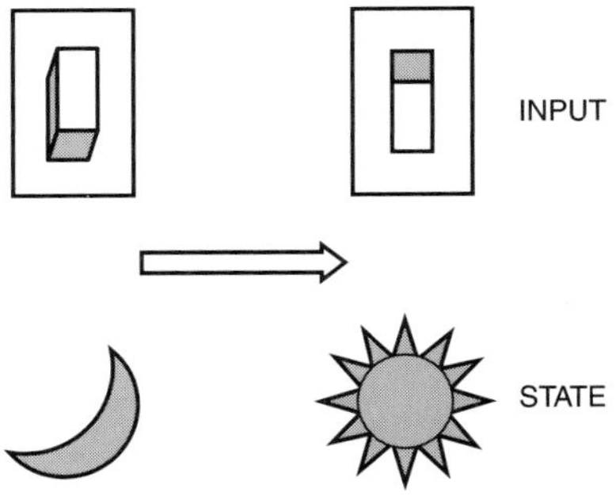

Finite state machines can be portrayed diagrammatically as shown in Figure 9.3 and in table format as shown in Table 9.1.

FIGURE 9.3
State diagram of a light switch FSM.

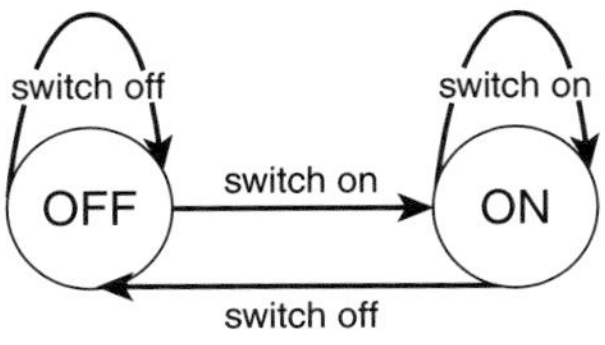

You can see in the diagram that in state S_0 (light off) the transition to state S_1 (light on) is made when input I_1 is received. Similarly, the transition from S_1 to S_0 is made when input I_0 is received.

TABLE 9.1 State Transition Table

	Input	
State	I_0	I_1
S_0	S_0	S_1
S_1	S_0	S_1

Generally, diagrams are more immediate and easier to understand than state transition tables. However, the transition table is useful for the production of C code.

Turning the FSM into Code

Now that we have the transition table, we can write the code as shown in Listing 9.1.

LISTING 9.1 LST9_1.C—Light Switch State Machine

```
/** light switch example: 2 states (off or on)
 **                        2 different inputs (switch on, switch off)
 **/

enum state { OFF,
             ON
           };

enum input { SWITCH_OFF,
             SWITCH_ON
           };

int main()
{
   enum state LightState;
   enum input LightInput;

   LightState = OFF;
   LightInput = SWITCH_ON;

   switch( LightState )
   {
      /* Light is currently OFF */
   case OFF:
      switch( LightInput )
      {
      case SWITCH_OFF:
```

LISTING 9.1 continued

```
         break;

      case SWITCH_ON:
         LightState = ON;
         break;
      }
      break;

      /* Light is currently ON */
   case ON:
      switch( LightInput )
      {
      case SWITCH_ON:
         break;

      case SWITCH_OFF:
         LightState = OFF;
         break;
      }
      break;
   }

   return 0;
}
```

At first inspection, the code appears to be overkill—all those lines to change states! However, the principle is well illustrated. When the machine is in a particular state, an input is handled according to that state, as shown in Listing 9.2.

LISTING 9.2 LST9_2.C—Light Switch State Machine Alternative Implementation

```
/* switch example: 2 states (off or on)
                            2 different inputs (turn on, turn off)
*/
enum state { OFF = 0,
             ON
           };

enum input { SWITCH_OFF = 0,
             SWITCH_ON
           };
```

LISTING 9.2 continued

```
#define NUM_STATES 2
#define NUM_INPUTS 2

int main()
{

   enum state LightState;
   enum input LightInput;

   enum state TransTable[NUM_STATES][NUM_INPUTS] = { { OFF, ON },
                                                      { OFF, ON } };

   LightState = OFF;
   LightInput = SWITCH_ON;

   LightState = TransTable[ LightState ][ LightInput ];

   return 0;
}
```

An alternative implementation would be to use a 2D array to represent the transitions.

Applications of Simulations and Controllers

Simulations are linked with controllers, except that they approach the problem from the opposite direction. Simulations are usually developed to mimic existing controller functionality. Simulations are worthwhile because of their potential to save money on real-world applications.

In mass-production areas such as oil, gas, and chemical refineries, a small efficiency improvement in one plant can result in millions of dollars saved.

Safety Critical Aspects of Controllers

Today, devices that previously were controlled by hardware and operated by human beings are under the control of software. In the case of vending machines and the like, this is no great worry. However, what if the software controls missiles, planes, or nuclear plants?

The following section illustrates some programming errors.

Common Programming Problems

Anyone who has been writing code for very long has his or her own share of coding blunder stories. Anyone who writes software in a team environment or who has to maintain another person's code soon finds his own "America's funniest coding mistakes." For example, Table 9.2 shows a few classics.

TABLE 9.2 Classic Errors

Example	*Error*
if (x=3)	Branch is always taken. Should be if (x==3)
if (x == 3);	; after the x should not be there, y = 4; y = 4 always executed
x==3;	x is not set to 3. This is perfectly legal in C. Try it!

C is a particularly unforgiving language in this respect. Other programming languages will pretty much hold your hand—C gives you enough rope to hang yourself.

Of course, there are many opportunities to minimize possible errors. Writing if(3==x) will catch accidental if (3=x) errors because it is not possible to assign a value to 3. Code reviews, thorough testing, and good programming methodologies all help.

In some cases, people have been harmed by software. In the following case, software directly caused the death of patients. Everybody in the software field should be aware of this tragic story.

The Tale of Therac-25

The Therac-25 was a medical linear accelerator designed and built in the early 1980s. It was installed in 11 hospitals in the U.S. and Canada.

The Therac-25 allowed the treatment of patients with tumors by destroying the tumor with doses of radiation. The Therac-25 had two modes of operation: an electron mode to treat shallow tissue and a photon/X-ray mode to treat deeper tissue. The two modes utilized the same beam of energy at varying power levels. In X-ray mode, the beam would operate at about 100 times the power level of that of the electron mode. This was due to the fact that a special filter target would be placed in front of the beam, causing X-rays to be produced.

It should be obvious that the modes and power levels are mutually exclusive. Without the X-ray mode filter being in place, the patient would receive massive doses of radiation. In previous linear accelerators, hardware interlocks existed in the design to prevent just such an occurrence. With the Therac-25, the software provided this safety functionality.

Unfortunately, on several occasions the X-ray mode filter was not in place, which resulted in massive radiation overdoses and the death of patients. The fault lay in a race condition whereby the user would accidentally set the mode to X-ray, which would default the energy level to high. The user could then correct the mode, setting it to electron. However, because of the time taken for the mechanical parts to move, the user's correction would be completed before the mechanics had finished moving.

This resulted in the energy level being left at high, and the X-ray filter not being in position. A second bug was later found. Treatment was allowed to proceed when a particular variable was set to 0. This signified that both the mode (filter targets) had been placed in position and the energy level had been set. This variable was incremented every time a specific subroutine was called during the setup phase of treatment. However, the variable was stored in only one byte (eight bits) and the subroutine would be frequently called. This caused an overflow within the variable, setting it to zero. If the operator started treatment at the moment that overflow occurred, the full beam strength would be given without any filter.

You can find a full, detailed account of the Therac-25 by Nancy Leveson, University of Washington, in *IEEE Computer,* Vol. 26, No. 7, July 1993.

The Moral of the Story

Take time to think about the way you write software and then remember that most software engineers probably code the same way. Then remember that this code is flying aircraft, treating patients, and controlling missiles.

Simulating a Simple Computer

In a way, a computer can be thought of as an advanced finite state machine. It has various states and inputs that determine the transition from one state to another. For a more complex example of simulations, let's simulate a simple computer with a cut-down 8-bit processor.

This computer will use the classic Von Neumann architecture. It has a shared memory for instructions and data (see Figure 9.4) and an ALU (Arithmetic Logic Unit).

Memory

For simplicity, this computer will have 65,536 bytes of memory. You may not be aware that in C a byte is not necessarily eight bits! By the ANSI standard, it is defined in `<limits.h>` as `CHAR_BIT` bits. `CHAR_BIT` is guaranteed to be at least eight bits but is permitted to be more. In most compilers it *is* eight bits, but it is important not to take this for granted. However, for the following simulation one byte equals eight bits.

FIGURE 9.4
Architecture of the simulated computer.

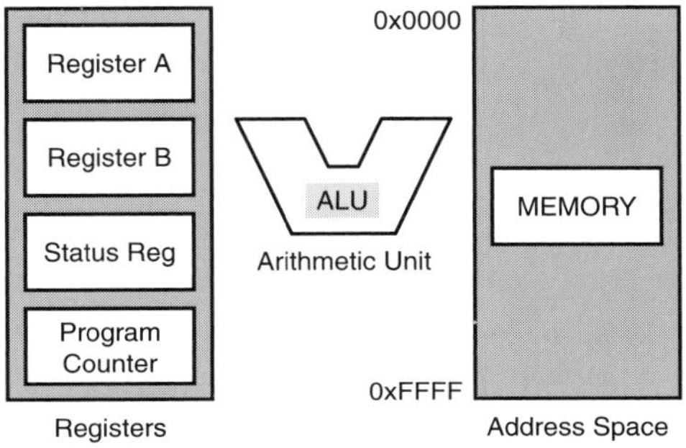

Registers

Our computer will have four registers (see Table 9.3). Again, this will keep the complexity to a minimum.

TABLE 9.3 Simulated Computer Instruction Set

Register	*Description*
Register A	An 8-bit general-purpose register.
Register B	An 8-bit general-purpose register.
PC Register	The program counter. This is a read-only file (from the user's perspective) register.
Status Register	This will hold the status of arithmetic operations, and will be the basis for deciding branch instructions.

For the computer simulation, the number of instructions will be kept to a minimum. However, even with a limited number of instructions, it will allow us to simulate the basic fundamentals of all computers.

Moreover, as with many things in computing, the phrase "what goes around, comes around" holds true. The first processors had very limited instruction sets. Then designers created processors with larger and larger instruction sets (Complex Instruction Set Chip, or CISC). The downside to this was that most programmers used only a small subset of the commands, and more commands led to a decrease in overall performance.

This introduced the Reduced Instruction Set Chip (RISC), which had (just like the first processors) a limited instruction set. The difference was that these new chips were designed to execute their small number of instructions in a short space of time. This was possible because fewer commands meant that the chips were more efficient.

In Table 9.4, memory addresses are 16 bits long (two bytes) and immediate, constant data is eight bits long (one byte).

TABLE 9.4 Simulated Computer Instruction Set

Instruction	*Argument*	*Description*
`LOADA`	Memory Address	Loads the contents of memory into the A register
`LOADB`	Memory Address	Loads the contents of memory into the B register
`LOADAI`	8-bit constant	Sets the A register = 8-bit constant
`LOADBI`	8-bit constant	Sets the B register = 8-bit constant
`NOP`		No operation for that cycle
`STOREA`	Memory Address	Stores the contents of register A into memory
`STOREB`	Memory Address	Stores the contents of register B into memory
`ADDA`	8-bit constant	Adds 8-bit constant to contents of register A
`ADDB`	8-bit constant	Adds 8-bit constant to contents of register B
`COMPAI`	8-bit constant	Compares register A with constant and sets the status of the status register
`COMPAI`	8-bit constant	Compares register B with constant and sets the status of the status register
`BLT`	Memory Address	Program jumps to address if status register < 0
`BGT`	Memory Address	Program jumps to address if status register > 0
`JUMP`	Memory Address	Program unconditionally jumps to memory address
`PRINTA`		Prints the contents of A on the console in hex format
`BREAK`		Tells the system to stop processing

This list covers the majority (functionality-wise) of the basic instructions used in most eight-bit processors. Although simple by today's standards, this was state-of-the-art in microprocessor technology in the 1970s.

Building the C Code

Now for a little bit of design. We will need the simulator to have the following functionality:

- To be able to read assembly code listing files and assemble them into memory

- To be able to run a program in memory
- To be able to step one instruction at a time through the program
- To be able to examine the contents of the registers
- To be able to examine the contents of memory (hex dump)
- To disassemble contents of memory (view assembly language)

For this simulator, we will have a command-driven interface (as opposed to menu-based).

Reading in the Assembly Listing

The assembly listing will be formed of the instructions in Table 9.4 in addition to comments and labels. The assembler for the simulation will be partially symbolic (that is, it will use `JUMP Label`, not `JUMP 0x00FF`) so the assembly user will not have to worry about calculating address offsets and the like (see Listing 9.3).

LISTING 9.3 LST9_3.ASM—Example Assembly Listing

```
* This is a comment, ignore me
:Loop1
 LOADAI    0
ADDA        1
COMPAI    9
BLT         Loop1
END
```

Comments should be stripped out. When a label is encountered, its memory address should be noted in a symbol table for later reference. Each instruction encountered should be entered into memory. We will add the restriction that references to labels can only be backward; that is, only those labels that have been declared (see Listing 9.4).

LISTING 9.4 LST9_4.C—Type Definitions

```
typedef enum {NONE, IMMEDIATE, ADDRESS} OPERAND_TYPE;

typedef struct
{
   char*         InstructionName;
   OPERAND_TYPE  Operand;
   unsigned char MachineCode;

} INSTRUCTION;
```

There are two possible approaches to parsing the data. The first is to parse each line via the use of individual string compares against each instruction name:

```
if ( 0 == strcmp (Token, "LOADB"))
```

Or, alternatively, to hash the `Token` via some method that would guarantee uniqueness for the domain of instructions and then perform a switch on the hash number. We would write several lines of code in order to handle each instruction. This approach gives maximum flexibility because each instruction can have custom operations associated with it. The disadvantage is that, in this case, very similar operations are performed for each instruction and thus almost identical code has to be written and maintained in multiple places.

The second approach is to maintain the instruction list in a data table, and then to write code to loop through the table. This means that there is less code to write and maintain.

The preceding tradeoff is a frequent occurrence in C programming. Programmers often find that they must decide between the flexibility of having individual code streams for each scenario, which results in duplication of code, or opting for a more generic solution that has less flexibility but results in less code to write and maintain.

In general, it is easier to write less code and maintain more data than the converse. However, this is not always true—the best approach can be chosen only with experience. See Listing 9.5.

LISTING 9.5 `LST9_5.C`—Instruction List

```
static INSTRUCTION InstructionTable[] = {"LOADA",  ADDRESS,   LOADA,
                                         "LOADB",  ADDRESS,   LOADB,
                                         "LOADAI", IMMEDIATE, LOADAI,
                                         "LOADBI", IMMEDIATE, LOADBI,
                                         "NOP",    NONE,      NOP,
                                         "STOREA", ADDRESS,   STOREA,
                                         "STOREB", ADDRESS,   STOREB,
                                         "ADDA",   IMMEDIATE, ADDA,
                                         "ADDB",   IMMEDIATE, ADDB,
                                         "COMPAI", IMMEDIATE, COMPAI,
                                         "COMPBI", IMMEDIATE, COMPBI,
                                         "BLT",    ADDRESS,   BLT,
                                         "BGT",    ADDRESS,   BGT,
                                         "JUMP",   ADDRESS,   JUMP,
                                         "PRINTA", NONE,      PRINTA
                                         "BREAK", NONE,      BREAK };
```

In Listings 9.4 and 9.5, the data tables for the instruction list are defined. The instruction table consists of a three-element structure: the instruction string, the type of instruction, and the code that will be inserted into memory (see Listing 9.6).

LISTING 9.6 LST9_6.C—Parsing the Assembly Listing

```
while (NULL != fgets (Line, MAX_LINE, Fp ))
{
    LineNo++;

    if ( '*' == Line[0] ¦¦ '#' == Line[0] ¦¦ '\n' == Line[0] )
    {
        /* discard comments */
        continue;
    }
    /* parse the line */
    Token = strtok (Line, Seps);

    if (NULL == Token)
    {
        continue;
    }

    /* check to see if this a label, if so then add to the symbol table */
    if (':' == Token[0])
    {
        Token++;
        Insert_Token (Token, SymbolTable, MemLocation);
    }
    else
    {
        /* assemble the token into memory */
        Instruction = FindInstruction (Token);
        Memory [MemLocation] = Instruction.MachineCode;
        MemLocation++;

        if (IMMEDIATE == Instruction.Operand ¦¦
             ADDRESS == Instruction.Operand)
        {
            /* Get the operand */
            Token = strtok (Line, Seps);
            if (NULL == Token)
            {
```

LISTING 9.6 continued

```
                printf("Error\n");
                break;
            }
        }

        /* We need to put one extra byte into memory */
        if ( IMMEDIATE == Instruction.Operand)
        {
            Memory [MemLocation] = strtol (Token, NULL, 16);
            MemLocation++;
        }

        /* We need to put two extra bytes into memory */
        if ( ADDRESS == Instruction.Operand)
        {
            Symbol = Find_Token (Token);
            /* the machine is big endian */
            Memory [MemLocation] = (Symbol.Location >> 8) & 0xFF;
            MemLocation++;
            Memory [MemLocation] = SymbolLocation &0xFF;
            MemLocation++;
        }
    }

}
```

Listing 9.6 shows how the assembly input file is to be parsed. Each line consists of either a label or an instruction along with optional comments. If a label is encountered, it is inserted into a symbol table along with the location in memory that it occupies.

The starting memory location is specified by the user (it defaults to hex 0x100).

Every instruction occupies one byte of memory. An instruction can have an optional operand, which can occupy one byte (in the case of `IMMEDIATE` types) or two bytes (in the case of `ADDRESS` types). An instruction with the operand type of `NONE` does not take an operand and therefore will occupy only one byte in total.

An `ADDRESS` is expected to be a label symbol. If the symbol has not already been encountered, this is flagged as an error.

The symbol table insertion effectively implements a version of `strdup`. This function is present in many C compilers, yet it is not an ANSI function. However, it is so useful that most programmers have their own version if it is not available. Note that the return from `malloc` should not be cast. Many C programmers write the following line:

```
x = (TYPE*) malloc ( n * sizeof(TYPE) );
```

However, the return type from `malloc` is `void *`, so there is no need to cast. Moreover, casting can be dangerous because it will mask the fact the you have forgotten to `#include <stdlib.h>` by casting away the default return type of `int`. This is a major difference between C and C++, where the return from `malloc` *must* be cast.

Running the Program

This is where the simulation really gets going. Basically, it means maintaining the four registers A, B, PC (Program Counter), and SR (Status Register) and reading and writing to memory. We really do get to "play computer" Again, there is the decision whether to use data tables to drive the program or to use custom code for each instruction. In this case, custom code is probably the better choice.

The user specifies the start address (in hexadecimal) of the first instruction. It is then merely a case of setting the Program Counter (PC) to that address. The instruction at the PC address is loaded, then decoded (via a switch statement), and the required operations are performed.

In its current state, the simulation will stop when it hits a `BREAK` statement or it encounters a statement that it does not recognize. Of course, in most real eight-bit microprocessors, this would result in undefined behavior, with the internal state of the system running wild.

Stepping Through Instructions

The ability to step one instruction at a time is useful, whether at assembly language level or at high-level language level. Fortunately, by modular design, we get this functionality almost for free. Both running and stepping use a common execution function, so we can minimize the amount of code duplication.

Examining the Contents of the Registers

This simply prints the contents of the registers A, B, PC, and SR.

Examining the Contents of Memory

Another simple function. This prints the contents of memory, 8 bytes per output line. It is given a start and end address.

Disassembling Contents of Memory

This is really just the opposite of option 1 (reading in a file and assembling it into memory). Given a start and end address, the function decodes an instruction in memory. This can be useful so that jump addresses can be inspected because the labels are resolved to addresses. For example, the line

```
JUMP    LABEL
```

will be transformed into

```
JUMP  1F0A
```

Tying It All Together

All the functions can now be tied together using a simple command line parser that utilizes `strtok`. If the ANSI standard library function `strtok` isn't already a tool that you use, it would be an excellent idea to familiarize yourself with the function. You will find it in `<string.h>`.

Summary

From this chapter, you should have a good ground-level understanding of finite state machines and state diagrams, at least enough to program simple examples. This chapter covered how simulations are used in industry.

It then covered the applications that controllers are used in and the very real potential that they have for harm. To demonstrate a more complex example of simulations, this chapter also covered the simulating of a simple Von Neumann computer.

Hopefully, you have gained an appreciation of the many ways C is useful in simulating real-world applications and, moreover, the way that C programs actually control real-world components.

CHAPTER 10

Recursion

In This Chapter

by Peter Seebach

"To understand recursion, you must first understand recursion." Most programmers have heard this expression. There's a certain amount of truth to it, but in this chapter, I'll try to help you get past the initial hump and start using recursion. This chapter gives you some exposure, not just to the basic questions (such as "What is recursion?"), but to ways of thinking about programs that will help you see whether recursion is the right solution to a problem.

The example code for this chapter, unlike the code in many of these chapters, isn't especially reusable. There's no need for a recursion library or other stock code for use in other recursive algorithms; instead, this sample code focuses on giving you hands-on experience with some of the classic examples, along with diagnostic output to let you watch how they work. (The one exception is an implementation of a function found in some C libraries, but which is not required by the standard; it's useful enough in recursive contexts to be worth supplying.)

This chapter covers

- How to implement recursive algorithms—This is pretty easy in C, but it never hurts to see it explained.
- How recursion works—We'll look at examples of different kinds of recursive algorithms, including some that are fairly inefficient.
- Some common pitfalls of recursive code—Not everything should be implemented recursively, and some recursive implementations are particularly inefficient.

What Is Recursion?

It's very easy to describe recursion, but it's very hard to explain it. The descriptions in this chapter might not make sense at first; give them a while to sink in. Play with the examples. Don't expect them to seem perfectly rational at first. Recursive code can be really hard to understand and can have a lot of surprising side effects. It's no surprise that a lot of the entries in the International Obfuscated C Code Contest are heavily, even abusively, recursive.

Note

The International Obfuscated C Code Contest, as the name suggests, is an annual contest where you write the weirdest possible code to perform the most mundane of tasks. You can find their Web site at `www.ioccc.org`.

Simply put, recursion is the process of a function calling itself. In C, this is really simple to do. You already know how to write a program in which a function calls another function, as shown in the most famous C program ever:

```
#include <stdio.h>

int
main(void) {
    printf("hello, world!\n");
    return 0;
}
```

In some languages, you have to do a lot of extra work to call a function if it will end up calling itself, even indirectly. In C, you don't. For instance, a particularly trivial example:

```
unsigned int
recurse_n_times(unsigned int n) {
    if (n == 0)
        return 0;
    else return recurse_n_times(n - 1) + 1;
}
```

This function returns its argument. But what a torturous path it takes! When you pass it a number greater than zero, the function calls itself that many times, only to end up returning the value you originally passed it.

This is not a particularly realistic example—no one would actually write this code in a real program—but it shows how easy it is to implement recursion in C. Quite simply, you don't have to "implement" recursion, it's just a language feature.

Getting beyond C in particular, recursion is the process of answering a question by answering a simpler version of the same question. How does this help you? You might have a difficult task to perform, but if you can easily break it down into a series of simpler tasks, and each of those can be easily broken down into still-simpler tasks, you can end up solving the "difficult" problem without ever actually doing anything difficult.

That's really it. Unfortunately, this simple concept can be hard to get the hang of. So, let's see some examples.

Factorials: A Traditional Example

Let's start with the traditional short example: a factorial function. (We'll see this one again, so watch carefully; if this doesn't make sense now, you might have a hard time with later examples referring back to it.)

For those who haven't encountered this term before, the *factorial of x* (written *x!*) is *x* times *x-1* times *x-2*... until you reach 1. Another way to write it is

```
x! = x * (x-1)!
```

with the special exception that

```
0! = 1
```

(And, as a side effect, it turns out that *1!*, being *1*0!*, is just 1.)

For instance, *4!* is *4*(3!)*, which is *4*(3*(2!))*, which is *4*(3*(2*(1!)))*. This is *(4*3*2*1)*, or 24. *5!* comes out to *5*4!*, or 120. As you can see, the value of *n!* is defined in terms of another factorial. This lends itself to a recursive implementation as we see in Listing 10.1.

LISTING 10.1 Factorial Function

```
01    long factorial(int x) {
02        if (x == 1)
03            return 1;
04        return x * factorial(x - 1);
05    }
```

How does this work? Let's look at what happens with factorial(4), as we trace through the code. (If you haven't gotten into the habit of tracing through your code "by hand," this is a great time to start; it makes recursion a lot more comprehensible.) It all starts when we call factorial(4).

We start on line 1, in the invocation of factorial(4). We get to line 2, and x is not 1, so we get to line 4, where we will return 4 * factorial(x - 1). Calculating this requires us to compute factorial(3).

We start factorial(3) on line 1. Again, x is not 1, so we will return 3 times factorial(2). That means we start another invocation.

We start factorial(2) on line 1. Again, when we get to line 2, x is not 1, so we will return 2 times factorial(1). We start that invocation.

We start factorial(1). This time, x *is* 1, so we just return 1.

Back on line 4 of factorial(2), we take that 1, multiply it by 2, and pass the result back up.

Back on line 4 of factorial(3), we take that 2, multiply it by 3, and pass the result back up.

Back on line 4 of factorial(4), we take that 6, multiply it by 4, and get our final result (24), which is the return value we started computing way back when.

And there we have it! Exactly the number I put in the previous paragraph, so we know the code must be right. (Authors don't make mistakes.)

What's really happening here? Let's introduce a term you've probably heard before: *stack*. A stack is really just any data structure that lets you push values and then pop the most recent values back off the stack. In C, people generally think of the sequence of functions calling other functions as occurring on a stack. (On some computers, there's actually a special region of memory called the stack, which is used to hold automatic variables, return values, and other parts of the C function call sequence. Others do this in other ways, but we don't care; it always *acts* like a stack.)

Recursion, in C, takes advantage of the *implicit* allocation of stack resources to handle nested function calls. You don't have to specifically ask for memory to hold the intermediate results of your calculation, you don't have to name variables, you just write your definition out, and you get the results you want.

For instance, looking back at our factorial(n) example, you'll notice that we end up with a handful of values that must be being stored somewhere—the multipliers that are used in the chain of returns at the end of the operation. Each

```
return n * factorial(n - 1);
```

statement is "storing" the local value of n on the stack. The nice thing about this is, no matter how many levels deep your function goes, you don't have to explicitly create variables with names such as "n5," "n6," and "n7," and you don't have to declare some huge array, or allocate it with `malloc()`; you just call yourself, and let the compiler sweat the details. (Later, we'll see what the code might look like if you allocated the array yourself.)

Often, the series of function calls from the top of the program (for example, `main()`) to the current point is referred to as a *call stack*, and the number of functions in it is referred to as *depth*, or *stack depth*.

Fibonacci: Another Traditional Example

Another popular example is the Fibonacci sequence. It's not a very "clean" example, though; read on before you actually write code like this. The Fibonacci sequence is one where each term is the sum of the two preceding terms. You start out with a pair of ones, and the sequence goes "1, 1, 2, 3, 5, 8, 13, 21, 34, ...". Let's see the naive recursive implementation in Listing 10.2.

LISTING 10.2 Fibonacci Sequence

```
int fib(int x) {
    if (x == 1 || x == 2)
        return 1;
    return fib(x - 2) + fib(x - 1);
}
```

Mathematically, this is precise and correct; indeed, this is how mathematicians are likely to describe the function. However, it turns out, in C, to be a horrible abuse of recursion. Why? Let's say you call `fib(9)`. The first thing it does is calculate `fib(7)`, which in turn calculates `fib(6)` and `fib(5)`. When it's finished with `fib(7)`, it calculates `fib(8)`. What does `fib(8)` do? It recalculates `fib(6)`, and then it recalculates `fib(7)`, which, of course, recalculates `fib(6)`, too. In short, it spends a huge amount of extra time calculating results it's already calculated. We'll analyze this in more detail later, but be aware that this algorithm is genuinely awful from a performance standpoint. (If all you want to do is *describe* the Fibonacci sequence, of course, it works just fine.)

Note

If you want to look at more examples of recursive algorithms right now, see Chapter 13, "Rapid Sorting Techniques." If you want a slightly heavier example, you can look at Chapter 19, "Expression Parsing and Evaluation." (Parsing is actually one of the best examples, but a parser is a heavy enough piece of code that I'd rather not duplicate the effort here.)

How to Use Recursion

Throughout this discussion, I'll assume you've read (or you will read) Chapter 3, "Optimization," which has a fair amount of information on performance analysis. We'll use fairly broad terms here, and when we do use the more technical terms, we won't go into a discussion of them; that material is covered elsewhere.

The first thing you have to do when writing a recursive algorithm is be sure that you really want to write a recursive algorithm. Sometimes, the best thing to do is not to write the recursive code in the first place. Recursion is a neat technique; it's not the only one worth knowing, though.

Many recursive algorithms will be characterized by a "divide and conquer" approach. At each layer of recursion, you should see a dramatic reduction in the size of the problem you're trying to solve. This isn't necessary, but it's generally a good sign.

Start by getting a feel for what you're trying to do. How are you solving this problem? If the first thing you think of doing is allocating some kind of stack to store temporary results, you are probably looking at a recursive operation.

Example Usage: Binary Search

An example of a reasonable use of recursion is the "binary search" algorithm. This algorithm takes a sorted array and finds a given value in the array (if it's present). The algorithm works like this. In the array you're looking at, compare the middle value to your search key. If you find it, you're finished. If your key is greater than the middle value, you search in the part of the array "above" the middle value; otherwise, you search below. Eventually, you get to an array with one item; if it's not your key, your key isn't in the array.

So, how would we write this? Let's assume we're just doing integers, and we're given an array of integers, the size of the array, and a search value. What should we return? My preference is to return a pointer to the member of the array we were searching for, or a null pointer if we didn't find it. So, the function must start out something similar to what you see in Listing 10.3.

LISTING 10.3 Search Function

```
/* search:  finds 'key' if it's in a[0]..a[asize-1] */
int *
search(int a[], int asize, int key) {
    int mid = asize / 2;

    /* sanity checks */
    if (a == NULL || asize == 0) {
        return NULL;
    }
    if (key > a[mid]) {
        /* key is greater than middle element */
        return search(a + mid + 1, asize - (mid + 1), key);
    }
    if (key < a[mid]) {
        /* key is less than middle element */
        return search(a, mid, key);
    }
```

LISTING 10.3 continued

```
18        /* not greater than, not less than - must be equal to! */
19        return &a[mid];
20    }
```

How does this work? If we end up trying to search in an array of zero elements, we return a null pointer; there can't be a match in that array. If you pass a null pointer, the search routine politely indicates failure, rather than trying to dereference it. Then, we have three possibilities:

First, we might have found our key; in this case, we return a pointer to it.

Second, the key may be greater than the middle element. In this case, we start with the element "after" the middle element. Since we're excluding elements `[0]` through `[mid]` of our array, the remainder must be `(mid + 1)` fewer elements than the original array. (Before you accept this, check the conditions out in your head. What happens if `mid` was the top element of the array? It works out, but you should always check things like this.)

Third, the key may be less than the middle element. In this case, there will be `mid` elements left (they're `[0]` through `[mid - 1]`). This was the source of a bug in my code before I tested it; without really thinking, I decided to subtract `mid + 1` from the array size again. This works with odd-sized arrays, but if the array has an even number of elements, this ends up skipping the element right below the original one. Again, check your boundary conditions. In this case, using `mid` as the size of the new array is easier to understand, too; since arrays go from `0` to `n-1` in C, if `a[mid]` is just outside the array, it's an array of `[mid]` items.

Now, let's trace this through a "real" execution. I've included the pathetically simple sample program as code on the CD. Open your CD to the little shiny spot about 3/4 inch out from the inside edge (this might vary in production); your file should be called `search.c`. Got that? Good. We're going to follow a binary search through an array. For the benefit of all three readers without CD-ROM drives, I'll reproduce the array here:

```
int a[] = { 0, 2, 4, 5, 7, 9, 10, 12 };
```

You'll notice the array is sorted. This search *will not work* if the array is not sorted! It might behave unpredictably, or it might get lost. It shouldn't do anything really destructive, but it will probably not be a very effective search algorithm; it might report that your key value isn't in the array, even if it is in the array.

So, what happens when we search for, say, 8? (Chorus: "We don't find it!") Well, that's right, we won't find it. But where do we look? We look in Figure 10.1.

We start in `search()`, with the array listed above as the array argument. `asize` is 8, and `key` is also 8. On line 04, we calculate `mid`, which will be `asize/2`, or 4. The sanity checks on line 7 don't stop us this time; we were passed an array, and it's not empty. So, we compare the key value to the "middle" object of the array. In this case, `a[mid]` is 7, so we go into the body of the `if` statement on line 10. Line 12 is

```
return search(a + mid + 1, asize - (mid + 1), key);
```

so we do just that. "`a + mid + 1`" is the address of the first element above `a[mid]`. Because we're removing `a[mid]` and all the elements below it from consideration, we will have `(mid + 1)` fewer elements left to search. This brings us into the next layer of our search.

FIGURE 10.1
Searching successively smaller parts of an array.

```
int a[] = { 0, 2, 4, 5, 7, 9, 10, 12 };

  [0   2   4   5   7   9    10   12]
                  mid

   0   2   4   5   7  [9    10   12]
                            mid

   0   2   4   5   7  [9]   10   12
                      mid

   0   2   4   5   7   9    10   12
```

At this layer, we have an array of 3 elements, ranging from 9 to 12. Because the new `asize` is 3, `mid` is 1. (You'll notice that, because we're using integer arithmetic, we round down. This is why some of the code looks asymmetrical.) Again, we pass through the sanity checks, so we compare `key` to the middle element, which is 10. This time, it's smaller, so we go past the first check, and end up following the body of the `if` statement on line 14. This time, we make the call to search on line 16. We'll start with the bottom of the array in the same place, but we'll only have the elements below `mid` in it, when we start a new invocation of `search()`.

Now we have an array of one element, starting with 9. `asize` is 1, so `mid` is zero. That means we end up looking at the "0th" element of the array: the only element it has. We compare `key` (still 8) to it. 8 is less than 9, so we try the same search again, but with `asize` of zero.

This time, our sanity check "fails." There are no elements left to search in, so we return a null pointer.

The higher-level search (in an array of one element) passes the null pointer back up.

The even-higher-level search (in an array of three elements) also passes the null pointer back up.

Finally, our initial search in the whole array returns the same null pointer. We're finished! We have found that the value 8 does not occur in the array.

Neat, huh? You'll notice that each search through the array had to handle about half as many elements as the previous one. This is why binary search is efficient; it's also why it's reasonable to implement it as a recursive function.

This is a "natural" application of recursion. At each stage, when you get around to calling `search()` again, you're doing exactly what you were doing at the top level—looking for a key in an array of known size. Because of this, we can keep using the same logic on smaller and smaller chunks of data, until we're finished.

Note

A "natural" application may not be the most appropriate one; this is an obvious way to write a binary search, but it may not be optimally efficient. It's a good example, not necessarily a good engineering decision.

The factorial example given at the beginning of the chapter doesn't make the same kind of sense. Why? Partially, because we aren't really *doing* anything at each level of recursion; we're just doing something over and over, without really "partitioning" the material we're working on. (You'll see more about this later in the chapter, when we talk about converting recursive implementations to iterative ones.)

How Not to Use Recursion

Restraint is sometimes the best answer. There are situations where, although recursion initially seems like a good idea, it's not. The Fibonacci sequence is a great example for this; although it does have the "recursive" trait, which is that each number is obtained by looking at "smaller" versions of the same problem, it looks at each one a number of times.

So, let's look at `fib1.c`. The `fib()` function has had a counter embedded in it. This way, we can see how much calculation we do. Before you run this, do some estimates. How many calls to `fib()` do you think will be made for `fib(10)`?

As you can see (if you've run the test program), the growth is fairly rapid; it rapidly gets to be much, much, larger than can possibly be rational. So, this is probably a bad candidate for a recursive implementation. (Later, we'll see ways to implement it so it won't have this problem.) If you're patient, try calculating `fib(40)` or so, but be aware that it can take a fairly long time. (By the time you read this, of course, processors will be faster; you might need to try `fib(50)` to see a substantial delay.)

There's another reason not to use recursive solutions for some problems, but it's much harder to quantify. Some problems simply aren't logically recursive. You might be able to pound them into working with a recursive algorithm, but the algorithm will always be a little ugly.

"Ugly." Wow, that's a really precise, technical-sounding term. Unfortunately, after a lot of talking with other programmers (and even a few non-programmers), I've found that most of us don't really *have* a clear set of rules for this. Good recursion is like good art; you know it when you see it.

One way of looking at it is to say that the underlying rule is that recursion makes sense when the recursive calls are each solving part of the "higher-level" instance that called them. It doesn't make sense at all if this is not the case. This won't always work, but it's a good rule.

An example: Someone once posted, to Usenet, an input-grabbing function that was implemented recursively. It looked like this:

```
void
read_input(void) {
    if (read_line()) {
        put_line_in_buffer();
        read_input();
    }
}
```

This just looks wrong to me. Why? Because the new call to `read_input()` isn't solving part of the higher-level problem; it's solving *another* problem just like the first one; this calls for iteration, not recursion. Even the awful Fibonacci example doesn't seem as confused as this. The `read_input()` function probably should have been written like this:

```
void
read_input(void) {
    while (read_line())
        put_line_in_buffer();
}
```

This way, we aren't creating a gigantic call stack for a long input file. It's still hard to quantify why this matters, especially if you know your input file is small; you'll have to develop a feel for this from your own experience. Just keep an eye out for things that don't really get simpler when you write them recursively.

Note

As mentioned earlier, function calls are implemented using some kind of a stack. There is no portable way of controlling the size of the stack, or even finding out if the next function call will fail because of running out of stack space. If you run out of stack space, the OS will probably just pull the plug on your program—if you're lucky. You don't generally have to worry about running out of stack space with normal function calls, but it becomes a possibility with recursive algorithms that go to a ridiculous depth, like the input-reading example.

That's usually *not* a real concern with an algorithm like binary sort, because even if you have as many as four billion elements in your array, you'll go to a depth of only $\log_2 n = 32$.

Understanding Recursion

Okay, now that we've got a broad overview, let's get into some detail. At the end of this section, you should have a good feel for how recursion really works.

One of the most important things to know, however, is that compilers will often do a fair amount of magic to make recursive programs more efficient, so all you know about how it "really" works won't tell you what actually happens inside the CPU. It just helps you understand what you're doing and what you might have wrong.

Another Example: Euclid's Algorithm

Let's add a couple of examples to our collection, and study them. The first is Euclid's algorithm for calculating the greatest common divisor of two numbers. Quick math refresher: The *greatest common divisor* of two numbers is the largest integer which divides both without any remainder. A sample implementation can be seen in Listing 10.4.

LISTING 10.4 Euclid's Algorithm

```
int
gcd(int x, int y) {
    if (x < y) {
        return gcd(y, x);
    } else if ((x % y) != 0) {
        return gcd(y, x % y);
```

LISTING 10.4 continued

```
    } else {
        return y;
    }
}
```

Since the result has to divide both numbers without a remainder, it doesn't matter which order we pass them in, but the algorithm likes to know which is larger. So, before we get into the real recursive part, we "recurse" calling `gcd()` with the values swapped. This is probably silly; we could just as well have written code to swap them in place, as follows:

```
if (x < y) {
    int tmp;
    tmp = x;
    x = y;
    y = tmp;
}
```

However, it turns out that this doesn't make a big difference. Although this isn't really an elegant use for recursion, it's shorter to write, and it's very clear that it won't add a lot of layers of recursion to our algorithm; after this, we'll always be sure that `x` starts out greater than `y`.

So, after we handle that, we end up with two cases. In one case, `y` divides `x` evenly; in this case, it's obviously their greatest common divisor. In the other case, there's a remainder. Here's where it gets cool: It turns out that, in that case, the greatest common divisor of the smaller number and the remainder are the same as the greatest common divisor of the smaller number and the larger number. Since we know that the remainder `(x % y)` is always strictly smaller than `y`, `gcd(y, x % y)` is guaranteed to have the property that the first argument is larger. So, we recurse.

The version of this program on the CD is a little more complicated, but all it really does is show you what recursion depth it's at when it's calling `gcd()`. This helps you get a picture for how the recursive algorithm is really working.

Example output is shown in Listing 10.5.

LISTING 10.5 Recursion Depth

```
two numbers? 25 15
calling gcd(25, 15):
 remainder 10, calling gcd(15, 10)
  remainder 5, calling gcd(10, 5)
   remainder 0, returning 5
```

LISTING 10.5 continued

```
  returning 5
 returning 5
```

You can establish for yourself that the output is what you should expect. Try this on a number of inputs; you will notice that the recursion rarely gets very deep.

Tail Recursion

Now, let's revisit our early "factorial" example. This example isn't especially favorable to recursion; it's really an iterative task. So, let's start by looking at the "simple" version, pretty much copied from the beginning of the chapter. However, we've added a variable named `count` to see how many levels of iteration we'll get. (The astute reader will already know what it will come out as.)

This example clearly "works"—it doesn't get nearly the kind of geometric growth that the Fibonacci calculator does—but it doesn't have the "homing in" feature that the binary search does, or that the GCD calculator does. The problem is that you can never "subdivide" the factorial program; you always end up going down the whole stack anyway.

This brings us to the definition of *tail recursion*, which is a special case where there's a single call to the recursive function at the end of that same function. (In fact, you'll notice that the GCD example works for this too, but it's not as clear-cut an advantage, there.)

Tail Recursion Elimination

In fact, many modern C compilers have fairly advanced optimization rules to cover tail recursion and are able to eliminate it with some consistency. Some don't, and you can do it yourself if you want to. Eliminating tail recursion involves transforming the function from one that calls itself to one that shoves variables around a little and jumps back to its start. Let's look at a nonrecursive factorial calculator.

This function is exactly the same as the previous one, except that it never calls itself; it just jumps back to the beginning. I used a `goto` rather than an explicit loop, to call attention to the fact that the compiler doesn't necessarily see this as a "loop" in the same way that it sees a `for` or `while` statement as a "loop." Certainly, a future reader of your code will see them differently. (In fact, you'd normally use a loop, but this is example code, not code for maintenance.)

You'll notice that suddenly there's no real question of recursion depth; we just accumulate values until something happens. Of course, you can measure "iterations," but since we aren't allocating new storage with every iteration, it's not as much a concern as depth might be.

You can do this to other functions, too. For instance, look at `gcd2.c` on the CD. The same thing is done to the `gcd` function—we convert it to use `goto` instead of calling itself. Again, it's the same until you're "done," at which point, instead of returning a value up the whole chain, you just return it directly to the caller. Again, we've replaced depth with iterations; code which used to call itself a number of times now goes through a loop a number of times (in this case, the same number).

Of course, this isn't code you'd want to write for real use; maintainers will lynch you if you use `goto` like this. Instead, you'd probably want to write a "proper" iterative version. So, let's look at those iterative versions.

With the `count` variable taken out, the factorial function is about the same size it used to be (see Listing 10.6).

LISTING 10.6 Rewritten Factorial Function

```
long
factorial(int x) {
    long accumulator = 1;
    while (x > 1) {
        accumulator *= x--;
    }
    return accumulator;
}
```

You'll notice that the algorithm really still does the same thing: If `x` is greater than one, we multiply (x-1 factorial) by `x`. However, in this case, we do it in place, rather than going down a nested chain of calls to `factorial()`.

Many compilers will end up generating pretty much the same code for these two variants; they both do the same thing, and it's not all that complicated.

Fibonacci Revisited

Let's eliminate the recursion from the Fibonacci program. Our first version is a little clumsy, but it's free of recursion. Feel free to try it yourself to get a feel for the performance. The version in Listing 10.7 is a *lot* faster than the recursive one.

LISTING 10.7 First Revision of Fibonacci Program

```
01    int
02    fib(int x) {
03        int i, *a, r;
04
05        if (x < 3)
06            return 1;
07
08        a = malloc(x * sizeof(int));
09
10        if (!a)
11            return -1;
12
13        a[1] = a[0] = 1;
14        for (i = 2; i < x; ++i) {
15            a[i] = a[i - 1] + a[i - 2];
16        }
17
18        r = a[x - 1];
19        free(a);
20        return r;
21    }
```

A few comments are in order. First off, you'll notice careful attention to boundary conditions. In fact, in my first draft of this, I got one of them wrong; I tested to see whether x was less than 2, rather than less than 3. I was thinking of the boundary correctly (it's at 2), but I forgot that the boundary condition was still a case where I wanted the immediate return. You'll also notice that we check the return from `malloc()`. Some example code doesn't do this; I think it's worth doing it, even in examples.

The main logic of this function is like this; we allocate enough memory for an array holding the first x numbers of the sequence. We fill in the first two numbers and then we loop through filling the rest in. When we're finished, we store the return value (line 18), because we want to free our memory (line 19) and then return a value that had been in the array.

This is actually a usable version, but it's pretty irritating having to allocate all this space when we really never use any number more than a couple of times. This leads us to the final version. Instead of allocating enough space for all the numbers, we'll just allocate enough space for three of them; the two we're adding, and the result of the addition. This gives us a new version in Listing 10.8.

LISTING 10.8 Final Version of Fibonacci Function

```
int
fib(int x) {
    int i, a[3];

    if (x < 3)
        return 1;

    a[1] = a[0] = 1;
    for (i = 2; i < x; ++i) {
        a[2] = a[0] + a[1];
        a[0] = a[1];
        a[1] = a[2];
    }

    return a[2];
}
```

Because we eliminated the array, we were also able to eliminate the need to make a copy of the last item in the array when we were finished with it. On the other hand, we have two extra copies per iteration as we "rotate" the values in the little array. Still, this manages to solve the problem, using substantially less time than the original, and less space than either of the other versions. Not a bad deal at all!

Just so you can see how this is supposed to work, I've included a "trace" of the runs through the array (see Table 10.1). We'll start with x = 6.

TABLE 10.1 Trace of Fibonacci Function

a[0]	*a[1]*	*a[2]*	*i*	*Where We Are*
1	1	N/A	2	initial setup
1	1	2	2	calculating a[2]
1	2	2	2	rotating values around
1	2	2	3	++i
1	2	3	3	calculating a[2]
2	3	3	3	rotating values around
2	3	3	4	++i
2	3	5	4	calculating a[2]
3	5	5	4	rotating values around
3	5	5	5	++i
3	5	8	5	calculating a[2]
5	8	8	5	rotating values around
5	8	8	6	++i

In this example, the function returns `8`.

You'll notice that each iteration takes only one more pass through the loop, whether it's the third iteration or the sixth. Compare this with the recursive implementation, which took three calls for x=3, nine for x=5, or 15 for x=6. In short, we've gone from geometric performance (each number takes about 1.6 times as many calculations as the one before it) to linear time. A massive improvement!

Unfortunately, this leaves us with the question of what we *should* use recursion for. The answer is, recursion makes sense when you can't do your work in a fixed-size scratch space—in other words, when you want an implicit stack. Even with the Fibonacci sequence, we were able to get everything done that we needed to do by using at most three values to store our results. When you do more complicated problems (such as language parsers), you can end up not having any way to know in advance how "deep" your analysis will get.

Of course, you can still convert to an iterative approach, but it starts being a pain to keep track of the allocation of your variables. This is where recursion can be really convenient: When it's necessary to allocate new variables for every iteration, the compiler simply does it for you. This is one area where C is a convenient language; the compiler takes care of calls from a function to itself just as easily as it takes care of calls from one function to another.

Recursion is often used in divide-and-conquer situations, such as sorting or tree traversal. In some of these cases, an iterative solution can be crafted, but the recursive code may be easy enough to understand to accept a small performance hit.

Indirect Recursion

In fact, because C handles calls from one function to another so naturally, it's possible for recursion to be "indirect." Rather than a function calling itself directly, it can call another function, which can call another function... and we may end up back at the first function. This isn't as common, but it's possible. Generally, it will only happen in more complicated contexts. For example, a parser might well end up with some indirect recursion.

You normally don't have to treat indirect recursion specially. However, it's worth remembering that it's still recursion, because recursive code can be subject to pitfalls that wouldn't have affected nonrecursive code, and this can bite you even if your recursion isn't immediately obvious. (Think about the `strtok()` example in the next section. Now think about what happens if you can't even figure out how you're getting back to the segment of code that uses `strtok()`!)

Recursion and Data Lifetime

One of the nicest things about writing recursive code in C is that the recursion "just happens." You don't have to do anything special or declare functions specially to mark them as recursive; the compiler just handles it.

Unfortunately, the compiler doesn't always take care of everything you want it to. In C, most objects have automatic storage duration, meaning they come into existence when the block they're in is entered, and they cease to exist when the block is finished.

For instance, function arguments behave like this: When you call a function, it is given storage space for copies of its arguments, and when the function returns, the space is automatically freed. You don't have to handle this; it's just part of the language.

However, objects with static storage duration don't behave this way. In the example programs, you'll notice that some variables are declared outside the recursive functions. In the recursive GCD calculator, `depth` is declared as a global variable and has static storage duration. Thus, even though every call to `gcd()` gets its own copies of `x` and `y`, they all share the depth variable.

This results in a common pitfall; functions that use objects with static storage duration might not work well in conjunction with recursion. As an example, consider the standard library function `strtok()`. `strtok()` has a static piece of data associated with it—the string it will "keep searching" if you pass it a null pointer. Let's look at a plausible-seeming function that breaks up lines of input, in Listing 10.9.

LISTING 10.9 Simple Tokenizer

```
void
tok(char *s, char *delim) {
    char *tmp;

    tmp = strtok(s, delim);
    while (tmp) {
        printf("token: %s\n", tmp);
        tmp = strtok(NULL, delim);
    }
}
```

Go ahead and compile the program from the CD, or write your own wrapper. This one's not very complicated, but it's sort of neat to see how easy it is to "parse" simple input. The code is quite straightforward—no tricks. Harmless, right? Now, let's make it a little more interesting. If it finds a "number" (a sequence of digits and commas), we want it to print the sets of digits separately.

Well, this will be easy! We've already got a routine to tokenize something using a given delimiter, so we try `tok2.c` (Listing 10.10), where we add a simple recursive call.

LISTING 10.10 Buggy Attempt at Adding a Feature

```
01    void
02    tok(char *s, char *delim) {
03        char *tmp;
04
05        tmp = strtok(s, delim);
06        while (tmp) {
07            /* strspn == length of initial substring containing
08             * only the characters in the 2nd argument
09             */
10            if (strspn(tmp, "0123456789,") == strlen(tmp) &&
11                strchr(tmp, ',')) {
12                tok(s, ",");
13            } else {
14                printf("token: %s\n", tmp);
15            }
16            tmp = strtok(NULL, delim);
17        }
18    }
```

The logic is simple enough; if we get a token consisting entirely of numbers and commas, and it contains a comma, we split it up using commas as the delimiter. (If it's got no comma, it's already been split up, and if it's got anything other than numbers or commas, it's some other kind of word.)

A couple of simple tests, and this appears to work; give it **`foo 123,456`**, and it comes out with tokens `foo`, `123`, and `456`. Isn't recursion powerful?

Now, let's try a slightly more complicated line: We'll give it **`123,456 foo`**. We'd expect `123`, `456`, and `foo`. Unfortunately, what we get is just `123` and `456`. The recursive calls have caused `strtok()` to step on its own feet, so to speak; the internal buffer used by `strtok()` gets overwritten by an "inner" call to `tok()`, so the "outer" call loses its place.

Let's trace the execution through. We start at the top:

```
tok("123,456 foo", " ");
```

On line 05, we set tmp to point to the "1" at the beginning of the string. At the same time, `strtok()` is saving a pointer to the "f" at the beginning of foo, and replacing the space before that with a null byte. Later, we expect that `strtok(NULL, "")` would return a pointer to the “f.”

Now we enter the loop on line 06. The first thing we do is check to see if our string (`tmp`) contains only numbers and commas, and if it contains at least one comma. It does, so we start another invocation of `tok` with this string, and a comma for a delimiter; this is as if we’d written

```
tok("123,456", ",");
```

We start our new invocation. The first thing we do is set our new variable named `tmp` (remember, because it’s an automatic variable, this isn’t the same as the `tmp` in the “outer” invocation of `tok()`). Again (we’re back to line 05, but in a deeper invocation), we use `strtok()` to split the string up. It returns a pointer to the “1,” while changing the comma to a null byte, and setting its internal pointer to point at the “4” so we can keep searching it.

We enter the loop on line 06. This time, the string pointed to by `tmp` doesn’t have a comma, so we just print it (line 14). Having printed the current token, we go on to line 16, where we call `strtok(NULL, ",")` so we can split out any more comma-separated fields. There’s no more, so `strtok()` sets its internal “next” pointer to a null pointer, to indicate that there’s no more fields (and that the next call should return nothing). It then returns a pointer to the “4.”

We go back to the start of the loop. We keep looping, because `tmp` is not a null pointer. Again, there’s no comma, so we print it out. Now, when we call `strtok()` again, `tmp` is set to a null pointer, because we’re finished parsing the “123,456” string we started on. So, we get to the top of the loop, but `tmp` is null, so we terminate, returning back to the top-level invocation.

Back here, we again reach the line where we call `strtok()` to set `tmp`. If you look back up to right before we called `tok()` a second time, you’ll see we’re expecting to get a pointer to the “f” of “foo.” Unfortunately, the buffer that `strtok()` was storing this in was overwritten during the other call to `tok()`! Instead of a pointer to the “f,” we get a null pointer. The loop is done, and we return to the calling routine, without processing the rest of the string. Oops!

What went wrong? Because `strtok()` only had one pointer, and it wasn’t preserved when we called `tok()` recursively, our “reasonable” recursive function actually failed to work as expected!

The problem here is that, when you use recursive functions like this, you generally need to make sure that anything you call isn’t going to be depending on static data that might be corrupted or, alternatively, that you save any such data.

Unfortunately, it's really hard to do this with `strtok()`, because the function doesn't provide a way to get at its internal buffer. Some systems offer an extension called `strsep()`, which is a function with similar functionality to `strtok()`, but which doesn't make use of a static buffer. Unfortunately, this function isn't in the C standard, but it is in the C libraries used on the various free UNIX-like systems, so you can always get a copy of their code, or you can use the work-alike provided on the CD.

An example of how to implement the `tok2` program correctly is provided, under the name `tok3.c`. It uses a function equivalent to the Berkeley `strsep()` function, under the innovative name of `sepstr()`. You're welcome to use this `sepstr()` function in your own code; it should be equivalent to the "standard" one, although it might not be quite as elegant as the version in the Berkeley version of the standard C Library. It's named `sepstr`, instead of `strsep`, because the C standard reserves names beginning with `str`, followed by any lowercase letter, for use by the implementation and, indeed, a number of systems do provide a `strsep()`. (Ones I know of include some Linux distributions and all the 4.4BSD-derived systems, such as BSD/OS or NetBSD.)

In general, this illustrates the way you create a function that can be used recursively; make sure it has no "internal state" that can get stepped on. It should rely entirely on its automatic variables and its arguments, and should return anything you'll need to know to use it again later.

If you haven't got the CD handy, Listing 10.11 shows a sample implementation of `sepstr()`.

LISTING 10.11 The `sepstr()` Function

```
char *
sepstr(char **s, char *delim) {
    char *ret;
    size_t n;

    /* sanity check */
    if (!s || !*s || !delim)
        return NULL;

    /* we return a pointer to the current value of s */
    ret = *s;

    /* first, we find out how much of '*s' is *not* in 'delim' - we'll
     * call that value 'n'.
     *
     * if (*s)[n] is a null byte, the entire string contains no instances
```

LISTING 10.11 continued

```
     * of any character in delim; otherwise, it's the first delimiter
     * found.
     */
    n = strcspn(*s, delim);
    if ((*s)[n]) {
        (*s)[n] = '\0';
        /* advance s to one past the first delimiter */
        *s += (n + 1);
    } else {
        /* no more strings to return */
        *s = NULL;
    }

    /* and we return the saved pointer to the old contents of *s. */
    return ret;
}
```

This function's interface is a little unusual for a standard library function, simply because it needs to return *two* values to the user. First, you need the address of the token you've just found; second, you need the address of the next token, so you know where to start up again. The way `sepstr()` handles this is to have the user provide storage for a pointer; thus, instead of passing in a string, you pass in the address of a pointer, so the new pointer can be stored back there. This sounds confusing, but it's really easy to use; you end up just looping through passing it the same value, until that value becomes a null pointer. Since this is such a nice interface, I copied it.

The first thing `sepstr()` does is a sanity check; if either of the arguments is a null pointer, or if the pointer the first one points to is a null pointer, the function can't do anything useful, so it returns a null pointer too. Remember that the logical-or operator in C "short-circuits"; if the first test fails, the second won't even be attempted. Thus, it's safe to test `*s` once we know that s is not a null pointer. After we make these checks, we store our return value. No matter what happens, the token we return will always start at the beginning of the string.

After this, we use a function called `strcspn()` to find out how much of the string doesn't use any characters in `delim`. The name comes from *complement span*; it returns the length of the initial substring of the first argument that is *spanned* (that is, consists entirely of members of the *complement* of the second argument). If the first character after that span is not a null byte, it's a character that was found in the delimiter string. So, we set that byte to be a null byte, and set the user's string pointer to point to the byte after it. Otherwise, there were no characters from the delimiter string to be found; there is no next token, so we set the user's string pointer to be a null pointer. Either way, we return the token we found (see Listing 10.12).

LISTING 10.12 Rewriting `tok()` to Use `sepstr()`

```
void
tok(char *s, char *delim) {
    char *tmp;

    tmp = sepstr(&s, delim);
    while (tmp) {
        if (strspn(tmp, "0123456789,") == strlen(tmp) &&
            strchr(tmp, ',')) {
            tok(tmp, ",");
        } else {
            printf("token: %s\n", tmp);
        }
        tmp = sepstr(&s, delim);
    }
}
```

Using `sepstr()` is pretty easy. The big difference is that you don't pass it a null pointer to tell it "keep working on that string." Every time you invoke it, you tell it where you want it to start, and it starts there. If you end up compiling this on a system with `strsep()` in the standard library, you'll find you can replace `sepstr()` with it, and nothing will need to change. (Unless you find a system where they provide a function named `strsep` that isn't at all like the one on other systems. This might sound crazy, but it happens occasionally with extensions.)

Applications for Recursion

Recursion generally makes sense for tasks which can be broken down into a number of smaller, similar tasks. If these "smaller" tasks are substantially different, you will probably find iteration more useful than recursion. Sometimes, the best way to handle something is a combination; a recursive algorithm which breaks a task down into parts, which are handled with iterative code.

The best application for recursion is probably parsing; simply put, parsing *is* a recursive task, by nature. Think about a C expression parser: You parse an expression such as 'x + (y + z)' by parsing an "expression" that looks like "x + <expression>", and then you parse the second expression using the same techniques. (For more on parsing, see Chapter 19.)

Searching is often handled recursively, especially if the original input is sorted. (You've seen a simple binary search above.) Note that not all searching is in a fixed, known array. Consider the problem of "searching" for a good move in a game of chess; this is frequently implemented as a recursive procedure, as a chess program looks through a tree of moves, each move taking up one "stack" level.

Sorting is another thing which is commonly recursive, although not all sorting algorithms are recursive. Quicksort, one of the most famous sorting algorithms, is generally explained as a recursive function, although you can force it into an iterative mold.

In general, recursion makes sense any time you find yourself planning to allocate space for each "level" of a problem that you solve. Play around with it. Don't be afraid to write a recursive solution that might be horribly inefficient at first; if it's really that bad, you might be able to find a way to improve it, but working with the recursive solution might help you understand the problem. Performance should be a secondary consideration; get the algorithm working and understood first, and then see if you need to improve it.

Summary

In this chapter, we've reviewed what recursion is, how it works, and what it's good for. We've looked at some examples of how it works, and some examples of how it can work really badly. We've seen a couple of pitfalls recursive code may run into. You should be able to make a reasonable decision on whether to implement something recursively or iteratively. If you want to learn more about this, you should definitely spend a little time writing test programs, and studying how they work. Also, of course, you should look at some of the standard literature, such as Knuth's *The Art of Computer Programming*.

I also recommend Douglas Hofstadter's book *Gödel, Escher, Bach*, if you want to get more exposure to the concept of recursion, including some noncomputer contexts in which it arises. The more familiar you are with recursion in general, the better you'll be able to use it in programming.

If you want a little more recursion-oriented thought, I leave you with a question: I have asserted that a recursive function to read input is bad style, and that a recursive parser is good style. If the recursive parser calls a function to read input, is this bad style? If not, how is it really different from the recursive input reader? I've tried this question on some fairly experienced programmers, and gotten some very interesting responses. Try it on your friends.

```
    }
  }
}
```

This looks perfectly ghastly. In fact, is it correct? Did you have to look twice to be sure? Would you like to have to maintain it? Neither would I.

If instead we revert to array notation, the code becomes much clearer. We can correct `PopulateLoadingArray()` (from the preceding code) simply by changing the function declaration:

```
void PopulateLoadingArray(double Loading[][NUM_GENDERS],
                          size_t MaxAge,
                          size_t NumGenders)
```

Note that we must indicate the size of all indices in the array, except the leftmost one (which is optional). This gives the compiler sufficient data to calculate the address information it needs.

One way in which we can simplify the task of passing an array to functions is to wrap it up in a `struct`, as shown in Listing 11.1.

LISTING 11.1 Passing an Array to a Function

```
#include <stdio.h>

typedef struct ARRAY_INT_4_6
{
  int array[4][6];
} ARRAY_INT_4_6;

int SumArray(ARRAY_INT_4_6 *);

int main(void)
{
  ARRAY_INT_4_6 Array =
  {
    {
      { 1, 2, 3, 4, 5, 6 },
      { 2, 3, 4, 5, 6, 7 },
      { 3, 4, 5, 6, 7, 8 },
      { 4, 5, 6, 7, 8, 9 }
    }
  };
  int Total;
```

LISTING 11.1 continued

```
  Total = SumArray(&Array);

  printf("Total is %d\n", Total);

  return 0;
}

int SumArray(ARRAY_INT_4_6 *a)
{
  size_t outer, inner;
  int Total = 0;

  for(outer = 0;
      outer < sizeof a->array / sizeof a->array[0];
      outer++)
  {
    for(inner = 0;
        inner < sizeof a->array[0] / sizeof a->array[0][0];
        inner++)
    {
      Total += a->array[outer][inner];
    }
  }
  return Total;
}
```

The advantages of this method are that it simplifies the parameter declaration syntax, and that it allows us to calculate the dimensions of the array within the function, as shown in the listing. The disadvantage is that we bind the function to a specific array size, making it difficult to apply this function to more general purposes. But then, with fixed array sizes, this is always going to be a problem no matter which way we do it. Whether you choose to wrap your array in a `struct` is, then, largely a matter of style.

Just to digress for a moment: We often deal with arrays of two (or more) dimensions by using nested loops. One mistake I make far too often is to copy and paste the outer loop to the inner loop, and forget to update *all* the elements of the loop control statement:

```
for(i = 0; i < OUTER; i++)
{
  for(j = 0; j < INNER; i++)
  {
```

```
      total += array[i][j];
    }
  }
```

This problem is less common if we use meaningful loop counter names, because the mistake seems to stand out more clearly.

N-dimensional Fixed-size Arrays

Two dimensions are enough for almost all needs. Even in 3D graphics programs, we can record the vertices of any figure using a 2D array. Each row represents one dimension, and each column represents one point. Each cell, then, represents the displacement of a given point from the origin along a given dimension. Thus, this 2D array

```
int Cube[3][8] =
{
  { 0, 1, 1, 0, 0, 1, 1, 0 },
  { 0, 0, 1, 1, 0, 0, 1, 1 },
  { 0, 0, 0, 0, 1, 1, 1, 1 }
};
```

represents the vertices of a 3D cube of unit side. We can even represent figures in four or more dimensions in this way, simply by increasing the number of rows.

Nevertheless, there are occasions when we do need to use more than two dimensions. In these cases, we may simply extend our 2D syntax, and ensure that we specify all indices (except that we may optionally omit the leftmost index) in the formal parameter declaration.

As previously mentioned, fixed-size arrays can be very limiting. The following sections look at the much more flexible concept of dynamically allocated, resizable arrays.

Resizable Arrays

Resizable arrays offer much more potential than fixed-size arrays; not only more potential for flexible, friendly, useful programs, but also more potential, alas, for bugs. We will endeavor to present techniques here for implementing resizable arrays in a safe and robust way.

One-dimensional Resizable Arrays

Making single-dimension resizable arrays is really simple. If we need an array of N objects of type T, this is how we do it:

```
#include <stdlib.h>

  /* ... */

  T *p;
  p = malloc(N * sizeof *p);
  if(p != NULL)
  {
    /* we have our array, and may now use it for storage */
  }
```

As you may have noticed, this code illustrates that there is no need to cast `malloc` in C programs and, in fact, doing so can disguise the accidental omission of `<stdlib.h>`.

Resizing the array is less simple, but is still fairly easy. We need another pointer, again of type "pointer to T":

```
#include <stdlib.h>

  /* ... */

  T *tmp;
  tmp = realloc(p, NewNumElems * sizeof *p);
  if(tmp != NULL)
  {
    /* the resizing worked */
    p = tmp;
  }
  else
  {
    /* The resizing didn't work, p still points to the
     * old data.
     */
  }
```

Note the use of the second pointer. This is essential whenever you call the `realloc` function. Many programmers simply use the same pointer `p`, on the assumption that all will be well. If all is *not* well, however, not only have they failed to get the extra memory they requested, but also they have lost the memory they previously had, because their only pointer to it, `p`, is now `NULL`!

The ability to resize arrays is very useful indeed, and can make our programs much more flexible.

We should not forget that, at some appropriate point, we must free the memory thus allocated when we are done with it.

Two-dimensional Resizable Arrays

This is where arrays start to be tremendous fun. Off-hand, I can think of three different ways to set up an array of M * N objects of type T. I've used `int`s in the sample code, but of course you can substitute any type.

Of the three, the first method occupies the least memory, but offers relatively slow access to elements in the array. The idea is to imitate a fixed-size array. We allocate `sizeof(T) * M * N` bytes, and can access a particular element `A[x][y]` at the address `A + N * x + y`. Remember that the compiler will take care of the size of each element for us (unless we are using `void *`) so we don't need to, and in fact should not, do this ourselves. Our final attempt at `PopulateLoadingArray()` illustrates this addressing technique nicely, so I won't repeat the code here.

Resizing such an array is tricky, because we have to do some complicated moving around of data if we are not to lose the information we've already stored in the array.

In the second technique, as in the first, we allocate a single block of memory. This time, however, the block is larger—we request enough extra memory for M pointers to T, a total memory requirement of `sizeof(T) * M * N + sizeof(T *) * M`. We set aside the first `sizeof(T *) * M` bytes for a series of pointers into the main array body. This allows us to use the notation `A[x][y]`. This is less obvious, so Listing 11.2 shows a fully working example.

LISTING 11.2 Two-dimensional Resizable Array

```
#include <stdio.h>
#include <stdlib.h>

typedef int T;

T **Allocate(size_t m, size_t n)
{
  T **a;
  T *p;
  size_t Row;

  a = malloc(m * n * sizeof **a + m * sizeof *a);
  if(a != NULL)
  {
    for(Row = 0, p = (T *)a + m; Row < m; Row++, p += n)
```

LISTING 11.2 continued

```
    {
      a[Row] = p;
    }
  }
  return a;
}


int main(void)
{
  T **array;
  int i;
  int j;
  int total = 0;
  int row = 4;
  int col = 7;

  array = Allocate(row, col);

  if(array != NULL)
  {
    /* Populating the array */
    for(i = 0; i < row; i++)
      for(j = 0; j < col; j++)
        array[i][j] = i + j;
    /* Accessing the array */
    for(i = 0; i < row; i++)
      for(j = 0; j < col; j++)
        total += array[i][j];

    printf("Total is %d\n", total);
    free(array);
  }

  return 0;
}
```

The cast in the `Allocate()` function is a (slight) weakness. Also, for a resizable array, this array isn't very resizable! It *can* be done, but the necessary housekeeping code to preserve the data is quite involved; we can resize the block easily enough, but we have to move data around in memory in quite complex ways. Listing 11.3 shows the code to resize the block. Note that we have to tell the function the old shape of the array as well as the new shape.

LISTING 11.3 Resizing a 2D Array with Pointers in Header Block

```
#include <stdlib.h>

typedef int T;

T **Reallocate(T **OldP,
               size_t oldm,
               size_t oldn,
               size_t newm,
               size_t newn)
{
  T **NewP = NULL;
  T *p;
  size_t Row;

  /* Do we need more memory? */
  if(newm * newn * sizeof **NewP + newm * sizeof *NewP >
     oldm * oldn * sizeof **OldP + oldm * sizeof *OldP)
  {
    /* Yes, so let's go get some */
    NewP = realloc(OldP,
                   newm * newn * sizeof **NewP +
                   newm * sizeof *NewP);
  }
  else
  {
    NewP = OldP;
  }

  if(NewP != NULL)
  {
    /* Now we have to set up the pointer table again */
    for(Row = 0, p = (T *)NewP + newm;
        Row < newm;
        Row++, p += newn)
    {
      NewP[Row] = p;
    }
  }
```

LISTING 11.3 continued

```
  return NewP;
}
```

You may care to try your hand at modifying this function to preserve as much data as possible from the original array. But I wouldn't.

The third method uses the same amount of memory as the second method, but does not require that memory to be in one contiguous block. It is also easier to resize.

We first allocate a block of memory to hold M pointers to T. Then we loop through that array and, in each iteration of the loop, we allocate a block of memory big enough to hold N objects of type T.

This means that we can no longer free the memory in a single call. We have to loop through the pointer array freeing each element, and then free the pointer array itself. (We can write a simple function to do this for us.) On the other hand, if we are using very large arrays, we don't need to worry so much about whether the allocation will succeed because it no longer has to be in one contiguous block. Naturally, we should still check whether it *has* succeeded, but the risk of failure is lower.

Figure 11.1 should help you to visualize this more easily.

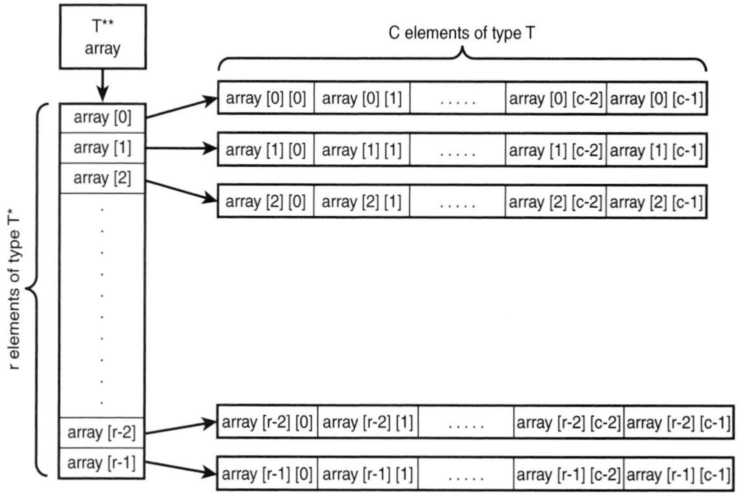

FIGURE 11.1
A resizable 2D array.

Listing 11.4 shows how we're going to do it.

LISTING 11.4 A Resizable Two-dimensional Array

```
#include <stdio.h>
#include <stdlib.h>

typedef int T;

void Release(T **a, size_t m)
{
  size_t Row;

  for(Row = 0; Row < m; Row++)
  {
    if(a[Row] != NULL)
    {
      free(a[Row]);
    }
  }
  free;
}

T **Allocate(size_t m, size_t n)
{
  T **a;
  size_t Row;
  int Success = 1;

  a = malloc(m * sizeof *a);
  if(a != NULL)
  {
    for(Row = 0; Row < m; Row++)
    {
      a[Row] = malloc(n * sizeof *a[Row]);
      if(NULL == a[Row])
      {
        Success = 0;
      }
    }
    /* If any inner allocation failed,
     * we should clean up
     */
```

LISTING 11.4 continued

```
    if(1 != Success)
    {
      Release(a, m);
      a = NULL;
    }
  }

  return a;
}

int main(void)
{
  T **array;
  int i;
  int j;
  int total = 0;
  int row = 4;
  int col = 7;

  array = Allocate(row, col);

  if(array != NULL)
  {
    /* Populating the array */
    for(i = 0; i < row; i++)
      for(j = 0; j < col; j++)
        array[i][j] = i + j;
    /* Accessing the array */
    for(i = 0; i < row; i++)
      for(j = 0; j < col; j++)
        total += array[i][j];

    printf("Total is %d\n", total);
    Release(array, row);
  }

  return 0;
}
```

This array is very flexible from a resizing point of view. We can add (or subtract) rows, we can make all the rows longer, or we can make *some* of the rows longer (which would give us a data structure known as a *ragged array*).

Such flexibility is extremely useful—especially the ability to have rows of different lengths. For example, if we were writing a text editor, we would be able to read the whole of a file into memory (subject to enough memory being available), with one line of the text file corresponding to one row of the array, with no wasted space.

To illustrate this, we'll write a routine to do just that—read a text file into memory. We'll assume that the text file comprises a reasonable number of lines of text, each separated from the next by a newline (`'\n'`). This may correspond to a single linefeed character (on, say, UNIX systems), a carriage return (on Macs), a combination of the two (DOS/Windows), or something else entirely. We don't need to code for this because, as long as we open the file in text mode, the standard library will do any necessary translation for us. The only stipulation is that the text file is in the format native to the operating system on which the code will run, whatever that may be.

We'll start off with the string array functions. (The complete code for Listing 11.5 is on the CD-ROM, and incorporates things like inclusions and prototypes, which I have omitted here for brevity.) First of all, we'd like to create an array of strings. To do this, we allocate space for an array of pointers, and then allocate some string space for that pointer.

LISTING 11.5 Reading a Text File into Memory

```
char **AllocStrArray(size_t NumRows, size_t Width)
{
  char **Array = NULL;
  size_t Row;
  int Success = 1;

  /* allocating 0 bytes is not a great idea, and
   * represents a logic error.
   */
  assert(NumRows > 0);
  assert(Width > 0);

  /* Just in case the zero allocation is NOT caught
   * in testing, we'll check for it here.
   */
  if(NumRows > 0 && Width > 0)
  {
    Array = malloc(NumRows * sizeof *Array);
```

LISTING 11.5 continued

```
    if(Array != NULL)
    {
      for(Row = 0; Row < NumRows; Row++)
      {
        Array[Row] = malloc(Width * sizeof *Array[Row]);
        if(NULL == Array[Row])
        {
          Success = 0;
        }
        else
        {
          /* Making this into an empty string is a quick
           * op which will almost invariably be The Right
           * Thing and can never be The Wrong Thing, so
           * we might as well do it.
           */
          Array[Row][0] = '\0';
        }
      }
      /* If any inner allocation failed,
       * we should clean up.
       */
      if(1 != Success)
      {
        FreeStrArray(Array, NumRows);
        Array = NULL;
      }
    }
  }

  return Array;
}
```

If the allocation cannot be completed in its entirety, the routine cleans up (by calling `FreeStrArray()`), and returns NULL. This presupposes the existence of `FreeStrArray()`, so here it is. As you would expect, it's a simple loop.

```
void FreeStrArray(char **Array, size_t NumRows)
{
  size_t Row;

  if(Array != NULL)
```

```
  {
    for(Row = 0; Row < NumRows; Row++)
    {
      if(Array[Row] != NULL)
      {
        free(Array[Row]);
      }
    }
    free(Array);
  }
}
```

Resizing one string is very simple. We need to know the row number and the new size.

```
int ResizeOneString(char **Array,
                    size_t Row,
                    size_t NewSize)
{
  char *p;
  int Success = 1;

  assert(Array != NULL);

  p = realloc(Array[Row], NewSize);
  if(p != NULL)
  {
    Array[Row] = p;
  }
  else
  {
    Success = 0;
  }

  return Success;
}
```

Notice how carefully we call `realloc()`. By using a spare pointer, we ensure that the original pointer is not lost even if the allocation fails.

We will certainly need the ability to add more rows (or remove rows). To instruct this function to remove rows, we simply pass a negative number in the `NumRowsToAdd` parameter.

```
int AddRowsToStrArray(char ***ArrayPtr,
                      size_t OldNumRows,
```

```
                        int NumRowsToAdd,
                        size_t InitWidth)
{
  char **p;
  int Success = 1;
  int Row;
  int OldRows;

  OldRows = (int)OldNumRows;
  if(NumRowsToAdd < 0)
  {
    for(Row = OldRows - 1;
        Row >= OldRows + NumRowsToAdd;
        Row--)
    {
      free((*ArrayPtr)[Row]);
    }
  }

  p = realloc(*ArrayPtr,
              (OldRows + NumRowsToAdd) *
               sizeof(**ArrayPtr));

  if(p != NULL)
  {
    *ArrayPtr = p;

    for(Row = OldRows;
        Success && Row < OldRows + NumRowsToAdd;
        Row++)
    {
      (*ArrayPtr)[Row] = malloc(InitWidth);
      if((*ArrayPtr)[Row] != NULL)
      {
        (*ArrayPtr)[Row][0] = '\0';
      }
      else
      {
        Success = 0;
      }
    }
  }
  else
```

```
  {
    Success = 0;
  }
  return Success;
}
```

Two points of interest arise from this code. First, if we are removing rows, we don't want to go into the loop that allocates new space for the new lines. The loop condition prevents this. Second, note the use of parentheses, such as `(*Array)[Row]`. Omitting the parentheses here would be disastrous because `[]` binds tighter (has a higher precedence) than `*`.

We now have all the code we *need*, but it would be *useful* to have a function that resizes each row to exactly the number of bytes required to hold the string which that row does in fact contain. We might argue that a little overhead doesn't matter that much, but there are cases in which it might. We don't *have* to use this function but, if we write it, it's there if we need it.

```
int ConsolidateStrArray(char **ArrayPtr,
                        size_t NumRows)
{
  size_t Row;
  size_t Len;
  int NumFailures = 0;

  for(Row = 0; Row < NumRows; Row++)
  {
    /* If the library has been correctly used, no
     * row pointer will ever be NULL, so we should
     * assert that this is the case.
     */
    assert(ArrayPtr[Row] != NULL);
    Len = 1 + strlen(ArrayPtr[Row]);
    if(0 == ResizeOneString(ArrayPtr, Row, Len))
    {
      ++NumFailures;
    }
  }
  return NumFailures;
}
```

Given those functions, the code for reading a file into memory is surprisingly short. We can simply loop through each line in the file, reading it into one row of the array. If the file is longer than our original guess, we can simply add more rows to the array. If any given line is longer than our initial guess, we can resize that row of the array. If this is the case, we may well find that our buffer is not big enough to read the entire line in one go using `fgets()`, so we need to add a little code to ensure that we collect the whole line, not just the first few bytes of it.

```
int ReadFile(char *Filename,
             char ***Array,
             int *NumRows)
{
  char Buffer[DEFAULT_LINE_LEN] = {0};
  char *NewLine = NULL;
  FILE *fp;
  int Error = 0;
  int Row = 0;
  size_t NumBlocks;

  *NumRows = 0;

  *Array = AllocStrArray(LINES_PER_ALLOC,
                         DEFAULT_LINE_LEN);
  if(NULL != *Array)
  {
    fp = fopen(Filename, "r");
    if(fp != NULL)
    {
      *NumRows = LINES_PER_ALLOC;
      NumBlocks = 1;

      /* fgets will give us no more than sizeof Buffer
       * bytes, including zero terminator and newline
       * if one is present within that number of bytes.
       * Therefore we need to cater for longer lines.
       * To do this, we call fgets again (and again
       * and again) until we encounter a newline.
       */
      while(0 == Error &&
            NULL != fgets(Buffer, sizeof Buffer, fp))
      {
        NewLine = strchr(Buffer, '\n');
        if(NewLine != NULL)
```

```
{
  *NewLine = '\0';
}
/* This strcat relies on the AllocStrArray()
 * function initialising rows to empty strings.
 */
strcat((*Array)[Row], Buffer);
if(NewLine != NULL)
{
  /* There was a newline, so the
   * next line is a new one.
   */
  NumBlocks = 1;
  ++Row;
  if(Row >= *NumRows)
  {
    /* Add another LINES_PER_ALLOC lines.
     * If it didn't work, give up.
     */
    if(0 == AddRowsToStrArray(Array,
                              *NumRows,
                              LINES_PER_ALLOC,
                              DEFAULT_LINE_LEN))
    {
      Error = ERR_ROWS_NOT_ADDED;
    }
    else
    {
      *NumRows += LINES_PER_ALLOC;
    }
  }
}
else
{
  ++NumBlocks;
  /* Make room for some more data on this line */
  if(0 ==
     ResizeOneString(*Array,
                     Row,
                     NumBlocks * DEFAULT_LINE_LEN))
  {
    Error = ERR_STRING_NOT_RESIZED;
  }
```

```
        }
      }
      fclose(fp);
      if(0 == Error && *NumRows > Row)
      {
        if(0 == AddRowsToStrArray(Array,
                                  *NumRows,
                                  Row - *NumRows,
                                  0))
        {
          Error = ERR_ALLOC_FAILED;
        }
        *NumRows = Row;
      }
    }
    else
    {
      Error = ERR_FILE_OPEN_FAILED; /* Can't open file */
    }
  }
  else
  {
    Error = ERR_ALLOC_FAILED; /* Can't allocate memory */
  }
  if(Error != 0)
  {
    /* If the original allocation failed,
     * *Array will be NULL. FreeStrArray()
     * correctly handles this possibility.
     */
    FreeStrArray(*Array, *NumRows);
    *NumRows = 0;
  }
  else
  {
    ConsolidateStrArray(*Array, *NumRows);
  }

  return Error;
}
```

Notice how we allocate *blocks* of new lines each time we run out of space, rather than just one line at a time, in an attempt to reduce the number of calls to `realloc()`. Memory allocation can be an expensive operation; allocating in batches may well improve the speed of the routine. Unfortunately, we can't *guarantee* this because each implementation is different, but it's a reasonable rule of thumb.

All we need now is to tie this all together with a `main()` driver to illustrate how the routine can be used in practice. I've chosen a very simple application, which just writes each string in the file to standard output, in reverse order. I've omitted headers for brevity. The full code can be found on the CD.

```
int main(int argc, char **argv)
{
  char **array = NULL;

  int rows;
  int thisrow;
  int error;

  if(argc > 1)
  {
    error = ReadFile(argv[1], &array, &rows);
    switch(error)
    {
      case 0:
        for(thisrow = rows - 1; thisrow >= 0; thisrow--)
        {
          printf("%s\n", array[thisrow]);
        }

        FreeStrArray(array, rows);
        break;
      case ERR_STRING_NOT_RESIZED:
      case ERR_ALLOC_FAILED:
      case ERR_ROWS_NOT_ADDED:
        puts("Insufficient memory.");
        break;
      case ERR_FILE_OPEN_FAILED:
        printf("Couldn't open %s for reading\n", argv[1]);
        break;
      default:
        printf("Unknown error! Code %d.\n", error);
        break;
    }
  }
```

```
  else
  {
    puts("Please specify the text file name.");
  }

  return 0;
}
```

Note that the string array allocation function is called via `ReadFile()`, but the `FreeStrArray()` function is called directly from `main()`. Is this a good idea? Many programmers think it would be better to write a function at the same level as `ReadFile()`, which would be responsible for releasing memory allocated via `ReadFile()`. This is a design decision which bears serious consideration, but I don't feel strongly about it one way or the other, so I won't prescribe an answer.

N-dimensional Resizable Arrays

Once we are fully up to speed on two-dimensional arrays, N-dimensional arrays are just an extension, with extra levels of indirection, each requiring another array of pointers. To illustrate this briefly, we'll write a simple function to allocate a five-dimensional array of type T (see Listing 11.6). Because I've already shown how to do full error checking in our two-dimensional example, I won't repeat that code here. A production-quality library routine should of course include it.

LISTING 11.6 A Five-dimensional Array

```
#include <stdlib.h>

typedef int T;

T *****Alloc5DArrayOfT(size_t m,
                       size_t n,
                       size_t p,
                       size_t q,
                       size_t r)
{
  T *****Array = NULL;
  int Success = 1;
  size_t a, b, c, d;

  Array =
      malloc(m * sizeof *Array);
  for(a = 0; a < m; a++)
  {
```

LISTING 11.6 continued

```
    Array[a] =
        malloc(n * sizeof *Array[0]);
    for(b = 0; b < n; b++)
    {
      Array[a][b] =
          malloc(p * sizeof *Array[0][0]);
      for(c = 0; c < p; c++)
      {
        Array[a][b][c] =
            malloc(q * sizeof *Array[0][0][0]);
        for(d = 0; d < q; d++)
        {
          Array[a][b][c][d] =
              malloc(r * sizeof *Array[0][0][0][0]);
        }
      }
    }
  }

  return Array;
}
```

This code may strike you as being rather clumsy. Surely a recursive solution would be much more elegant? Well, not really. The trouble is, what pointer type would a recursive solution use? ANSI does *not* guarantee that `sizeof(T*) == sizeof(T**)`, for any particular T.

If this were a big problem, we'd find a solution. But it's not a big problem because multi-dimensional arrays are actually rarely needed (in fact, they are used more often than they should be). If we find ourselves using multi-dimensional arrays as a matter of habit, we really ought to be questioning our design.

Arrays of Pointers

Naturally, arrays can be used to store anything, including objects of any size, subject to any limits enforced by the implementation. Nevertheless, it's sometimes a better idea to store not the objects themselves, but pointers to those objects.

We gain several advantages by storing pointers in our arrays instead of objects. First, we may be more likely to get the memory we need to store the objects if we don't need that memory to be all in one chunk. Second, we can move the objects around more easily. If, for example, we need to sort the array, we can swap pointers to the objects around much more efficiently than the objects themselves; or we can split the array into two or more pieces, much more conveniently and quickly, simply by copying pointers rather than objects.

These advantages only pertain, however, if the objects are large in size in comparison to pointers. There's no particular benefit in having an array of `int *`, each element of which points to a single `int`. This qualification also applies, as we will see, to other kinds of data structure.

Arrays of Pointers to Function

One marvelously powerful way in which we can use arrays is to store pointers to functions. Bjarne Stroustrup, creator of the C++ language, writes that an "array of pointers to functions is often useful. For example, the menu system for my mouse-based editor is implemented using arrays of pointers to functions to represent operations." Although the implementation of this idea may be quite complex, the idea itself is simple. Each operation is implemented within a single function (or, more likely, a single interface function that calls other functions to help it achieve its purpose), and each menu in the editor is represented internally by an array of pointers to these functions.

We could also use this technique to loop through a series of functions. This may seem pointless (why don't we unroll the loop by calling the functions explicitly?), but when we bear in mind that we could, *within the loop*, vary the functions pointed to, it becomes apparent that this is a powerful mechanism indeed.

The possibilities are endless. We'll illustrate the technique, however, with a very simple and common use for arrays of pointers to function—a finite state machine. I don't want to go into too much detail here, because finite state machines are covered elsewhere in the book. Finite state machines are usually deterministic, but here's an FSM with a slight difference: a random walk. As shown in Listing 11.7, the program has five states—up, down, left, right, and stop. As each action is performed, the next state is determined randomly.

LISTING 11.7 Using an Array of Pointers to Function

```
#include <stdio.h>
#include <time.h>
#include <stdlib.h>

int Random(int i)
```

LISTING 11.7 continued

```
{
  double d;

  d = rand() / ((double)RAND_MAX + 1.0);
  d *= i;
  return (int)d;
}

int go_left(int *x, int *y)
{
  --*x;

  printf("Going left!\n");

  return Random(5);

}

int go_right(int *x, int *y)
{
  ++*x;

  printf("Going right!\n");
  return Random(5);

}

int go_down(int *x, int *y)
{
  --*y;

  printf("Going down!\n");

  return Random(5);

}

int go_up(int *x, int *y)
{
  ++*y;

  printf("Going up!\n");
```

LISTING 11.7 continued

```
  return Random(5);

}

int stop(int *x, int *y)
{
  printf("End of the road: (%d, %d)\n", *x, *y);

  return -1;
}

int main(void)
{
  int (*action[])(int *, int *) =
  {
    go_left, go_right, go_down, go_up, stop
  };

  int state = 0;
  int x = 0;
  int y = 0;

  srand((unsigned)time(NULL));

  do
  {
    printf("Currently at (%d, %d)\n", x, y);
    state = (*action[state])(&x, &y);
  } while(state != -1);

  return 0;
}
```

Our declaration for the function pointer array is relatively simple, so I have refrained from defining any new types. If, however, the functions to which I want to point have more complicated types (if, for example, they themselves take pointers to function as arguments), the syntax can get positively scary. In these situations, we'd use `typedef` to simplify the code by using intermediate types.

When I compile this program, I get four diagnostics, all warning me about unused variables. This is the price I pay for type safety. All the objects in my array must be of the same type. Because I wanted to fully prototype my functions, I had to make them all the same type. In fact, each function (except `stop()`) needs only one integer; but two of them need that integer to be `x`, and the other two need it to be `y`. The `stop()` function needs them both.

This problem of differing argument lists commonly faces us when we want to treat functions similarly in this way.

One solution is the one we adopted—add extra arguments so that all the functions have the same type. Another way is to abandon type safety, and declare all the functions as `int()`; that is, functions with no specified parameter list, returning `int`. This prevents the compiler from doing prototype checking, which means we can use our array to point to different kinds of functions, but it also removes an important safety net—so we had better be pretty sure that we exactly know what we're doing.

Another solution is to use ellipsis notation to allow as many arguments as we like after the first. This is little better than declaring the functions as `int()`—it still removes most of the compiler's prototype checking ability for the specified functions.

Finally, we could simply pass a pointer to a structure (disguised as `void *`) to all the functions concerned, and simply cast to a pointer to a structure of the correct type inside each function. This goes against the spirit (although not the letter) of prototype checking, however; the whole point of type safety is to prevent us passing in, say, an `int` and treating it as a `double` by mistake, and cavalier use of `void *` sidesteps this safety net. (We could reduce the risk by always adding a type tag to the structure. More of this later.)

None of these solutions are really satisfactory. Unless we are singularly fortunate and only ever want to point to functions that are genuinely of the same type within our array, we necessarily compromise on the type safety issue, so we should take extra care when checking our code.

Arrays of Heterogeneous Objects

The requirement that all elements of an array are the same type can seem restrictive. Wouldn't it be nice if we could keep lots of different kinds of objects in the same array? The capability to treat a group of related but different objects *as* a group, while still retaining the ability to deal with them individually according to their kind, would give us a lot of flexibility.

It's perfectly possible to do this, and in fact relatively simple. In so doing, we must play games with type safety, but we can mitigate that to some extent by using type tags. We first declare a structure with a type tag and a pointer to the object; if we want, we can also store a function pointer, giving us a tempting taste of encapsulation (see Listing 11.8).

LISTING 11.8 Array of Objects

```
typedef struct HETEROBJECT
{
  int tag;
  void *obj;
  int (*func)();
} HETEROBJECT;
```

We can see immediately that the overhead is quite significant for small objects; we probably wouldn't want to adopt this solution if most of our objects were *very* small.

Note also that we will get some compilation warnings from most good compilers because we have abandoned type checking on our encapsulated function. These warnings are not to be taken lightly. There are ways to get rid of them, as pointed out in the previous section, but such tricks only get rid of the warning itself, not the underlying problem—this is like trying to put out a fire by turning off the fire alarm. We'll instead take note of the warnings, check that the danger of which they warn us does not apply here, and proceed with caution.

I've chosen to use an enumerated type for the tags, to ensure that we don't get duplicate types. `INVALID_TAG` is the first tag, with the default enumerated type value 0, to ensure that a declaration such as `HETEROBJECT Bag[6] = {0}` will correctly mark each element in the array as (currently) invalid. We will assign an appropriate tag value at some time soon after the declaration, of course.

Also, I've written a little helper function, to simplify the initialization of the array.

```
enum
{
  INVALID_TAG,
  FOO_TAG,
  BAR_TAG,
  BAZ_TAG
} TAG;

typedef struct FOO
{
  char data;
```

```
  char foo[80];
} FOO;

typedef struct BAR
{
  char bar[80];
  long data;
} BAR;

typedef struct BAZ
{
  double data_a;
  char baz[80];
  double data_b;
} BAZ;

void BagInsert(HETEROBJECT *bag,
               size_t Item,
               int Tag,
               void *Address,
               int (*Function)())
{
  bag[Item].tag  = Tag;
  bag[Item].obj  = Address;
  bag[Item].func = Function;
}

int DoFoo(FOO *foo)
{
  printf("%s [%c]\n", foo->foo, foo->data);
  return 0;
}
int DoBar(BAR *bar)
{
  printf("%s [%ld]\n", bar->bar, bar->data);
  return 0;
}
int DoBaz(BAZ *baz)
{
  printf("%s [%f, %f]\n", baz->baz, baz->data_a, baz->data_b);
  return 0;
}
```

```
int main(void)
{
  FOO fa = {'a', "I'm the first foo"};
  FOO fb = {'b', "I'm the second foo"};
  BAR ba = {"I'm the first bar", 6 };
  BAR bb = {"I'm the second bar", 42 };
  BAZ za = { 1.414, "I'm the first baz", 1.618 };
  BAZ zb = { 2.718, "I'm the second baz", 3.141 };

  HETEROBJECT Bag[6] = {0};

  int i;

  BagInsert(Bag, 0, BAR_TAG, &bb, DoBar);
  BagInsert(Bag, 1, BAZ_TAG, &za, DoBaz);
  BagInsert(Bag, 2, BAR_TAG, &ba, DoBar);
  BagInsert(Bag, 3, FOO_TAG, &fb, DoFoo);
  BagInsert(Bag, 4, BAZ_TAG, &zb, DoBaz);
  BagInsert(Bag, 5, FOO_TAG, &fa, DoFoo);

  for(i = 0; i < sizeof Bag / sizeof Bag[0]; i++)
  {
    (*Bag[i].func)(Bag[i].obj);
  }

  return 0;
}
```

I would have liked to adopt a more formal approach, and to provide a complete library for you to use, but there's little that can be standardized here. I can't even say for certain that a function pointer return type of `int` will suit your purposes. You might, in fact, prefer not to use function pointers at all (a switch inside the main `for` loop would have done just as well in this rather artificial example). And besides the helper function `BagInsert()`, which may or may not suit your needs, there is no real need for a function library; simple array syntax is perfectly adequate.

We saw here how tags can be used to allow us to put different kinds of data into the same array. We'll use the same technique again and again in the rest of the code presented in this chapter. Now that you know how to use tags, however, we won't trouble you with further illustrations of their use. The code handles them if you want it to—if you always use one particular kind of object in your data structure, don't worry about the tag; simply pass, say, zero as the tag value, to satisfy the compiler.

Of course, those tags are not as typesafe as, say, a C++ template. No compiler is going to tell you that you've used the *wrong* tag for a data structure. (On the other hand, C++ templates produce a complete new set of object code for each different type, which some people view as a bit wasteful.) This chapter relies quite heavily on pointers to unknown types, and places the responsibility for type discipline firmly on the user-programmer's shoulders. That's as it should be. Some people think type safety is critical, others think it's a straitjacket, and yet others think that type safety should be a guide but not a prison. A good library should serve all these kinds of user-programmer.

I am a great fan of `typedef`. Many C programmers think `typedef` is an unnecessary obfuscation, which gets between the programmer and the information that he needs if he is to do his job properly. Whether you agree with this point of view depends on how you perceive the task of programming.

It's not unreasonable to see C as a kind of portable assembly language—you shove numbers into memory, trawl through them doing calculations, and spit out the answer. C is pitched at a low enough level to encourage this kind of programming.

On the other hand, it's equally valid to consider each new problem to be likely to occur again at some point, and to plan against that day. So we try to make our code reusable. All C programmers do this to a greater or lesser extent, even if it's only by finding an old program and yanking out some old source code to paste into their new program. There, undoubtedly, they will hack it around to do something slightly different, and end up with several dozen slightly different versions of the same code!

I have found that code is easier to reuse if it is written in a way that doesn't expose you to the nitty-gritty details of the sub-problem which that code solves. When I am writing a TCP/IP client, it doesn't really matter to me whether the `SOCKET` type is an `int` (as is in fact the case) or a complicated structure. All I'm really interested in at that point in time is declaring one, initializing it correctly, and passing it to the right functions. This concept of data abstraction ties in neatly with the functional abstraction that C provides in its standard library. I'm not saying that we should be blind to the inner workings of our libraries. But we shouldn't have to focus on *how* they work, *every single time* we use them. Once we are confident that we understand what they do, we should be able to reuse them without having that knowledge shoved in our faces over and over. The cleaner the interface, the better. The `typedef` keyword helps us to store the low-level details of the library interface where we can get at them if we have to, but which we can ignore if we choose.

If you take this idea to its illogical conclusion, of course, you can end up with C++. Nevertheless, a realistic level of abstraction can help us to focus on what is important, and to trust that our libraries are doing their job correctly and get on with doing our job—writing the applications that use those libraries.

For the rest of this chapter, we'll be looking at classical data structures. I have used `typedef` in quite a few cases, in an attempt to make the meaning and usage of each data structure crystal clear.

Single-linked Lists

A single-linked list is a way of joining objects together, such that each object has associated with it some way of indicating the next object in the list. The order is application-dependent, and is usually just the order in which the program encounters the data. Lists are most useful when the order of the items within them is not important. If we need to order the list by some key, so that we can search it for a particular item, we'd be better off with a more ordered data structure, such as a heap (which I'll be explaining later in this chapter) or a tree (covered in Chapter 12, "Binary Search Trees").

Lists are especially useful when we need to store a lot of data in memory at once but don't know in advance how much data we can expect to receive, or when we need to rearrange data arbitrarily.

We can implement a single-linked list very simply (and naively), using an array as shown in Listing 11.9.

LISTING 11.9 An Array-based Single-linked List

```
#include <stdio.h>

typedef struct ITEM
{
  char Title[30];
  char Author[30];
  int Next;
} ITEM;

int main(void)
{
  ITEM List[] =
  {
    {"UNIX Unleashed", "Burk and Horvath", 2},
    {"Algorithms in C", "Sedgewick", 9},
    {"Builder Unleashed","Calvert", 10},
    {"C++ Unleashed", "Liberty", 12},
    {"Linux Unleashed", "Husain and Parker", 8},
    {"Teach Yourself BCB", "Reisdorph", 1},
    {"Data Structures & Algorithms", "Lafore", 3},
```

LISTING 11.9 continued

```
    {"DOS Programmers Reference", "Dettmann & Johnson", 11},
    {"C Programming Language", "Kernighan & Ritchie", 6},
    {"C++ Programming Language", "Stroustrup", 13},
    {"C: How to Program", "Deitel & Deitel", 7},
    {"C : A Reference Manual", "Harbison & Steele", 15},
    {"The Standard C Library", "Plauger", 5},
    {"C Programming FAQs", "Summit", 14},
    {"Expert C Programming", "van der Linden", -1},
    {"C Unleashed", "Heathfield & Kirby", 4}
  };

  int Current = 0;

  while(Current != -1)
  {
    printf("Read %s, by %s.\n",
           List[Current].Title,
           List[Current].Author);
    Current = List[Current].Next;
  }

  return 0;
}
```

This list is linked in such a way as to give the books by alphabetical order of author if they are iterated in list order. (This was an arbitrary decision, purely to illustrate the ordering of the list. In practice, simple lists are generally not appropriate for sorting data arriving in random order. Binary trees are better at this.)

The key to understanding the linked list is in the line that assigns `Current` a new value; that value is the index of the next item in the list. In order to ensure that the list terminates, we need a *sentinel* value; I chose -1, but it could be any value, as long as it's detectably illegal for a real index value. (If the last item in the list indicates the index of the first item, we have a circular list. More on this later.)

Although it is possible, as we have just seen, to implement linked lists using an array, it is a little clumsy. If the array is full, we must reallocate its space when a new item arrives. If we want to add a new item to the front of the list, we must either move every item up one place to make room, or introduce a new variable to indicate which item is at the start of the list.

Also, we have embedded within our data definition the knowledge that it is part of a list. Do we really need to do that? Is it not possible to have a list of items that don't have such knowledge? This would be very useful if we have predefined structs that we now want to store in a list, despite the fact that they were not designed with that knowledge in mind. For example, can we not have a list of objects of type `struct tm`?

We already know the answer to the latter problem. When we were dealing with arrays, we saw how simple it is to embed a pointer in a structure, which can point at anything we like. As a result, we can separate the idea of a list and the idea of application data, and treat them separately. This makes it possible and, in fact, desirable to write a set of library routines to manage a linked list of... of... anything!

We can solve the former problem quite easily too. Although a structure cannot contain an instance of itself (where would it all end?), it *can* contain a *pointer* to an instance of itself. If we use this pointer to point to the next item in our list, we can build the list quickly and simply, and we can add new items wherever we like, including the beginning of the list. We will need a sentinel value to mark the end of the list, and `NULL` suits this purpose admirably. Figure 11.2 may help you to visualize this more easily.

FIGURE 11.2
A single-linked list with three items.

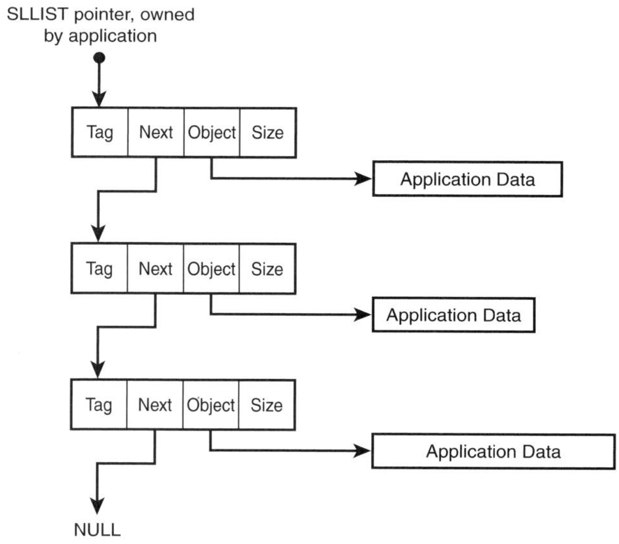

Isolating the list itself from the items in that list has another important advantage. When we want to store our list on a disk or other offline storage medium, we are able to save just the items, not the list information itself. If the list structure information were embedded in the application data structure, we'd have to pick our way gingerly through the structure, saving only selected members and skipping over the list pointers. Alternatively, we could write out the list information too, but this would cost unnecessary storage space. We'd have to be really careful when reading information back from the storage device, too, because we'd be reading misleading pointer information that we would have to conscientiously correct. Life *doesn't* have to be that messy.

In order to generalize our list as much as possible, let's not assume that we are going to be storing objects that are all of the same type. Therefore, we'll use a tag field. Also, it may be useful to store within our structure the size of the item pointed to. (The application may, or may not, require this information. Let's keep it flexible.) The full source code for Listing 11.10 can be found on the CD, in the files `sllist.h` and `sllist.c`; the test driver is stored in `sllistmn.c`.

First of all, we need a suitable data structure.

LISTING 11.10 A Simple Single-linked List Library

```
typedef struct SLLIST
{
  int Tag;
  struct SLLIST *Next;
  void *Object;
  size_t Size;
} SLLIST;
```

Here we have a pointer to the next item in the list, a pointer to the data itself, a tag field, and a size (which we don't use in the linked list code itself; they are there purely as conveniences to the user-programmer).

Adding Items

A list can only have a new item placed at the beginning, the end, or somewhere in the middle. We'll start off with a function to add an item somewhere in the middle; the other two functions are really special cases of this function.

The first addition defines the list. To start a list off, we simply define a pointer to `SLLIST`, assign `NULL` to it, and pass it to one of the `Add` functions. What we must *not* do in the calling code is declare an instance of `SLLIST`; we just want a pointer. The `Add` functions get the required memory themselves, and the deletion functions rely on being able to `free` up the memory occupied by an item—if they do this on an instance of `SLLIST` not allocated via `malloc` (or `realloc` or `calloc`), the result is undefined. Just a quick reminder—if we release memory not allocated in one of these ways, our implementation is free, at run-time, to do anything it likes, including but by no means restricted to releasing the lions from their cages in the zoo just over the road. That can get messy, and the paperwork is a real bind.

With the second addition, we start to build the list. Each item in the list points to the next item, with the last item pointing to `NULL`.

```
int SLAdd(SLLIST **Item,
          int Tag,
          void *Object,
          size_t Size)
{
  SLLIST *NewItem;
  int Result = SL_SUCCESS;

  assert(Item != NULL);

  if(Size > 0)
  {
    NewItem = malloc(sizeof *NewItem);
    if(NewItem != NULL)
    {
      NewItem->Tag    = Tag;
      NewItem->Size   = Size;
      NewItem->Object = malloc(Size);

      if(NewItem->Object != NULL)
      {
        memcpy(NewItem->Object, Object, Size);
        /* Handle empty list */
        if(NULL == *Item)
        {
          NewItem->Next = NULL;
          *Item = NewItem;
        }
        else /* Insert just after current item */
        {
          NewItem->Next = (*Item)->Next;
          (*Item)->Next = NewItem;
        }
      }
      else
      {
        free(NewItem);
        Result = SL_NO_MEM;
```

```
      }
    }
    else
    {
      Result = SL_NO_MEM;
    }
  }
  else
  {
    Result = SL_ZERO_SIZE;
  }

  return Result;
}
```

If there is insufficient memory to store the object, we fail safe by freeing the memory we allocated for the `SLLIST` structure, so that no memory at all is allocated for the new item. This kind of housekeeping is essential, but does tend to make our code considerably longer than a naive implementation. The payoff is that we will be able to use the code with a considerable amount of confidence that it will withstand heavy applications.

This function will insert an item just after the item whose address is passed to it. We'd also like to be able to insert a new item before the item passed in. The next function does this. With a single-linked list, however, this raises a difficulty. We can only do this at the *front* of the list, because we have no way of getting to the previous item, to reset its `Next` pointer. In fact, we have no way of knowing that the user-programmer has given us the first item in the list! We must trust that he has. I don't know about you, but I hate trusting my user-programmers, even though they are splendid people and undoubtedly know exactly what they are doing (most of the time). I'd rather be absolutely sure that my code can't break. Having said that, we trust our user-programmers whenever we write a library function that takes a `char *`. We can check for `NULL`, but we can't check, for instance, for a completely uninitialized pointer, or that enough space has been allocated for the operation our function performs.

```
int SLFront(SLLIST **Item,
            int Tag,
            void *Object,
            size_t Size)
{
  int Result = SL_SUCCESS;

  SLLIST *p = NULL;
```

```
  assert(Item != NULL);

  Result = SLAdd(&p, Tag, Object, Size);
  if(SL_SUCCESS == Result)
  {
    p->Next = *Item;
    *Item = p;
  }

  return Result;
}
```

This function, for all its problems, is gratifyingly short because we were able to reuse the code from `SLAdd()`.

If the user-programmer gives us the address of an item in the middle of the list, the result will be a split list. There will be two beginnings to the list, one of which will be the item we just added. Temptingly innovative as this split list idea may be, it is fraught with peril, and we should avoid it.

This problem disappears with double-linked lists (more on those later) because by their very nature they allow us to go backwards through the list.

Adding items to the front of the list is useful because it's quick. Sometimes, however, our application may require that we place them at the end.

```
int SLAppend(SLLIST **Item,
             int Tag,
             void *Object,
             size_t Size)
{
  int Result = SL_SUCCESS;
  SLLIST *EndSeeker;

  assert(Item != NULL);

  if(NULL == *Item)
  {
    Result = SLAdd(Item, Tag, Object, Size);
  }
  else
  {
    EndSeeker = *Item;
    while(EndSeeker->Next != NULL)
    {
```

```
      EndSeeker = EndSeeker->Next;
    }
    Result = SLAdd(&EndSeeker, Tag, Object, Size);
  }

  return Result;
}
```

We have no choice but to iterate through the list, looking for the last node, which makes this an expensive operation for long lists. Actually, that's not strictly true. We *do* have a choice. We could have a controlling struct that contains a pointer to the head and the tail of the list. This would also allow us to solve the problem of ensuring that `SLFront()` is not called for any item except the one at the front. It would, however, complicate the model somewhat and I don't propose to explore that route here, especially because it's fairly obvious how to modify the supplied code.

Updating an Item

There are times when we need to modify the data stored in a particular position. We can do this easily, using the following code:

```
int SLUpdate(SLLIST *Item,
             int NewTag,
             void *NewObject,
             size_t NewSize)
{
  int Result = SL_SUCCESS;

  void *p;

  if(NewSize > 0)
  {
    p = realloc(Item->Object, NewSize);
    if(NULL != p)
    {
      Item->Object = p;
      memmove(Item->Object, NewObject, NewSize);
      Item->Tag = NewTag;
      Item->Size = NewSize;
    }
    else
    {
      Result = SL_NO_MEM;
    }
```

```
  }
  else
  {
    Result = SL_ZERO_SIZE;
  }

  return Result;
}
```

As you can see, we allow the user-programmer to provide us not only with different data, but also with a completely different object, with a new tag and a new size. There is no particular need for the user-programmer to store only *one* type of object in our list. By judicious use of the tag, he can control a large number of different kinds of objects within the same list. This can be of considerable benefit in non-trivial applications that need to deal homogeneously with heterogeneous data. Allowing one object to be replaced with a different kind of object adds to this flexibility.

Retrieving Data

How does the user-programmer gain access to the data stored in a particular item of the list? He could simply dereference the `SLLIST` structure's `Object` pointer, but we'd rather he didn't do that because by so doing he binds his code tightly to our particular implementation of the single-linked list. (We can't *stop* him from doing that without making the code a lot more complicated, and such a course would make the library harder to use, penalizing user-programmers who play by the rules.) If we provide a simple mechanism to allow him access to the data in a more object-oriented way, however, we can reasonably expect him to do the decent thing.

```
void *SLGetData(SLLIST *Item,
                int *Tag,
                size_t *Size)
{
  void *p = NULL;

  if(Item != NULL)
  {
    if(Tag != NULL)
    {
      *Tag = Item->Tag;
    }
    if(Size != NULL)
    {
      *Size = Item->Size;
```

```
    }
    p = Item->Object;
  }

  return p;
}
```

We could have returned a copy of the data, but that would have placed the responsibility on the user-programmer for releasing the memory for that copy when he'd finished with it, and we're trying to make his job easier, not harder. It does mean, however, that we have to trust him with a pointer to the data.

If you're a C++ fan, you might be looking smug at this point. Remember, then, that any C++ object's data hiding can be blown away by a cast to `char *`.

Deleting an Item

Removing an item from the list is simple enough if all we want to do is free up the memory. That's not all we have to do, however. The problem is list integrity. We can easily remove the item after the one we're given but, because we don't have a pointer to the previous item, we can't remove the one we're given and still ensure that the list remains correctly linked. The best we can do is return a pointer to the next item, and trust the user-programmer himself to link up the list correctly. That's not an ideal situation. Again, this difficulty vanishes into the mist with double-linked lists.

```
SLLIST *SLDeleteThis(SLLIST *Item)
{
  SLLIST *NextNode = NULL;

  if(Item != NULL)
  {
    NextNode = Item->Next;

    if(Item->Object != NULL)
    {
      free(Item->Object);
    }
    free(Item);
  }

  return NextNode;
}

void SLDeleteNext(SLLIST *Item)
```

```
{
  if(Item != NULL && Item->Next != NULL)
  {
    Item->Next = SLDeleteThis(Item->Next);
  }
}
```

Again, we are able to re-use code to minimize redundancy.

Destroying the List

Once we've finished with our list, we need to be able to destroy it completely. This is relatively trivial:

```
void SLDestroy(SLLIST **List)
{
  SLLIST *Next;
  if(*List != NULL)
  {
    Next = *List;
    do
    {
      Next = SLDeleteThis(Next);
    } while(Next != NULL);
    *List = NULL;
  }
}
```

I was quite tempted to make this function recursive. It would, however, have been a mistake. If the list had several thousand elements, a stack-based implementation could easily have run out of resources, and failed. The iterative solution is almost certainly quicker too.

Walking the List

The final function in our single-linked list library gives us the ability to perform some operation on all the items in the list in one fell swoop. To do this, we borrow a trick from the standard library functions, `qsort` and `bsearch`, which take pointers to function as part of their parameter list. `SLWalk` requires a pointer to a function taking three parameters: a tag, a pointer to an object of some kind, and a pointer to a struct containing arguments (this final pointer may be `NULL` if you don't need arguments). The tag allows us to do some kind of switch within the function in case we want to deal with different kinds of objects. `SLWalk` simply iterates through the list, calling the function for each item in turn, passing it the tag, the object, and the arguments. It assumes your function returns 0 on success, and will halt the walk if any call to your function fails (returns non-zero). It will return the result of the most recent call (which, unless an error has occurred part of the way through the walk, will be the result of the call to the last item in the list).

```
int SLWalk(SLLIST *List,
           int(*Func)(int, void *, void *),
           void *Args)
{
  SLLIST *ThisItem;
  int Result = 0;

  for(ThisItem = List;
      0 == Result && ThisItem != NULL;
      ThisItem = ThisItem->Next)
  {
    Result = (*Func)(ThisItem->Tag,
                     ThisItem->Object,
                     Args);
  }

  return Result;
}
```

And that's it. We now have all we need to manage single-linked lists generically and powerfully. So, how do we use this library? Let's find out, by writing a test driver.

Test Driver

Here is a quick example. You will see that I have to use a temporary variable when I want to pick up an element partway through the list. That's because I dare not let go of the pointer to the start of the list (a problem we will solve later on by using double-linked lists):

```
#include <stdio.h>
#include <stdlib.h>
#include <assert.h>

#include "sllist.h"

typedef struct BOOK
{
  char Title[30];
  char Author[30];
} BOOK;
```

```
typedef struct FIELD_INFO
{
  int TitleWidth;
  int AuthWidth;
} FIELD_INFO;

int PrintBook(int Tag, void *Memory, void *Args)
{
  BOOK *b = Memory;
  FIELD_INFO *f = Args;

  assert(Tag == 0);

  printf("Read %*s, by %*s\n",
         f->TitleWidth,
         b->Title,
         f->AuthWidth,
         b->Author);

  return 0;
}


int main(void)
{
  BOOK Book[] =
  {
    {"Expert C Programming", "van der Linden"},
    {"C Programming FAQs", "Summit"},
    {"C++ Programming Language", "Stroustrup"},
    {"Algorithms in C", "Sedgewick"},
    {"Teach Yourself BCB", "Reisdorph"},
    {"The Standard C Library", "Plauger"},
    {"C++ Unleashed", "Liberty"},
    {"Data Structures & Algorithms", "Lafore"},
    {"C Programming Language", "Kernighan & Ritchie"},
    {"Linux Unleashed", "Husain and Parker"},
    {"C Unleashed", "Heathfield & Kirby"},
    {"C : A Reference Manual", "Harbison & Steele"},
    {"DOS Programmers Reference", "Dettmann & Johnson"},
    {"C: How to Program", "Deitel & Deitel"},
    {"Builder Unleashed", "Calvert"},
    {"UNIX Unleashed", "Burk and Horvath"}
```

```
};

SLLIST *List = NULL;
SLLIST *Removed = NULL;

BOOK *Data;

FIELD_INFO FldInfo = { 30, 30};
size_t NumBooks = sizeof Book / sizeof Book[0];

size_t i;

/* Populate the list */
for(i = 0; i < NumBooks; i++)
{
  if(SL_SUCCESS !=
        SLFront(&List, 0, Book + i, sizeof(BOOK)))
  {
    puts("Couldn't allocate enough memory.");
    SLDestroy(&List);
    exit(EXIT_FAILURE);
  }
}

/* Print the list */
SLWalk(List, PrintBook, &FldInfo);

/* Remove one item */
Removed = List;

for(i = 0; i < NumBooks / 2; i++)
{
  Removed = Removed->Next;
}

Data = SLGetData(Removed->Next, NULL, NULL);
printf("\nRemoving title %s\n\n", Data->Title);
SLDeleteNext(Removed);

/* Print the list again to confirm deletion */
SLWalk(List, PrintBook, &FldInfo);
```

```
  /* Destroy the list */
  SLDestroy(&List);

  return 0;
}
```

Our use of the `FIELD_INFO` structure in this code is rather artificial; the information it contains is actually available within the `BOOK` structure; all we need to do is use `sizeof`. It does, however, illustrate the mechanics of how to use the `Args` parameter.

Double-linked Lists

We have seen that single-linked lists suffer from a number of problems, most of which stem from our inability to backtrack through the list. We can solve all of these difficulties by adding backtracking pointers. When we add these links into the single-linked list, it becomes a double-linked list.

Double-linked lists differ from single-linked lists in that they contain not only a pointer to the next item but also a pointer to the previous item. This adds extra overhead to the list structure, but this extra overhead is nearly always worth it because it gives us a lot of extra power, flexibility, and robustness. We can see how this works in Figure 11.3.

FIGURE 11.3
A double-linked list with three items.

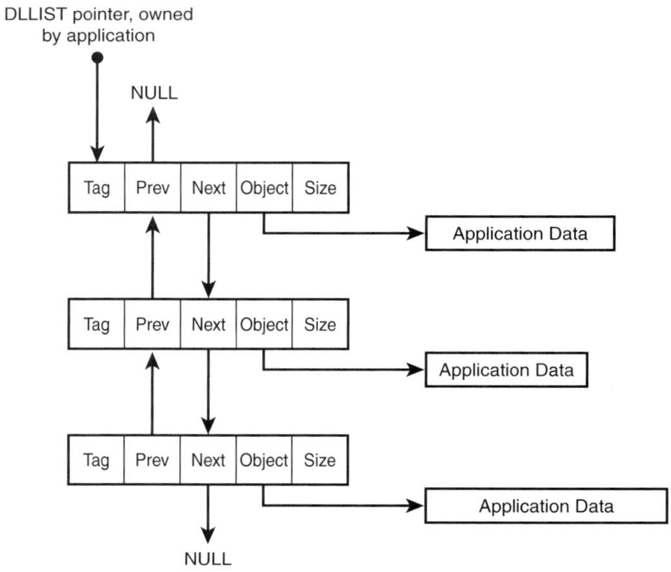

Here, I have compromised on literal accuracy (each Prev and Next pointer should really point to the *base address* of the structure, not into the middle of it somewhere) to more clearly illustrate the logic of the list. We can follow the pointers all the way along the list and, in fact, can legally refer to some Item in the list using the notation Item->Next->Prev or even Item->Next->Prev->Prev->Prev->Next->Next if we so choose. (Providing only that all of the items involved in that rather bizarre expression do actually exist; if any of the sub-expressions resolves to NULL, the code breaks.)

We have seen how we can use resizable arrays to store a text file in memory, and I suggested that we might use this kind of data structure when writing a text editor. That approach is fraught with problems, however. Although we can easily read a file in such a way, we hit difficulties the moment we try to edit the data. If, for example, our user hits the Return key, he expects to create a new line in the file he's editing. That requires us to insert a new row in our array—not at the end (which would be trivial to do) but somewhere in the middle. Because we have an array of pointers, all we need do is create a new row at the end, and memmove all the pointers along one place. But this memmove would have to take place every time the user hits Return; it would be better if we could insert the new line in place, without having to move anything else around. The double-linked list solves this problem.

You will find the source code for this library (see Listing 11.11) in dllist.h and dllist.c, on the CD.

Creating a Double-linked List

To create a double-linked list, all we need is a single item. Given an appropriate data structure (which, as you can see, is practically identical to SLLIST, with the single addition of a Prev pointer):

LISTING 11.11 A Double-linked List Library

```
typedef struct DLLIST
{
  int Tag;
  struct DLLIST *Prev;
  struct DLLIST *Next;
  void *Object;
  size_t Size;
} DLLIST;
```

we can write a simple function to create a new item, with its Prev and Next pointers set to NULL.

```
DLLIST *DLCreate(int Tag, void *Object, size_t Size)
```

```
{
  DLLIST *NewItem;

  NewItem = malloc(sizeof *NewItem);
  if(NewItem != NULL)
  {
    NewItem->Prev = NewItem->Next = NULL;
    NewItem->Tag = Tag;
    NewItem->Size = Size;
    NewItem->Object = malloc(Size);
    if(NULL != NewItem->Object)
    {
      memcpy(NewItem->Object, Object, Size);
    }
    else
    {
      free(NewItem);
      NewItem = NULL;
    }
  }

  return NewItem;
}
```

The user-programmer can call this function to create the first item in a list if he wants, but he doesn't have to. The various `Add` functions will call it as required.

Before we get too heavily into double-linked list insertion routines, here are a few simple navigational functions that will save us some work later on.

```
DLLIST *DLGetPrev(DLLIST *List)
{
  if(List != NULL)
  {
    List = List->Prev;
  }

  return List;
}

DLLIST *DLGetNext(DLLIST *List)
{
  if(List != NULL)
  {
```

```
    List = List->Next;
  }

  return List;
}

DLLIST *DLGetFirst(DLLIST *List)
{
  if(List != NULL)
  {
    while(List->Prev != NULL)
    {
      List = DLGetPrev(List);
    }
  }
  return List;
}

DLLIST *DLGetLast(DLLIST *List)
{
  if(List != NULL)
  {
    while(List->Next != NULL)
    {
      List = DLGetNext(List);
    }
  }
  return List;
}
```

Now, many of our functions need to insert an item into a list, where the item already exists. For example, the item may have just been created, using the `DLCreate()` function, and now needs to be inserted into the correct place. We could place all the pointer code into each function needing it, but it makes sense to move it into its own function. The user-programmer can call it directly if he wants, but most of the time he won't need to. Actually, we'll have two such functions—one to insert the new item before an existing item, and one to insert it after the existing item. Because the two functions are very similar, we'll just show one of them here.

Note

Because we often want to do *something* either before or after an existing item, whatever that something may be, we find that many of our functions exist in two flavors. We could have merged them, at the cost of an extra parameter; there are arguments for and against each method. I selected the method I believe to be clearest.

```
int DLInsertBefore(DLLIST *ExistingItem, DLLIST *NewItem)
{
  int Result = DL_SUCCESS;

  if(ExistingItem != NULL && NewItem != NULL)
  {
    NewItem->Next = ExistingItem;
    NewItem->Prev = ExistingItem->Prev;
    ExistingItem->Prev = NewItem;
    if(NewItem->Prev != NULL)
    {
      NewItem->Prev->Next = NewItem;
    }
  }
  else
  {
    Result = DL_NULL_POINTER;
  }

  return Result;
}
```

There are four different places in which a new item can be added—right at the start, right at the end, just before *this* item, and just after *this* item. When the list is short, some of these places are in fact the *same* place, but that doesn't really matter, as we will discover.

Insertion at Start

To insert an item at the start of the list, we must first *find* the start of the list. (We could trust the user-programmer to give us the start of the list, but there is no need, and it's best to be robust whenever we can.) We can use the `DLGetFirst()` function for this.

```
int DLPrepend(DLLIST **Item,
              int Tag,
```

```
               void *Object,
               size_t Size)
{
int Result = DL_SUCCESS;

  DLLIST *p;
  DLLIST *Start;

  assert(Item != NULL);

  p = DLCreate(Tag, Object, Size);

  if(p != NULL)
  {
    if(NULL == *Item)
    {
      *Item = p;
    }
    else
    {
      Start = DLGetFirst(*Item);
      DLInsertBefore(Start, p);
    }
  }
  else
  {
    Result = DL_NO_MEM;
  }

  return Result;
}
```

Insertion at End

To insert an item at the very end of the list, we need only call `DLGetNext()`, which returns a pointer to the last element in the list. The code for `DLAppend()`, which adds an item at the end of the list, is so similar to `DLPrepend()` that repeating it here would achieve little; it's on the CD, of course.

Insertion in the Middle

When we want to insert an item somewhere other than the beginning or the end, we begin to earn our corn. We have four pointers to take care of; the `Prev` and `Next` pointers for the new item, the `Next` pointer of the item that precedes it, and the `Prev` pointer of the item that follows it. Since you can't get big lists without starting with little lists, some of these items may not exist, so we have to be careful about `NULL` pointers.

Given an existing member of a list, we can insert our new item just before it or just after it. Both are justifiable, and it's hard to choose between them without knowing the specifics of the application. Thus, we provide both. (They are so similar that only one is shown here.)

```
int DLAddAfter(DLLIST **Item,
               int Tag,
               void *Object,
               size_t Size)
{
  int Result = DL_SUCCESS;
  DLLIST *p;

  assert(Item != NULL);

  p = DLCreate(Tag, Object, Size);

  if(p != NULL)
  {
    if(NULL == *Item)
    {
      *Item = p;
    }
    else
    {
      DLInsertAfter(*Item, p);
    }
  }
  else
  {
    Result = DL_NO_MEM;
  }

  return Result;
}
```

Updating and Retrieving Data

The functions `DLUpdate()` and `DLGetData()` provide us with the same kind of data access we showed for single-linked lists and, apart from the fact that they take a `DLLIST *` instead of an `SLLIST *`, are more or less identical to `SLUpdate()` and `SLGetData()`.

Extracting an Item

We may want to remove an item from the list without deleting it (that is, without freeing its memory); for example, we may want to move items from one list to another. This is easily done, but it does place the onus on the user to clean up properly.

```
DLLIST *DLExtract(DLLIST *Item)
{
  if(Item != NULL)
  {
    if(Item->Prev != NULL)
    {
      Item->Prev->Next = Item->Next;
    }
    if(Item->Next != NULL)
    {
      Item->Next->Prev = Item->Prev;
    }
  }
  return Item;
}
```

Deleting an Item

We had problems with list integrity when deleting an item from a single-linked list. We have no such difficulty with the double-linked list, and we need only one function to delete, not two. Here it is:

```
void DLDelete(DLLIST *Item)
{
  if(Item != NULL)
  {
    DLExtract(Item);

    if(Item->Object != NULL)
    {
      free(Item->Object);
    }
    free(Item);
  }
}
```

This function calls `DLExtract()` to splice the list before releasing the item's memory.

Exchanging Items

There will be times when we want to exchange the positions of some of the items in the list. For example, we might want to sort the list by some data-dependent key. The exchange would be relatively simple, except for the awkward case where the two nodes to be exchanged are adjacent. We need to check carefully to see if they are. If so, the easiest solution is simply to remove one of them from the list altogether, and then reinsert it in the appropriate place.

```
int DLExchange(DLLIST *ItemA, DLLIST *ItemB)
{
  int Result = DL_SUCCESS;
  DLLIST *t0;
  DLLIST *t1;
  DLLIST *t2;
  DLLIST *t3;

  if(ItemA != NULL && ItemB != NULL)
  {
    if(ItemA->Next == ItemB)
    {
      DLExtract(ItemA);
      DLInsertAfter(ItemB, ItemA);
    }
    else if(ItemB->Next == ItemA)
    {
      DLExtract(ItemB);
      DLInsertAfter(ItemA, ItemB);
    }
    else
    {
      t0 = ItemA->Prev;
      t1 = ItemA->Next;
      t2 = ItemB->Prev;
      t3 = ItemB->Next;

      DLExtract(ItemA);
      DLExtract(ItemB);

      if(t2 != NULL)
      {
        DLInsertAfter(t2, ItemA);
      }
```

```
      else
      {
        DLInsertBefore(t3, ItemA);
      }

      if(t0 != NULL)
      {
        DLInsertAfter(t0, ItemB);
      }
      else
      {
        DLInsertBefore(t1, ItemB);
      }
    }
  }
  else
  {
    Result = DL_NULL_POINTER;
  }

  return Result;
}
```

Counting Items

Sometimes it's useful to know how many items there are in the list. This is very simple, and illustrates a good use of the `DLGetPrev()` and `DLGetNext()` functions:

```
int DLCount(DLLIST *List)
{
  int Items = 0;

  DLLIST *Prev = List;
  DLLIST *Next = List;

  if(List != NULL)
  {
    ++Items;
    while((Prev = DLGetPrev(Prev)) != NULL)
    {
      ++Items;
    }
    while((Next = DLGetNext(Next)) != NULL)
    {
```

```
      ++Items;
    }
  }

  return Items;
}
```

Cut and Paste

The ability to chop lists up and join them back together in new and interesting ways would be extremely useful in many kinds of applications. This is not hard to do, once you have a basic understanding of how to manipulate the pointers. But we run into questions of implementation design. How do we specify the section of the list that we want to cut, for example? Do we say "start here and cut N items"? Or "cut from *this* item to *that* item," or some other way that I haven't considered? Which method is most convenient really depends on the application. For example, a text editor would probably work on a "cut from here to there" basis, whereas a simulation program may well be better suited to a "cut from here for N items" method. Also, it makes for an interesting exercise, and I'd hate to deprive you of that, so I haven't included code for it. Should you want to investigate this idea further, you may well find `DLExtract()` and `DLInsertAfter()` to be of considerable use.

To get you started, here's code to paste one list onto the end of another. Joining two lists together is something we can reasonably expect a user-programmer to want to do, and the interface admits of few variant possibilities. Given functions we have already written, the code is gratifyingly simple.

```
void DLJoin(DLLIST *Left, DLLIST *Right)
{
  if(Left != NULL && Right != NULL)
  {
    Left = DLGetLast(Left);
    Right = DLGetFirst(Right);

    Left->Next = Right;
    Right->Prev = Left;
  }
}
```

Destroying the Whole List

This is very easy to do and, interestingly, we don't need to have the first item in the list given to us. Any item will do. Because of the double link, we can go backward and forward from the link we are given, until we hit `NULL`. We could use the `DLGetFirst()` function to roll back to the start of the list, but it's slightly more efficient simply to delete backward, then delete forward, especially if the pointer we are given happens to be some distance from the beginning of the list.

```
void DLDestroy(DLLIST **List)
{
  DLLIST *Marker;
  DLLIST *Prev;
  DLLIST *Next;

  if(*List != NULL)
  {
    /* First, destroy all previous items */
    Prev = (*List)->Prev;
    while(Prev != NULL)
    {
      Marker = Prev->Prev;
      DLDelete(Prev);
      Prev = Marker;
    }

    Next = *List;
    do
    {
      Marker = Next;
      DLDelete(Next);
      Next = Marker;
    } while(Next != NULL);
    *List = NULL;
  }
}
```

Walking the List

For completeness, I've included `DLWalk()`. Because it contains little we haven't already seen in `SLWalk()`, however, I won't list it here. The only difference is that it seeks the first item in the list before iterating through the items.

Test Driver

To illustrate some of the flexibility of the double-linked list, let's take a quick holiday. We'll need to plan our route carefully, of course, to take in some of the major tourist resorts of the world. We'll start off with a hefty itinerary, and then slowly cut back our schedule (at random) until we're left with just one place to go. For brevity, I've snipped some of the code (including some of the error checking and most of the includes!), but you can find the full source on the CD, together with a file, `cityloc.txt`, which contains the latitude and longitude of 300 major cities. It also contains some not quite so major villages (which don't actually have an international airport, but *ought* to). The file is in comma-separated variable format.

```
/* standard headers snipped */

#include "dllist.h"

#define PI 3.14159265358979323846

typedef struct CITY
{
  char Nation[30];
  char CityName[25];
  double Latitude;
  double Longitude;
} CITY;

int CompCities(const void *p1, const void *p2)
{
  const CITY *c1 = p1, *c2 = p2;

  return strcmp(c1->CityName, c2->CityName);
}

int ParseCity(CITY *c, char *Buffer)
{
  char *Token;
  char *endp;

  Token = strtok(Buffer, ",\n");
  strcpy(c->Nation, Token);
  Token = strtok(NULL, ",\n");
  strcpy(c->CityName, Token);
  Token = strtok(NULL, ",\n");
```

```
  c->Latitude = strtod(Token, &endp);
  Token = strtok(NULL, ",\n");
  c->Latitude += strtod(Token, &endp) / 60.0;
  Token = strtok(NULL, ",\n");
  if('S' == toupper(*Token))
  {
    c->Latitude *= -1.0;
  }

  c->Latitude *= PI;
  c->Latitude /= 180.0;
  Token = strtok(NULL, ",\n");
  c->Longitude = strtod(Token, &endp);
  Token = strtok(NULL, ",\n");
  c->Longitude += strtod(Token, &endp) / 60.0;
  Token = strtok(NULL, ",\n");
  if('E' == toupper(*Token))
  {
    c->Longitude *= -1.0;
  }

  c->Longitude *= PI;
  c->Longitude /= 180.0;

  return 1;
}

/* Calculate the distance between two points on the earth's
 * surface (accurate to within around +/- 30 miles).
 */
int CalcGreatCircleDistance(CITY *City1, CITY *City2)
{
  return (int)(3956.934132687      *
    acos((sin(City1->Latitude)      *
          sin(City2->Latitude))     +
        ((cos(City1->Latitude)      *
          cos(City2->Latitude))     *
        ((cos(City1->Longitude)     *
          cos(City2->Longitude))    +
         (sin(City1->Longitude)     *
          sin(City2->Longitude))))));
}
```

```
int Random(int n)
{
  double d;

  d = rand() / (RAND_MAX + 1.0);
  d *= n;

  return (int)d;
}

/* The test file cityloc.txt may be passed as argv[1]. */
int main(int argc, char *argv[])
{
  DLLIST *List = NULL;
  DLLIST *Safe = NULL;
  CITY *City = NULL;
  CITY ThisCity = {0};
  CITY *TempCity = NULL;
  CITY *First;
  CITY *Second;
  long TotalDistance;
  int Distance;

  int i;
  int j;
  int k;

  int NumCities = 0;
  int MaxCities = 0;

  char Buffer[80] = {0};

  FILE *fp = NULL;

  srand((unsigned)time(NULL));
  if(argc > 1)
  {
    fp = fopen(argv[1], "r");
    /* snipped error checking */
  }
  else
  {
    puts("Please specify a cities file.");
```

```
    exit(EXIT_FAILURE);
  }

  while(NULL != fgets(Buffer,
                      sizeof Buffer,
                      fp))
  {
    if(ParseCity(&ThisCity, Buffer))
    {
      if(++NumCities >= MaxCities)
      {
        ++MaxCities;
        MaxCities *= 3;
        MaxCities /= 2;

        TempCity = realloc(City,
                           MaxCities * sizeof *TempCity);

        /* snipped error checking */

        City = TempCity;
      }
      memcpy(City + NumCities - 1,
             &ThisCity,
             sizeof *City);
    }
  }

  fclose(fp);

  TempCity = realloc(City, NumCities * sizeof *TempCity);
  if(NULL == TempCity)
  {
    puts("Something odd is happening. realloc returned");
    puts("NULL for a /reduction/ in storage.");
  }
  else
  {
    City = TempCity;
  }

  j = Random(NumCities - 6) + 6;
```

```
/* Build a random list of cities */
for(i = 0; i < j; i++)
{
  k = Random(NumCities);

  if(DL_SUCCESS != DLAddAfter(&List,
                              0,
                              City + k,
                              sizeof *City))
  {
    /* snipped error checking */
  }
}

Safe = List;

while(j > 1)
{
  TotalDistance = 0;
  First = DLGetData(List, NULL, NULL);

  while(DLGetNext(List) != NULL)
  {
    List = DLGetNext(List);
    Second = DLGetData(List, NULL, NULL);

    Distance =
      CalcGreatCircleDistance(First, Second);

    printf("%s - %s : %d miles.\n",
      First->CityName, Second->CityName, Distance);

    TotalDistance += Distance;

    First = Second;
  }

  printf("Total distance for this route: %ld miles.\n",
         TotalDistance);

  if(j > 2)
  {
```

```
      printf("---- Removing one city ----\n");
    }

    k = Random(j - 1);
    for(i = 0; i < k; i++)
    {
      List = DLGetPrev(List);
    }
    DLDelete(List);

    List = Safe;
    --j;
  }

  /* Destroy the list */
  DLDestroy(&List);

  free(City);

  return EXIT_SUCCESS;
}
```

This code illustrates how items can be added to the list, and how they can then be removed. It also shows, most importantly, how you can traverse the list in either direction.

Circular Lists

Circular lists are either single- or double-linked lists that chase their own tail; A points to B points to C points to D points to E points to A. They are best suited to circular data. For example, consider a train timetable for a route with a 24-hour period (the timetable repeats itself every 24 hours). If a customer asks, at 9 p.m., which trains will be leaving in the next six hours, he presumably would like to be informed not only of the 21:38 train, but also of the 01:19. A circular list is nicely suited to this task. Because of its circular nature, there is no start item or end item in a circular list. It's useful, therefore, to have the concept of a current position, through which all operations are conducted (this can be seen clearly in Figure 11.4). If the item we want isn't at the current position, we can rotate the list until we have the item we want. Typically, the application will rotate the list one item at a time but it should be able to rotate through more than one item if it needs to. Rotations are very fast because no data actually moves around in memory—all we need to do is re-assign a pointer. Figure 11.4 shows how the list pointers co-operate to form a ring, with each element in the list storing a pointer to the application's data.

FIGURE 11.4
A circular list.

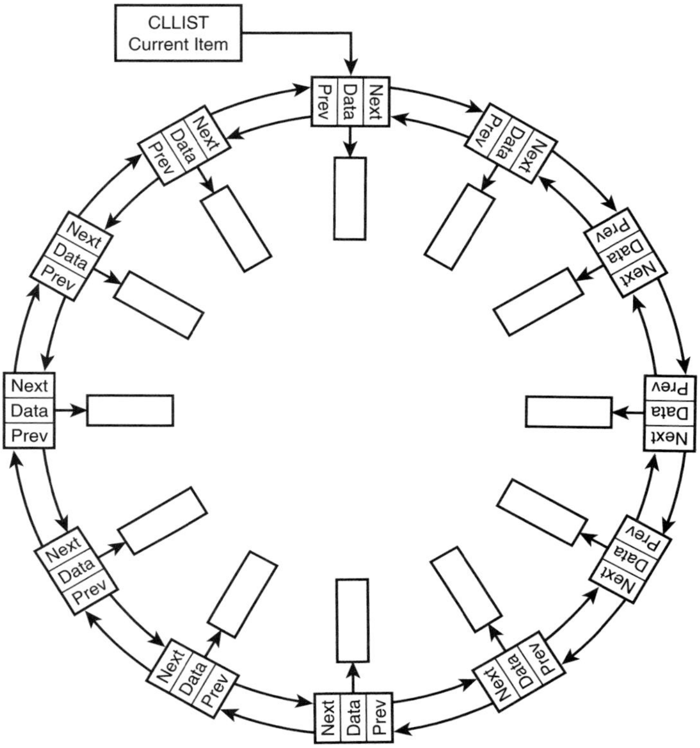

Header Node

A header node is by no means essential for a circular list, but it can simplify the code immensely. Some circular list implementations point the tail pointer back to the header node. This can have the opposite effect and make the code more complicated. It somehow seems more appropriate for the tail pointer to point to the first pointer, in true circular fashion.

We will use a header node (see Listing 11.12) to minimize the user-programmer's overhead in keeping track of the current item. All he need do is look after the header node, and the circular list will more or less look after itself. This allows us to keep extra information too—information associated not with any one item on the list, but to do with the list itself. We will take advantage of this flexibility to keep a count of the number of items in the list.

LISTING 11.12 A Circular List Library

```
typedef struct CL_ITEM
{
  int Tag;
  struct CL_ITEM *Prev;
  struct CL_ITEM *Next;
  void *Object;
  size_t Size;
} CL_ITEM;

typedef struct CLIST
{
  CL_ITEM *CurrentItem;
  size_t NumItems;
} CLIST;
```

To use the single-linked and double-linked list libraries, we needed to declare a pointer to an item, and assign `NULL` to it. Our header node is slightly different; in our application code, we will define an instance of it, rather than a pointer to an instance of it. To ensure that it is correctly initialized, we should define it as follows:

```
CLIST Clist = {0};
```

This initialization will guarantee that `CList.CurrentItem` is `NULL`, and `CList.NumItems` is 0.

Note

We can't use `memset` for the same purpose, because we can't guarantee that the target machine will use all-bits-zero to represent `NULL`.

Inserting the First Node

The first node is a special case because it will point to itself. To detect whether it's the first node is trivial. We need only check the `NumItems` field of the `CLIST` structure.

Inserting Subsequent Nodes

For subsequent nodes, we have to consider where in the list they are to be inserted. One sensible strategy is to add the new node to the end of the list. Where, though, is the end of a circular list? Perhaps the end is the item pointed to by the `Prev` pointer of the current item.

It's as good a definition as any, so we will use it, and insert a new item after it, so that the new item becomes the current item's `Prev` target.

Consider the second item to be added to the list. We want to add it as `Current->Prev->Next`. Now, with only one item in the list, `Current->Prev` points to `Current`! So we will actually be pointing `Current->Next` to the new item, as well as `Current->Prev`! When we consider the circular nature of the situation, however, we can see that this is in fact the correct behavior.

Here, then, is code to insert items into the list:

```
int CLAddItem(CLIST *List,
              int Tag,
              void *Object,
              size_t Size)
{
  CL_ITEM *NewItem;
  int Result = CL_SUCCESS;

  assert(List != NULL);

  NewItem = CLCreate(Tag, Object, Size);
  if(NULL == NewItem)
  {
    Result = CL_NO_MEM;
  }
  else
  {
    ++List->NumItems;

    if(NULL == List->CurrentItem)
    {
      /* First item in the list, so
       * it points to itself in
       * both directions.
       */
      List->CurrentItem = NewItem;
      List->CurrentItem->Next = NewItem;
      List->CurrentItem->Prev = NewItem;
    }
    else
    {
      /* We'll place this item just
       * behind the current item
```

```
        */
        NewItem->Prev = List->CurrentItem->Prev;
        NewItem->Next = List->CurrentItem;
        List->CurrentItem->Prev->Next = NewItem;
        List->CurrentItem->Prev = NewItem;
      }
    }

  return Result;
}
```

As you can see, this code calls a function, `CLCreate()`, which I haven't shown here but which is on the CD, in the `cllist.c` file. Its task is to create a new node, which `CLAddItem()` can then add into the list.

Retrieving and Updating Data

If we discipline ourselves to retrieve only the item in the current position, retrieval is simple. We need only return a pointer to the current item's data. Likewise, update is very easy. We've already covered the general idea in this chapter; to see the source code, check out `cllist.c` on the CD.

Rotating the List

Efficient list rotation is an interesting exercise in optimization. Because the list is circular, it shares some properties with modulo arithmetic. We want to rotate the list `P` places, and there are `N` items in the list. The first optimization to spring to mind is that we could reduce `P` to be in the range `0` to `N—1`. This is easily done using C's modulo operator. Before we do that, though, it would be wise to ensure that `P` is non-negative. If it *is* negative, we should bring it into the positive range. We can do this, without affecting `P`'s meaning, by adding a multiple of `N` to it.

To get the appropriate multiple `M`, we can do this:

```
M = (N – 1 – P) / N
```

This calculation takes advantage of the fact that integer division results in an integer result.

We add this to `P`:

```
P = P + (M * N)
```

This will make `P` positive, without changing the net result of the rotation request. We only need to do this if `P` is negative, of course. We can now reduce `P` modulo `N` to get the minimum number of places we need to rotate. Except that it may not be the minimum!

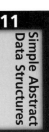

Our next optimization draws on the fact that moving `P` places forward in a circle is the same as moving `N—P` places backward. So, if `P > N / 2`, we can move `N—P` places backward instead of `P` places forward. Here's the code:

```
void CLRotate(CLIST *List, int Places)
{
  int Multiple;
  int i;

  assert(List != NULL);

  if(List->NumItems > 0)
  {
    if(Places < 0)
    {
      Multiple = (List->NumItems - 1 - Places) /
                   List->NumItems;
      Places += Multiple * List->NumItems;
    }

    Places %= List->NumItems;

    if(Places > (int)List->NumItems / 2)
    {
      Places = List->NumItems - Places;
      for(i = 0; i < Places; i++)
      {
        List->CurrentItem = List->CurrentItem->Prev;
      }
    }
    else
    {
      for(i = 0; i < Places; i++)
      {
        List->CurrentItem = List->CurrentItem->Next;
      }
    }
  }
}
```

Deleting Nodes

Since we have adopted the convention that we will only address the list via the item at its current position, deletion should be quite simple and, indeed, it is. The only minor problem arises when the item to be deleted is the only item in the list:

```
int CLDelete(CLIST *List)
{
  int Deleted = 0;
  CL_ITEM *PrevItem;
  CL_ITEM *ThisItem;
  CL_ITEM *NextItem;

  assert(List != NULL);

  if(List->NumItems > 0)
  {
    Deleted = 1;

    ThisItem = List->CurrentItem;
    free(ThisItem->Object);
    NextItem = ThisItem->Next;
    PrevItem = ThisItem->Prev;

    if(1 == List->NumItems)
    {
      List->CurrentItem = NULL;
    }
    else
    {
      List->CurrentItem = NextItem;
      NextItem->Prev = PrevItem;
      PrevItem->Next = NextItem;
    }

    free(ThisItem);

    --List->NumItems;
  }

  return Deleted;
}
```

We've returned an integer to indicate whether an item was in fact deleted. This makes the `CLDestroy()` function trivial. This is one of those rare cases when I use the `continue` statement, as a way of documenting that I did indeed intend the loop control statement to do all the work. Any optimizing compiler worth its salt will remove the `continue` statement.

```
void CLDestroy(CLIST *List)
{
  assert(List != NULL);

  while(CLDelete(List))
  {
    continue;
  }
}
```

Walking the List

Because we know exactly how many items there are in the list, walking the list can be done in a simple loop:

```
int CLWalk(CLIST *List,
           int(*Func)(int, void *, void *),
           void *Args)
{
  CL_ITEM *ThisItem;
  int Result = 0;
  int i;

  assert(List != NULL);

  for(ThisItem = List->CurrentItem, i = 0;
      0 == Result && i < (int)List->NumItems;
      ThisItem = ThisItem->Next, i++)
  {
    Result = (*Func)(ThisItem->Tag,
                     ThisItem->Object,
                     Args);
  }

  return Result;
}
```

Solving The Josephus Problem

For our demonstration program, what better example of a circular data structure than the Josephus Problem?

According to legend, the Jewish historian Flavius Josephus (37 AD–c. 100 AD) was caught up in some fighting between Jews and Romans, and was hiding in a cave with some 40 other people. The cave was surrounded by Roman soldiers. Discovery and capture seemed inevitable. To most there, death was a more honorable option, and the group thus resolved to commit suicide by standing in a circle, counting round it, and killing every third person, until there was only one person left, who would then be expected to kill himself. Josephus and a friend of his were more sympathetic to the concept of capture than the rest of the party; they quickly (and, I suspect, feverishly) worked out where to place themselves in the circle so that they could be sure of being the last two standing.

Generally speaking, the Josephus Problem comprises eliminating every Kth member of a group originally comprising N items, until only one or (if you are a stickler for detail) two members remain. A circular list lends itself well to solving this problem:

```
#include <stdio.h>
#include <stdlib.h>
#include <string.h>
#include <time.h>

#include "clist.h"

int main(void)
{
  char *Intro[] =
  {
    "The Josephus Problem",
    "--------------------",
    " ",
    "Consider a ring of N items. If the Kth item",
    "is eliminated, there will now be N - 1 items.",
    "If this procedure is performed iteratively,",
    "eventually there will be just one item",
    "remaining. Which is it?",
    " ",
    "This program provides the answer.",
    " ",
    NULL
  };
  char **Text;
```

```
    char buffer[32];
    char *endp;
    CLIST Circle = {0};
    int Result = EXIT_SUCCESS;
    unsigned long N;
    unsigned long K;
    unsigned long i;

    for(Text = Intro; *Text != NULL; ++Text)
    {
      puts(*Text);
    }

    puts("\nHow many items in the ring?");

    if(NULL == fgets(buffer, sizeof buffer, stdin))
    {
      puts("Program aborted.");
      exit(EXIT_FAILURE);
    }
    N = strtoul(buffer, &endp, 10);
    if(endp == buffer || N == 0)
    {
      puts("Program aborted.");
      Result = EXIT_FAILURE;
    }
    else
    {
      puts("Count how many items before removing one?");

      if(NULL == fgets(buffer, sizeof buffer, stdin))
      {
        puts("Program aborted.");
        exit(EXIT_FAILURE);
      }

      K = strtoul(buffer, &endp, 10);
      if(endp == buffer || K == 0)
      {
        puts("Program aborted.");
        Result = EXIT_FAILURE;
      }
    }
```

```
  for(i = 0; EXIT_SUCCESS == Result && i < N; i++)
  {
    if(CL_SUCCESS !=
          CLAddItem(&Circle,
                    0,
                    &i,
                    sizeof i))
    {
      printf("Insufficient memory. Sorry.\n");
      Result = EXIT_FAILURE;
    }
  }

  if(EXIT_SUCCESS == Result)
  {
    while(Circle.NumItems > 1)
    {
      CLRotate(&Circle, K);
      printf("Removing item %lu.\n",
                *(unsigned long *)CLGetData(&Circle,
                                            NULL,
                                            NULL));
      CLDelete(&Circle);
      /* Removing an item makes the next current,
       * which puts our count out by one, so roll
       * the circle back one node.
       */
      CLRotate(&Circle, -1);
    }

    printf("The last item is %lu.\n",
                *(unsigned long *)CLGetData(&Circle,
                                            NULL,
                                            NULL));
  }

  CLDestroy(&Circle);
  return Result;
}
```

Well, okay, we don't need to solve too many Josephus Problems in our day-to-day programming! But the concept of a circular list is equally applicable to other kinds of simulation, to music sequencing software, and even to operating system time-slicing routines.

Stacks

All of the data structures presented in this chapter are in common use in applications and systems software around the world, but perhaps none is used quite as often as the *stack*, which has (rightly or wrongly) become almost synonymous with parameter passing conventions in modern languages. But what *is* a stack? Let's find out.

At heart, a stack is simply a list, but with two rules associated with it. The first rule is that you can only place items on the top of the stack (this is known as *pushing* an item). The second rule is that you can only take items from the top of the stack (known as *popping*). These rules are summed up in the acronym LIFO (Last In, First Out). Figure 11.5 illustrates this idea. Stacks are frequently used by compilers to keep track of functions and function parameters—so frequently that many programmers talk of "placing arguments on the stack" as if compilers *always* use stacks for holding arguments. Like so many truisms, this isn't universally true—for example, many optimizing compilers place arguments in registers if doing so will improve performance.

FIGURE 11.5
A stack.

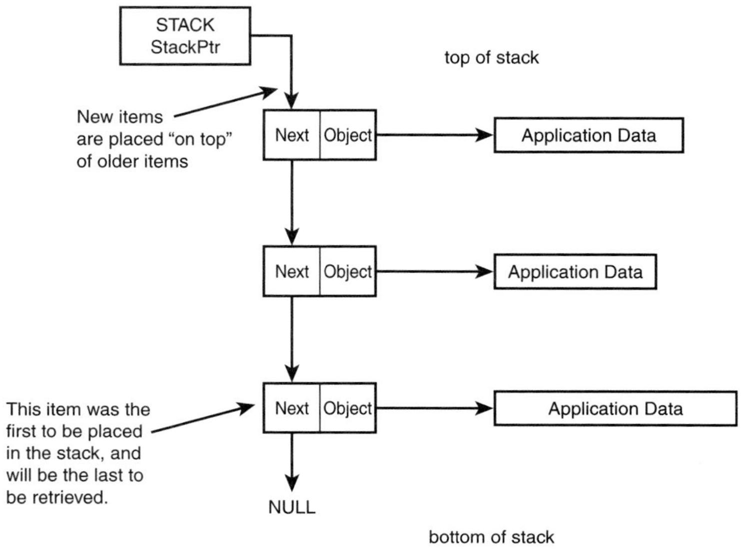

We don't have to be compiler writers to find stacks useful, however. Stacks have a place in Reverse Polish Notation calculators, expression evaluation, and a plethora of application-specific solutions. We will be looking at one such application as our example program.

Most of the stacks I have seen in application code have been poorly implemented. Almost invariably, the code has been written as part of the application, rather than as a standalone reusable library. (Code reuse is the Holy Grail of C++; aficionados of that language constantly seek code reuse and never quite seem to find it. C devotees, on the other hand, have been quietly reusing code for years; they just don't feel the need to shout about it. But for some odd reason this excellent history of reuse doesn't seem, at least in my own experience, to include stacks.) Programmers usually code their stack as a `static` array with file scope, so that both the `push()` function and the `pop()` function can have access to the stack. That's good data-hiding, but poor abstraction. This technique restricts the access functions to being used only for one stack (unless they have taken a lot more trouble than most programmers do in fact take).

Furthermore, the array is bound to one type; if we want to stack up variables of some other type, we have to write a new set of functions.

Finally, the stack is not infinitely extensible (subject to machine- and operating system-imposed limits), but is restricted to some arbitrary maximum that is judged good enough by the implementer at the time the code is written. This always seems like a good idea, and almost invariably isn't, because any arbitrarily imposed limit is doomed to be exceeded at some point.

When designing a general stack library, then, we'd like to solve these problems. Unfortunately, we can't easily keep the data hiding without using static variables, and we don't want to use those if we can possibly avoid it because it's difficult to keep them thread-safe (especially as ANSI C provides no support for threads).

Because a stack is simply a special kind of list, it makes sense to reuse some of the list code we've already written. In this case, we don't particularly need a double-linked list, so we will reduce the overhead for our stack by using a single-linked list. We'll wrap this up in a new structure, a `STACK`, whose address we will pass to the functions that will do the pushing and popping.

Creating the Stack

Our stack structure is very simple (see Listing 11.13).

LISTING 11.13 Hacking a Stack

```
typedef struct STACK
{
#ifndef NDEBUG
  int CheckInit1;
#endif

  SLLIST *StackPtr;
  size_t NumItems;

#ifndef NDEBUG
  int CheckInit2;
#endif
} STACK;
```

The `NumItems` field is purely for convenience. We also define a couple of debugging fields, which are for use in assertion statements.

Notice that because we are using the `SLLIST` structure, we must `#include "sllist.h"` before the compiler reaches this `STACK` type definition. We have three choices.

The first choice is to abandon `SLLIST` and re-implement the functions we need. As a fully paid-up member of the Lazy Programmers' Association, I'd like to avoid the extra work involved here.

Instead, we could include the `sllist.h` header inside the `stack.h` header. I don't like this option; nesting headers is not a good idea, in my opinion.

Third, we could insist that the user-programmer include `sllist.h` in any translation unit in which he includes `stack.h`, making sure that `sllist.h` is above `stack.h`. I don't like this option either because it seems to defer extra work until later (never make yourself do something every day for years, if you can instead do something else today, only once).

So none of the options is ideal (at least, not from my purist point of view), and thus we will have to compromise on a less-than-perfect solution. The first option is definitely out because C programmers reuse code whenever possible. The third option seems like hard work, and has another drawback; it makes our application programs reliant on our stack library reusing `SLLIST`. At the moment this seems like a great idea but, just maybe, in a year's time we'll come up with something even better. If so, it's bad enough having to recompile and relink everything. (If we change the `STACK` structure's contents, that implies the necessity for a recompilation of anything using functions from the stack library.) Having to edit the application code too would be annoying and potentially costly. If we simply include `sllist.h` in `stack.h`, though, we avoid this problem, and shield the user-programmer from the normally unnecessary knowledge that the stack implementation uses the list code.

It is with some reluctance, then, that we include `sllist.h` in `stack.h`, but at least we have the satisfaction of knowing that it's the least bad solution.

Once we have our structure definition, all our application code need do is define an instance of it properly. This is very simple:

```
STACK Stack = {0};
```

This definition will correctly initialize the stack pointer to `NULL`, and the `NumItems` variable to zero. If `NDEBUG` is not defined, such a definition will, naturally, also initialize the check fields to zero. (If `NDEBUG` *is* defined, these fields will be preprocessed out of existence.)

Pushing Items

Pushing items, also, is very easy. We need only call the `SLFront()` function defined in the single-linked list library code:

```
int StackPush(STACK *Stack,
              int Tag,
              void *Object,
              size_t Size)
{
  int Result = STACK_PUSH_FAILURE;
  int ListResult;
  assert(Stack != NULL);
  assert(0 == Stack->CheckInit1 && 0 == Stack->CheckInit2);

  ListResult = SLFront(&Stack->StackPtr, Tag, Object, Size);

  if(SL_SUCCESS == ListResult)
  {
    Result = STACK_SUCCESS;
    ++Stack->NumItems;
  }

  return Result;
}
```

That was wonderfully easy. All we had to do was call code we'd already written. As you may have noticed, we've defined a new set of error macros for the stack code because we don't want our user-programmers to be forced to write code that depends on our having used `SLLIST` for the underlying implementation.

The assertions don't guarantee that the stack has been initialized properly (especially because they disappear when NDEBUG is defined), but they give us a reasonable degree of safety against accidentally sloppy initialization.

Popping Items

Popping items should be as easy as pushing them. The code is already more than half-written for us. We have two tasks to perform: We must retrieve the object from the stack, in such a way that the calling application can get at the data, and we must remove the data from the stack.

The problem here is one of responsibility. When an item is pushed onto the stack, the library code allocates memory for the item. (It's actually the single-linked list code that does the allocation, but the point is that the user-programmer didn't allocate the memory.) It should, then, be the library code's responsibility for releasing the memory for the item too. But the user-programmer presumably wouldn't be popping the stack if he didn't want to access the data, and he can't do that if we've just released it. (Those people who think you *can* do this should spend a little less time writing broken programs and a little more time reading the Standard.)

We solve this problem by requiring the user-programmer to pass us a pointer to sufficient memory to store the object. We will copy the object into that memory, and then release the memory for our copy of the item. The user-programmer is presumed to know how much space he requires in order to store the top item on the stack.

```
int StackPop(void *Object, STACK *Stack)
{
  size_t Size;
  void *p;
  int Result = STACK_SUCCESS;

  assert(Stack != NULL);
  assert(0 == Stack->CheckInit1 && 0 == Stack->CheckInit2);

  if(Stack->NumItems > 0)
  {
    p = SLGetData(Stack->StackPtr, NULL, &Size);
    if(p != NULL && Object != NULL)
    {
      memcpy(Object, p, Size);
    }
    else
    {
```

```
      Result = STACK_POP_FAILURE;
    }
    Stack->StackPtr = SLDeleteThis(Stack->StackPtr);
    --Stack->NumItems;
  }
  else
  {
    Result = STACK_EMPTY;
  }

  return Result;
}
```

Peeking at the Top Item

In popping the stack, I handwaved my way past an important problem. I said that the user-programmer "is presumed to know how much space he requires in order to store the top item on the stack," but I didn't say how he was supposed to discover that information. Here's a function that provides him access to all the information he needs:

```
void *StackGetData(STACK *Stack, int *Tag, size_t *Size)
{
  assert(Stack != NULL);
  assert(0 == Stack->CheckInit1 && 0 == Stack->CheckInit2);

  return SLGetData(Stack->StackPtr, Tag, Size);
}
```

Counting the Items on the Stack

About the only other property of the stack that we haven't covered is the number of items on it. This is easily retrieved:

```
size_t StackCount(STACK *Stack)
{
  assert(Stack != NULL);
  assert(0 == Stack->CheckInit1 && 0 == Stack->CheckInit2);
  return Stack->NumItems;
}
```

Preserving the Stack Nature

It's important not to cheat by either adding an item or removing an item other than at the top. This is because the concept of a stack is widely known; it's not unreasonable for a maintenance programmer to expect that the normal rules of stacks have been followed. Keeping to the LIFO paradigm ensures that your code is more easily understood. If you want to add items to, or remove items from, the middle or bottom of the stack, use a linked list instead.

If the user-programmer updates a stack strictly in accordance with the manufacturer's instructions (that is, only through the published interface functions `StackPush` and `StackPop`), the library code will observe the rules of LIFO.

Stack Example: HTML Syntax Checker

To illustrate our stack library, we're going to write a rudimentary HTML syntax checker. Our program's job will be to ensure that each HTML opening tag is matched by a corresponding closing tag. To do this, we simply read the whole file into memory (reusing the `ReadFile` function from earlier in the chapter) and check each line for opening tags and closing tags (a tag is enclosed by < and > characters, and a closing tag begins with the `/` character). Each time we encounter a new tag, we first check to see if it is one of those tags that doesn't need to be closed (some HTML tags, such as `<hr>`, fall into this category). If it isn't, we push it onto the stack. When we come across a closing tag, we pop the stack and compare. If the two tags are not the same, we conclude that there is a syntax error in the HTML script. There isn't space here to show you the complete source code, which you can find on the CD. Here's `main()`, though:

```
int main(int argc, char *argv[])
{
  STACK Stack = {0};
  char Filename[FILENAME_MAX] = {0};
  char *HTMLTag = NULL;
  char *Temp = NULL;
  size_t CurrSize = 0;
  char *p; /* find < */
  char *q; /* find > */

  char **array = NULL; /* HTML file */

  int Count = 0;
  int Error;
  int rows;
```

```
int thisrow;

int Status = EXIT_SUCCESS;

if(argc > 1)
{
  strcpy(Filename, argv[1]);
}
else
{
  printf("HTML syntax checker\n");
  printf("Please type in the name of the file\n");
  printf("to check or EOF (^Z in DOS/Win, ^D\n");
  printf("in Unix) to quit: ");

  fflush(stdout);

  if(NULL == fgets(Filename, sizeof Filename, stdin))
  {
    printf("Exiting program.\n");
    Status = EXIT_FAILURE;
  }
  else
  {
    p = strchr(Filename, '\n');
    if(NULL != p)
    {
      *p = '\0';
    }
  }
}
if(EXIT_SUCCESS == Status)
{
  Error = ReadFile(Filename, &array, &rows);

  if(Error != 0)
  {
    printf("Couldn't read file %s.\n", Filename);
    Status = EXIT_FAILURE;
  }
  else
  {
```

```
printf("\nChecking file %s\n\n", Filename);
for(thisrow = 0;
    EXIT_SUCCESS == Status && thisrow < rows;
    thisrow++)
{
  p = strchr(array[thisrow], '<');

  while(EXIT_SUCCESS == Status && p != NULL)
  {
    q = strpbrk(p + 1, "\t >\n");

    if(NULL == q)
    {
      printf("Syntax error, line %d"
             " (no tag closure).\n", thisrow);
      ++Count;
    }
    else
    {
      if(q - p > (int)CurrSize)
      {
        CurrSize = q - p;
        Temp = realloc(HTMLTag, CurrSize);
        if(Temp != NULL)
        {
          HTMLTag = Temp;
        }
        else
        {
          printf("Memory loss.\n");
          Status = EXIT_FAILURE;
        }
      }
      memcpy(HTMLTag, p + 1, q - 1 - p);
      HTMLTag[q - 1 - p] = '\0';
      DownString(HTMLTag);
    }

    if(p[1] != '/')
    {
      if(!Exempt(HTMLTag))
      {
```

```
          if(STACK_SUCCESS != StackPush(&Stack,
                                        0,
                                        HTMLTag,
                                        q - p))
          {
            printf("Stack failure: %s on line %d\n",
                   HTMLTag,
                   thisrow);
            Status = EXIT_FAILURE;
          }
        }
      }
      else
      {
        Temp = StackGetData(&Stack,
                            NULL,
                            NULL);

        if(0 != strcmp(HTMLTag + 1, Temp))
        {
          printf("%s closure expected,"
                 " %s closure found on line %d.\n",
                 Temp,
                 HTMLTag,
                 thisrow);
          ++Count;
        }

        StackPop(NULL, &Stack);
      }
      p = strchr(p + 1, '<');
    }
  }

  printf("%d syntax error%s found.\n",
         Count,
         Count == 1 ? "" : "s");

  FreeStrArray(array, rows);
 }
}
```

```
  StackDestroy(&Stack);

  return Status;
}
```

To test this code, I gave it all the pages on my Web site. At first, I thought the code had a bug, because it reported several HTML syntax errors in Web pages that have been up and about on the Web for quite a while now (always suspect your own code before anything else!). But I was wrong. On further investigation, it turned out that the Web pages in question did in fact have errors in them. So, this is a useful demo program indeed.

Queues

The most useful data structures are the ones that are easy to picture in your head. A stack is a good example of this; anyone can imagine a pile of boxes (which is what a stack really is). Queues, too, are very simple to visualize, and this ease of understanding makes the queue a very powerful part of the programmer's toolkit.

Queues are similar to stacks in principle, but follow another set of rules, known as FIFO (First In, First Out). Under this regimen, we may only add items to the end of the queue, and may only remove items from the front of the queue. This works in exactly the same way as a queue in a shop or post office (see Figure 11.6).

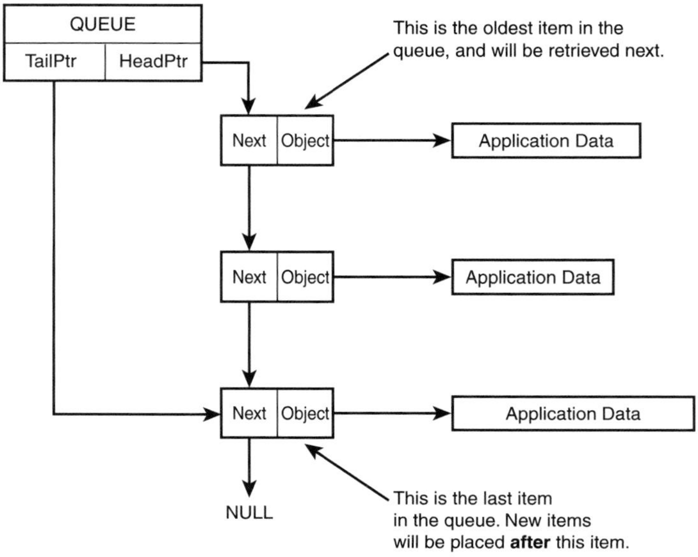

FIGURE 11.6
A queue.

Queues are frequently used in simulations. For a very vivid example, imagine writing a supermarket simulation; queues are ideal for modeling the line of people waiting to see the cashier. They can also be useful in systems programming. For example, multi-tasking operating systems often keep events or messages in a queue or, more commonly, lots of queues—one for each current process.

The queue library is slightly more awkward to code using single-linked lists than the stack was, but it can be done. The trick is to maintain two pointers—one to the head of the queue, and one to the tail.

Actually, we can save a few miserly bytes of memory by implementing the queue with just one pointer, but only at the expense of having to iterate through the entire queue every time we want to retrieve an item from it. This is time-costly for large queues because it requires an O(n) operation instead of an O(1) operation. Also, I suspect that the extra code required more than offsets the memory saved for one queue; program code can't be stored in zero bytes, after all. If we were writing an application in circumstances where we had to support thousands or millions of queues, however, we might yet consider this memory optimization (and its associated performance cost) to be worthwhile.

Creating the Queue

The data structure shown in Listing 11.14 is what we'll use for the queue.

LISTING 11.14 Creating a Queue

```
typedef struct QUEUE
{
#ifndef NDEBUG
  int CheckInit1;
#endif

  SLLIST *HeadPtr;
  SLLIST *TailPtr;
  size_t NumItems;

#ifndef NDEBUG
  int CheckInit2;
#endif
} QUEUE;
```

We expect our user-programmer to define an instance of `QUEUE` correctly, just as for the `STACK` code:

```
QUEUE Queue = {0};
```

Adding Items to the Queue

We have two scenarios here: adding an item into an empty queue, and adding an item into a queue that already contains at least one item. In each case, our job is simply to ensure that we keep the pointers straight.

```
int QueueAdd(QUEUE *Queue,
             int Tag,
             void *Object,
             size_t Size)
{
  int Result = QUEUE_ADD_FAILURE;
  int ListResult;
  assert(Queue != NULL);
  assert(0 == Queue->CheckInit1 && 0 == Queue->CheckInit2);

  ListResult = SLAdd(&Queue->TailPtr, Tag, Object, Size);

  if(SL_SUCCESS == ListResult)
  {
    if(0 == Queue->NumItems)
    {
      Queue->HeadPtr = Queue->TailPtr;
    }
    else
    {
      Queue->TailPtr = Queue->TailPtr->Next;
    }

    Result = QUEUE_SUCCESS;
    ++Queue->NumItems;
  }

  return Result;
}
```

From this listing we can see that the head pointer always points to the first item in the list, and the tail pointer always points to the last item.

Removing Items from the Queue

We have the same dual situation when removing items as we had when adding them. Either the first item in the queue is the only item remaining, or it isn't. In the former case, we need to fix the tail pointer (to NULL). Also, we face the same problem that we had with the stack with regard to allowing the user-programmer access to the data we are about to free; it is therefore perhaps not entirely unnatural that we should adopt the same solution.

```
int QueueRemove(void *Object, QUEUE *Queue)
{
  size_t Size;
  void *p;
  int Result = QUEUE_SUCCESS;

  assert(Queue != NULL);
  assert(0 == Queue->CheckInit1 && 0 == Queue->CheckInit2);

  if(Queue->NumItems > 0)
  {
    p = SLGetData(Queue->HeadPtr, NULL, &Size);
    if(p != NULL)
    {
      memcpy(Object, p, Size);
    }
    else
    {
      Result = QUEUE_DEL_FAILURE;
    }
    Queue->HeadPtr = SLDeleteThis(Queue->HeadPtr);
    --Queue->NumItems;
    if(0 == Queue->NumItems)
    {
      Queue->TailPtr = NULL;
    }
  }
  else
  {
    Result = QUEUE_EMPTY;
  }

  return Result;
}
```

Needless to say, we also need to provide a `QueueGetData()` function, which you will find on the CD. (To all intents and purposes it's identical to the `StackGetData()` function.)

Preserving the Queue Nature

For precisely the same reasons that we shouldn't cheat on stacks, we shouldn't cheat on queues either. The concept of a queue is even more clearly understood than that of a stack, so we should stick to the FIFO rules.

Queue Library Application

This queue library is really easy to use, having only two functions of note—one to add an item to the queue, and one to remove it—so I won't show example source here. On the CD, however, you'll find (in `queuemn.c`) a program that simulates a supermarket queue. Customers arrive at the queue with a number of items they want to buy. When a cashier becomes available, they go to that cashier to be served. The number of cashiers at work is controlled by the user, the idea being to maximize profit by using as many cashiers as necessary (and no more—cashiers do tend to insist on being paid, for some reason).

Priority Queues

We've already begun to look at ordered data structures, such as the stack and the queue. Sometimes, though, we have to re-order our data structures as new data arrives. The priority queue is a classic example of this requirement.

A priority queue is a data structure that facilitates the storage of items in priority order. They are typically used in task-scheduling applications. They wouldn't be completely out of place in multi-tasking operating systems, either. The rule is simple: First In, Largest Out (or, if you prefer, First In, Smallest Out—it all depends how you define priority).

There are various ways to implement a priority queue, the most obvious of which is a sorted list. The idea here is to use a normal list, inserting a new item by first searching along the list for the correct place for that item (based on some kind of priority key), and then adding the item into that position.

This is a beguilingly simple idea. It is also seriously flawed. It works fine for low numbers of items, but begins to creak and groan as the list grows. The time complexity of a sorted list is $O(N^2)$, and we can do much better than that. But how?

As happens so often, *The Art of Computer Programming*, by Donald E Knuth, the single most useful programming reference work in history, comes to our rescue. In Volume III, *Sorting and Searching*, Knuth discusses priority queues, and shows us an algorithm called `heapsort`. Knuth defines an array of items K to be a `heap` if the keys of those items are used to order them such that $1 <= \lfloor j/2 \rfloor < j <= N$, $K[j/2] >= K[j]$. `Heapsort`, naturally enough, turns an array into a heap. Knuth also provides a method for keeping the array sorted when items are added or removed.

In Figure 11.7, the objects have simple integers as keys, where a high number indicates a high priority. The solid lines indicate pointer relationships (for example, the object stored at element 0 of the heap contains a pointer to the object whose key is 317). The dotted lines indicate logical relationships. As can be clearly seen, therefore, a heap is a kind of tree.

FIGURE 11.7
A heap.

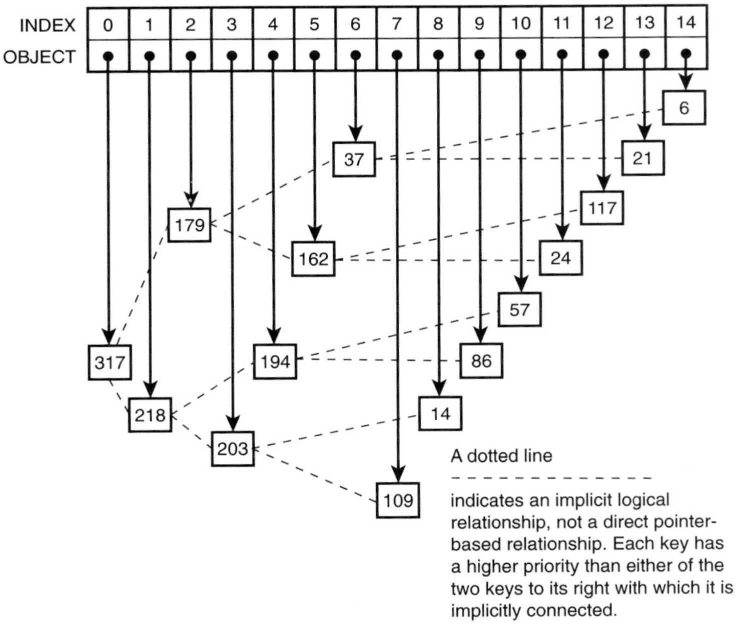

Because heaps are so involved (check out the source code if you don't believe me!), our library idea is particularly useful. You need never code a heap in the whole of the rest of your career, because what follows is a completely general heap library capable of handling any and all kinds of objects, separately or together (subject only to their being comparable to each other in some way). The source code presented here is firmly based on Ben Pfaff's GNU code (he's a good chap really), but I've adapted it to take objects of any kind.

Creating the Priority Queue

We define two data structures: a heap control structure and a heap element. They are shown in Listing 11.15.

LISTING 11.15 Creating a Priority Queue

```
typedef struct HEAP_ELEMENT
{
  int Tag;
  size_t Size;
  void *Object;
} HEAP_ELEMENT;

typedef struct HEAP
{
  size_t Count;             /* Number of elements in heap. */
  size_t MaxCount;          /* No. of elems allocated. */
  HEAP_ELEMENT *Heap;       /* Heap elements. */
} HEAP;
```

As you can see, the HEAP structure will store general information about the heap. Strictly speaking, the heap itself is the array of HEAP_ELEMENT structures, which is why the pointer to them is also named Heap.

```
HEAP *HeapCreate(size_t MaxCount)
{
  HEAP *Heap = malloc(sizeof *Heap);
  if(Heap != NULL)
  {
    Heap->Count = 0;
    Heap->MaxCount = MaxCount;
    Heap->Heap = malloc(Heap->MaxCount *
                        sizeof *Heap->Heap);
    if(Heap->Heap == NULL)
    {
      free(Heap);
      Heap = NULL;
    }
  }
  return Heap;
}
```

We need to ensure that we place no arbitrary limits on the user-programmer. Therefore, we dynamically allocate space for the heap, based on an initial guess of how many items are likely to be required, but which we can resize as necessary.

Adding Items to the Priority Queue

This is where it starts to get scary. Knuth's algorithm is reproduced here in all its glory.

```
int HeapInsert(HEAP *Heap,
               int Tag,
               size_t Size,
               void *Object,
               HEAP_COMPARE Comp)
{
  int i, j;

  int Done = 0;
  int Okay = 1;

  void *NewObject = NULL;

  assert (Heap != NULL);

  NewObject = malloc(Size);
  if(NULL == NewObject)
  {
    Okay = 0;
  }
  else
  {
    memcpy(NewObject, Object, Size);
  }

  if(Okay && Heap->Count >= Heap->MaxCount)
  {
    Heap->Heap = realloc(Heap->Heap,
                         2 * Heap->MaxCount *
                           sizeof *Heap->Heap);
    if(Heap->Heap != NULL)
    {
      Heap->MaxCount *= 2;
    }
    else
    {
      Okay = 0;
      free(NewObject);
    }
  }
```

```
  if(Okay)
  {
    /* Knuth's Algorithm 5.2.3-16.  Step 1. */
    j = Heap->Count + 1;

    while(!Done)
    {
      /* Step 2. */
      i = j / 2;

      /* Step 3. */
      if (i == 0 || (*Comp)(Heap->Heap[i - 1].Object,
                            Heap->Heap[i - 1].Tag,
                            Object,
                            Tag) <= 0)
      {
        Heap->Heap[j - 1].Tag = Tag;
        Heap->Heap[j - 1].Size = Size;
        Heap->Heap[j - 1].Object = NewObject;
        Heap->Count++;
        Done = 1;
      }
      else
      {
        /* Step 4. */
        Heap->Heap[j - 1] = Heap->Heap[i - 1];
        j = i;
      }
    }
  }

  return Okay;
}
```

A few implementation details need to be highlighted. First, it is possible that there is insufficient room in the heap to insert a new item. If this happens, we simply double the amount allocated to the heap. If our initial guess is reasonable, this is unlikely to happen more than once.

Second, we are dealing with objects that we need to compare. Much of the time, these objects may not be numerically comparable. Therefore, we need the user-programmer to provide a way to compare objects. The standard library functions, `qsort` and `bsearch`, have exactly this problem, so let's borrow their solution—a pointer to a comparison function. This comparison function needs to work in more or less the same way as qsort's, except that we have to bear in mind that we may be dealing with objects of different types. This is fine as long as they can be compared meaningfully. Therefore, we need to pass tags to the comparison function. As a result, the function is of the type pointer to function taking two pointers to void and two ints, and returning int. This is sufficiently long-winded to deserve its own typedef, so here we are:

```
typedef int (*HEAP_COMPARE)(const void *Left,
                            int LeftTag,
                            const void *Right,
                            int RightTag);
```

You will notice that, when I call a pointer to function, I use the syntax (*foo)(), rather than simply foo(). Both are legitimate, and some people prefer the latter because they think it keeps the code looking simple, a worthy objective indeed. I like to see the asterisk, though, because it reminds me that I am dealing with a pointer to a function, and saves me from going looking for the (non-existent) function body to foo().

Removing Items from the Priority Queue

As each item is inserted, it is marshalled into its correct place in the heap. When we remove an item, then, we simply take the first one. Unfortunately, however, it's not quite as simple as that. We have to ensure that we leave the heap intact. Here's how:

```
int HeapDelete(HEAP   *Heap,
               int    *pTag,
               size_t *pSize,
               void   *pObject,
               HEAP_COMPARE Comp)
{
  /* Knuth's Algorithm 5.2.3H-19. */
  int r, i, j;
  int Done;
  int KeyTag;
  void *KeyObject = NULL;

  void *OldItem;


  if (Heap->Count == 0)
    return -1;
  if(pTag != NULL)
  {
```

```
    *pTag = Heap->Heap[0].Tag;
  }
  if(pSize != NULL)
  {
    *pSize = Heap->Heap[0].Size;
  }
  if(pObject != NULL)
  {
    memcpy(pObject,
           Heap->Heap[0].Object,
           Heap->Heap[0].Size);
  }

  OldItem = Heap->Heap[0].Object;

  KeyTag = Heap->Heap[Heap->Count - 1].Tag;
  KeyObject = Heap->Heap[Heap->Count - 1].Object;

r = Heap->Count - 1;

  j = 1;

  Done = 0;
  while(!Done)
  {
    i = j;
    j *= 2;
    if (j > r)
    {
      Done = 1;
    }
    else
    {
      if (j != r)
      {
        if((*Comp)(Heap->Heap[j - 1].Object,
                   Heap->Heap[j - 1].Tag,
                   Heap->Heap[j    ].Object,
                   Heap->Heap[j    ].Tag) > 0)
        {
          j++;
        }
      }
```

```
      if((*Comp)(KeyObject,
                 KeyTag,
                 Heap->Heap[j - 1].Object,
                 Heap->Heap[j - 1].Tag) <= 0)
      {
        Done = 1;
      }
      else
      {
        Heap->Heap[i - 1] = Heap->Heap[j - 1];
      }
    }
  }

  Heap->Heap[i - 1].Object = KeyObject;
  Heap->Heap[i - 1].Tag = KeyTag;

  free(OldItem);

  --Heap->Count;

  return 0;
}
```

On the CD, you can find the helper functions necessary for completing the priority queue library.

Priority Queue Application

Here's a simple to-do list display program. Feel free to modify it to suit your own purposes (perhaps you don't fancy running for President this week). To save space in a chapter already on the long side, I've removed everything except `main()` but, naturally, you can find the full program on the CD.

```
int main(void)
{
  TASK TaskList[] =
  {
    {"Run for president", 30},
    {"Wash the dog", 20},
    {"Take children to school", 15},
    {"Write a sonnet", 16},
    {"Mow the lawn", 7},
    {"Drink coffee", 6},
```

```
    {"Do Usenet", 7},
    {"Read a good book", 17},
    {"Check email", 4},
    {"Buy flowers", 1},
    {"Install new OS", 9},
    {"Pour coffee", 5}
  };

  TASK ThisTask = {0};

  size_t NumTasks = sizeof TaskList / sizeof TaskList[0];
  size_t i;

  HEAP *Heap;
  int BadCount;

  Heap = HeapCreate(8);

  if(NULL != Heap)
  {

    for(i = 0; i < NumTasks; i++)
    {
      HeapInsert(Heap,
                 0,
                 sizeof TaskList[0],
                 TaskList + i,
                 CompareTasks);
    }

    /* Now let's check that the heap really is a heap. */
    printf("Is this a heap?\n");

    BadCount = HeapVerify(Heap, CompareTasks, stdout);
    if(BadCount > 0)
    {
      printf("Number of errors: %d\n", BadCount);
    }
    else
    {
      puts("Good heap.");
    }
```

```
    puts("Here's a heap dump.");
    HeapDump(Heap, PrintTasks, stdout);

    while(HeapGetSize(Heap) > 0)
    {
      HeapDelete(Heap,
                 NULL,
                 NULL,
                 &ThisTask,
                 CompareTasks);
      printf("Time to %s\n", ThisTask.JobName);
    }

    HeapDestroy(Heap);
  }
  return 0;
}
```

Deques

The word *deque* (pronounced "deck") is a rather charming computer science neologism; it is derived from double-ended queue, a phrase that exactly describes its purpose. There is no well-established acronym for deques as there was for queues and stacks; the best I can come up with is FOLIFOLO (First Or Last In, First Or Last Out), a suggestion that is unlikely to win a "Best Acronym of the Year" award. Be that as it may, the rules are simple: we may add items to either end of the deque, and we may remove items from either end of the deque, but we may not add items to, or remove items from, any other part of the deque (see Figure 11.8).

Creating the Deque

This must be familiar ground by now! The code is shown in Listing 11.16.

LISTING 11.16 Creating a Deque

```
typedef struct DEQUE
{
#ifndef NDEBUG
  int CheckInit1;
#endif
```

LISTING 11.16 continued

```
  DLLIST *HeadPtr;
  DLLIST *TailPtr;
  size_t NumItems;

#ifndef NDEBUG
  int CheckInit2;
#endif
} DEQUE;
```

FIGURE 11.8
A deque.

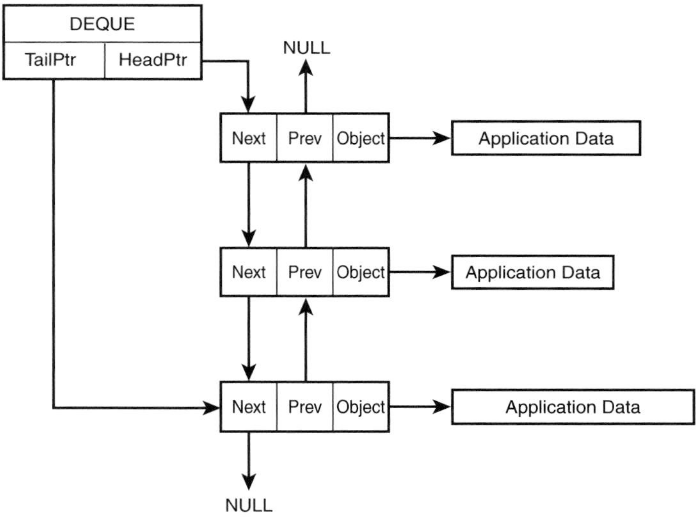

As you can see, we're going to use a double-linked list as the underlying mechanism. A single-linked list is impractical because we would need to constantly iterate through it whenever we removed an item from the tail of the list. Again, I've embedded the necessary inclusion statement into `deque.h`, for the same reasons already covered earlier in the chapter.

Adding Items to the Head

Because the double-linked list code is doing most of the work, the code for adding items is fairly short:

```
int DequeAddAtFront(DEQUE *Deque,
                    int Tag,
                    void *Object,
```

```
                    size_t Size)
{
  int Result = DEQUE_ADD_FAILURE;
  int ListResult;
  assert(Deque != NULL);
  assert(0 == Deque->CheckInit1 && 0 == Deque->CheckInit2);

  ListResult = DLAddBefore(&Deque->HeadPtr,
                           Tag,
                           Object,
                           Size);

  if(DL_SUCCESS == ListResult)
  {
    if(0 == Deque->NumItems)
    {
      Deque->TailPtr = Deque->HeadPtr;
    }
    else
    {
      Deque->HeadPtr = Deque->HeadPtr->Prev;
    }

    Result = DEQUE_SUCCESS;
    ++Deque->NumItems;
  }

  return Result;
}
```

Adding Items to the Tail

Not surprisingly, there is a degree of symmetry in the code to add an item to the tail of the deque. Here is the part of the code that differs from the previous function:

```
  /* ... */
  ListResult = DLAddAfter(&Deque->TailPtr,
                          Tag,
                          Object,
                          Size);

  if(DL_SUCCESS == ListResult)
  {
    if(0 == Deque->NumItems)
```

```
    {
      Deque->HeadPtr = Deque->TailPtr;
    }
    else
    {
      Deque->TailPtr = Deque->TailPtr->Next;
    }
  /* ... */
```

Removing Items from the Head

It's not too difficult to remove an item from the head of the deque, but we do have to use a temporary pointer to save the address of the new head:

```
int DequeRemoveFromFront(void *Object, DEQUE *Deque)
{
  size_t Size;
  void *p;
  DLLIST *Temp;
  int Result = DEQUE_SUCCESS;

  assert(Deque != NULL);
  assert(0 == Deque->CheckInit1 && 0 == Deque->CheckInit2);

  if(Deque->NumItems > 0)
  {
    p = DLGetData(Deque->HeadPtr, NULL, &Size);
    if(p != NULL)
    {
      if(Object != NULL)
      {
        memcpy(Object, p, Size);
      }
      Temp = Deque->HeadPtr->Next;
      DLDelete(Deque->HeadPtr);
      Deque->HeadPtr = Temp;

      --Deque->NumItems;
      if(0 == Deque->NumItems)
      {
        Deque->TailPtr = NULL;
      }
    }
    else
```

```
    {
      Result = DEQUE_DEL_FAILURE;
    }
  }
  else
  {
    Result = DEQUE_EMPTY;
  }

  return Result;
}
```

Removing Items from the Tail

Again, the symmetry of the deque is evident in the source to remove an item from its tail end. Here is the code that differs:

```
/* ... */
p = DLGetData(Deque->TailPtr, NULL, &Size);
if(p != NULL)
{
  if(Object != NULL)
  {
    memcpy(Object, p, Size);
  }
  Temp = Deque->TailPtr->Prev;
  DLDelete(Deque->TailPtr);
  Deque->TailPtr = Temp;

  --Deque->NumItems;
  if(0 == Deque->NumItems)
  {
    Deque->HeadPtr = NULL;
/* ... */
```

Preserving the Deque Nature

Once more (and, I promise, for the last time), I'd like to draw attention to the importance of maintaining the deque paradigm. If we start inserting items into or removing items from the middle of the deque (and it's not hard to do), we may solve an immediate coding problem but we also call our design into question. If we have to hack the deque, was a deque the right solution in the first place? Furthermore, we make the task of maintenance more difficult. If you need a list, use a list, not a deque.

Deque of Cars

Some people are fortunate enough to be able to afford to transport their cars long distances by rail. Cars are driven onto either end of the transporter, and then just sit there until the train arrives at wherever it is the cars are going.

It's not a good idea to have all the short-haul cars in the middle of the transporter! Ideally, we'd like all the long-haul cars in the middle, with the short-haul cars on either end.

The transporter is a good example of a deque, because the only way you're going to get a car onto (or off) the transporter without that car being at one end or the other is with a lifting device such as a crane. Far easier to drive them on and drive them off.

To achieve this, the cars must be sorted. Dann Corbit points out in Chapter 13, "Rapid Sorting Techniques," that we must *never* use `qsort`. I hope he'll forgive me for using it here. Bear in mind that `qsort` isn't *necessarily* an implementation of the Quicksort algorithm. The Standard requires only that `qsort` sorts the data—it doesn't specify how. (Admittedly, vendors who implement `qsort` using a Bubble Sort aren't going to sell many copies of their compiler.) Be that as it may, I'm going to use `qsort` because it's quick to write calling code for it, and thus it doesn't distract too much from the point of the example, which is to demonstrate the deque library functions.

In Listing 11.16, the cars are all loaded onto the transporter at Dover (on the southeast coast of England). Some of the cars are going as far as Scotland. How can we ensure that they get there with the minimum amount of effort? Here's how:

```
int main(void)
{
  DEQUE Transporter = {0};

  char *City[NUM_CITIES] =
  {
    "London",
    "Watford",
    "Luton",
    "Milton Keynes",
    "Northampton",
    "Leicester",
    "Derby",
    "Chesterfield",
    "Sheffield",
    "Leeds",
    "Newcastle",
```

```
  "Edinburgh"
};

size_t NumCities = sizeof City / sizeof City[0];

CAR LeftCar[LNUM_CARS] = {0};
CAR RightCar[RNUM_CARS] = {0};
CAR *Car;

int i;

srand((unsigned)time(NULL));

for(i = 0; i < LNUM_CARS; i++)
{
  RandomiseCar(LeftCar + i);
}
for(i = 0; i < RNUM_CARS; i++)
{
  RandomiseCar(RightCar + i);
}

qsort(LeftCar,
      LNUM_CARS,
      sizeof LeftCar[0],
      CompareCarsByDest);
qsort(RightCar,
      RNUM_CARS,
      sizeof RightCar[0],
      CompareCarsByDest);

puts("Welcome to Dover. The automatic car-loading");
puts("process is about to begin.\n");

for(i = 0; i < LNUM_CARS; i++)
{
  if(DEQUE_SUCCESS != DequeAddAtFront(&Transporter,
                                      0,
                                      LeftCar + i,
                                      sizeof LeftCar[i]))
  {
    puts("Car crash? Insufficient memory.");
    exit(EXIT_FAILURE);
```

```
    }
    printf("%s, bound for %s, added at front.\n",
           LeftCar[i].RegNumber,
           City[LeftCar[i].Destination]);

  }

  for(i = 0; i < RNUM_CARS; i++)
  {
    if(DEQUE_SUCCESS != DequeAddAtBack(&Transporter,
                                       0,
                                       RightCar + i,
                                       sizeof RightCar[i]))
    {
      puts("Crunch! Insufficient memory.");
      exit(EXIT_FAILURE);
    }
    printf("%s, bound for %s, added at back.\n",
           RightCar[i].RegNumber,
           City[RightCar[i].Destination]);

  }

  printf("Okay, we're on our way to %s!\n", City[0]);

  for(i = 0;
      DequeCount(&Transporter) > 0 && i < NUM_CITIES;
      i++)
  {
    puts("Deedle-dee-DEE, Deedle-dee-DAH...");
    printf("Okay, we've arrived at %s.\n", City[i]);

    Car = DequeGetDataFromFront(&Transporter, NULL, NULL);

    if(Car == NULL)
    {
      puts("We seem to have run out of cars,");
      puts("so I guess the journey is over.");
      exit(0);
    }

    while(Car != NULL &&
          DequeCount(&Transporter) > 0 &&
```

```
         Car->Destination == i)
    {
      printf("Unloading %s from front.\n", Car->RegNumber);
      DequeRemoveFromFront(NULL, &Transporter);
      Car = DequeGetDataFromFront(&Transporter, NULL, NULL);
    }

    Car = DequeGetDataFromBack(&Transporter, NULL, NULL);

    while(Car != NULL &&
          DequeCount(&Transporter) > 0 &&
          Car->Destination == i)
    {
      printf("Unloading %s from back.\n", Car->RegNumber);
      DequeRemoveFromBack(NULL, &Transporter);
      Car = DequeGetDataFromBack(&Transporter, NULL, NULL);
    }

    if(i < NUM_CITIES - 1)
    {
      printf("All done, so we're off to %s!\n",
             City[i + 1]);
    }
  }

  printf("That's it - journey's end.\n");

  return 0;
}
```

As you can see, I've stripped down the printed source; the full source is available on the CD, in the file `dequemn.c`.

In this example, I've used the peek functions, `DequeGetDataFromFront` and `DequeGetDataFromBack`, to check whether I want to remove the data before I actually get it off the deque. This is not necessary if we know in advance that we want to remove the item in question irrespective of the data contained therein. In such a case, we would pass the address of an appropriately sized object to `DequeRemoveFromFront` or `DequeRemoveFromBack`. If we are using mixed object types, however, we will need to peek at the data, even if only to determine which kind of data is at the end of the deque.

Heterogeneous Structures and Object Trees

The real world is a complex beast, and can be difficult to model. Life doesn't always fall neatly into arrays, or circular lists, or stacks. If, however, we consider using classical data structures in combination, we can build up an appropriate level of complexity fairly quickly.

What is an appropriate level of complexity? We don't want our code to be complicated, but we do want it to describe reality as closely as is necessary to solve the problem at hand. "Things should be made as simple as possible, but not any simpler," says Einstein; sometimes we need to accept complexity so that we can solve complex problems. Those who say "You can't do that in C" should really be saying, much of the time, "You can't do that *easily* in C."

For example, consider a railway marshalling yard. What kind of data structure is it? It's not an array. It's not a list, either. In fact, it doesn't seem to be adequately described by any of the classical data structures, not even if we include trees. A graph, perhaps, would be the single most appropriate data structure for modeling a marshalling yard, but it wouldn't be completely adequate.

But who says we have to use just *one* data structure?

What is a siding, if not a stack? What is a double-ended siding, if not a deque? Main lines, distinguished from double-ended sidings by the inclusion of points that connect them to other main lines, are double-linked lists. Even a turntable can be described classically as a circular list. And, of course, we can have arrays of all of these if we want.

Thus, by using many different kinds of data structures in combination, we can build up the appropriate level of complexity required by whatever problem it is that we currently face. I'm not saying a marshalling yard simulator would be easy to write. But we can make life a little easier by breaking the problem down into manageable sub-problems, and then tying the solutions to those sub-problems together in an appropriate way. This is the essence of programming.

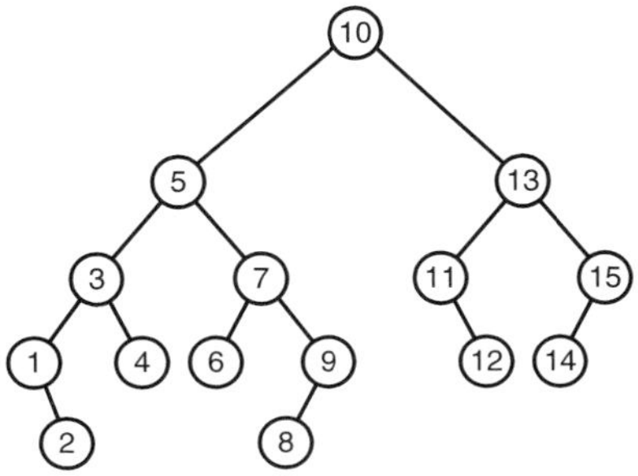

FIGURE 12.2
Another tree containing the integers from 1 to 15. Compare its structure to that of Figure 12.1.

C Structure for a Node

Enough theory. It's time to dive in and see what we can do with binary trees. Let's start with their nodes.

Looking back at our definition of a node, we can directly write an analogous C structure definition as shown in Listing 12.1.

LISTING 12.1 `bin.c`—Node Structure for Binary Tree

```
struct bin_node {
  int data;
  struct bin_node *left;
  struct bin_node *right;
};
```

Note the exact correspondence between the abstract definition of a binary tree and the structure above: `struct bin_node` contains a value, `data`, a pointer to a left subtree, `left`, and a pointer to a right subtree, `right`.

For the purposes of this chapter, we define `bin_node`'s value as an integer. Extending the code to handle generic data types is an interesting exercise left to the reader.

C Structure for a Tree

In addition to keeping track of individual nodes, we need to handle entire trees. Most of the time, this boils down to keeping track of the tree's root node. It would be easy enough to pass this to tree functions. But sometimes we want to keep other information about the tree along with it. The easiest way to do this is to define another structure for the tree itself, putting the root pointer and auxiliary information into it, like so:

```
struct bin_tree {
  struct bin_node *root;
  int count;
};
```

`root` is defined as a pointer to a node. Alternatively, it could be declared as a node itself, but this would complicate many operations. On the whole, it's easier to declare the root as a pointer.

The `count` field is an example of extra information about the tree itself. Some applications of binary trees often want to know the number of nodes in the tree. For this purpose, it's convenient to update `count` rather than to count nodes each time.

Operations

This is the really exciting part. Now that we've figured out why we'd want to use binary tree data structures and how we can represent them in C, we can write code to perform operations on them. Let's do it.

Creation

Creating an empty binary tree is straightforward. First, we allocate memory for a `struct bin_tree` with `malloc()`. If `malloc()` fails, we return a null pointer to alert the caller. Alternatively, we could print an error message and terminate, or free unneeded memory and try again, or use any number of other error-recovery strategies. Otherwise, the allocation is successful. We initialize the new tree and return a pointer to it to the caller.

```
struct bin_tree *bin_create(void)
{
  struct bin_tree *tree = malloc(sizeof *tree);
  if (tree == NULL)
    return NULL;
  tree->root = NULL;
  tree->count = 0;
  return tree;
}
```

Search

Empty binary trees by themselves aren't very useful. Now that we have code to create an empty binary tree, we'll want to put some data into it. As it turns out, the first step in inserting a node (and many other tree operations) is searching for a node with the same value, so we'll take a look at searching first on our way to insertion.

```
57 int bin_search(const struct bin_tree *tree, int item)
58 {
59   const struct bin_node *node;
60
61   assert(tree != NULL);
62   node = tree->root;
63   for (;;) {
64     if (node == NULL)
65       return 0;
66     else if (item == node->data)
67       return 1;
68     else if (item > node->data)
69       node = node->right;
70     else
71       node = node->left;
72   }
73 }
```

We declare `bin_search()` to take a tree `tree` to search and a value `item` to search for as its arguments. The function will return nonzero if `item` is in the tree, zero if it is not.

The function begins with an assertion (line 61), always a good idea in functions that make assumptions about their arguments (which is just about every function). In this case, we require that `tree` points to a valid `struct bin_tree`. Although we can't test for that directly, we can and do verify that it is not a null pointer.

Note that `!= NULL` is required here, even though it is optional in tests for non-null pointers in `if` and `while` statements and many similar contexts. Many compilers will treat `assert(tree);` and `assert(tree != NULL);` identically, but the behavior of the former is technically undefined. Better safe than sorry.

The actual binary search follows the assertion, using the algorithm discussed in depth at the beginning of this chapter. We start the search from the tree's root (line 62).

In each step, we first test whether we're out of nodes (line 64). If so, the target item is not in the tree, and we return 0 to alert the caller (line 65). If not, we compare this node's data to `item`. If they are equal, we return 1 to report it to the caller (lines 66 and 67).

If item is bigger than node's value, item must be in node's right subtree (if it is in the tree at all), so we move to the right subtree and repeat the entire process (lines 68 and 69). Otherwise, item must be less than node's value, so we move to its left subtree and repeat (lines 70 and 71).

Let's examine bin_search()'s behavior for the boundary condition of an empty tree. It is always a good idea to check boundary conditions because they have a way of sneaking up on careless programmers and filling the code with bugs. At any rate, we are safe in this case: If tree is empty, tree->root will be a null pointer, so bin_search() will return 0 the first time through the loop.

Insertion

As hinted in the preceding section, insertion into a binary tree is a simple extension to searching. The difference is that, if the target item turns out not to be in the tree, we graft a new node onto the tree at the point where we expected it to be.

```
 78 int bin_insert(struct bin_tree *tree, int item)
 79 {
 80   struct bin_node *node, **new;
 81
 82   assert(tree != NULL);
 83   new = &tree->root;
 84   node = tree->root;
 85   for (;;) {
 86     if (node == NULL) {
 87       node = *new = malloc(sizeof *node);
 88       if (node != NULL) {
 89         node->data = item;
 90         node->left = node->right = NULL;
 91         tree->count++;
 92         return 1;
 93       }
 94       else
 95         return 0;
 96     }
 97     else if (item == node->data)
 98       return 2;
 99     else if (item > node->data) {
100       new = &node->right;
101       node = node->right;
102     }
103     else {
```

```
104         new = &node->left;
105         node = node->left;
106       }
107     }
108 }
```

We declare `bin_insert()` to take a binary tree and an item to insert into it as arguments. `bin_insert()` will return 1 if the item was successfully inserted, 2 if an item of the same value already existed in `tree` (binary search trees, as we've defined them, cannot contain duplicate values), or 0 if the item did not exist in the tree but could not be inserted due to a memory allocation error. As a consequence, the caller can check for success by testing for a nonzero return value.

As before, `node` points to the node that we're currently looking at. A new variable, `new`, a double pointer, points to the pointer that we followed to arrive at `node`. This is an important point, so keep it in mind when reading the code.

At the beginning of the function, we verify that `tree` is not a null pointer, then initialize `node` to the tree root and `new` to the address of the pointer to the tree root (lines 82—84).

The function's main loop (lines 85—105) is repeated once for every level of the tree traversed. The tests are analogous to those used in `bin_search()`.

The biggest difference from `bin_search()` appears in the behavior when a null pointer is encountered, indicating that `item` is not in the tree. We want to add an item at the proper point in the tree by replacing the null pointer that we followed to get to this point with a new node containing `item`. Fortunately, we know where this null pointer is located because we've used `new` to keep track of it. We simply allocate a new node and store it into `*new`, checking that the memory allocation succeeded (lines 87 and 88).

In addition, we store the new node into `node` for easier access. We initialize the new node with `item` and set its subtree pointers to null pointers (lines 89 and 90). Finally, we increment the node count for the tree and return 1 to indicate that a new node was inserted (lines 91 and 92).

The traversal code has changed slightly to maintain the value of `new`, and the return value used when `item` is found has changed. Apart from that, the remaining code in the function is the same as that in `bin_search()`.

Deletion

Now that we have code for constructing a binary tree and adding items to it, we will probably want to delete items from it as well. This is a little more complicated than insertion. Let's take a look at the code.

```
int bin_delete(struct bin_tree *tree, int item)
{
  struct bin_node **q, *z;

  assert(tree != NULL);
  q = &tree->root;
  z = tree->root;
  for (;;) {
    if (z == NULL)
      return 0;
    else if (item == z->data)
      break;
    else if (item > z->data) {
      q = &z->right;
      z = z->right;
    }
    else {
      q = &z->left;
      z = z->left;
    }
  }

  if (z->right == NULL)
    *q = z->left;
  else {
    struct bin_node *y = z->right;
    if (y->left == NULL) {
      y->left = z->left;
      *q = y;
    }
    else {
      struct bin_node *x = y->left;
      while (x->left != NULL) {
        y = x;
        x = y->left;
      }
      y->left = x->right;
      x->left = z->left;
      x->right = z->right;
      *q = x;
    }
  }

```

```
155    tree->count--;
156    free(z);
157    return 1;
158 }
```

We declare `bin_delete()` to take a binary tree, `tree`, and a value to delete, `item`, as arguments. `bin_delete()` will return 0 if `item` was not in the tree or 1 if `item` was successfully deleted. (The function cannot fail, so it does not have a failure return value.)

The loop at the beginning of the function (lines 119–132) should now look familiar. It is the same algorithm for searching in a binary tree that we've implemented twice before, but `node` has been renamed to `z` and `new` has been renamed to `q`. In addition, finding `item` causes the loop to terminate (using `break`) instead of inserting an item.

When the loop terminates, we know that `item` exists in `tree` because that's the condition to terminate the loop. In addition, `z` points to the node to be deleted, and `q` points to the pointer that was followed to arrive at `z`. Now, we must examine `z` to find out how we can delete it from the tree. As it turns out, there are three cases, two of which are simple and one of which is more complicated. Each case is illustrated in Figure 12.3 and discussed in the following paragraphs.

Case 1 (Figure 12.3a; lines 134 and 135): Node `z` has no right child, so it can be deleted by replacing it with its left child. We simply replace the pointer to `z` (`*q`) by a pointer to `z`'s left child. If `z` has no left child, `*q` is replaced by a null pointer, which is also okay. This is all that is necessary for this case.

Case 2 (Figure 12.3b; lines 137–141): Node `z` has a right child, but its right child has no left child. `z`'s right child `y` receives `z`'s left subtree, then replaces `z`. We replace `z` with `y` by setting `*q`. In addition, we copy `z`'s left subtree pointer into `y` so that `z`'s left subtree doesn't get lost.

Case 3 (Figure 12.3c; lines 142–151): In the remaining case, `z` is replaced by its successor `x`, then `x` is deleted directly since it does not have a left child. We know that `z` has a right child and that right child has a left child, which we save in `x`. A loop then runs along the left-side child pointer of `x`, until it runs into a node with no left child (lines 144–147). At that point, `x` is the successor of `z` in `tree`. That is, `x` has the smallest value in `tree` greater than `z`. `y` is `x`'s parent node.

Why is `x` the successor of `z`? Consider it logically. First, all the nodes in `z`'s left subtree are less than `z`, so `z`'s successor must be in its right subtree. Specifically, it must be the smallest value in `z`'s right subtree. Because values in a binary tree become smaller as the tree is descended to the left, the way to find the smallest value is to visit nodes farther to the left until there are no more left descendants. At no point is it useful to move to the right because the right child of a node is always bigger than the node.

Now, x is the successor of z in the tree and y is x's parent node. To effectively delete z, we replace z by x, and reduce the problem of deleting z to the problem of deleting the node where x was originally located. x had no left child (otherwise it wouldn't have been z's successor), so deleting it is easy.

FIGURE 12.3a
Deleting a node from a binary tree.

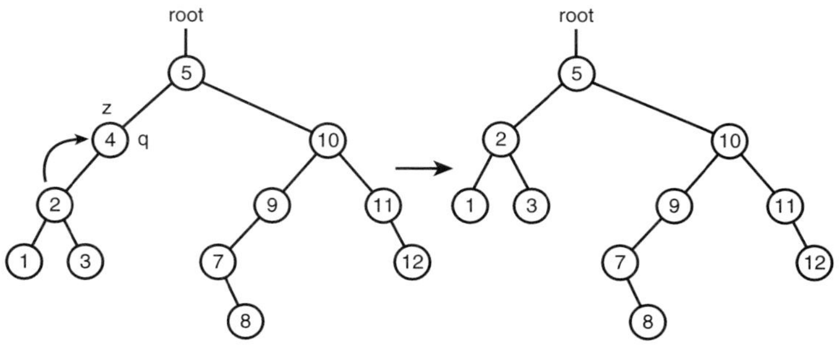

FIGURE 12.3b

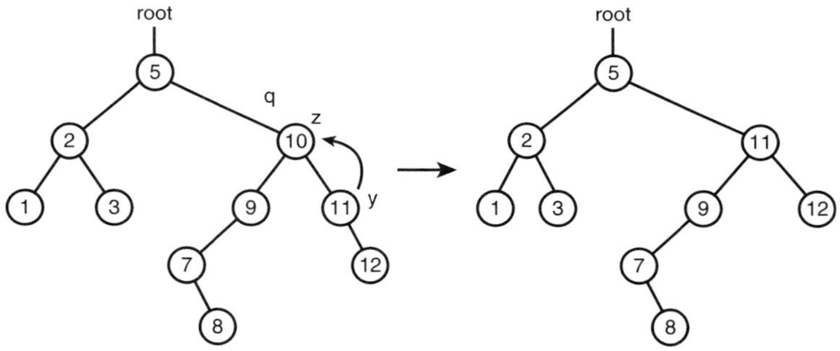

FIGURE 12.3c

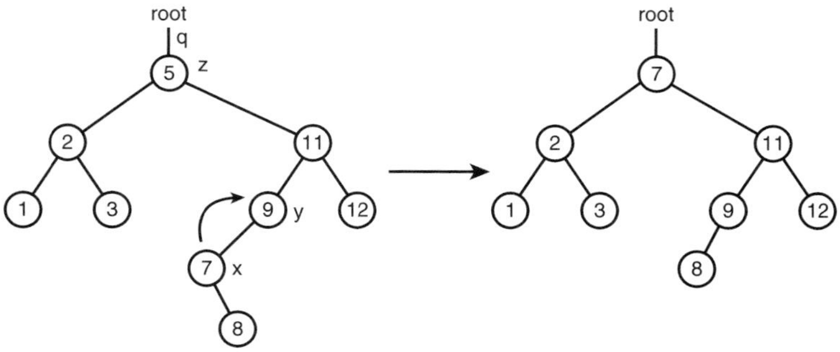

First, x is removed from the tree by replacing y's left subtree pointer (which points to x) by x's right subtree (line 148). Then x's subtrees are replaced by z's subtrees and `*q` is set to point to x rather than z, completing the deletion (lines 148–151).

The number of nodes in the tree has decreased by one as a result of the deletion, so `tree->count` is decremented (line 155). `t` is no longer in use, so it is freed (line 156). Finally, `bin_delete()` returns to the caller, indicating that a node was successfully deleted (line 157).

For completeness, consider boundary conditions. What if the node to be deleted is the only node in the tree? If that happens, `z` becomes the node, it is recognized in the first loop iteration, and the loop exits immediately. Because `z` is a leaf node, it has no right subtree, so it is handled by case 1. Everything is well.

In-order Recursive Traversal

One advantage of binary search trees over some other data structures is that the data in them can be easily accessed in sorted order. In structures such as *hash tables*, it's necessary to perform a slow, expensive sort each time this is done.

Recursion provides the easiest way to write a routine to print out, in order, the values of all of the nodes in a binary search tree. The algorithm follows directly from the structure of a binary search tree. For each node, its value is greater than the nodes in its left subtree and less than the nodes in its right subtree. Therefore, to print out the tree's contents, first print the contents of the root's left subtree, then the contents of the root, and then contents of the root's right subtree.

But how should the subtrees be printed? Remember, the subtrees are binary trees themselves, so their contents can be printed out the same way: by printing the contents of the subtree's root node's left subtree, then the subtree's root, and then its right subtree. In other words, the subtrees are printed out recursively in the same manner as the root.

We can write code directly from this description:

```
162 static void walk(const struct bin_node *node)
163 {
164   if (node == NULL)
165     return;
166   walk(node->left);
167   printf("%d ", node->data);
168   walk(node->right);
169 }
```

`walk()` takes as an argument a pointer to a node in binary search tree, `node`. It prints the contents of the tree rooted at `node` in sorted order.

Notice that `walk()` is the first function we've defined so far that takes a node pointer as an argument. This isn't really something that we want to do. In writing a library of functions, it's best not to require users to know more about the library's internals than necessary. This is the principle of *information hiding* or *abstraction*. This is also why `walk()` is declared `static`, preventing code outside the file in which it is defined from seeing it. We'll define a more convenient public function later for walking a tree that takes a tree pointer rather than a node pointer.

The function's code is simple: If `node` is a null pointer, there is nothing to print (lines 164 and 165). Otherwise, the left subtree of the node is printed (line 166), then the value of the node itself (line 167), and then the right subtree (line 168), just as described above.

Now let us define a public function for using `walk()`, as promised:

```
void bin_walk(const struct bin_tree *tree)
{
  assert(tree != NULL);
  walk(tree->root);
}
```

This function should be largely self-explanatory. It checks for a non-null `tree` argument and calls `walk()` to do the real work.

In-order Iterative Traversal

Recursion is an easy way to implement an in-order walk of the values in a binary tree, but it's often inconvenient. For instance, suppose that we want to write a function `tree_sum()` to sum the values in a binary search tree and return this value. If we modified `bin_walk()` into `bin_walk_action()` to take a pointer to a function to call for each node, we'd end up with code something like this:

```
static void sum_walk_function(int value, void *sum)
{
  *(int *) sum += value;
}

int tree_sum(struct bin_tree *tree)
{
  int sum = 0;
  bin_walk_action(tree, &sum);
  return sum;
}
```

There are several objections to this method. First, it uses two functions to do a job that logically requires only one, which separates the logic into too-small pieces, making the program harder to understand. Second, passing data between `tree_sum()` and `sum_walk_function()` is difficult. Third, passing data is dangerous because it requires casts, which are best avoided by cautious programmers.

An iterative binary search tree traversal routine could avoid these problems. `tree_sum()` could then be written more like this:

```
int tree_sum(struct bin_tree *tree)
{
  struct bin_iterator iter;
  int sum = 0, addend;

  bin_for_each_init(&iter);
  while (bin_for_each(tree, &iter, &addend))
    sum += addend;

  return sum;
}
```


This version of the code avoids many of the pitfalls involved in the former version. It does not require two functions to do the work of one, it keeps the logic in one place, and it doesn't require intricate and dangerous work to pass data around.

Now that we see the utility of writing an iterative traversal function, let's get into the meat of writing one. For brevity and simplicity, we won't implement the full functionality of `bin_for_each()` as used above.

We could just design an iterative tree traverser from ground up, but it's more fun and perhaps more instructive to "factor out" the recursion in the recursive iterator that we have already. Consider the guts of the `walk()` function from the previous section:

```
if (node == NULL)
  return;
walk(node->left);
printf("%d ", node->data);
walk(node->right);
```

Notice that the final recursive call to `walk()` doesn't do anything after it returns. This is called *tail recursion* and it can always be replaced by a jump back to the beginning of the function, after changing any function arguments as necessary. So as a first step in eliminating recursion, rewrite the code as follows:

```
for (;;) {
  if (node == NULL)
    return;
  walk(node->left);
  printf("%d ", node->data);
  walk(node->right);
}
```

Only one recursive call remains, but eliminating this one is tougher. Think about what really happens when `walk(node->left)` is executed: the current value of `node` is saved, then it is replaced by `node->left`, and then the function starts over from the beginning. If `node` is null, and the function returns, the previous value of `node` is restored and execution resumes from immediately after the call.

We can simulate this process without actually calling `walk(node->left)` if we save and restore the value of `node` ourselves. For this purpose, a stack data structure is ideal. (In fact, many C implementations use a stack internally to keep track of function calls.) It is easy to incorporate a stack:

```
struct bin_node *stack[32];
int count = 0;
for (;;) {
  while (node != NULL) {
    stack[count++] = node;
    node = node->left;
  }
  if (count == 0)
    return;
  node = stack[--count];
  printf("%d ", node->data);
  node = node->right;
}
```

`stack` is an array of pointers to nodes composing the stack contents. `count` is the number of node pointers on the stack at any given time. (Therefore, if `count` is greater than zero, the topmost node pointer is in `stack[count - 1]`.)

The new code inside the loop implements the explicit saving of the current value of `node`. When `node` is not null, it is saved on the stack and `node` is replaced by `node->left`, then the function effectively starts over from the beginning by going back to the beginning of the loop. If the value of `node` is null, the function restores the previous value of `node` and continues. If there is no previous value of `node`, as indicated by an empty stack, that means that we're done, so we return.

Now we've written a complete replacement for `walk()`. However, if you've been following closely, you might have noticed that now there's no reason to break traversing the tree into two functions. We can easily merge our modified `walk()` with `bin_walk()` to produce a new function, `bin_traverse()`:

```
void bin_traverse(const struct bin_tree *tree)
{
  struct bin_node *stack[32];
```

```
  int count;

  struct bin_node *node;

  assert(tree != NULL);
  count = 0;
  node = tree->root;
  for (;;) {
    while (node != NULL) {
      stack[count++] = node;
      node = node->left;
    }
    if (count == 0)
      return;
    node = stack[--count];
    printf("%d ", node->data);
    node = node->right;
  }
}
```

Note that in practice the preceding implementation should be avoided unless the maximum height of the tree is known to be bounded and less than the size of the stack. A practical implementation would allocate the stack dynamically and expand it on demand.

Destruction

Eventually, every tree outlives its usefulness. When that happens, it's time to destroy it. That job includes destroying each node in the tree and the tree structure itself. Destroying each node in the tree is a job for another recursive function. This time, we need to make sure that we don't access a node after we've destroyed it. The easiest way to do this is to use postorder traversal, as opposed to the in-order traversal used in `avl_walk()` and `avl_traverse()`. In postorder, we first perform an action recursively on each subtree of a node, then on the node itself. This is easy to do:

```
static void destroy(struct bin_node *node)
{
  if (node == NULL)
    return;
  destroy(node->left);
  destroy(node->right);
  free(node);
}
```

First, `destroy()` checks whether the pointer to a node it has been handed for destruction, `node`, is null. If it is, there is nothing to do and the function returns (lines 206 and 207). Otherwise, `destroy()` calls itself recursively for `node`'s left and right subtrees, then frees `node` itself (lines 208–210).

We want to be able to destroy a tree without knowing about its internal structure. In addition, the `struct bin_tree` must be destroyed as well as the nodes. For this reason, we define a convenience function that calls `destroy()` internally:

```
void bin_destroy(struct bin_tree *tree)
{
  assert(tree != NULL);
  destroy(tree->root);
  free(tree);
}
```

Count

Way back when we defined `struct bin_tree`, we put a member called `count` into it to keep track of how many nodes were in the tree. So far, we haven't provided any way to get at that information other than to access the members of `struct bin_tree` directly. Requiring users of a library to know what is inside a structure, instead of letting them treat it as a "black box," is poor practice, especially when the library is likely to be useful outside of the original code it is used by.

Let's provide a simple function for obtaining the number of nodes in a specified binary tree:

```
int bin_count(const struct bin_tree *tree)
{
  assert(tree != NULL);
  return tree->count;
}
```

This code should be self-explanatory.

Analysis

At the beginning of this chapter, the reason that we started looking at binary trees was because searching lists was too slow in some circumstances. Now we should take another look at the speed of binary trees to make sure that they're everything we expected them to be.

In the guessing game example, there were always two choices at every level of the tree. This meant that the number of possibilities was halved after each step. This is what we want.

But what happens if there aren't two choices at each level? In that case, the number of choices doesn't get halved at each step. Instead, only one possibility has been eliminated (the item that was compared against). This is as bad as linear search, where only one possibility is eliminated at each step.

We need some more terminology now in order to make the discussion easier. The *height* of a tree is the maximum number of nodes that can be visited, starting from the tree's root, if one is permitted only to move down the tree from parent to child, never from child to parent. By this definition, the height of a leaf is 1, and the height of a non-leaf node is 1 plus the greater of its subtrees' heights.

The maximum search time for a binary tree depends on its height. If a tree has a height of 5, then at most five comparisons need be made to determine whether a particular target item is in the tree. A binary tree with n nodes has height of at least $\log_2 n$, but its height can be as high as n if it was carelessly constructed.

Obviously, since the maximum search time is based on the height of the tree, we want our trees to have heights as small as possible. Let's look first look at how a normal binary tree would be constructed, then look at how this can degenerate into a linked list, and then examine strategies for minimizing tree height.

Constructing a Binary Tree in Random Order

At the beginning of the chapter we considered constructing a binary tree from a sorted list. When we did that, we always ended up with a minimum-height binary tree. But that's not a realistic way to construct a binary tree: In real life, we will always want to add and delete nodes. If we didn't need that ability, we would simply use a sorted list because that's easier to do.

So, assume that we begin with an empty binary tree, to which we add nodes until the tree contains what we want it to. Suppose that we add the nodes in random order. Think about what this means for `bin_insert()`: At each step into the tree, there is a 50% chance that the item to be inserted is greater than the node's value and a 50% chance that it is less. Logically, this means that inserting a node with a random value into a binary tree will end up at a random location at the bottom of the tree. So inserting items into a binary tree in random order should result in a tree that can be searched quickly, because there's no tendency for nodes to "pile up" at any given point in the tree.

Deleting nodes from a tree in random order also tends to keeps the tree height at a minimum. This is more difficult to see, because `bin_delete()` has three different cases, but rest assured that it is so.

You may not be satisfied with these informal arguments. In that case, take a look at *The Art of Computer Programming, Vol. 3* or *Introduction to Algorithms*, referenced in Appendix

B, "Selected Bibliography." Both of these books give formal proofs that insertion into and deletion from a binary tree in random order tend to keep the height of the tree at a minimum. The mathematics that they use is beyond the scope of this book, but it is not really difficult.

Constructing a Binary Tree in Nonrandom Order

What happens when values aren't inserted into a binary tree in random order? In that case, the tree may degenerate into a linked list. For instance, as a worst case, consider Figure 12.4a as an example of what happens when items are inserted in sorted order. Figure 12.4b, a "zig-zag" tree, is more unusual but just as bad for searching.

FIGURE 12.4a
Two forms of degenerate binary tree.

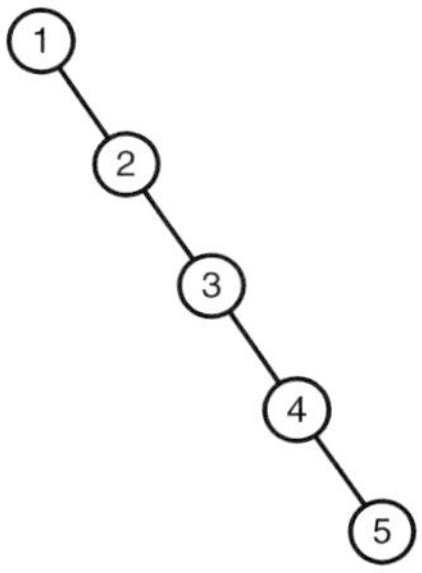

FIGURE 12.4b

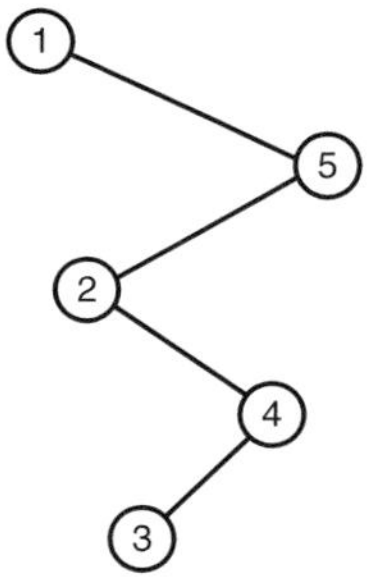

There aren't any simple solutions to this problem. If your application is likely to insert items into a binary tree in sorted order, it's best not to use a simple binary tree. Instead, you can use one of the "balanced" tree data structures discussed in the second half of this chapter, or adopt a different data structure entirely.

In practice, many applications may do just fine with plain binary trees, which have the advantage of being simpler than balanced trees. The pathological case of a binary tree degenerating into a linked list doesn't come up very often in those applications. In the end, figure out what works best for your application and use that.

Advanced Topics

There are several ways to implement binary trees, and so far only one of them has been shown in this chapter. It's worth looking at some of these alternate techniques. In the following sections, we'll take a look at parent pointers and threading in binary trees.

Parent Pointers

When we wrote the function for iterative traversal of a binary tree, `avl_traverse()`, we had to keep track of the nodes that we needed to return to on a stack because we had no other way of moving back up the tree. Wouldn't it be nice if we could find the successor of a node without having to keep track of its parent node? Then we wouldn't have to keep a stack when we're traversing the tree because we'd be able to get from any node to its successor with ease.

One way to solve this problem is by storing an additional pointer in each node that points to the node's parent. If the node is the tree's root, the parent pointer is a null pointer.

Doing this requires that we modify `struct bin_node`. The change is easy to make as shown in Listing 12.2.

LISTING 12.2 `pbin.c`—Node Structure for Binary Tree with Parent Pointers

```
struct pbin_node {
  int data;
  struct pbin_node *left;
  struct pbin_node *right;
  struct pbin_node *parent;
};
```

We've named our modified node `struct pbin_node`. In addition, `struct pbin_tree` can be defined in a manner analogous to `struct bin_tree`. For a demonstration of how to use the `parent` field, let's implement a function for finding the successor of a given node in a binary tree with parent pointers:

```
static struct pbin_node *successor(struct pbin_node *x)
{
  struct pbin_node *y;

  assert(x != NULL);
  if (x->right != NULL) {
    y = x->right;
    while (y->left != NULL)
      y = y->left;
```

```
203     }
204     else {
205       y = x->parent;
206       while (y != NULL && x == y->right) {
207         x = y;
208         y = y->parent;
209       }
210     }
211
212     return y;
213   }
```

`pbin_successor()` takes a pointer to a node, `x`, as an argument and returns the node's successor as the result. If the node contains the largest value in the tree, it returns a null pointer.

Case 1 (lines 199–203): If `x` has a right child, its successor is the smallest value in its right subtree. Compare this to the code for case 3 in `bin_delete()`. Note that so far the parent pointers haven't come into play at all.

Case 2 (lines 204–210): This is trickier conceptually. Consider finding the successor of node 7 or node 11 in Figure 12.1 for examples of case 2. It is easier to think of this case backwards. If `x` has a successor `y`, then `x` is the predecessor of `y`. If we were going to find `y`'s predecessor, we'd take the maximum value in `y`'s left subtree, just as to find the successor of a node we find the minimum value in its right subtree. To do this, we'd move down to the left from `y`, then down to the right until we couldn't move right any further.

We can reverse this process by moving up to the left in the tree until we've moved up to the left as far as we can go, then move up to the right once. Note that at each step there's only one choice for where we move up to, so we just examine which direction we in fact moved and if it was to the right, we're done. We're also done if we ran out of nodes, because that indicates that `x` is the item in the tree with the greatest value.

Parent pointers make traversing a tree easier, as we've shown, but they complicate and slow down inserting into and deleting from the tree because more fields in each node have to be updated. In addition, trees with parent pointers take up more memory than ordinary binary trees.

All the other operations shown for plain binary trees can be implemented for binary trees with parent pointers. For brevity, code for these operations is not included in the text, but it can be found in `pbin.c` on the accompanying CD-ROM.

Threading

Parent pointers are one way to simplify traversal of a binary tree; threading is another. The idea of threading starts from the observation that, in binary tree nodes that have empty left or right subtrees, the subtree fields are wasted storing null pointers. In a *threaded binary tree*, subtree pointers that would otherwise be null are used to store pointers to other parts of the tree.

Specifically, a potentially null left subtree pointer is used to point to the node's predecessor, and a potentially null right subtree pointer points to the node's successor. These otherwise-null pointers are called *threads*. In this section, non-thread pointers are called *links*.

The left thread of the node having the smallest value in the tree is a null pointer; similarly for the right thread of the largest valued node. These are the only null pointers in the tree.

Of course, it's necessary to be able to tell the difference between an ordinary link and a thread. As a result, two extra bits must be added to the node to allow links to be distinguished from threads.

We can easily define a threaded binary tree node based on this description as we see in Listing 12.3.

LISTING 12.3 `tbin.c`—Node Structure for Threaded Binary Tree

```
struct tbin_node {
  int data;
  struct tbin_node *left;
  struct tbin_node *right;
  unsigned l_thread:1;
  unsigned r_thread:1;
};
```

In the structure above, `l_thread` is set to 0 when `left` is a link and to 1 when it is a thread, and similarly for `r_thread`. `l_thread` and `r_thread` are declared as bit fields with a width of one bit, so only a single bit is used for each. If memory is not at a premium, it may be faster to declare each of them as type `char` because many compilers optimize bit fields poorly.

Let's write a function to find the successor to a node in a threaded tree:

```
static struct tbin_node *successor(struct tbin_node *x)
{
  struct tbin_node *y;

  assert(x != NULL);
```

```
287
288   y = x->right;
289   if (x->r_thread == 0)
290     while (y->l_thread == 0)
291       y = y->left;
292   return y;
293 }
```

Again, there are two cases. Case 1 (lines 288—291) is the same as for `pbin_successor()`: If the node has a right subtree, find the minimum value in that subtree. Note that instead of checking for non-null pointers, the code checks that the pointers are links instead of threads. Case 2 (line 288) is even simpler: If the node's `right` pointer is a thread, it points directly to the node's successor. (Either way, we start by moving right, so line 288 is shared between the two cases.)

A tree threaded in this way is a fully threaded tree. We can also define a *right-threaded* binary tree, in which the right child of each node is threaded as described above, but left children are not threaded. In a fully threaded tree, a function `predecessor()` analogous to `successor()` can be written, but such a function cannot be written efficiently for a right-threaded tree. The advantage of a right-threaded tree is that operations modifying the tree are slightly faster because left threads need not be maintained.

Threaded trees can take up slightly less memory than trees with parent pointers. Both solutions solve the same problems in traversal, and both solutions take extra time for tree insertions and deletions compared to ordinary binary trees. Threaded binary trees have slightly faster traversal time. Choosing one or the other can be difficult. If a tree with their properties is needed, it may come down to which type you understand better when deciding which to implement.

Code for threaded trees for all the operations shown for plain binary trees is available as `tbin.c` on the CD-ROM. It is omitted here for brevity.

Balanced Binary Trees

Back when we were analyzing the performance of binary trees, we noted that if items are inserted into a binary tree in sorted order, the tree's performance degenerates to that of a linked list. We also noted that there is no easy way to avoid this behavior.

There is a way if we're willing to deal with some complexity. After each operation that changes the tree, we can *rebalance* it, so that its height is the smallest possible. That way, any searches in the tree will take their minimum possible time. Because insertions and deletions also involve searching, this speeds those operations up as well.

Unfortunately, there is no known way to quickly rebalance a tree to its minimum height. But rebalancing is a great idea, and we don't have to let it go to waste. We can't rebalance a tree to its minimum height, but we can come close by defining criteria for the maximum amount that a tree can be "unbalanced" before it is rearranged to meet the criteria. This way, although we don't necessarily have a minimum-height tree at any given time, we still get something that's pretty close.

AVL trees and *red-black trees* specify different sets of criteria for considering trees balanced. The following sections take a look first at AVL trees, then at red-black trees. For each type of balanced tree, we'll learn their balance criteria, then define their node structure and write functions for insertion and deletion. Although code for the other operations isn't listed here, it is included on the CD-ROM in files `avl.c` and `rb.c`.

The following sections give an overview of how insertion and deletion in balanced trees work, but the best way to understand balanced trees is to work with them by hand on paper. Try drawing a tree, then inserting or deleting a node. After the operation, perform rebalancing if necessary for the type of tree you're dealing with. Figure out how the code would perform the same operation, and compare the results. No amount of explanation can match this type of learning by doing.

AVL Trees

AVL trees are one of the oldest known types of balanced binary search trees, and they are still one of the most popular. The term AVL comes from the initials of the inventors, Russian mathematicians G. M. Adel'son-Vel'skiĭ and E. M. Landis.

In an AVL tree, the *balance factor* of a node is defined as the height of the node's right subtree minus the height of its left subtree. To be an AVL tree, the balance factor of every node in the tree must be between -1 and +1. Thus, every part of an AVL tree is "almost balanced," because each node's left and right subtrees have similar height.

A binary tree with n nodes has a height of $\log_2(n+1)$, rounded up to the nearest integer, if it is perfectly balanced. On the other hand, an AVL tree with n nodes always has a height between $\log_2(n+1)$ and $1.4404\log_2(n+2) - 0.328$ (for proof, see *The Art of Computer Programming, Vol. 3*, referenced in Appendix B). So, the AVL balance condition doesn't always result in trees as good as a perfectly balanced tree, but it comes pretty close.

We can easily design a C structure for an AVL tree node as shown in Listing 12.4.

LISTING 12.4 `avl.c`—Node Structure for AVL Tree

```
struct avl_node {
  struct avl_node *link[2];
  int data;
```

LISTING 12.4 continued

```
    short bal;
};
```

There are a few changes between this and the structures for nodes that we've used previously, so let's take a closer look. First, note that where we previously had `left` and `right` links, we now have an array of two pointers to `avl_node` structures, called `link`. `link[0]` corresponds to the `left` member seen previously, and `link[1]` corresponds to `right`. This will make it easier to store a reference to one of a node's children—we can simply store a 0 or 1 and use that value as an index into the `link` array.

In addition, `link` has been moved up in the structure to be its first member. There is a good reason for this. ANSI C guarantees that a pointer to a structure is a pointer to its first member, and vice versa, if we perform an appropriate cast. In some of the code below, we will want to pretend that the `root` pointer in an `avl_tree` structure is an `avl_node`, as opposed to the pointer to `avl_node` that it is declared as. When we do this, we will only be interested in accessing the first element of `link`. As a result, we can simply take the address of the tree's `root` member and cast it to `avl_node *` and use the result.

The final change is the addition of `bal`. `bal` is used to keep track of the node's balance factor. It will always have a value of -1, 0, or +1. `bal` is given type `short` in the code presented here, but a possibly smaller signed type such as `signed char` or even a signed bit-field type could also be used.

`struct avl_tree` corresponds exactly to `struct bin_tree`. Most of the `bin_*()` routines for dealing with binary trees can be used in their original form, as long as we change references to `bin_tree` and `bin_node` to refer to `avl_tree` and `avl_node`, respectively. The exceptions are the functions that actually modify the tree because they now need to maintain the nodes' `bal` members and rebalance the tree when necessary. These are, in our code, the functions for tree insertion and deletion. The following sections take a look at how these can be implemented for AVL trees.

Insertion

Insertion into an AVL tree is more complex than insertion into a simple binary search tree. The process can be divided into four distinct phases:

1. *Searching*. This is similar to the same step in insertion into an ordinary binary search tree. In addition, we need to keep track of some more information as we move down the tree.
2. *Insertion*. We actually add a new node to the tree.

3. *Adjust balance factors.* The balance factors of the nodes above the new node have changed. We adjust them to their proper new values.
4. *Rotation.* If the new node would otherwise cause the tree to become unbalanced, we move some nodes around in the tree to maintain the balance condition. This is called a *rotation*.

Let's jump right into the code and see how it works:

```
int avl_insert(struct avl_tree *tree, int item)
{
  struct avl_node **v, *w, *x, *y, *z;

  assert(tree != NULL);
  v = &tree->root;
  x = z = tree->root;
  if (x == NULL) {
    tree->root = new_node(tree, item);
    return tree->root != NULL;
  }

  for (;;) {
    int dir;
    if (item == z->data)
      return 2;

    dir = item > z->data;
    y = z->link[dir];
    if (y == NULL) {
      y = z->link[dir] = new_node(tree, item);
      if (y == NULL)
        return 0;
      break;
    }

    if (y->bal != 0) {
      v = &z->link[dir];
      x = y;
    }
    z = y;
  }

  w = z = x->link[item > x->data];
  while (z != y)
```

```
    if (item < z->data) {
      z->bal = -1;
      z = z->link[0];
    }
    else {
      z->bal = +1;
      z = z->link[1];
    }

  if (item < x->data) {
    if (x->bal != -1)
      x->bal--;
    else if (w->bal == -1) {
      *v = w;
      x->link[0] = w->link[1];
      w->link[1] = x;
      x->bal = w->bal = 0;
    }
    else {
      assert(w->bal == +1);
      *v = z = w->link[1];
      w->link[1] = z->link[0];
      z->link[0] = w;
      x->link[0] = z->link[1];
      z->link[1] = x;
      if (z->bal == -1) {
        x->bal = 1;
        w->bal = 0;
      }
      else if (z->bal == 0)
        x->bal = w->bal = 0;
      else {
        assert(z->bal == +1);
        x->bal = 0;
        w->bal = -1;
      }
      z->bal = 0;
    }
  }
  else {
    if (x->bal != +1)
      x->bal++;
    else if (w->bal == +1) {
```

```
170         *v = w;
171         x->link[1] = w->link[0];
172         w->link[0] = x;
173         x->bal = w->bal = 0;
174       }
175       else {
176         assert(w->bal == -1);
177         *v = z = w->link[0];
178         w->link[0] = z->link[1];
179         z->link[1] = w;
180         x->link[1] = z->link[0];
181         z->link[0] = x;
182         if (z->bal == +1) {
183           x->bal = -1;
184           w->bal = 0;
185         }
186         else if (z->bal == 0)
187           x->bal = w->bal = 0;
188         else {
189           assert(z->bal == -1);
190           x->bal = 0;
191           w->bal = 1;
192         }
193         z->bal = 0;
194       }
195     }
196     return 1;
197 }
```


We begin by declaring a number of variables and handling the special case of insertion into an empty AVL tree (lines 94—102). It is easier to handle this special case by itself than to try to include it in the general algorithm.

`new_node()` refers to a helper function that tries to allocate a new `struct avl_node`. If it is successful, it initializes the new node's `item`, sets its child pointers to null pointers, sets its `bal` field to zero, increments `tree`'s `count` field, and returns the new node. Otherwise, it returns a null pointer.

The code in lines 104—123 handles both the search and insertion phases of inserting a node into an AVL tree. It is similar to the corresponding code from `bin_insert()`, but there are some new aspects as well. Variable `z` is used to keep track of the node being examined. If node `z` has the same value as the item to be inserted, we return (lines 106 and 107). Otherwise, `dir` is assigned the index into `z->link` of the child of `z` to examine next (line

109). If `item` is greater than `z->data`, `item > z->data` has a value of 1, meaning the right child; otherwise, `item` is less and `item < z->data` is 0, meaning the left child.

`y` is assigned the next node to inspect, the child of `z` on side `dir` (line 110). If `y` is a null pointer, this is the point at which to insert the new node. A new node is created with `new_node()`, inserted as `z`'s child, and assigned to `y`, then the loop is exited with `break` (lines 111–116). If the new node cannot be allocated, the function exits unsuccessfully (lines 113 and 114).

`x` is used to keep track of the last node encountered with a nonzero balance factor, and `v` records the pointer that was followed to arrive at `x` (lines 118–121). Node `x` is the point at which we may need to rebalance: If a node has a zero balance factor, adding a new node under it can change that node's balance factor to +1 or -1, but it will never force a rebalancing operation.

Inserting the new node `y` necessitates change in the balance factors of the nodes above it. The code segment in lines 125–134 updates balance factors for the nodes between `x` and `y`. All of these nodes had balance factors of 0 before this code ran because `x` points to the node with nonzero balance factor that is closest to `y` along the path from the root. All of them have nonzero balance factors afterward because inserting `y` increases the height of the tree.

After the balance factors of the nodes between `x` and `y` have been updated, it's time to update the balance factor of `x` itself. It's easiest to divide this into two variants: one where `y` is in the left subtree of `x` (lines 136–166), and one where `y` is in the right subtree of `x` (lines 166–195). These variants are exactly analogous, so only the code for the former will be examined.

If the balance factor of `x` is +1 or 0, it's easy. We can simply update `x->bal` to have the new balance factor (line 138). After that, we're done.

Otherwise, the balance factor of `x` is -1, meaning that its left subtree was already taller than its right subtree, and we've made it even taller. So we have to rearrange nodes in order to keep the AVL property of the tree. There are two ways that we can rearrange the nodes when that happens.

Figure 12.5 illustrates each possibility. In the figure, balance factors are shown inside nodes and arbitrary subtrees are shown as capital letters above their relative heights. A new node has been inserted at `w`, which has led `x` to have an effective balance factor of -2, disallowed by the AVL balance criterion.

Case 1 (Figure 12.5a; lines 139–144): `w`, the left child of `x`, has a balance factor of -1, as shown on the left side of the figure. The code performs a *right rotation* on `w` and `x`, by moving `w` to the place formerly occupied by `x`. `x` becomes `w`'s right child and `w`'s former right child becomes `x`'s left child. In this way, the total height of the subtree remains the same as it was before the insertion of y, but the AVL balance condition is now satisfied. The results of the rotation can be seen on the figure's right side.

FIGURE 12.5a
Cases requiring rebalancing upon insertion into an AVL tree.

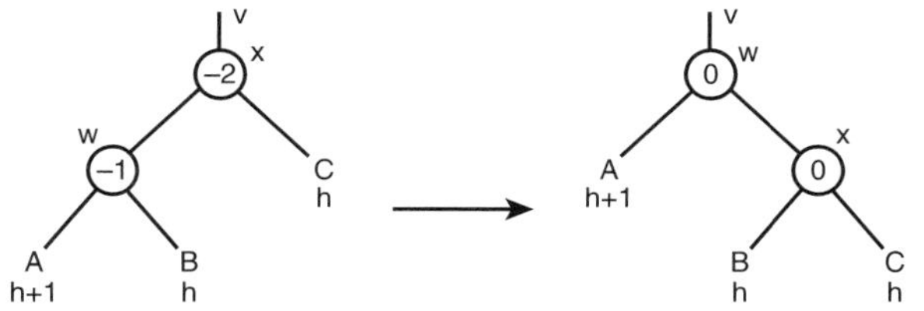

FIGURE 12.5b

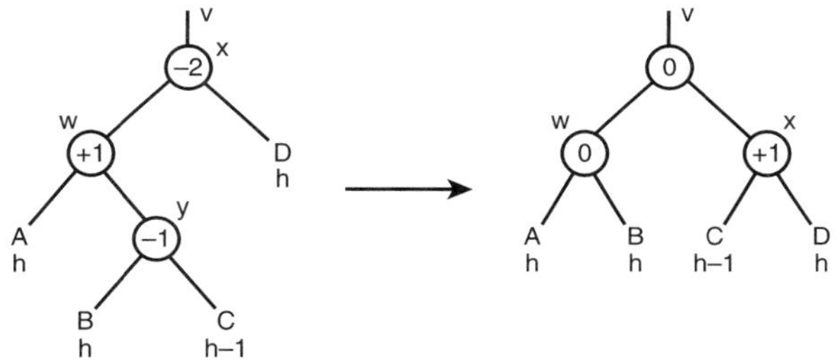

Case 2 (Figure 12.5b, lines 145—163): w has a balance factor of +1. When this occurs, we perform a *double rotation* composed of a *left rotation* on y and w, then a *right rotation* on y and x (lines 147—151).

There are three subcases of this case that are distinguished by the balance factor of w's right child, only one of which is illustrated. These subcases determine the balance factors of x and w after the double rotation is performed. Refer to the code for details (lines 152—162).

After rebalancing, we're done, and we return successfully (line 196).

Deletion

Deletion in an AVL tree is also more complicated than the corresponding operation in a plain binary tree. It's also more complicated than insertion into an AVL tree. Let's divide it up into phases as for insertion:

1. *Searching*. We search down the tree to find the node to delete. We keep track of the nodes that we've visited along the way, because we may need to know them for later phases.
2. *Deletion*. The node is deleted. We adjust the list of visited nodes to make it consistent with the changes in the tree.
3. *Rebalancing*. We adjust balance factors and perform rebalancing as needed.

Let's jump right in:

```
int avl_delete(struct avl_tree *tree, int item)
{
  struct avl_node *ap[32];
  int ad[32];
  int k = 1;

  struct avl_node **y, *z;

  assert(tree != NULL);

  ad[0] = 0;
  ap[0] = (struct avl_node *) &tree->root;

  z = tree->root;
  for (;;) {
    int dir;
    if (z == NULL)
      return 0;
    if (item == z->data)
      break;

    dir = item > z->data;
    ap[k] = z;
    ad[k++] = dir;
    z = z->link[dir];
  }

  tree->count--;
  y = &ap[k - 1]->link[ad[k - 1]];
  if (z->link[1] == NULL)
    *y = z->link[0];
  else {
    struct avl_node *x = z->link[1];
    if (x->link[0] == NULL) {
      x->link[0] = z->link[0];
      *y = x;
      x->bal = z->bal;
      ad[k] = 1;
      ap[k++] = x;
    }
    else {
```

```
    struct avl_node *w = x->link[0];
    int j = k++;

    ad[k] = 0;
    ap[k++] = x;
    while (w->link[0] != NULL) {
      x = w;
      w = x->link[0];
      ad[k] = 0;
      ap[k++] = x;
    }

    ad[j] = 1;
    ap[j] = w;
    w->link[0] = z->link[0];
    x->link[0] = w->link[1];
    w->link[1] = z->link[1];
    w->bal = z->bal;
    *y = w;
  }
}

free(z);
assert(k > 0);
while (--k) {
  struct avl_node *w, *x;

  w = ap[k];
  if (ad[k] == 0) {
    if (w->bal == -1) {
      w->bal = 0;
      continue;
    }
    else if (w->bal == 0) {
      w->bal = 1;
      break;
    }

    assert(w->bal == +1);

    x = w->link[1];
    assert(x != NULL);

```

```
      if (x->bal > -1) {
        w->link[1] = x->link[0];
        x->link[0] = w;
        ap[k - 1]->link[ad[k - 1]] = x;
        if (x->bal == 0) {
          x->bal = -1;
          break;
        }
        else
          w->bal = x->bal = 0;
      }
      else {
        assert(x->bal == -1);
        z = x->link[0];
        x->link[0] = z->link[1];
        z->link[1] = x;
        w->link[1] = z->link[0];
        z->link[0] = w;
        if (z->bal == +1) {
          w->bal = -1;
          x->bal = 0;
        }
        else if (z->bal == 0)
          w->bal = x->bal = 0;
        else {
          assert(z->bal == -1);
          w->bal = 0;
          x->bal = +1;
        }
        z->bal = 0;
        ap[k - 1]->link[ad[k - 1]] = z;
      }
    }
    else {
      assert(ad[k] == 1);
      if (w->bal == +1) {
        w->bal = 0;
        continue;
      }
      else if (w->bal == 0) {
        w->bal = -1;
        break;
      }
```

```

      assert(w->bal == -1);

      x = w->link[0];
      assert(x != NULL);

      if (x->bal < +1) {
        w->link[0] = x->link[1];
        x->link[1] = w;
        ap[k - 1]->link[ad[k - 1]] = x;
        if (x->bal == 0) {
          x->bal = +1;
          break;
        }
        else
          w->bal = x->bal = 0;
      }
      else if (x->bal == +1) {
        z = x->link[1];
        x->link[1] = z->link[0];
        z->link[0] = x;
        w->link[0] = z->link[1];
        z->link[1] = w;
        if (z->bal == -1) {
          w->bal = 1;
          x->bal = 0;
        }
        else if (z->bal == 0)
          w->bal = x->bal = 0;
        else {
          assert(z->bal == 1);
          w->bal = 0;
          x->bal = -1;
        }
        z->bal = 0;
        ap[k - 1]->link[ad[k - 1]] = z;
      }
    }
  }

  return 1;
}
```

The code in lines 214—226 should look pretty familiar. All we are doing is searching down the tree with `z`, comparing each node visited with `item`. The nodes we visit are added to the stack, with the nodes stored in array `ap[]` and the direction we moved from each of them stored in array `ad[]` (lines 223 and 224). When we encounter `item`, the loop exits (lines 229 and 220).

Now we move into the deletion phase (lines 228—264). There are the same three cases here as for deletion in a binary tree, but they are complicated by the need to maintain the list of nodes above the one being deleted.

To start out, `y` is assigned the pointer that was followed to arrive at `z`, using the stack of node pointers (line 229). The first case (lines 230 and 231) is as simple as binary tree deletion.

The second case (lines 233—240) is almost as simple as binary tree deletion, but notice that we have to copy `z`'s balance factor to `x` and add `x` to the stack of nodes.

The third case (lines 241—261) is a bit more complicated. As we traverse nodes to find the successor of `z` in the tree (lines 247—252), we have to add those nodes to the stack (lines 250 and 251). There's another subtlety: Since we're replacing node `x` by node `w` in the tree, we also have to replace `x` by `w` in the stack (lines 254 and 255).

Now it's time to move into the rebalancing phase (lines 265—366). This is somewhat analogous to the rebalancing phase for AVL tree insertion, but it is sometimes necessary to perform more than one rotation.

We loop as long as there are nodes still on the stack. `w` is assigned the top node on the stack at the top of each loop (line 269). `ad[k]` is the index into `w->link[]` of the subtree from which the node was deleted.

As in insertion, there are two symmetric cases. We'll take a look at the case where `ad[k]` is 0 (lines 270—317); that is, where the node deleted was from `w`'s left subtree.

There are two simple cases. If `w`'s balance factor is -1, the deletion from `w`'s left subtree has caused `w` to become more balanced, and we set its balance factor to 0 (lines 271—274). However, this means that the total height of `w` has decreased, so it might be necessary to rebalance the tree of which `w` is a child. So, we go to the next iteration of the loop using `continue`.

The second simple case (lines 275—278) is when `w`'s balance factor is 0. In this case, deleting a node from `w`'s left subtree has caused its right subtree to become taller than its left, so its balance factor becomes +1. Its overall height does not change, so there's no need to trickle this change further up the tree, and we're done, so `break` is used to exit the loop.

Figure 12.6 illustrates the more complicated cases that require a rotation. The notation used in the figure is the same as for Figure 12.5. In each case, a node has been deleted from the left subtree of node `w` having balance factor +1, leaving `w`'s new balance factor to effectively be +2, disallowed by the AVL balance criterion.

FIGURE 12.6a
Cases requiring rebalancing upon deletion from an AVL tree.

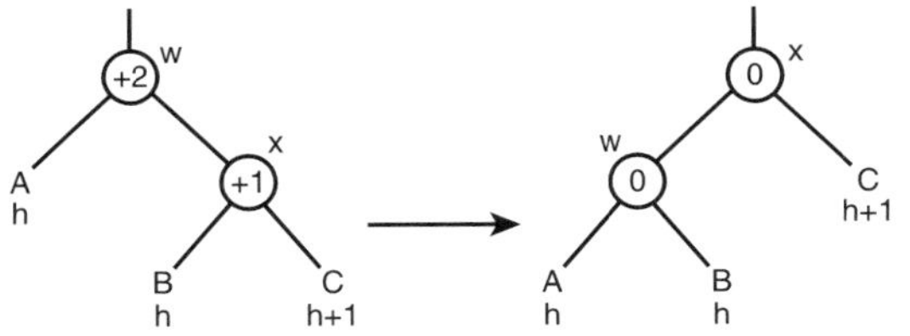

FIGURE 12.6b

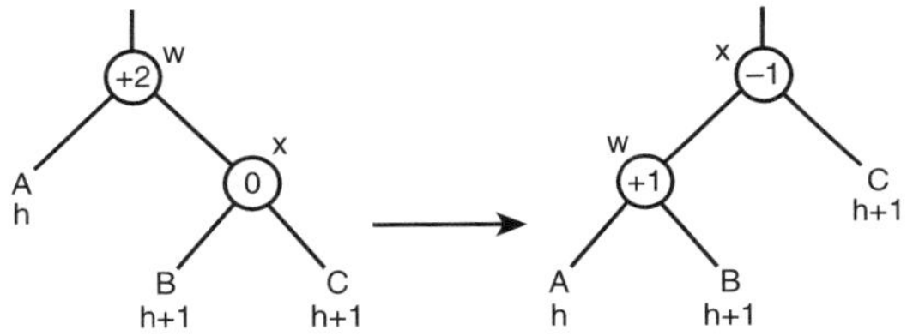

FIGURE 12.6c

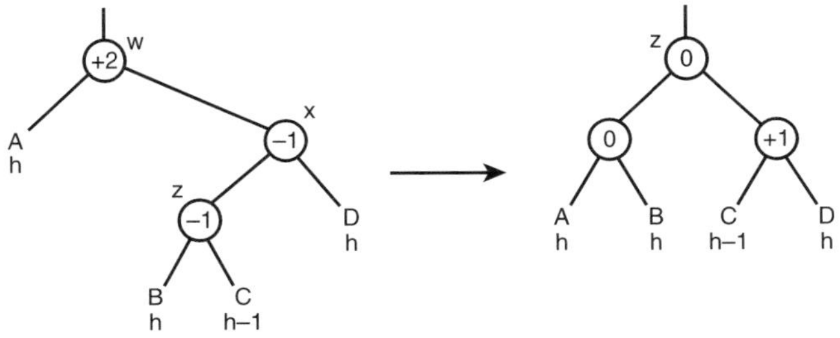

Case 1 (Figure 12.6a; lines 285—288 and 293 and 294): `x`, `w`'s right child, has a +1 balance factor. A left rotation restores `x` and `w` to full balance. The loop continues.

Case 2 (Figure 12.6b; lines 285—292): `x` has a balance factor of 0. A left rotation restores the AVL balance criterion. Afterward, `x` has a balance factor of -1 and `w` of +1. The loop terminates.

Case 3 (Figure 12.6c; lines 296—316): `x`'s balance factor is -1, requiring a double rotation to restore balance. `x`'s left child `z` may have any balance factor before the rotation, leading to three subcases. This code is similar to that used to perform a double rotation for insertion in an AVL tree.

Observe how cases 1 and 2 here resemble case 1 in insertion and how case 3 resembles case 1 in insertion. This can be seen easily, for instance, by comparing Figure 12.6a and b with Figure 12.5a, and Figure 12.6c to Figure 12.5b.

After this, we're all done, and we return successfully.

Red-black Trees

Red-black trees are a newer form of balanced tree structure than AVL trees, first devised by Bayer in 1972 under the name of "symmetric binary B-trees." The present terminology was introduced by Guibas and Sedgewick in 1978.

In a red-black tree, every node is associated with a *color*: either red or black. The balance condition is maintained by constraining the way nodes can be arranged, based on their color. The precise rules are as follows:

1. Red nodes may have only black children.
2. All the paths from a node to any leaf node below it contain the same number of black nodes.

In addition, the red-black trees in this chapter will always have a black node at the root, in order to simplify some of the code. General red-black trees may have roots of either color.

The *black-height* of a node, for our purposes, is the number of black nodes in a path from it down to a leaf, not including the node itself.

A red-black tree with n nodes has height between $\log_2(n+1)$ and $2\log_2(n+1)$.

We can define an enumerated type to keep track of node colors, as shown in Listing 12.5.

LISTING 12.5 `rb.c`—Enumerated Type for Node Colors in Red-black Tree

```
enum color {
  RB_RED,
  RB_BLACK
};
```

Using `enum color`, we can design a C structure for a red-black tree node:

```
struct rb_node {
  struct rb_node *link[2];
  int data;
  enum color color;
};
```

`struct rb_node` follows the same pattern as our AVL tree node. Instead of a balance factor, it contains `color`, which takes one of the enumerated constant values `RB_RED`, for a red node, or `RB_BLACK`, for a black node. Alternatively, `color` could be declared as a particular integer such as `short` or `char` or even an unsigned bit-field type.

As with AVL trees, many of the routines for handling binary trees can easily be adapted for use with red-black trees. Again, routines that modify the tree are the exception. The following sections take a look at implementing insertion and deletion in red-black trees.

Insertion

Without further prelude, let's examine the code for insertion into a red-black tree.

```
int rb_insert(struct rb_tree *tree, int item)
{
  struct rb_node *ap[48];
  int ad[48];
  int ak;

  struct rb_node *x, *y;

  assert(tree != NULL);
  if (tree->root == NULL) {
    tree->root = new_node(tree, item, RB_BLACK);
    return tree->root != NULL;
  }

  ad[0] = 0;
  ap[0] = (struct rb_node *) &tree->root;
  ak = 1;

  x = tree->root;
  for (;;) {
    int dir;

    if (item == x->data)
      return 2;
    dir = item > x->data;

    ap[ak] = x;
    ad[ak++] = dir;
    y = x->link[dir];
    if (y == NULL) {
      x = x->link[dir] = new_node(tree, item, RB_RED);
```

```
      if (x == NULL)
        return 0;
      break;
    }
    x = y;
  }

  while (ap[ak - 1]->color == RB_RED)
    if (ad[ak - 2] == 0) {
      y = ap[ak - 2]->link[1];
      if (y != NULL && y->color == RB_RED) {
        ap[--ak]->color = y->color = RB_BLACK;
        ap[--ak]->color = RB_RED;
      }
      else {
        if (ad[ak - 1] == 1) {
          x = ap[ak - 1];
          y = x->link[1];
          x->link[1] = y->link[0];
          y->link[0] = x;
          ap[ak - 2]->link[0] = y;
        }
        else
          y = ap[ak - 1];

        x = ap[ak - 2];
        x->color = RB_RED;
        y->color = RB_BLACK;

        x->link[0] = y->link[1];
        y->link[1] = x;
        ap[ak - 3]->link[ad[ak - 3]] = y;

        break;
      }
    }
    else {
      y = ap[ak - 2]->link[0];
      if (y != NULL && y->color == RB_RED) {
        ap[--ak]->color = y->color = RB_BLACK;
        ap[--ak]->color = RB_RED;
      }
      else {
```

```
174         if (ad[ak - 1] == 0) {
175           x = ap[ak - 1];
176           y = x->link[0];
177           x->link[0] = y->link[1];
178           y->link[1] = x;
179           ap[ak - 2]->link[1] = y;
180         }
181         else
182           y = ap[ak - 1];
183
184         x = ap[ak - 2];
185         x->color = RB_RED;
186         y->color = RB_BLACK;
187
188         x->link[1] = y->link[0];
189         y->link[0] = x;
190         ap[ak - 3]->link[ad[ak - 3]] = y;
191         break;
192       }
193     }
194
195   tree->root->color = RB_BLACK;
196
197   return 1;
198 }
```


At the start of the function, we declare some necessary variables (lines 102–106). The special case of insertion into an empty tree is also handled in order to simplify the general algorithm (lines 109–112).

This code uses a helper function `new_node()` that allocates and initializes a new `struct rb_node`. `item` and `color` are set as requested by the caller, both child pointers are set to null, `tree`'s `count` is incremented, and the new node is returned. If memory cannot be allocated, `new_node()` returns a null pointer.

Lines 118–136 are familiar code for searching a binary tree and inserting a new node. In addition, each node visited is added to a stack used later in rebalancing (lines 126 and 127).

The new node, `x`, is always colored red initially. Consider the constraints on the red-black tree that adding this node may have violated. Adding a red node cannot violate constraint 2 because it does not change the number of black nodes along any path. But it may violate constraint 1: If `x`'s parent node is red, making `x` red is not allowed, and we need to fix up the structure.

The loop in lines 138–193 repeats as long as constraint 1 is not satisfied. At the beginning of each iteration, consider `x` to be a red node whose parent `ap[ak - 1]` is also red. (Actually, `x` is not maintained by the loop. Instead, it is figured out from the information on the top of the stack when necessary.)

During each iteration, we figure out what needs to be changed at this level of the tree to satisfy constraint 1. Then we perform the change and continue to the loop's next iteration if it's possible that more changes are necessary, or exit the loop if the changes fixed the tree.

As before, there are two symmetric cases. We'll examine the case in lines 139–166, where `x`'s parent is the left child of its own parent, `x`'s "grandparent." We first designate `y` as `x`'s "uncle"; that is, `x`'s grandparent's right child (line 140). (`y` may be a null pointer, in which case `x` has no uncle.)

The three cases are illustrated in Figure 12.7. In the figure, black nodes are filled in and red nodes are empty. Nodes not named in the program source code are labeled *a* and *b* for convenience. Capital letters designate arbitrary subtrees. In each case, a red node has been inserted on the left side of *a* as the child of another red node, violating red-black constraint 1.

FIGURE 12.7a
Cases requiring rebalancing upon insertion into a red-black tree.

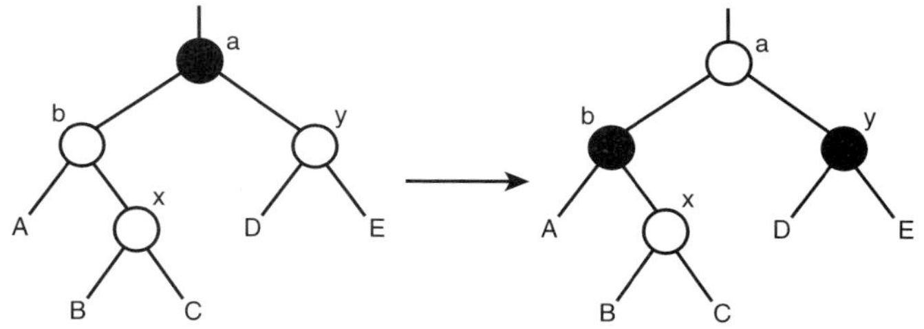

FIGURE 12.7b

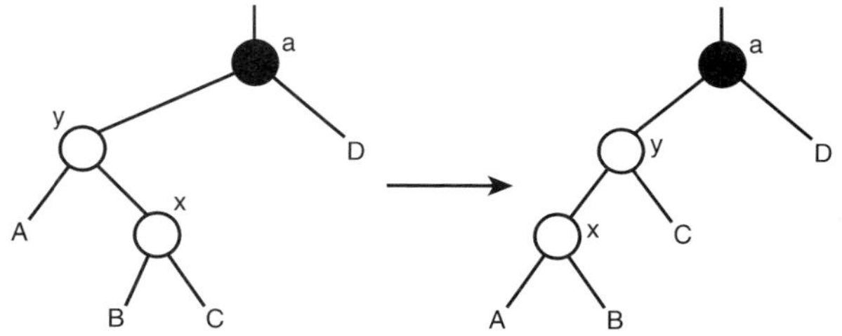

FIGURE 12.7C

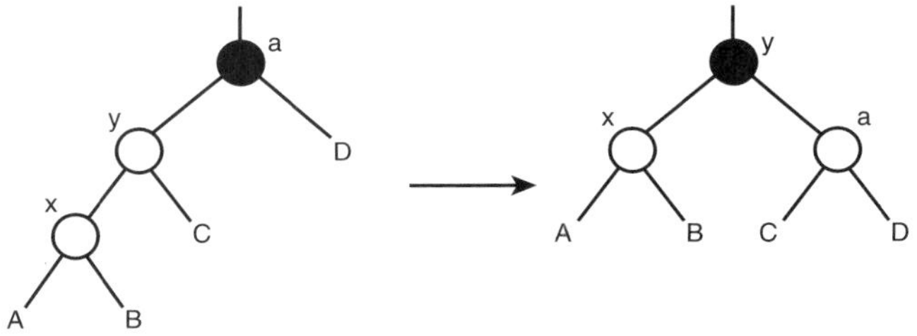

Case 1 (Figure 12.7a; lines 141–144): If `y` exists and it is red, we can simply change `b` and `y`'s colors to black and `a`'s color to red. Notice that this keeps the black-height of the tree rooted at `x`'s grandparent the same, preserving constraint 2. However, there's the possibility that `a` is the child of a red node. This is the situation that the loop is designed to handle. So, we go through the loop again with `x` replaced by `a`'s parent. (Again, `x` is maintained implicitly; it is not actually reassigned.)

The figure shows only the case where `x` is the right child of `b`, but it applies equally if `x` is the left child of `b`.

Case 2 (Figure 12.7b; lines 146–152): If `x` is the right child of its parent, we transform it through a left rotation. This transforms case 2 into case 3, handled later. Whether a rotation is made or not, this code sets `y` as the parent of `x` (line 148 or 154).

Case 3 (Figure 12.7c; lines 156–164): We have `x` as the red left child of red node `y`, which in turn is the left child of its black parent `a`. We perform a right rotation. Notice that the steps taken in cases 2 and 3 maintain the black-height of the tree, satisfying constraint 2, and they restore constraint 1 by separating the two red nodes. Because the tree's red-black property constraints are now satisfied, the loop is exited.

As a final step, we set the color of the tree's root to black (line 195). This is always allowed because it will never lead to a violation of either constraint.

Deletion

Now let's look at how to delete a node. As usual, we'll start with a code listing.

```
202 int rb_delete(struct rb_tree *tree, int item)
203 {
204   struct rb_node *ap[48];
205   int ad[48];
206   int k;
207
208   struct rb_node *w, *x, *y, *z;
```

```

assert(tree != NULL);

ad[0] = 0;
ap[0] = (struct rb_node *) &tree->root;
k = 1;

z = tree->root;
for (;;) {
  int dir;

  if (z == NULL)
    return 0;

  if (item == z->data)
    break;
  dir = item > z->data;

  ap[k] = z;
  ad[k++] = dir;
  z = z->link[dir];
}
tree->count--;

if (z->link[0] == NULL || z->link[1] == NULL) {
  y = z;

  x = y->link[0];
  if (x == NULL)
    x = y->link[1];
}
else {
  ap[k] = z;
  ad[k++] = 1;
  y = z->link[1];

  while (y->link[0] != NULL) {
    ap[k] = y;
    ad[k++] = 0;
    y = y->link[0];
```

```
    }

    x = y->link[1];
    z->data = y->data;
  }
  ap[k - 1]->link[ad[k - 1]] = x;

  if (y->color == RB_RED) {
    free(y);
    return 1;
  }

  free(y);

  while (k > 1 && (x == NULL || x->color == RB_BLACK))
    if (ad[k - 1] == 0) {
      w = ap[k - 1]->link[1];

      if (w->color == RB_RED) {
        w->color = RB_BLACK;
        ap[k - 1]->color = RB_RED;

        ap[k - 1]->link[1] = w->link[0];
        w->link[0] = ap[k - 1];
        ap[k - 2]->link[ad[k - 2]] = w;

        ap[k] = ap[k - 1];
        ad[k] = 0;
        ap[k - 1] = w;
        k++;

        w = ap[k - 1]->link[1];
      }

      if ((w->link[0] == NULL || w->link[0]->color == RB_BLACK)
          && (w->link[1] == NULL || w->link[1]->color == RB_BLACK)) {
        w->color = RB_RED;
        x = ap[k - 1];
        k--;
      }
      else {
```

```
        if (w->link[1] == NULL || w->link[1]->color == RB_BLACK) {
          w->link[0]->color = RB_BLACK;
          w->color = RB_RED;

          y = w->link[0];
          w->link[0] = y->link[1];
          y->link[1] = w;

          w = ap[k - 1]->link[1] = y;
        }

        w->color = ap[k - 1]->color;
        ap[k - 1]->color = RB_BLACK;
        w->link[1]->color = RB_BLACK;

        ap[k - 1]->link[1] = w->link[0];
        w->link[0] = ap[k - 1];
        ap[k - 2]->link[ad[k - 2]] = w;

        x = tree->root;
        break;
      }
    }
    else {
      w = ap[k - 1]->link[0];
      if (w->color == RB_RED) {
        w->color = RB_BLACK;
        ap[k - 1]->color = RB_RED;

        ap[k - 1]->link[0] = w->link[1];
        w->link[1] = ap[k - 1];
        ap[k - 2]->link[ad[k - 2]] = w;

        ap[k] = ap[k - 1];
        ad[k] = 1;
        ap[k - 1] = w;
        k++;

        w = ap[k - 1]->link[0];
      }

```

```
331       if ((w->link[0] == NULL || w->link[0]->color == RB_BLACK)
332           && (w->link[1] == NULL || w->link[1]->color == RB_BLACK)) {
333         w->color = RB_RED;
334         x = ap[k - 1];
335         k--;
336       }
337       else {
338         if (w->link[0] == NULL || w->link[0]->color == RB_BLACK) {
339           w->link[1]->color = RB_BLACK;
340           w->color = RB_RED;
341
342           y = w->link[1];
343           w->link[1] = y->link[0];
344           y->link[0] = w;
345
346           w = ap[k - 1]->link[0] = y;
347         }
348
349         w->color = ap[k - 1]->color;
350         ap[k - 1]->color = RB_BLACK;
351         w->link[0]->color = RB_BLACK;
352
353         ap[k - 1]->link[0] = w->link[1];
354         w->link[1] = ap[k - 1];
355         ap[k - 2]->link[ad[k - 2]] = w;
356
357         x = tree->root;
358         break;
359       }
360     }
361
362   if (x != NULL)
363     x->color = RB_BLACK;
364
365   return 1;
366 }
```

rb_delete() begins as do many functions that we've looked at, with declarations of local variables, including a stack, and appropriate assertions (lines 204–210).

The code in lines 212–230 is similar to that seen in `avl_delete()` and `rb_insert()`. It searches down the tree with `z` for a node containing data matching `item`, pushing nodes on the stack as it encounters them. When a match is found, the loop exits. When the loop terminates, `z` is the item to delete, `pa[k - 1]` is `z`'s parent, and so on.

The technique used for deletion in `rb_delete()` is slightly different from that in `avl_delete()` and `bin_delete()`, so it will be described in some detail here.

If `z` has fewer than two children, the pointer to it from its parent is replaced by `z`'s left child, if it exists, otherwise by its right child (lines 233–239). As a consequence, if `z` is a leaf, it is replaced by a null pointer.

Otherwise, `y` is used to find `z`'s successor in the tree, pushing nodes on the stack as they are visited (lines 240–253. Because `z`'s successor cannot have a left child, it can be easily deleted through replacement by its right child (if any). Its data is copied into `z` (line 252). This is different from the method presented earlier, where pointers were manipulated to move the deleted node's successor rather than copying the data field.

`y` is the node that is deleted (line 254). If `y` is red, it can be removed without violating either red-black constraint, and we return successfully (lines 256–259). Either way, storage for `y` is released using `free()` (line 257 or 261).

Now it's time to fix the tree's red-black properties. We just deleted a black node, so constraint 2 has been broken, and it is our job to repair it. At this point, `x` is the root of the tree that has one fewer black node than it should, and the stack contains its parent nodes all the way up to `tree`'s root.

The loop condition (line 263) tests whether `x` is red. If it is, we're done and exit the loop, since we can simply change its color to black. We also exit the loop if tree adjustments have trickled all the way up to the tree root, as judged by the value of `k` because that also indicates that the tree is now a proper red-black tree again.

Once again, there are two symmetric cases. We will examine the case where `x` is the left child of its parent (lines 264–312). As a first step, take `w` to be the right child of `x`'s parent (line 265). Then look at each possibility, as illustrated in Figure 12.8.

In Figure 12.8, black nodes are filled in and red nodes are empty. Nodes shaded gray may be either red or black. Nodes not named in the program source code are labeled *a, b,* and *c* for convenience. Capital letters designate arbitrary subtrees.

Case 1 (Figure 12.8a; lines 267–281): This case, when `w` is red, is easier to handle by transforming it into one of the other cases than by handling it directly. This is done by rotating `w` left, into the spot occupied by `a`, and keeping the stack updated. Notice that this transformation doesn't change the black-height of the subtree's children.

FIGURE 12.8a
Cases requiring rebalancing upon deletion from a red-black tree.

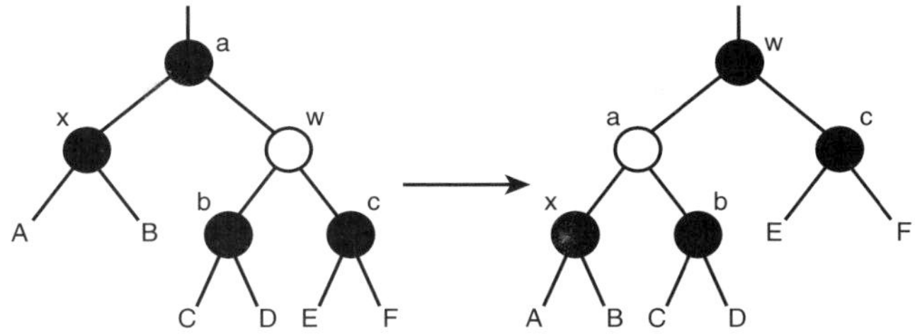

FIGURE 12.8b

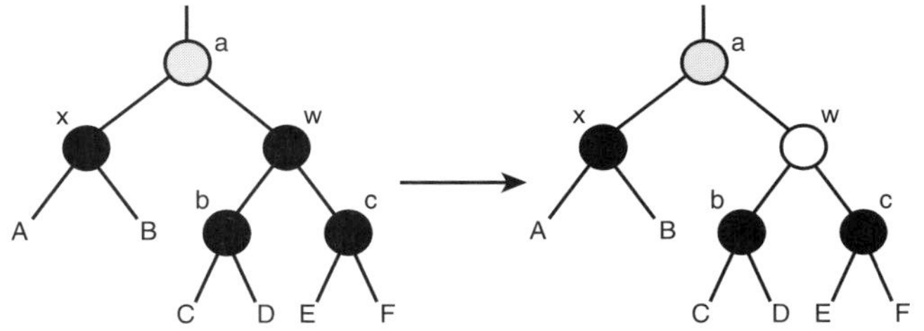

FIGURE 12.8c

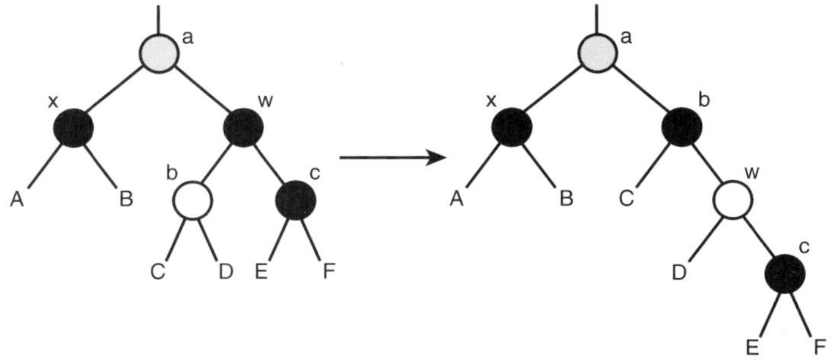

FIGURE 12.8d

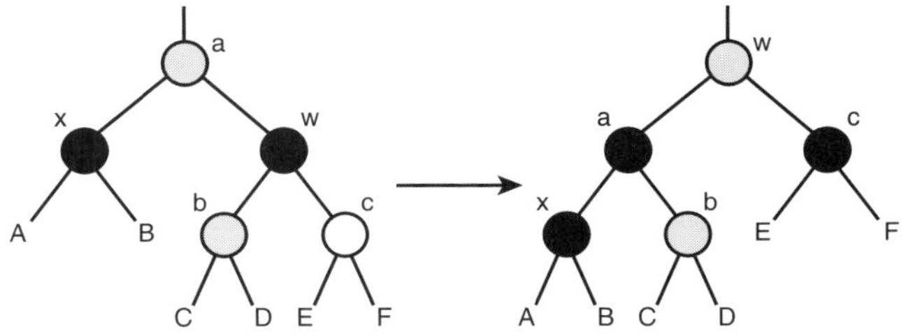

Case 2 (Figure 12.8b; lines 283–288): If w has no red children (b and c may be black nodes or nonexistent), it can simply be re-colored as red. This eliminates a black node from the right subtree of x's parent, matching the black node eliminated at x. This restores constraint 2 for the subtree. It is still necessary to propagate the change up the tree because the black-height of the subtree as a whole has changed, so the stack is popped and the loop continues.

Case 3 (Figure 12.8c; lines 290–299): If b is red and c is black or does not exist, then we transform it into Case 4 by performing a right rotation at w and exchanging the colors of w and b.

Case 4 (Figure 12.8d; lines 301–310): w has a red right child. We perform a left rotation and re-color some of the nodes. This increases the black-height on the left side of the subtree, fully satisfying constraint 2. We assign tree's root node to x to ensure that tree will have a black root, then exit the loop.

If x isn't a null pointer, we set its color to black, as required by the loop condition (lines 362 and 363). Finally, we return successfully (line 365).

Comparison of AVL and Red-black Trees

AVL and red-black trees are comparable in practice. Some points to note:

- Insertion and deletion are $O(\log_2 n)$ for both AVL and red-black trees.
- Insertion into an AVL tree requires at most one rotation, but deletion may require up to $\log_2 n$ deletions. On the other hand, insertion into a red-black tree may require two rotations, but deletion never requires more than three.
- The maximum height of an AVL tree for a tree of n nodes is smaller than the maximum height of a red-black tree of n nodes.

Besides comparisons between different types of balanced trees, it's worth comparing balanced trees to a few other well-known data structures:

- *Hash tables* offer O(1) search, insertion, and deletion, on average. However, it is possible to encounter pathological cases that reduce their performance to $O(n)$ for n elements. Devising a proper hash function can be difficult and time-consuming. In addition, hash tables cannot be easily or quickly traversed in order of the elements stored in them.
- *Skip lists* offer the same performance as binary trees for the operations covered here. In addition, they can speed iterating through the nodes in order by storing the nodes in order in memory. Skip lists also have pathological cases as do hash tables. It is

possible to reduce the likelihood of these cases to a negligible level, however. Skip lists are a relatively recent invention, so they are not as well known as other methods.

- *2-3 trees*, *splay trees*, and other types of *multiway trees* all allow for branching in more than two directions at each point in a tree. These methods all have disadvantages that make them less suitable than balanced trees in general situations, but they have areas of applicability, such as in storage and searching of disk-based data archives.

As a final note, keep in mind that AVL and red-black trees can include parent pointers or threads just like ordinary binary trees. It is a good test of your understanding of binary tree structures to construct insertion and deletion routines for these augmented forms of trees.

Summary

This chapter discussed the basics of binary tree manipulation. We began with a description of linear search, then binary search for a sorted list. We discovered that binary trees were a more efficient alternative for use with large, dynamically changing lists. We examined the details of a number of algorithms for manipulating and searching binary trees, and implemented them in C. We also looked at the advantages and disadvantages of binary trees with parent pointers and threaded binary trees. We implemented two types of balanced binary trees, AVL trees and red-black trees, that avoid the pathological cases of ordinary binary trees at the cost of additional complication. Finally, we briefly compared the properties and merits of binary trees to those of some other types of data structure.

CHAPTER 13

Rapid Sorting Techniques

by Dann Corbit

In This Chapter

This chapter takes a look at sorting techniques. First, we'll define the basic terms and algorithms, and then we will explain their inner workings. We will also present implementations of some of the most useful algorithms. Finally, we will present a compound algorithm that presents many of the useful techniques and can be used for sorting very large collections of data. Some of the ideas presented in this chapter are entirely new. They have never been presented before anywhere else (to the best of my knowledge) and may prove enormously beneficial for those who have never considered them.

Classifying Data

Sorting is an act of classification. If we have a pile of unordered data, one of the first things we should consider is classifying that data. With rapidly advancing computer systems and the advent of the information superhighway, we can obviously locate and store more data than we ever dreamed possible in the past. But a giant pile of unordered data is of low value. In order to extract meaning from the data, we must first classify it by some important or key characteristics. The more order we introduce, the more valuable the data becomes because we can answer more questions from it. "Yes, sales are up, but which region is doing the best and which is doing the worst? Which salesman has the highest volume? Which equipment makes our salesmen more effective and which has little or no effect? Which training seems to have the most impact?" We can answer these questions without sorting, but we can answer them many times faster by sorting. And time is money. If we have an unordered pile of twenty million records, answering questions about the data would be horrible. If we classify the data, we will be able to answer questions on a timely basis.

Steven S. Skiena, in *The Algorithm Design Manual*, notes the following on pages 33 and 34:

- Sorting is the basic building block around which many other algorithms are built. By understanding sorting, we obtain an amazing amount of power to solve other problems.

- Historically, computers have spent more time sorting than doing anything else. A quarter of all mainframe cycles are spent sorting data [Knu73b]. Although it is unclear whether this remains true on smaller computers, sorting remains the most ubiquitous combinatorial algorithm problem in practice.

- Sorting is the most thoroughly studied problem in computer science. Literally dozens of different algorithms are known, most of which possess some advantage over all other algorithms in certain situations. To become convinced of this, the reader is encouraged to browse through [Knu73b], with hundreds of pages of interesting sorting algorithms and analysis.
- Most of the interesting ideas used in the design of algorithms appear in the context of sorting, such as divide and conquer, data structures, and randomized algorithms.

Note

[Knu73b] is a reference to *The Art of Computer Programming, Volume 3: Sorting and Searching,* D. E. Knuth, Addison-Wesley, Reading MA, 1973.

Types of Sorting Algorithms

Here is a list of some common sorting algorithms used in various applications:

- An *internal sort* is an algorithm that only uses in-core (also called RAM or primary) main memory during the sort other than a single pass to read the data and a single pass to write the sorted output.
- An *external sort* is a sort algorithm that uses external memory, usually disk (occasionally tape on older systems), during the sort and generally performs multiple reads and writes. External sorts are designed to process lists of data that cannot fit into main memory all at once.

  Whether a sort is internal or external is an algorithm design decision rather than a physical reality. An internal sort might use virtual memory and actually operate using disk most of the time. An external sort might be able to load all the data at once and require only a single pass.
- A *comparison sort* is a sort algorithm that makes comparisons between keys to arrange items in a prearranged order.
- A *distributive sort* is a sort algorithm that operates directly on some characteristic of the keys.

- An *in-place sort* is a sort algorithm where the algorithm requires only a small, fixed amount of additional memory to complete the sort. This is often called *in-situ* sorting in the literature.
- A *stable sort* is an algorithm that preserves the original ordering of items with equal keys. An unstable sort can always be converted to a stable sort by the addition of a key item such as the original position in the list.

When to Use a Sort Routine

If faced with a sorting problem, the first thing to decide is whether to write a sort routine or not. Most of the time, the answer will be not to write one. For a large pool of data, where we ask repeated questions, it is much smarter to just store the data in a database. The database company has undoubtedly spent hundreds of thousands or even millions of dollars figuring out the most effective ways to order your data. It may also be possible that you have a selection problem rather than a sorting problem. Selection is a much easier operation than sorting. However, sometimes you will have to write a sort. Perhaps you are the employee of the database company tasked with creating a fantastic way to order data on-the-fly, such as when a client issues an order-by clause on data with no index associated with it. Perhaps you are writing a routine that drives a graphics card and you must order polygons in multiple dimensions. Because this must obviously happen as fast as possible, storing to and from a database is clearly out of the question. There are many other factors, pro and con, which must always be weighed before making such a decision. Supposing that the decision is to write a sort routine, let's consider the fundamentals of what is needed.

Sorting Fundamentals

Sorting is really just math operations on sets. In the long run, we end up sorting either by subtraction or by division. Imagine two sets. The first set is called unknown, and the second is called sorted. Our initial set may or may not have some kind of order in it. To create a sorted set, we can take an item from the first set and put it into the second set. We can continue this process until the first set is empty and the second set is full. This is an example of sorting by subtraction.Bubble-sort, selection-sort, and insertion-sort are typical examples that work this way.

In Figure 13.1, notice how each operation on the unordered set transfers a single object to the ordered set. Hence, we are subtracting from the set of unknown order and adding to the ordered set. Typically, we will have to examine or move a majority of the items in the unknown set or the ordered set (or possibly both) during each set operation.

FIGURE 13.1
Sorting by subtraction.

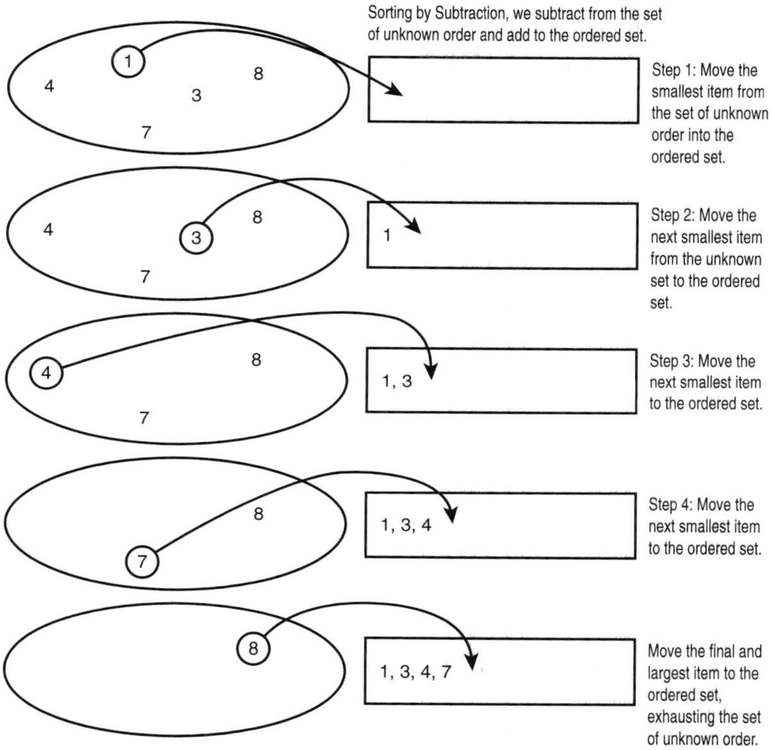

Sorting by Subtraction, we subtract from the set of unknown order and add to the ordered set.
Step 1: Move the smallest item from the set of unknown order into the ordered set.
Step 2: Move the next smallest item from the unknown set to the ordered set.
Step 3: Move the next smallest item to the ordered set.
Step 4: Move the next smallest item to the ordered set.
Move the final and largest item to the ordered set, exhausting the set of unknown order.
1
1, 3
1, 3, 4
1, 3, 4, 7

We may also try dividing our unknown set in half. We can perform this division in a number of ways. We could pick an item and divide into things that are smaller and things that are larger. We could divide the set into "winners" and "losers." If we keep dividing, eventually our unknown set will be completely classified. Quick-sort and heap-sort work in this way.

In Figure 13.2, notice how each operation on the unordered set divides the set or a subset by two. Hence, we divide the problem into smaller and smaller pieces until it vanishes.

Perhaps we would like to divide by a number larger than two. If we know what the data looks like, we can fragment it into classes by any number of different means. Bucket-sort and counting-sort work in this manner. It might seem that we should always divide by a big number to make things go faster, but that is not always true. Imagine a set with only three things in it. It won't make much difference if we subtract, divide by two, or divide by one thousand as far as the number of steps needed is concerned. And the simple operations like subtract tend to be easier to perform than division.

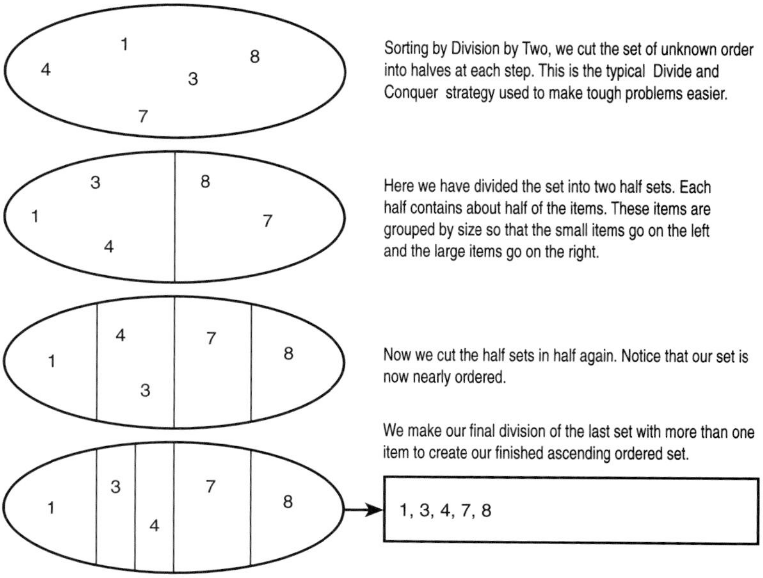

1
4
8
3
7
Sorting by Division by Two, we cut the set of unknown order into halves at each step. This is the typical Divide and Conquer strategy used to make tough problems easier.
3
8
1
7
4
Here we have divided the set into two half sets. Each half contains about half of the items. These items are grouped by size so that the small items go on the left and the large items go on the right.
4
7
1
8
3
Now we cut the half sets in half again. Notice that our set is now nearly ordered.
We make our final division of the last set with more than one item to create our finished ascending ordered set.
3
7
1
8
4
1, 3, 4, 7, 8

FIGURE 13.2
Sorting by division by two.

In Figure 13.3, notice how each operation on the unordered set divides the set by some number N. This method divides the unordered set into subsets much faster than dividing by two.

Sorting by division by a large number will vary by the number we choose to divide by. In Figure 13.3, if we choose the number 9, we can finish the whole job in a single step.

Notice that we will need at least as many bins as the number we choose to divide by. Notice also that if we choose a very large number, we may have a lot of empty bins, which may waste time as we inspect them.

In the lower portion of Figure 13.3, we see that if we go from the most significant digit to the least significant digit, our method of separation into groups does not have to be stable. If we go from the least significant digit to the most significant digit, our method of separation into groups must be stable or the routine will not work. That is why counting-sort is often used for least significant digit radix-sort. Counting sort is a stable algorithm.

FIGURE 13.3
Sorting by division by some number N.

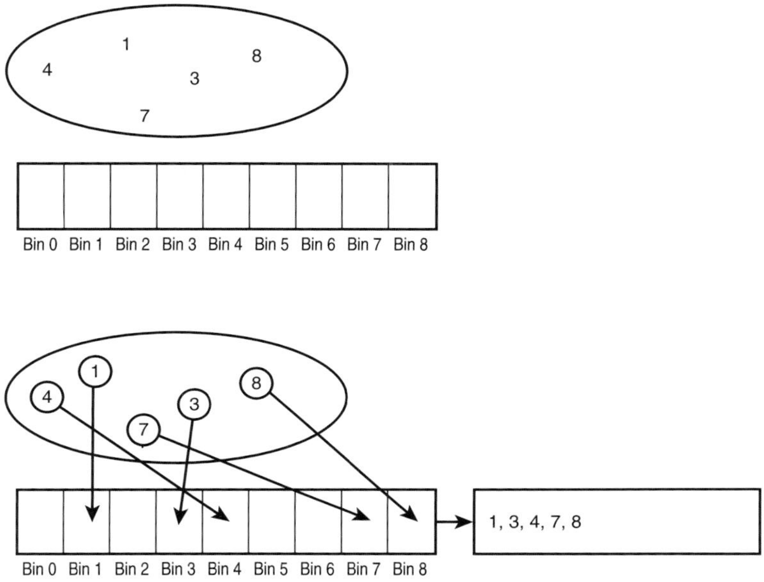

O(n²) Algorithms

We will begin with a discussion of internal sorting, starting with $O(n^2)$ algorithms. Keep in mind something important about optimality—optimal does not mean "fastest." It might seem as though we should always sort in linear time by dividing by large N. Indeed, if our set is large enough, we should. But remember that big-O notation talks about the asymptotic behavior of algorithms and not actual performance. It is counter-intuitive, but $O(n^2)$ is the fastest way to sort very tiny sets of data. This is very important to understand because algorithms with superior big-O performance often break a large set into tiny sets and then use an $O(n^2)$ algorithm to clean up. So if I sort ten million items, this may become one million sets of ten items. As you can well imagine, in such a situation, the performance of our $O(n^2)$ algorithm can dominate the total time of the sort.

Routines to Avoid and Why

Rather than starting with what $O(n^2)$ algorithm we ought to use, let's start with the routines to avoid and why we should avoid them.

Selection-Sort

Selection-sort is probably the most obvious sorting strategy. As an experiment, suppose I give you a list of five numbers and ask you to put them in order: 100, 8, 2, 20, and 9. I am sure that you selected 2, 8, 9, 20, and 100, but how did you arrive at that particular order? Quite likely, you just picked the smallest, then the next smallest, and so on. Selection-sort orders items by repeatedly looking through the unsorted items to find the smallest one and moving it to its final location. With selection-sort (like any other), we start with a set of unknown order. We gradually create an ordered set, which grows as the unknown set shrinks. The algorithm successively finds the element in the unsorted section that belongs in the position next to the sorted section, followed by an interchange of elements to put the proper element into place at the end of the ordered list.

The idea behind selection-sort is that each shift of data moves an item directly into its final, correct place. First, we find the smallest element in the array and swap it with the element in the first position. Then we find the second smallest element and exchange it with the element in the second position. We continue in this way until the entire array is sorted. This method is called selection-sort because it repeatedly selects the smallest element in the yet unsorted part of the array.

Bi-directional selection-sort (sometimes called shaker-sort) is a simple variation of selection-sort that finds both the smallest and the largest items on each pass and then moves them to their final correct places. We can gain a small efficiency by searching for the minimum and maximum in a special way. Instead of comparing the minimum and maximum that we have found thus far with each element of the unordered list, we will instead compare the unordered list items against each other two at a time. Then we compare the minimum against the smaller of the two, and the maximum against the larger of the two. Thus, instead of four comparisons per two unordered items, it takes only three. Although this is a dandy way to find minimum and maximum, it is still a horrible way to sort. Don't do it.

Selection-sort is among the worst algorithms in numbers of comparisons as it is $O(n^2)$ but is very efficient in terms of exchanges since it is O(n). This virtue is often cited as a reason to choose selection-sort for large data objects. Don't do it. It's a bad idea. Selection-sort is as slow as bubble-sort in general, and if you use a pointer-based sort instead of sorting the objects themselves, the size of the object does not matter. In short: Don't ever use selection-sort for any kind of sorting. It is useful for understanding how heap-sort works, but it simply is not a good way to sort.

Bubble-Sort

Bubble-sort is a technique in which pairs of neighboring values in the list to be sorted are compared and exchanged if they are out of order. Therefore, an item bubbles upward in the list until it reaches one that compares smaller. If a complete pass is made without any exchanges being made, the data must already be sorted so we can stop the algorithm without going through all passes if this should occur.

A bi-directional bubble-sort (sometimes also called shaker-sort) can also be created. The first iteration is done like a standard bubble-sort and the second iteration moves upward. An upward iteration allows a large element to sink only one place, but allows a small element to bubble up faster. This is a benefit only if smaller elements happen to be located at the bottom to begin with. Complexity is $O(n^2)$ both in number of comparisons and number of exchanges. The best case is when the distribution is almost sorted, with no small items at the end of the array. Sedgewick and Knuth both ridicule bubble-sort for good reason. It is a horrible $O(n^2)$ algorithm both in number of comparisons and number of exchanges. For some reason, it is often found in introductory programming books and in programming homework assignments. Bubble-sorts work best (less horribly) only when the distribution is almost sorted, with no small items at the end of the array. Don't use bubble-sort. It's simply horrible.

A Costly Lesson

Now for a horror story: In 1989, I was working on a large software project for a large corporation in the Pacific Northwest. They were writing a front-end package for their corporate library. The back-end database was SQL*Server, and the library package was called Dynix Marquis. The Dynix people had only written an OS/2 front end, and the corporation I was working for was not about to install OS/2 on nine thousand desktops. My job was to write a parser for ALA library rules, which describe how to preprocess a string so that queries can find it in a uniform manner. I was looking at someone else's code and noticed that he was doing a disk-based bubble-sort of the bibliographies, since people could request the bibs in any of a myriad of different orders. "This is a bubble-sort!" I said.

"Well," he said, "Even Knuth said that there is a time and a place for bubble-sort. The query sets are very small and the operations on the data are very complicated. This routine is very easy to understand and debug. Come try some sample queries and I will show you that performance is always acceptable and within project guidelines."

I sat down and ran a large number of queries and sure enough, he was right. Or so I thought. It turned out that the machines the developers were using were 486s with 16 megs of RAM, which was pretty much top of the line at the time. Most people who actually used it had 386s with about 4 megs of RAM. Even so, it passed the performance tests, but just barely. There were a lot of user complaints about the speed. Now we might imagine that with the exponential increase in computer power over time, the situation would rapidly get better and better. The opposite is true. The problem is that the library collection also grew exponentially. So a query for something like ''Show all videos on C or C++ ordered by date'' would result in only eight videos in 1989, but by 1994 it was more like 800. Eventually, they replaced the system with something much less capable. A bubble-sort had scuttled a one million-dollar project. Dynix Marquis had written a Windows front end by that time, but the feature set of the old front end was so much richer that I dearly missed it. (I was one of the heaviest users of the library system. I held the record for most items checked out in a day, in a week, in a month, in a quarter, and in a year.) My conclusion: Don't use bubble-sort. Not ever, for any reason. The alternatives are vastly superior. The chance for real, serious damage is much too great. You might imagine that there would never be enough items to make a difference, but that is a very dangerous proposition. Quite frankly, binary insertion is just as easy to visualize and program as bubble-sort. Bubble-sort is evil. Now, it's true that men like Jon Bentley, P. J. Plauger, Robert Sedgewick, or Donald Knuth might know good times to use some of these inferior algorithms. But for most of us mere mortals, the advice is ''stay away—far, far away."

Useful Sorting Techniques

Now that we have determined that we should not use selection-sort and we should not use bubble-sort, let's consider the $O(n^2)$ algorithms that should be at the top of our list: insertion-sort and its relatives.

Insertion-Sort

To get a clear understanding of how some sorting algorithms work, let's do a series of mind experiments involving a fabled family named Jones. Any apparent linkage to persons real or imaginary (including my mother's family) is purely coincidental. First, let me introduce you to the Jones family. The father is named Roscoe Richard, but everyone calls him Dick. The mother's name is Rhea, but Dick calls her "Mud." The children (by ascending age) are named Marilyn, Karen, Anita (called Nita), Judy, and Vicky. Dick is quite a practical joker. He once filled a coffee cup two-thirds full of mercury, floated a few nuts and bolts in it, and then poured one-quarter inch of coffee on top. Pointing out the nuts and bolts to Rhea, he said, "Hey Mud! You made the coffee too strong again."

One day the Jones girls were sitting on the front step eating their breakfast. They had fried eggs for breakfast, and none of them cared for the yolk part. So they took out the yolks and threw them up into the air. "Hey Mr. Sun, go back into your sky where you belong!" they chimed together.

Dick was looking out the window. "Playing with your food again! We'll see about that," he said. Dick went and got a special pair of reading glasses. They were so potent that when wearing them you could not see anything clearly that was more than a foot or so away. (Dick just got the glasses because it made the girls look funny and made the job a lot harder. But it helps in the computer analogy because computers only examine one or two items at a time. They can't look at a big pile and see the matches like we can.) While wearing these glasses, beyond one foot, all that could be discerned was a fuzzy blur. "All right girls," said Dick, "time to sort the socks, but the one doing the sorting will have to wear these glasses, and you can't say where to put the sock if you are not wearing the glasses."

Now, the Jones family has many different sized feet. Dick has size 10. Rhea has size 8. As for the children, Marilyn has size 7, Karen size 6, Nita size 5, Judy size 4, and Vicky size 3. To simplify things, they keep only white socks. That way they don't have to hunt as hard for pairs, and it won't matter as much if one or more gets lost. But since they are different sizes, they still need to be matched for length. Marilyn figures out a way to sort the socks into order (see Figure 13.4). Here is how she solves it:

Algorithm Linear Insertion

1. Pick up a sock from the basket.
2. For each sock on the floor (if any), pick it up to see if the one she is holding is larger.
3. When she finds that the sock from the basket is smaller than the one on the floor, she moves all the socks on the floor down, from that place forward, leaving a spot on the floor for the new sock.
4. She puts this sock into the open spot she just created.
5. If there are more socks still in the basket, she goes back to step 1 and continues until the basket is empty.

This is shown more formally in Listing 13.1.

FIGURE 13.4
Sorting socks.

LISTING 13.1 Linear Insertion Sort

```
/*
Straightforward linear insertion.  Binary insertion is better, and
Shell-sort is better yet.
*/
void            LINEARINSERTION(Etype a[], unsigned long n)
{
    unsigned long   i,
                    j;
    Etype          tmp;

    for (i = 1; i < n; i++) /* look for insertion point. */
        for (j = i; j > 0 && GT(a[j - 1], a[j]); j--) {
            /* Move the others down and insert it. */
            tmp = a[j];
            a[j] = a[j - 1];
            a[j - 1] = tmp;
        }
}
```

This is actually a fairly efficient way to do the classification of socks. Since each family member has seven pairs, there are only 7 people * 7 pairs * 2 socks/pair = 98 socks.

Let's figure out how long it takes to sort the socks, on average. The number of socks on the floor begins with one and ends with 98. There will be exactly 98 executions of the steps 1–5, since one sequence is executed for each step. Remember that the list changes in size, starting from one sock and ending with 98 socks. At some arbitrary point "t", we will have to look at half the socks (on average) to find the insertion point. We will also have to move half the pile down. So the sum of operations (on average) is as follows:

Compares: 0 + 1+ 1.5 + 2 + 2.5 +...+ 49 = 2425.5 comparisons (approximately $(n^2)/4$, which is 2401).

The number of sock moves is exactly the same on average, 2425.5.

Since the girls can make about one examination or move per second, it takes 4,851 seconds to do the job (about 1 hour and 20 minutes). It is interesting that if moves and compares take about the same amount of time, the algorithm always takes about the same time to complete. The reason is that if we find the insertion spot early, we have to move more socks. And if we find the insertion spot late, we have to move fewer socks. If we insert in the first spot, we move all the socks down. If we insert at the end, we move none of the socks.

"Well done," says Dick. "Now it's Karen's turn." He picks up the socks, puts them back in the basket, and stirs them up thoroughly. Suddenly, the girls realize that they are all going to have to sort the socks.

"It is going to take more than five hours before we all finish," laments Nita.

"I have an idea," Judy offered.

"What is it?" Marilyn wondered aloud. After all, if she had said something earlier, maybe it would not have taken her so long to complete the task.

"Well, it has to do with pretending," said Judy. "When you look at the socks on the floor, they are already where they are supposed to be. The smallest one is on the left, and the biggest one is on the right. First, we will have Vicky stand next to the smallest sock, and Marilyn stand next to the biggest. Why don't we look at the middle sock first? Now, if the one you are holding is bigger than the sock you pick up, we will have Vicky stand next to the sock you checked, on account of she's the smallest. Then, we'll pretend that the sock next to Vicky is the smallest sock, and look halfway between the pretend smallest sock and the largest. Now, if the one you are holding is not bigger than the sock you pick up, we will have Marilyn stand next to the sock you checked, because she's the biggest. Then, we'll pretend that the sock next to Marilyn is the largest sock, and look halfway between the pretend largest sock and the smallest. If we have Vicky and Marilyn keep doing this, we'll only have to look at a few socks."

Algorithm Binary Insertion

1. Marilyn and Vicky stand at the big and small end of the sock pile (together to start off with).
2. Karen picks up a sock from the basket.
3. Karen looks at the sock on the floor halfway between Vicky and Marilyn (if any).
4. If the sock in Karen's hand is bigger than the sock from the floor, move Vicky to the spot where the sock on the floor came from. Otherwise, move Marilyn there.
5. Repeat step 2 until Marilyn and Vicky are standing on the same spot.
6. Karen moves all the socks on the floor down, from that place forward, leaving a spot on the floor for the new sock.
7. Then she puts this sock into the open spot she just created.
8. If there are more socks still in the basket, she goes back to step 1 and continues until the basket is empty.

Listing 13.2 shows the implementation in C.

LISTING 13.2 Binary Insertion Sort

```
/*
This is a straightforward binary insertion sort.
Binary insertion is much faster on average compared to linear insertion.
Shell-sort is even better, according to my calculations.  You might
want to benchmark both binary insertion and shell-sort, but I suspect
shell-sort will outperform binary insertion on most systems.
*/
void            INSERTIONSORT(Etype array[], unsigned long count)
{
    unsigned long   partition;  /* The end of a new partition */
    long            beg;        /* Search beginning here (this moves toward
                                 * ipg) */
    long            ipg;        /* Current guess for the insertion point
                                 * (average of beg+end) */
    long            end;        /* Search ending here */
    Etype           temp;       /* Hold one element of the array in
                                 * temporary storage */
    /* * One element is sorted by definition. * Form larger and larger
     * ordered partitions * until the entire array is correctly ordered */

        for (partition = 1; partition < count; partition++) {
            /* inline binary search to find point of insertion */
            beg = ipg = 0;      /* The first element of the ordered part of
```

LISTING 13.2 continued

```
                          * the array is element 0 */
            end = partition - 1;/* The last element already ordered is
                          * element partition-1 */

            /* Without this check, loop terminates only if an equal element
             * is already sorted */
            while (end >= beg) {
                /* insertion point guess of halfway between beginning and
                 * ending */
                ipg = ((end + beg) >> 1);       /* BUGBUG: we can't sort sets
                                                 * > (MAX_LONG)/2 elements */
                /* However, this sort should *NEVER* be used for anything but
                 * tiny partitions */

                /* The element sitting at the end of the partition is the one
                 * we will insert */
                /* It is not ordered yet, but all the array to the left of it
                 * is in sort. */
                if (GT(array[ipg], array[partition]))
                    end = ipg - 1;
                else
                    beg = ++ipg;
            }
            /* make room at array[ipg] for array[i] */
            /* It might already be in the right place */
            if (partition != (unsigned long) ipg) {
                temp = array[partition];        /* Save the new element we
                                                 * are ready to insert */
                /* Move the data from the insertion point downward.  We can't
                 * use memcpy()! */
                memmove(&array[ipg + 1], &array[ipg],
                        (partition - ipg) * sizeof(Etype));
                array[ipg] = temp;      /* Put the new element in its sorted
                                         * order */
            }

    }
    return;
}
```

Compares: 0 + 1+ log2(2)+ ... + log2(98) = 512.5 comparisons (approximately 0.79 * n * log2(n) which is 0.79 * 648.24 for n=98).

The average number of sock moves is exactly the same as for linear insertion, 2425.5.

The total number of operations on average is much less, about 2,938 total compares and moves. With this algorithm, the number of compares is always the same regardless of the order of the incoming socks. Fortunately, this number is very small. However, the number of moves, while just like linear insertion, changes the performance of the algorithm quite a bit. If we had to move them all down each time, we would be doing just as much work as before. But if the list is already ordered correctly each time, we don't have any moves at all. We just append the sock to the end of the list. So the total of sock operations could be as small as 512 and a half. So the sock ordering will probably take about 49 minutes, but it could be as quick as eight and one half minutes.

As we can see, algorithm binary insertion is much better than linear insertion. In fact, for teeny-tiny sets (perhaps 20 items or so) binary insertion is probably the only algorithm you should ever use. It's much better than linear insertion. There is yet another improvement we can make to insertion-sort.

Shell-Sort

Shell-sort was the most optimal sort in terms of complexity before Hoare's quick-sort algorithm. That's not true any more, but it is an excellent algorithm for small sets. Shell-sort is a generalization of insertion-sort. This sorting algorithm was invented by Donald Shell, and is inspired by the insertion-sort's ability to work very fast on an array that is nearly ordered. It is also known as *diminishing increment* sort. Unlike insertion-sort, shell-sort does not sort the entire array at once. Instead, it divides the array into distant segments, which are separately sorted by using insertion-sort.

For some increment h, consider the array as a set of h different arrays. Each set contains the elements that are congruent to n modulo h. Once all of the segments are sorted, shell-sort re-divides the array into fewer segments and repeats the algorithm until the final sort, when the spacing is one. It is interesting that *any* sequence of increments will work, as long as the final segment is one. However, some increments work much better than others. The best possible increment sequence may yet be undiscovered. Although the shell-sort is easy to understand, formal analysis is hard. For shell-sort, the average case complexity is not precisely known, but is about $O(n^{(4/3)})$ for a judicious choice of h-increment. So, what's the explanation for why we need shell-sort? It's because of Big Daddy and his brothers. Big Daddy is the biggest, tallest guy in the set to be sorted. All the other elements are afraid of him, so he stands wherever he likes. Sometimes, he stands in the very first position. When that happens, insertion-sort will move him one single space right on each succeeding pass. Big Daddy gets moved n–1 times. But that's not the worst of it. Sometimes his tall brothers stand next to him. They also slide along slowly, just like Big Daddy. Once in a great while (just to be a pest), Big Daddy orders all the elements to stand in reverse order. This really takes the zip out of insertion-sort.

Here is how shell-sort comes to the rescue. Suppose, at some point in time, the h-increment is ten. What we do on this pass is essentially an insertion-sort on every tenth element. Now elements in our h-subset will still shift only one space right in our h-subset, but that is *ten* spaces right in the actual list. So we have figured out a way to throw the heavy guys to the right much faster than one space at a time. Shell-sort still does much better on nearly ordered sets than on nearly reversed sets. But it is a tremendous improvement over regular insertion-sort. Even with this wonderful improvement, shell-sort is only appropriate for small sets. Listing 13.3 shows what shell-sort looks like.

LISTING 13.3 Shell-Sort

```
/*
** The h-constants for this version of Shell-sort come from:
** Handbook of Algorithms and Data Structures in Pascal and C
** By Gaston Gonnet, Ricardo Baeza-Yates
** Addison Wesley; ISBN: 0201416077
** These h-increments work better for me than Sedgewick's under
** full optimization.  Your mileage may vary, so I suggest you
** try Sedgewick's suggestions as well.  The h-increment arena
** is a rich environment for exploration.  I suggest attempting
** all possible permutations below 20, since that is where a
** good shell-sort is crucial.  If you find something wonderful
** you may get your name up in lights.
*/
void            SHELLSORT(Etype array[], size_t count)
{
    size_t          i,
                    inc,
                    j;
    Etype           tmp;

    switch (count) {
    case 0:
    case 1:
        return;
    case 2:
        INSERTTWO(array);
        return;
    case 3:
        INSERTTHREE(array);
```

LISTING 13.3 continued

```
            return;
        case 4:
            INSERTFOUR(array);
            return;
default:

        for (inc = count; inc > 0;) {
            for (i = inc; i < count; i++) {
                j = i;
                tmp = array[i];
                while (j >= inc && (LT(tmp, array[j - inc]))) {
                    array[j] = array[j - inc];
                    j -= inc;
                }
                array[j] = tmp;
            }                   /* Calculate the next h-increment */
            inc = (size_t) ((inc > 1) && (inc < 5)) ? 1 : 5 * inc / 11;
        }
    }
}
```

Notice that there are special optimizations for when the count of elements is less than five. This only speeds up the routine a few percent, but it is worth it. Shell-sort will be used for many purposes when dealing with small partitions, and other sort routines will frequently call shell-sort. So any little tweak to get a hair more speed should be carefully considered.

Quick-Sort

Now, on to our next adventure for the Jones girls. I can't tell you what they did wrong, because it's a bit embarrassing. Suffice it to say it involved ice cream. Anyway, it was time for Dick to mete out a new punishment. When the girls saw Dick with the thick glasses, they said, "We know—the socks!" But he said, "Nope. I've got something different in mind." Now Dick liked to play penny-ante poker. He used to play with his buddies from the Department of Highways all the time. Dick tended to win a lot more than he lost and had amassed quite a collection of small change. He brought out a gallon jar full of coins. "Sort these into order..." said Dick, "and don't forget to wear the glasses. The rules stay the same. Only the one wearing the glasses can put them where they belong. The others can't say a word."

"There are thousands of them! Maybe hundreds of thousands! We'll never get it done with our sock tricks," said Marilyn. Then Nita got her great idea. "We'll cut them in half," said Nita.

"I'll go get a saw," said Vicky.

"No, no..." said Nita, "nothing like that. We will just split the gallon jar of coins into smaller and smaller piles. Here's how we will do it:"

Algorithm Quick-Sort

1. Pour the coins into a pile.
2. Grab a coin from the pile.
3. For any coins that are worth more, put them into a pile on the right.
4. For any coins that are worth less, put them into a pile on the left.
5. Go back to step 2 for each pile until all the piles have one coin in them. Since we put piles of bigger things on the right and smaller things on the left, when we get down to piles of one coin each, everything is perfectly in order.

Listing 13.4 shows the implementation in C.

LISTING 13.4 Primitive Quick-Sort

```
/*
Primitive quicksort.  This is a bad algorithm for general purposes.
Don't use it.
*/
void            QSORTB(Etype * A, int l, int r)
{
    int             loc;

    if (l < r) {
        int             i = l,
                        j = r;
        Etype           tmp,
                        pivot = A[l];
        /* Divide piles into partitions */
        for (;;) {
            while ((A[j] >= pivot) && (j > l))
                j- -;
            while ((A[i] < pivot) && (i < r))
                i++;
            if (i < j) {
                tmp = A[i];
```

LISTING 13.4 continued

```
                A[i] = A[j];
                A[j] = tmp;
            } else {
                loc = j;
                break;
            }
        }
        /* Recurse */
        QSORTB(A, l, loc);
        QSORTB(A, loc + 1, r);
    }
}
```

That's just what they did. It took quite a while—nearly five hours, but not bad considering how many coins they started out with and having to wear those stupid glasses.

Disadvantages of Quick-Sort

For nicely random data, the quick-sort algorithm described does a wonderful job; but it will go perverse with many common inputs. As Jon Bentley explains in "Software Exploratorium: History of a Heapsort" (*Unix Review,* Vol. 10, 8, August, 1992), many popular implementations of quick-sort have severe defects that cause degeneration to quadratic behavior for fairly common inputs such as already ordered, reverse ordered, and organ-pipe so that "sorting half a million elements, a run that should take a few minutes, takes a few weeks." Unmodified quick-sort is so dangerous that it should not be used for anything except perhaps teaching purposes. Once the simple algorithm is understood, a few small changes can render it many, many times safer for general use.

Singleton's Sort

The Association for Computing Machinery (ACM) algorithm 347 is a much safer variation of the basic quick-sort algorithm. So let's go back to the Jones household and see how our friends are getting along.

Naturally, when Dick came to see how the girls were doing, he was surprised that they had finished the job. Rhea said that she had been in the room the whole time and nobody cheated. "Well," said Dick, "now it is time for the next person to take their turn."

"We'll never finish!" lamented Judy.

"Let's think about what went wrong," said Marilyn. "One thing I noticed is that sometimes we grab something stupid like a penny and nothing is lower than that. But we can't just say 'Don't pick a penny' because the pile might have nothing but pennies in it. So why don't we stir up the pile and pick a few coins. Then we will take the middle from the ones we grab, and divide the piles using that."

Nita said, "I notice that sometimes a pile has all the same thing in it so it's already in order. Why don't we fly through the pile one time first to see if it does not need to be sorted?"

Rhea had the best idea yet, "I notice that you spend an awful lot of time on the small piles. Why don't you use your sock trick when you get to the tiny piles? I'll bet it will save a ton of time."

Here's what they did:

Algorithm Singleton's Sort (Quick-Sort Modified)

1. Pour the coins into a pile.
2. Check to see if the pile is already ordered. If not:
3. Stir up the coins and grab a few from the pile. Pick the middle coin from this batch.
4. For any coins that are worth more, put them into a pile on the right.
5. For any coins that are worth less, put them into a pile on the left.
6. If the pile is small, use the sock trick (Algorithm Binary Insertion). Else:
7. Go back to step 2 for each pile until all the piles are sorted. Since we put piles of bigger things on the right and smaller things on the left, when we get down to piles of one coin each, everything is perfectly in order.

Note

The listing for ACM Algorithm 347 is fairly lengthy. Please examine the file `allsort.h` on the CD for relevant details of the actual implementation.

It wasn't all punishment in the Jones household. Sometimes, they liked to have fun. They were very talented with musical instruments and sometimes Dick would play the harmonica or the accordion and Rhea would play the piano. They played old familiar songs that everybody knew and the girls would sing along.

Heap-Sort

One time, the Joneses decided to have a checkers tournament. Everybody knew Dick was the best player, so he sat out the first game. For the other players, they tried to pit the oldest (and probably the best) players against the youngest (and probably the worst.) Rhea played against Vicky, Marilyn played against Judy, and Karen played against Nita. As expected, Rhea, Marilyn, and Karen won (though Karen had quite a time of it!) Now Karen played Dick, and Rhea played Marilyn. Dick won as expected, but Marilyn had the first upset of the night. In the final game, much to everyone's surprise, Marilyn came out the winner. Now, the reason that real tournaments are often held in this format is to find out (on a given day) who the best player is. The best players bubble up toward the top. In computer science terms, this structure is called a *heap*. Maybe because tournaments can be heaps of fun!

Running a tournament is the equivalent of a build-heap operation. There are some interesting properties about a heap. One thing we may notice is that only a few games had to be played to find out who the best player was. The basic efficiency of a heap is O(n*log(n)), just like quick-sort. A second thing is that a heap is not very deep from bottom to top. In fact, the depth is ceil(log2(n)). Put another way, if we find the highest order bit in the number of things to count, that's about how deep our heap will be. So, for instance, if we have two to the twentieth power items in our heap, it will be exactly twenty levels deep. Heaps are also nice and simple, and they have an important property. It's easy to get the top item from a heap. In the case of our checkers contest, it was Marilyn. We can also take things out and put new things in with very little work and it remains heap ordered.

Now, there are many kinds of heaps, and some are more efficient than others. There even exist heaps for which all operations are O(1) except operation "delete the smallest item," which is O(log(n)). However, I would not advise using those heaps. The reason is that they have great asymptotic behavior (when the number of things is enormous) but for simply large sets of data (which is where we should use heaps), the fancy heaps do not do as well as simpler formats. So shall we sort with heaps? We could form a heap and then pick the top item until it is empty. But it turns out that sorting with heaps in this way is just not as good as quick-sort. And the rare case when quick-sort goes berserk can be made so infrequent that heap-sort is really not worth it.

If we look at the average case behavior of quick-sort compared to heap-sort, heap-sort is simply much, much slower (on average) by a large constant factor. Here is the damage that could occur from using heap-sort to sort data. Imagine a special grid that is distributed to 40,000 employees. This grid has employee information. We might want to find someone by his first name or his last name. Or maybe we remember his phone number but not his name and we want to use his name when he picks up the phone so we won't sound stupid when he answers. So the employee should be able to reorder the data by any combination he sees fit. We may use a sort to do that. If these 40,000 employees use the list twice a week and it averages ten seconds from using heap-sort instead of two seconds from using quick-sort, in one year that is (40,000 employees * 2 times / week * 52 weeks / year * (10—2) seconds) = 33,280,000 seconds wasted. Since there are 86,400 seconds in one day, that's 385 days of employee time wasted. Over one full man-year, from that tiny eight-second difference, has been wasted. Add to that the frustration of waiting ten seconds for something to happen and you can see that it might impact productivity. Worst of all, if it was annoying enough, they might abandon the tool altogether and the whole project will have been for nothing. Tools should make people more productive, but if badly designed, they can make people less productive.

However, we won't abandon heaps. Heaps are enormously useful for sorting, as we will see later in the form of a priority queue. We will use a priority queue (which is nothing more than a heap where we are mostly interested with picking out the top item and adding and subtracting things from it) to help us combine things later on.

Counting-Sort

Well, after another misadventure, it's back to the jar. But this time Dick brought out a five-gallon bucket full of coins to go along with it!

"We'll never see daylight again," lamented Vicky.

This time, before they even got started they sat and thought for a long time. "It may as well be a bathtub full," said Marilyn, "We'll never sort them all."

Then Karen had her bold stroke. "Cans! We need lots and lots of cans!" said Karen.

"What for?" asked Judy.

"The one who looks at the coin will call out for a can. Then we will bring her the right one, and she can drop the coin in," said Karen. "It's not breaking the rules, because the one with the glasses still puts the coin where it belongs and tells us where it should go."

Marilyn saw a problem, "Well, we have a lot of cans out in the barn, but how will we know what size to use? We only have one more five-gallon bucket and some one-gallon pails and a lot of quart-sized ones and a whole bunch of tiny ones."

"I thought of that already," said Karen, "We'll count the coins once first. Then for those that we have the most of, we use the big cans. For those we only have a few of, we use the smallest cans."

Here's what they did:

Algorithm Counting-Sort

1. Count all the coins in the pile by type.
2. Arrange the buckets by number of coins expected.
3. For each coin left in the big pile, call out the can name.
4. Drop the coin into the can and go to step 3.

FIGURE 13.5
Sorting coins.

Amazingly, it was so fast that they actually finished faster than when they counted just one gallon of coins instead of six times as many.

Dick was astonished. "Three hours and forty-five minutes to sort out all those six gallons of coins and the sorter didn't peak!? Mud, did they break the rules?"

"Well, it was a little iffy, but I would have to say no. They did not break the rules."

"OK," said Dick, "I'll just have to get Walter then."

Now Walter had played penny-ante poker all his life. And he inherited a pile of coins from his dad, who had inherited a pile of coins from his dad. After a quick phone call, Walter showed up with a giant gunnysack loaded with coins.

"Now we'll see how long it takes," said Dick.

Once again the girls put their thinking caps on. "Any ideas?" said Vicky. Nothing but silence.

Now Rhea said something, "Dick, will you make me a board?"

"Sure Mud," he said, "What kind of a board?"

"One with holes in it. One hole for each size of coin that there is. Even those old two-cent pieces and the twenty-dollar gold pieces. Every kind you might possibly have."

"OK," said Dick, "I'll be back in five minutes."

Finally, Dick showed up with the board and asked Rhea what she was going to do with it.

"Well first," she said, "I'm going to run out to the shed and get some pipe."

About ten minutes later, Rhea came in the door with a wheelbarrow full of pipe sections of all shapes and sizes, a roll of duct tape, and a bunch of gunnysacks. After about fifteen more minutes, she had built a contraption that looked like some kind of insane multi-headed bagpipe collection. She had taped one end of a piece of pipe of the appropriate size to the board where a hole came out. The other end of the pipe was taped to a gunnysack. She had written on the board the denomination of the coin next to each hole. She handed her contraption to Marilyn. Here's how it worked:

Algorithm Multiple List Insertion

1. Pick up a coin from the pile until empty.
2. Look at the board to find where it goes.
3. Put it into the right hole.
4. Go to step 1.

Did you notice that we have basically a single operation for every coin? And you don't even have to count them first. In a manner of speaking, we are still using divide and conquer, but we are dividing many sets at once. Essentially, we are using a hash to perform the divisions—but we are using a magic hash. We choose the unique hash that will put the data in its proper order after its operation.

Now, at first blush, it might seem that we ought to sort everything this way. But remember all the work that had to happen first—making the contraption to separate the coins in the first place? We'll call that thing a *map* function. Well, you will need to build a map function for each and every data type that you plan to sort with multiple list insertion. There is a second problem also—memory. Now, in the Jones girl's solution (yes, Rhea is the mother, but she's also a girl) we had sacks at the end of the pipes that just happened to be big enough. But on a computer if we have a million things to sort, we don't want one million sacks all of size one million. That would be a horrible waste. Instead, we will probably use a linked-list structure of some kind. This will add an overhead of at least one pointer for each item to be sorted. If we have a really large collection of things (too large to fit into memory), we might unnecessarily limit the number of things we can sort at once. Since disk seeking and reading is much more expensive than memory access, we will want to keep as much data in memory as possible.

FIGURE 13.6
Sorting coins with multiple list insertion.

In general, these fastest techniques are only fastest for large sets. So we can do a trick like we did with quick-sort. We can sort really large lists with counting-sort on part of the key if the list is stupendous in size. We can sort with multiple list insertion on part of the key if it is not quite as horribly large. Then, when we have divided the piles into something more manageable, we can switch to Singleton's sort (which in turn switches to binary insertion automatically). So, as the saying goes, we use the right tool for the right job.

The counting-sort algorithm is a stable two-pass sorting method that operates directly on the keys. The first pass counts the occurrences of each key into an array of offsets, and then makes a running total so each offset entry is the starting point for insertion of the new item. The second pass puts each item in its final place according to the offset entry for that key. In counting-sort, we assume that the keys are integers between 0 and k, for some fixed integer k. We often choose `k = UCHAR_MAX` so that the counts will run one character of data at a time. This choice is arbitrary, and could just as well be `USHRT_MAX`, but that would require much more auxiliary storage and may also waste a great deal of time examining empty buckets. Counting-sort costs O(n + k), which is O(n) if k is O(n). This gives us a very fast way of sorting items in a restricted range. Notice that it beats our "optimal" lower bound of O(n*log(n)). This is not a contradiction that optimal sorting requires n*log(n) comparisons, because counting-sort is not a comparison-based sort. Counting-sort is not terribly useful all by itself because we seldom want to sort single characters.

For example, if we have an array of four things to sort, and the first one has first byte 7, the second has first byte 0, the third has first byte 5, and the last has first byte 4, we will have the following counts in our counts array:

1, 0, 0, 0, 1, 1, 0, 1

Then we figure out the offsets by adding all previous bins to our current bin, so our offsets look like this:

0, 1, 1, 1, 1, 2, 3, 3, 4

Now, when we insert our data in the target array, if we see a zero, we put it at offset zero, and if we see a 5 it goes at offset 2, and so on. That way, we can put the object exactly where it goes as soon as we see it.

LSD Radix-Sort

LSD radix-sorting stands for Least Significant Digit radix-sorting. We proceed from the right to the left, one character (or bin) at a time. LSD radix-sorting was used with mechanical card sorters even before computers were invented. For each digit or character, there is a container. That container is calculated by performing a count, as above, for counting-sort. On each subsequent pass, the current character determines which container in which to transfer the record. We repeat this process for each character of the key least significant to most significant. This works only because counting-sort is stable. We don't have to use counting-sort. We could also use merge-sort, as it is a stable algorithm. In practice, however, we will never do that. The places where we want to employ radix-sort are where the keys are small or the amount of data is simply enormous. For enormous amounts of data, merge-sort is not a great idea. At least not as good as counting-sort.

LSD Radix-Sort Modified for Speed

Since we always know in advance how many passes we will take, we may as well count all the buckets at once. Let's suppose we have an eight-character key and our buckets hold one character. If we don't count the characters all at once, we will have eight counting passes and eight distribution passes. If we count them all at once, we will have only one counting pass and eight distribution passes. If our keys are long, we will save a lot of time. The additional storage is pretty moderate, since we only need one extra set of counting bins for each chunk of the key to process.

MSD Radix-Sort

In MSD radix-sort (Most Significant Digit), we proceed from the left to the right instead of from the right to the left. This means that we can no longer count all the bins at once. However, there is a new benefit. We can sort only those sections that need it. If, for instance, the entire set consists of a single character, we would be done in one pass. If we were using LSD radix-sort, we would process all the bins anyway. In a more realistic sense, we only spend the energy to process the significant characters of the key. If (for instance) we have a 256-character key, it is very unlikely that we will need to scan the whole key from left to right to put all of the items in sequence. Another big advantage is that MSD radix-sort does not require a stable sorting algorithm like LSD radix-sort does. That means that we can switch off to quick-sort or shell-sort or some other algorithm if we so choose to put any subset into order.

There are some recent advances in radix-sorting, such as adaptive radix-sort and forward radix-sort, which bear investigation. Stefan Nilsson has done some remarkable work in this area.

Radix-Sorting with Arbitrary Data Types

I suspect that every book on sorting you read will tell you that you can't use radix-sorting techniques in an arbitrary way like you can with comparison sorts. This is simply not true. Counting-sort–based radix-sort operations can be just as generic as any comparison-based sort. Now, how is it that we sort generically with comparison-based sorting? We pass in a comparison function that tells us if one object is bigger, smaller, or the same size as a similar object. But in order to render this information, we must know the significance of the bits. For instance, with floating point numbers, the most significant bit is the sign bit, followed by the sign of the exponent. Then comes the exponent bits, followed by the mantissa bits. For an unsigned short, we have the most significant byte up to the least significant byte. So how can we communicate this information to the sorting function? We simply provide a chunk function that returns the bits in chunks by order of significance. This function is the radix analog to the comparison function for comparison sorts. Since there are only a small number of native data types in the C language, it is not at all difficult to produce chunk operators for all of them.

The Danger of Linear Time Algorithms

The real danger of linear time algorithms is application toward large keys. Suppose that we want to sort records that have as a key 256-character strings. It may also be the case that the leading characters are all the same. It is not nearly so unthinkable as you might imagine. Consider a report where things are being grouped by company divisions. We might have keys that start off "Amalgamated Computer Consulting—Western Division" at the start of each and every record. That means that we will waste a horrible amount of time counting and distributing those bytes. Now let's consider some much shorter keys. Suppose that we have 24-character keys. Since radix-sorting is a function of the key length, we will have about 25*n passes for our clever one-pass counting LSD radix-sort. But if we used an n*log(n) sort, this would mean log(n) [base 2] would have to be more than 25. Since 2^{25} is 33,554,432, that is the approximate number of items we would have to sort to break even with a less "optimal" O(n*log(n)) sorting method! In other words, linear time sorting is a horrible idea when the keys are even moderately large. We can, of course, choose a hybrid strategy or use radix-methods only for small keys (see Listings 13.5 and 13.6).

LISTING 13.5 MSD Radix-Sort

```
/*
Most significant digit radix sort.
The outline of these sorts comes from "Algorithms in C"
by Robert Sedgewick, ISBN:0-201-31452-5.

I have added a generic CHUNK operator.  This operator
s analogous to the compare operator for a standard sort.
Besides just peeling out the digit, CHUNK performs whatever
transforation is needed in order to put the bits in the
proper order of significance.
*/
#ifndef RADIX_MISSING

#define bin l+count[A]

void            RADIXMSD(Etype a[], long l, long r, unsigned w)
{
    if (w > KEYSIZE || r <= l)
```

LISTING 13.5 continued

```
        return;
    if (r - l <= LargeCutoff * COST) {
        IQSORT5(a + l, r - l + 1);
        return;
    } else {
        long            i,
                        j,
                        count[R + 1] = {0};
        Etype          *b = malloc((r - l + 1) * sizeof(Etype));

        /* Use standard comparison sort if allocation fails */
        if (b == NULL) {
            IQSORT5(a + l, r - l + 1);
            return;
        }
        /* increment the starting place for the next bin */
        for (i = l; i <= r; i++) {
            count[CHUNK(a + i, w) + 1]++;
        }

        /* Add the previous bin counts to find true offset */
        for (j = 1; j < R; j++)
            count[j] += count[j - 1];

        /* Distribute according to bin positions */
        for (i = l; i <= r; i++) {
            b[count[CHUNK(a + i, w)]++] = a[i];
        }
        /* Transfer back to the original array */
        for (i = l; i <= r; i++)
            a[i] = b[i - l];
        free(b);

        /* Process the next chunk of the key for the first bin */
        RADIXMSD(a, l, bin(0) - 1, w + 1);
        for (j = 0; j < R - 1; j++) {
            /* Process the next chunk of the key for the rest of the  bins */
            RADIXMSD(a, bin(j), bin(j + 1) - 1, w + 1);
        }

    }
}
```

A least significant digit radix-sort is shown in Listing 13.6.

LISTING 13.6 LSD Radix-Sort

```
/*
Least significant digit radix sort.
The outline of these sorts comes from "Algorithms in C"
by Robert Sedgewick, ISBN:0-201-31452-5.

I have added a generic CHUNK operator.  This operator
is analogous to the compare operator for a standard sort.
Besides just peeling out the digit, CHUNK performs whatever
transforation is needed in order to put the bits in the
proper order of significance.
There is also a CHUNKS operator that finds all single chunks
in the data object at once.
*/
void            RADIXLSD(Etype a[], long l, long r, size_t keysize)
{
    int             i,
                    j,
                    w;
    Etype          *b;

    if (r - l <= LargeCutoff * COST) {
        IQSORT5(a + l, r - l + 1);
        return;
    }
    /* For long keys, LSD Radix sort is too expensive */
    if (KEYSIZE > 8) {
        RADIXMSD(a, l, r, 0);
        return;
    } else {
        unsigned long   cnts[R + 1][8] = {0};
        b = malloc((r - l + 1) * sizeof(Etype));

        /* Use standard comparison sort if allocation fails */
        if (b == NULL) {
            IQSORT5(a + l, r - l + 1);
            return;
        }
        /* Count the bins all at once */
        for (i = l; i <= r; i++)
```

LISTING 13.6 continued

```
            CHUNKS(a + i, cnts);
        for (w = KEYSIZE - 1; w >= 0; w- -)
            /* Add the previous bin counts to find true offset */
            for (j = 1; j < R; j++)
                cnts[j][w] += cnts[j - 1][w];


        for (w = KEYSIZE - 1; w >= 0; w- -) {
            long            count[R + 1] =
            {0};

            /* Distribute according to bin positions */
            for (i = l; i <= r; i++) {
                b[cnts[CHUNK(&a[i], w)][w]++] = a[i];
            }
            /* Transfer back to the original array */
            for (i = l; i <= r; i++)
                a[i] = b[i];
        }
        free(b);
    }
}
```

Merge Strategies

Suppose that we can't fit the whole pile of data into memory, no matter what we try. We'll just have to sort it in chunks then, and combine the chunks when we are done. To do that, we will use a technique called merging.

To understand merging, we will first consider a simple example, and then a couple wacky applications of it. Finally, we will use a priority queue as a multiple set merge algorithm as our primary sorting technique to sort sets of any size.

Binary Merge-Sort

Binary merging (merging of two sets and sometimes referred to as simply "merging") is probably the simplest thing to understand of all the techniques discussed.

Algorithm Binary Merge

1. With two lists already in order (nevermind how they got here—it's magic), you pull out the item that is the smaller of the two you are looking at.

2. You keep doing that until one list is empty.
3. Write out the rest of the remaining list (if any) since it is already in order.

Listing 13.7 shows a horrible, but easily understandable merge-sort that uses binary merge.

LISTING 13.7 Merge-Sort

```
/*
** The following routines are for a horrible but easily understandable
** form of merge-sort.  Here, we actually join the ordered data
*/
void
MMERGE (Etype A[], Etype B[], size_t l, size_t m, size_t r)
{
  size_t i = l;
  size_t j = m + 1;
  size_t k = l;
  /* Put the smallest thing into array B */
  while ((i <= m) && (j <= r))
    {
      if (LT (A[i], A[j]))
        B[k++] = A[i++];
      else
        B[k++] = A[j++];
    }
  /* Copy leftover (if any) */
  while (i <= m)
    {
      B[k++] = A[i++];
    }
  while (j <= r)
    {
      B[k++] = A[j++];
    }
  /* Transfer back to original array */
  for (k = l; k <= r; k++)
    {
      A[k] = B[k];
    }
}

/* Helper function for icky(tm) merge sort */
void
MSORT (Etype A[], Etype B[], size_t l, size_t r)
```

LISTING 13.7 continued

```
{
  size_t m; /* The middle */
  if (l < r)
    { /* Cut problem to half size until 1 unit */
      /* Divide partition by 2, sort and merge */
      m = ((l + r) >> 1);
      MSORT (A, B, l, m);
      MSORT (A, B, m + 1, r);
      MMERGE (A, B, l, m, r); /* A single element is ordered */
    }
}
/*
This is a really bad merge sort.  Please don't use it.
It is for educational purposes only.
*/
void
MERGESORTB (Etype A[], size_t count)
{
  Etype *B;
  if ((B = malloc(count * sizeof(Etype))))
  {
    MSORT (A, B, 0, count-1);
    free(b);
  }
  else /* Hopefully, we will fail and use a good sort. ;-) */
    IQSORT5(A, count);
}
```

Disadvantages of Binary Merge-Sort

The simple binary merge-sort algorithm has one benefit—it is stable. Merge-sort requires extra memory proportional to the number of items to be sorted. If the memory allocation fails, it resorts to quick-sort, which is not stable. In other words, you can't count on it being stable. Either that, or you can't count on it working. It also requires extra memory. Not only that, it is much slower than quick-sort. Mike Lee has written a merge-sort that does a lot better than this one, but it is still not nearly as fast as quick-sort (you can find Mike's merge-sort at `http://www.ontek.com/mikey/flogger.tar.uu`). And it still requires extra memory. You can do some things to speed up merge-sort. You can divide the long sections of data into chunks to see if you can skip some comparisons. You can do some fancy gyrations to reduce the extra storage requirement to a constant extra amount. But after all of these workarounds, you still end up with an algorithm that is not as good as quick-sort.

Partition Discovery Merge-Sort

Now, let's think about a stream of data—any stream of data. What properties does it have? One thing we know about it is that the data coming along gets larger, gets smaller, or stays the same. That's called *trichotomy* (which is a funny word for something that everybody already knows). Anyway, let's suppose that we scan the data once. As long as the data does not reverse direction, we keep adding to our current partition. So if it keeps going up or stays the same, we keep on adding to an ascending partition. Or if it keeps going down or stays the same, we add it to a descending partition. When we think about it, there are only these two types of partitions. Now, we might have only ascending partitions if we have a saw tooth wave with teeth going forward. Or we might have only descending partitions if we have a saw tooth wave with teeth going backward. Most likely, we will have both kinds of partitions. This is something like the "Natural merge" used by Von Neumann. However, Von Neumann only looked for ascending sequences. Using an idea like that, we might find only partitions of size 1 (if, for instance the data was reverse-ordered). But using both kinds of partitions, we can find all the order that already exists in the data. We would have a single descending partition for reverse-ordered data. But how do we merge these already sorted up and/or down sequences into one final ordered set?

It is fairly obvious that we can pull from the front of ascending sequences and from the back of descending sequences to extract items in order. We could then use our simple (and icky) merge algorithm to combine the sets two at a time. Then we could combine these sets in the same way, and so forth until we have a single set. If we call k=(total set size)/(average partition size), we would only have about k/2+k/4...+1 merge steps. Sounds pretty efficient. But let's revisit our priority queue.

Since we are sorting block by block (because the whole file won't fit into memory), we have a list of files that contain sorted blocks. If we put the small end of each list into a priority queue and pull the top item out of our priority queue until it becomes empty, we will have sorted all items in a single step. "SMOKE AND MIRRORS! Horse feathers! Pickle smoke!" you may be shouting inside your head (hopefully not out loud because people will think you are odd). After all, the priority queue is doing all the same work that our individual merge steps would have done using two lists at a time. But there is an important difference. With sorting lists two at a time where not all lists fit in memory, we will have to make all of those runs to and from disk. With this kind of merging, we have:

Algorithm Partition Discovery Merge-Sort Using Priority Queues

1. Form partitions by scanning the data (to discover them) or by opening a set of pre-ordered files from disk (to discover them the easy way—by magic).
2. Insert the smallest element of each partition into a priority queue.
3. Remove the smallest item from the priority queue and write it out to disk.

4. If the smallest item's removal has not exhausted that partition, add the next item from that partition into our priority queue.
5. Go to step 3.

It should be obvious that this method only reads and writes in one single pass, no matter how many files are needed to create the final run. This is a wonderful mother lode of value. Formerly, large files were sorted with an algorithm called replacement selection. Replacement selection is a slow algorithm, but it doubles the normal length of runs. Since binary merging requires many read and write passes to order all the data, doubling the size of the run is worthwhile even though the fundamental algorithm is a dog. However, now that we know how to merge with a priority queue, I like to think that we have a more elegant replacement.

But there is a problem. Let's think a minute about the worst case. Perhaps on scanning the data, we have all the data going up-down-up-down... so that all partitions are of size two. In this case, we will have two problems. First of all, our partition information consumes memory. We need to mark the start and the end of each partition and also tag whether it is ascending or descending. Likely, this data will consist of two unsigned longs and a char for each partition. If the keys are small, we are wasting a lot of memory. Not only that, but with tiny partitions like this, our algorithm behaves like ordinary heap-sort. That's too bad, since we noted before that it is a lot worse than quick-sort on average.

Cookie-Cutter Merge-Sort

To solve that particular problem, I present a novel idea I call cookie-cutter merge-sort. Let's say we start scanning the data and from our initial analysis we can see that it will have far too many partitions. Instead, let's use our cutoff sort on tiny segments all the same size and stamp out even-sized cookies from our array. If the last segment does not evenly fit, we will just hold onto it until later. By using this technique we have achieved a whole bunch of partitions that are all the same size and all the same direction. Now we can use our other merge algorithm. In summary:

Algorithm Cookie-Cutter Merge

1. Divide the list into smaller sets of size t=n/k, where n is the set size and k is some size efficient for cutoff files.
2. Sort the cutoff files using a cutoff routine such as shell-sort.
3. Perform Algorithm Partition Discovery Merge-Sort.

Listing 13.8 shows the implementation in C.

LISTING 13.8 Partition Discovery Merge-Sort

```
/*
** The purpose of this routine is to discover partitions in the data.
** This is a two state FSM.
** Ascend = 1, Descend = 0.
**
** This is a vastly improved version of my ugly code.
** The large improvement was from Kang Su Gatlin.
**
*/
int PARSCAN(Etype * array, unsigned long n, partition ps[], long max_par)
{
    unsigned long   i;
    char            direction;
    long            pcount = 0;

    ps[pcount].start = 0;
    ps[pcount].ascending = GE(array[1], array[0]);
    for (i = 1; i < n; i++) {
        direction = GE(array[i], array[i - 1]);
        if (ps[pcount].ascending != direction) {
            ps[pcount].end = i - 1;
            pcount++;
            if (pcount > max_par)
                return -max_par;
            ps[pcount].start = i;
            if (i == n - 1)
                ps[pcount].ascending = 1;
            else
                ps[pcount].ascending = GE(array[i + 1], array[i]);
        }
    }
    ps[pcount].end = n - 1;
    pcount++;
    return pcount;
}

/*
** Remove the smallest item from a partition.
*/
Etype           PDELETEMIN(partition * p, char *end, Etype data[])
{
    Etype           e;
```

LISTING 13.8 continued

```
    if (p->start < p->end) {
        *end = 0;
    } else {
        *end = 1;
        if (p->start > p->end)
            puts("Error! Deletion from empty partition");
    }
    if (p->ascending) {
        e = data[p->start++];
    } else {
        e = data[p->end- -];
    }

    return e;
}

/*
** Retrieve the smallest item from a partition.
*/
Etype           PGETMIN(partition p, Etype data[])
{
    Etype           e;
    if (p.ascending) {
        e = data[p.start];
    } else {
        e = data[p.end];
    }
    return e;
}

/*
** This shell-sort operates on partitions of data, rather
** than on simple data elements.
*/
void            PSHELLSORT(partition array[], size_t count, Etype * data)
{
    size_t          i,
                    inc,
                    j;

    partition       tmp;
    Etype           etmp;
```

FIGURE 13.9
Sorting routine mathematical analysis Theoretical Average Performance—Small element count; near origin view.

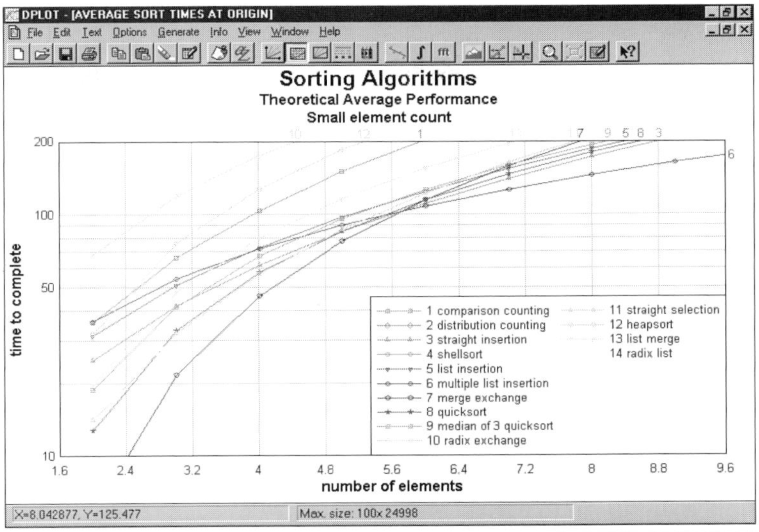

FIGURE 13.10
Sorting routine mathematical analysis Theoretical Average Performance—Small element count.

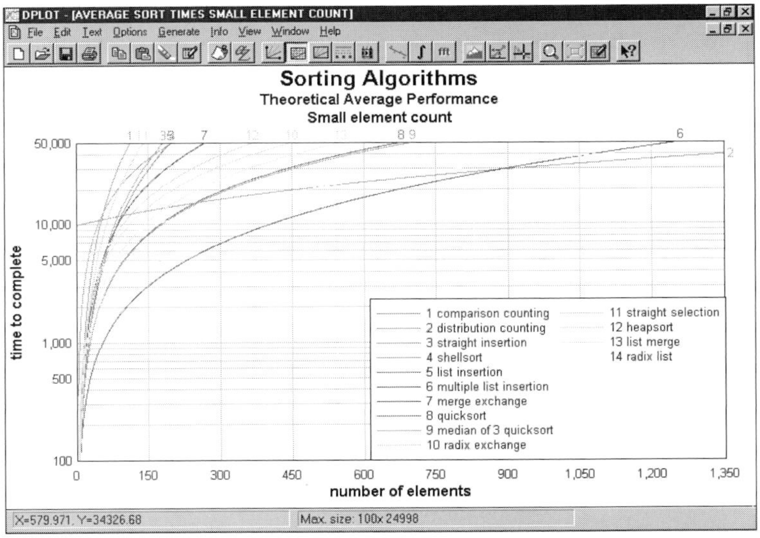

These figures are from mathematical calculations and do give a fair overall picture of how sorting operations will behave. However, it is essential to actually benchmark the sort routines on your compiler. How they perform on my compiler on my machine may be different from what they do on yours. So we need to know how each sort performs under various conditions. We should generate all kinds of different data patterns to throw at it. That's because all these different data patterns really do happen in real life. We should also benchmark it on real, live data. That's because real life data will have patterns we have not thought of. Listing 13.9 is a program to do rough timing studies.

LISTING 13.9 Timing Studies for Sorting Routines

```
#include <limits.h>
#include <float.h>
#include <stdio.h>
#include <stdlib.h>
#include <time.h>
#include <assert.h>
#include <string.h>
#include <math.h>
#include "inteltyp.h"
#include "distribs.h"
#include "genproto.h"
#include "mtrand.h"

#ifdef WIN32
#define CDECL __cdecl
#else
#define CDECL
#endif


#ifdef ASSERT
#undef ASSERT
#endif

#ifdef _DEBUG
#define ASSERT(x) assert((x))
#else
#define ASSERT(x)
#endif


static const char *dlist[] =
{
    "constant",
    "five",
    "perverse",
```

LISTING 13.9 continued

```
    "ramp",
    "random",
    "reverse",
    "sorted",
    "ten",
    "trig",
    "twenty",
    "two",
    NULL
};


/*
   **  Functions to time another function
   **  WARNING: Static variables are modified, so this code is NOT REENTRANT!
   **  Do not use this code in multi-threading programs!
 */

static clock_t  c_start,
                c_now;
static time_t   start,
                now;
static const double dclocks_per_sec = CLOCKS_PER_SEC;
void            reset_timer()
{
    start = time(NULL);
    c_start = clock();
}

double          dTotal = 0;
double          elapsed_time_since_reset(const char *message)
{
    double          delta;
    double          fract;
    now = time(NULL);
    c_now = clock();
    delta = difftime(now, start);
    fract = (c_now - c_start) / dclocks_per_sec;
    if (delta > 10000) {
        if (*message)
            printf("%s:%g\n", message, delta);
        dTotal += delta;
```

LISTING 13.9 continued

```
    } else {
        if (*message)
            printf("%s:%g\n", message, fract);
        dTotal += fract;
    }
    start = now;
    c_start = c_now;
    return delta;
}


void            dup(int la[], double da[], int count)
{
    int             i;
    for (i = 0; i < count; i++)
        da[i] = (double) la[i];
}

#define MAX_PAR 100
int
                CDECL
                gmain(int argc, char **argv)
{
    int             k;
    double          dt[512];
    int             it[512];
    long            COUNT = 1000000L;
    long            pmin,
                    pmax;
    size_t          cmax = COUNT;
    unsigned long   cycles = 0;
    long            iterations;
    size_t          count;
    size_t          pass;
    char            pause[3];
    int             which = 0;
    int             sorttype;
    int             iseed = 7;
    int            *iarray;
    double         *darray;
    double          bd = 0,
                    hd = 0,
```

LISTING 13.9 continued

```
                    sd = 0,
                    id = 0,
                    qd = 0,
                    ld = 0,
                    pd = 0,
                    md = 0;
    double          bi = 0,
                    si = 0,
                    hi = 0,
                    ii = 0,
                    qi = 0,
                    li = 0,
                    pi = 0,
                    mi = 0;

    partition       pset[MAX_PAR] = {0};

    enum distribution_type d = constant;
    if (argc > 1) {
        COUNT = atoi(argv[1]);
        if (COUNT < 1) {
            puts("Count must be >= 1");
            exit(EXIT_FAILURE);
        }
    }
    iarray = malloc(COUNT * sizeof(int));
    darray = malloc(COUNT * sizeof(double));
    if (!iarray || !darray) {
        puts("Error allocating arrays for sort tests.");
        exit(EXIT_FAILURE);
    }
    if (argc > 3) {
        pmin = atol(argv[2]);
        pmax = atol(argv[3]);
    } else {
        pmin = 2;
        pmax = cmax;
    }
    mtsrand(4357U);
    printf("pmin = %ld, pmax = %ld\n", pmin, pmax);
    printf("Sort type            (n) Batch Shell Insert "
           " Quick RadixL RadixM  Heap Merge\n");
```

LISTING 13.9 continued

```
    for (pass = pmin; pass <= pmax;) {
#ifdef _DEBUG
        iterations = 1;
#else
        iterations = /* (long) (1e3 / (log(pass))); */ 1;
#endif
        if (iterations < 1)
            iterations = 1;
#ifdef _DEBUG
        printf("pass = %ld, iterations = %ld\n", pass, iterations);
#endif
        count = pass;
        while (d < unknown) {
#ifdef _DEBUG
            printf("type=%s, element count = %ld, interations = %ld\n",
                    dlist[which], count, iterations);
#endif

            for (sorttype = 0; sorttype < 5; sorttype++) {
                cycles++;
                make_distrib(darray, iarray, pass, d);
                if (count <= 64) {
                    memcpy(dt, darray, count * sizeof dt[0]);
                    memcpy(it, iarray, count * sizeof it[0]);

                    switch (sorttype) {
                    case 0:
#ifdef _DEBUG
                        if ((cycles + 1) % 2000 == 0)
                            putchar('i');
#endif
                        for (k = 0; k < iterations; k++) {
                            memcpy(dt, darray, count * sizeof dt[0]);
                            memcpy(it, iarray, count * sizeof it[0]);
                            reset_timer();
                            InsertionSort_si(it, count);
                            ii += elapsed_time_since_reset("");

                            reset_timer();
                            InsertionSort_d(dt, count);
                            id += elapsed_time_since_reset("");
                            if (!ArrayIsDefinitelySorted_si(it, count - 1))
```

LISTING 13.9 continued

```
                    puts("NOT SORTED");
                if (!ArrayIsDefinitelySorted_d(dt, count - 1))
                    puts("NOT SORTED");
            }

            break;
        case 1:
#ifdef _DEBUG
            if ((cycles + 1) % 2000 == 0)
                putchar('b');
#endif
            for (k = 0; k < iterations; k++) {
                memcpy(dt, darray, count * sizeof dt[0]);
                memcpy(it, iarray, count * sizeof it[0]);
                reset_timer();
                Batcher_si(it, count);
                bi += elapsed_time_since_reset("");
                reset_timer();
                Batcher_d(dt, count);
                bd += elapsed_time_since_reset("");
                if (!ArrayIsDefinitelySorted_si(it, count - 1))
                    puts("NOT SORTED");
                if (!ArrayIsDefinitelySorted_d(dt, count - 1))
                    puts("NOT SORTED");
            }
            break;
        case 2:
#ifdef _DEBUG
            if ((cycles + 1) % 2000 == 0)
                putchar('s');
#endif
            for (k = 0; k < iterations; k++) {
                memcpy(dt, darray, count * sizeof dt[0]);
                memcpy(it, iarray, count * sizeof it[0]);
                reset_timer();
                Shellsort_si(it, count);
                si += elapsed_time_since_reset("");
                reset_timer();
                Shellsort_d(dt, count);
                sd += elapsed_time_since_reset("");
                if (!ArrayIsDefinitelySorted_si(it, count - 1))
                    puts("NOT SORTED");
```

LISTING 13.9 continued

```
                if (!ArrayIsDefinitelySorted_d(dt, count - 1))
                    puts("NOT SORTED");
            }
            break;
        }
    }
    switch (sorttype) {
    case 0:
        for (k = 0; k < iterations; k++) {
            make_distrib(darray, iarray, pass, d);
            reset_timer();
            Iqsort5_si(iarray, count);
            qi += elapsed_time_since_reset("");
            reset_timer();
            Iqsort5_d(darray, count);
            qd += elapsed_time_since_reset("");
            if (!ArrayIsDefinitelySorted_si(iarray, count - 1))
                puts("NOT SORTED");
            if (!ArrayIsDefinitelySorted_d(darray, count - 1))
                puts("NOT SORTED");
        }
        break;
    case 1:
        for (k = 0; k < iterations; k++) {
            make_distrib(darray, iarray, pass, d);
            reset_timer();
            RadixLsd_si(iarray, 0, count - 1, 0);
            li += elapsed_time_since_reset("");
            reset_timer();
            RadixLsd_d(darray, 0, count - 1, 0);
            ld += elapsed_time_since_reset("");
            if (!ArrayIsDefinitelySorted_si(iarray, count - 1))
                puts("NOT SORTED");
            if (!ArrayIsDefinitelySorted_d(darray, count - 1))
                puts("NOT SORTED");
        }
        break;
    case 2:
        for (k = 0; k < iterations; k++) {
            make_distrib(darray, iarray, pass, d);
            reset_timer();
            heapsort_si(iarray, count);
```

LISTING 13.9 continued

```
            hi += elapsed_time_since_reset("");
            reset_timer();
            heapsort_d(darray, count);
            hd += elapsed_time_since_reset("");
            if (!ArrayIsDefinitelySorted_si(iarray, count - 1))
                puts("NOT SORTED");
            if (!ArrayIsDefinitelySorted_d(darray, count - 1))
                puts("NOT SORTED");
        }
        break;

    case 3:
        for (k = 0; k < iterations; k++) {
            make_distrib(darray, iarray, pass, d);
            reset_timer();
            merge_sort_si(iarray, count, pset, MAX_PAR);
            pi += elapsed_time_since_reset("");
            reset_timer();
            merge_sort_d(darray, count, pset, MAX_PAR);
            pd += elapsed_time_since_reset("");
            if (!ArrayIsDefinitelySorted_si(iarray, count - 1))
                puts("NOT SORTED");
            if (!ArrayIsDefinitelySorted_d(darray, count - 1))
                puts("NOT SORTED");
        }
        break;

    case 4:
        for (k = 0; k < iterations; k++) {
            make_distrib(darray, iarray, pass, d);
            reset_timer();
            RadixMsd_si(iarray, 0, count - 1, 0);
            mi += elapsed_time_since_reset("");
            reset_timer();
            RadixMsd_d(darray, 0, count - 1, 0);
            md += elapsed_time_since_reset("");
            if (!ArrayIsDefinitelySorted_si(iarray, count - 1))
                puts("NOT SORTED");
            if (!ArrayIsDefinitelySorted_d(darray, count - 1))
                puts("NOT SORTED");
        }
    }
```

LISTING 13.9 continued

```
            }
            which++;
            d++;
        }
        which = 0;
        d = constant;
        printf("Integral sorts %9lu %5.1f %5.1f  %5.1f "
               " %5.1f  %5.1f  %5.1f %5.1f %5.1f\n",
                pass, bi, si, ii, qi, li, mi, hi, pi);
        printf("Double   sorts %9lu %5.1f %5.1f  %5.1f "
               " %5.1f  %5.1f  %5.1f %5.1f %5.1f\n",
                pass, bd, sd, id, qd, ld, md, hd, pd);
        bi = si = ii = qi = li = mi = hi = pi = 0;
        bd = sd = id = qd = ld = md = hd = pd = 0;
        if (pass < 64)
            pass++;
        else
            pass = pass * 2;

    }

    free(darray);
    free(iarray);
    printf("Press enter to continue.\n");
    fgets(pause, sizeof pause, stdin);

    return 0;
}
```

To get really accurate times, you should use a profiler. Many compilers come with a profiler, or you may want to purchase an after-market profiler such as Vtune.

For each kind of data we might want to sort, we will make a sort object. The sort object will have a compare function (required) and a map function (if possible). Hopefully, we will have both. Now, we will have an array of function pointers that are located according to the algorithm that works best at a particular size. No matter what the problem size is, we will be able to sort it with a good deal of efficiency. We may even have more than one set of function pointers because we might want to use different techniques for different types of data. Then we will load as big a chunk of data as will fit into memory at once. We will sort it and write it to a temp file. We will continue until all chunks are ordered. Then we will combine the chunks with our priority queue into a single output file.

Algorithm Lightning-Sort

1. Read a chunk that is as large as random access memory will allow (not virtual memory).
2. Sort that chunk and write it to disk as a run using the best algorithm for that set size.
3. If the original file is not exhausted, go to step 1.
4. Insert the heads of all temp files into a priority queue and perform a priority queue merge until all temp files are empty.

Listing 13.10 shows the implementation in C.

LISTING 13.10 Lightning-Sort

```
/*
** This test driver is for a merge sort you have never heard about.
** It is a very important idea.  That's because we can now merge as
** many subfiles as we like in a single pass.  It could be made a lot
** better, but this file demonstrates the concept nicely.
*/
#include <stdio.h>
#include <string.h>
#include <stdlib.h>
#include <math.h>
#include <float.h>
#include "inteltyp.h"
#include "distribs.h"
#include "genproto.h"
#include "mtrand.h"

#include "barproto.h"

/*
** This is set to 40 megs, but it can be whatever you like.
*/
static const unsigned long max_buffer = 40000000L;

#define MAX_STR_LEN 8192        /* make this anything you like */

#define MAXLINES 1500000        /* max #lines in input file */

static char    *backup[MAXLINES]; /* Array to hold a subsection of input */
static FILE    *fout; /* the output file */
```

LISTING 13.10 continued

```
/*
   Read from stdin and create an array with one element
   per line. Return the number of lines.
 */

/* Your operating system will probably have some limit */
#define MAX_TEMP_FILES 256

/* How many partitions are there? */
static int      count = 0;

/* This object defines our set of ordered subsets */
/* We will sort the file in chunks.  The sorted   */
/* chunks are described here. */
static fileset  fset[MAX_TEMP_FILES] = {0};     /* about 2 megs */

/* Read the next item from a file set */
int             fgetitem(fileset * p)
{
    char           *pc;
    pc = fgets(p->buffer, sizeof(p->buffer), p->fin);
#ifdef _DEBUG
    if (!pc) {
        if (!feof(p->fin))
            puts(strerror(errno));
    }
#endif
    p->empty = (pc == NULL);
    return p->empty;
}


/*
** remove the smallest item from a fileset and indicate EOF
*/
char            *fdeletemin(fileset * p, char *end)
{
    if (p->empty || p->fin == NULL) {
        puts("error! deletion from empty fileset");
        exit(EXIT_FAILURE);
    }
    p->empty = *end = fgetitem(p);
```

LISTING 13.10 continued

```
    return p->buffer;
}

/*
** Shell-sort a list of filesets.  This is not sorting the data
** in the file.  We are sorting the fileset objects by their
** current smallest object (which will be the first item, since
** we are using sorted subsets of the original data.
*/
void            fshellsort(fileset fset[], size_t count)
{
    size_t          i,
                    inc,
                    j;
    fileset         tmp;
    char           *etmp;
    for (inc = count; inc > 0;) {
        for (i = inc; i < count; i++) {
            j = i;
            tmp = fset[i];
            etmp = tmp.buffer;
            while (j >= inc && (lt(etmp, fset[j - inc].buffer))) {
                fset[j] = fset[j - inc];
                j -= inc;
            }
            fset[j] = tmp;
        }                       /* calculate the next h-increment */
        inc = (size_t) ((inc > 1) && (inc < 5)) ? 1 : 5 * inc / 11;
    }
}


/*
** Normalize is needed after we remove an item to ensure that the
** set is still ordered.  This will take O(log(q)) operations, where
** q is the number of filesets [NOT the number of data items].
*/
void            fnormalize(fileset * fset, size_t count)
{
    long            beg;        /* search beginning here (this moves toward
                                 * ipg) */
    long            ipg;        /* current guess for the insertion point */
```

LISTING 13.10 continued

```
    long            end;        /* search ending here */

    fileset         temp;       /* hold one fileset in temporary storage */
    long            i;

    char           *mcguffin = fset[0].buffer;
    /* maybe we don't need to do anything (i'm an optimist) */
    if (count < 2 || le(mcguffin, fset[1].buffer))
        return;

    /* inline binary search to find point of insertion */
    beg = ipg = 1;              /* the first element of the ordered part of
                                 * the data is element 0 */
    end = count - 1;            /* the last element already ordered is
                                 * element fileset */
    /* without this check, loop terminates only if an equal element is
     * already sorted */
    while (end >= beg) {
        /* insertion point guess of halfway between beginning and ending */
        ipg = ((end + beg) >> 1);
        if (ge(fset[ipg].buffer, mcguffin))
            end = ipg - 1;
        else
            beg = ++ipg;
    }
    /* make room at fset[ipg] for fset[0] */
    temp = fset[0];             /* save the new element we are ready to
                                 * insert */
    for (i = 0; i < ipg; i++)
        fset[i] = fset[i + 1];
    fset[ipg - 1] = temp;       /* put the new element in its sorted order */
    return;
}

/*
** Is a string greater than or equal to another one?
*/
int             ge(char *l, char *r)
{
    return (strcmp(l, r) >= 0);
}
```

LISTING 13.10 continued

```
/*
** Is a string less than or equal to another one?
*/
int             le(char *l, char *r)
{
    return (strcmp(l, r) <= 0);
}

/*
** Is a string strictly less than or equal to another one?
*/
int             lt(char *l, char *r)
{
    return (strcmp(l, r) < 0);
}

/*
** Read a block of lines from a file.
*/
static int      readlines(
char *file_name,
char *lines[],
int maxlines,
size_t * offset
)
{
    int             nlines = 0;
    size_t          size;
    static size_t   limit;
    char           *newline;
    static FILE    *in_file;
    static char    *basep,
                   *cur;

    if (*offset == 0) {
        if (!(in_file = fopen(file_name, "rb"))) {
            perror(file_name);
            exit(EXIT_FAILURE);
        }
        fseek(in_file, 0, SEEK_END);
        size = ftell(in_file) + 10000;
        limit = size - *offset > max_buffer ? max_buffer : size - *offset;
```

LISTING 13.10 continued

```
        fseek(in_file, *offset, SEEK_SET);
        if (!(basep = calloc((limit + 1), 1)))
            return -1;
    }
    fseek(in_file, *offset, SEEK_SET);
    cur = basep;
    while (fgets(cur, limit - (cur - basep), in_file)) {
        lines[nlines] = cur;
        if ((newline = strchr(lines[nlines], '\n'))) {
            cur = newline + 2;
        } else {
            puts("warning -- text in file should end in newline");

            cur[strlen(cur)] = '\n';
            cur[strlen(cur)] = 0;
            cur += strlen(cur) + 1;
       }
        nlines++;
        if (nlines == maxlines || limit - (cur - basep) < MAX_STR_LEN) {
            *offset = ftell(in_file);
            break;
        }
    }
    if (feof(in_file))
        *offset = 0;
    return nlines;
}
/*
** Write the subset of the original data held in array t.
*/
void            writelines(char *t[], int nlines, FILE * fout)
{
    int             i;

    for (i = 0; i < nlines; i++)
        fprintf(fout, "%s", t[i]);
}

/*
** Test driver
*/
int             main(int argc, char *argv[])
```

LISTING 13.10 continued

```
{
    int             nlines;
    int             i;
    char            end = 0;
    char           *e;
    size_t          offset = 0;
    char           *name;
    int             savecount;
    fileset        *fs = fset;
    mtsrand(4357U);
    if (argc != 3) {
        fprintf(stderr, "Usage: %s input_file output_file\n", argv[0]);
        return 1;
    }
    fout = fopen(argv[2], "wb");
    if (fout == NULL) {
        printf("Count not open %s\n", argv[2]);
        exit(EXIT_FAILURE);
    }
    fprintf(stderr, "\nFile: %s\n", argv[1]);

    do {
        /* Read a block from the input file */
        if ((nlines = readlines(argv[1], backup, MAXLINES, &offset)) >= 0) {
            /* Sort that block we just read */
            Iqsort5_str(backup, nlines);
#ifdef _DEBUG
            if (!ArrayIsDefinitelySorted_str(backup, nlines)) {
                puts("rats");
                exit(EXIT_FAILURE);
            }
#endif
            /* Write the sorted block to disk */
            if ((name = tmpnam(NULL)) != NULL) {
                strcpy(fset[count].filename, name);
                fset[count].fin = fopen(fset[count].filename, "wt");
                writelines(backup, nlines, fset[count].fin);
                count++;
            } else {
                puts("error creating output file");
                exit(EXIT_FAILURE);
            }
```

LISTING 13.10 continued

```
        }
    /* Loop until the file is empty */
    } while (offset > 0);

    /* flush to disk all open files */
    fflush(NULL);
    /* Close temp files (originally opened in write mode)
    ** and reopen in read mode.  Then get the first item.
    */
    for (i = 0; i < count; i++) {
        fclose(fset[i].fin);
        fset[i].fin = fopen(fset[i].filename, "rt");
        fseek(fset[i].fin, 0, SEEK_SET);
        fgetitem(&fset[i]);
    }
    /* Shell sort our partitions.  If the number is huge, perhaps
    ** quick-sort or radix-sort should be used instead.
    */
    fshellsort(fset, count);
    savecount = count; /* Remember how many paritions we had */

    /* Merge the partitions using our strange priority queue */
    while (count > 0) {
        e = fs[0].buffer;
        fprintf(fout, "%s", fs[0].buffer);
        fdeletemin(fs, &end);
        if (end) {
            fs++;
            count- -;
        }
        fnormalize(fs, count);
    }
    /* Flush all open files to disk */
    fflush(NULL);
    /* Close and remove all temp files */
    for (i = 0; i < savecount; i++) {
        fclose(fset[i].fin);
        if (remove(fset[i].filename) != 0) {
            printf("unable to delete file %s\n", fset[i].filename);
            puts(strerror(errno));
        }
    }
```

LISTING 13.10 continued

```
    return 0;
}
```

The reason that this technique is so valuable is that disk I/O dominates sort time. With this technique, we must:

- Read the file in chunks in a single pass.
- Write out the sorted chunks in a single pass.
- Read the sorted chunks using our priority queue model.
- Write out the merged data.

In doing so, we have to read and write exactly twice, no matter how big the file is and no matter how little memory is available. If we were to use an ordinary merge, we would have to read and write the file many times. If, for instance, we have eight subfiles generated, we would have one read/write pass to generate them. Then we would read/write the eight subfiles in a merge pass to create four subfiles. Then, we would again read/write the four subfiles to create two subfiles, and finally read/write the two subfiles to create a single ordered file. As you can easily see, if we had hundreds of subfiles, we would do a lot of reading and writing. That's the reason that replacement selection sorting is often performed. The algorithm is a slow one, but it creates runs that are twice as long as normal, on average. This allows for a reduced number of sort/merge passes. But with this priority queue model-based merge, we don't have to use replacement selection.

Note

There is something strange in my interface design.

You may notice that some of my routines don't look like routines at all. Here is one example:

```
/*
** Believe it or not, this is a complete routine to sort arrays of strings.
** The define ETYPE_STRING will cause allsort.h to generate functions that
** operate on array of strings.
**
** Why all this bother and not just use a comparison function?
** Because the qsort() style interface is slow.  This is a bit more painful,
** but the payoff in speed is worth it.
*/
```

```
#define ETYPE_STRING
#include "allsort.h"
```

Where's the code!? In this routine, what I am actually doing is creating something like a template in C++. The reason I bother with that technique rather than just using an interface like `qsort()` is that we gain a significant speedup. The `qsort()` interface demands that `memcpy()` be used to exchange elements, since we do not know what size they are. The fake template metaphor allows us to operate more efficiently and more naturally.

Summary

Sorting, like many other computer science tasks, is a combination of art and science. Some experimentation is needed to find out what really does work best. The interface for `qsort()` as defined in `<stdlib.h>` has a high cost due to calls to `memcpy()`, and a simpler array-based metaphor can be introduced that reduces the shortcomings of the `qsort()` interface model at a cost of increased code space. From my experience, the standard solution of switching to algorithm linear insertion-sort for small sub-files is a mistake. Binary insertion-sort is faster and shell-sort is faster yet. So for small subfiles, it is shell-sort that should be used and not linear insertion-sort. The speed can be augmented somewhat by especially optimal sorts for the very smallest of subfiles. For larger files, quick-sort is probably better than merge-sort or heap-sort for most real-world applications. Some necessary modifications to keep quick-sort safe for general use include probabilistic choice of median, checking for in-order and reverse-order partitions, changing algorithm to shell-sort when the partitions become small, and always sorting the smaller partition before the larger one. Some of these techniques are commonly found in sorting libraries, but frequently one or more will be left out, causing a sort to be less efficient than it could be or even downright dangerous to use. That is a terrible shame because sorting is one of the most important and frequently performed computer activities. It is often said that radix-sorting algorithms are not suited to arbitrary data. Yet with a metaphor similar to that used for comparison sorting, we can sort with exactly the same generality. A function to map the most significant bits in chunks of the size of our radix is exactly what is needed. Even generalized radix sorting is not a panacea, since long key lengths will rapidly throw away any performance advantage over standard comparison based algorithms like quick-sort. Finally, disk-based sorting frequently uses multiple merge passes. This is a serious mistake because a priority queue–based approach is much more efficient. Even replacement selection pales in contrast. The priority queue model merges all the sub-files in a single pass. Every rule of thumb (such as those that I have presented) has exceptions. However, the rules will bear out much more frequently than the exceptions. It is always good to explore alternatives. Each of the techniques I have described can be improved. It is my fond hope that some readers of this book will not only improve them, but also pass their new ideas on to others.

CHAPTER 14

Tries

by Scott Fluhrer

IN THIS CHAPTER

The data structures described in the previous chapters are excellent workhorses that are quite handy. However, there is another data structure that is sometimes useful. It can sometimes solve problems—mostly problems that are solved by searching—a bit more efficiently. This data structure is known as a *trie*.

This chapter looks at the trie data structure. First, it explains what a trie is and shows its basic properties. Then, it takes a look at some example code that implements a trie and examines how this code can be adjusted to meet the needs of an application. Lastly, this chapter compares the trie data structure with other data structures.

The Trie Data Structure

To illustrate this approach, consider this sample problem: You want to look up a word in a computerized dictionary extremely quickly. One approach would be to take the first letter of the word, say *S*, and consider only those words that start with the letter *S*. If more than one word in the dictionary starts with the letter *S*, you look at the next letter in the word, say *T*, and consider only those words that start with *ST*. You go through the letters of the word until you have considered enough letters to uniquely identify the word.

This is exactly the approach used in a trie. The key you are searching on is broken up into pieces (in the preceding example, the various letters that make up the word), and each piece is used in succession to determine which branch of the tree to follow. This is different from the binary search tree described in Chapter 12, "Binary Search Trees"; you use bits extracted from the key to direct the search rather than comparing the search key with a key contained in the node.

Formally, a trie is a structure composed of zero or more *nodes*. Each node might have no children, in which case it is called a *leaf*, or it might have several other nodes as children, in which case it is called a *subtrie*. Each leaf corresponds to a key that has been added to the trie. You require that the key in each leaf directs the path to that leaf. You also require that a subtrie has at least two leaves underneath it.

Note

It has been suggested that because a tree has leaves, a trie should have lieves. I think that pun is too silly to be taken seriously.

This approach has several differences from the more typical binary search tree. For one, there is no reason why each node has to have only two subnodes. By extracting N bits of the key at once and using all of them to select the next node, you speed up the search because you are stepping down a 2^N-ary tree. Of course, if you make N large, you also increase the size of each node rather dramatically, so there is a time/memory tradeoff here.

One property that a trie has is that its shape is determined only by the keys it currently contains. The search scans enough of the key to uniquely identify the key from all other keys in the trie, and never any farther. This means that, unlike most other data structures, the time a trie takes is not influenced by the order of inserts and deletes—there is no need to have fancy rebalancing logic.

When Do You Use It?

Tries are good at searching for exact matches. However, you must be careful about a few things:

- Tries tend to use more memory than other data structures. That's because each subtrie has a full table of pointers to the subnodes. In comparison, a binary tree contains only twice as many pointers within the tree as there are nodes (plus one). Of course, with a trie, you can reduce the memory usage by decreasing the number of bits of key you examine at a time, but that also reduces the speed of the trie search.
- The routines to maintain the trie tend to be a bit more complex than other data structures, such as trees or hash tables. Of course, they are not nearly as complex as, say, an AVL tree.
- Tries look at the keys as sequences of bits. That means that, unless you have an exact bitwise match, the search will not find the entry. One unobvious implication of this is that you need to be careful if the key is actually a structure; C allows implementations to insert padding after structure members, and this padding might not have a consistent value. If you really want to use a structure as the key, you need to modify the `key_walker` object (defined later in the chapter) so that it walks down the various members of the structure, avoiding any unnamed padding.

How to Use Tries

Now, let's go on to examine an implementation of a trie, and see how it works.

Before we talk about the routines, we need to talk about what the data structures look like. And, before we can talk about the structures, we need to talk about how they work together. When we have a pointer to a node, we really don't care whether it's a leaf or a subtrie, until it comes time to examine it. We will make leaves and subtries distinct structures. Normally, pointers to different structures are incompatible. However, we can make the first element of each structure the same type. Then, C allows us to cast a pointer to a structure to a pointer to the first member, and so the casted pointers to leaves and to subtries are now compatible. In addition, if that first member gives us the type of the structure, we can examine that member and then know which structure to cast it back to. And so, this structure looks like the following:

```
enum trie_node_type { TRIE_LEAF, TRIE_SUBTRIE };
typedef enum trie_node_type *trie_pointer;
```

A `trie_pointer` is a pointer that can point to any type of node. All leaves will have a `TRIE_LEAF` as the contents of the first member, and all subtries will have `TRIE_SUBTRIE`. We define two types of nodes; alternative implementations will quite often define several others.

Then, starting from the definition of a trie, a subtrie corresponds to a prefix of a key that at least two distinct keys actually share. We then know that the trie search needs to know which node to go to for the next symbol, which is the `next_level` array. Because we also want to be able to handle the case that one key is actually the prefix of another, we also need to know what happens if the key ends here—the `exact_match` points to that leaf, if any. It also turns out to be useful to keep track in `count` of the number of keys for which this node is a prefix—it simplifies the delete function. And so, our structure for a node looks like the following:

```
#define LOG_TRIE_BRANCH_FACTOR 4
#define TRIE_BRANCH_FACTOR (1<<LOG_TRIE_BRANCH_FACTOR)
struct trie_subtrie {
  enum trie_node_type type; /* TRIE_NODE */
  struct trie_leaf *exact_match;
  int count;
  trie_pointer next_level[TRIE_BRANCH_FACTOR];
};
```

Here, we define `LOG_TRIE_BRANCH_FACTOR` to be the number of bits of key we read for each subtrie, and `TRIE_BRANCH_FACTOR` is the resulting factor at each subtrie. These can be tuned to adjust the speed and memory usage of the trie.

Similarly, a leaf stands for a unique key, and when the search routine hits it, it knows that that key is the only possible match. So, when we actually hit a leaf, we need to know the key this leaf actually stands for. When the search routine hits it, it needs to check that we actually got that key (it might not match any key in the trie). We use the `key` and the `len_key` fields for that. It actually points to a copy that we allocate, so someone outside this module doesn't need to maintain it. In addition, we need to remember what the insert routine was told to return when this key was entered—the `result` field. Since the application may need the type of the `result` field be a specific type, we'll make this field of type `type_result`, which we can `typedef` later when we know what type the application needs. This gives us the following:

```
struct trie_leaf {
  enum trie_node_type type; /* TRIE_LEAF */
  unsigned char *key;
  size_t len_key;
  trie_result result;
};
```

We also need to define the object that stands for an entire trie. We need to keep track of the root (the node that corresponds to the empty prefix). And so, we have:

```
struct trie {
  trie_pointer root;
};
```

Creation and Destruction

The first thing we need to do is create our trie. The creation routine is fairly trivial:

```
struct trie *trie_create(void)
{
  struct trie *trie = malloc( sizeof(*trie ) );

  if (trie) {
    trie->root = 0;
  }
  return trie;
}
```

This simply attempts to allocate a trie structure and, if successful, initializes it to empty.

The routine to destroy a trie and free up all the memory it uses is a bit more complicated. First, we have the recursive routine that frees up a node and everything beneath it. It has a structure that will be repeated several times in this module: It takes a generic pointer, switches on the type of object it points to, and then handles the object based on the type. For a leaf, we make a specific routine to free that; it'll come in handy in other places. For a subtrie, we also free up the other associated nodes: the exact match leaf (if any) and the subnodes. Here is how to free a node:

```
static void destroy_node(trie_pointer node)
{
  if (node == 0)
    return;
```

```
  switch (*node) {
    case TRIE_LEAF: {
      struct trie_leaf *p = (struct trie_leaf*)node;
      destroy_leaf(p);
      break;
    }
    case TRIE_SUBTRIE: {
      struct trie_subtrie *p = (struct trie_subtrie*)node;
      int i;
      destroy_leaf(p->exact_match);
      for (i=0; i<TRIE_BRANCH_FACTOR; i++)
        destroy_node(p->next_level[i]);
      free(p);
      break;
    }
    default: assert(0);
  }
}

static void destroy_leaf(struct trie_leaf *leaf)
{
  if (leaf) {
    free(leaf->key);
    free(leaf);
  }
}
```

This routine's handling of a node is common to several of the trie routines; it knows that it is a pointer to either a `trie_subtrie` or a `trie_leaf`, but it doesn't know which. So, it switches on the type field, and based on what that is, handles it as either a node or a leaf.

After we have that, the routine to free up an entire trie is easy—we just free up the nodes that make up the trie, and then free up the space for the trie structure itself:

```
void trie_destroy(struct trie *trie)
{
  if (trie) {
    destroy_node(trie->root);
    free(trie);
  }
}
```

Extracting Bits

Tries work by extracting bits from the key to direct the search. We also need to extract bits in exactly the same way while inserting or deleting a key. So, we put together an object to do the work for us. We call the object a `key_walker` (because it walks down a key extracting bits), and provide an `initialize_walker` macro to start it down a key and an `extract_next` macro to extract the next set of bits. It turns out that the insert routine also can use an `extract_at_offset` macro to extract the Nth set of bits from a key. We make these macros because they are used in the search routine, and the whole point of this module is to do fast searches.

Normally, we would include this type of functionality within a function, which would be called from several places in the program. Functions tend to be easier to understand than macros, easier to debug, and are less prone to weird side effects. However, the whole point of the trie is to be able to do searches extremely quickly, and when used carefully, macros can often give better performance. In this case, the potential for extra performance outweighs the other considerations.

The `key_walker` that we define just treats the key as an array of `unsigned char`s with an explicit length. Some applications can use a `key_walker` that knows considerably more about the actual structure of the key.

For our version, these macros are easy to write if each set of bits we extract is actually an `unsigned char` as shown in Listing 14.1.

LISTING 14.1 Extracting Bits from a Key

```
typedef struct key_walker {
  const unsigned char *key;
  size_t len;
} key_walker;
#define initialize_walker(walker, key, len_key) \
  (void)(                                       \
    (walker).key = (key),                       \
    (walker).len = (len_key)                    \
  )
#define extract_next(walker)                    \
  ((walker).len == 0 ? -1 : ((walker).len -= 1, *(walker).key++))
#define extract_at_offset(key, len_key, offset) \
  ((len_key) <= (offset) ? -1 : ((key)[offset]))
```

The `key` member points to the next byte of key, and `len` gives the number of bytes left—when that reaches zero, we report the end of the key.

However, having a set of bits that large is not always desirable. Extracting at least eight bits requires sizable subtries. In addition, some compilers have unsigned chars significantly larger than eight bits, which makes the space usage even worse.

So, we need to provide an alternative implementation that is able to iteratively extract bits from the individual unsigned chars that make up the key. Fortunately, we can have the preprocessor select the implementation.

```
#define LEVEL_PER_UCHAR  ((CHAR_BIT+TRIE_LOG_BRANCH_FACTOR-1) /         \
                                                TRIE_LOG_BRANCH_FACTOR)


typedef struct key_walker {
  const unsigned char *key;
  size_t len;
  int bit_offset;
} key_walker;
#define initialize_walker(walker, key, len_key)                  \
  (void) (                                                       \
    (walker).key = (key),                                        \
    (walker).len = (len_key),                                    \
    (walker).bit_offset = -TRIE_LOG_BRANCH_FACTOR                \
  )
#define extract_next(walker)                                     \
  ((walker).len == 0 ? -1 :                                      \
    ((walker).bit_offset >= CHAR_BIT-TRIE_LOG_BRANCH_FACTOR ? \
      (((walker).len -= 1) ? ((walker).bit_offset=0,             \
          *++(walker).key & (TRIE_BRANCH_FACTOR-1)) : -1) :      \
      ((walker).bit_offset += TRIE_LOG_BRANCH_FACTOR,            \
          (*(walker).key >> (walker).bit_offset)                 \
                  & (TRIE_BRANCH_FACTOR-1))))
#define extract_at_offset(key, len_key, offset)                  \
   ((len_key)*LEVEL_PER_UCHAR <= (offset) ? -1 :                 \
    ((((key)[ (offset)/LEVEL_PER_UCHAR ]) >>                     \
         (TRIE_LOG_BRANCH_FACTOR*((offset)%LEVEL_PER_UCHAR))) \
                 & (TRIE_BRANCH_FACTOR-1)))
```

These macros look considerably more intimidating, but they are really only slightly more complex. The key member now points to the next byte of key, and len gives the number of bytes left. However, now bit_offset gives the bits (minus TRIE_LOG_BRANCH_FACTOR) we need to shift that byte to obtain the next set of times. The extract_next macro first checks whether we have run out of key (if len is zero). Then, it checks whether we have extracted the last set of bits from the current byte, and if we have it steps to the next byte (if any). If there are more bits in this byte, it steps the bit_offset to the next set of bits and extracts those bits. We always extract a set of bits from a single `unsigned char`; this prevents the awkward situation where we need to get the next group of bits from the key, and the key ends in the middle.

Searching

To search on a particular key (which really is the goal of a trie), we start at the root node, and start extracting bits of the key to determine which path to take. We keep on going until we hit a `NULL` (which means that nothing matched), a leaf (which means that that specific leaf is the only possible match), or run out of key bits. In the last case, where we run out of key while within a subtrie, we handle that by checking whether there was a leaf that corresponded to an exact match. Putting all this together, we get the code in Listing 14.2.

LISTING 14.2 Searching a Trie

```
trie_result trie_search(const struct trie *trie,
                              const unsigned char *key, size_t len_key)
{
  trie_pointer node;
  key_walker walker;
  const struct trie_leaf *leaf;

  if (trie == 0)
    return 0;

  initialize_walker(walker, key, len_key);
  node = trie->root;
  for (;;) {
    const struct trie_subtrie *q;
    int n;

    if (!node) {
      return 0;
    }
    if (*node != TRIE_SUBTRIE)
      break;

    q = (const struct trie_subtrie*)node;
    n = extract_next(walker);
    if (n < 0) {
      return compare_leaf( q->exact_match, key, len_key );
    } else {
      assert( n < TRIE_BRANCH_FACTOR );
```

LISTING 14.2 continued

```
        node = q->next_level[n];
      }
    }

    assert( *node == TRIE_LEAF );
    leaf = (const struct trie_leaf*)node;
    return compare_leaf( leaf, key, len_key );
}
```

This scans down the key, indexing the various subtries, until it either runs out of key, or it runs out of subtrie. At that point, it examines the node it found and determines whether this is the right key. Of course, this assumes another routine to determine whether it is the right key and get either the result value or a "not found" value. We could do that inline in the main search routine, except we need to do it in two places, and there's little point in duplicating code needlessly. If we wanted a little additional speed, we could convert it into a macro as follows:

```
static trie_result compare_leaf( const struct trie_leaf *leaf,
                                  const unsigned char *key, size_t len_key )
{
  if (!leaf || len_key != leaf->len_key ||
      0 != memcmp( key, leaf->key, len_key)) {
    return 0;
  } else
    return leaf->result;
}
```

Insertion

Of course, searching for values won't work very well unless we can insert values for the search to find. We declare `trie_insert` to take the trie to insert into, the key (and the size of the key) to search on, and the value to return if that key is found.

What we can do is posit a routine that will insert a leaf into a node. It will need the node to insert into, the leaf, and the engine to extract bits from the key we're inserting. It also turns out to be necessary to explicitly pass in the depth of the node we're inserting. It'll handle failures by returning `NULL` and not changing anything; because a successful insert cannot result in a `NULL`, this cannot be ambiguous. After we have that routine, all we need to do is allocate our leaf (and our copy of the key the leaf refers to) and insert it into the root node as shown in Listing 14.3.

LISTING 14.3 Inserting a Key into a Trie

```
int trie_insert(struct trie *trie, const unsigned char *key, size_t len_key,
            trie_result result) {
  if (trie) {
    trie_pointer p;
    key_walker walker;
    struct trie_leaf *leaf;

    leaf = malloc( sizeof( *leaf ) );
    if (!leaf)
      return 0;
    leaf->key = malloc( len_key > 0 ? len_key : 1 );
    if (!leaf->key) {
      free(leaf);
      return 0;
    }
    memcpy( leaf->key, key, len_key );
    leaf->type = TRIE_LEAF;
    leaf->len_key = len_key;
    leaf->result = result;

    initialize_walker( walker, key, len_key );

    p = insert_node( trie->root, &walker, 0, leaf );

    if (p) {
      trie->root = p;
      return 1;
    }

    destroy_leaf( leaf );
  }
  return 0;
}
```

Of course, we now need to write the routine to insert a leaf. To insert a leaf into a node, we need to handle three cases: when the node is empty, when the node is a leaf, and when the node is a full node. The empty case is the easiest. When we add a leaf to an empty node, we know that if the search reached this part of the trie, this leaf is the only possible match, and we use the leaf itself as the node as seen in Listing 14.4.

LISTING 14.4 Inserting a Leaf into a Node

```
static trie_pointer insert_node( trie_pointer old_node, key_walker *walker,
                                               int level,
                                               struct trie_leaf *leaf )
{
  if (!old_node) {
    return (trie_pointer)leaf;
  }
```

Inserting into a full node is the next easiest. If we run out of key, we install this as the exact match. (Unless there already is one. If there is, this routine rejects it as an error; your application might want to handle inserts of already existing keys differently.) If more key bits are available, we insert the leaf into that node on the next level (making sure, of course, that we handle errors from the insert correctly).

```
  switch (*old_node) {
    case TRIE_SUBTRIE: {
      struct trie_subtrie *node = (struct trie_subtrie*)old_node;
      int n;

      n = extract_next( *walker );

      if (n < 0) {
        /*
         * If we ran out of key, then install this as an exact match, unless
         * there's already one there
         */
        if (node->exact_match) {
          return 0;
        }
        node->exact_match = leaf;
      } else {
        /*
         * The next set of bits is n -- recursively call insert_node to insert
         * the leaf into the n-th next_level node
         */
        assert( n < TRIE_BRANCH_FACTOR );
        if (node->next_level[n]) {
          trie_pointer next_level = insert_node( node->next_level[n],
                                     walker, level+1, leaf );
          if (!next_level) {
            return 0;
```

```
      }
      node->next_level[n] = next_level;
    } else
      node->next_level[n] = (trie_pointer)leaf;
  }
  /*
   * In either case, if we reach here, we succesfully added the leaf.
   */
  node->count += 1;
  return (trie_pointer)node;
}
```

The most difficult case is when we're inserting a leaf into another leaf. However, we can handle this by expanding the existing leaf into a full node and then using the existing routine (that we're currently writing) to insert the new leaf into the newly expanded node. This gives us

```
case TRIE_LEAF: {
  struct trie_subtrie *new_node;
  struct trie_leaf *previous_leaf = (struct trie_leaf*)old_node;
  trie_pointer result;
  int i, n;

  new_node = malloc( sizeof( *new_node ));
  if (!new_node) return 0;

  new_node->type = TRIE_SUBTRIE;
  new_node->exact_match = 0;
  for (i=0; i<TRIE_BRANCH_FACTOR; i++)
    new_node->next_level[i] = 0;

  n = extract_at_offset( previous_leaf->key, previous_leaf->len_key,
                                                           level );
  if (n < 0) {
    new_node->exact_match = previous_leaf;
  } else {
    assert( n < TRIE_BRANCH_FACTOR );
    new_node->next_level[n] = (trie_pointer)previous_leaf;
  }
  new_node->count = 1;

  result = insert_node( (trie_pointer)new_node, walker, level, leaf );

  if (!result) {
```

```
        free(new_node);
        return 0;
      }

      return result;
    }
    default:
      assert(0);
      return 0;
  }
}
```

Deletion

It is also at times necessary to be able to delete entries from the trie. To do so, we first create a routine to delete a leaf from a node. Exactly as we have done before, we switch on the type of node. Handling the case where the node happens to be a leaf is easy—we check whether the leaf is for the key we are deleting, and if so, we delete it and set the pointer the caller passed in to NULL. Deleting a leaf is shown in Listing 14.5.

LISTING 14.5 Deleting a Leaf from a Trie

```
static int delete_node( trie_pointer *node, key_walker *walker,
             const unsigned char *key, size_t len_key )
{
  if (!*node)
    return 0;

  switch (**node) {
    case TRIE_LEAF: {
      struct trie_leaf *p = (struct trie_leaf*)*node;
      if (len_key != p->len_key || 0 != memcmp( key, p->key, len_key ))
        return 0;

      destroy_leaf(p);
      *node = 0;
      return 1;
    }
```

The case where the node is a full node is a bit trickier. First, we examine the next bits from the key to find out where the leaf would be, and delete the leaf from that subnode, handling the case where the key ends here:

```
case TRIE_SUBTRIE: {
  struct trie_subtrie *p = (struct trie_subtrie*)*node;
  int n;
  n = extract_next( *walker );
  if (n < 0) {
    if (p->exact_match == 0)
      return 0;

    assert( len_key == p->exact_match->len_key &&
                     0 == memcmp( key, p->exact_match->key, len_key ) );
    destroy_leaf( p->exact_match );
    p->exact_match = 0;
  } else {
    if (!delete_node( &p->next_level[n], walker, key, len_key ))
      return 0;
  }
```

However, then we need to consider whether to collapse the subtrie. This is where we use the count: we want to collapse the subtrie if there is only one remaining leaf underneath it. If there is, we want to replace the node with that leaf. After we realize what we want to do, the code to do so is straightforward: It searches for the key (which is either an exact match or on the next level because any subnodes would have already been collapsed), free the node, and replace the node with the remaining leaf:

```
p->count -= 1;
assert( p->count > 0 );
if (p->count == 1) {
  trie_pointer leaf;
  int i;

  /*
   * We need to collapse the node.  Fortunately, we know that the
   * sublevels must also be collapsed, and so we can just scan through
   * all our children for a non-NULL subnode
   */
  leaf = (trie_pointer)p->exact_match;
  for (i=0; i<TRIE_BRANCH_FACTOR; i++)
    if (p->next_level[i]) {
      assert( leaf == 0 );
      leaf = p->next_level[i];
    }

  /* We must have found a child which must be a leaf */
  assert( leaf != 0 );
```

```
        assert( *leaf == TRIE_LEAF );

        /* We can use that leaf as the new node, free up the old subtrie */
        free(p);
        *node = leaf;
      }
      return 1;
    }

    default:
      assert(0);
      return 0;
  }
}
```

After we have that routine, it becomes easy to write the routine to delete the leaf from the entire trie—just remove the leaf from the root as follows in Listing 14.6.

LISTING 14.6 Deleting a Leaf from a Trie

```
int trie_delete( struct trie *trie, const unsigned char *key, size_t len_key )
{
  if (trie) {
    key_walker walker;

    initialize_walker( walker, key, len_key );
    return delete_node( &trie->root, &walker, key, len_key );
  }
  return 0;
}
```

Possible Trie Modifications

There are a number of possible variations you can make on the preceding code, depending on the exact requirements of the application. You can vary the value of `LOG_TRIE_BRANCH_FACTOR` to change the tradeoff between time and memory. Here is a list of other ideas that might be appropriate for your application:

- Your application may never have one key being a prefix of another. For example, your application can make all keys be the same length. In this case, you can eliminate the `exact_match` data member, and all the logic associated with it.

- The preceding routines assume that attempting to insert a key that already exists is an error. Depending on what the application wants, you might prefer either to silently ignore the key insert, or to have it update the result. In either case, you can modify the `insert_node` routine to handle this case. Note that this is slightly trickier than it looks; the easiest method is to add code to compare the two leaves when you attempt to insert into a leaf, and handle it there.

- One method to save space is to modify the node format. You can collapse all nodes with fewer than N leaves into a special format that has a list of the matching leaves. When the search routine hits one of these special nodes, it does a sequential scan through the list to find a match. This can save a large amount of space because, in a normal trie, most of the room is taken up in the lower levels, and those are exactly the levels this collapses.

- A rather more ambitious modification to save space (which is probably less effective; if you need to do this one, you probably should have done the previous one already) is to change the node format to use a two-level table. The first level is an array of `TRIE_BRANCH_FACTOR` `unsigned chars`. The value is used to index into an array of pointers. The trick is that you allocate only as many entries in the second array is there are distinct entries, and so all the `NULL` pointers have only one entry allocated to them. Because most pointers are usually `NULL`, and on most compilers pointers take up rather more space than `unsigned chars`, this results in a space savings. A node with `NumChildren` child nodes underneath it uses `TRIE_BRANCH_FACTOR + (NumChildren+1)*sizeof(TriePointer)` bytes, rather than `TRIE_BRANCH_FACTOR* sizeof(TriePointer)` bytes. The insert routine becomes rather more tricky, though, especially if you have to handle the case where you can have `UCHAR_MAX` distinct children.

- On the other hand, there are a few things you can do to speed the search routine. You can define a static `TRIE_NULL` node, which is used to indicate that there are no leaves with the given prefix (the current implementation uses an explicit `NULL` to indicate that). By replacing all occurrences of `NULL` with pointers to the distinguished node, you can eliminate the `NULL` pointer check from `trie_search`, replacing it with a check if the node type when the search finally hits a non-node value. On many CPUs, potential branches are rather expensive, and so this can save a considerable amount of time.

- Another approach to attempt to gain speed at the expense of space is to change the definition of a trie so that the leaves always occur in the position that the full key expansion gives. For example, the leaf corresponding to "ABC" would always be found in a character-based trie by following the "A" branch, then the "B" branch, and then the "C" branch. This is a timesaving because when the search routine hits the leaf, it does not need to double-check whether this is a false hit—if you took the path to get to the leaf, it must be the right key. Word of warning: this can chew up a lot of memory if you have long keys.

- By making even more ambitious changes, you can also extend the trie to handle searches for ambiguous patterns. An example of an ambiguous pattern match would be checking whether the input pattern matched "AB*", "A*C", or "*BC", where * can be any character.

To allow for ambiguous matches, several modifications must be done. They include

- Modifying the format of a leaf node to allow for the possibility that several different patterns might match. You can decide which pattern should be credited with the match at insert time.
- Modifying the node format so that a node corresponds to a specific list of potential matching leaves at a specific level. This implies that the trie will no longer have a strict tree structure, but instead that a particular node can have pointers from several parent nodes (this is a *directed acyclic graph* structure).

Note

For more detailed coverage of directed acyclic and other types of graphs, see Chapter 16, "Working with Graphs."

- The insert and delete routines must be modified to handle this changed data structure. In particular, if they need to change a pointer by adding or removing a leaf, they should check if that particular node is already in existence, and if it is, reuse that.

This problem, quite frankly, doesn't come up very often and, as you can see, involves a bit of work to do properly. However, if you need to do those searches extremely quickly, a trie is one of your few alternatives.

Comparison of Tries with Binary Trees and Hash Tables

Tries attempt to solve the same types of problems as binary trees and hash tables. Here's how tries compare with these more conventional data structures:

- Tries do searching on a trie in O(1) time, worst-case, as long as the key size is fixed. Hash tables can do O(1) average case time, but their worst-case time is significantly worse. Tree structures that hold n elements take O(log(n)) time.
- In contrast to hash tables, tries can be quickly traversed in the order of the elements stored in them. This does take modification of the key walker, which would need to traverse the key in most significant bit first order. Of course, a binary tree can do this and more.
- Tries tend to use significantly more space than either trees or hash tables. The latter two have space overhead proportional to the number of nodes within the data structure. A trie, by contrast, takes up space proportional to the number of nodes times the number of elements that need to be examined on average before you get a match times the size of each subtrie. If you tend to have many keys with long common prefixes, this can add up to a lot of memory. You really need to know your data before you can say whether a trie is appropriate.

Summary

This chapter discussed the basics of trie manipulation. It began by defining a trie and discussing the basics of a trie search and some of their fundamental properties. We then implemented a trie and discussed a number of ways to modify this implementation. Finally, this chapter briefly compared the properties and merits of tries to those of some other data structures.

CHAPTER 15

Sparse Matrix

by William Fishburne

In This Chapter

This chapter examines one of the most versatile data structures ever conceived. The sparse matrix is a memory economical structure for storing data that is spread over a vast logical region. A sparse matrix functions much like a standard array, but carries with it the versatility of list and tree structures while maintaining the spatial awareness associated with an array. Sparse matrices are used to store a proportionally small amount of data that is situated in a large data space. There is significant overhead associated with the implementation of a sparse matrix that makes it increasingly impractical as the data space fills up with meaningful values. Thus, there is a rather well defined subset of problems that find their solution in the sparse matrix data structure.

The construction of a sparse matrix is really a process of associating several multiply-linked lists. These linked lists form a logical array of values wherein only non-zero values are stored. Due to the logical complexity of the relationships between lists, it is necessary to build functions that ease the traversal of the array and remove this complexity from the main areas of programming and encapsulate the functionality within a library. Finally, practical uses of the library are examined.

What Is a Sparse Matrix?

Before getting into the detail of the construction of the sparse matrix, it is important to understand its nature. A sparse matrix is a complicated data structure that requires careful administration to maintain. The sparse matrix mimics the function of an array without the memory overhead associated with a large array that has mostly empty cells. Although a sparse matrix is not generally full, Figure 15.1 shows a fully allocated 6×6 array.

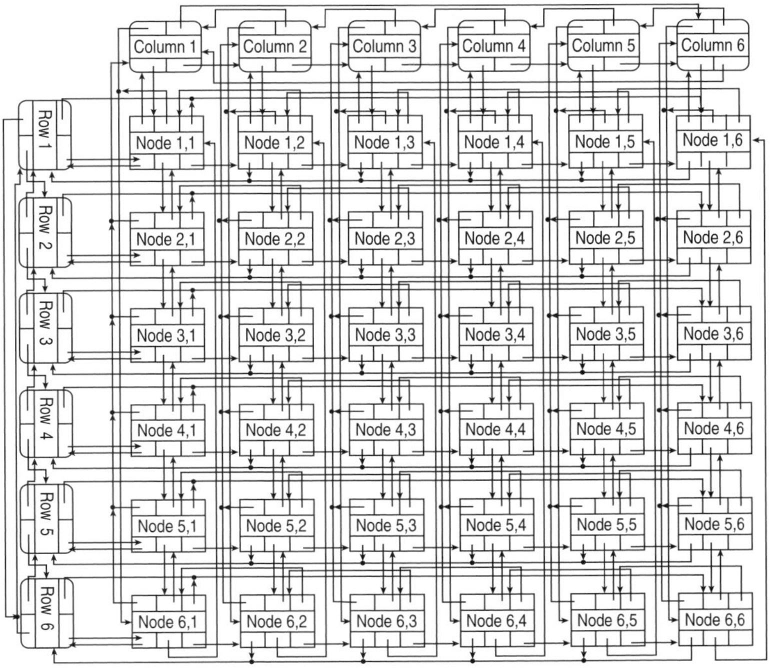

FIGURE 15.1
A fully allocated 6×6 sparse matrix.

Not Just Another Array

Note

It is not unusual for the terms "standard array" and "C language array" to be used interchangeably in this chapter. The use of the term "standard array" once denoted the array as defined in the standard C libraries, but the use of the term "standard" today connotes rules established by a recognized standards body. For this reason, "standard array" has generally been replaced by "C language array."

Another archaic term, "Pascal Array," was once used to describe arrays in C because the arrays were stored in the same manner as was used in the Pascal language. Historically, Pascal was used in educational institutions, so many programmers were familiar with the details of the language and referring to a "Pascal Array" was very descriptive. Today, fewer and fewer schools are teaching Pascal, so the term is no longer descriptive. For this reason, the term has not been used in this chapter.

A sparse matrix can be differentiated from a standard array in the following ways:

- Physical storage
- Access method
- Retrieval speed

Each of these distinctions is investigated in detail in the rest of this section.

Physical Storage

A C array is usually physically stored as a sequence of values. In a one-dimensional array (for example, a[depth]), the *depth* of the array represents the number of offsets minus one from the beginning position of the array to the end of the array. So, the fourth element of a one-dimensional array is offset from the beginning of the array by a distance of three times the size of each array element. This is shown graphically in Figure 15.2.

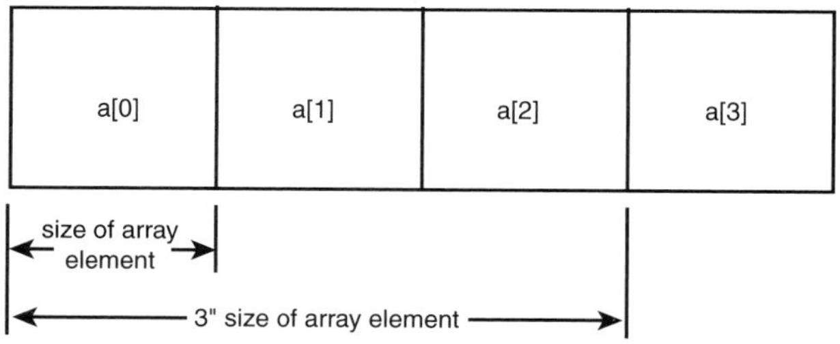

FIGURE 15.2
Finding the fourth element of a 1 × 4 standard array.

A multidimensional array is slightly more complicated and stored in a variety of ways depending upon the nature of the C implementation, but the general approach is that additional dimensions are stored as offsets within each other. Thus, to find the location of a two-dimensional array element, a[1][3], it would be necessary to find the pointer for the beginning of the array subset a[1], then go to three times the size of each array element as shown in Figure 15.3.

The space required by a traditional array, therefore, can be calculated as the maximum size of each array dimension times the size of each element. It is clear from this sizing exercise that the storage for a standard array increases geometrically as the number of dimensions increase. In addition, the storage space required for a standard array increases algebraically as the size of any given dimension is increased.

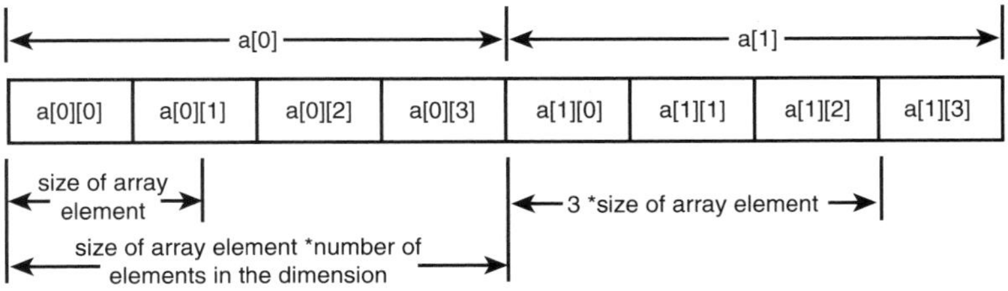

FIGURE 15.3
Finding the fourth element of the second dimension of a 2 × 4 standard array.

A sparse matrix, however, only stores the cells that have values. There are headers associated with the sparse array and pointers for each dimension, as will be detailed later, but the storage space required for a sparse matrix increases linearly as the number of cells with values increases, *regardless of any changes in the number or size of any dimension!* This is the critical attribute of a sparse matrix that makes it a valuable tool for analysis of vast data systems with a minimal number of values.

Access Method

In standard C, the array is a built-in component of the language and uses the reserved characters [] to indicate the existence of an array and tuple reference into the array. Because a sparse matrix is not an integral component of the C language, it is necessary to make function calls to reference the different components of the sparse matrix. This clutters the code when compared with the use of standard array notation.

Retrieval Speed

Because a standard C array is basically an offset from the starting point of the array, access to any given array cell is very quick. A sparse matrix, on the other hand, is basically a collection of linked lists, so accessing a cell requires traversal of a series of pointers. Thus, the access time for any given cell in a sparse matrix is variable depending on the number of links that need to be traversed. Generally, a sparse matrix has a slower retrieval speed than a comparable standard array.

Header Lists

As stated earlier, a sparse matrix is composed of a collection of linked lists. One portion of the collection defines the dimensions of the array. A sparse matrix has one header list structure for each dimension in the array. Each header list is composed of header list elements that represent a specific instance of a dimension that is populated with data. The header lists are doubly-linked lists to allow movement in either direction. Figure 15.4 is a close-up look at the header list element.

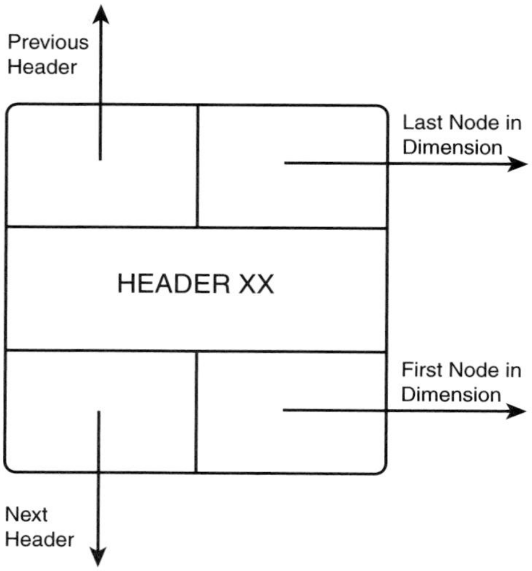

Figure 15.4
An element of a header list.

For example, consider a two-dimensional 6 × 6 sparse matrix as fully diagramed in Figure 15.1. Suppose further that only two nodes have values: [1][4] and [2][3]. In this case, the row header list would be composed of the headers Row 2 and Row 3, which represent the second and third rows of the array. The column header list would be composed of the headers Column 4 and Column 5, which represent the third and forth columns of the array. Because there are no values in the other columns or rows, they are not present in the sparse matrix. A query for the value associated with [0][0], for example, would return 0 (remember an unpopulated value in a sparse matrix is considered to be 0) without ever having to look at the data because there is no row and no column with these values in the appropriate header lists.

Matrix Nodes

The next portion of a sparse matrix is the collection of linked lists that serve as the nodes of the matrix. The nodes contain the data stored within the sparse array and the basic structure of each node is shown in Figure 15.5. Please note that this basic structure does not show all of the detail of the node structure; that will be fleshed out in the following sections.

Using the example given in the previous section, there would only be two node values. The node at [1][4] would point to the headers for Row 2 and Column 5 and the node list pointers would all point back to itself. The node at [2][3] would point to the headers for Row 3 and Column 4 and the node list pointers would again all point back to itself. The complete sparse matrix for this example is shown in Figure 15.6.

FIGURE 15.5
A node element.

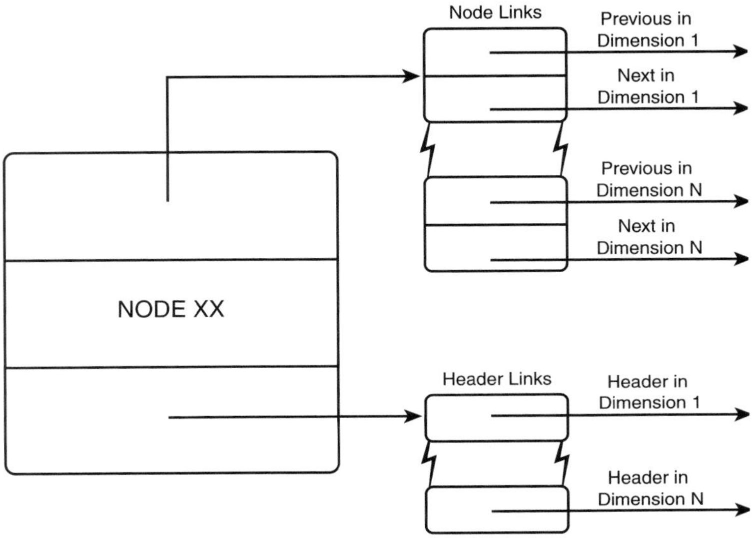

FIGURE 15.6
A 6 × 6 sparse matrix with two nodes.

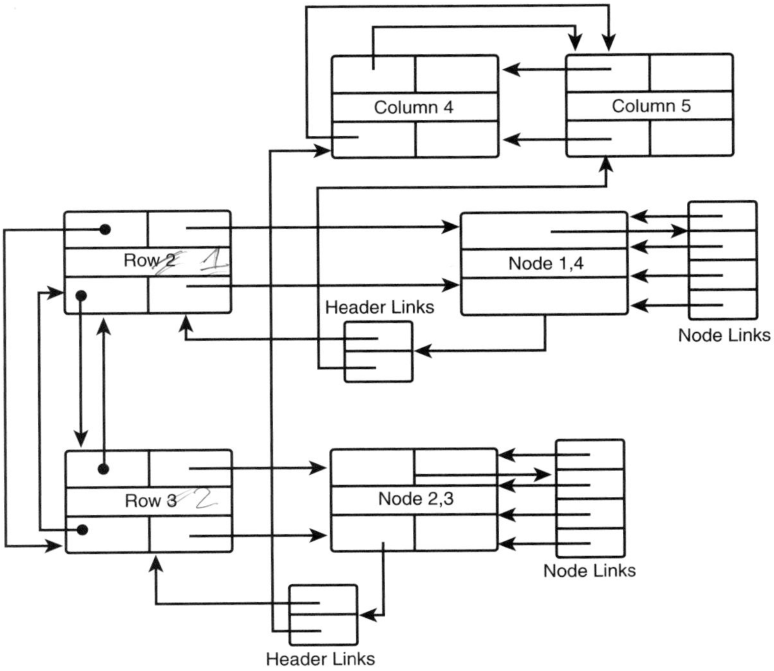

Dimensionality

The number of header lists used to make up the matrix itself determines the number of dimensions in a sparse matrix. Often, sparse matrices are defined with fixed dimension constraints, but in this chapter an N dimensional array will be developed. Because each header list stands on its own, the header list structures are not affected by the effort to develop an N dimensional array. Each node, however, must point back to its associated headers, so the variable number of pointers required adds an interesting wrinkle to the implementation. In addition, nodes need to point forward and backward to neighbor nodes in each dimension. Again, the need for a variable number of pointer pairs complicates the implementation of the sparse matrix.

Because there is a tendency for data to become increasingly sparse as more dimensions are considered, it makes sense to develop a sparse matrix implementation that allows for any dimensional size. In addition, the storage benefit of a sparse array increases significantly as the number of dimensions increase.

Why Sparse Data?

Having a library for managing a sparse matrix on hand, why should the library only be used for sparse data sets? All of the advantages that come from using sparse matrices derive from the fact that the data in the matrix is sparse. If the data set is not sparse, then using a sparse matrix can actually be a bad thing. Manipulating a sparse matrix is not as comfortable to most programmers as a standard array, so if the data set is not sparse, most programmers would not choose the extra effort implied by a sparse matrix implementation and would use a standard array instead. Additionally, performance may be an issue. In some ways, using a sparse matrix can be complex when attempting tasks that are straightforward in standard arrays. Finally, the storage advantages that dictate the use of a sparse matrix when a sparse data set is available diminish dramatically, as the data becomes more and more dense.

What Is Sparse Data?

Sparse data is traditionally considered data for which there are predominantly null, or empty, values. In some cases, the fact that a data set is sparse is intuitively obvious. Consider, for example, an effort to map every visible star in the night sky. Obviously there are many more empty spaces in the night sky than there are stars visible to the naked eye (or the night sky would be very bright). Although the number of stars in the night sky is huge (so you might be inclined to think the data set would not be sparse), they are spread over an enormous area. Thus, the number of visible stars compared to the number of places visible stars could be is an example of sparse data.

What makes data sparse, then, is not the quantity of data, but the degree to which potential data positions actually hold values. The ratio of actual values to possible values is how sparseness is measured. In order to determine the appropriateness of a sparse array, it is necessary to evaluate the appropriate level of performance, code complexity, and storage impact.

Complexity Issues

Sparse matrices are complex data structures by nature. If the problem to be solved is simple, it doesn't make sense to add the complexity of a sparse matrix. In addition, if memory is not an issue, adding the complexity of a sparse matrix again does not make sense. The programmer has to weigh the value of the flexibility of a sparse matrix against the added complexity (and implied code bulk) that comes with it.

Another consideration is code reusability. Creating, employing, and using a library of sparse matrix utilities is difficult work. Not all programmers are capable of maintaining, much less modifying, code developed for sparse matrices. This makes the code that much more difficult for a new programmer to assimilate and modify. Clearly, code should be as simple as possible to facilitate reusability and maintainability. Using sparse matrices just because you can is rarely a good idea.

There are operations that are actually simplified by using a sparse matrix. This is particularly true if it is necessary to search through a matrix looking for values and then modify those values by examining the neighboring cells for values. An application that is almost made for sparse matrices is Conway's Game of Life (see the sidebar). This application can be found in numerous screen savers today, so this chapter will not address its implementation. However, a quick look at the concepts used will show how a sparse matrix can actually reduce complexity.

Conway's Game of Life

The Game of Life invented by John H. Conway is not a game at all, but a study of cellular automata (a branch of artificial life) which was first published in *Scientific American* in April of 1970. The game is quite simple and the rules are easily understood. The game is played on a grid (usually two-dimensional), which is the living space for each cellular automaton. An initial (usually random) configuration is inserted into the grid and then populations are allowed to evolve over time. The rules for whether a cell lives or dies are

Occupied Neighbors	*Activity*
0	Death
1	Death
2	Survive
3	Survive or Birth
4	Death
5	Death
6	Death
7	Death
8	Death

Conway's Game of Life is traditionally used to teach students how to use sparse matrices because it is such an uncommonly good fit for the sparse matrix data type. In general, cellular automata exercises mesh well with the requirements for a sparse matrix data type.

In Conway's Game of Life, a cell is considered alive if it has a value of 1. The game is usually played on a two-dimensional matrix, but is not limited to two dimensions. The matrix is set up with an initial configuration (which may be random) of 1s liberally spaced throughout the matrix space. Each "generation" of the game is a pass through the matrix. Cells that have a value may lose that value based on the number of neighbors (too many neighbors and a cell "dies" of overpopulation; too few neighbors and a cell "dies" of starvation). In addition, cells can cause a neighboring empty cell to become alive (a sufficient number of neighbors adjacent to an empty cell causes the empty cell to become alive).

In a screen saver, a typical board would have 640×480 cells for a total of 307,200 cells. Some screens, however, could support 1280×1024 cells for a total of 1,310,720 cells. Keep in mind that the population is dynamic and could have as few as 15 or so active cells to thousands of active cells. Because activity is always within one cell of an active cell, hundreds of thousands of cells may be unnecessarily evaluated in a standard array implementation. In a sparse implementation, however, it would be simple to find the "living" cells and perform operations around them. This is one example of an instance where a sparse matrix would actually reduce the complexity of the implementation.

Storage Advantages

If the data is sparse, a sparse matrix offers significant storage advantages over a standard array because only the active data members are stored. The overhead associated with the sparse matrix implementation in this chapter is fairly straightforward to estimate. For each header value there are 4 pointers. For each node value there are 3 × dimensions pointers (where dimensions is the number of dimensions in the matrix). To calculate the overhead on this basis:

```
Overhead = (headers_used * 4 * pointer_size) +
           (nodes_used * 3 * dimensions * pointer_size)
```

Consider a two-dimensional matrix, with 100 header values in each dimension. Within this matrix, no more than 250 integer values are stored. Each of the headers actually uses no more than 70 of its possible header values. If integers are 4 bytes and pointers are 4 bytes long then the Overhead would be a total of 7,120 bytes. The 250 values would require 250 × 4 bytes of storage, or 1,000 bytes. Thus, the total storage would be 8,120 bytes. The comparable storage requirement for a standard array would be 100 × 100 × 4=40,000 bytes. Thus the sparse matrix would offer almost a five-fold reduction in storage space.

Note

Bear in mind that the preceding analysis is only an estimate because the actual structures of the header elements and sparse matrix nodes have not yet occurred. This estimate uses the information currently presented to estimate the overhead cost of the sparse matrix. A more complete overhead cost will be presented later in the chapter.

When to Use a Sparse Matrix

Having examined the nature of a sparse matrix and the nature of the data ideally represented by a sparse matrix, it is time to consider when a sparse matrix is appropriately used. There are a variety of general problem types that lend themselves to a sparse matrix, and several of the problem types will be explored. Additionally, there are computations that are appropriate for a sparse matrix and computations that are inappropriate, in general, for a sparse matrix.

This section is not a comprehensive listing of all appropriate environments for sparse matrices; rather, it is an effort to provide some guidelines and a starting point for examining a particular problem's appropriateness. By looking at some sample areas where sparse matrices are appropriate, it is possible to evaluate a particular application and determine if the use of sparse matrices is warranted.

Types of Problems

Earlier in this chapter, Conway's Game of Life was shown to be an almost perfect match for a sparse matrix data type. There are other types of problems that lend themselves to a sparse matrix implementation. Just as Conway's Game of Life was a specific type of problem within the field of cellular automata, this section will examine some specific problems within broader problems that naturally lend themselves to a sparse matrix implementation.

Directed Graphs

A graph shows a relationship between nodes. A directed graph shows not only how nodes connect, but in which direction. In some cases, it is also possible to put a "weight" on the connection between nodes, which describes, in some way, the nature of the connection.

A good example of a weighted, directed graph is a road map. Cities or road junctions would be nodes in the graph and the roads that connect the nodes would be the connectivity. The weighting might be the distance between nodes. Direction would come into play if some of the roads were only one-way. This logical construct is shown in Figure 15.7.

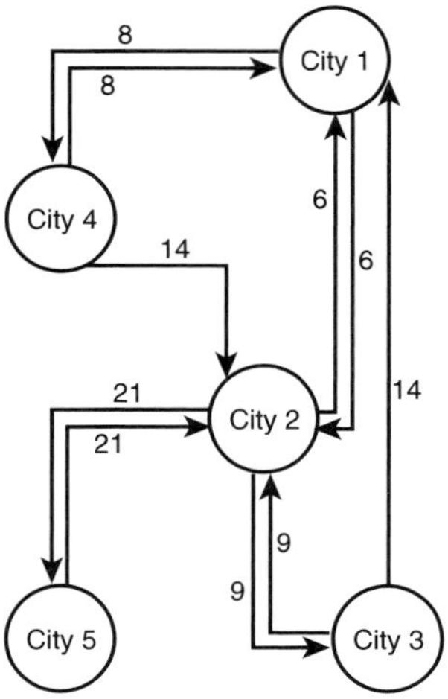

FIGURE 15.7
A map showing a sample directed, weighted graph.

The directed graph can be shown in a sparse array by creating two dimensions (one for the starting point and one for the ending point), which each contain the list of cities. In traditional parlance, the rows would be the starting point of a journey, and the columns would be an ending point. The weights for each journey (or the distance between cities) would be recorded as the value stored in the node of the sparse matrix.

The routes between cities are directed by virtue of the dimensions selected with which to represent them. Each city is considered an ordered pair, whereby (City 4, City 2) does not necessarily result in the same value as (City 2, City 4). In fact, in the example given, (City 4, City 2) results in 14, but (City 2, City 4) is not possible and fails.

Because a sparse matrix can easily grow dimensions (add or remove cities), and does not store information about city combinations that don't have a direct route between them (City 4 and City 5, for example), a sparse matrix is a memory-efficient means of storing the map. Of course, a map as simple as the one given in the example wouldn't make sense as a sparse matrix, but even a mildly complicated map would see dramatic storage benefits over a traditional array.

The headers of the sparse matrix can make the sparse matrix easier to traverse than the multi-linked list with which traditional directed graphs are built. So, depending upon the application, a sparse matrix implementation may provide performance benefits that are not available from a more traditional approach.

Clustered Data

Data that is clustered together in several groups over a broad area but that needs to be related is another type of problem handled well by sparse matrices. Because the sparse matrix only stores the data that is actually there, the space between entries does not matter very much.

Consider an effort to monitor the water flow across a broad landscape that serves as a watershed for a lake or river. Near the lake or river, water volume would be quite high leading to values in virtually all the cells that represent this area. As the watershed is mapped toward its edges, the data points would taper as major tributaries are tracked back to their sources. At the outside edges, there would be very few cells with values. As a whole, the data would tend to cluster around the major areas of flow into the lake or river.

The clustering effect of the data is terribly important in this kind of mapping. In addition, however, it is very important to be able to look at general areas and determine in a broad sense what the sources of water are in order to facilitate conservation efforts, or monitor the health of the watershed. Using a sparse structure, it is possible to collect individual density clusters and it is possible to track volumes across broad areas without having to perform calculations on cells that have no water flow.

Multiply-Linked Nodes

Graphs that contain a certain style of multiply-linked nodes are also handled well by sparse matrices. If the graph can be considered to have layered connections between nodes, each layer of the graph can be considered as an element of an additional dimension. Earlier in this section, a weighted, directed graph was discussed. This was a two-dimensional method for handling multiply-linked nodes. There is an entire class of problems, however, that have multiple two-dimensional solutions and this type of problem can be represented by a three-dimensional sparse matrix.

Flight paths for airplanes are of this form. Flight paths are extremely complicated and can be viewed from many different dimensions. Three of the most critical include source city, destination city, and flight position over time. Several additional dimensions are leg number, flight number, jet number, and seats sold. Examining just the three dimensions noted first, it would be possible to use source city as one header, destination city as another header, and time as the third header. Thus, flights between cities are layered by time slots.

Typically, multiply-linked nodes would be stored using a tree structure of some sort.

In some cases, however, tree structures do not work well. This case, in particular, makes it very hard to pick the head of the tree. Additionally, how should the tree be traversed? By time slot? By source city? By destination city? A matrix, naturally, allows the data to be traversed in whatever fashion is most appropriate for any given user. Moreover, the degree to which flight data is sparse (it is rare that every city is connected to every other city by a direct flight and it is rare that all flights are in the air at once), a sparse matrix makes very good sense and economical use of resources.

Computations That Are Appropriate

In addition to the basic structure of the data in a given problem, there are computations that may themselves justify the use of a sparse matrix. Taking advantage of the natural array style functions inherent in a sparse matrix is an obviously appropriate computation. There are a variety of others addressed in the body of this section.

Graph Traversal

Traversing a graph from a known starting point and searching for a known ending point is a natural for a sparse matrix. The linked list structure within the sparse matrix is very similar to the structures normally used to handle graphs with the addition of known start and destination points built in to the header information of the sparse matrix. In the case of a directed graph, the traversal is very straightforward. For an undirected graph, the traversal is more difficult because multiple sparse matrix nodes must be visited for each node in the graph.

Parallel Node Operations

If the same operation needs to be performed on each valued cell, a sparse matrix structure can farm the valued nodes out to any group of parallel processors. Because a sparse matrix only records cells with values, there is no chance that a cell without a value could be sent to a processor. If a row (or header list) of columns is sent to a processor, it is economically traversed using only the meaningful values. Should a neighboring cell be needed, it is a link away without having to calculate array indexes. For these reasons, sparse matrices are often used in intensive engineering calculations on enormous parallel machines.

Pivot Matrices

A unity matrix is a matrix with all 0s except the diagonal from the top-left corner to the bottom-right corner. A unity matrix is obviously sparse in all but the most trivial of cases.

> **Note**
>
> A *unity matrix* and an *identity matrix* are the same thing. Both describe a two-dimensional matrix that has a zero in every cell except for ones, which run along the diagonal from the upper left to the lower right.

A variant on the unity matrix is a pivot matrix. A pivot matrix is a unity matrix in which one pair of rows has been exchanged. Pivot matrices are often used to perform Gaussian elimination.

Gaussian elimination is a method for solving N simultaneous equations of N variables. The process for performing Gaussian elimination is beyond the scope of this chapter.

Because one of the many uses of a matrix is to solve simultaneous equations, it is valuable to be able to efficiently store and manipulate identity and pivot matrices.

Simple Matrix Manipulations

Basic matrix operations include addition, subtraction, multiplication, inversion, and reduction to row echelon form (Gaussian elimination is a method of performing this task). These simple matrix manipulations are handled in a straightforward manner despite the complexity of a sparse matrix implementation. All of these operations are reviewed in Chapter 18, "Matrix Arithmetic."

In addition to these standard matrix manipulations, other simple matrix manipulations include searching for specific values and traversing the matrix for local maximums and minimums as well as global values for the same. Again, these are all quite basic and reasonable functions for which the use of a sparse matrix is appropriate.

Computations to Avoid

While looking at the capabilities of a sparse matrix and the types of computations that are appropriate, it is also worthwhile to consider the types of computations that are seriously complicated by a sparse matrix. This section examines a variety of computations that are made more complex by virtue of the data format being a sparse matrix.

Just because something is complex or difficult is no reason it can't or shouldn't be done. In the spirit, however, of simple is best, it is worthwhile to review computations that are hampered (and why) by sparse matrix structures so that the programmer can make an informed decision. In some cases, the complexity simply cannot be avoided and that is fine. In others, there may be another approach that is more appropriate and by looking at the shortcomings of sparse matrices, these situations can be readily identified.

Complex Matrix Manipulations

Complex matrix manipulations include calculating Eigen values, matrix transpositions, calculating determinates, and tensor products. It may be surprising that something so basic as calculating determinates actually falls under a complex matrix manipulation. In fact, the determinate involves multiplying values that are related to each other (in two dimensions) on a diagonal. A sparse matrix has no link along the diagonal, so finding diagonal values is difficult and time consuming.

A quick study would point out that unity matrices only have values on the diagonal. So what is the difference? A unity matrix only has one value in each row/column pair. This makes it very easy to validate a unity matrix despite the fact that the values lie along a diagonal. This is not so for the determinate that multiplies diagonal values *ad nauseum*.

All of these operations involve traversing the array more than once and none of them derive direct benefit from having null values in the array. Thus, if these are the types of operations anticipated, it is generally better to steer clear of the sparse matrix data structure unless it is absolutely necessary.

Inversions

Inversions represent a special case, not because of the process, of inverting a matrix, but because of the process for determining whether a matrix can be inverted. Typically, a determinate is calculated and only if the determinate is not zero is an inversion possible. It is possible to determine that an inversion is not possible in other ways, but it can be quite costly particularly on a large matrix. For this reason, it is generally not a good idea to use a sparse matrix when building an inversion.

"Null" Value Searches

Searching for something that isn't there is generally considered difficult in the computing community. This holds true of sparse matrices.

> **Note**
>
> There is a distinction between a `NULL` value and a 0 in C. "Null" is quoted above to distinguish it from the C reserved word `NULL`. The reference to a "Null" value in this section is literally the absence of a value. Sparse data sets are simply missing lots of values in lots of cells (that is why they are sparse). In a sparse matrix an empty cell is returned as 0. Thus a search for empty cells in a sparse matrix ("Null" values, not `NULL` values) equates to a search for 0.

If, for some reason, there is a need to find "Null" or 0 values, a sparse matrix is probably not the right data structure. This is true for a large number of reasons of which only a small subset will be visited:

- If the data is sparse, the result of a "Null" search will be larger than the sparse matrix that is being searched!
- Searching for "Null" values means that positions must be interpolated between actual values within the sparse matrix. This is a complicated and exhausting programming process fraught with error.

- Both nodes and headers must be searched because an entire header could be missing.
- The memory saved by using a sparse matrix structure will rarely outweigh the processing time added by the same.

In general, it is worthwhile to remember that sparse matrices were invented to ease the manipulation of values within a matrix while effectively ignoring "Null" values. If the point of a sparse matrix is to ignore "Null" values, does it really make sense to use this structure when searching for them?

Constructing a Sparse Matrix

Finally! The meat of the chapter! Now that the concepts behind a sparse matrix are well understood and the advantages and shortcomings have been examined, it is time to consider the process of building a sparse matrix.

The sparse matrix implementation, which follows, allows for a dynamically defined N-dimensional matrix. Most sparse matrix implementations are specifically two or three dimensions (one or the other, not both) and this design can be modified to limit to these dimensions, but the design is intended to handle as many dimensions as the user cares to define.

It should be clear from the start that trying to handle an arbitrary dimension matrix significantly complicates the effort. The anticipation, however, is that this will be of more use to you simply because it is more complicated and can be simplified without much effort. So, buckle up and prepare to charge into the code!

Because memory is generally allocated dynamically, it is important that routines be available to clean up memory allocation before a pointer to a sparse matrix is dropped. Thus, this section addresses both the creation and deletion of sparse matrix components.

The data structure for the sparse matrix itself is deceptively simple:

```
typedef struct sparse_matrix {
  SP_HDR_ELEMENT *hdr_stack;
  int error_no,
      dimensions,
      *hdr_ranges;
} SPARSE_MATRIX;
```

The `hdr_stack` pointer does not point to one header list pointer, but points to a stack of header list pointers, one for each dimension. Similarly, the `hdr_ranges` pointer does not point to one range, but a stack of high and low sequence number values for each dimension.

`dimensions` is the number of dimensions in the sparse matrix. `Error_no` is set whenever the sparse matrix encounters an error. The possible values for `Error_no` are shown in Table 15.1.

TABLE 15.1 Error Values

Value	*Meaning*
0	No Error
1	Out of Memory
2	Broken Header Link
3	Broken Node Link
4	Below Minimum Dimension Value
5	Above Maximum Dimension Value
6	Invalid Dimension
7	Insert Failed
8	No Value Found
9	Not Enough Dimensions
10	Node List Not Empty

The error numbers and defines associated with the errors are defined in the file `sparse.h`, which is found on the CD that accompanies this book.

The stack pointers are discussed in the following sections.

Building Header Lists

The header lists are used in the sparse matrix to define the components of a dimension. There is one header list per dimension, and each header list may have as many components as appropriate. Each component of a header list is called a *Header List Element*.

In standard arrays, elements are integers ranging from 0 to the dimension size – 1. Thus, a three-dimensional standard array with four elements in each dimension would be declared as:

```
int my_array[4][4][4];
```

This array would have array elements 0–3 in each dimension.

In an N-dimensional sparse array, the only component that needs to be defined at creation is the number of dimensions. Thereafter, header list elements can be defined explicitly (particularly if the header has a character data value) or implicitly (by inserting values into the sparse matrix).

Each header list is stored in the SPARSE_MATRIX structure. The lists are stacked one atop the other within the structure. To find the header list associated with a particular dimension, simply add ((dimension – 1) to the pointer for the stack. The function that performs this activity is sp_get_header_list. This function returns a SP_HDR_ELEMENT pointer and is passed the SPARSE_MATRIX pointer and the dimension that is being requested. The following call shows an attempt to request the second dimension header from the sparse matrix my_matrix.

```
#include <sparse.h>
...
SP_HDR_ELEMENT *header_requested;
SPARSE_MATRIX the_matrix;
int the_dimension;
...
the_dimension = 2;
header_requested = sp_get_header_list(&the_matrix, the_dimension);
if (header_requested == (SP_HDR_ELEMENT *)NULL)

  if(the_matrix.error_no != SP_NOERR)

    fprintf(stderr, " sp_get_header_list:  Error %d on request for
➥dimension header %dn" ,
                     matrix.error_no, the_dimension);
    exit(matrix.error_no);

  else

    fprintf(stdout, " No values currently in the sparse matrixn" );


else

  fprintf(stdout, " Successfully retrieved the header for dimension %d" ,
                  the_dimension);

...
```

Generally, it won't be necessary to invoke this function directly, but it is frequently used internally to the sparse matrix library discussed throughout the rest of this chapter.

Defining Header List Elements

The C structure used to represent a header list element is slightly more complicated than has been presented so far. On occasion, it is helpful to be able to define arrays that have character strings as dimension values. In a standard C array, this is done using enumerated types.

Because the effort in this chapter is to design a very versatile, highly reusable sparse matrix implementation, the header elements contain a pointer to a user defined type that specifies the data which defines the header element. If the user does not specify a type a type of integer will be supplied. Although it is possible that a user would want a wide variety of types for different dimensions, the practical implementation of a different data type for each possible dimension is beyond the scope of this book. Thus, header elements may be associated with only one user defined type: `SP_HEADER_DATA`. The default structure used for `SP_HEADER_DATA` is

```
typedef struct sp_header_data {

  int header_label;
} SP_HEADER_DATA;
```

If a user defines a structure for `SP_HEADER_DATA`, it is important that the user also define (at compile time) the variable `SPHDUD`.

This is done by inserting the following line before the definition of the users version of `SP_HEADER_DATA`:

```
#define SPHDUD
```

The use of this variable to preclude the default definition is shown in the file `sparse.h`, which is included in the CD that goes with this book.

In addition, the header data element structure contains a sequence number. Thus, the structure of a header element is

```
typedef struct sp_hdr_element {

  struct sp_hdr_element *previous, *next;
  struct sp_node *first, *last;
  int sequence;
  SP_HEADER_DATA *detail;
} SP_HDR_ELEMENT;
```

The `previous` and `next` pointers are the pointers used to construct the doubly-linked list for the header list. The `first` and `last` pointers are used to construct the doubly-linked list for the nodes of the sparse matrix, which are in this dimensional element. The `detail` pointer, of course, is used for the user-defined type associated with the header.

Static Versus Dynamic Allocation

It is possible to allocate the header data ahead of time if the maximum size of the header dimensions are known and the overhead involved is not a concern. This type of allocation is static and means that the dimensions do not change over the course of program execution.

The programs presented in this chapter assume dynamic allocation, again, to increase the flexibility of the sparse matrix library. Dynamic memory allocation, however, does come at a price. Because the memory is allocated dynamically, it is possible that the memory used is not properly returned to the available memory pool, causing *memory drain*. In addition, it is necessary to monitor return values from any function that may allocate memory in case the memory is not available or the allocation fails for some other reason. For this reason, the sparse matrix data type, as described, incorporates an error field, which is set whenever there is an error involving the sparse matrix. Each function should reset the error field at the beginning of execution to prevent the `error_no` field from returning errors from a previous function.

Singly-Versus Doubly-Linked Lists

This implementation of the sparse matrix uses doubly-linked lists to facilitate traversal of the matrix in any direction. Because the lists are doubly linked and circular, there should never be a NULL link. Discovering a NULL link would indicate that an error has occurred in the process of creating the sparse matrix.

Having doubly-linked lists in the header lists is particularly valuable because it is not unusual to travel back and forth between header elements in the process of manipulating a matrix. To have to traverse the entire dimension to move backwards can be draining on performance, particularly for large dimensional spaces. Because it is a fundamental concept of the sparse matrix that there be a small amount of data in proportion to the space available for that data, it seems particularly wise to use doubly-linked lists on the header lists.

Using a singly-linked implementation can significantly reduce the overhead of a sparse matrix. In general, however, the overhead of the sparse matrix is trivial in comparison to the data set even with doubly-linked lists. Although having doubly-linked lists complicates the list maintenance, it seems like a more judicious use of time to examine the complicated case and leave simplifying it as an exercise for you as opposed to the reverse.

Adding Additional Dimensions

Prior to inserting data into the sparse matrix, dimensions can be added at will. Once data has been inserted into the matrix, it does not make sense to be able to add another dimension. The matrix would have no way of determining the appropriate new dimensional value for existing data.

To add a new dimension to an existing sparse matrix (without data), the function `sp_add_header_dimension` is invoked. This function returns a `SPARSE_MATRIX` pointer and is passed the `SPARSE_MATRIX` pointer, the dimension that is being added, and the minimum and maximum ranges for the dimension. The following call shows an attempt to insert the second dimension into the sparse matrix `my_matrix`.

```
#include <sparse.h>
...
SPARSE_MATRIX the_matrix, *matrix_ptr;
int the_dimension, dim_min, dim_max;
...
the_dimension = 2;
dim_min = 0;
dim_max = 5000;
matrix_ptr = &the_matrix;
matrix_ptr = sp_add_header_dimension(&the_matrix,
                                     the_dimension,
                                     dim_min, dim_max);
if (the_matrix.error_no != SP_NOERR)

  fprintf(stderr, " sp_add_header_element: Error %d received
➥trying to add dimension %dn" ,
                  the_matrix.error_no, the_dimension);
  return(the_matrix.error_no);

...
```

Adding a header to an existing sparse matrix involves inserting an entry into the `sp_hdr_stack` field of a `SPARSE_MATRIX` structure. The algorithm for this process is shown here (less the parameter validations):

```
if the new dimension is larger than the number of dimensions
   in the existing array
  reallocate the stack for the header lists
  initialize the header stack entries
```

```
  copy the old header stack into the new header stack
  reallocate the stack for the header range entries
  initialize the range stack entries
  copy the old range stack entries into the new range stack
  free the old range stack and old header stack
allocate space for the new detail portion of the header
assign the header element detail to the pointer just created
initialize the new header pointers to point back to itself
set the sequence number to the minimum value
insert the new range values
return the SPARSE_MATRIX
```

The code to perform this function is found in `sparse.c` in the CD at the end of this book. The portion of the code that implements this algorithm is

```
/* Check to see if this new dimension is within the existing range
     of the dimensions for the matrix */
  if (dim > sp->dimensions)
  {
    /* Attempt to allocate a new header stack of the appropriate size */
    new_hdr_stack = (SP_HDR_ELEMENT *)malloc(sizeof(SP_HDR_ELEMENT)*dim);
    if (new_hdr_stack == (SP_HDR_ELEMENT *)NULL)
    {
      sp->error_no = SP_MEMLOW;
      return(sp);
    }

    /* Attempt to allocate a new range stack of the appropriate size */
    new_rng_stack = (int *)malloc(sizeof(int)*dim*2);
    if (new_rng_stack == (int *)NULL)
    {
      free(new_hdr_stack);
      sp->error_no = SP_MEMLOW;
      return(sp);
    }

    /* Copy the old header stack values into the new stack */
    (void *)memcpy((void *)new_hdr_stack, (void *)(sp->hdr_stack),
                   sizeof(SP_HDR_ELEMENT) * (sp->dimensions));

    /* Copy the old range stack values into the new stack */
    (void *)memcpy((void *)new_rng_stack, (void *)(sp->hdr_ranges),
                   sizeof(int) * (sp->dimensions) * 2);
```

```
    /* Initialize the new elements */
    for (curr_dim = 0; curr_dim < dim; curr_dim++)
    {
      new_header = (SP_HDR_ELEMENT *)(new_hdr_stack + curr_dim);
      new_header->previous = new_header;
      new_header->next = new_header;
      new_header->first = (SP_NODE *)NULL;
      new_header->last = (SP_NODE *)NULL;
      if (curr_dim >= sp->dimensions)
      {
        new_header->sequence = 0;
        new_rng = (int *)(new_rng_stack + (2 * curr_dim));
        *new_rng = 0;
        new_rng ++;
        *new_rng = 0;
      }
      new_header->detail = (SP_HEADER_DATA *)NULL;
    }

    /* insert the new values */
    sp->dimensions = dim;
    free(sp->hdr_ranges);
    free(sp->hdr_stack);
    sp->hdr_ranges = new_rng_stack;
    sp->hdr_stack = new_hdr_stack;
  }

  /* Insert the information for the added dimension */
  new_header = (SP_HDR_ELEMENT *)(sp->hdr_stack + (dim - 1));
  new_header->sequence = dim_min;
  new_rng = (int *)(sp->hdr_ranges + (2 * (dim - 1)));
  *new_rng = dim_min;
  new_rng ++;
  *new_rng = dim_max;
```

Of particular interest in this section of code are the calls to `malloc`, which allocate space for the header lists and the header ranges.

Adding Header List Elements

Once the dimensions have been specified and properly allocated within the array, specific header list elements can be inserted or appended to the existing list. It is not necessary to manually perform this function immediately after creating the sparse matrix because these header list elements are added implicitly when a new node is inserted into the sparse matrix for which there is no prior header.

Another reason for adding the list elements specifically would be to populate the list header detail field with a user-defined value.

Inserting

Header list elements can be inserted in any order. Thus, inserting a header list element implies that there may already be a list value on either side of the element to be inserted. Because the 0th element is inserted by default at the time of the creation of the dimension, there will always be at least one other element to consider. Since the process of inserting a node in a doubly-linked list has already been covered, the code for this function will not be reviewed, but it appears in `sparse.c` in the CD at the end of the book.

To insert a header list element, the `sp_ins_header_element` function is called. This function returns a modified `SPARSE_MATRIX`. The function is sent a `SPARSE_MATRIX`, the dimension in which the header is to be inserted, a sequence number within the dimension, and a pointer to the `SP_HEADER_DATA` detail information. The following call shows an attempt to insert a header for the third element in the second dimension into the sparse matrix `my_matrix`.

```
#include <sparse.h>
...
SPARSE_MATRIX the_matrix, *matrix_ptr;
int the_dimension, the_sequence;
SP_HEADER_DATA *the_detail = (SP_HEADER_DATA *)NULL;
...
the_dimension = 2;
the_sequence = 3;
matrix_ptr = &the_matrix;
matrix_ptr = sp_ins_header_element(&the_matrix, the_dimension,
                                   the_sequence, the_detail);
if (the_matrix.error_no != SP_NOERR)
{
  fprintf(stderr, "sp_ins_header_element: Error %d received
```

```
➥trying to add header element %d\n",
                   the_matrix.error_no, the_sequence);
  return(the_matrix.error_no);
}
...
```

Appending

Appending a header element is the same process as inserting a header element for a doubly-linked list. For a singly-linked list, however, the process would be slightly different, so it would probably be useful to write a program that would append header element entries. This exercise is left to you, but it devolves to a very slight modification to the insertion program, `sp_ins_header_element`.

Deleting Header List Elements

Because header list elements are allocated using a call to `malloc`, it is important that these elements be deleted properly to prevent memory drain. This is done using `free` and rebuilding the link structure for the doubly-linked list. As a practical matter, the link structure is traditionally modified before the memory of the offending list element is removed. In some ways it is helpful to have the list element available so that its pointer can be reassigned directly before it is eliminated. The algorithm used for this function follows (less the parameter validations):

```
get the header list for the appropriate dimension
search the header list for the appropriate sequence number
if the sequence number is not found
  return the sparse matrix as there is nothing to delete
if the header list element has nodes associated
  return the sparse matrix with an error
set the next pointer for the previous element to the next
 pointer for the current element
set the previous pointer for the next element to the previous
 pointer for the current element
free the space used by the header detail
free the header list element
return the sparse matrix
```

The source code for `sp_del_header_element` is in the file `sparse.c` located in the CD at the end of this book. The portion of the source code, which handles the algorithm listed above, is

```
/* Find the header to be deleted */
  list_top = sp_get_header_list(sp, dim);
```

```
if (sp->error_no != SP_NOERR)
{
  return(sp);
}

/* The first value is definitely not the one to be deleted,
   so search for subsequent values */
old_header = list_top;
do
{
  old_header = old_header->next;
}
while ((old_header->sequence < seq) &&
       (old_header != list_top));

/* if the old_header doesn't have the sequence number
   being sought, then there is no header element with
   that value */
if (old_header->sequence != seq)
{
  return(sp);
}

/* Make sure that there are no nodes associated with
   the header */
if ((old_header->first != (SP_NODE *)NULL) ||
    (old_header->last != (SP_NODE *)NULL))
{
  sp->error_no = SP_NFULL;
  return(sp);
}

/* Adjust the pointers for the previous node */
old_header->previous->next = old_header->next;

/* Adjust the pointers for the next node */
old_header->next->previous = old_header->previous;

/* Free the allocated space */
free(old_header->detail);
free(old_header);
return(sp);
```

Caution

It is very important that the `SP_HEADER_ELEMENT` variables be deleted using this type of programming and not just by reassigning the pointer. If the pointer is reassigned, the stack fields within `SP_HEADER_ELEMENT` will remain allocated and be unreferenced. This could lead to loss of available memory for the program, and eventually these lost pointers will consume the entire memory space.

Rebuilding Links

The last part of the code portion shown in the preceding section rebuilds the doubly-linked list around the header element that is to be deleted. The integrity of the list must be maintained as the elements from the list are inserted or deleted. This means that the previous and next pointers of existing header elements must be rebuilt so that there is not a hole in the list.

Links to nodes are not considered because it is impossible to delete a header element if nodes remain in the sparse matrix. The nodes would need to be reassigned to a new header element and that wouldn't make any sense at all. Thus, if the header element has pointers to nodes, the header element cannot be deleted and an error is returned from `sp_del_header_element`.

Memory Warnings

Because the memory for the sparse matrix is dynamically assigned, memory is taken from the heap as components of the sparse matrix are added. This memory must be made available back to the heap if some or the entire sparse matrix is deleted. If the memory is not returned to the heap, it will not be available to other assignments within the program. Eventually, the memory will fill and program execution will halt. For this reason, it is important to have functions that return the memory to the heap associated with any data structure that makes dynamic memory allocations.

It is also worth noting that if memory is not available when an attempt is made to allocate it from the heap, the functions that build the sparse matrix return errors. The errors described in Table 15.1 include memory errors that should be checked after each allocation. Examples of this type of checking can be seen throughout the code for the functions that build the sparse matrix.

Building Matrix Node Lists

At this point the sparse matrix has headers, but no place in which to place actual data. So, great, it is possible to build an N dimensional sparse matrix, but it is useless without somewhere to actually store data values! Enter the node. The node contains the data associated with values that are inserted into the sparse matrix.

Although it may have seemed that the header structures were a tad involved, the node structures are actually N-doubly-linked lists. That is to say that they link doubly in N directions to the N dimensions of the sparse matrix. Once again, the use of stacks of links is going to be critical to performing this function.

Retrieving a list of nodes is generally done in association with a header element. Thus, passing a `SPARSE_MATRIX`, a dimension, and a sequence number to the function `sp_get_node_list` retrieves the node list. The algorithm for retrieving node lists is

```
retrieve the header list
step through the header list looking for the sequence number
if the sequence number is found
  return the pointer to the first node from the header element
else
  return NULL
```

The only tricky part to this simple algorithm is the process of stepping through the header list. Because the header list is in the order of the sequence number, it is tempting to step through the list until a sequence number that is larger than the one for which you are looking appears. The problem with this approach is that if all the sequence numbers in the header list are below the sequence number for which the search was made, the search will loop endlessly through the circular list. Thus, it is important to check for the top of the list and halt the search if it is encountered.

Tip

Whenever searching through the doubly-linked lists in the sparse matrix, it is worthwhile to monitor for the list header (or starting point) so that the list is not traversed endlessly.

The code, which retrieves a node list, is `sp_get_node_list` and is found on the CD at the end of the book. Here is the portion of the code that implements the preceding algorithm:

```
/* Retrieve the header list associated with the dimension */
  header_list = sp_get_header_list(sp, dim);
```

```
  if ((sp->error_no != SP_NOERR) ||
      (header_list = (SP_HDR_ELEMENT *)NULL))
  {
    return((SP_NODE *)NULL);
  }

/* Search the header list for the requested sequence */
  header_element = header_list;
  while ((header_element->next->sequence < seq) &&
         (header_element->next != header_list))
  {
    header_element = header_element->next;
  }

  /* If the header_element is not the same sequence number
     as passed in, then the sequence number is not in the
     list */
  if (header_element->sequence != seq)
  {
    return((SP_NODE *)NULL);
  }
  else
  {
    return(header_element->first);
  }
```

Although it is nice to be able to retrieve a list of nodes, the process for actually creating matrix nodes has yet to be defined.

Defining Matrix Nodes

The matrix node lists hang off of the header list element as shown in Figure 15.1 and described in the code sequence and algorithm in the previous section. The structure for the matrix node is also deceptively simple:

```
typedef struct sp_node {

  SP_HDR_ELEMENT **hdr_stack;
  struct sp_node **dimension_stack;
  int value;
} SP_NODE;
```

The `hdr_stack` within the `SP_NODE` structure is different from the `hdr_stack` within the `SPARSE_MATRIX` structure. The name is the same because the structure of the data is the same. The hdr_stack is a stack of SP_HDR_ELEMENT pointers, one for each dimension. These pointers refer to the header list elements that are associated with the node.

The dimension_stack field is used to store the pointers for the doubly-linked list in each dimension. Like the other stack structures in the sparse matrix, dimension_stack does not point to one SP_NODE structure, but to two per dimension. The next pointer in each dimension comes first, followed by the previous pointer for that dimension. The dimensions are stored in order.

The value field holds the value associated with the node.

Static Versus Dynamic Allocation

It is possible to allocate the node data ahead of time if the maximum number of nodes is known and the overhead involved is not a concern. This type of allocation is static and means that the number of nodes does not change over the course of program execution. Although this is reasonable for headers, it is extremely rare that this makes sense for nodes. A rare exception might be creating an identity matrix that is used over and over throughout the program. Generally, however, it is a bad idea to constrain the size of the matrix in this way.

The programs presented in this chapter assume dynamic allocation, again, to increase the flexibility of the sparse matrix library. Dynamic memory allocation, however, does come at a price. Because the memory is allocated dynamically, it is possible that the memory used is not properly returned to the available memory pool, causing *memory drain*. In addition, it is necessary to monitor return values from any function that may allocate memory in case the memory is not available or the allocation fails for some other reason. For this reason, the sparse matrix data type, as described above, incorporates an error field, which is set whenever there is an error involving the sparse matrix. Each function should reset the error field at the beginning of execution to prevent the error_no field from returning errors from a previous function.

Linking to Header List Elements

Each node links to a single header list element for each dimension. In this way it is possible to start from a node and traverse node values in nearby positions in any given dimension. Although nodes are directly linked to each other, nodes that are neighbors in one dimension might be greatly removed from each other in another dimension.

The links to the header list elements are stored in the hdr_stack field of the SP_NODE structure. There is one entry in the stack for each dimension and the dimensions are stacked in order. Putting entries into this stack uses the same formulas employed in the hdr_stack in the SPARSE_MATRIX structure.

Singly-Versus Doubly-Linked Lists

This implementation of the sparse matrix uses doubly-linked lists to facilitate traversal of the matrix in any direction. Because the lists are doubly-linked and circular, there should never be a NULL link. Discovering a NULL link would indicate that an error has occurred in the process of creating the sparse matrix.

Having doubly-linked lists in the node lists is critical. It is rare that an application, which is appropriate for a sparse matrix, would not benefit from being able to swiftly access neighbors in any dimension. Conway's Game of Life, for example, is constantly moving between neighbors and doing calculations. With a singly-linked list, it would be necessary in some cases to traverse the entire linked list to move back one entry.

If you choose to implement the node lists with a single link, it would be wise to consider using trailing pointers and recursive approaches to traversing the links so that the effect of having links in only one direction is mitigated.

Inserting Additional Dimensions

Once nodes have been added to the sparse matrix, the number of dimensions cannot be changed. Imagine for a moment a two-dimensional graph that has only one point at (3,5). Suppose that suddenly the graph was changed to three dimensions. Where would the point lie along the third dimension? An argument could be made that all the points currently in the graph would be at the 0 position, (3,5,0), on the new graph, but this is, at best, a waste of the third dimension.

Caution

Dimensions cannot be added to the sparse matrix once node values have been inserted. This makes sense if you consider what would have to happen to the nodes. If a new dimension were created, what would be the node value along that dimension? Suppose that a two-dimensional matrix were made three-dimensional. Are the existing nodes planer? Are they at the 0 point on the new dimension? There is no way to accurately answer these questions.

This is not to say that header list elements cannot be added. In fact, header list elements are implicitly added whenever a node is created for which there was no previous header list element in any given dimension. This means that the first few nodes are going to take longer to insert because one or more header list elements are inserted at the same time.

Inserting Matrix Nodes

Matrix nodes are added by specifying the header element list sequence numbers, which position the node within the sparse matrix. This ordered set of numbers, or tuple, has to match the number of dimensions in the matrix. Because the matrix can have N dimensions, the tuple that represents the position of the node in the matrix needs to be able to have N dimensions. In order to look at inserting nodes to the matrix, it will be necessary to find a way to store these tuples.

The structure used for storing a tuple will seem very familiar:

```
typedef struct sp_tuple {

  int *seq_stack, dimensions;
} SP_TUPLE;
```

The `dimensions` field contains the number of dimensions that the tuple is supposed to represent. The `seq_stack` field is a pointer to a stack of sequence numbers in dimension order. Because this is basically a stack, the functions that manipulate the tuple are `sp_tuple_dim` and `sp_add_tuple`. Of course, the structure needs to be deleted using `sp_del_tuple`. Because the use of stacks is already discussed in Chapter 11, "Simple Abstract Data Structures," and elsewhere in this chapter, the code for these functions will not be reviewed, but is available in the CD at the end of the book.

Once the tuple has been defined, nodes can be inserted into the sparse matrix.

Inserting

The first step in inserting a node is to make sure that the node has not already been inserted. If the node has already been created within the sparse matrix, the user may just be trying to change the value. Thus, the first step is to see if the node already exists. The algorithm for retrieving a node is as follows:

```
Check the values in the passed tuple against the valid
 ranges for the given dimensions
Get the node list associated with the first dimension value
For each dimension in the tuple retrieve the corresponding
 header list element pointer
  Incorporate the element into a stack
Compare the built stack to the hdr_stack values of the node
 list looking for a match
If a match is found
  Return the node
Else
  Return NULL
```

Normally, in the algorithms, the necessary parameter validations are assumed. In this algorithm, it is so important to remember to check a passed tuple against the valid ranges for the tuple dimensions within the sparse matrix that it has been included explicitly.

Because the tuple's first dimension is easily accessible and it is necessary to start somewhere, the node list associated with the first dimension is pulled from the sparse matrix. At this point, the nodes in the list have a pointer to a header stack which is itself a stack of pointers that point back to header list elements. The tuple, on the other hand, has a stack of sequence numbers that correspond to header list elements. Although both point to the same thing in principle, they cannot be directly compared. It is necessary to convert one to the other, then perform the comparison. Thus, the next step is to convert the tuple sequence number stack into a header list element stack.

Now that the tuple stack has been converted, it is possible to do a direct comparison between the newly generated stack and the stack stored in the nodes. This is executed as a direct bit-for-bit memory comparison.

Once a match for the stacks has been found, it is a straightforward process of returning the first node that matches. Because it is only possible for one node to match the tuple exactly, if a match is found, it must be the correct match.

The code that implements this process is shown in its entirety in Listing 15.1. The program, `sp_retrieve_node`, is found in the file `sparse.c` on the CD in the back of this book.

The entire listing for this function is presented here to reinforce the importance of checking parameters and because some of the functions performed by the code are unclear without all of the variable declarations.

LISTING 15.1 Retrieves a Node from a Sparse Matrix

```
/****************************************************************
**  SP_RETRIEVE_NODE                                          **
**                                                            **
**    Retrieves a node from a sparse matrix.                  **
**                                                            **
**  INPUT:                                                    **
**    sp -- The sparse matrix into which the node is to be    **
**          inserted.                                         **
**    tuple -- The tuple used to define the location of       **
**             the node.                                      **
**                                                            **
**  OUTPUT:                                                   **
**    SPARSE_MATRIX * -- A pointer to the modified sparse     **
                         matrix                               **
```

15

Sparse Matrix

LISTING 15.1 continued

```
**                                                           **
**  SIDE EFFECTS:                                            **
**    The error_no field of the sparse matrix can be set    **
**  to an error if an error is encountered.  Whenever an    **
**  error is encountered, this value is set and a NULL      **
**  pointer is returned.  Thus, if a NULL pointer is        **
**  returned from this function it is important to          **
**  examine the error_no of the associated sparse matrix.   **
**                                                           **
**  NOTES:                                                   **
**                                                           **
*************************************************************/

#include <stdio.h>
#include <stdlib.h>
#include <string.h>
#include "sparse.h"

SP_NODE *sp_retrieve_node(SPARSE_MATRIX *sp, SP_TUPLE *tuple)
/* SPARSE_MATRIX *sp  The sparse matrix from which the node
                        is to be retrieved */
/* SP_TUPLE *tuple    The tuple used to define the location
                        of the node */
{
  SP_NODE *new_list, *node_pos;
  SP_HDR_ELEMENT **new_hdr_list, *hdr_pos, *hdr_list;
  int curr_dim, *curr_seq, node_found=0;

  /* If the sparse matrix is empty, then a node cannot be
     retrieved */
  if (sp == (SPARSE_MATRIX *)NULL)
  {
    return((SP_NODE *)NULL);
  }

  sp->error_no = SP_NOERR;

  /* If the tuple is empty, then no node can be retrieved */
  if (tuple == (SP_TUPLE *)NULL)
  {
    sp->error_no = SP_BADDIM;
    return((SP_NODE *)NULL);
```

LISTING 15.1 continued

```
}

/* Make sure that the number of dimensions in the tuple
   matches the number of dimensions in the sparse matrix */
if (sp->dimensions != tuple->dimensions)
{
  sp->error_no = SP_BADDIM;
  return((SP_NODE *)NULL);
}

/* Make sure that the tuple specified is legal */
for(curr_dim = 0; curr_dim < sp->dimensions; curr_dim++)
{
  curr_seq = (int *)(tuple->seq + (curr_dim));
  if ((*curr_seq < sp_get_range_min(sp, curr_dim + 1)) ||
      (sp->error_no != SP_NOERR))
  {
    sp->error_no = SP_DLOW;
    return((SP_NODE *)NULL);
  }
  if ((*curr_seq > sp_get_range_max(sp, curr_dim + 1)) ||
      (sp->error_no != SP_NOERR))
  {
    sp->error_no = SP_DHIGH;
    return((SP_NODE *)NULL);
  }
}

/* Get the node list associated with the first dimension */
new_list = sp_get_node_list(sp, (int)1, *(tuple->seq));
if ((new_list == (SP_NODE *)NULL) ||
    (sp->error_no != SP_NOERR))
{
  return((SP_NODE *)NULL);
}

/* Build a header stack */
new_hdr_list =
  (SP_HDR_ELEMENT **)malloc(sizeof(SP_HDR_ELEMENT *) *
                            sp->dimensions);
if (new_hdr_list == (SP_HDR_ELEMENT **)NULL)
{
```

LISTING 15.1 continued

```
    sp->error_no = SP_MEMLOW;
    return((SP_NODE *)NULL);
  }

  /* For each dimension in the tuple, seek out the
     corresponding header list element */
  for (curr_dim = 0; curr_dim < sp->dimensions; curr_dim++)
  {
    /* Get the sequence number associated with the current
       dimension */
    curr_seq = ((int *)(tuple->seq + (curr_dim)));

    /* Get the header list element */
    hdr_pos = sp_hdr_list_element_get(sp, curr_dim + 1,
                                      *curr_seq);
    if ((hdr_pos == (SP_HDR_ELEMENT *)NULL) ||
        (sp->error_no != SP_NOERR))
    {
      free(new_hdr_list);
      return((SP_NODE *)NULL);
    }

    /* Insert this header into the list */
    *((SP_HDR_ELEMENT **)(new_hdr_list + (curr_dim))) =
      hdr_pos;
  }

  /* Search for a matching tuple in the node list */
  node_pos = new_list;
  node_found = 1;
  if (memcmp((void *)node_pos->hdr_stack,
             (void *)new_hdr_list,
             (sizeof(SP_HDR_ELEMENT *) * sp->dimensions)))
  {
    do
    {
      /* The first pointer in the dimension_stack points to
         the next node in the first dimension, since that is
         what we want, we can use the shorthand below */
      node_pos = *(node_pos->dimension_stack);
      node_found = !memcmp((void *)node_pos->hdr_stack,
                           (void *)new_hdr_list,
```

LISTING 15.1 continued

```
                              (sizeof(SP_HDR_ELEMENT *) *
                               sp->dimensions));
    }
    while ((node_pos != new_list) && (!node_found));
  }

  free(new_hdr_list);
  if (node_found)
  {
    return(node_pos);
  }
  else
  {
    return((SP_NODE *)NULL);
  }
}
```

Nodes can be inserted in any order. Thus, inserting a node implies that there may already be another node in any of the other dimensions that has one or more of the same header list elements. On some occasions, however, a needed header list element may not exist, so as a precaution, an attempt is made to insert the header list element required. In this manner, if the header list element is needed, it is created; if not, the insert fails. Because inserting a node involves inserting the node into many doubly-linked lists, it is worthwhile to review the algorithm for performing this kind of insert.

The insertion of a node is complicated, so the analysis of the algorithm will be broken up into manageable chunks. The first thing to consider is whether the node even needs to be inserted. If the node already exists, an attempt to insert could simply be an effort to change the value. This is the simplest case and will be evaluated first:

```
if the node already exists
  insert the passed value into the value field of the node
```

To see if the node already exists, the function `sp_retrieve_node` is sent the `SPARSE_MATRIX` and the tuple for the location of the new node:

```
  /* Attempt to retrieve the node in case it already exists */
  new_node = sp_retrieve_node(sp, tuple);
  if (sp->error_no != SP_NOERR)

    return(sp);
```

```
/* If the node exists, just update the value */
if (new_node != (SP_NODE *)NULL)

  new_node->value = node_val;
  return(sp);
```

Usually, the node will not already exist, so it is necessary to search for where the node should be inserted. It is also necessary to start building up the pointers that will be part of the node. In addition, if header list elements do not exist which the node needs, the header list elements should be created. All of this can be done at the same time using the following algorithm:

```
Allocate space for the header stack
Loop through each dimension
  Retrieve the sequence number from the tuple for this dimension
  Attempt to insert the header list element
  Get the header list element that corresponds to this dimension
   and sequence number
  Store the pointer to the header list element in the node hdr_stack
```

The algorithm is implemented using the following code:

```
/* Since the node doesn't exist, check to make sure all the
   headers exist and if they don't, then insert them.  In the
   process, build up the header list stack needed by the
   node */
  new_hdr_stack = (SP_HDR_ELEMENT **)malloc
                  (sizeof(SP_HDR_ELEMENT *) *
                   (sp->dimensions - 1));
  for (curr_dim = 0; curr_dim < sp->dimensions; curr_dim++)
  {
    /* Set the current sequence number to the sequence number
       in the tuple stack associated with the current
       dimension */
    curr_seq = (int *)(tuple->seq + (curr_dim));

    /* Insert the header element, if appropriate */
    sp_res = sp_ins_header_element(sp, curr_dim + 1,
                                   *curr_seq,
                                   (SP_HEADER_DATA *)NULL);
    if (sp->error_no != SP_NOERR)
    {
      free(new_hdr_stack);
      return(sp);
```

```
    }

    /* Retrieve a pointer to the header list element */
    header_pos = sp_hdr_list_element_get(sp, curr_dim + 1,
                                          *curr_seq);
    if ((header_pos == (SP_HDR_ELEMENT *)NULL) ||
        (sp->error_no != SP_NOERR))
    {
      free(new_hdr_stack);
      return(sp);
    }
    *(new_hdr_stack + (curr_dim)) = header_pos;
  }
```

At this point, it is time to create the new node and `dimension_stack` structure. The `dimension_stack` structure should be initialized to point to the new node, so that if the node is the first node in the sparse array, the pointers are properly configured. This process is easily understood. The last portion of the procedure is the most difficult.

Stepping through each dimension, the pointers for the node to other nodes need to be assigned and the node needs to be inserted into a doubly-linked list for each dimension. Once again, this is all performed in the same loop. The algorithm for performing these functions is

```
Loop through each dimension
  Get the header list element associated with the new node for this dimension
  Get the node list associated with the header list element
  If the node list is empty
    Insert the new node into the list
  Else
    Loop through the dimensions again (sub_dimension)
      Get the sequence number from the tuple for the sub_dimension
      While the sequence number for the node in the node list is < the
       tuple sequence number and the whole node list has not
       been traversed
        Go to the next node in the node list
      If the node list sequence number > the tuple sequence number
        Put a pointer to the node from the node list into the new
         node's next  field for this dimension
        Put a pointer to the node from the node list's previous
         node into the new node's previous field for this
         dimension
```

```
Put the new node into the previous node of the node in the node list
Put the new node into the next node of the node before the
 current  node in the node list
Leave the sub_dimension loop
```

The success of this loop depends on the order of the nodes in a node list. The order of the nodes within any node list is from the 1st dimension to the Nth dimension. Thus, whenever searching through the nodes, as long as the search is ordered by dimension from the least to the largest dimension, the node sequence number values will increase in size. The code that performs the function described in the preceding algorithm is

```
/* insert the node into the node lists associated with each
   header list element */
  for (curr_dim = 0; curr_dim < sp->dimensions; curr_dim++)
  {
    /* Get the header list element associated with this
       dimension */
    header_pos = *(SP_HDR_ELEMENT **)(new_node->hdr_stack +
                                  curr_dim);

    /* Get the list of nodes associated with this header list
       element */
    node_head = header_pos->first;

    /* The list of nodes is ordered by the dimension sequence
       numbers, left to right, so traverse the list starting
       with the first dimension of the tuple until the correct
       position in the list is found */
    node_pos = node_head;
    back_to_top = 0;
    pos_found = 0;

    /* If there were no other nodes in this list, then the
       position is automatically the first position */
    if (node_pos == (SP_NODE *)NULL)
    {
      pos_found = 1;
      header_pos->first = new_node;
      header_pos->last = new_node;
    }
```

```
for (sub_dim = 0;
     (sub_dim < sp->dimensions) && (!pos_found) &&
      (!back_to_top);
     sub_dim++)
{
  /* skip the current dimension, because all nodes in the
     list match the current dimension by default */
  if (sub_dim != curr_dim)
  {
    /* Get the sequence number for the tuple in this
       dimension */
    curr_seq = (int *)(tuple->seq + (sub_dim));

    /* search for an entry which is equal to or greater
       than the sequence number of the node */
    next_sub_dim = 0;
    do
    {
      /* Get the sequence number for this node in this
         sub-dimension */
      node_seq = ((SP_HDR_ELEMENT *)*
                  ((node_pos->hdr_stack) +
                   (sub_dim)))->sequence;

      /* If this sub dimension sequence number is larger
         than the tuple sequence number, then the node
         should be inserted before the current node */
      if (node_seq > *curr_seq)
      {
        pos_found = 1;
      }
      else
      {
        /* If the sub dimension sequence number is equal
           to the tuple sequence number, then the next
           dimension needs to be checked */
        if(node_seq == *curr_seq)
        {
          next_sub_dim = 1;
        }

        else
        {
```

```
                /* If the sub dimension sequence number is
                   smaller than the tuple sequence number,
                   check the next node */
                node_pos = sp_next_node(sp, curr_dim+1,
                                        node_pos);
                if (sp->error_no != SP_NOERR)
                {
                  free(new_hdr_stack);
                  free(new_node);
                  free(node_stack);
                  return(sp);
                }
                back_to_top = (node_pos == node_head);
              }
            }
          }
          while ((!back_to_top) && (!pos_found) &&
                 (!next_sub_dim));
        }
      }

      /* If a node has been found which is larger than the
         current node, set up the pointers */
      if (node_pos != (SP_NODE *)NULL)
      {
        /* At this point, node_pos points to the node which
           belongs after the current node.  Since this node
           belongs after the current node in the doubly linked
           list, set up the next pointer in the dimension
           stack */
        next_node = node_pos;
        *((SP_NODE **)(new_node->dimension_stack +
                      (2 * curr_dim))) =
          next_node;

        /* The previous pointer is the previous pointer held
           by the old node */
        prev_node = sp_previous_node(sp, curr_dim+1, node_pos);
        if ((sp->error_no != SP_NOERR) ||
            (prev_node == (SP_NODE *)NULL))
        {
          free(new_hdr_stack);
          free(new_node);
```

```
        free(node_stack);
        return(sp);
      }
      *((SP_NODE **)(new_node->dimension_stack +
                     (2 * curr_dim) + 1)) = prev_node;

      /* Now insert the node into the existing link
         structure */
      *((SP_NODE **)(prev_node->dimension_stack +
                    (2 * curr_dim))) = new_node;

      *((SP_NODE **)(next_node->dimension_stack +
                     (2 * curr_dim) + 1)) = new_node;
    }

    /* Update the first and last pointers as appropriate */
    if (node_pos == node_head)
    {
      /* If the whole list has been checked, then node_pos
         should be the last node in the header link */
      if (back_to_top)
      {
        header_pos->last = new_node;
        header_pos->first = next_node;
      }
      else
      {
        /* If the new node is smaller than the header node,
           then the first node of the header link should
           point to node_pos */
        header_pos->first = new_node;
        header_pos->last = prev_node;
      }
    }
  }
```

The function that inserts a node into a sparse matrix is `sp_ins_node`. This function is in `sparse.c`, which can be found on the CD at the end of the book. `sp_ins_node` is sent the `SPARSE_MATRIX` structure, a tuple describing the position of the node, and the value that is to be assigned to the node.

Appending

Appending nodes to the sparse matrix is the same as inserting when using doubly-linked lists. It would significantly complicate the code (which is already a tad convoluted) to use singly-linked lists for the node lists with the number of trailing pointers that would be required. Unless singly-linked lists are used, the concept of appending nodes is not really relevant.

Deleting Matrix Nodes

Deleting a matrix node is not as complicated as inserting the node. The primary effort in the `sp_del_node` function is to rebuild the links that are broken when the node is removed. This function is passed a `SPARSE_MATRIX` structure and a `SP_TUPLE` structure, which identifies the position of the node in the matrix. Once the node has been retrieved, the next step is to rebuild the linked lists around the node. Finally, any links in the header that pointed to the node, which is being deleted, need to be redirected.

Because of all this pointer rearrangement, it is necessary to remember that the nodes should only be deleted using a deletion function and not a direct call to `free`. The direct call to `free` will leave memory unreferenced (the stacks in the node are built using `malloc`) and the doubly-linked lists broken.

> **Caution**
>
> Always use the delete function associated with a structure built using `malloc` to be sure that all the memory is recovered.

Rebuilding Links

The delete function, `sp_del_node`, can be found in the file `sparse.c` on the CD at the end of this book. The function uses the following algorithm to rebuild links of a node that is to be deleted:

```
Retrieve the node to be deleted
Loop through the dimensions
  Set the next pointer on the previous node to the next pointer on the deleted node
  Set the previous pointer on the next node to the previous pointer on the deleted
   node
  If this node is the only node in the header's node list
    Set the header list element's first and last pointers to NULL
  If this node is in the header list element's first pointer
```

```
  Set the header list element's first pointer to the next pointer on the deleted
   node
If this node is in the header list element's last pointer
  Set the header list element's last pointer to the previous pointer on the deleted
   node
```

Note

It is important to remember that the header list element *for each dimension* needs to have the pointers to node lists updated whenever the node list changes. It is easy to forget with the number of pointers that need to be managed, but it is critical because these pointers are likely to be used and must not fall out of date. If the node list is updated and the header list element pointers are not, attempts to traverse the node list may fail. If nodes are removed (particularly nodes that are the top of the node list) and the header list is not updated, attempts to access the node list would fail.

The actual code that implements this algorithm is shown below without any of the parameter checks that are included in sp_del_node:

```
/* retrieve the node to be deleted */
  del_node = sp_retrieve_node(sp, tuple);
  if ((del_node == (SP_NODE *)NULL) ||
      (sp->error_no != SP_NOERR))
  {
    return;
  }

  /* rearrange the pointers around this node in the existing
     lists in each dimension */
  for (curr_dim = 0; curr_dim < sp->dimensions; curr_dim++)
  {
    next_node = *((SP_NODE **)(del_node->dimension_stack +
                               (2 * curr_dim)));
    prev_node = *((SP_NODE **)(del_node->dimension_stack +
                               (2 * curr_dim) + 1));

    /* Set the next pointer on the prev_node to next_node */
    *((SP_NODE **)(prev_node->dimension_stack +
                  (2 * curr_dim))) = next_node;
```

```
    /* Set the previous pointer on the next_node to
       prev_node */
    *((SP_NODE **)(next_node->dimension_stack +
                   (2 * curr_dim) + 1)) = prev_node;

    /* The pointers in the header may be effected */
    header = *(SP_HDR_ELEMENT **)(del_node->hdr_stack +
                                  curr_dim);

    /* If this is the last node in the list then the first
       and last pointer in the header should be set to NULL */
    if ((next_node == prev_node) && (next_node = del_node))
    {

      header->first = (SP_NODE *)NULL;
      header->last = (SP_NODE *)NULL;
    }
    else
    {
      /* Adjust the first pointer if del_node was the head of
         the list */
      if (header->first == del_node)
      {
        header->first = next_node;
      }

      /* Adjust the last pointer if del_node was the tail of
         the list */
      if (header->last == del_node)
      {
        header->last = prev_node;
      }
    }
  }
```

Once the links have been rebuilt, all of the structures associated with the node can be freed and the node itself can be freed. This function doesn't return a value because there is nothing meaningful to return.

FIGURE 16.1
A graph of a simple Web site.

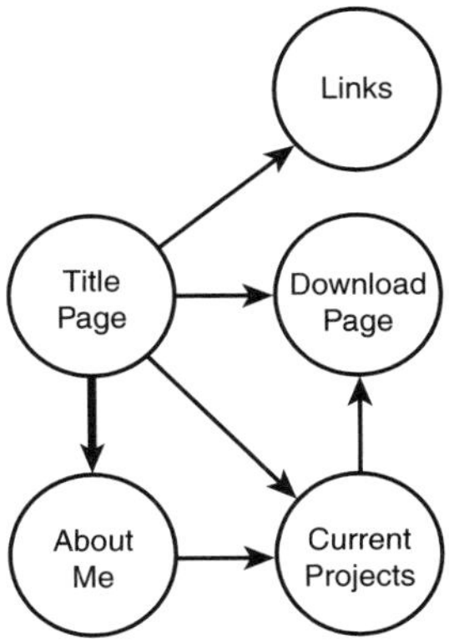

It is usually obvious that something is graph-like. Road maps, computer networks and electronic circuit diagrams all exhibit graph like properties. The general rule is that if it looks like a graph, it usually is one!

Directed Graphs

A *directed graph* is simply a graph where the edges between vertices have direction (see Figure 16.2). Each edge is one way, from source to destination vertex. An edge is defined as being comprised of a pair of vertices. In a directed graph, the order of the pair is important—typically an edge (v,w) is traversable from v to w only. Edges which are directed are drawn with an arrow on them showing the direction in which the vertices are connected.

FIGURE 16.2
A directed graph.

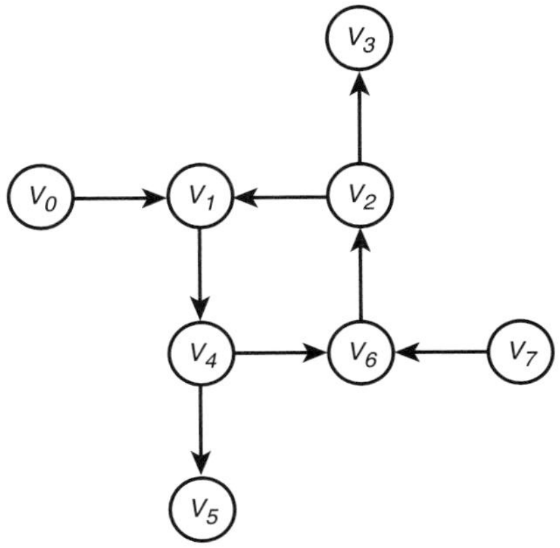

Undirectd Graphs

An *undirected graph* has edges which are traversable from either of the two vertices it lies between (see Figure 16.3). That is, an edge (v,w) implies that there is an edge (w,v). Edges in an undirected graph are not marked with an arrow, implying that the can be traversed in either direction. The indegree of a vertex in an undirected graph is the same as its degree.

FIGURE 16.3
An undirected graph.

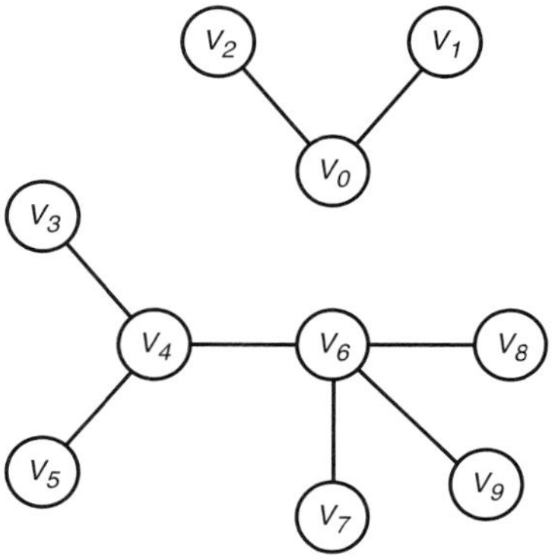

Undirected graphs can be described as being *complete* if every vertex in a complete graph has an edge to all other vertices as shown in Figure 16.4.

FIGURE 16.4
A complete undirected graph.

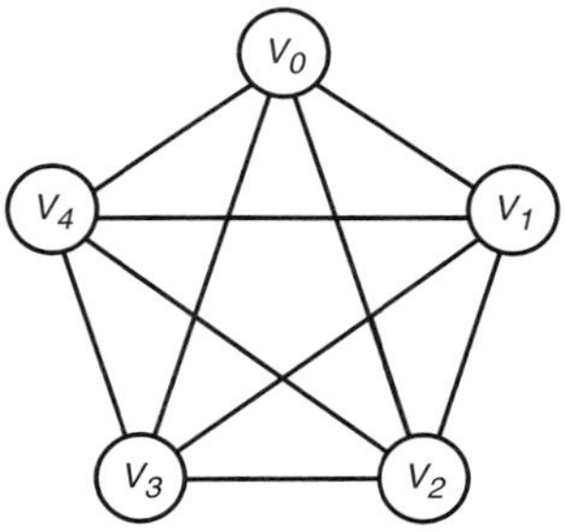

Connected Graphs

An undirected graph is said to be *connected* when there is a path, using any number of edges, from any one vertex to all other vertices. The example in Figure 16.5 has this property.

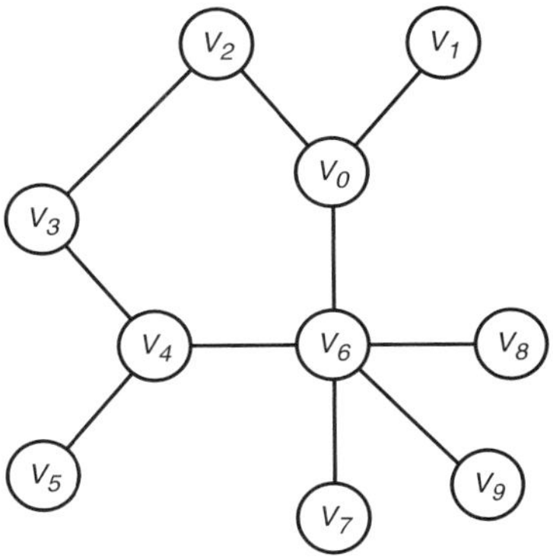

FIGURE 16.5
An undirected connected graph.

For directed graphs, it is a little more convoluted. When, like with an undirected connected graph, there is a path from any one vertex to all other vertices, the graph can be described as being *strongly connected* (see Figure 16.6).

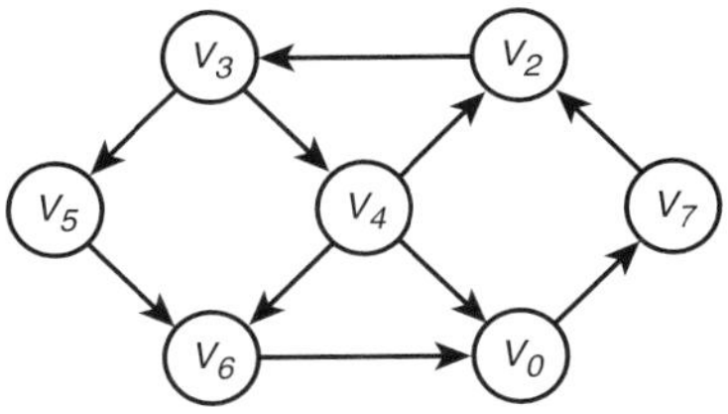

FIGURE 16.6
A directed strongly connected graph.

A directed graph can be described as being *weakly connected*. Directed weakly connected graphs do not have a path from every vertex to every other, but when the direction of the edges is ignored (that is, if it were treated as an undirected graph) the graph would be connected (see Figure 16.7).

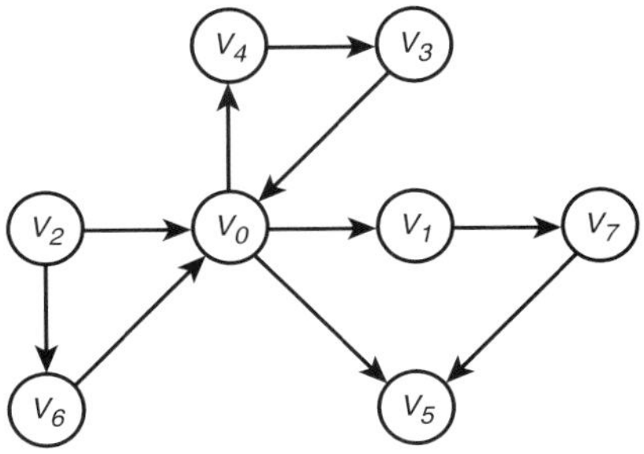

FIGURE 16.7
A directed weakly connected graph.

Graphs that are not undirected connected graphs or directed graphs which are strongly or weakly connected are simply described as being unconnected graphs.

Dense and Sparse Graphs

An important property of a graph is how *dense* or *sparse* it is. A graph in which every vertex is connected to only a small proportion of the vertices present in the graph is known as a sparse graph. The opposite of this, where each vertex is connected to a large proportion of the other vertices is dense.

For a known graph it is easy to determine how dense or sparse it is. You can do this by examining the average degree of the vertices. In a graph that is built dynamically it is more difficult. How dense or sparse the graph is affects how it can best be stored in memory and the running time of any algorithms that will work upon it. Predicting whether a graph would be best considered as being dense or sparse depnds on what the graph will represent. Real-life networks are typically sparse.

Note

For more detailed information on sparse matrices, see Chapter 15, "Sparse Matrix."

When implementing graphs, it is important to be able to determine or predict how dense a graph will be before it is used. If adjacency lists are used, more memory will be required to store dense graphs. If the graph is likely to be dense, it is usually more efficient to store the graph as an adjacency matrix.

Cyclic and Acyclic Graphs

A *cycle* is a path that begins and ends at the same vertex. A graph in which there is a cycle is said to be a *cyclic graph*. The opposite is an *acyclic graph*, which is a graph containing no cycles. Both directed and undirected graphs can be described as cyclic and acyclic. Undirected graphs that don't contain any cycles are trees (see Figures 16.8 and 16.9). Cycles are also known as circuits.

Euler circuits are cycles where every edge of a graph is traversed exactly once. There is a technique using a depth-first search to find such cycles. Most people are aware of this kind of cycle: They are commonly used as simple puzzles where a wireframe picture must be drawn without removing pen from paper. Similarly, *Euler paths* are paths that traverse every edge of a graph exactly once but not beginning and ending at the same vertex. A solution to finding an Euler circuit or path in a graph is presented later in this chapter.

FIGURE 16.8
An undirected cyclic graph.

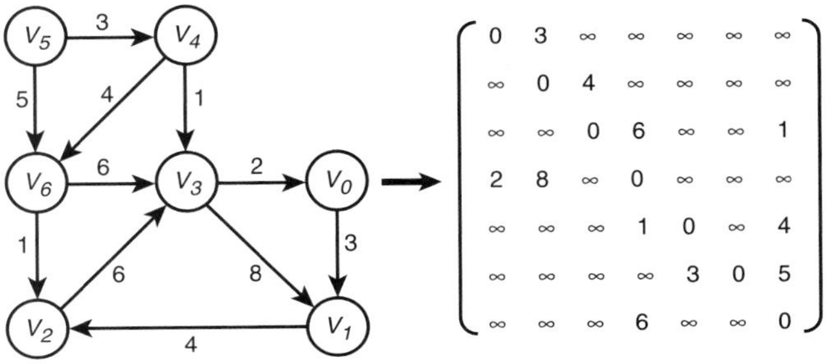

FIGURE 16.9
An undirected acyclic graph.

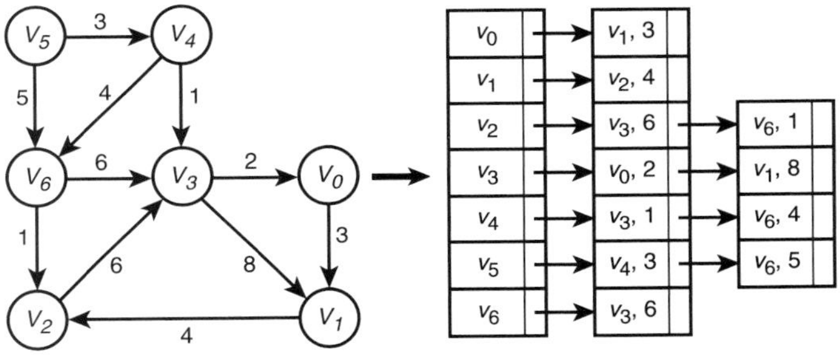

Representing Graphs

How a graph is best represented as a data structure depends heavily on how dense the graph will be. There are two main approaches: adjacency matrices and adjacency lists. Neither work well for all graphs.

For dense graphs, an adjacency matrix uses considerably less memory than an adjacency list of the same graph. For sparse graphs it is reversed, with the adjacency lists being more efficient.

It is, therefore, important to be able to predict how dense or sparse a graph is going to be before a representation is picked.

Adjacency Matrices

An *adjacency matrix* can be used to represent a graph. Simply, it is a two-dimensional array with a row and column for each vertex. Edges between vertices are made by manipulating the contents of the array.

In order to create an edge (v,w) with a cost c, we simply make M[v,w]=c. An edge with a cost of infinity is the equivalent of no edge. M[v,v] are typically 0, there is no cost in moving from one vertex back to itself (see Figure 16.10).

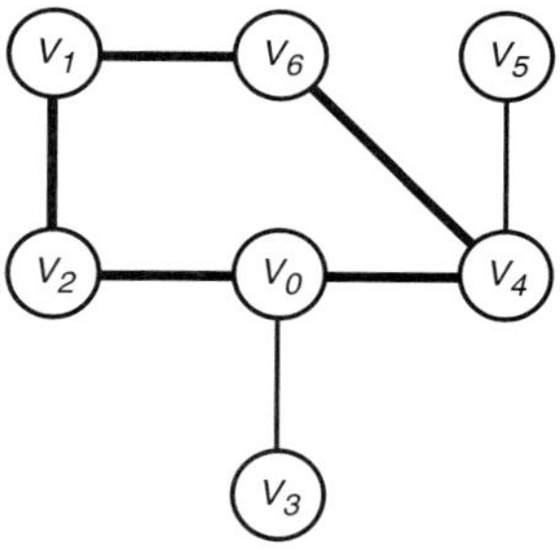

FIGURE 16.10
A sample graph and its adjacency matrix.

Adjacency Lists

Adjacency lists are a dynamic solution to graph representation. It is more efficient for sparse graphs because only the edges present in the graph are stored. All the memory allocated is used for present edges.

For each vertex in the graph, a linked list is maintained. Each element of the linked list represents a single edge and stores the cost and the destination. When adding an edge, a new element is added to the linked list (see Figure 16.11). The technique is similar to that used for sparse arrays.

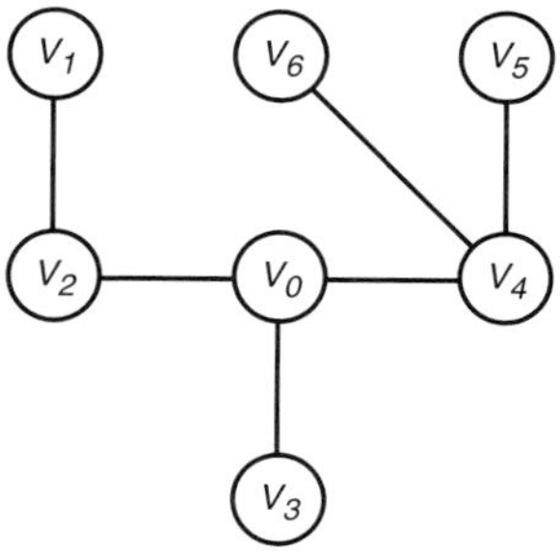

FIGURE 16.11
A sample graph and its adjacency list.

The companion CD-ROM contains a graph library including both of these representations. One of the aims of the library is to enable the same code to work with either representation. All the code examples in this chapter will work with either representation unmodified, unless the operation only makes sense for a particular kind of graph.

The `Graph` structure is the top-level structure that defines a graph to the library. This structure keeps track of all the vertices and edges that exist in a graph, whether it is represented as an adjacency matrix or as adjacency lists.

```
struct Graph
{
        int NumVertices;
        struct Graph_Vertex ** Vertices;
        struct Graph_Spec * Private;                    /* internal value */
};
```

There are two functions that relate only to this structure.

```
struct Graph * MakeGraph(enum GraphType T);
```

This function creates a new empty graph, and returns the pointer to the `Graph` structure, or `NULL` if memory cannot be allocated for it. The single parameter determines the way in which the graph is represented: `List` for adjacency lists or `Matrix` for an adjacency matrix.

```
int FreeGraph(struct Graph * G);
```

This function frees the memory allocated to a Graph structure, including all vertices and edges that have been added to it.

Vertices are represented using a `struct Graph_Vertex`. These structures can hold a tag that can either be of type `int` or `void *`. Graph vertices typically represent real things, and this tag value allows each vertex to be connected with the information of what it represents.

```
int AddVertex(struct Graph * G);
```

A `Graph` structure without vertices is completely useless. This function adds a single vertex to the graph structure and returns the index value, or an error code which is <0. The returned index is then used to identify the vertex in the graph. The index returned is only valid if no vertices are removed since the index was first set. The following snippet of C code shows how a graph can be made, a vertex created, and its tag value set.

```
int i;
struct Graph * G;

G=MakeGraph(List);
if (!G)
{
    /* not enough memory to create a graph structure */
}
i=AddVertex(G);
if (i<0)
```

```
{
    /* failed to add a vertex */
}
```

```
G->Vertices[i]->Tag.Num=42;
int RemoveVertex(struct Graph * G, int Index);
```

It is also necessary to be able to remove vertices. Any edges that lead to or from the vertex to be removed are also removed. When a vertex is removed, the vertices are re-indexed so that there is no hole where the newly removed vertex used to be.

```
int ConnectVertex(struct Graph * G, int Source, int Destination, int Cost);
```

This function adds a directed edge from the source vertex to the destination vertex of the given cost. This edge is one-way from the source to the destination. Adding an undirected edge can be done simply by adding an edge from `Source` to `Destination`, and then a second edge from `Destination` to `Source`. Connecting from a `Source` to a `Destination` vertex which already have an edge between them changes the cost of the previous edge to the `Cost` parameter.

```
int DisconnectVertex(struct Graph * G, int Source, int Destination);
```

This function removes an edge between `Source` and `Destination`. In an undirected graph you must also remember to remove the edge from `Destination` to `Source` as well.

Most of the algorithms that can be applied to graphs require some examination of edges between vertices. The way in which an edge is represented is dependent upon how the graph is represented. Adjacency matrices and adjacency lists store edges in a very different manner. In order to be able to examine the list of edges for both representations, these functions are provided. They work identically for both adjacency matrices and adjacency lists and they allow a single function to operate on both representations.

The `EdgeScan` structure holds the information for a single edge, as well as the information required by the `EdgeScanNext()` function to locate the next edge in the list.

```
struct EdgeScan
{
    struct Graph * G;
    int Cost;
    int Source;
    int Dest;
    union
    {
        void * Ptr;
        int Index;
```

```
    } Internal;    /* used internally to record position */
};
```

```
int EdgeScanStart(struct Graph * G, int Index, struct EdgeScan * EScan);
```

This function initializes an `EdgeScan` structure in preparation of listing the edges for a particular vertex determined by its index.

```
int EdgeScanEnd(struct EdgeScan * EScan);
```

This function brings an edge scan operation to its end, freeing up any resources inside the `EdgeScan` structure. Once this has been performed, the contents of the `EdgeScan` structure are no longer valid.

```
int EdgeScanNext(struct EdgeScan * EScan);
```

This function retrieves information for the next edge (or the first if `EdgeScanStart` just called) and sets the members of the `EdgeScan` structure. If the last edge has already been returned in this way, then >0 is returned. On success, 0 is returned.

The following code snippet shows how to examine the list of edges for a particular vertex.

```
/* G is a graph containing a number of vertices with edges between them */
struct EdgeScan E;

EdgeScanStart(G,i,&E);
while (EdgeScanNext(&E)==0)
{
    /* do something with the members of E */
}
EdgeScanEnd(&E);
```

Topological Sorting

Directed acyclic graphs can be used to represent events or states that must be reached in order, as shown in Figure 16.12. A typical use is a task network, used to define the required order of a number of tasks. In order to progress to a new task, its prerequisites must have been completed.

The vertices of such a graph are most likely not to be labeled in the order in which they need to be traversed. A *topological sort* will discover the order of traversal. Usually, the order determined will not be unique.

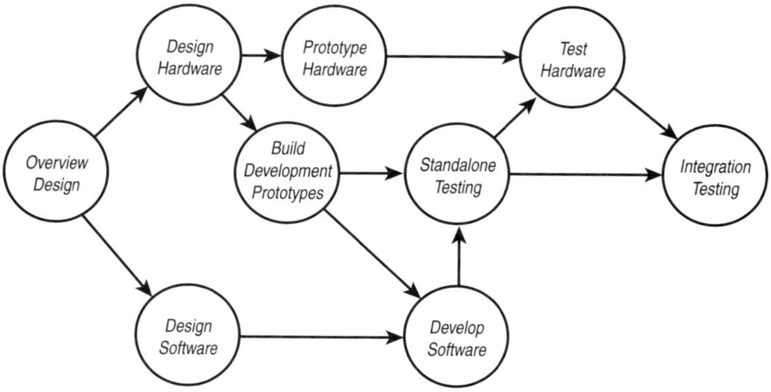

FIGURE 16.12
A task network.

Performing a topologic sort on a graph is fairly simple. A vertex with no incoming edges is a valid root vertex. This vertex and any edges leading away from it are then removed from the graph. We then look for another vertex without incoming edges. If none can be found, the graph contains a cycle and cannot be topologically sorted. The order in which the root vertices are selected is the result of the sort.

This algorithm can be implemented so that it is non-destructive and efficient when useful data structures are used effectively.

A root vertex has an indegree of 0. Removing a root vertex has the effect of reducing the indegree of any adjacent vertices by 1, potentially creating new root vertices. The most time-consuming part of this algorithm is finding root vertices. A linear search of the vertices would be very slow because it must be performed every time a vertex is removed.

A better approach is to use a queue of vertices of indegree 0. As edges are removed and new root vertices are created, they can be added to the queue as well. The order in which vertices are added to this queue is also the result of the topological sort.

First, we must create a table of the indegree of each vertex (see Listing 16.1). This can be done simply by examining the destination of every edge in the graph and incrementing a counter. This will take E, the number of edges in the graph, iterations to complete.

The table can now be examined to find the vertices we can use as the first root. Any vertices with indegree 0 are added to a queue. For this implementation, I have chosen to implement the queue in an array. This array is used to hold the new root vertices to be stepped through and to return the result.

LISTING 16.1 Building an Indegree Table

```
void InitIndegreeTable(struct Graph * G, int * itable)
{
  /*
    Build an indegree table from graph G
    itable must be at least G->NumVertices in length
  */

  int i;
  struct EdgeScan E;

  for (i=0;i<G->NumVertices;i++) {
    EdgeScanStart(G,i,&E);
    while (EdgeScanNext(&E)==0)
    {
      itable[E.Dest]++;
    }
    EdgeScanEnd(&E);
  }
}


int TopologicalSort(struct Graph * G, int ** sorted)
{
  /*
    Perform a topological sort on graph G, creating
    an array of G->NumVertices integers and returning
    it in *sorted.

    Returns 0 on success,
    <0 on error (GRAPH_BADPARAM, GRAPH_OUTOFMEM, GRAPH_BADGRAPH)
  */

  int first, last, i;
  int * queue;
  int * itable;
  struct EdgeScan E;

  if (!G || !sorted) return GRAPH_BADPARAM;
  queue=malloc(sizeof(int)*G->NumVertices);
  itable=malloc(sizeof(int)*G->NumVertices);
  if (!queue || !itable)
  {
```

LISTING 16.1 continued

```
    free(queue);free(itable);
    return GRAPH_OUTOFMEM;
  }

  InitIndegreeTable(G,itable);
  last=0;first=0;

  /* search for vertices with indegree 0 */
  for (i=0;i<G->NumVertices;i++)
  {
    if (itable[i]==0) Enqueue(i);
  }

  /* while there are still vertices with indegree 0... */
  while (last!=first)
  {
    Dequeue(i);
    EdgeScanStart(G,i,&E);
    while (EdgeScanNext(&E)==0)
    {
      itable[E.Dest]--;
      if (itable[E.Dest]==0) Enqueue(E.Dest);
    }
    EdgeScanEnd(&E);
  }

  free(itable);

  /* if we haven't dequeued G->NumVertices elements, we have a cyclic graph */
  if (first!=G->NumVertices)
  {
    free(queue); return GRAPH_BADGRAPH;
  }

  *sorted=queue;
  return 0;
}
```

This implementation is reasonably efficient requiring O(V+E) iterations to complete. It is somewhat wasteful because a lot of time is spent building the indegree table and finding the first root vertices and adding them to the queue. Adding the indegree of each vertex to the graph data structure would improve the running time of this algorithm at the cost of slightly greater memory usage and a slight speed reduction when adding or removing edges.

Matching

One of the more common problems which can be solved using graphs is that of matching elements from one set to elements in another distinct set. The data are modeled using a specialized graph to simplify the problem. A *bipartite graph* is a graph where the vertices are separated into two distinct sets A and B such that edges connect each vertex in A to vertices in B. The edges represent some relationship between the two sets, like "v_a likes v_b" or "v_a is skilled in v_b."

A matching is any graph which connects set A to set B. The number of matchings which are valid depends on the data being represented. Not all the possible edges may be valid because an edge represents a relationship between vertices of the two sets. A *maximum matching* is a matching which connects the largest number of vertices in set A to the largest number of vertices in set B.

For instance, a project will contain a number of different tasks, each requiring different skills. There will be a number of people on the team with varying skills available to work on this project. The problem would be to allow every task to be completed in such a way that all the staff are working on tasks which suit their skills. This would be a maximum matching.

The staff members are each represented as a vertex, as are the tasks to be completed. Although both sets are represented by vertices in the bipartite graph, they are distinct sets, shown in the diagrams as two columns. Edges are added from staff members to tasks for which they have the skills to complete (see Figure 16.13).

The algorithm works by using an initial matching which might not be optimal. It begins by examining all the vertices in set A to determine whether any do not have any edges and if so labels them (see Figure 16.14). If there are none, the matching is already optimal. In the example, the initial matching has only one vertex in set A without any edges. This is "Steve" and is marked with an asterisk.

For every newly labeled vertex V, every unlabeled vertex in set B to which there is an edge not in the initial matching is labeled with V. The first time this is done, any vertex marked with an asterisk (any vertex in set A that does not have any edges) is classed as newly labeled.

FIGURE 16.13
A bipartite graph of staff and tasks.

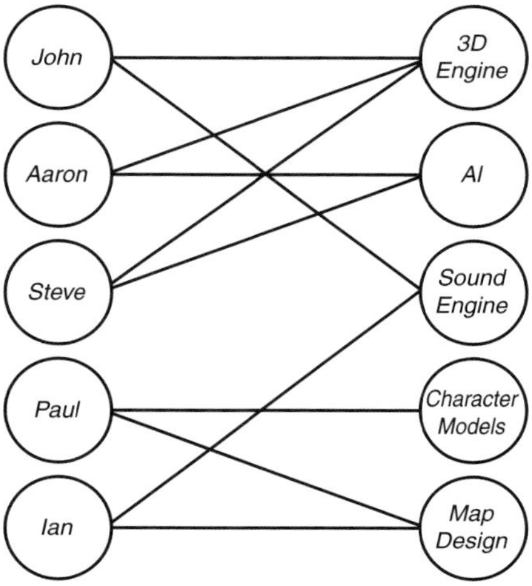

FIGURE 16.14
An initial matching.

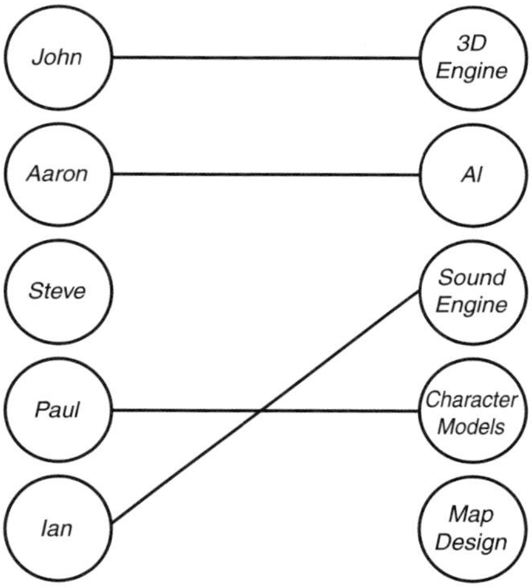

We do something similar with the newly labeled vertices in B. For every newly labeled vertex V, every unlabelled vertex in set A to which there is an edge in the initial matching is labeled with V (the sequence of Figures 16.15a through 16.15e shows this process). These two steps are repeated until no more labeling can be done.

If there is a vertex in B which is labeled but does not have any edges going to it in the initial matching then it isn't optimal. If the matching is optimal, we simply stop here.

FIGURE 16.15a
The stages of labeling—Diagram a.

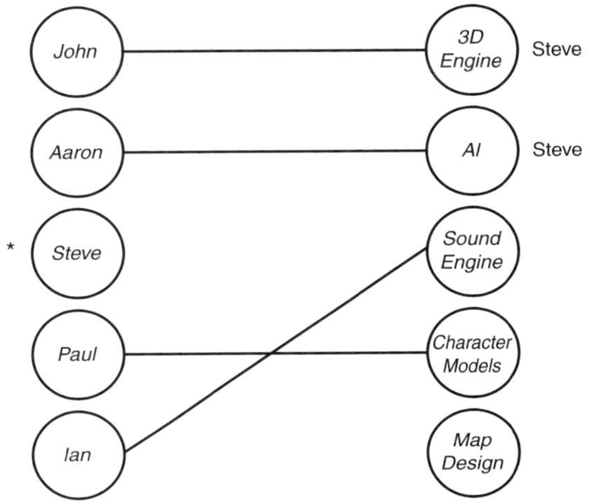

FIGURE 16.15b
The stages of labeling—Diagram b.

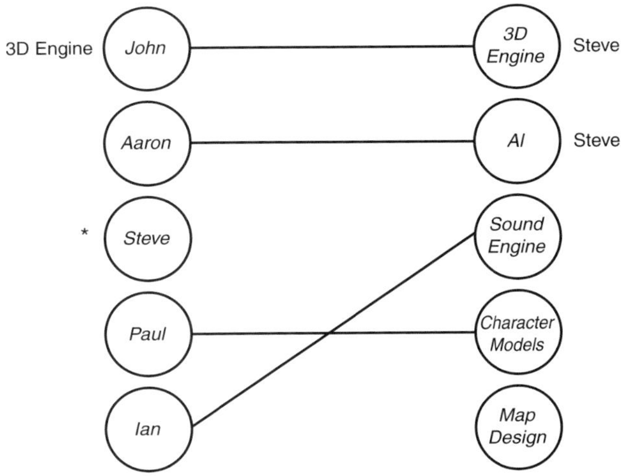

An alternating path can be found by traversing vertices starting from the vertex in B which is labeled but not in the initial matching as in Figure 16.16. The path moves from a vertex to its label, stopping when an unlabelled vertex is reached.

A maximum matching can be found using the initial matching and this alternating path. The solution is made up of all the edges in the initial matching that are not in the alternating path, and all the edges in the alternating path that are not in the initial matching, as you see in Figure 16.17.

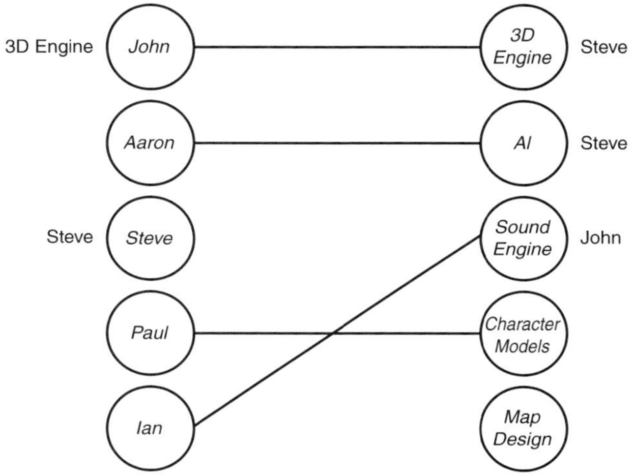

FIGURE 16.15C
The stages of labeling—Diagram c.

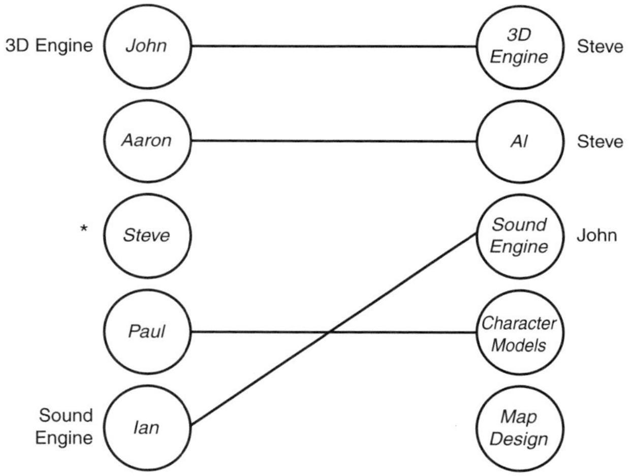

FIGURE 16.15D
The stages of labeling—Diagram d.

A good approach to implementing this algorithm is to use a pair of stacks and a pair of tables. The stacks are used to efficiently identify newly labeled vertices. Elements are popped off one stack and newly labeled vertices are simply pushed onto the other. Two stacks are used because we need to differentiate between newly labeled vertices in set A and set B. The tables are used to hold the initial matching and the labeling for each vertex.

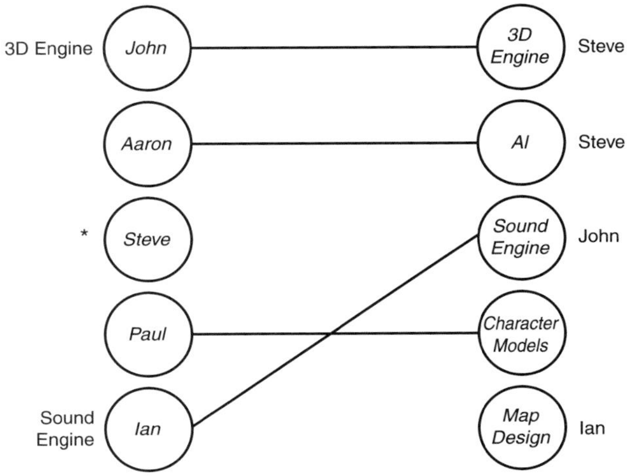

FIGURE 16.15e
The stages of labeling—Diagram e.

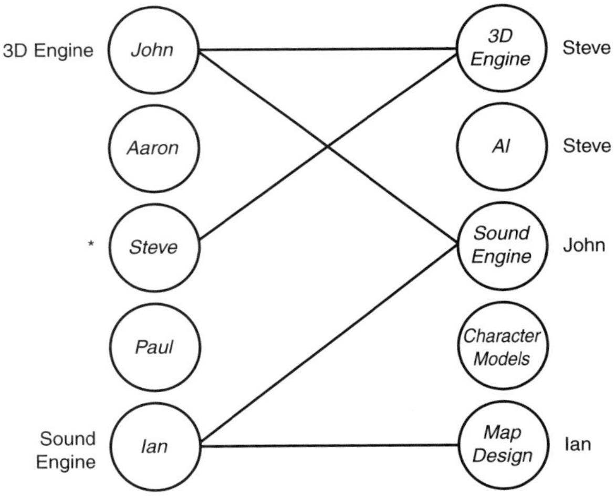

FIGURE 16.16
The alternating path.

A fairly decent initial matching can be found by adding as many edges as possible (see Table 16.1). The nearer to an optimal solution the initial matching is, the sooner the solution will be found. One approach to this is to linearly select every vertex in the graph and add any edge from that vertex to any other vertex which doesn't already have an edge going to it. At most, this will take E (the number of edges in the graph) iterations. This is likely to be fairly close to an optimal matching.

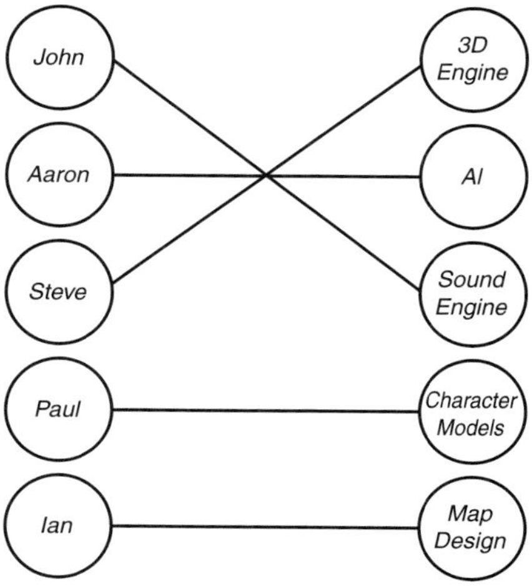

FIGURE 16.17
A maximum matching.

TABLE 16.1 Initial Matching

Vertex	*Dest*	*Vertex*	*Dest*
John	3D engine	3D engine	John
Aaron	AI	AI	Aaron
Steve	none	Sound engine	Ian
Paul	Models	Models	Paul
Ian	Sound engine	Levels	none

Labeling is performed using the stacks. The table to hold the labels is initialized so that each vertex is unlabelled. The initial matching is examined and any edges in set A that aren't connected to another vertex are pushed onto the first stack and labeled with some null value.

First, vertices are popped off the first stack and any connected vertices not in the initial matching without labels are pushed onto the second stack and labeled. Then, vertices are popped off the second stack and any connected vertices in the initial matching without labels are pushed onto the first stack and labeled.

This continues until both stacks are empty. At this point, no more labeling is possible (see Table 16.2). In the worst case almost every vertex would be pushed onto one of the stacks. In practice it depends on the initial matching selected and the graph. The closer the initial matching is to the maximum matching, the fewer vertices need to be processed.

TABLE 16.2 Result of Labeling

Vertex	*Dest*	*Vertex*	*Dest*
John	3D engine	3D engine	Steve
Aaron	AI	AI	Steve
Steve		Sound engine	John
Paul		Models	
Ian	Sound engine	Levels	Ian

The initial matching can then be examined for unlabeled vertices in set B to which there is no edge. Using the label table, the path can be found (see Table 16.3). A simple but a little inefficient approach is to follow the path and create a new table holding only the path.

TABLE 16.3 Alternating Path

Vertex	*Dest*	*Vertex*	*Dest*
John	3D engine	3D engine	Steve
Aaron	–1	AI	–1
Steve	3D engine	Sound engine	John
Paul	–1	Models	–1
Ian	Sound engine	Levels	Ian

The maximum matching is now simple to find. The initial matching table and the path table can be compared. Where the destination vertex in the path table is –1 (as in, not in the path) the edge indicated by the initial matching is added to the solution. Where the destination vertex in the path table is different from that for the corresponding vertex in the initial matching, that edge is added as well (see Table 16.4). These edges are all undirected.

TABLE 16.4 Maximum Matching

Vertex	*Dest*	*Vertex*	*Dest*
John	Sound engine	3D engine	Steve
Aaron	AI	AI	AI
Steve	3D engine	Sound engine	John
Paul	Models	Models	Paul
Ian	Levels	Levels	Ian

Depth First Search

Many useful operations that can be performed on graphs require a search of the vertices in the graph by following edges. Typically, this is done in a fashion similar to exhaustive searches in trees.

A depth-first search (DFS) on a graph is essentially the same to preorder traversal in a tree. A root vertex is selected, and processing is performed on the root. Then, every vertex adjacent to the root is recursively processed in the same way. The difference is that we must make sure that a vertex that has already been visited is not revisited later. This is achieved by maintaining a table of vertices which have been visited. An adjacent vertex is passed into the recursive function only if it has not already been visited. The following code is a template for a depth-first search. Although it successfully traverses a depth-first search tree through a graph, it does no processing.

```
void GenericDepthFirstSearch(struct Graph * G,int Index,int * Visited)
{
  /* Visited points to an array of integers with G->NumVertices
     elements, initialized to 0 before the first call
  */
  struct EdgeScan EScan;

  Visited[Index]=true;
  /* do processing here! */
  EdgeScanStart(G,Index,&EScan);
  while (!EdgeScanNext(&EScan))
  {
    if (!Visited[EScan.Dest]) DepthFirstSearch( G, EScan.Dest, Visited);
  }
  EdgeScanEnd(&EScan);
}
```

The running time for a depth-first search on a graph is typically O. Each edge is examined to determine whether its destination has been visited.

In actuality, the depth-first search follows a tree structure through the graph. Figure 16.18 shows a possible depth-first search. The solid lines are edges which have been traversed by the depth-first search. The broken lines are edges which have been examined but not traversed because the destination vertex has already been visited. The depth-first search begins at v_0 which has a single outgoing edge going to v_1. The edge from v_1 to v_3 is then traversed. The edge from v_3 to v_0 is drawn as a broken line because v_0 has already been visited and that edge is examined but not traversed. The tree can easily be seen if you ignore the untraversed edges (the broken lines). The search continues down through the tree until all vertices have been visited.

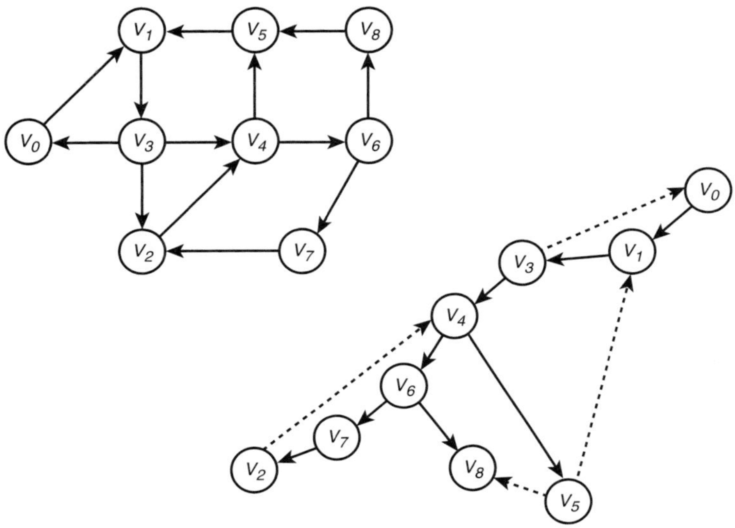

FIGURE 16.18
A tree traversed in a graph using DFS.

The problem with the generic depth-first search function above is that in an unconnected undirected graph or a weakly connected directed graph, there will be some vertices that are not reached. Also, from a software perspective the passing of Visited on the first invocation and trusting that it is allocated and initialized are far from desirable. Both problems can be solved with a wrapper function.

This top-level function allocates Visited and performs the first invocation of the function that performs the actual depth-first search. When the function returns, each vertex in the tree from the root vertex has been processed. If the graph is connected, all vertices will have been marked as visited.

If the graph isn't connected (or strongly connected), another depth-first search can be performed by the wrapper function starting from an unvisited vertex. This can be performed as many times as required until all vertices have been visited.

This operation could become very expensive. The worst way in which it can be performed is to do a linear search of Visited, starting from index 0 every time. Even if the graph were connected, V iterations would be required to prove that there were no unvisited vertices. There are two simple improvements for these problems.

The first is to maintain a count of vertices that have been visited in addition to the Visited array. The depth-first search function would increment this counter. The wrapper function can now easily verify that each vertex has been visited. This keeps the run time on connected graphs down to O(E).

The second improves the running time in the case of very unconnected graphs. Instead of resetting a counter to 0 and examining the Visited array to find unvisited vertices, the counter is set to 0 initially. On subsequent calls to the depth-first search function, the counter is not reset, and the search for unvisited vertices continues from the next index after the previous root vertex. This ensures that even in the worst case for this check (where there are no connections in the graph) only V iterations are required. This makes the overall worst-case running time to be O(V+E).

The two simplest uses of depth-first searches are to determine whether a graph is connected (or strongly connected for directed graphs) and to determine whether there is a path between two vertices. The first, determining connectedness, is a simple modification of a generic depth-first search wrapper. The depth-first search function shown in Listing 16.2 should only be invoked once. After it has returned, either all vertices will have been visited and the graph is connected or there are unvisited vertices and the graph is not connected. Directed graphs, when used with this technique, will return true when they are strongly connected. Weakly connected and unconnected directed graphs will both fail this test.

Determining whether there is a path between two vertices using a depth-first search is equally simple. In many situations, knowing whether there is a path from vertex u to v is useful. Using a depth-first search will be completed in less than O time. A shortest path algorithm could be used to determine if there is a path from vertex u to v but would take much longer to execute—they are ill suited to this simple task.

LISTING 16.2 Depth-First Search

```
/* An implementation of a depth-first search to determine if there is a
   path (of any length) from S to D. Visited is required to avert infinitely
   moving around cycles, must be sizeof(int)*NumberOfVertices), and be
   initialised with zeros before first executing.
*/
int AVC_Inner(struct Graph * G, int S, int D,int * Visited)
{
  int retval;
  struct EdgeScan EScan;

  retval=0;
  Visited[S]=1;
  EdgeScanStart(G,S,&EScan);
  while (EdgeScanNext(&EScan)==0 && retval==0)
  {
    if (EScan.Dest==D) retval=0;
    else if (!Visited[EScan.Dest]) retval=AVC_Inner(G,EScan.Dest,D,Visited);
  }
```

LISTING 16.2 continued

```
  EdgeScanEnd(&EScan);
  return retval;
}

int AreVerticesConnected(struct Graph * G,int Source, int Dest)
{
  int * Visited;
  int i, retval;

  if (!G || Source<0 || Dest<0 ||
      Source>=G->NumVertices || Dest>=G->NumVertices) return GRAPH_BADPARAM;

  Visited=malloc(sizeof(int)*G->NumVertices);
  if (!Visited) return GRAPH_OUTOFMEM;
  for (i=0;i<G->NumVertices;i++) Visited[i]=0;

  retval=AVC_Inner(G,Source,Dest,Visited);
  free(Visited);

  return retval;
}
```

The wrapper function is used to initialize the Visited structure. The depth-first search function is invoked using u as the root. The destination vertex is passed. As each vertex is visited by the depth-first search function, it is compared to v. The worst case running time of this technique is O(E), as is typical with depth-first search functions.

A breadth-first search could also be used for this task. Such a search adds destination vertices to a queue. Adjacent vertices are added to the back of the queue. This, too, has an O(E) running time. In practice, it is unlikely to have a noticeable improvement over a depth-first search. Where u and v are close together, a breadth-first search is likely to locate v in fewer iterations than a depth-first search. The opposite is also true.

Non-Recursive Depth-First Search

Recursive functions are not ideal in many situations. For a deep recursion, a lot of the executables stack can be used. There is also the overhead of pushing and popping parameters the compiler deems necessary at each level; the more information passed, the more stack space is required. In most cases, the overhead is small, and so the simpler recursive implementation is adequate. In situations where stack space is limited or the depth of the recursion is very large, it is definitely more sensible not to use recursion at all. A depth-first search, like any recursive function, can be performed without having the function call itself (eating up stack).

This is achieved by maintaining a stack in main memory. Many computer architectures have specific features to access one or more stacks. Operating systems and programs that run on them use these features. They are usually limited in size, much smaller than the total memory available. Writing portable code is never as easy as it might appear, because it usually requires much general understanding of the limitations of most platforms. This is one such case: Some systems might allow immense stacks, whereas others will not. This can, of course, be worked around by implementing a stack of your own in main memory.

The largest concern is that for very large graphs with many thousand vertices the programs stack can overflow. Some modern compilers and operating system combinations do not have a very large stack at all. The number of recursions before the stack overflows can be as small as 80,000 or as large as several million. On less recent systems (such as 16-bit MS-DOS and similar platforms) the stack could even be limited to less than 3 or 4 thousand deep recursion, depending on the number of arguments passed. The total amount of memory in most systems is sufficient to contain a stack of millions of elements, typically much larger than the stack space available to the program.

Stacks can be implemented both simply and efficiently, and main memory is usually large compared to the program stack available. The search is performed by pushing onto the stack the index of each vertex adjacent to the current vertex. The next root is selected simply by popping a vertex from the stack. If the stack is empty, a new root is selected that has not been visited and the search continues from there until all vertices have been visited. The function below is a template for performing a depth-first search using a stack data structure instead of recursion. This function does no actual processing except traversing the depth-first search tree.

```
void Stack_DFS(struct Graph * G)
{
    int V;
    int * Visited;
    struct EdgeScan E;
    struct Stack * S;

    InitStack(S);
    Visited=malloc(sizeof(int)*G->NumVertices);
    if (!Visited) return;
    for (V=0;V<G->NumVertices;V++) Visited[V]=0;
```

```
for (V=0;V<G->NumVertices;V++)
{
do {
        if (Visited[V]) continue;
        Visited[V]=1;

        /* do processing for V here */

        EdgeScanStart(G,V,&E);
        while (EdgeScanNext(&E)==0)
        {
            if (!Visited[E.Dest]) Push(E.Dest,S)
        }
        if (IsEmpty(S)) V=-1;
        else V=Pop(S);
    } while (V!=-1);
}
free(Visited);
FreeStack(S);
}
```

Strongly Connected Components

Weakly connected directed graphs have subgraphs which are strongly connected. These are referred to as strongly connected components. A directed graph with only one strongly connected component is strongly connected.

It is possible to locate the strongly connected components of a directed graph, or determine if it is strongly connected using two depth-first searches.

The first search is performed on G. Each vertex is numbered in the order it is traversed. Whenever a dead end is reached, the search is continued at any unvisited vertex and number continues from there. Figure 16.19 shows the result of the depth-first spanning forest and the numbering on G.

The graph G is then transformed to make a new graph G_t by reversing the direction of every edge. A depth-first search on G_t is performed starting from the vertex with the smallest number given in the previous search. When a dead end has been reached, the search begins from the vertex with the smallest number until all vertices have been visited.

Each tree in the depth-first spanning forest found by the search on G_t, shown in Figure 16.20, is a strongly connected component.

FIGURE 16.19
The graph G and its DFS spanning forest.

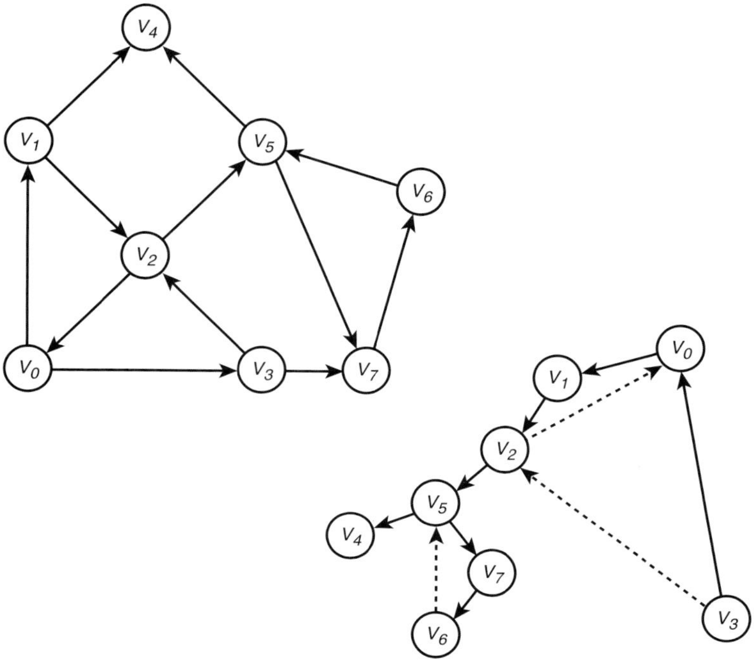

For two vertices to be strongly connected there must be a path from u to v and from v to u in both G and G_t. The depth-first spanning forest for G and G_t determine whether that is the case.

The depth-first search on G, which numbers the vertices, produces a depth-first spanning forest. Each strongly connected component must exist in the same depth-first spanning tree. Furthermore, if there is a path from a vertex u to a vertex v, u was traversed before v was, and so u has a smaller number than v.

Traversing an edge in G_t from a vertex u to a vertex v is the same as traversing an edge from v to u in G. Again, a depth-first spanning forest is produced, and again each vertex in a strongly connected component must be in the same depth-first spanning tree. But there is a subtle difference.

The depth-first search on G_t begins with the smallest numbered vertex. If we reach a vertex after this in the same depth-first spanning tree, we know there is not only a path from u to v in G, but also a path from u to v in G_t. G_t is the transpose of G, and so there must be a path from u to v and from v to u in G (re-reversing the edge traversed in G_t). Therefore, u and v must be strongly connected.

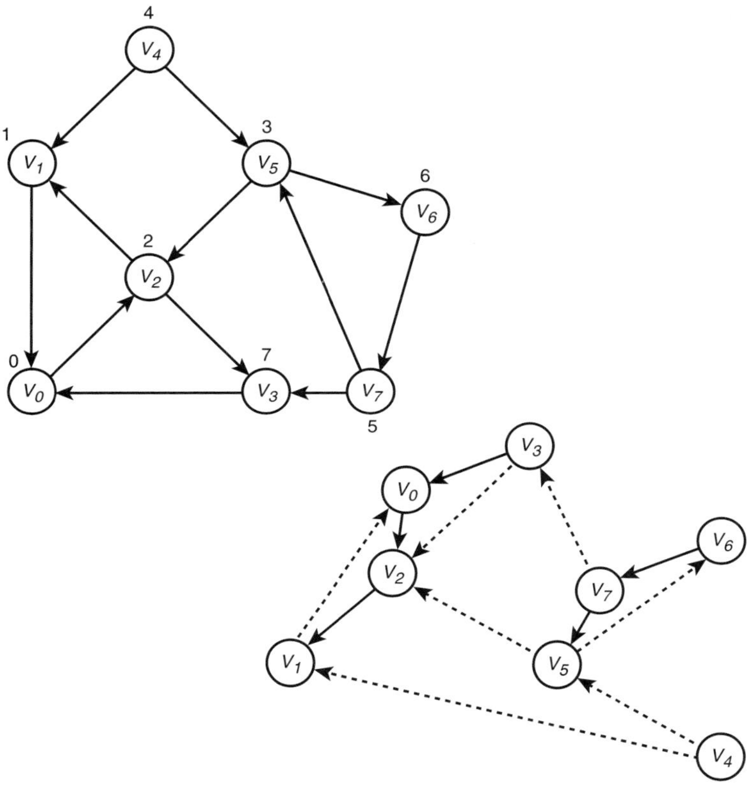

FIGURE 16.20
The graph Gt and its DFS spanning forest.

This means that the depth-first spanning forest in G_t identifies all the strongly connected components in G.

Finding Euler Paths and Circuits

An Euler path traverses every edge in a graph once. An Euler circuit traverses every edge in a graph once and begins and ends at the same vertex (see Figure 16.21). Most people are familiar with this concept through a simple puzzle—drawing a shape made out of lines without removing the pen from the paper.

More seriously, finding Euler paths and circuits does have more practical applications. It can be used to locate a route through some real-life network in such a way that it touches each edge, which might represent a road for instance, exactly once. There are some properties which a graph must satisfy in order for there to be an Euler path or circuit.

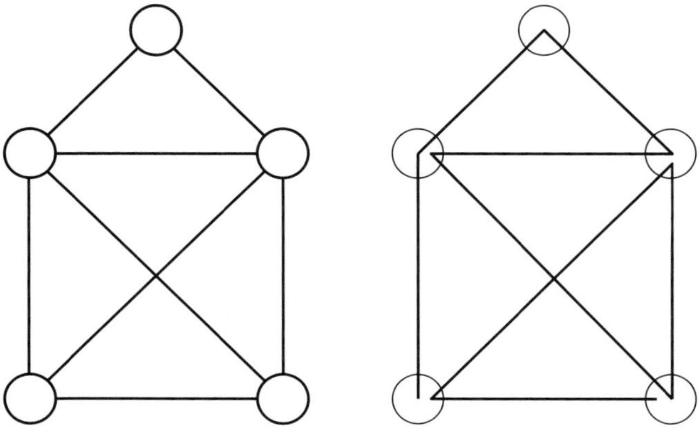

FIGURE 16.21
A graph which has an Euler path, and the path itself.

For an Euler circuit, every vertex must have an even degree. If any vertex has an odd degree, it is impossible to form an Euler circuit. Every vertex must be entered and left using only untraversed edges. This can never happen with an vertex of odd degree because it can be entered, but all edges leading from it will have already been traversed.

For an Euler path to be possible, there must be exactly two vertices with odd degree. The path must begin and end at a vertex with odd degree because only those vertices can be visited an odd number of times.

A further obvious restriction is required. The graph need not be connected. The graph must contain only one connected subgraph however. If more than one exists, there cannot be either an Euler circuit or a path because some of the edges can never be reached.

Any graph which satisfies the preceding conditions must have an Euler path or Euler circuit. Such a graph is described as being Eulerian.

Finding an Euler circuit or path can be done using something similar to a depth-first search. The following algorithm is used to find an Euler circuit, but it can be modified simply to find an Euler path in any graph that satisfies the conditions for their presence.

Figures 16.22 to 16.25 show an example of this algorithm. The algorithm works by locating cycles within the graph using something similar to a depth-first search. These cycles can then be combined to form a single cycle which traverses all edges in the graph—an Euler cycle. The algorithm can be described as the following steps:

1. Initialize a list of cycles.
2. Perform a depth-first search, until all edges have been removed from the graph. Add the current vertex number to the current path. Traverse an edge performing the search

and remove it. If there is no edge to traverse, add the current path to the list of cycles, and continue to search from the first vertex with an untraversed edge.

3. Combine the paths and cycles together to form a single Euler circuit.

FIGURE 16.22
Original graph.

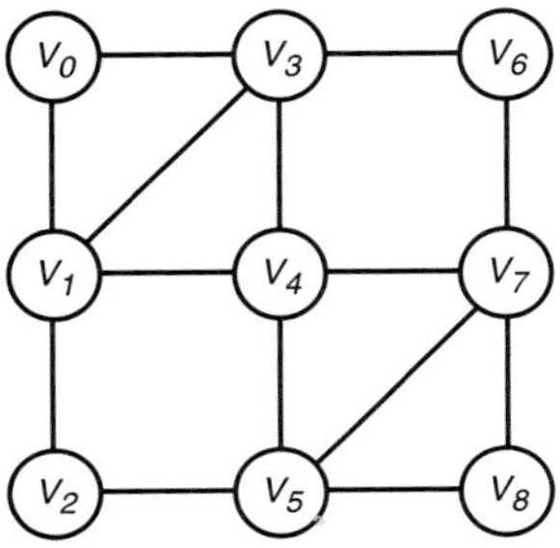

The cycles selected have been chosen to highlight the algorithm. The depth-first search begins at v_0 and on successive iterations visits v_1 and v_3. After v_3, v_0 is reached and a cycle is found. The cycle v_0, v_1, v_4, v_3, v_0 is stored.

FIGURE 16.23
The graph with the path 0→1→4→3→0 removed.

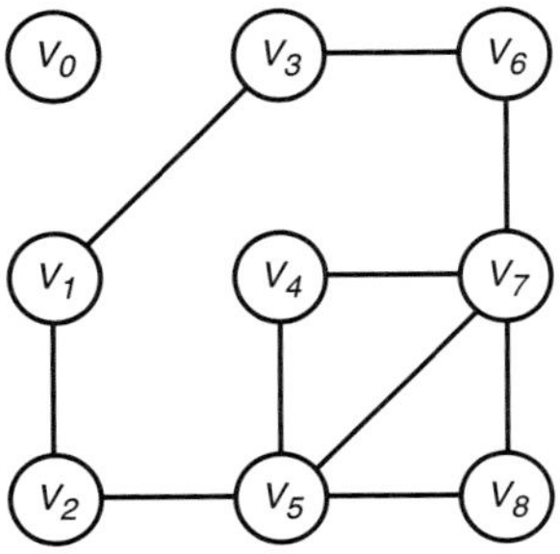

The depth-first search is then continued at the first vertex which has edges leading away from it. In this case it is v_1. The depth-first search can find the cycle v_1, v_2, v_5, v_4, v_7, v_6, v_3, v_1 which is added to the list of cycles. Figure 16.24 shows the graph without the second cycle found.

The next depth-first search will begin at v_5 and will find the cycle v_5, v_7, v_8, v_5. At this point, there are no more edges which have not been traversed and we have three cycles.

FIGURE 16.24
The graph with the path 1→2→5→4→7→6→3→1 removed.

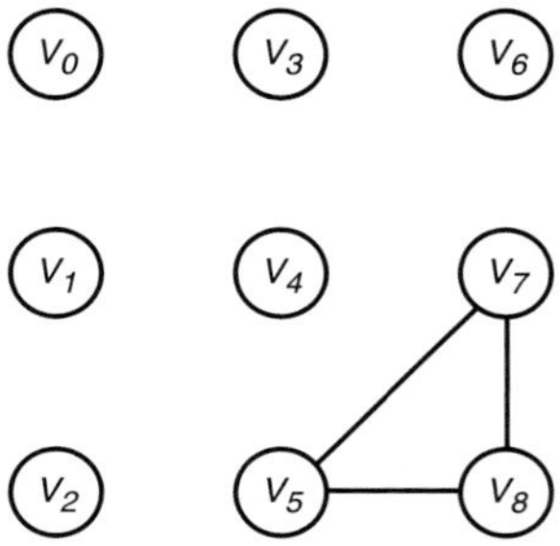

The complete cycle can be found by inserting the cycles into one another. A cycle which begins and ends at a vertex can be inserted into another cycle or path in place of that vertex. In this case, the cycle $v_1, v_2, v_5, v_4, v_7, v_6, v_5, v_1$ can be inserted into the cycle v_0, v_1, v_4, v_3, v_0 in place of the v_1. The same can be done with the remaining cycle in order to get the complete Euler circuit.

FIGURE 16.25
The Euler circuit found.

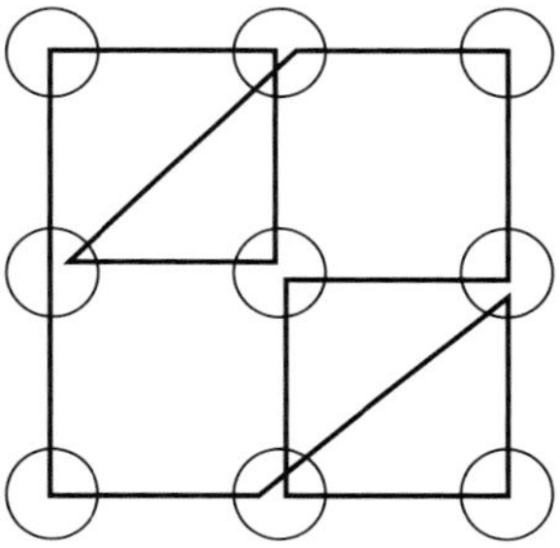

The same algorithm can be used to find Euler paths as well, with some slight amendments. The difference lies in the result of the first search. Any graph that satisfies the conditions for an Euler circuit will produce a cycle after the first search. To find an Euler path, the first search must be performed from one of the two vertices with an odd degree. The output of this search will be a path from the first vertex with odd degree to the second. All subsequent searches will produce cycles, which can be inserted into the first path in the same fashion as used for the Euler circuit.

Implementing this algorithm efficiently can be a little cumbersome. Undirected graphs pose a potential problem because of the way they are usually represented. Even though in the graph the edge is a singular entity it is abstracted as two directed edges one from u to v and one from v to u.

Traversing the adjacency matrix or adjacency list to check for edges is the bulk of the processing time required by this algorithm. Generally, it is desirable to only move forward through the list of edges. When an edge has been traversed it can either be removed or it lies behind the edge pointer for that vertex and so never crops up again.

That is certainly true for directed graphs; after an edge is passed it is never examined again. Undirected graphs complicate the algorithm a little because we must cater to the fact that each edge is represented by two directed edges. This means that it is possible to examine an undirected edge twice effectively moving both forward and backward through each edge, making for incorrect results. Clever use of data structures solves these problems.

The Travelling Salesperson Problem

The Travelling Salesperson Problem (TSP) is encountered every day in various forms, and not all of the people involved are actually selling anything. A salesperson is to visit a number of cities beginning and ending at his home. The aim is to find the cycle with the smallest length.

We can represent this problem using graphs. The cities are simply represented as vertices and routes from one city to another are represented by edges. The cost of traversing an edge could be metric whether it be money, distance, time, or some combination of these factors.

The TSP can be solved by finding Hamiltonian cycles in a graph that represents the real network. A Hamiltonian cycle is a cycle that visits every vertex only once and then returns to the starting vertex. The optimum solution to the TSP is simply the shortest length Hamiltonian cycle in the graph.

Solving the TSP on a graph appears to be fairly trivial. The brute force method is simply to calculate all possible Hamiltonian cycles and compare them. The cycle with the least total cost is the solution. This approach guarantees that the optimum solution will be found. This technique does have a major flaw, however.

The problem with the brute force method is that the time required for it to complete is easily beyond the lifetime of the person requiring the result. For a complete graph of V vertices there are $(V-1)!/2$ possible Hamiltonian cycles. Assuming we used a 25 vertex graph and that the computer running the algorithm could process a billion permutations every second, we would require close to 10 million years to calculate a solution.

Fortunately, for most practical purposes a close approximation is all that is required. The result doesn't need to be perfect—it only needs to be good enough. A close approximation can be performed considerably faster and return a result soon enough to be of use.

The first stage is to create an approximation quickly that can be improved upon later. What we are aiming for is a Hamiltonian cycle, or as close as we can get to one, of the shortest possible length. Finding this isn't practical, but we can get very close in a short amount of time. All complete graphs are Hamiltionian: there is always at least one Hamiltionian cycle. Graphs that are not complete may or may not be Hamiltonian. In order to simplify the problem and to make it operate on graphs that are not Hamiltonian, we need to transform the original graph into a complete graph. This way we can guarentee that there will be a Hamiltonian cycle to be found.

A complete graph can be made from the original graph by adding edges between from each vertex to all other vertices with a cost equal to the length of the shortest path between them. A good technique is to use Floyd's all pairs shortest path algorithm and to use the result table to create a new complete graph. Figure 16.26 shows a graph and a complete graph that has been created from it.

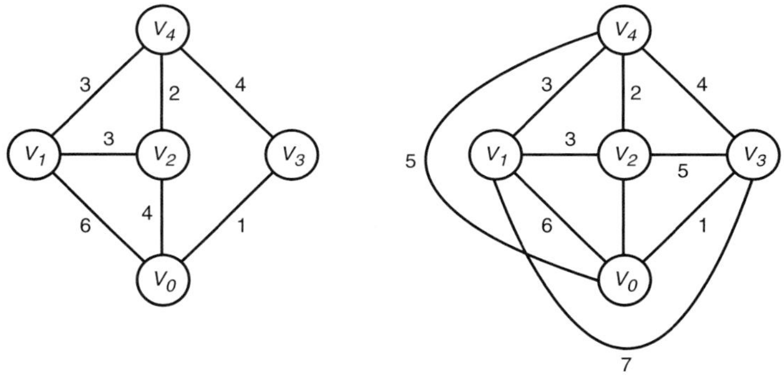

FIGURE 16.26
A graph and a complete graph created from it.

We can find an initial cycle using a straightforward nearest neighbor algorithm. Beginning at the "home" vertex, the nearest neighboring vertex that has not already been visited is added to the initial cycle. Once all vertices have been visited, the cycle is completed by traversing the edge to the "home" vertex. Figure 16.27 shows the result of the nearest neighbor algorithm on the example complete graph, starting at v_0, the "home" vertex.

The length of this initial Hamiltonian cycle must be equal to or greater than the optimum Hamiltonian cycle. The cycle found is likely to be close to the length of the optimum Hamiltonian cycle but it is unlikely to be exact.

Now that we have a cycle somewhat near to the minimum Hamiltonian cycle length, it is possible to improve the cycle that we have already found. This is a done by altering the cycle according to a set of rules and then comparing the length of the newly created cycle against the previous cycle.

FIGURE 16.27
Result of the nearest neighbor algorithm.

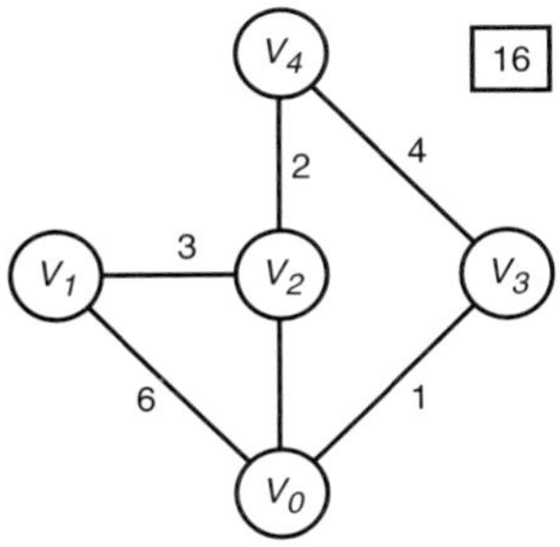

A good approximation or even an exact cycle can be found by manipulating the edges of the best known cycle. Disconnecting a pair of edges such that the cycle is split into two paths (of more than one vertex) and reconnecting these edges differently is a good mechanism to alter the best known cycle. For any such pair of edges there is only one combination to which they can be set that creates a cycle which differs from the best known. If one or several newly created cycles have a lower total cost than the best known, then it becomes the best known cycle and the process is repeated with each pair of edges being tried again until no permutations improve on the best known.

Once finished, the best known cycle should be either greater than but close to the actual optimum total cost or is the exact optimum cost. Figure 16.28 shows the cycles produced on the first pass. The number in the square box near each cycle is the total length. Only one new cycle has a lower total length than the original. On the second pass, none of the new cycles are any improvement and the algorithm finishes with the cycle $v_0 \rightarrow v_3 \rightarrow v_4 \rightarrow v_1 \rightarrow v_2 \rightarrow v_0$, which has a total length of 15.

The cycle that has been determined is not in the same context as the original input graph but that of the complete graph that was made from the original input graph. The cycle must now be processed to put it back into the context of the original graph. When applied to the original graph, each element of the cycle is in fact the shortest path between two vertices and not a list of vertices to traverse. In simple terms, the cycle $v_0 \rightarrow v_3 \rightarrow v_4 \rightarrow v_1 \rightarrow v_2 \rightarrow v_0$ in the context of the original graph is the shortest path from v_0 to v_3 followed by the shortest path from v_3 to v_4 followed by the shortest path from v_4 to v_1 and so on. In the case of the example, all the paths happen to be one edge long but will not be true of all graphs.

For almost all purposes, this technique will produce reasonably accurate results in a small amount of time. Application of such an algorithm doesn't only apply to travelling salespeople and delivery routes.

FIGURE 16.28
The cycles produced.

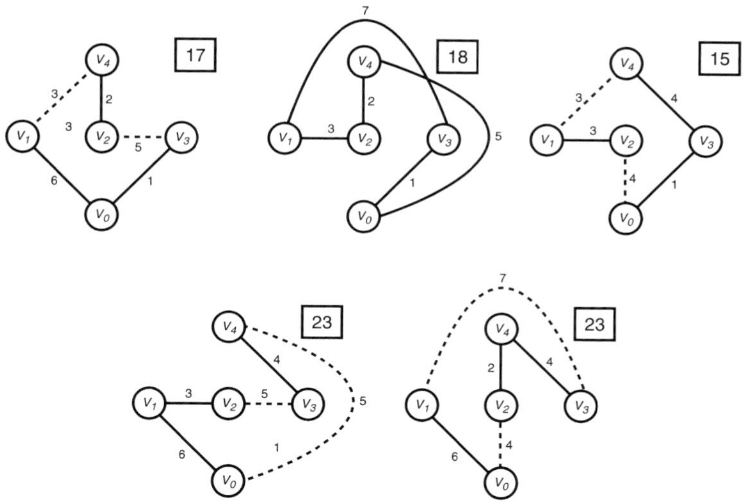

Shortest Path Algorithms

One of the principal uses of graph theory is to discover the "best" of several routes. This is determined by means of calculating the lowest-cost path between vertices in a graph. This cost could be anything: the price of a ticket, distance in miles, some measure of time, or anything else you can quantify numerically. The important thing is that it measures how "good" a connection is between two vertices. For the shortest-path algorithms, the smaller the cost the better the route.

Many problems in the real world are soluble by determining the shortest path. The obvious candidates are problems involved with the shortest time, distance, or price to move from one place to another. Discovering the shortest path can be applied to anything that you can represent as a graph.

Dijkstra's Algorithm: Single Source

Dijkstra's algorithm calculates the total cost of the shortest path from any single vertex in a graph to all other vertices. It works in progressive stages. At each iteration, the lowest total cost to one vertex is determined.

Dijkstra's Algorithm: Iterations

For each vertex in the graph, two values are stored. The total cost of the path from the start vertex to each vertex is used to keep track of the cost of the best path so far, and at the end of the algorithm the actual cost of the shortest path. To trace this path, for each vertex the preceding vertex in the shortest path is stored and can be used to move backwards along that path. Dijkstra's algorithm can be described as the following steps:

1. Initially, the start vertex is given a total cost of 0. All other vertices have a total cost of infinity. The previous vertex for all the vertices is cleared. The start vertex is V, the current vertex.
2. Mark V as visited. Its total cost is final.
3. Adjust the total cost of all the vertices adjacent to V that have not been visited. If the total cost to V plus the cost of the edge to an adjacent vertex is less than the total cost to the adjacent vertex, the path through V is of a lower cost than the best found so far. Set the new total cost of the adjacent vertex, and set V as the vertex which comes before it in the path.
4. Select the vertex which has not been visited with the smallest total cost to be the current vertex, V.
5. Repeat from step 2 until all the vertices have been visited.

When the algorithm has finished, the previous vertex member of the table can be used to move backward along the shortest path from any vertex.

Figures 16.29 through 16.36 and Tables 16.5 through 16.12 demonstrates Dijkstra's algorithm in action. In the diagrams, the vertices that have been visited are filled and those that haven't been visited are not. The number floating near each vertex is the smallest-cost path to that vertex at that point. After a vertex is visited, the total cost from the start is not altered. v_1 is the start vertex.

The first graph (Figure 16.29) shows the state after stage 1. The total cost of the path to start vertex, v_1, is set to 0, and infinity for all other vertices.

TABLE 16.5 Dijkstra's Algorithm—Stage 1

v_n	*Visited*	*Total Cost*	*Previous Vertex*
1	no	0	none
2	no	∞	none
3	no	∞	none
4	no	∞	none
5	no	∞	none
6	no	∞	none
7	no	∞	none

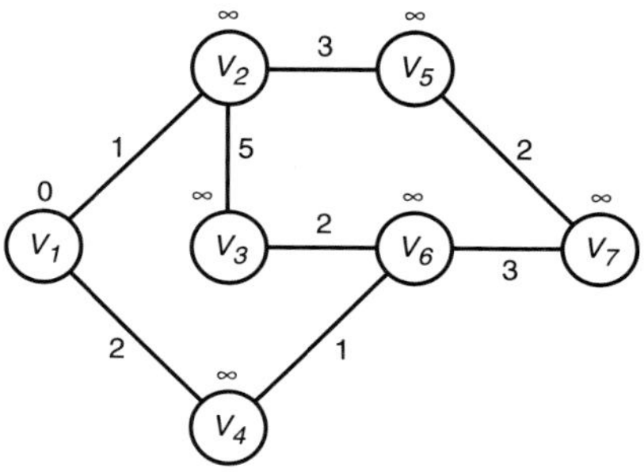

FIGURE 16.29
Initial table and initial diagram.

After one iteration, the total cost to v_1 has been completed and the total costs to v_2 and v_3 have been adjusted.

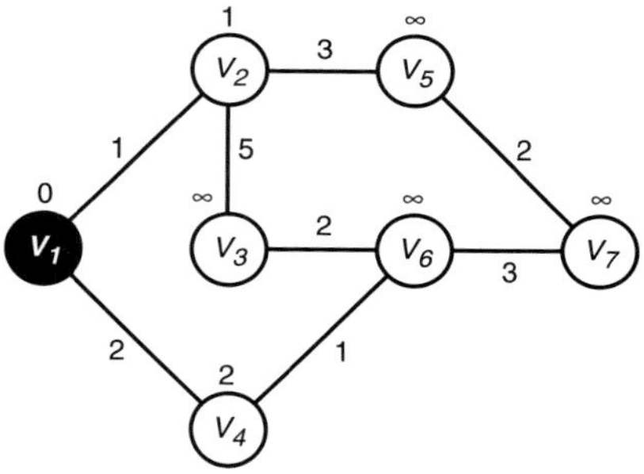

FIGURE 16.30
Dijkstra's algorithm—Stage 2 diagram.

TABLE 16.6 Dijkstra's Algorithm—Stage 2

v_n	*Visited*	*Total Cost*	*Previous Vertex*
1	yes	0	none
2	no	1	v_1
3	no	∞	none
4	no	2	v_1
5	no	∞	none
6	no	∞	none
7	no	∞	none

The vertex with the smallest total cost which has not been visited is select, v_2. It is marked as being visited, the total costs to v_3 and v_5 are adjusted.

FIGURE 16.31
Dijkstra's algorithm—Stage 3 diagram.

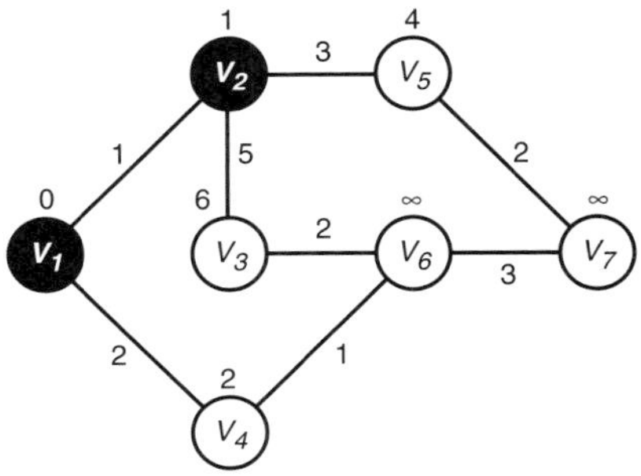

TABLE 16.7 Dijkstra's Algorithm—Stage 3

v_n	*Visited*	*Total Cost*	*Previous Vertex*
1	yes	0	none
2	yes	1	v_1
3	no	6	v_2
4	no	2	v_1
5	no	4	v_2
6	no	∞	none
7	no	∞	none

Next, v_4 is selected. Because v_1 has been visited, only v_6 is updated.

TABLE 16.8 Dijkstra's Algorithm—Stage 4

v_n	*Visited*	*Total Cost*	*Previous Vertex*
1	yes	0	none
2	yes	1	v_1
3	no	6	v_2
4	yes	2	v_1
5	no	4	v_2
6	no	3	v_4
7	no	∞	none

Vertex v_6 is then selected. v_7 is updated. The path from v_6 to v_3 is of a lower cost, 5, than the path found so far, 6. The total cost for v_3 is updated, and v_6 is set as the previous vertex in the path.

FIGURE 16.32
Dijkstra's algorithm—Stage 4 diagram.

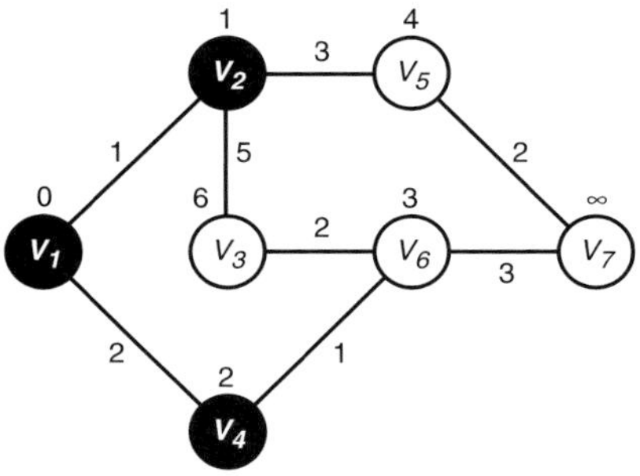

FIGURE 16.33
Dijkstra's algorithm—Stage 5 diagram.

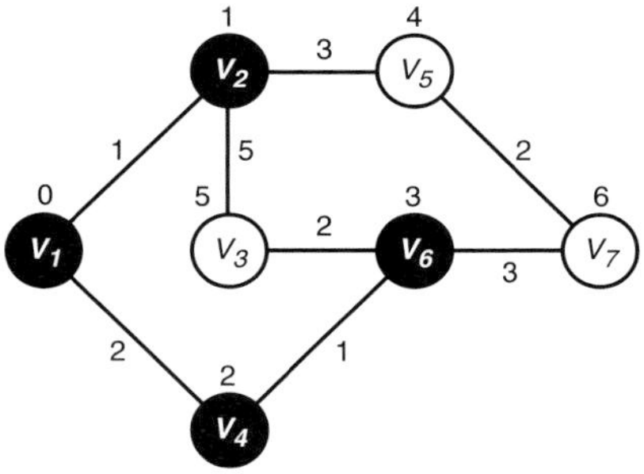

TABLE 16.9 Dijkstra's Algorithm—Stage 5

v_n	Visited	Total Cost	Previous Vertex
1	yes	0	none
2	yes	1	v_1
3	no	5	v_6
4	yes	2	v_1
5	no	4	v_2
6	yes	3	v_4
7	no	6	v_6

Then, v_5 is selected. The adjacent vertex v_7 is not updated because the path via v_5 is no improvement over the one found so far.

After each vertex is visited, its adjacent vertices are inserted into the prioritized queue. The queue ensures that the elements are removed in ascending order of their total cost.

Exactly how the queue structure functions has a massive bearing over the efficiency of the algorithm. For a normal prioritized queue, there are two approaches.

The first involves a prioritized queue which does not allow repetitions of the same vertex. When an already-present vertex is added to it, the lowest cost of the two survive and the other is discarded. In the main algorithm, vertices are simply removed from the queue in the correct order, without repetitions. Typically, a search of the queue is required to determine if the new vertex is already present. Listing 16.4 is an implementation of this technique for sparse graphs.

LISTING 16.4 Dijkstra's Algorithm For Sparse Graphs

```
int Dijkstra_Sparse(struct Graph * G, int Source, struct Dijkstra_Table * Table)
{
  int V;    /* V is the index of the current vertex */
  int i;
  struct PQueue Q;
  struct Dijkstra_Row * Results;
  struct EdgeScan E;    /* holds information about an edge */

  PQ_Initialise(&Q);
  InitResults(&Results, G->NumVertices);

  Results[Source].Total=0;        /* Step 1 */
  Results[Source].Previous=-1;    /* no previous vertex */
  V=Source;

  do {
    Results[V].Visited=TRUE;    /* Step 2 */

    EdgeScanStart(G, V, &E);    /* Step 3 */
    while (EdgeScanNext(&E)==0)
    {
      if (Results[E.Dest].Visited) continue;
      if (E.Cost<0) return GRAPH_BADGRAPH;

      if (Results[V].Total + E.Cost < Results[E.Dest].Total )
      {
        Results[E.Dest].Total = Results[V].Total + E.Cost;
        Results[E.Dest].Previous=V;
        PQ_Enqueue(&Q,Results[E.Dest].Total,E.Dest);
```

LISTING 16.4 continued

```
        }
      }
      EdgeScanEnd(&E);

      V=PQ_Dequeue(&Q);              /* Step 4 */
    } while (V!=-1);

    Table->G=G;
    Table->Source=Source;
    Table->Results=Results;

    return 0;
}
```

The second involves a queue which does allow repetitions of the same vertex. In this case, each time a vertex is removed from the queue, it must be checked to see if it has already been visited. This is simply done with a loop which removes vertices from the queue until there are either no more or an unvisited vertex is found.

So what's the difference? The second approach is likely to have a considerably larger value of N, the number of elements in the queue which potentially can become as large as the number of edges in the graph. This equates to greater memory usage, and all that is involved with the allocation and freeing of each element of the queue. The first will use considerably less memory.

The first technique will generally be faster, even though a search of the queue must be performed. The number of edges in a graph is potentially very large and the overhead of adding, removing, and examining each element in the queue is often larger than searching through the queue.

The data structure used as the prioritized queue has a large bearing on the running time. A simple linked list implementation produces terrible results, each search taking up to V iterations resulting in $O(V^2)$ running time. Although this is the same as the simple implementation previously described, it will take longer because maintaining the linked list would take more time.

Use of a binary heap can dramatically improve the time bound for sparse graphs. Binary heap operations typically run in O(log N), and improve the running time of Dijkstra's algorithm to O(V log V). Performing a search in a binary heap can be very time consuming, however, and any gains which are made from their use are lost in this extra overhead. Other heap structures on which find operations are less difficult will fare considerably better.

Dijkstra's algorithm has a major draw back, which limits its usefulness. It does not work when there are negative cost edges. Consider Figure 16.37.

When this algorithm is used, the shortest path from v_1 to v_2 is reported as being v_1, v_3, v_2 with a total cost of 3. In reality, the shortest path is v_1, v_3, v_4, v_2 with a total cost of –4.

The failure occurs because the algorithm assumes that the total cost to reach a vertex will only ever be increased. After a vertex has been visited, it is assumed that there are no other paths by which it can be reached that are of lower cost. This is true only for positive cost

FIGURE 16.37
A graph with a negative cost edge.

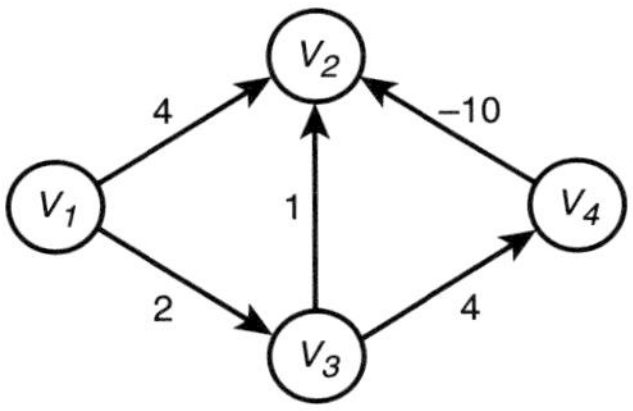

edges. Any route back to an already-visited vertex must have a total cost greater than or equal to the path already found.

When there is a negative edge, this is not the case as the preceding example shows. There might be a path back to an already visited vertex which has a cost less than that already found. There is, however, a solution: the Bellman-Ford algorithm.

Bellman-Ford Algorithm: Single-Source, Negative-Cost Edges

Bellman-Ford algorithm is much like Dijkstra's algorithm. The fundamental difference is that where Dijkstra assumes that you never return to an already visited vertex, the Bellman-Ford algorithm does not.

There are two notable problems. The first is that it takes longer to run than Dijkstra's algorithm. Dijkstra's algorithm only processes each vertex once. In contrast the Bellman-Ford algorithm potentially visits each vertex up to V–1 times (for example, in a complete graph).

The second problem is peculiar to graphs which have one or more negatively weighted cycles. In such graphs it is possible that the algorithm will never exit. It will just go around and around the cycle indefinitely. This problem can be overcome with a little effort.

Consider a vertex to which all other vertices are adjacent, like any vertex of a complete graph. When the algorithm runs, the central vertex will be queued at most a total of V–1 times, V being the number of vertices in the graph. When a cycle occurs involving that vertex, it will be queued many times, many more than V–1. By trapping this condition (when a vertex is enqueued more than V–1 times) it is possible to make the function exit. In such a situation, it is impossible to carry on with the algorithm and so no results which can be trusted are produced.

For the vertices which are part of the cycle, the shortest path between them becomes infinitely negative because it is possible to move around the cycle forever getting a path of lower and lower cost. Any path which can be made which contains a vertex in a negative cost cycle will similarly have an infinitely negative cost. It is generally better to simply discard any results found in graphs with negative cycles, because in practice they are not meaningful.

In practical situations, negative cost edges (and therefore negative cost cycles) are extremely rare. Take for example a graph that represents a rail network in which the cost of an edge is the actual cost in dollars to make that journey. In this context, a negative cost edge would be where the rail company paid its passengers to use that particular line. In almost all other real-life situations represented as a graph, negative cost edges do not occur. Listing 16.5 shows the Bellman-Ford algorithm.

LISTING 16.5 Bellman-Ford Algorithm

```
int Bellman(struct Graph * G, int Source, struct Dijkstra_Table * Table)
{
  int V;    /* V is the index of the current vertex */
  int i;
  struct PQueue Q;
  struct Dijkstra_Row * Results;
  struct EdgeScan E;    /* holds information about an edge */

  PQ_Initialise(&Q);
  i=InitResults(&Results, G->NumVertices);
  if (i) return i;    /* report any errors */

  Results[Source].Total=0;       /* Step 1 */
  Results[Source].Previous=-1;    /* no previous vertex */
  V=Source;

  do {
    Results[V].Visited++;       /* Step 2 */
    if (Results[V].Visited==G->NumVertices) return GRAPH_BADGRAPH;
```

LISTING 16.5 continued

```
    /* if we have visited a vertex once for each vertex,
       then we must be in a negatively weighted cycle. Return
       an error to prevent infinite loop
    */

    EdgeScanStart(G, V, &E);     /* Step 3 */
    while (EdgeScanNext(&E)==0)
    {
      if (Results[V].Total + E.Cost < Results[E.Dest].Total )
      {
        Results[E.Dest].Total = Results[V].Total + E.Cost;
        Results[E.Dest].Previous=V;
        PQ_Enqueue(&Q,Results[E.Dest].Total,E.Dest);
      }
    }
    EdgeScanEnd(&E);

    V=PQ_Dequeue(&Q);            /* Step 4 */

  } while (V!=-1);

  Table->G=G;
  Table->Source=Source;
  Table->Results=Results;

  return 0;
}
```

Floyd's Algorithm: All Pairs

The Floyd's algorithm calculates the shortest path between all pairs of vertices in a graph, unlike those covered previously. Such a task can be achieved by running a single source shortest path algorithm V—1 times and collating the results. In the case of Dijkstra's algorithm, this would require near V^3 iterations. The same is true for Floyd's algorithm.

The difference lies in how difficult each iteration is to perform. Floyd's algorithm can be implemented very simply such that each iteration takes very little time to execute. In almost all circumstances, it is much faster than performing many single-source shortest-path functions.

Suppose we have a path between vertices v_i and v_j, which visits a number of intermediate vertices. We can express this path by listing the sequence of vertices which comprise it so the path is v_i, i_0, i_1, i_2 ... i_n, v_j. D[u,v] is the shortest path between two vertices. c[u,v] is the cost of the immediate edge from u to v, that is the cost of any edge if u and v are adjacent, or infinity when they are not adjacent.

In Dijkstra's algorithm, we apply a rule recursively to find the shortest path between two vertices D[u,v]:

$D[u,v] = \min(D[u,v], D[u,i_n]+c[i_n,v])$

In English, the minimum cost from u to v is the shortest cost found so far or is the cost to an intermediate vertex plus the edge connecting the intermediate to v. By moving through all vertices that can be used as an intermediate, the shortest path to all vertices can be calculated. This is what makes Dijkstra's algorithm "single source"—u is never changed.

Floyd's algorithm is based on the same rule but works differently. Like Dijkstra's algorithm it calculates the shortest path in stages by iterating through the variables in the rule. The difference is the way in which this is done.

Instead of having a path found up to the intermediate i_n, we treat the path from u to v as two separate paths, split at i_k, some intermediate vertex. We are now interested in the path from i_k to v, rather than just examining if there is an edge from i_n to v.

As Floyd's algorithm is performed, the lengths of unknown paths are found by using the lengths of paths which are already known. After the shortest path between u and v is calculated it can be used to find paths from u through v to other vertices.

Initially, the known shortest paths are the edges in the graph. As the algorithm progresses, more shortest paths are found. An array is used to store the current known shortest paths and initially is identical to the adjacency matrix of the graph.

We select an intermediate vertex (k). For each pair of vertices (i,j) we apply the rule:

$D[i,j] = \min(D[i,j] , D[i,k] + D[k,j])$

As each value of k is used, every possible path between two vertices is examined, and the shortest found. The following example shows how the algorithm works in practice.

Instead of presenting the results as an adjacency matrix, the most common way they are stored when implemented, Figure 16.38 and Table 16.13 shows the results in a more human-friendly manner. This makes it much clearer as to what is going on in Floyd's algorithm.

The first column of the table is the list of all possible paths which can exist in the example graph. The next column is the initial values for the cost of these paths, and each subsequent column is the costs after each value of k has been tried. The costs in bold are the minimum costs which have been calculated for the specified value of k—that is, the current cost of i→j is greater than that of i→k + k→j.

TABLE 16.13 Floyd's Algorithm

Path	*Initially*	*k=0*	*k=1*	*k=2*	*k=3*
$v_0 \rightarrow v_0$	0	0	0	0	0
$v_0 \rightarrow v_1$	–1	–1	–1	–1	–1

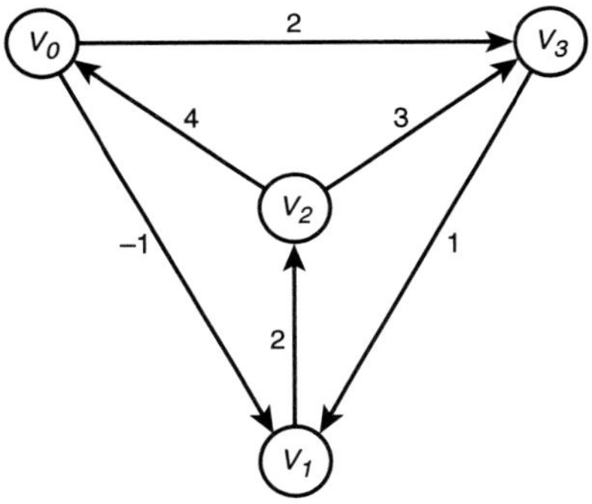

FIGURE 16.38
Floyd's algorithm.

TABLE 16.13 continued

Path	*Initially*	*k=0*	*k=1*	*k=2*	*k=3*
$v_0 \rightarrow v_2$	∞	∞	**1**	1	1
$v_0 \rightarrow v_3$	2	2	2	2	2
$v_1 \rightarrow v_0$	∞	∞	∞	**6**	6
$v_1 \rightarrow v_1$	0	0	0	0	0
$v_1 \rightarrow v_2$	2	2	2	2	2
$v_1 \rightarrow v_3$	∞	∞	∞	**5**	5
$v_2 \rightarrow v_0$	4	4	4	4	4
$v_2 \rightarrow v_1$	∞	**3**	3	3	3
$v_2 \rightarrow v_2$	0	0	0	0	0
$v_2 \rightarrow v_3$	3	3	3	3	3

TABLE 16.13 continued

Path	Initially	k=0	k=1	k=2	k=3
$v_3 \rightarrow v_0$	∞	∞	∞	**7**	7
$v_3 \rightarrow v_1$	1	1	1	1	1
$v_3 \rightarrow v_2$	∞	∞	**3**	3	3
$v_3 \rightarrow v_3$	0	0	0	0	0

First, v_0 is used as the intermediate vertex. For every i and j, we use the rule to determine whether the path from i to j using the intermediate vertex is shorter than that currently known. In the example, it finds that the path $v_2 \rightarrow v_1$ is shorter than that known when it uses v_0 as an intermediate. In other words, the path $v_2 \rightarrow v_0 \rightarrow v_1$ is shorter than the shortest path $v_2 \rightarrow v_1$ currently known.

During the next iteration, when k=1, the same operation is performed again. However, this time we find that the paths $v_0 \rightarrow v_1 \rightarrow v_2$ and $v_3 \rightarrow v_1 \rightarrow v_2$ are shorter than the currently known paths $v_0 \rightarrow v_1$ and $v_3 \rightarrow v_2$, respectively. After all values of k have been used, the final values are the length of the shortest paths. Listing 16.6 is an implementation of Floyd's algorithm.

It is also possible to determine the actual path, not just its length between any pair of vertices. This is a little more complex than with Dijkstra's algorithm, but not by much. The information required is the value of k which is the shortest path. From this, we can break down each path into two paths, the first ending and the next beginning with the intermediate vertex. The same operation can be applied to each of the paths until each has been broken down completely: The path is direct from u to v without any intermediate vertices.

For instance, the path $v_3 \rightarrow v_0$ can be found. By examining the table, the shortest path from $v_3 \rightarrow v_0$ uses v_2 as an intermediate vertex—k=2 for the shortest path. The path now becomes $v_3 \rightarrow v_2 \rightarrow v_0$. We apply the same logic to the path $v_3 \rightarrow v_2$. This shortest path uses v_1 as an intermediate. The path so far is $v_3 \rightarrow v_1 \rightarrow v_2 \rightarrow v_0$.

Further steps will find that each part of the path cannot be broken down any further because there is no associated value of k.

This technique breaks the path down as if it is a binary tree. Figure 16.39 clearly shows how the path $v_3 \rightarrow v_0$ was broken down. The same is true for any path.

FIGURE 16.39
The path from v3→v0.

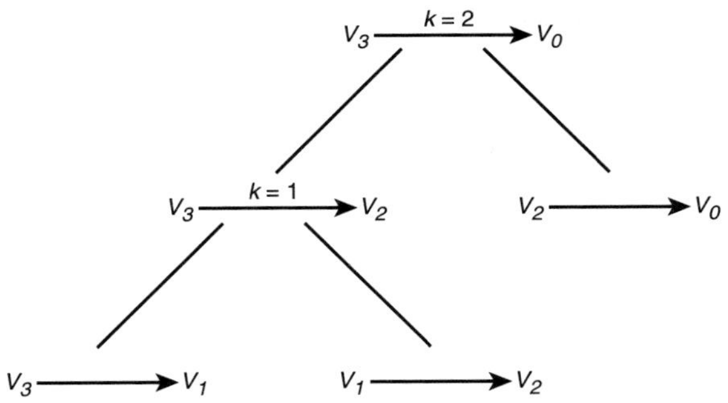

LISTING 16.6 Floyd's Algorithm

```
int Floyd(struct Graph * G,struct Floyd_Table * Table)
    /* Uses Floyds algorithm to calculated the shortest path for all pairs.
       Returns 0 on succes, or <0 on error (GRAPH_OUTOFMEM, GRAPH_BADPARAM)
       Passing a graph containing a negative cost cycle will produce spurious
       results but will not result in segmentation fault, infinite loops
       or similar
    */
{
  int i,j,k;

  /* for every pair of vertices i and j find the shortest path
     D[i,j]. D[i,j] is determined as the minimum of D[i,j] and
     the path through every intermediate vertex k. That is
     min( D[i,j], D[i,k]+D[k,j] )
  */

  struct Floyd_Result **  R;
  struct EdgeScan EScan;

  if (!G || !Table || !G->NumVertices) return GRAPH_BADPARAM;

  /* Create the 2 dimensional array of results */
  R=MakeResults(G->NumVertices);
  if (!R) return GRAPH_OUTOFMEM;

  /* Initialise the results table */
  for (i=0;i<G->NumVertices;i++)
  {
    EdgeScanStart(G,i,&EScan);
```

LISTING 16.6 continued

```
    while (EdgeScanNext(&EScan)==0)
    {
      R[i][EScan.Dest].Total=EScan.Cost;
    }
    EdgeScanEnd(&EScan);
  }

  for (k=0;k<G->NumVertices;k++)
    for (i=0;i<G->NumVertices;i++)
      for (j=0;j<G->NumVertices;j++)
      {
        /* Because, in practice, GRAPH_NOTCONNECTED is INT_MAX we must
             ensure we do not overflow */
        if (R[i][k].Total==GRAPH_NOTCONNECTED || R[k][j].Total==
             GRAPH_NOTCONNECTED) continue;
        if (R[i][j].Total > R[i][k].Total + R[k][j].Total)
        {
          R[i][j].Total=R[i][k].Total + R[k][j].Total;
          R[i][j].Previous=k;
        }
      }

  Table->G=G;
  Table->Results=R;

  return 0;
}
```

Floyd's algorithm will produce correct results for graphs with negative cost edges. If a negative cost cycle is encountered, the algorithm will not loop infinitely, but the results produced cannot be trusted. This condition can be determined by examining the paths from every vertex back to itself. If a negative cost cycle is present, the cost to get from a vertex back to itself will be a negative value after the algorithm has finished. Normally, the distance from any vertex back to itself would be 0.

As can be clearly seen, Floyd's algorithm requires V^3 iterations to be completed, the same as performing Dijkstra's algorithm for each vertex. The difference is the amount of time taken to perform each iteration.

The implementation of Floyd's algorithm has a very tight inner loop. A good optimizing compiler will make exceptionally fast executable code from it. Implementations of Dijkstra's algorithm usually have a more complex inner loop, and so each iteration takes longer to execute.

In fact, the preceding implementation is not as efficient as it could be. This is because of the value selected to use for unconnected edges, `GRAPH_NOTCONNECTED`. This is defined to be `INT_MAX` (in the file "graphs.h" on the CD). Adding `INT_MAX` to itself typically results in an overflow. Under ANSI/ISO C, overflowing a variable causes undefined behavior. Practically, it would make spurious results in directed graphs which are not connected graphs and directed graphs which are not strongly connected. On most computer systems vertices to which there is no path will report values very close to, but not the same as `GRAPH_NOTCONNECTED`.

The check prevents this overflow from occurring but at the cost of performance. The inner loop is so tight that such a check will increase the running time considerably. There are a number of ways in which it can be overcome.

One technique is to assume that the graph is connected (or strongly connected in the case of directed graphs). The check is then unnecessary because the condition it is there to protect against could never happen.

A second technique is not to use `GRAPH_NOTCONNECTED`, but to pick a value that will not overflow when doubled (that is, `INT_MAX > 2*n`). Any total cost for the graph would have to be less than n, at least halving the range for the longest path in a graph.

The function on the CD and presented here is designed to be generic, to work with any sensible graph on which you care to use it, and so the check has been left in. If performance is a major issue, it can be removed and other concessions made.

When trying to find the shortest paths for all pairs of a dense graph, a good implementation of Floyd's algorithm is almost certainly faster than applying an implementation of Dijkstra's algorithm many times. For a sparse graph, using an implementation of Dijkstra's algorithm that uses a binary heap, the speed increase would be less pronounced.

Theoretically, there is a technique based on Floyd's algorithm which will perform better for large sparse graphs. This algorithm checks every possible intermediate vertex for every pair of vertices in the graph. For a sparse graph, the number of known paths between pairs is small compared to the number of possible pairs.

While performing Floyd's algorithm on paper, it becomes obvious that it is only necessary to work with known vertices. Simply, if $v_i \rightarrow v_k$ isn't known (it is infinity) then any path from $v_i \rightarrow v_k \rightarrow v_j$ will be infinity, and no improvement. The same idea can be applied to the second part of the path $v_k \rightarrow v_j$.

The idea of known paths can be used to reduce the number of iterations required. The difficulty lies in the implementation of such an algorithm. It is likely that it would be slower than performing the normal implementation Floyd's algorithm because of the processor time taken to maintain the various data structures required.

Minimum Spanning Trees

A spanning tree is a tree formed from the edges of an undirected graph which connects all the vertices present. A minimum spanning tree is the spanning tree that has the lowest total cost (the sum of the cost of each used edge). Only connected graphs can have minimum spanning trees.

Minimum spanning trees are often used to solve a specific kind of problem. Imagine setting up a WAN (wide area network) between a number of distant locations. The aim is to find the shortest length of cable to connect all the required locations together. This can be determined by producing a graph where vertices are locations and the edges between them are potential cable connections weighted relative to distance or cost (see Figure 16.40). The minimum spanning tree of such a graph is the answer to the problem; it is the smallest total cost connecting all vertices.

FIGURE 16.40
A graph and a minimum spanning tree of the graph.

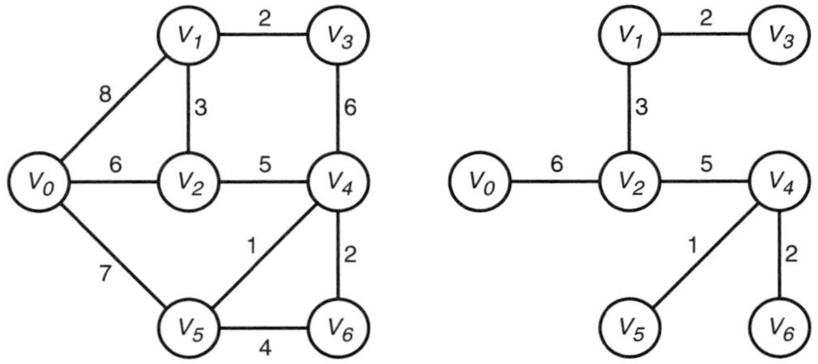

Any spanning tree has V–1 edges, which is the minimum number of edges by which V vertices can be connected. Adding an edge to a spanning tree will create a cycle, and it will no longer be a tree. Removing any edge within the cycle removes the cycle and returns it to being a tree. The total cost of the edges of the tree is lowered if the cost of the edge removed is greater than the cost of the new edge added.

A spanning tree has minimum cost when the adding of an edge and removal of another will always increase the total cost of the edges in the tree.

Two techniques are commonly used to produce a minimum spanning tree of a graph. The first covered here, Kruskal's algorithm, constructs the tree by adding edges in order of cost. The second, Prim's algorithm, works by building the tree by adding a vertex to it at each stage.

Kruskal's Algorithm

This algorithm produces a minimum spanning tree of a graph by adding an edge to the tree each iteration, until all vertices are connected. Any edges which would form a cycle are ignored. Figure 16.41 shows the minimum spanning tree at each stage for the sample graph in Figure 16.40. Kruskal's algorithm can be performed as follows:

1. Create the data structure to hold the tree while it is built. It is initialized to contain all the vertices which exist in the graph without any edges connecting them.
2. List all the edges in the graph in order of cost. Select the first (lowest-cost) edge.
3. Select the next edge in the list.
4. If the current edge does not form a cycle, add it to the tree.
5. Repeat from step 3 until all vertices in the tree have been connected.

The most computationally expensive part of any implementation of this algorithm is the way in which edges are selected. Graphs are typically stored in a way which makes it difficult to create a list of edges for the whole graph. Both of the representation techniques suffer this problem, but they have advantages in other areas.

A good approach is to produce a prioritized queue of edges. The dequeue operation is automatically the smallest cost edge which has not been examined. After this is done, stages 3 to 5 are completed in at most E iterations, the number of edges in the graph. The way in which the queue is implemented has the greatest bearing on running time.

One approach is to use a binary heap, a somewhat complex but efficient data structure. Prioritized queues using a binary heap as its underlying data structure typically does a single enqueue operation on O(log N) time making the time taken to build the prioritized queue of edges O(E log E).

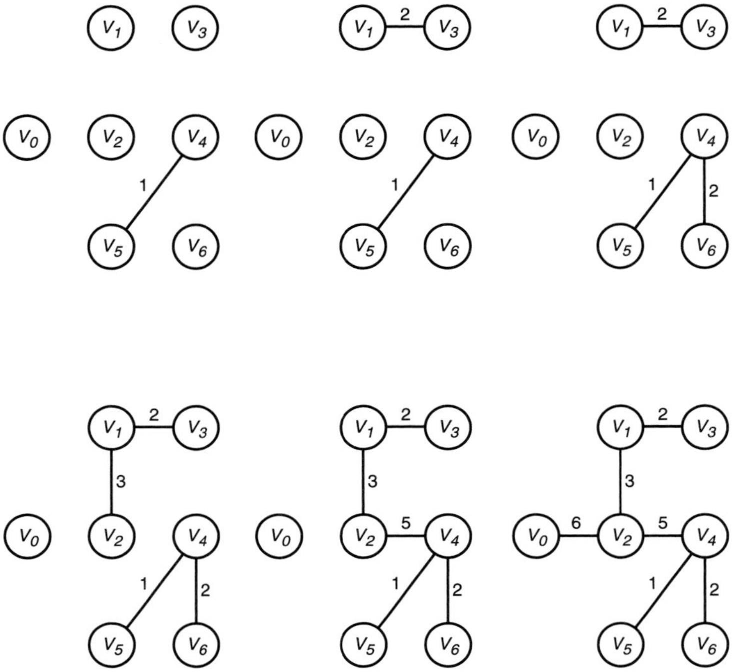

FIGURE 16.41
The stages of Kruskal's algorithm.

LISTING 16.7 Kruskal's Algorithm

```
int Kruskal_Undirected(struct Graph * G,struct Graph ** TreePtr)
{
  /* The graph G is examined to produce a new graph, which is
     a minimum spanning tree and the struct Graph * denoted
     by TreePtr is assigned the new value.
     return 0 on success, <0 on error (GRAPH_BADPARAM, GRAPH_OUTOFMEM)
  */

  int i, j, numadded;
  struct Graph * Tree;
  struct PEdgeQueue * Q;
  struct EdgeScan EScan;

  if (!G || !TreePtr) return GRAPH_BADPARAM;

  PEQ_Initialise(Q);
  Tree=MakeGraph(List);
  if (!Tree) return GRAPH_OUTOFMEM;
```

LISTING 16.7 continued

```
/* step 1 and 2: order the edges in the graph by cost
   also, duplicate the vertices in G into Tree
   (only because it's generally faster to have one
   loop doing 2 things, than 2 loops doing 1)
*/

for (i=0;i<G->NumVertices;i++)
{
  j=AddVertex(Tree);
  if (j<0)
  {
    /* error, clean up and return */
    PEQ_Free(Q);
    FreeGraph(Tree);
    return j;
  }
  Tree->Vertices[j]->Tag=G->Vertices[i]->Tag;

  EdgeScanStart(G,i,&EScan);
  while (!EdgeScanNext(&EScan))
  {
    /* adjust EScan such that we do not repeat the reverse
       edge since we're dealing with undirected graphs only
       This means that we only use half the required memory,
       and we only ever traverse any edge once. The cost
       is the processing we need to do here.
    */
    if (EScan.Source>EScan.Dest) SWAP(EScan.Source,EScan.Dest,int);

    if (PEQ_Enqueue(Q,&EScan))
    {
      /* error - out of memory. Clean up and return */
      PEQ_Free(Q);
      FreeGraph(Tree);
      return GRAPH_OUTOFMEM;
    }
  }
  EdgeScanEnd(&EScan);
}

numadded=0;
```

LISTING 16.7 continued

```
  /* step 3, select the next edge in the list */
  while (numadded<G->NumVertices-1 && !PEQ_Dequeue(Q,&EScan))
  {

 /* step 4, if the current edge does not form a cycle
    add the current edge to the tree
    */

    if (!AreVerticesConnected(Tree,EScan.Source,EScan.Dest))
    {
      /* if there is no path from source to dest, then the
         current edge will not make a cycle when added */
      j=ConnectVertex(Tree,EScan.Source,EScan.Dest,EScan.Cost);
      if (!j) j=ConnectVertex(Tree,EScan.Dest,EScan.Source,EScan.Cost);
      if (j)
      {
        /* an error occured, clean up and return */
        PEQ_Free(Q);
        FreeGraph(Tree);
        return j;
      }
      numadded++;
    }
  }

  *TreePtr=Tree;
  PEQ_Free(Q);

  return 0;
}
```

Prim's Algorithm

Prim's algorithm creates a minimum spanning tree by adding a single edge (and thus a vertex) to the tree over a number of iterations. The vertices in the graph are split into two sets: those which are part of the tree and those which are not. At each iteration, the lowest-cost edge connecting any vertex which is part of the solution to any vertex which is not yet in the solution is added. This is performed until there are no more vertices left to be added. To put it another way, until V–1 edges have been selected.

This algorithm can be seen to be similar to Dijkstra's algorithm. The difference is that Prim's algorithm stores the lowest-cost edge whereas Dijkstra's algorithm stores the lowest-cost path. Prim's algorithm can be described as the following steps:

1. Select a root vertex, V.
2. Mark V as visited.
3. For every vertex adjacent to V, adjust the shortest edge cost.
4. Select the vertex that has not been visited with the smallest edge cost to be the current vertex, V, and add the connecting edge to the spanning tree.
5. Repeat from step 2 until all the vertices have been visited.

Tables 16.14 through 16.21 and Figure 16.42 demonstrate Prim's algorithm. Figure 16.42 shows the minimum spanning tree at each stage for the example graph in Figure 16.40.

TABLE 16.14 Prim's Algorithm—Stage 1

v_n	*Visited*	*Edge Cost*	*Previous Vertex*
0	no	∞	none
1	no	∞	none
2	no	∞	none
3	no	∞	none
4	no	∞	none
5	no	∞	none
6	no	∞	none

TABLE 16.15 Prim's Algorithm—Stage 2

v_n	*Visited*	*Edge Cost*	*Previous Vertex*
0	yes	∞	none
1	no	8	v_0
2	no	6	v_0
3	no	∞	none
4	no	∞	none
5	no	7	v_0
6	no	∞	none

TABLE 16.16 Prim's Algorithm—Stage 3

v_n	*Visited*	*Edge Cost*	*Previous Vertex*
0	yes	∞	none
1	no	3	v_2
2	yes	6	v_1
3	no	∞	none
4	no	5	v_2
5	no	7	v_0
6	no	∞	none

TABLE 16.17 Prim's Algorithm—Stage 4

v_n	*Visited*	*Edge Cost*	*Previous Vertex*
0	yes	∞	none
1	yes	3	v_2
2	yes	6	v_0
3	no	2	v_1
4	no	5	v_2
5	no	7	v_0
6	no	∞	none

TABLE 16.18 Prim's Algorithm—Stage 5

v_n	*Visited*	*Edge Cost*	*Previous Vertex*
0	yes	∞	none
1	yes	3	v_2
2	yes	6	v_0
3	yes	2	v_1
4	no	5	v_2
5	no	7	v_0
6	no	∞	none

TABLE 16.19 Prim's Algorithm—Stage 6

v_n	Visited	Edge Cost	Previous Vertex
0	yes	∞	none
1	yes	3	v_2
2	yes	6	v_0
3	yes	2	v_1
4	yes	5	v_2
5	no	1	v_4
6	no	2	v_4

TABLE 16.20 Prim's Algorithm—Stage 7

v_n	Visited	Edge Cost	Previous Vertex
0	yes	∞	none
1	yes	3	v_2
2	yes	6	v_0
3	yes	2	v_1
4	yes	5	v_2
5	yes	1	v_4
6	no	2	v_4

TABLE 16.21 Prim's Algorithm—Stage 8

v_n	Visited	Edge Cost	Previous Vertex
0	yes	∞	none
1	yes	3	v_2
2	yes	6	v_0
3	yes	2	v_1
4	yes	5	v_2
5	yes	1	v_4
6	yes	2	v_4

Although Prim's algorithm is similar to Dijkstra's algorithm, it does not suffer from some of the problems which Dijkstra's algorithm does. The operation performed by Prim's algorithm will not be different if negative cost edges are present. Negative cost cycles are not a problem either: no cycles are made in the result of the algorithm (it is a tree) and the algorithm cannot infinitely loop.

The similarity in the algorithms is also reflected in their implementations. All the implementation and performance issues pertaining to Dijkstra's algorithm are equally valid when applied to Prim's algorithm. An implementation of Prim's algorithm for undirected graphs is shown in Listing 16.8.

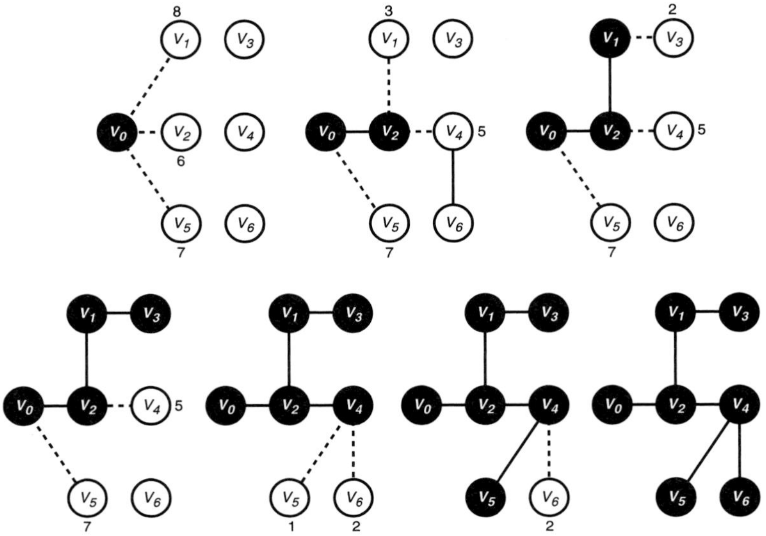

FIGURE 16.42
The stages of Prim's algorithm.

LISTING 16.8 Prim's Algorithm

```
int Prim_Undirected(struct Graph * G,struct Graph ** TreePtr)
{
  /* The graph G is examined to produce a new graph, which is
     a minimum spanning tree and the struct Graph * denoted
     by TreePtr is assigned the new value.
     return 0 on success, <0 on error (GRAPH_BADPARAM, GRAPH_OUTOFMEM)
  */

  struct Graph * Tree;
  struct Prim_Working * W;
  struct EdgeScan EScan;
  int NumVisited, V, i, j, lowest;

  if (!G || !TreePtr) return GRAPH_BADPARAM;

  Tree=MakeGraph(List);
  if (!Tree) return GRAPH_OUTOFMEM;

  W=malloc(sizeof(struct Prim_Working)*G->NumVertices);
  if (!W)
  {
    FreeGraph(Tree);
```

LISTING 16.8 continued

```
    return GRAPH_OUTOFMEM;
  };

  for (i=0;i<G->NumVertices;i++)
  {
    W[i].Visited=FALSE;
    W[i].LowestCost=GRAPH_NOTCONNECTED;
    W[i].Prev=-1;

    j=AddVertex(Tree);
    if (j<0)
    {
      /* error, clean up and return */
      FreeGraph(Tree);
      free(W);
      return j;
    }
    Tree->Vertices[j]->Tag=G->Vertices[i]->Tag;
  }

  NumVisited=0;

  /* Tree is an empty graph,
     Visited is an array of integers G->NumVertices long initially zeroed */

  /* step 1, select a root vertex V*/
  V=0;

  for (;;)
  {
    /* step 2, mark V as visited */
    W[V].Visited=TRUE;
    NumVisited++;

    if (NumVisited==G->NumVertices) break;  /* we're finished */

    /* step 3. for every vertex adjacent to V, adjust
       the lowest edge cost
    */

    EdgeScanStart(G,V,&EScan);
    while (!EdgeScanNext(&EScan))
```

LISTING 16.8 continued

```
    {
      if (EScan.Cost<W[EScan.Dest].LowestCost)
      {
        W[EScan.Dest].LowestCost=EScan.Cost;
        W[EScan.Dest].Prev=V;
      }
    }
    EdgeScanEnd(&EScan);

    /* step 4, select the vertex with the lowest cost
       edge which has not been visited and add the edge
       to the minimum spanning tree
    */

    lowest=GRAPH_NOTCONNECTED;V=-1;
    for (i=0;i<G->NumVertices;i++)
    {
      if (W[i].Visited) continue;

      if (V==-1) V=i;
      if (W[i].LowestCost<lowest)
      {
        lowest=W[i].LowestCost;
        V=i;
      }
    }

    if (W[V].Prev!=-1)
    {
        i=ConnectVertex(Tree,V,W[V].Prev,W[V].LowestCost);
        if (!i) i=ConnectVertex(Tree,W[V].Prev,V,W[V].LowestCost);
        if (i)
        {
            /* error occurred, tidy up and return */
            free(W);
            FreeGraph(Tree);
            return i;
        }
    }

    /* The first 'V=i' in the for loop above is used to preserve
       the index of a vertex which has not been visited. This is
```

LISTING 16.8 continued

```
        to neatly handle the situation where all the visited
        vertices do not have any edges to any vertices which have
        not been visited (that is, the graph is unconnected). If
        the graph is unconnected, then V is set to an unvisited
        vertex and a minimum spanning forest is made instead of a
        minimum spanning tree. If it is connected, then V would be
        the index of the vertex with the lowest cost edge known.
    */
  }

  free(W);
  *TreePtr=Tree;

  return 0;
}
```

The worst-case running time for Prim's algorithm is $O(V^2)$. This can be reduced for sparse graphs by using a prioritized queue of vertices. Using a binary heap as the underlying structure for the queue, the running time for sparse graphs can be reduced to be O(E log V).

When Prim's algorithm is used on an unconnected graph, some vertices will not be visited. A minimum spanning tree is not possible in such a graph, but it is possible to produce a forest of minimum spanning trees for each connected part of the graph.

Optimization: A Final Note

As a data structure, graphs are fairly complex and can easily become very large. Working with such complicated structures consumes processing time. The key to optimization is to alter the data structures used to represent a graph in order to reduce the number of iterations of common algorithms.

With most computational algorithms such as sorting and searching, selecting suitable data structures will improve performance, but usually it is the algorithm that is employed which has the greatest increase in performance. For any algorithm working on a graph, the number of iterations (and therefore the running time) is much more dependant on the speed of examining the graph data structure.

The first matter that must be taken into account is whether or not the graph is dense or sparse. This is very dependent on what the graph is modeling. Generally, the larger the data structure (in terms of its physical memory usage) the longer it will take to access and complete a task. The more memory there is to process, the more memory must be examined and this inevitably lengthens the running time of an algorithm. Selecting the most memory-efficient representation will normally reduce the running time by a sizable proportion.

The second matter to consider is determining whether the data structure is well suited to the algorithms that will be used in your particular application. If, for instance, you had a graph that was updated slightly but frequently, a large amount of processing time could be freed up simply by maintaining the list of edges as and when edges were changed, added, or removed.

There are no hard and fast rules when it comes to optimizing graph algorithms. The general approach is simply to keep frequently required data easily accessible, and the only way of doing this is through good use of data structures.

Summary

This chapter has introduced some elementary graph theory, shown some techniques for representing a graph as a data structure, and presented some algorithms that can be used practically. The graph library used in all the code examples in the chapter is flexible enough to be used in all but the most time-critical of applications.

The basic matrix operations are all simple; in fact, except for initializing variables and setting up loops, the core calculations can be implemented in C with a single line of code for each operation.

Note

The practical matters of initializing variables, setting up loops, dealing with memory management, and error detection increase the complexity, but no programmer should legitimately be intimidated by matrix arithmetic. The basics are simple and straightforward; even the medium complexity issues can be readily understood. The really complex matters may require the assistance of a specialist in numerical analysis—matters not dealt with extensively in this chapter.

Calculating determinants and inverting matrices are more involved, but there are straightforward and easily understood methods for doing the operations and for implementing them in C. In addition, when an inverse matrix is calculated (something that is frequently done while solving simultaneous linear equations), error propagation is a major problem. Error propagation and correction are discussed later in the chapter.

In a very real sense, the most complex part of doing matrix arithmetic with the C programming language is the implementation of the design details. These include initializing variables, determining what language structures and components to use to represent a matrix, memory management (including handling of temporary variables), passing complex structures as arguments, and using pointers to efficiently address individual elements of a matrix.

Simple Matrix Arithmetic Operations

The standard mathematical notation for representing a matrix with an abstract symbol is with a bold capital letter such as *A*, which represents a rectangular array of numbers with a typical element a_{ij} at row *i* and column *j*. Since we are talking about how to implement matrix arithmetic using the C programming language, when it is natural, we will simply refer to the element `a[i][j]` using the standard C representation for a 2D array.

Although many of the matrices that are of interest for problems like solving equations are square matrices (2×2 or 3×3 matrices), a matrix is, in general, a rectangular array of numbers and does not have to be a square array.

Two matrices with the same rectangular dimensions can be added to give a new matrix with the same rectangular dimensions. For instance, two 3×4 matrices can be added to give a new 3×4 matrix. The elements of the new matrix are simply the sum of the corresponding elements of the two matrices being added (in C notation):

```
sum_ab[i][j] = a[i][j] + b[i][j];
```

(which must be enclosed in the proper `for` loops to actually implement). Likewise, subtraction is

```
diff_ab[i][j] = a[i][j] - b[i][j];
```

Addition and subtraction should be familiar.

Another simple matrix operation is transposition; it literally transposes the elements from rows to columns. It is represented symbolically with a superscript T for transpose (A^T) and is pronounced *A-transpose*. For a square matrix, the transpose "flips" the matrix across the main diagonal. More generally, the transpose of an $M \times N$ matrix is an $N \times M$ matrix, as shown in Figure 17.1.

FIGURE 17.1
The transpose of an $M \times N$ matrix results in a new matrix, $N \times M$.

$$\begin{bmatrix} 1 & 2 & 3 & 2 \\ 4 & 5 & 6 & 1 \\ 7 & 8 & 9 & 4 \end{bmatrix}^T = \begin{bmatrix} 1 & 4 & 7 \\ 2 & 5 & 8 \\ 3 & 6 & 9 \\ 2 & 1 & 4 \end{bmatrix}$$

In C notation:

```
a_transpose[i][j] = a[j][i];
```

Although it is not needed or used further in this chapter, the transposition operation is implemented because it is so widely used in broader matrix arithmetic operations. Similarly, the matrix library will have a function to multiply a matrix by a constant; it is also a common matrix operation, though not one that is needed explicitly for this chapter.

There are two other terms that are important when discussing matrix arithmetic. The first is a *diagonal matrix* (see Figure 17.2), which is a square matrix that has 0s on all of the off-diagonal elements.

FIGURE 17.2
A diagonal matrix.

$$\begin{bmatrix} a_{11} & 0 & 0 & 0 \\ 0 & a_{22} & 0 & 0 \\ 0 & 0 & a_{33} & 0 \\ 0 & 0 & 0 & a_{44} \end{bmatrix}$$

The other term is a *triangular matrix* (see Figure 17.3), a square matrix that has 0s on the elements either below the diagonal (an *upper triangular* matrix since the non-zero elements are in the upper half) or above the diagonal (in this case, a *lower triangular* matrix since the non-zero elements are in the lower half of the matrix).

FIGURE 17.3
A triangular matrix.

$$\text{lower triangular} \implies \begin{bmatrix} 3 & 0 & 0 & 0 \\ 7 & 8 & 0 & 0 \\ 6 & 7 & 11 & 0 \\ 3 & 8 & 9 & 10 \end{bmatrix} \qquad \text{upper triangular} \implies \begin{bmatrix} 3 & 7 & 6 & 3 \\ 0 & 8 & 7 & 8 \\ 0 & 0 & 11 & 9 \\ 0 & 0 & 0 & 10 \end{bmatrix}$$

This chapter does not make extensive use of triangular matrices, but they are a staple of some kinds of analysis, so the definitions are worthwhile. Upper triangular matrices will also be a useful descriptive terminology in the section "Determinants and the Euclidean Norm" later in the chapter.

Implementing a Matrix Structure in C

The obvious question is "What could be simpler?" After all, a rectangular array is simply (as stated at the very beginning of the chapter):

```
double a[M][N];
```

where M and N are literal constants (probably defined by a macro statement `#define M 3`). And, if you do not mind embedding the details of matrix arithmetic at every place in your code that any operation is carried out, this approach can be used. This might be the right approach for some situations. Another approach might be to set aside global variables (or, if they need to be hidden, static variables) that are large enough to bound the maximum dimensions of any matrix you want to work with. Then your specific routines simply work with only a portion of these variables. For example, if you are going to handle a few 2×2 or 4×4 or larger matrices, but never larger than 10×10, you could set aside a number of 10×10 global arrays and do all of your calculations in those arrays (and certainly you can define functions to do things with that approach).

If, however, you want to write functions that handle the matrix arithmetic in a way where the details are hidden, where arbitrary size matrices (within the reasonable limits imposed by your system memory) can be handled, and where you do not necessarily know in advance how many matrices you may need to deal with, there is a need to define an appropriate C structure to house a matrix.

There are a number of practical questions. The 1990 ANSI C language is the implementation language for the matrix library. This standard only allows arrays to be declared using compile time constant dimensions. It is legal to declare `a[3][4]` but not to declare `a[m][n]` where m and n are calculated during program operation.

Note

The new 1999 ANSI Standard on the C programming language allows declarations of arrays using runtime calculated variables. Some earlier compilers also offered this as a non-standard extension. However, many compilers do not yet offer this feature. For purposes of maintaining compatibility both with the earlier C standard and with current C compilers, which do not yet offer runtime calculated dimensions, the matrix library implements matrix arithmetic without depending on this feature.

Pointer Arithmetic and Array Indices

One of the first issues to think about is the pointer arithmetic that underlies C's implementation of arrays. When you define a 2D array like the one above, you can pass the name of the array as an argument to a function, but the information about the dimensions of the array is not passed automatically. When you then use the double square bracket notation to reference the array, the compiler has no way to address individual elements. The simplest way to handle this is to make use of the following facts:

- 2D arrays are stored "row-wise."
- Pointer arithmetic and array indices are equivalent.

The C expression `a[i]` can be written equivalently as `*(a+i)`. When the compiler is automatically tracking the dimensions of a 2D array, the expression `a[i][j]` is equivalent to `*(a+i*numrows+j)`.

The C statements

```
double a[4] = {1,2,3,4};
```

and

```
double a[2][2] = {{1,2},{3,4}};
```

result in the same internal storage in the machine.

The simplest solution for passing an array to a function is to simply pass the address of the first element of the array (namely `&a[0]` for a 1D array or `&a[0][0]` for a 2D array) and then do the index arithmetic inside the function. Likewise, when allocating an array, simply allocate a 1D array and do the index arithmetic separately.

This will result in code that looks generally one of two ways. The first is

```
index = 0;
for ( i = 0; i < rows; i++) {
    for ( j = 0; j < cols; j++) {
        a[index] = 0.0;
        index++;
    }
}
```

The calculation of `index` by starting with 0 and incrementing throughout simply avoids the issue of doing detailed arithmetic by taking advantage of the row-wise storage. This is because the first element of a subsequent row of storage immediately follows the last element of the current row. This will be particularly useful where matrix calculations for a single element of a matrix depend on only a single element of another matrix. (This is true for matrix addition and subtraction.)

The second general form involves actually calculating the index explicitly:

```
for ( i = 0; i < rows; i++) {
    for ( j = 0; j < cols; j++) {
        a[mdx(i,j)] = 0.0;
    }
}
```

where `mdx()` is a macro or a function:

```
int mdx( int i, int j) {
    return i*rows+j;
}
```

Note

`mdx()` is simply an abbreviation for matrix index. Keeping the name short is important because of the frequency of the use of this function (which is implemented as a static function usable only inside the matrix library itself). The definition as a function was used throughout development to simplify debugging and testing. Upon completion of development, the `mdx()` function was replaced with an equivalent macro.

What Is the Initial Index?

Another issue, and one that is likely to cause confusion, is the conflicting practice of the initial index. The first element of a 2D C array is `a[0][0]`, whereas the mathematical convention is that the first element of a 2D matrix is a_{11}. Sooner or later, someone will forget the distinction (quite likely you as the programmer or implementer). Some other matrix libraries explicitly recalculate all indices to allow using the mathematical convention even inside the implementing code. Unfortunately, sooner or later, this extra step can also cause confusion. The matrix library follows the C convention of `[0][0]` being the first element. This chapter uses both the C convention to discuss the implementing code and the mathematical convention when discussing the mathematics or equations.

Note

The practice of forcing array indices to start with 1 instead of 0 is sometimes implemented with a dependence on very questionable C code; in addition, it can be a source of major confusion to experienced C programmers who expect the first element of an array to have an index of 0. If for some reason this is an absolute necessity, you should reimplement the code with some notation that suggests the difference. For example, consider addressing elements with a function notation so that the index is wrapped in parentheses rather than brackets. Generally, this approach is very un-C-like and should be avoided for the sake of future code maintenance.

Using the C convention in implementing code has little effect on the final user of a program where the focus is on the result and not on the hidden details of how calculations are being done.

The Matrix Type Structure MATRIX_T

The appropriate generic approach is to describe a C `struct` that can be dynamically allocated that will hold all of the information needed to allow a matrix calculation to be done on the contents of the structure. The number of rows and columns is needed (the dimensions of the matrix) as well as the values of the matrix elements. (The individual values such as a_{23} are referred to as the *elements* of the matrix.) Conceptually, we would like to have the structure shown in Figure 17.4.

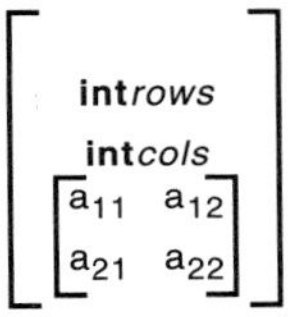

FIGURE 17.4
A generic matrix type structure.

However, one extra level of indirection is needed (to enable dynamic allocation of the array whose size is not known until program runtime). Instead, use the structure shown in Figure 17.5.

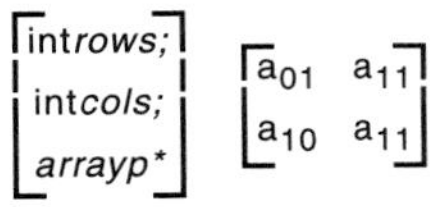

FIGURE 17.5
A matrix type structure with dynamic allocation of the array.

In C terminology, a basic matrix type can be defined as

```
typedef struct {
    int rows;
    int cols;
    double *val;
} MATRIX_T;
```

When the structure is dynamically allocated, then, based on the size of the matrix, the pointer to `val` will point to a dynamically allocated array of doubles (allocated at the same time that the structure is allocated based on the values of `rows` and `cols`).

With all of that said, let's begin the real implementation of a set of matrix routines with dynamic allocation and freeing of a `MATRIX_T`, as shown in Listing 17.1.

LISTING 17.1 Implementing a Matrix with Dynamic Allocation

```
/* allocates a new matrix, elements not initialized */
MATRIX_T *
m_new(int nrows, int ncols)
{
    double *temp;
    MATRIX_T *m = NULL;
    if ((temp = malloc(nrows * ncols * sizeof(double)))
              == NULL) {
        mmerrcode = ALLOCFAIL;
        return NULL;
    }
    if ((m = malloc(sizeof(MATRIX_T))) == NULL) {
        mmerrcode = ALLOCFAIL;
        free(temp);
        return NULL;
    }
    m->rows = nrows;
    m->cols = ncols;
    m->val = temp;
    return m;
}

/* frees matrix */
void
m_free(MATRIX_T * m)
{
    if ( m == NULL) return;
  /* not an error; used for recovery in
     other matrix library routines */
    free(m->val);
    free(m);
}}
```

These listings are the beginnings of the `m_matrix.c` file, which is included on the CD-ROM. The `m_new()` function first allocates an appropriately sized array of doubles. If this fails, `NULL` is returned immediately indicating failure. Then the `MATRIX_T` itself is allocated and initialized. If the allocation fails, the previously allocated array of doubles is freed and `NULL` is returned indicating failure. Otherwise, the result is an allocated `MATRIX_T` with initialized `rows` and `cols` variables and uninitialized values for the array of doubles. The `m_free` function frees the allocated `MATRIX_T` and the associated array of doubles. In addition, an error code is set to the `#defined` constant `ALLOCFAIL`.

Note

The proper way to declare `MATRIX_T` pointers is

```
MATRIX_T *a = NULL; /* NULL will cause uninitialized */
                    /* pointers to be detected in    */
                    /* the error detection code in   */
                    /* the matrix library            */
a = m_new(3,4);
```

Error Handling

A major issue in doing any kind of sophisticated calculations in C (or most other programming languages, for that matter) is how to handle failures. The decision I have made is to set an error value that can be tested by the programmer (see Listing 17.2). This is done by using a static variable `mmerrcode`, which can be set, reset, or tested with the functions `m_seterr()`, `m_reseterr()`, and `m_errcode()`. There is also a function `m_errmsg()`, which returns a descriptive string.

Note

Use of static variables with file scope (such as `mmerrcode`) is a potential problem. In this case, it is a natural way to handle the requirement of retaining the error state. The problem is that this usage will not cause failure if you are coding threads, but it can lead to a spurious value for `mmerrcode` for one thread because the value was set in another thread. If you are coding a threaded application that uses the matrix library, you will need to modify the library to find another way to keep track of error codes.

LISTING 17.2 Error Handling

```
static int mmerrcode = 0;

void
m_seterr(int errcode)
{
    mmerrcode = errcode;
}

void
```

LISTING 17.2 continued

```
m_reseterr(void)
{
    mmerrcode = 0;
}

const char *
m_errmsg(int errcode)
{
    switch (errcode) {
        case RMISMATCH:
            return "row mismatch";
        case CMISMATCH:
            return "column mismatch";
        case NOTSQUARE:
            return "not a square matrix";
        case ALLOCFAIL:
            return "allocation failure";
        case FILEREADFAIL:
            return "file read failure";
        case ROWPARSEFAIL:
            return "row parse failure";
        case COLPARSEFAIL:
            return "column parse failure";
        case RCMISMATCH:
            return "row-column mismatch";
        case INDEXOUTOFRANGE:
            return "index out of range";
        case LENMISMATCH:
            return "length mismatch";
        case NULLARG:
            return "NULL argument";
        default:
            return NULL;
    }
}

int
m_errcode(void)
{
    return mmerrcode;
}
```

Other Design Principles for the Matrix Library

Writing a consistent library requires making a series of design decisions.

What kind of convention will be used for returning values and passing arguments? The matrix library will pass pointers to `MATRIX_T` structures for both the result and the arguments. Generally, the return value will be a `MATRIX_T` pointer to the result. This supports a style of writing code that bears at least a minimal similarity to writing the equations. For example, a matrix sum can be coded as follows:

```
result = m_add( result, a, b);
```

Only the "result" argument will be modified. The "input" arguments will not be changed. As a matter of good practice, the user of the matrix library should not write code where the "result" argument is the same as one of the "input" arguments. In some cases, this will give correct results, but it cannot be depended upon.

Will memory allocation be primarily under the control of the library or the calling program? To the extent feasible, memory allocation will be under the direct control of the calling program. Temporary variables will be allocated and freed only when absolutely necessary.

Should the library encourage programmers to directly access or modify the contents of data structures, or should there be functions to allow the manipulation safely under library control? Access functions are provided to return the number of rows, columns, and the values of individual elements as well as to set the value of individual elements.

> **Note**
>
> It is virtually impossible to prevent a determined programmer from directly accessing the internal elements of data structures, but if you provide functions that allow it to be done safely, it encourages programmers not to undertake dangerous tasks on their own.

What kinds of specialized input/output routines are needed to serve the purposes of the matrix library? Functions are provided to allocate `MATRIX_T`s, to initialize them from files, from 1D or 2D arrays, or to set them equal to the identity matrix. Output functions include a function to print to `stdout` and to write comma-separated values (CSV) format to file.

How are functions and variables to be named? Generally, public functions have an `m_` prefix. Static variables have an `mm` prefix. Static functions are named descriptively but do not have a special prefix.

It is commonly accepted practice that variable names should be meaningful. For example, `row` is a more descriptive name than `i` for a row index. The variable naming conventions within matrix library functions use meaningful names to some extent. However, the mathematical literature discussing matrices makes such pervasive use of single letter indices such as `i`, `j`, and `k` that is natural for the matrix library to use such single letter index names also.

Initializing from Arrays

The matrix library has two functions for initializing a `MATRIX_T` from arrays—one for initializing from 1D arrays and another for 2D arrays. As discussed previously, the internal representation for 1D and 2D arrays with the same total number of elements is the same. As a result, the function for initializing from 2D arrays simply calculates the total number of elements and calls the function for initializing from a 1D array. Listing 17.3 shows the two functions.

LISTING 17.3 Initializing Arrays

```
MATRIX_T *
m_assign_arr2(MATRIX_T * a, int nrows,
              int ncols, double *arr)
{
    int len;
    if (a == NULL) {
        mmerrcode = NULLARG;
        return a;
    }
    if (nrows != a->rows) {
        mmerrcode = RMISMATCH;
        return a;
    }
    if (ncols != a->cols) {
        mmerrcode = CMISMATCH;
        return a;
    }
len = nrows * ncols;
    return m_assign_arr1(a, len, arr);
}

MATRIX_T *
m_assign_arr1(MATRIX_T * a, int alen, double *arr)
{
```

LISTING 17.3 continued

```
    int i, j, index;
    if (a == NULL) {
        mmerrcode = NULLARG;
        return a;
    }
    if (alen != a->rows * a->cols) {
        mmerrcode = LENMISMATCH;
        return a;
    }
    index = 0;
    for (i = 0; i < a->rows; i++) {
        for (j = 0; j < a->cols; j++) {             a->val[index] = arr[index];
            index++;
        }
    }
    return a;
}
```

The error detection code in these functions is fairly typical. Check to be sure that none of the MATRIX_T pointer arguments are NULL. Check to be sure that the number of rows and columns is consistent between the arguments.

Getting a Matrix from a File

One of the more complicated operations is the basic input of initializing a MATRIX_T from a file. The function m_fnew() is the matrix library function to allocate and initialize MATRIX_T objects from files.

It is convenient to allow comments to be embedded in data files (for which the file extension .mat is used in this chapter). Comments are lines that begin with a # character. Matrix data is then given on a line which, for a four-row matrix, reads "rows,4". Likewise, for a five-column matrix, the column data is given on a line by itself as "cols,5". Note that there are no spaces before or after the comma. Matrix element values are then given on subsequent lines with commas separating each value. Comment lines can be embedded anywhere in the file. Lines of the .mat files are read individually with the function m_getline(), which ignores comment lines. Subsequent lines can contain data for another matrix. Opening and closing the file containing the matrix data is the responsibility of the calling program.

Note

The function `m_getline()` makes use of a static char array variable `line` with file scope. It has the same disadvantages as the `mmerrcode` static variable discussed previously. Because `m_getline()` is the only function that uses `line`, there is less likelihood of a problem, but the code is not re-entrant. Because `line` has a nominal length of 4096 characters, using a static variable keeps the stack smaller for the function `m_getline()`. If re-entrant code is an issue, you can determine what maximum length you actually need and declare `line` internally to `m_getline()`.

The row and column data and the element value data is parsed with the `strtok()` standard library function.

Note

`Strtok()` has a reputation for being tricky to use, but for this application it is ideal. The parsing of each line into individual fields is unambiguous. There are no empty fields (one of the things that `strtok()` does not handle). Using `strtok()` also causes code that is not re-entrant. My recommendation to programmers who need to do simple parsing of strings is to read the `strtok()` documentation carefully. It is, despite its bad reputation and limitations, an excellent tool to use when the circumstances are right. (Indeed, my personal opinion is that the criticisms of `strtok()` closely resemble the criticisms an amateur carpenter might make: "Hammers are dangerous; I really hurt my thumb the first time I tried to use one." But try to drive a nail without a hammer. On the other hand, hammers are virtually useless for driving in wood screws. Use the right tool for the job.)

One other potential disadvantage of using `strtok()` in `m_fnew()` is that users are precluded from using `strtok()` in code that spans a call to `strtok()`.

An example matrix data file is shown in Listing 17.4.

LISTING 17.4 Example of a Matrix Data File

```
# This is a comment line
# Another comment line
rows,2
cols,3
1.1,2.0,3.0
```

LISTING 17.4 continued

```
4.6,5.3,9.1
# Another set of matrix data follows
rows,3
cols,2
1.1,2.5
3.0,4.2
4.0,5.1
```


The functions `m_fnew()` and `m_getline()` are shown in Listing 17.5.

LISTING 17.5 Allocating and Initializaing a Matrix from a File

```
char *
m_getline(FILE * fp)
{
    do {
        if (!fgets(line, LINELEN, fp)) {
            mmerrcode = FILEREADFAIL;
            return NULL;
        }
    } while (*line == '#');
    return line;
}

MATRIX_T *
m_fnew(FILE * fp)
{
    int i, j, rows, cols, index;
    char *tok;
    char *lineptr;
    MATRIX_T *a;

    /* get number of rows */
    if (!m_getline(fp)) { return NULL;}
    if (!(tok = strtok(line, ","))) {
        mmerrcode = ROWPARSEFAIL;
        return NULL;
    }
    if (strcmp(tok, "rows")) {
        mmerrcode = ROWPARSEFAIL;
        return NULL;
    }
```

LISTING 17.5 continued

```
    if (!(tok = strtok(NULL, ","))) {
        mmerrcode = ROWPARSEFAIL;
        return NULL;
    }
    rows = atoi(tok);
    if (!rows) {
        mmerrcode = ROWPARSEFAIL;
        return NULL;
    }
    /* get number of columns */
    if (!m_getline(fp)) { return NULL;}
    if (!(tok = strtok(line, ","))) {
        mmerrcode = COLPARSEFAIL;
        return NULL;
    }
    if (strcmp(tok, "cols")) {
        mmerrcode = COLPARSEFAIL;
        return NULL;
    }
    if (!(tok = strtok(NULL, ","))) {
        mmerrcode = COLPARSEFAIL;
        return NULL;
    }
    cols = atoi(tok);
    if (!cols) {
        mmerrcode = COLPARSEFAIL;
        return NULL;
    }
    /* allocate new matrix */
    if (!(a = m_new(rows, cols)))
        return NULL;           /* error checking done in
                                * m_new */
    index = 0;
    for (i = 0; i < rows; i++) {
        if (!m_getline(fp)) {
            m_free;
            return NULL;
        }
        lineptr = line;
        for (j = 0; j < cols; j++) {
            if (!(tok = strtok(lineptr, ","))) {
                m_free;
```

LISTING 17.5 continued

```
                return NULL;
            }
            a->val[index] = atof(tok);
            index++;
            lineptr = NULL;     /* NULL arg to strtok after
                                 * 1st pass */
        }
    }
    return a;}
```


Writing MATRIX_T Objects to stdout or a File

Two very straightforward functions are provided to write matrix objects to output. The first is `m_printf`, which sends a formatted print to `stdout`. The second is `m_fputcsv`, which writes a matrix object to a file in comma-separated value format. These functions are shown in Listing 17.6.

LISTING 17.6 Output Functions

```
void
m_printf(char *label, char *format, MATRIX_T * a)
{
    int i, j;
    if (a == NULL) {
        printf("m_printf NULL argument error\n");
        return;
    }
    printf("%s\n", label);
    printf("rows = %d, cols = %d\n", a->rows, a->cols);
    for (i = 0; i < a->rows; i++) {
        for (j = 0; j < a->cols; j++) {
            printf(format, a->val[mdx(a,i,j)]);
        }
        printf("\n");
    }
}

void
m_fputcsv(FILE * fp, MATRIX_T * a)
```

LISTING 17.8 continued

```
{
    int i, j;
    char *sep;
    char comma[] = ",";
    char nocomma[] = "";
    if (a == NULL) {
        mmerrcode = NULLARG;
        return;
    }
    fprintf(fp, "rows,%d\n", a->rows);
    fprintf(fp, "cols,%d\n", a->cols);
    for (i = 0; i < a->rows; i++) {
        sep = nocomma;
        for (j = 0; j < a->cols; j++) {
            fprintf(fp, "%s%f", sep, a->val[mdx(a,i,j)]);
            sep = comma;
        }
        fprintf(fp, "\n");
    }}
```

Function `m_printf()` accepts arguments for a label and for the numeric format of the elements to allow programmer control over the display format.

Function `m_fputcsv()` is less flexible in that regard. It uses the default numeric format `%f`. If this is not suitable, it can be easily modified. It is important, however, to suppress leading spaces in the format. The only tricky thing about either function is the method of assuring that there is no leading or trailing comma in the rows of numbers. This is done by preceding each value with the string `sep` (containing either `comma` or `nocomma`).

Full Implementation of Addition and Transposition

Listing 17.7 shows example code for implementing addition and transposition.

LISTING 17.7 Matrix Addition and Transposition

```
MATRIX_T *
m_add(MATRIX_T * sum, MATRIX_T * a, MATRIX_T * b)
{
    int i, j, index;
    if (sum == NULL || a == NULL || b == NULL) {
```

LISTING 17.7 continued

```
        mmerrcode = NULLARG;
        return sum;
    }
  if (a->rows != b->rows) {
        m_seterr(RMISMATCH);
        return sum;
    }
    if (sum->rows != b->rows) {
        m_seterr(RMISMATCH);
        return sum;
    }
    if (a->cols != b->cols) {
        m_seterr(CMISMATCH);
        return sum;
    }
    if (sum->cols != b->cols) {
        m_seterr(CMISMATCH);
        return sum;
    }

    index = 0;
    for (i = 0; i < sum->rows; i++) {
        for (j = 0; j < sum->cols; j++) {
            sum->val[index] =
                a->val[index] + b->val[index];
            index++;
        }
    }
    return sum;
}

MATRIX_T *
m_transpose(MATRIX_T * trans, MATRIX_T * a)
{
    int i, j;
    if (trans == NULL || a == NULL) {
        mmerrcode = NULLARG;
        return trans;
    }
  if (trans->rows != a->cols) {
        mmerrcode = RCMISMATCH;
        return trans;
```

LISTING 17.7 continued

```
    }
    if (trans->cols != a->rows) {
        mmerrcode = RCMISMATCH;
        return trans;
    }

    for (i = 0; i < a->rows; i++) {
        for (j = 0; j < a->cols; j++) {
            trans->val[mdx(trans, j, i)] =
                a->val[mdx(a, i, j)];
        }
    }
    return trans;
}
```

As promised, the basic operation is done in a single line of code although (as also promised) initialization, error detection, and setting up loops takes much more code. The relevant two lines of code are the ones starting `sum->val` and `trans->val` buried in the second level of the `for` loops.

To improve clarity and focus on the essential matrix operations, most of the listings later in this chapter do not show the full error detection code that is contained in the file `m_matrix.c` on the CD-ROM. The code contained in the functions for addition and transposition are fairly typical of the error checks that are done. The code for subtraction and multiplication by a constant are also not shown in listings but are included in the complete matrix library on the CD-ROM.

Complex Matrix Concepts

The basic operations—error handling, allocation, and input/output—are now complete. The more complex matrix operations in this chapter are calculating the determinant and the inverse of a matrix.

Complex Matrix Math

The primary motivation (at least initially) for learning matrix arithmetic is to solve simultaneous equations. A single linear equation is at the heart of linear algebra. Figure 17.6 shows a single linear equation and its solution.

FIGURE 17.6
Solving a simple linear equation.

$$ax = b \text{ or } x = \frac{b}{a}$$

This solution is obtained by multiplying both sides of the original equation by *1/a* or a^{-1}, which is simply the inverse of the number *a*. In fact, the intermediate step to finding the solution can be written as shown in Figure 17.6.

FIGURE 17.7
Intermediate step to solving a simple linear equation.

$$a^{-1}ax = x = a^{-1}b = \frac{b}{a}$$

This simplest linear equation has no practical involvement with the subject of matrices. However, when you begin to deal with sets of equations where you have several unknowns such as in Figure 17.8, then matrix terminology becomes especially useful.

FIGURE 17.8
Sets of linear equations.

$$a_{11}\, x_1 + a_{12}\, x_2 = b_1$$
$$a_{21}\, x_1 + a_{22}\, x_2 = b_2$$

Mathematicians rewrite the equations in Figure 17.8 as the matrix product seen in Figure 17.9.

FIGURE 17.9
A set of linear equations in matrix form.

$$\begin{bmatrix} a_{11} & a_{12} \\ a_{21} & a_{22} \end{bmatrix} \bullet \begin{bmatrix} x_1 \\ x_2 \end{bmatrix} = \begin{bmatrix} b_1 \\ b_2 \end{bmatrix}$$

or

$$Ax = b$$

In Figure 17.9, *A* is a 2×2 matrix and *x* and *b* are 1×2 matrices (or vectors).

Just as for the first equation (with only one unknown), the solution can be written as shown in Figure 17.10.

This example is, for now, just the motivation. It glosses over the details such as matrix multiplication and the identity matrix.

FIGURE 17.10
The solution for a set of linear equations using matrix notation.

$x = A^{-1}b$

where A^{-1} is the matrix inverse of A.

Matrix Multiplication

The motivational example previously discussed and shown in Figures 17.8 and 17.9

$Ax=b$

hints at the definition of the matrix product. The example is for a 2 × 2 matrix multiplying a 2 × 1 matrix. In general, the product is not limited to a single column. The number of columns of the left-hand matrix in the product must be the same as the number of rows of the right-hand matrix. The elements of the product are the sum of the row-column elements. Mathematically, this is shown in Figure 17.11.

FIGURE 17.11
Matrix multiplication.

$$\text{product}_{ij} = \sum_{k=1}^{n} a_{ik}b_{kj}$$

In Figure 17.11, *a* is an M × N matrix, *b* is an N × P matrix, and the resulting product is an M × P matrix.

In C, this is written (neglecting all the outer loops and initialization):

```
product[i][j] = 0.0;
for (k = 0; k < COLS; k++) {
    product[i][j] += a[i][k]*b[k][j];
}
```

An important note about matrix multiplication is that the product *AB* is usually not the same as the product *BA* (although there are a few important exceptions). Mathematicians would say that matrix multiplication is not *commutative*, but most of the time you will not need to worry about the fancy terminology. It should be clear that, since rectangular matrices can be multiplied with only one common dimension, the fact that the product *AB* is defined does not mean that the product *BA* is defined. For example, the product of a 3 × 4 matrix (as the left multiplicand) and a 4 × 5 matrix is defined, but not vice versa.

The matrix library code for multiplying matrices is shown in Listing 17.8.

LISTING 17.8 Multiplying Matrices

```
MATRIX_T *
m_mup(MATRIX_T * prod, MATRIX_T * a, MATRIX_T * b)
{
    int i, j, k;
    if (prod == NULL || a == NULL || b == NULL) {
        mmerrcode = NULLARG;
        return prod;
    }
    if (prod->rows != a->rows) {
        mmerrcode = RMISMATCH;
        return prod;
    }
    if (prod->cols != b->cols) {
        mmerrcode = CMISMATCH;
        return prod;
    }
    if (a->cols != b->rows) {
        mmerrcode = RCMISMATCH;
        return prod;
    }
    for (i = 0; i < a->rows; i++) {
        for (j = 0; j < b->cols; j++) {

            prod->val[mdx(prod,i,j)];
            for (k = 0; k < a->cols; k++) {
                prod->val[mdx(prod,i,j)] +=
                    a->val[mdx(a,i,k)] * b->val[mdx(b,k,j)];
            }
        }
    }
    return prod;}
```

The Identity Matrix

The identity matrix is defined as the square matrix, with zeros for its off-diagonal elements and ones for its diagonal elements. The identity matrix is typically shown symbolically as *I*. A 3×3 example is shown in Figure 17.12.

FIGURE 17.12
The identity matrix.

$$I = \begin{bmatrix} 1 & 0 & 0 \\ 0 & 1 & 0 \\ 0 & 0 & 1 \end{bmatrix}$$

The identity matrix, when multiplied by any other matrix (of the correct size), results in that same matrix. In other words, the identity matrix is the matrix arithmetic equivalent to the ordinary number 1 or at least as far as multiplication goes. The identity matrix is one of the important exceptions to matrix multiplication since

$$AI = IA$$

It should be noted that matrix notation can sometimes be sloppy with regard to the identity matrix. For example, if the matrix A shown in the preceding equation is square, then the identity matrix is understood to be the same size as A. But if A is not a square matrix, say an $m \times n$ matrix, the notation implies that the I in the term AI is an $n \times n$ matrix while the I in the term IA is an $m \times m$ matrix. Though this sounds confusing, in practice it simply means that the identity matrix is taken to be whatever size it needs to be for the equation to work.

A more precise way to handle this (when it is important) is to use the alternate notation I_n to denote an $n \times n$ identity matrix.

Sometimes (especially in engineering terminology) the identity matrix is called a *unitary* matrix and denoted by U.

One of the C functions included in the matrix library is `m_assign_identity()`, which assigns the elemental values of the identity matrix to the array passed as the argument (and the result).

Determinants and the Euclidean Norm

One of the most important topics in matrix arithmetic is matrix inversion, but before covering matrix inversion, it is convenient to cover determinants. In a very loose (and distinctly non-mathematical) fashion, a determinant is a measure of the magnitude of a square matrix (and only a square matrix—non-square matrices do not have determinants). If the determinant of a matrix is zero, it means the matrix cannot be inverted. Further, if the determinant is nearly zero, there is a higher likelihood that the matrix is *ill-conditioned*, which simply means that the inverse matrix is likely to have larger inherent errors resulting from the calculation itself.

The idea of a determinant being zero is mathematically exact, but in writing programs that do numerical analysis using floating point numbers (whether C floats, doubles, long doubles, or any other kind of floating point construct) there is a real possibility that a number that should calculate to be exactly zero will calculate instead to be a very small non-zero number.

The sense in which a determinant is like a magnitude is best understood in the context of our standby equation *Ax=b*. The solution to this turns out (in a fairly natural way) to be as shown in Figure 17.13.

FIGURE 17.13
Solution to a determinant.

$$x_{ij} = \frac{const_{ij}b}{detA}$$

This chapter doesn't use the approach shown in Figure 17.13 to solve the equation, but most textbooks on linear algebra and matrices discuss solving the equation this way. (Then they don't use it because it is less than efficient.) Another approach is shown in Figure 17.14.

FIGURE 17.14
Finding the determinant of a matrix.

A 2x2 matrix has a determinant equal to the quantity:

$$a_{11}a_{22} - a_{12}a_{21}$$

A 3x3 matrix has a determinant equal to the quantity:

Larger matrices have determinants that consist of much more involved sums and differences of products of the elements. Rather than try to calculate determinants using such an involved set of definitions (which can also be very inefficient), this chapter makes use of some known properties of determinants to simplify the calculation.

The determinant of a triangular (or diagonal) matrix is the product of the diagonal elements, as shown in Figure 17.15.

Note

The numbers x, y, and z are used in the upper part of the example triangular matrix (see Figure 17.15). The determinant does not depend on the values of x, y, and z.

FIGURE 17.15
The determinant of a triangular (or diagonal) matrix is the product of the diagonal elements.

$$\det \begin{bmatrix} 2 & x & y \\ 0 & 3 & z \\ 0 & 0 & 4 \end{bmatrix} = 2 \bullet 3 \bullet 4 = 24$$

If a row of a matrix is multiplied by a constant, the determinant of the new matrix is the constant times the determinant of the original matrix, as you can see in Figure 17.16.

FIGURE 17.16
The determinant of a matrix when a row is multiplied by a constant.

$$\det \begin{bmatrix} 2 & x & y \\ 0 & 3 & z \\ 0 & 0 & 3 \bullet 4 \end{bmatrix} = 3 \bullet \det \begin{bmatrix} 2 & x & y \\ 0 & 3 & z \\ 0 & 0 & 4 \end{bmatrix} = 3 \bullet (2 \bullet 3 \bullet 4) = 72$$

Note

For directly calculating determinants, the matrix library does *not* use the property that multiplying a row by a constant multiplies the determinant by a constant. Later in the chapter, however, the determinant is also calculated indirectly during matrix inversion, and this property will be used there.

If two rows of a matrix are interchanged, the determinant of the resulting matrix is the same absolute value as the original, but the sign is changed as in Figure 17.17.

FIGURE 17.17
The determinant of a matrix when two rows are interchanged.

$$\det \begin{bmatrix} 0 & 0 & 4 \\ 0 & 3 & z \\ 2 & x & y \end{bmatrix} = (-1) \bullet \det \begin{bmatrix} 2 & x & y \\ 0 & 3 & z \\ 0 & 0 & 4 \end{bmatrix} = (-1) \bullet 2 \bullet 3 \bullet 4 = -24$$

If a multiple of one row is added to or subtracted from another row of the matrix, the determinant is unchanged, as shown in Figure 17.18.

By making use of these properties, a square matrix can be manipulated into a triangular or diagonal matrix for which the determinant can easily be calculated.

FIGURE 17.18
If a multiple of one row is added to or subtracted from another row of the matrix, the determinant is unchanged.

$$\det\begin{bmatrix} 2 & x & y \\ 0 & 3 & z \\ 0 & 0 & 4 \end{bmatrix} = \det\begin{bmatrix} 2 & x & y \\ 0 & 3 & z \\ 0+2 & 0+x & 4+y \end{bmatrix} = 2 \cdot 3 \cdot 4 = 24$$

An example calculation of a determinant using this method is shown in Table 17.1. Multiples of the first row are added or subtracted from the remaining rows to put 0s in every first column except the first row. Then multiples of the second row are added or subtracted from the remaining lower rows to put 0s in every second column below the diagonal. When finished, you have an upper triangular matrix. This method is referred to as *Gaussian elimination*. The determinant is simply the product of the diagonal elements. The particular element on the diagonal that you are working with to eliminate the lower elements is called the *pivot element*.

Note

There is a temptation to ignore the fancy terminology like Gaussian elimination. Gauss was a famous mathematician who originated this method of calculating determinants (and the corresponding way of solving linear equations). The terminology is so common that you are likely to find yourself feeling left out in any conversation involving linear algebra if you don't have some feeling for it. But like so many other things in mathematics, it is just a name.

TABLE 17.1 Gaussian Elimination

	Original Matrix		
1.00	2.00	3.00	4.00
5.00	6.00	7.00	8.00
1.00	4.00	5.00	7.00
2.00	3.00	-3.00	4.00
	row 0: swaprows		
5.00	6.00	7.00	8.00
1.00	2.00	3.00	4.00
1.00	4.00	5.00	7.00
2.00	3.00	-3.00	4.00

TABLE 17.1 continued

	row 0, column 0: make lower column zero		
5.00	6.00	7.00	8.00
0.00	0.80	1.60	2.40
0.00	2.80	3.60	5.40
0.00	0.60	-5.80	0.80
	row 1: swaprows		
5.00	6.00	7.00	8.00
0.00	2.80	3.60	5.40
0.00	0.80	1.60	2.40
0.00	0.60	-5.80	0.80
	row 1, column 1: make lower column zero		
5.00	6.00	7.00	8.00
0.00	2.80	3.60	5.40
0.00	0.00	0.57	0.86
0.00	0.00	-6.57	-0.36
	row 2: swaprows		
5.00	6.00	7.00	8.00
0.00	2.80	3.60	5.40
0.00	0.00	-6.57	-0.36
0.00	0.00	0.57	0.86
	row 2, column 2: make lower column zero		
5.00	6.00	7.00	8.00
0.00	2.80	3.60	5.40
0.00	0.00	-6.57	-0.36
0.00	0.00	0.00	0.83
	result		
det =	76.00		

There is a temptation to ignore the possibility of swapping rows. If you do, sooner or later, by applying these operations naively, you will encounter a matrix that has a zero on the diagonal and that will not allow you to proceed with the generation of a triangular matrix (at least not without doing row swaps). An example is the 3×3 matrix shown in Figure 17.19.

FIGURE 17.19
Example of a matrix showing the need for swapping rows.

$$\begin{bmatrix} 0 & 0 & 1 \\ 1 & 1 & 1 \\ 1 & 2 & 2 \end{bmatrix}$$

The matrix in Figure 17.19 has a determinant of -1 but cannot be put into diagonal or triangular form without swapping rows.

Another reason for swapping rows is to improve accuracy. If the pivot element being considered is the element in the column with the maximum absolute value, there will be improved accuracy in the calculation of the determinant. When row swapping is used to put the maximum element in the lower half of the matrix into the pivot position, the method is referred to as *Gaussian elimination with partial pivot maximization* (again, merely a name).

The matrix library provides the function `m_det()` to calculate the determinant. Helper functions `swaprows()` and `set_low_zero()` are used, respectively, to swap rows between the specified row and the pivot row and to add or subtract multiples of the pivot row to make each element below the diagonal in the appropriate column equal to zero.

The code is shown in Listing 17.9; the actual testing for singularity is done using the concept of the *normalized determinant* discussed in the next section.

LISTING 17.9 Calculating a Determinant

```
double
m_det(MATRIX_T * a, double epsilon)
{
/* calculates the determinant of matrix a using Gaussian
 * elimination with partial pivot maximization */

/* error checking code not shown */

    int row, col, swap, sign;
    double pivot, e_norm, det;
    e_norm = m_e_norm;
    det = 1.0;
    sign = 1;

    /* allocate a "scratch" matrix to work with */
    if (!(t = m_new(a->rows, a->cols))) return 0.0;
    t = m_assign(t, a);

    /* for each row */
    for (row = 0; row < t->rows; row++) {
        /* find largest element below diagonal in column */
        swap = maxelementrow(t, row);
        /* swap rows to put largest element on pivot */
        if (swap != row) {
            sign = -sign;
```

LISTING 17.9 continued

```
            swaprows(t, row, swap);
        }
        /* multiply running product of det by the pivot
         * element */
        pivot = t->val[mdx(t, row, row)];
        det *= pivot;
        if ((fabs(det) / e_norm) < epsilon) {
            return 0;          /* potentially singular
                                * matrix */
        }
        /* subtract a multiple of the pivot row from each
         * row (below the diagonal) to put 0's in all
         * elements of the pivot column below the diagonal */
        col = row;
        set_low_zero(t, col);
    }
    m_free(t);
    if (sign < 0)
        det = -det;
    return det;
}

static void
set_low_zero(MATRIX_T * t, int col)
{
    int i, j;
    double pivot, factor;
    pivot = t->val[mdx(t, col, col)];
    for (i = col + 1; i < t->rows; i++) {
        factor = t->val[mdx(t, i, col)] / pivot;
        for (j = col; j < t->cols; j++) {
            t->val[mdx(t, i, j)] -=
                factor * t->val[mdx(t, col, j)];
        }
    }
}

static void
swaprows(MATRIX_T * t, int row, int swap)
{
    int j;
    double temp;
```

LISTING 17.9 continued

```
    for (j = 0; j < t->cols; j++) {
        temp = t->val[mdx(t, row, j)];
        t->val[mdx(t, row, j)] = t->val[mdx(t, swap, j)];
        t->val[mdx(t, swap, j)] = temp;
    }}
```

One of the design principles for the matrix library is to leave arguments to functions unchanged (unless they are actually results). A second principle is to minimize the allocation of temporary variables. This conflict between design principles led to the decision to allocate and free a temporary `MATRIX_T` as part of the calculation in `m_det()`.

The Euclidean Norm and the Normalized Determinant

If the determinant of a matrix is zero, it is singular. If it is nearly zero, the matrix is likely to be ill-conditioned and the calculation of the matrix is likely to be error prone. Because calculations with floating point numbers have a tendency to lose precision, it is useful to have a test for "nearly zero." The difficulty is that a 3×3 diagonal matrix with diagonal elements equal to 10^{-6} has a determinant of 10^{-18}, whereas a 3×3 diagonal matrix with diagonal elements equal to 1000 has a determinant of 1,000,000,000 (or 10^9). Yet the two matrices are basically equivalent, so there is no reason to think that calculations involving either the matrices or their determinants should result in fundamentally poorer precision simply because one has a determinant 27 orders of magnitude smaller than the other. The real measure of how near the determinant is to zero depends on the magnitude of the elements of the matrix.

> **Note**
>
> This example of differences in the value of determinants has been deliberately fabricated. (And is, thus, a fairly peculiar example.) Calculations for diagonal matrices are not likely to be difficult in any case, but there are other cases far more severe involving non-diagonal matrices. Any pair of similar matrices with all elements multiplied by a common factor that differs by a large amount will suffer from a similar apparent disparity that has nothing to do with the properties of the matrices.

One measure is to compare the absolute value of the determinant to the absolute value of the largest magnitude element. If the determinant is orders of magnitude smaller than that element, the matrix is likely to be ill-conditioned.

A more systematic approach is to make use of the Euclidean Norm of the matrix, which is defined to be the square root of the sum of the squares of each element of the matrix (see Figure 17.20). A C function `m_e_norm` is provided to calculate the Euclidean Norm. Then the normalized determinant is defined to be the absolute value of the determinant divided by the Euclidean Norm. If this value is much less than 1, the matrix is ill-conditioned. The normalized determinant provides a more objective measure of how near the determinant is to zero and how likely the matrix is to be ill-conditioned. This method works well in most cases, but the user should be aware that there are cases where even this approach can give a misleading result. Checking the Euclidean Norm of the inverse matrix can be useful in these cases (although this is not implemented in the matrix library with this book).

FIGURE 17.20
The Euclidean Norm.

$$\frac{|\text{det(A)}|}{\sqrt{\sum_{j=1}^{\text{rows}} \sum_{j=1}^{\text{cols}} a_{ij}^2}} << 1$$

Note

The terms Euclidean Norm and Normalized Determinant are just more fancy names; once again, it should not cause intimidation. The terminology is the precise terminology used by specialists, but is not as widely used as some of the other terminology mentioned in the chapter.

Even this test needs to be applied with some caution. The C Standard requires that a double have at least 10 digits of precision. Depending on the particular matrix, a normalized determinant value could legitimately be as low as 10^{-9} (10^{-14} for IEEE-compliant compilers) and still leave an order of magnitude for the accumulation of errors that results from a matrix being ill-conditioned. The actual situation depends heavily on the variation in ranges of the values of elements of the matrix and how the ingrained error propagation happens in a particular case. As a practical matter, it is probably wise to make any tests based on the normalized determinant as large as possible without interfering with the calculation at hand. In the C function to compute the matrix, the running product that will eventually become the determinant is compared with a comparison argument, *epsilon*, passed to the function. If at any point the running product divided by the Euclidean Norm is smaller than *epsilon*, the calculation is terminated and a value of zero is returned.

Note

The 1990 ANSI C Standard requires that a float have at least 6 digits of precision and that doubles and long doubles have at least 10 digits of precision. It further suggests that compilers which choose to comply with IEEE Standard 754 (on numeric representation) should have doubles with at least 15 digits of precision.

The Inverse Matrix

Calculating the inverse matrix is done in a manner similar to the calculation of the determinant. The inverse of matrix A is defined as the matrix A^{-1} that when multiplied by A yields the identity matrix (see Figure 17.21). This is another of the exceptions to the order of matrix multiplication.

FIGURE 17.21
Properties of the inverse matrix.

$$AA^{-1} = A^{-1}A = I$$

Drop back to our set of linear equations, as shown in Figure 17.22.

To solve this set of equations, if you know A^{-1}, then multiply both sides of the equation by A^{-1} resulting in Figure 17.23.

So, if you apply the same row multiplication, row-swapping, and elimination of the off-diagonal elements to A and to I, you can simultaneously convert A to I and I to A^{-1}. If you keep a running product of the diagonal elements (before they are transformed to 1), you get the determinant more or less painlessly.

FIGURE 17.22
Recognizing the implicit identity matrix on the right side of the equation.

$$Ax = b \text{ or } Ax = Ib$$

FIGURE 17.23
Solving linear equations with the inverse matrix.

$$A^{-1} Ax = A^{-1}Ib \text{ or } x = A^{-1}b$$

The differences in this process and the calculation of the determinant is that the elements above and below the diagonal are forced to zero. This process is called *Gauss-Jordan elimination*. Again, it is important to maximize the pivot elements. (Actually, this is still what is called partial pivot maximization. Full pivot maximization would involve swapping columns as well. However, swapping columns results in a calculated inverse matrix that is scrambled in order. Rather than deal with the complexity of "unscrambling" the result, partial pivot maximization based only on row swapping is used. In addition, the extra accuracy gained by full pivot maximization rather than partial pivot maximization is usually small.)

Listing 17.10 shows the C code to implement the matrix inversion code (and its helper functions). Again, a test is done for the normalized determinant being less than a comparison value, and, if so, the determinant is set equal to zero and the inversion function returns. Table 17.2 shows the steps in inverting a matrix.

LISTING 17.10 Matrix Inversion

```
MATRIX_T *
m_inverse(MATRIX_T * v, MATRIX_T * a,
          double *det, double epsilon)
{
/* calculates the inverse of matrix a using Gauss-Jordan
 * elimination with partial pivot maximization */
    int row, col, swap, sign;
    double pivot, e_norm;
    MATRIX_T *t = NULL;
    /*** error checking code not shown ***/
    e_norm = m_e_norm(a);
    *det = 1.0;
    sign = 1;

    /* allocate a "scratch" matrix to invert */
    t = m_new(a->rows, a->cols);
    t = m_assign(t, a);

    /* set target matrix to the identity matrix */
    v = m_assign_identity(v);

    for (row = 0; row < t->rows; row++) {
        /* find largest element below diagonal in column */
        swap = maxelementrow(t, row);
        /* swap rows to put largest element on pivot */
        if (swap != row) { sign = -sign; }
```

LISTING 17.10 continued

```
            swaprows2(t, v, row, swap);
        }
        /* divide each element on pivot row by pivot
         * element putting a 1 in the pivot element */
        pivot = t->val[mdx(t, row, row)];
        *det *= pivot;
        if ((fabs(*det) / e_norm) < epsilon) {
            return v;          /* potentially singular
                                * matrix */
        }
        t = m_muprow(row, 1. / pivot, t);
        v = m_muprow(row, 1. / pivot, v);

        /* subtract a multiple of the pivot row from each
         * row to put 0's in all elements of the pivot
         * column except the pivot row */
        col = row;
        set_col_zero(t, v, col);
    }
    m_free(t);
    if (sign < 0)
        *det = -*det;
    return v;
}

static void
set_col_zero(MATRIX_T * t, MATRIX_T * v, int col)
{
    int i, j;
    double pivot, factor;
    pivot = t->val[mdx(t, col, col)];
    for (i = 0; i < t->rows; i++) {
        if (i == col) {
            continue;
        }
        factor = t->val[mdx(t, i, col)] / pivot;
        for (j = 0; j < t->cols; j++) {
            t->val[mdx(t, i, j)] -=
                factor * t->val[mdx(t, col, j)];
            v->val[mdx(v, i, j)] -=
                factor * v->val[mdx(v, col, j)];
        }
```

LISTING 17.10 continued

```
    }
}

static void
swaprows2(MATRIX_T * t, MATRIX_T * v, int row, int swap)
{
    int j;
    double temp;
    for (j = 0; j < t->cols; j++) {
        temp = t->val[mdx(t, row, j)];
        t->val[mdx(t, row, j)] = t->val[mdx(t, swap, j)];
        t->val[mdx(t, swap, j)] = temp;
        temp = v->val[mdx(v, row, j)];
        v->val[mdx(v, row, j)] = v->val[mdx(v, swap, j)];
        v->val[mdx(v, swap, j)] = temp;
    }
}
```

Table 17.2 shows a sample of intermediate and final results from the preceding listing.

TABLE 17.2 Matrix Inversion, Step By Step

Original Matrix and Identity Matrix								
1.00	2.00	3.00	4.00	**	1.00	0.00	0.00	0.00
5.00	6.00	7.00	8.00	**	0.00	1.00	0.00	0.00
1.00	4.00	5.00	7.00	**	0.00	0.00	1.00	0.00
2.00	3.00	-3.00	4.00	**	0.00	0.00	0.00	1.00
row 0: swaprows								
5.00	6.00	7.00	8.00	**	0.00	1.00	0.00	0.00
1.00	2.00	3.00	4.00	**	1.00	0.00	0.00	0.00
1.00	4.00	5.00	7.00	**	0.00	0.00	1.00	0.00
2.00	3.00	-3.00	4.00	**	0.00	0.00	0.00	1.00
row 0, column 0: make column zero								
1.00	1.20	1.40	1.60	**	0.00	0.20	0.00	0.00
0.00	0.80	1.60	2.40	**	1.00	-0.20	0.00	0.00
0.00	2.80	3.60	5.40	**	0.00	-0.20	1.00	0.00
0.00	0.60	-5.80	0.80	**	0.00	-0.40	0.00	1.00
row 1: swaprows								
1.00	1.20	1.40	1.60	**	0.00	0.20	0.00	0.00
0.00	2.80	3.60	5.40	**	0.00	-0.20	1.00	0.00
0.00	0.80	1.60	2.40	**	1.00	-0.20	0.00	0.00
0.00	0.60	-5.80	0.80	**	0.00	-0.40	0.00	1.00

TABLE 17.2 continued

row 1, column 1: make column zero								
1.00	0.00	-0.14	-0.71	**	0.00	0.29	-0.43	0.00
0.00	1.00	1.29	1.93	**	0.00	-0.07	0.36	0.00
0.00	0.00	0.57	0.86	**	1.00	-0.14	-0.29	0.00
0.00	0.00	-6.57	-0.36	**	0.00	-0.36	-0.21	1.00
row 2: swaprows								
1.00	0.00	-0.14	-0.71	**	0.00	0.29	-0.43	0.00
0.00	1.00	1.29	1.93	**	0.00	-0.07	0.36	0.00
0.00	0.00	-6.57	-0.36	**	0.00	-0.36	-0.21	1.00
0.00	0.00	0.57	0.86	**	1.00	-0.14	-0.29	0.00
row 2, column 2: make column zero								
1.00	0.00	0.00	-0.71	**	0.00	0.29	-0.42	-0.02
0.00	1.00	0.00	1.86	**	0.00	-0.14	0.32	0.20
0.00	0.00	1.00	0.05	**	0.00	0.05	0.03	-0.15
0.00	0.00	0.00	0.83	**	1.00	-0.17	-0.30	0.09
row 3, column 3: make column zero Results in Completed Identity Matrix and Inverse								
1.00	0.00	0.00	0.00	**	0.86	0.14	-0.68	0.05
0.00	1.00	0.00	0.00	**	-2.25	0.25	1.00	0.00
0.00	0.00	1.00	0.00	**	-0.07	0.07	0.05	-0.16
0.00	0.00	0.00	1.00	**	1.21	-0.21	-0.37	0.11

Once again, this function allocates and frees temporary variables to avoid modifying arguments other than the result. The helper functions are `set_col_zero()` and `swaprows2()`, which are analogous to the helper functions used in calculating determinants. Both of the functions work on both the matrix being inverted and the target inverse.

Solving Linear Equations

To solve linear equations, the easiest approach given the code implemented so far is to calculate the inverse of the matrix and multiply it times the known vector, as shown in Figure 17.24.

FIGURE 17.24
Solving linear equations using matrix inversion.

$$Ax = b \Rightarrow x = A^{-1}b$$

There are slightly more direct ways to solve linear equations (as discussed in the section on determinants), but this method has a major advantage of allowing an easy and straightforward extension to correct errors.

A C function to solve linear equations is shown in Listing 17.11.

LISTING 17.11 Solving Linear Equations

```
MATRIX_T *
m_solve(MATRIX_T * x, MATRIX_T * a, MATRIX_T * b,
        double epsilon)
{
/* solves linear equation Ax = b for x using matrix
 * inversion NOTE: no explicit error checking; (except for
 * allocation failures) all potential errors are checked in
 * called functions */
    MATRIX_T *ainv = NULL;
    double det = 0.0;
    if ((ainv = m_new(a->rows, a->cols)) == NULL) {
        return x;
    }
    if ((ainv = m_inverse(ainv, a, &det, epsilon)) == NULL)
        return x;
    x = m_mup(x, ainv, b);
    m_free(ainv);
    return x;
}
```

Since what is desired from this function is the solution to a set of linear equations, the inverse function that is calculated is of no interest once the calculation is complete. This function allocates and frees a temporary `MATRIX_T` to hold the inverse function. In addition, it calls the `m_inverse()` function, which also allocates and frees temporary variables.

Error Propagation in Matrix Calculations

All floating point errors are subject to inaccuracies. Integer values that are represented as floating point values are represented exactly (if they are in the representable range and precision of the floating point type being used), but most other numbers do not have an exact representation. Representing one third to 10 (or 15) digits of precision seems to be more than enough for ordinary purposes. That is, it seems like enough until you conduct a series of multiplications, divisions, additions, and subtractions of widely varying numbers.

Floating point errors accumulate and can mask the correct results of involved calculations like inverting a matrix. Subtracting two numbers that are nearly equal, for example, results in a loss of precision. Likewise, adding or subtracting two numbers that differ in order of magnitude by nearly the underlying precision used by the compiler also results in loss of precision. Chapter 24, "Arbitrary Precision Arithmetic," discusses the propagation of floating point errors in substantial detail.

Note

For example, if the maximum precision of numbers is four digits, the difference in 100.0 and 99.95 could result (depending on how the operation is handled by the math library) in a difference of 0 or a difference of 0.1; neither being what is wanted. (It is of course possible that a particular math library might carry additional digits of precision for internal calculations and return a result of 0.05, but there is no guarantee, and, in general, such libraries are a rarity.) Likewise, the sum of 100.0 and 0.01 is 100.0 with only four digits of precision. With at least 10 or 15 digits of precision in an ANSI-compliant compiler, the situation is mproved. Ultimately, however, any specific limit in the number of digits will result in errors in either the precision or the number of significant figures of the result of floating point calculations. Needless to say, matrix calculations (and most other calculations that involve a significant number of divisions, multiplications, additions, and subtractions to get a result) would benefit from the use of arbitrary or extended precision arithmetic as discussed in Chapter 24. This benefit will be most pronounced for calculations of determinants and the inverse of matrices.

Error Correction in Solving Linear Equations

If there is reason to believe that there are substantial errors in the solution of a set of linear equations, there is a straightforward iterative approach to correct errors.

Note

A substantial error is in the eye of the beholder. For some purposes, a couple of percent accuracy (or worse) may be more than adequate. In other cases, the 10 or 15 digits of precision guaranteed by the C Standard may not be enough even if there is no error propagation.

The "solution" x returned by `m_solve()` is not exact. Substituting x back into the original equation results in a new vector b, which is different than the original b.

To understand the error correction method, use the notation that x is the desired exact solution and x' is the calculated result. When x' is substituted back into the original equations the result is b', which is different than b (see Figure 17.25).

FIGURE 17.25
Error correction in solving linear equations.

$Ax^1 = b^1$

Subtract this equation from the original equation and the result is

$A(x - x') = b - b'$ or $A \bullet xadj = b - b'$

But if the adjustment to x is known (and it can be calculated directly by multiplying A^{-1} times b-b'), the true x should be simply x+*xadj*.

This error correction will not give an exact solution for x since the calculated values *xadj* and the differences in the known and calculated b's will have errors for the same reasons that the calculated x originally had an error. It makes sense to apply the method iteratively, but the very presence of errors will keep it from converging in an absolute sense. Iterating while the magnitude (in some sense) of *xadj* is decreasing is effective. Tests for decreasing error terms could be the maximum absolute value of an element of *xadj* or the Euclidean Norm of *xadj*. One or two iterations may be enough, though several more may continue to improve the result. Eventually, the process will fail to bring about any further improvement.

The C function `m_ecsolve()` implements this process. Iterations are continued while the Euclidean Norm is decreasing. (A limit of 10 iterations is hard coded into this function to prevent the potential of a runaway calculation. In practice, 10 iterations should never be needed; however, if this limit needs to be increased, the `for` loop incorporating the limit is identified in a comment.) The code is shown in Listing 17.12.

Note

Many specialists suggest that one or two iterations is sufficient for this error correction technique. There is no harm in applying it until some specific criteria is attained (such as continued decreases in the Euclidean Norm). Other criteria could be used as well; for example, continued decreases in the maximum absolute value of an `xadj` term.

Error correction techniques can be useful for small matrices, but 10×10 matrices and larger especially benefit from the use of error correction.

LISTING 17.12 Error Correction in Solving Linear Equations

```
MATRIX_T *
m_ecsolve(MATRIX_T * x, MATRIX_T * a, MATRIX_T * b,
          double epsilon)
{
/* solves linear equation Ax = b for x using matrix
 * inversion and a followup iterative approach for error
 * correction */
    MATRIX_T *ainv = NULL;
    MATRIX_T *bprime = NULL;
    MATRIX_T *adj = NULL;
    MATRIX_T *newx = NULL;
    MATRIX_T *newadj = NULL;
    MATRIX_T *err = NULL;
    int iteration;
    double adjenorm, newadjenorm, det;
    if (!(ainv = m_new(a->rows, a->cols))) {
        mmerrcode = ALLOCFAIL;
        goto ending;
    }
    if (!(bprime = m_new(b->rows, b->cols))) {
        mmerrcode = ALLOCFAIL;
        goto ending;
    }
    if (!(adj = m_new(x->rows, x->cols))) {
        mmerrcode = ALLOCFAIL;
        goto ending;
    }
    if (!(newx = m_new(x->rows, x->cols))) {
        mmerrcode = ALLOCFAIL;
        goto ending;
    }
    if (!(newadj = m_new(adj->rows, adj->cols))) {
        mmerrcode = ALLOCFAIL;
        goto ending;
    }
    if (!(err = m_new(x->rows, x->cols))) {
        mmerrcode = ALLOCFAIL;
        goto ending;
    }
    /* calculate the first try at a solution including
     * calculation of first adjustment */
    ainv = m_inverse(ainv, a, &det, epsilon);
```

17 Matrix Arithmetic

LISTING 17.12 continued

```
    x = m_mup(x, ainv, b);
    bprime = m_mup(bprime, a, x);
    err = m_sub(err, b, bprime);
    adj = m_mup(adj, ainv, err);
    adjenorm = m_e_norm(adj);


    /* iteratively calculate new solutions while accuracy
     * improves do no more than 10 iterations to prevent a
     * runaway calculation */
    for (iteration = 0; iteration < MMAXITERATIONS; iteration++) {
        newx = m_add(newx, x, adj);
        bprime = m_mup(bprime, a, newx);
        err = m_sub(err, b, bprime);
        newadj = m_mup(newadj, ainv, err);
        newadjenorm = m_e_norm(newadj);
        /* this is a test to see if complete else clause
         * operates to break out of loop if no improvement
         * since previous iteration; otherwise try again */
        if (newadjenorm < adjenorm) {  /* still improving */
            adjenorm = newadjenorm;
            x = m_assign(x, newx);
            adj = m_assign(adj, newadj);
        } else {
            break;
        }
    }
  ending:
    m_free(err);
    m_free(newadj);
    m_free(newx);
    m_free(adj);
    m_free(bprime);
    m_free(ainv);
    return x;}
```

Like `m_solve()`, the inverse matrix is not a part of the desired result for `m_ecsolve()`, so a temporary variable is allocated for use inside the function. Since the inverse function is also called, there are further indirect allocations of temporary `MATRIX_T` variables. Several other temporaries are allocated and later freed as well to hold interim results.

Note

If you didn't look closely at the listing for `m_ecsolve()`, look again. Normally, when programming in a structured language, the `goto` statement is discouraged. There is an old adage that says, "You can write spaghetti code in any language." And it is definitely true. Why then, you may ask, does `m_ecsolve()` use `goto`? Because the function must clean up its prior memory allocations in the event of an allocation failure, the allocation failure portion of the code would involve code for each test that had as many as five calls to `m_free()`. Yet these same calls are made at the end of the function. In this case, using `goto` actually shortens the code and simplifies cleaning up the allocations in the event of failure. Should you avoid `goto`? Absolutely, but when its use can actually simplify code (without making it harder to understand), then use `goto` sparingly.

This completes the technical topics treated in this chapter. The remaining material is a set of thoughts on improvements a programmer might want to think about for the matrix library and a brief comment on what other software is available that may be useful.

Where Do You Go from Here?

The matrix library developed in this chapter is a good basic library, but there are many possible improvements. A few of these are listed for those who may be inclined to make some changes and would like a starting point to think about possible projects:

- Extend the library to cover other matrix functions such as `eigenvalues`, `eigenvectors`, `cofactors`, and so forth.
- Modify the algorithm used for inverting matrices. A possible suggestion is an algorithm that uses lower and upper triangular matrices. This method reduces the number of additions and multiplications and thus reduces error propagation in the calculation.
- Implement an algorithm to solve linear equations directly rather than using matrix inversion. A good starting point is the Gaussian elimination method used for calculating determinants, which yields (internally) an upper triangular matrix that can be used to solve for the bottom row, then the next to bottom row, and so forth.
- Explicitly pass in or use global variables for temporary storage in `m_det()`, `m_inverse()`, `m_solve()`, and so on.

- Make provisions for an error handling function and provide a default error handler. Alternatively, change return convention to always return an error code and return results via modification of the result arguments.
- Optimize the index calculation arithmetic to the extent feasible.
- Make use of the new capability to dynamically allocate 2D arrays to make references to elements more natural. Alternatively, modify the dynamic allocation following one of the several methods listed in the `comp.lang.c` FAQ to accomplish the same thing.
- Rewrite the library to use a numeric type other than doubles for the floating point calculations. Doing this for floats or long doubles would be especially easy. Other possibilities include any numeric type that supports the four basic arithmetic operations (addition, subtraction, multiplication, and division). Examples that you can implement fairly easily include fixed point numbers, complex numbers or rational numbers (admittedly, *easy* may be in the eye of the beholder). Arbitrary precision arithmetic is somewhat harder (primarily because the process of defining the basic operations is more involved).
- Rewrite the library to generically use arithmetic routines for another numeric type by passing in an array of function pointers for needed mathematical operations. Note that although this will result in a very general library, there may be significant performance degradation depending on how the newly defined numeric type handles temporary variables.
- Rewrite the library to use sparse arrays. (Sparse arrays are discussed in Chapter 15, "Sparse Matrix.")
- Rewrite the library to use sparse arrays of a generic numeric type (such as arbitrarily precise values).
- Use a completely alternate approach and find a commercial or freely available library and implement a way to use it on your platform.

Other Approaches

There is a freely available package called *linpack*, written many years ago in FORTRAN. It is considered in many senses to be the measuring stick for linear algebra calculations. If you have access to a FORTRAN compiler and your C compiler supports calling object code written in other languages, it is possible to implement a set of wrapper functions and call the linpack routines directly.

This chapter discusses several applications of C interfacing to real-world digitized signals with the emphasis on standard C programming techniques rather than the mathematical theory involved.

It should be noted that much of the example code in this section makes heavy use of C's bitwise and shift operators. If you are not familiar with these language features, you should review Chapter 5, "Playing with Bits and Bytes," before experimenting with the code here.

Data Compression

Data compression is one of the key technologies of the Internet today. Other than the raw HTML of Web pages themselves, almost all data that passes through the Net is compressed in some format or other. Table 18.1 describes just a few of the most common compressed formats found on the Net.

TABLE 18.1 Some Common Compressed File Types

File Type	*Data*
GIF	Graphics
PNG	Graphics
JPEG	Graphics
MPEG	Video and Sound
AVI	Video and Sound
PDF	Text and Graphics
MP3	Music
ZIP	Anything
GZ	Anything

Some of the latest Web technology, such as Web Cams, live audio, and video broadcasts depend on live, real-time compression of the audio or video data at its source and decompression on the destination computer.

Note

An excellent source of information on many different file formats, including graphics and compressed types, is *Wotsit's Programmer's File Format Collection* at `http://www.wotsit.org`.

Data compression is used to save both storage space and transmission time. Compressed data takes up less space on hard disk drives, backup tapes, and other storage media. It also takes less time to copy or transmit, which can save time when transmitting or receiving through a communications medium with limited bandwidth, such as using a modem to connect to the Internet.

Compression algorithms work by recognizing patterns and repetitions in the original uncompressed data. If data is to be both encrypted and compressed, the end result is usually smaller if the compression is applied before the encryption. This is because encryption removes the patterns and repetitions that compression algorithms need to be effective.

Types of Compression

All compression formats can be divided into two types: lossless and lossy.

- *Lossless* compression is completely reversible. When the compressed representation of the data is decompressed, the result is an exact duplicate of the original data before compression. One important fact to remember is that no lossless compression technique can guarantee to reduce the size of any and all arbitrary data items. Any algorithm can be defeated by worst-case input, ending up with a "compressed" output that is actually larger, not smaller, than the input.
- *Lossy* compression is not completely reversible. When the compressed representation of the data is decompressed, the result is an approximation of the original data, not a bit-by-bit duplicate.

Both types of compression are widely used today, for different purposes.

When compressing your data to back up on a tape, CD, or Zip drive, you want to use lossless compression. If you can't create an exact duplicate from the backup, there is no point to backing up at all. Likewise, when you download a compressed file from the Internet containing an executable program image, you need to be able to decompress it to an exact copy of the original or you won't be able to run the program.

Lossy compression is often used on audio and video data to achieve greater compression ratios. This takes advantage of the fact that there are limitations to our senses, especially in their ability to distinguish very small differences in color, brightness, pitch, or volume.

All compression formats can be divided into two other types: adaptable and fixed.

- *Adaptable compression* algorithms adapt themselves to the actual data they are processing. They revise their encoding based on the patterns and repetitions in the data being encoded. These algorithms can provide the best overall compression ratios for arbitrary data formats.

- *Fixed compression* algorithms are based on predetermined assumptions about the data to be encoded. When applied to just any arbitrary data format, they do not tend to produce compression ratios as high as adaptable algorithms can. But when fixed algorithms are applied to the type of data they were designed for, they can often achieve higher compression ratios than a general-purpose adaptable technique.

Most Used Compression Algorithm

Probably everyone who is reading this book has sent or received at least one fax. The Group 3 Digital Facsimile standard was issued by the Comité Consultatif International Téléphonique et Télégraphique (CCITT) working group of the International Telecommunications Union (ITU) in 1983. This led directly to the fax machine revolution of that decade and the early 1990s.

There are two CCITT standards pertinent to fax transmissions. One of them, T.4, describes the format for encoding and compressing image data for fax transmission. Another CCITT standard involved with faxing is discussed later in the chapter.

The T.4 fax encoding format is a good choice for illustrating some of the concepts and code used for programming compression algorithms in C. It is a widely used, real-world standard, not a made up example. In addition, it combines two important methods used in many types of compression algorithms: run length encoding and fixed Huffman encoding. Finally, it is a lossless compression format, so if you implement both the encoding and decoding routines properly you can encode and then decode a file and expect to get back exactly what you started with. This allows experimentation with T.4 code using simple binary data files, without actually requiring a fax machine or phone line.

Ordinary, everyday fax machines perform T.4 encoding and decoding in real time, on real-world video signals from the document they are scanning and transmitting or receiving and reproducing. Many features of the T.4 protocol were designed to allow relatively inexpensive machines to be developed in the days when processors were much more expensive and less powerful, and memory more costly than today. A fax machine can be made with only a few thousand bytes of memory. While not important on today's typical desktop computer, memory is a scarce commodity in typical embedded systems like a standalone fax machine. In the example programs for T.4 encoding and decoding, I will illustrate some of the techniques used to minimize memory usage in these applications.

The Fax Image

All fax images are scanned at the same horizontal resolution. Each horizontal scan line consists of 215 millimeters +/– 1% encoded as 1,728 pixel elements (pixels), for a horizontal resolution of approximately eight pixels per millimeter or 200 pixels per inch. Each scan line starts on the left and continues pixel-by-pixel to the right.

Group 3 defines two resolutions: standard and higher. The vertical resolution is what varies between these two resolutions. "Standard" scans 3.85 horizontal lines per millimeter (approximately 98 scan lines per inch), whereas "higher" uses twice as many, 7.7 scan lines per millimeter (approximately 195 per inch). Fax machines built to inch, rather than metric, dimensions may scan or print at 200 pixels per inch horizontally and either 100 or 200 vertically with no adjustment required.

Standard fax machines can handle metric A4 or the common U.S. size, 8.5-inch-by-11-inch, paper. The standard length is based on A4 paper, which has a nominal length of 297 millimeters. That translates to approximately 1,143 scan lines per page at the standard resolution, or about 2,287 at the higher resolution. Usually not all of the possible scan lines are transmitted, due to scanner and printer cut-off areas. Typical pages on typical machines generally send between 1,000 to 1,100 standard resolution scan rows or 2,000 to 2,200 at higher resolution.

The first step in understanding T.4 fax encoding and compression is seeing what the image of the page looks like to the fax machine as it is scanned. We'll take a small excerpt from the world's most famous C program, "Hello World," and see it as the fax machine does. Figure 18.1 shows what the word Hello, printed and scanned or rendered into higher fax resolution in a 9-point fixed-pitch font, looks like to the fax machine or software.

For the moment, let's assume that this is literally the upper left-hand corner of a page we are going to transmit as a fax, and the rest of the page is completely blank white paper. The top two scan lines are margin and completely blank, as are the leftmost two columns, even in the rows that contain text pixels.

Image to Encoded Stream

Each scan line of a fax image contains exactly 1,728 pixels, each of which can be either black or white. Since there are only two possible values for a pixel, it can be represented as a single bit, 1 for white or 0 for black. That means an entire scan line can be stored in 216 unsigned chars, each holding the value of eight pixels. C requires that an unsigned char contain at least eight bits and that there are no invalid bit patterns or trap representations, so we can store any combination of 1 and 0 bits, representing white and black pixels in an unsigned char, without problems. Even if a particular implementation has character types with more than eight bits, it is convenient to store eight bits of data in each unsigned char because devices such as UARTs involved in fax communications typically accept eight bits at a time.

FIGURE 18.1
The word Hello in 9-point type at "higher" fax resolution.

Fax scanners and other digital video devices, such as desktop scanners and digital cameras, typically use *Charge Coupled Devices* (CCDs) to digitize an image. Fax machines in particular often use a device called a *Contact Image Scanner* (CIS) specifically made for fax applications, but this is just a specific type of CCD. A CCD device outputs an analog voltage signal for each pixel in the image, proportional to the brightness of the pixel. This signal can be applied to a device known as an *Analog to Digital Converter* (ADC), which generates a digital value proportional to the analog voltage. Software can read the digital word for the brightness of each pixel, compare it to a preset threshold value, and decide whether the pixel is white or black. Another method that can be used for fax scanning is an analog device called a *comparator*, which has two analog inputs and a single digital output. The two inputs are connected to a voltage representing the brightness threshold and the analog pixel signals from the CCD. The digital output goes to 1 or 0 depending on which input voltage is higher. This effectively makes the comparator a single-bit ADC, and requires less processing overhead and less expensive circuitry than a real ADC and a software comparison of the brightness of each pixel.

The sample code discussed in this section and included on the companion CD does not go into the hardware-specific detail of reading and digitizing the image pixels. Instead, it starts by assuming that its input file contains 216 `unsigned chars` per scan line, eight pixels per `unsigned char`. Bit 7 (0X80) of the first `unsigned char` represents the very first (leftmost) pixel in the image. Bit 6 (0X40) represents the second pixel, bit 7 of the second byte of the array represents the ninth pixel, and so on until bit 0 (0X01) of the final (216th) `unsigned char` represents the value of the very last image pixel on the far right.

We could transmit the scanned fax image as a series of raw binary scan lines as described above—216 octets per row, which take a total of 246,888 octets, or 1,975,104 bits, per maximum A4 size page of 1,143 scan rows—at standard resolution. At the typical fax transmission rate of 9,600 bps (bits per second), it would require approximately 205 seconds, almost three-and-a-half minutes, to transmit the image. Even at the 14,400 bps transmission rate of newer fax machines, the time is still about 137 seconds, roughly two-and-a-quarter minutes. The octet count, bit count, and transmission time would each double for a higher resolution image.

The actual transmission time for the fax image of a typical typewritten page at 9,600 bps is about 30 seconds, which means that T.4 encoding compresses the image to about 288,000 bits, or 36,000 octets. Even allowing for the fact that not all possible scan rows are actually used, the compression for a typewritten page on the average reduces the 216 octets per scan row to about 36 octets, a compression ratio about 6 to 1.

The Encoding Format

Looking back at Figure 18.1, we can see that the first and second scan lines will contain nothing but white pixels. The 216 unsigned chars in the array representing the scan data will each contain the value 0xFF. When we get to the third scan line, the first that contains character data, we start to see some variation. Table 18.2 shows the contents of the scan data array for this scan line.

TABLE 18.2 Scan Image Data for the Third Row of Hello

Unsigned Char Offset	*Contents (binary)*	*Contents (hex)*
0	11000011	0xC3
1	11000111	0xC7
2	11111111	0xFF
3	11111111	0xFF
4	00000001	0x01
5	11111110	0xFE
6	00000111	0x07

The remaining 209 `unsigned chars` all contain 0xFF for the rest of the blank white scan line.

The first step of encoding each scan line is run length counting. We start at the leftmost pixel of each scan line and count the number of continuous white pixels in a row, until either the end of the line or a black pixel is found. We can describe the pixels in a row by a series of numbers of pixels of the same color, each number followed by a W for white pixels or a B for black pixels.

For the first two scan lines, in the upper margin above the text, we would count 1,728 white pixels, which we can represent as 1728W. In the third line, where the scanner sees the tops of the "H" and the two "l" characters, we could describe the first 7 `unsigned chars` of the scan line shown in Table 18.2 as containing

2W, 4B, 4W, 3B, 19W, 7B, 8W, 6B, 3W

Since the remaining 1,672 pixels in the remaining 209 `unsigned chars` in the array all contain all 1 bits for all white pixels, the actual encoding of this complete scan row is

2W, 4B, 4W, 3B, 19W, 7B, 8W, 6B, 1675W

It is these run lengths of alternating white and black pixels that are actually encoded and transmitted. A fax scan line always starts with a white pixel run count, so if a line is scanned that starts with the very first pixel black, the first run on that line is counted as 0W.

The actual format used to encode the run lengths is a modified Huffman encoding. In more common Huffman usage, the data being encoded consists of fixed-size values, such as characters, and variable length codes (called "code words" in T.4 fax protocol) are assigned so that the most frequently occurring values are represented by the shortest code words and the least frequently occurring by the longest. In T.4 fax encoding, the code words represent the run lengths, so both the raw data and the encoded output represent variable length bit strings. As in all types of Huffman encoding, all code words must be unique. No code word can start with the same bit sequence of a shorter code word.

Note that despite the phrase "code words" the T.4 codes have variable lengths between 2 and 13 bits, and have no relation at all to processor word size or any other fixed-length value.

One possible way to assign T.4 code words to pixel runs would be to have 1,729 code words for each run length of white pixels between 0 and 1,728, and another 1,728 code words for black runs. This would lead to some extremely long code runs and limit the amount of compression achieved. Instead, T.4 specifies a two-level approach to encoding the pixel runs.

This is somewhat similar to the concept we use in decimal numbers where the digits 0 through 9 are put together in combinations to represent numbers in the hundreds or thousands in base 10. In hex we use 0 through 9 and A through F to represent values in base 16.

The T.4 protocol uses a form of base 64 encoding. There are 64 code words each for black and white pixels, indicating run lengths from 0 to 63, called "terminating code words," as shown in Table 18.3. When a run length within this range is found in a scan line, the corresponding code word is added to the encoding for the scan line.

TABLE 18.3 T.4 Fax Terminating Code Words for 0 Through 63 Pixel Runs

Run Length	*White Code Word*	*Black Code Word*
0	00110101	0000110111
1	000111	010
2	0111	11
3	1000	10
4	1011	011
5	1100	0011
6	1110	0010
7	1111	00011
8	10011	000101
9	10100	000100
10	00111	0000100
11	01000	0000101
12	001000	0000111
13	000011	00000100
14	110100	00000111
15	110101	000011000
16	101010	0000010111
17	101011	0000011000
18	0100111	0000001000
19	0001100	00001100111
20	0001000	00001101000
21	0010111	00001101100
22	0000011	00000110111
23	0000100	00000101000
24	0101000	00000010111
25	0101011	00000011000
26	0010011	000011001010
27	0100100	000011001011

TABLE 18.3 continued

Run Length	White Code Word	Black Code Word
28	0011000	000011001100
29	00000010	000011001101
30	00000011	000001101000
31	00011010	000001101001
32	00011011	000001101010
33	00010010	000001101011
34	00010011	000011010010
35	00010100	000011010011
36	00010101	000011010100
37	00010110	000011010101
38	00010111	000011010110
39	00101000	000011010111
40	00101001	000001101100
41	00101010	000001101101
42	00101011	000011011010
43	00101100	000011011011
44	00101101	000001010100
45	00000100	000001010101
46	00000101	000001010110
47	00001010	000001010111
48	00001011	000001100100
49	01010010	000001100101
50	01010011	000001010010
51	01010100	000001010011
52	01010101	000000100100
53	00100100	000000110111
54	00100101	000000111000
55	01011000	000000100111
56	01011001	000000101000
57	01011010	000001011000
58	01011011	000001011001
59	01001010	000000101011
60	01001011	000000101100
61	00110010	000001011010
62	00110011	000001100110
63	00110100	000001100111

If a run of pixels is longer than 63, such as a blank white row of 1,728 pixels, a second set of code words comes into use. These are called "make-up code words," and each make-up code word stands for a multiple of 64 black or white pixels, again with a different set of codes for each color. When a make-up code word appears in a fax transmission, it is always immediately followed by a terminating code word for the same color. The make-up codes are shown in Table 18.4.

TABLE 18.4 T.4 Fax Make-Up Code Words for 64 Through 1,728 Pixel Runs

Run Length	*White Code Word*	*Black Code Word*
64	11011	0000001111
128	10010	000011001000
192	010111	000011001001
256	0110111	000001011011
320	00110110	000000110011
384	00110111	000000110100
448	01100100	000000110101
512	01100101	0000001101100
576	01101000	0000001101101
640	01100111	0000001001010
704	011001100	0000001001011
768	011001101	0000001001100
832	011010010	0000001001101
896	011010011	0000001110010
960	011010100	0000001110011
1024	011010101	0000001110100
1088	011010110	0000001110101
1152	011010111	0000001110110
1216	011011000	0000001110111
1280	011011001	0000001010010
1344	011011010	0000001010011
1408	011011011	0000001010100
1472	010011000	0000001010101
1536	010011001	0000001011010
1600	010011010	0000001011011
1664	011000	0000001100100
1728	010011011	0000001100101

There's only one other code word we need to complete T.4 encoding of a fax image: EOL, the end-of-line code word. This code word has the bit pattern 000000000001, and has several special properties.

The first is its pattern. It starts with 11 leading zeros, a sequence of zeros that never appears anywhere but at the end of a scan row. If you examine the other code words in Table 18.4, you will see that none of them start with more than six consecutive zeros or end with more than three, so the greatest possible number of zeros in the combination of any two consecutive code words is nine.

The other special property of the EOL code is that it can be extended with more 0 bits. There can be any number of extra 0 bits added before the final 1 bit of the EOL code word. No padding is allowed in or between any other code words.

Now we can go back to the top three scan lines of Figure 18.1 and see how the actual encoding is accomplished. We will change the notation used above to add a final letter T or M for terminating or make-up code word, respectively. The first two all-blank rows each contain 1,728 white pixels in a single run. Since 1,728 is greater than 64, and is in fact an exact multiple of 64, these blank lines can each be described as

1,728WM, 0WT, EOL

That is, white make-up code word 010011011 for 1,728 white pixels followed by white terminating code word 00110101 followed by EOL code word 000000000001. Since the variable length codes are strung together one after another without regard for higher-level boundaries, the final encoding for each of the first two scan lines is

010011011 00110101 000000000001

In other words, a scan line of 1,728 pixels, reduced to 1,728 bits of ones and zeros, is encoded by the T.4 protocol to 29 bits, a compression ratio of 1728:29 or almost 60:1! It is a common technique used by many fax machines and computer fax programs to always pad out a line to an octet boundary by adding leading zeros to the EOL code word:

010011011 00110101 000000000000001

The compression ratio is now 1728:32, or exactly 54:1!

The blank line of all white pixels has the best compression ratio. The average typewritten or printed page contains quite a few blank white scan lines between rows of text, so this contributes greatly to the overall compression of a typical fax transmission.

The third row in Figure 18.1 can now be expressed in our two-level description as

2WT, 4BT, 4WT, 3BT, 19WT, 7BT, 8WT, 6BT, 1664WM, 11WT, EOL

The encoded bit stream becomes

000111 011 1011 10 0001100 00011 10011 0010 011000 000000000001

With two 0 padding bits added to the EOL code word to end the line on an octet boundary, it becomes

000111 011 1011 10 0001100 00011 10011 0010 011000 00000000000001

The compression ratio with padding is 1728:56, still over 30:1.

Each transmission of a fax page begins with a single EOL sequence, followed immediately by the first scan row. Each scan row in a fax transmission is encoded into the variable length codes shown in Tables 18.3 and 18.4 and transmitted as a continuous bit stream without regard for octet or any other boundaries. There are no start, stop, parity, or any other bits in the stream. Each scan row ends with the EOL code word consisting of at least 11 consecutive 0 bits. This allows the receiver to resynchronize with the transmitter in the event of transmission errors as any sequence of more than nine consecutive 0 bits will be part of an EOL sequence. Each scan row except for the last is immediately followed by the beginning code word of the next row, again without regard for octet boundaries, although it may begin a new octet if the preceding line naturally ended on an octet boundary or was padded to do so, as in the second example above.

The final scan row of the page is followed by six consecutive EOL code words, with no pixel data code words in between, indicating that the end of the page has been reached.

One More Twist

Before we can begin encoding and decoding T.4 fax format data, there is just one more twist, literally, that needs to be taken into account. The T.4 code words are described as a stream of bits from left to right, and the first, leftmost bit of each code word immediately follows the last, rightmost bit of the preceding code word. These bits are required to be transmitted sequentially from the sender to the receiver in precise left-to-right order. Fax machines and fax modems use standard serial port devices, however, and when an 8-bit octet is written to the transmitter of such a device it sends out the bits in a serial stream starting with the least significant, rightmost bit first and working toward the most significant, leftmost bit.

To illustrate this, let's return to the encoding for a blank white line, with two padding bits added to the EOL code word to round it up to an octet boundary:

010011011 00110101 00000000000001

We can illustrate this by separating the line into 8-bit octets:

01001101 10011010 10000000 00000001

If we write these four octet values one after another to the transmitter of a standard serial device, the serial bit stream that will result in time sequence will be

10110010 01011001 00000001 10000000

The octets will be in the proper sequence, but the bits in each octet will be reversed. The applications to encode binary data to the T.4 protocol, and decode T.4 back to binary, will perform this bit reversal on-the-fly.

The T.4 Compression Program: `encode.c`

The companion CD contains complete source code for a standard C program that reads binary data from a file in chunks of 216 unsigned characters, treats the low eight bits as scan line pixels, and generates the T.4 encoding for each scan line and writes it to another binary file. The program is built from a single source file named `encode.c`. I will save space by not showing most of the file contents here.

The header `fax.h` defines some numeric constants to avoid hard coded numbers in the source. It is also included by `decode.c`, which performs the opposite operation and turns a T.4 encoded representation of a fax page back into a raw binary scan image. The contents of `fax.h` are as follows:

```
#define PIXELS_PER_ROW    1728
#define PIXELS_PER_OCTET  8
#define OCTETS_PER_ROW    (PIXELS_PER_ROW / PIXELS_PER_OCTET)
#define MAXIMUM_ROWS      1024
#define T4_BUFFER_SIZE    1024
#define EOL_LENGTH        12
#define OCTET_MASK        0xff
```

`encode.c` defines a data type for storing and using T.4 code words, and defines four constant arrays of this type, one each for white and black terminating code words and white and black make-up code words. Here is the data type definition:

```
typedef struct
{
  unsigned char code_length;
  unsigned char bit_pattern;
} T4_ENCODE;
```

The lookup tables for all of the code words are four arrays of `T4_ENCODE` structures. You might find values for the contents of these structures puzzling at first glance. Both members of the structure are `unsigned char` types, which are only guaranteed to contain eight bits and hold a range of values from 0 through 255 inclusive. There is no problem holding the number of bits in a code word, which is always between 2 and 13, in the `code_length` member. But the code words themselves can contain up to 13 bits and yet we represent them in the `bit_pattern` member. We need to do this in standard C, on any processor with a C compiler, not just on some particular platform where `unsigned char` happens to contain 13 or more bits.

To see how this can be done, take another look at Tables 18.3 and 18.4. Even though some of the code words use 9, 10, 11, 12, or 13 bits, all of the 1 bits are within the rightmost 8 bits. All of the bits before the last 8 in the longer code words are 0 bits. No matter what size unsigned integer type we store the bit pattern in, the actual numeric value is less than 255, since the leading 0 bits do not contribute any value. So we can store the value of any code word in an `unsigned char`. In fact, even if the platform and compiler provide more than eight bits in an `unsigned char`, only the lowest eight are used by the T.4 encoding and decoding programs. If there are any higher bits, they are totally unused.

Here are the first few lines from `encode.c`, which contains the arrays of lookup tables:

```
static cost T4_ENCODE white_terminate[] =
{
  { 8, 0XAC }, /*    0 white pixels */
  { 6, 0XE0 }, /*    1 white pixels */
  { 4, 0XE0 }, /*    2 white pixels */
  { 4, 0X10 }, /*    3 white pixels */
```

If you compare them to the first few code words for runs of white pixels in Table 18.3, you are probably still puzzled. Even though I explained above how each code word can be stored in an `unsigned char`, the `bit_pattern` members in the array elements do not seem to match those in the table at all. This is because the table entries are already reversed to accommodate the bit order of serial device transmission.

Figure 18.2 shows two examples of how the table values are derived, one for a code word less than eight bits, and one for one longer than eight bits. The code word for a run of four white pixels, 1011, is placed right justified into the four lowest bits of an octet (`unsigned char`) in row A. The higher bits of the octet are filled with 0 bits in row B. Then the eight bits are reversed left-to-right in row C, and this value is used for the `bit_pattern` member. If you check `encode.c` you will see that the `bit_pattern` member for `white_terminate[4]` is 0xD0.

Row D shows the make-up code word for a run of 512 black pixels, 000001101100. Row E shows the octet remaining after all bits higher than the lowest eight, which are always 0, are discarded. Again the eight bits retained are reversed right-to-left, resulting in row F, so the `bit_pattern` member for `black_makeup[7]` (which holds the code word for this run) is initialized to 0x36.

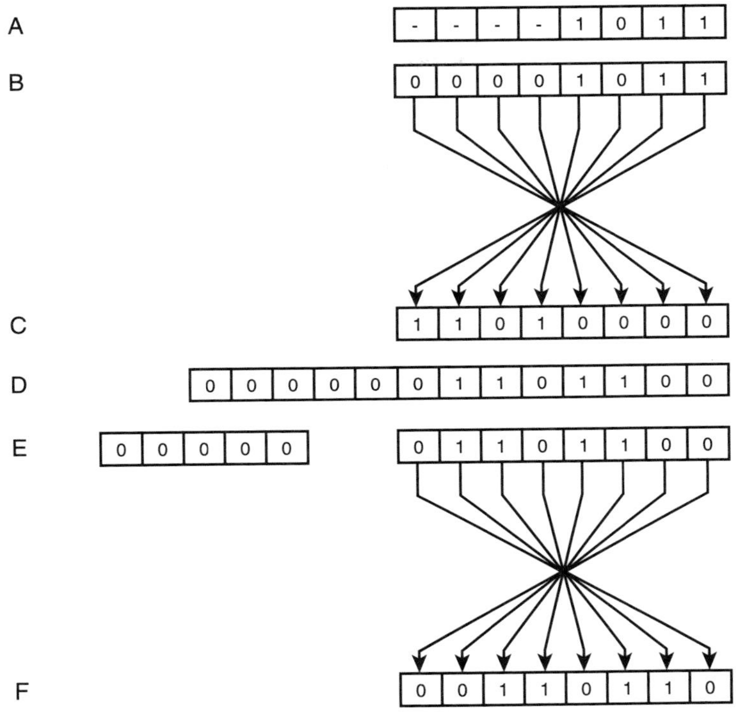

FIGURE 18.2
Encoding T.4 codes into 8-bit values.

The `main()` Function

The `main()` function in the file `encode.c` is a simple driver for the actual compression code. It parses the command-line arguments to find two file names, one for an input file containing binary pixel data to encode, the second for an output file to hold the T.4 encoded result. The files are opened in binary mode.

It also defines a buffer large enough to hold the T.4 output generated by any possible scan line. Since the code words used are fixed, it is easy to calculate the longest possible encoded output. The worst case scan line is one containing alternating white and black pixels. The code for a run of one white pixel contains six bits, and the code for a run of a single black pixel contains three bits. So each combination of one white and one black pixel generates nine bits of code words. A 1,728 pixel row can contain 864 pair of alternating pixels, resulting in 7,776 bits of code words (927 octets). If the row starts with a black pixel, an initial 8-bit code word must be added, and finally two bytes for the EOL bringing the total up to 975 octets. I defined `T4_BUFFER_SIZE` to be 1,024 in `fax.h`, but in an embedded system with limited memory, exactly 975 bytes might be used.

The EncodePage() Function

main() calls the function EncodePage(), passing the two FILE pointers, a pointer to the array, and a copy of the name of the output file, for error messages. This function is presented in Listing 18.1.

LISTING 18.1 EncodePage() Function

```
static int
EncodePage(FILE *fin, FILE *fout,
           unsigned char *buff,
           char *output_name)
{
  int size;
  int scan_lines;
  size_t written;

  /* write required initial EOL code word to file */
  if (sizeof EOL != fwrite(EOL, 1, sizeof EOL, fout))
  {
     printf(wr_err, output_name);
     return EOF;
  }

  for (scan_lines = 0;  scan_lines< MAXIMUM_ROWS; )
  {
    size = EncodeLine(buff, fin);

    if (size < 0)
    {
       break;
    }
    ++scan_lines;

    written = fwrite(buff, sizeof *buff, size, fout);
    if ((int)written != size)
    {
      printf(wr_err, output_name);
      return EOF;
    }
  }

  /* write the required six consecutive EOL code words  */
  /* to indicate end of page                            */
```

LISTING 18.1 continued

```
  if (sizeof EOP != fwrite(EOP, 1, sizeof EOP, fout))
  {
    printf(wr_err, output_name);
    return EOF;
  }

  return scan_lines;
}
```

The `EncodeLine()` Function

`EncodePage()` calls `EncodeLine()` up to `MAXIMUM_ROWS` times, or until the end of the input file is reached in the process of trying to read 216 `unsigned char`s from the source file (see Listing 18.2). It writes the T.4 encoded version of each line to the output file and returns an integer indicating its success. It can return 0 or a positive number of scan lines generated and written, or the standard C macro `EOF`, which is a negative integer on error.

LISTING 18.2 `EncodeLine()` Function

```
int
EncodeLine(unsigned char *t4_out, FILE *fin)
{
  int scan_count = PIXELS_PER_ROW;
  int run_count;
  unsigned char *t4_ptr = t4_out;
  PIXEL_BITS color = WHITE_PIXEL;

  while (scan_count > 0)
  {
    run_count = CountPixelRun(color, scan_count, fin);
    if (run_count == EOF)
    {
      return EOF;
    }

    if (color == BLACK_PIXEL)
    {
      if (run_count > 63)
      {
        t4_ptr = OutputCodeWord(
          black_makeup + (run_count / 64) - 1,
          t4_ptr);
```

LISTING 18.2 continued

```
      }
      t4_ptr = OutputCodeWord(
        black_terminate + (run_count % 64),
        t4_ptr);
      color = WHITE_PIXEL;
    }
    else
    {
      if (run_count > 63)
      {
        t4_ptr = OutputCodeWord(
          white_makeup + (run_count / 64) - 1,
          t4_ptr);
      }
      t4_ptr = OutputCodeWord(
        white_terminate + (run_count % 64),
        t4_ptr);
      color = BLACK_PIXEL;
    }

    scan_count -= run_count;
  }

  t4_ptr = OutputCodeWord(NULL, t4_ptr);
  return (int)(t4_ptr - t4_out);
}
```

The `CountPixelRun()` Function

`EncodeLine()` calls `CountPixelRun()` (see Listing 18.3) to alternately extract runs of white and black pixels from the binary image source file. This function returns either a number between 0 and 1,728, indicating the length of a run of the specified color found, or `EOF` if the input file runs out in the middle of a scan line. As it extracts pixel runs it keeps a running total of the number of pixels remaining in the scan line, always passing this value to `CountPixelRun()`. This is needed because the input file contains raw binary data with no delimiters to indicate the end of the scan lines.

`EncodeLine()` then calls `OutputCodeWord()` to store the code words for each run in the buffer passed to it by `EncodePage()`. If a run is greater than 63 pixels, it requires both a make-up and a terminating code word.

If `EncodeLine()` runs into an input or output error it returns `EOF`, otherwise it returns an integer indicating the number of bytes of code generated. The last line casts the value computed by subtracting two pointers into the output buffer array to `int`. This is advisable because the difference between two pointers in C has the type `ptrdiff_t`, defined in `<stddef.h>`, which must be at least as large as an `int` but might be larger. The compiler will automatically convert this to `int` if necessary, and it will fit without overflow because we already know that the largest value we can generate is 975, but it is always best to make this type of cast explicit.

LISTING 18.3 `CountPixelRun()` Function

```
static int
CountPixelRun(PIXEL_BITS wanted, int maximum, FILE *fin)
{
  int run_count = 0;
  int input;
  static int raw_pixels = 0;
  static int bits_used = 8;
  static int EOF_flag = 0;

  for ( ; ; )
  {
    if (bits_used >= PIXELS_PER_OCTET)
    {
      if (maximum >= 8)
      {
        if (EOF_flag)
        {
          return EOF;
        }
        else if ((input = fgetc(fin)) == EOF)
        {
          EOF_flag = 1;
          break;
        }
        raw_pixels = input & OCTET_MASK;
        bits_used = 0;
      }
      else
      {
        break;
      }
    }
```

LISTING 18.3 continued

```
    if (wanted == (raw_pixels & PIXEL_TEST))
    {
      ++run_count;
      ++bits_used;
      --maximum;
      raw_pixels <<= 1;
    }
    else
    {
       break;
    }
  }

  return run_count;
}
```

`CountPixelRun()` receives a `PIXEL_BITS` value to indicate which color run is being sought, a count of the remaining pixels in the current scan line, and a pointer to the input file for reading data. Since pixel runs can begin and end at any point, without regard to octet boundaries, `CountPixelRun()` retains some persistent data in static variables.

`Unsigned int raw_pixels` contains the contents of the most recent octet from the input file across calls to the function in the event that a pixel run ends in the middle of an octet. It is initialized to 0 by default because it has static storage duration, but the explicit initializer serves as a reminder of this fact.

`bits_used` counts the number of pixels already extracted from `raw_pixels`. When `bits_used` reaches `PIXELS_PER_OCTET`, defined as 8 in `fax.h`, all the pixels have been used and another octet must be read from the input file when more pixels are needed. Initializing it to `PIXELS_PER_OCTET` causes `CountPixelRun()` to read the first octet from the input file the first time it is called.

Finally, `EOF_flag` is used by `CountPixelRun()` to remember that it has already received an error reading the input file. When a call to `fgetc()` first returns `EOF`, this flag is set and the current run is terminated and the run count already accumulated is returned to `EncodeLine()`. If `EncodeLine()` calls `CountPixelRun()` again, it merely returns `EOF`.

The local variable `input` is defined as a signed `int` to receive the value returned by `fgetc()`. If the `unsigned int raw_pixels` were used, the code might not correctly recognize `EOF` on all C implementations.

The actual run-counting algorithm checks the highest used bit in `raw_pixels` by performing a bitwise AND with `PIXEL_MASK`, an enumerated constant with the value of 0x80, and testing the result against the `PIXEL_BITS` argument wanted, which is 0x80 for white pixels or 0 for black. As long as the result matches, the run continues and `raw_pixels` is shifted left by 1 to bring the next bit into testing position.

The `OutputCodeWord()` Function

The next function, `OutputCodeWord()` (see Listing 18.4) illustrates the fact that inserting arbitrary length bit patterns into an output bit stream is much simpler than recognizing arbitrary bit patterns in an input stream. Since the length of the output bit pattern is known, `OutputCodeWord()` can handle it in chunks up to the size of a full octet, depending on length and alignment. The length of an input pattern is not known until all its bits are read. It is possible to write code where an entire octet is tested as it is read to see if all its pixels are the current color. This could result in a time savings when counting white pixel runs (remember all of those blank scan lines) but not for black pixel runs, where eight or more continuous black pixels are not common in typical faxed documents.

LISTING 18.4 `OutputCodeWord()` Function

```
static unsigned char
*OutputCodeWord(const T4_ENCODE *code, unsigned char *t4_ptr)
{
  int length;
  static int free_bits = 8;
  static unsigned long current_output = 0;

  /* if the pointer argument is NULL, output EOL code word  */
  if (NULL == code)
  {
    current_output &= OCTET_MASK;
    current_output >>= free_bits;
    *t4_ptr++ = (unsigned char)(current_output & OCTET_MASK);
    if (free_bits < 4)
    {
      *t4_ptr++ = 0;
    }
    *t4_ptr++ = 0x80;
    free_bits = PIXELS_PER_OCTET;
    current_output = 0;
  }
  /* otherwise output the code word in the structure       */
  else
```

LISTING 18.4 continued

```
  {
    length = code->code_length;
    current_output |=
      ((unsigned long)code->bit_pattern << length);

    while (length >= free_bits)
    {
      current_output >>= free_bits;
      *t4_ptr++ = (unsigned char)(current_output & OCTET_MASK);
      length -= free_bits;
      free_bits = PIXELS_PER_OCTET;
    }

    if (length != 0)
    {
      current_output >>= length;
      free_bits -= length;
    }
  }
  return t4_ptr;
}
```

`OutputCodeWord()` is called by `EncodeLine()` two different ways, to output the code word for a run of pixels or to output the EOL code word. In the former case, the argument code indicates the reason. If code is `NULL`, it indicates than an EOL should be generated. If code is not `NULL`, it points to one of the `T4_DECODE` structures and the code word that structure contains is output. In either case, `OutputCodeWord()` returns the destination pointer it receives once it has finished, by which time it might have been incremented once or twice.

`OutputCodeWord()`also needs internal static variables to retain information between calls. Since a code word might end up partially filling an octet, `current_output` might be partially filled when the function returns so it needs to be static to remember the value. The `free_bits` value remembers how many bits of the next code word can still be placed in `current_output`.

Figure 18.3 illustrates the step-by-step operation of inserting an arbitrary length code word beginning on an arbitrary bit boundary. Specifically, adding a 13-bit long code word to the five remaining bits of previous code words.

FIGURE 18.3
Inserting variable length code word.

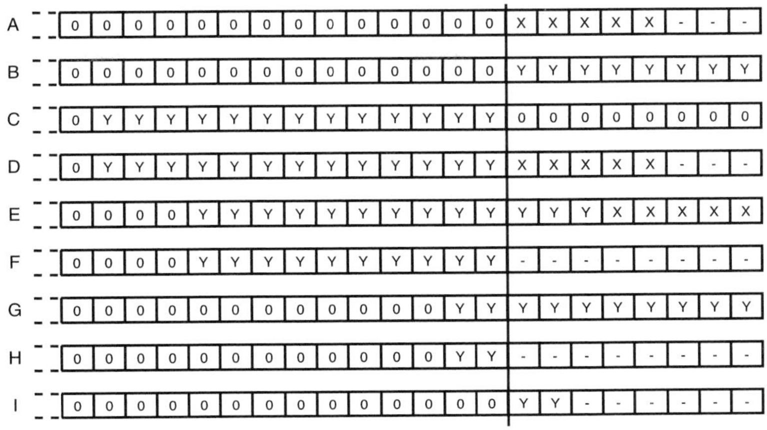

Displaying actual 1 and 0 characters for each bit position makes it difficult to tell the used bits from the unused ones, and the bits of the new code word from those left over from a previous one. So the illustration takes a step back from the actual bit contents and uses a different notation. The letter `X` indicates a bit in the `current_output` variable from previous code word insertions, regardless of whether each bit is actually a 1 or a 0. Likewise, the letter `Y` represents a bit in the new code word to be inserted, regardless of its actual value. An `0` in the figure indicates a bit that is specifically a 0 bit and is not part of the output. Finally a `-` stands for a "don't care" bit which has already been moved to the output buffer in memory and will be discarded, so its value no longer matters. The vertical bar in the illustration shows where the low octet, containing the least significant bits of `current_output`, lies.

Assume that `free_bits` contains the value 3, meaning that the rightmost three bits of `current_output` are "don't care" and the leftmost five bits contain prior code word bits. We can represent the contents of code word as `XXXXX---`. All bits above the lowest eight are 0. This is shown in row A. The dashed lines to the left indicate that there are more 0 bits, since `current_output` is an `unsigned long` and actually holds at least 32 bits.

Row B shows the `bit_pattern` member of `T4_ENCODE` structure, an octet stored in an `unsigned char` containing eight bits. If the implementation's `unsigned char` contains more than eight bits, the higher bits are all 0. Any or all of the bits to the left of the vertical bar might not exist.

These three lines of code expand the new code word to its full length and merge it into `current_output`:

```
length = code->code_length;
current_output |=
  ((unsigned long)code->bit_pattern << length);
```

This operation is shown in rows B, C, and D. The first step in evaluating the expression is casting the `bit_pattern` member to `unsigned long`. Casting a value from a narrower to a wider unsigned type fills the higher bits with 0, so once the cast is performed the intermediate value is exactly like row B.

The parentheses force the left shift operation to be performed next. The `unsigned long` value is left shifted 13 places in our example, and the results are shown in row C. Shifting left always shifts 0 bits in from the right, regardless of whether the value being shifted is signed or unsigned. In the process, the five final bits of the new code, which are all 0 bits, are re-created, and the entire code word is shifted past the first eight bits of the temporary value, leaving the low eight bits all 0.

The final step in the expression is to bitwise inclusive OR the temporary unsigned long value into `current_output`. Since `current_output` has all 0 bits above the lowest octet and the temporary value has all 0 bits in the lowest octet, the result of the logical merge is straightforward and is shown in row D.

Now we come to the loop beginning with

```
while (length >= free_bits)
```

Since length is 13 and unused output is only 3, the first time the condition is evaluated, the body of the loop is executed. The line

```
current_output >>= free_bits;
```

shifts `current_output` by three, and the result is shown in row E. Since `current_output` is an unsigned type, right-shifting always shifts 0 bits in from the left. The low octet of current output is now completely filled by eight bits of code words, so the octet can now be stored in the output buffer. The line

```
*t4_ptr++ = (unsigned char)(current_output & OCTET_MASK);
```

performs this task, and increments the output pointer to the next location in the output buffer to be filled. The bitwise AND with `OCTET_MASK`, defined as 0xff, ensures that only the low eight bits of the `unsigned char` are used. It is not necessary on implementations with 8-bit chars, but makes the program portable to platforms with wider characters. The cast to `unsigned char` is not required because `OCTET_MASK` has already made sure that the value is within the range of an unsigned char, but explicit casts when assigning to a smaller type are always a good idea and eliminate compiler and lint warnings.

Once the eight bits have been moved to the output buffer, they are no longer needed and so become "don't care" bits as shown in row F.

The final two lines in the body of the loop are

```
length -= free_bits;
      free_bits = PIXELS_PER_OCTET;
```

We just shifted free_bits (in this case 3) bits of the new pattern into the low octet, so we subtract that 3 from the length to leave 10 bits yet to be dealt with. Since all the bits in the low octet are now "don't care" and available for use, we set free_bits to PIXELS_PER_OCTET, defined as 8.

Since length (10) is greater than free_bits (8), we execute the while loop body a second time. current_output is shifted right by free_bits (8), resulting in row G. In the process, all of the "don't care" bits that were already stored in the output buffer are shifted off the right end of current_output and disappear. The low octet is filled with eight new bits, so it is again stored into the output buffer, and its contents flagged as "don't care" in row H. Finally, the loop subtracts free_bits (8) from length (10), leaving length with a value of 2. free_bits is set to 8 again.

The while condition is evaluated a third time, but now length (2) is not greater than or equal to free_bits (8), so the body of the loop is skipped. Execution reaches the conditional expression:

```
if (length != 0)
```

In the case we are walking through length is 2, so the body is executed.

```
    {
      current_output >>= length;
      free_bits -= length;
    }
```

current_output is shifted left by two in row I, and that two is subtracted from free_bits, resulting in a value of 6, indicating that there are six remaining "don't care" bits in the low octet to be replaced with bits from the next code word.

The other point of interest in this function is its handling of the EOL code word when the code parameter is NULL. The T.4 protocol does not require that scan lines end and new scan lines start on an octet boundary, but it is a very common practice because it simplifies buffer management for writing to a file, as in this program, or sending to a serial device, as in a fax machine.

Encoded Stream to Image

Decoding a T.4 encoded page back into raw binary pixels is more complex than encoding it was in the first place. This is generally true of most compression algorithms and many encryption methods as well. The specific reasons in the case of T.4 encoding are

- We know when encoding that each raw scan line consists of exactly 216 octets containing 1,728 bits representing image pixels. When decoding we do not know in advance how long any line is until we find code words adding up to 1,728 bits and the final EOL code word.
- Any arbitrary sequence of pixels can appear in a valid image; there are no illegal or invalid values so no error checking is required. But not every sequence of arbitrary bits represents a valid T.4 encoded image. In fact, there are far more invalid sequences than valid ones, so the decoding program must do considerable error checking.

The T.4 Decompression Program: `decode.c`

The companion CD contains complete source code for a standard C program that reads T.4 encoded data from a file and writes the decoded raw binary image to another file. If you start with a properly built binary image file, encode it with the encode program, and decode the result with the decode program, the output of decode will be identical to the original binary file. Other than the same `fax.h` header used in the encoding program, `decode.c` includes only standard C headers and is contained in a single source file.

Again, a structure data type is defined at the beginning of the file to represent T.4 code words, but both the structure type and the arrangement of the lookup table arrays are quite a bit different from the encoding program. The structure is defined:

```
typedef struct
{
  unsigned char bit_pattern;
  unsigned char run_length;
} T4_DECODE;
```

Looking at the first array containing some of these structures:

```
static const T4_DECODE t4_white_04[] =
{
  { 0x07, 0x02 }, /*    2 white pixels */
  { 0x08, 0x03 }, /*    3 white pixels */
  { 0x0B, 0x04 }, /*    4 white pixels */
```

```
    { 0x0C, 0x05 }, /*    5 white pixels */
    { 0x0E, 0x06 }, /*    6 white pixels */
    { 0x0F, 0x07 }  /*    7 white pixels */
};
```

The first thing you will probably notice is that the code words are not reversed and left-justified in the `bit_pattern` member. Instead they are stored as they appear in Tables 18.3 and 18.4, and are right-justified. The pattern matching code is much more straightforward this way, so the left-to-right reversal is done before the lookup tables are searched.

The discussion of the encoding program lookup tables explained how code words with lengths of up to 13 bits can be held in eight bits without loss, because all higher bits are 0 and do not contribute to the numerical value.

On the other hand, the `run_length` member has to indicate every possible value between 0 and 1,728, inclusive, in eight bits, which can only directly represent values up to 255. This trick is accomplished with a little help from the fact that there are only 91 distinct code words of each color, so we really only need 91 different values. The first obvious step is to use the values 0 through 63 to represent the run length for terminating codes. There are several possible methods of representing make-up code words. The one used here takes advantage of the fact that make-up code words always represent exact multiples of 64 with no remainder. If the length represented by a make-up code word is divided by 64, the result is between 1 and 27, inclusive. To distinguish a value of 1 representing the code word for a 64 pixel run and the 1 representing a single pixel, the `run_length` member for make-up codes has 0x80 bitwise ORed into it.

So terminating code words for 0 through 63 pixel runs have `run_length` member values of 0x00 through 0x3f, inclusive, and make-up codes for runs of 64 through 1,728 (1 x 64 through 27 x 64) have values of 0x81 through 0x9b, inclusive.

In a program for a desktop machine, I would just use a short int to hold the actual value of each run length, but in an embedded system a representation like this would quite likely be used to save memory.

The `T4_DECODE` structures are separated into more arrays than the `T4_ENCODE` structures in the encode program were. There is a separate array for all code words of the same length for each color. Within each array the structures are sorted in ascending order by the numerical value of their code word.

The decode algorithm also uses a second data type. The type definition and part of the array are shown here:

```
typedef struct
{
  const T4_DECODE *token;
  int search_length;
} CODE_TABLE;

static const CODE_TABLE code_table[12][2] =
{
  {
    { t4_black_02, sizeof t4_black_02/sizeof *t4_black_02 },
    { NULL       , 0                                      }
  },

  {
    { t4_black_03, sizeof t4_black_03/sizeof *t4_black_03 },
    { NULL       , 0                                      }
  },

  {
    { t4_black_04, sizeof t4_black_03/sizeof *t4_black_03 },
    { t4_white_04, sizeof t4_white_04/sizeof *t4_white_04 }
  },
```

As the program builds a potential code word bit-by-bit from the input file, the `CODE_TABLE` structure for the appropriate color and code word length is selected from this array.

Finally, two enumerated data types are defined, one to represent pixel colors and the other to express things that can be found instead of a code word indicating a pixel run:

```
typedef enum
{
  BLACK_WANTED,
  WHITE_WANTED
} PIXEL_WANTED;

typedef enum
{
  T4_EOF         = -1, /* end of input file encountered  */
  T4_EOL         = -2, /* end of line code word found    */
  T4_INVALID     = -3  /* invalid T.4 valid code word    */
} T4_RESULTS;
```

The main() Function

Here again the `main()` function is a simple driver. It defines an output buffer to hold a full line of binary pixel data. Decoding is just the opposite of encoding in that the exact size of each output line is known but the length of the input line needs to be determined. `main()` also parses the command-line arguments to obtain the source and output filenames, and opens the two files in binary mode. The two `FILE` pointers and a pointer to the data buffer are passed to the `DecodePage()` function.

The DecodePage() Function

`DecodePage()`, shown in Listing 18.5, includes the individual line as well as the complete page handling code. There is no separate `DecodeLine()` function, as there was an `EncodeLine()` function in the encode program, because that would complicate the end-of-page sequence recognition.

LISTING 18.5 `DecodePage()` Function

```
int
DecodePage(FILE *fin,
           FILE *fout,
           unsigned char * const buff)
{
  PIXEL_WANTED wanted;     /* color currently sought       */
  int pixel_run;           /* length of current color run  */
  int eop_count = 0;       /* use to recognize end of page */
  int fax_lines;           /* count of lines decoded       */
  int pixel_count;         /* total pixels in current line */
  int total_run;           /* total pixels in current run  */
  unsigned char *out_ptr;  /* pointer into output buffer   */

  /* first code word in the file must be an EOL */
  pixel_run = GetPixelRun(WHITE_WANTED, fin);
  if (pixel_run != T4_EOL)
  {
    puts("missing initial EOL");
    return EOF;
  }

  /* read, decode, and output encoded scan lines one-by-one */
  for (fax_lines = 0; fax_lines < MAXIMUM_ROWS; )
  {
    wanted = WHITE_WANTED;   /* lines start with white runs  */
    out_ptr = buff;          /* output starts at beginning   */
```

LISTING 18.5 continued

```
pixel_count = 0;         /* have no pixels in new line    */

do
{
  pixel_run = GetPixelRun(wanted, fin);
  if (pixel_run >= 0)
  {
    eop_count = 0;       /* pixel runs since last EOL     */
    if ((total_run = pixel_run) > 63)
    {
      /* if the pixel run just decodes is greater than  */
      /* 63, it is a make-up code and they are always   */
      /* followed by a terminating code for the same    */
      /* color, so call GetPixelRun again with the same */
      /* color to get the total run length              */
      pixel_run = GetPixelRun(wanted, fin);
      if (pixel_run >= 0)
      {
        total_run += pixel_run;
      }
      else
      {
        puts("decode: make-up code missing");
        return EOF;
      }
    }

    /* before inserting the new run of pixels into the  */
    /* output buffer, check to make sure that it will   */
    /* not exceed the proper number of pixels per row   */
    /* as this could cause writing past the end of the  */
    /* memory space belonging to the buffer, causing    */
    /* undefined behavior                               */
    if ((pixel_count += total_run) > PIXELS_PER_ROW)
    {
      puts("decode: line too long");
      return EOF;
    }
    else
    {
      /* the new run of pixels will fit in the buffer   */
      /* so insert it                                   */
```

LISTING 18.5 continued

```
        out_ptr = OutputPixels(total_run, wanted, out_ptr);
        /* since white and black pixel runs alternate we  */
        /* now want to look for the opposite color of the */
        /* last run                                       */
        if (wanted == WHITE_WANTED)
        {
          wanted = BLACK_WANTED;
        }
        else
        {
          wanted = WHITE_WANTED;
        }
      }
    }
  } while (pixel_run >= 0);

  /* a value which does not represent a pixel run has     */
  /* been returned by GetPixelRun(), decided what to do   */
  /* next based on its exact value                        */
  switch (pixel_run)
  {
    case T4_EOF:
      puts("decode: unexpected end of file");
      return EOF;
    case T4_EOL:
      /* there are two correct circumstances for finding  */
      /* an EOL code word, the first after decoding the   */
      /* code words for exactly the 1728 pixels...        */
      if (PIXELS_PER_ROW == pixel_count)
      {
        ++fax_lines;
        fwrite(buff, 1, OCTETS_PER_ROW, fout);
        ++eop_count;
      }
      /* ...and the second is after decoding 0 pixels     */
      /* after the preceding EOL code, since six          */
      /* consecutive EOL codes in a row with no pixels at */
      /* all in between signal the end of the page        */
      else if (0 == pixel_count)
      {
        if (++eop_count >= 6)
        {
```

LISTING 18.5 continued

```
            return fax_lines;
          }
        }
        /* if an EOL code word is found after some number   */
        /* of pixels less than 1,728 it is an error         */
        else
        {
          puts("decode: invalid line length");
          return EOF;
        }
        break;
      case T4_INVALID:
        /* if GetPixelRun() detected a pattern of bits that */
        /* don't correspond to any T.4 code word...         */
        puts("decode: invalid t.4 code");
        return EOF;
      default:
        /* for safety sake there is a default case...       */
        puts("decode: program error");
        return EOF;
    }
  }

  return fax_lines;
}
```

After verifying that the file contains the required initial EOL code word, `DecodePage()` executes a loop for each scan line until it has decoded `MAXIMUM_ROWS`, it finds the end of page sequence, or an error occurs.

In the loop for each line it calls the `GetPixelRun()` function, looking for runs of white and black pixels alternately. When a make-up code is returned for either color, `DecodePage()` calls `GetPixelRun()` again with the same color to get the following terminating code. The values of the two codes are added together and sent to the `OutputPixels()` function as a single run.

As it decodes pixel runs, `DecodePage()` keeps a running count of the total pixels in the current line. Each new run length is checked with the running total to make sure that erroneous input does not cause it to exceed `PIXELS_PER_ROW`. If that happened and `OutputPixels()` was called, the bounds of the output buffer array would be exceeded invoking undefined behavior. If the total run lengths found for a scan line exceed the proper length, the program halts with an error.

DecodePage() does not check for zero length runs of white pixels when a scan line actually starts with a black pixel. It just passes the value to OutputPixels(), which is written to do absolutely nothing when presented with a zero length run of either color.

The variable eop_count is used to recognize the end-of-page sequence composed of six consecutive EOL code words with no intervening pixel data. This value is incremented each time an EOL sequence is found, and set back to zero when any pixel data is extracted. If eop_count ever reaches six, the page is finished.

GetPixelRun()returns a value between 0 and 1,728, inclusive, when it finds a valid run of the proper color pixels. Negative return values are defined in the T4_RESULTS enumeration for conditions other than a run of pixels.

If pixel_run receives a negative value from GetPixelRun(), none of the remaining code inside the do..while() loop is executed and the loop exits because the while() condition is false. The enumerated value is then handled by the switch() statement.

If DecodePage() is successful it returns the number of lines decoded and stored to main(), otherwise it returns EOF to indicate an error. Actually, it gives up at the very first error, which would probably generate customer complaints in a real fax machine. A better approach would be to scan the encoded stream for at least 11 consecutive 0 bits, indicating that the next 1 bit to arrive signals an EOL. In many cases, one or more scan lines might be lost but the bulk of the page image is rescued.

The GetPixelRun() Function

GetPixelRun(), shown in Listing 18.6, is called with a PIXEL_WANTED parameter to specify the color sought and a pointer to the input file that it passes along to the GetNextBit() function. It initializes several variables.

code_word is set to 0, since no bits have been read from the input file and placed into it yet. bits, which represents the length of code_word, is also set to 0.

Code words for black pixels can contain any number of bits between 2 and 13, but white code words are all between 4 and 9 bits in length, so GetPixelRun() sets the variables min_bits and max_bits to the proper values for the current pixel color.

Then GetPixelRun() enters its main loop, which continues until a code word is recognized or an error occurs.

LISTING 18.6 `GetPixelRun()` Function

```
static int
GetPixelRun(PIXEL_WANTED color, FILE *fin)
{
  unsigned int code_word = 0;
  int bits = 0;
  int pixel_run, next_bit, min_bits, max_bits;
  const T4_DECODE *t4p;

  /* treat wanted as a Boolean, BLACK_WANTED indicates    */
  /* black, any other value indicates white               */
  if (BLACK_WANTED == color)
  {
    min_bits = 2;     /* minimum length black code word   */
    max_bits = 13;    /* maximum length black code word   */
  }
  else  /* WHITE_PIXEL wanted */
  {
    color = WHITE_WANTED;
    min_bits = 4;     /* minimum length white code word   */
    max_bits = 9;     /* maximum length white code word   */
  }

  for ( ; ; )         /* until code word found or error   */
  {
    do
    {
      /* because a do..while loop has the test at the end */
      /* it always executes at least once so on each pass */
      /* the GetNextBit() function will always be called  */
      /* even if the length of the code word under        */
      /* construction is greater than the minimum value   */
      if ((next_bit = GetNextBit(fin)) == T4_EOF)
      {
        return T4_EOF;
      }
      else
      {
        code_word = (code_word << 1) ¦ next_bit;
      }
    } while (++bits < min_bits);

    /*  check for EOL once code word is long enough */
```

LISTING 18.6 continued

```
    if (bits >= EOL_LENGTH && code_word == 1)
    {
      return T4_EOL;
    }

    /* if already past maximum bit length and not   */
    /* EOL must be all zero bits on the way to EOL  */
    if (bits > max_bits)
    {
      if (code_word != 0)
      {
        return T4_INVALID;
      }
    }
    else if (NULL != (t4p =
      code_table[bits - 2][color].token))
    /* this condition has to be in an else if clause to the */
    /* one above it because if bits > max_bits the access   */
    /* to the code_table array will be beyond the end of    */
    /* array causing undefined behavior                     */
    {
      t4p = bsearch(&code_word, t4p,
            code_table[bits - 2][color].search_length,
            sizeof *t4p, T4Compare);

      if (NULL != t4p)
      {
        pixel_run = t4p->run_length;
        /* here the packing of make-up codes into unsigned  */
        /* chars is undone and the run length expanded back */
        /* to its full value                                */
        if (pixel_run & 0x80)
        {
          pixel_run &= ~0x80;
          pixel_run <<= 6;
        }
        return pixel_run;
      }
    }
  }
}
```

The do..while() loop at the top of the main loop will call GetNextBit() twice for black or four times for white pixel runs initially. The returned bits are shifted into code_word from the right. Once code_word contains min_bits bits, the loop terminates. On each additional pass through the outer loop, the do..while() will add one more bit to code_word even though bits is already greater than or equal to min_bits.

The next test is for the EOL code word. If 11 or more 0 bits have already been assembled into code_word, the final 1 bit which finishes EOL will make the test true and the enum value T4_EOL is returned.

If EOL is not detected, a test is performed for erroneous input data. If code_word already contains more than max_bits (9 for white or 13 for black), the only valid possibility is that it is partially through an EOL code word, having extracted a string of 0s on the way to the final 1 bit. If code_word is already longer than max_bits for the current color and does not equal 0, GetPixelRun() has detected an invalid T.4 sequence and an error value is returned.

If execution passes this test, code_word contains a valid length for a code word for the current color. The color and length are combined to access the code_table array, retrieving a pointer to the first element of the array of CODE_TABLE structures containing all valid code words of the current length for the current color. All code words have a length of at least 2, so the code_table array starts with code word length 2 in its first pair of elements. This is accommodated by using bits-2 as an index value.

After verifying that the T4_DECODE pointer is not NULL as a sanity check, GetPixelRun() uses the pointer and the search_length member to call the standard library function bsearch() to search the sorted array for a bit_pattern value equal to the current value of code_word.

If bsearch() returns a match, GetPixelRun() checks to see whether the run_length member of the T4_DECODE structure is a simple terminating length (0 to 63) or a make-up length, by checking bit 7. If it is a make-up length, it is unpacked into a normal int value between 64 and 1,728. Then the run length is returned.

The T4Compare() Function

This very brief function has a signature matching the callback function required by bsearch(). The first pointer to void parameter is an alias for a pointer to the code_word variable in `GetPixelRun()`. The second is an alias to an element of the `T4_DECODE` array containing code words of the appropriate color and the same length as `code_word`.

```
static int T4Compare(const void *x, const void *y)
{
  return *(int *)x - (int)((T4_DECODE *)y)->bit_pattern;
}
```

The pointers must be cast to appropriate types for the underlying data before dereferencing. In the case of `code_word`, which is actually an `unsigned int`, the value is always positive and less than 4096, so accessing it through a pointer to `signed int` is well defined and results in a `signed int` of the same value. The second pointer is explicitly cast to a pointer to a `T4_DECODE` structure, used to access the `bit_pattern` member, and the value is then cast to `signed int`.

Both values are cast to `signed`, rather than `unsigned int`, so a single subtraction can generate an accurate return value. Without the cast they might promote to unsigned int on some relatively rare platforms, and the subtraction of two `unsigned int`s can never yield a negative result.

The `GetNextBit()` Function

The `GetNextBit()` function shown in Listing 18.7 works very much the same as part of the `CountPixelRun()` function in the encode program. It maintains static variables containing the octet most recently read from the input file and the number of bits already extracted from the octet. It is in a function of its own to emphasize that this is where the left-to-right reversal takes place in the decoding program. `GetNextBit()` shifts octets left to right and always returns the rightmost bit. `GetPixelRun()` left shifts its `code_word` variable and moves the returned bit in from the right.

LISTING 18.7 `GetNextBit()` Function

```
static int
GetNextBit(FILE *fin)
{
  static int bits_used = PIXELS_PER_OCTET;
  static unsigned int t4_in;
  int input;

  /* see if there are bits remaining in the current octet */
  if (bits_used >= PIXELS_PER_OCTET)
  {
    /* none left, get a new octet from the source file    */
    if ((input = fgetc(fin)) == EOF)
```

LISTING 18.7 continued

```
    {
      return T4_EOF;
    }
    else
    {
      /* have new octet, mask to 8 least significant bits */
      t4_in = input & OCTET_MASK;
      /* haven't use any bits from this octet yet         */
      bits_used = 0;
    }
  }
  else
  {
    /* more bits in current octet, shift the last one     */
    /* off the right end and bring the next one to bit 0  */
    t4_in >>= 1;
  }

  ++bits_used;                  /* using a bit, count it  */
  return t4_in & 1;             /* return bit 0 of octet  */
}
```

The `OutputPixels()` Function

The `OutputPixels()` function, shown in Listing 18.8, receives a color, a count, and a pointer to the output buffer to store the results. Because it deals with variable length bit streams that are not required to start and end on octet boundaries, it keeps static internal variables for the current partially filled octet and the number of free bits still available in it.

Its operation is very similar to the `OutputCodeWord()` function in the encode program, again illustrating that inserting known length bit patterns into an output stream is much simpler than extracting unknown length patterns from an input stream.

LISTING 18.8 `OutputPixels()` Function

```
static unsigned char
*OutputPixels(int length,
              PIXEL_WANTED wanted,
              unsigned char *out_ptr)
{
  unsigned int mask;
  static int outbits_left = PIXELS_PER_OCTET;
```

LISTING 18.8 continued

```
    static unsigned int pixel_out = 0;

    if (BLACK_WANTED == wanted)
    {
      mask = 0;
    }
    else
    {
      mask = 0xff;
    }

    while (length >= outbits_left)
    {
      pixel_out <<= outbits_left;
      *out_ptr++ = (unsigned char)(pixel_out
        | (mask >> (PIXELS_PER_OCTET - outbits_left)));
      pixel_out = 0;
      length -= outbits_left;
      outbits_left = PIXELS_PER_OCTET;
    }

    if (length)
    {
      pixel_out <<= length;
      pixel_out |=
        mask >> (PIXELS_PER_OCTET - length);
      outbits_left -= length;
    }

    return out_ptr;
  }
```

Character Generation

If you have ever received a fax, you probably noticed a header across the top of each page. The headers usually include the name of the sender's company and the phone number connected to the fax machine. A page number is also common. Even if the rest of the page is jagged and distorted, the header is crisp and precise.

These headers are generated by the fax machine or fax transmission software directly. They are not part of the image on paper fed to the scanner, so they are straight and unblemished even if the paper does not feed smoothly or evenly.

The headers are generated from information entered into the fax machine or software by the user as part of the initial set up. The fax encodes these strings into T.4 codes and transmits them before the actual image content of the page.

It is not possible to directly generate T.4 encoding from text strings, or even from the individual bit patterns used for each character. Due to the way runs of white and black pixels are encoded, the entire line of text must be converted to pixels in the equivalent of a scan line.

The companion CD contains a source file named `text2bin.c`, which reads plain old ASCII text files and generates binary image files equivalent to printing the text on paper in a 10-point fixed-pitch font and scanning it with a fax machine. The character generator is based on the PC text mode "extended" characters so it has glyphs for all characters with numeric values from 0 through 255.

The output files are raw binary images encoded in 216 unsigned chars per scan row, with eight pixels stored in the least significant bits of each `unsigned char`. They can be used as source files for the `encode.c` program. Details are included in the `chap18.txt` file on the CD.

There is also a "bonus" program on the CD named `lj300.c`. This program reads a binary file as produced by `decode.c` or `text2bin.c` and generates a binary file to print the image on a Laser Jet or compatible with 300 DPI raster graphics. If you have another type of printer with graphics capabilities, you can use this as a starting point for converting the images for your printer.

To actually print the images to a compatible printer, you will need to know how to send a raw binary file directly to your printer without modifications by the operating system's printer driver. Further details are in the `chap18.txt` file on the CD.

Error Detection and Correction

Data is valuable, but vulnerable. Information that costs a great deal in money and effort needs to be stored and retrieved, and transmitted and received. Just ask anyone whose hard disk has crashed with files that weren't backed up anywhere. Information, in digital or any other form, represents a high degree of organization and a low degree of entropy. But the physical laws of the world decree that entropy will always increase unless energy is expended to prevent it.

This section looks at applying C to the task of detecting and correcting inevitable errors in data storage or transmission. To avoid repeating the phrase "data storage or transmission" over and over again, I will use the phrase "data handling" to refer to any situation where errors might creep into data.

Combating Chaos

The enemies of our data never rest. Electrical storms and even sunspots constantly try to garble transmissions. Hard disk drives and other storage media degenerate with age and sometimes fail to return what was stored. In the real world, it is impossible to guarantee that data will never be corrupted or damaged when it is stored or transmitted. With the application of appropriate techniques, however, we can reduce the probability of harm by data damage to a very small value.

There are two separate but related ideas involved here: error detection and error correction. Error detection involves recognizing that data, whether received by transmission or retrieved from storage, has been changed or corrupted. Error correction, which necessarily requires error detection, consists of methods of recognizing what the data should be and restoring it to its original condition.

If I receive the text "Hello Worle" in an electronic message from another C programmer, I can quickly deduce that he most likely meant "Hello World" and there was either a transmission error or he made a simple typographical error. Once I've detected the error I can correct it almost instantly.

Most problems are not that simple, however. Consider the yearly financial records for a major corporation being sent to their accounting firm. There might be literally millions of bytes of data, much of it in binary in spreadsheets. First it is compressed, then encrypted for security. The final data stream bears no resemblance at all to the actual information, and a single bit error can render it impossible to decrypt and decompress back into usable form.

Redundancy

The key to error detection and correction is redundancy, adding extra information beyond the bare minimum needed to convey the information. The "Hello World" example already has a large amount of redundancy. There are only eight different characters in the string—"H", "e", "l", "o", "W", "r", "d", and the space character. Since three bits can hold eight different combinations, we could assign 3-bit substitutions for the characters in the order listed above. If my programmer friend and I have agreed that we will only use these eight characters, and we also have already agreed on their encoding, we could replace "Hello World" with the binary digit string 000001010010011111100011101010110, requiring only 33 bits instead of at least 88 bits it occupies as 11 characters.

Now a transmission error could change the last 3-bit character representation from the code for "d" to the code for "e", resulting in 00000101001001111110001101010001. I certainly could not tell from looking at the bit string that the information was garbled. After decoding it I could still recognize the error, but only because it is a short and very familiar phrase.

When complex data is stored or transmitted in a form that is not humanly recognizable, there may be no way to tell from the data itself that it has been garbled. In some cases we can, however; for example, a changed bit or two in the binary representation of a floating-point number might result in a processor error when processed later or an obvious error in calculations, but also it might not.

If errors crop up in binary data stored as a stream of unsigned characters, we can't depend on an exception or trap when we access the data in a C program, because every combination of bits in an unsigned char is a valid value.

There are many ways of adding redundancy to data handling to allow error detection and possibly correction. We'll look at some of the most common ones, beginning with the earliest.

The simplest way to add redundancy to any data handling situation is duplication. In fact, that is the whole point behind making backup copies. This is a good technique for long-term storage, but it is less satisfactory for communications and real-time handling of critical data.

Consider duplication in communications. Instead of sending you a single copy of a file electronically, I send two copies separately. You compare the two copies and if they match exactly you have a very good probability that both are correct.

But what if they don't match? Most likely one is correct and the other has errors, but which is which? Want to flip a coin?

All right, I'll send three separate copies. If all three are identical there's an extremely good probability that they are all correct. If two agree and the third does not, majority rules. Of course, if all three are different we're back to square one.

The problem with duplication in communications is that it is costly in time and bandwidth.

Parity

In the early days of computers, data was mostly text and text was mostly ASCII. Most computers had word sizes that were multiples of eight bits, or at least could interface to 8-bit peripheral devices. Standard interfaces such as parallel printer ports, serial communication UARTs, and many others were developed that allowed data to be read or written to them in 8-bit chunks, or octets.

One of the earliest error detection techniques was parity, quickly implemented in UART hardware. The entire ASCII character set covered a range of values from 0 through 127. In C notation for hex values, this was 0x00 through 0x7F. The most significant bit was always 0 and never changed. If the contents of that last bit were set in some way based on the value of the other seven bits, an error that flipped the value of one of the bits could be detected.

In binary terms, the word *parity* is used to describe the number of 1 bits in a binary value.

An octet containing the binary value 0x1 contains the eight bits 00000001. A quick glance reveals that the octet contains a single 1 bit, and since 1 is an odd number we say that this octet has odd parity. Note that even and odd parity has nothing to do with whether the value of the number is even or odd. An octet containing the even number 2 is 00000010 in binary and still has odd parity.

Suppose we can adopt the convention that when we handle ASCII text using one octet per character, we will examine the low seven bits to determine if they contain an even or odd number of 1 bits. Then we will set the otherwise unused highest bit so that the overall 8-bit octet has a specified parity, even or odd. It doesn't really make any difference whether even or odd is selected, as long as everyone agrees on which it is.

How do we check and set parity? It is quite simple to do in hardware, and many UARTs and some processors, such as the Intel x86 series, can do it for you, but it is not difficult to do in C. Simply use the bitwise exclusive OR operator to combine all the bits together one by one. If the final result bit is 1, the series of bits has odd parity. If it is 0, they are even.

The simple program in Listing 18.9 (included on the CD) illustrates parity testing and setting in C. The low seven bits of a value are checked and the eighth bit is then set so that the full eight bits will have even parity.

LISTING 18.9 `Parity.c`—Adds Even Parity to Characters Read from `stdin`

```
#include <stdio.h>
#include <string.h>

unsigned int even_parity(unsigned int ch)
{
```

LISTING 18.9 continued

```
  int temp = 0;
  int count;

  /* trim to 7 bit ASCII  */
  ch &= 0x7f;

  /* set temp to 0 for even parity or 1 for odd parity  */
  for (count = 0; count < 8; ++count)
  {
      temp ^= ((ch >> count) & 1);
  }

  if (temp)
  {
    ch |= 0x80;
  }

  return ch;
}

int main(void)
{
  char buff[22];
  char *cp;

  for ( ; ; )
  {
    printf("\nEnter up to 20 characters: ");
    fflush(stdout);

    if (fgets(buff, sizeof buff, stdin) == NULL ||
          buff [0] == '\n')
    {
      puts("Goodbye!");
      return 0;
    }

    /* remove newline from string if present  */
    if ((cp = strchr(buff, '\n')) != NULL)
    {
      *cp = '\0';
```

LISTING 18.9 continued

```
    }

    for (cp = buff; *cp != '\0'; ++cp)
    {
      printf("%02X is %02X with even parity\n",
        *cp & 0x7f, even_parity(*cp & 0x7f));
    }
  }
}
```

If you run the parity and enter the digits 0 through 9 at the prompt you will see the following output, assuming your system uses the ASCII character set:

```
Enter up to 20 characters: 0123456789
0x30 is 0x30 with even parity
0x31 is 0xB1 with even parity
0x32 is 0xB2 with even parity
0x33 is 0x33 with even parity
0x34 is 0xB4 with even parity
0x35 is 0x35 with even parity
0x36 is 0x36 with even parity
0x37 is 0xB7 with even parity
0x38 is 0xB8 with even parity
0x39 is 0x39 with even parity
```

Half of the digit values will be unchanged, and the other half will have the extra bit turned on.

When parity is used, any single-bit error is detectable. The four lower bits of the ASCII code for the digit 0 are all 0 bits. If any one of them were to be changed to a 1 by a data handling error, the result would be 0x31, 0x32, 0x34, or 0x38. Each of these is ASCII code for a different digit, but none of them has the proper parity as you can see from the preceding program output.

In fact, a system using parity will detect any odd number of bit errors, three or five or seven. Consider all three of the lowest bits of ASCII 0, 0x30, being flipped to 1s. The result is 0x37, which is ASCII 7 but has wrong parity. This is error detection only, with no possibility of correction because a parity error only tells us that an odd number of bits have been changed, not how many or which ones.

The weakness of a parity bit is that it can't detect any number of even bit errors. Suppose the two lowest bits of 0 are both toggled by an error. 0x30 becomes 0x33, which is ASCII 3, and does not display an error.

So a parity bit by itself is weak insurance. You might think that the possibility of two errors in a single octet is relatively small, but some situations, especially certain transmission noise conditions, tend to cause burst errors, where several successive bits are garbled, and it is still used in some common applications, such as serial communications.

Checksums

One way to add error checking to data is to produce checksums. This takes advantage of the fact that all data can be viewed as an array of unsigned chars in memory, or as a stream of unsigned chars when writing to, or reading from, a stream, which can include disk files or communications channels. In addition, unsigned chars are just small integral types in C; that is, they are numbers. So we can add up as many of them as we like, and as long as we use unsigned types the result is always well defined.

The simple program in Listing 18.10 (included on the companion CD as `chekline.c`) illustrates a method for computing checksums.

LISTING 18.10 `Chekline.c`—Computes Checksums on Strings Read from `stdin`

```
#include <stdio.h>
#include <string.h>

int main(void)
{
  char buff[100];
  unsigned int count, sum;
char *nl;

  for ( ; ; )
  {
    printf("Enter a string: ");
    fflush(stdout);
    if ( fgets(buff, sizeof buff, stdin) == NULL
        || buff[0] == '\n')
    {
      return 0;
    }
    if ((nl = strchr(buff, '\n')) != NULL)
      *nl = '\0';

    for (count = 0, sum = 0; buff[count] != '\0'; ++count)
    {
      sum += (unsigned char)buff[count];
```

LISTING 18.13 `Hamming.c`—Illustrates the Use of Hamming Codes

```
int main(void)
{
  unsigned long value;
  unsigned long modified;
  long the_bit;
  int ham;
  int mod_ham;
  char buff[50];

  for ( ; ; )
  {
    printf("Enter a value between 0 and 255 in C notation: ");
    fflush(stdout);
    if (NULL == (fgets(buff, sizeof buff, stdin)))
    {
      break;
    }
    else if (*buff == '\n')
    {
      break;
    }
    value = strtoul(buff, NULL, 0);
    if (value > 255)
    {
      puts("Value too large");
      continue;
    }
    printf("Enter the bit (0 - 7) to change: ");
    fflush(stdout);
    if (NULL == (fgets(buff, sizeof buff, stdin)))
    {
      break;
    }
    else if (*buff == '\n')
    {
      break;
    }
    the_bit = strtol(buff, NULL, 0);
    if (the_bit > 7 || the_bit < 0)
    {
      puts("Bit number out of range");
      continue;
```

LISTING 18.13 continued

```
    }
    ham = hamming[value];
    modified = value ^ (1 << the_bit);
    mod_ham = hamming[modified];
    printf("Original value 0x%02X Hamming Code 0x%X\n",
            value, ham);
    printf("Modified value 0x%02X Hamming Code 0x%X\n",
            modified, mod_ham);
    printf("Exclusive OR of the Hamming Codes is 0x%X\n",
            ham ^ mod_ham);
    printf("Correction mask is 0x%02X\n",
            corrections[ham ^ mod_ham]);
    printf("Corrected value is 0x%02X\n\n",
            modified ^ corrections[ham ^ mod_ham]);
  }
  printf("\nGoodbye\n");
  return 0;
}
```

The program prompts for a valid value for an octet (0 through 255) and a bit number (0 through 7). If a newline is entered without any data at either prompt, the program exits. After verifying the entered data, the program inverts the specified bit number in the entered value. It obtains the Hamming code for both the original and modified, and exclusive ORs them together. The result of the exclusive OR is used to index the corrections table, which relates the C numbers to the bits in the data octet. The corrections value is exclusive ORed with the "corrupted" octet to restore the original data.

RAID Technology

At the start of the discussion of Hamming codes, I mentioned the issue of a hard drive crash on a server storing critical data. Any disk drive is a wear part and it is only a question of when, not if, it will fail. If a drive fails before data stored on it has been copied or backed up somewhere else, that data is lost.

One of the techniques used for dealing with the possibility of drive failure is RAID (Redundant Array of Independent Disks) technology. There are different levels of RAID technology, some of which provide data protection and others which do not.

One RAID technique is called *drive mirroring*. The server contains two identical disks, operated in parallel either by special hardware in the computer or operating system–level driver software, transparent to the application program storing the critical data. The same data is written in parallel to both drives. If one drive fails, all the data is still intact on the second drive.

If you think back to the concept of transmitting two copies of data, you might wonder how drive mirroring avoids the same pitfalls. When a drive fails, it is often completely unreadable so there is no doubt which one is down. Even if the drive responds, disk controllers automatically compute CRC checks on data as they write it, and recompute and check them when reading back. So there is generally no problem recognizing which drive has failed when the data read back from does not match.

With one disk down, however, the system no longer has the protection afforded by mirroring. If it must keep operating, new data is stored on the remaining drive only. If the second drive fails before the first failed drive can be replaced and the drives mirrored again, data will be lost.

There are other levels of RAID that use more than two drives, and use Hamming codes to reconstruct the data. Extreme implementations actually generate a (7,4) Hamming code on each 4-bit nibble of data and use up to seven drives, one for each data bit and one for each Hamming bit. The technique of splitting a single data value across multiple drives is called *striping*.

There are intermediate levels that can provide more security than simple mirroring during a drive failure, but are less expensive than the seven drive approach.

Consider a system that uses a (12,8) Hamming code. There are 12 bits of encoded data that can be split into three nibbles of four bits each. These three nibbles can be striped across three different drives. During a drive failure, the system can fall back on drive mirroring with the other two drives to protect new data until the third drive is replaced.

A natural thought would be split the data octet into its high and low four bits. Each of these 4-bit nibbles would be stored on one drive, with the 4-bit Hamming code stored on the third drive. Unfortunately, this will not work. If the drive storing the high nibble fails, it is not possible to uniquely derive it from the low nibble and Hamming bits.

Altogether there are 35 different ways to split an 8-bit octet into two 4-bit nibbles. Twelve of these splits do provide the quality we need; that is, with either nibble and the four Hamming code bits they can re-create the missing data nibble and restore the original data. One of these 12 combinations is illustrated in Figure 18.5.

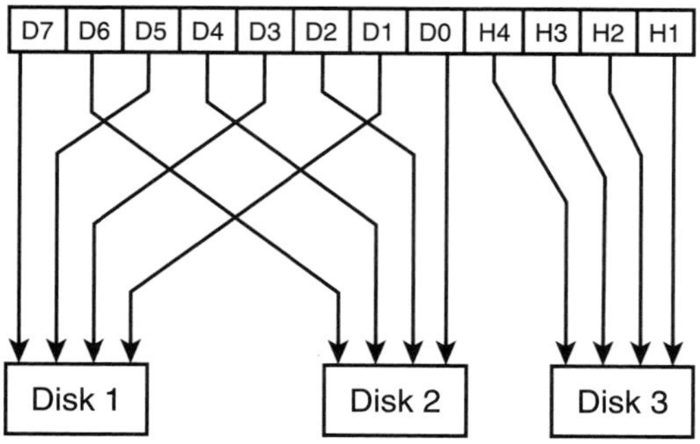

FIGURE 18.5
Drive striping with Hamming codes.

PID Control Algorithms

One reason for programs to capture, digitize, and process external signals is to control the real-world process that the signal represents. One of the most widely used programming techniques in control implementations is the PID algorithm in its many variations and adaptations.

All control mechanisms, from the simple light switch to the most sophisticated automated machinery, can be classified into one of two categories: closed loop and open loop. These are illustrated in Figure 18.6. The closed loop control gets its name from the circular feedback path on the right-hand side of the diagram. The control output goes from the controller to the processes being controlled. The feedback input travels from the process back to the control, closing the loop. The open loop control on the left-hand side gets its name from the absence of the feedback half of the loop.

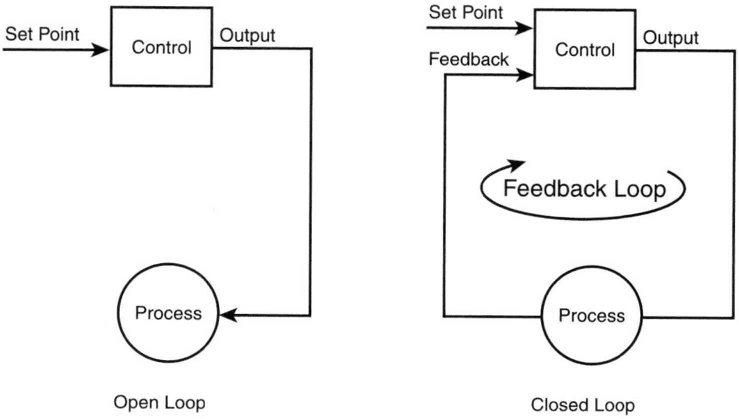

FIGURE 18.6
Open and closed loops.

There is an entirely different method for dividing all control mechanisms into another two categories, and that is the nature of the output mechanism they control. These two categories are continuously variable and on/off. A continuously variable control can modify its output from zero to some maximum value, or in some cases from some negative minimum value, through zero, to some maximum positive value. An on/off control, sometimes referred to as a "bang bang" control, only has two settings: all the way on or all the way off.

There is no direct correlation between the two sets of categories. All four combinations are possible: open loop on/off, open loop continuous output, closed loop on/off, and closed loop continuous output. It is the fourth category, the closed loop continuous output control, that is the most interesting.

Table 18.5 presents some terms used in control terminology and their definitions.

TABLE 18.5 Control Term Definitions

Control Term	*Definition*
Process Variable	This is the digitized feedback signal representing the real-world processing being controlled.
Set Point	This value is an input to the control mechanism and indicates the desired value of the Process Variable.
Output	This value is calculated by the control and sent to some real-world mechanism that has an effect on the process being controlled.
Error	The error is the difference between the set point and the Process Variable at any particular instant in time. The object of the control algorithm is to maintain the error as close as possible to zero at all times.
Interval or Ticks	Almost all control algorithms include a time factor. The Process Variable is sampled at each Interval (or on each Tick) and the algorithm computes a new Output value.
Disturbance	This is a change in external factors other than the controller Output that affects the Process Variable. Going up or down hill would be a disturbance to an automobile cruise control attempting to maintain a constant speed.
Transfer Ratio	The inputs and outputs of the controller might have very different scales. For example, a Set Point input of 10 milliamps might indicate an output of 1 amp. The Transfer Ratio is a simple scalar constant to allow different signal levels to be directly compared.
Gain	This is a general term applied to the overall transfer ratio of the controller and to the individual terms making up the control algorithm. A control that outputs 1 amp for 10 milliamps of input would have an overall Gain of 100. Any Gain may be zero, in which case it has no effect on the Output, or it may be greater than, less than, or equal to one.

Table 18.5 continued

Control Term	*Definition*
Proportional Gain	The "P" in PID stands for a proportional term. On each pass through the loop, the current Error (difference between Process Variable and Set Point) is multiplied by the Proportional Gain (or P Gain) to compute the P Term that participates in calculating the Output.
Integral Gain	The "I" in PID stands for Integral, as the term is pronounced and used in calculus, not in C programming. The Error is summed, or integrated, over time and this sum is multiplied by the Integral Gain (I Gain) to produce the I Term that participates in calculating the Output.
Derivative Gain	The "D" in PID stands for Derivative, another calculus term. The term has the same meaning in control theory, the rate of change of a function. In this case, rate of change in the Error from one Interval to the next is the Derivative, and this value is multiplied by the Derivative Gain (D Gain) to produce the D Term that participates in calculating the new Output.
Bias	A Bias is a constant term added into calculating the Output, independent of the Set Point or feedback from the Process Variable.
Lag	Some controlled processes have no time lag between a change in Output and a corresponding change in the Process Variable, or at least the change is fully completed by the next interval. Examples might be volume or light intensity, where the electronics being controlled react very quickly. Most physical control processes such as motion, temperature, pressure, and others have considerable inertia. It takes some time for the Process Variable to fully settle after a change in Output.
Dead Time	This is related to, but different from, Lag. In some systems, due to distance or other factors, a change in Output might not produce any change in the Process Variable at all for some length of time. Eventually the Output change starts to have an effect. The `pidloop` program on the companion CD for this section does not simulate Dead Time.
Acceleration Rate	In many control situations the requirement is to bring the Process Variable to the Set Point as quickly as possible. In other situations it is important that the Process Variable change at a specific rate, called the Acceleration Rate. The acceleration rate may be positive when increasing the Process Variable and negative when decreasing it.
Stiction	This term is a contraction of "stationery friction." It is a physical fact that there is more friction between stationery objects than there is between those in relative motion. The effect of stiction on a system is to make it non-linear at very low levels of Output. When starting from a standstill, there will be no change in the Process Variable at all until the Output reaches some minimum level. The `pidloop` program on the companion CD does not simulate Stiction.

TABLE 18.5 continued

Control Term	Definition
Feed Forward	An algorithm incorporates Feed Forward when it anticipates some effect that will increase the Error and modifies the Output in advance to prevent or reduce the increase. Each Feed Forward is another type of gain.
Acceleration Feed Forward	This Feed Forward term is sometimes used in control algorithms when there is a change in the Set Point, either immediate or gradually, at a specified Acceleration Rate. If the current Output is maintaining a satisfactorily small Error at the current Set Point, a change in Set Point will require the Error to increase before the P, I, and D terms will react. A change in Set Point is multiplied by the Acceleration Feed Forward Gain and applied to the Output immediately, to change the Output before the error increases.
Velocity Feed Forward	Velocity Feed Forward is a modified form of the Bias defined above. It is computed by applying a constant factor to the Set Point, but is still independent of feedback from the Process Variable.
Friction Feed Forward	This Feed Forward is sometimes used in systems with enough Stiction to produce a measurable effect on the Process Variable under ordinary circumstances. It is generally implemented as an additional term added to the Output when the Process Variable is in the region where Stiction causes the greatest non-linearity.
Hold Time	Some mechanism driven by controller Output to in turn control the Process Variable cannot operate beyond a certain frequency, or might even be damaged if operated too quickly. An example would be the compressor in refrigeration or air conditioning equipment. This is common with control mechanisms which can only be switched all the way on or all the way off, and are not continuously variable. Hold time is the length of time, expressed in Intervals or Ticks, after the Output has been switched on or off, before it can be switched again.
Slew Rate	Sometimes the nature of the process being controlled dictates a maximum rate of change in the controller Output. Examples would include a motor gearbox that could be damaged if the speed of the driving motor changed too rapidly and exceeded its torque rating, or any motion controller with passengers where too rapid a change in velocity would cause an uncomfortable jerk.

The `pidloop.c` Program

The control algorithm itself consists of deriving and computing values from the process variable and error measurements, then multiplying these values by gain coefficients to produce products. The products are then summed together to calculate the new output.

Not all control systems use all of the gain and feed forward terms defined in Table 18.5. In fact, very few would use them all. It is still possible to write a generic program that incorporates all the possible terms. Setting the coefficient for any term to 0 keeps it from having any effect on the output.

The source file `pidloop.c` is on the companion CD. Most of the functions in this file pertain to the simulator, parsing command-line input and running in single-cycle interactive or automated mode. Only the function `ComputePID()` and part of `main()` are actually part of the control algorithm itself.

The file `pidloop.txt` on the companion CD explains how to run `pidloop` after you build it in interactive mode, or controlled by scripts. The CD also contains scripts for all the examples here (files with an extension of `.pid`). With the directions in the text file and the supplied samples it should be easy to figure out how to modify these scripts or conduct new ones for experimentation.

For simplicity, all of the scripts assume that the output can go from -100% to 100%, and the transfer ratio between output and process variable is unity.

If you do not have an easy ability to graph the outputs of the `pidloop` program, you can experiment with the effects of changing gains, feed forwards, and lag by noting the change in the RMS error value output at the end. The lower the RMS value, the lower the average error.

The `PID_PARAMS` Structure

The `PID_PARAMS` structure in Listing 18.14 contains all of the variables for the PID loop itself, plus a few related to the simulation grouped together for convenience.

LISTING 18.14 `PID_PARAMS` **Structure from** `pidloop.c`

```
typedef struct
{
  double p_gain;       /* 'P' proportional gain         */
  double i_gain;       /* 'I' integral gain             */
  double d_gain;       /* 'D' derivative gain           */
  double acc_ff;       /* 'A' acceleration feed forward */
  double fri_ff;       /* 'F' friction feed forward     */
  double vel_ff;       /* 'V' velocity feed forward     */
  double hold;         /* 'H' output Hold               */
  double bias;         /* 'B' bias                      */
  double accel;        /* 'R' acceleration rate         */
  double setpt;        /* 'S' set point                 */
  double trans;        /* 'T' transfer ratio            */
```

LISTING 18.14 continued

```
  double lag;         /* 'L' lag in output change       */
  double min;         /* 'N' minimum output value       */
  double max;         /* 'M' maximum output value       */
  double cycles;      /* 'Y' repeat cycle count         */
  double slew;        /* 'W' maximum slew rate          */
} PID_PARAMS;
```

The File Scope Variables

The variables `this_target` and `next_target` are used in PID calculation but are defined at file scope (see Listing 18.15) so they can be used in outputting the simulation results. `event_index` and `rms_error` are only part of the simulation.

LISTING 18.15 File Scope Variables from `pidloop.c`

```
static int          event_index         = 0;
static double       this_target         = 0.0;
static double       next_target         = 0.0;
static double       rms_error           = 0.0;
```


The `ComputePID()` Function

The `CoumptePID()` function in Listing 18.16 contains a full implementation of the control algorithm using most of the common techniques.

The first section of code handles acceleration and deceleration. If the current target for the process variable is not equal to the set point, it is adjusted by adding or subtracting the acceleration value to it on each pass until it does reach the final set point. This value is saved in `next_target` and the difference between it and the current target is calculated and stored in `accel`.

`this_error` is calculated by subtracting the current process variable `PV` from `this_target`. The error derivative (rate of change in the error) is calculated in `deriv` by subtracting `last_error` from `this_error`. The same value is also added to the running total of the integral error in `integral`.

This completes all the calculations based on the current and past values of the process variable. The `this_output` calculation multiplies each of these values by the corresponding gain, and adds up the products of the multiplications. If any gain is set to 0 it produces a product of 0 and does not contribute to the sum.

The function then performs limit checks on the new `this_output` value. If a slew rate is specified, it limits the amount `this_output` can differ from `last_output` regardless of all other factors. If the output has absolute minimum and maximum limits, `this_output` must be checked against them and forced to stay within the allowed range.

Additional housekeeping makes sure that the `last_output` and `last_error` values are updated with the results of the current calculation so the values will be available on the next pass through the loop.

LISTING 18.16 `ComputePID()` Function from `pidloop.c`

```
static double
ComputePID(double PV)
{
  /* the three static variables are required to retain  */
  /* information between passes through the loop        */
  static double     integral                 = 0.0;
  static double     last_error               = 0.0;
  static double     last_output              = 0.0;

         double     this_error;
         double     this_output;
         double     accel;
         double     deriv;
         double     friction;

  /* the desired PV for this iteration is the value     */
  /* calculated as next_target during the last loop     */
  this_target = next_target;

  /* test for acceleration, compute new target PV for   */
  /* the next pass through the loop                     */
  if (params.accel > 0 && this_target != params.setpt)
  {
    if (this_target < params.setpt)
    {
      next_target += params.accel;
      if (next_target > params.setpt)
      {
        next_target = params.setpt;
      }
    }
    else /* params.target > params.setpoint */
```

LISTING 18.16 continued

```
    {
      next_target -= params.accel;
      if (next_target < params.setpt)
      {
        next_target = params.setpt;
      }
    }
  }
  else
  {
    next_target = params.setpt;
  }

  /* acceleration is the difference between the PV      */
  /* target on this pass and the next pass through the  */
  /* loop                                                */
  accel = next_target - this_target;

  /* the error for the current pass is the difference   */
  /* between the current target and the current PV      */
  this_error = this_target - PV;

  /* the derivative is the difference between the error */
  /* for the current pass and the previous pass         */
  deriv = this_error - last_error;

  /* a very simple determination of whether there is    */
  /* special friction to be overcome on the next pass,  */
  /* if the current PV is 0 and the target for the next */
  /* pass is not 0, stiction could be a problem         */
  friction = (PV == 0.0 && next_target != 0.0);

  /* the new error is added to the integral             */
  integral += this_target - PV;

  /* the square of the error is accumulated in          */
  /* rms_error, for reporting at the end of the program */
  /* it has no part in the PID loop calculations        */
  rms_error += (this_error * this_error);

  /* now that all of the variable terms have been       */
  /* computed they can be multiplied by the appropriate */
```

LISTING 18.16 continued

```
  /* coefficients and the resulting products summed     */
  this_output = params.p_gain * this_error
              + params.i_gain * integral
              + params.d_gain * deriv
              + params.acc_ff * accel
              + params.vel_ff * next_target
              + params.fri_ff * friction
              + params.bias;

  last_error   = this_error;

  /* check for slew rate limiting on the output change  */
  if (0 != params.slew)
  {
    if (this_output - last_output > params.slew)
    {
      this_output = last_output + params.slew;
    }
    else if (last_output - this_output > params.slew)
    {
      this_output = last_output - params.slew;
    }
  }

  /* now check the output value for absolute limits     */
  if (this_output < params.min)
  {
    this_output = params.min;
  }
  else if (this_output > params.max)
  {
    this_output = params.max;
  }

  /* store the new output value to be used as the old   */
  /* output value on the next loop pass                 */
  return last_output = this_output;
}
```

Putting It Together, PID

Figure 18.10 shows the result of running the `pid.pid` script, combining all three gains that give the PID algorithm its name. The RMS error has been reduced to 8.43 and the graph shows less oscillation and quicker settling.

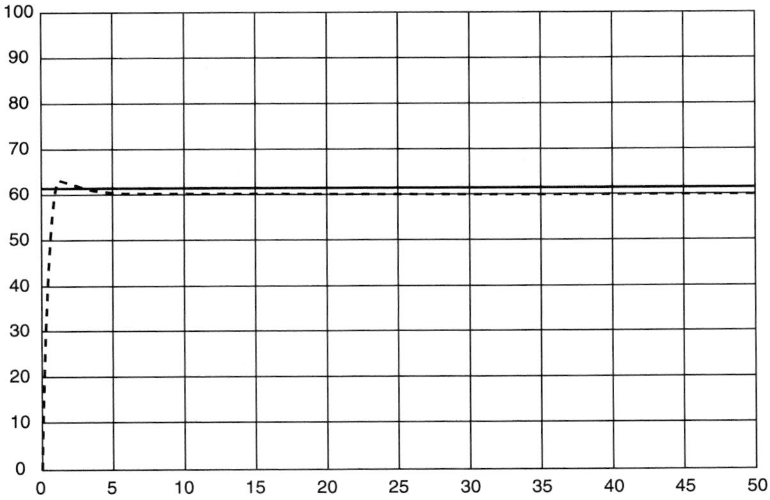

FIGURE 18.10
Graph of full PID control.

Profiles

The examples of various components of the PID algorithm so far have operated on the assumption that the process variable starts some distance away from the set point when the control algorithm starts, and that the desired outcome is for it to reach the set point as quickly as possible and stay there. This is not always the case. There are times when we want to control the change in the process variable closely.

Consider controlling the temperature inside a chemical vat where a reaction is taking place. If the temperature rise is too slow, time is wasted and perhaps the result of the reaction is less than optimal. If the temperature rise is too rapid, pressure could build up in the reactor and risk damage.

One type of control where the controlled rate of process variable change is important is motion control. When controlling the motion of an elevator, for example, we want to control the acceleration to avoid jerking passengers. Another is coordinating multiple motions. Consider a machine tool that cuts out parts. To cut two-dimensional shapes it has two motors, X and Y. To cut a 45 degree angle, both motors must accelerate at the same rate to the same speed, and decelerate again. If one accelerates or decelerates faster than the other, the cut will not be straight.

There is often a need in motion control to move from one position to another by accelerating at a specific rate to a commanded velocity. Once the appropriate distance to the destination is reached, the motion slows down again at the same rate it used to accelerate, coming to a smooth stop at the final location.

If you plot a graph of the velocity versus time, the result is a trapezoid and is often referred to as a *profile*.

Figure 18.11 shows such a profile, although the simulator uses a specific time to begin the deceleration rather than a position. It is run with the script `accel1.pid`, using the same settings as the last graph, and illustrates the trapezoidal profile shape.

It accelerates at a rate of 3% of full travel per interval until it reaches a velocity of 70%. At the specified time, it decelerates at 3% (or accelerates at -3%) per interval back to a full stop. The RMS error is approximately 1.69.

Feed Forwards

The PID algorithms examined so far have all been reactive. They take action after an error has developed. Even the derivative term, which acts to limit future overshoots, is based on two past error values.

Consider a system in a stable state with its process value equal to its set point. These could both be zero, or it could be stable at some value. When it is time for the system to accelerate, the set point is raised by some amount each iteration. This change doesn't cause an error until after it was supposed to happen, so the response lags behind and the overall error increases. Since the control is applying the controlled set point change, it can anticipate the error change that will result and take anticipatory action ahead of time to reduce or eliminate the future error.

This is the basis of acceleration feed forward. The profile in Figure 18.11 starts with both its process variable and set point at zero, then an acceleration of 3% is added. Since there is still no error, the output and process variable remain at zero for the current cycle. On the next iteration, the 3% acceleration shows up fully as an error. The normal PID algorithm acts to correct this error, but another 3% is added next time to create more error.

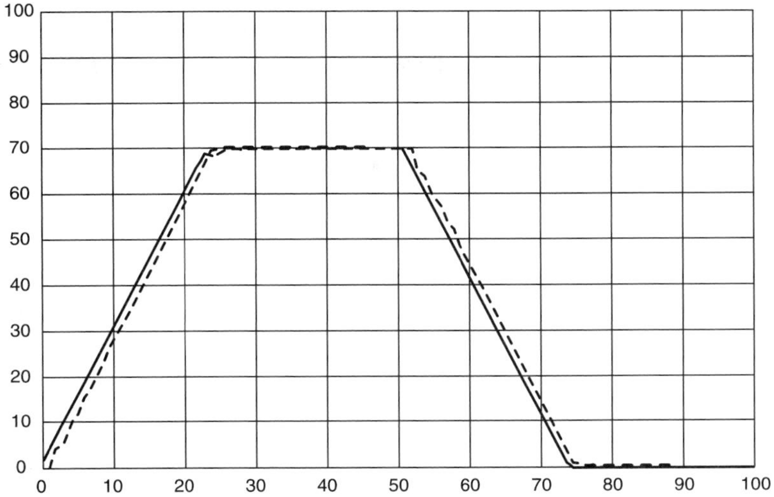

FIGURE 18.11
Motion Profile.

Acceleration feed forward adds an output term based on the acceleration at the time it is added, before it becomes an error.

The other feed forward illustrated here is velocity feed forward. This improves the response of the process variable to changes in the set point, whether they are single jumps or controlled acceleration.

Under ordinary PID control, the integral builds up until it exactly reaches the value necessary to hold the output at the set point when multiplied by the I gain. When the set point changes and the control tries to respond, that built-up integral resists the change, trying to maintain the old set point until accumulated errors adjust it to the new set point.

Reducing the integral gain can improve the response to set point changes. If nothing replaces the I gain, however, it will increase the time it takes for the process variable to settle.

Velocity feed forward replaces some of the I gain. It is computed by multiplying the set point itself by a gain factor. Like friction feed forward, it is applied to the new set point as a change is made, to anticipate and try to eliminate a future error.

Figure 18.12 graphs the results of the script `accel2.pid`. The script has the same acceleration and final set points as `accel1.pid`, but has acceleration and velocity feed forwards added, and the integral gain reduced to compensate.

It is almost impossible to see the dashed set point line under the solid process variable line. The 1.69 RMS error of `accel1` decreases to approximately 0.168, a decrease by more than an order of magnitude.

FIGURE 18.12
Motion profile with feed forwards.

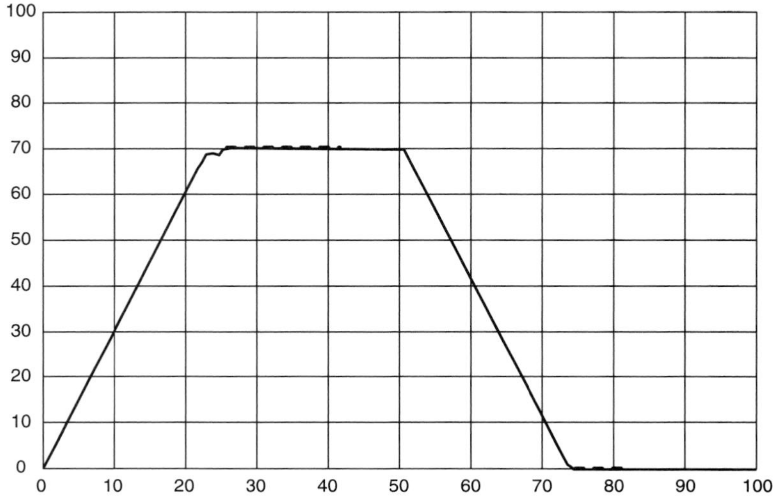

Other PID Modifications and Experiments

None of the sample scripts use the friction feed forward parameter, a small value added to very low process variable levels to overcome stiction, because the simulator does not support it.

Try modifying values in the various script files and seeing how the changes affect the results. Small changes, especially in the lag parameter, can have big effects. If you have a text editor that supports column mode selection and copy, and a spreadsheet program that can draw graphs, you can see the results graphically quite easily. I used this technique initially, but used a different method to create the originals for the graphs in the book.

Included on the companion CD is a program named `script.c` that I used as a tool to help generate the graphs. It reads an output file captured from `pidloop` and generates a text file containing an AutoCAD script. It is not up to the caliber of code for inclusion in the book, but I've included it on the CD to serve as a starting point in case you have a graphic program that can run scripts.

Dedicated Digital Signal Processors

The computational part of any digital signal processing application can be programmed in standard C, and executed on any platform that has a standard C compiler available. But general-purpose processors used in desktop computers are not optimized for maximum performance on these calculations, whereas a type of processor called a *Digital Signal Processor* (DSP) is.

Following are some of the special hardware features of DSPs that make them highly efficient at digital signal processing computations. Not all DSPs have all of these features.

The MAC Instruction

The MAC (Multiply Accumulate) instruction is the signature feature of a DSP. Many signal processing algorithms perform sum of product calculations, like the calculation of the new output value in the `pidloop` code. In a normal processor, it would require at least two instructions for each step. First the two terms such as a value and a gain are multiplied together, then their product is added to the running total of the sum. DSPs have a MAC instruction that multiplies two values and adds their product to an accumulator in a single step.

Summing Squares

Accumulating a running total of the squares of values is another common DSP code technique, as in the RMS calculation in `pidloop`. Many DSPs have single instructions that square a value and add or subtract the square to an accumulator in a single step.

Array Indexing

DSPs often operate on large arrays of data samples, either one- or two-dimensional arrays. They must often access elements in a specific, but not sequential, order. An array of 1,024 samples might need to be accessed like this: element 0, element 512, element 1, element 513, and so on. Many DSPs have special indexing hardware features to accommodate this. Special registers are preloaded with increment values for indexing, and the value is added to an index after each use.

Circular Buffers

DSPs often operate on streams of data held at least temporarily in circular memory buffers. In ordinary C, an index would need to be incremented, then checked for passing the end and wrapped back to zero. Many DSPs have special hardware features to handle this wraparound in hardware.

Saturating Arithmetic

In many applications, a large array of data may need to be modified by multiplying, dividing, adding, or subtracting the same value to each element. If the values are of one of the signed integer types, overflow or underflow produces undefined behavior. If they are unsigned types, the behavior is well defined, but not what is wanted. The desired behavior is to set the result to its minimum or maximum value if the calculation would overflow. This must be done by code on conventional processors, but many DSPs have special saturating arithmetic instructions that do this in hardware.

Zero Overhead Loops

DSP computations often involve looping over large arrays of data. Due to their special computational instructions, such loops often consist of a single instruction, such as a MAC. Many DSPs have a special loop register. When an instruction loads a value into that register the next instruction, provided that it is a repeatable instruction, is repeated that many times at full speed.

Multiple Address Spaces and Data Buses

On a conventional processor like a Pentium or Power PC, there is only one data bus. All instructions and data come into the processor through it. DSPs often have two or three separate data buses, such as one for code memory to fetch instructions and two to data memory to fetch operands simultaneously.

Large Internal Memories

DSPs have benefited from the same advances in semiconductor technology that conventional processors have, including large amounts of on-chip memory. Rather than use such memory as a cache, DSPs use it as fixed memory holding code and data for the fastest possible execution.

Why Not a DSP On the Desktop?

DSPs have much higher performance than conventional processors like the Pentium or Power PC for certain types of calculations. This might raise the question of why they are not used in desktop computers. The answer is that their optimizations for number crunching come at a price. The transistors used to implement DSP features are not available to provide many common features needed by desktop operating systems and applications.

Multitasking Limitations

Today's conventional processors have hardware features such as hardware memory managers to support virtual memory and memory protection for multiple tasks and threads. DSPs do not have such hardware, and do not do well at multitasking at all.

Limited Data Types

DSPs typically have a single type to represent real numbers, a fixed or floating-point type. On 32-bit DSPs, this type typically is a 32-bit type similar to the IEEE 754 single precision type used as a float by C implementations on most modern processors. In some instances, the real type is not IEEE compatible and requires conversion if the IEEE type is needed. Most do not support a longer floating-point type and so do not actually meet the requirements for a standard C `double` or `long double`.

Limited Memory Accessibility

Most DSPs address memory in one size only. A 32-bit DSP has 32-bit registers and reads, writes, and operates on 32-bit words at a time. On several of the most common 32-bit DSP families, `char`, `short`, `int`, and `long` are all 32-bit values with exactly the same ranges, and a byte in C is 32 bits as well. If you stored four characters per 32-bit word to save space, a DSP would have to read the word and use bitwise operations to change the value of one character in a string.

Missing Instructions

Despite the high-speed computational features of DSPs, they are missing some hardware instructions needed for efficient translation of many common programming chores. For example, most DSPs do not have a divide instruction. Division must be performed by a software subroutine.

DSP Extensions in Mainstream Processors

Despite the fact that DSPs would not perform well running modern desktop operating systems like Windows or Linux and their applications, some of their features are finding their way into more conventional processors.

Probably the best known examples are Intel's MMX and SIMD extensions for later members of its Pentium family of processors. Perhaps less well known are Motorola's AltiVec instructions added to Power PC processors. All of these are based on Single Instruction, Multiple Data operations, where a special register holds up to four integer or single precision floating-point types, and a single instruction executes the same operation on all four values simultaneously. They feature such DSP features as saturating arithmetic, and increase the performance of the computer for audiovisual tasks, like playing DVD movies or MP3 music, and other applications.

Processors for embedded control applications are joining this trend as well. Many embedded systems use a conventional processor and either a DSP or custom hardware to perform their tasks, and benefit from integration of DSP features into the main processor.

One member of Intel's MCS96 series of controllers, popular in embedded automotive applications, has added a 32-bit accumulator and special new instructions to use it.

The same technology that allows desktop processors to have multiple integer and floating-point units executing in parallel has enabled some of the newest processors targeted at the embedded market to integrate a full-featured DSP on the same chip with a standard processor.

Summary

This chapter examined some of the concepts of Digital Signal Processing from a C programming, rather than a mathematical, point of view. We have looked at examples every C programmer encounters every time he or she uses their computer. If you boot from your hard disk drive, log onto the Internet, and open a Web page with even one graphic on it, your computer has executed PID control for the disk drive operation, error detection and correction techniques on the transmitted and received data, and data decompression to reproduce the graphic.

The C language provides all of the tools and functions necessary for any signal processing task, from the low-level bitwise AND shift operations used in compression and error handling to complex floating-point calculations in applications like the PID control algorithm.

Finally, we looked at something most C programmers do not write code for directly, the dedicated Digital Signal Processor. We examined the ways it differs from more familiar desktop processors, and how the compromises in DSP processor design improve performance in certain specialized calculations often used in signal processing at the expense of overall efficiency in more operations used in more general-purpose programs.

CHAPTER 19

Expression Parsing and Evaluation

by Dr. Ian D. K. Kelly

In This Chapter

There are certain expressions you can make in C, and there are rules for understanding these expressions. Expressions that do not match these rules are in error and are not part of C. Error messages from a C compiler, for example, request that we change such statements that are in error.

This chapter looks at how we can describe expressions—our syntax notation. It then shows how we can write a translator that reads a syntax definition and then parses input against that definition. This is code that matches our input against rules, and tells us when it does not match.

Within a C program we may come across statements containing expressions, such as

```
x+=x*g*((p[0]*g+p[1])*g+p[2])/(((q[0]*g+q[1])*g+q[2])*g+q[3]);
```

or

```
ps[L3]=ps[L3]<<1 | ps[L4]>>15;
```

or

```
sexp=lexp<SHRT_MIN?SHRT_MIN:lexp<SHRT_MAX?(short)lexp:SHRT_MAX;
```

and we know that there is a fixed order in which such expressions are to be evaluated. From the rules that specify this order, we can understand these expressions, no matter how obscure. The rules for parsing such expressions are part of the specification of the C language and include the syntax rules (what you can say) and semantics rules (what it means when you've said it).

If we want to write expressions, we have to apply those rules to produce expressions of the correct form: If an expression does not match the rules, it is not legal and cannot be used. However, there is an extremely large number of legal expressions, and we need to be able to unravel them and decide what they mean.

Statement of the Problem

We are going to try to construct part of a compiler. It will be a simple expression parser that will take as input some text that we believe to be an expression. It also will produce as output two things:

- Either a description of the form of the expression (its syntax) or error messages
- A chunk of code that, when embedded in the correct program environment, will evaluate the expression

We also have some requirements for error handling, timing, and accuracy.

- *Error handling*: We have to be able to cope with attempted expressions that are illegal—that have an incorrect form—and produce sensible error messages. It is no good having a compiler that simply points to a statement containing an error and issues an incomprehensible or unhelpful message.
- *Timing*: We want our parser and code generator to run in reasonable time. As expressions get longer, compilers have to do more work. We do not want the time this work takes to increase exponentially with the length of the expression (which did happen with some early compilers). Ideally, we would like a second expression, twice as long as the first, to compile in only about twice the time—we would like timing to be linear, if possible.
- *Accuracy*: Whereas we want to detect errors, we do not want good expressions marked as being bad or bad expressions marked as good, and we really would like the code produced for evaluating the expression to match the real meaning of the expression. Code that always produces the answer `42` is unlikely to be very useful.

When we have produced this code for processing expressions, we should understand more deeply how some parts of compilers are written, why they sometimes take so long to compile our code, and why their error messages are sometimes infuriatingly obscure.

Statement of the Solution

We need to look at the rules that describe the syntax (what you can say) and the process of parsing (discovering what was said).

Syntax Notation

Within the definition of C, whether you look at the ANSI standard or the definitive K&R, there are rules that describe the syntax, and there are descriptions of what the various rules mean. The syntax rules are written in a formal notation. For example:

multiplicative-expression:

cast-expression
*multiplicative-expression * case-expression*
multiplicative-expression / case-expression
multiplicative-expression % case-expression

additive-expression:

multiplicative-expression

additive-expression + *multiplicative-expression*

additive-expression - *multiplicative-expression*

The meaning in English is "The binary operator `*` denotes multiplication. The binary operator `/` yields the quotient, and the `%` operator the remainder of the division of the first operand by the second; if the second operand is 0, the result is undefined..."

This notation is often called BNF (Bakus-Naur Form) and was first used when describing the language Algol 60. There are several different ways that BNF can be written, and a little later in this chapter I will be using a slightly different notation from the one used in K&R.

Each syntax rule has a *name*. This is written on the first line, followed by a colon. On each subsequent line there is an *alternate*. Each alternate is a sequence of items. Each item is either a character string (meaning that this character must appear in the thing being parsed) or a name (meaning that something of that description must appear in the input). Names are always written in *italic*.

Sometimes the subscript $_{\text{opt}}$ is placed next to a name. This means that the entity is optional—it occurs zero or one time.

Sometimes there are so many short alternates that they are all written on one line, and following the name and the colon is the phrase *one of*.

Some sample rules from K&R are

parameter-declaration:

declaration-specifiers declarator

declaration-specifiers abstract-declarator$_{opt}$

unary-operator: one of

& * + - ~ !

type-specifier: one of

void char short int long float double signed

unsigned struct-or-union-specifier enum-specifier typedef-name

You can see that occasionally (such as in the definition of *type-specifier* above) this notation leaves us having to split a single line into two or more lines, without meaning we are offering an alternate.

In summary, this notation says

- Each thing in *italic* represents something else in this syntax.
- Each thing in clear represents itself.
- Alternates are represented *either* by being placed on separate lines *or* by placing the phrase *one of* after the node name.
- The subscript *opt* indicates that the item is optional.

Understanding the Syntax

One way a person could go about understanding an expression would be to take a copy of K&R in one hand and try to build up the syntax diagram for the expression. Starting with the expression

```
b * c2 + xyz
```

a person might reason: "This is made up of five distinct symbols: the three identifiers `b`, `c2`, and `xyz`, and the two binary arithmetic operators `*` and `+`. The value in `b` is multiplied by the value in `c2` and to their product is added the value in `xyz`."

In this reasoning the person has used

- Lexical rules, recognizing, for example, `b`, `c2`, and `xyz` as identifiers and `*` and `/` as operators
- Semantic rules, interpreting `+` as addition and `*` as multiplication
- Precedence rules, knowing that multiplication binds tighter than addition and hence will be performed before the addition

Our code must contain an implementation of all of these sorts of rules. We have to see both how rules in each of these categories can be represented and how code can implement them.

Syntax Rules

The syntax rules are quite long. I have constructed a subset of the rules for C. This subset does not contain assignment expressions or enumeration constants and is very limited as to the type of names that can be used within a cast. It is also limited as to the types of integer constants supported, and omits the bitwise not operator. However, it does contain all the major elements of an expression in C. It is to this set of rules that we will be writing our sample code.

The syntax notation used in this subset is more compressed than the BNF notation described previously and used in the official (K&R) definition. Alternatives are separated by a vertical bar (|) rather than being placed on separate lines. The name being defined is separated from its definition by "colon colon equals" (::=) rather than just a colon, and each rule is terminated with a hash mark (#) rather than having no termination at all. Words in *italic* are the names of syntax entities, and characters that are quoted (and often, for emphasis, in **bold**) represent themselves (these are called *terminal characters*). The subscript $_{opt}$ (for optional) is not used, but *empty* is used instead. Some of the suggestions for implementation that are included in paragraph A13 of K&R have been instantiated in this expression of expression syntax.

You should get used to syntaxes expressed in different forms of the BNF notation. There is nothing magic about any one form—but all forms have to be able to express references to other syntactic descriptions, terminal characters, and alternates. The compressed form of BNF used here is, by the way, much closer to the original form used in the Algol 60 Report: it has good historical precedent.

empty ::= #

primary-expression ::= *identifier* | *constant* | (*expression*) #

identifier ::= *letter identifier-tail* #

identifier-tail ::= *letter identifier-tail* | *digit identifier-tail* | "_" *identifier-tail* | *empty* #

constant ::= *integer-constant* | *character-constant* | *floating-constant* #

character-constant ::="**L**" *small-character-constant* | *small-character-constant* #

small-character-constant ::= "'"*single-character*"'" | "'"*escaped-character*"'" #

digit ::= "**0**" | "**1**" | "**2**" | "**3**" | "**4**" | "**5**" | "**6**" | "**7**" | "**8**" | "**9**" #

octal-digit ::= "**0**" | "**1**" | "**2**" | "**3**" | "**4**" | "**5**" | "**6**" | "**7**" #

optional-octal-digit ::= *octal-digit* | *empty* #

hex-digit ::= *digit* | *upper-hex-digit* | *lower-hex-digit* |

upper-hex-digit ::= "**A**" | "**B**" | "**C**" | "**D**" | "**E**" | "**F**" #

lower-hex-digit ::= "**a**" | "**b**" | "**c**" | "**d**" | "**e**" | "**f**" #

escaped-character ::= "\" *escape-sequence* #

escape-sequence ::= "**n**" | "**t**" | "**v**" | "**b**" | "**r**" | "**d**" | "**a**" | "\" | "**?**" | "'" | *octal-digit*
optional-octal-digit optional-octal-digit | "**x**" *hex-digit hex-digit* #

integer-constant ::= *digit integer-constant* | *digit* #

floating-constant ::= *integer-part fraction-part E-part exponent F-part* #

integer-part ::= *integer-constant* | *empty* #

fraction-part ::= point integer-part | empty #

point ::= "." #

E-part ::= **"e"** | **"E"** | *empty #*

F-part ::= **"f"** | **"F"** | **"l"** | **"L"** | *empty #*

exponent ::= optional-sign integer-constant | empty #

optional-sign ::= "+" | "-" | empty #

postfix-expression ::= primary-expression | postfix-expression "++" | postfix-expression "--" #

unary-expression ::= postfix-expression | "++" unary-expression | "--" unary-expression | unary-operator cast-expression #

unary-operator ::= "-" | "!" #

cast-expression ::= unary-expression #

multiplicative-expression ::= cast-expression | multiplicative-expression "" cast-expression | multiplicative-expression "/" cast-expression | multiplicative-expression "%" cast-expression #*

additive-expression ::= multiplicative-expression | additive-expression "+" multiplicative-expression | additive-expression "-" multiplicative-expression #

shift-expression ::= additive-expression | shift-expression "<<" additive-expression | shift-expression ">>" additive-expression #

relational-expression ::= shift-expression | relational-expression "<" shift-expression | relational-expression ">" shift-expression | relational-expression "<=" shift-expression | relational-expression ">=" shift-expression #

equality-expression ::= relational-expression | equality-expression "==" relational-expression | equality-expression "!=" relational-expression #

AND-expression ::= equality-expression | AND-expression "&" equality-expression #

exclusive-OR-expression ::= AND-expression | exclusive-OR-expression "^" AND-expression #

inclusive-OR-expression ::= exclusive-OR-expression | inclusive-OR-expression"|" exclusive-OR-expression #

logical-AND-expression ::= inclusive-OR-expression | logical-AND-expression "&&" inclusive-OR-expression #

logical-OR-expression ::= logical-AND-expression | logical-OR-expression "||" logical-AND-expression #

expression ::= logical-OR-expression #

The class *single-character* is not defined formally. It means "any single printable character other that single quote, double quote, question mark or backslash." This includes all the upper- and lowercase letters, the digits, and the characters , . # £ | % ^ & * ( ) - _ + = { } [ ] : ; @ | ~ # , . < > and / (forward slash). In the context of this code we will not allow for the invisible ASCII characters for which there is no explicit escape sequence, though some compilers allow these to be in strings or expressed as character constants.

The class *letter* is not defined formally, but means any upper- or lowercase letter from *a* to *z*, or from *A* to *Z*.

Note also that at least the syntax classes *expression*, *cast-expression*, *unary-operator*, *postfix-expression*, *type-name*, and *constant* in our syntax are different from the official C definitions, which are larger and would make our code very much longer if we used them. There is nothing difficult in extending this code to the full definitions—but there is a limited number of pages in this book! Also, an *identifier* in this syntax cannot begin with an underscore but must begin with a letter, and we have removed arrays and pointers.

This (reduced) syntax similarly assumes that all superfluous whitespace has already been removed from the text being parsed, so it contains no blanks, newlines, tabs, formfeeds, or comments.

Parsing (With No Discussion of Error)

When we parse a string of characters that we think might be an expression, we want to be able to split it into substrings, so we can say "from here to there is an identifier," "from here to there is an additive-expression," and so on. As an example, consider the expression

```
b*c2+xyz
```

If we number each of these characters

0	b
1	*
2	c
3	2
4	+
5	x
6	y
7	z

then during the parsing process we will come up with the information in Table 19.1.

TABLE 19.1 Simple Parse Table

No.	Syntax Item	Starts at Character	Ends at Character	Starts at Syntax	Ends at Syntax
1	*identifier*	0	0	0	0
2	*identifier*	2	3	0	0
3	*identifier*	5	7	0	0
4	*primary-expression*	0	0	1	1
5	*primary-expression*	2	3	2	2
6	*primary-expression*	5	7	3	3
7	*postfix-expression*	0	0	4	4
8	*postfix-expression*	2	3	5	5
9	*postfix-expression*	5	7	6	6
10	*unary-expression*	0	0	7	7
11	*unary-expression*	2	3	8	8
12	*unary-expression*	5	7	9	9
13	*cast-expression*	0	0	10	10
14	*cast-expression*	2	3	11	11
15	*cast-expression*	5	7	12	12
16	*multiplicative- expression*	0	0	13	13
17	*multiplicative-expression*	0	3	16	14
18	*multiplicative-expression*	5	7	15	15
19	*additive-expression*	0	3	17	17
20	*additive-expression*	0	7	19	18
21	*shift-expression*	0	7	20	20
22	*relational- expression*	0	7	21	21
23	*equality-expression*	0	7	22	22
24	*AND-expression*	0	7	23	23
25	*exclusive-OR- expression*	0	7	24	24
26	*inclusive-OR- expression*	0	7	25	25
27	*logical-AND- expression*	0	7	26	26
28	*logical-OR- expression*	0	7	27	27
29	*expression*	0	7	28	28

Figure 19.1 is the diagram of the parse. Such diagrams can also be drawn as tree-structures, as shown in Figure 19.2. Both figures are a representation of part of Table 19.1.

Although I find the tree in Figure 19.2 much easier to read than the table, we shall stick to producing just the table in our sample code.

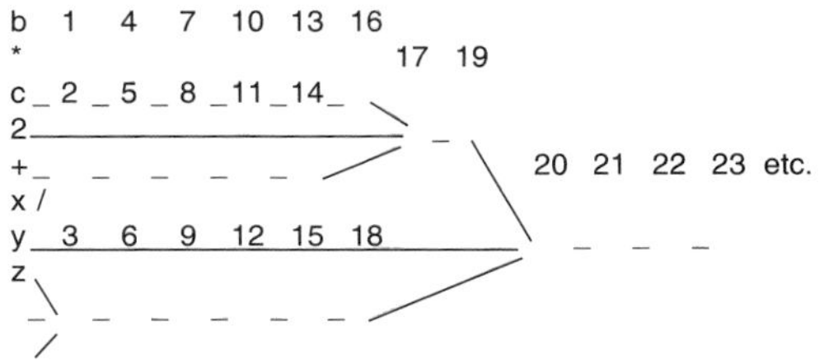

FIGURE 19.1
Expression syntax.

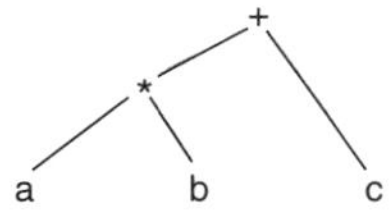

FIGURE 19.2
A simple parse tree.

Parsing Techniques

There are several methods of parsing: *top-down recursive descent*, *bottom-up*, *island-collision*, *LALR*, *simple precedence*, and many more. For an excellent introduction to some of these, look at the classic *Principles of Compiler Design* by Alfred V. Aho and Jeffry D. Ullman (Addison-Wesley, 1977). The method described here is a modified top-down recursive descent with look-ahead and initial lexical scan.

Bottom-up parsing means that you begin by looking at the smallest parts of the syntax, the parts that are nearest the incoming text, and gradually build up complex structures from simpler ones. This is roughly the order in which Table 19.1 is listed. You begin by reasoning "This is a letter followed by another letter: That could be an identifier. This is an identifier followed by a multiply sign followed by another identifier, so this could be a multiplicative expression," and so on, moving up toward "expression," which is what we are trying to recognize. If there is an error in the incoming text and it does not match the possible syntax, then that is detected as early as possible and usually very close to the error in the text.

Top-down parsing means that you start with the part of the syntax you ultimately want to recognize—your final target—and gradually wind down toward the characters in the text. This method sometimes means that you get all the way down to the input text to find that it does not match, so you have to backtrack and take another alternative. Top-down parsing can take much longer than bottom-up, but such parsers are much easier to write. If there is an error in the text that is being parsed, this is not certain until all possibilities have been tried, and often we have no clue as to where in the statement the error is.

We can get the advantage of "easy to write" and avoid the disadvantage of "slow to run" by adding two features to the parse. One is a lexical scan, and the other is look-ahead. A lexical scan is rather like applying some of the syntax bottom-up. You choose some syntax classes and make the decision that these are so common and easy to recognize, irrespective of context, that it is worthwhile to scan for these first. This means that things like identifier are sought only once.

When a syntax rule has several alternatives, these may be tried in any order. The best order to use is to try the longest possible alternative first. For example, if we are looking for a *conditional-expression*, it is worthwhile looking forward in the text to see if there is a question mark anywhere. If there is, we should try the second alternative first and go back to the first alternative only if that fails. If there is no question mark, we should try the first alternative first, and if this fails we know that the second alternative must also fail.

We can add to every alternative two sparse tables: "must contain" and "can start with." The "must contain" table indicates what the previous parsing or lexical stages must have identified as occurring in the following text, if that particular alternative is to succeed. So for the second alternative of conditional-expression, the "must contain" table would indicate that at least the characters "?" and ":" must be present in subsequent text.

The "can start with" table is also a sparse array and indicates what characters and syntax entities may occur at the start of any alternative. This means that an alternative can be quickly bypassed if there is no possibility of it being true, according to the first few characters. A "can start with" table is equally useful in bottom-up parsing. It can be constructed automatically from the syntax itself, as can the "must contain" table. Code for this is included on the CD in file `Ch19Par2.c`.

Semantics

The semantics we will implement is simply the generation of a chunk of code, also written in C, that will evaluate the expression. The C code will be completely different from the expression, however, and will emulate simple assembler code for an imaginary CPU. For a description of an assembly language for a real CPU you could look at *Assembly Language for the PC* by John Socha and Peter Norton, which may give you a clue as to why I have chosen the kind of instructions I have. Our imaginary CPU has two *accumulators* into which values may be loaded, from which values may be stored, and between which arithmetic operations may be performed. It also has a simplified *stack*, which is a large array that can be accessed only at the element whose subscript is in the index. The *index* is a simple `int` variable whose value is known to be initially zero.

All other variables are of type `double`. The only operations that we will allow are set out in Table 19.2 (some of which have been marked as doubtful with a double question mark).

The "doubtful" items, if included, make the generated code shorter, though they are not strictly necessary. At the end of the evaluation we want the first accumulator to contain the value and the value of index to have returned to zero.

TABLE 19.2 Operations Allowed on the Imaginary CPU

Operation	*Description*
`label:`	No action—just a place for a `goto` label.
`A1 = constant;`	Load the value *`constant`* into accumulator 1.
`A2 = constant;`	Load the value *`constant`* into accumulator 2. (??)
`A1 = name;`	Load the contents of *`name`* into accumulator 1.
`A2 = name;`	Load the contents of *`name`* into accumulator 2. (??)
`name = A1;`	Store accumulator 1 in *`name`*.
`name = A2;`	Store accumulator 2 in *`name`*. (??)
`A1 = A2;`	Copy accumulator 2 into accumulator 1. (??)
`A2 = A1;`	Copy accumulator 1 into accumulator 2.
`A1 = A1 op A2;`	Perform operation *op* between the contents of accumulator 2 and accumulator 1, putting the answer in accumulator 1. The allowed operations are +, -, *, /, %, |, & and ^.
`A1 = op A1;`	Perform the unary operation *op* on the contents of accumulator 1. The allowed operations are - and !.
`A1 = stack[index--];`	Pop the top stack item into accumulator 1.
`A2 = stack[index--];`	Pop the top stack item into accumulator 2.
`stack[index++] = A1;`	Push accumulator 1 onto the stack.
`stack[index++] = A2;`	Push accumulator 2 onto the stack. (??)
`goto label`	Transfer control to *`label`*.
`if (A1 op A2) goto label`	Transfer control to *`label`* if the *op* relation is true. The relation may be any of ==, !=, >=, <=, > and <.

As an example of using just these operations, the evaluation of the expression

```
b * c2 + xyz
```

would be the code

```
A1 = b;
A2 = c2;
A1 = A1 * A2;
A2 = xyz;
A1 = A1 + A2;
```

A more complex expression might require the use of the stack. Thus, the expression

```
(a * b + c * d ) / (e + f)
```

would require the code:

```
A1 = a;
A2 = b;
A1 = A1 * A2;
stack[index++] = A1;
A1 = c;
A2 = d;
A1 = A1 * A2;
A2 = stack[index--];
A1 = A1 + A2;
stack[index++] = A1;
A1 = e;
A2 = f;
A1 = A1 + A2;

stack[index++] = A1;
A2 = stack[index--];
A1 = stack[index--];
A1 = A1 / A2;
```

Other expressions will require the use of labels and branch instructions. So the expression

```
( a > b ) ? c + d : e * f
```

could be represented as

```
A1 = e;
A2 = f;
A1 = A1 * a2;
stack[index++] = A1;
A1 = c;
A2 = d;
A1 = A1 + A2;
stack[index++] = A1;
A1 = a;
A2 = b;
if (A1>A2) goto L1;
```

```
A1 = stack[index--];
A2 = stack[index--];
goto L2:
L1:
A2 = stack[index--];
A1 = stack[index--];
L2:
```

Precedence Rules and Order of Evaluation

The sample expressions whose translations are shown above clearly illustrate that the operations have to be performed in what can be a quite different order from that in the original expression. This order depends on the precedence rules of the C language and what operations can be performed in the final CPU (in our case, the imaginary machine).

Some of the order of evaluation comes quite naturally as a result of the syntax analysis. The way in which the syntax is written brings together those items that bind tightest. The order of evaluation of operations of the same degree of binding is stated in the order of precedence table on page 53 of the second edition of K&R. This shows us that the multiplicative operators, for example, are evaluated left to right, but the conditional operator ?: is evaluated right to left.

In order to make some sense of all this, we often use what is called *Polish notation,* which is covered in the next section.

Polish Notation

Polish notation (named after Poland, the country, not the wax that makes furniture shine) is a means of writing arithmetic expressions entirely without parentheses. If we examine the possible operations on our imaginary machine, we see that it contains no parentheses either—no machine does.

Brief History

The Polish mathematician and logician Jan Łukasiewicz (and, yes, that initial L *does* have a slanted bar through it) typed his doctoral thesis in 1920 on an old German typewriter that had not just two shift positions but three: lowercase letters and punctuation, uppercase letters, and (in the third shift) all the brackets and other special characters. Rather than have to use all three shifts (the, clattery old machine frequently stuck when changing shifts), Łukasiewicz invented a notation that did not require the use of parentheses. This was done by changing the notation from the ordinary *operand operator operand* to *operator operand operand*. Thus the ordinary $A + B$ became $+ A B$.

Examples of Polish and Reverse Polish

Quite complex expressions requiring many parentheses in their ordinary form reduce to simple strings in Polish notation—simple, but not easy for the untrained eye to read. So

```
( a * ( c + d ) + ( e + f ) * g ) / ( j + i)
```

in Polish notation becomes

```
/ + * a + c d * + e f g + j i
```

The order *operator operand operand* could equally well be *operand operand operator*. That is, we can put the operator after its operands rather than before it. This is called *Reverse Polish* notation. As an example, the above expression in Reverse Polish would be

```
a c d + * e f + g * + j i + /
```

Note

"Polish notation" is also called "prefix notation," and "Reverse Polish Notation" is also called "postfix notation." The "normal" notation is called "infix."

Why Polish Notation Is Useful

Although Reverse Polish notation is not intuitive for us poor humans, it is very close to the order that is required for expression evaluation on our imaginary machine. The expression

```
a * b + c
```

becomes, in Reverse Polish

```
a b * c +
```

We could interpret this, using a subset of our machine instructions, as

```
load A1 with a
push A1 onto the stack
load A1 with b
push A1 onto the stack
pop the stack into A2
pop the stack into A1
perform multiplication
push A1 onto the stack
load A1 with c
push A1 onto the stack
```

```
pop the stack into A2
pop the stack into A1
perform addition
```

In code this would be

```
A1 = a;
stack[index++] = A1;
A1 = b;
stack[index++] = A1;
A2 = stack[index--];
A1 = stack[index--];
A1 = A1 * A2;
stack[index++] = A1;
A1 = c;
stack[index++] = A1;
A2 = stack[index--];
A1 = stack[index--];
A1 = A1 + A2;
```

The subset of instructions we will allow for the moment are just those that are not marked with the double question mark in Table 19.2.

Transformation from Ordinary Form to Reverse Polish Form

Both ordinary Polish and reverse Polish can be constructed from the syntax analysis of an expression. If that analysis is drawn as a tree, we can imagine a balloon around the tree from which the air is slowly taken, so that the balloon wraps around the root and branches and twigs and leaves, as illustrated in Figure 19.3.

FIGURE 19.3
Polish and reverse Polish notation can be constructed from syntax analysis.

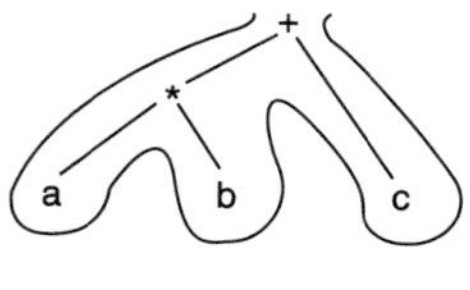

If you follow the skin of the balloon you will trace through the whole tree. You will visit more than once each point where there is a branch. So, for example, in the above tree if we start at the top (the root) and go left, the order in which we visit the nodes of the tree is: `+ * a * b * + c +`. If in this sequence you record the name of the node the *first* time you encounter it—as you go down toward it (for example `++*abc`), you have the ordinary Polish notation. If you record the name of the node the *last* time you encounter it—as you go up from it— you have reverse Polish: `ab*c+`. This one tree form is the basis of both notations. The scan for ordinary Polish notation could be called "children after parents," and the scan for reverse Polish could be called "parents after children." The more formal names are preorder traversal and postorder traversal, respectively.

This description works no matter how complex the expression or its analysis.

Simplified Version

Our parsing engine needs to be able to do two things:

- Read the syntax of the expressions we are going to parse and build up interior structures that will allow parsing to take place.
- Parse an expression according to that syntax, producing the appropriate output.

One way of building the parse engine would be to compile the syntax into the program. This has the disadvantage of inflexibility: If an error is discovered in the syntax, the program must be changed. Our way is to read in the syntax, which means it can be changed easily without modification to the program proper. For a beautifully elegant implementation of a compiler with the syntax written into the code, see *Algorithms + Data Structures = Programs* by Niklaus Wirth (Prentice Hall, 1976). This is a lovely example of how to write programs—and shows a clear reason why the syntax should *not* be in the code itself!

Reading the Syntax

The code on the CD in files `Ch19Pars.c` and `Ch19Pars.h` expects the syntax to be written according to the following rules:

- Every syntax definition is on one "line" (ends with a hash sign, and a newline).
- Every syntax definition starts in the first position with the name of the syntax entity being described.
- After the name, each syntax definition consists of one or more alternates, each alternate being separated from the next by a vertical bar.
- Each alternate consists of a sequence of items.

- An item is a name (the name of some syntax entity), a character string, a routine name in parentheses, a routine name in curly brackets, or a routine name in square brackets. We will describe these routines later in the section "Full Version."
- Each explicit character or character string expected in the input being parsed is enclosed in double quotes, with the same rules as standard C notation for backslash, question mark, quotes, and so on.

This notation is similar to that used in Table 19.1 but even more terse.

The syntax is read in and built up into a series of structures. Each syntax rule produces a structure of the following form:

- `NULL` pointers indicate the ends of the chains. In addition, when the whole syntax has been read, the structures are scanned to fill in the following tables:
  - **Syntax Names Table**—There is one entry for each syntax definition (line) in the syntax input. Each entry records the name of the item and a pointer to the head element that defines the item. There also are some flags used during the construction process. The subscript (row number) for each entry is the number that is subsequently used for referring to this syntax definition. This table is `MAX_SYNTAX_ITEMS` elements long, where `MAX_SYNTAX_ITEMS` is the maximum number of syntax definitions supported by this program.
  - **Must Contain Table**—There is one entry for each syntax alternate. The length of each entry is 256 + `MAX_SYNTAX_ITEMS` elements long. Each element is a single `char` that has either the value (binary) `0` or the value (character) `Y`. The `0` indicates that this alternate need not contain that specific character or syntax item. The `Y` indicates that this alternate must contain this particular character or syntax item. The first 256 elements represent the characters, and the remaining elements represent syntax items.
  - **Starts With Table**—There is one entry for each syntax alternate and one entry for each syntax head. The length of each entry is 256 + `MAX_SYNTAX_ITEMS` + `MAX_ALTERNATE_ITEMS` elements long. `MAX_ALTERNATE_ITEMS` is the maximum number of supported alternates in all syntax rules taken together. Each element is a single `char` that has either the value (binary) `0`, or the value (character) `Y` to indicate that this alternate or head may or may not start with that specific character (the first 256 elements), or that syntax item—just like the Must Contain table.

The code for allocating and constructing the syntax tree (see Listing 19.1) is mirrored by code that frees the tree. That is, for every routine that allocates a part of the syntax tree, there is a routine that frees that same part.

LISTING 19.1 Reading the Syntax Definition

```
#include <stdio.h>
#include <stdlib.h>
#include <string.h>
#include <ctype.h>

#ifndef TRUE
#define TRUE 1
#endif
#ifndef FALSE
#define FALSE 0
#endif


#define SYNTAX_LINE_LIMIT 1024
#define MAX_SYNTAX_ITEMS 128
#define MAX_ALTERNATE_ITEMS 1024
#define MAX_ROUTINE_NAMES 30
#define SYNTAX_NAME_LENGTH 32
#define ROUTINE_NAME_LENGTH 16
#define PARSE_BUFFER_LENGTH 4096

struct sSyntaxHead;
struct sSyntaxAlt;
struct sSyntaxBody;
struct sSyntaxHead* SyntaxRoot;

struct sSyntaxHead {
    char SyntaxName [SYNTAX_NAME_LENGTH+1];
    struct sSyntaxHead* pNextHead;
    struct sSyntaxHead* pPreviousHead;
    struct sSyntaxAlt* FirstAlternate;
    int iSyntaxNumber;
    int iStartsWith;
    int iMustContain;
    int (*LexRoutine) ( void* );
    int iIsLexical;
};

struct sSyntaxAlt {
    struct sSyntaxBody* ThisBody;
    struct sSyntaxAlt*  NextAlt;
    struct sSyntaxAlt*  PreviousAlt;
```

LISTING 19.1 continued

```
    struct sSyntaxHead* ParentHead;
    int iSyntaxNumber;
    int iAlternateNumber;
    int iStartsWith;
    int iMustContain;
};

struct sSyntaxBody {
    struct sSyntaxBody* NextBody;
    struct sSyntaxBody* PreviousBody;
    struct sSyntaxAlt*  ParentAlt;
    struct sSyntaxHead* BodyHead;
    char* BodyContents;
    int (*BodyCheck) ( void* );
    int (*LexCheck) ( void* );
    int (*CodeGenerate) ( void* );
    int iSyntaxNumber;
    int iAlternateNumber;
    int iStartsWith;
    int iMustContain;
};



int ReadSyntax ( struct sSyntaxHead** pRoot )
{
extern char *_sys_errlist[];
    int iStatus = TRUE;

    fSyntaxFile = fopen ( sSyntaxFileName, "r" );
    if (fSyntaxFile==NULL)
    {
        /* ERROR - the syntax file could not be opened */
        iStatus = FALSE;
        return iStatus;
    }

    while (!feof(fSyntaxFile))
    {
        iStatus = ProcessSyntaxLine ( );
        if ( *pRoot == NULL )
        {
```

LISTING 19.1 continued

```
            *pRoot = SyntaxTable[0].pSyntaxPointer;
        }
    }

    fclose(fSyntaxFile);

    return iStatus;
}

int FindSyntaxName ( char* SyntaxName )
{
    int iReturn = 0;
    int i;
    int j;

    j = iNextSyntax;
    if (j>0)
    {
        for (i=0;((iReturn==0)&&(i<iNextSyntax));i++)
        {
            if (strcmp(SyntaxName,SyntaxTable[i].SyntaxName)==0)
            {
                iReturn = i;
            }
        }
    }

    if (iReturn==0)
    {
        iReturn = CreateSyntaxTableEntry ( SyntaxName );
}

    return iReturn;
}

int CreateSyntaxTableEntry (char* pSyntaxName)
{
    int iStatus;

    strcpy(SyntaxTable[iNextSyntax].SyntaxName,pSyntaxName);
    SyntaxTable[iNextSyntax].pSyntaxPointer  = NULL;
    SyntaxTable[iNextSyntax].iMustContain = 0;
```

LISTING 19.1 continued

```
    SyntaxTable[iNextSyntax].iStartsWith  = 0;
    iStatus = iNextSyntax;
    iNextSyntax++;

    return iStatus;
}

void FreeWholeSyntax ( void )
{
    int i;

    for (i=0;(i<iNextSyntax);i++)
    {
        if ( SyntaxTable[i].pSyntaxPointer!=NULL )
        {
            FreeSyntaxHead ( SyntaxTable[i].pSyntaxPointer );
            SyntaxTable[i].pSyntaxPointer = NULL;
        }
    }

    return;
}

int GetSyntaxName ( char* SyntaxLine, int* j )
{
    struct sSyntaxHead* pNewSyntaxHead;
    char SyntaxName[SYNTAX_NAME_LENGTH+1];
    int i;
    int m;
    int iMySyntaxNumber;

    strcpy(SyntaxName,"");
    m = 0;
    for (i=0; (m==0); i++)
    {
        if (isidchar(SyntaxLine[i + *j]))
        {
            SyntaxName[i] = SyntaxLine[i + *j];
            SyntaxName[i + 1] = '\0';
        }
        else
        {
```

LISTING 19.1 continued

```
            m = i;
            *j += i;
        }
    }

    iMySyntaxNumber = FindSyntaxName ( SyntaxName );
    if (SyntaxTable[iMySyntaxNumber].pSyntaxPointer==NULL)
    {
        pNewSyntaxHead = malloc ( sizeof (struct sSyntaxHead) );
        SyntaxTable[iMySyntaxNumber].pSyntaxPointer  = pNewSyntaxHead;
        strcpy(pNewSyntaxHead->SyntaxName,SyntaxName);
        pNewSyntaxHead->iSyntaxNumber   = iMySyntaxNumber;
        pNewSyntaxHead->iStartsWith     = 0;
        pNewSyntaxHead->iMustContain    = 0;
        pNewSyntaxHead->FirstAlternate = NULL;
        pNewSyntaxHead->LexRoutine      = NULL;
        pNewSyntaxHead->iIsLexical      = FALSE;
        pNewSyntaxHead->pNextHead       = NULL;
        if (iMySyntaxNumber>0)
        {
          pNewSyntaxHead->pPreviousHead =
                        SyntaxTable[iMySyntaxNumber-1].pSyntaxPointer;
            (SyntaxTable[iMySyntaxNumber-1].pSyntaxPointer)->pNextHead =
                        pNewSyntaxHead;
        }
        else
        {
            pNewSyntaxHead->pPreviousHead  = NULL;
        }
    }
    return iMySyntaxNumber;
}

int isidchar ( char testchar )
{
    int iStatus;

    if ((isalpha(testchar))||(isdigit(testchar)||(testchar=='-')))
        iStatus = TRUE;
    else
        iStatus = FALSE;
```

LISTING 19.1 continued

```
    return iStatus;
}

int GetIdentifier ( char* InputBuffer, char* Identifier, int* j )
{
    int iStatus = FALSE;
    int i = 0;

    while ((isidchar(*(InputBuffer+*j))) && (i<ROUTINE_NAME_LENGTH))
    {
        Identifier[i++] = *(InputBuffer+*j);
        (*j)++;
        iStatus = TRUE;
    }

    Identifier[i] = '\0';

    return iStatus;
}

int GetLexName ( char* SyntaxLine, char* Identifier, int* j,
➥int iMySyntaxNumber )
{
    int     iMyLexNumber = -1;

    while (SyntaxLine[*j]==' ')
        (*j)++;

    if ((SyntaxLine[*j]=='{') || (SyntaxLine[*j]=='(')
    ||  (SyntaxLine[*j]=='['))
    {
        (*j)++;
        iMyLexNumber = GetIdentifier ( SyntaxLine, Identifier, j );
        (*j)++;
        while ((SyntaxLine[*j]==' ') || (SyntaxLine[*j]=='\t'))
        {
            (*j)++;
        }
    }

    if (strncmp(&SyntaxLine[*j],":L:=",4)==0)
    {
```

The code in Listing 19.1 for reading the syntax definition does not support lexical scanning and does not construct the "must contain" and "starts with" tables. That is code that is straightforward to create.

Parsing the Expression

In the sample parser in files `Ch19Pars.c` and `Ch19Pars.h`, the expressions to be read are in a file. Each expression is read and parsed, and the code generated at the end of a successful parse is written to an output file. If another form of output is needed, it is easy to change that, too.

The parser puts one pointer at the start of the expression and another pointer at the top of the abstract (possible) syntax tree. It then tries to match the characters pointed to by the first pointer with the syntax rules pointed to by the second. The syntax rules eventually lead to an individual item that contains a pointer to a character string. That character string either matches the input characters or it does not. If it matches, we have found a (possible) syntax match, and we can then go on to try the next syntax item. If it does not match, this syntax rule is no good, so we try the next alternative. If this is the last alternative, then we have to go up the tree one level and try the next alternative at that level. Eventually we will come back to the top of the abstract syntax tree, and we have either found a complete match (hooray!) or we know that the input is incorrect (boo!).

That's all a bit abstract. Let me give an example. Suppose we are trying to match the syntax name *element*, for which the syntax definitions are

element ::= metal | non-metal #

metal ::= A-metal | C-metal | N-metal #

*A-metal ::= "**A**" A-metal-end #*

*C-metal ::= "**C**" C-metal-end #*

*N-metal ::= "**N**" N-metal-end #*

non-metal ::= A-non-metal | C-non-metal | N-non-metal #

*A-non-metal ::= "**A**" A-non-metal-end #*

*C-non-metal ::= "**C**" C-non-metal-end #*

*N-non-metal ::= "**N**" N-non-metal-end #*

*A-metal-end ::= "**u**" | "**g**" #*

*C-metal-end ::= "**o**" | "**u**" | "**r**" #*

*N-metal-end ::= "**i**" #*

*A-non-metal-end ::= "**r**" #*

*C-non-metal-end ::= "**l**" | empty #*

*N-non-metal-end ::= "**e**" | empty #*

This allows us to recognize the metals Au, Ag, Co, Cu, Cr, and Ni (gold, silver, cobalt, copper, chromium, and nickel, respectively) and the non-metals Ar, Cl, C, Ne, and N (argon, chlorine, carbon, neon, and nitrogen, respectively).

Suppose the input stream is

```
Au
```

then the parser starts by asking "Is this an *element*?"

The parser asks "Is this a metal?"

Then the question is "Is this an *A-metal*?"

So to be an *A-metal* there must be a letter **A**...

Hmm. This illustration is taking up a lot of paper. We can compress this by writing each diagram as one line. The answer to any question will be lined up with the start of the question but on a subsequent line. The character in the input that we are pointing at with the end pointer will be **bold**, and the character being pointed at with the start pointer will be *italic*. So all the above becomes

Element	**A**u
metal	**A**u
A-metal	**A**u
A	**A**u
yes—it is **A**	**A**u
A-metal-end	A**u**
u	A**u**
yes—it is **u**	A**u**
yes—it is A-metal-end	A**u**
yes—it is A-metal	A**u**
yes—it is metal	A**u**
yes—it is element	A**u**

That was quick and easy. Gold is OK. Now suppose the input is

```
Cu
```

The series of questions and answers will be rather longer:

element	**C**u
metal	**C**u

A-metal	Cu
A	Cu
no—not **A**	Cu
no—not A-metal	Cu
C-metal	Cu
C	Cu
yes—it is a **C**	Cu
C-metal-end	Cu
o	Cu
no—it is not **o**	Cu
u	Cu
yes—it is **u**	Cu
yes—it is C-metal-end	Cu
yes—it is C-metal	Cu
yes—it is metal	Cu
yes—it is element	Cu

You can see that the start and end pointers have moved backward and forward across the input, and several potential parses were built and destroyed before the real answer was found. Copper is OK, too. If you build a trace like this for parsing nitrogen (N) you will see a much longer and more convoluted path, which eventually gives a "yes" answer.

Now suppose that the input is

```
Cs
```

The trace for this will be

element	Cs
metal	Cs
A-metal	Cs
A	Cs
*no—not **A***	Cs
no—not A-metal	Cs
C-metal	Cs
C	Cs
*yes—it is a **C***	Cs

C-metal-end	C**s**
... (lines tracing not **o**, not **u**, not **r**)	...
no—not a C-metal-end	C**s**
no—not a C-metal	C**s**
N-metal	**C**s
...	...
no—not C-non-metal-end	C**s**
no—not C-non-metal	C**s**
N-non-metal	**C**s
N	**C**s
*no—not **N***	**C**s
no—not N-non-metal	**C**s
no—not non metal	**C**s
no—not element	**C**s

This has traced through the whole of the syntax tree and not found a match. This syntax did not allow cesium.

We have also seen that we need to remember at each stage both the start and the end pointers. That is, for each bit of the syntax as we recognize it, we need to know which is the first character that this part matches and which the last. Thus, when we have an error, we know how far we have to go back to try again, and we can also indicate to the user which bits of the expression were recognized as what.

Simplified Syntax for Expressions

The simplified syntax that we will consider is the one written in Figure 19.1. This is the full syntax that we are going to use throughout this chapter. The only reason it is simplified here is that we are not going to look at the lexical analysis yet, nor are we going to consider the "can start with" and "must contain" options. The parsing process thus will reparse several times any items that can start different alternatives, so that each identifier (for example) will be rescanned several times before its proper context is found. It is not necessarily efficient, but it is easy to explain.

Intuitive Rules in English

Each of the syntax rules has a simple English interpretation, such as "an additive-expression is either a multiplicative-expression, an additive-expression followed by a plus sign followed by a multiplicative-expression, or an additive-expression followed by a minus sign followed by a multiplicative-expression." This can also be expressed as

additive-expression ::= *multiplicative-expression* | *additive-expression* "+" *multiplicative-expression* | *additive-expression* "-" *multiplicative-expression* #

These are not, alas, the kind of sentences we exchange cheerfully over pints of beer or seductively over glasses of wine—but they are clear and simple. Now would be a good time to read again the contents of Figure 19.1 to remind yourself of the (reduced) expression syntax we are aiming for.

Strict Rules in C

The code in files `Ch19Pars.c` and `Ch19Pars.h` on the CD contains the simple parsing mechanism. This code is in three main parts: the control, which opens the files, requests the loading of the abstract syntax, reads the expressions to be parsed, and calls for parsing and code generation; the syntax loading, which sets up the control structures for the parsing; and the parsing and code generation.

In the sample code it is assumed that the abstract syntax is in a specific file whose filename is explicitly quoted in the code (you will obviously want to change this to match your own particular environment). It is also assumed that the expressions to be parsed and the output to be generated are again in files whose names are explicitly quoted in the code. Your mileage *will* vary.

There are two main structures that are set up: the abstract syntax (what can be recognized) and the concrete parse (what actually has been recognized).

The abstract syntax matches the contents of Figure 19.1 in that each rule is expressed in a connected tree structure. Each node has a name (the equivalent of the left side of the syntax rule) and a set of one or more alternates (the parts of the right side that are separated by vertical bars). Each alternate points to a chain of items. Each item is a pointer either to a syntax node (a named item) or to a character string. There are other elements within the items that we will discuss later.

The concrete parse is a single tree. Each of its nodes points to one specific abstract syntax node and an alternative within that node. Each node also contains a sequence (chain) of items. Each item is either a pointer to another concrete parse node or a pointer to an explicit character string.

logical-OR-expression ::= *logical-AND-expression* | *logical-OR-expression* "||" *logical-AND-expression #*

expression ::= *logical-OR-expression #*

The parser commences with the start pointer pointing to the first character of the input buffer and the end pointer set to `NULL` (not pointing at anything). It tries to match the input buffer against the root syntax rule of the abstract syntax tree. In our case the parser starts looking for `expression`. The first (and only) alternative for `expression` is `logical-OR-expression`. The parser constructs a concrete parse node for `expression` and then another node for `logical-OR-expression`. The first alternative for `logical-OR-expression` is `logical-AND-expression`. The parse continues, constructing more concrete parse nodes. Eventually the parser will reach either the end of the input buffer or an abstract syntax item that it simply cannot match. If the parser reaches the end of the expression at the same time as it reaches the end of all the outstanding abstract syntax items, then the parse has been successful. In that case, we go through the code-generation step.

However, if there is a non-recognition, or there are more items in the outstanding abstract syntax items that have not yet been recognized, then we have a failure. The parser has to undo its last decision and make an alternative choice. The last decision of the parser was that in which a particular alternative within the abstract syntax was chosen. The bottommost item is rejected, the corresponding parse node is removed, and the next abstract syntax alternative is tried. This process of going up and down the trees continues until either there is a definitive failure (there are no more possible alternatives and no match has been found) or there is a success.

That description is a little dry. Let's look at a concrete example. Suppose that the input buffer contains

```
abc5 + xyz6
```

Then the parser will try

expression

logical-OR-expression (1st alternate)

logical-AND-expression (1st alternate)

inclusive-OR-expression (1st alternate)

exclusive-OR-expression (1st alternate)

AND-expression (1st alternate)

equality-expression (1st alternate)

relational-expression (1st alternate)

shift-expression (1st alternate)

additive-expression (1st alternate)

multiplicative-expression (1st alternate)

cast-expression (1st alternate)

unary-expression (1st alternate)

postfix-expression (1st alternate)

primary-expression (1st alternate)

identifier (1st alternate)

At this point we have to scan for *identifier* which, in our definition, starts with *letter* followed by *identifier-tail*.

identifier ::= *letter identifier-tail #*

identifier-tail ::= *letter identifier-tail* | *digit identifier-tail* | "_" *identifier-tail* | *empty #*

The class *letter* matches the initial letter *a*, and for the next item (*identifier-tail*) the start pointer is advanced to point to the letter *b* in the input buffer. So the parse continues:

letter ('a')

identifier-tail (1st alternate)

letter ('b')

identifier-tail (1st alternate)

letter ('c')

identifier-tail (1st alternate)

letter

At this point we have an error. The start pointer is pointing at the character '5', which is definitely not a *letter*. So this branch is deleted all the way back to where the last choice was made, and the second alternate is tried instead. Thus, the end of the parse given above becomes

letter ('a')

identifier-tail (1st alternate)

letter ('b')

identifier-tail (1st alternate)

letter ('c')

~~*identifier-tail (1st alternate)*~~

~~*letter*~~

identifier-tail (2nd alternate)

digit ('5')

The strikethrough lines, here and below, show some of the false trails taken by the parser in reaching the correct conclusion.

The next syntax item is again *identifier-tail*, which fails on the first alternate (because '+' is not a *letter*) and on the second alternate (because '+' is not a *digit*). It succeeds on the third alternate (*empty*):

letter ('a')

identifier-tail (1st alternate)

letter ('b')

identifier-tail (1st alternate)

letter ('c')

~~*identifier-tail (1st alternate)*~~

~~*letter*~~

identifier-tail (2nd alternate)

digit ('5')

~~*identifier-tail (1st alternate)*~~

~~*letter*~~

~~*identifier-tail (2nd alternate)*~~

~~*digit*~~

identifier-tail (3rd alternate)

empty

Now we look for the next syntax item expected, which is the rest of the parse of *primary-expression*. Eventually the parse will produce the structure in Table 19.3.

TABLE 19.3 Parsing of Primary-Expression

Parse Name	*Part of Expression*
expression	abc5 + xyz6
logical-OR-expression (1st alternate)	abc5 + xyz6
logical-AND-expression (1st alternate)	abc5 + xyz6
inclusive-OR-expression (1st alternate)	abc5 + xyz6
exclusive-OR-expression (1st alternate)	abc5 + xyz6
AND-expression (1st alternate)	abc5 + xyz6
equality-expression (1st alternate)	abc5 + xyz6
relational-expression (1st alternate)	abc5 + xyz6

TABLE 19.3 continued

Parse Name	Part of Expression
shift-expression (1st alternate)	abc5 + xyz6
additive-expression (2nd alternate)	abc5 + xyz6
additive-expression (1st alternate)	abc5
multiplicative-expression (1st alternate)	abc5
cast-expression (1st alternate)	abc5
unary-expression (1st alternate)	abc5
postfix-expression (1st alternate)	abc5
primary-expression (1st alternate)	abc5
identifier (1st alternate)	abc5
letter	a
identifier-tail (1st alternate)	bc5
letter	b
identifier-tail (1st alternate)	c5
letter	c
identifier-tail (2nd alternate)	5
digit	
identifier-tail (3rd alternate)	
empty	5
'+'	+
multiplicative-expression (1st alternate)	xyz6
cast-expression (1st alternate)	xyz6
unary-expression (1st alternate)	xyz6
postfix-expression (1st alternate)	xyz6
primary-expression (1st alternate)	xyz6
identifier (1st alternate)	xyz6
letter	x
identifier-tail (1st alternate)	yz6
letter	y
identifier-tail (1st alternate)	z6
letter	z
identifier-tail (2nd alternate)	6
digit	6
identifier-tail (3rd alternate)	empty

Recursion

All of this process uses recursive routines—that is, routines that call themselves, either directly or indirectly. There is nothing wrong with recursion, but we must be sure that we avoid infinite recursion, which can happen very easily. Consider this syntax with just one rule:

```
alpha ::= alpha "b" ¦ "a" #
```

An `alpha` is a string of the letter `a`, followed by a single `b`. The parser looks at the input buffer and says "Is this an `alpha`?" and decides that it will go down one level and ask "Is this an `alpha`?" and then it recurses down another level and asks "Is this an `alpha`?" and decides that...

To avoid that kind of *left recursion* we could rewrite the above rule as a pair of rules:

alpha ::= *alphahead* "b" #

alphahead ::= "a" *alphahead>* | "a" #

In this pair we know that every branch tries to examine at least one character in the input buffer before it decides on success or failure. Thus, this syntax can never recurse infinitely.

But what about the much longer syntax for C expressions? Can a parse using that syntax ever recurse infinitely? The answer is not obvious at first glance and, though you can examine the syntax to see if there are any possible dangerous branches, perhaps there should be something in the parser that warns you whenever it comes across this unwanted situation. If this warning is raised, it has two effects. The first is that it stops your parser from running uselessly for an infinite amount of time, and the second is that it warns you of an error in the original syntax.

To detect an infinite recursion, as the parser adds a new header (node) to the parse tree at each stage, it can look back at all the previous nodes to see if there is a node with both the same name and the same values for the input and output pointers. If there is, then we are about to go into the same state that we were in at a previous point in the parsing process, and we can raise the error.

Recursive rules may be hidden. Consider the following syntax:

alpha ::= *alphahead* "b" | *betahead* "c" #

alphahead ::= *betahead* "a" | "b" *alphahead* #

betahead ::= *alphahead* "b" | "a" *betahead* #

Can you see the recursion at first glance? Here it is the last pair of rules. When the parser is trying to see if something is an `alphahead`, it first asks "Is this a `betahead`?" To determine this it asks "Is this an `alphahead`?" and to determine this it asks "Is this a `betahead`?" and to determine this...

Even if the alternates are inverted, the recursion still exists:

alpha ::= *alphahead* "b" | *betahead* "c" #

alphahead ::= "b" *alphahead* | *betahead* "a" #

betahead ::= "a" *betahead* | *alphahead* "b" #

Here, if the parser is given a buffer containing just the character `c`, it asks "Is this an `alpha`?" and to determine this it asks "Is this an `alphahead` *(first alternate)*?" and to determine this it looks at the first character and finds it is not a `b`. So it asks instead "Is this an `alphahead` *(second alternate)*?" To determine this it asks "Is this a `betahead` *(first alternate)*?" So the parser looks at the first character, finds that it is not an `a`, and replaces that question with "Is this a `betahead` *(second alternate)*?" To answer that, the parser then asks "Is this an `alphahead` *(first alternate)*?" and we are back where we were earlier.

Errors in the Syntax

It gets worse than that. Have you noticed that these last two syntaxes have another very serious error? There is in fact *no* character string that matches them. The pair of definitions for `alphahead` and `betahead` can never end, even in the abstract. How can we be sure that we do not have this error in our much more complex syntax for C expressions?

You will be pleased to learn that when we guarantee that there are no infinitely recursive paths through the syntax, then we know that it must always terminate. So it becomes quite important to be sure that we have no infinite recursion possible within our syntax. For a short syntax this can be done by eye. For a longer syntax there are tools that can check the quality of the syntax.

It is easy to check that every syntax name used is also defined—but as you write a syntax, that is an error that is easy to make and important to remove. It is equally easy—and as important—to verify that no name is defined twice.

Simple Parser in C

The simple parser in Listing 19.2 constructs a parse tree from the given input and the syntax definition that has been read. The parse routine is recursive, taking three arguments: a pointer to the part of the input buffer in which we are currently interested, the abstract syntax node we are trying to match against, and the parent (previous) parse node in the parse tree we have already built up. If this last pointer is `NULL`, then this is the start of the parse, and a new root parse element needs to be allocated.

LISTING 19.2 Simple Parser

```
struct sParseNode;

struct sParseNode {
    struct sParseNode*  ParentParse;
    struct sParseNode*  NextParse;
    struct sParseNode*  PreviousParse;
    struct sParseNode*   ThisParse;
    struct sSyntaxHead*  ThisHead;
    struct sSyntaxBody*  ThisBody;
    int (*CodeGenerate) ( void* );
    int iFirstChar;
    int iLastChar;
};

struct sSyntaxTableElement {
    char SyntaxName[SYNTAX_NAME_LENGTH+1];
    struct sSyntaxHead* pSyntaxPointer;
    int iStartsWith;
    int iMustContain;
};

struct sAlternateTableElement {
    struct sSyntaxAlt* pAlternatePointer;
    int iSyntaxNumber;
    int iStartsWith;
    int iMustContain;
};

struct sRoutineNameTableElement {
    char sNameBody[ROUTINE_NAME_LENGTH+1];
    int (*BodyRoutine) ( void* );
};

/* ------------------------ GLOBAL VARIABLES ---------------------- */

struct sSyntaxHead* pRootSyntax;
struct sParseNode*  pRootParse;
struct sRoutineNameTableElement RoutineNameTable[MAX_ROUTINE_NAMES];
struct sSyntaxTableElement SyntaxTable [MAX_SYNTAX_ITEMS];
struct sAlternateTableElement AlternateTable [MAX_ALTERNATE_ITEMS];
int globLabel;
int globMaxName;
```

LISTING 19.2 continued

```
int iNextSyntax;
int iNextAlternate;
char SyntaxLine[SYNTAX_LINE_LIMIT+1];
char ParseBuffer[PARSE_BUFFER_LENGTH+1];
FILE * fSyntaxFile;
char sSyntaxFileName[257];
FILE * fInputFile;
char sInputFileName[257];
FILE * fOutputFile;
char sOutputFileName[257];

/* ---------------------- END GLOBAL VARIABLES -------------------- */

/* ------ Prototypes ---------------------------------------------*/

int ReadSyntax        ( struct sSyntaxHead** pRoot );
int FindSyntaxName    ( char*  SyntaxName );
int ProcessSyntaxLine ( void );
void FreeWholeSyntax  ( void );
int GetNewSyntaxHead  ( struct sSyntaxHead** ppNewSyntaxHead,
                        char*  Identifier );
int CreateSyntaxTableEntry (char* pSyntaxName);
void FreeSyntaxHead   ( struct sSyntaxHead*  pFreeHead );
int GetAlternates     ( int*   j,
                        struct sSyntaxHead*  pNewSyntaxHead );
int GetOneAlternate   ( int*   j,
                        struct sSyntaxAlt*   pNewAlternate );
void FreeAlternates   ( struct sSyntaxAlt**  pFreeAlt );
int GetSyntaxItem     ( int*   j,
                        struct sSyntaxBody*  pNewBody );
void FreeSyntaxItem   ( struct sSyntaxBody** pFreeBody );
void SkipSpaces       ( int*   j );
int GetSyntaxName     ( char*  SyntaxLine,
                        int*   j );
void RemoveSpaces     ( char*  InputBuffer );
int TryMatchParse     ( char** ppInputBuffer,
                        int*   k,
                        struct sSyntaxBody*  pSyntaxP,
                        struct sParseNode**  ppParseBody );
int GetNewParseBody (   struct sParseNode*   pParentHead,
                        struct sParseNode*   pPreviousBody,
                        struct sParseNode**  ppNewBody );
```

LISTING 19.2 continued

```
int BuildNewParseBody ( struct sParseNode*   pParentHead,
                        struct sParseNode*   pPreviousBody,
                        struct sParseNode**  ppNewBody,
                        int    iFirstChar,
                        int    iLastChar );
int Parse             ( char** ppInputBuffer,
                        int*   k,
                        struct sSyntaxHead*  pRootS,
                        struct sParseNode**  ppRootP );
int GenerateOutputCode( struct sParseNode*   pRootP );
int GetNextSyntax     ( struct sSyntaxBody**  ppSyntaxP );
int SkipNextSyntax    ( struct sSyntaxBody**  ppSyntaxP );
void PrintSyntaxTree  ( void );
int isidchar          ( char   testchar );
int GetIdentifier     ( char*  InputBuffer,
                        char*  Identifier,
                        int*   j );
int GetLexName        ( char*  SyntaxLine,
                        char*  Identifier,
                        int*   j,
                        int    k );
int ProcessOutputNode ( struct sParseNode** ppParseHead,
                        struct sParseNode** ppParseBody );
int GetRoutinePointer ( char*  pszRoutineName,
                        int    (**FoundRoutine) (void*) );
int parletter         ( void* );
int pardigit          ( void* );
int paroctal          ( void* );
int parchar           ( void* );
int gencomparison     ( char* pszComparator );
int genlt             ( void* );
int genle             ( void* );
int gengt             ( void* );
int genge             ( void* );
int geneq             ( void* );
int genne             ( void* );
int genAND            ( void* );
int genOR             ( void* );
int genXOR            ( void* );
int genLAND           ( void* );
int genLOR            ( void* );
int genoperate        ( char*  pszOperator );
```

LISTING 19.2 continued

```
int genadd           ( void* );
int gensubtract      ( void* );
int genmutiply       ( void* );
int gendivide        ( void* );
int genmodulus       ( void* );
void SetupRoutineNames ( void );


void RemoveSpaces ( char* InputBuffer )
{
   int in,out,bInSpaces;

   bInSpaces = FALSE;
   out = 0;

   for (in=0;((in<PARSE_BUFFER_LENGTH)&& (InputBuffer[in]!='\0'));in++)
   {
       if (bInSpaces)
       {
           if (!isspace(InputBuffer[in]))
           {
               InputBuffer[out++] = InputBuffer[in];
               bInSpaces = FALSE;
           }
       }
       else
       {
           if (isspace(InputBuffer[in]))
           {
              bInSpaces = TRUE;
              InputBuffer[out++] = ' ';
           }
           else InputBuffer[out++] = InputBuffer[in];
       }
   }   /* end of "for/in" loop along input buffer */

   InputBuffer[out] = '\0';
}

int parletter ( void* one )
{
```

LISTING 19.2 continued

```
    int iStatus;

    if (isalpha(*(char*)one))
    {
        iStatus=TRUE;
    }
    else
        iStatus = FALSE;

    return iStatus;
}

int pardigit ( void* one )
{
    int iStatus;

    if (isdigit(*(char*)one))
    {
        iStatus=TRUE;
    }
    else
        iStatus = FALSE;

    return iStatus;
}

int paroctal ( void* one )
{
    int iStatus;

    if ((isdigit(*(char*)one)) && (*(char*)one!='8')
    &&  (*(char*)one!='9'))
    {
        iStatus=TRUE;
    }
    else
        iStatus = FALSE;

    return iStatus;
}
```

LISTING 19.2 continued

```
int parchar ( void* one )
{
    int iStatus;

    if ((*(char*)one=='\'') || (*(char*)one=='\\')
    ||  (*(char*)one=='\?') || (*(char*)one=='\"'))
    {
        iStatus = FALSE;
    }
    else
        iStatus=TRUE;

    return iStatus;
}

int BuildNewParseBody ( struct sParseNode*  pParentHead,
                        struct sParseNode*  pPreviousBody,
                        struct sParseNode** ppNewBody,
                        int    iFirstChar,
                        int    iLastChar )
{
    int iStatus;

    iStatus = GetNewParseBody ( pParentHead, pPreviousBody, ppNewBody );
    if (iStatus==TRUE)
    {
        (*ppNewBody)->iFirstChar = iFirstChar;
        (*ppNewBody)->iLastChar  = iLastChar;
    }

    return iStatus;
}

int GetNewParseBody ( struct sParseNode*  pParentHead,
                      struct sParseNode*  pPreviousBody,
                      struct sParseNode** ppNewBody )
{
    int iStatus = TRUE;

    *ppNewBody = malloc(sizeof (struct sParseNode));
    if ((*ppNewBody)!=NULL)
    {
```

LISTING 19.2 continued

```
        (*ppNewBody)->ParentParse   = pParentHead;
        (*ppNewBody)->NextParse     = NULL;
        (*ppNewBody)->PreviousParse = pPreviousBody;
        if (pPreviousBody!=NULL)
        {
            pPreviousBody->NextParse = *ppNewBody;
        }
        (*ppNewBody)->ThisParse  = NULL;
        (*ppNewBody)->iFirstChar = 0;
        (*ppNewBody)->iLastChar  = -1;
    }
    else
    {
    }

    return iStatus;
}

int TryMatchParse ( char** ppInputBuffer,
                    int* k,
                    struct sSyntaxBody* pSyntaxP,
                    struct sParseNode** ppParseBody )
{
    int iStatus = TRUE;
    int iBodyStringLength;
    int kLocal;
    struct sParseNode* pNewParse = NULL;
    char *pInputBuffer;

    if (pSyntaxP->BodyContents!=NULL)
    {
        iBodyStringLength = strlen(pSyntaxP->BodyContents);
        if ((iBodyStringLength + k)>PARSE_BUFFER_LENGTH)
        {
            iStatus = FALSE;
            return iStatus;
        }
        pInputBuffer = *ppInputBuffer;
        if (strncmp(*pInputBuffer+k,pSyntaxP->BodyContents,
                    iBodyStringLength)!=0)
        {
            iStatus = FALSE;
```

LISTING 19.2 continued

```
                return iStatus;
            }
        } else {
            pNewParse = NULL;
            kLocal = *k;
            if (!BuildNewParseBody ( *ppParseBody, NULL, &pNewParse, kLocal, -1))
            {
                iStatus = FALSE;
                return iStatus;
            }
            if((pSyntaxP->BodyHead)!=NULL)
               iStatus = Parse ( &pInputBuffer, &kLocal, pSyntaxP->BodyHead,
                              &pNewParse );
            else
               iStatus = TRUE;
            *k = kLocal;
        }

        return iStatus;
}

int Parse ( char** ppInputBuffer,
            int*   k,
            struct sSyntaxHead* pRootS,
            struct sParseNode** ppRootP )
{
    int    iStatus                  = FALSE;
    int    iWorkStatus              = TRUE;
    int    bNextExists              = FALSE;
    struct sSyntaxBody*  pSyntaxP    = NULL;
    struct sSyntaxBody** ppSyntaxP   = &pSyntaxP;
    struct sParseNode*   pParseBody  = NULL;
    struct sParseNode**  ppParseBody = &pParseBody;

    if ((*ppRootP)==NULL)
    {
        *ppRootP = malloc(sizeof (struct sParseNode));
        if ((*ppRootP)==NULL)
        {
            iStatus = FALSE;
            return iStatus;
        }
```

LISTING 19.2 continued

```
        (*ppRootP)->ParentParse   = NULL;
        (*ppRootP)->NextParse     = NULL;
        (*ppRootP)->PreviousParse = NULL;
        (*ppRootP)->ThisHead      = pRootS;
        (*ppRootP)->ThisBody      = NULL;
        (*ppRootP)->ThisParse     = NULL;
        (*ppRootP)->CodeGenerate  = NULL;
        (*ppRootP)->iFirstChar    = 0;
        (*ppRootP)->iLastChar     = -1;
    }
    else
    {
    }

    pSyntaxP = pRootS->FirstAlternate->ThisBody;
    ppSyntaxP = &pSyntaxP;
    bNextExists = (pSyntaxP!=NULL);

        while (bNextExists && iWorkStatus)
        {
    if (pSyntaxP==NULL)
    {
        iStatus = TRUE;
        return iStatus;
    }   /* this was a finished parse */
        bNextExists = TRUE;
            iWorkStatus = TryMatchParse ( ppInputBuffer, k, pSyntaxP,
                                          ppParseBody );
            if (iWorkStatus)
            {
                bNextExists = GetNextSyntax ( ppSyntaxP );
            }
            else
            {
                iWorkStatus = SkipNextSyntax ( ppSyntaxP );
            }
    if ((*ppSyntaxP)!=NULL)
    {
        pSyntaxP = *ppSyntaxP;
    }
        }   /* end of "while" there is another node to check */
        iStatus = iWorkStatus;
```

LISTING 19.2 continued

```
    return iStatus;
}

int GetNextSyntax ( struct sSyntaxBody** ppSyntaxP )
{
    int iReturn = FALSE;

    *ppSyntaxP = (*ppSyntaxP)->NextBody;
    if ((*ppSyntaxP)!=NULL)
        iReturn = TRUE;
    return iReturn;
}

int SkipNextSyntax (struct sSyntaxBody** ppSyntaxP )
{
    int iReturn = FALSE;

    if (((*ppSyntaxP)->ParentAlt->NextAlt)!=NULL)
    {
        *ppSyntaxP = (*ppSyntaxP)->ParentAlt->NextAlt->ThisBody;
    }
    if ((*ppSyntaxP)!=NULL)
        iReturn = TRUE;
    return iReturn;
}

void PrintParseTree ( struct sParseNode* pInput, int depth )
{
    struct sParseNode* pParseNode;
    int    newDepth;

    newDepth = depth+1;
    pParseNode = pInput;
    while (pParseNode!=NULL)
    {
       if (pParseNode==NULL)
           return;
       sp(depth); printf("At :%p: points :%p:%p:%s:\n",pParseNode,
       pParseNode->ThisHead,pParseNode->ThisBody,
       pParseNode->ThisHead->SyntaxName);
       sp(depth); printf("   :%p:%p:%p:  :%p:%p:%p:\n",
       pParseNode->ParentParse,pParseNode->NextParse,
```

LISTING 19.2 continued

```
        pParseNode->PreviousParse,
        pParseNode->ThisParse,pParseNode->ThisHead,
        pParseNode->ThisBody);

        if (pParseNode->ThisParse!=NULL)
        {
            PrintParseTree ( pParseNode->ThisParse, newDepth);
        }

        pParseNode = pParseNode->NextParse;
    }

    return;
}

void PrintSyntaxTree ( void )
{
    struct sSyntaxHead* pSyntaxHead;
    struct sSyntaxAlt*  pSyntaxAlt;
    struct sSyntaxBody* pSyntaxBody;
    int iHead = 0;
    int iAlt  = 0;
    int iBody = 0;
    int i = 0;
    /* Start from the root syntax head  */
    pSyntaxHead = pRootSyntax;
    printf("-----------------START---------------------\n");
    /* Loop round the syntax heads      */
    while ((pSyntaxHead!=NULL) && (iHead<20))
    {
        iHead++;
        printf("Head name :%s: address  :%p:",pSyntaxHead->SyntaxName,
               pSyntaxHead);
        printf("\n");
        printf("Syntax counter in head  :%d:\n",pSyntaxHead->iSyntaxNumber);
        printf("First Alternate in Head :%p:\n",pSyntaxHead->FirstAlternate);
        pSyntaxAlt = pSyntaxHead->FirstAlternate;
        iAlt = 0;
        while ((pSyntaxAlt!=NULL) && (iAlt<10))
        {
            iAlt++;
            printf("    Start of alternate :%p:",pSyntaxAlt);
```

LISTING 19.2 continued

```
        printf("\n");
        printf("    Alternate counter  :%d:\n",
               pSyntaxAlt->iAlternateNumber);
        printf("    Syntax Counter in Alternate :%d:\n",
               pSyntaxAlt->iSyntaxNumber);
        printf("    Body pointer in Alternate   :%p:\n",
               pSyntaxAlt->ThisBody);
        /* For this syntax head, loop round the alternates */
        /* For this alternate, loop round the body items   */
        pSyntaxBody = pSyntaxAlt->ThisBody;
        iBody = 0;
        while ((pSyntaxBody!=NULL) && (iBody<20))
        {
          printf("        Start of body  :%p:",pSyntaxBody);
          printf("\n");
          printf("        parent alt     :%p:\n",pSyntaxBody->ParentAlt);
          printf("        Body Contents  :%p:\n",pSyntaxBody->BodyContents);
          if (pSyntaxBody->BodyContents!=NULL)
              printf("        == :%p: :%s:\n",pSyntaxBody->BodyContents,
              (pSyntaxBody->BodyContents));
          printf("        Syntax Head    :%p:\n",pSyntaxBody->BodyHead);
          printf("        Syntax Number  :%d: alternate :%d:\n",
              pSyntaxBody->iSyntaxNumber,pSyntaxBody->iAlternateNumber);
          printf("        End of body    :%p:\n",pSyntaxBody);
          pSyntaxBody = pSyntaxBody->NextBody;
          iBody++;
        }    /* End of body loop */
        printf("    End of alternate   :%p:\n",pSyntaxAlt);
        pSyntaxAlt = pSyntaxAlt->NextAlt;
    }   /* End of alternate loop */
    printf("End of Head %s\n",pSyntaxHead->SyntaxName);
    pSyntaxHead = pSyntaxHead-> pNextHead;
}  /* End of syntax head loop */
printf("--------------TABLES--------------------\n");
printf("iNextSyntax=:%5.5d: iNextAlternate=:%5.5d:\n",iNextSyntax,
        iNextAlternate);
for (i=0;(i<iNextSyntax);i++)
{
    printf("%5.5d :%p: :%s:\n",i,SyntaxTable[i].pSyntaxPointer,
           SyntaxTable[i].SyntaxName);
}
printf("   .................................\n");
```

LISTING 19.2 continued

```
    for (i=0;(i<iNextAlternate);i++)
    {
        printf("%5.5d :%p: :%5.5d:\n",i,AlternateTable[i].pAlternatePointer,
               AlternateTable[i].iSyntaxNumber);
    }
    printf("-----------------END--------------------\n");
    return;
}

oid SetupRoutineNames ( void )
{
    strcpy(RoutineNameTable[0].sNameBody,"genadd");
    RoutineNameTable[0].BodyRoutine = genadd;
    strcpy(RoutineNameTable[1].sNameBody,"gensubtract");
    RoutineNameTable[1].BodyRoutine = gensubtract;
    strcpy(RoutineNameTable[2].sNameBody,"genmultiply");
    RoutineNameTable[2].BodyRoutine = genmultiply;
    strcpy(RoutineNameTable[3].sNameBody,"gendivide");
    RoutineNameTable[3].BodyRoutine = gendivide;
    strcpy(RoutineNameTable[4].sNameBody,"genmodulus");
    RoutineNameTable[4].BodyRoutine = genmodulus;
    strcpy(RoutineNameTable[5].sNameBody,"genmolt");
    RoutineNameTable[5].BodyRoutine = genlt;
    strcpy(RoutineNameTable[6].sNameBody,"genle");
    RoutineNameTable[6].BodyRoutine = genle;
    strcpy(RoutineNameTable[7].sNameBody,"gengt");
    RoutineNameTable[7].BodyRoutine = gengt;
    strcpy(RoutineNameTable[8].sNameBody,"genge");
    RoutineNameTable[8].BodyRoutine = genge;
    strcpy(RoutineNameTable[9].sNameBody,"geneq");
    RoutineNameTable[9].BodyRoutine = geneq;
    strcpy(RoutineNameTable[10].sNameBody,"genne");
    RoutineNameTable[10].BodyRoutine = genne;
    strcpy(RoutineNameTable[11].sNameBody,"genAND");
    RoutineNameTable[11].BodyRoutine = genAND;
    strcpy(RoutineNameTable[12].sNameBody,"genOR");
    RoutineNameTable[12].BodyRoutine = genOR;
    strcpy(RoutineNameTable[13].sNameBody,"genXOR");
    RoutineNameTable[13].BodyRoutine = genXOR;
    strcpy(RoutineNameTable[14].sNameBody,"genLAND");
    RoutineNameTable[14].BodyRoutine = genLAND;
    strcpy(RoutineNameTable[15].sNameBody,"genLOR");
```

LISTING 19.2 continued

```
    RoutineNameTable[15].BodyRoutine = genLOR;
    strcpy(RoutineNameTable[16].sNameBody,"parletter");
    RoutineNameTable[16].BodyRoutine = parletter;
    strcpy(RoutineNameTable[17].sNameBody,"pardigit");
    RoutineNameTable[17].BodyRoutine = pardigit;
    strcpy(RoutineNameTable[18].sNameBody,"paroctal");
    RoutineNameTable[18].BodyRoutine = paroctal;
    strcpy(RoutineNameTable[19].sNameBody,"parchar");
    RoutineNameTable[19].BodyRoutine = parchar;
    strcpy(RoutineNameTable[20].sNameBody,"genid");
    RoutineNameTable[20].BodyRoutine = NULL;
    strcpy(RoutineNameTable[21].sNameBody,"genconst");
    RoutineNameTable[21].BodyRoutine = NULL;
    strcpy(RoutineNameTable[22].sNameBody,"genplusplus");
    RoutineNameTable[22].BodyRoutine = NULL;
    globMaxName = 22;

    return;
}


int main ( int argc, char * argv[])
{
    int iStatus     = EXIT_SUCCESS;
    int bGoodSyntax= FALSE;
    int bGoodParse = FALSE;
    int bGoodOutput= FALSE;
    int k           = 0;
    char* p         = NULL;
    char* pParseBuffer = NULL;

    printf("Parser: Version 1.0 20000325.20:47\n");

    iNextSyntax     = 0;   /* Zeroth item is special */
    iNextAlternate = 0;   /* Zeroth item is special */
    SyntaxTable[0].SyntaxName[0]   = '\0';
    SyntaxTable[0].pSyntaxPointer = NULL;
    SyntaxTable[0].iStartsWith    = 0;
    SyntaxTable[0].iMustContain   = 0;
    AlternateTable[0].pAlternatePointer = NULL;
    AlternateTable[0].iSyntaxNumber     = 0;
    AlternateTable[0].iStartsWith       = 0;
```

LISTING 19.2 continued

```
    AlternateTable[0].iMustContain      = 0;
    pRootSyntax     = NULL;
    pRootParse      = NULL;
    fSyntaxFile     = NULL;
    strcpy(sSyntaxFileName,"Syntax.txt");
    fInputFile      = NULL;
    strcpy(sInputFileName, "TestInput.txt");
    fOutputFile     = NULL;
    strcpy(sOutputFileName,"GeneratedCode.txt");

    SetupRoutineNames ( );
    globLabel = 0;

    bGoodSyntax = ReadSyntax ( &pRootSyntax );
    fInputFile = fopen(sInputFileName,"r");
    if (fInputFile==NULL)
    {
        iStatus = EXIT_FAILURE;
        return iStatus;
    }

    fOutputFile = fopen(sOutputFileName,"w");
    if (fOutputFile==NULL)
    {
        iStatus = EXIT_FAILURE;
        return iStatus;
    }

    while (!feof(fInputFile))
    {
        p = fgets(ParseBuffer,PARSE_BUFFER_LENGTH,fInputFile);
        if(p!=NULL)
        {
            RemoveSpaces(ParseBuffer);
            /* LexicalAnalyse(ParseBuffer) */
            k = 0;
            pParseBuffer = &ParseBuffer[0];
            bGoodParse = Parse ( &pParseBuffer, &k, pRootSyntax, &pRootParse );
            if (bGoodParse)
            {
                bGoodOutput = GenerateOutputCode ( pRootParse );
            }
```

LISTING 19.2 continued

```
        }   /* end of "if/then" found a new line to parse */
    }       /* end of "while" reading the input expression file */

    if (fSyntaxFile!=NULL)
    {
        fclose(fSyntaxFile);
    }
    if (fInputFile!=NULL)
    {
        fclose(fInputFile);
    }
    if (fOutputFile!=NULL)
    {
        fclose(fOutputFile);
    }

    return iStatus;
}
```

Listing 19.2 illustrates the basic parser code. For further comments, see the files `Ch19Pars.c` and `Ch19Pars.h` on the accompanying CD. The code in this illustration may take a very long time to discover that some input is in error—and it may also take a very long time to discover the correct parse for correct input. It does not use the "must contain" and "starts with" tables. This is code that would be straightforward to add.

Full Version

Now that we have seen how we can parse an expression, there are two more things to consider: how we can parse efficiently, and what we can generate as output.

Parsing efficiently means, in our example, that we have to indicate which items can be looked at in the initial lexical scan. If you look back at the sample parse for the expression

```
abc5 + xyz6
```

you will see that *identifier* was tried and retried several times. If these *identifier* tokens had been found by an initial scan, there would have been no need to rescan them in each alternate. In our notation we can use the symbol `:L:=` rather than `::=` for each item that is to be preprocessed by the lexical scan. There do not have to be many of these items, provided they are deep enough in the syntax to avoid numerous repetitions.

Generating output means that we have to have some series of action associated with each parsed item. In our notation we can add the name of a C function in square brackets (such as `[name]`) to indicate a function to be called when the parse is complete, which will generate the output relevant to that particular branch of the parse.

Sometimes a syntax rule may be better expressed or more efficiently implemented by a specific function called to apply that one rule. If a C function name in curly braces (such as `{name}`) is specified immediately after the defining name, then that lexical C function will be used instead of the general parsing mechanism.

It might also be helpful to add other "short circuit" routines to be called during parsing. Specifying these in ordinary parentheses is possible, as in `(name)`, but it is not illustrated here. Such routines can be used to bypass the general parser at specific points in the syntax where the more general powers of the slower full parser are not required. Consider this *only* if execution of your parser is time critical.

Thus, we could have

identifier :L:= *letter identifier-tail* #

identifier-tail {*lexidtail*} ::= *letter identifier-tail* | *digit identifier-tail* | "_" *identifier-tail* | *empty* #

additive-expression ::= *multiplicative-expression* | *additive-expression* "+" *multiplicative-expression* [*genadd*] | *additive-expression* "-" *multiplicative-expression* [*gensub*] #

Note that each of the functions called by the syntax will have to be available to the parser to use.

These functions are in addition to the general syntax notation. They certainly are not the only means of generating output code from a parse—just one convenient way that is described here and illustrated in the code accompanying this chapter on the CD.

Full Syntax for Expressions

The following syntax is implemented by the code in the files `Ch19Par2.c` and `Ch19Par2.h` on the accompanying CD. The syntax is in file `ExpSynt2.txt`.

> *empty* ::= #
>
> *primary-expression ::= identifier [genid] | constant [genconst] | "(" expression ")"* #
>
> *identifier :L:= letter identifier-tail* #
>
> *identifier-tail {lexidtail} ::= letter identifier-tail | digit identifier-tail | "_" identifier-tail | empty* #

letter (parletter) :L:= "x" #

single-character (parchar) :L:= "x" #

constant ::= integer-constant | *character-constant* | *floating-constant #*

character-constant ::="**L**" *small-character-constant* | *small-character-constant #*

small-character-constant :L:= "'"*single-character* "'" | "'"*escaped-character* "'" #

digit (pardigit) :L:= "**0**" | "**1**" | "**2**" | "**3**" | "**4**" | "**5**" | "**6**" | "**7**" | "**8**" | "**9**" #

octal-digit (paroctal) :L:= "**0**" | "**1**" | "**2**" | "**3**" | "**4**" | "**5**" | "**6**" | "**7**" #

optional-octal-digit ::= octal-digit | *empty #*

hex-digit ::= digit | *upper-hex-digit* | *lower-hex-digit* |

upper-hex-digit ::= "**A**" | "**B**" | "**C**" | "**D**" | "**E**" | "**F**" #

lower-hex-digit ::= "**a**" | "**b**" | "**c**" | "**d**" | "**e**" | "**f**" #

escaped-character {lexescchar} :L:= "\" *escape-sequence #*

escape-sequence ::= "**n**" | "**t**" | "**v**" | "**b**" | "**r**" | "**d**" | "**a**" | "****" | "**?**" | "**'**" | *octal-digit optional-octal-digit optional-octal-digit* | "**x**" *hex-digit hex-digit #*

integer-constant {lexintcon} :L:= digit integer-constant | *digit #*

floating-constant {lexflpcon} :L:= integer-part fraction-part E-part exponent F-part #

integer-constantNL ::= digit integer-constant | *digit #*

integer-part ::= integer-constantNL | *empty #*

fraction-part ::= point integer-part | *empty #*

point ::= "**.**" #

E-part ::= "**e**" | "**E**" | *empty #*

F-part ::= "**f**" | "**F**" | "**l**" | "**L**" | *empty #*

exponent ::= optional-sign integer-constant | *empty #*

optional-sign ::= "**+**" | "**-**" | *empty #*

postfix-expression ::= primary-expression | *postfix-expression* "**++**" *[genplusplus]* | *postfix-expression* "**--**" *[genminusminus] #*

unary-expression ::= postfix-expression | *[genplusplus]* "**++**" *unary-expression* | *[genminusminus]* "**--**" *unary-expression* | *unary-operator cast-expression [genunary] #*

unary-operator ::= "**-**" | "**!**" #

cast-expression ::= unary-expression #

19

Expression Parsing and Evaluation

multiplicative-expression ::= cast-expression | multiplicative-expression "" cast-expression [genmultiply] | multiplicative-expression "/" cast-expression [gendivide] | multiplicative-expression "%" cast-expression [genmodulus] #*

additive-expression ::= multiplicative-expression | additive-expression "+" multiplicative-expression [genadd] | additive-expression "-" multiplicative-expression [gensubtract] #

shift-expression ::= additive-expression | shift-expression "<<" additive-expression [genleftshift] | shift-expression ">>" additive-expression [genrightshift] #

relational-expression ::= shift-expression | relational-expression "<" shift-expression [genlt] | relational-expression ">" shift-expression [gengt] | relational-expression "<=" shift-expression [genle] | relational-expression ">=" shift-expression [genge] #

equality-expression ::= relational-expression | equality-expression "==" relational-expression [geneq] | equality-expression "!=" relational-expression [genne] #

AND-expression ::= equality-expression | AND-expression "&" equality-expression [genAND] #

exclusive-OR-expression ::= AND-expression | exclusive-OR-expression "^" AND-expression [genXOR] #

inclusive-OR-expression ::= exclusive-OR-expression | inclusive-OR-expression "|" exclusive-OR-expression [genOR] #

logical-AND-expression ::= inclusive-OR-expression | logical-AND-expression "&&" inclusive-OR-expression [genLAND] #

logical-OR-expression ::= logical-AND-expression | logical-OR-expression "||" logical-AND-expression [genLOR] #

expression ::= logical-OR-expression #

The definitions for *letter* and *single-character* given above rely entirely on the code routines for implementation—the right sides above do *not* represent what they mean.

Intuitive Rules in English

Each of the relevant syntax rules has been augmented with a call on a routine that will plant the code for that particular arithmetic operator. Where the calls are placed indicates that the whole of the subexpression must have been parsed before the operation can take place. Each operator is applied starting from the bottom of the parse tree (the point furthest from the root), moving upward towards the root. In fact, the operators are applied in the "parents after children" order described earlier (postorder traversal).

For every subexpression, there is exactly one point at which an evaluation function is called. If there were more than one, then there would be extraneous code planted—not serious, perhaps, but not efficient. This is not a deep discussion: Those of you who are concerned with writing compilers containing optimization should be researching elsewhere.

The lexical items, which do not need to be rescanned every time, are *identifier*, *small-character-constant*, *escaped-character*, *digit*, *integer-constant* and *floating-constant*. Because the first part of a *floating-constant* (the *integer-part*) may look like an *integer-constant*, this pair of lexical items has to be sought in the order *floating-constant* followed by *integer-constant*. This syntax has been altered to indicate that we have two different sorts of *integer-constant*: the sort for which we want lexical analysis, and the sort that lies within another definition (*integer-constantNL*), for which no lexical analysis is required.

Strict Rules in C

The various routines whose names are now referred to in the syntax need to be known to the parser. As the syntax tree is loaded, the identifiers are matched against the known list, and pointers to the real routines are placed in the syntax tree. If the routine is not known, an error message can be issued: In the sample code a simple `NULL` pointer is placed. The code for this is on the accompanying CD in files `Ch19Par2.c` and `Ch19Pars.h`.

Transformation from Polish Form to Evaluation

The Polish form of the expression exists in this parse as the tree. We have shown how scanning a tree can generate either the Polish form or the Reverse Polish form. The code generation part of this analyzer scans the tree in "parents after children" order, applying the routines for code generation at each node that contains a request. The requests to generate code are placed at the end of their alternates, so that they are the last thing encountered in processing the branch. This emphasizes the Reverse Polish that is being used. Each code-generation routine is specific for the kind of operator being processed.

English Description of the Process

The abstract syntax is read in, and an internal description of the abstract syntax (what can be said) is built up. Then, for each line of real input, there is first a parse (finding out "what was actually said") and a code generation, which scans the parse tree, applying the code-generation operations, in Reverse Polish order. The actions of the various routines are as in Table 19.4.

TABLE 19.4 Code Generation Routines

Code Routine	*Action*	*Description*
x [genid]	A1 = x; stack[index++] = A1;	Load the contents of the identifier into register A1 and push it onto the stack.
x [genconst]	A1 = x; stack[index++] = A1;	Load the constant into register A1 and push it onto the stack.
[genplusplus]	A1 =stack[index--]; A2 = 1; A1 = A1 + A2; stack[index++]= A1;	Add 1 to the top element on the stack.
[genminusminus]	A1 =stack[index--]; A2 = 1; A1 = A1 - A2; stack[index++]= A1;	Subtract 1 from the top element on the stack.
[genmultiply]	A1 =stack[index--]; A2 =stack[index--]; A1 = A1 * A2;	Multiply the top two stack elements. This code is very similar to that for other arithmetic operations.stack[index++]Just the single= A1;operation character must be changed for [genadd], [gensubtract], and [genmodulus].
[genlt]	A1 =stack[index--]; A2 =stack[index--]; if (A1 < A2)goto M2; A1 = 0; goto L2; M2:A1 = 1; L2:	Determine whether the top two stack elements have a relationship of "less than." Note that the other comparison operators are almost identical ([gengt], [genle], [genge], [geneq], and [genne]), with just the comparison operator changed.
t [genunary]	A1 =stack[index--]; A1 = t A1; stack[index++]= A1;	Apply unary operator `t` to the top stack element.
[genAND]	A1 =stack[index--]; A2 =stack[index--]; A1 = A1 & A2; stack[index++]= A1;	Apply AND operator to the top two stack elements. This code is almost identical for the other logical operators ([genOR], [genXOR], [genLAND], and [genLOR]). In fact, this code is very similar to that planted for the arithmetic operators, too.

The code in Table 19.4 is not the most efficient that can be generated. For example, there will be many occurrences in the final sequence of the instruction pair:

```
stack[index++] = A1;
A1 = stack[index--];
```

which can always be optimized out. This can be achieved by simple cooperation between the code generation routines or by a second pass over the generated code, removing redundant code pairs. Real compilers do more than this—loops are optimized, common subexpressions are eliminated, register usage is organized to reduce the number of store accesses, and so on.

Example Code for Some of the Process

The code in Listing 19.3 shows some of the code-generation routines. This example parser and code generator does not actually evaluate the expressions itself. It would be very simple to replace these code-generation routines with evaluation routines. The code is planted in the same order in which it would be evaluated, so rather than plant the instructions, an evaluation version of this parser would simply run the instructions.

LISTING 19.3 Some Code-Generation Routines

```
int GenerateOutputCode ( struct sParseNode* pRootP )
{
    int  iStatus = TRUE;
    struct sParseNode* pParseHead;
    struct sParseNode* pParseBody;

    pParseHead = pRootP;
    pParseBody = pParseHead->ThisParse;
    while ((pParseHead!=NULL) && (iStatus==TRUE))
    {
        iStatus = ProcessOutputNode( &pParseHead, &pParseBody );
    }

    return iStatus;
}

int ProcessOutputNode ( struct sParseNode** ppParseHead,
                        struct sParseNode** ppParseBody )
{
    int iStatus = TRUE;

    if ((*ppParseBody)==NULL)
    {
        if (/*((*ppParseHead)->ThisBody!=NULL) && */
            (((*ppParseHead)->CodeGenerate)!=NULL))
        {
            (*ppParseHead)->CodeGenerate ( NULL );
```

LISTING 19.3 continued

```
        }
    }
    else
    {
        *ppParseBody = (*ppParseBody)->NextParse;
    }
    if((*ppParseBody)!=NULL)
    {
        *ppParseHead = (*ppParseBody)->ParentParse;
    }
    else
    {
        *ppParseHead = NULL;
    }
    return iStatus;
}


int gencomparison ( char* pszComparator )
{
    int iStatus = TRUE;

    fprintf(fOutputFile,"A1 = stack[index--];\n");
    fprintf(fOutputFile,"A2 = stack[index--];\n");
    fprintf(fOutputFile,"if (A1 %s A2) goto M%4.4d;\n",
                        pszComparator,++globLabel);
    fprintf(fOutputFile,"A1 = 0;\n");
    fprintf(fOutputFile,"goto L%4.4d;\n",globLabel);
    fprintf(fOutputFile,"M%4.4d:\n",globLabel);
    fprintf(fOutputFile,"A1 = 1;\n");
    fprintf(fOutputFile,"L%4.4d:\n",globLabel);
    return iStatus;
}


int genlt ( void* one )
{
    int iStatus;
    iStatus = gencomparison("<");
    return iStatus;
}
```

LISTING 19.3 continued

```
int gengt ( void* one )
{
    int iStatus;
    iStatus = gencomparison(">");
    return iStatus;
}

int genle ( void* one )
{
    int iStatus;
    iStatus = gencomparison("<=");
    return iStatus;
}

int genge ( void* one )
{
    int iStatus;
    iStatus = gencomparison(">=");
    return iStatus;
}

int geneq ( void* one )
{
    int iStatus;
    iStatus = gencomparison("==");
    return iStatus;
}

int genne ( void* one )
{
    int iStatus;
    iStatus = gencomparison("!=");
    return iStatus;
}

int genoperate ( char* pszOperator )
{
    int iStatus = TRUE;

    fprintf(fOutputFile,"A1 = stack[index--];\n");
    fprintf(fOutputFile,"A2 = stack[index--];\n");
    fprintf(fOutputFile,"A1 = A1 %s A2;\n",pszOperator);
```

LISTING 19.3 continued

```
    fprintf(fOutputFile,"stack[index++] = A1;\n");

    return iStatus;
}

int genadd ( void* one )
{
    int iStatus;

    iStatus = genoperate("+");

    return iStatus;
}

int gensubtract ( void* one )
{
    int iStatus;
    iStatus = genoperate("-");
    return iStatus;
}

int genmultiply ( void* one )
{
    int iStatus;
    iStatus = genoperate("*");
    return iStatus;
}

int gendivide ( void* one )
{
    int iStatus;
    iStatus = genoperate("/");
    return iStatus;
}

int genmodulus ( void* one )
{
    int iStatus;
    iStatus = genoperate("%");
    return iStatus;
}
```

LISTING 19.3 continued

```
int genAND ( void* one )
{
    int iStatus;
    iStatus = genoperate("&&");
    return iStatus;
}

int genOR ( void* one )
{
    int iStatus;
    iStatus = genoperate("||");
    return iStatus;
}

int genXOR ( void* one )
{
    int iStatus;
    iStatus = genoperate("^");
    return iStatus;
}

int genLAND ( void* one )
{
    int iStatus;
    iStatus = genoperate("&");
    return iStatus;
}

int genLOR ( void* one )
{
    int iStatus;
    iStatus = genoperate("|");
    return iStatus;
}

void sp(int depth)
{
    int i;
    for (i=0;i<depth;i++)
```

LISTING 19.3 continued

```
        printf(" ");
    return;
}
```

Parsing Erroneous Input

Your typing is perfect, not like mine. You never make an error, so a parser for your expressions does not need to handle errors. But my typing is dubious (and I omit brackets, I misspell, I put leading plus signs on integers, and by forgetful extension I create operators like "!>" (meaning "not greater than"). So parsers for my expressions certainly need to handle errors and give me a clue where I have gone wrong.

Aristotle said that correct reasoning is finite but that there are infinite ways of reasoning incorrectly. Every sort of parse error is possible, but the best we can do in an automated parser is to point to the first error detected and let the user work out what is really wrong. We have to assume, when handling errors, that the input text is close to a correct expression in the language—we should not expect a C compiler to produce very coherent error messages if it is presented a COBOL program or the text of *Finnegans Wake*!

A top-down parser determines that there is an error only when it reaches the end of the input, and that does not really give you a clue as to where exactly the error was. A bottom-up parser can often point more nearly to the origin of the input error—but not always. For a language like C and expressions with a syntax like that of expressions in C, a reasonable guess can usually be made of the point of error. If your input language is like FORTRAN IV, for instance, then the point of error may be very hard to find indeed, because of the design of the language.

One method of making a parser handle errors more helpfully is to split the input during an initial pass into subexpressions that can be determined by lexical inspection. Within the C language, a first pass could pair up brackets and parentheses and then call a separate parse process for each of the contents of these.

For more discussion on error handling, see *Principles of Compiler Design* by Alfred V. Aho and Jeffry D. Ullman (Addison-Wesley, 1977), as recommended earlier.

Write careful code, and enjoy parsing!

Summary

In this chapter, we looked at an alternative—and older—form of BNF, and indicated some extensions to make for more efficient syntax expression.

We then looked at a sample translator that reads a grammar and then parses against that grammar, producing semantic output—an interpretation. This is one example of the most general case of a translator. Finally, we observed that even in this book, the sample code cannot do everything—there is more to be learned about parsing.

CHAPTER 20

Making Software Tools

by Richard Heathfield

In This Chapter

There are three kinds of software tools:

- The kind we write for other people to use.
- The kind other people write for us to use.
- The kind we write for ourselves.

(Professional toolsmiths, such as compiler writers, will argue that tools, like compilers, fall into all three categories.)

We all write tools for other people. We normally just call them programs but, for our users, those programs are tools that make their lives easier. That's the theory, anyway.

We all use tools written for us by other people: Operating systems, compilers, linkers, profilers, Relational Database Management Systems, code analyzers, text editors, version control systems, and so forth. If we insisted on writing all these for ourselves, we'd never get anything else done. (Someone writes them, of course. If you are one of those people, I think you'll agree that those products keep you busy.)

This chapter is about the third kind of tool—the kind we write for ourselves to make our own job easier. From now till the end of this chapter, I use the term solely with this meaning in mind.

It's sometimes hard to explain to a project manager that it is worth writing a tool that is not a "deliverable," which the end user will never see, and which will cost hard cash to produce. Nevertheless, writing such software can produce real cost savings in the medium or long term.

The Right Tool for the Job

A couple of years ago I found myself on a Year 2000 project. My first task was to do a vendor assessment on a Y2K tool by a specialist software tool supplier. We spent a couple of weeks trying to get this tool to do what we wanted it to do, but it insisted on (and excelled at) doing what it was designed for, which was definitely not Y2K work!

It was the closest product we could find to what we needed (which was basically a fancy form of `grep`). It cost around £25000 (roughly $40,000) *per copy*, and we wanted five copies at least. We were on the point of spending a vast amount of money on this software, not because it did what we wanted but because it was the closest to it that we could find.

At this point in the story, you're probably expecting me to say "Well, I got to thinking, and I figured..." and I'd hate to disappoint you.

Well, I got to thinking, and I figured that we could write a better tool than that, and we could do it fast, and we could do it cheap.

And that's we did. First, we found a DOS version of `grep` (not difficult these days). Next, we wrote a few data formatting routines in C, a primitive code generator to produce a DOS batch file packed full of `grep` calls (hundreds of them), and a Visual Basic front end. We wrote another code generator that took the output from `grep` and reformatted it as `#pragma message` statements, which we bound into a "Hello world" source. Each message was put into exactly the same format as a Visual C++ 1.5 compiler warning message. Finally, we shelled out from Visual Basic to Visual C++ 1.5, automatically sending it the keystrokes that would tell it to load and compile our generated file. Visual C++ would then produce the contents of all the `#pragma message` statements in its output window. Since they were in its own warning format, it reacted as if they were warnings. So when we double-clicked on a `grep` hit, the Visual C++ IDE took us straight to the file where the hit occurred so that we could examine the source, in context, for problems relating to the use of two-digit year fields.

Of course, it was all duct tape and piano wire, and was never going to be a commercial competitor to the tool we'd been assessing. But that wasn't the intention. The purpose was to get a tool that did *exactly* what *we* wanted, and that's exactly what it did. (The last time I heard, the client is still using it for other purposes.) Furthermore, it saved the client an awful lot of money. And it was tremendous fun to write, too.

In *The Mythical Man-Month*, Fred Brooks discusses a suggested ideal programming team structure, as proposed by Harlan Mills. In that team, he reserves a special place for the toolsmith. "Each team will need its own toolsmith, regardless of the excellence and reliability of any centrally provided service... The tool-builder will often construct specialized utilities, catalogued procedures, [and] macro libraries."

I've never met a toolsmith, in the sense that Fred Brooks was discussing. That is, I have never met anyone who was brought into a programming team *specifically* to write tools for the rest of the team to use. That's a pity. (Maybe you have been more fortunate.) The implication is clear, though—nobody else is going to write our tools for us, so either we write them ourselves or they don't get written. So, if we're going to write some tools to make our life easier, we may as well write them properly.

Characteristics of Good Software Tools

Writing tools properly, rather than quickly, may seem like a waste of programming resource. That's a short-term view, though, because good tools can be used again and again. Let's look now at what makes a good software tool.

User Interface

Because the tools we write aren't intended to be used or even seen by those people whom we normally think of as users, they don't have to be pretty. They don't even have to be GUI-based. In fact, it's often better to provide a command-line interface to the more general tools we write, partly because this makes it a lot easier to use them in combination, by way of pipes and filters, and partly because I can write an ANSI C program and be sure that you have a fighting chance of understanding it at first sight. This would be far less likely to be true if I were using a GUI library with which you were not familiar. All the tools we develop in this chapter are intended to be run in a command-line environment, but it would not take a tremendous amount of effort to modify them for use in GUI programs.

When writing a new programming tool, it's tempting to assume that its user knows what it is for, especially if you only ever intend to use it yourself. Imagine that, six months ago, near the end of Phase 1 of your product, you wrote a tool to help with, say, testing. And very useful it was too. You haven't used it since then. Now Phase 2 is nearly done, and you need that tool again. So, how does it work? (It's no good asking me. I don't know either.)

To avoid this problem, make it a rule of thumb that all the tools you write should include some standard way to provide a gentle reminder of how to use them! One strategy is to add an `-h` switch to all your programs (or, if you prefer, `-?`), which is interpreted as a cry for help. Another is to require some kind of command-line argument in order for the program to work, with the default (`argc == 1`) being to print a short memory-jogging instruction list. It doesn't matter which strategy you adopt, as long as you are consistent.

As far as possible, let your programs work with standard input and output. If you have to manipulate a binary file, so be it, but many project-specific problems relate to text files. Using standard I/O allows you to take full advantage of pipes and filters to join tools together in new and creative ways.

Making Tools Work Together

A few years ago, when I was working for a UK insurance company on a large new business quotations system, I was given the task of checking that the project makefiles were up-to-date. It sounds easy enough, but there were dozens of them, and they were all huge!

It started off as an essentially manual task, but I kept finding little ways in which I could automate some of the more painful aspects of the job. By the time I had finished, I had a little string of tools—about a dozen of them altogether. They all used standard I/O and, as a result, I was able to hook them all together in one long line, something like this:

```
a < makefile | b | c | d | e | f | g | h | i | j > reportfile
```

This saved me a lot of work, and sped up the task considerably. On one occasion a colleague of mine, who was not above a little shoulder-surfing occasionally, saw me typing in that command (with, I should add, rather more useful program names than I have shown here). I heard a gasp, and turned round. He'd gone very pale indeed. I think I *might* have been overdoing the standard I/O just a little. But the point, I hope, is clear. Simple tools, designed to work together, can save you a lot of work. This is the philosophy behind most of the UNIX tools.

Robustness

In theory, I should tell you that it's vital to make your tools just as robust as your production programs. In practice, though, you will probably pay no heed; if you're like many programmers, you'll make your programs robust in approximate proportion to the number of times you expect them to be used. (Beware! Good habits are hard to find, and easy to lose.)

When you code up a one-shot file hack, though, you're probably not going to be checking to see whether a `malloc()` of a few bytes worked, no matter how loudly I tell you to, unless you're already the kind of person who does that anyway. So I won't nag you anymore about it. Well, perhaps I'll bang one drum—always, always, *always* check `fopen()`'s return value, and print some kind of meaningful message if it fails. It'll save you time in the long term, I promise.

Flexibility

The more flexible your tools are, the more likely you are to be able to reuse them for some other purpose. On the other hand, it does mean they take longer to write, which may be an issue for you. But if you have time to take a simple problem, generalize it to the hilt, and then write a program to solve the general problem, you will find it to be one of the most interesting and rewarding aspects of toolcraft.

Simplicity

This objective is, to some extent, in conflict with the objective of flexibility. It's a trade-off. The simpler your program, the more likely it is to work the first time. (Okay, second time.) The more flexible it is, the better the chance that you will be able to reuse it, under slightly different circumstances, in the future. If you can write it simply and flexibly, you're onto a winning combination.

Portability

All the best programs eventually get ported. The closer your software tool is to ANSI C, the simpler it will be to port to another compiler or operating system. If the problem is inherently non-portable, see if you can break it into two problems, one portable and one non-portable. For example, if your requirement is to report the number of lines in each file in a directory tree, you could write a program to read a directory tree, writing all the relevant filenames to a file (without bothering to read the files themselves), and have a second program read that file as input. It can then portably use `fopen()` on each filename in turn, without having to know anything at all about directory structures. This makes porting it to some other environment very simple indeed, because you need only rewrite the first program. Furthermore, some operating systems provide commands at the user interface level for walking file systems in this way, which is all to the good because it means that, at least for those operating systems, you don't need to rewrite that part of the tool at all.

Code Libraries

Code reuse is the *sine qua non* of productive programming. At the simplest level, we reuse code every time we call `printf()` or `strcpy()`. Higher up the scale, we are in the fortunate position of being able to amass many useful routines over the course of our careers. Regrettably, we don't always take the trouble to arrange them in an easily reusable way. All too often, when faced with a familiar problem, we think to ourselves, "Ah yes, I did something like this a few months ago." Then we go and dig out the source to an old program, copy a bunch of routines, paste them into our new program, and hack them around a bit until they do exactly what we need.

It doesn't have to be that way. Any C implementation worth its salt will allow us to build libraries of useful routines, and to link those libraries into our applications. Techniques for doing this differ from one implementation to the next, but it is always possible somehow. Consult your implementation's documentation for local information on how to build libraries.

Careful programming will help us here. When we solve a problem, if we try to solve it generally rather than in an application-specific way we can make our future lives much easier (at the cost of taking a little more trouble in the present). If we get into this good habit, it won't be long before we have a powerful collection of useful routines that we can use over and over again. This can make many tools a lot quicker to write. (Quick example: file filter. Using a binary tree library, you can filter a text file for duplicate lines in three steps: read `stdin` into a tree keyed on text, copy into a second tree keyed on line number, write a second tree to `stdout`. Job done. The source comprises about 15 lines of non-library code.)

File scope variables are a major obstacle to such reuse, by the way. The more a function is coupled to the program in which it lives, the harder it is to rip it out and plug it into another program. This is one of the reasons that I do my very best not to use file scope variables (be they `static` or `extern`) at all.

A word about library organization may be in order. Good linkers will do their best, when linking library code into a program, to access only the routines that are actually *used* by that program. This has two clear benefits, which are related to each other. First, the final program is smaller than if the whole library had been linked in. Second and consequently, our program's performance may well benefit from the smaller code size because small programs are less likely to be swapped in and out of memory by the operating system's memory manager, a process which can sometimes reduce performance significantly. We can assist the linker by placing as few functions into each source file as possible, the ideal being one function per source file. This is because it's very difficult to correctly extract code from an object file at the functional level (consider, for example, the case where a function uses file scope variables), so linkers tend to grab entire object files from the library.

Note

On the CD-ROM that accompanies this book, we have tended not to separate out each function into a separate file. Had we done so, you would have been faced with a bewildering number of new source files, which can be quite disconcerting, to say the least. But it wasn't an easy decision to make.

General Purpose Filters and Tools

The best tools are those that are useful over and over again, even if they only do something very simple. Following is a quick tour of some of the most common tools around.

Tabs to Spaces Conversion

Many C programmers hold passionate views on indentation. Some insist that tabs are evil, and others are adamant that tabs are the Right Thing. I'm easy either way. Some environments (especially in the mainframe world), however, do present problems for source code containing tabs, so it's useful to have a way of converting these tabs to spaces—and back. It's so simple a tool to write that I won't show source here. If you are in lazy mode, you can find a tabs-to-spaces conversion utility in Bob Stout's Snippets collection at `http://www.snippets.org` (an excellent bunch of general-purpose C tools, and well worth a look). If you're in interested mode, though, you may find it diverting to write your own program to do this conversion and its inverse.

EBCDIC to ASCII Conversion

Yes, EBCDIC is still used on many sites. Most terminal emulators provide a conversion utility that does the necessary translations between ASCII and EBCDIC for us when we need to transfer files between a mainframe platform and a PC or UNIX box. It's not difficult to imagine circumstances, however, when you might want to do this yourself. If you were developing a mainframe-based Web browser, for example, you might well find it valuable to do your own conversions. Again, Snippets has a perfectly workable conversion program. On the CD-ROM, you'll find an ASCII-EBCDIC conversion table (`ascebc.txt`) stored in a program-friendly format (CSV), which may be of use to you if you decide to implement your own translation tool. It's probably best to use `unsigned char` in such a program. On the mainframe, `char` is `unsigned` by default, because EBCDIC is an 8-bit code. ASCII is only a 7-bit code, and is typically represented by `signed char`, but ASCII characters may still legally be stored in an `unsigned char`. A further consequence of this difference is that not all EBCDIC codes have ASCII equivalents, so you would need to consider carefully what would constitute appropriate behavior for an EBCDIC-ASCII conversion program that encountered an EBCDIC character with no ASCII equivalent, given the particular circumstances of your project.

Tee Time

In environments that provide a command line, it's very common to redirect program output to a file. But some people, including me, like to see what's going on while the program is running. For example, in MS-DOS the `dir` command produces a directory listing that can easily be used for generating lists of files for input to a program, simply by redirecting its output to a file (for example, `dir *.c /b > clist`). It's more convenient, though, if you can see its output at the same time (if only to satisfy yourself that the command is working on the right files!); there's no provision for this in MS-DOS. But we can write a simple program that will achieve the desired effect, as shown in Listing 20.1.

LISTING 20.1 Splitting Output into Two Streams

```
#include <stdio.h>

void tee(FILE *fp)
{
  char buffer[2048];
  while(fgets(buffer, sizeof buffer, stdin))
  {
    fprintf(stdout, "%s", buffer);
    if(NULL != fp)
    {
      fprintf(fp, "%s", buffer);
    }
  }
}

int main(int argc, char *argv[])
{
  FILE *fp = NULL;
  if(argc > 1)
  {
    fp = fopen(argv[1], "w");
    if(NULL == fp)
    {
      fputs("Error opening output stream.", stderr);
    }
  }
  tee(fp);
  if(NULL != fp)
  {
    fclose(fp);
  }

  return 0;
}
```

The program in Listing 20.1 copies its standard input to standard output, but also writes it to the file named in `argv[1]` (if present). It's so simple, and so useful, that I find it hard to understand why Microsoft didn't include one in MS-DOS as a standard utility. Be that as it may, this program enables us, by modifying our command slightly (`dir *.c /b ¦ tee clist`), to see the results instantly and have them tucked safely away in the file. (UNIX users will naturally prefer to use `ls` rather than `dir`, and MVS users are probably wringing their hands in frustration at this point because most of their tools execute in batch mode, out of sight.) This is just an example usage, by the way. You'll find plenty of other ways to benefit from this little program.

A Simple Line Splitter

Some environments impose line length limitations that make porting code to them more painful than we might like. For example, it's not uncommon for mainframe program source files to be stored in a Partitioned Data Set (PDS) with a record length of 80 bytes (which is why mainframe programmers are sometimes accused of having an "80-column mind"). As a result, a mainframe C project's Coding Standards document will often insist that lines are no longer than 80 columns or even, in some cases, 72 columns. This allows for the whole source to be seen in the ISPF editor, which displays eight-digit line numbers for your comfort and convenience. That's fine if you're writing code on that platform because the editor makes it quite difficult for you to forget the limitation. If, however, your code already exists on another platform and you want to port it, the chances are high that you will have many lines of code that exceed the specified limit. In such cases, the right solution is to edit your source into a shape suitable for porting. That's the medium term view. In the short term, though, perhaps you just want to quickly test whether your source will work unmodified on the new platform. Also, you'd like to put off all that tedious editing for now, especially if the portability test reveals that there is much work to be done on the source before it will operate correctly on the new platform. In such circumstances, a program that will edit your code for you (however inelegantly) will be of significant help. (UNIX programmers will use `indent` for this task, and might like to skip ahead to the end of this listing.)

Listing 20.2 shows how such a program might look.

LISTING 20.2 A Simple Line-Splitting Routine

```
#include <stdio.h>
#include <stdlib.h>
#include <string.h>

void help(void)
{
```

LISTING 20.2 continued

```
  char *helpmsg[] =
  {
    "limn",
    "Usage: limn <n>",
    "Example: limn 72",
    "Copies standard input to standard output,",
    "ensuring that no line exceeds n characters",
    "in length. Longer lines are split, and a",
    "terminating \\ character is added to the",
    "line at the split point. n must be at least 3."
  };

  size_t i, j = sizeof helpmsg / sizeof helpmsg[0];

  for(i = 0; i < j; i++)
  {
    puts(helpmsg[i]);
  }
}

int main(int argc, char **argv)
{
  int status = EXIT_SUCCESS;

  char *endp;
  int thischar;
  size_t lim;
  size_t currline = 0;

  if(argc < 2 || strcmp(argv[1], "-?") == 0)
  {
    help();
    status = EXIT_FAILURE;
  }
  else
  {
    lim = (size_t)strtoul(argv[1], &endp, 10);

    if(endp == argv[1] || lim < 3)
    {
      help();
      printf("\nInvalid arg %s\n", argv[1]);
```

LISTING 20.2 continued

```
      status = EXIT_FAILURE;
    }
    else
    {
      while((thischar = getchar()) != EOF)
      {
        if(thischar == '\n')
        {
          currline = 0;
        }
        else if(++currline == lim)
        {
          putchar('\\');
          putchar('\n');
          currline = 1;
        }
        putchar(thischar);
      }
    }
  }

  return status;
}
```

To see just how inelegant this solution is, let's try filtering a C source file (such as the program itself) through it with a command-line argument of 10. Here's a fragment from the resulting output:

```
int main(\
int argc,\
 char **a\
rgv)
{
  int sta\
tus = EXI\
T_SUCCESS
;

  char *e\
ndp;
  int thi\
schar;
```

```
  size_t \
lim;
  size_t \
currline \
= 0;
```

Horrible. Of course, with a limit of 80 rather than 10 it wouldn't look quite so bad, but even so, it's not exactly pretty.

If you're lazy (perhaps through lack of time), you'll put up with that kind of output, at least temporarily. If, however, you have the time to be interested, you may want to rewrite it to split lines at more appropriate places. String literals make such a task slightly involved, but it's not too difficult.

Tip

You can split string literals into chunks. For example, this

```
"The system has detected that you pressed a key - press [RESET]
 to effect this change"
```

becomes

```
"The system has detected " "that you pressed a key - press [RESET]"
 " to effect this change"
```

The line can now be split between the newly inserted quotation marks which, as you may have noticed, should *not* be separated by commas.

Byte Search and Replace

I suppose it's a consequence of my background in mainframe C programming that I have developed quite a few tools specifically to assist me in porting source code from PC to mainframe. If you've ever used a mainframe text editor, you'll perhaps understand why I prefer to write my code on the PC!

Under some terminal emulation programs, the characters `[` and `]` are not supported. The characters `0xBA` and `0xBB` are the EBCDIC equivalents of ASCII's `0x5B` (left square bracket) and `0x5D` (right square bracket). In practice, however, these values frequently (depending on how your terminal emulation is set up) don't work because the compiler rejects them as illegal characters. For C programmers, this presents something of a problem. One solution, if you can call it that, is to use trigraphs instead of brackets. For example:

```
char MyArray??(??) = "Hello world";
char YourArray??(100??) = {0};
```

This works, but it's hard to read.

As it happens, EBCDIC does contain a pair of characters that the compiler treats as if they were `[` and `]`. The EBCDIC codes for the two characters in question are `0xAD` and `0xBD`.

Wouldn't it be nice if we could write a program to convert all the square brackets in a C program to the ASCII values which, when the file is converted to EBCDIC, will become the EBCDIC values that trick the compiler into thinking that the square brackets really are square brackets?

Wouldn't it be even nicer if we could write a program to convert all occurrences of any arbitrary byte value within a file to some other value that we specify?

I've called this program `sandra`. (I should hasten to add that I don't know anyone called Sandra!) It stands for **S**earch **AND** **R**epl**A**ce, and can be found on the CD-ROM as `sandra.c`. But beware. As you will see, all is not well with `sandra`. Have a look at the `HexToInt()` function (Listing 20.3), for instance.

LISTING 20.3 Byte Search and Replace

```
#include <stdio.h>
#include <stdlib.h>
#include <string.h>
#include <ctype.h>

int HexToInt(char *s)
{
  int IntVal = 0;
  char Hex[] = "0123456789ABCDEF";
  char *p = NULL;

  while(*s != '\0')
  {
    IntVal <<= 4;
    p = strchr(Hex, toupper(*s));
    if(NULL != p)
    {
      IntVal |= (p - Hex);
    }
    else
    {
      printf("Can't convert hex value %s.\n", s);
```

LISTING 20.3 continued

```
      exit(EXIT_FAILURE);
    }
    ++s;
  }
  return IntVal;
}
```

If we use it carefully, this routine works just fine. Unfortunately, if it is given an invalid input (that is, a string that it doesn't recognize as being in hexadecimal format), it scribbles on `stdout` and exits the program. This makes it impractical to include `HexToInt()` in a code library. That's a shame, because it's an otherwise useful routine. Fortunately, that's very easy to fix, simply by passing an extra parameter—either a pointer to an error value or a pointer to an object in which the result can be stored (leaving the return value free for use as an error code).

Regrettably, that isn't the only problem with this routine. Did you see the bug? If it is given a sufficiently long input string, it will overflow `IntVal`, resulting in undefined behavior. (This can be obviated by changing its type to `unsigned int`. It won't stop the result being incorrect if an excessively long string is passed in, but it will at least be predictably incorrect.)

When we write software tools for our own use, it's easy to get careless and take shortcuts that we wouldn't dream of taking in production code; remember, undefined behavior can bite us just as hard as it can bite our users.

Let's look at the rest of the program. Our troubles are not yet over...

```
void Sandra(char *filename, int in, int out)
{
  FILE *fp = NULL;
  unsigned long count = 0;
  unsigned char c;

  fp = fopen(filename, "r+b");
  if(NULL == fp)
  {
    printf("Can't open file %s for update.\n", filename);
    exit(EXIT_FAILURE);
  }
  while(fread(&c, 1, 1, fp))
  {
if(c == (unsigned char)in)
```

```
    {
      c = (unsigned char)out;
      fseek(fp, -1L, SEEK_CUR);
      count++;
      if(1 != fwrite(&c, 1, 1, fp))
      {
        puts("Can't write to file.");
        fclose(fp);
        exit(EXIT_FAILURE);
      }
      if(EOF == fflush(fp))
      {
        puts("fflush failed.");
        fclose(fp);
        exit(EXIT_FAILURE);
      }
    }
  }
  fclose(fp);
  printf("The byte was replaced %lu time%s.\n",
         count,
         count == 1UL ? "" : "s");
}
```

This function, too, has its problems. Fortunately, this time they are minor ones.

First, the name of the function, although cute, is not as descriptive as, say, `SearchAndReplaceByte()` would be. Giving functions and variables cute names always seems like harmless fun at first. Six months after the event, though, this practice can cause serious hair loss as you struggle to remember what on earth the function does. You have now been warned, so don't blame me if you go bald.

The second problem is similar to `HexToInt()`'s weakness. The function is too tightly coupled to the specific application, for much the same reasons as in `HexToInt()`.

Before we leave this function, it might be worth pointing out the `fflush()` call. In C, if you read from a stream and then write to it, you must call a file positioning function (one of `fseek`, `fgetpos`, `rewind`) in between those two operations. If you write to a stream and then read from it, you must call a file positioning function or `fflush()` in between those two operations. If you don't, the program invokes undefined behavior, and you shouldn't act surprised when it formats your hard disk or declares nuclear war on your dog.

One of the technical reviewers for this book, using Turbo C++ 3 in ANSI C mode under Windows 98, found that this program didn't work as it should, and suggested replacing fflush(fp) with fseek(fp, 0L, SEEK_CUR). This is a reasonable workaround, but should not be necessary if you are using a truly ANSI-compliant compiler.

Finally, let's look at main(). The important point here is the behavior if too few arguments are supplied. ANSI does not guarantee that argv[0] contains the program name. It is perfectly legal for an implementation to provide the program with an argc value of 0, in which case argv[0] will be NULL. If your operating system always provides an argc value of at least 1, and you aren't concerned about portability, this isn't an issue for you.

```
int main(int argc, char *argv[])
{
  if(argc < 4)
  {
    printf("Usage: %s filename searchbyte replacebyte\n",
           argc > 0 ? argv[0] : "sandra");
  }
  else
  {
    Sandra(argv[1], HexToInt(argv[2]), HexToInt(argv[3]));
  }
  return 0;
}
```

Rewriting sandra in a more robust way is left as a simple exercise. It's probably worth your while to do this if you ever use more than one platform, and especially if you work on mainframe systems.

Hex Dump

Many C programmers believe that data is best stored in text files. Text files are easy to create with a text editor, easy to read, easy to modify with a text editor, and easy to port to other operating systems. Binary files are more awkward. For a start, they're often impossible to read because they contain unprintable characters. They are also difficult to modify correctly and very awkward to port because different operating systems use different alignment strategies and even different byte ordering. Nevertheless, we sometimes have to use binary data, even if it's only because we arrived on the project too late to affect the design decision on data storage. In these circumstances, it's very useful to be able to dump the hexadecimal output of a binary file to stdout.

Several utilities already do this, and they are very useful. Unfortunately, they tend to display the hexadecimal output in 16-column format. That's fine if all your records have a length that is a multiple of 16 bytes. Of course, most records don't.

So let's have a go at writing our own (see Listing 20.4). We'll default to 16 bytes per line too because this makes for a reasonably efficient output on an 80-column screen, but we will provide an override to allow the column width to be anything required. I've taken particular care to make this code as portable as possible, so it should run quite happily on any platform, even those with 32-bit bytes. When you are writing tools for multiple platforms, taking care to be portable is well worth the effort.

LISTING 20.4 Hex Dump

```
#include <stdio.h>
#include <stdlib.h>
#include <string.h>
#include <ctype.h>
#include <limits.h>

/* Help() function snipped from book text. See hd.c */

int HexDump(char *Filename, size_t Width)
{
  int Status = EXIT_SUCCESS;

  FILE *InFilePtr;
```

In C, a `char` is defined to be the same size as a byte. Most systems have 8-bit bytes. In fact, this is so prevalent that many programmers find it hard to believe that other byte sizes are possible. Nevertheless, architectures do exist that use 16- or even 32-bit bytes. Since we want to display each hexadecimal digit (or *hexit*) in a byte, it's quite important to know how many hexits to display! We can calculate this fairly simply. If there are `CHAR_BIT` bits (defined in `<limits.h>`) in a byte, and four bits to a hexit (this is always true), `CHAR_BIT / 4` hexits are needed to represent a byte. Well, almost. Actually, there's no requirement for `CHAR_BIT` to be a multiple of 4, so in fact we need to add 3 before the division. For example, if `CHAR_BIT` were 9 or 10 or 11, two hexits would not suffice, but `(CHAR_BIT + 3) / 4` hexits would.

```
 int HexitsPerByte = (CHAR_BIT + 3) / 4;

  unsigned char *TextBuffer;
  unsigned char *HexBuffer;

  size_t BytesRead;
  size_t ThisByte;
  size_t HexBuffWidth;
```

```
InFilePtr = fopen(Filename, "rb");
if(NULL == InFilePtr)
{
  printf("Can't open file %s for reading.\n",
         Filename);
  Status = EXIT_FAILURE;
}
else
{
  HexBuffWidth = Width * (HexitsPerByte + 1);

  TextBuffer = malloc(Width + 1);
  if(NULL == TextBuffer)
  {
    printf("Couldn't allocate %u bytes.\n",
           (unsigned)(Width + 1));
    Status = EXIT_FAILURE;
  }
  else
  {
    HexBuffer = malloc(HexBuffWidth + 1);
    if(NULL == HexBuffer)
    {
      printf("Couldn't allocate %u bytes.\n",
             (unsigned)(HexBuffWidth + 1));
      Status = EXIT_FAILURE;
    }
    else
    {
```

We process `Width` bytes at a time. By storing the number of bytes actually read (which we obtain by specifying a block size of 1 and a count of `Width`), we can handle the last few bytes of a file that isn't an exact multiple of the specified width, in the same loop as the bulk of the file.

```
      while((BytesRead = fread(TextBuffer,
                               1,
                               Width,
                               InFilePtr)) > 0)
      {
        for(ThisByte = 0;
            ThisByte < BytesRead;
            ThisByte++)
        {
```

```
            /* Insert hex code into hex buffer
             * at the appropriate offset
             */
            sprintf((char *)(HexBuffer +
                             ThisByte *
                             (HexitsPerByte + 1)),
                    "%0*X ",
                    HexitsPerByte,
                    (unsigned)TextBuffer[ThisByte]);
```

For obvious reasons, we don't want to print unprintable characters. A common convention is to display some other character in their place, such as `'.'`, so we'll do that too.

```
            if(!isprint(TextBuffer[ThisByte]))
            {
              TextBuffer[ThisByte] = '.';
            }
          }

          TextBuffer[ThisByte] = '\0';

          printf("%-*.*s ¦ %s\n",
                 HexBuffWidth,
                 HexBuffWidth,
                 HexBuffer,
                 TextBuffer);
        }
        if(ferror(InFilePtr))
        {
          printf("Warning: read error on file %s.\n",
                 Filename);
          Status = EXIT_FAILURE;
        }

        /* release memory resource */
        free(HexBuffer);
      }

      /* release memory resource */
      free(TextBuffer);
    }

    /* release file resource */
    fclose(InFilePtr);
```

```
  }

  return Status;
}


int main(int argc, char **argv)
{
  int Status = EXIT_SUCCESS;
  size_t NumChars = 16;
  char *EndPointer;
  int FilenameArg = 1;

  if(argc < 2 ||  strcmp("-?", argv[1]) == 0)
  {
    Help();
    Status = EXIT_FAILURE;
  }
  else
  {
    if(memcmp(argv[1], "-c", 2) == 0)
    {
      FilenameArg = 2;
      NumChars = (size_t)strtoul(argv[1] + 2,
                                 &EndPointer,
                                 10);
```

When converting from string to numeric format, always use the `strtox` family of functions: `strtod()`, `strtol()`, `strtoul()`, and so on. They give you much more information about the conversion than `atoi()` and `atof()`. Specifically, they tell you which was the first character not to be convertible.

```
if(EndPointer == argv[1] + 2 || NumChars < 1)
      {
        Help();
        puts("\nInvalid or missing argument.");
        Status = EXIT_FAILURE;
      }
    }
  }

  if(EXIT_SUCCESS == Status)
  {
    Status = HexDump(argv[FilenameArg], NumChars);
```

```
    }

    return Status;
}
```

A more adventurous hex dump program might accept a header record size as an additional, possibly optional, argument, and either display that many bytes separately or skip them altogether. That way, if the header record were of a different size than the other records, it wouldn't stop them from appearing in the way we'd like. If that modification sounds useful to you, feel free to hack the source around.

Automatic Test Data Generation

Testing is every programmer's pet hate. Debugging, despite its apparently negative connotations, can actually be quite enthralling. There's a sense of challenge, of a mystery to be solved, and many developers get tremendous satisfaction from finally nailing a bug. But testing is boring, or at least it should be. There shouldn't be any surprises in testing because, in theory, all the bugs have been found. Also, completely thorough testing is mindlessly repetitive. Still, it has to be done, so why not try to make it a bit easier and quicker? If we can automate at least some of the tasks associated with testing, we can save a lot of time and tedium.

One aspect of testing that is relatively easy to automate is that of test data generation. Simply thinking up test data can be annoyingly time-consuming, and it wears out your fingers too. Perhaps we can save ourselves some typing, though. If we can write a program to think up our test data for us, we can substantially cut the time we have to spend on what most of us regard as a less than fascinating process.

Writing Test-friendly Applications

The best way to auto-generate test data is by writing a program that produces a file, or files, which the application will then read. To facilitate this, it makes sense to write our application in such a way that it can read a test data file, and use it in the same way (as nearly as possible) as it would use live data. Now it may be that our application would normally expect input directly from the user, perhaps via a graphical API. Depending on the application, it may be desirable to test the input routines separately, while the automatically generated test data file is read into the application purely to test underlying algorithms. It may, on the other hand, be necessary to use a commercial testing tool to drive the user interface. In the latter case, it's sensible to design the test data generator in such a way that it produces test data files that the main test tool can read. This way, all the testing can be done in one cycle, without any manual intervention at all. If that's not an issue, the format of our files is up to us, in which case I recommend CSV format.

In case you haven't come across CSV, it stands for "comma-separated values" and means exactly that—a list of values separated by commas (unless a comma is inside quotation marks, in which case it is read as part of the string the quotation marks delimit). Such a format is trivial to generate and relatively easy to read (using `strtok()` or some similar technique). Furthermore, most spreadsheet programs can read and write CSV files. Thus, if we like the data we've produced automatically but want to make a few tweaks to it (perhaps adding a few specific tests that our generator didn't provide, editing existing tests and so on), we can just load the file into our spreadsheet, edit it in place, and save it again. If no spreadsheet is conveniently at hand, we can just as quickly use a text editor to tweak the data (although not quite as easily because a text editor is unlikely to tabulate the data).

Another advantage of using a spreadsheet-readable format for our test data files is that we can use the power of any modern spreadsheet program to check our results. We create the files in CSV format. We load the inputs into the spreadsheet, and write formulae to calculate our expected results. When we test the program, we can then compare its results against the spreadsheet's results. If the program being tested produces a CSV file as output, we're in seventh heaven, because we can electronically compare the results against those provided by the spreadsheet—a big time savings. In passing, I should add that if you adopt this suggestion, don't automatically blame all mismatched results on the program you are testing. The fault could be in the spreadsheet formulae. Which is in error can only be discovered by careful checking of both or (better) by calculating the correct result in some other way.

How does your application respond to failure? Does it self-destruct, carrying faulty data down with it in a cataclysmic firework display of error messages and assertion failures? Or does it provide some technique for recording the error, and then quietly move on to the next set of data?

The firework technique isn't always avoidable. Sometimes we do have to halt processing on error. Most of the time, though, we don't. If a bank's overnight run at its national data center stalled because some clerk in Manchester had typed a 3 instead of a 2 on an account number, the economy would soon grind to a halt. Nowadays we have to write programs that, wherever possible, recover from errors rather than give in to them. If we can do this, it will certainly help our testing. If we can't, we must resign ourselves to finding no more than one problem per test run.

Designing Test Data

When we write test data generators, we have to consider all the usual criteria for test data. We will generally need tests for off-by-one errors, overflow, divide-by-zero, and so on, as well as the normal, run-of-the-mill test cases that you don't mind dating but wouldn't want to marry. It's worth spending some time on this. The more comprehensive your test data, the more assured you can be that your program is going to be tested properly.

Automatic test generators are best used for the ordinary cases. Your special cases should really be handcrafted. Having said that, a test generator can produce an awful lot of ordinary cases; it may serendipitously come up with a few special cases of its own. If they break your application, so much the better (always look on the bright side).

Writing Test Data Generation Code

A comprehensive test data generator would be a most challenging, if not impossible, program to write, so I'm not going to try. Instead, I've chosen a relatively simple hypothetical application, which processes a transaction log comprising a reference number, a date, an account name, and an amount. How can we generate test data for this program?

It's not difficult to produce relatively realistic-looking data. This non-existent transaction log processor expects to see reference numbers in `AA9999/aaa` format (that is, two uppercase letters, a four-digit number, a `'/'`, and three lowercase letters, such as `"BD4392/rjh"`). It would like its dates to be in international date format `yyyy/mm/dd` (for example, `"2000/06/28"`), for easy sorting. Then it needs an account name (as this is a business, it needs business-like names), and a transaction amount, to two decimal places. If the transaction is a spend, the amount is negative. Otherwise, it's positive.

Random numbers can be a big help here. (Of course, C's standard library doesn't actually provide random numbers; they are merely pseudo-random. But they're random enough for rock 'n' roll, so we'll use them anyway, and we'll call them "random" too, even if that isn't, strictly speaking, true.) Random numbers can give us random data. That is a good thing, but it can also be a problem. What if we need to reconstruct our datafile exactly at a later date?

In C, the values you get from `rand()` are based on a seed value that initializes the internal implementation of some pseudo-random number generation algorithm or other. You can select that seed value yourself, by passing it to `srand()`. If you pass a constant value, you'll always get the same results from `rand()`. If, instead, you send a random value, you will get different results every time. (How do you get a random value for giving to `srand()` in the first place, then? Easy. `srand(time(NULL));` will do it nicely.)

The driver routine for our test data generator example passes `srand()` either a constant value or a random value, depending on a command-line parameter. I won't show the driver here, but you can find it on the CD-ROM in `datagen.c`.

Here, then, are a couple of handy functions for generating random doubles in the range `0.0 <= R < 1.0` and integers in the range `0 <= R < N`. Many people use the `%` operator for getting random integers into a range (for example, `rand() % N`). That's fine if the particular random number generator being used by that implementation is a good one. Most are only mediocre, and are not always as random in the low bits as they ought to be. The techniques outlined in Listing 20.5 are considerably better because they place more significance on the higher bits, which most commercially available random number generators are quite good at.

LISTING 20.5 Random Test Data Generation

```
double RandDbl(void)
{
  return rand() / ((double)RAND_MAX + 1.0);
}

int RandInt(int n)
{
  return (int)(n * RandDbl());
}
```

Now we're ready to generate some data. There's nothing complicated about the following function, but there are one or two points of interest to note. First, as you can see, I've defined a couple of pointers to the alphabet (one for lowercase and one for uppercase). If your system uses ASCII, you could obtain a random letter of the alphabet using a simple expression such as `RandInt(26) + 'A'`, and that would work fine. It would not, however, work on systems using some other collating sequences, such as EBCDIC. The technique outlined here is portable across all collating sequences (although not across all languages; for simplicity's sake, I've used the normal English 26-letter alphabet).

To make matters clearer and simpler, I've defined a couple of arrays to hold the two elements of a typical company name. A real-world implementation would probably read these from file, and would have a considerably wider range. Be that as it may, the technique is the same; we combine them at random to get a good spread of company names.

```
int GenerateData(FILE *fp, size_t MaxRecs)
{
```

```
char *Lower = "abcdefghijklmnopqrstuvwxyz";
char *Upper = "ABCDEFGHIJKLMNOPQRSTUVWXYZ";

char *Name[] =
{
  "Arrow",          "Bizarre",
  "Complete",       "Drastic",
  "Eagle",          "Fiddleyew",
  "Gilbert",        "Havago",
  "Ingenious",      "J Random Loser",
  "Kludgit & Runn", "Lightheart",
  "Mouse",          "Neurosis",
  "Objective",      "Paradigm",
  "Quality",        "Runaway",
  "Systemic",       "Terrible",
  "Underwater",     "Value",
  "Wannabee",       "YesWeWill"
};

char *Business[] =
{
  "Advertising",      "Building",
  "Computers",        "Deliveries",
  "Engineering",      "Foam Packing",
  "Garage",           "Hotels",
  "Industries",       "Janitorial",
  "Knitwear",         "Laser Printers",
  "Mills",            "Notaries",
  "Office Cleaning",  "Printers",
  "Questionnaires",   "Radio",
  "Systems",          "Talismans",
  "Upholstery",       "Van Hire",
  "Waste Disposal",   "Yo-yos"
};

size_t NumNames = sizeof Name / sizeof Name[0];
size_t NumBuses = sizeof Business / sizeof Business[0];

time_t date_time_t;
struct tm date = {0};
struct tm *pd;
```

```
size_t ThisRec;

date_time_t = time(NULL);

pd = localtime(&date_time_t);
if(pd != NULL)
{
  memcpy(&date, pd, sizeof date);
}
else
```

What we really don't want is for our test data generator to generate unintentionally bad data. When we call `localtime()`, we are not given any guarantee that we will get a valid result. We might be handed a `NULL` pointer instead. We don't want that to stop us, so we handle the possibility and set up an alternative date instead. I chose 1 January 2000 as the base date to use in an emergency. Normally, today's date would be used.

```
{
  date.tm_mday = 1;
  date.tm_mon = 0;
  date.tm_year = 100;
}

fprintf(fp, "Reference,Date,Account,Amount\n");

for(ThisRec = 0; ThisRec < MaxRecs; ThisRec++)
{
  fprintf(fp,
          "%c%c%04d/%c%c%c,",
          Upper[RandInt(26)],
          Upper[RandInt(26)],
          RandInt(10000),
          Lower[RandInt(26)],
          Lower[RandInt(26)],
          Lower[RandInt(26)]);

  fprintf(fp,
          "%d/%02d/%02d,",
          date.tm_year + 1900, /* NB: NOT a Y2K bug! */
          date.tm_mon + 1,
          date.tm_mday);

  fprintf(fp,
          "%s ",
```

```
            Name[RandInt(NumNames)]);    fprintf(fp,
            "%s Ltd,",
            Business[RandInt(NumBuses)]);
```

To get a good range of debits and credits, I've picked a random number and subtracted a smaller number from it. That way, we can be reasonably assured that some numbers will be positive, and others negative. We're unlikely to get 0.00 in a short run, however; that's the kind of exception testing we should add by hand.

```
    fprintf(fp,
            "%.2f\n",
            (RandDbl() * 5000.0) - 2250.0);

    if(RandInt(2) == 0)
    {
```

Periodically, we should change the date. I've chosen to increment the date by 1 on the toss of a coin (`RandInt(2) == 0`), but you might prefer to add N days, with N being chosen, perhaps, at random. You might even consider making the date go backwards, to test sort validation routines.

The technique for changing the date is simple enough, but is interesting because it makes use of a function that few people seem to know about—`mktime()`. This function converts a `struct tm` into a `time_t`, which sounds boringly simple. The interesting part is that, in doing the conversion, `mktime()` will *normalize* the date, and therefore we don't have to. We can simply add 1 to the day number, and trust `mktime()` to sort out situations where we've added 1 to a day that's already at the highest legal setting for the month in question.

The Y2.038K Bug

On some systems, `time_t` is represented internally as a `long int` *and* the difference between two successive `time_t` values represents one second *and* the value represents the time since some date about 30 years ago (1 January 1970 is not uncommon). (The ANSI Standard doesn't say this must be so, but it doesn't forbid it either). On such systems, including those I use most often, `time_t`'s days are, quite literally, numbered. An implementation like this, using a base date of 1/1/1970, is going to run out of `time_t` values in January 2038. If you are using such a system, you might get strange results if you produce enough records using the `GenerateData()` function. (Solution? Get a new compiler, with a more sensible `time_t` strategy. But ask before you buy!)

```
      ++date.tm_mday;
      date_time_t = mktime(&date);
      if(date_time_t != (time_t)-1)
      {
        pd = localtime(&date_time_t);
        if(pd != NULL)
        {
          memcpy(&date, pd, sizeof date);
        }
      }
    }
  }

  return 0;
}
```

As you can see, automatic test data generation tools are very simple to write, once you've decided you want to write them, despite the occasional snag (such as the date issue in this example). Let's now turn our attention to something a bit scarier!

Code Generators

If we can automate the production of at least some of our software, we can save a lot of time. Furthermore, writing a code generator is one of the most fascinating aspects of software development.

Quines

The simplest form of code generator to explain (although by no means the simplest to write) is the *quine*. A quine is a program that generates its own source code as output. I like to think of it as a self-documenting program with attitude. Here's a well-known quine, which I lifted from the Jargon File when nobody was looking:

```
char*f="char *f=%c%s%c;main(){printf(f,34,f,34,10);}%c";
main(){printf(f,34,f,34,10);}
```

I don't know who first wrote this program, I'm afraid, but I do know that he or she has a warped mind. You really have to run it to see what I mean. You'll find the code on the CD-ROM (`quine.c`). (By the way, I should warn you that it only works on machines that use ASCII.)

I introduced a line break to meet the line length requirements of this book, but the quine doesn't mind. It will quietly "mend" itself the first time you run it so, if you redirect its output to a file, you will have the true quine.

Since it doesn't give a prototype for the variadic function `printf()`, it invokes undefined behavior, but I think its sheer hack value should earn it a pardon. If you ever have an hour to spare and don't mind getting a headache, you may want to have a go at writing your own quine.

Now, I showed you the quine for a reason, so I'd better explain why before I forget. It's all to do with appropriateness. When should we write code generators?

When Is Code Generation Appropriate?

Despite its obvious cleverness, the quine has a fairly easy time of it. It knows exactly what output is required; it doesn't have to rely on any input to tell it what to do. In the real world, things aren't as simple. We want to generate *useful* code. If the output were the same all the time, we wouldn't need a code generator; it would nearly always be quicker simply to write the program we need.

Code generators are rarely used to write complete programs. The problem they solve is one of repetitiveness, either within the program itself or across a large collection of programs. Let me give you an example. A few years ago, I was working on a large cross-platform project which we were developing for use on Microsoft Windows (version 3.1, if you'll cast your minds back) and on MVS, a mainframe operating system. The program could be considered to be split into two modules—a database access module and a calculations module. We'd written and debugged the calculations code (but not the database module) on the PC, but it had to be *tested* on the mainframe, where debugging facilities were somewhat primitive. So, whenever testing revealed a bug, we had a problem.

The solution is simple enough to state, but was rather harder to implement. If we could somehow intercept the data after it had been through the database access module, and ship it down to the PC, we could feed it into the PC version of the calculations module, and debug it there.

The answer? A code generator. I wrote code to read the module's header files (where, to my disgust, practically all of the variables were defined) and produce source code that could store the name and value of every single variable of interest. That was the hard bit. The easy bit was to write routines to dump that information to a file (in text format, of course, because the two platforms did not use the same byte order), and to read the information from the file after it had been shipped to the PC. Naturally, whenever a new variable had to be introduced, we simply ran the code generator again to pick that variable up and include it in the output code, which was then recompiled and plugged back into the process.

On a more recent but very similar project, a colleague of mine wrote a code generator that read COBOL copybooks and turned them into C header files. Whenever the mainframe people fiddled with their copybooks, we reran the code generator, so that the C bits of the program were using the same data definitions as the COBOL bits.

In both those cases (and several more), we were saved a lot of time and effort by automating our programming. Moreover, in both those cases, the code generator had to read source code so that it could do its job. This is known as *parsing*, and we had a close look at parsing already in Chapter 19, "Expression Parsing and Evaluation," so I promise you I won't go into too much detail on parsing theory.

Since we have to write a parser as part of our code generation application, we might as well save ourselves further parsing work in the future if we can. So let's write a parser for a program that will produce a parsing program. I hope that didn't sound too confusing! Allow me to explain.

When I sit down to write a program, my first step is completely automatic. My fingers know what to do without my telling them:

```
#include <stdio.h>

int main(void)
{
  return 0;
}
```

Well, it may not be much, but it's a good start, and it means I'm ready to rock. Unfortunately, my next step is usually to realize that I am going to need to capture some information on the command line. So a quick edit is in order, to add `int argc` and `char *argv[]` (or `char **argv`) to the `main()` declaration. And then my heart sinks into my boots, because I know—I just *know*—that I have a tedious task ahead of me: command-line argument parsing. I'm going to have to check that there are enough arguments. I may need to check that there aren't too many, as well. Do the arguments validly represent the kind of data I was expecting? What about switches? It's not difficult work, but it's hardly exciting, is it?

It would be wonderful if I could just run a code generator to produce some of that code for me. The UNIX people among you will, at this point, be rolling their eyes and yelling, "`getopt()`, you fool! `getopt()`!", to which I have just three things to say. First, `getopt()` is not an ANSI C function, and therefore it is not guaranteed to be available on all platforms. The four C compilers I use most often at home are `gcc` (Linux), `gcc` (DJGPP), Microsoft Visual C++ (in C mode), and Borland C++ (likewise). The last-named two, both mainstream compilers in wide use, don't support `getopt()` as far as I can tell (after wide-ranging and exhaustive research, consisting primarily of a quick dip into the help files). Second, `getopt()` doesn't take enough work out of the task; just using it is quite an intensive process in itself. And third, the manpage (UNIX documentation) for `getopt()` on my Linux system says in the Bugs entry, "This manpage is confusing." That just about sums it up.

No, what I really want is a program that will write the command line bits of my program for me, and give me easy access to everything the user has specified. I'd like to be able to write something like this:

```
int ApplicationMain(char *infile, char *outfile, int optflag)
{
  /* ... */
}
```

and have the code generator worry about the rest. Of course, the arguments to `ApplicationMain()` will vary from program to program. That's awkward. Can a code generator do that?

Well, yes it can. But, to do that, we need to have a way of telling it exactly what to do for each program, and that way has to be simpler (for the user of the code generator) than writing the code ourselves. Effectively, we need to write a new language. That's not quite as scary as it sounds. To give you a comfortable example of what I mean, the `printf()` format string constitutes a language; but we're so accustomed to using that language that we don't often stop to think that it *is* a language.

Designing Data Input Grammar and Syntax

Our code generator will need input if it is to be anything more than a curiosity piece. Therefore, we need to parse an input stream of some kind. How exactly we do this will depend heavily on the nature of the application, and especially on whether we have control over the input specification. If we are writing, say, a Pascal-to-C conversion utility, we have no such control; we have to be able to parse Pascal in order to meet the specification. If, however, we are able to define the input grammar ourselves, we can make life relatively easy.

Since we're going to write a command-line parser generator, we can choose our own syntax for it—we are not constrained by the syntax of an existing language.

What do we want to tell our code generator? Let's keep it simple, and settle for a list of variables of type `long`, `double`, or `char *`. That shouldn't be too hard to manage. Also, since switches are so useful, let's add the facility to handle simple (on/off) switches.

Here's a sample grammar in rough-and-ready Backus-Naur Form:

```
infile:
  specifier
  infile specifier

specifier: one of
  switchspecifier
  doublespecifier
  longspecifier
  stringspecifier

switchspecifier:
  -identifier

doublespecifier:
  identifier D

longspecifier:
  identifier L

stringspecifier:
  identifier S length

identifier:
  letter
  identifiertail letter

identifiertail:
  letterorunderscore identifiertail
  digit identifiertail
  letterorunderscore
  digit

letterorunderscore:
  letter
  _

letter: one of
  A B C D E F G H I J K L M N O P Q R S T U V W X Y Z
  a b c d e f g h i j k l m n o p q r s t u v w x y z
```

```
digit: one of
  0 1 2 3 4 5 6 7 8 9

length:
  1 to 255
```

What that means is that the code generator's parsing engine should be able to accept four different kinds of specifiers from the input stream:

- `-foo` means that `foo` is an optional switch. If specified by the end user, it should be set to 1, but otherwise it should be left at 0. This support for switches is somewhat limited but, after all, we're trying to keep things simple for now.
- `bar L` means that `bar` is a `long int`, and is mandatory. (Only switches are not mandatory.)
- `baz D` means that `baz` is a `double`.
- `quux S 35` means that `quux` is a string that may not exceed 35 bytes in length (not including the null terminator).

Any number of specifiers may be supplied, although you should bear in mind that a conforming implementation need not support function parameter lists with more than 127 parameters. But that should be plenty.

If we gave the code generator these example inputs, we would like it to produce code that reads and understands `argv`, passing `argv`'s information on to us in the form of a function call:

```
int ApplicationMain(int foo, long bar, double baz, char *quux)
```

We are going to write a program that must parse our input, so that it can produce code that can parse input and hand us the results of the parsing so that we can use that input in our program. Code generators often involve us in this kind of twisted thinking, I'm afraid, but it's worth it in the long run for the sheer power and flexibility they can provide.

A Simple Parser

To parse our grammar fully would require a considerable amount of validation, so we're going to focus on the higher-level aspects of the grammar. Specifically, we are not going to validate any of the identifiers we are given. We will simply read and accept them in good faith. Since they will eventually be submitted to a C compiler, we can assume that they will be validated at that point. We will not be distinguishing between `FileName` (which is a legal identifier in C) and `Fil$name` (which isn't).

To implement our parser, we will use a Finite State Machine (or FSM). Our state machine is very simple, having just four states—Get Variable, Get Type, Get Length, and Stop, as shown in Listing 20.6.

LISTING 20.6 A Simple Parsing Routine

```
#include <stdio.h>
#include <stdlib.h>
#include <string.h>
#include <assert.h>

#include "dllist.h"
```

Wait a minute—`"dllist.h"`? Yes, we're going to reuse some of the code we developed earlier in the book. We need to store our variables somehow. The order of the variables is significant, and we are likely to want to walk the list of variables several times, making a double-linked list seem appropriate. So we may as well dig out and use the library we developed in Chapter 11, "Simple Abstract Data Structures."

```
#define INDENT_2  "  "
#define INDENT_4  "    "

#define MAX_IDENT_LEN 32
#define MAX_STR_LEN   255

#define LINES_PER_SCREEN 23

#define BOOL   'B'
#define DOUBLE 'D'
#define LONG   'L'
#define STRING 'S'

/* Arguments of type 'B' are switches,
 * which are either On or Off, so they
 * don't need a data type or a length.
 */
#define NON_SWITCH_TYPES "DLS"


#define GET_VARIABLE   'V'
#define GET_TYPE       'T'
```

```
#define GET_LEN        'L'
#define STOP           'S'

#define SWITCH_CHAR    '-'
```

The indent macros are used by the code generator later on.

`MAX_IDENT_LEN` and `MAX_STR_LEN` limit the size of our identifier names and our string arguments, respectively. The limits are arbitrary; they could easily be adjusted if you felt the need.

`LINES_PER_SCREEN` is used by the `Help()` generator. `BOOL` and its fellows represent the type indicators in our grammar, `B`, `D`, `L`, and `S`. `BOOL` types (optional switches, which may be either on or off) are awkward, because they aren't like the other three types. I decided to design the grammar in this way simply to show that awkward grammars may be handled if you're careful. You may find it diverting to "fix" the grammar and edit the parser accordingly (which will result in a slightly simpler parser and, perversely, an even more useful program).

Now we come to storage. The parser must put the information it gains into some kind of container. A simple structure is all that is required.

```
typedef struct ARGUMENT
{
  char Name[MAX_IDENT_LEN];
  int Type;
  size_t Len; /* for strings */
} ARGUMENT;

int ParseInput(DLLIST **ArgList,
               FILE *InStream,
               FILE *LogStream)
{
  int Status = EXIT_SUCCESS;

  ARGUMENT Arg = {0};

  char InBuff[256];
  char *VarName;
  char *VarType;
  char *VarLen;
  char *EndPtr;

  const char Delims[] = " ,\t\n";
```

```
char *Data;
char *NextToken;
int HaveData = 0;
int State = GET_VARIABLE;
```

This is where we initialize our state machine. The first state is `GET_VARIABLE`. While we're at it, we initialize the `HaveData` variable to 0 because, at present, we haven't read any data from the input stream.

```
while(EXIT_SUCCESS == Status &&
      State != STOP)
{
  fprintf(LogStream,
          "Status report: Data? %s\n",
          HaveData ? "Yes" : "No");
```

As an aid to debugging, I dumped a few strings into a logfile, so that I could follow the progress of the state machine easily and quickly. I've removed them from this listing (except the one we've just seen), but they are still in the source on the CD-ROM (`genargs.c`).

If we don't have any data at this point (for example, on the first time into the loop), we ought to go and get some. To do this we use `fgets()`. This function is robust; we are guaranteed that it will not overflow our input buffer. What it might do (and usually does, the exception being when the available data exceeds the space to store it) is leave a `'\n'` on the end of the output but, in this case, we don't mind because we can simply include `'\n'` in our string of tokenization delimiters.

```
    if(!HaveData)
    {
      Data = fgets(InBuff, sizeof InBuff, InStream);
      if(Data != NULL)
      {
        fprintf(LogStream,
                "Status report: Got data %s\n",
                InBuff);
        HaveData = 1;
        NextToken = InBuff;
      }
      else
      {
```

If we found some data, all is well. If we didn't, we have to consider our grammar. The only place in which we can legitimately run out of data is between specifiers; that is, just at the place where we would otherwise expect a variable identifier. Therefore, if we are in any other state, we have a syntax error, so we should stop the state machine.

```
        if(State != GET_VARIABLE)
        {
          Status = EXIT_FAILURE;
        }
        State = STOP;
      }
    }
```

Here is the state engine itself. Remember, the first state we'll encounter under normal circumstances is `GET_VARIABLE`. If it's `STOP`, which it might be if there were no data, the state engine stops immediately. Giving the engine an empty input data stream such as a zero length file is worth trying, actually, because it will result in a program shell that resembles an empty snail shell in many ways, the most significant of which is that it has no snails in it. Such experimentation indicates very clearly and graphically which parts of the code generator rely on the input you provide. Normally, however, our opening state is `GET_VARIABLE`.

```
    switch(State)
    {
      case STOP:
        break;

      case GET_VARIABLE:
        VarName = strtok(NextToken, Delims);
        NextToken = NULL;
```

When we want to get a token from the data buffer, we need to know, for `strtok()`'s benefit, whether we have just replenished the buffer. Hence, the use of `NextToken` here—its job is to point to the new data buffer, or to nowhere, depending on which is currently most appropriate. `NextToken` is pointed at the data buffer again near the top of the loop, whenever new data is received.

If the tokenization fails, we set `HaveData` to 0, thus formally registering a complaint with the top of the loop, which will then get some more data for us.

```
        if(VarName == NULL)
        {
          HaveData = 0;
        }
```

```
        else
        {
          if(VarName[0] == SWITCH_CHAR)
          {
            if(strlen(VarName + 1) > MAX_IDENT_LEN)
            {
              Status = EXIT_FAILURE;
              State = STOP;
            }
            else
            {
              strcpy(Arg.Name, VarName + 1);
              Arg.Type = BOOL;
              Arg.Len = 0;
```

This is where the syntax is a little awkward. We have to check separately for switch variables. If we find one, we need to check that its name isn't too long, and then add it to the double-linked list of variables, using `DLAppend()`.

When we find a switch variable, there is no change of state because the whole variable is dealt with in one token.

```
              if(DL_SUCCESS != DLAppend(ArgList,
                                        0,
                                        &Arg,
                                        sizeof Arg))
              {
                Status = EXIT_FAILURE;
                State = STOP;
              }
            }
          }
          else
          {
            if(strlen(VarName) > MAX_IDENT_LEN)
            {
              Status = EXIT_FAILURE;
              State = STOP;
            }
            else
            {
```

When the variable is not a switch, we need to do two things. First, we need to safeguard our copy of the variable name, and second, we need to change the state of the machine from `GET_VARIABLE` to `GET_TYPE`.

The `strcpy()` into the argument structure is required, by the way. In the event of the type specifier being on a separate line of input, the variable name will be overwritten by `fgets()`, so we should grab it while we can.

```
              strcpy(Arg.Name, VarName);
              State = GET_TYPE;
            }
          }
        }
        break;

      case GET_TYPE:
        VarType = strtok(NextToken, Delims);
        NextToken = NULL;
        if(VarType == NULL)
        {
          HaveData = 0;
        }
        else
        {
```

Having obtained our type using `strtok()`, we can validate it. It must be a string containing just one non-null character, which must be one of `"D"`, `"S"`, or `"L"`: If it is none of these, then it is wrong, and we should stop processing.

```
          if(VarType[1] != '\0' ||
             strchr(NON_SWITCH_TYPES, VarType[0]) == NULL)
          {
            State = STOP;
            Status = EXIT_FAILURE;
          }
          else
          {
```

The type has passed our validation, so we can carry on. We save the type in our structure, and set the variable's length to zero. If the variable is of string type, we set the state to `GET_LEN`, so that this default length can be overwritten next time around the loop. Otherwise, we can add the variable to the list immediately; then we are ready for the next variable, so we set the type to `GET_VARIABLE`.

```
          Arg.Type = VarType[0];
          Arg.Len = 0;
          if(VarType[0] == STRING)
          {
            State = GET_LEN;
          }
          else
          {
            if(DL_SUCCESS != DLAppend(ArgList,
                                      0,
                                      &Arg,
                                      sizeof Arg))
            {
              Status = EXIT_FAILURE;
              State = STOP;
            }
            else
            {
              State = GET_VARIABLE;
            }
          }
        }
      }
      break;
    case GET_LEN:
      VarLen = strtok(NextToken, Delims);
      NextToken = NULL;

      if(VarLen == NULL)
      {
        HaveData = 0;
      }
      else
      {
        Arg.Len = (size_t)strtoul(VarLen, &EndPtr, 10);
        if(EndPtr == VarLen ||
           Arg.Len == 0     ||
           Arg.Len > MAX_STR_LEN)
        {
          State = STOP;
          Status = EXIT_FAILURE;
        }
        else
```

We convert the length to numeric format, and check it against a few basic constraints (does the string represent a number between 1 and MAX_STR_LEN?). If all is well, we can add the string to the list of variables immediately using DLAppend(), and go hunting for the next variable by setting the state to GET_VARIABLE.

```
          {
            if(DL_SUCCESS != DLAppend(ArgList,
                                      0,
                                      &Arg,
                                      sizeof Arg))
            {
              Status = EXIT_FAILURE;
              State = STOP;
            }
            else
            {
              State = GET_VARIABLE;
            }
          }
        }
        break;
      default:
        /* D */
```

If we reach the default, we're in trouble because our states are controlled internally; an unknown state therefore represents a broken program.

```
        assert(0); /* This program is broken */
        State = STOP;
        State = EXIT_FAILURE;
        break;
    }
  }

  return Status;
}
```

When this function ends, the double-linked list will contain a number of variable descriptors. A more complex grammar might result in a longer function. It might even result in more detailed variable descriptors. But it will still produce a list. We will use this list in the code generator.

Sample Code Generator Output

If we had an example of the kind of file we were trying to produce, we could get a clear sight of our objective. On this occasion, we can see an exact example because I was able to take a quick trip into the future and grab the output from the program we're going to write while the time police weren't looking. You, however, won't usually be in that most fortunate position. Fear not, because the solution is simple enough. Just knock up an example in a text editor. Then make a few copies of it, and change the copies slightly, in appropriate ways. The ways in which you change it represent the value of the code generator you are trying to write; it will be making those changes instead of you, in due course.

What we're about to see is an output file. It's easy to forget that because it looks just like source code, but it was produced by a C program. Let's look at this output, then, and identify certain features that are of general importance to code generation. At this stage, we're not too concerned with what the output code does.

The first thing to notice in Listing 20.7 is that the code contains a comment indicating its origin. That's important, as we'll see in a short while. It's easy to forget to add comments to generated code and, on the whole, they aren't quite as important as in normal code, but if there is only one comment in your generated source, let it be one that says "this is generated source."

LISTING 20.7 Generated Source Code Output

```
/* argproc.c */
/* automatically generated file. Do not
 * modify this file by hand. Change
 * genargs.c and regenerate the file
 * instead.
 */
#include <stdio.h>
#include <stdlib.h>
#include <string.h>

#define SWITCH_CHAR '-'

typedef struct ARG
{
  int    internal;
  char   InFile[256];
  char   OutFile[256];
  char   LogFile[256];
```

LISTING 20.7 continued

```
  char   HelpFile[256];
} ARG;
```

This particular run was for a program expecting two input filenames, two output filenames, and an optional switch. The exact contents of the ARG structure (which, if you remember, is built automatically) will vary depending upon the instructions given to the generator.

Automatic creation of abstract data types is a typical use of code generators. Normally, those abstract data types are intended for use by the programmer. In this particular case, ARG variables are only meant for use by the generated code itself.

```
int GetArgs(int argc, char **argv, ARG *argp)
{
  int ThisArg;
  int CompArg;

  if(argc <= 4)
  {
    return -1;
  }
  if(argc > 6)
  {
    return -2;
  }
```

The hard-coded values 4 and 6 are specific to this application. In general, "magic numbers" of this kind constitute bad programming practice because they make the program harder to change. Since, however, they should only change if the argument syntax for the program changes, and since that would entail regenerating the code (and thus updating the numbers automatically), the reasons why magic numbers are bad don't really apply. Still, it would be relatively simple to sort out this difficulty if we had a specific reason to be concerned about it.

```
  for(ThisArg = 1, CompArg = 0; ThisArg < argc; ThisArg++)
  {
    if(argv[ThisArg][0] == SWITCH_CHAR)
    {
      if(strcmp("-internal", argv[ThisArg]) == 0)
      {
        argp->internal = 1;
      }
      else
      {
```

```
        printf("Unknown switch %s\n", argv[ThisArg]);
        return ThisArg;
      }
    }
    else
    {
```

By this point in the code, we can clearly see that the code's layout is neat and readable. It could be argued that, since we're never going to edit this code, it doesn't matter whether it's readable. (It's the same argument as I gave for magic numbers earlier.) That's a fair point, but keeping the code legible has benefits when you are trying to debug the code generator itself.

```
      switch(CompArg)
      {
        case 0:
        {
            if(strlen(argv[ThisArg]) > 255)
            {
              return ThisArg;
            }
            strcpy(argp->InFile, argv[ThisArg]);
            break;
        }
        case 1:
        {
            if(strlen(argv[ThisArg]) > 255)
            {
              return ThisArg;
            }
            strcpy(argp->OutFile, argv[ThisArg]);
            break;

        case 2:
        {
            if(strlen(argv[ThisArg]) > 255)
            {
              return ThisArg;
            }
            strcpy(argp->LogFile, argv[ThisArg]);
            break;
        }
        case 3:
        {
```

```
                if(strlen(argv[ThisArg]) > 255)
                {
                  return ThisArg;
                }
                strcpy(argp->HelpFile, argv[ThisArg]);
                break;
            }
          }

          ++CompArg;
        }
      }
      return 0;
    }
```

The switch block is interesting. Take a closer look at those case statements. Each declares a local scope using { and }, even though these are not required by the syntax of case. Why? It could just be a style issue; many programmers enclose their case blocks in braces because it looks good, and some do it so that they can use their programming editor's brace-matching ability to make it easier to find their way around switches that have large case blocks. In the present case (if you'll forgive the pun), there's a good, solid, and completely invisible reason for it.

This example of the output code is for an application that needs only one switch and a few strings as arguments. Other applications might require long or double arguments. In such circumstances, the output code would need to provide calls to conversion functions (strtol and strtod) that require the address of a char * variable. We could just declare one at function scope, but that would mean a warning on some compilers, in outputs (such as this one) where the variable is not used. Instead, we use a local scope, and declare the char * variable inside that local scope if it's needed. It would have been possible to omit the local scope from those case blocks that don't need it, but local scopes, if done correctly, tend not to produce diagnostics even if they are superfluous, so removing them would have unnecessarily complicated the code generator. How far you are prepared to put up with unnecessary code in your output is largely determined by how long and difficult you want the code generator development process to be.

```
int ApplicationMain(int internal,
                    char * InFile,
                    char * OutFile,
                    char * LogFile,
                    char * HelpFile);
```

```
void Help(void);

int main(int argc, char **argv)
{
  int Status;
  int ArgResult;
  ARG ArgList = {0};

  ArgResult = GetArgs(argc, argv, &ArgList);
  if(ArgResult != 0)
  {
    Help();
    Status = EXIT_FAILURE;
  }
  else
  {
    /* Calling your program... */
    Status = (ApplicationMain(ArgList.internal,
                              ArgList.InFile,
                              ArgList.OutFile,
                              ArgList.LogFile,
                              ArgList.HelpFile) == 0) ?
     EXIT_SUCCESS :
     EXIT_FAILURE;
  }

  return Status;
}
```

And now we can see how it all fits together. The `main()` function calls `GetArgs()`, which populates the `ArgList` structure, and then calls `ApplicationMain()`, passing each individual item in that structure as a separate argument. It's clear that the prototype of `ApplicationMain()` will vary from one application to another because the members of the `ArgList` structure will be different each time. It's equally clear that the code generator can work out that prototype for itself, and write that prototype, on a program-by-program basis, to its output file (the generated C program).

If `GetArgs()` returns a non-zero value, the program calls the `Help()` function and quits the program. The code generator produces the `Help()` function too, but I won't show it here. It comprises a large number of `printf()` calls, interspersed with an occasional `fgets()` to make the help a bit easier to read. We could have made this part of the process a lot simpler. We will, after all, be providing the code generator with a text file containing the text that we want it to provide in `Help()`, so why could we not have simply arranged matters so that the help file itself was available at our own program's runtime? The problem with that solution is that it assumes that the help file will be available at runtime. What if it isn't? By embedding the file into the generated code, we ensure that the text is available when we need it most.

Maintaining Control

If you need to change the output of a code generator, always change the generator, never the output code itself. If you change the output code instead, you will lose your changes the next time you run the generator. That's why it's so important for the code generator to "sign" the file, indicating its origins and saying "do not modify" in clear, authoritative tones. I once included a comment that I thought was much more polite; something like "please don't change this code unless you really, really have to; it's better to change the generator if you have time." Naturally, various people decided that they really, really had to change the code itself and, equally naturally, this caused me some major headaches later on. Be clear, be authoritative. Automatically generated code should be changed only by changing the generator, not by fiddling with the output code.

Unfortunately, whenever I am dogmatic about something, an exception rears its ugly head and proves me wrong. *In the particular case of this code generator and others that produce template listings*, it is acceptable to modify the source code in one particular way *if and only if* the `-internal` switch is used. This switch will build a skeleton `ApplicationMain()` function in the generated code, the idea being to provide a template that you can fill out yourself. In this particular case, the whole point of the switch is so that you can use the generator for simple, one-off programs which reside entirely in one translation unit. You don't really have much choice but to edit the generated code—otherwise, where will you put your functionality? If you don't specify the `-internal` switch, however, the skeleton function is not generated; it is assumed that you will provide that function in some other translation unit.

A Simple Code Generator

A C program can, at a high level, be divided into three parts: preprocessor directives, type definitions, and functions. We have two functions we want to generate, so the code generator will consist of four primary routines—one for preprocessor directives, one for types, and two for functions.

The `WriteHeaders()` function is responsible for preprocessor directives. Its first task, though, is to label the output code with its (the output's) filename, together with a warning that it is automatically generated. To do this, naturally, it uses comment syntax.

After that, it's a simple matter of writing a few `#include` statements and a `#define`. The precise inclusions required will vary from one generator to the next. It's even possible that you won't want to use any `#includes` at all, such as when you are generating a header file.

You may find it helpful to print out the file `argproc.c` from the CD-ROM, and keep it close at hand while studying the code in Listing 20.8, which generates `argproc.c`.

LISTING 20.8 Header Generation Routine

```
int WriteHeaders(FILE *OutStream, char *OutFile)
{
  fprintf(OutStream, "/* %s */\n", OutFile);
  fprintf(OutStream,
          "/* automatically generated file. Do not\n");
  fprintf(OutStream,
          " * modify this file by hand. Change\n");
  fprintf(OutStream,
          " * genargs.c and regenerate the file\n");
  fprintf(OutStream,
          " * instead.\n");
  fprintf(OutStream,
          " */\n");

  fprintf(OutStream, "#include <stdio.h>\n");
  fprintf(OutStream, "#include <stdlib.h>\n");
  fprintf(OutStream, "#include <string.h>\n\n");

  fprintf(OutStream,
          "#define SWITCH_CHAR '%c'\n\n",
          SWITCH_CHAR);

  return EXIT_SUCCESS;
}
```

The preprocessor directives were easy—just one `fprintf()` after another. The next stage is to generate our `typedef` code. Because we have each element of the structure in our double-linked list, it's relatively simple to create the `ARG` type; it's an ordinary loop through the list.

At two points we need to take special care; both have to do with the `STRING` case. First, we need to remember to allocate a length one greater than the value stored for us by the parser, to allow for the null terminating character. Second, this value is a `size_t`; we know it is an unsigned integer type but we don't know exactly what kind it is, so we do need to cast it before sending it to `fprintf()`.

Mainframe users please note: Depending on how clueful your terminal emulation software is, you may wish to substitute `"char  %s[%u];\n"` with `"char  %s??(%u??);\n"`.

```
int WriteTypedef(FILE *OutStream, DLLIST *ArgList)
{
  ARGUMENT *Arg;
  fprintf(OutStream, "typedef struct ARG\n{\n");

  while(ArgList)
  {
    Arg = DLGetData(ArgList, NULL, NULL);

    fprintf(OutStream, "  ");

    switch(Arg->Type)
    {
      case BOOL:
        fprintf(OutStream, "int    %s;\n", Arg->Name);
        break;
      case LONG:
        fprintf(OutStream, "long   %s;\n", Arg->Name);
        break;
      case DOUBLE:
        fprintf(OutStream, "double %s;\n", Arg->Name);
        break;
      case STRING:
        fprintf(OutStream, "char   %s[%u];\n",
               Arg->Name,
               (unsigned)(Arg->Len + 1));
        break;

    }

    ArgList = DLGetNext(ArgList);
  }

  fprintf(OutStream, "} ARG;\n\n");

  return EXIT_SUCCESS;
}
```

Now we need to write the code that will generate the `GetArgs()` function. This is where we have to pay particular attention to detail, but there's nothing too difficult here. Just before we launch into it, allow me to point out that `CountBools()` is simply a helper function that counts the number of optional command-line arguments in the list of variables passed in via the `ArgList` parameter. I haven't shown the code for `CountBools()` here, but it's on the CD-ROM, in `genargs.c`.

```
int WriteFunction(FILE *OutStream, DLLIST *ArgList)
{
  DLLIST *Start;
  ARGUMENT *Arg;
  int CompArgs;
  int OptArgs;
  int ThisArg;
  int ThisCompArg;

  char *Indent = INDENT_2;

  OptArgs = CountBools(ArgList);
  CompArgs = DLCount(ArgList) - OptArgs;

  Start = DLGetFirst(ArgList);
```

Our first task is to generate the function definition. It will be passed `argc` and `argv` from `main()`, together with a pointer to an `ARG` structure. Since we have already calculated that there are `CompArgs` compulsory arguments, and since we know that there are `OptArgs` optional arguments, it's quite simple to generate code to detect whether there are sufficient arguments, and also whether there are too many. By dealing with these cases first, we leave ourselves free to concentrate on the more involved task of checking the arguments themselves.

```
  fprintf(OutStream,
          "int GetArgs(int argc,"
          " char **argv, ARG *argp)\n");
  fprintf(OutStream, "{\n");  fprintf(OutStream, "  int ThisArg;\n");
  fprintf(OutStream, "  int CompArg;\n");

  fprintf(OutStream, "\n");
  fprintf(OutStream, "  if(argc <= %d)\n", CompArgs);
  fprintf(OutStream, "  {\n");
  fprintf(OutStream, "    return -1;\n");
  fprintf(OutStream, "  }\n");
```

```
fprintf(OutStream, "  if(argc > %d)\n", CompArgs +
                                        OptArgs + 1);
fprintf(OutStream, "  {\n");
fprintf(OutStream, "    return -2;\n");
fprintf(OutStream, "  }\n");

fprintf(OutStream, "  for(ThisArg = 1, CompArg = 0;"
       " ThisArg < argc; ThisArg++)\n");
fprintf(OutStream, "  {\n");
```

Optional arguments need special handling, but *only* if there are any optional arguments specified in the grammar; hence the test for `OptArgs > 0`. The following code will embed checking for each optional argument into the generated code, one optional argument after the other.

```
if(OptArgs > 0)
{
  fprintf(OutStream, "    if(argv[ThisArg][0] == "
                     "SWITCH_CHAR)\n");
  fprintf(OutStream, "    {\n      ");

  do
  {
    Arg = DLGetData(ArgList, NULL, NULL);
    if(Arg->Type == BOOL)
    {
      fprintf(OutStream,
              "if(strcmp(\"%c%s\","
              " argv[ThisArg]) == 0)\n",
              SWITCH_CHAR,
              Arg->Name);

      fprintf(OutStream, "      {\n");

      fprintf(OutStream,
              "         argp->%s = 1;\n",
              Arg->Name);

      fprintf(OutStream, "      }\n");
      fprintf(OutStream, "      else ");
    }

    ArgList = DLGetNext(ArgList);
  } while(ArgList != NULL);
```

We know we want to handle unrecognized arguments with an `else`, so it makes sense to use `if ... / else if ... / else if ... / else` syntax, as this construct lends itself easily to iteration. Even if we didn't have a default condition, this would probably be the wisest course, even if it meant us ending with an empty `else {}`.

```
    fprintf(OutStream, "\n");
    fprintf(OutStream, "      {\n");

    fprintf(OutStream,
            "        printf(\"Unknown switch "
            "%%s\\n\", argv[ThisArg]);\n");

    fprintf(OutStream, "        return ThisArg;\n");
    fprintf(OutStream, "      }\n");

    ArgList = Start;

    fprintf(OutStream, "    }\n");
    fprintf(OutStream, "    else\n");
    fprintf(OutStream, "    {\n");

    Indent = INDENT_4;
  }
```

At the top of the generated `GetArgs()` function, we pointed the `Indent` pointer at a string literal containing two spaces. If there are no optional arguments, it will still be pointing there. If there are optional arguments, it's just been redirected to a string literal containing four spaces, to preserve indenting. It may seem like a minor point of style, but it does make things so much clearer if you can read the generated code easily.

Having dealt with the optional arguments, now we can look at the compulsory arguments. Since we know in which order they appear, we can use a `switch` to jump right to the code to handle any one of them.

```
  fprintf(OutStream, "%s  switch(CompArg)\n", Indent);
  fprintf(OutStream, "%s  {\n", Indent);

  for(ThisArg = 0, ThisCompArg = 0;
      ThisCompArg < CompArgs;
      ThisArg++)
  {
    Arg = DLGetData(ArgList, NULL, NULL);
```

```
if(Arg->Type != BOOL)
{
  fprintf(OutStream,
          "%s    case %d:\n",
          Indent,
          ThisCompArg);

  fprintf(OutStream,
          "%s    {\n",
          Indent);
```

We discussed this seemingly spurious opening brace earlier in the chapter. If we have a `long` or a `double` argument, we need a new variable, `char *EndPtr`, for use by `strtol` or `strtod`. Why not just use `atol()` and `atof()`, which don't need this extra pointer? Because they can't tell the difference between 0 (or 0.0) and random non-numeric text, that's why. We'd like to return an error if the argument cannot be correctly converted.

```
  switch(Arg->Type)
  {
    case LONG:
      fprintf(OutStream,
              "%s        char *EndPtr;\n",
              Indent);

      fprintf(OutStream,
              "%s        argp->%s = "
              "strtol(argv[ThisArg]"
              ", &EndPtr, 10);\n",
              Indent,
              Arg->Name);

      fprintf(OutStream,
              "%s        if(EndPtr =="
              " argv[ThisArg])\n",
              Indent);

      fprintf(OutStream,
              "%s        {\n",
              Indent);

      fprintf(OutStream,
              "%s          return ThisArg;\n",
              Indent);
```

```
        fprintf(OutStream,
                "%s        }\n",
                Indent);
```

Most of the time, we can't get away with only generating the minimum code that will do the job. We have to create the code that will do the job properly, and that involves generating error-checking code too.

```
        break;
      case DOUBLE:
        fprintf(OutStream,
                "%s        char *EndPtr;\n",
                Indent);

        fprintf(OutStream,
                "%s        argp->%s = strtod"
                "(argv[ThisArg], &EndPtr);\n",
                Indent,
                Arg->Name);

        fprintf(OutStream,
                "%s        if(EndPtr "
                "== argv[ThisArg])\n",
               Indent);

        fprintf(OutStream,
                "%s        {\n",
                Indent);

        fprintf(OutStream,
                "%s          return ThisArg;\n",
                Indent);

        fprintf(OutStream,
                "%s        }\n",
                Indent);
        break;
      case STRING:
```

Our string type presents no such conversion problems. It does, however, introduce one further problem—that of storage. We have to ensure that the string will fit into the ARG structure to which we've been passed a pointer. Fortunately, we've already got the maximum length of the string available to us, so we can simply call `strlen()` to do the checking for us, and compare the return value against the length we have stored. If all is well, we can use `strcpy()` to copy the user's data into our structure.

```
        fprintf(OutStream,
                "%s        if(strlen(argv"
                "[ThisArg]) > %d)\n",
                Indent,
                Arg->Len);
        fprintf(OutStream,
                "%s        {\n",
                Indent);
        fprintf(OutStream,
                "%s          return ThisArg;\n",
                Indent);

        fprintf(OutStream,
                "%s        }\n",
                Indent);

        fprintf(OutStream,
                "%s        strcpy(argp->%s, "
                "argv[ThisArg]);\n",
                Indent,
                Arg->Name);
        break;
      default:
        /* Unsupported type, already validated. */
        assert(0);
        break;
    }
    fprintf(OutStream,
            "%s        break;\n",
            Indent);

    fprintf(OutStream,
            "%s    }\n",
            Indent);

    ++ThisCompArg;
  }

  ArgList = DLGetNext(ArgList);
```

```
  }

  fprintf(OutStream, "%s  }\n", Indent);
  fprintf(OutStream, "\n");
  fprintf(OutStream, "%s  ++CompArg;\n", Indent);
```

Whether we have optional arguments or not, we are now approaching the point of commonality, so we can end the `if()` statement with a closing brace and forget about `Indent` from now on.

```
  if(OptArgs > 0)
  {
    fprintf(OutStream, "    }\n");
  }

  fprintf(OutStream, "  }\n");

  fprintf(OutStream, "  return 0;\n");
  fprintf(OutStream, "}\n\n");

  return EXIT_SUCCESS;
}
```

Up until now, all our `fprintf()` statements have been relatively simple. Now it starts to get a bit more involved, mainly because we will be printing `printf()` statements, which means we are going to run into the problem of *escape characters*.

Consider an expression as simple as this: `printf("Hi\n");`—if we want to print that expression on the screen or other standard output device, we have to escape three of the characters in the string, like this:

```
  printf("printf(\"Hi\\n\");\n");
```

This looks rather odd, but it's necessary. This is something to watch out for whenever you are writing programs that write programs.

```
int WriteMain(FILE *OutStream,
              FILE *HelpStream,
              DLLIST *ArgList,
              int InternalApp)
{
  DLLIST *Arg;
  ARGUMENT *Data;
```

The easiest way to generate `main()` is to define an array of pointers to the text we want to print. We can then simply iterate through those pointers, printing as we go. This works for almost the whole function. There are, however, four places in which it isn't good enough. Three of these are to do with `ApplicationMain()`; the prototype, the call, and (if `-internal` is specified) the function body. The fourth is the generation of the `Help()` function. To enable us to use the simple technique for most of the output, and customized code for the exceptions, we use a placeholder in some of the string literals in the pointer array. In this case, I've chosen `%` for the place where the prototype should go, `^` for the call, `!` for the `Help()` function, and `&` for the function body (if appropriate). Thus, a switch on `MainText[i][0]` will enable us to handle these special cases, with the default being a simple call to `fprintf()`.

```
char *MainText[] =
{
  "",
  "%", /* write prototype for ApplicationMain() */
  "",
  "void Help(void);",
  "",
  "int main(int argc, char **argv)",
  "{",
  "  int Status;",
  "  int ArgResult;",
  "  ARG ArgList = {0};",
  "",
  "  ArgResult = GetArgs(argc, argv, &ArgList);",
  "  if(ArgResult != 0)",
  "  {",
  "    Help();",
  "    Status = EXIT_FAILURE;",
  "  }",
  "  else",
  "  {",
  "    /* Calling your program... */",
  "^", /* Write function call for ApplicationMain() */
  "  }",
  "",
  "  return Status;",
  "}",
  "",
  "void Help(void)",
  "{",
  "!",
  "}",
  "",
```

```
    "&", /* Write function body for ApplicationMain() */
    NULL
  };

  int i;
  int j;
  char buffer[MAX_STR_LEN];
  char *p;

  for(i = 0; MainText[i] != NULL; i++)
  {
    switch(MainText[i][0])
    {
      case '!':
```

Here's our first special case, the `Help()` function. This is really quite simple. We read from the help file provided by the user, strip the newline (if present), and dump the contents of that file into a `printf()` statement. A more subtle implementation would probably write code to define an array of `char *` for `Help()`, in exactly the same way as in the function that generates `Help()`, and would add loop code to print it. If you want to change the code to do that, you may.

In case there is a lot of `Help()` output, we ensure that the display is halted every few lines, so that the user can keep up, pressing Enter when he is happy to continue.

```
        /* Generate the Help() function */
        fprintf(OutStream, "  char buffer[8];\n\n");

        j = 0;

        while(fgets(buffer, sizeof buffer, HelpStream))
        {
          p = strchr(buffer, '\n');
          if(p != NULL)
          {
            *p = '\0';
          }
          fprintf(OutStream,
                  "  printf(\"%s\\n\");\n",
                  buffer);

          ++j;

          if(j == LINES_PER_SCREEN)
```

```
          {
            fprintf(OutStream,
                    "  fprintf(stderr, \"Press ENTER to"
                    " continue...\\n\");\n");
            fprintf(OutStream,
                    "  fgets(buffer, sizeof buffer, "
                    "stdin);\n");
            j = 0;
          }
        }
        break;
      case '%':
      case '&':
```

The function prototype and the function definition are so closely related that we can deal with them, for the most part, in the same way. The differences are slight. First, we don't want to generate a function body if the `-internal` flag has not been specified. Second, we need a semicolon on the prototype, but not on the function definition. Third, we want a function body to follow the definition but not the prototype. Each of these is dealt with simply, using `if()`.

If we could guarantee that the user always wanted an internal function body, we wouldn't need a separate prototype. We could simply define the function above `main()`, and it would act as its own prototype. But to insist that the user have `ApplicationMain()` internal to the generated code would place severe limitations on him or her; I don't think the slightly simpler code would justify those limitations.

```
        if(MainText[i][0] == '&')
        {
          if(!InternalApp)
          {
            break;
          }
          fprintf(OutStream,
                  "/* Write, or call, your"
                  " application here.\n");
          fprintf(OutStream,
                  " * ApplicationMain must"
                  " return int. 0 indicates\n");
          fprintf(OutStream,
                  " * success. Any other value "
                  "indicates failure.");
          fprintf(OutStream,
                  " */\n\n");
```

```
}

/* Generate the prototype */
fprintf(OutStream, "int ApplicationMain(");

j = 0;
```

Yet again, we have to loop through our argument list. This time, it's to produce the prototype and function definition for `ApplicationMain()`. There's one more such loop after this one, too.

As a matter of portability, we place each parameter after the first on a separate line. The ANSI C Standard requires compliant compilers to support at least 127 parameters in a function call; it also does *not* require them to support source lines more than 509 characters long (at least in the C89 Standard, and many of us still use C89 compilers). Since parameters take at least six characters each (three for `int`, one for a space, one for a comma, and one for the identifier, rising to two after all one-character identifiers are used up), failing to split parameters onto separate lines could result in a line well over 700 characters long. A C89-compliant compiler could legitimately refuse to compile such source code.

Note the use of `j` to keep track of whether the current argument is the first argument. If it is, we shouldn't lead with a comma; that would result in a syntax error when we compiled the generated code.

```
for(Arg = ArgList;
    Arg != NULL;
    Arg = DLGetNext(Arg))
{
  Data = DLGetData(Arg, NULL, NULL);
  switch(Data->Type)
  {
    case BOOL:
      fprintf(OutStream,
              "%sint    ",
              j == 0 ?
                   "" :
                   ", \n            "
                   "            ");
      break;
    case LONG:
      fprintf(OutStream,
              "%slong   ",
              j == 0 ?
                   "" :
```

```
                    ", \n          "
                    "              ");
          break;
        case DOUBLE:
          fprintf(OutStream,
                  "%sdouble ",
                  j == 0 ?
                    "" :
                    ", \n          "
                    "              ");
          break;
        case STRING:
          fprintf(OutStream,
                  "%schar * ",
                  j == 0  ?
                    "" :
                    ", \n          "
                    "              ");
          break;
        default:
          fprintf(stderr,
                  "program error in fun"
                  "ction WriteMain()\n");
          assert(0);
          break;
      }

      ++j;

      fprintf(OutStream, "%s", Data->Name);
    }

    fprintf(OutStream,
            ")%s\n",
            MainText[i][0] == '%' ? ";" : "");

    if(MainText[i][0] == '&')
    {
      fprintf(OutStream, "{\n  return 0;\n}\n\n");
    }

    break;
```

Notice how we wrap up this case. If we are generating a prototype, we end with a semicolon. Otherwise, we end with a function body (only if one is required, of course—the test for that is near the top of this case block).

Now it's time to generate the call to the function. This must be done irrespective of whether there is a supporting function body. (As a consequence, the function body must be written elsewhere when -internal is not defined, or this program will never link properly.)

This time, we don't have to worry about the type of the variable—we need only specify its name, prefixed with the name of the structure, and the dot operator.

```
      case '^':
        /* Generate the call */
        fprintf(OutStream,
                "    Status = (ApplicationMain(");

        j = 0;

        for(Arg = ArgList;
            Arg != NULL;
            Arg = DLGetNext(Arg))
        {
          Data = DLGetData(Arg, NULL, NULL);

          fprintf(OutStream, "%sArgList.%s",
                  j == 0 ?
                  "" :
                  ",\n                              ",
                  Data->Name);
          ++j;
        }

        fprintf(OutStream,
                ") == 0) ?\n     EXIT_SUCCESS "
                ":\n     EXIT_FAILURE;\n");

        break;
      default:
        fprintf(OutStream, "%s\n", MainText[i]);
        break;
    }
  }

  return EXIT_SUCCESS;
}
```

We now have all the code we need to generate our output file. All we need is to tie it together. To do this, we need a function that can:

- Accept command-line arguments for the `internal` flag and the names of the four files we require—the grammar file, the output file, the log file (for the parser), and the help file.
- Open the files for reading or writing, as appropriate.
- Call the parser function and the code generation functions.

I've edited this function by replacing the file-handling and argument-walking code with comments, but of course the complete source is on the CD-ROM.

```
int ApplicationMain(int internal,
                    char * InFile,
                    char * OutFile,
                    char * LogFile,
                    char * HelpFile)
{
  int Status;

  DLLIST *ArgList = NULL;

  FILE *fpIn, *fpOut, *fpLog, *fpHelp;

  /* code to open all four files goes here. */

  Status = ParseInput(&ArgList, fpIn, fpLog);

  if(EXIT_SUCCESS == Status)
  {
    DLWalk(ArgList, WalkArgs, fpLog);

    Status = WriteHeaders(fpOut, OutFile);
  }
  if(EXIT_SUCCESS == Status)
  {
    Status = WriteTypedef(fpOut, ArgList);
  }
  if(EXIT_SUCCESS == Status)
  {
    Status = WriteFunction(fpOut, ArgList);
```

- Problems that are difficult to conceptualize can often be solved with reasonable efficiency by a genetic algorithm. So long as the solutions can be compared against each other to distinguish the better from the worse, a perfect solution can be sought.
- The processes of evolution scale very well to large parallel systems. The larger the population, the faster the evolution. Subpopulations can be evaluated independently of each other, then split, duplicated, and merged again with very few restrictions.
- The solutions generated can be very far from those expected. A wide variety of correct solutions to certain problems may exist, and sometimes it takes such a randomized search to discover them. This can lead to revolutionary (or evolutionary!) new approaches when the program discovers a solution never before considered, but likely to be as good or better than that currently employed. Creative processes can be modeled well by genetic algorithms, where similar stages of brainstorm, reapply, criticize, and refine (called mutation, recombination, and selection in evolutionary terms) are used.

The following is a list of terms frequently used with genetic data structures and algorithms:

- *Gene*—A section of genetic code that represents a single parameter to a potential solution.
- *Allele*—The value stored in a gene.
- *Chromosome*—A collection of genes, sufficient to completely describe a possible solution to a program. Specifies a single point in the solution space.
- *Genome*—All the chromosomes of an individual organism.
- *Genotype*—The values of a genome.
- *Problem Space*—The area of all possible problem instances, with each independent parameter defining another dimension.
- *Solution Space*—Similar to the problem space, but defined by the solution parameters, not the problem parameters. Every point inside the solution space represents a valid, but possibly suboptimal solution to the specified problem.

Genetic Structure

The fundamental genetic data structure is the gene. A gene is simply a section of genetic code representing a single parameter to the potential solution. Genes can be any size; they are commonly no more than a single bit long.

Tip

Only the solution parameters should be present in the genetic code. Other variables, including problem space parameters, should not be represented.

Although any scheme can be used to represent alleles in the genes, a binary Gray code is most common, because evolutionary operators, especially those for mutation, seem to be more effective at making incremental changes in Gray codes than in sequential encodings. Gray codes, named after their inventor Frank Gray, are any numerical ordering systems wherein all adjacent integers differ in their digital representation by exactly one digit. Such representations are useful for genetic applications because small alterations, such as from mutation, usually tend to create only small changes in value. Table 21.1 provides an example binary Gray code of three bits, contrasted with conventional sequential binary ordering.

TABLE 21.1 Gray Code Binary Ordering Example

Gray	*Sequential*
000	000
001	001
011	010
010	011
110	100
111	101
101	110
100	111

Although Gray codes have many interesting properties, their most beneficial feature to a genetic system is their digital proximity. By keeping the modified values near each other, the undesirable effects of randomization can be minimized. Large value changes are less likely to result from small digital changes when a Gray encoding is used.

Conversions to and from simple Gray encodings are easy, as demonstrated by Listing 21.1.

LISTING 21.1 Converting Gray Code to Conventional Binary Representations

```
unsigned int bin_to_Gray(unsigned int n)
{
    return n ^ (n >> 1);
}
```

LISTING 21.1 continued

```
unsigned int Gray_to_bin(unsigned int n)
{
    int i;
    for(i=0; (1 << i) < sizeof(n) * CHAR_BIT; i++)
    {
        n ^= n >> (1 << i);
    }
    return n;
}
```

Genes are grouped into chromosomes. A single chromosome contains a sufficient number of genes to fully describe a solution, and to be evaluated independently for solution fitness. With most implementations, each individual of the population contains only a single chromosome. Secondary chromosomes can be used to store dormant traits or other data not directly related to the primary problem.

A chromosome's structure can vary greatly. Flat, single-dimensional, statically sized bit or character arrays are the simplest chromosomal structures, yet are quite sufficient for most applications. More elaborate chromosomes can be constructed, including multidimensional arrays, trees, and even hash tables. These structures are more costly to manipulate, unless they better mirror the solution space.

An individual's full complement of chromosomes comprises the organism's genome. Genomes can freely use very simple structures, very complex structures, or anything in between to organize their component chromosomes. Nature uses a pretty simple method: just string everything together into one long array (or two duplicate arrays for DNA).

How do you determine how best to organize the genetic data? First, consider the operations to be done on it. The genome will be copied, combined with other genomes, mutated, spliced, and evaluated for fitness to determine how well it solves the specified problem. The genome will probably not be searched or displayed. Consider also the data it will store. This varies between implementations and between problem goals. Sometimes a particular encoding will not work well with certain structures. Sometimes a single, scalar integer will suffice to encode the entire genome. For the most efficiency and logical clarity, every gene, every chromosome, and every genome should be designed such that every possible arrangement and order lies within the solution space at a unique point, with no points unaccounted for. Eliminating known "bad solutions" from the solution space can also positively impact performance. If x can only be optimal when between 0 and 10, do not define the x range as 0 to 100. Of course, you should be certain you understand x well, or else you may exclude some non-obvious good solutions. The final point you should consider is the evolution process. You should ensure that your genetic structure can effectively be recombined for evolution. The child chromosomes should inherit as many fitness advantages as possible from their parent(s). If the genetic structure makes this unlikely, difficult, or impossible, the genetic algorithm degrades quickly to a random walk through the solution space. In some cases, the problem itself makes genetic inheritance undesirable. For those problems, such an approach is a poor solution.

Mutation Operations

Populations can eventually suffer from stagnation if a little new genetic material is not mixed in now and then. The population gradually becomes filled with many very similar genotypes. Maintaining a ratio of few generations to many individuals can reduce stagnation, but this is a poor general solution. Genetic drift stagnates the population as the organisms repeatedly intermix within the same gene pool from generation to generation. Even natural selection plays a part in stagnation, as the fittest organisms tend to replace the least fit. Under extreme conditions, such as when only a tiny percentage of the population survives or reproduces each generation, this can cause uniformity, and only a single, superior genotype will remain.

Mutation operations serve to keep a population from stagnating by gently adding some random elements to some of the chromosomes. Sometimes either genetic drift or natural selection will eliminate critical alleles useful for creating more powerful organisms. Mutation enables a population to occasionally experiment with entirely original alleles, rather than simply trying more combinations of alleles from existing genotypes.

Caution

Mutation must be kept low. Too much mutation will eradicate the benefits gained from inheritance and evolution. Mutation is poison to a genetic algorithm unless administered in small doses.

Recombination

Recombination is the process of creating a new population from the old. There are many ways to do this. The only requirement is that new chromosomes be constructed and that some characteristics of the parent chromosomes remain in the children.

Single Parents

Shuffling alleles within the same chromosome has an effect similar to simple mutation. This form of recombination involves only swapping allele gene positions, such as changing ABC into ACB. The child variations seldom retain advantages from this type of inheritance. Recombination techniques that involve more than a single parent are more effective at producing superior genotypes.

Gene Crossover

Gene crossover is a very simple recombination technique. The child takes alleles from more than one parent chromosome, randomly selecting which parent will provide the next allele. The child genes still map directly to the parent genes (no allele changes position), but the combination is a blend of alleles from each parent. For example, combining the parent sequences ABC and XYZ this way can produce eight different possible child combinations: ABZ, AYC, AYZ, XBC, XBZ, XYC, and the two original parent sequences.

Constraints can be imposed on the mixture. For example, you could require that a larger proportion of alleles come from the more successful parent(s). If one strong and two weak chromosomes are mated together, it may be desirable to have more of the alleles come from the single strong parent than the two weak parents. Another possibility is a requirement that each parent contribute an equal share of alleles.

Gene crossover is most effective when used on relatively independent genes.

Gene Sequence Crossover

This very common technique copies whole sequences of alleles from each parent. Splicing points are chosen along the child chromosome, dividing the shares between the parents. ABCD crossed with WXYZ in this manner can produce eight possible child combinations, depending on which splicing point is chosen, and which parent gets which side: ABCZ, ABYZ, AXYZ, WXYD, WXCD, WBCD, and the original two parent sequences. This method of recombination is more stable, in that valuable characteristics are more likely to be passed to the next generation, and that children are more likely to closely resemble their parents. However, sequential crossover produces less variety than crossing individual genes.

Caution

Splicing points should be chosen at gene boundaries. Cutting individual alleles in two can destroy advantageous characteristics.

Gene Merging

It is possible for a child chromosome to inherit an allele not found in any parent, but created by the combination of the alleles themselves. Several operations can be used to merge the alleles, such as exclusive OR, averaging, and so on. For genes that represent continuous parameters, merging can greatly speed the search for an optimum value.

Note

Gene merging is not useful for discrete values. If combining two alleles to form a unique allele does not make sense for a particular gene, exclude that gene from the process. Some chromosomes are designed to contain only discrete values, in which case merging is not helpful.

Selection

Because each new generation should contain genomes superior to those of the prior generations, a means must be employed to include the better fit chromosomes more often than the less fit chromosomes. One simple method includes only the best few organisms in the reproduction phase, and lets the inferior genomes die quietly. This choice can be made rigid, using so-called "hard" selection, ensuring those most inferior will always die and those most superior will always survive. Or the choice can be probabilistic, using "soft" selection, allowing some more favorable chromosomes to become extinct in the hopes that some less fit parents will produce exceptional offspring.

Caution

Allowing too few genomes to survive and participate in the creation of the next generation can lead to very rapid stagnation.

Each member genome of a population must first be ranked by a fitness function. This simply determines how well each genetically encoded solution solves the problem goal. Because several candidates must be compared with each other, the fitness function should return an accurate, finely grained judgement, easily ranked and compared with each other. It is always easiest to work with a single fitness value, but some problems can be reduced to no fewer than several values. For example, a search for the best possible job may find some jobs that pay more, some that are in better locations, and some that are more fun. However, it is probably not feasible to have the program decide how to convert all these criteria into a single "better job" indicator. In these cases, the fitness function will have many values that are roughly equal, as when one chromosome finds a good paying job, but another chromosome has found a better work environment. Only when all fitness values are higher can a chromosome safely be considered superior to another.

The designer must choose how to handle surviving parents each generation. A generation can either serve as a loud punctuation, totally regenerating the population each round, or certain select individuals may survive into the following generations. These strategies are respectively called the *Comma Strategy* and the *Plus Strategy*. Disallowing a parent to compete with its offspring is often written (parent, child), indicating a death of the parent and the replacement by the child, whereas (parent + child) joins the parents and children together into the same population as opponents, peers, and potential mates. Plus Strategies tend to perform better, but the results of using a Comma Strategy can be useful for judging the performance of the selection and recombination techniques.

Occasionally, genes within the population converge onto a single value. All or most of the chromosomes have the same allele value for a gene. While this is often a good thing, indicating the best possible allele for that gene, sometimes a strong but false optimum is realized. Mutation will eventually push the population beyond any undesirable stability, but until then evolution cannot continue to improve the population on its natural course. A means of producing greater variety without sacrificing the necessary benefits of stability and progressive improvement is *speciation*. By dividing a population into subpopulations from which genomes rarely or never migrate, distinct species develop. Although one subpopulation may lose its vitality, another may still continue to evolve. An occasional introduction of one or a few foreign organisms can shake up a stalemate and free the population to move forward again. Sometimes two subpopulations will evolve at very different rates and a single foreign genome from the more advanced subpopulation can infest and quickly dominate the weaker, making the two species suddenly very similar. The gentlest way to introduce foreign genomes is to cross the foreign organism(s) with one or more residents. This tames the impact the newcomers can create.

Species can also be segregated by similar but not identical problem spaces. Sometimes chromosomes will evolve more rapidly when faced with a problem that is just a little different from the real thing. After the modified problem has been solved well, only a little more evolution is usually necessary to convert the solution to a similar problem. These small genetic changes necessary for the minor specialization to the modified problem can often be inherited from an existing, resident population that has already been working on the target problem for a few generations.

Opening the Black Box

Genetic algorithms are easily implemented. They intuitively make sense. Programmers can understand how to do it properly, yet know very few details of the underlying theoretical foundations. The mathematics upon which genetic algorithms rely is not simple, and it is not easily digested. Because most programmers only care about implementing the algorithm to reap the benefits, and not about proving or completely understanding the principles, there is a widespread tendency to make decisions empirically by trying it out, seeing if it seems to work, and then using it. This often works well enough, but when a program does not behave as it should, this lack of deep understanding can become a big problem.

Consider the genetic functions in your program highly experimental. Make the control variables easily changeable. Make it easy to try different strategies. Report a lot of statistical data as you experiment. Report the condition of the population, the success of the recombination, the number of unique individuals, the number of generations, and so on. Try to report broad overviews and summaries as well as a few sample close-ups of individuals undergoing various operations. If possible, try to make your experimental program very interactive, so that you can easily observe the effect each control parameter has on the program's performance.

Remember that it is far easier to get a single simple function to work correctly than an entire program. Genetic algorithms depend on several interrelated operations to perform properly. It is very unlikely that you will be able to identify the cause of incorrect behavior by only observing the end result. "My population is very chaotic," for example, is not a very specific symptom. Understand what each function is designed to do, then test it by itself to ensure it does so.

Make your source code as easy to navigate as possible. Use long, descriptive identifiers. Consistently use your metaphors. Labels like "mu" and "lambda" probably do not help as much as "parents" and "children." If a metaphor no longer seems to help, drop it. If you prefer to say "DNA" instead of "genome," do so. If you envision mutation as a rainstorm, feel free to rename your "mutation_factor" variable to "inches_of_precipitation." The computer science community seems to prefer the genetics and evolution metaphor, but there is no reason you cannot use another. If you are not comfortable with words like "allele" and "genotype," don't use them. But try to use some kind of metaphor because it is easier that way to give each element a unique, meaningful label. If you use several different operations, try to give each its own name. Don't number them and call them something like "RepOp27" because these are more likely to be confused with each other and to force anyone looking at the code to find the definition and usage before understanding the meaning. And, of course, insert enough comments to explain what you are doing and why, referring to your metaphors often.

Optimization

Randomized searches are slow. The more randomized they are, the more slowly they find what they are looking for. Genetic algorithms are a class of randomized search techniques. Luckily, genetic algorithms have some unusual properties that are well suited to certain forms of optimization.

Parallelism

Genetic algorithms are easily run in parallel. One way this can be accomplished is by having each process develop an independent subpopulation. Periodically, representative genomes are exchanged between subpopulations, so that the benefits discovered by one process can be used to speed the progress of another process. This creates multiple parallel species, all with the same end goal.

There are ways to evolve the same species in parallel too. The evolutionary process, consisting of potentially several mutation, recombination, and selection operations, can be split lengthwise, with each process dedicated to a single operation along the pipeline. It can also be split widthwise by dividing the population into independent segments for many operations, such as fitness evaluation and mutation, then reunited once every generation.

Finding Effective Genetic Operators

Every problem and every implementation has a different set of optimal operators. Sometimes using only two parents in sequential crossover works best, while other times a hillclimbing mutation works better. By testing your populations with different operations, and with different controls, you can discover what works best for that problem.

Remember also that genetic algorithms make pretty good general-purpose optimizers. As an alternative to statically optimizing your search, meta-evolutionary functions can be used to evolve the evolutionary strategy itself. The fitness of the strategy would be a measure of how quickly the population improves. The genotype would represent a solution of the available operations, perhaps as simple as a single bit for each gene to switch an operation on and off.

Dividing the Problem Space

Genetic algorithms work much faster searching multiple small solution spaces than one large, combined solution space. Do not combine many small problems into one. This can be tempting, but it will almost definitely require longer to solve many problems at once rather than independently.

Example: Mr. Rich wants to have the most luxurious transport possible to carry him around the city. He needs to hire a well-groomed chauffeur and purchase a very expensive car. Because we can assume any chauffeur under consideration can drive any car under consideration, the two problems should be split. The same population should not be tasked with finding the combination of best chauffeur and best car. Each population should be specialized, one to find a driver, and the other to find a car.

In the most extreme situations, splitting the problem in two like this can reduce the solution space to only double the square root of the combined problem. Instead of a million possibilities, only two thousand need be searched. The problem should be split into as many subproblems as possible. If the subproblems really are interrelated, such as when each chauffeur drives each car differently, and it affects the fitness of the solution, the problem cannot appropriately be split into smaller problems.

Rejecting Past Failures

A program can keep a record of each grossly suboptimal chromosome so that if the same chromosome is ever generated again, it can be immediately eliminated. This can save a little time because genetic algorithms have no inherent guarantee that the same evolutionary trail will not be tried multiple times. Care must be taken not to exclude good routes to superior combinations. Usually, a very poor chromosome will not lead to a better one before a fitter chromosome will. For most problems, good chromosomes are more likely to produce record-breaking offspring than bad chromosomes.

Error Correction

Some applications devote a sizeable share of resources to error detection and/or correction. Communications programs, in particular, deal with connection failures, traffic problems, and device errors. Many times using a genetic algorithm reduces or eliminates the need for these safeguards because it has a remedy already built in. Genetic programs are essentially unaffected by a few erroneous genomes, missing or late genomes, repeated copies of genomes, and so on. So long as it is "mostly good," the problems are usually not even noticed. Even if the non-evolving portion of the program is slightly damaged—for example, causing the fitness evaluation to be not quite right, or a small part of the recombination code to be ignored—the algorithm is likely to continue to function almost as well as if there had been no errors. Unlike most other algorithms, genetic algorithms are flexible enough that errors often become small handicaps, not critical system failures. Errors that arise tend to be evolved away along with the suboptimal solutions.

Incomplete Solutions and Changing Resource Constraints

Sometimes speed is critical. On a real-time system, problems must be solved within the given timeframes, or terrible things happen. By incrementally seeking the best possible solution, a genetic algorithm can provide a good solution on demand. It may not be able to guarantee just how good a solution it will have, but it can offer the best it has found so far. If an immediate answer is required, one is available. If later there is a chance to replace the solution again, another greatly superior solution may be ready. The current population can even be frozen and saved for more evolution later.

It may be that a problem will need to be solved, but the resources available for the task change continually. A genetic algorithm can easily adjust the size of the population to fit within the available memory space. As more space becomes available, larger populations can be used. Even if memory is reclaimed away from the genetic algorithm while evolution is in progress, the lost genomes do not become a fatal problem. And if CPU time is cut short, a solution representing the best so far is always ready and waiting. Even with very limited memory and time constraints, genetic algorithms can offer pretty good solutions, although they obviously do best when resources are plentiful.

Outgrowing the Metaphors

Metaphors are great aids for understanding and can even point research in new directions. A model of Mother Nature often works well. Some of the most basic fundamentals are universal, working equally well for bacteria and computer programs. Other aspects are not universal. Just as modern aircraft use metal instead of feathers, a programmer should discard elements of natural genetics and evolution whenever more advanced techniques become available. Nature can be a good starting place, providing observable proofs of viability, but do not assume that the natural methods are the best possible, or even the most interesting. Jets can fly much higher and much faster than any bird, bat, or insect can. Current research into evolutionary algorithms is breaking away from the original natural models and using newer, more powerful ideas.

Example Application: A Genetic Stock Advisor

A stock trader turns a profit by selling shares of stock for more than the purchase price. At the most basic level, a stock trader must decide when to buy shares, when to sell shares, and when to hold the shares acquired earlier.

Stock analysis is a good application for a genetic algorithm because it is often difficult to determine exactly what factors are useful for predicting future stock prices, and there are likely to be many equally good, but not necessarily obvious solutions. Sometimes stock prices seem to hold true to a certain pattern, while other times they seem entirely random. Using a genetic algorithm, we can evolve a roughly optimal solution and find when best to buy shares, and when best to sell them.

Note

The complete example program is not included in this chapter, but can be found on the CD along with some recent stock price data to try it on.

Analysis of the Problem

The input will consist of a two-dimensional array of price histories, covering a year. Each column will be a unique ticker symbol, and each row will be another day. The output will be a recommendation for each column, one of buy, hold, or sell. Listing 21.2 defines these structures.

LISTING 21.2 The Input and Output Types for a Genetic Stock Advisor

```
/* The datatype used for input */
typedef struct
{
    unsigned int price[NUM_STOCKS][HISTORY_LENGTH];
```

LISTING 21.2 continued

```
} history_t;

/* The datatype used for output */
typedef enum
{
    SELL = -1,
    HOLD = 0,
    BUY = 1
} recommendation_t;
```

The Genetic Structure

Our solution requires only a recommendation, but our fitness function requires that each chromosome have encoded within it a plan for producing recommendations from a price history. We don't want just any buy, sell, or hold recommendation, but one that is likely to be the most profitable recommendation. All we need to do is design a chromosome that can be interpreted as a recommendation generator.

Fixed-length chromosomes are far simpler to implement, and we probably do not require a variable number of genes, so we will try to ensure we have a fixed number of genes.

Recommendations will be generated by comparing the current price with the current average price for that stock, using genetically encoded buy and sell points. Each chromosome will contain only two genes: one describing the price (proportionate to the current average price) when a buy will be triggered, and the second similarly describing the price when sell recommendations are triggered. When neither buy nor sell recommendations are triggered, a hold recommendation is generated.

Because each of our genes is a simple integer value, we will use a Gray encoding for the values.

See Listing 21.3 for the genetic structures used with our genetic stock advisor, ranging from individual genes to whole populations.

LISTING 21.3 Genetic and Input Structures for the Genetic Stock Advisor

```
typedef unsigned int gene_t;

typedef struct
{
    gene_t buy_price;
    gene_t sell_price;
```

LISTING 21.3 continued

```
} chromosome_t;

typedef struct
{
    chromosome_t individual[SPECIES_POPULATION];
} species_t;

typedef struct
{
    species_t species[NUM_STOCKS];
} population_t;
```

Measuring Fitness

We want to get the recommendation most likely to make us the most money. We will define this as the system for generating recommendations that prove most profitable when applied to the available price histories. Therefore, a genotype will be considered most fit that produces the recommendation plan that, had it been followed every day to date, would have resulted in the most profit. We would then have reason to believe the genotype's system for producing recommendations is sound. We will use a single, signed fitness value representing the profit the genotype would have produced had it been applied every day in the price history. See Listing 21.4 for a description in C.

LISTING 21.4 The Function Responsible for Measuring How Well Each Organism Does at Stock Trading

```
long fitness(
    /* The chromosome to be judged */
    chromosome_t* c,
    /* Historic prices */
    unsigned int* history
  )
{
    long total_price = 0;
    long avg_price;
    long price;
    long shares = 0;
    long cash = 0;
    unsigned int t;

    for(t = 0; t < HISTORY_LENGTH; t++)
    {
```

LISTING 21.4 continued

```
        price = history[t];
        total_price += price;
        avg_price = total_price / (t + 1);

        /* Make price relative to average */
        price -= avg_price;

        /* Convert price to percentage value */
        price = price * 100 / avg_price;

        if(-price >= (long)Gray_to_bin(c->buy_price))
        {
            /* Buy another share */
            ++shares;
            cash -= (long)history[t];
        }
        else if(price >= (long)Gray_to_bin(c->sell_price))
        {
            /* Sell another share */
            --shares;
            cash += (long)history[t];
        }
    }

    /* Cash out of holdings for net worth comparison */
    cash += shares * (long)history[t-1];

    return cash;
}
```

The Selection Process

Because each stock has similar but potentially independent factors affecting its price, we will assign a species to each stock ticker symbol. Migration will enable any general advantages to surface and become widespread, while individual necessary differences can be maintained. Each ticker symbol will receive a recommendation from a specialized expert organism, evolved only for that symbol, yet these organisms will collaborate with each other, trading useful ideas with neighbor subpopulations assigned to other stocks.

Each subpopulation will have a fixed size. Every generation, new genotypes will replace older ones. Listing 21.5 uses a Plus Strategy, enabling the parent genotypes to survive indefinitely from generation to generation.

LISTING 21.5 A Simple Selection Function for Deciding Who Lives and Who Dies

```
unsigned int select_survivors(
    /* Existing species */
    species_t const* before,
    /* The surviving organisms */
    species_t* after,
    /* The fitness value of each organism */
    long* fit
  )
{
    unsigned int i;
    unsigned int j;
    long record;
    long temp;

    /* Copy 1/4 of the most fit to after[] */
    for(i = 0; i < SPECIES_POPULATION / 4; i++)
    {
        record = i;
        for(j = i+1; j < SPECIES_POPULATION; j++)
        {
            if(fit[j] > fit[record])
            {
                record = j;
            }
        }

        /* Swap fitness values */
        temp = fit[record];
        fit[record] = fit[i];
        fit[i] = temp;

        after->individual[i] = before->individual[record];
    }

    return i;
}
```

Initializing the Population

We will begin with an entirely random population each session. Listing 21.6 contains the initialization functions.

LISTING 21.6 Both the Chromosome's Genes are Set to Random Values

```
void initialize_chromosome(chromosome_t* c)
{
    c->buy_price = bin_to_Gray(rand() % MAX_PRICE);
    c->sell_price = bin_to_Gray(rand() % MAX_PRICE);
}

void initialize_species(species_t* s)
{
    int i;
    for(i = 0; i < SPECIES_POPULATION; i++)
    {
        initialize_chromosome(&s->individual[i]);
    }
}

void initialize_population(population_t* p)
{
    int i;
    /* There is one species for every stock */
    for(i = 0; i < NUM_STOCKS; i++)
    {
        initialize_species(&p->species[i]);
    }
}
```

The Mutation Strategy

We will use only light mutation for this task. Simple, random bit flipping will suffice, as demonstrated by Listing 21.7.

LISTING 21.7 Bit Flipping, Among the Simplest of Mutation Functions

```
void mutate_gene(gene_t* g)
{
    /* Flip a random bit in the gene */
```

LISTING 21.7 continued

```
    *g ^= 1 << rand() % (sizeof (gene_t) * CHAR_BIT);

}

void mutate_chromosome(chromosome_t* c)
{
    switch(rand() & 1)
    {
        case 0:
            mutate_gene(&c->buy_price);
            break;
        case 1:
            mutate_gene(&c->sell_price);
            break;
    }
}

void mutate_species(species_t* s)
{
    unsigned int i;

    for(i = 0; i < SPECIES_POPULATION; i++)
    {
        /* Mutate only one in every MUTATION_FACTOR */
        if(rand() % MUTATION_FACTOR == 0)
        {
            mutate_chromosome(&s->individual[i]);
        }
    }
}
```

The Recombination Strategy

Each gene can logically be merged with the same gene of another chromosome, so we will employ merging to allow two extremes to meet in the middle. Simple crossover also makes sense in this case.

Because there are so few genes, only two parents at a time will combine to produce offspring. Parent selection will be done randomly (see Listing 21.8).

LISTING 21.8 The Recombination Functions Responsible for Creating New Organisms from the Old

```
void mate_genes(
    gene_t* parent_1,
    gene_t* parent_2,
    gene_t* child
  )
{
    switch(rand() % 3)
    {
        case 0:
            /* Inherit from parent 1 */
            *child = *parent_1;
            break;
        case 1:
            /* Inherit from parent 2 */
            *child = *parent_2;
            break;
        case 2:
            /* Inherit from both parents */
            *child = *parent_1 + *parent_2 >> 1;
            break;
    }
}

void mate_chromosomes(
    chromosome_t* parent_1,
    chromosome_t* parent_2,
    chromosome_t* child
  )
{
    mate_genes(
        &parent_1->buy_price,
        &parent_2->buy_price,
        &child->buy_price
      );
    mate_genes(
        &parent_1->sell_price,
        &parent_2->sell_price,
        &child->sell_price
      );
}
```

LISTING 21.8 continued

```
void recombine(
    species_t* s,
    unsigned int num_survivors
  )
{
    unsigned int i;
    unsigned int parent_1;
    unsigned int parent_2;

    /* Replenish the species population with children */
    for(i = num_survivors; i < SPECIES_POPULATION; i++)
    {
        /* Select two random parents from the survivors */
        parent_1 = rand() % num_survivors;
        parent_2 = rand() % num_survivors;

        /* Create the child from the two parents */
        mate_chromosomes(
            &s->individual[parent_1],
            &s->individual[parent_2],
            &s->individual[i]
          );
    }
}
```

The Results and Conclusion

Populations of a hundred seem to consistently find the best possible values in less than fifty generations. Because the chromosomes are so simple, all but the largest changes in the recombination have no discernable effect.

Using this very simple algorithm for finding good stock trading envelopes seems to be adequate. It can quickly find the best possible fitness values, and seems to beg to explore larger solution spaces, beyond simple buy/sell points. Use of more complex fitness strategies, such as pattern matching, should take longer, but result in more optimal recommendations.

It can come as a bit of a shock to discover that some of our most-loved functions are actually not portable. Inexperienced DOS and Windows programmers tend to think that `getch()`, `kbhit()`, `clrscr()`, and so on are part of the C language, and are in for a rude awakening when they port their code to another compiler, perhaps for another operating system. Many UNIX programmers find it hard to believe that ANSI makes no mention of `bzero()`. And everyone knows that`strdup()` and `stricmp()` are standard C functions. Except, of course, that they aren't.

When we deal with hardware, we are frequently obliged to write non-portable code. But it is possible to write this non-portable code in a way that minimizes the problems we face when porting that code to another environment. The trick, as is so often the case in programming, is to divide and conquer. By dividing our program into portable and non-portable parts, we can reduce the amount of rework required when the time comes to port. Isolating the non-portable code into its own modules means that we need rewrite only those modules for each new platform.

Abstraction Layers

An abstraction layer is a function or group of functions whose task is to isolate an application from the functions it would normally call (see Figure 22.1). For example, a programmer may, instead of calling `getch()` from his application, choose to call `GetKey()` instead. He then writes `GetKey()` so that it calls `getch()` for him. `GetKey()` is an abstraction. It doesn't actually do any work itself (or at least, very little). It passes that task on to `getch()`. One day, the program will be ported to a system that doesn't support `getch()`, but that's okay—only the `GetKey()` function needs to be re-coded, not the entire application. The application simply calls `GetKey()` and neither knows nor cares how `GetKey()` gets a keypress, so long as a keypress is indeed retrieved. Thus, the application source itself remains completely portable. Only the abstraction functions need be re-coded on each platform.

The benefits of abstraction layers, and the best way to write them, only become really clear in relatively large programs. This is usually an author's excuse for not dealing in full detail with the issue at hand (and I have every sympathy). Just for a change, then, let's look really thoroughly at a real-world problem involving non-portable code, and let's see if we can make that code portable after all (or, at least, more portable).

The real-world problem we are going to solve is that of communications. How do we write a program that talks to another program running on a different computer? Specifically, how do we write such a program in a way that minimizes the difficulty of porting that program to another environment?

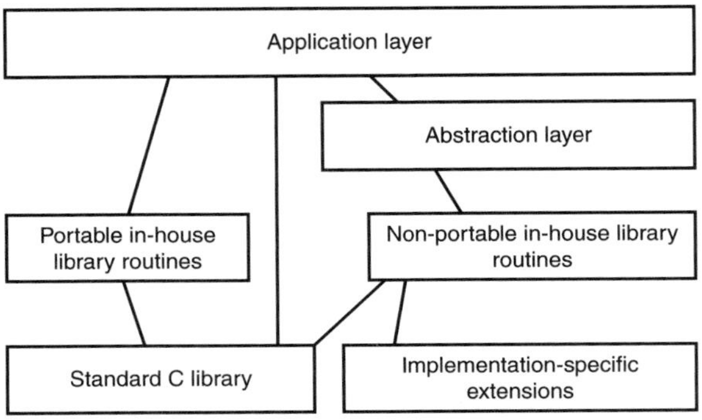

FIGURE 22.1
Isolating library functions with abstraction layers.

Before we tackle the problem of portability, let's tackle the first problem: the communications technique itself.

This is a huge subject, so we will have to gloss over a few things that are in themselves the subject of entire books. By the end of this chapter, we should be able to get two programs, possibly running on different machines, to talk to each other. To get to our destination that quickly, we may have to put up with the fact that the scenery will be a little blurred. To mitigate this problem, you'll find a list of further reading for this chapter in Appendix B, "Selected Bibliography."

Sockets

To get our programs to talk to each other, we are going to use a communications library known as Berkeley Sockets. This is not just a library but also a paradigm. The general idea is similar to telephony. Given a telephone, a hole in the wall to which the telephone lead connects, and an account with the Phone Company, I can make a phone call to anyone in the world who has a similar arrangement at his end. I don't need to know how my voice gets to my friend, or how his voice gets to me. All I need to know is how to talk to that hole in the wall, which is commonly called a socket. Berkeley Sockets is based more or less on this idea.

The Internet offers us two primary transmission protocols; each is useful in its own way. The simplest protocol is UDP (User Datagram Protocol). This protocol is commonly also called IP (Internet Protocol). The other transmission mechanism is TCP (Transmission Control Protocol). These together are abbreviated TCP/IP. How, then, do they differ, and which should we use in which circumstances?

TCP is a bidirectional connection-oriented stream protocol. This means that it can offer a reliable stream of data that is guaranteed to be sequenced and error-free. Every packet will be acknowledged using sequencing numbers within the header of the packet.The error checking is done by performing a CRC (Cyclic Redundancy Check) algorithm on the packet to guarantee that it arrived intact and uncorrupted. This is all provided by the TCP process running on the operating system—our applications do not have to do anything special to take advantage of this.

UDP is the complete opposite; it is a best effort transmission mechanism. This simply means that the packets may arrive out of order, may arrive with errors, or may of course not arrive at all. TCP's reliability comes at a cost—the overhead is quite significant. TCP sockets employ what is commonly called the 3-Way Handshake. In this process the initiating machine, usually called the client, sends an Acknowledgment Request to the server (the machine accepting client requests). The server then begins to set up the resources needed to maintain a connected socket. It replies to the ACK with an acknowledgment and a synchronize request. This packet is referred to as ACK/SYN. The client machine will accept this packet and reply one more time to complete the 3-Way Handshake. The final packet contains an acknowledgment of the previous packet and a synchronize (SYN) reply. Once this packet arrives on the server, the session setup is complete. Each host can then begin sending or receiving data.

UDP has no concept of a session or connection; the steps that TCP employs are, therefore, not necessary for UDP sockets. Datagram sockets can send and receive data from any machine at any time. With no acknowledgments or error checking, these tend to be very fast in nature, especially over slow WAN lines.

TCP/IP is commonly compared to the mail system. TCP corresponds to registered mail. When you send a package with registered mail, it is guaranteed to arrive intact and in the same condition in which it was sent. If for some reason it was undeliverable, you will be notified so that you can resolve the problem and try again.

UDP, on the other hand, is more like a postcard. When you send a postcard, you are taking a best effort approach to sending your message. It may arrive perfectly. It may be torn en route. It may arrive six months after it was sent, or of course it may get lost in the mail system and never arrive. When determining which method is most appropriate for your programs, you need to consider the nature of your data. Is every single byte, indeed every bit, critical? Can you afford to lose any data?

When you are dealing with financial systems or navigation systems, the answer to whether you can afford to lose data is clearly a resounding "No." But there are circumstances in which the answer might be "Yes."

What about streaming video? The primary consideration with video transmissions is speed. It is vital to transmit live video data as quickly as possible to provide smooth frame transition. If one pixel in one frame is wrong, and will be viewed for considerably less than a second, will it even be noticeable? Probably not.

Sometimes, then, we will want to use the full error checking of TCP, and sometimes we will want the raw speed of UDP. The choice is yours. Berkeley Sockets fully supports both of these protocols.

The Sockets library is widely available on UNIX systems. Microsoft has implemented it in a slightly different way; it calls the end result *Winsock*. IBM has a version of the Sockets library available for its mainframe systems, too. Unfortunately, all these versions differ slightly from each other. That's our problem. We'll solve it later on in the chapter. For now, let's have a look at two different flavors of Sockets—UNIX and Windows.

> **Note**
>
> If you want to write code on an IBM mainframe or a Mac, you'll have a little research to do—but you'll be glad to hear that the concept of an abstraction layer is just as relevant and useful to you as to the rest of us.

Our first case study, for which we will be using the TCP transport mechanism, involves a small retail chain. It has a head office and a number of branch offices. At the end of each day, each branch office computer needs to send the sales total for that branch to the head office computer. In return, the head office computer will send to the branch computer the total sales for the previous day across all the branches. For the purposes of this illustration, we are not concerned with security.

We will first develop a UNIX solution, and then a Windows solution. These solutions will be very similar, but not identical. We will then show how we could have eased the porting process by writing an abstraction layer for the non-portable parts of the program.

Sockets Using TCP Under UNIX

We have two programs to write: the server (which is the program we want to run on the head office computer) and the client (one copy of which is installed on each branch computer). We'll start with the server.

A UNIX Server Program

The server's job is mainly to listen. It needs to be aware of when clients are requesting a connection with it. It needs to accept each connection, conduct a conversation with the client, and close the connection when the conversation is over.

An IP address is an unsigned 32-bit quantity (currently in the slow process of being upgraded to 128 bits) that uniquely identifies a machine within a given network. That network may be the Internet, of course, which is why we need such a big identifier. To contact the server, the client needs to know the server's IP address. The server, however, does *not* need to know the client's IP address in advance. (The client will tell it.)

Note

The new upcoming 128-bit IP is called IPv6 or IPng for Internet Protocol, Next Generation. In time it will replace the 32-bit IP version 4 we currently use.

Because more than one network-aware program might be running on the head office computer, we need a method to distinguish between programs so that when a packet of data arrives at the computer, the underlying system knows for which program the packet is intended. For a real-world example, we need look no further than an average Internet server. Such a machine would commonly be running any or all of these programs: email services, an HTTP Web Server, an FTP or File Transfer Protocol server, chat servers, e-commerce services, and many more. Just using the IP address of the machine will get it as far as the machine, but we then need to ensure that the data will be delivered to the correct service. The simplest way is to associate each packet of data with a particular number, where the number identifies the program for which the packet is intended. This number is known as a *port number*.

We need to choose a port number that is unlikely to conflict with other programs running on our computer. Port numbers are stored in a 16-bit unsigned integer type, so we have values in the range 0 to 65535 to play with. Everything from 0 to 1023 is reserved, however, so we can't use those for this particular program (in fact, on many UNIX boxes you can't use these numbers *at all*, even for their intended purpose, unless you are logged in as root). When selecting a port or socket number to use, you should check the current standards base (formalized in a group of documents known as Requests For Comment (RFCs)) to be certain that your selected number is not currently being used by another well-known application. With only a few exceptions, almost all other numbers are up for grabs; all we have to do is to choose a number that will ensure that we don't have two programs on the same computer waiting for data on the same port at the same time. This is a local machine management issue. Our client needs to know the port number on which the server will be listening. For this reason, we need to use the same port number for the server every time. We'll choose 1091 as the port number for this application, on the simple grounds that it's as good a random number as any, and is not currently in use by any applications local to this network.

Listing 22.1 shows the complete source code for the UNIX server.

LISTING 22.1 Source Code for a UNIX TCP Server

```
#include <stdio.h>
#include <stdlib.h>
#include <string.h>
#include <signal.h>
#include <sys/time.h>
#include <sys/select.h>
#include <sys/types.h>
#include <sys/socket.h>
#include <netinet/in.h>
```

As you can see, we need to include quite a few header files just to write a small server. The first four are simply required by this particular program, but the last five all have to do with the socket library. `sys/time.h` is used by `select()`, `sys/select.h` is needed by `select()` and the FD* macros, `sys/types.h` is needed for the `htons()` macro, `sys/socket.h` holds the prototypes for the socket calls (such as `recv()`), and `netinet/in.h` defines the structs for the socket calls.

```
#define DEFAULT_FILE_NAME "sales.dat"

volatile sig_atomic_t done;

void inthandler(int Sig)
{
 done = 1;
}

int CheckForData(int sockfd)
 {
  struct timeval tv;
  fd_set read_fd;
  tv.tv_sec=0;
  tv.tv_usec=0;
  FD_ZERO(&read_fd);
```

```
  FD_SET(sockfd, &read_fd);
  if(select(sockfd+1, &read_fd,NULL, NULL, &tv)== -1)
   {
    return 0;
   }
  if(FD_ISSET(sockfd, &read_fd))
   {
    return 1;
   }
 return 0;
}
```


Note

Specifying the `volatile` qualifier instructs a compiler to make no assumptions about a variable's contents when optimizing. For example, in this code:

```
volatile int i;
i = 5;
i++;
i++;
```

the `volatile` qualifier warns the compiler not to replace these three instructions with

```
i = 7;
```

because it tells the compiler that, in theory at least, the value of `i` could be changed by some other factor outside the compiler's control.

This little routine is the networking equivalent of `kbhit()`. Those of you who have heard of `kbhit()` (which is not an ANSI C function, by the way) will know that it is used to determine whether information about a keypress is waiting in the keyboard buffer, without collecting that keypress information. This `CheckForData()` function determines, using a Berkeley Sockets function called `select()`, whether there is data waiting to be collected, but it doesn't actually collect that data.

Tip

In fact, the `select()` function just monitors file descriptors; in a UNIX environment, the file descriptor value 0 is considered to be `stdin`, so by passing this value in a set to `select()`, you can turn it into a literal equivalent of `kbhit()`.

```
int main(int argc, char **argv)
{
  int sockfd=0;
  int new_fd=0;
  struct sockaddr_in my_addr;
  struct sockaddr_in their_addr;
  socklen_t sin_size=0;
  char data[255]={0};
  char *endp;

  FILE *fp;
  char Filename[FILENAME_MAX] = DEFAULT_FILE_NAME;
  unsigned long currenttotal = 0;
  unsigned long  newtotal = 0;
```

In the UNIX environment, almost everything is treated as if it were a file. If you already know UNIX, you already know this, and if you don't, you probably don't care. Suffice it to say, then, that a UNIX socket is no different, and has a file descriptor associated with it. This descriptor can be written to or read from for data input-output. The variable `sockfd` is such a file descriptor, and we will use it to keep track of one of our sockets (we'll be using two; this one will listen for new connections). Whenever we get a new connection request, we'll use `new_fd` to accept the connection request. The structure `my_addr` contains our local server information and `their_addr` is a struct containing our client's address information.

Before we get to actually set up the socket, we need to do a little housekeeping at the application level. Remember that we are going to tell all our clients the total sales for yesterday. So we need to find yesterday's file (with luck, it'll be in the file named by `argv[1]`), open it, and grab the number.

```
if(argc < 2)
{
  printf("No file specified. Using \"%s\"\n",
         DEFAULT_FILE_NAME);
}
else
{
  strcpy(Filename, argv[1]);
}

fp = fopen(Filename, "r");
if(fp != NULL)
{
  if(NULL != fgets(data, sizeof data, fp))
  {
    currenttotal = strtoul(data, &endp, 10);
  }

  fclose(fp);
}
else
{
  printf("Couldn't read file %s\n", Filename);
}
```

So that our user can easily stop the server program, we'll install an interrupt handler, using `signal()`. Strictly speaking, just about the only thing the ANSI Standard allows us to do in a signal handler (portably) is to modify the value of a `sig_atomic_t` variable. So that's what we do. The variable we modify is the one that controls the loop. When we interrupt the program, the variable is set to 1, which ends the loop on the next time around.

```
if(signal(SIGINT, SIG_IGN) != SIG_IGN)
{
  signal(SIGINT, inthandler);
}
```

```
if(signal(SIGTERM, SIG_IGN) != SIG_IGN)
{
  signal(SIGTERM, inthandler);
}
```

Now we can start setting up the socket. We use the `my_addr` structure to give some information about how we are going to use the socket. We're using a family value of `AF_INET`, which basically means we want to use the Internet domain (TCP/IP network transmissions).

`INADDR_ANY` is a value which means "I am quite happy for this socket to talk to any IP address on the planet (or, indeed, off it)."

The `htons()` routine (it is, in fact, a macro) ensures that our port number information will be stored in network byte order (high byte, low byte) irrespective of whether our local architecture is *big-endian* (most significant byte stored first, as on the IBM 370 family, the PDP-10, Motorola microprocessors, and many RISC-based machines) or *little-endian* (least significant byte stored first, as on the PDP-11, VAX, and Intel machines).

Next, we open the socket by calling the `socket()` function. This function returns a file descriptor for us to use in subsequent sockets library function calls.

`SOCK_STREAM` indicates that we want this socket to use the TCP transport mechanism rather than UDP.

```
my_addr.sin_family = AF_INET;
  my_addr.sin_addr.s_addr = INADDR_ANY;
  my_addr.sin_port = htons(1091);

  memset(my_addr.sin_zero, 0,sizeof my_addr.sin_zero);

  if ((sockfd = socket(AF_INET, SOCK_STREAM, 0)) == -1)
  {
    printf("Unexpected error on socket()\n");
    return EXIT_FAILURE;
  }
```

Now that our socket is open, we can use it to establish communication by binding it to the appropriate port, which we have already set up in the `my_addr` structure. If the server doesn't do this, the client has no way to get in touch.

Once the server is ready, it can start to listen out for clients. Appropriately enough, the function we need to call is `listen()`. This function's first argument is the file descriptor that specifies which socket to listen on. The second argument indicates how many clients we would like the system to keep in the queue to connect (that is, for how big a backlog we want provision to be made).

```
if(bind(sockfd,
          (struct sockaddr *)&my_addr,
          sizeof(struct sockaddr))== -1)
  {
   printf("Unexpected error on bind()\n");
   return EXIT_FAILURE;
  }

  if(listen(sockfd, 4) == -1)
  {
    printf("Unexpected error on listen()\n");
    shutdown(sockfd,2);
    return EXIT_FAILURE;
  }
```

The `accept()` function (which we are about to meet) is blocking; that means that it will wait until a connection request turns up before returning control to our program. That's why we have our `CheckForData()` function; we only call `accept()` when we think there's something worth accepting.

If we do call it, it means there is a packet waiting to be processed. Because we shut down each new connection after reading it, it must be a new connection—after all, we don't let old connections live long enough to give us a second packet. So, `accept()` will give us a new socket descriptor for use with that new connection. We can then use that socket descriptor to pass to `recv()`, along with a buffer to collect the actual data.

The `recv()` call receives data from the socket. To do its job, it needs to know which socket to look at, where to place the data, and how much data to accept. The final parameter is for certain flags that need not concern us here. A value of 0 will tell `recv()` to use default values, which will suit our example application perfectly.

```
while(!done)
  {
    if(0 != CheckForData(sockfd))
    {
      sin_size = sizeof(struct sockaddr_in);
      if((new_fd = accept(sockfd,
                          (struct sockaddr *)&their_addr,
                          &sin_size)) == -1)
      {
```

```
        printf("Unexpected error on accept()\n");
        continue;
      }

      memset(data, 0, sizeof data);

      if(recv(new_fd, data, sizeof data, 0) == -1)
      {
       printf("Unexpected error on recv()\n");
      }
      else
      {
        newtotal += strtoul(data, &endp, 10);
        printf("Received data: %s\n", data);
      }
```

Finally, we send our reply back to the client. The `send()` function is syntactically similar to the `recv()` function. Once we've sent our data, we don't need to talk to this client anymore, so we shut down the temporary socket.

```
      sprintf(data, "%lu\n", currenttotal);      if(send(new_fd, data, sizeof data, 0)
== -1)
      {
       printf("Unexpected error on send()\n");
      }
      shutdown(new_fd, 2);
    }
  }
```

This process continues as long as necessary. The user signals the program when it's time to stop by pressing Ctrl+C. Our signal handler sets the loop control variable at that point, so that the loop terminates on the next test. At that point, we can shut down our listening socket and write our data to the output file.

```
  shutdown(sockfd,2);
  printf("User requested program to halt.\n");
  fp = fopen(Filename, "w");
  if(fp != NULL)
  {
    fprintf(fp, "%lu\n", newtotal);
    fclose(fp);
  }
  else
```

```
  {
    printf("Couldn't write total %lu to file %s\n",
           newtotal,
           Filename);
  }

  return EXIT_SUCCESS;
}
```


That's it. As you can see, the code is reasonably short, given that this program is capable of talking to another computer halfway around the world. As you can also see, the code is as portable, more or less, as the equator is square.

On its own, this program is useless. We're going to need a client for it to talk to.

A UNIX Client Program

Writing the client is a little more complicated because we need to tell the client where the server is. We can do this using a DNS (Domain Name Service). We tell the DNS the name of the computer running the server program (commonly called a hostname), and it then tells us that computer's IP address. If you don't have a DNS, or if your machine is set up not to use it, it will use the hosts file instead. This is a list of hostnames and their corresponding IP addresses.

Listing 22.2 shows the client implementation. Note that we've added a new header, `netdb.h`, which has the prototype for the `gethostbyname()` function.

LISTING 22.2 Source Code for a UNIX TCP Client

```
#include <stdio.h>
#include <stdlib.h>
#include <errno.h>
#include <string.h>
#include <netdb.h>
#include <netinet/in.h>
#include <sys/socket.h>

int Random(int n)
{
  return (int)(n * (rand() / (1.0 + (double)RAND_MAX))); }

int main(int argc, char *argv[])
{
```

LISTING 22.2 continued

```
int sockfd=0;
char data[255]={0};
struct hostent *he;
struct sockaddr_in their_addr;

srand(time(NULL));

if (argc < 2)
{
  fprintf(stderr,"usage: application hostname\n");
  return EXIT_FAILURE;
}

if((he = gethostbyname(argv[1])) == NULL)
{
  printf("Error with gethostbyname()\n");
  return EXIT_FAILURE;
}

if ((sockfd = socket(AF_INET, SOCK_STREAM, 0)) == -1)
{
  printf("Error with socket()\n");
  return EXIT_FAILURE;
}

their_addr.sin_family = AF_INET;
their_addr.sin_port = htons(1091);
their_addr.sin_addr = *((struct in_addr *)he->h_addr);
memset(their_addr.sin_zero,
       0,
       sizeof their_addr.sin_zero);
```

So far, this is pretty similar to the server code. One exception you may have noticed is that, instead of using `INADDR_ANY` for the IP address, we've used the address returned to us by the `gethostbyname()` function.

The next difference is that we don't `listen()` or `accept()`. Those are server functions. Instead, we need to `connect()` to the server. Here's how:

```
if(connect(sockfd,
           (struct sockaddr *)&their_addr,
           sizeof(struct sockaddr)) == -1)
```

```
  {
    printf("Error with connect()\n");
    return EXIT_FAILURE;
  }
  sprintf(data,
          "%lu Branch %d",
          (unsigned long)Random(10000),
          Random(100));

  if(send(sockfd, data, sizeof data, 0) == -1)
  {
    printf("Error with send()\n");
    return EXIT_FAILURE;
  }

  memset(data, 0, sizeof data);
  if (recv(sockfd, data, sizeof data, 0) == -1)
  {
    printf("Error with recv()\n");
    return EXIT_FAILURE;
  }

  printf("Received: %s\n", data);

  shutdown(sockfd,2);
  return EXIT_SUCCESS;
}
```

That wasn't so bad, was it? But, again, this code is non-portable to a significant degree. Neither this program nor the server program would ever compile under a typical Windows-based compiler. So, how would we do this under Windows?

Sockets Using TCP Under Windows

Windows sockets programs use the Winsock library, which is very closely related, but (alas!) not identical, to Berkeley Sockets. Unfortunately, we don't have space to discuss all the differences. But we can at least develop a Windows server and client. So, without further ado, let's have a look at the server program.

A Windows Server Program

As you can see from Listing 22.3, Windows likes to do things its own way. `WSAStartup()` and `WSACleanup()` are perhaps the most obvious differences from the UNIX code. Also, the Windows version uses different header files and has a plethora of different types, such as SOCKET, WORD, and so forth, which we ought to use to protect ourselves to some extent against future changes to the underlying library.

LISTING 22.3 Source Code for a Windows TCP Server

```
#include <stdio.h>
#include <stdlib.h>
#include <string.h>
#include <winsock.h>
#include <signal.h>

#define DEFAULT_FILE_NAME "sales.dat"

volatile sig_atomic_t done;

void inthandler(int Sig)
{
  done = 1;
}

int CheckForData(int sockfd)
{
  struct timeval tv;
  fd_set read_fd;
  tv.tv_sec=0;
  tv.tv_usec=0;
  FD_ZERO(&read_fd);
  FD_SET(sockfd, &read_fd);
  if(select(sockfd+1, &read_fd,NULL, NULL, &tv)== -1)
  {
   return 0;
  }

  if(FD_ISSET(sockfd, &read_fd))
  {
    return 1;
  }
  return 0;
}

int main(int argc, char **argv)
{
  WORD          wVersionRequested = MAKEWORD(1,1);
```

LISTING 22.3 continued

```
WSADATA     wsaData;
SOCKET      sock;
SOCKET      new_sock;
SOCKADDR_IN my_addr;

char data[255]= {0};

char *endp;

FILE *fp;
char Filename[FILENAME_MAX] = DEFAULT_FILE_NAME;
unsigned long currenttotal = 0;
unsigned long newtotal = 0;
if(argc < 2)
{
  printf("No file specified. Using \"%s\"\n",
         DEFAULT_FILE_NAME);
}
else
{
  strcpy(Filename, argv[1]);
}

fp = fopen(Filename, "r");
if(fp != NULL)
{
  if(NULL != fgets(data, sizeof data, fp))
  {
    currenttotal = strtoul(data, &endp, 10);
  }

  fclose(fp);
}
else
{
  printf("Couldn't read file %s\n", Filename);
}

if(signal(SIGINT, SIG_IGN) != SIG_IGN)
{
  signal(SIGINT, inthandler);
```

LISTING 22.3 continued

```
  }

  if(signal(SIGTERM, SIG_IGN) != SIG_IGN)
  {
    signal(SIGTERM, inthandler);
  }

  my_addr.sin_family = AF_INET;
  my_addr.sin_addr.s_addr = INADDR_ANY;
  my_addr.sin_port = htons(1091);

  WSAStartup(wVersionRequested, &wsaData);
  if(wsaData.wVersion != wVersionRequested)
  {
    printf("\n Wrong version of Winsock\n");
    return EXIT_FAILURE;
  }

  if((sock = socket(AF_INET, SOCK_STREAM, 0)) ==
      INVALID_SOCKET)
  {
    printf("Unexpected error on socket()\n");
    return EXIT_FAILURE;
  }

  if(bind(sock,
          (LPSOCKADDR)&my_addr,
          sizeof(struct sockaddr)) == SOCKET_ERROR)
  {
    printf("Unexpected error on bind()\n");
    shutdown(sock,2);
    return EXIT_FAILURE;
  }

  if (listen(sock, SOMAXCONN) == SOCKET_ERROR)
  {
    printf("Unexpected error on listen()\n");
    shutdown(sock, 2);
    return EXIT_FAILURE;
  }
```

LISTING 22.3 continued

```
  while(!done)
  {
    if(0 != CheckForData(sock))
    {
      new_sock = accept(sock, NULL, NULL);
      if(new_sock == INVALID_SOCKET)
      {
        printf("Unexpected error on accept()\n");
      }

      memset(data, 0, sizeof data);

      if(recv(new_sock, data, sizeof data,0) ==
         SOCKET_ERROR)
      {
        printf("Unexpected error on recv()\n");
      }

      memset(data, 0, sizeof data);

if (recv(new_sock, data, sizeof data,0) == SOCKET_ERROR)
      {
       printf("Unexpected error on recv()\n");
      }
      else
      {
        newtotal += strtoul(data, &endp, 10);
        printf("Received data: %s\n", data);
      }
      sprintf(data, "%lu", currenttotal);
      if (send(new_sock, data, sizeof data,0) == SOCKET_ERROR)
      {
       printf("Unexpected error on send()\n");
      }

    shutdown(new_sock,2);
    }
   }


   shutdown(sock, 2);
   WSACleanup();
```

LISTING 22.3 continued

```
  printf("User requested program to halt.\n");
  fp = fopen(Filename, "w");
  if(fp != NULL)
  {
    fprintf(fp, "%lu\n", newtotal);
    fclose(fp);
  }
  else
  {
    printf("Couldn't write total %lu to file %s\n",
           newtotal,
           Filename);
  }
  return EXIT_SUCCESS;
}
```

It could have been a lot worse. The Windows code is sufficiently close to the UNIX code to make an abstraction layer look relatively easy. This is not always the case. If, for example, we had written a fully GUI Windows program instead of a console application, our abstraction layer would have had to cope not just with the sockets code, but with the whole Windows GUI concept. That's possible, but by no means easy. (In fact, I was sorely tempted to set it as an exercise!)

A Windows Client Program

Now that we've seen the Windows native TCP Server program, Listing 22.4 shows the Client routine.

LISTING 22.4 Source Code for a Windows TCP Client

```
#include <stdio.h>
#include <string.h>
#include <time.h>
#include <winsock.h>

int Random(int n)
{
  return (int)(n * (rand() / (1.0 + (double)RAND_MAX)));
}

int main(int argc, char *argv[])
{
```

LISTING 22.4 continued

```
WORD wVersionRequested = MAKEWORD(1,1);
SOCKADDR_IN their_addr;
WSADATA wsaData;
SOCKET sockfd;
LPHOSTENT he;
char data[255]={0};
int nRet=0;

srand(time(NULL));
if (argc < 2)
 {
  printf("usage: application hostname\n");
  return EXIT_FAILURE;
 }

nRet = WSAStartup(wVersionRequested,
                  &wsaData);
if (wsaData.wVersion != wVersionRequested)
 {
  printf("\n Wrong version of Winsock\n");
  return EXIT_FAILURE;
 }

he = gethostbyname(argv[1]);
if (he == NULL)
 {
  printf("Error in gethostbyname().\n");
  return EXIT_FAILURE;
 }

sockfd = socket(AF_INET,
                SOCK_STREAM,
                IPPROTO_TCP);
if (sockfd == INVALID_SOCKET)
 {
  printf("Error on call to socket()\n");
  return EXIT_FAILURE;
 }

their_addr.sin_family = AF_INET;
their_addr.sin_addr = *((LPIN_ADDR)*he->h_addr_list);
```

LISTING 22.4 continued

```
  their_addr.sin_port = htons(1091);

  nRet = connect(sockfd,
                 (LPSOCKADDR)&their_addr,
                  sizeof(struct sockaddr));
  if (nRet == SOCKET_ERROR)
   {
    printf("Error on connect().\n");
    return EXIT_FAILURE;
   }

  sprintf(data, "%lu Branch %d",
         (unsigned long)Random(10000),
         Random(100));

  nRet = send(sockfd, data, strlen(data), 0);
  if (nRet == SOCKET_ERROR)
   {
    printf("Err on send()\n");
    return EXIT_FAILURE;
   }

  memset(data, 0, sizeof data);

  nRet = recv(sockfd,    data, sizeof data, 0);
  if (nRet == SOCKET_ERROR)
   {
    printf("Error on recv()\n");
      return EXIT_FAILURE;
   }

  printf("Received: %s\n", data);

  shutdown(sockfd,2);
  WSACleanup();
  return EXIT_SUCCESS;
}
```

Cross-platform Application

The trouble with this program is that we had to write the whole thing twice, once for each platform. For such a small, simple program, it was no real bother. For a large, complicated program, it would be a serious trial to have to rewrite the whole thing for the new platform.

Two possible solutions to this problem spring to mind. We could litter our code with `#ifdef` preprocessor directives, or we could write an abstraction layer.

Let's examine the conditional compilation option first.

Using the Preprocessor as a Porting Tool

The idea of conditional compilation is to identify some unique directive that is defined by each compiler for which we plan to write code. In this case, we need only distinguish between Windows and UNIX. If we are using a recent Microsoft or Borland C compiler, we are relatively safe in guessing that `_WIN32` is defined. (Does the word "relatively" worry you? It worries me...)

In Listing 22.5, we can see an example of using the preprocessor to create a cross-platform version of the servers shown in previous listings.

LISTING 22.5 Using Preprocessing Directives as a Porting Tool

```
#include <stdio.h>
#include <stdlib.h>
#include <string.h>
#include <signal.h>

#ifdef _WIN32
#include <winsock.h>
#else
#include <sys/time.h>
#include <sys/select.h>
#include <sys/types.h>
#include <sys/socket.h>
#include <netinet/in.h>
#endif

#define DEFAULT_FILE_NAME "sales.dat"

volatile sig_atomic_t done;

void inthandler(int Sig)
```

LISTING 22.5 continued

```
{
done = 1;
}

int CheckForData(int sockfd)
{
  struct timeval tv;
  fd_set read_fd;
  tv.tv_sec=0;
  tv.tv_usec=0;
  FD_ZERO(&read_fd);
  FD_SET(sockfd, &read_fd);
  if(select(sockfd+1, &read_fd,NULL, NULL, &tv)== -1)
  {
    return 0;
  }
  if(FD_ISSET(sockfd, &read_fd))
  {
    return 1;
  }
return 0;
}

int main(int argc, char **argv)
{
#ifdef _WIN32

  WORD wVersionRequested = MAKEWORD(1,1);
  WSADATA wsaData;
  SOCKET  sock;
  SOCKET  new_sock;
  SOCKADDR_IN my_addr;

#else
  int sock=0;
  int new_sock=0;
  struct sockaddr_in my_addr;
  struct sockaddr_in their_addr;
  socklen_t sin_size=0;

#endif
```

LISTING 22.5 continued

```
char data[255]= {0};
char *endp;

FILE *fp;
char Filename[FILENAME_MAX] = DEFAULT_FILE_NAME;
unsigned long currenttotal = 0;
unsigned long newtotal = 0;

if(argc < 2)
{
  printf("No file specified. Using \"%s\"\n",
         DEFAULT_FILE_NAME);
}
else
{
  strcpy(Filename, argv[1]);
}

fp = fopen(Filename, "r");
if(fp != NULL)
{
  if(NULL != fgets(data, sizeof data, fp))
  {
    currenttotal = strtoul(data, &endp, 10);
  }

  fclose(fp);
}
else
{
  printf("Couldn't read file %s\n", Filename);
}

if(signal(SIGINT, SIG_IGN) != SIG_IGN)
{
  signal(SIGINT, inthandler);
}

if(signal(SIGTERM, SIG_IGN) != SIG_IGN)
{
  signal(SIGTERM, inthandler);
```

LISTING 22.5 continued

```
  }

  my_addr.sin_family = AF_INET;
  my_addr.sin_addr.s_addr = INADDR_ANY;
  my_addr.sin_port = htons(1091);

#ifdef _WIN32
  WSAStartup(wVersionRequested, &wsaData);
  if (wsaData.wVersion != wVersionRequested)
  {
    printf("\n Wrong version of Winsock\n");
    return EXIT_FAILURE;
  }


  if ((sock = socket(AF_INET, SOCK_STREAM, 0)) ==
      INVALID_SOCKET)
#else
  memset(my_addr.sin_zero, 0,sizeof my_addr.sin_zero);

  if ((sock = socket(AF_INET, SOCK_STREAM, 0)) == -1)
#endif
  {
    printf("Unexpected error on socket()\n");
    return EXIT_FAILURE;
  }

#ifdef _WIN32
  if (bind(sock, (LPSOCKADDR)&my_addr,sizeof(struct sockaddr)) ==SOCKET_ERROR)
#else
  if (bind(sock,(struct sockaddr *)&my_addr, sizeof(struct sockaddr))== -1)

#endif
  {
    printf("Unexpected error on bind()\n");
    shutdown(sock,2);
    return EXIT_FAILURE;
  }

#ifdef _WIN32
  if (listen(sock, SOMAXCONN) == SOCKET_ERROR)
#else
```

LISTING 22.5 continued

```
  if (listen(sock, 4) == -1)
#endif
  {
    printf("Unexpected error on listen()\n");
    shutdown(sock,2);
    return EXIT_FAILURE;
  }


  while(!done)
  {
    if(0 != CheckForData(sock))
    {

#ifdef _WIN32
      new_sock = accept(sock, NULL, NULL);
      if (new_sock == INVALID_SOCKET)
#else
      sin_size = sizeof(struct sockaddr_in);
      if((new_sock = accept(sock,
                            (struct sockaddr *)
                            &their_addr,&sin_size)) == -1)
#endif
      {
        printf("Unexpected error on accept()\n");
      }
#ifndef _WIN32
      memset(data, 0, sizeof data);
#endif

#ifdef _WIN32
      if(recv(new_sock, data, sizeof data, 0) ==SOCKET_ERROR)
#else
      if(recv(new_sock, data, sizeof data, 0) == -1)
#endif
      {
        printf("Unexpected error on recv()\n");
      }
      else
      {
        newtotal += strtoul(data, &endp, 10);
        printf("Received data: %s\n", data);
```

LISTING 22.5 continued

```
      }

      sprintf(data, "%lu", currenttotal);
#ifdef _WIN32
      if (send(new_sock, data, sizeof data, 0) == SOCKET_ERROR)
#else
      if (send(new_sock, data, sizeof data, 0) == -1)
#endif
      {
        printf("Unexpected error on send()\n");
      }
      shutdown(new_sock, 2);     }
  }
  shutdown(sock , 2);
#ifdef _WIN32
  WSACleanup();
#endif
  printf("User requested program to halt.\n");
  fp = fopen(Filename, "w");
  if(fp != NULL)
  {
    fprintf(fp, "%lu\n", newtotal);
    fclose(fp);
  }
  else
  {
    printf("Couldn't write total %lu to file %s\n",
           newtotal,
           Filename);
  }
  return EXIT_SUCCESS;
}
```

It looks ghastly, doesn't it? Worse, it's hard to follow and therefore hard to maintain. If you make a change, the odds are good that you will have to make that change in two places.

What if we were writing code that had to work on three compilers? Or five? Or nine? Imagine what the code would look like. Fortunately, there's a better way.

Writing an Abstraction Layer

An abstraction layer isolates platform-specific functionality and data types into a separate module (or modules) from portable code. The platform-specific modules are then rewritten specifically for each platform. This involves the writing of a new header file to contain platform-specific `typedefs` and `#defines`, together with function prototypes for the abstracted functions (and it's vital to understand that these function prototypes must be identical on all the target platforms). The application module itself will include this new header, and will be linked to whichever platform-specific module is appropriate.

We will call our abstraction layer CUPS ("C Unleashed Portable Sockets"). Cute, huh?

Listing 22.6 shows our UNIX version of `cups.h`.

LISTING 22.6 Header for UNIX Version of Portable Sockets Library

```
/* this is the Unix version of cups.h */
#ifndef CUPS_H__
#define CUPS_H__

#include <sys/types.h>
#include <netinet/in.h>
#include <sys/socket.h>
#include <sys/time.h>
#include <sys/select.h>
#include <netdb.h>
#include <stdlib.h>

#define CUPS_SHUTDOWN_RECEIVE     0
#define CUPS_SHUTDOWN_SEND        1
#define CUPS_SHUTDOWN_BOTH        2

typedef struct CUPS_INFO
{
  int Dummy; /* placeholder: Windows needs
              * init info, Unix doesn't.
              */
} CUPS_INFO;

typedef struct CONNECTION
{
  int address_length;
  struct sockaddr_in my_addr;
  struct sockaddr_in their_addr;
```

LISTING 22.6 continued

```
  struct hostent *he;
  socklen_t sin_size;
  int Socket;
} CONNECTION;
```

This CONNECTION structure is key to our abstraction layer. It contains instances of all the data structures we're going to need for the UNIX version of the code. The idea is to remove any trace of Berkeley Sockets from the application layer's source code. Encapsulating the Sockets data in a structure means that, although the general socket paradigm remains, we no longer depend on any single aspect of Berkeley Sockets at the application layer.

```
void CUPSInit(CUPS_INFO *pInfo);
int CUPSStartup(CUPS_INFO *pInfo);
int CUPSGetHostByName(CONNECTION *Connection, char *);
int CUPSConnect(CONNECTION *Connection);
int CUPSCheckForData(CONNECTION *Connection);
int CUPSInitTCPConnection(CONNECTION *Connection,
                          unsigned long Address,
                          unsigned short Port);
int CUPSInitUDPConnection(CONNECTION *Connection,
                          unsigned long Address,
                          unsigned short Port);
int CUPSBind(CONNECTION *Connection);
int CUPSListen(CONNECTION *Connection);
int CUPSShutDown(CONNECTION *Connection,
                 int ShutdownType);
int CUPSAcceptConnection(CONNECTION *NewSocket,
                         CONNECTION *ServerConnection);
int CUPSRecv(CONNECTION *Connection,
             char *data,
             size_t size);
int CUPSRecvFrom(CONNECTION *Connection,
                 char *data,
                 size_t size);
int CUPSSendTo(CONNECTION *Connection,
               char *data,
               size_t size);
int CUPSSend(CONNECTION *Connection,
             char *data,
             size_t size);
int CUPSShutdownClientConnection(CONNECTION *Connection,
```

LISTING 22.9 continued

```
  int Result = 0; /* 0 = success */
  WSADATA wsaData;
  WSAStartup(pInfo->VersionRequested, &wsaData);

  if(wsaData.wVersion != pInfo->VersionRequested)
  {
    Result = 1;
  }
  return Result;
}

int CUPSGetHostByName(CONNECTION *Connection,
                      char *Host)
{
  int Result=0;
  if((Connection->he=gethostbyname(Host)) == NULL)
  {
    Result = 1;
  }
  return Result;
}

int CUPSInitTCPConnection(CONNECTION *Connection,
                          unsigned long Address,
                          unsigned short Port)
{
  int Result = 0;
  if(!Connection->he)
  {
   Connection->my_addr.sin_family = AF_INET;
   Connection->my_addr.sin_addr.s_addr = Address;
   Connection->my_addr.sin_port = htons(Port);
  }
  else
  {
   Connection->their_addr.sin_family = AF_INET;
   Connection->their_addr.sin_addr =
       *((LPIN_ADDR)*Connection->he->h_addr_list);
   Connection->their_addr.sin_port = htons(Port);
  }
   Connection->Socket = socket(AF_INET, SOCK_STREAM, 0);
   if(Connection->Socket == INVALID_SOCKET)
```

LISTING 22.9 continued

```
  {
    Result = 1;
  }
  return Result;
}

int CUPSInitUDPConnection(CONNECTION *Connection,
                          unsigned long Address,
                          unsigned short Port)
{
  int Result = 0;
  Connection->address_length = sizeof(struct sockaddr_in);
  if(!Connection->he)
  {
   Connection->my_addr.sin_family = AF_INET;
   Connection->my_addr.sin_addr.s_addr = Address;
   Connection->my_addr.sin_port = htons(Port);
  }
 else
  {
   Connection->their_addr.sin_family = AF_INET;
   Connection->their_addr.sin_addr =
      *((LPIN_ADDR)*Connection->he->h_addr_list);
   Connection->their_addr.sin_port = htons(Port);
  }
   Connection->Socket = socket(AF_INET, SOCK_DGRAM, 0);
   if(Connection->Socket == INVALID_SOCKET)
  {
    Result = 1;
  }
  return Result;
}

int CUPSConnect(CONNECTION *Connection)
{
 return connect(Connection->Socket,
               (LPSOCKADDR)&Connection->their_addr,
                sizeof (struct sockaddr));
 }

int CUPSBind(CONNECTION *Connection)
{
```

LISTING 22.9 continued

```
  int Result = 0;
  if(bind(Connection->Socket,
          (LPSOCKADDR)&Connection->my_addr,
          sizeof(struct sockaddr)) == SOCKET_ERROR)
  {
    Result = 1;
  }
  return Result;
}

int CUPSListen(CONNECTION *Connection)
{
  int Result = 0;
  if(listen(Connection->Socket, SOMAXCONN) ==
     SOCKET_ERROR)
  {
    Result = 1;
  }
  return Result;
}

int CUPSShutdown(CONNECTION *Connection, int ShutdownType)
{
  if(ShutdownType != CUPS_SHUTDOWN_RECEIVE &&
     ShutdownType != CUPS_SHUTDOWN_SEND)
  {
    ShutdownType = CUPS_SHUTDOWN_BOTH;
  }
  shutdown(Connection->Socket, ShutdownType);
  return 0;
}

int CUPSAcceptConnection(CONNECTION *NewSocket,
                         CONNECTION *ServerConnection)
{
  int Result = 0;
  *NewSocket = *ServerConnection;
  NewSocket->Socket = accept(ServerConnection->Socket,
                             NULL, NULL);
  if(NewSocket->Socket == INVALID_SOCKET)
  {
    Result = 1;
```

LISTING 22.9 continued

```
  }
  return Result;
}

int CUPSRecv(CONNECTION *Connection,
             char *data, size_t size)
{
  int Result = 0;
  if(recv(Connection->Socket,
          data, (int)size, 0) == SOCKET_ERROR)
  {
    Result = 1;
  }
  return Result;
}

int CUPSRecvFrom(CONNECTION *Connection,
                 char *data, size_t size)
{
 int Result = 0;
 if(recvfrom(Connection->Socket, data, size, 0,
      (struct sockaddr *)&Connection->their_addr,
      &Connection->address_length) == SOCKET_ERROR)
  {
    Result = 1;
  }
  return Result;
}

int CUPSSend(CONNECTION *Connection,
             char *data, size_t size)
{
  int Result = 0;
  if(send(Connection->Socket, data,
          (int)size, 0) == SOCKET_ERROR)
  {
    Result = 1;
  }
  return Result;
}

int CUPSSendTo(CONNECTION *Connection,
```

LISTING 22.9 continued

```
               char *data, size_t size)
{
  int Result = 0;
  if(sendto(Connection->Socket,
            data,
            size,
            0,
            (struct sockaddr *)&Connection->their_addr,
            (int) sizeof (struct sockaddr)) ==
            SOCKET_ERROR)
  {
    Result = 1;
  }

  return Result;
}

int CUPSShutdownClientConnection(CONNECTION *Connection,
                                 int ShutdownType)
{
  if(ShutdownType != CUPS_SHUTDOWN_RECEIVE &&
     ShutdownType != CUPS_SHUTDOWN_SEND)
  {
    ShutdownType = CUPS_SHUTDOWN_BOTH;
  }
  shutdown(Connection->Socket, ShutdownType);
  return 0;
}

int CUPSCleanup(CUPS_INFO *CupsInfo)
{
  WSACleanup();
  return 0;
}

int CUPSCheckForData(CONNECTION *Connection)
{
  struct timeval tv;
  fd_set read_fd;
  tv.tv_sec=0;
  tv.tv_usec=0;
  FD_ZERO(&read_fd);
```

LISTING 22.9 continued

```
  FD_SET(Connection->Socket, &read_fd);
  if(select(Connection->Socket+1, &read_fd,
            NULL, NULL, &tv)== -1)
  {
    return 0;
  }
  if(FD_ISSET(Connection->Socket, &read_fd))
  {
    return 1;
  }
 return 0;
}
```

The CUPS library lays the groundwork on which we can write the preceding applications. We simply link in the object code of the correct `cups.c` file for our architecture.

Let's see how such an application would look. Listing 22.10 shows the same server we coded earlier, but now using the CUPS library to abstract non-portable functionality away from the primary application source. The question is, "Is this source file for Windows or UNIX?"

LISTING 22.10 Cross-platform Server Application Using the CUPS Library

```
/* application (server program) */

#include <stdio.h>
#include <stdlib.h>
#include <string.h>
#include <signal.h>

#include "cups.h"

#define DEFAULT_FILE_NAME "sales.dat"

volatile sig_atomic_t done;

void inthandler(int Sig)
{
  done = 1;
}

int main(int argc, char **argv)
```

LISTING 22.10 continued

```
{
  CUPS_INFO CupsInfo = {0};

  CONNECTION ServerConnection = {0};
  CONNECTION ConnectionToClient = {0};

  char data[255] = {0};
  char *endp;
  FILE *fp;
  char Filename[FILENAME_MAX] = DEFAULT_FILE_NAME;
  unsigned long currenttotal = 0;
  unsigned long  newtotal = 0;

  if(argc < 2)
  {
    printf("No file specified. Using \"%s\"\n",
           DEFAULT_FILE_NAME);
  }
  else
  {
    strcpy(Filename, argv[1]);
  }

  fp = fopen(Filename, "r");
  if(fp != NULL)
  {
    if(NULL != fgets(data, sizeof data, fp))
    {       currenttotal = strtoul(data, &endp, 10);
    }

    fclose(fp);
  }
  else
  {
    printf("Couldn't read file %s\n", Filename);
  }

  if(signal(SIGINT, SIG_IGN) != SIG_IGN)
   {
    signal(SIGINT, inthandler);
   }
```

LISTING 22.10 continued

```
  if(signal(SIGTERM, SIG_IGN) != SIG_IGN)
   {
    signal(SIGTERM, inthandler);
   }

  srand(time(NULL));
  CUPSInit(&CupsInfo);
  if(CUPSStartup(&CupsInfo) != 0)
  {
    printf("Initialization failed.\n");
    fgets(data, sizeof data, stdin);
    return EXIT_FAILURE;
  }

  if(0 != CUPSInitTCPConnection(&ServerConnection,
                                INADDR_ANY, 1091))
  {
    printf("Call to socket() failed\n\n");
    return EXIT_FAILURE;
  }

  if(0 != CUPSBind(&ServerConnection))
  {
    printf("Can't bind().\n");
    return EXIT_FAILURE;
  }

  if(0 != CUPSListen(&ServerConnection))
  {
    printf("Unexpected error while calling listen().\n");
    CUPSShutdown(&ServerConnection, CUPS_SHUTDOWN_BOTH);
    return EXIT_FAILURE;
  }

  while(!done)
{
  if(0 != CUPSCheckForData(&ServerConnection))
    {
    if(0 != CUPSAcceptConnection(&ConnectionToClient,
                                 &ServerConnection))
    {
      printf("Unexpected error on accept()\n");
```

LISTING 22.10 continued

```
    }
    else
    {
      memset(data, 0, sizeof data);

      if(0 != CUPSRecv(&ConnectionToClient,
                       data, sizeof data))
      {
        printf("Unexpected error on recv()\n");
      }
      else
      {
        newtotal += strtoul(data, &endp, 10);
        printf("Received data: %s\n", data);
      }

      sprintf(data, "%lu\n", currenttotal);
      if(0 != CUPSSend(&ConnectionToClient,
                       data, sizeof data))
      {
        printf("Unexpected error on send()\n");
      }

      CUPSShutdownClientConnection(&ConnectionToClient,
                                   CUPS_SHUTDOWN_BOTH);
    }
  }
}
CUPSShutdown(&ServerConnection, CUPS_SHUTDOWN_BOTH);
CUPSCleanup(&CupsInfo);

printf("User requested program to halt.\n");

fp = fopen(Filename, "w");
if(fp != NULL)
{
  fprintf(fp, "%lu\n", newtotal);
  fclose(fp);
}
else
{
  printf("Couldn't write total %lu to "
```

LISTING 22.10 continued

```
           "file %s\n", newtotal, Filename);
  }
  return 0;
}
```

No prizes. The answer is "Yes." The beauty of using the CUPS library is that this single file will suffice on both of our key architectures for this chapter, UNIX and Microsoft Windows.

We will take one more look at it in action (see Listing 22.11), this time in the client.

LISTING 22.11 Cross-platform Client Application with CUPS Library

```
#include <stdio.h>
#include <stdlib.h>
#include <string.h>

#include "cups.h"

int Random(int n)
{
  return (int)(n * (rand() / (1.0 + (double)RAND_MAX)));
}

int main(int argc, char *argv[])
 {
   CUPS_INFO CupsInfo = {0};
   CONNECTION ClientConnection = {0};
   char data[255]={0};

   if (argc != 2)
    {
     printf("usage: application hostname\n");
     return EXIT_FAILURE;
    }

   srand(time(NULL));
   CUPSInit(&CupsInfo);
   if(CUPSStartup(&CupsInfo) != 0)
    {
     printf("Initialization failed.\n");
     fgets(data, sizeof data, stdin);
```

SERVER_PROTOCOL

The SERVER_PROTOCOL variable is very similar to the GATEWAY_INTERFACE variable. It specifies the version and protocol to which the Web server adheres.

```
SERVER_PROTOCOL=HTTP/1.1
```

SERVER_SOFTWARE

The SERVER_SOFTWARE variable consists of the name and version information of the Web server.

```
SERVER_SOFTWARE = Apache/1.3.6 (Unix) (Red Hat/Linux)
```

Retrieving Input

When discussing the FORM tag previously, we briefly mentioned the METHOD attribute. This attribute determines which of two completely different methods the Web server will use when sending data to the CGI application. You will recall that the two possible values for METHOD are GET and POST.

When METHOD is set to GET, the Web server will invoke the process stipulated by the ACTION attribute and use the data from the form to populate an environment variable named QUERY_STRING. It will also display the data string in the browser address bar, just as if it were a URL (uniform resource locator), which might be a problem if your data contains, say, password information. This is not specific to a particular browser; it's a consequence of the HTTP protocol. Furthermore, there is a limit to the number of characters a URL may contain. This limit is specific to the Web server being used. In some cases it can be as high as 8192 bytes or as low as 255 bytes, but the important thing is that there is a limit.

Fortunately, there is an excellent alternative. By setting the METHOD attribute to POST, we can tell the Web server to pass the data to the CGI application via its standard input stream. The Web server will also tell the CGI process the exact number of bytes to accept, in an environment variable named CONTENT_LENGTH; this sidesteps the arbitrary Web server limitation on data length. As a final bonus, POST will also not display the query string on the URL bar in the same way that GET does. Still, you shouldn't consider this to be secure, merely more secure. The information is still sent from the browser to the Web server "in clear" (unencrypted).

The first task our CGI application must perform is to determine where to get its data. To do this, we examine the REQUEST_METHOD environment variable, which will, as we have seen, be set to either GET or POST.

If the method is `GET`, we can find the data in the contents of the `QUERY_STRING` environment variable. If the method is `POST`, we may find out how much data there is to read by checking the `CONTENT_LENGTH` environment variable. We can then allocate that much data (the `malloc()` function is good for this) and then read that number of bytes from the standard input stream.

Let's look at some source code that achieves all this (see Listing 23.1). You'll notice that the code uses a handful of macros. These are defined in the file `cgi.h`, which you will find on the CD-ROM.

LISTING 23.1 `ReadCGIData`—Reads CGI Input from an Input Stream

```
char *ReadCGIData(int *Error)
{
  char *Buffer = NULL;
  char *RequestMethod = NULL;
  char *ContentLength = NULL;
  char *CGIData = NULL;

  size_t Size = 0;

  *Error = CGI_SUCCESS;

  RequestMethod = getenv("REQUEST_METHOD");
  if(NULL == RequestMethod)
  {
    *Error = CGI_NULL_REQ_METHOD;
  }

  if(0 == *Error)
  {
    if(strcmp(RequestMethod,"GET") == 0)
    {
      /* GET */
      CGIData = getenv("QUERY_STRING");
      if(NULL == CGIData)
      {
        *Error = CGI_NO_QUERY_STRING;
      }
      else
      {
        Buffer = DupString(CGIData);
        if(NULL == Buffer)
```

LISTING 23.1 continued

```
        {
          *Error = CGI_NO_MEMORY;
        }
      }
    }
    else if(strcmp(RequestMethod,"POST") == 0)
    {
      /* POST */
      ContentLength = getenv("CONTENT_LENGTH");
      if(NULL == ContentLength)
      {
        *Error = CGI_BAD_CONTENT_LENGTH;
      }
      if(0 == *Error)
      {
        Size = (size_t)atoi(ContentLength);
        if(Size <= 0)
        {
          *Error = CGI_BAD_CONTENT_LENGTH;
        }
      }
      if(0 == *Error)
      {
        ++Size;
        Buffer = malloc(Size);
        if(NULL == Buffer)
        {
          *Error = CGI_NO_MEMORY;
        }
        else
        {
          if(NULL == fgets(Buffer, Size, stdin))
          {
            *Error = CGI_NO_DATA;
            free(Buffer);
            Buffer = NULL;
          }
        }
      }
    }
    else
    {
```

LISTING 23.1 continued

```
      *Error = CGI_UNKNOWN_METHOD;
    }
  }

  return Buffer;
}
```

This source may be found in `cgi.c`, which, again, is on the CD-ROM.

You may have noticed that there is absolutely nothing application-specific in this function, and perhaps you're wondering whether it will suit all CGI C programs. The answer is yes. It doesn't even mind whether you use `GET` or `POST`. Therefore, you don't have to write any of this, ever. You can just hijack it from the CD-ROM. (That's okay; don't mention it.)

Parsing the Query String

The `ReadCGIData()` function returns a pointer to a copy of the query string passed to the CGI application by the Web server. It is a string of text that contains all the data from the Web page form. It is in the format *`variable=value`* and, if there is more than one data item, they are separated by ampersands (for example, *`variable=value&variable=value`*). The variable name in question will depend on the `NAME` value we used for that variable in our HTML form.

Also in the string you may notice some odd characters. For example, `message=this+is+a+test&message2=wow+%21`.

Let's take a careful look at what this data is and why it is in this format. As you will undoubtedly recall, the query string is passed as a valid URL when we use the `GET` method of data transfer. It follows, therefore, that this string must follow the rules of the URL syntax. For example, there can be no spaces or punctuation. Imagine a URL that read `http://w!^w.$%.com`; it simply would not work. But what if we need to pass that exact string of data to our CGI? We can, thanks to the Web server's data encoding mechanism.

We have two distinct decoding tasks to perform (although there's nothing to stop us doing them in parallel). The first is to convert any "+" characters we find into " " (space) characters. The second is to translate hex-encoded characters into their ASCII equivalents. They are represented by `%xx`, where `%` is a token to let us know to handle this specially. The `xx` is the hex value of the ASCII equivalent. For example, `%21` equates to 0x21 in hex, which is 33 in decimal. The ASCII character "!" is represented as 33.

Note

If you're a mainframe programmer, you may be bridling a little at this point. What about EBCDIC and all the other collating sequences out there? Whatever happened to portable programming? Well, HTTP uses ASCII and there's no two ways about it. ASCII is the de facto Web alphabet.

This description may seem a little complex. It's a lot easier to show than to tell, so let's have a look at some C source in Listing 23.2.

LISTING 23.2 `CGIHexToAscii`—Converts Hex Encoded Data to Printable ASCII Data

```
int CGIHexToAscii(char *s)
{
  /* Set Error to non-zero on error */
  int Error = 0;

  /* It's going to be very convenient to
   * have all the hexadecimal digits in
   * a contiguous, ordered string
   */
  static const char *Hex = "0123456789ABCDEF";

  /* We'll use this to store an offset
   * into the Hex array.
   */
  unsigned int Ascii = 0;

  /* This is basically a spare pointer.
   * We walk it along the list, using
   * it as the current place for storing
   * characters.
   */
  char *p;

  /* non-NULL if a valid hexadecimal digit was found */
  char *Match;

  /* For each character in the string... */
  for(p = s; !Error && *s != '\0'; s++)
  {
    /* Is it a hex-coded character? */
```

LISTING 23.2 continued

```
    if(*s == '%')
    {
      /* Yes. Leaving p behind, move s on to
       * the first byte of the encoding.
       */
      s++;

      /* It had better be in the Hex string.
       * If not, that's an error in the data.
       */
      if((Match = strchr(Hex, *s)) != NULL)
      {
        /* We can now calculate the high nybble of the
         * ASCII equivalent of the coded character.
         */
        Ascii = (unsigned int)(Match - Hex);

        /* And now we do the whole thing
         * again for the low nybble.
         */
        s++;
        if((Match = strchr(Hex, *s)) != NULL)
        {
          /* Move the high nybble out of the way */
          Ascii <<= 4;
          Ascii |= (unsigned int)(Match - Hex);

          /* Now we can update the string.
           * Note that p lags behind s by two characters
           * for each hex-encoded character in the data.
           */
          *p++ = (char)Ascii;
        }
        else
        {
          Error = 1;
        }
      }
      else
      {
        Error = 1;
      }
```

LISTING 23.2 continued

```
    }
    /* If it's not a hex-encoded character, could it
     * be a +, which needs to become a space?
     */
    else if(*s == '+')
    {
      *p++ = ' ';
    }
    /* No? In which case we just copy the character. */
    else
    {
      *p++ = *s;
    }
  }
  if(!Error)
  {
    /* Let's not forget to zero-terminate the string. */
    *p = '\0';
  }
  return Error;
}
```


Again, this code is on the CD-ROM in `cgi.c` and, again, it's necessary and sufficient—you need never write it yourself.

You might be thinking that we send the entire query string to this function. We don't. You will recall that our data is formatted as *`variable=value`* pairs, separated by ampersands. If an ampersand is part of the user data (and converted into hex code by the browser), converting the whole string from hex to ASCII could be a really bad move. It makes sense to tokenize it into *`variable=value`* pairs first and then decode each pair.

Also, we need to think about storing the variables and their values. The way that immediately springs to mind is a list. So our first requirement is a data structure suitable for making into a linked list. Here's a quote from `cgi.h`:

```
typedef struct CGI_LIST
{
  char *Variable;
  char *Value;
  struct CGI_LIST *Next;
} CGI_LIST;
```

Nothing complicated; this is a very straightforward single-linked list. We are going to walk along our query string, breaking it apart at the ampersands, decoding it, and then splitting it into variable and value (using the first "=" character we find as the delimiter between the two). Unfortunately, we are in the awkward situation that we don't know how much memory to allocate to the value and how much to the variable. One method would be to iterate through the string to find the first "=" character, then return to the start of the string and iterate through it again to do the actual copying of data. This is a little clumsy.

As it turns out, we don't need to know this. We can simply point both `Variable` and `Value` at the same place (the variable), then walk the `Value` pointer forward until it hits an "=" character, set that to the null character (\0), and then point to the character just past it. As long as we remember that `Value` doesn't point to its own space, but into `Variable`'s (and thus we don't try to `free()` it twice by mistake), all will be well and, in fact, it turns out to be a rather neat solution.

Listing 23.3 shows the function that builds the list.

LISTING 23.3 `CGICreateList`—**Create and Populate Linked List with User Data**

```
CGI_LIST *CGICreateList(char *Data)
{
  /* The list base pointer */
  CGI_LIST *CGIList;
  /* Our current position within the list */
  CGI_LIST *CurrItem = NULL;

  /* If we get any error, however slight, ditch
   * the whole list and walk off the pitch.
   */
  int Error = 0;

  /* One field. Tokenised from Data using '=' */
  char *Field;

  /* Get some memory for the base node */
  CGIList = malloc(sizeof *CGIList);
  if(CGIList != NULL)
  {
    /* Point travelling pointer to base of list */
    CurrItem = CGIList;

    /* Get the first field. Because strtok modifies its
     * input, we can't use the query string directly in
```

LISTING 23.3 continued

```
     * case it was stored in the environment variable
     * (GET method) which is why we made a copy earlier.
     */
    Field = strtok(Data, "&\n");
    if(NULL == Field)
    {
      Error = 1; /* No data! */
    }

    /* For each field */
    while(0 == Error && Field != NULL)
    {
      /* Convert encoded characters (eg %21 to '!') */
      if(CGIHexToAscii(Field) != 0)
      {
        Error = 1;
      }
      else
      {
        /* Ensure that default values are in place
         * NB can't use memset because we have no
         * assurance from the ANSI Standard that
         * NULL has a bit pattern of all bits zero.
         */
        CurrItem->Value    = NULL;
        CurrItem->Next     = NULL;

        /* Copy the field data for safe keeping */
        CurrItem->Variable = DupString(Field);
        if(NULL == CurrItem->Variable)
        {
          Error = 2;
        }
        else
        {
          /* Start at Variable */
          CurrItem->Value = CurrItem->Variable;

          /* Keep going unti we hit '=' */
          while(*CurrItem->Value != '\0' &&
                *CurrItem->Value != '=')
          {
```

LISTING 23.3 continued

```
          ++CurrItem->Value;
        }
        if('\0' == *CurrItem->Value)
        {
          Error = 3;
        }
        else
        {
          /* Zero-terminate Variable */
          *CurrItem->Value = '\0';
          /* Point to first byte of value */
          ++CurrItem->Value;
        }
      }
    }

    if(0 == Error)
    {
      /* Get next token */
      Field = strtok(NULL, "&\n");
      if(Field != NULL)
      {
        /* allocate memory for next node */
        CurrItem->Next = malloc(sizeof *CurrItem->Next);
        if(NULL == CurrItem->Next)
        {
          Error = 1;
        }
        else
        {
          CurrItem = CurrItem->Next;
        }
      }
    }
  }
  /* If anything went wrong, bin the whole list */
  if(Error != 0)
  {
    CGIDestroyList(CGIList);
    CGIList = NULL;
  }
}
```

LISTING 23.3 continued

```
  return CGIList;
}
```

The code in Listing 23.3 builds a linked list with each node representing one variable and its associated value, with NULL indicating the end of the list. This list will quite happily hold variables with the same name, so we won't have any problem with radio buttons or drop-down lists set to `MULTIPLE`.

We also need code to destroy the list. Fortunately, it's quite simple, as shown here:

```
void CGIDestroyList(CGI_LIST *List)
{
  CGI_LIST *Next = NULL;

  while(List != NULL)
  {
    Next = List->Next;
    if(List->Variable != NULL)
    {
      free(List->Variable);
    }
    /* Note: we don't free Value because
     * it is pointing into the Variable
     * area anyway.
     */
    free(List);
    List = Next;
  }
}
```


Sample Application: Function Prototype Lookup

All of the C code we have seen so far in this chapter has been totally generic, and may be used in any CGI program. Now let's look at a particular application. You may recall that our sample application will allow the user to look up the function prototype for any function in the ANSI C standard library. If the user prefers, he may look up the version number of the CGI application by using `version` as his search string. In either case, it would be tidier if the user didn't have to move back to the original page in order to repeat the search. Therefore, our CGI application will not only display the function prototype or version number, but also a brand new form, so that the user may seamlessly continue his research into C's rich function library.

To make your future CGI programming as effortless as possible, I've placed all the application functionality into a function called `App()`, except for one helper function that is specific to this application. Consider `App()` to be the entry point to the CGI program. (It isn't, of course, and there's nothing magical about the name `App()`, in CGI terms; that's just a name I chose. Feel free to change it to something else if you like, as long as you make the corresponding change to `main()`.) If you want a different CGI application, you need only rewrite this one function. Of course, you may use additional helper functions if you want. We use one such function here, as shown in Listing 23.4.

LISTING 23.4 App—Application-Specific Code to Display Prototypes from the ANSI C Standard Library

```
void App(CGI_LIST *List)
{
  char *Proto = NULL;
  int GettingVersionInfo = 0;
  char *VersionInfo =
    "C Unleashed CGI Demo v1.05";
  char *ScriptName = getenv("SCRIPT_NAME");

  /* We are only expecting one item in the list,
   * so let's use it.
   */

  if(strcmp(List->Value, "version") == 0)
  {
    GettingVersionInfo = 1;
  }

  printf("<HTML>\n");
  printf("  <HEAD>\n");
  printf("    <TITLE>\n      ");
  if(GettingVersionInfo)
  {
    printf("Version information for CGI Demo\n");
  }
  else
  {
    printf("Function prototype for %s", List->Value);
  }
```

LISTING 23.4 continued

```
printf("    </TITLE>\n");
printf("  </HEAD>\n");
printf("  <BODY>\n");


if(GettingVersionInfo)
{
  printf("<H1>Version information for CGI Demo<H1>\n");
  printf("<P><P><H2>%s</H2>\n", VersionInfo);
}
else
{
  printf("  <H1><B>%s</B></H1><P>\n", List->Value);

  Proto = GetPrototype(List->Value);
  if(NULL == Proto)
  { source file>
    printf("<I>%s not found. Please"
           " check spelling.</I>\n",
           List->Value);
  }
  else
  {
    printf("<I>%s</I>\n", Proto);
  }
}

if(ScriptName != NULL)
{
  printf("    <BR>\n");
  printf("    <FORM METHOD=\"POST\""
              " ACTION=\"%s\">\n",
              ScriptName);

  printf("      <BR><HR><BR>\n");
  printf("      <CENTER>\n");
  printf("        <FONT SIZE=4>\n");
  printf("          Next search:\n");
  printf("          <BR>\n<BR>\n");
  printf("          Please type in the name "
                    "of the function\n");
  printf("          whose prototype you"
```

LISTING 23.4 continued

```
                    " wish to see.\n");
    printf("        </FONT>\n");

    printf("        <BR><BR>\n");
    printf("        <INPUT TYPE=\"text\" NAME="
           "\"function\" SIZE=\"20\">\n");
    printf("        <BR><BR>\n");

    printf("        <INPUT TYPE=\"submit\">\n");
    printf("      </CENTER>\n");
    printf("    </FORM>\n");
  }

  printf("  </BODY>\n");
  printf("</HTML>\n");
}
```

As you can see, all we need to do to create our output is to call `printf`! The Web server will pick up our standard output stream and send it to the user's browser, just as if the user had requested a normal Web page (which, in a way, he did).

The helper function `GetPrototype()` returns an HTML encoding of the function prototype, together with the appropriate header file and, in a couple of cases, a useful comment. It returns NULL if it doesn't have information about the supplied function name. There's little point in quoting the source here. It's on the CD-ROM, in the `proto.c` source file. Basically, it's a simple lookup table. A "real" CGI application might query a text file or an SQL database at this point, but for simplicity, portability, and (perhaps) speed, `GetPrototype()` holds all its information in memory.

All we need now is to tie all this code together with a `main()` function (see Listing 23.5), and we're done.

LISTING 23.5 `main()`—Entry Point of Our CGI Application

```
int main(void)
{
  CGI_LIST *List = NULL;
  char *CopyOfQueryString = NULL;
  int ErrorCode = 0;

  /* The next line is required, for HTTP
   * protocol reasons. It will not appear
```

LISTING 23.5 continued

```
 * on your output HTML page.
 */
printf("Content-Type: text/html\n\n");

CopyOfQueryString = ReadCGIData(&ErrorCode);

if(NULL == CopyOfQueryString)
{
  switch(ErrorCode)
  {
    case CGI_NULL_REQ_METHOD:
      printf("No CGI request method "
             "could be identified.\n");
      break;
    case CGI_UNKNOWN_METHOD:
      printf("Unsupported CGI request method.\n");
      break;
    case CGI_NO_QUERY_STRING:
      printf("No CGI query string found.\n");
      break;
    case CGI_NO_MEMORY:
      printf("Memory allocation failure.\n");
      break;
    case CGI_BAD_CONTENT_LENGTH:
      printf("Missing or invalid CONTENT_LENGTH.\n");
      break;
    case CGI_NO_DATA:
      printf("No CGI input data could be found.\n");
      break;
    default:
      printf("Unknown CGI Error.\n");
      break;
  }

  /* We can't proceed, so we might as well exit. */
  return EXIT_FAILURE;
}

List = CGICreateList(CopyOfQueryString);
```

LISTING 23.5 continued

```
  /* Whether that worked or not, we don't need
   * CopyOfQueryString any more, so let's dump it.
   */
  free(CopyOfQueryString);

  if(NULL == List)
  {
    printf("Can't parse CGI data.\n");
    return EXIT_FAILURE;
  }

  /****************************
   *                          *
   * This is where your CGI   *
   * application gets called! *
   *                          *
   ****************************/
  App(List);

  /* Let's not forget to clean up */
  CGIDestroyList(List);

  return 0;
}
```

As you probably worked out already, this source code is stored on the CD-ROM, in `proto.c`.

By now, I hope you're wondering where the catch is. This all seems too simple! Well, there is no catch. It really is that simple, and I hope you'll agree it's even simpler, now that all the setup code is written for you. All you need do to write your own CGI applications is to replace the `App()` function with your own.

Figures 23.2 and 23.3 show our sample CGI application in action.

Figure 23.2 shows how our HTML form is displayed and accepts user input.

In Figure 23.3 we can see the CGI results as displayed in the Internet Explorer Web browser.

FIGURE 23.2
Proto Web page.

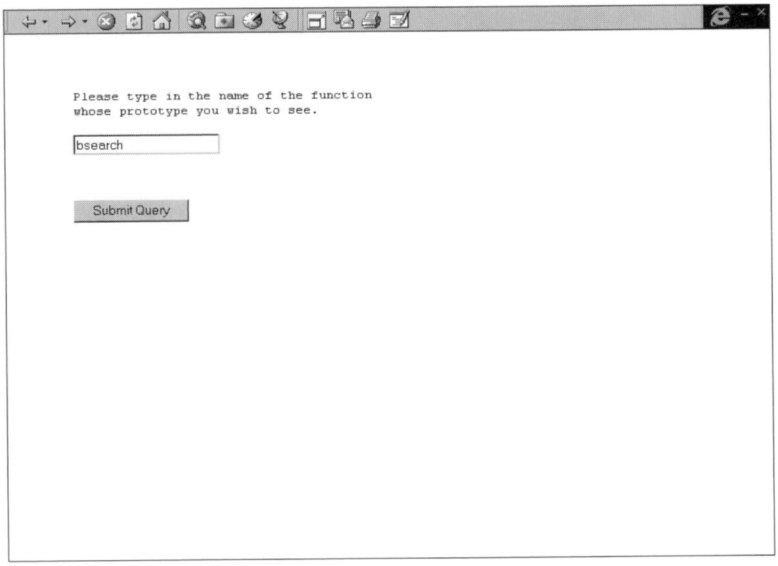

FIGURE 23.3
Proto CGI application.

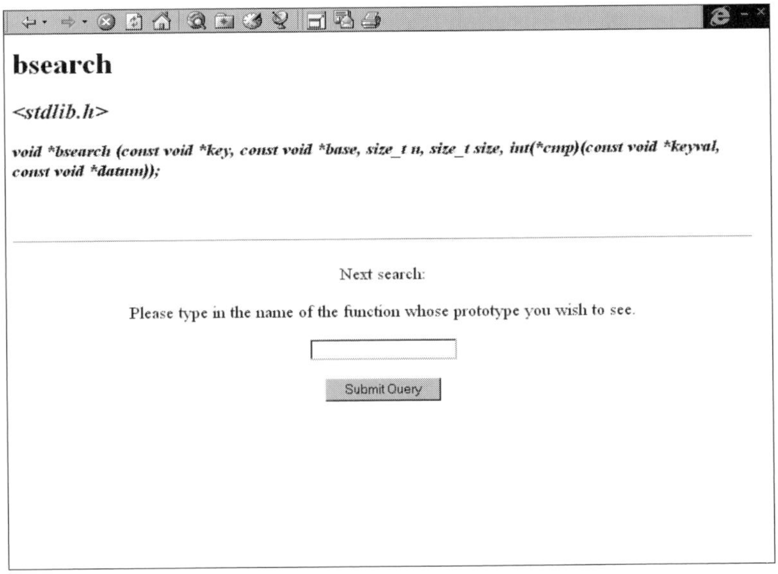

Security Concerns

There are a few security matters we need to consider when writing CGI programs. Generally speaking, there are no exploitable "holes" in the CGI process. The most common issues stem from poor programming.

Running External Processes

The CGI process is owned by the same process ID as the Web server. This could lead to possible security compromises if the end user were allowed to execute commands on our server.

Let's take a specific example. We have a form that runs as a ping server. Its sole job is to get a hostname or IP address from an HTTP form and try to ping that device, echoing the results back to the screen.

```
<FORM METHOD="POST" ACTION="/cgi-bin/ping.cgi">
<INPUT TYPE=TEXT NAME=host>
</FORM>
```

Now let's say we parse the query string and extract the data corresponding to that entry in the HTML form, assigning it to `char *name`. How would we go about doing the rest of it?

```
char cmd[255]={0};
sprintf(cmd, "/bin/ping -c4 %s", name);
system(cmd);
```

This would do exactly what we want and does seem like a reasonable approach. But alas, we have a cunning user. What if he enters this name into the form?

```
"www.mcp.com;cat%20/etc/passwd"
```

It would be run through the `system()` command as `ping -c4 127.0.0.1; cat /etc/passwd`. (`%20` is the hex code of the ASCII space character.)

This particular Web server happens to be running on a UNIX machine. In UNIX, the ";" tells the shell to execute the next command, the next command in this case being to echo sensitive data back through the Web browser.

Our CGI program can run any command that the owner of the Web server can run, potentially opening up severe security holes.

Now it's perfectly true that you are highly unlikely to write a ping server! Nevertheless, date/time servers are quite common, and it's not unknown for them to fetch the date using a `system()` call, rather than `time()` and `localtime()`. And some CGI programs call `sendmail` to deliver the CGI's output via email. If the `system()` call is written naively, we have a security breach just sitting there, probably waiting for the worst possible time to happen.

HTML Source Is Not a Secret

Almost every browser allows the user to read our HTML source and/or save it to file. This information can be useful to a cracker in his quest to compromise our security. Let's take a common CGI application—sending an email to a Webmaster.

```
<INPUT TYPE=HIDDEN NAME=sendto VALUE=webmaster@mcp.com>
```

What are we giving away here? If nothing else, we see two things. First, the output will be mailed to the address `webmaster@mcp.com`. Second, the user may be able to change that value! This applies to all of our HTML code. A cracker can save our HTML document to his local disk and edit it so that it will now read `VALUE=me@mybadsite.com`. When he executes this, it will send the new data to the CGI application, and the email will go to the address he substituted. Even if no other harm is done, we have just created a potential email gateway for spammers.

Let's look at another possibility. We are writing a CGI database application, and our HTML contains the names of the database and table we need to consult. We might even specify the account name and password to use for making the connection to the database! Let's say we took this approach:

```
<INPUT TYPE=HIDDEN NAME=db VALUE=2000q1>
<INPUT TYPE=HIDDEN NAME=table VALUE=sales>
```

This is actually quite a common sight. We just published the database name and the table name, two items of information that really should be kept very secret. This gives crackers (curious, mischievous, or downright malicious individuals) the opportunity to try brute force techniques in an attempt to crack (break into) your database. What happens if they save the HTML source, edit it, and try the same search on `<INPUT TYPE=HIDDEN NAME=dbVALUE=2000q2>` or your current quarter and year? Will they have access to unreleased data? It depends on your implementation, but it is certainly possible, and in fact it is one of the first things to look for.

So, how can you secure your CGI applications?

It is really very simple; trust nothing. Always assume every piece of data they submit is riddled with errors, or even potentially an offensive attack against your server. You need to validate everything.

Don't use `GET` for sending data to a server unless you are completely and utterly convinced that the information has no bearing on security. Remember that the entire `QUERY_STRING` will be displayed in the URL line on your client's browsers, if there is the possibility of over-the-shoulder reading being detrimental to your CGI, circumvent it by using the `POST` method.

Be aware of what you reveal in your HTML. Keep in mind that even hidden values can be changed and used against you.

Use the Secure Sockets Layer (SSL) or Secure HTTP (SHTTP) to encrypt sensitive data.

Treat everything as if it were open source. Any calls to perform system applications need to be fully validated to be sure they imply no potentially harmful problems. Don't fall into the trap of thinking that your source is secret because only your company's own personnel will ever see it. Inside attacks are by far the most common in the computing industry. Can your company survive a determined attack against its systems by a cracker armed with inside information from a disgruntled employee (or ex-employee)?

Let's be careful out there.

Summary

This chapter looked at the common gateway interface programming environment. We discussed in detail the process of creating dynamic Web pages using standard HTML and the C programming language. We created utility code that can be used in all of our CGI applications, and we then created an example application and examined its usage on a Web server. Finally, we took a closer look at some potential security risks associated with programming CGI applications and explained methods to prevent misuse of this technology.

CHAPTER 24

Arbitrary Precision Arithmetic

by Dr. Ian D. K. Kelly

In This Chapter

Dr. Johnson asked a lady her age. On being told that it was twenty-five and a quarter he observed that the answer was very precise, though its accuracy was questionable, and in any case had very little significance. As you compute, you are concerned with maintaining a particular precision (the number of figures you want to represent) and a known accuracy (the confidence that they are the correct figures).

This chapter discusses how you can find out what precision your calculations already have, and how you can write code with huge precision (and accuracy). To do this, you have to look at what causes arithmetic error, and how to avoid it. This chapter also presents some code that illustrates several different ways of representing extremely precise values (up to 10,000 digits), and of performing the ordinary arithmetic operations on these numbers. Finally, it gives some hints as to how and when to choose which method(s) to use yourself.

Mathematicians have a habit of giving names to strange numbers, such as *pi* and *gamma* and *aleph-null* and *C-zero*. There is a number that mathematicians call *e*. This is the number shown in Figure 24.1 (and don't be frightened by the formula).

FIGURE 24.1
Irrational numbers.

$$\sum_{n=0}^{\infty} \frac{1}{n!}$$

The formula in Figure 24.1 can also be represented as

1 + 1/1! + 1/2! + 1/3! + 1/4! + 1/5! + 1/6! + ...

or

1 + 1/1 + 1/(1*2) + 1/(1*2*3) + 1/(1*2*3*4) + 1/(1*2*3*4*5) + 1/(1*2*3*4*5*6) + ...

and its value is approximately 2.718.

The number *e* is an *irrational* number because there are no two integers *a* and *b* such that *e* = *a* / *b*, so it cannot be expressed as a ratio. After you have finished reading this chapter, you may come to the conclusion that mathematicians who think about such things are irrational too. My irrational desire is to see what the first ten thousand decimal places of *e* look like. Listing 24.1 is an example of a short program to calculate and display *e*.

Order of Computation

In abstract mathematics, it does not matter in what order you perform a calculation—the result is always the same. Thus, $A-B+C-D+E-F$ is always equal to $A+C+E-B-D-F$, which is always equal to $(A+C+E)-(B+D+F)$, and $(A*B)/C$ is always equal to $(A/C)*B$. But this is not the case when computing—we have to remember that each arithmetic operation propagates error differently, and that some orders of computation will give rise to underflow or very large proportionate error, and other orders will not.

For example, consider the calculation of $A-B+C$, where we know that A and B are always close in magnitude. This means that the subtraction of B from A will yield a value that is small in comparison to the values we started with, and consequently the error of the difference will be much higher in proportion than the errors we started with. So if we compute $(A-B)+C$ we are constructing a term with a known high error $(A-B)$ and adding C to it. If instead we computed $(A+C)-B$, we are performing a subtraction of two elements that are further apart in magnitude, and the proportional error is not increased as much.

For a further example, consider the calculation of $A-B+C-D+E-$F, where we know that A and B are very close together in magnitude, and C and D are close, as are E and F. The same proportional-error increase will be true for the pair C and D, and the pair E and F as is true for the pair A and B. So if we compute $(A-B)+(C-D)+(E-F)$, we have this same increase of proportionate error three times. If, however, we changed this to $(A+C+E)-(B+D+F)$, we have this unavoidable increase in error only once.

With multiplication and division, you are usually better off doing all the multiplications before doing any of the divisions because you tend to lose less significance. Thus, use $(A*B)/C$ rather than $(A/C)*B$.

The Sizes of Integers

There are several types in C that allow us to store integers: `char`, `short int`, `int`, and `long int`. The C standard is very careful not to dictate very much about how many bits each of these has to contain, but it does indicate some minima. A `char` must contain at least 8 bits. A `short int` must be no shorter than a `char` and must have at least 16 bits. An `int` must be no shorter than a `short int`, and also must contain at least 16 bits. A `long int` must be no shorter than a `short int` and no shorter than an `int`, and it must have at least 32 bits. It *can* be longer, but the standard does not say that it *has* to be longer!

The other thing the standard does not dictate is whether `char` is the same as `unsigned char` or is the same as `signed char`—it may be either. It does, however, say that `int` is the same as `signed int` and `long int` is the same as `signed long int`. If you need to be sure that a `char` can be signed, though, you must remember to declare it as `signed char`. Similarly, if you need to be sure that a `char` is unsigned, you have to declare it as `unsigned char`.

Usually you will find that `char` is 8 bits, `short int` is 16 bits, and `long int` is 32 bits—but you cannot depend upon this. If the compiler writer chooses to make `char` 11 bits, and `short int`, `int`, and `long int` all 67 bits, according to the C Standard that is perfectly all right. More realistically, you may find in some implementations that `char` is 16 bits, `short int` and `int` are both 32 bits, and `long int` is 64 bits. On a Cray, `char` is 8 bits, and `short int`, `int`, and `long int` are all 64 bits.

The number of bits determines the largest value (the furthest from zero) that can be held. For unsigned 8-, 16-, and 32-bit integers, these values are 255, 65535, and 4294967295; for signed 8-, 16-, and 32-bit integers, the positive values are 127, 32767, and 2147483647, and 64 bits give the impressive value 9223372036854775807. The negative values are probably –128, –32768, and –2147483648 and, of course, the astounding –9223372036854775808. They are not *certainly* these values—they might be the same as the positive values, but with the negative sign—it depends on whether negative numbers are held in twos complement notation (which is the usual form) or ones complement (less usual now, but still possible). Examples of both ones complement and twos complement are shown in Table 24.2.

TABLE 24.2 Making Negative Numbers by Ones Complement and Twos Complement

Ones Complement	Twos Complement
Consider the number +105 in decimal, which is 01101001 in 8-bit binary (typically a signed char), and consider how to represent –105:	
Rule for making negative:	Rule for making negative:
"Flip the bits," so 01101001 becomes 10010110	"Flip the bits and add one," so 01101001 becomes first 10010110, then we add one to get 10010111
Consider the number 1 in decimal, which is 00000001 in 8-bit binary:	
–1 is 11111110	–1 is 11111111
Consider the number zero, which is 00000000 in 8-bit binary:	
–0 is 11111111, so there is both a +0 and a –0	Flip the bits to get 11111111 and add one to get 00000000 (and a carry, which is ignored), so –0 is the same as +0

One of the consequences of using ones complement is that there is both a plus zero and a minus zero, which have different representations. In ones complement, the most distant from zero negative number is exactly the same magnitude (but opposite sign) as the most distant from zero positive number. So for 8-bit signed integers, the limits are –127 to +127. Another disadvantage of ones complement negation is that you cannot determine the even/odd status by simply looking at the last bit of the representation.

Twos complement has only one sort of zero (which seems much more like the real world to me). It also allows you to represent a negative number that is greater in magnitude than the largest positive number you can represent in the same number of bits. So for 8-bit integers, the limits are –128 to +127.

Precision of Integer Operations

Integers are easy numbers. They start from zero and go up and down in steps of one. Any integer operation—provided it is subject to no errors like overflow—is precisely accurate. And that's that.

Ah, no it isn't.

Provided that no part of a series of operations using add, subtract, and multiply ever overflows, all is well. But when there is division, we have to beware.

Two and three are integers, but two divided by three (2/3) is not. It is also, as it happens, not representable precisely in binary, and its storage internally necessarily has some error. So what can we say about the code in Listing 24.2 (and on the CD in file `Ch24inti.c`), where two is divided by three in various ways?

LISTING 24.2 Integer Division

```
#include <stdio.h>

int main (int argc, char * argv[])
{
    int iTwo = 2;
    int iThree = 3;
    int iA;
    double dB;
    double dC;
    double dD;

    iA = iTwo / iThree;
    dB = iTwo / iThree;
```

LISTING 24.2 continued

```
    dC = (double) iTwo / iThree;
    dD = (double) (iTwo / iThree);

    printf("ia = %d dB=%f dC=%f dD=%f\n",iA,dB,dC,dD);

    return 0;
}
```

Because the integral part of two divided by three is zero, we should not be surprised that `iA` takes the value zero. But surely all the others should give us the answer 0.6666667?

To get the value 0.666666... there has to be some type conversion. That is, the manner in which numbers are represented has to change from the `int` (integer) type to the `double` (floating-point) type. The C language contains some type-conversion rules, and compilers may add to these—the exact rules are detailed in *The C Programming Language* (K&R). These rules boil down to a sequence starting:

> If either operand is `long double`, convert the other to `long double`
>
> Otherwise, if either operand is `double`, convert the other to `double`
>
> Otherwise, if either operand is `float`, convert the other to `float`
>
> Otherwise...

(You can find the full details in K&R.)

These rules of type conversion for arithmetic expressions also depend upon what is an expression. In the sample program in Listing 24.2, these conversion rules may have different effects according to bracketing, and according to whether a compiler includes the left-hand side of an assignment in its consideration of the scope of an expression. For MSVC Release 4.2 under Windows NT 4.0, the results of this sample program were:

```
iA = 0   dB = 0.000000    dC = 0.666667   dD=0.000000
```

These results show that two divided by three is zero, when that result is at any time placed into an `int`. So in the statements

```
iA = iTwo / iThree;
```

and

```
dB = iTwo / iThree;
```

the right-hand side is an expression that contains just `int` fields. Hence it is evaluated as an `int`, giving zero, and this `int` value is then converted to the appropriate type to be stored in the target variable. Even though `dB` in the example is of type `double`, it still gets the answer zero.

The statement

```
dC = (double) iTwo / iThree;
```

has an expression on the right-hand side that contains one `int` and one `double`. The cast `(double)` converts the numerator into type `double` *before* the operation takes place. Hence, this statement gives the answer 0.666667.

But how do we explain the fact that

```
dD = (double) (iTwo / iThree);
```

also gives an answer of zero? Surely here we have also cast to `double`?

Yes, we have cast to `double`—but the thing cast is a complete expression; the contents of the parentheses. This expression, which contains only `int` terms, will be cast *after* being evaluated. This, as you can see, is too late: the all-`int` expression produces an `int` zero, which is then cast to type `double` for assignment to the left-hand side.

Type Conversions Between `long` and `int`

The C language allows you to assign an `int` to a `long int`. This is unexceptional, and should not produce any errors. But the language also allows you to assign a `long int` to an `int` and this may produce problems. A good compiler may warn you of these assignments; pay attention to these warnings.

The Sizes of Floating Point

For representing non-integral numbers, computers use a format known as floating point. The computer hardware will support one or more floating-point sizes, ranging from 16 bits (possible, but unusual), 32 bits (the most common), 64 bits (now becoming common), 128 bits, and so on. There are even some machines with intermediate sizes, such as 80 bits and 96 bits.

How Floating Point Is Represented

In the computer, a floating-point number is made up of two or three sub-fields:

- The sign (which does not always exist)
- The exponent (sometimes called the *characteristic*)
- The value (sometimes called the *mantissa*)

The mantissa can be thought of as a binary fraction. Its most significant bit represents 2^{-1} or a half, its next bit is 2^{-2} or a quarter, and so on. The exponent is the power of the *floating base*, *b*, by which the mantissa fraction must be multiplied to get the value. If *c* is the value of the characteristic (which is an integer) and *m* is the value of the mantissa (which is always less than one), the value in the floating-point field is $m * b^c$.

Phew! What does that mean? Assume, for this example, that the floating base is 16. This is a number chosen by the hardware engineers when the particular computer was designed, and is not something you can control. So in our case the value of a floating-point field is $m * 16^c$. So the number 112.0 would be binary fraction .11100000 and exponent 2 because $112.0 = (7/16) * 16^2$. The number 112.25 would be binary fraction (mantissa) .11101000 and exponent 2.

The floating base might be 2 or 8 or 16. If you are using the IBM 390, it is 16. If you are using a processor of the Intel x86 range, it is 2. There is no theoretical reason for the floating base being a power of two—but for practical reasons it always is. If you are an expert in hardware design, you could amuse yourself by sketching a floating-point arithmetic unit that uses base 37, even though nobody will want to use it!

If the values of the three fields sign, exponent, and value are the positive integers *s*, *e*, and *v* respectively, then the value of the floating-point number expressed by them will be of the form:

$(-1)^s * b^{(e-M)} * 0.v$ or $(-1)^s * b^{(e-M)} * 1.v$

where *M* is the value expressed by just the top bit of the exponent field, and *b* is the exponent base. So for IBM floating point this is

$(-1)^s * 16^{(e-64)} * 0.v$

and for IEEE standard format it is

$(-1)^s * 2^{(e-128)} * 1.v$

Maximum Precision

Each of the parts of a floating-point number has a length, a certain number of bits of which it is composed. The number of bits in the mantissa determines how precisely the number can be represented. The number of bits in the characteristic (the exponent) determines how wide a range of numbers can be represented.

One of the formats of floating point on IBM's System 390 (and related machines) has 1 bit for the sign field, 7 bits for the exponent, and 24 bits for the mantissa. The floating base is 16, which means that you can only guarantee 21 of those 24 bits (this is explained in the following section, "Normalization"). Hence, the maximum precision of these numbers is one part in 2^{21} or one part in just over two million.

The 7 bits of the exponent (characteristic) are interpreted as a signed 8-bit, and hence range from –64 to +63. This gives a range from numbers as small as 16^{-64} to 16^{+63}, or from about 8.6×10^{-78} to $7.2 \times 10^{+75}$. Since the mantissa may have any fractional value from just under one down as far as a sixteenth, the low end of the range actually goes down as far as 5.4×10^{-79}.

If we can find a format with more bits in each field, we get more precision (if there are more bits in the mantissa) and a wider range (if there are more bits in the characteristic).

When we looked at integers, we saw the overflow error for the first time. For floating-point numbers, an overflow error occurs when we try to represent a number that is greater in magnitude than the maximum exponent that we can represent. In the format of the IBM System 390 example, this would be beyond plus or minus $7.2 \times 10^{+78}$.

However, now we can see the possibility of a new kind of error—the *underflow* error. This happens when we try to represent a number that is closer to zero than the smallest exponent we can represent. In the same environment, this would be a number lying within the range plus or minus 5.4×10^{-79}. This is a species of error that cannot exist in integer arithmetic: the nearest integers to zero are plus one and minus one—and these are easy to represent.

There is another new kind of error as well, which also did not exist in integer arithmetic: *loss of precision*. No matter what we do, if the numbers with which we are computing have a mantissa length of 24 bits, we can never be any more precise than 1 in 2^{+24}, and in practical terms probably no better than 1 in 2^{+21}.

In our sample problem of wanting to compute *e* to ten thousand places, we certainly need to use fractions much closer to zero than allowed by an exponent of 7, 63, or even 1023 bits. We will definitely have underflow (unless our exponents can be more than 32000 bits), and loss of precision (unless each mantissa can also have more than 32000 bits).

Normalization

The number 0.001953125 (or one five-hundred-and-twelfth, 1/512) can be expressed in a number of ways:

$16^{-2} \times 1/2$

$16^{-1} \times 1/32$

$16^{0} \times 1/512$

$16^{+1} \times 1/8192$

and so on. Of all of these representations, the one with the largest mantissa is the first one on our list. If you look at this value in binary, you will see that it has the fewest number of leading zeros. This is called the *normalized* value. In general, the normalized representation for any floating-point number is the one with the fewest leading zeros, and hence the largest number of significant bits in the mantissa. If the floating base is 16, this implies that at least one bit in the top nibble (four bits) is a 1 (one); if the floating-base is 8, at least one bit from the top three is a 1 (one); if the floating base is two, then the top bit itself should be a 1 (one).

Floating-point operations may give rise to either normalized or un-normalized results. In general, you should assume that the results will be normalized, but allow for losing some bits of precision. For example, if the floating base is 16, you must assume that every floating-point operation will lose you at least three bits of precision. In fact, some operations will lose fewer—but always assume the worst.

Precision of Floating-Point Operations

How precise, in fact, are floating-point operations?

On modern machines, there is an extension of the number of bits in the mantissa that is made during the calculation process, so that the hardware does not lose as many bits as has been hinted before, but you must not assume that your hardware is modern in this respect. You would be better finding out precisely. How?

Find the Precision of Floating Point

There are lots of different facts about the representation of numbers in your environment that you would like to know. How can you discover what they actually are?

There are a number of constants defined as part of the standard C language, whose values are given in the libraries `<float.h>` and `<limits.h>`. These values differ from machine to machine and from compiler to compiler, which is why you should always be careful to refer to their symbolic names. Never let your code assume that you know the values of these numbers. The sample program in Listing 24.3 (and on the CD in file `Ch24cnst.c`) shows how you can (inelegantly) list these values in your environment.

LISTING 24.3 How to List the Standard Arithmetic Limits

```
#include <stdio.h>
#include <limits.h>
#include <float.h>

int main (int argc, char* argv[])
{
    printf("    Characters and integers:\n");
    printf("CHAR_BIT=%d  CHAR_MAX=%d  CHAR_MIN=%d\n",
            CHAR_BIT,CHAR_MAX,CHAR_MIN);
    printf("INT_MAX=%d      INT_MIN=%d\n",INT_MAX,INT_MIN);
    printf("LONG_MAX=%ld    LONG_MIN=%ld\n",LONG_MAX,LONG_MIN);
    printf("SCHAR_MAX=%d    SCHAR_MIN=%d\n",SCHAR_MAX,SCHAR_MIN);
    printf("SHRT_MAX=%d     SHRT_MIN=%d\n",SHRT_MAX,SHRT_MIN);
    printf("UCHAR_MAX=%d UINT_MAX=%u ULONG_MAX=%ul USHRT_MAX=%d\n",
            UCHAR_MAX,UINT_MAX,ULONG_MAX,USHRT_MAX);

    printf("    Floating point:\n");
    printf("FLT_ROUNDS=%d FLT_RADIX=%d FLT_MANT_DIG=%d FLT_DIG=%d\n",
            FLT_ROUNDS,FLT_RADIX,FLT_MANT_DIG,FLT_DIG);
    printf("FLT_MIN_EXP=%d FLT_MIN_10_EXP=%d\n",FLT_MIN_EXP,
           FLT_MIN_10_EXP);
    printf("FLT_MAX_EXP=%d FLT_MAX_10_EXP=%d\n",FLT_MAX_EXP,
            FLT_MAX_10_EXP);
    printf("FLT_MAX=%e FLT_EPSILON=%e FLT_MIN=%e\n",FLT_MAX,
            FLT_EPSILON,FLT_MIN);

    printf("    Double precision:\n");
    printf("DBL_MANT_DIG=%d DBL_DIG=%d\n",
            DBL_MANT_DIG,DBL_DIG);
    printf("DBL_MIN_EXP=%d DBL_MIN_10_EXP=%d\n",DBL_MIN_EXP,
            DBL_MIN_10_EXP);
    printf("DBL_MAX_EXP=%d DBL_MAX_10_EXP=%d\n",DBL_MAX_EXP,
            DBL_MAX_10_EXP);
    printf("DBL_MAX=%e DBL_EPSILON=%e DBL_MIN=%e\n",DBL_MAX,
            DBL_EPSILON,DBL_MIN);

    printf("    Long Double precision:\n");
    printf("LDBL_MANT_DIG=%d LDBL_DIG=%d\n",
            LDBL_MANT_DIG,LDBL_DIG);
    printf("LDBL_MIN_EXP=%d LDBL_MIN_10_EXP=%d\n",LDBL_MIN_EXP,
            LDBL_MIN_10_EXP);
    printf("LDBL_MAX_EXP=%d LDBL_MAX_10_EXP=%d\n",LDBL_MAX_EXP,
```

LISTING 24.3 continued

```
          LDBL_MAX_10_EXP);
    printf("LDBL_MAX=%e LDBL_EPSILON=%e LDBL_MIN=%e\n",LDBL_MAX,
          LDBL_EPSILON,LDBL_MIN);
    return 0;
}
```

These values tell you exactly, for your environment, how numbers are represented. The meanings of these constants are listed in Table 24.3 and Table 24.4.

TABLE 24.3 The Arithmetic Precision Limits for Integers

Symbolic	*Meaning*
`CHAR_BIT`	The number of bits in a `char`. This must be at least 8.
`CHAR_MAX`	The maximum integer value in a `char`. This must be at least 127. It may be the same as `SCHAR_MAX` or `UCHAR_MAX`—but which it is depends on the environment.
`CHAR_MIN`	The minimum integer value in a `char`. This must go down at least as far as –127. It may be the same as `SCHAR_MIN` or `UCHAR_MIN`—but which it is depends on the environment.
`INT_MAX`	The maximum value in a `signed int`. This must be at least 32767.
`INT_MIN`	The minimum value in a `signed int`. This must go down at least as far as –32767.
`LONG_MAX`	The maximum value in a `long int`. This must be no less than `INT_MAX`, and must be no less than 2147483647, though it may be more.
`LONG_MIN`	The minimum value in a `long int`. This must go down at least as far as `INT_MIN`, and must be at least as low as –214783647, though it may be even further from zero.
`SCHAR_MAX`	The maximum value in a `signed char`. This must be at least 127.
`SCHAR_MIN`	The minimum value in a `signed char`. This must be at least as low as –127.
`SHRT_MAX`	The maximum value for a `short int`. This must be at least 32767.
`SHRT_MIN`	The minimum value for a `short int`. This must be at least as low as –32767.
`UCHAR_MAX`	The maximum value in an `unsigned char`. This must be at least 255.
`USHRT_MAX`	The maximum value for an `unsigned short int`. This must be at least 65535, and no smaller than `SHRT_MAX`.
`UINT_MAX`	The maximum value for an `unsigned int`. This must be at least 65535 and no smaller than `USHRT_MAX`.
`ULONG_MAX`	The maximum value for an `unsigned long int`. This must be at least 4294967295 and no smaller than `UINT_MAX`.

TABLE 24.4 The Arithmetic Precision Limits for Floating Point

Symbolic	*Meaning*
`FLT_ROUNDS`	The model for floating-point rounding for addition: –1—Indeterminable 0—Toward zero 1—Toward nearest 2—Toward positive infinity 3—Toward negative infinity
`FLT_RADIX`	The exponent within floating-point representation. This may be 2 or 16—or any other value that hardware engineers dream up. It must be at least 2.

`FLT_MANT_DIG`
`DBL_MANT_DIG`
`LDBL_MANT_DIG`
	The number of base-`FLT_RADIX` digits in the floating-point representation (`float`, `double`, `long double`).

`FLT_DIG`
`DBL_DIG`
`LDBL_DIG`
	Precision in decimal digits of the floating-point representation (`float`, `double`, `long double`). It must be at least 6 for `float` and 10 for `double` and `long double`.

`FLT_MIN_EXP`
`DBL_MIN_EXP`
`LDBL_MIN_EXP`
	The minimum base-`FLT_RADIX` floating- point exponent (`float`, `double`, `long double`).

`FLT_MIN_10_EXP`
`DBL_MIN_10_EXP`
`LDBL_MIN_10_EXP`
	The minimum decimal floating-point exponent (`float`, `double`, `long double`).

`FLT_MAX_EXP`
`DBL_MAX_EXP`
`LDBL_MAX_EXP`
	The maximum base-`FLT_RADIX` floating- point exponent (`float`, `double`, `long double`).

`FLT_MAX_10_EXP`
`DBL_MAX_10_EXP`
`LDBL_MAX_10_EXP`
	The maximum decimal floating-point exponent (`float`, `double`, `long double`).

`FLT_MAX`
`DBL_MAX`
`LDBL_MAX`
	The maximum normalized floating-point number (`float`, `double`, `long double`).
	This is the largest quantity (the one furthest from zero) that can be represented. It must be at least 1E+37.

`FLT_EPSILON`
`DBL_EPSILON`
`LDBL_EPSILON`
	The smallest detectable difference between 1 and the least value less than 1 representable in floating- point (`float`, `double`, `long double`). It must be no greater than 1E-5 (one hundredth-thousandth) for `float` and 1E-9 for `double` and `long double`.

`FLT_MIN`
`DBL_MIN`
`LDBL_MIN`
	The minimum normalized floating-point number (`float`, `double`, `long double`).
	This is the tiniest quantity (the one nearest to zero) that can be represented. It must be no greater than 1E-37.

The meanings given in Tables 24.3 and 24.4 are not quite the same as the official definitions of these constants—for the exact details you should refer to the standard itself. But the meanings given here are definitely good enough for all practical use.

In each environment (a particular C compiler on a particular machine, running under a particular operating system) each of these constants has a value. That value may well be different from the minima stated in Tables 24.3 and 24.4. Table 24.5, Table 24.6, Table 24.7, and Table 24.8 show some sample values from five different environments on the same piece of hardware.

TABLE 24.5 Sample Values for Integer limits

Symbolic	*Values*
`CHAR_BIT`	8
`CHAR_MAX`	127
`CHAR_MIN`	-127, -128
`UCHAR_MAX`	255
`UCHAR_MIN`	-255, -256
`SCHAR_MAX`	127
`SCHAR_MIN`	-128
`SHRT_MAX`	32767
`SHRT_MIN`	-32767, -32768
`INT_MAX`	2147483647, 32767
`INT_MIN`	-2147483647, -2147483648, -32767, -32768
`LONG_MAX`	2147483647
`LONG_MIN`	-2147483647, -2147483648
`USHRT_MAX`	65535
`UINT_MAX`	4294967295, 655351
`ulong_max`	4294967295, 655351

TABLE 24.6 Sample Values for Float Limits

Symbolic	*Values*
`FLT_ROUNDS`	1
`FLT_RADIX`	2
`FLT_MANT_DIG`	24
`FLT_DIG`	6
`FLT_MIN_EXP`	-125
`FLT_MIN_10_EXP`	-37
`FLT_MAX_EXP`	128

TABLE 24.6 continued

Symbolic	*Values*
FLT_MAX_10_EXP	38
FLT_MAX	3.404823E+38
FLT_EPSILON	1.192093E-07
flt_min	1.175494e-38

TABLE 24.7 Sample Values for Double Limits

Symbolic	*Values*
DBL_MANT_DIG	53
DBL_DIG	15
DBL_MIN_EXP	-1021
DBL_MIN_10_EXP	-307
DBL_MAX_EXP	1024
DBL_MAX_10_EXP	308
DBL_MAX	1.797693E+308
DBL_EPSILON	2.220446E-16
dbl_min	2.225074e-308, 0

TABLE 24.8 Sample Values for Long Double Limits

Symbolic	*Values*
ldbl_mant_dig	53, 64
ldbl_dig	15, 18, 19
ldbl_min_exp	-1021, -16381
ldbl_min_10_exp	-307, -4931
ldbl_max_exp	1024, 16384
ldbl_max_10_exp	308, 4932
ldbl_max	1.797693e+308, NAN
ldbl_epsilon	2.220446e-16, 2.121398e-314, 5.342539-318, 1.618855e-319
ldbl_min	2.225074e-308, 3.464203e-310, 5.284429e-315, 7.588354e-320

All of the five environments in Tables 24.5, 24.6, 24.7, and 24.8 were run on the same Intel processor—the same machine—but under different operating systems, and using different C compilers and runtime libraries. One combination even stated that `DBL_MIN` was 0.0, which is a rather improbable actual value! The symbol "NAN" in these tables means "Not A Number"; that is, the value cannot be represented using the standard techniques.

Never Make Assumptions About the Environment

When results are not a precise binary fraction (and they very rarely are!), there may well be some rounding. Do not assume that the rounding will be done the way you were taught at school ("if the last digit is below five, round down; if the last digit is five or above, round up"). There are four possible regular methods of rounding that may occur in your particular environment, plus "don't know." Different compilers and different runtime libraries may well use different protocols on the same machine. Although it is not specified in the possible values for `FLT_ROUNDS`, one method of rounding exact midpoints is *round always to even* or *round always to odd*. This is an attempt to remove some of the inherent bias in always rounding midpoints up. Knuth discusses this in some detail, together with an instructive example of drift.

Drift is experienced when biased rounding gradually pulls the result of a series of computations further and further from its true value. For example, if *A*=0.55555555 and *B*=1.0, then *A*+*B* may well be rounded to the value 1.5555556. If we subtract *B* from this, we get a value very slightly different from the *A* with which we started: 0.555556, so that *(A+B)*—B—A actually has a non-zero value. So the loop

```
int i;
double A=0.55555555;
double B=1.0;
double C=0.0;
for (i=0;(i<32000);i++)
{
    C = ((C + (A + B)) - B) - 0.55555555;
}
```

may well end up with a sizeable—and erroneous—value in *C*. You may experiment in your environments with other values for *A* and *B* to find whether drift can be a problem for the values that interest you. For some more sample code to test drift, look at the file `Ch24Drft.c` on the CD.

Negative Numbers Need Not be Twos Complement

We tend to assume that negative numbers are expressed using the twos complement method. But that is not always so: there are machines that still use ones complement.

Consequently, we also often assume that the negative end of a range is one greater in magnitude than the positive end of the range: but that, too, is not always so. If you examine the possible values given in the examples for `INT_MAX` and `INT_MIN`, you will see that sometimes `INT_MIN` = –(`INT_MAX` + 1) and sometimes `INT_MIN` = –`INT_MAX`. Don't make the assumption about the representation of negative numbers in your code: tilde (~) means flip the bits and minus (–) means negate. Any code that maps between these two operators is machine- or environment-dependent.

Big-endian and Little-endian Representations

In what order are the bits of a number stored within the hardware? Consider the decimal number 4660. This is, in hexadecimal, 1234. In our environment, if a `short int` has 16 bits, and we place this value in a `short int`, can we expect to see somewhere in the machine two consecutive bytes of which the one with the lower address has the value 12 and the one with the higher address has the value 34?

Alas, no. On some machines, we will find two bytes that read 12 | 34, but on other machines this number will be stored as 34 | 12. These representations are called *big-endian* and *little-endian* (a reference to *Gulliver's Travels*).

How about larger numbers, stored in 32 bits? If in your environment the type `long int` occupies 32 bits, and you set a `long int` variable to have the decimal value 305419896, how will that be stored? The hexadecimal for this number is 12345678 and according to the architecture of the machine, all of the following are possible:

12 | 34 | 56 | 78

34 | 12 | 78 | 56

78 | 56 | 34 | 12

That is, none of the bytes are inverted, only pairs of bytes are inverted, or the whole quadruple is inverted. Thus, it is important never to construct code that associates machine addresses with values except in steps of the size of those values. So never, for example, get the least significant byte in a `long int` by manipulating a pointer to that `long int` so as to extract its fourth `char`: you will often get something other than you expect—and what you get depends upon the machine.

Examples of Enormous Precision—and the Opposite

One of the occupations considered fun by mathematicians is to compute enormous numbers of decimal places. Every time I look to see how many places we now have for π (pi), it grows and grows. It is not, it seems, enough just to take a circle and divide the length around it by the width across it. We now have π to many hundreds (nay, *thousands*) of millions of decimal places. We also know e to many million places—though I (for the purposes of this chapter) would rather calculate it than look it up.

When we make physical measurements, however, we are lucky if we can get ten places of accuracy, and usually have to make do with fewer. We can discover the distance of the moon at any time to a precision of about 10 centimeters, which is slightly better than one part in 10^{10}—so that is something we know very precisely: we have only a one in ten thousand million error. We have ten figures of precision.

We know the number of molecules in 12 grams of carbon to be about $6.02217 * 10^{23}$—but this figure is accurate only to about one part in 10^6 so we have at least a one in a million error. We have only five figures of precision.

At noon on 1st June 1995, the human population of Europe was estimated to be about 498 million—but we know that figure only to an accuracy of plus or minus three million, which is worse than a one in a hundred error. We have just two figures of precision.

The distance from the Earth of the Great Nebula in Andromeda is, arguably, somewhere between two million light-years and five million light-years: that is between $1.9 * 10^{22}$ and $4.7 * 10^{22}$ meters, which is an error of 250%.

Various Methods for Representing Enormous Precision

Since the sizes of integers and the precisions of floating point are limited by the computer hardware, we have to be able to represent highly precise numbers in some other way.

We, as humans, using pencil and paper, have no problem: we just write down long strings of figures. We can multiply together two-digit numbers, and we can (although with a bit more effort) multiply together 100-digit numbers.

So how can we represent, within a program, very long strings of digits?

Strings of Integers

When we use pencil and paper, the strings of integers that we write are normally the ordinary 0 1 2 3 4 5 6 7 8 and 9. This set arises (ultimately) from the arbitrary biological fact that human beings tend to have ten digits: fingers and thumbs. But ten is no different from any other whole number greater than one: we could have chosen any other number at all. We chose ten simply because it is convenient as a number base. Other peoples have made other choices: in classical Greece, where they wore open-toed sandals, the number base was twenty (which still has an effect on the way numbers between 50 and 100 are represented in French), and in Babylon it was sixty.

We use a *positional* notation. In the number 532, the meaning of the 2 is two units, the meaning of the 3 is three tens, and the meaning of the 5 is five ten-by-tens (hundreds).

Base-10 Representation

In our normal base-ten numbers we have ten different symbols, which are arranged in order (reading from right to left) starting with units (ten to the power zero), then tens (ten to the power one), then hundreds (ten to the power two), then thousands (ten to the power three), and so on.

For those of you with an interest in human spoken languages, the Arabic numerals that we use are perfectly constructed—if you are writing in Arabic, which is written from right to left, the reverse of English writing. The numbers are still written with the least significant on the right and the most significant on the left. When we try to read out a string of numbers in an English text, we have to scan ahead to the end (least significant end) of the number, and count backwards to find out what name to give to the first digit. Quickly say this number out loud: 968374215. Was it obvious to you, without going to the end and counting, that the 9 was actually "nine hundred million" rather than "ninety million" or "nine thousand million"?

Whether that was obvious or not, it *was* obvious that whatever there were nine of, they were each ten-times as large as whatever there were six of because the 9 was immediately to the left of the 6, and we are using base-10 notation.

Base-16 Representation

If we adopted the convention when counting of using both our fingers and toes, but leaving out our thumbs and great toes, we would have 16 digits. We could then use a positional notation which, reading from right to left, would give us the number of units (sixteen to the power zero), sixteens (sixteen to the power one), 256s (sixteen to the power two), 4096s (sixteen to the power three), and so on, in a gloriously unmemorable—but perfectly logical—sequence.

This would be base-16 representation—hexadecimal. To use it, we would have to have 16 different digits, and by convention these are 0 1 2 3 4 5 6 7 8 9 A B C D E and F.

By now you are perhaps feeling insulted, that I should be explaining something that you already know perfectly well—after all, the C language has `printf` format control fields for all of base-10 decimal (`%d`), base-8 octal (`%o`), and base-16 hexadecimal (`%x`) representations. Please do not feel insulted: I am merely introducing the fact that we can use *anything* greater than one as our number base. How about something non-intuitive, something very large indeed?

Base-32768 Representation

We could use base-32768 representation. This would require 32,768 different symbols, and each position would represent units (32768 to the power zero), 32,768s (32768 to the power one), 1,073,741,824s (32768 to the power two), and so on, in an even more unmemorable sequence. This would be perfect, in C, as an array of `short int`.

Because human beings don't read numbers to that base very easily, we could instead choose 10,000 (ten thousand) as our number base, then each array element would contain exactly four decimal digits of the number we are representing, making it much easier to print out and/or read in these values. Or we could use arrays of `long int`, relying on the fact that a `long int` can always hold a value of at least 2,147,483,647 and choose 1,000,000,000 (one thousand million) as our number base. Every position here would contain nine decimal digits.

There is some sample code later that uses 10,000 (ten thousand) as the number base.

Strings of Characters

We can go back to base-10 again, but this time represent numbers as strings of characters (`char`) exactly the way that we write them. This would mean that the routines for add, subtract, and so forth would have to deal with the digits one at a time, catering for "carry" and "borrow," in just the way that we ourselves do when using pencil and paper.

Sample Code for Operating on Strings of Characters

Although you cannot rely upon the ASCII character set being used (you might be running on an EBCDIC machine, for example), you *can* rely on the representations for the characters `'0'` through `'9'` being consecutive, and `'0'` being lower in collating sequence than `'9'`. Thus if `c` is a variable of type `char` and you know that it contains a digit, then `(c-'0')` is the decimal value of that digit. This, at least, is guaranteed by the C language definition.

Addition

If we have set a limit for accuracy within our system of, say, twelve thousand digits, all number variables would be declared as

```
#define MAX_PRECISION 12000
char aSample[MAX_PRECISION+1];
```

To perform addition you have to deal with "carry." Assume that we want to compute the sum of two number variables; the following routine might be of help:

```
#define MAX_PRECISION 12000
int cAdd ( char * aOne, char * aTwo, char * aThree )
{
    int iStatus = 0;
    int carry = 0;
    int i = 0;
    int j = 0;

    for (i=MAX_PRECISION-1;(i>=0);i--)
    {
        j = *(aOne+i) + *(aTwo+i) + carry - '0' - '0';
        carry = j / 10;
        j = j % 10;
        *(aThree+i) = j + '0';
    }
    return iStatus;
}
```

For more comments on the preceding code, see the file `Ch24Add.c` on the CD.

Similarly, we could extend our number representation to arrays of `int`, where the first element of each array indicated how many more elements there were in that array. That is, not all arrays are of the same length.

Multiplication

The code in Listing 24.4 indicates that multiplication is rather more complex. The (copious!) comments on this code will be found in files `Ch24AOK.c` and `Ch24AOK2.c` on the CD. This method of multiplication splits the problem into four parts:

1. Multiply a pair of digits
2. Multiply two strings of digits
3. Allocate space
4. Normalize an amount

By "digits" here we mean "base ten thousand" digits—more than human beings tend to have on their hands.

The reason we have to consider separately a "simple" multiplication of one word by one word is that a product is potentially longer than the operands. So, for example, 9876 (which is a single "base ten thousand" digit) multiplied by 4567 (which is again just one "base ten thousand" digit) gives 45103692, which is the two "base ten thousand" digits "4510" followed by "3692."

LISTING 24.4 Multiplication to Base 10,000

```
#include <stdlib.h>
#define BASE 10000
#define SQRT_BASE 100
#define INT int

int pairMultiply ( INT iOne, INT iTwo, INT * pAnswer)
{
    INT iStatus = 0;
    INT iOneTop = 0;
    INT iOneBot = 0;
    INT iTwoTop = 0;
    INT iTwoBot = 0;
    INT iAnsTop = 0;
    INT iAnsBot = 0;

   if (iOne>SQRT_BASE)
    {
```

LISTING 24.4 continued

```
        iOneTop = iOne / SQRT_BASE;
        iOneBot = iOne % SQRT_BASE;
    }
    else
    {
        iOneTop = 0;
        iOneBot = iOne;
    }

    if (iTwo>SQRT_BASE)
    {
        iTwoTop = iTwo / SQRT_BASE;
        iTwoBot = iTwo % SQRT_BASE;
    }
    else
    {
        iTwoTop = 0;
        iTwoBot = iTwo;
    }

    iAnsBot = (iOneBot * iTwoBot) +
        (iOneBot * iTwoTop * SQRT_BASE) +
        (iOneTop * iTwoBot * SQRT_BASE);
    iAnsTop = (iOneTop * iTwoTop);
    if (iAnsBot>BASE)
    {
        iAnsBot = iAnsBot % BASE;
        iAnsTop = iAnsTop + (iAnsBot / BASE);
    }
    pAnswer[0] = iAnsTop;
    pAnswer[1] = iAnsBot;
    return iStatus;
}

int aMultiply ( INT * aOne, INT * aTwo, INT ** aAnswer)
{
    int iStatus = 0;
    int i = 0;
    int j = 0;
    int k = 0;
```

LISTING 24.4 continued

```
    int m = 0;
    INT * pInt;
    INT ** ppInt = &pInt;
    INT w[2];

    if ((aOne==NULL) || (aTwo==NULL) || (aAnswer==NULL))
       iStatus = 1;
    else
    {
        i = abs(aOne[0]) + abs(aTwo[0]) + 1;
        j = aAllocate(i, ppInt);
        if (j!=0)
            iStatus = 1;
        else
        {
            for (k=abs(aTwo[0]);(k>0);k--)
            {
                for (j=abs(aOne[0]);(j>0);j--)
                {
                    m = pairMultiply ( aOne[j], aTwo[k], w);
                    pInt[i + 1 - k - j] += w[1];
                    pInt[i - k - j] += w[0];
                }
            }
            if (((aOne[0]>0)&&(aTwo[0]<0))
            ||  ((aOne[0]<0)&&(aTwo[0]>0)))
                pInt[0] = - pInt[0];
            m = aNormalise (ppInt, aAnswer);
            if (m!=0)
                iStatus = 1;
        }
    }
    return iStatus;
}

int aNormalise ( INT ** aUnNormal, INT ** aNormal )
{
    int iStatus = 0;
    int i = 0;
    int j = 0;
```

LISTING 24.4 continued

```
    int k = 0;
    int m = 0;
    int s = 1;

    if ((aUnNormal==NULL) || (aNormal==NULL)
                          || ((*aUnNormal)==NULL))
        iStatus = 1;
    else
    {
        *aNormal = *aUnNormal;
        k = abs((*aUnNormal)[0]);
        if ((*aUnNormal)[0]<0)
            s = -1;
        if (k>0)
        {
            j = (*aUnNormal)[1];
            m = 0;
            for (i=1;((j==0)&&(i<=k));i++)
            {
                j = (*aUnNormal)[i];
                m++;
            }
        }
        if (m>0)
        {
            k = abs((*aUnNormal)[0]) - m;
            j = aAllocate(k, aNormal);
            for (i=1;(i<(k+1));i++)
            {
                j = i + m;
                (*aNormal)[j] = (*aUnNormal)[i];
            }
            if (s<0)
                (*aNormal)[0] = - (*aNormal)[0];
            free(*aUnNormal);
            *aUnNormal = NULL;
        }
    }
```

LISTING 24.4 continued

```
    return iStatus;
}

int aAllocate ( int iCount, INT ** aAnswer )
{
    int iStatus = 0;
    INT * pInt = NULL;
    int i = 0;

    pInt = calloc ( sizeof (INT), iCount + 1);

    if (pInt==NULL)
    {
        iStatus = 1;
        return iStatus;
    }
    else
    {
        for (i=1;(i<=iCount);i++)
            pInt[i] = 0;
        *pInt = iCount;
    }
    if (aAnswer!=NULL)
        *aAnswer = pInt;
    return iStatus;
}
```

Fractional Numbers

None of the code presented here for very large numbers has considered non-integral numbers. But the extension from integers to fractions is, in fact, very simple. There is just one other piece of information that you need to carry around with each number, which is the position of its decimal point.

Prior to addition and subtraction, the operands have to be aligned; that is, extra leading or trailing zeros have to be added to ensure that the number of digits in both operands are the same, and that the decimal point is at the same place in each. The subsequent normalization of the answer will have to remove both leading and trailing zeros.

Multiplication and division may take place exactly as if the operands were in fact integers, and only after the operation do we have to consider where to place the decimal point in the answer, prior to its being normalized. The position can be calculated as described in the following section.

Decimal Position for Multiplication

If we are multiplying two numbers, the first of which has a digits before the decimal point, and b digits after it (so the total number is $(a+b)$ digits long, and the second number has c digits before the decimal point and d digits after it (so the whole number is $(c+d)$ digits long), the product will have $(b+d)$ positions after the decimal point. So we simply add up the number of places after the point for the two operands, and that is the number of places after the point for the product.

Decimal Position for Division

This is not quite so straightforward as multiplication. If the numbers are as in the paragraph for multiplication, $a.b$ divided by $c.d$, if we consider just the first $(a+b-c-d)$ digits prior to normalization, of those the last $(b-d)$ follow the point.

General Arithmetic Routines

In the files `CH24Abad.c` and `CH24AOK.c` on the CD, there is a set of routines for performing the four main arithmetic operations on extremely large integers. The first of these files (`CH24Abad.c`) contains correct but incomplete code, which you are welcome to use as an assistance pushing you to consider some further problems. The file `Ch24AOK.c` gives sample solutions to all those problems that were explicitly set.

The routines shown in Table 24.9 exist.

TABLE 24.9 Arithmetic Operations on Very Large Integers

Name of Routine	*Function*
`aAdd`	Adds a very large number (an *addend*) to another very large number, allocating space for the *sum*.
`aSubtract`	Subtracts a very large number (the *subtrahend*) from another very large number (the *minuend*), allocating space for the difference.

TABLE 24.9 continued

Name of Routine	*Function*
`aMultiply`	Multiplies a very large number (a *multiplicand*) by another very large number, allocating space for the *product*.
`aDivide`	Divides a very large number (the *numerator*) by another very large number (the *denominator*), allocating space for the *quotient*. The code comments indicate how the remainder can also be calculated.

The utility routines shown in Table 24.10 are used within the four main routines from Table 24.9.

TABLE 24.10 Utility Routines for Arithmetic Operations on Very Large Integers

Name of Routine	*Function*
`pairMultiply`	Multiplies a single word by another single word to produce their product in a pair (*array*) of words. All the operands must have been pre-allocated by the caller.
`cascMultiply`	Multiplies a very large number by a single word, allocating space for the product.
`oneDivide`	Divides a single word by another single word, giving the quotient and the remainder in an array. All of the operands must have been pre-allocated by the caller.
`pairDivide`	Divides a pair of words (*array*) by a single word, giving the quotient and remainder in an array. All of the operands must have been pre-allocated by the caller.
`cascDivide`	Divides a very large number by a single word, allocating space for the quotient. The remainder is not calculated.
`aDivNormalize`	Normalizes for division, allocating space for the normalized answer.
`aNormalize`	Normalizes a very large number, both allocating space for the answer and freeing the space of the given argument.

In the file `CH24AOK2.c`, all of the preceding routines are repeated, but with the additional possibility of having a decimal point within the numbers (that is, true non-integral numbers).

In all of those files, the following routines allocate space that must be freed by their callers: `aAdd`, `aSubtract`, `aMultiply`, `aDivide`, `cascMultiply`, `cascDivide`, `aDivNormalize`.

In the file `ChSafe.c`, there is a set of routines for all the base arithmetic operations upon type `double`. These routines are shown in Table 24.11.

TABLE 24.11 Routines for Base Arithmetic Operations on Type `double`

Name of Routine	*Function*
`flpSafeDivideSensitive`	Divides a numerator with a given precision by a denominator with a given precision, to give a quotient, calculating its precision, and raising any necessary error signals.
`flpSafeDivide`	Divides a numerator by a denominator to give a quotient. This routine calls `flpSafeDivideSensitive` to perform its inner calculations.
`flpSafeMultiplySensitive`	Multiplies a multiplicand with a given precision by another multiplicand, with its given precision, giving the product, calculating its precision, and raising any necessary error signals.
`flpSafeMultiply`	Multiplies a multiplicand by another multiplicand, giving the product. This routine calls `flpSafeMultiplySensitive` to perform its inner calculations.
`flpSafeAddSensitive`	Adds an addend with a given precision to another addend with a given precision, giving the sum, calculating its precision, and raising any necessary error signals.
`flpSafeAdd`	Adds an addend to another addend, giving the sum. This routine calls `flpSafeAddSensitive` to perform its inner calculations.
`flpSafeSubtractSensitive`	Subtracts a subtrahend with a given precision from a minuend with a given precision, giving the difference, calculating its precision, and raising any necessary error signals. This routine calls `flpSafeAddSensitive` to perform its inner calculations.
`flpSafeSubtract`	Subtracts a subtrahend from a minuend, giving the difference. This routine calls `flpSafeSubtractSensitive` to perform its inner calculations.
`flpcmp`	Compares two floating-point numbers, to the best accuracy appropriate for the type.
`flpSetEquivalent`	If the variables provided are equivalent according to epsilon (precision limit), both are set to the variable with the highest absolute value. If the variables are not equivalent, the function returns false.

Some of the naming of variables within these routines depends upon the English terminology:

Addend plus Addend equals Sum

Minuend minus Subtrahend equals Difference

Multiplicand times Multiplicand equals Product

Numerator divided by Denominator equals Quotient (and Remainder)

The arguments to these routines are all in the same sequence. For the "non-sensitive" routines (flpSafeAdd, flpSafeSubtract, flpSafeMultiply, and flpSafeDivide), there are always just two operands, and the routine returns the result of applying the operation. All results and operands are of type double. So instead of writing

```
double dA, dB, dC;
...
dA = dB + dC;
```

you can write

```
double dA, dB, dC;
...
da = flpSafeAdd ( dB, dC );
```

The "sensitive" routines (which are flpSafeAddSensitive, flpSafeSubtractSensitive, flpSaveMultiplySensitive, and flpSaveDivideSensitive) also take the same argument sequence, which is rather longer. The value returned is the result of applying the operation. There are seven arguments, which are

- The first operand, type double.
- The precision of the first operand, type double. If the value of this precision is zero, the first operand is being declared as having no known error.
- The second operand, type double.
- The precision of the second operand, type double.
- A pointer to a double, which is to receive the precision of the result. If this pointer is NULL, it is ignored.
- An int flag, which indicates whether or not this routine is to raise errors. If the value is zero, no raise will be issued.
- A pointer to an int, which will be given the value of the error that would have been raised. This pointer will be used only if the sixth parameter has the value zero, indicating that errors must not actually be raised, and it is not a NULL pointer.

The exact equivalent of

```
dA = flpSafeAdd ( dB, dC );
```

is

```
dA = flpSafeAddSensitive ( dA, 0.0, dC, 0.0, NULL, 0, NULL);
```

which is exactly what this call is converted into.

The two remaining routines in this set are the range compare, `flpcmp`, and the set equivalent, `flpSetEquivalent`.

Routine `flpcmp` takes three parameters. The first and third are double and the second is a character string. That string contains an explicit comparison operator: one of ==, !=, >, <, <=, or >=. The routine `flpcmp` performs the stated comparison on the first and third arguments, and returns the Boolean result of that comparison. The comparisons are made, however, within a certain precision range: two items are considered equal if they are within `COMPARE_EPSILON` of each other, where `COMPARE_EPSILON` has been defined earlier.

Routine `flpSetEquivalent` takes two parameters, each of which is a pointer to a double. If these are equal (as determined by `flpcmp`), the one with the smallest absolute value is set equal to the one with the largest absolute value.

Using Standard Types

If we cannot break away from the built-in types of `float`, `double`, and `long double`, how can we be sure that we are performing "safe" arithmetic? That is, how can we know the precision with which we can regard our results after calculation? On the CD in the files `Ch24Safe.c` and `Ch24Safe.h` there is a complete set of routines that deal with all the arithmetic operations on type `double`. These routines could be easily extended to cover type `long double`. They are listed in Listing 24.5—the bulk of the comments have been removed in the listing here, but can be found on the CD.

LISTING 24.5 Safe Arithmetic Routines, Type `double`

```
#include <stdio.h>
#include <signal.h>
#include <math.h>
#include <limits.h>
#include <float.h>
#include <string.h>

#include "Ch24Safe.h"

#ifndef TRUE
#define TRUE (0==0)
#endif

#ifndef FALSE
#define FALSE (1==0)
#endif
```

LISTING 24.5 continued

```
/* Macro constant required for flpcmp() */
#define COMPARE_EPSILON DBL_EPSILON

/* ARITHMET_ACCEPT_PRECISION is the limit of acceptable     */
/* precision after any arithmetic operation. This has been  */
/* set to one percent (0.01), but may be altered to any     */
/* value considered appropriate. This must be a long double */
/* (hence the trailing L):                                  */
#define ARITHMET_ACCEPT_PRECISION (0.01L)

#define ARITHMET_DENOMINATOR_ZERO SIGILL
#define ARITHMET_PRECISION_BAD    SIGINT
#define ARITHMET_BEYOND_RANGE     SIGFPE

double flpSafeDivideSensitive (
                  double flpNumerator,
                  double flpNumeratorPrecision,
                  double flpDenominator,
                  double flpDenominatorPrecision,
                  double * pflpResultPrecision,
                  int RaiseError, int * pErrorRaised )
{
   double flpReturnValue            = 0.0;
   double flpZero                   = 0.0;
   double flpLocalResultPrecision   = 0.0;
   double flpLocalNumPrecision      = 0.0;
   double flpLocalDenomPrecision    = 0.0;
   long double flpLocalReturnValue = 0.0;

   if ( pflpResultPrecision != NULL )
   {
      flpLocalNumPrecision=DBL_EPSILON * fabs( flpNumerator );
      if ( DBL_EPSILON > flpLocalNumPrecision )
         flpLocalNumPrecision = DBL_EPSILON;
      if ( flpNumeratorPrecision > flpLocalNumPrecision )
         flpLocalNumPrecision = flpNumeratorPrecision;
      flpLocalDenomPrecision = DBL_EPSILON *
                        fabs( flpDenominator );
      if ( DBL_EPSILON > flpLocalDenomPrecision )
         flpLocalDenomPrecision = DBL_EPSILON;
      if ( flpDenominatorPrecision > flpLocalDenomPrecision )
         flpLocalDenomPrecision = flpDenominatorPrecision;
```

LISTING 24.5 continued

```
        flpLocalResultPrecision = ( flpLocalNumPrecision   *
                                    fabs ( flpDenominator ) )
                                + ( flpLocalDenomPrecision *
                                    fabs ( flpNumerator ) );
        if ( flpLocalResultPrecision < DBL_EPSILON )
             flpLocalResultPrecision = DBL_EPSILON;
        *pflpResultPrecision = flpLocalResultPrecision;
    }

    if ( pErrorRaised != NULL )
        *pErrorRaised = 0;

    if ( flpcmp ( flpNumerator, "==", flpZero ) )
        return ( flpReturnValue );

    if ( flpcmp ( flpDenominator, "==", flpZero ) )
    {
        if ( pflpResultPrecision != NULL )
            *pflpResultPrecision = DBL_MAX;

        if ( pErrorRaised != NULL )
            *pErrorRaised = ARITHMET_DENOMINATOR_ZERO;

        if ( RaiseError )
           raise ( ARITHMET_DENOMINATOR_ZERO );
        flpReturnValue = DBL_MAX;
        return ( flpReturnValue );
    }

    flpLocalReturnValue = (long double) flpNumerator /
                          (long double) flpDenominator;
    if ( flpLocalResultPrecision < DBL_EPSILON *
                       fabs ( flpLocalReturnValue ) )
         flpLocalResultPrecision = DBL_EPSILON *
                       fabs ( flpLocalReturnValue ) ;

    if ( fabs ( flpLocalReturnValue ) > DBL_MAX )
    {
        if ( pflpResultPrecision != NULL )
            *pflpResultPrecision = DBL_MAX;
        if ( pErrorRaised != NULL )
            *pErrorRaised = ARITHMET_PRECISION_BAD;
```

LISTING 24.5 continued

```
      if ( flpLocalReturnValue < 0.0L )
         flpReturnValue = - DBL_MAX;
      else flpReturnValue = DBL_MAX;
      if ( RaiseError )
         raise ( ARITHMET_PRECISION_BAD );
      return ( flpReturnValue );
   } else {
      flpReturnValue = flpLocalReturnValue;
      if ( pflpResultPrecision != NULL )
          *pflpResultPrecision = flpLocalResultPrecision;
      if (  flpLocalResultPrecision  >
           ( fabs ( flpReturnValue ) > DBL_EPSILON ?
               ( fabs ( flpReturnValue ) *
                 ARITHMET_ACCEPT_PRECISION ) : DBL_EPSILON ) )
      {
         if ( pErrorRaised != NULL )
             *pErrorRaised = ARITHMET_BEYOND_RANGE;
         if ( RaiseError )
            raise ( ARITHMET_BEYOND_RANGE );
      }
   }
   return ( flpReturnValue );
}

double flpSafeDivide (double flpNumerator,
                      double flpDenominator)
{
  double flpReturnValue = 0.0;

  flpReturnValue = flpSafeDivideSensitive (flpNumerator, 0.0,
                                           flpDenominator, 0.0,
                                            NULL, FALSE, NULL);
  return (flpReturnValue);
}

double flpSafeMultiplySensitive (
             double flpFirstMultiplicand,
             double flpFirstMultiplicandPrecision,
             double flpSecondMultiplicand,
             double flpSecondMultiplicandPrecision,
             double * pflpResultPrecision,
             int RaiseError, int * pErrorRaised )
```

LISTING 24.6 continued

```
/* CAUTION: there are limits on the reliable actions with */
/* this size of base.                                     */
#if (INT_MAX>(ILIMIT*100000))
#define NUMBER_BASE 100000
#define DIGS_IN_BASE 5
#else
#define NUMBER_BASE 10
#define DIGS_IN_BASE 1
#endif

#if (DIGS_IN_BASE==5)
#define NUMBER_WIDTH 2001
#else
#define NUMBER_WIDTH 10001
#endif

int LongDivide ( int * Numerator, int * Denominator,
                 int * Answer );
int LongAdd ( int * iFirst, int * iSecond, int * iAnswer );

int main(int argc, char * argv[])
{
    int aResult[NUMBER_WIDTH+1];
    int aWork[NUMBER_WIDTH+1];
    int i;
    int j;

    aResult[0] = NUMBER_WIDTH;
    aResult[1] = 1;
    aWork[0] = NUMBER_WIDTH;
    aWork[1] = 1;
    for (i=2;(i<=NUMBER_WIDTH);i++)
    {
        aResult[i] = 0;
        aWork[i] = 0;
    }
    for (i=1;(i<ILIMIT);i++)
    {
        j = LongDivide ( aWork, &i, aWork );
        if (j<=0)
            i = ILIMIT + 1;
        LongAdd ( aWork, aResult, aResult );
```

LISTING 24.6 continued

```
    }
    printf("e = ");
    printf("%1.1d.",aResult[1]);
    for (i=2;(i<NUMBER_WIDTH);i++)
    {
#if (DIGS_IN_BASE==5)
        printf("%5.5d ",aResult[i]);
#endif
#if (DIGS_IN_BASE==1)
        printf("%1.1d",aResult[i]);
        if ((i % 5)==1)
           printf(" ");
#endif
        if ((i % 10)==0)
        {
            printf("\n");
            if ((i % 100)==0)
                printf("\n");
        }
    }
    printf("\n");
    return 1;
}

int LongDivide ( int * Numerator, int * Denominator,
                 int * Answer )
{
    int iStatus = 0;
    int j = 0;
    int k = 0;
    int m = 0;
    int d = 0;

    d = *Denominator;
    Answer[0] = Numerator[0];
    for (j=1;(j<=Numerator[0]);j++)
    {
        if (k>0)
            m = Numerator[j] + (k * NUMBER_BASE);
        else
            m = Numerator[j];
        Answer[j] = m / d;
```

LISTING 24.6 continued

```
        if (Answer[j] !=0)
            iStatus = 1;
        k = m % d;
    }
    return iStatus;
}

int LongAdd ( int * iFirst, int * iSecond, int * iAnswer )
{
    int iStatus = 0;
    int i = 0;
    int j = 0;
    int k = 0;
    int m = 0;

    i = iFirst[0];
    k = 0;
    for (j=i;(j>0);j- -)
    {
        if (iFirst[j]!=0)
            iStatus = 1;
        m = iFirst[j] + iSecond[j] + k;
        k = 0;
        while (m>=NUMBER_BASE)
        {
            m -= NUMBER_BASE;
            k += 1;
        }
        iAnswer[j] = m;
    }
    return iStatus;
```


What is the answer that we get when we run this program to calculate *e*? The start of the output is shown here, and all of it is in file `Ch24BigE.txt` on the CD.

```
e = 2.71828 18284 59045 23536 02874 71352 66249 77572 47093
69995 95749 66967 62772 40766 30353 54759 45713 82178 52516
64274 27466 39193 20030 59921 81741 35966 29043 57290 03342
95260 59563 07381 32328 62794 34907 63233 82988 07531 95251
01901 15738 34187 93070 21540 89149 93488 41675 09244 76146
06680 82264 80016 84774 11853 74234 54424 37107 53907 77449
```

92069 55170 27618 38606 26133 13845 83000 75204 49338 26560
29760 67371 13200 70932 87091 27443 74704 72306 96977 20931
01416 92836 81902 55151 08657 46377 21112 52389 78442 50569
53696 77078 54499 69967 94686 44549 05987 93163 68892 30098

79312 77361 78215 42499 92295 76351 48220 82698 95193 66803
31825 28869 39849 64651 05820 93923 98294 88793 32036 25094
43117 30123 81970 68416 14039 70198 37679 32068 32823 76464
80429 53118 02328 78250 98194 55815 30175 67173 61332 06981
12509 96181 88159 30416 90351 59888 85193 45807 27386 67385
89422 87922 84998 92086 80582 57492 79610 48419 84443 63463
24496 84875 60233 62482 70419 78623 20900 21609 90235 30436
99418 49146 31409 34317 38143 64054 62531 52096 18369 08887
07016 76839 64243 78140 59271 45635 49061 30310 72085 10383
75051 01157 47704 17189 86106 87396 96552 12671 54688 95703

50354 02123 40784 98193 34321 06817 01210 05627 88023 51930
33224 74501 58539 04730 41995 77770 93503 66041 69973 29725
08868 76966 40355 57071 62268 44716 25607 98826 51787 13419
51246 65201 03059 21236 67719 43252 78675 39855 89448 96970
96409 75459 18569 56380 23637 01621 12047 74272 28364 89613
42251 64450 78182 44235 29486 36372 14174 02388 93441 24796
35743 70263 75529 44483 37998 01612 54922 78509 25778 25620
92622 64832 62779 33386 56648 16277 25164 01910 59004 91644
99828 93150 56604 72580 27786 31864 15519 56532 44258 69829
46959 30801 91529 87211 72556 34754 63964 47910 14590 40905
86298 49679 12874 06870 50489 58586 71747 98546 67757 57320
56812 88459 20541 33405 39220 00113 78630 09455 60688 16674
00169 84205 58040 33637 95376 45203 04024 32256 61352 78369
51177 88386 38744 39662 53224 98506 54995 88623 42818 99707
73327 61717 83928 03494 65014 34558 89707 19425 86398 77275
47109 62953 74152 11151 36835 06275 26023 26484 72870 39207
64310 05958 41166 12054 52970 30236 47254 92966 69381 15137
32275 36450 98889 03136 02057 24817 65851 18063 03644 28123
14965 50704 75102 54465 01172 72115 55194 86685 08003 68532
28183 15219 60037 35625 27944 95158 28418 82947 87610 85263

98139 55990 06737 64829 22443 75287 18462 45780 36192 98197
13991 47564 48826 26039 03381 44182 32625 15097 48279 87779
96437 30899 70388 86778 22713 83605 77297 88241 25611 90717
66394 65070 63304 52795 46618 55096 66618 56647 09711 34447
40160 70462 62156 80717 48187 78443 71436 98821 85596 70959
10259 68620 02353 71858 87485 69652 20005 03117 34392 07321

```
13908 03293 63447 97273 55955 27734 90717 83793 42163 70120
50054 51326 38354 40001 86323 99149 07054 79778 05669 78533
58048 96690 62951 19432 47309 95876 55236 81285 90413 83241
16072 26029 98330 53537 08761 38939 63917 79574 54016 13722

36187 89365 26053 81558 41587 18692 55386 06164 77983 40254
35128 43961 29460 35291 33259 42794 90433 72990 85731 58029
09586 31382 68329 14771 16396 33709 24003 16894 58636 06064
58459 25126 99465 57248 39186 56420 97526 85082 30754 42545
99376 91704 19777 80085 36273 09417 10163 43490 76964 23722
29435 23661 25572 50881 47792 23151 97477 80605 69672 53801
71807 76360 34624 59278 77846 58506 56050 78084 42115 29697
52189 08740 19660 90665 18035 16501 79250 46195 01366 58543
66327 12549 63990 85491 44200 01457 47608 19302 21206 60243
30096 41270 48943 90397 17719 51806 99086 99860 etc. etc.
```

Summary

This chapter looked at some of the ways in which, using standard C, you can support increased precision, and created code to perform operations on numbers with many digits. It also looked at how error (that all-pervasive demon) creeps in and propagates in manners that are often unexpected. As a final example, we computed *e* to a ridiculous number of places. Ridiculous? Both *e* and *pi* (π) are already known to hundreds of millions of places: should you want to do the same yourself you will have to invent even more ways of representing extremely precise numbers than we have seen here. Happy calculating!

CHAPTER 25

Natural Language Processing

by Dr. Ian D. K. Kelly

In This Chapter

"Mistah Kurtz—he dead." (*Heart of Darkness, Joseph Conrad.*)

"Here's looking at you, kid." (*Casblanca, Julius P. Epstein.*)

"Who done it?" (*anon.*)

There are certain expressions we can make in English, and rules for understanding these expressions. Expressions that do not match these rules are in error, and are not part of English. So far, this is the same as what was said for C arithmetic expressions in Chapter 19, "Expression Parsing and Evaluation." But with English utterances, we cannot go back and get them changed when they do not match our rules—we have to either change our rules or cope with the errors. And, curiouser and curiouser, that is one of the ways in which English, as a language, has changed historically. Expressions that do not match these rules sometimes *are* part of English, or become part of it.

There are many computer systems that take natural language input, as opposed to artificial or algorithmic language input. This chapter examines some of the techniques that can be used in processing natural language. English is a natural language, and it is the one from which most of the examples will be drawn—but there is nothing special about English; French, German, Swahili, Tamil, Mandarin, Arabic, Urdu, Spanish—all of them are complex. All natural languages are complex.

Computer systems that handle natural language also may have to be complex, and this chapter discusses both simple systems (such as command processors) and highly complex systems (such as machine translation systems). You'll discover what natural language processing means, and learn the various kinds of natural language processing that a computer might do. This chapter compares the syntax and semantics of English with those of an algorithmic language, and discusses how you could write C code for natural language processing.

Human Language Syntax and Semantics

Just like algorithmic languages, natural languages have syntax and semantics: *what you can say* and *what it means when you have said it*. But human syntax is much more complex than algorithmic syntax, and much more flexible. The semantics of natural languages depends upon the real world, not an artificial world in which everything is measured. For example, at this moment I am typing this chapter on a portable PC. I am sitting on a train. Opposite me there is a tall, youngish man with slightly receding blond hair. He is reading intently a softbound book, folded back with disregard for the integrity of its spine. Book-ravishing, blond, balding youth sits intently.

Newspapers have many examples like that last sentence, and we accept them. You also now have a mental image—but not a precise one—of a man whose age you do not know exactly, and of whose hairline you are not completely certain (but know a little), doing something to a book (whose size and color have not been stated). Each reader's mental image will be different, and different from the reality in front of me. Any system that processes natural language must be able to cope with these imprecisions, and must be able to preserve them, where relevant. A politician once complained that his intentional ambiguities were lost in translation: Programs may not be ambiguous, but their data may have to be.

Natural Language Syntax

Can we write a complete, descriptive grammar of a language like English? The quick answer to that question is "No, we cannot." It is possible to write a descriptive grammar of some parts of English, as it is spoken (or written) in some places. But a complete grammar would have to allow the recognition "Mistah Kurtz—he dead," while simultaneously suggesting that this form should not normally be used. Observation of what we actually say (as opposed to the more formal language that we write), shows that the bulk of what comes from our mouths—and is accepted by all listeners—is incomplete and can be understood only from its context. "Fancy a coffee? Pass me the ... thanks ... with or without?"

In the fourth century BC (or it may have been the sixth—or some other—there is a great deal of academic argument on the point) a man called Panini wrote down the syntax of the Sanskrit language (and yes, the first letter n in his name should have a dot beneath it). You probably do not speak Sanskrit—unless, perhaps, you have chosen to study Hindu religious texts, or Indo-European linguistics—but it was the ordinary, everyday language of the time. Panini's grammar (the Astadhyayi) is as close as we have ever gotten to a complete description of a human, spoken language. For its description there had to be a syntax notation, and this was one of the things Panini invented. It was not too dissimilar to BNF: immensely powerful, and immensely unreadable.

You were probably taught at school about nouns and adjectives and verbs in English, and how to determine what is the subject of a sentence, and what is the predicate. You will know words like "singular" and "plural" and expressions like "future tense" and "subordinate clause." You may even know that English is, by preference, a "subject-verb-object" language. But have you ever encountered diagrams like

$[[[[\mathit{The}]_{\text{Det}}[\mathit{cat}]_{\text{Nn}}]_{\text{NP}}]_{\text{Subj}}[[\mathit{sat}]_{\text{Vb}}[[\mathit{on}]_{\text{Prep}}[[\mathit{the}]_{\text{Det}}[\mathit{mat}]_{\text{Nn}}]\text{NP}]_{\text{PrpP}}]_{\text{Pred}}]_{\text{S}}$.

which indicates one possible syntax for *The cat sat on the mat.*? This is exactly equivalent to the diagram in Figure 25.1.

FIGURE 25.1
English language syntax for a simple sentence.

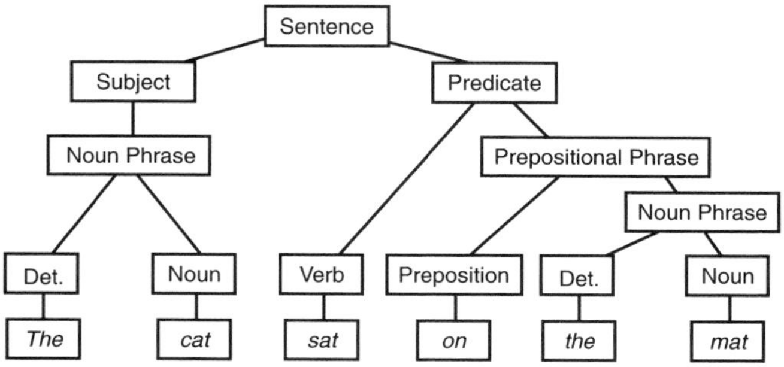

Both of these indicate that the sentence is made up of a subject followed by a predicate, that the predicate consists of a verb followed by a prepositional phrase, that a noun phrase consists of a determiner followed by a noun, and so on.

There are other models for language, and linguists are far from agreed on which are the most representative, or which are the most useful. For example, a *Dependency Analysis* would give the format shown in Figure 25.2.

FIGURE 25.2
Dependency analysis for a simple sentence.

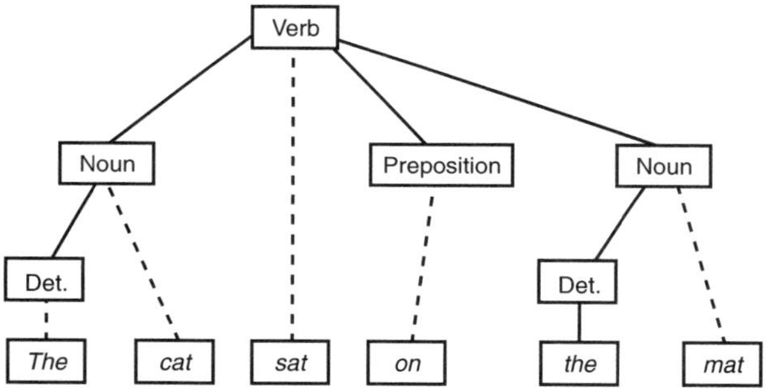

So there is no one correct way to parse English. It all depends on your point of view, and (ultimately) what you are going to use the parse for.

Contrast with Algorithmic Languages

A language like C (or Cobol or Fortran or Ada) is very much defined by its syntax. The syntax is known in advance, and is known to be both complete and correct. Languages like English (or French or Arabic or Tamil) grow and change, without any one body deciding what the correct syntax is.

If you speak American English, you will hopefully understand what I am about to say. If you speak British English, you will possibly have picked up the American usage of "hopefully" in the previous sentence. That "American usage" has now also become "British usage"—but only after many letters were written to *The Times* complaining that it was bad, explaining that it was good, observing that it came from a German phrase via Yiddish, and so on. And if you want to understand—or in any way process—sentences that contain the word "hopefully," you will have had to change those processes for handling British English in the 1980s. Natural languages do not just gain new words, they gain new ways of using those words. This is easy to deal with: *Not.*

Sample Rules for Subset of English

Table 25.1 shows a small grammar for a tiny subset of English. This grammar allows many good sentences using the words in the set *boy girl dog cat table chair old young green heavy intelligent living kisses hits puts gives runs barks sits talks lies decays glows never soon on by with to the a no every.* The grammar is in the compressed, original version of BNF that was introduced in Chapter 19.

TABLE 25.1 A First Tiny Grammar

Syntax Rules
sentence ::= subject predicate #
subject ::= noun-phrase #
predicate ::= verb-structure | verb-structure objects adverb-string #
objects ::= direct-object | indirect-object | direct-object adverb-string indirect-object #
verb-structure ::= adverb-string verb adverb-string #
adverb-string ::= adverb adverb-string | adverb | empty #
direct-object ::= noun-phrase #
indirect-object ::= preposition noun-phrase #
noun-phrase ::= determiner adjective-string noun #
adjective-string ::= adjective adjective-string | adjective | empty #
empty ::= #
determiner ::= "the" | "a" | "no" | "every" #
noun ::= "boy" | "girl" | "cat" | "dog" | "table" | "chair" #
adjective ::= "old" | "young" | "green" | "heavy" | "intelligent" | "living" #
adverb ::= "never" | "soon" #
preposition ::= "on" | "by" | "with" | "to" #
verb ::= "kisses" | "puts" | "gives" | "runs" | "lies" | "barks" | "sits" | "talks" | "hits" | "decays" | "glows" #

The grammar in Table 25.1 allows sentences like *the boy kisses a girl*, *a dog never barks*, *the boy soon gives a heavy cat to a young girl*. These are unexceptional, and correct: they are good English sentences. It also allows bizarre sentences like *the green dog kisses a young table*, *a heavy chair barks*, *every old chair soon lies on the green cat*. These are possible English sentences, but unlikely because of facts about the real world (dogs are not green, chairs do not bark). But it is good that the grammar allows these sentences—they might, after all, in some strange circumstance be useful.

This grammar also allows sentences like *every heavy green heavy green green green heavy heavy young old cat barks with a table*. This is not good. It is extremely hard to think of any real-world circumstance that would allow that sentence to have sense, and *no girl soon never puts soon never* is completely beyond the pale—but allowed by this grammar. This grammar, he dead.

Ah, no it isn't.

The sentences that have been criticized above are actually perfectly good English sentences, and the argument has merely been that we would never need to use them in this real world. They are observations about this universe (the "real world"), but not all the possible universes we can think of. The useful circumstances may be hard to think of, but they are not impossible. The grammar does not, on the other hand, allow us to say truly non-English things like *barks green with puts*, for which no interpretation is possible in any universe.

Table 25.2 contains a slightly more restrictive grammar, which more closely limits the number of sentences that will be allowed.

TABLE 25.2 A More Restrictive Tiny Grammar

Syntax Rules
sentence ::= personal-subject personal-predicate | animate-subject animate-predicate | inanimate-subject inanimate-predicate #
subject ::= noun-phrase #
personal-subject ::= personal-noun-phrase #
animate-subject ::= animate-noun-phrase #
inanimate-subject ::= inanimate-noun-phrase #
predicate ::= verb-structure | verb-structure objects adverb-string #
personal-predicate ::= personal-verb-structure | personal-verb-structure objects adverb-string #
animate-predicate ::= animate-verb-structure | animate-verb-structure objects adverb-string #
inanimate-predicate ::= inanimate-verb-structure | inanimate-verb-structure objects adverb-string #
objects ::= direct-object | indirect-object | direct-object adverb-string indirect-object #

TABLE 25.2 continued

Syntax Rules
verb-structure ::= adverb-string verb adverb-string #
personal-verb-structure ::= adverb-string personal-verb adverb-string #
animate-verb-structure ::= adverb-string animate-verb adverb-string #
inanimate-verb-structure ::= adverb-string inanimate-verb adverb-string #
adverb-string ::= adverb adverb-string | adverb | empty #
direct-object ::= noun-phrase #
indirect-object ::= preposition noun-phrase #
personal-noun-phrase ::= determiner personal-part #
animate-noun-phrase ::= determiner animate-part #
inanimate-noun-phrase ::= determiner inanimate-part #
noun-phrase ::= determiner personal-part | determiner animate-part | determiner inanimate-part #
personal-part ::= personal-adjective-string personal-noun #
animate-part ::= animate-adjective-string animate-noun #
inanimate-part ::= inanimate-adjective-string inanimate-noun #
adjective-string ::= adjective adjective-string | adjective | empty #
personal-adjective-string ::= personal-adjective personal-adjective-string | personal-adjective | empty #
animate-adjective-string ::= animate-adjective animate-adjective-string | animate-adjective | empty #
inanimate-adjective-string ::= inanimate-adjective inanimate-adjective-string | inanimate-adjective | empty #
general-adjective-string ::= general-adjective general-adjective-string | general-adjective | empty #
empty ::= #
determiner ::= “the” | “a” | “no” | “every” #
inanimate-noun ::= “table” | “chair” #
animate-noun ::= “cat” | “dog” | personal-noun #
personal-noun ::= “boy” | “girl” #
noun ::= inanimate-noun | animate-noun #
general-adjective ::= “old” | “young” | “heavy” #
personal-adjective ::= general-adjective | animate-adjective | “intelligent” #
animate-adjective ::= general-adjective | “living” #
inanimate-adjective ::= general-adjective | “green” #
adjective ::= general-adjective | personal-adjective | inanimate-adjective #
adverb ::= “never” | “soon” #
preposition ::= “on” | “by” | “with” | “to” #
general-verb ::= “stands” | “lies” #

TABLE 25.2 continued

Syntax Rules
inanimate-verb ::= "decays" | "glows" | general-verb #
animate-verb ::= "barks" | "sits" | "puts" | "runs" | general-verb #
personal-verb ::= "kisses" | "gives" | "talks" | "sits" | "puts" | "runs" | general-verb #
verb ::= inanimate-verb | animate-verb | personal-verb #

The grammar in Table 25.2 still allows *the boy kisses a girl*, *a dog never barks*, and *the boy soon gives a heavy cat to a young girl*. But it does not allow anything containing *green cat* or *green dog*; only the *boy* or *girl* can be the subject of *talks* and *kisses*, and it allows *the green table glows* but does not allow *a dog glows*. We can have *the dog runs* but not *the table runs*.

As grammars like that in Table 25.2 grow, they become very unwieldy, and we soon have to think of other techniques of achieving the same ends. Also, these grammars are too restrictive—we *do* sometimes (but rarely) want to be able to talk about *the green dog*. Perhaps we should not be using the grammar exclusively, but making multiple passes across the natural language input, declaring some structures to be more or less probable, depending on what we know about the real world and how particular words correlate together.

We have also placed into the grammar the complete vocabulary. This is not what is needed for extensive language recognition: We need to have dictionaries, probably contained in files, to which words can be added. And each dictionary entry should say about the word it describes whether it is a noun or adjective or adverb, and so on, and whether it is personal or animate or inanimate or in some other set of classes that we may think up.

Context Recognition

The grammar in Table 25.2 has included some of the properties of the semantics as part of the grammar. This is inevitable for natural languages. In fact, we have tried to build in some *context recognition* into our grammar. Noam Chomsky divided grammars into four groups:

Type 3 grammars are *regular* or *finite state* grammars.

Type 2 grammars are *phrase structure* or *context free* grammars.

Type 1 grammars are *context sensitive* grammars.

Type 0 grammars are completely *general* grammars.

Most computer language grammars are expressed as Type 2 grammars, *context free*, though some context sensitivity is built into the interpretation mechanism (the semantic element) of compilers (for example,the C statement `j = 34000;` usually implies that the variable `j` should not be of type `short int`). Natural languages are at least of Type 1, *context sensitive*. Some of the context sensitivity arises from our knowledge of the real world, and some merely relates to the language itself. Some analysts declare that natural languages are of Type 0—completely *general*.

When you look at the rejected utterances in Table 25.3, you can see that real-world knowledge is not a good reason for rejecting a linguistic structure.

TABLE 25.3 Rejected Utterances

Forbidden Utterance	*Reason*
The green dog	Real-world knowledge: Dogs are never green. But then, I *might* dye a dog green—it is possible.
The boys has spoken	Linguistic knowledge: *the boys* is plural, but *has spoken* requires a singular subject.
Colorless green ideas sleep furiously	Real-world knowledge: It is so difficult to imagine a possible world in which this has a meaning that we reject it. But if this is interpreted as "unexciting ecological concepts do nothing very much, with a great deal of noise," then in this world the sentence does have an interpretation. This utterance, by the way, is one of Chomsky's examples of a grammatical sentence that is not in the language.
Man flies to the moon	Real-world knowledge: this is completely impossible. Oops! In 1969 our state of knowledge changed: This sentence has now become a possible, legal sentence of English.

Mixing the vocabulary (the dictionary) and the grammar into one structure makes both less transparent. One technique that has been used is to state the grammar very simply (like that in Table 25.1), but to add two sorts of markers to terms in the dictionary. The first set of markers is the simple grammatical categories: *boy* and *table* are NOUNS, *green* and *intelligent* are ADJECTIVES. The second set of markers indicates what sort of properties the term has, and to what extent. Thus, for example, *boy* and *girl* are ANIMATE and PERSONAL, *cat* and *dog* are ANIMATE, and *table* is INANIMATE; the verbs *talks* and *kisses* are PERSONAL to a large extent, but ANIMATE to a small extent. The parser can then be extended to prefer pairings whose properties match; that is, to pair PERSONAL verbs with PERSONAL subjects or (to a lesser extent) with ANIMATE subjects, INANIMATE adjectives with inanimate nouns, and so on.

Another analysis that has been made by examining very large bodies of text has been to measure what words appear with (correlate with) what other words. For example, the word *table* often appears close to the word *leg*, but not so often close to the word *chlorine*. These correlation tables are very helpful when there is some doubt as to the correctness of the natural language text being processed, or to determine which particular meaning to ascribe to a given word. There is more discussion of this later, in the section "Machine Translation."

The grammars of computer languages are fixed, and the edges are known. It is always possible to determine whether a given utterance is in the language or is not. But with natural languages the boundaries continually change, and at any time there are some utterances that are "on the edge," and it is difficult to determine whether they are in the language or not. Natural language processing systems must cope with this, and not classify its input into "good English" and "bad English," but instead into *natural language input this system can process*, and *other input—sorry.*

The parser introduced in Chapter 19 could be used with any of the preceding grammars to produce an analysis tree of some English sentences. The code for expression evaluation, however, would have to be changed to something appropriate for a natural language system: You would have to decide what the semantic really is for your input.

Natural Language Semantics

> *The cat sat on the mat. Lots of cats do that, everybody knows. And nothing strange comes of it. But once a cat sat on a mat and something strange did come of it.*
>
> (Joan Aitken, "*The Cat Sat on the Mat*" in "*Stories for Under-Fives*," eds. Sara and Stephen Corrin, Faber and Faber, 1974).

But what *is* the meaning of a text?

When you encounter a simple sentence such as *The cat sat on the mat* you say "I know what that means," but do you? Very much depends upon the intention of the sentence in the first place. Was it intended to state that at some particular moment in the real or recounted past a specific individual of the species *felis felis* seated itself on a small piece of carpet in front of a door? Was it intended to be an example of a simple sentence such as any child still learning to read could yet understand? Was it chosen for its assonance of repeated *at* sounds?

In context this may be easy to decide—for us humans. In the opening paragraph from Joan Aitken's delightful little children's story, quoted just above, the meaning of the sentence is not just its primary one but also a literary reference that even very small children would recognize. The only other context in which I have actually met this sentence is as an illustration for syntactic analysis.

There is a problem with determining the meaning of just one word, let alone a whole sentence. Words are frequently *polysemes*, having more than one meaning. For example, the word *table* might be a concrete noun (the thing that goes with chairs), or an abstract noun (as in *table of the elements*), or an adjective (as in *Table Mountain*), or a verb concerning a proposal at a meeting. In this latter context its meaning is very different in the two sorts of English spoken on opposite sides of the Atlantic, or again, a verb meaning to place in an array (*table these figures*). It is only from the context that the meaning and part of speech of *table* can be determined. And this is true for a very high proportion of English words. In this paragraph alone, the following additional words can easily be seen to be polysemous: *abstract, array, concrete, determined, goes, high, just, let, meeting, part, place, proposal, sentence, sorts, speech*.

In the sentences *Time flies like an arrow.* and *Fruit flies like an apple.* we know that the words *flies* and *like* have completely different meanings. This comes from our real-world knowledge, and the consequential lexical knowledge, such as there exists in English such a term as *fruit fly* (so that these two words go together, with *fly* being a noun, and *fruit* being an adjective that describes it), but that there is no single lexical term *time fly*.

For us, as we design and write computer systems, we have to think "What do we want this natural language input and output for? What do we want it to do?" And on the basis of the answers to these questions we can define narrow grammars of a subset of English (or Spanish or Welsh or Cherokee or Japanese, and so on) suitable for our purpose.

In an algorithmic language, there is a strict interpretation for every statement. With natural languages the meanings can be very fluid. Remember that in the computer interpretation of natural language we always have to ask "What do we want it to do?" before we can begin to create an interpretation. Are we seeking commands or seeking descriptions or giving information or analyzing authorship or what?

If we take the simplest sort of natural language system—one that selects from a limited set of statements (such as a command parser for a computer system)—then it is easy to discuss semantics. If we consider a very large system, such as one for machine translation, then semantics can be extremely complex.

Complexities of Natural Language Input

I personally would like to be able to talk to my computer. My wife tells me that I *do* actually talk to my computer, but I would like the computer to understand my speech and to answer back. Since we do not yet have HAL (from Kubrick's *2001*) anywhere in the world, why might we even now want natural language input to a computer or machine system?

Processing Commands

You are probably already familiar with computer languages other than C. These may be the languages of the various UNIX command scripts (Bourne shell, Korn shell, awk, perl) or the control languages for other systems (JCL under MVS, MS-DOS batch commands, and so on). The commands that are issued are of a very restricted set: to delete files, inquire about disk space, create directories, request that certain events happen at certain times, and things like that. A small subset of English can be chosen to represent many of these commands. Thus instead of:

```
cd /home/syzygy
ls -l *.c
rm test.c
rm *.tmp
```

you could "say" or type:

> *Go to directory syzygy under home under the root directory. Show me the names and details of all files of type little C. Delete the file test dot little C. Delete all files of type little Tee Em Pee.*

This same set of English commands might, under a different system, translate into:

```
cd \home\syzygy
dir *.c
erase test.c
erase *.tmp
```

This allows a user to avoid learning the more terse command languages, which differ from system to system. English, unfortunately, is rather more long-winded than shell scripting.

Playing Games

Go north. Take rod. Put bird in cage. Fight dragon with sword. These are commands familiar to all who have played *Adventure* (sometimes called *Colossal Cave*). Other games (such as *Zork*) allow even more complex input. Some of the many different MUDs (Multi-User Dungeons) have natural language understanding and production systems that are more complex still.

Within a game there is a small, well-defined universe. All the items of language being used refer to just that universe. Most of the human input can be interpreted as an imperative verb (do something: *go*, *take*, *fight*), followed by a direct object (the thing to do it to: *bird*, *dragon*), and sometimes an indirect object (the thing to do it by or with: *in cage*, *with sword*).

The processing of input does not have to exercise many subtle arguments to determine what the input means: If the player says *eat banana* and at that point in the game there is no *banana*, or the game does not consider *eat* as one of the supported actions, then the game can cheerfully tell the user that his request is not understood (and perhaps induce an imaginary dwarf to pop up and fling an axe at him).

The syntax for natural language game input is likely to be very restricted, and the processing does not have to deal with polysemes—*bear* will only mean a grizzly, *table* will only be the furniture.

Machine Translation

At completely the opposite pole is Machine Translation (MT); that is, using a computer to translate between two human languages. The input to an MT system is absolutely any text, about almost any subject you can imagine, and the output desired is an adequate (though perhaps not stylish) and correct translation. If the MT system cannot process the text, it does not have *Colossal Cave*'s option of throwing an axe at you. The syntax for MT is extremely complex.

MT and Machine Assisted Translation (MAT) have been under development since the start of electronic computing, and there are many commercial systems available. These systems are used by large language users; for example, the European Commission, the Ford Motor Company, the United States Air Force, and NASA. MT systems are also used by small language users; that is, individuals. There are Web sites that will give a first translation of Web pages between the most common European languages.

MT works best with information text, and tends not to work well with stylistic and idiomatic text. For example, the following are easy to translate: *Use the 15 mm. open-end spanner to remove the topmost nut.*; *The control-flow statements of a language specify the order in which computations are performed.*; *Draw ellipse with horizontal diameter* d1 *and vertical diameter* d2, *with left edge at current position.* But these utterances are more difficult: *How sweet the moonlight sleeps upon this bank* (Shakespeare); *No time like the present* (trad.); *After us the deluge* (Marie Antoinette); *Give him a flea in his ear* (trad.); *But where are the snows of yesteryear?* (Villon); *Go down to the shop and get us half a pigs head, with two eyes, to see us through the week* (London Cockney saying).

Why are they more difficult? Consider *Give him a flea in his ear.* This has nothing to do with real fleas (the insect *pulex irritans*), nor with real ears; rather, it means to scold. It is an idiomatic expression. But if this phrase were translated, word by word, into French, without regard to its English idiomatic meaning, you would get a perfectly good French idiom that means *whisper to him*. So an MT system seeking to translate from English into French must know both the idiom in English and also the (different) idiom in French. Consider *Go down to the shop...see us through the week.* This is a play on the meanings of the word "see." *How sweet the moonlight sleeps...* upon what sort of bank? a bank of credit? a bank of earth? a river bank? And is it really sleeping, or is this a metaphor?

A dictionary for MT needs to be particularly rich because it must contain not just the raw individual words of the language, but also the idioms and the expressions and the multi-word terms. So, for example, it must contain the word *magnetic*, and it must contain the word *tape*, and it must contain the word *unit*, but also it must contain the term *magnetic tape unit*. The French for *magnetic* is *magnétique*, the French for *tape* is *étape,* and the French for *unit* is *unité*, but the French for *magnetic tape unit* is *dérouleur.*

There is no detectable limit to the potential length of a term: *myocardial infarction* is a single term built from two specialist words; *magnetic tape unit* is a jargon term built of three reasonably common words. Neil Tomkinson (in *Reflections on English Usage*, Language Monthly, July 1984) quotes the monster *Reserve Band guaranteed Atlas Aircraft Corporation Limited bearer U.S. dollar ten year Certificates* as a single unitary term—the equivalent of one word—in the particular context in which it was used.

There are even more terms in a language than there are words, and we have already mentioned idioms. An *idiom* is a unit of discourse that means more than (or different from) the sum of its parts. A single-word idiom is a polysemous word or metaphor—such as using the word *tongue* to mean *language*. Multiple-word idioms may be metaphors that are still living, such as *we have not closed the door on negotiations*, or proverbial and long-since dead, such as *closing the stable door after the horse has bolted*. The English *pig in a poke* is the Russian *cat in a bag*, but to *let the* (English) *cat out of the bag* is different again. And woe betide the translator of the euphemism *tired and emotional* who does not know that what it really means (in English newspapers) is *drunk*.

Knowing what to translate and what to leave untranslated is also a difficulty: proper names are a particular problem. *Jean-Loup Chiflet* points out that he is *John Wolfwhistle* in English; *Dr. Peter Toma*, who was responsible for turning the research at Georgetown into a commercially working MT system, was surprised to read his name as *Dr. Peter Divided into [several] volumes*. Toma is the past-historic of the rather rare—but real—French verb *tomer*, meaning "to divide into [several] volumes."

There is also the problem of identifying which parts of the input actually are idioms, and which are literal. For example, he who *kicks the bucket* very rarely taps with his leg a portable container for liquid; just prior to that he is *on his last legs* in English, but *beating the garlic* in French. Responsibility does not sit on your literal shoulders, but on your figurative (metaphorical) ones; a *pain in the neck* is not always a reference to discomfort from the cervical vertebrae. The Russian *na ulitsa bolshoi dvijenie* literally says *on street large motion*, but what it means is *there is a lot of traffic in the street.*

Resolving polysemes will sometimes involve reasoning from the general subject matter of the text (this is about furniture, so *table* is furniture; this is about financial performance, so *table* is a multi-dimensional display of figures), and sometimes from the possible grammatical forms of sentences (this sentence has only one possible verb, so *bear* is a verb; this sentence has two possible verbs, but only one possible subject, so *bear* is a noun).

Many books have been written on MT. I recommend to you as good introductions *Machine Translation, Ten Years On*, eds. Douglas Clarke and Alfred Vella, Cranfield University Press, 1998, and the superb *Machine Translation, Past, Present, Future* by W.J. Hutchins, Ellis Horwood, 1986.

There are a huge number of MT and MAT systems in use and development, including Globalink, Metal, Systran, AppTek, PC-Transfer, PARS, SPANAM/ENGSPAN, ATLAS, Transcend, LOGOS, and Eurotra. For a larger list, search the Web.

To see an MT system in action, go to the Web page `http://babelfish.altavista.com/` and you will be able to see Systran in action. There is an unnamed MT system being used at `http://www.t-mail.com/` and information on some other systems and their theoretical underpinnings, together with a lot of helpful discussion, may be seen at `http://www.lim.nl/eamt/` (and those of its sister organizations), and `http://www.bcs.org.uk/nalatran/nalatran.htm` and links from these pages.

This Equals That

It is when we have large quantities of natural language text that we realize comparison is difficult. The C function `strcpy` indicates equality only for exact character-for-character equivalence. But wee often make errrors, sometimes we use incorrectly grammar, more extra words get inserted and words get left. A natural language system must be able to cope with this. So string comparison in a natural language system must yield not a triple *greater/equal/less than* but a degree of measure as to how similar two strings are. One possibility is to assign a weight to each character position, with the leading positions having the highest weight. Listing 25.1 is a sample string comparison function. The caller can decide whether to simply accept the positive/zero/negative return, or to look at its magnitude.

LISTING 25.1 String Comparison

```
#include <string.h>
int strlike(char *s, char *t)
{
    int i;
    int j;
    int r = 0;
    int w = 16384;
    r = strcpy(s,t);
    if (r==0)
        return r;
    if (r<0)
        w = -w;
    j = min(strlen(s),strlen(t));
    for (i=0; (i<j); i++)
    {
        if (s[i]==t[i])
           r += w;
        w = w / 2;
    }
    return r;
}
```

This is a fuzzy string compare. The section “Parsing Natural Language Input” later in this chapter talks about how we can have fuzzy parsers.

Artificial Intelligence

John McCarthy, the inventor of the LISP programming language, first coined the term *Artificial Intelligence* (AI) in 1956. The term and the subject it names have been a source of debate ever since. The various extreme views include

- Artificial intelligence is impossible. Only human beings (or other beings with souls) can have intelligence; machines cannot have souls and therefore machines can never think. AI is artificial in the same way that plastic flowers are artificial: bearing only a superficial similarity to the original, without any of the essential qualities.
- *Of course* machines can be made to think: Man himself is only a machine, after all. AI is artificial only in the sense that a helicopter is an artificial bird: the flight is real,

even though its superficial appearance and the principles whereby it is realized are different.

- AI is ultimately artificial only in the same way that a man-made lake is artificial—in all its essential features and in appearance they are identical. They differ only in historic origin, and after a while the relevance (and detectability) of that fades away. Manufactured intelligence is just the next step in the natural evolution of increasingly specialized and adapted life-forms on Earth.

Each of these extreme views (and many of the intermediate positions) have been used as justification for the conclusions:

- And therefore research into AI is at worst harmless, and at best a possible source of useful artifacts.
- And therefore research into AI is pointless, being doomed to failure.
- And therefore research into AI is one of the most important tasks that should be undertaken by any civilized society.
- And therefore AI research should be rejected as being grounded in sinful hubris.

Whether or not machines can be made to *think* (and I make no personal comment on that here), AI research is certainly giving them more to *do*. As we learn more, the boundaries of the AI field keep moving: I personally think that AI is everything about computers that we don't yet fully understand. The well-known ELIZA computer conversation model is an example of what used to be thought of as AI, but is now thought of as an amusing—but illustrative—toy.

To understand speech requires a lot of intelligence (some illustrations are given in the "Speech Recognition" section later in this chapter) and AI certainly has a part to play in natural language processing.

Determination of Authorship

Stylistic analysis of language *as she is spoke* yields something quite different from what is normally printed in dictionaries. For example, as an English speaker you know the verb *to see*, and you know that its primary meaning is involved with the action performed by the eyes. What you are probably not aware of is that you are three times more likely to use *see* to mean *understand* than any other use. So you see that we have to make *understand* its primary (most common) meaning for computer translation, and in parsing text.

The individual words in a text can be counted, and the patterns of the most common words can be drawn up. In one text by myself that I examined, in the first 8000 words of text the most common words I used were *the of to a/an and in is* and *that*. The counts for these words were 489, 332, 225, 212, 182, 150, 136, and 119. But the first 8000 words in another text, by a different author, but on the same subject gave for these words the counts 540, 263, 219, 200, 178, 226, 185, and 59. For this author, his most popular words were in the order *the of in to a/an is* and *be*. A third author on the same subject had counts 684, 229, 248, 175, 136, 232, 126, and 59. His most popular words, in order, were *the to in of for a/an be* and *is*. You cannot, on the basis of this one examination, guarantee that all my texts will produce the same counts (489, 332, 225, 212...), but you can be fairly certain that because of the way I think and write, my most popular words will always be *the of to a* in that order.

The ratios of the counts for these small words are very significant markers of who wrote a text, and have been used as the basis of authorship studies. For example, the Pauline Epistles have been analyzed in their original Greek showing that they were not all written by the same author (which accepted scholarship had known for years).

Measuring the use ratio of *of* to *the* does not tell you what the text is about, but it *is* meaningful to ask at what level does a pair (or triple...) of words become a significant term to be entered into the lexicon. And it can begin to give you clues as to the existence of multi-word terms, where these words are separated.

If you want to write code that counts the words in a text and displays their frequencies, be sure to read the "Morphology" section in this chapter. You may want to class related words together—you may want to count both *a* and *an* as a single word, or you may want to consider *love*, *loves*, *loved*, and *loving* all in the same count.

Electronic Toys

Last Christmas I was given a Furby. This is a cuddly toy, with batteries, that talks. It reacts to sound and light in the outside world, can detect when it is upside-down, or being patted, or being tickled, or when it is being fed. You can only feed a Furby imaginary food, by pressing down on its real tongue with a spoon. My Furby speaks English (a little). I gather that there are Spanish-speaking and French-speaking Furbies too, and there is no real reason for there not being a version that supports any human language.

The language generated by Furby is flexible, and is drawn from a vocabulary of about a hundred "words," not all of which are in English. These words are combined into multi-word utterances. As time passes, the average length of these utterances grows—the sentence structure becomes more complex.

Listing 25.2 is some sample code for generating random, but syntactically correct, English text.

LISTING 25.2 Generating Random Text

```
#include <stdio.h>
#include <string.h>
#include <stdlib.h>
#include <time.h>

char* pRandWord ( char* WordList[], int ListLength, int NullChances)
{
    char* pReturn = NULL;
    int   iMaximum;
    int   iFound;

    iMaximum = ListLength + NullChances;
    iFound = rand() % iMaximum;
    if (iFound<ListLength)
        pReturn = WordList[iFound];
    return pReturn;
}

void WordList( char* WordList[], int ListLength)
{
    int iProbNull;
    char* pW;

    iProbNull = ListLength;
    pW = WordList[0];
    while (pW!=NULL)
    {
        pW = pRandWord (WordList, ListLength, iProbNull);
        iProbNull += iProbNull;
        if (pW!=NULL)
            printf("%s ",pW);
    }
}

int main (int argc, char* argv[])
{
    int i = 0;
    int j = 0;
    char* pW;

    char *Nouns[] = { "table", "chair", "boy", "girl", "dog", "cat",
         "bottle", "clarinet", "candle", "sofa", "father", "mother",
```

LISTING 25.2 continued

```
        "television", "telephone", "flower", "book", "cup" };
    int  CountNouns = 17;
    char *Verbs[] = { "eats", "kisses", "loves", "orders", "sees",
        "understands", "takes", "answers", "moves", "ignores" };
    int  CountVerbs = 10;
    char *Adjectives[] = { "tall", "small", "pretty", "flat", "tuneless",
        "different", "green", "plastic", "delicate", "pompous" };
    int  CountAdjectives = 10;
    char *Determiners[] = { "a", "the", "no", "every" };
    int  CountDeterminers = 4;
    char *Adverbs[] = { "quickly", "slowly", "twice", "evenly", "thus" };
    int  CountAdverbs = 5;

    time_t thistime;

    thistime = time(NULL);
    srand (thistime);

    pW = pRandWord (Determiners, CountDeterminers, 0);
    printf("%s ",pW);

    WordList(Adjectives, CountAdjectives);

    pW = pRandWord (Nouns, CountNouns, 0);
    printf("%s ",pW);

    WordList(Adverbs, CountAdverbs);

    pW = pRandWord(Verbs, CountVerbs, 0);
    printf("%s ",pW);

    pW = pRandWord (Determiners, CountDeterminers, 0);
    printf("%s ",pW);

    WordList(Adjectives, CountAdjectives);

    pW = pRandWord (Nouns, CountNouns, 0);
    printf("%s.\n",pW);

    return 0;
}
```

Speech Recognition

My wife declares that my car phone is a toy. It certainly recognizes my voice when I ask it to dial particular phone numbers. We are so used to recognizing speech that often we do not consider how very complex it is. If someone speaks to you in a language that you know, you have no difficulty in splitting the stream of sounds into words and phrases, and constructing meaning from the result. If you hear speech in a language that you do not know, however, you cannot even begin to guess where the word boundaries are. *Weactuallyspeakinonecontinuousstreamofsound*. Consider the complexities set out in the following sections.

Sound Processing

Each language contains its own sounds. There is only one sound that exists in all human spoken languages, and that is the Ah sound (as in "f**a**ther," "Ahhh"). There are many hundreds of other sounds that we can make. In any one language there are between twelve and sixty different sounds used, a selection from this large set. In English there are about forty-five sounds used. These sounds are called *phonemes*. Our spelling when we write is only an approximation to these sounds.

Phoneme Recognition

To recognize a spoken sound, we have to have a model of the sounds in that language. The model is different for each language, even for languages that are very similar to each other, and is different for the various dialects of the one language. Your accent, if you speak American English, is very different from my southern British accent. In my own family, my mother speaks with a strong Irish accent, and my father-in-law, who is from Scotland, sounds rather like Mr. Scott in *Star Trek*. But we all understand each other's voices perfectly.

To remind you how important accent is, the standard Australian English pronunciation of the word "basin" sounds exactly like the standard American pronunciation of the word "bison": Any speech-processing system that cannot cope with these variations is a non-starter—an inevitable failure.

So consider *The cat sat on the mat*: What are the phonemes in this?
They are: [ɵɜkatsatɒnɵɜmat] or, one by one
/ɵ/ /ɜ/ /k/ /a/ /t/ /s/ /a/ /t/ /ɒ/ /n/ /ɵ/ /ɜ/ /m/ /a/ /t/. Eek!
What does this mean? The symbols that do not look like proper letters are part of the IPA, the International Phonetic Alphabet. This is a book on C, so I can only direct you to books on linguistics (or the prefaces of large dictionaries) to get a complete listing of the IPA and what all the symbols mean. But the meaning of that weird

string of characters is simply "the sound /th/ is followed by the sound /er/ is followed by the sound /k/" and so on.

To know what sounds are in the language, you can record large quantities of it and analyze those recordings, or you can refer to the linguistic textbooks for the research already done.

Sandhi

As we speak we make modifications to the basic sounds, depending on context. Consider the word "sit." This has three phonemes: [sit]. Consider the word "down." This has four phonemes: [down]. But when we say *sit down* the "t" at the end of *sit* and the "d" at the beginning of *down* are brought together to make just one "d" sound. So what we actually say is [sidown] or *sid-down*. This modification of sounds when they appear together is called *sandhi*. (This is one of the few Sanskrit words we have in English. It is pronounced "Sun-dhee.") The design of any speech-recognition system has to have some basic knowledge of the sandhi rules for the language being spoken. The rules are different for each language.

Word Recognition

Once a system has split the input sound into its separate phonemes and then applied the rules of sandhi for that language, it is easy to recognize the words, isn't it?

Alas, no. There are several problems in word recognition. Among these are knowing where the words start and end, and morphology.

In the phrase *six sailors seek cattle*, the system has to be able to reject *sick sailor see cat `le* and *six sail or sea-cat `le* to get to the right combination. In this case we know that "`le" is not a valid English word, and being able to eliminate that helps us home in on the correct analysis. But what about the sentence *Can he be famous?*: This is exactly the same set of sounds as the (nonsense) *canny beef a mouse*. In fact there *is* a difference—but it is one of *stress*. The first syllable of *famous* is stressed, but in *a mouse* it is the word *mouse* that receives the stress. Although you may not be aware of it, this sort of thing is extremely important for your own understanding of spoken English.

Morphology

Consider the English word "love." This gives rise to *loves*, *loved*, *loving*, *lovely*, *unlovingly*, *unloved*, *lover*, and so on. The "extra parts" added to "love" in this list are all *morphemes*, and the part of grammar that looks at the structure of words is called *morphology*.

Each human language has its own way of putting morphemes together, and of inflecting words. English is rather simple in this area: We are used to adding "s" to make a plural (*cat, cats*), or adding "ed" to make a past tense (*love, loved*), and "ing" to make an adjective or participle from a verb (*love, loving*), or "ly" to make an adverb from an adjective (*delicious, deliciously*). Other languages have huge numbers of inflections (changes) on their words. If a dictionary contained all the forms of a word it would be huge, and we are used to looking up the *root* of a word when we seek its meaning. The same process can be used with computer dictionaries—but this must be supported by morphological analysis.

Morphological generation can sometimes be done by rule, and sometimes requires dictionary information. Consider Listing 25.3, which tries to generate the parts of a verb in English. Consider the verb *to open* as in *I open this book*. We can say *Yesterday I opened this book* and *I have opened this book* and *I am opening this book*.

LISTING 25.3 Morphological Generation

```
#include <stdio.h>
#include <string.h>

void MorphVerb1(char* verb)
{
    printf("%s %sed %sed %sing\n",verb,verb,verb,verb);
    return;
}

int main(int argc, char* agv[])
{
    MorphVerb1("open");
    MorphVerb1("love");
    return 0;
}
```

The output for the verb *love* has too many letter *e*s. We can correct that by examining the last character of the verb: if it is an *e* then we just add a *d* and not an *ed*, and when we add the *ing* we have to remove the *e*. So Listing 25.4 is perhaps a bit better.

LISTING 25.4 Morphological Generation—Second Attempt

```
#include <stdio.h>
#include <string.h>

void MorphVerb1(char* verb)
{
    int LengthVerb;
    int EPosition;
    LengthVerb = strlen(verb);
    EPosition = LengthVerb - 1;
    if (verb[EPosition]=='e')
        printf("%s %sd %sd %*.*sing\n",verb,verb,verb,
               EPosition,EPosition,verb);
    else printf("%s %sed %sed %sing\n",verb,verb,verb,verb);
    return;
}

int main(int argc, char* agv[])
{
    MorphVerb1("open");
    MorphVerb1("love");
    MorphVerb1("tap");
    return 0;
}
```

Well that's correct for the verbs *to open* and *to love*, but it gives the wrong spelling for the verb *to tap*. For this we have to add the rule that if the verb ends with a single consonant preceded by a single vowel, the consonant is doubled—*tap, tapped*. If the final consonant is preceded by a pair of vowels, though, there is no such doubling—*clean, cleaned*. Listing 25.5 shows this rule applied.

LISTING 25.5 Morphological Generation—Third Attempt

```
#include <stdio.h>
#include <string.h>

int isVowel (char cTestLetter)
{
    int iReturn = 0;
    if ((cTestLetter=='a') || (cTestLetter=='e')
    ||  (cTestLetter=='i') || (cTestLetter=='o')
    ||  (cTestLetter=='u'))
        iReturn = 1;
```

LISTING 25.5 continued

```
    return iReturn;
}

void MorphVerb1(char* verb)
{
    int LengthVerb;
    int LastPosition;
    LengthVerb = strlen(verb);
    LastPosition = LengthVerb - 1;
    if (verb[LastPosition]=='e')
        printf("%s %sd %sd %*.*sing\n",verb,verb,verb,
               LastPosition,LastPosition,verb);
    else if ((!isVowel(verb[LastPosition]))
         &&  ( isVowel(verb[LastPosition-1]))
         &&  (!isVowel(verb[LastPosition-2])))
         printf("%s %s%ced %s%ced %s%cing\n",verb,
                verb,verb[LastPosition],
                verb,verb[LastPosition],
                verb,verb[LastPosition]);
    else printf("%s %sed %sed %sing\n",verb,verb,verb,verb);
    return;
}

int main(int argc, char* agv[])
{
    MorphVerb1("open");
    MorphVerb1("love");
    MorphVerb1("tap");
    MorphVerb1("clean");
    MorphVerb1("look");
    MorphVerb1("see");
    return 0;
}
```

Now, with the program in Listing 25.5, we have *love*, *tap*, *clean*, and *look* correct—but we have lost correctness on the verb *to open* (our last rule tampered with that, when it should not). Worse than that, we cannot find an algorithm that will correctly compute the forms of the verb *to see* (*see*, *saw*, *seen*, *seeing*), and the verb *to shake* (*shake*, *shook*, *shaken*, *shaking*), and all the other most common English irregular verbs and strong verbs. We will just have to use a dictionary.

Utterance Recognition

So now we can look at an *utterance*; that is, one spoken sentence or command. We have seen that we have to be able to get some sound input (here we have to consider the appropriate hardware and sound processing software). We have to split the input into its phonemes, and make any sandhi adjustments for the language being spoken. We have to look up dictionaries for the language, to remove doubt about possible sound ambiguities, and to present a possible string of words (or, more probably, a list of alternative possible strings of words) to be processed. This is all a complex, interleaved task, much of which is still poorly understood. No wonder it does not happen much!

Once the utterance has been input, it must be processed—but this processing phase may well have to interact with the input stage to come to a decision as to "what was actually said."

The simplest systems are those that take the narrowest range of input; for example, my car phone, which expects only numbers and a very small set of one- or two-word commands.

Utterance Processing

If the system is a game, then the game progresses. If the natural language system is a command processor (for a phone or computer), then the command is translated into the internal format for that operating system or machine, and is executed. If the system is a spoken-language translation system (and these are being created for multi-national phone conversations), then the translation process is commenced from the input as perceived. Whatever the system, there is a possibility that it will proceed well, or that there will be errors.

Handling Errors

The method of handling errors depends upon what the system is for, and at what level the errors occur. This is hardly original—natural language systems are the same as all other computer systems in this regard.

The errors might be in the recognition of the input; for example, too much background noise (*set date to wendsssssschch 14th schlshclember*), unrecognized accent (*libel desk* for *label disk*), or words used that are not in the dictionary (*phone: dial marmalade*). The errors might be in what is requested; for example, the user asks to delete a file that does not exist or cannot be removed (*erase dot dot*), or this user makes a request for which he does not have the rights (*go to the root directory and delete all files*), or the user does not give enough information for the command to be issued (*delete it*), or the game-player requests an impossible action (*hit dragon with mountain*). Each of these will need handling in the usual manner, depending on the system. Perhaps this is to discover whether there is a similar utterance that could be used, and offer it as an alternative (*do you mean 'erase all files in parent directory'?*); or reject the utterance (*Command not issued*), or take some appropriate default action (*Dragon scornfully consumes you. Please play again soon.*)

Text Recognition

It is much more likely that you will want to consider text recognition. That is, most natural language systems take textual input. This has the huge advantage that at least the system can be sure of what the input actually is (even though there are still error processing requirements). There are fewer requirements for determining the real input, except where the text has been corrupted, or was incorrect to start with. We are familiar with spell-checking software, which tries to determine the intended text from what was actually typed. An example was given in Listing 25.1 of a fuzzy string comparison, detecting *string similarity* rather than *string equivalence*.

Similar algorithms exist for complex parsing, where the input does not match the grammar, but is close (in some meaning of that word) to a possible legal input.

Parsing Natural Language Input

In Chapter 19 there is an example of a parser. Can we extend this sort of parser to deal with natural language input, and if so, what modifications do we have to make to it?

There is no one correct parse of natural language—each system has to decide the grammar it is going to use based on what the system is for. For an MT system, the parse will probably have to be deep; for a game, the parse may be shallow. The numerous Web pages on MT may give you a clue as to how complex a question this is. But we will assume in what follows that what we are doing is constructing a parser for game input. Thus the parse need only be shallow, and across a small dictionary. The dictionary in our example need not be external, but can be part of the grammar.

Parsing Techniques

Just as for algorithmic languages, there are different techniques that may be used for parsing natural language. One grammar and one linguistic model may be implemented in several different ways.

We tend to think of analysis as being top-down, but the final parse tree need not have been built in that way—it may be built from the bottom up. The same observations apply to natural language parsing as apply to algorithmic language parsing: Top-town analyzers are easy to write, but slow to run, and bottom-up analyzers are harder to write, but faster to run.

For natural languages we have another possibility, called *island collision* parsers. The individual units of natural language input are easy to identify as units—they are, basically, the words. Each word may be examined in the lexicon, and parsing information attached to it. Then pairs and triples of partially parsed items may be taken, to see whether there are any higher-level syntactic entities that match these groupings. As long as there is success, we carry on accumulating larger and larger parsed sub-groups, till finally we have just one group, which is the complete parse of the whole input. It is as if from the sea of the unknown small islands of definiteness arise, and these islands grow larger, adjacent islands merging into larger islands, as if they were colliding—hence the name *island collision*.

Fuzzy Parsing

We have seen the contrast between the strict comparison *this string is equal to that* and the fuzzy comparison *this string is like that*. Parsers used in compilers make strict comparisons with the syntax. Parsers used for natural language have to make fuzzy, probabilistic comparisons with the language syntax. One way of achieving this is to replace all the strict string compares with fuzzy compares. Thus, we do not ask questions such as *is this word a noun?* But instead *is this word like a noun, within the acceptable limits?*

Each piece of input may be parsed several times. The first time, all the limits are set to require exact equality. If that parse fails, the allowed error is increased and the parse is attempted again. This can be repeated as often as is appropriate for the application in hand, determining first *this is a sentence*, and then *this is very like a sentence* and then *this is somewhat like a sentence*, and so on.

Complexities of Natural Language Output

The output from a computer can include pictures (images), printout (text), sound, or actions (process control). The printed output and the sound output could be in natural language form.

The simplest natural language output is the selection of one or more stock phrases, already part of the program. This is what we are used to—the error-messages from compilers, the status reports of systems, the headings on tables. This, however, is not what is meant by natural language output.

When you generate a sentence, you do not take one of a stock of sentences you already know. Instead, you take words that you already know and put them together in a structure you have selected, modifying the words at the same time, to generate a sentence that you have very probably never before spoken or written—and never will again. Most of our experience of sentences is with singular examples. This is what is needed for natural language output—a system that can generate utterances from a dictionary (lexicon) and grammar rules, making the necessary modifications to the words—and these modifications can be rather complex.

If we take the small dictionary *banana cream mustard like he* and we want to convey the idea that some other person had, at some time in the past, a predilection for plantains together with the fatty part of milk, we might build up as follows:

> somebody *like* (past) something
>
> somebody=*he like* (past) something=(*banana, cream*)
>
> *he like* (past) (*banana, cream*)

At this point we have to start adding extra words, changing (*banana, cream*) to *banana and cream*. The word *and* was not part of what we wanted to say, but is required by English syntax (and other words would be possible here). So now we have

> *he like* (past) *banana and cream*

But there are still two more modifications to make to word forms. The first is due to the necessity of marking the past tense. We do this by changing *like* to *liked*. And the other change is because when expressing a general class, we often use the plural form in English, so *banana* becomes *bananas*. Thus

> *He liked bananas and cream.*

Suppose, by contrast, we want to indicate that this person detested plantains when administered with that tangy yellow relish. Then the sequence might go:

> somebody negative *like* (past) something
>
> somebody=*he* negative *like* (past) something=(*banana, mustard*)
>
> *he* negative *like* (past) (*banana, mustard*)

We can now change (*banana, mustard*) either to *banana and mustard* or *banana with mustard*. Because the sentence is negative, and it is the two together that are disliked and not each separately, we would probably choose *banana with mustard* (but this is not certain—just probable). So

> *he* negative *like* (past) *banana with mustard*
>
> *he* negative *like* (past) *bananas with mustard*

In some languages we would now produce

he not like (past) *banana with mustard*

but English does not work like that. We have to add some part of the verb "to do," giving

he do not like (past) *banana with mustard*

and we also have the oddity that to mark the past tense here we do not change the verb *like* (which we did in the previous example), but the verb *do,* giving us, finally:

he did not like bananas with mustard

As you can see, the modifications are not trivial. Moreover, they are different for each language. If you think in Italian you may wonder why English adds an extra verb when making a negative; if you think in French you may wonder how the English can get away without bracketing the verb that is being negated. If you write programs you will now be realizing just how difficult natural language output can be.

Sound Output

Producing sound output is much simpler than recognizing sound input. It is still not an easy problem as there have to be a series of facilities. First, there must be a means of choosing what, in general structure, to output (utterance generation). Then the system must make the choice of which words to use (word generation), constructing the correct forms of those words (morphology). Then we have to choose the pronunciation and stress in context, which includes applying the sandhi rules, making the output recognizable by choosing the pacing and pitch, and coping with error situations.

Dr. Margaret Masterman suggested that all human speech could be analyzed in terms of breath groups. A *breath group* is the set of syllables that are said without a gap, and hence have to be said in one breath. These sets are rather small, usually having fewer than twenty syllables. Sentences are long, being composed of several breath groups. If the inter-group gaps are missing, comprehension is impaired. If the inter-group gaps are wrongly placed, comprehension might be destroyed. A perfect example of this is the speech starting *If we offend, it is with our good will.* in *A Midsummer Night's Dream*. This is written with the punctuation showing the actor where to place the breath groups, which completely (and comically) mangles the meaning:

Our true intent is. All for your delight
we are not here. That you should here repent you.

This becomes rather dull if rephrased in the correct breath groups:

Our true intent is all for your delight.

We are not here that you should here repent you.

A sound output system must produce the correct breath groups, or it, too, will mangle the meaning.

Text Output

Producing output text is also not entirely simple. We are used to certain layout in documents, and the various word-processing programs help us achieve that with our human-selected texts. In Machine Translation, for example, it is important to preserve not just the meaning of the text, but indications of which parts of the text are headings, which are the body, and which words or phrases were emphasized in the original (by being in **bold** or *italic*). In text layout it is important to use correct rules of hyphenation and line breaking, which are specific to the language and to the text.

Summary

It is clear from the enormous amounts of research world-wide that machine language understanding and processing will be among the next major achievements of computer technology. My friends who are translators, who are powered by fish-and-chips, can only wait the day—not far distant—when they can be replaced by translators powered by electricity. We have yet to reach the take-off point envisaged by I. J. Good in 1962, when he observed that the ultra-intelligent computer would be the last invention that man would ever need to make—for the computers themselves would take over the inventing once they were as clever as ourselves. But we are not far from that point—it should arrive within the lifetimes of most readers of this book.

It is still too early to discuss whether artificially intelligent computers should be given the vote or accorded moral rights—and possibly not meaningful. As yet we can create only the intelligence (approximately) of a cockroach. According to accepted theories, this took nature at least 1500 million years to achieve. Machines have achieved it in 50 years. If machines continue to evolve at the same rate (which is 30 million times faster than organic life), we will have our first machine as intelligent as a human in just 13 years time—the equivalent of 400 million years. I am reminded that there are "pi by ten to the seven" seconds in a year—just over 31 million—so one second in computer evolution is roughly equivalent to one year in biological evolution. It seems that Arthur C. Clarke's *2001* was not so very far off target in its timing.

CHAPTER 26

Encryption

by Mike Wright

In This Chapter

Of all a program's typical components, probably none so commonly has unseen problems as those responsible for security. A failure to protect data is unique in that it is almost invisible, very unlike performance limitations, functional inaccuracies, or even compatibility problems. It is even commonplace for a product to have gaping security holes that never reach the attention of the designer. These holes remain for more expert users to exploit or publicize.

It is therefore necessary for any software engineer to have a certain minimum understanding, sufficient to guarantee at least the level of security he requires.

C is an ideal language for encryption because it is widely understood, very portable, and highly efficient. These three attributes are all extremely desirable for encryption applications.

This chapter examines how to create secure computer systems. Because there is no such thing as medium or mild security (there are only the quick and the dead), it concentrates entirely on the strongest technology available. It takes a tour through each step of planning, design, and final implementation. It clearly defines the terms used with encryption, and highlights each of the requirements for strong security. This chapter suggests good solutions to the common problems and takes careful note of the tricky and difficult areas where so many programmers make their worst mistakes. It focuses more on how to get the job done right today than on studying historic landmarks. This chapter doesn't cover novelties or trivia, but keeps close to those techniques that are valid, useful, and trustworthy.

Assessing Security Risks

Encryption is useful specifically to defend against enemies. If the only threats are incompetent users, unreliable devices, or other situations where there is no perceived malice, do not use encryption. Other, better suited solutions exist for ensuring data integrity, removing patterns, and so on that do not provide for intentional intrusion. These solutions are often far more efficient and sometimes more effective.

Define the Threat

Define, in detail, who you are afraid of. Completely unknown, unforeseen attackers are invincible. Categorize your threats into meaningful groups according to intent, resources, and other relevant criteria. For some applications, it is appropriate to include every user as a potential threat.

Assess the Attacker's Resources

Next, each attacker's resources should be examined and listed. How much time and money do they have? How much computing power do they have? Do they have access to any keys (such as public keys in a two-key system)? Can they communicate with legitimate users, and are they capable of coercing, persuading, tricking, or stealing more access or information from them?

While evaluating a potential attacker's resources, it is better to estimate too high than too low. As technology marches forward, less is required to obtain the same result. Computing power tends to cost less, better algorithms tend to appear and become widespread, processing and communication tend to take less time, and better experts tend to become available. This is well demonstrated by the fact that the well-known DES algorithm is no longer considered sufficient for even very short time periods and is quickly being discarded in favor of solutions many orders of magnitude more powerful. Even so-called "casual" attackers now have access to powerful hardware and dedicated, cleverly designed software enabling them to crack messages recently thought to require "all the computers in the world working for longer than the age of the universe" in no more than a few hours.

Identify the Target

After deciding what each attacker has, you must determine what each attacker wants. Why would they attack your system? What are their motives? How determined are they likely to be? What, specifically, are they seeking? Be careful not to blindly assume that your attackers will be logically seeking a meaningful reward. Sometimes someone will simply want a challenge or will be in a very bad mood. Consider how many computer viruses have been written with no reward to the programmer but the damage caused and a risk of legal punishment. The biggest, tastiest carrot is not always the one the rabbit eats.

Define the Attackers' Weapons and Tactics

Next on the list should be each avenue of attack available to each attacker. Be specific and be thorough. If it is not impossible for the attacker to cause damage using a certain approach or tool, that attack should be on your list. Try to think from your hypothetical attackers' position and envision how you would proceed. It may be tempting to give up and conclude that no attack is possible, but try to be resourceful. Sometimes it is helpful to pretend certain safeguards are removed, or that a few rules are changed. If an attacker is able to easily circumvent some of the rules or presumptions you rely upon, you may find yourself very exposed. Keep in mind, for example, that not all secrets must always be discovered. Passwords may be guessed. An operating system or other program may be making copies of your data you aren't considering, such as in freed memory, backups, and swap files. By being able to reduce the number of unknown secrets, even a little, an attacker may be capable of using brute force to find the remainder. Sometimes castles with very strong walls are conquered by a few good climbers with blow darts, despite the walls' ample immunity to blow darts.

Know the Users

Very often the most exploitable element of a system is the system's users. These users often have a great deal of access, but all too often too little respect or knowledge for the system's optimal security. Unless you know they will behave otherwise, plan for very foolish users. Even if your users are not malicious, they can and often do inadvertently enable others to compromise the system. You are safest to assume that many of your users will not follow any guidelines at all unless they are forced upon them. If you don't forcefully require a new random password periodically, they will use their favorite pet's name throughout all eternity, regardless of your instructions. That's just the way users are. If their behavior could compromise the system, especially if it could affect more than only that one user, you should take steps to force the users to adhere to proper protocol.

Focus on the Weakest Link

This next point cannot be emphasized enough: The weakest link is always the only one requiring improvement. Your system cannot be made more secure by sealing a hole no attacker uses. If all your users post their passwords on their personal Web pages, it is pointless to upgrade your encryption algorithm. Fix first what is most broken. Carefully evaluate your list of attackers and your current system design to detect what is most easily exploitable by each of your attackers. Your attackers will do much the same thing: They will look at your system, find the vulnerabilities they are capable of exploiting, and then select the easiest they can find. They will only give up when the easiest is too difficult. Any other vulnerabilities do not matter—only the easiest one matters.

Do not forget, however, that some attackers may find one thing easy and others another. An attacker who can gain physical access to a critical terminal will likely choose a much different approach than one who must access it remotely, for example.

Why Not Create New Encryption Algorithms?

Good encryption algorithms are hard to come by. They are exceptionally difficult to invent, and even when a new one is created, it is often quickly laden with patents and export restrictions, making it inconvenient or even impossible for others to reuse.

This bleak situation has encouraged programmers to design their own encryption algorithms, sometimes with drastic results. Because so many programmers are accustomed to focusing on observable program characteristics, such as memory footprint and execution time, they often do not give enough thought to the security of the encryption. After only a few moments of contemplating possible vulnerabilities, algorithms are promoted from thin air to "sufficiently secure." Very presumptuous programmers will even compare their naive algorithms with currently popular algorithms in literature, and perhaps even claim to be their equal.

What Is Wrong with New Ciphers?

The problem is that faulty ciphers are not easily detected by non-cryptographers. Garbled text is very easy to produce. Most pseudorandom number sequences appear at first to be quite random. Output from a very weak encryption algorithm looks very much the same as output from a very strong encryption algorithm.

The result of this similarity is that faults become all but invisible. Whereas output from a faulty sorting algorithm will be clearly incorrect, output from a faulty encryption algorithm looks perfectly fine. Gibberish is expected and gibberish is produced.

Consider the following naive algorithm:

```
char encrypt(char p)
{
  return ~p;
}
```

Such an algorithm will often produce output that looks a little garbled. It will most likely foil keyword searches, but any half-wit could crack it. It is no more secure than Caesar's "shift by three" rule. A more sophisticated algorithm may turn to the C Standard Library for help, something such as

```
void encrypt(char* p, unsigned key)
{
  srand(key);
  while(*p)
  {
    *p++ ^= rand();
  }
}
```

This is more secure than the first, but not by much. This basic algorithm, with a few variations, is the most common "home grown" encryption algorithm. The first problem is that the `rand()` function is not guaranteed to produce random values—in fact, it is intended to produce pseudorandom values. Although truly random values are quite secure, pseudorandom values contain detectable patterns. Additionally, the seed is only a single `unsigned int` value. It takes only a minute or two to try every possible key value, even on a slow computer. The messages could be decoded and the key discovered very easily without even invoking elementary cryptanalysis. Still another reason to frown on this code is that differences in `rand()` implementations make it very nonportable. Any other library implementations are likely to be incompatible and fail to properly decrypt another's ciphertext.

Keep the Outer Wall in Plain View

Sometimes a programmer will keep the encryption algorithm itself a secret, in an attempt to further secure it from would-be attackers. This is no better than refusing to allow torches along the outside wall of your castle in the hopes that approaching attackers will stumble in the dark. There is only one situation when this helps anything at all: when the code is never accessible to the attackers, not even in binary form, and both the algorithm employed and the attackers are exceptionally weak. Any moderately able attacker can discover the algorithm from a binary executable, almost without regard to how well it is hidden. Analysis of the ciphertext alone can be sufficient to discover, or even circumvent, the original algorithm, especially for weaker ciphers. You should always keep the approach to your castle well lit to better detect those sneaky intruders. Remember that it's only to their advantage to feel around in the dark for holes in the wall. Archers can't shoot an enemy they can't see and the builders can't repair a defect they never discover.

The disadvantage to keeping the source code a secret is huge. It prevents analysis and criticism by others. Even the most respected, most expert cryptographers worldwide publish their ideas for review before putting trust in them. Outsiders often quickly find things the designers overlooked. Fresh perspectives are worth a lot, and attackers always have fresh perspectives because they are not the designers of the system. By keeping the algorithm secret, you give any potential attackers that much advantage. No worthwhile cipher relies upon the algorithm itself being secret to maintain its security. The keys should be secret, not the algorithm. If your cipher does rely on the algorithm's secrecy, you should quickly rethink your design—it is very vulnerable.

Consider how much time and other resources are devoted to developing a good cipher. If a secret algorithm can be exposed to more than one individual, all the secrecy of the algorithm faces very serious risks of being lost to attackers. A single defector or a single leak can destroy the secret. If any appreciable portion of the cipher's security relied upon this secrecy, an entirely new algorithm must be immediately formulated, even if the keys are safe. This becomes a very bad situation.

Complexity Is Not Security

You may try to make your algorithm more secure by adding several shifts and prime numbers, adding substitution tables, and perhaps adding so many unrelated jumbled operations that it becomes so complex it is certain to be secure. Unfortunately, all this could only help by the most remote chance. If your plan is to confuse your attackers by confusing yourself, adding many operations you cannot otherwise justify simply to complicate the process, you will accomplish very little. You may confuse yourself enough that you will hesitate to cryptanalyze your own algorithm, and you may make your algorithm so horrendously inefficient that no reasonable person would want to try full key searches, but your attacker will probably find the very same exploitable patterns in the very same places. The use of unjustified or weakly justified operations may be compared to casting strange spells on your castle's bricks. If you have no idea what the spells may do, you have no guarantee that they will help more than they will hurt. Many jumbled operations often reduce to only a very few simple, fast operations, making it unnecessary for your attacker to discover the exact sequence originally used. It then becomes very likely that your attackers will be capable of cracking your messages in less time than it takes you to encrypt or decrypt them yourself! It is a sad sight to see a castle's wall crumble with less effort than it takes an ally to open the gate.

Do not smugly think that only people with superior intellects can crack your homemade encryption. You are a C programmer, so naturally you are far more intelligent than the average human. Any encryption algorithm you invent is all but guaranteed to protect against everyone but perhaps government spy agencies, right? Wrong! You may be surprised to see the tools available to casual attackers. General-purpose solvers are available for free download, some capable of breaking most naive encryption algorithms without any user input whatsoever. Armed with a few words of guessed plaintext and one of the very user-friendly solver programs, even your kid sister could crack most of these poorly protected secret messages within minutes.

If you are really intent on designing your own encryption algorithms, you will need more than this chapter provides. Cryptographers need to do a lot of reading, practice cracking ciphers on their own, and develop a lot of patience before being capable of creating respectable algorithms. Multiply the time and effort it took you to learn the C language inside and out by about ten and you will have my estimate of what it takes to become a beginning cryptographer. Cryptography is no small undertaking—the math is very demanding, and a great deal of formal logic is employed.

Selecting an Encryption Algorithm

The vast majority of programmers are best advised to implement existing encryption algorithms.

This is not meant to be an exhaustive, or even a very representative, list of algorithms. I will describe a few solutions that are fairly good, safe bets. Most of the algorithms I list here are or can be made into so-called strong encryption algorithms that may be subject to export restrictions. Check applicable laws before exporting them across borders.

There are a few different uses for encryption technology. Although all involve hiding information from attackers, there is a variety of ways to do it, each with its own applications. You must understand well what security needs your system has and select an appropriate solution for the task.

Single-Key Encryption

Single-key encryption currently offers greater security and speed than two-key encryption can, given the same key sizes. It is most useful when there is only one friendly party involved, making key distribution unnecessary. Because the same key is used to encrypt and decrypt, problems can quickly arise when other parties must be included. This is the most conventional form of encryption and provides confidentiality from outsiders. It also provides some authentication, in that it is usually difficult for a party not holding the secret key to forge encrypted messages.

Single-key encryption algorithms are further subdivided into block ciphers and stream ciphers. As their names imply, block ciphers are intended to be applied to fixed-length data blocks, whereas stream ciphers are designed to be used with continuous data streams. Generally, stream ciphers are a little more flexible and a little less secure than block ciphers. The basic idea behind stream ciphers is to generate a very good pseudorandom number sequence, using the key as the seed, and combine it with the plaintext.

RC4 is a widely used stream cipher developed by RSA Data Security, Inc. It was originally protected as a trade secret of RSA, but it has since become a well-known algorithm. RC4 is not patented, but the name, "RC4," itself is a trademark of RSA Data Security, Inc. This cipher's popularity can be largely attributed to its simplicity (see Listing 26.1). It uses only 2064 bits of state with no predefined constants, and is considered quite secure. This is an excellent choice if you want high performance and fair to good security, but don't want to spend a lot of time with complications like block sizes, huge tables, and sophisticated operations.

LISTING 26.1 The RC4 Encryption/Decryption Functions

```
typedef struct
{
  byte_t table[256];
  byte_t index[2];
} RC4_key_t;

/* called before encryption/decryption */
void RC4_setup_key(
  byte_t const key_text[],
  size_t len,
  RC4_key_t* key)
{
  int i;
  byte_t temp, e;

  /* Initialize key table */
  for(i = 0; i < 256; i++)
  {
    key->table[i] = i;
  }

  /* Initialize indices */
  key->index[0] = 0;
  key->index[1] = 0;

  /* Prepare key table */
  for(i = 0, e = 0; i < 256; i++)
  {
    /* Find e index */
    e += key_text[i%len] + key->table[i];

    /* Exchange values */
    temp = key->table[i];
    key->table[i] = key->table[e];
    key->table[e] = temp;
  }
}

/* You can encrypt and decrypt with this function */
void RC4_encrypt(
  byte_t const plaintext[],
  byte_t ciphertext[],
```

LISTING 26.1 continued

```
  size_t len,
  RC4_key_t* key)
{
  int i;
  byte_t temp;

  for(i = 0; i < len; i++)
  {
    /* Update indices */
    key->index[1] += key->table[++key->index[0]];

    /* Swap table entries */
    temp = key->table[key->index[0]];
    key->table[key->index[0]] = key->table[key->index[1]];
    key->table[key->index[1]] = temp;

    /* Create ciphertext (Output Feedback Mode) */
    ciphertext[i] =
      plaintext[i] ^
      key->table[
        key->table[key->index[0]] +
        key->table[key->index[1]]
      ];
  }
}
```

There are a great variety of block ciphers to choose from. Here are some of the best and most popular:

- **DES (Data Encryption Standard):** The official NIST encryption algorithm for unclassified data from 1976 to 1997, adopted as FIPS 46. This algorithm is largely outdated. The 64-bit (56-bit effective length) keys DES uses are too small for today's purposes. However, DES is still used to implement Triple-DES, a far more secure algorithm. There is likely no other encryption algorithm so well studied as DES.
- **Triple-DES:** As its name implies, Triple-DES uses three different DES passes with three different keys over the same data. This algorithm is much stronger than ordinary DES, but obviously much slower. Some people prefer to use Triple-DES as a safer alternative, given the depth of analysis devoted to DES, while others avoid it for the same reason, fearing secret shortcuts and dedicated hardware.

- **Blowfish:** A cipher developed by Bruce Schneier of Counterpane Systems. Blowfish is unpatented, uncopyrighted, and explicitly declared free for all uses. This is a popular encryption algorithm, offering high security and fast execution times.
- **CAST** (after the designers, Carlisle Adams and Stafford Taveres)**:** A secure encryption algorithm popularized by later versions of PGP (Pretty Good Privacy). Although patented by Northern Telecom Ltd., it may be used freely without special permission, and without payment.
- **Rijndael** (after the designers, Vincent Rijmen and Joan Daemen)**:** This cipher offers fast key setup, making it more attractive for applications needing to encrypt or decrypt using many different keys. Its speed and strength are also good. Rijndael is not patented.
- **Serpent:** This cipher is a slow, but very secure algorithm. It does not require much memory and can resist timing attacks well. It is designed to allow for an unusual "bitslicing" implementation, potentially enabling very efficient parallel computation of its S-boxes.
- **Twofish:** A cipher developed by Counterpane Systems, the developer of Blowfish. Like Blowfish, Twofish is unpatented, uncopyrighted, and explicitly declared free for all uses. Twofish is very secure and very fast. It is quite flexible and can be modified to make space/time tradeoffs and use many different key sizes.

For detailed descriptions and example source code of these algorithms, you are encouraged to refer to *Applied Cryptography—Protocols, Algorithms, and Source Code in C* by Bruce Schneier. It is a great cryptographic reference book for C programmers implementing encryption. Here are a couple good Web sites to start a hunt for source code:

`http://www.counterpane.com/`

`http://www.pgpi.org/`

Two-Key Encryption

Two-key encryption involves the use of a key pair: one public key and one private key. It enables more distrust than single-key encryption, making key distribution to multiple parties easier. The public key can be freely distributed, even to the unfriendly parties, whereas the private key needn't be distributed at all, not even to any of the friendly parties. This capability is immensely useful for many applications, especially network applications involving communication over insecure channels. Techniques related to two-key encryption are also used for creating digital signatures.

Because secure two-key encryption is both trickier to develop and a more recent concept, there are not many truly unique algorithms. There are currently only three commonly used basic ideas: those involving discrete logarithms, factoring, and elliptic curves. The following and most others rely on one of these three techniques.

- **Diffie-Hellman** (after its designers)**:** A key exchange system relying upon discrete logarithms in the finite fields generated by large prime numbers. This was the first system proposed and is the most commonly employed technique. It is the basis for several other cryptosystems, including the ANSI standard, X9.42.
- **RSA** (after its designers, Rivest, Shamir, and Adleman)**:** A complete two-key cryptosystem, performing both key distribution and digital signature operations. The RSA system relies upon the difficulty of finding the prime factors of large integers.
- **DSS (Digital Signature Standard):** A variation of the digital signature algorithm discovered by El Gamal. It provides only digital signature operations and is commonly used with the Diffie-Hellman system.
- **ECC (Elliptic Curve Cryptosystem):** A promising new idea first proposed independently by Koblitz and Miller. Their technique is essentially the same as the Diffie-Hellman system, but it uses elliptic curves over a finite field instead of ordinary discrete logarithms. This method may enable greater security for smaller key sizes, but has not been studied as much as the more conventional systems.

One-Way Hashes

Hashing is also commonly associated with encryption and especially digital signatures. Although it is a little dissimilar to conventional encryption, it still protects plaintext from discovery. Unlike conventional encryption, there is no distinct key involved, and it is very difficult to obtain the plaintext from only the ciphertext (called the hash or message digest).

Hashing is commonly used in other applications having nothing to do with securing data, such as the popular hash table structure. In common with other hashes, security hashes rely on the results being evenly distributed. Security hashes are different in that they are focused upon making the hash operation unidirectional. It is intentionally very difficult to derive the original input value from the hash, or to find a second input value that will produce the same hash value.

The U.S. National Security Agency developed SHA-1 (Secure Hash Algorithm-1) as part of the Secure Hash Standard. Although SHA-1 is a rather complex algorithm, it is probably the best choice for almost all applications requiring a secure hash function.

SHA-1 produces a 160-bit digest and operates on fixed-sized blocks of 512 bits (see Listing 26.2). Because it requires the input message be partitioned into fixed blocks, some amount of padding often needs to be done. SHA-1 defines a special and rather unusual padding function that entails appending a "1" bit, many zeros, and finally a 64-bit message length integer.

LISTING 26.2 The SHA-1 Padding Function

```
void SHA_1_pad_msg(
  uint32_t* padded,
  uint64_t num_blocks,
  byte_t const* unpadded,
  uint64_t len
)
{
  uint64_t zeros;
  uint64_t extra_len;
  uint64_t p_len;
  uint64_t i;
  byte_t* b_ptr;

  b_ptr = (byte_t*)padded;

  p_len = num_blocks * 64;

  extra_len = p_len - len;

  memset(b_ptr + len, 0, extra_len);

  memcpy(padded, unpadded, len);

  zeros = extra_len - 8;
  if(zeros > 0)
  {
    --zeros;
    for(i = 0; i < zeros; i++)
    {
      b_ptr[p_len - i - 9] = 0;
    }
    b_ptr[p_len - i - 9] = 0x80;
  }

  /* big endian to native byte order */
```

LISTING 26.2 continued

```
  native_byte_order(padded, len/4+1);

  /* End with message length */
  padded[num_blocks * 16 - 2] = len >> 29;
  padded[num_blocks * 16 - 1] = len << 3;
}
```

Thankfully, SHA-1 has only a handful of "magical" constants and only three permutation functions. The overall operation is pretty simple: Each block is fed into the main hashing function for processing, and the message's digest is the sum of each component block's digest (see Listing 26.3).

LISTING 26.3 An Implementation of the SHA-1 Algorithm

```
/*
 * Declare type SHA_1_F as a pointer to a function
 * operating on three 32-bit words.
 */
typedef uint32_t (*SHA_1_F)(
  uint32_t a,
  uint32_t b,
  uint32_t c);

uint32_t SHA_1_F0(
  uint32_t a,
  uint32_t b,
  uint32_t c)
{
  return c ^ a & (b ^ c);
}

/* Same function for F1() and F3() */
uint32_t SHA_1_F1F3(
  uint32_t a,
  uint32_t b,
  uint32_t c)
{
  return a ^ b ^ c;
}

uint32_t SHA_1_F2(
  uint32_t a,
```

LISTING 26.3 continued

```
  uint32_t b,
  uint32_t c)
{
  return a & b | c & (a | b);
}

uint32_t SHA_1_rot(uint32_t x, int n)
{
  return x << n | x >> 32-n;
}

void SHA_1_main(
  uint32_t const msg[16],
  uint32_t digest[5])
{
  uint32_t const K[4] =
  {
    0x5A827999,
    0x6ED9EBA1,
    0x8F1BBCDC,
    0xCA62C1D6
  };

  /* The 4 SHA-1 F functions */
  SHA_1_F const F[4] = {
    &SHA_1_F0,
    &SHA_1_F1F3,
    &SHA_1_F2,
    &SHA_1_F1F3
  };

  uint32_t table[80];
  uint32_t offset[5];
  uint32_t temp;
  int i, j;

  /* Initialize offset */
  for(i = 0; i < 5; i++)
  {
    offset[i] = digest[i];
  }
```

LISTING 26.3 continued

```
  /* Initialize table */
  for(i = 0; i < 16; i++)
  {
    table[i] = msg[i];
  }
  for(; i < 80; i++)
  {
    table[i] =
      SHA_1_rot(
        table[i - 3] ^
          table[i - 8] ^
          table[i - 14] ^
          table[i - 16],
        1
      );
  }

  /* Calculate digest offset */
  for(j = 0, i = 0; j < 4; j++)
  {
    for(; i < j * 20 + 20; i++)
    {
      temp =
        SHA_1_rot(offset[0], 5) +
        (*F[j])(offset[1], offset[2], offset[3]) +
        offset[4] +
        table[i] +
        K[j];
      offset[4] = offset[3];
      offset[3] = offset[2];
      offset[2] = SHA_1_rot(offset[1], 30);
      offset[1] = offset[0];
      offset[0] = temp;
    }
  }

  /* Update digest */
  for(i = 0; i < 5; i++)
  {
    digest[i] += offset[i];
  }
}
```

LISTING 26.3 continued

```
/* Returns 0 on error */
int SHA_1_full(
  byte_t const* msg,
  uint64_t len,
  uint32_t digest[5]
)
{
  uint32_t const origin[5] =
  {
    0x67452301,
    0xEFCDAB89,
    0x98BADCFE,
    0x10325476,
    0xC3D2E1F0
  };
  uint32_t* padded;
  uint64_t num_blocks;
  uint64_t i;

  /* Pad msg out to 512-bit blocks */
  num_blocks = (len + 8) * 8 / 512 + 1;
  padded = (uint32_t*)malloc(
    num_blocks * 64
  );
  if(padded == NULL)
  {
    errno = ENOMEM;
    return 0;
  }
  SHA_1_pad_msg(padded, num_blocks, msg, len);

  /* Initialize digest */
  for(i = 0; i < 5; i++)
  {
    digest[i] = origin[i];
  }

  /* Hash digest with each block */
  for(i = 0; i < num_blocks; i++)
  {
    SHA_1_main(padded + i * 16, digest);
```

LISTING 26.3 continued

```
  }

  free(padded);

  return 1;
}
```

Implementing Encryption

Even after an algorithm has been chosen, great care must be used in implementing it to ensure the protection provided by the encryption is not nullified by a poor implementation. There are many choices to be made and many opportunities to make mistakes.

Modes of Operation

Ciphers can be used in any of several different modes. Each mode specifies operations to be performed on the plaintext or ciphertext before and after the primary encryption process itself. These operations serve to add further protection to the data, alongside the encryption algorithm. The strongest of encryption algorithms is almost worthless if used in a very weak mode.

Four standard modes of operation are described in FIPS 81 (mirrored in ANSI X3.106-1983). Several non-standard modes have been proposed, but I strongly suggest avoiding any of them unless you have overwhelming reason not to.

The following labels will be used to describe each mode. I detest the single-letter variable names used by most reference texts, so I will use full-length names. Hopefully they will be clearer.

- `BLOCKSIZE`—The number of bits in each block. The block size is usually between 64- and 256-bits long.
- `ELEMENTSIZE`—For feedback modes, the length, in bits, of each text array element. This is usually constant, not variable for each message. `ELEMENTSIZE` can be any value from 1 to `BLOCKSIZE`.
- `block_t`—The type used for each block. Every block cipher algorithm defines a block and possible block sizes. They are simply fixed-size, contiguous sequences of bits. A block is the required input to and output from a block cipher function.

- `element_t`—The type of text array elements in the feedback modes. Each `element_t` variable is `ELEMENTSIZE` bits long. For the common case when `ELEMENTSIZE == BLOCKSIZE`, `element_t` is equivalent to `block_t`.
- `plaintext[]`—The array of blocks to be encrypted. Each element of the array is a unique block, of type `block_t` (or `element_t` in feedback modes). This is the information being hidden from your attackers.
- `ciphertext[]`—The array of encrypted blocks, also of type `block_t` (or `element_t` in feedback modes). This is the input to decryption and the output of encryption. It is the information being hidden from your attackers, after being protected by encryption.
- `key`—The secret value used to encrypt or decrypt the text. The algorithm and/or the block size determine its size.
- `origin`—The initialization vector. This is a salt value, required for most modes before encryption or decryption can begin. The origin is always of type `block_t` and must be unique.
- `encrypt()`—The basic encryption function. It takes one block of plaintext and the key as input, returning one block of ciphertext as output. This function is implemented as defined by the chosen encryption algorithm (whether DES, Twofish, and so on).
- `decrypt()`—The basic decryption function, performing the reverse operation of the `encrypt()` function. It takes one block of ciphertext and the key as input, returning one block of plaintext as output.

Electronic Code Book (ECB) Mode

ECB mode is the least secure, most simple, and most naive encryption implementation (see Listing 26.4). Because fewer operations are performed, it is also the fastest and smallest, but the resources consumed by mode operations are very miniscule compared to those of the encryption code. The ECB mode should not be used when security is desired. This mode should only be used to make tests, verify correct implementation of the encryption algorithms, and other similar uses, never in the product software itself.

LISTING 26.4 The Electronic Code Book (ECB) Mode

```
void encryption(
  block_t const plaintext[],
  block_t ciphertext[],
  size_t len,
  key_t key)
```

LISTING 26.4 continued

```
{
  int i;
  for(i = 0; i < len; i++)
  {
    ciphertext[i] = encrypt(plaintext[i], key);
  }
}

void decryption(
  block_t const ciphertext[],
  block_t plaintext[],
  size_t len,
  key_t key)
{
  int i;
  for(i = 0; i < len; i++)
  {
    plaintext[i] = decrypt(ciphertext[i], key);
  }
}
```

Cipher Block Chaining (CBC) Mode

CBC is a secure mode but still quite simple (see Listing 26.5). It XORs each plaintext block with the last ciphertext block, helping to ensure that each identical plaintext block does not result in an identical ciphertext block.

LISTING 26.5 The Cipher Block Chaining (CBC) Mode

```
void encryption(
  block_t const plaintext[],
  block_t ciphertext[],
  size_t len,
  key_t key,
  block_t origin)
{
  int i;
  ciphertext[0] = encrypt(plaintext[0] ^ origin, key);
  for(i = 1; i < len; i++)
  {
    ciphertext[i] =
      encrypt(plaintext[i] ^ ciphertext[i - 1], key);
```

LISTING 26.5 continued

```
  }
}

void decryption(
  block_t const ciphertext[],
  block_t plaintext[],
  size_t len,
  key_t key,
  block_t origin)
{
  int i;
  plaintext[0] = decrypt(ciphertext[0], key) ^ origin;
  for(i = 1; i < len; i++)
  {
    plaintext[i] =
      decrypt(ciphertext[i], key) ^ ciphertext[i - 1];
  }
}
```

Output Feedback (OFB) Mode

The two feedback modes are more complex (see Listing 26.6). Note that the `decrypt()` function is not used by the feedback modes. The `encrypt()` function is used for both encryption and decryption. In some situations, this can save valuable code space, and come debugging time, it always helps to have one very complex function instead of two very complex functions.

LISTING 26.6 Output Feedback (OFB) Mode

```
void encryption(
  block_t const plaintext[],
  block_t ciphertext[],
  size_t len,
  key_t key,
  block_t origin)
{
  int i;
  block_t temp;

  temp = origin;

  for(i = 0; i < len; i++)
```

LISTING 26.6 continued

```
  {
    temp = encrypt(temp, key);
    ciphertext[i] = plaintext[i] ^ temp;
  }
}

void decryption(
  block_t const ciphertext[],
  block_t plaintext[],
  size_t len,
  key_t key,
  block_t origin)
{
  int i;
  block_t temp;

  temp = origin;

  for(i = 0; i < len; i++)
  {
    temp = encrypt(temp, key);
    plaintext[i] = ciphertext[i] ^ temp;
  }
}
```

Note

The output feedback mode shown in Listing 26.6 assumes `BLOCKSIZE` is equal to `ELEMENTSIZE`. The standard allows the OFB mode to be used with other element sizes, but this is always both less secure and more complicated.

Cipher Feedback (CFB) Mode

CFB mode is quite similar to the Output Feedback (OFB) mode, but uses the ciphertext as the feedback to mask the message instead of repeatedly encrypting the origin independently from the text (see Listing 26.7).

Note

Remember, the blocks are defined by the encryption algorithm as the units input to and output from the `encrypt()` and `decrypt()` functions, whereas the elements are the units composing the text. With the previously described modes, the text was simply composed of blocks, leaving no distinction between elements and blocks, but there can be an important distinction with the more complex feedback modes.

LISTING 26.7 Cipher Feedback (CFB) Mode

```
void encryption(
  element_t const plaintext[],
  element_t ciphertext[],
  size_t len,
  key_t key,
  block_t origin)
{
  int i;
  block_t temp;

  temp = origin;
  ciphertext[0] =
    plaintext[0] ^
    encrypt(temp, key) >> BLOCKSIZE - ELEMENTSIZE &
      (1 << ELEMENTSIZE) - 1;

  for(i = 1; i < len; i++)
  {
    temp = temp << ELEMENTSIZE | ciphertext[i - 1];
    ciphertext[i] =
      plaintext[i] ^
      encrypt(temp, key) >> BLOCKSIZE - ELEMENTSIZE &
        (1 << ELEMENTSIZE) - 1;
  }
}

void decryption(
  element_t const ciphertext[],
  element_t plaintext[],
  size_t len,
```

LISTING 26.7 continued

```
  key_t key,
  block_t origin)
{
  int i;
  block_t temp;

  temp = origin;
  plaintext[0] =
    ciphertext[0] ^
    encrypt(temp, key) >> BLOCKSIZE - ELEMENTSIZE &
      (1 << ELEMENTSIZE) - 1;

  for(i = 1; i < len; i++)
  {
    temp = temp << ELEMENTSIZE | ciphertext[i - 1];
    plaintext[i] =
      ciphertext[i] ^
      encrypt(temp, key) >> BLOCKSIZE - ELEMENTSIZE &
        (1 << ELEMENTSIZE) - 1;
  }
}
```

When `ELEMENTSIZE` is equal to `BLOCKSIZE`, this all gets considerably simpler, eliminating the need for a distinct `element_t` type and making both the shifting and one temporary variable unnecessary as shown in Listing 26.8. But note that unlike OFB, using an `ELEMENTSIZE` other than `BLOCKSIZE` is not known to be less secure, only more complicated.

LISTING 26.8 Cipher Feedback (CFB) Mode when `ELEMENTSIZE == BLOCKSIZE`

```
void encryption(
  block_t const plaintext[],
  block_t ciphertext[],
  size_t len,
  key_t key,
  block_t origin)
{
  int i;

  ciphertext[0] = plaintext[0] ^ encrypt(origin, key);

  for(i = 1; i < len; i++)
  {
```

LISTING 26.8 continued

```
    ciphertext[i] =
      plaintext[i] ^ encrypt(ciphertext[i - 1], key);
  }
}

void decryption(
  block_t const ciphertext[],
  block_t plaintext[],
  size_t len,
  key_t key,
  block_t origin)
{
  int i;

  plaintext[0] = ciphertext[0] ^ encrypt(origin, key);

  for(i = 1; i < len; i++)
  {
    plaintext[i] =
      ciphertext[i] ^ encrypt(ciphertext[i - 1], key);
  }
}
```

I generally suggest using the Cipher Feedback (CFB) Mode and using it with `ELEMENTSIZE` equal to `BLOCKSIZE`. This is a moderately simple solution, allowing fast software encryption/decryption, and it requires that only the `encrypt()` function be implemented for both encryption and decryption. Removing the `decrypt()` function makes one less very complex function to debug.

Changing the value of `ELEMENTSIZE` to something other than `BLOCKSIZE` adds more complexity and makes software implementations much slower. Hardware implementations are also made slower, but not so drastically, because the bit manipulation can usually be done more efficiently in hardware.

All of the four standard modes (ECB, CBC, OFB, CFB) have undergone extensive analysis for many years. The ECB mode has been found to be insecure for too many reasons to list. The other three modes are much better.

In the Output Feedback (OFB) Mode, the `encrypt()` operation can be precomputed or computed in parallel with the reception of the plaintext or ciphertext. Because this operation is usually quite slow, this can add very significant speed advantages. Please note that the key and origin values must be known before any work can begin.

Byte Order

Practically all encryption-related functions operate on multibyte blocks used as integers. To ensure interoperability between different implementations, care should be taken when converting data between representation as integer blocks and representation as sequences of bits.

> **Tip**
>
> Whenever bit manipulation is called for, only unsigned integer types should be used. The sign bit only gets in the way.

The de facto standard byte order is big-endian ("ABCD"), meaning that the most significant byte(s) come before all byte(s) of lesser significance. In big-endian byte order, the 32-bit value 0x0A0B0C0D would be represented as a sequence of the four bytes 0x0A, 0x0B, 0x0C, 0x0D, in that order. Some processors (among them the very popular Intel 80x86 processors) use other byte orders and may require conversions.

If any interoperability is desired, all blocks should be translated to and from big-endian. Often even implementation verification requires proper byte ordering to match the reference samples.

Here is a simple function illustrating the conversion of a message of 32-bit blocks from big-endian to the native byte order:

```
void native_byte_order(
  uint32_t* msg,
  size_t num_blocks)
{
  byte_t* b_ptr;

  while(num_blocks--)
  {
    b_ptr = (byte_t*)(msg + num_blocks);
    msg[num_blocks] =
      (uint32_t)b_ptr[0] << 24 |
      (uint32_t)b_ptr[1] << 16 |
      (uint32_t)b_ptr[2] << 8 |
      (uint32_t)b_ptr[3];
  }
}
```

The reverse is done to translate the output back into big-endian:

```
void big_endian(
  uint32_t* msg,
  size_t num_blocks)
{
  byte_t* b_ptr;
  uint32_t temp;

  while(num_blocks--)
  {
    b_ptr = (byte_t*)(msg + num_blocks);
    temp = msg[num_blocks];
    b_ptr[0] = temp >> 24;
    b_ptr[1] = temp >> 16;
    b_ptr[2] = temp >> 8;
    b_ptr[3] = temp;
  }
}
```

Ensuring Public Key Authenticity

In two-key cryptosystems, having an attacker know the public keys used is not usually a big problem. However, under some circumstances, it is possible for an attacker to intercept the public keys as they are being exchanged and substitute other keys in their stead. If the attacker can convince another party that they have received a public key from a different, trusted party, the attacker could masquerade as that party, receiving all messages intended for it and be able to forge any message from the party. Therefore, participants in such a system require a means to prove to each other the identity of their respective public keys.

One solution is to use certifying authorities. Every participant gets the public key of all trusted certifying authorities by some trusted, secure means (usually outside the protocol), so they can be assured that the public keys of the certifying authorities are actually the correct keys. Thereafter, any party that needs to have a key associated with their identity can turn to one of the certifying authorities and receive a certificate, after proving somehow to the certifying authority that the identity and key are held by the same party. The certificate is simply a digital signature of the identifying information combined with the public key.

Too Much Speed

Secure encryption is a relatively slow operation. This will very probably remain a universal truth forever. Although it is very easy to make an insecure encryption algorithm perform slowly, it is quite another task to make a very secure encryption algorithm perform quickly. Secure encryption algorithms often rely on very complex operations or on repeating operations many times to make the results very complex.

Encryption algorithms, in common with any other algorithms, can be optimized. Using precomputed tables, parallel execution, reused intermediate states, and other common techniques can vastly improve the runtime performance. One often finds, however, that many common optimizations cannot properly be applied to a secure encryption algorithm. For example, a very secure encryption scheme cannot generally benefit as much from a parallel architecture because security is often gained by using many operations that absolutely must be performed sequentially, containing many important dependencies from step to step.

Be careful sacrificing security for speed. There is no question that weaker encryption can be much faster than stronger encryption, but the level of security sacrificed by doing so is very often underestimated. If you are confident that a certain algorithm is secure enough, feel free to optimize it and make it faster so long as you do not alter the output or the operation in a way that could jeopardize its defenses. Although some optimizations produce obvious hazards, others may not be quite so clear. Rearranging the order of operations, for example, can have disastrous consequences if it affects the output in any way. Try to verify that your output is exactly what it should be, that your method for generating keys is correct, and so on. I would strongly discourage you from inventing new algorithms, inventing new modes of operation, or modifying existing ones unless you are more a cryptographer than a programmer.

Some encryption algorithms have been specially coded to reduce their susceptibility to timing and power attacks. With many operations, an attacker can more accurately guess the value of a key by knowing how long the operation took to complete, or how many resources were used during the operation. For example, exponentiation with a large exponent often takes substantially longer than the same operation with a smaller exponent. Any operation that takes different lengths of time for different operand values is susceptible to timing attacks. Take this into consideration while optimizing your code if these attacks pose a threat.

Remember that the inherent slowness of an encryption algorithm contributes to its protection from brute force attacks, wherein the attacker simply tries all possibilities. If you have stumbled upon a lightning fast algorithm, ask yourself how long it would take to successfully crack it using brute force. Sometimes just a few iterations (in the range of a few billion) are enough to enable an attacker to compromise the entire message or key. Just because a cipher uses a 256-bit key does not necessarily mean that an attacker needs to try every possible permutation of 256 bits. Chances are that a fast algorithm is fast because it does very little, affording little if any protection. The fastest encryption of all is also the least secure of all, simply: `ciphertext[i] = plaintext[i]`.

Too Much Strength

It may seem strange, but you can use encryption with too much strength. When is it too strong? When you have no understanding of what you are doing or how it should be done. Blindly copying code is a sure way to introduce vulnerabilities. You should look at examples of strong encryption algorithms, try to understand them, and then implement them after understanding them well. Some may be disappointed to learn that those incapable of understanding strong encryption software are probably incapable of properly implementing it.

Now, don't misunderstand. Programmers can certainly happen upon algorithms that are brilliantly designed and far superior to anything they could ever invent themselves. You could fail to understand some of the properties it has, yet reap its benefits. However, the program is still limited by its designer's own understanding. If something needs to be adapted to your particular situation, you may be incapable of doing it, or even unaware that such an adaptation is necessary without a firm understanding of what is going on and why. If you don't have an appreciation for why a certain algorithm is considered so strong, you may implement this superior algorithm so poorly that the properties providing its great strength vanish.

If you are torn between a weaker algorithm you understand and a stronger algorithm you do not understand, study the stronger algorithm longer until you start to understand it. Any other choice will result in a potentially insecure implementation. Imagine you cannot swim, and you are jumping from atop a very high cliff. Below, you have two choices: a 200-foot-deep sea on one side and an ankle-deep pond on the other. If the shallowness does not kill you, your inability to handle the depth will. The solution is not only to dive into the deep end, but to learn to swim as well.

If the time and effort cannot be spared to become acquainted with the strong encryption yourself, at least have your implementation reviewed by someone who is familiar with the technology. That way you can discover any glaring weaknesses that may have crept in.

Just Add Salt

Any secret data operated on by a security function, whether to encrypt it, hash it, sign it, or any other purpose, should be coated with salt first. Salt is a unique value added to the secret to ensure that the resulting sequence is very unlikely to ever be repeated. The salt's primary requirement is uniqueness. You can use random values, timestamps, indices, or any other value easily made unique. A constant value does not make good salt because it is not unique after its first use. All the standard encryption modes, with the exception of the simple ECB mode, require at least one block of salt for their origin values.

Why use salt? If no salt is added, the data is susceptible to a variety of attacks exploiting the redundancy of the encrypted data. If an attacker can see several blocks repeating themselves, or if he can reliably associate ciphertext output with plaintext input, your defenses have been foiled. There is no need to discover the key if the attacker already knows that "We have been discovered!" always encrypts to 0xABCDEF123456. He will know that every time that block occurs, the same message is being used, and he can begin to compose a dictionary of all the messages you use. In fact, almost all methods of cryptanalysis are made harder for your attacker when there is salt added.

You must ensure that the same data is never encrypted with the same key, or that the same data encrypted with the same key always becomes a different ciphertext. It is not necessary that the salt be secret. Even if the attacker knows the salt value you used, the salt has still done its work so long as it is unique. Making the salt a secret along with the key is even more secure, but usually not worth the trouble. Remember that the salt must be unique for every message, so storing it with your key is no more efficient than using a one-time pad (a random key that is used once, then replaced by a new random one). Most implementations record the salt in the clear (not encrypted) beside the encrypted message it was added to. This is an acceptable practice. Having a salt value your attackers can see is far more secure than having no salt at all. Having a secret salt helps a little more, but if you can do that, you may as well have a larger key because a big key helps more.

The Persistence of Memory

With such facilities as caches, virtual memory, and automated backups now commonplace, attackers have a much easier time finding confidential data by looking for a mirror image of the secret data in an insecure location.

To protect against this, precautions should be taken involving a firm understanding of the worst possible scenarios under which your program will execute. This may mean assuming all your program's runtime data is copied to an unprotected swap file and that interprocess communication may be transmitted in the clear over the Internet. It may also mean that system calls and their arguments may be monitored, that your program may be executed in an emulated environment that does not fully support all the same security measures or guarantees, and so on.

As very general precautions, do not keep sensitive data for longer than necessary. Wipe the structures clean immediately after their use. Avoid sending sensitive data to or through external shared libraries. Also, be very careful what is displayed to your users and how. What may be intended only for a single user's view may actually be transmitted through hundreds of streams, none offering any guarantees of privacy. A call to `printf()`, for example, will copy the data to `stdin`, which may in turn be redirected to any number of other streams, including pipes, files, and sockets, perhaps ending up transmitted as plain text via telnet across 50 other computers. Do not assume your users will be wise enough to recognize the danger because users never do until it is an evening news story, and even then they sometimes do not.

Try not to overlook data that should be kept confidential. Intermediate variable states, random seed information, and so on can all help make an attacker's job very easy. If you do not need it, and it has anything to do with your security functions, destroy it immediately after use. Don't only call `free()` and `fclose()`, but reset the value to a constant so its previous state is no more.

In Search of Noise

Encryption keys must be unguessable to any potential attackers. Encryption can be no stronger than the randomness of its keys. The only way to make the keys unguessable is to make the keys absolutely random. The less random the keys, the fewer keys are likely, making the key size effectively smaller and easier to use brute force attacks against. The odds of a key being one value must be no greater than it being any other valid value. (Some algorithms have a few especially weak keys, which should always be excluded by the key generation process.) Although pseudorandom number generators are commonplace (like the standard `rand()` function), truly random numbers are much more difficult to come by.

A pseudorandom number generator works by taking an initial, presumably random value and expanding it into many values with a complex pattern. The pattern is intended to be sufficiently complex that it is not detected, making all the values appear to be random. Pseudorandom number streams are not good substitutes for truly random number streams. For example, seeding a 256-bit key with pseudorandom numbers seeded by a random 8-bit value results in a 256-bit key with an 8-bit effective length, because only 8 bits are actually unknown. Seeding a pseudorandom number generator with pseudorandom numbers accomplishes very little and only results in more pseudorandom numbers with basically the same seed.

Some hardware is designed such that truly random measurements are periodically available to the running programs. Be careful when relying upon these measurements because they may be less random than they first appear. Simply because the specification calls it random does not mean that it is sufficiently random to be useful for encryption. Unreliable or unpredictable data streams are not necessarily useful random streams.

Most programs turn to their users for random input. The fine-grained timing of user events, such as the millisecond counter when the program was started, seems to work well enough as a small source of data. Collecting more than a byte or two of random data from timing the user's actions can take a long time and possibly irritate the user. As with any random data source, timing does not work well when it is likely that an attacker can guess the times. For example, timing keystrokes does not work well if an attacker is or could be intercepting keystrokes.

One bad solution that is very often relied upon is to ask the user to enter random data directly himself. Users are very poor random number generators. They tend to think that everything they think up is random and unguessable, then reuse it at every opportunity. Although many users enjoy the opportunity to invent their own passwords, they almost always abuse it by selecting actual words or other easily guessed data in an attempt to make the passwords easier to remember. Taking a hash of a user's password (or passphrase) does not always help. User-supplied random data is of such poor quality that it takes a great deal of it (more than a user is likely to remember) to seed a good, random hash value.

The arts of cryptography and computer science have advanced far enough that taking full advantage of strong encryption requires more random data than typical users are capable of memorizing. There are approximately two hundred thousand words, including names, learned in a typical adult's lifetime. Choosing one word out of those two hundred thousand with equal probability provides less than 18 bits of data. A DES key then requires more than three words, whereas a 256-bit AES key requires more than 14 words. Current two-key ciphers require larger keys for equivalent security, meaning a user may be asked to memorize a sequence of more than a hundred truly random words. These are the same users that have trouble remembering telephone numbers. The conclusion is that only users with exceptional memories can use strong encryption, or that strong encryption requires augmenting natural memory with recordable media, such as computer disks.

Less Is More

No matter how good the encryption, security can always be improved by generating less ciphertext. Most cryptanalytic attacks require or prefer a large quantity of ciphertext to analyze. Even after a message has been cracked, every attacker prefers to be rewarded with a large message.

Keys should be discarded and replaced often so that little is encrypted by each unique key. Do not generate many keys at once and simply store them for later. The longer a key is stored, the more likely it is that someone has stolen it. When a new key is desired, generate a fresh one from fresh random data. Always destroy old keys completely, wiping them to constants when they are no longer needed.

Because two-key encryption is generally slower and requires larger keys for security equivalent to single-key encryption, using both together is usually preferred. The two-key encryption process can be used to encrypt only the key of the single-key encryption algorithm, potentially making the message both more secure and faster to process than using only two-key encryption by itself.

Another very helpful technique that should be applied wherever practical is to compress the data before encrypting it. Compression helps in several ways. It serves to remove revealing patterns and shrink the resulting ciphertext. This presents less to the attacker for analysis. Compression also speeds the encryption and decryption processes by feeding the slower cryptographic functions fewer blocks. Of course, a smaller ciphertext is also more efficient to store and transmit.

Leave No Clues

Sometimes the "meat" of the messages is not the only valuable part. Sometimes the contents of the message can even be ascertained from the time of transmission, the length of the transmission, the sender, the receiver, and any other publicly available information. Any properties of the message that are likely to be valuable to an attacker should be protected, or even removed if possible. Move any sensitive header information (such as the subject) into the encrypted body whenever possible. If that is not possible, encrypt the fields separately. When using only one key, it is always better to have one big encrypted field than many different encrypted fields.

If the transmission time is important, the transmissions should be made periodic. If the important message must be received within one minute of sending it, send dummy messages every minute so that the real message will not be detected. Carefully construct the fake messages so they are indistinguishable from the real thing; make them close to the same length and contain close to the same contents. If the length and contents are not known beforehand, simply randomize them using truly random values. Each receiving party should decrypt and verify each fake message, perhaps looking for an index count or signature. This prevents an attacker from substituting different fake messages.

Alternatively, transmission timing can be obscured by delaying the outgoing message by a sufficiently long, truly random amount. Of course, this slows the reception of the message by the intended party.

Anonymity can be accomplished by having multiple parties all periodically exchanging largely fake or meaningless encrypted messages with each other, substituting a real message only when there is a real conversation in progress.

Steganography

The greatest single advantage an attacker can get is to find something to attack. Therefore, the best protection is gained by having potential attackers completely unaware of the messages.

Steganography really becomes useful when combined with conventional encryption techniques. An attacker discovering only hidden ciphertext is much more likely to move on and look elsewhere, thinking the data too random to be meaningful. For steganographic purposes, it becomes necessary that the ciphertext not only be protected from unauthorized translation back to plaintext form, but it is very desirable to have the ciphertext blend in with the surrounding data and context. This makes it far more likely to be overlooked and may influence the choice of algorithms.

The most obvious steganographic strategy is to hide a message where no attacker is looking. Using this approach, it is often possible to hide very large messages. Some frequent hiding places include unallocated memory, including memory on disks; document encoding (usually HTML or XML); unused, reserved, or ignored header fields, especially comment fields; unconventionally accessed disk sectors; and disk sectors marked "bad."

A less-used strategy is to hide data atop other data, with the two messages occupying the same space. Many formats are flexible enough that small variations in a file can make no difference in its interpretation. For example, C compilers ignore whitespace in source code, so encoding another message in a C file's source would go unnoticed by the compiler. By appending only 0 to 3 spaces to the end of every line of C code, you could hide 2 bits per line and probably go undetected, even by programmers carefully reviewing the file. In fact, even attackers trying to find encrypted messages are unlikely to look very hard in a plain C file. By hiding the message in another message, you gain another advantage: you can encrypt the carrier message itself. This way, you can even feed your attackers misinformation, should they manage to crack the carrier message. After going through the trouble to crack a difficult message, they will be so happy to see a secret message that they will not think about looking through it for other hidden meanings. Even if they do look, the hidden message should be sufficiently random-looking to appear not to be a message at all, only their own imagination.

Because only small, plausible variations are likely to go unnoticed, the carrier message is usually much larger than the embedded hidden message. Most steganographers use larger media for their carrier messages, such as image and sound files. These media usually provide enough space for simple text messages. Changes in the least significant bit of each sample or of each pixel can easily go undetected.

The Final Touches

The last stage in designing any encryption application should be to break it. You should break your program at least once. Take the hat of the attacker and seek out weaknesses. When it starts to get too difficult, try making it a little easier on yourself by making your pretend users break rules, reducing or removing your encryption algorithm, and so on. Sometimes shortcomings are more obvious when the program or environment is crippled in some unrelated respect.

After the thrill of breaking your own program wears down, hand it off to others and have them break it for you. If they can't break it, at least ask them to offer suggestions and point out potential problems. Give them your pertinent source code so they can quickly see how you are doing things.

Then, after fixing all the vulnerabilities you discovered from repeatedly breaking your program, play what-if. Ask yourself exactly what could happen if the system was compromised somehow. Imagine you have both very malicious and very foolish users. Imagine someone takes your source code and distributes modified, Trojan Horse versions of it. Determine how one serious breach can affect any other accounts or programs. Don't take these issues lightly and casually dismiss all the possibilities. If you are using encryption at all, you expect attackers, and if you expect attackers, you should anticipate what happens when they succeed. You should take steps to ensure that one successful attack does not destroy the entire system or make further attacks easier.

Not only should you try to limit the maximum extent of a security breach, but you should also plan for means of secure recovery from possible problems. Issues ranging from forgotten passwords to corrupted key files to total system failure should be carefully planned for before the security model is complete. Leaving them for later introduces risks, possibly enabling attackers to circumvent all other defenses simply by invoking an insecure failure recovery system. It is fearfully common to be able to break into a largely secure system by forcing it to recover from a problem, or even by pretending to be a troubled user in need of help.

Lastly, after you have completed your program, be careful not to promise more than you have provided. Do not boast of how impenetrable your program is. So very few programs are perfect; you should be cautious claiming yours is one of them. Plainly and honestly describe your weaknesses so that your users can work around and properly adjust to them. Users will not love you for giving them a false sense of security. Describe exactly which algorithms are used and how, along with your source of random data and other pertinent information. Hiding this information does little to protect your software, but makes it more likely that problems will be caught early, and that expert users will trust your product. If the experts trust your program, they will advise the non-experts and the whole user community will trust it.

Summary

You have seen that software encryption is usually a C issue. Other languages seem to always be just a little too high-level or a little too low-level to be good languages for implementing encryption.

Almost every modern application must be concerned with security. Employers are becoming more and more oriented toward making money using computer software and entrusting very important information to computer software. You've seen why it is ever more important for C programmers to have a firm understanding of pertinent security issues and technologies such as data encryption. Successful computerized privacy, authentication, and commerce would all be impossible without it.

This chapter has gone over how to measure and classify threats. You have seen that sometimes the greatest dangers are the very users you are protecting. You've learned the pitfalls of developing new encryption ciphers without sufficient devotion to cryptographic concerns.

This chapter looked over the current cryptographic landscape to get a good feel for the algorithms that should be employed and when.

A look at the minimum requirements for an embedded system shows that we are dealing with a very basic type of computer system. All we need is a processor, some readable memory with the program to execute, and a connection to the machine or object we are supposed to control. Add some low order electronic circuitry (power supply, quartz, and so on) and that's it. The processor itself will provide some writable memory locations (registers, for instance). Anything beyond that is added only if needed, for instance add-ons such as the following:

- RAM
- Interrupt controllers
- Memory-mapped devices
- Serial or parallel ports
- A bus system for connecting more complex peripherals

Depending on the task that the microprocessor is needed for, a manufacturer can decide to either design and build his own computer system from the components mentioned previously, or look for prefabricated computer modules that he might use. There is in fact a growing market for prefabricated embeddable modules with a number of obvious advantages, including the following:

- Standardization through mass production
- No need to develop and test complex computer circuitry
- Support for hardware integration and software development

The main goal is to provide a flexible yet simple, small, and powerful computer module that a company can fit into its product.

This chapter concentrates on the key aspects of cross-platform software development and how they relate to programming embedded systems in C:

- Getting started: compiler and tools
- Getting the program to run: program startup code
- Getting feedback: basic input and output facilities

Programming Embedded Systems in C

Most embedded systems nowadays are programmed in either Assembler or C, with C leading the field. The C language elegantly combines low-level programming with high-level language features. Low-level programming (that is, programming very close to the hardware) is required due to the rudimentary nature of embedded systems. High-level language features mainly improve readability and maintainability of the code.

C has become the standard programming language for embedded systems. C compilers are available for every microprocessor and every prefabricated embedded system module, where they form an integral part of the software development package for the module. If you are designing your own system, you can either get a C compiler for your microprocessor from the manufacturer of the processor or you can see if the GNU-C compiler supports your processor. The free GNU project supports a wide range of target processors and it includes more than just the GNU-C compiler: linker, library manager, and a wide range of software development tools are all part of the project. In fact, many C compilers distributed by manufacturers of processor or embedded modules are based on the GNU-C compiler.

No matter what compiler you use, programming an embedded system always means cross-platform software development. Your software development system typically will differ considerably from the target hardware that will run the program you create. In some instances the difference might not be all that large, but the result will be the same. You cannot run the program for the embedded system on the platform where you created it. A cross compiler is needed along with a set of cross software development tools.

Getting Started

Getting started with software development for an embedded system is easiest if you can obtain a full set of cross compiler and tools from the company that produces your processor or your embedded module. You will get a set of instructions to guide you through the process of setting up the host system, install all the tools, and so on. In the end, your host system is ready for producing programs that will run on the target hardware.

GCC (the GNU-C compiler) and its tools (the BINUTILS) are the typical alternative if there is no software package available for your hardware. GNU has been ported to a wide range of target processors and processor architectures. The compiler, the tools, and lists of supported host and target systems can be found at `http://www.gnu.org`.

The basic requirement is a host system with an existing C compiler capable of creating C programs for the host. Step one is to unpack the source code for the BINUTILS and build them for the target system. This will create an assembler, a linker, a library manager for object files, and assorted other tools. All GNU software packages use the same three-step mechanism for building the software:

1. Configure the source code for the given host and target system types and the host system directory structure. This will create the `make` files required.
2. Use the `MAKE` utility to build the program or programs from the source code. The resulting programs will run on the host, but support the target hardware.
3. Install the programs created to the host system directory structure using `MAKE` a second time.

After building `BINUTILS`, you unpack the GCC source code and build it using the same three-step mechanism. At this point, you should have a working C cross compiler with a working set of build tools.

Running an Embedded System Program

One of the major problems with embedded systems is transferring the program from the host system to the embedded system where it will run. The basic technique for program startup is the same for most microprocessors: when the power is switched on or a reset is enabled, the processor will go into a specific initial state and will start executing commands at a specific predefined memory address. The actual program or an appropriate loader or starter program must be available at that memory address to execute. Furthermore, the program must include all code required to initialize the processor and all hardware it uses.

The simplest approach to providing the program at the address where the processor expects it to be is to use replaceable or programmable memory modules, like ROM, PROM, EPROM, EEPROM, and so on. These memory modules represent read-only memory for storing a program. The program is executed by plugging the module into its socket on the embedded system and switching on the power. The EEPROM, and its more modern variant the Flash-ROM, are special because they can be reprogrammed in place, without having to be removed, by using special electronic circuitry. It is therefore a bit weak on the read-only aspect. Indeed, it can be wired in such a way that a program can rewrite the EEPROM at runtime; for instance, for storing parameter information or for in-field update of the program itself. In case those acronyms are unknown to you, here is a short guide to what they mean:

- ROM—Read Only Memory
- PROM—Programmable ROM

- EPROM—Erasable PROM
- EEPROM—Electrically Erasable PROM
- Flash-ROM—A modern variant of the EEPROM where whole blocks of memory can be cleared (flashed) and rewritten very fast, other advantages include faster memory read access and larger memory capacities with smaller chips.

Those chip types represent the most typical method for storing programs on an embedded system. Systems where hard disks are available for storing program code are quite rare. What remains to be done, before the program can be started, is to write the program into the chips. Removable chip solutions require plugging the chip into a special programmer device and putting the (re)programmed chip back into the embedded system. Modern EEPROM or Flash-ROM solutions can be reprogrammed on-board and in-system. To do this, the existing software must include special routines to operate the hardware features for erasing and rewriting the memory chip contents. The new program written into the EEPROM or Flash-ROM can, for instance, be obtained via a communication connection from a host system.

If the embedded system has sufficient RAM and a fixed communication connection to a suitable host system, we can implement an alternate and more dynamic approach. The (EEP)ROM just contains a simple boot loader program that uses the communication connection to request the actual program to run from the host system. The program code is loaded into RAM via the communication connection and the last action of the boot loader is to start it.

The preceding section describes the most basic form of an embedded program, where the program must initialize the processor and all hardware before it can begin with the main task. In other words, the software must provide a lot of very basic and complex functionality before it can perform even the simplest tasks. For the most part, this is not a major problem. For most microprocessors, basic initialization code is available through the Internet. An Internet search or some research in the relevant Usenet newsgroups can save a lot of time and work. With most I/O hardware, the situation is similar: If it is not too unusual, you should be able to find source code that either does what you want or serves as a good basic example.

Finally, I want to mention a few cases where the software situation is even less critical. Yet again the prefabricated embedded system module has the most to offer. If the module is well supported, it will come with a full set of adjustable startup code and with additional I/O libraries for accessing all the hardware it has to offer. Some systems might have or can be equipped with BIOS modules or at least with a boot PROM. A BIOS is a sort of onboard software library for the system. It contains basic startup code and additional but very basic

I/O support (BIOS means Basic Input Output Software). A boot PROM offers even less functionality: mainly the basic processor initialization and typically a minimal mechanism for loading the program from an input device, like the serial port, a network connection, or a storage device.

Basic Input and Output Facilities

A program without access to any I/O facilities whatsoever is pretty useless. It cannot obtain input data and it cannot submit results or take actions. I/O hardware is required that is connected to the processor in a way that allows the processor to control it. Essentially, the only way a microprocessor can interface with its environment is by reading or altering the contents of memory locations. Processors with I/O devices right on the chip form an exception: They will have assembler instructions for using these devices.

Memory-mapped hardware is programmed by writing code bytes or bit combinations into memory locations. To do this in C, you will have to assign the memory address to a pointer variable. For instance, let's assume that we want to set bit 3 at address 0x80004242:

```
unsigned char *adr = 0x80004242;  /* just an irrelevant sample address /*
*adr = *adr | 0x04;
```

Code like that is inherently compiler- and hardware-specific. For one thing, the memory address will very likely be invalid for any system besides the one the code was written for. For another, the concept of assigning integer values to pointer variables in C is by definition compiler-specific. On some C compilers it can be illegal and on others it might require a special syntax. The preceding example, however, uses the most common syntax employed by most C compilers.

For most of the hardware in an embedded system, you will require a list of memory addresses connected to the hardware and a detailed description of what can be read from those addresses and what writing to the addresses will do. The main problem of programming an embedded system is that these descriptions tend to be highly complex. Even the seemingly simplest tasks, such as using a serial port, require highly complex functions to perform them. The rule of thumb is that programming hardware directly through a memory-mapped interface is very complex. That's why having even the most basic software support is an enormous advantage, and this should not be underestimated.

Let's look at a simple practical example of programming a memory-mapped output device: a seven-segment display, like the ones used in digital watches. There are seven lines for each single digit, which can be switched on or off individually and that form the number 8 if all are switched on. For our example, let's say the display consists of four digits and there is a colon between the first two and the last two digits. The display looks like this:

```
 -     -         -     -
| |   | |   *   | |   | |
 -     -         -     -
| |   | |   *   | |   | |
 -     -         -     -
```

Each digit is mapped to one byte in memory. The bits 0 to 6 of each byte control the seven segments; bit 7 is unused. There is a fifth control byte offering two simple functions: bit 0 toggles whether the display is switched on or off and bit 1 toggles whether the colon is on or off. We will write a simple basic driver function that changes the contents of the display by doing the following:

- Switching off the display
- Setting the new contents
- Switching the display back on

```
/*
** setDisplayContents
**
** digits : the bytes to write to the four digits in the display
**          byte 0 is the rightmost digit
** colon : flag for controlling the colon: 0 = off, 1 = on
**
** Macro DISPLAY_BASE_ADR is used to obtain the display base
** address. The offset 0 is assumed to be the display control
** register. Offsets 1 to 4 are assumed to be the digits 1 to
** 4 (rightmost to leftmost respectively).
*/
void setDisplayContents( unsigned char digits[4], int colon )
{
   unsigned char *display = DISPLAY_BASE_ADR;
   int i;

   /* switch display off */
   display[0] &= 0xFE;

   /* write the 4 digits */
   for ( i=0 ; i < 4 ; i++ )
      display[i+1] = digits[i];
```

```
   /* set the colon status */
   if ( colon == 0 )
      display[0] &= 0xFD;
   else
      display[0] |= 0x02;

   /* switch display back on */
   display[0] |= 0x01;
}
```


`setDisplayContents()` does not even have to know what the bit combinations will look like. It is just a rudimentary driver function. A function at a higher level of logic, let's call it `displayTime()`, could now use `setDisplayContents()` to display a real-time value like "12:00" on the display. If you think about what `displayTime()` would look like, you will notice that it is still hardware dependent. The function must know how the bit positions in the digit byte correspond to the lines of the number. Without a table like this, the function `setDisplayContents()` is useless:

```
      0
      -
   6 | | 1
      -  2
   5 | | 3
      -
       4
```

A function like

```
int displayTime( int hours, int minutes, int colon );
```

is a good example of a high-level end user interface. It can be used without specific hardware knowledge, and it is tailored to a well-defined task.

The example shows how to control an output device and write driver functions for it. Reading an input device is done with similar basic memory access operations. For instance, the hardware manual for one of my digitizer cards states that reading at a specific `FIFO_DATA_ADR` will give you the bottom element of the hardware FIFO (FIFO is the First In First Out storage concept) where the digitizer stores the results of digitizing an analog input line in regular intervals. Another address `FIFO_STAUS_ADR` can be read to obtain hardware FIFO status information. The individual bits correspond to states such as FIFO empty, FIFO half full, and FIFO overflow. Here's a short and simple example of how those addresses can be used to obtain new input:

```
int readFifo( unsigned char *pData )
{
```

```
    int status;
    status = *((unsigned char*)FIFO_STAUS_ADR);
    if ( (status & 0x03) == 0 )
       *pData = *((unsigned char*)FIFO_DATA_ADR);
    return status & 0x03;
}
```

Printing Messages and Debugging

Debugging a program for and on an embedded system is a highly complex task, mainly because there is rarely a device for displaying text or support for connecting to an interactive debugger. Interactive debuggers on source code level are the best tools for debugging your software, but they require a very complex mechanism for interacting with the running program. With a typical embedded system there is either no way to use a debugger, or at least no easy way. If the system is powerful enough to support an RTOS (Real Time Operating Systems), and if the RTOS supports debugging, we have found a way to access host-based debugging, quite likely even on a C source code level.

Printing messages on some kind of terminal or screen is one of the most basic ways of debugging a program, and quite often it is the only way available. If the embedded system does not have a display device, it absolutely requires some hardware for communicating with the host system. Without this communication support, debugging becomes very difficult and will have to rely on exploiting any hardware data output mechanism available.

Being able to send data to the host includes being able to send text to the host. Quite often a serial interface is available on the embedded system and can be used for sending data to the host. On the host system, a receiver program is needed that receives the incoming text and displays it on the screen in a suitable way. From personal experience, I can relate that it is possible to debug even the most complex highly parallel real-time applications using little more than a simple `printf()` function.

In situations where you do not have the chance to resort to text output functions, debugging gets complicated. Some way of generating optical or acoustical feedback must be found to generate basic feedback of program progress. Examples of such situations include

- Program startup code
- Interrupt handlers functions
- Highly time-critical functions

Typical solutions include using, if present, a speaker or an LED, or a seven-segment display. If neither of these things is available, a weapon of last resort is to hook up an oscilloscope to the embedded system to catch changes to specific memory or I/O locations.

Embedded C Programming and ANSI C

After all this discussion of how embedded systems programming is so hardware-specific, you may be surprised by the title of this section. I have explained carefully that an embedded system is programmed at a very low and hardware-specific level, whereas ANSI C by definition is a highly hardware-independent programming language.

A closer look reveals that ANSI C can become a very important part of writing software for an embedded system. Fast, complex, and powerful computing hardware is becoming cheaper with every year (some might say every month), which drastically increases the computing power available in embedded systems. Software for an embedded system benefits the most from the advantages of ANSI C when there is a considerable amount of hardware-independent processing. Having a powerful processor will almost automatically increase the amount of hardware-independent processing on the system.

Have another look at the example in the previous section. All hardware dependencies for setting the seven-segment display are encapsulated in the simple function `setDisplayContents()`. The larger and more complex function `displayTime()` can be written completely in ANSI C.

The ANSI C standard describes two concepts for writing a conforming C compiler: hosted and freestanding (non-hosted) implementation. The term *hosted implementation* means that the full standard is supported, whereas a *freestanding implementation* will support a subset of the standard, where mainly the I/O facilities of `<stdio.h>` are missing. But even a freestanding system will support all language constructs, such as expressions, data types, or functions in exactly the way that ANSI C describes.

Abstraction and encapsulation are the key aspects of using ANSI C in an embedded system. The hardware dependencies and the system-specific code must be extracted and encapsulated into simple low-level driver functions, building the basic interface for accessing the hardware. The high-level ANSI C code will use (only) the driver interface to access the hardware. If this concept is used consequently and if some planning was put into building a good driver interface, porting the software to a new system is limited to porting the driver interface and the functions to the new hardware.

Porting software for an embedded system is not that far fetched with hardware changing as fast as it does today, and it might not be as drastic as you might expect. Maybe you just want to use the new and faster processor model, or add a new device that will impact memory layout, or use a new more powerful interrupt controller. The possibilities of minor or major changes are numerous, and each change will have a minor or major impact on the corresponding interface functions.

If the concept of having a low-level driver interface for all hardware devices is implemented consequently, you will actually implement a concept very similar to what modern operating systems use. On a more basic level, maybe, and certainly on a smaller scale, but it is the same principle. The similarity was so striking, it made many a programmer wonder whether it could be turned into the concept for a very simple operating system for embedded systems, and that is how the Real Time Operating Systems were born.

Real Time Operating Systems

Embedded systems represent the main target for Real Time Operating Systems (RTOS). An RTOS will mainly attempt to satisfy the real-time needs of an embedded application. It will attempt to give as much of the computing power as possible to the active tasks; in other words, the RTOS itself will consume as little as possible. Also, it offers a standardized function-level interface to the hardware of the embedded system, thereby reducing the task of porting embedded system applications to porting the RTOS. Last, but not least, an RTOS will implement high-level operating system features such as multitasking, multithreading, and interprocess communication, using a standardized function interface; it will also have integrated debugging support for the RTOS applications.

Dealing with hardware on a very direct level often results in very strict timing conditions that have to be met. Hardware interrupts must be dealt with as fast as possible, that is, immediately, or devices have to be tended at fixed intervals with very high precision. High precision is the key aspect here. Normal operating systems, such as Windows or UNIX, cannot guarantee specific and accurate response times for interrupts or hardware timers. An RTOS, on the other hand, will specify that for a specific target system it guarantees responding to an interrupt within, for instance, 12 microseconds. For most operations of the RTOS, you get a guaranteed maximum execution or response time. Generally an RTOS is a devoted minimalist: All operations are executed as fast and as efficiently as possible to consume a minimum of processing time.

Important hardware features such as hardware timers, interrupt controllers, memory access, or serial port communication are accessed through interface functions of the RTOS. If the RTOS has been ported to a specific target system and if that hardware is available on the target system, it can be accessed by the application in a standardized way. The application becomes considerably less hardware dependent and can be programmed on a much higher level of logic.

Multitasking and process communication are central features of any modern operating system. They are very complex to implement, and within an RTOS there is the added complexity of real-time efficiency. If you had to implement this for a given hardware, you would in fact end up with your own small, self-written operating system.

All in all, it is a great plus to have an RTOS available for a given embedded system. Considering all the features that it offers, it is almost always worth the effort of porting it to a given hardware, if it has not been ported already. Popular RTOSes come equipped with ports to a wide variety of different hardware platforms. These ports will include popular embedded system boards, important hardware architectures, and typical embedded system microprocessors. If you've got a prefabricated embedded system module and the RTOS is available for that module, you will just have to build it for that target, or it is part of the software development environment that comes with the module.

If your target hardware is supported at the level of processor type or hardware architecture, you will have to port parts of the RTOS source code yourself to adapt it to your specific hardware layout. Because this is standard procedure for an RTOS, it is (or should be) well documented, and existing ports serve as examples for adding new ones. The RTOS was created with flexibility and portability in mind. Porting it to new hardware is part of the design. And as I said before, it is almost always worth the effort because reimplementing what the RTOS offers will cost considerably more time.

RTEMS as a Typical Sample RTOS

RTEMS (Real Time Executive for Military Systems) is a typical example of a powerful and flexible RTOS. Originally invented for the U.S. military, it was implemented with general utility for embedded systems and real-time environments in mind. The RTEMS operating system is available for free, and it is based on the free GNU software development tools. The GNU tools are by design cross system software development tools, where a host system is used to create applications for a differing target system. RTEMS makes full use of this concept by adding its own target type "rtems" for all targets that RTEMS supports.

The central Web page for RTEMS is `http://www.rtems.com`.

Here is a list of what RTEMS supports and what any good RTOS will (or should) support in a similar way:

- Support for homogenous and heterogeneous multiprocessor systems
- Multitasking
- Event driven, priority based, preemptive scheduling
- Optional rate monotonic scheduling
- Intertask communication and synchronization
- Priority inheritance
- Responsive interrupt management
- Dynamic memory allocation
- Support for a large number of processors and specific embedded boards
- High level of user configurability
- High level of user extendibility
- Reentrant ANSI C library
- POSIX support
- TCP/IP stack and BSD sockets implementation

Reading through that list shows the advantages of having an RTOS like RTEMS. Most of the features are very complex to implement, especially with real-time considerations in mind. Yet RTEMS manages to be very resource efficient. It will only occupy approximately 60 to 120 kilobytes, depending on the number of features being used for an application.

All hardware-dependent parts of RTEMS are encapsulated in the so-called Boards Support Package, or BSP. Porting RTEMS to a new target hardware is reduced to writing a new BSP for the target hardware, either based on a generic template or by adapting an existing similar BSP. The BSP includes device drivers for all hardware devices to implement a set of well-defined interface functions, thus adding a level of abstraction that will make an application more hardware independent.

Summary

This chapter introduced the basic concepts of embedded systems—how they represent a very specific and dedicated piece of programmable hardware and how each one is quite unique in its own way. A very important step in programming embedded systems is to obtain a good software development environment with reliable debugging support. The preferred and most common programming language is C, and most prefabricated embedded system modules will include a C compiler and a set of build tools.

For the larger and more powerful systems, specific real-time operating systems can be used to get a powerful and flexible environment for the application to run on.

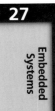

CHAPTER 28

Parallel Processing

by Stephan Wilms

In This Chapter

This chapter introduces important concepts of parallel processing and gives some examples of how to do parallel processing in C. The first section, "Basic Concepts," is a beginner's introduction to the subject of parallel processing.

Basic Concepts

Parallel processing means doing things simultaneously. Let's look at an example first. If it takes one man one hour to wash a car, two men can wash two cars in the same amount of time. Both men can wash one car in about half an hour. The result is that by doubling the number of workers, you get twice the efficiency. Faster and more efficient production is indeed one of the main goals of parallel processing. Applying this concept to computers would lead us to the simple formula that increasing the number of computers and programs working on the same problem will lower the time it takes to solve the problem or complete a calculation by the same magnitude. It is not that simple, though, as the example can show us. Imagine telling six people, or maybe even ten, to wash a car. Would you get the car washed in one tenth of the time? Probably not, because there is a maximum number of people that can effectively partake in washing one car. The general rule is that there usually exists a maximum limit for the degree of parallelization that can be applied to a given problem. To illustrate another aspect of parallelization, ten people can efficiently be used to wash ten cars in parallel, but only if there is a sufficient (and constant) supply of dirty cars to keep them occupied. Again, the efficiency of parallelization depends on the nature of the problem.

What you have learned so far are two basic ways of parallel processing:

- In depth parallelization, where multiple workers work on one instance of the problem and finish it before continuing with the next one.
- Broad parallel processing, where multiple workers work on multiple instances of the problem independent of one another.

Both concepts can be combined to form a new concept similar to a production line. Each worker is assigned one specific subtask that he performs on every instance of the problem. When he's finished with his subtask, he moves on to the next instance. If we apply this concept to the example of washing a car, it might mean that the first worker washes just the roof, the second worker washes the windows, the third worker washes the sides, and so forth. The example even shows another important aspect of production line parallelization (also called *pipelining*): the importance of the order of execution. The steps must be executed in the right order to get the desired result. For example, washing the roof after having cleaned the windows is not a good idea.

Computers and Parallel Processing

You will find two types of parallelism with computers: real and simulated parallel processing. *Real* parallel processing requires having several microprocessors being able to communicate with one another or share a common set of data. *Simulated* parallel processing uses just one microprocessor for executing a number of programs that seem to run in parallel. A *round robin* mechanism is used to share processing time between the parallel programs. There is a scheduler, usually in the form of an operating system, which gives a certain amount of processing time to each program one after another. True simulated parallel processing is also called *preemptive multitasking*. The parallel programs are called *tasks*, and preemptive means that the operating system performs the scheduling independent of the task. A task gets activated, is allowed to execute for a certain time slice, and is put back into a dormant state until the scheduler gets back around to it. Often, priorities are used to reflect the importance of tasks. Tasks with higher priority might get bigger time slices or get activated more often.

You might ask yourself, "Why simulated multitasking?" The operating system and the scheduling add considerable overhead to the processing. Well, there are a number of important reasons:

- The operating system uses the scheduling mechanism to run system services as a set of parallel tasks, thus creating a high level of modularization.
- The operating system uses the scheduling to run the programs started for and by multiple users in parallel, thus sharing processing time between the users on a fair basis.
- A program can use parallelism to achieve a higher degree of modularization by separating a complex problem into simpler subproblems; as, for instance, in the simple washing a car example from the preceding section. The simpler subproblems must be independent enough to be executed on a parallel basis.
- A program can use parallel processing to make use of the powerful scheduling features of the operating system. Often, more complex programs have to implement features that are supposed to implement parallel features. For instance, think of a word processor that has to read user input and check the spelling at the same time, or a program that has to receive input data, process the data, and send or store the results. Those programs could implement their own scheduling to make sure that input data doesn't get lost, especially if it can arrive with varying speed, but nevertheless make sure that data processing gets as much time as it needs. Using

parallel tasks and letting the operating system do the scheduling is usually much more powerful, though, and saves the programmer the enormous effort of having to implement complex scheduling routines.

- A program with a well-planed degree of parallelism, as indicated by the previous points, becomes highly scalable with regard to real parallel hardware. If the program consists of rather independent parallel tasks with well-designed interfaces for passing information and data from one task to the next, the program can become highly independent of whether all tasks run on the same processor or whether the tasks get distributed across multiple processors. Adding more hardware will speed up the program without having to change the program itself.

Preemptive Multitasking

Preemptive multitasking as a concept is more than just having a scheduler for distributing CPU time between parallel tasks. Encapsulation and virtualization are other aspects that the preceding list only hinted at. Each task can, by design, assume it has a whole processor to itself. The operating system makes sure that tasks do not interfere with one another. The concept requires all tasks to access ("see") all hardware resources through the operating system. Thus, the operating system can run multiple tasks, where all tasks can safely assume that they have full access to all hardware.

One more word on scheduling and preemptive multitasking: both get attributed to the operating system, which is indeed correct in most cases. Modern microprocessors usually do have built-in multitasking support, but an operating system is needed to control and operate this mechanism. There are some admittedly rare exceptions, though. Some microprocessors feature built-in preemptive multitasking with hardware scheduling. Microprocessors like that do not need an operating system for multitasking. The INMOS Transputer processor is a popular example of this genre. Nevertheless, because this is quite out of the ordinary, the text will continue to refer to the operating system as the main scheduling instance. Special hardware like the Transputer is typically found in the area of embedded systems, which is covered in Chapter 28 "Embedded Systems."

Cooperative Multitasking

For completeness, I will also mention cooperative multitasking, which is occasionally referred to as "poor man's multitasking." Preemptive multitasking is complex to implement for an operating system—it requires considerable administrative overhead, for one thing. Cooperative multitasking is a simpler approach to parallelism. The concept is to continue executing the current program until control returns to the operating system, whereupon it will switch to the next program. A program can either return control voluntarily by calling a special *descheduling* function, or involuntarily if the operating system intercepts any call to an operating system function for the purpose of descheduling. The obvious disadvantage is that any program can monopolize CPU resources by rarely or never relinquishing control. That's why it is called cooperative—it only works if all programs cooperate. One single non-cooperative program is enough to effectively block the operating system. For example, Win3.x uses cooperative multitasking. A single task that does not return control to the OS can freeze up all tasks. Win9x and WinNT use preemptive multitasking.

Interprocess Communication

Separating a program into parallel tasks requires that those tasks either share data or exchange data to work toward a common goal. With multitasking, the tasks should be independent to the degree of assuming that they all run on their own processor. Therefore, sharing data is usually out of the question. Multithreading is the conceptual solution for parallel programs that require shared data. Parallel tasks, on the other hand, use communication connections to exchange data and information.

Interprocess communication is a basic mechanism that an operating system has to implement along with multitasking. A communication channel can be seen as a unidirectional connection between two tasks for either sending or receiving data. For the sake of clarity, it is best to have dedicated channels for specific purposes. Let's look at a general data processing task as an example. The task is part of a bigger program and has to process incoming data in some specific way before sending the data on to some other task. A typical set of communication channels includes

- One channel for receiving the data to be processed.
- One channel for sending the data on after it has been processed.
- One channel for receiving control commands (such as processing parameters or start/end commands). This channel is typically connected to a controlling task responsible for controlling data flow and data processing in a large data-processing application.
- One channel for sending notifications, command acknowledgements, progress or status information, or error messages sent back to the controlling process. Several dedicated channels might be used here, if this is advantageous to program design.

Threads, Multithreading, and Synchronization

Tasks offer a high level of independence up to being able to place them on different processes, but there is a price:

- They do not have much in common and considerably complex communication mechanisms must be used to exchange data.
- They represent a rather static mechanism for parallel processing.

On both accounts, there is an alternative called *threads*. Threads share the same data and code area in memory, and they can easily be started and stopped within one task. Imagine a thread as being a function that, when called, runs parallel to the calling function. Threads represent parallel subcomponents of a task. The disadvantage is, of course, that threads are restricted to running in the same environment that the parent task runs in. In other words, a thread cannot be placed on a different processor or run with different multitasking options.

Threads can be seen as logical components of a task, very similar to functions. If the program logic of a task indicates things that could happen in parallel, threads can represent this parallelism and efficiently use the powerful parallel scheduling of the operating system. For instance, think of a task that has to receive input data via two channels, process the data, and send the result on via a third output data channel. The solution might be a task consisting of four threads:

- A receiver thread for the first input data channel that places the incoming data into a buffer
- A receiver thread for the second input data channel that places the incoming data into either the same buffer that the other receiver uses or into a separate second input data buffer
- A data processing thread that takes input data from the input buffer(s), processes the data, and places the results into an output data buffer
- A sender thread that takes the output data from the output data buffer and sends it via the output channel

This concept uses the data-sharing ability of threads and actually uses the threads to implement a full separation of channel communication from data processing. Accessing shared data from multiple parallel threads leads to the problem of data access synchronization.

Two threads writing to the same object in memory will, quite obviously, cause a collision. In the case of a buffer, both might end up writing into the same slot of the buffer, causing a disastrous mix-up of data. The solution is called *access synchronization*: shared memory objects should only be accessed by one thread at one time. There must be an instance where the threads can look up whether the buffer is currently available for writing to or reading from, and it must be possible for the threads to reserve access to the buffer as long as they are using it.

The synchronization mechanism itself must be *thread safe*. In other words, suppose two threads both ask for a write permission at almost the same time. In that case, the synchronization mechanism must prevent these threads from both getting the information that the buffer is available for writing. This type of synchronization instance is called a *semaphore*, and the uniquely accessible object is typically called a *resource*. Semaphores are generally used to synchronize parallel access to uniquely accessible resources. Two basic operations suffice for using semaphores:

- Waiting for a semaphore to become available. The semaphore is reserved to the waiting task. As soon as it becomes available the corresponding resources can be accessed, but only after the semaphore reservation function has returned, not before.
- Releasing the semaphore as soon as the corresponding resource is no longer required. For efficient multithreading, a semaphore should not be kept reserved longer than is absolutely necessary because other threads might already be waiting for it.

Parallel Processing in C

The ANSI-C programming language itself, as has repeatedly been mentioned, does not support system-specific features, and parallel processing is such a feature.

Each operating system or software development toolkit features its own concept for supporting parallel programming. The C programmer accesses these features using special support functions of the operating system and a special set of C callable functions. Functions, data structures, and other definitions form a parallel programming API (application programmer's interface). This section uses one specific API as an example to demonstrate how such an API can be used to utilize the main features of parallel programming in C. I am going to use the INMOS ToolSet for my source code examples. It might not be a very widespread API, but it is very simple and straightforward in implementing the basic and advanced concepts of parallel programming.

The concepts demonstrated in this section are

- Multitasking
- Multithreading

- Interprocess communication
- Process synchronization

Multitasking in C

Tasks are independent parallel programs. Each task forms a separate program in its own right, and consequently has its own `main()` function. Creating and starting does not require special effort on most operating systems. The system itself supports starting programs in parallel. For instance, with a GUI-oriented system you use simple mouse clicks to start as many programs as you like and they will all run as parallel tasks. Interprocess, or in this case intertask, communication is what makes a set of tasks special. Communication makes tasks form a large program with a common goal. Because this is an important aspect, I'll discuss it in the section "Interprocess Communication in C" later in the chapter.

Having an operating system command shell that supports starting tasks means that you can also use C to start tasks from within a program by simply passing the appropriate shell command to the `system()` function. For instance, this function call will start a program called `hello` as a parallel task and return immediately for a UNIX `bash` shell:

```
system( "&hello" );
```

The following line does the same thing for Windows:

```
system( "start /m hello.exe " );
```

More typically, shell scripts are used to start up all tasks of a large parallel application for an operating system. Special programming environments, however, often form an exception, especially if there is no operating system on the target hardware or if the operating system is a special implementation for embedded systems. They implement special solutions for starting the tasks of an application. Some support special functions for starting tasks and others use special build tools for combining tasks to form a program.

The INMOS ToolSet system, which I will mainly use for source code examples, belongs in the second category. Hardware and software require that all tasks for all processors form single binary files. A compiler and linker are used to create the tasks as separate programs (called *linked units*), and a configuration and collection tool is used to combine the tasks into a single binary, along with information about which tasks run on which processor and how they intend to communicate with one another. A loader and starter program will copy the resulting binary onto the target hardware and handle task distribution and the startup procedure.

Multithreading in C

Multithreading is more closely related to C programming than multitasking. A well-defined function interface is required to create and start C functions as parallel threads. Because this is not supported by ANSI-C, each programming environment supplies its own interface. The general concept is typically the same, or at least very similar, across all systems. However, the programmer must research the specific details anew for each system. I will be using INMOS ToolSet interface syntax to present those basic concepts.

Assume that threads are represented by an opaque data structure called `Process` and that any function that I want to start as a thread must at least have a pointer to `Process` as its first parameter. Furthermore, there is a function called `ProcAlloc()` to create a process from a function and `ProcRun()` to start a process that has been created. Consider the simple sample program in Listing 28.1, which uses a thread to print an arbitrary number of greetings.

LISTING 28.1 Using a Thread to Print an Arbitrary Number of Greetings

```
#include <stdio.h>
#include <process.h>   /* C extensions for threads */

void MyFirstProcess( Process *p, int numberOfHellos, int *pFinished )
{
   int i;
   for ( i=0 ; i < numberOfHellos ; i++ )
   {
      printf( "'Hello World' number %d from process %p\n", i, p );
   }
   *pFinished = 1;
}

int main( void )
{
   int finished = 0;
   Process *procHello;

   procHello = ProcAlloc( MyFirstProcess,  /* the thread function */
                          1000,            /* amount of stack memory */
                          2,               /* no. of arguments */
                          5,               /* the first argument */
                          &finished );     /* the second argument */

   if ( procHello != NULL )
```

LISTING 28.1 continued

```
    {
        ProcRun( procHello );
        while ( finished == 0 )
        {
            printf( "main is waiting ...\n" );
        }
        printf( "main: end of thread detected\n" );
        ProcAllocClean( procHello );
    }
    else
    {
        printf( "ERROR: unable to allocate process\n" );
    }

    return 0;
}
```

Allocating the thread requires specifying the stack memory for the thread function and the number of actual arguments in addition to the `Process*`, followed by the argument values to pass to the thread function. A non-NULL thread pointer indicates that the allocation was successful. An integer variable `finished` is used to show one (admittedly simple and rudimentary) way for `main` to detect when the process `procHello` has reached its end. This also shows how `main()` keeps on running parallel to `MyFirstProcess`. `ProcAllocClean()` releases all memory allocated for `MyFirstProcess()`. The output of this program follows:

```
main is waiting ...
'Hello World' number 1 from process 8000c374
main is waiting ...
'Hello World' number 2 from process 8000c374
main is waiting ...
'Hello World' number 3 from process 8000c374
main is waiting ...
'Hello World' number 4 from process 8000c374
main is waiting ...
'Hello World' number 5 from process 8000c374
main is waiting ...
main: end of thread detected
```

Interprocess Communication in C

Communication channels can be used at any point where tasks or threads want to exchange data. They form the main data-exchange mechanism for tasks, whereas threads can choose whether to use channels or shared data. An advantage of a communication channel is the automatic built-in synchronization. When data has been received, it can be processed immediately because it is a full copy of the data that has been sent.

The INMOS ToolSet uses the data type `Channel` to represent a communication connection between two parallel processes. A `Channel` is always unidirectional; that is, it has one fixed sending end and one fixed receiving end. Bidirectional communication requires two dedicated unidirectional `Channel` connections. Here are two simple functions that handle the sending and receiving of data via a `Channel`:

```
int ChanOut( Channel *pOutChan , void *pDataToSend, int numBytesToSend );

int ChanIn( Channel *pInChan , void *pStoreHere, int numBytesToReceive );
```

Both functions will return when the operation has been completed. ToolSet implements a fully synchronous `Channel` communication. When `ChanOut()` returns, the receiver can safely assume that the data has been received completely and successfully. This might be different for other programming environments, though. Other systems might have a sending function that returns as soon as all the data is on its way, which does not necessarily mean that it has arrived.

Obtaining the `Channel` instances for communication differs between tasks and threads. The following sections cover these two aspects.

`Channel` Communication for Tasks

The main problem for tasks is how to acquire the `Channel` instances for communicating with one another. As independent programs, they do not share data and cannot pass information from one to another. Usually, this problem is solved with support from the operating system or software development environment. One common solution supported by many operating systems is called pipes or named pipes. The tasks request a communication channel from the operating system, and the system notices when two requests match and supplies a direct connection.

INMOS ToolSet is a more static system. There is a static distribution of tasks onto processors at program build time via a configuration text file. Specifying communication connections between tasks is an additional important feature of the configuration file. Commands like the following can be used to connect two tasks:

```
connect  task1.dataInput  to  task2.dataOutput;
```

`task1`, `task2`, `dataInput`, and `dataOutput` are names defined by the programmer at other points in the configuration file. Within the task, there is a special function called `getparam()` for obtaining channels (and other parameters) from the program configuration:

```
Channel *myInputChannel;
/* ... */
myInputChannel = (Channel*)getparam( 1 );
```

The number `1` simply indicates that the first parameter from the task configuration is used as a channel pointer.

Channels are used uniformly in tasks and threads once they have been obtained. The next section includes some sample code using channel communication.

Channel Communication for Threads

Within a task, channels can be created dynamically as needed and passed along to functions and threads as normal function arguments. INMOS ToolSet supplies a specific function, `ChanAlloc()`, to allocate a channel. `ChanFree()` can be used to release the channel after it has been used. Combine those two with `ChanOut()` and `ChanIn()` described earlier and you've got the basic functionality for powerful channel communication. Listing 28.2 demonstrates the concept of using channel communication.

LISTING 28.2 Using Channel Communication

```
#include <stdio.h>
#include <stdlib.h>
#include <process.h>   /* C extensions for threads and channels */

/*
** This thread will add 2 to the integer it receives via the input
** channel and send the result via the output channel.
** Receiving the number 0 will terminate the thread.
*/
void AddTwoProc( Process *p, Channel *input, Channel *output )
{
   int number = 1;

   while ( number != 0 )
   {
      ChanIn( input, &number, sizeof(int) );
      printf( "AddTwoProc: received number %d\n", number );
      if ( number != 0 )
      {
```

LISTING 28.2 continued

```
         number += 2;
      }
      ChanOut( output, &number, sizeof(int) );
   }
   printf( "AddTwoProc: end of thread reached\n" );
}

int main( void )
{
   int i, newValue;
   Process *procAddTwo = NULL;
   Channel *chanToThread = NULL;
   Channel *chanFromThread = NULL;

   /*
   ** simplified allocation and error handling: attempt to allocate
   ** all itmes and check if this succeeded.
   */
   chanToThread   = ChanAlloc();
   chanFromThread = ChanAlloc();
   procAddTwo = ProcAlloc( AddTwoProc, 1000, 2,
                           chanToThread, chanFromThread);
   if ( chanToThread == NULL || chanFromThread == NULL
        || procAddTwo == NULL )
   {
      printf( "ERROR: allocting data failed\n" );
      return EXIT_FAILURE;
   }

   /* start the thread */
   ProcRun( procAddTwo );

   for ( i = 10 ; i >= 0 ; i-- )
   {
      ChanOut( chanToThread, &i, sizeof(int) );
      ChanIn( chanFromThread, &newValue, sizeof(int) );
      printf( "main: send %d and received %d\n", i, newValue );
   }

   return EXIT_SUCCESS;
}
```

Here's the program output:

```
AddTwoProc: received number 10
main: send 10 and received 12
AddTwoProc: received number 9
main: send 9 and received 11
AddTwoProc: received number 8
main: send 8 and received 10
AddTwoProc: received number 7
main: send 7 and received 9
AddTwoProc: received number 6
main: send 6 and received 8
AddTwoProc: received number 5
main: send 5 and received 7
AddTwoProc: received number 4
main: send 4 and received 6
AddTwoProc: received number 3
main: send 3 and received 5
AddTwoProc: received number 2
main: send 2 and received 4
AddTwoProc: received number 1
main: send 1 and received 3
AddTwoProc: received number 0
AddTwoProc: end of thread reached
main: send 0 and received 0
```

The sample program uses allocated channels as parameters to `AddTwoProc()` and handles the communication in `main()`. The uniformity of channel communication would also allow an implementation where the channels are obtained via calls to `getparam()` and where a separate task communicates with the `AddTwoProc()` thread. Also note that calls to `ChanFree()` and `ProcAllocClean()` were omitted for brevity. Automatic deallocation on program termination is assumed.

Data Access Synchronization in C

Threads can easily share access to the same data objects. To prevent collisions, the threads must synchronize access to those shared data objects. Have another look at the code in Listing 28.1. Both the `main()` thread and the `MyFirstProcess()` thread access the variable `finished` declared in `main`. A pointer to `finished` is passed to the `MyFirstProcess()` thread that actually writes a new value to this variable. In this specific case, synchronization is not used and not required. One thread only writes to the variable and one thread only reads the variable.

If two threads were to write to the same variable in parallel, the thread scheduling would decide on a rather random basis which value is available at which time. Let's concentrate on an example I mentioned earlier: Imagine two threads adding data objects in one shared buffer. Such a buffer might, for instance, have an array for storing the data objects in sequential order and a location counter specifying the next available array index for storing the next data object. Storing a data object is done in three steps:

1. Check if there is still room in the buffer.
2. Store the data object in the array at the current free location.
3. Increment the location counter by one.

Let's look at a simplified C implementation:

```
int AddDataToBuffer( Buffer *pBuf, Data *pData )
{
   int returnCode = 0;  /* default code for successful operation */
   if ( pBuf->location < pBuf->maximum )
   {
      pBuf->dataArray[pBuf->location] = *pData;
      pBuf->location += 1;
   }
   else
      returnCode = -1;

   return returnCode;
}
```

Now think what happens if two threads attempt to execute those three steps at almost the same time. A fatal data access collision can happen at any step. For instance, if one thread just begins with step 2, while the other thread has just finished step 2 but has not executed step 3 yet, the first thread will overwrite the data item written by the second thread because the second thread has not come around to incrementing the location counter.

Here's the code for what those two threads could look like:

```
/*
** simplified receive and store thread: there is no ending condition
** and error handling is very rudimentary
*/
void RecAndStoreProc( Process *p, Channel *pRecChan, Buffer *pBuf )
{
   int returnCode;
   Data dataObject;
```

```
    while ( 1 )
    {
        /* receive one data object */
        ChanIn ( pRecChan, &dataObject, sizeof(dataObject) );

        /* attempt to store the data obect in the buffer */
        returnCode = AddDataToBuffer( pBuf, &dataObject );
        if ( returnCode != 0 )
        {
            printf( "ERROR: buffer store failed => data object lost\n" );
        }
    }
}
```

A synchronization mechanism is required to reserve buffer access before actually accessing the buffer. The concept of semaphores, explained at the beginning of this chapter, represents exactly what is needed for this problem. Parallel programming environments all have their own implementation of semaphores, but the basic mechanism is something that must be provided by the programming environment. Most importantly, semaphores are guaranteed to work exclusively. INMOS ToolSet offers these functions for supporting semaphores:

```
Semaphore *SemAlloc( int initialState );
void SemFree( Semaphore *pSemaphore );
void SemWait( Semaphore *pSemaphore );
void SemSignal( Semaphore *pSemaphore );
```

The first two functions simply allocate and release `Semaphore` objects. Semaphores can have two states: reserved (value 1) and available (value 0), and that's what can be set with `initialState`. `SemWait()` will wait until a given semaphore is available and reserve access to that semaphore in one go. `SemSignal()` will relinquish access to the semaphore, thereby marking is as available.

If you assume that the `Buffer` data structure has a component of type `Semaphore*` called `pAccessSync`, you simply have to change the `AddDataToBuffer()` function like this to get full parallel thread safe synchronization:

```
/*
** Example definition for "Data" and "Buffer" data types.
*/
typedef int Data;

typedef struct buffer_s
{
```

A lot of the changes in C99 are simply attempts to clarify or correct wording from the previous standard. When complaints (called "defect reports") were filed on the C89 standard, many received a response stating only that these defects would be reviewed or addressed in a future revision of the C standard. Many have now been addressed.

New Types

C99 has a vast array of generically-named integer types, a Boolean type, a 64-bit integer type, and new complex arithmetic types. It also introduces variable length arrays and structures with a last member of variable size.

Basic Types

The C99 standard introduces a new type called `_Bool`, which is a Boolean type. Normally, you'll want to include `<stdbool.h>` and refer to it as `bool`. The only reason the type isn't named `bool` to begin with is that a lot of existing code already provides macros with names like that. The Boolean type has all the features you'd probably want; a conversion to `_Bool` will yield the true value (`1`) from any non-zero value, and the false value (`0`) otherwise. This doesn't change the C language's underlying rule that any expression which evaluates equal to zero will be "false" for purposes of `if`, `while`, or `for` statements.

Note

The macro that defines `bool` to mean `_Bool` is not in any of the old headers because this might break existing code; you have to explicitly request the new feature.

C99 introduces three complex types, corresponding to the three floating point types you're familiar with. The complex types allow you to do all sorts of horrid physics. Of course, for the same reason that `bool` is called `_Bool`, the keyword which introduces a complex type is `_Complex`, unless you include `<complex.h>`, in which case it's just `complex`. The `<complex.h>` header also provides a value `I`, which corresponds to the mathematical constant *i*. As an example:

```
#include <complex.h>
    complex float f = { 1, 0 };
    f *= I;     // f now contains { 0, 1 };
```

Last, but not least, C99 expanded the range of integer types, potentially dramatically. The most famous new type is `long long`. The name is a little inconsistent with the rest of the language (normally, a qualifier does not get applied twice, or at least, has no additional effect the second time), but the existing practice was overwhelming. This type is found in a number of compilers already, and is the "at least 64 bit" integer type. Note that all platforms must provide this type, but on many, performance will be substantially worse than that of 32-bit or smaller types.

The introduction of `long long` creates a problem for a number of existing programs; they might have been written to assume that any integer-typed value can be cast to `long` and printed with `%ld`. However, on systems where `long long` is larger than plain `long`, this won't always work anymore. The impact from this is expected to be limited, but, nonetheless, the need for a guaranteed-maximal integer type has been noted, so C99 introduced a largest integer type, called `intmax_t`. This type must exist on all systems and must be at least as large as every other type. Likewise, the language now contains a type called `intptr_t`, which is an integer type that can hold a pointer, if one is available. Some platforms will not have an integer type large enough to represent arbitrary pointer values, in which case `intptr_t` will not exist. There's a new `printf` format flag corresponding to `intmax_t`; it is discussed in the section "New Library Features," later in this chapter.

The C99 standard also introduced a large family of types with names that look like `int`*`N`*`_t`—for example, `int64_t`, `int32_t`, and so on. The base types are "exact" types; `int32_t` has exactly 32 bits. However, a system need not provide all these types; most will provide the ones that they have corresponding hardware for. So, you still can't write portable code that gets a 32-bit integer, but you can write code that will, without using `#ifdef`, get a 32-bit integer on every platform where one is available.

In addition to the exact-width types, there are a number of types with names like `int_least32_t`. These types allow the implementation to give you a possibly larger type that is natural to the system; thus, while `int32_t` must be exactly 32 bits, `int_least32_t` could be 36 or even 128. There are also "fast" types, such as `int_fast32_t`, which are expected to represent the "fastest" type of at least N bits available in the environment.

Implementations can also offer additional integer types other than those listed, although the standard requires `intmax_t` to be the integer type with the largest range. The set of additional types offered is potentially huge, but in general, the assumption is that such types would correspond to native word sizes or the types used for system interfaces (such as the possible range of file sizes or an argument to a particular system call).

To support all the new integer types, the integer promotion rules have been changed substantially to work in generic terms rather than being described only in terms of the types explicitly enumerated in the standard. In general, you can assume that the "widest" type in an expression will be the one everything promotes to.

The huge family of integer types was added to allow people to use standard names for commonly desired features. In existing code, a huge number of programs have deeply nested `#ifdef` constructs trying to specify "a 32 bit integer" or "an integer with at least 32 bits"; these are now done for you by the compiler. The fast and least types are provided to let programmers whose requirements are not as specific get a type that will suit their needs, without relying on the popular 8-bit-byte.

Derived Types

C99 introduces three new array-style declarations: variable-length arrays, variable structure members, and some weird ways to modify "array" parameters to functions.

Variable-length arrays: There, I said it. VLAs change a number of things about the C language. The most surprising, to an experienced programmer, is likely to be their interaction with the `sizeof` operator. Because an array's size can vary at runtime, the `sizeof` operator, when applied to a variable length array, *is no longer a constant*. This also means that the operand of `sizeof` will be evaluated in such cases (and only in such cases), which it would not be if there were no VLA type in the operand. Watch your step.

Variable-length arrays are a surprisingly powerful expressive feature. However, there are some pitfalls. One of these is the use of size expressions that have side effects. In some cases, you can create a situation where the `sizeof` operator has side effects. You can safely assume that future maintainers will curse your name if you do this.

Variable length arrays can't be used everywhere; for example, structure members can't be VLAs. However, structure declarations also have a new form that can be "variable." Many older C programmers will remember the "`struct` hack." The original form of this was the following structure declaration:

```
struct foo {
    int len;
    char data[1];
};
```

The programmer would allocate more space for this structure than expected and then treat data as if it were a much larger array. The C committee, when asked about this, indicated that it was not a correct practice, but did not offer an alternative. So, in C99, a way to implement this was provided. In C99, you write the previous code snippet as

```
struct foo {
    int len;
    char data[];
};
```

and it has a size determined as if the last member were not present. However, if you allocate additional space, you can use it through that last member.

New Library Features

The standard library grew dramatically in size in C99. You'll want to review the library section of the standard or your compiler's documentation, when it becomes available. There are a whole bunch of new floating point functions, many of which are intended to provide hints to the compiler that a given optimization is allowable or desirable.

The standard added a number of new functions that make it easier for programmers to write stable, maintainable code. For example, the new `snprintf()` function allows a programmer to indicate the maximum number of characters that can be safely written into a string. It still returns the number of characters it would have written had there been enough room, allowing you to check the amount of room you'll need before allocating it. This function came from 4.4BSD, so all the BSD-derived systems already provide it, and most of the Linux implementations you'll see probably do too.

The new standard includes a header, `<tgmath.h>`, which does some serious magic with the floating point functions. In general, any function in `<math.h>` which takes a double argument (or more than one) becomes "generic" when you include `<tgmath.h>`. If you pass it a float, it returns a float; if you pass it a long double, it returns a long double. This also applies to the functions on complex numbers provided in `<complex.h>`.

Corresponding to the new `intmax_t` type is a new `printf` flag. The format specifier for an `intmax_t` is `%jd`. It is now possible to print any signed integer value you encounter in a C program as follows:

```
printf("%jd\n", (intmax_t) n);
```

(If you're wondering why it's not something intuitive, like `%md`, it's because an existing implementation had used `%m` as an extension.)

Preprocessor Syntax

The preprocessor has gained a number of small features. One of the most wished-for is the addition of variable length macros. In C99, variable-length macros look something like this:

```
#define PERR(format, ...) fprintf(stderr, format, __VA_ARGS__)
```

This will tragically eliminate one of the most frequently asked questions on Usenet.

The new language introduces a new form of `pragma`, designed to be used in macro expansions. It looks like `_Pragma("args")`, and is generally equivalent to `#pragma args`. Note that the arguments are in quotes.

New predefined macro names have been added; most of these will be used for feature tests. (You can test whether or not a macro is defined to determine whether or not an implementation supports the corresponding feature.)

The preprocessor now does all math in `intmax_t`, not `long`.

Macro arguments might now be empty; the macro expansion simply inserts nothing where the missing argument would have gone. For example:

```
#define P(x) x ## printf
// expands to fprintf(stdout, "hello, world!\n");
P(f)(stdout, "hello, world!\n");
// expands to printf("hello, world!\n"); - but invalid in C89
P()(stdout, "hello, world!\n");
```

In C89, the `P()` macro invocation would have been invalid, because the macro requires an argument; in C99, you're allowed to just leave the argument out.

Finally, the feature you've all been waiting for: `//` comments. These work just like the similar comments in C++, and many, if not all, compilers in regular use today already have an option to enable them.

Declarations

The most visible change in C99 declarations is where you can put them; declarations can now be mixed with code. In general, anywhere you can have a statement, you can also have a declaration. (One exception is that only statements can have labels in front of them; declarations can't.) Additionally, a value can be declared (and optionally initialized) in the first clause of a for statement, in which case its scope goes to the end of the loop (not the end of the enclosing block). An example would be

```
for (int i = 1; i <= 10; ++i) {
    printf("simple example. [line %d]\n", i);
```

```
}
// i is out of scope here
```

Compound literals are a kind of very temporary declaration. In C99, you no longer need to declare a variable to create (and even initialize) an object. You can simply put a type name in front of a brace-enclosed list; this looks like a cast, although it's not the same thing. For example, given the following declarations:

```
struct bar { int a, b, c; char *s; };
struct bar value1, value2;
```

In C89, you could put values into a structure one at a time, like this:

```
value1.a = 0;
value1.b = 1;
value1.c = 3;
value1.s = "twenty three";
```

In C99, you can set them all at once, like this:

```
value2 = (struct bar) { 0, 1, 3, "twenty three" };
```

instead of having to initialize the members separately. There is a nameless object of type `struct bar` declared here; it is treated as though it has automatic storage duration, and you can take its address and even modify the contents!

The following example isn't very portable, but it's a good example of what compound literals are useful for. The UNIX system call `select` takes as arguments an integer, three (possibly null) pointers to arrays of integers, and a pointer to a `struct timeval`. Many people use `select` as a quick way to sleep for a small amount of time, say, less than a second. An example of how to do this in C89 (still assuming a UNIX-style environment) would be

```
void millisleep(int n) {
    struct timeval t;
    t.tv_sec = 0;
    t.tv_usec = n * 1000;
    select(0, 0, 0, 0, &t);
}
```

In C99, this could be written

```
void millisleep (int n) {
        select(0, 0, 0, 0, &((struct timeval) { 0, n * 1000 }));
}
```

On some systems, the `select` call modifies its last argument to indicate the time remaining, if any time was left before the call timed out; this code will work anyway, although it won't provide a way to check the time remaining.

This feature becomes even more powerful in conjunction with designated initializers, explained later in this chapter.

The C99 standard also introduces the concept of "restricted pointers." People who remember the last standard will doubtless be thinking, with horror, of the `noalias` specifier that was briefly seen in a draft of the previous standard. However, `restrict` is substantially different.

The basic idea of restricted pointers is to provide additional information about potential aliasing to compilers, to allow them to better optimize programs. Essentially, when you define a function, if you believe it is nonsensical for two pointers passed to the function to point to the same place, you might use the restrict qualifier when declaring them. In general, if you take a program, and remove `restrict` from it, it will continue to work. However, if you add `restrict`, you are making promises to the compiler that certain objects are distinct, so you can introduce undefined behavior.

You mostly need to know about `restrict` because the arguments to some standard library functions are now restrict-qualified, meaning they are declared with the `restrict` keyword. In general, this means you must not pass these functions multiple pointers to the same object; for a more technical (and accurate) explanation, read the standard.

C99 introduces one more qualifier: `inline`. The `inline` qualifier can only be used on functions and does about the same thing in C that it does in C++. In C, `inline` is considered to be a pure hint; the compiler is never required to inline functions. A number of compilers have already implemented the `inline` keyword, since it's used in C++. There are subtle differences, but for most purposes, you can ignore them and just use `inline` to hint to the compiler that a given function should be as fast as possible. Be aware that inlining does not *always* increase performance; you might find examples of programs that perform worse when you declare functions with `inline`.

In C99, qualifiers can be repeated; this was introduced because people wanted to be able to use `volatile` in a `typedef` and later declare a `volatile` object of the defined type. So, type qualifiers can now be duplicated, and the extra copies have no effect.

Finally, the keyword `static` has yet another meaning in C99. If a function parameter is declared with an array type, the size of the array can have type qualifiers. If one of those qualifiers is `static`, any pointer passed to the function must point to at least the given number of elements. For example

```
void foo(int a[static 10]);
```

declares a function whose first argument is a pointer to at least 10 values of type int. It wouldn't be a new C standard if it didn't give a new meaning to the word `static`.

Initialization

Several aspects of variable initialization have changed. One is that (partially because of compound literals), the requirement that the initializers for an aggregate (an array, structure, or union) must be constant has been dropped.

C99 also introduces "designated initializers," allowing you to specify which member of an aggregate an initializer is intended for. In general, you can now initialize the specific members of an array, structure, or even array of structures that you want to. For instance, if you had a structure

```
struct foo {
    int a, b;
};
```

you could initialize it by writing

```
struct foo f = { .b = 3; };
```

which would be equivalent to writing

```
struct foo f = { 0, 3 };
```

What makes this particularly desirable, of course, is that you no longer need to initialize members in order, and you no longer need to go rewrite initializers when you add members, change their order, or otherwise alter the original structure definition; as long as all the fields you attempt to initialize exist, you're good. Fields not initialized explicitly are initialized to zero, just like they used to be.

Designated initializers also make it possible to initialize a specific member of a union other than the first named member (eliminating yet another frequently asked question on Usenet).

You can also use these in conjunction with compound literals; for instance, you can write the previous example (involving `select`) like this:

```
select(0, 0, 0, 0, &((struct timeval) { .tv_usec = n * 1000 }));
```

It is now permitted to add a comma at the end of the list of values for an `enum` type. This is intended to make it easier for programs to write other programs and is consistent with the general rule that extra commas at the end of lists are often allowed.

Other New Features

Every function has an implicit variable called `__func__`, which is a string containing the name of that function. This feature is found in a number of compilers (although the spelling is often different), and is primarily useful for debugging purposes. On some implementations, a similar feature is available through a preprocessor macro, but the version that made it into the final standard is an identifier, and can't be used in preprocessor hacks.

It is now possible to write floating point constants in hexadecimal. I am not making this up. The spelling looks like this:

```
float f = 0x2.fp10;
```

The "p" serves to introduce an exponent, which is written in decimal, and indicates the binary exponent. This representation is intended to correspond to the way floating point numbers are typically stored, with a number of bits of represented value and a binary exponent indicating the scale. If you haven't been missing this feature, you probably won't be using it much.

There are now "standard pragmas"—things you can put in a `#pragma` directive which have a consistent behavior across compilers, all of which start with the token `STDC`.

There is now a standard specification for IEEE arithmetic in C; not all implementations will provide it, but if they do, there's a standard specification for testing the availability of IEEE math (through one of the feature test macros referred to earlier).

What Did We Lose?

Implicit `int`. Programs that depend on the assumption that something with no declared type will have type `int` are no longer correct. This feature had not been flagged as obsolescent in C89, but it's easy enough to fix, and many compilers already warn about it. If you've been guilty of the bad style of not declaring things explicitly, you're about to pay for it. Note that this also means that `static i;` is no longer a declaration of a static integer; it is now a syntax error.

It is no longer allowed to return a value from a function declared to return `void` or to execute a return statement with no value from a function with non-void return type.

The description of `main` now makes it clearer that the return type of `int` is not optional. The committee members had previously felt that this was obvious enough, but the widespread use of `void main(void)` in C books has made it clear that the existing text was not quite sufficiently clear. Note that a specific implementation is still allowed to choose to accept additional forms of main other than the two listed (one with arguments, one without); however, only those two are expected to be portable.

In C89, it was confirmed (through a defect report) that `long` was the largest integer type; this guarantee went away in C99. Debates over this continue to rage on Usenet.

Not everything that was suggested made it into the language. Two common string-related library functions, `strdup` and `strsep`, didn't make the cut.

However, for the most part, features were added, not removed. This sounds great until you try to carry a full-sized printout of the standard around for a day.

What Changes?

There are a variety of subtle changes in the C language. Most changes will not affect most programs. Furthermore, in general, compilers should be able to give warnings about any surprises caused by changes in how a given implementation handles the language. Mostly, you should find that existing programs continue to compile and run as expected with the new language spec.

Mostly, changes should be a result of programmers choosing to replace code using C89 idioms with code using C99 idioms. Changes that affect existing code have been kept to a minimum, and wherever possible, such changes will elicit warning or error messages.

A lot of clarifications have been made, and errors in the standard fixed. In a number of cases, the wording in the C89 standard had undesired implications or didn't say what the committee originally thought it meant. In some cases, boundary conditions that hadn't been considered have been addressed; for example, `tmpnam` now returns a null pointer if it can't generate a suitable name. This was previously only possible after at least `TMP_MAX` calls to `tmpnam` had occurred. Aliasing rules are substantially cleaned up and clarified.

The C99 standard altered the definitions of implementation-defined, unspecified, and undefined behavior. The boundaries between them have shifted and been clarified significantly. This should not affect most programs, although a few things have changed; for example, integer division involving negative numbers is now fully defined by the standard. (It used to be possible for an implementation to round either up or down.)

In the C89 standard, there was a fairly broad mention, in the definition of undefined behavior, that access to indeterminately valued objects might yield undefined behavior. In C99, this is clarified with the introduction of "trap representations." A trap representation is a sequence of bits that, when interpreted as being of a given type, do not correspond to a value. If you access stored data through an `lvalue` with a type for which that data is a trap representation, you get undefined behavior. In English, this means that certain data can't have certain types—for example, a given sequence of bits might not be a valid `float`. In general, it is assumed that a valid value of one type might be a trap representation for any other noncharacter type. Also, when an object's value is indeterminate (for example, anything uninitialized), it is possible that it is a trap representation. So, if you declare a pointer, but it is not initialized, not only is it undefined behavior to dereference the pointer, it is undefined behavior to access it at all—say, to cast it to another type, print it, or assign its value to another pointer. Character types do not have trap representations, so you can access any data as a sequence of bytes, without worrying about trap representations.

The trap representation wording isn't supposed to really change the way the language works, only to clarify, but it will come as a surprise to people who didn't know that simply *reading* an invalid value could cause core dumps or other surprises. Don't access uninitialized memory; you'll be happier.

If `main` is declared with a return type of `int` (as it must be, in portable code), "falling off the end" of `main` is equivalent to returning 0. Many careless programmers have been returning random values to their environment for years; this is now fixed.

The standard has clarified that only the precise mode strings (for `fopen`) given in the standard have defined meanings. The C89 standard has been read by some people to suggest that additional text might follow the mode string (especially in the common `"rt"` seen in some books for "text mode" on some systems, which would just be `"r"` in standard C, since text mode is the default), but the C99 standard either changes this or clarifies the intent, depending on whom you ask.

Overall, you should find the changes harmless; nonetheless, you might want to make sure you have an older compiler around in case you run into trouble at first, just as many people felt the need to keep a pre-ISO C compiler around through the early part of the 1990s.

Summary

C99 is a substantial change in the C language; the changes are no less dramatic than the changes between the language described in the 1978 edition of Kernighan and Ritchie's *The C Programming Language* and the language described in the 1989 ISO standard. No short summary (such as this chapter) will give you the full story; I've tried to focus on features which interested me, but you might find that other features are more important to you. Don't expect a major language revision to be a one-week conversion; it will take you time to get comfortable with the new features, and you'll make plenty of mistakes as you get used to the new language. Enjoy the learning experience.

The best source for information on the new language is, for now, the new standard; by the time you read this, it should certainly be possible for you to buy the new language spec in PDF format from the ISO Web site. National bodies (such as ANSI) might not adopt it as quickly, but initial implementations are already cropping up all over. The gcc compiler will probably have most of the language features by the time you read this; indeed, many of the features in C99 parallel features in gcc.

Steve Summit's excellent FAQ (frequently asked questions) list for the Usenet newsgroup `comp.lang.c` has a substantial amount of initial information on C99; it remains recommended reading. As of this writing, his FAQ can be found at:

`http://www.eskimo.com/~scs/C-faq/top.html`

Discussion of the C standard can also be found on Usenet, in the newsgroup `comp.std.c`, which discusses the various incarnations of the ISO standard. The discussion tends toward the esoteric, but if you want to learn the fine points of the language or discuss questions you have, no finer resource exists.

The C committee is still having meetings, and there is some talk of a C0X language spec being released in the future, probably in around ten years. If you want to get involved, go right ahead! Membership is open to people who are interested in participating, and the committee is always happy to have more people available to do the work. The official home page of the committee is, as of this writing:

`http://anubis.dkuug.dk/JTC1/SC22/WG14/`

Appendixes

Part IV

In This Part

APPENDIX A

GNU GENERAL PUBLIC LICENSE

TERMS AND CONDITIONS FOR COPYING, DISTRIBUTION AND MODIFICATION

This License applies to any program or other work which contains a notice placed by the copyright holder saying it may be distributed under the terms of this General Public License. The "Program", below, refers to any such program or work, and a "work based on the Program" means either the Program or any derivative work under copyright law: that is to say, a work containing the Program or a portion of it, either verbatim or with modifications and/or translated into another language. (Hereinafter, translation is included without limitation in the term "modification".) Each licensee is addressed as "you".

Activities other than copying, distribution and modification are not covered by this License; they are outside its scope. The act of running the Program is not restricted, and the output from the Program is covered only if its contents constitute a work based on the Program (independent of having been made by running the Program).

Whether that is true depends on what the Program does.

1. You may copy and distribute verbatim copies of the Program's source code as you receive it, in any medium, provided that you conspicuously and appropriately publish on each copy an appropriate copyright notice and disclaimer of warranty; keep intact all the notices that refer to this License and to the absence of any warranty; and give any other recipients of the Program a copy of this License along with the Program.

   You may charge a fee for the physical act of transferring a copy, and you may at your option offer warranty protection in exchange for a fee.

2. You may modify your copy or copies of the Program or any portion of it, thus forming a work based on the Program, and copy and distribute such modifications or work under the terms of Section 1 above, provided that you also meet all of these conditions:

   a)You must cause the modified files to carry prominent notices stating that you changed the files and the date of any change.

   b)You must cause any work that you distribute or publish, that in whole or in part contains or is derived from the Program or any part thereof, to be licensed as a whole at no charge to all third parties under the terms of this License.

   c)If the modified program normally reads commands interactively when run, you must cause it, when started running for such interactive use in the most ordinary way, to print or display an announcement including an appropriate copyright notice and a notice that there is no warranty (or else, saying that you provide a warranty) and that

APPENDIX B

Selected Bibliography

This appendix provides a list of books and resources suggested by the contributing authors for advanced material on C programming.

Books

The Algorithm Design Manual, Steven S. Skiena, Springer-Verlag New York, Inc., ISBN 0-387-94860-0

Algorithms in C Parts 1-4, Fundamentals, Data Structures, Sorting, Searching 3rd Edition, Robert Sedgewick, 1997 ISBN 0-201-31452-5

The Art of Computer Programming Volume 1, Donald E Knuth, Addison-Wesley, ISBN 0-201-89683-4

The Art of Computer Programming Volume 2, Donald E Knuth, Addison-Wesley, ISBN 0-201-89684-2

The Art of Computer Programming Volume 3, Donald E Knuth, Addison-Wesley, ISBN 0-201-89685-0

C: A Reference Manual, 4th Ed., Harbison & Steele, Prentice Hall, ISBN 0-13-326224-3

C: How to Program, 2nd Ed., Deitel, H.M. & Deitel, P.J., Prentice Hall, ISBN 0-13-226119-7

C Programming: A Modern Approach, K. N. King, W. W. Norton & Company, Softcover ISBN 0-393-96945-2

C Programming FAQs, Steve Summit, Addison-Wesley, ISBN 0-201-84519-9

The C Programming Language, 2nd Ed., Brian W Kernighan and Dennis M Ritchie, Prentice Hall, ISBN 0-13-110362-8

C *Traps and Pitfalls*, Andrew Koenig, Addison-Wesley, ISBN 0-201-17928-8

Code Complete, Steve McConnell, Microsoft Press, ISBN 1-55615-484-4

Data Structures and Algorithm Analysis in C, Mark Allen Weiss, Addison-Wesley, ISBN 0-201-49840-5

Data Structures Using C, Aaron M. Tenenbaum, Yedidyah Langsam, Moshe J. Augenstein, Prentice-Hall, Englewood Cliffs, NJ, 1990 (ISBN 0-13-199746-7).

Expert C Programming, Peter van der Linden, Prentice Hall, ISBN 0-13-177429-8

Introduction to Algorithms, Thomas H. Cormen et al., MIT Press, ISBN 0-262-03141-8

The New Hacker's Dictionary, Eric S Raymond, MIT Press, ISBN 0-262-68092-0

The Practice of Programming, Brian W Kernighan and Rob Pike, Addison-Wesley, ISBN 0-201-61586-X

The Standard C Library, P.J. Plauger, Prentice Hall, ISBN 0-13-131509-9

Sorting and Sort Systems, Harold Lorin, Addison-Wesley, ISBN 0-201-14453-0

Networking

These books aren't strictly about C, but if you want to learn more about networking you may find them useful. Where these books provide example code, it tends to be in C.

TCP/IP Illustrated, W. Richard Stevens

Published by Addison-Wesley

Volume 1 Details the TCP/IP protocols

ISBN 0201633469

Volume 2 Details the TCP/IP stack in 4.4BSD-Lite

ISBN 020163354X

Volume 3 Details many TCP/IP Services

ISBN 0201634953

UNIX Network Programming, W. Richard Stevens, Prentice Hall, *Volume 1 Networking APIs: Sockets and XTI*, ISBN 013490012X

Windows Sockets Network Programming, Bob Quinn and Dave Shute, Addison-Wesley, ISBN 0201633728

Online Resources

Robert Sedgewick's analysis of Shellsort:

`http://www.cs.princeton.edu/~rs/talks/shellsort.ps`

Stefan Nilsson's home page (radix sorting):

`http://www.nada.kth.se/~snilsson/`

Karim Ratib's Codepage (algorithms galore):

`http://www2.iro.umontreal.ca/~ratib/code/`

Priority Queue information by Lee Killough:

`http://members.xoom.com/killough/heaps.html`

The following selection of Internet programming sites should prove useful if you want to learn more about network programming:

The IETF is the authoritative source for RFCs, FYIs, and other informational documents regarding TCP/IP.

`http://www.ietf.org/`

Internet Assigned Numbers Authority home page:

`http://www.iana.org/`

Internet Societal Task Force home page:

`http://www.istf.isoc.org/`

Internet Society home page:

`http://www.isoc.org/`

Internet Architecture Board home page:

`http://www.iab.org/`

Internet Engineering & Planning Group:

`http://www.iepg.org`

Usenet

For discussing ANSI C: `comp.lang.c`

For networking: the `comp.protocols.tcp-ip` and `alt.winsock` newsgroups are both excellent.

Please, always be sure to read a newsgroup's FAQs before posting to that newsgroup.

INDEX

SYMBOLS

A

B

D

E

F

J

K

L

M

N

O

P

Q

S

T

U

X - Z

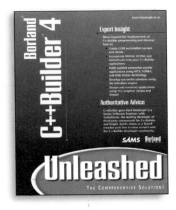

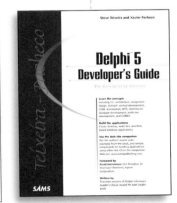

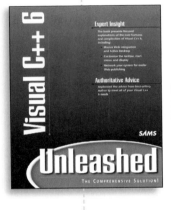